CW00429645

THE BUILDINGS OF ENGLAND

FOUNDING EDITOR: NIKOLAUS PEVSNER

LANCASHIRE: LIVERPOOL AND THE SOUTH-WEST

RICHARD POLLARD AND NIKOLAUS PEVSNER

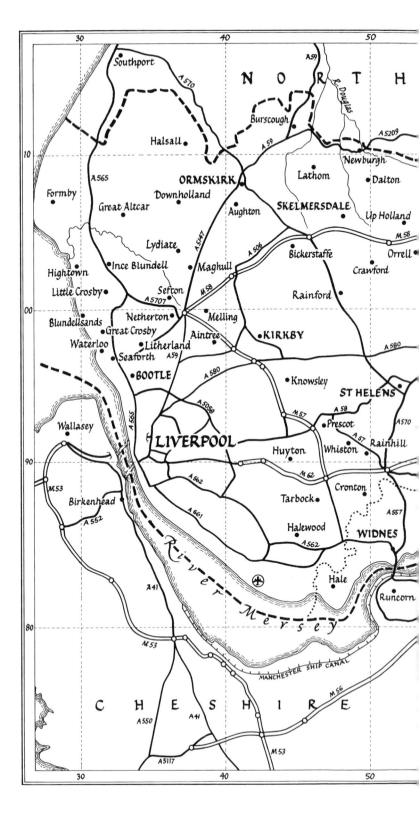

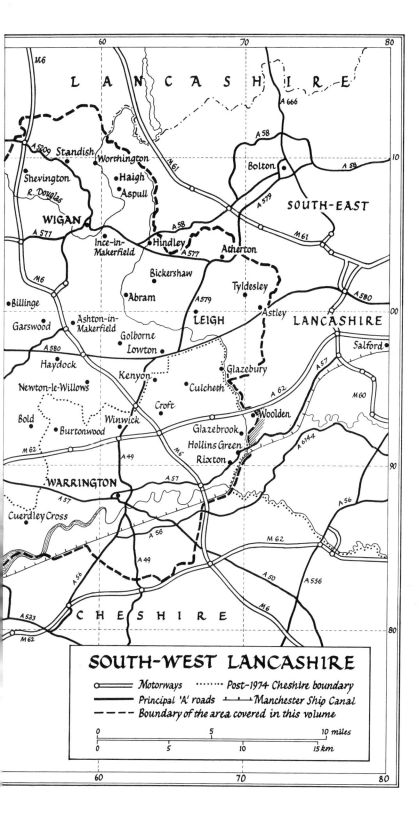

PEVSNER ARCHITECTURAL GUIDES

The Buildings of England series was created and
largely written by Sir Nikolaus Pevsner (1902–83).
First editions of the county volumes were published by
Penguin Books between 1951 and 1974. The continuing
programme of revisions and new volumes has been
supported by research financed through
the Buildings Books Trust since 1994

THE BUILDINGS BOOKS TRUST

was established in 1994, registered charity number 1042101.
It promotes the appreciation and understanding
of architecture by supporting and financing
the research needed to sustain new and revised volumes of
The Buildings of England, Ireland, Scotland and *Wales*

The Trust gratefully acknowledges
a major grant from

ENGLISH HERITAGE

towards the cost of research and writing,
as well as assistance with photography

and an additional grant towards the cost of maps
and other illustrations from

THE C.J. ROBERTSON TRUST

Lancashire: Liverpool and the South-West

BY

RICHARD POLLARD

AND

NIKOLAUS PEVSNER

WITH CONTRIBUTIONS

FROM

JOSEPH SHARPLES

THE BUILDINGS OF ENGLAND

YALE UNIVERSITY PRESS
NEW HAVEN AND LONDON

YALE UNIVERSITY PRESS
NEW HAVEN AND LONDON
302 Temple Street, New Haven CT 06511
47 Bedford Square, London WC1B 3DP
www.pevsner.co.uk
www.lookingatbuildings.org
www.yalebooks.co.uk
www.yalebooks.com
for
THE BUILDINGS BOOKS TRUST

Published by Yale University Press 2006
2 4 6 8 10 9 7 5 3 1

ISBN 0 300 10910 5

Printed in China
through World Print
Set in Monotype Plantin

CONTENTS

LIST OF TEXT FIGURES AND MAPS   x

PHOTOGRAPHIC ACKNOWLEDGEMENTS   xiv

MAP REFERENCES   xv

EDITOR'S FOREWORD   xvi

ACKNOWLEDGEMENTS   xvii

INTRODUCTION   1

    GEOLOGY AND BUILDING STONES   3
    BY FRED BROADHURST

    PREHISTORIC SOUTH-WEST LANCASHIRE   9
    BY R.W. COWELL

    SOUTH-WEST LANCASHIRE FROM THE
    ROMAN CONQUEST TO THE MIDDLE AGES   14
    BY ROBERT A. PHILPOTT

    CHURCH ARCHITECTURE TO THE
    SEVENTEENTH CENTURY   22

    DOMESTIC AND OTHER SECULAR ARCHITECTURE
    TO *c.* 1700   29

    THE EIGHTEENTH CENTURY   39

    SOUTH-WEST LANCASHIRE IN THE
    INDUSTRIAL REVOLUTION   49

    ARCHITECTURE IN THE EARLY NINETEENTH
    CENTURY   59

    VICTORIAN AND EDWARDIAN DEVELOPMENTS   68

    THE INTER-WAR YEARS   97

    SOUTH-WEST LANCASHIRE FROM 1945   104

    FURTHER READING   116

SOUTH-WEST LANCASHIRE   121

    LIVERPOOL   242

GLOSSARY   687

INDEX OF ARCHITECTS, ARTISTS, PATRONS AND
RESIDENTS   713

INDEX OF PLACES   729

LIST OF TEXT FIGURES AND MAPS

Every effort has been made to contact or trace all copyright holders. The publishers will be glad to make good any errors or omissions brought to our attention in future editions.

Liverpool, the Calderstones, drawing by William
  Lathom, 1825 (Transactions of the Historical Society
  of Lancashire and Cheshire, 1915)   12
Lathom, reconstruction of roundhouse excavated at
  Duttons Farm, c. C1–C2 (National Museums Liverpool
  Field Archaeology Unit courtesy of Mark Faulkner)   13
Newton-le-Willows, Castle Hill, drawing, 1843
  (Memoirs of the Literary and Philosophical Society of
  Manchester, 1843)   19
Warrington, Bewsey Old Hall, plan showing moat
  (Dr Jennifer Lewis, The Medieval Earthworks of the
  Hundred of West Derby, 2000)   21
Warrington Priory, plan based on excavation (Transactions
  of the Historical Society of Lancashire and Cheshire, 1936)   24
Winwick, St Oswald, brass of Sir Peter Legh (†1527) and
  wife (James L. Thornely, Monumental Brasses of
  Lancashire and Cheshire, 1893)   27
Ince-in-Makerfield, Peel Hall, sections (G. Miller,
  Historic Houses in Lancashire: The Douglas Valley, 2002)   32
Wigan, Winstanley Hall, drawing of the east front in 1817
  (M. Gregson, A Portfolio of Fragments relating to the History
  of the County Palatine and Duchy of Lancaster, 1869)   35
Haskayne (Downholland), Stock Cottage, School Lane,
  plan and cutaway view   37
Liverpool, St Paul, 1763–9 (demolished), engraving by
  E. Rooker after P.P. Burdett, 1773 (Liverpool Record
  Office)   39
Bold, Bold Hall, c. 1732 (demolished), lithograph by
  C.J. Greenwood, after Isaac Shaw, c. 1845
  (Warrington Library, Museum and Archives Service)   44
St Helens, British Plate Glass Company works, 1773–6
  (demolished), engraving by Sly, after Anelay
  (The Pictorial History of the County of Lancaster, 1844)   56
Widnes, West Bank, extract from the Ordnance Survey
  County Series, 6 inch 1st edition, 1849 (Crown
  Copyright and Landmark Information Group)   59
Liverpool, court housing, plan by W.H. Duncan, 1840
  (Liverpool Record Office)   61

Liverpool, Albany Building, Old Hall Street, 1856–8,
    lithograph from W. Herdman, *Views in Modern
    Liverpool*, 1864   68
Liverpool, NatWest Bank (originally Parr's), Castle
    Street, 1898–1901, section (*Architectural Review*, vol. 10,
    1901)   70
Liverpool, Royal Infirmary, Pembroke Place, 1887–90   77
Liverpool, Wavertree, St Bridget, 1868–72
    (*The Builder*, vol. 29, 1871)   90
Liverpool, suburban housing by Liverpool Corporation
    Housing Department, standard plans, 1930s
    (Liverpool Record Office)   101
Liverpool, city centre redevelopment proposals by
    Liverpool City Council/Liverpool City Centre
    Planning Group, 1965   104

Aintree Racecourse, grandstand, 1829 (demolished),
    elevation by John Foster Jun. (Liverpool Record Office) 123
Atherton Hall, 1723–43 (demolished) (C. Campbell,
    Vitruvius Britannicus vol. 3, 1725)   140
Aughton, St Michael, plan (*Victoria History of the
    Counties of England: Lancaster*, vol. 3, 1907)   143
Aughton, Moor Hall, engraving, early C19 (Liverpool
    Record Office)   146
Billinge, St Aidan, 1716–18, contract drawing by Henry
    Sephton (Wigan Archives Services)   149
Bootle, Stanley Precinct, town centre development as
    envisaged in the 1960s (Sefton Metropolitan Borough
    Council)   159
Crawford, Manor House, 1728, ground-floor plan
    (G. Miller, *Historic Houses in Lancashire: The Douglas
    Valley*, 2002)   164
Golborne, Lightshaw Hall, *c.* 1553, section (courtesy of
    Dr Jennifer Lewis)   178
Haigh Hall, 1827–*c.* 1844, ground-floor plan   184
Halsall, St Cuthbert, plan (*Victoria History of the
    Counties of England: Lancaster*, vol. 3, 1907)   193
Ince Blundell Hall, plan (*Country Life*, 10 April 1968)   205
Kirkby, town plan (Liverpool City Council pamphlet,
    1961)   214
Knowsley Hall, block plan   218
Lathom House, *c.* 1725–40 (largely demolished),
    engraving by R. Sears after G. Pickering, 1832
    (Liverpool Record Office)   225
Leigh, houses on Beech Grove, drawing and plans for
    J.C. Prestwich & Son, *c.* 1914 (courtesy of Brian Kay) 235
Liverpool, Old Dock, 1710–16, and Dry Dock, detail from
    map by J. Chadwick, 1725 (Liverpool Record Office)   260
Liverpool, Albert Dock warehouses, 1843–7, transverse
    section (Ken Worrall)   265
Liverpool Town Hall, first-floor plan (*The Kaleidoscope*,
    c. 1820; Liverpool Record Office)   287

Liverpool, St George's Hall, 1841–54, plan (*The Builder*, vol. 13, 1855) 292

Liverpool, Compton House, Church Street, 1867, C19 print (Liverpool Record Office) 314

Liverpool Exchange Buildings, 1803–8 (demolished) and Nelson's Monument, 1813, lithograph by W. Crane after Robert Barrow, early C19 (Liverpool Record Office) 323

Liverpool Anglican Cathedral, 1904–78, plan 349

Liverpool Metropolitan Cathedral, crypt, 1933–*c.* 1940, plan 355

Liverpool Metropolitan Cathedral, 1962–7, section 356

Liverpool, Allerton, New Heys, 1861–5, watercolour by Alfred Waterhouse, 1862 (RIBA) 390

Liverpool, Croxteth Hall, axonometric view (Liverpool City Council) 406

Liverpool, Edge Hill, the Moorish Arch over the Liverpool & Manchester Railway, engraving by A.B. Clayton, 1831 (Liverpool Record Office) 414

Liverpool, Newsham Park, Seamen's Orphan Institution 1870–5 (*The Builder*, vol. 30, 1872) 425

Liverpool, Speke, view of 1936 development plan (Liverpool Record Office) 460

Liverpool, Speke Hall, ground-floor plan (The National Trust) 464

Liverpool, Walton, St Mary, drawing, 1811 (Liverpool Record Office) 488

Ormskirk, St Peter and St Paul, drawing, 1811 (Liverpool Record Office) 533

St Helens, Beechams Factory, 1884–7, engraving (*Building News*, vol. 49, 1886) 558

St Helens, Alexandra Park, Pilkington Glass headquarters, 1956–65, block plan 573

Sefton, St Helen, screens, drawing by Richard Bridgens, 1822 (Richard Bridgens, *Sefton Church with part of the interior decorations*, 1822) 581

Skelmersdale New Town, plan (F.J. Osborn, *New Towns: Their Origins, Achievements and Progress*, 1977) 586

Warrington, St Elphin, monument to Sir John Boteler (†1463) and wife, engraving by Birrit after Moses Griffith, before 1819 (Warrington Library, Museum and Archives Service) 605

Warrington, St Ann, 1866–8 (*Building News*, vol. 17, 1869) 622

Warrington, Greenhall's Brewery, C19 advertisement (Warrington Library, Museum and Archives Service) 626

Warrington New Town, Winwick Quay 4 industrial unit, 1979, detail, by Grimshaw Architects, 1983 (courtesy of the architects) 641

Wigan, a north-east view, drawing, early C19 (Wigan Heritage Service) 659

Winwick, St Oswald, Anglo-Saxon cross fragment, drawing (*Victoria History of the Counties of England: Lancaster*, vol. 1, 1906) 680

MAPS

Geological map   4
Bootle   158
Liverpool Docks, south   264
Liverpool Docks, north   275
Liverpool, centre   282
Liverpool, cathedral area   346
Liverpool suburbs   381
Ormskirk   532
Prescot   541
St Helens, town centre   554
St Helens, outer   562
Warrington   603
Widnes   647
Wigan   669

PHOTOGRAPHIC ACKNOWLEDGEMENTS

We are grateful to English Heritage and its photographers Bob Skingle, Tong Perry and Keith Buck for taking most of the photographs in this volume (© English Heritage Photo Library) and also to the sources of the remaining photographs as shown below. We are grateful for permission to reproduce them as appropriate.

John Benbow: 1
Martin Charles: 62
English Heritage (National Monuments Record): 77, 80, 86, 117
Richard Pollard: 2, 25, 40, 58, 101, 103, 104, 108, 122, 123, 124, 125, 126
Urban Splash: 81, 127
Courtesy of the Rt Hon. Earl of Derby & Jarrold publishing 2005: 31, 107

MAP REFERENCES

The numbers printed in italic type in the margin against the place names in the gazetteer of the book indicate the position of the place in question on the index map (pp. 2–3), which is divided into sections by the 10-kilometre reference lines of the National Grid. The reference given here omits the two initial letters (formerly numbers) which in a full grid reference refer to the 100-kilometre squares into which the county is divided. The first two numbers indicate the *western* boundary, and the last two the *southern* boundary, of the 10-kilometre square in which the place in question is situated. For example, Abram (reference 6000) will be found in the 10-kilometre square bounded by grid lines 60 (on the *west*) and 00, and 00 (on the *south*) and 10; Widnes (reference 5080) in the square bounded by the grid lines 50 (on the *west*) and 60, and 80 (on the *south*) and 90.

The map contains all those places, whether towns, villages, or isolated buildings, which are the subject of separate entries in the text.

EDITOR'S FOREWORD

*This is the second part of a planned three-volume survey of the build-
ings of Lancashire, revised and expanded from Nikolaus Pevsner's
two books of 1969. Its sister volume for the southern part is Clare
Hartwell and Matthew Hyde's* Lancashire: Manchester and the
South-East *(2004). The division of the southern part of Lancashire
into two, necessary in order to do justice to the great cities of Liverpool
and Manchester, has also allowed both volumes to expand northwards.
The boundary between northern and southern parts is therefore different from that of the first series. This volume also includes a small
area of the historic county of Cheshire, now absorbed into Warrington.
A third Lancashire volume is under way to cover the north of the
county, and this will be followed by revised volumes on the Lake Counties and on Cheshire, including those areas formerly part of the
Metropolitan County of Merseyside. The* Buildings of England's *re-
survey of the North West will then be complete.*

*The challenges of assessing such a heavily urbanized county are con-
siderable; indeed, Pevsner considered South Lancashire 'the most difficult area I have had to describe'. To make matters worse, he undertook his tour at a time when plans for comprehensive urban redevelopment were at their zenith. Since that period the pace of change in
the area has been swift. The task of assessing the present architectural
state of South-West Lancashire began with the paperback Pevsner City
Guides'* Liverpool *(2004), written by Joseph Sharples with contributions from Richard Pollard. In this more comprehensive hardback
volume the authors' roles are reversed, for the Liverpool paperback text,
suitably adapted, forms the heart of the account of the city. Where possible, the 1960s text served as a basis for accounts of the areas beyond,
but in most cases these descriptions are Mr Pollard's own. Many essential themes which were previously skimmed over – vernacular traditions, gentry houses and industrial buildings, to name but three – are
now explored in depth, and placed in the context of the industrial and
commercial history of the area. A wholly new Introduction, including
specially commissioned accounts of the geology and archaeology, completes the text. The book also follows recent* Buildings of England *tra-
ditions in its numerous maps and text illustrations, along with splendid
colour photographs, generously supplied by English Heritage. The
results are a vindication of the special interest of this densely inhabited but under-explored area of England.*

ACKNOWLEDGEMENTS

This book is based on sections of Nikolaus Pevsner's *South Lancashire* and *North Lancashire*, both published in 1969. Our greatest debt therefore is owed to him. We also reused the research notes prepared for Pevsner by the late Edward Hubbard, and can only repeat Sir Nikolaus's praise for their thoroughness and precision. Edward Hubbard was also the author of *Cheshire*, a small part of which forms the basis of sections of the Warrington entry. Pevsner was helped by many others too, including Donald Buttress who supplied a great deal of information on churches, John H.G. Archer, Jeffrey Howarth, A.W. Sewter, Denis Evinson and Ivan Hall.

Lancashire: Liverpool and the South-West would not have been possible without a major grant from English Heritage to cover the costs of research and writing. We are further indebted to English Heritage for its generosity in providing most of the photographs; plaudits for these are due to their photographers, especially Tony Perry and Bob Skingle. A number of English Heritage investigators have generously shared their thoughts and findings from various projects, amongst them Sarah Brown, John Cattell, Peter de Figueiredo, Colum Giles, Ian Goodall and Elain Harwood. We have also made use of research carried out for the University of Liverpool's Mercantile Liverpool Project, funded by the Leverhulme Trust, English Heritage, the Philip Holt Trust and Liverpool City Council's World Heritage Site.

A book such as this depends to a great extent on the co-operation of numerous librarians and archivists. The staff of Liverpool Record Office and Liverpool Central Library were extremely helpful, as were those at St Helens Local History Library, especially Peter Sergeant, who went out of his way to answer obscure inquiries. Thanks are also extended to Mark Sargant at Crosby Library, who like Peter Sergeant kindly looked through parts of the typescript, and to the staff of the Wigan History Shop, and Wigan Borough Archives in Leigh, the Warrington Local History Library, and the Cheshire and Lancashire record offices. At the University of Liverpool library, Maureen Watry and the Special Collections and Archives staff were generous with their time, as was the University Archivist, Adrian Allan. Thanks are also due to the Maritime Archives and Library at the Merseyside Maritime Museum; to the Walker Art Gallery; and to Meg Whittle of the Liverpool Archdiocesan Archives. Help also came from the British Architectural Library; the V&A Print Room; Fr James Hodkinson SJ of the Jesuit archives; Mike

Chrimes of the Institute of Civil Engineers; Ian Leith of the National Monuments Record; Jessie Campbell and Nicholas Webb of Barclays Group Records; Tina Staples of HSBC Midland Group archives; Laura Taylor of Lloyds TSB Group archives; and Sarah Millard of the Bank of England.

The contributions of three experts enhance the early parts of the introduction: Fred Broadhurst on geology, R.W. Cowell on prehistoric archaeology, and Robert Philpott on the archaeology of the Roman and medieval periods. Another archaeologist, Norman Redhead at the Greater Manchester Archaeology Unit, contributed to descriptions of archaeology in the Greater Manchester sections, and made the Sites and Monuments Record available. Sarah Jane Farr and the staff of the Merseyside Sites and Monuments Record dug out files and supported the research throughout the project.

Local authority planning and conservation staff have been a generous source of advice and assistance, and a mine of observation and unpublished information. In particular, we want to single out Philip Powell of Wigan Metropolitan Borough Council, who contributed immensely to our understanding and knowledge of all aspects of architecture within that borough; he read through parts of the typescript with many beneficial results. We would also like to thank David Innes, formerly of St Helens Borough Council, Joe Martin of Salford City Council, and John Hinchliffe, Glynn Marsden, John Flynn and Wendy Morgan of Liverpool City Council. We are also grateful to the many staff at the University of Liverpool and National Museums Liverpool who gave assistance.

A number of other people have contributed specialist knowledge to areas both geographical and typological, many of whom kindly read parts of the manuscript. Dr Jen Lewis generously made available her knowledge of medieval moated sites, and of her home town of Formby. Miles Broughton and the late Quentin Hughes shared their wide knowledge of Liverpool architecture. So did James Darwin, Janet Gnosspelius, Florence Gersten, John Vaughan and Mike Chitty. Adrian Jarvis was always happy to draw on his remarkable knowledge of the Liverpool docks, which, through his research and publications, forms the basis of much of our account. Gary Miller's detailed research and his advice on the halls and houses in the Douglas Valley area were invaluable, and enhance many gazetteer entries. Mary Presland proffered information, checked entries and chased queries. Janice Hayes at Warrington Museum was constantly helpful, particularly in respect of Bewsey Old Hall. Many of the observations on the work of A.W.N. Pugin would not have been possible without the advice of Timothy Brittain-Catlin. Michael Hall offered the fruits of his research on Bodley; Patrick Farman's encyclopedic knowledge of brasses was very welcome; Dr Jennifer Freeman answered queries about W.D. Caröe, and opened up the Historic Chapels Trust's files on St Benet, Netherton. Bill Halsall answered questions on community architecture and housing co-ops in Liverpool. Alyson Pollard and Dave Moffat gave access to their work on the Audsleys, and supplied information on stained glass. Lynn Pearson shared her findings on the Mersey Brewery, and she and Penny Beckett helped with tiles and architectural ceramics. Other unpublished research and theses, frequently a source of otherwise unknown information, include Douglas Wall's on Thomas Shelmerdine's libraries, Jane Longmore's on the Liverpool Corporation Estate, Gillian Moore's on Peter Ellis, John Baily's on Thomas Rickman, and Penny Hebgin-Barnes's on medieval stained glass.

Other individuals we would like to thank include Geoffrey Brandwood, Anthony Grimshaw, Robin Wolley, Ian Taylor, Peter Cormack, Ian Dungavell, Colin Stansfield, Sharman Kadish, Neil Burton, Peter Howell, Gavin Stamp and David Walker.

It would be impossible to thank individually all those kind owners, managers, custodians, clergy and members of staff who made themselves or others available so that we could poke about in buildings, and who offered us information. We are very grateful to every one of them, but special mention must be made of Fr Michael Friar at St Dunstan, Liverpool, Canon Malcolm Forrest for Wigan Hall, Canon Roger Wikeley of St Mary, West Derby, Dr Cecil Moss of the Princes Road Synagogue, Liverpool, Julia Carder at Croxteth Park, the Earl of Derby and his archivists at Knowsley Hall, Simon Osborne and his staff at Speke Hall, Nicholas Blundell of Crosby Hall, Tim Sharratt at Haigh Hall, the staff of Warrington Town Hall, Sister Mary Laura at Ince Blundell, Mr Duffy of St Edward's College, Liverpool, and Shirley Tonge of Morley's Hall.

Clare Hartwell and Matthew Hyde were occasional but always enjoyable and invigorating visiting companions, and shared insights and information from the preparation of their sister volume, on SE Lancashire. The structure of the introduction owes a huge debt to them too. Tom Wesley, who was behind the wheel with Pevsner in 1967, made many valuable comments after enthusiastically test-walking our text for central Liverpool.

This book would not have been possible without the unwavering support and guidance of Simon Bradley at Yale University Press. His acute editing was a constant source of marvel, and enhanced the volume immeasurably. Emily Lees and Emily Wraith co-ordinated the illustrations, and Emily Winter did the page layouts, with unruffleable efficiency. Sally Salvesen oversaw the whole project. Bernard Dod copyedited the text, and Charlotte Chapman proof-read it. Reg Piggott drew the county map, and Alan Fagan the others. Judith Wardman and Christine Shuttleworth compiled the remarkable indexes. Gavin Watson and everyone at the Buildings Books Trust were always supportive.

To all these people the authors are indebted.

As ever, the authors and publishers will be very grateful for information on errors or omissions.

RP, JS
January 2006

INTRODUCTION

There is a tendency to imagine Lancashire entirely carpeted in mills and terraced houses. But whilst S E Lancashire is indeed one of the most densely developed regions in Europe, the S W of the county has quite a different character. Even late in the C19 much of it was still sparsely populated mosses and meres or rolling farmland, and large expanses are still rural today. From the summit of Ashurst Beacon, the most westerly outpost of the hills that fall down from the Pennines, you can survey the whole of this area, the West Derby Hundred of Lancashire. Away to the W is the Irish Sea, and beside it the flat coastal plain, a windswept, waterlogged land of few and scattered villages until the marshes were drained and the railway created genteel dormitories out of places like Great Crosby and Blundellsands. Side by side just N of Great Crosby are the landscaped parks of Crosby and Ince Blundell halls, two wooded islands where for centuries two Blundell families lived, and after the Reformation kept the old faith alive, like so many of the gentry and aristocracy in Lancashire. A low ridge inland from here has at its N end Ormskirk, and at the S Aughton, two of only thirteen medieval parishes in the whole area covered by this guide, a measure of the then small size of the population. S of all this is Liverpool, a vast semicircular fan of bricks and mortar spreading inland from the Mersey estuary. Liverpool, of course, dominates economically, culturally and architecturally. It has merged imperceptibly – at least to the outsider – with once-independent satellites to the N and S, such as Waterloo, established as a fashionable watering place on the nearest bit of coast to the city, and Bootle, an industrial town made by the Stanleys, Earls of Derby. The Stanleys have been the pre-eminent family of S Lancashire since the C15, and their sprawling Knowsley Hall still stands in the midst of a vast medieval deer park despite the encroachment of the conurbation.

The River Mersey was far from being a perfect harbour, but it was an excellent highway to the new industrial areas of Lancashire, only thirty miles away; so Liverpool became one of the world's great ports and commercial power-houses. Constant improvement of communications was key to the economic expansion of S W Lancashire: turnpikes and improved river navigation in the late C17 and early C18, then came the county's first canals, then in 1830 the world's first modern railway, linking Liverpool and Manchester. Its route crosses the Sankey Brook Navigation, a canal that predates the more celebrated Bridgewater Canal. Within a few decades the Navigation had attracted a plate-glass manufactory, so starting an industry that created a new town, St Helens. The sprawling *ad hoc* character of St Helens, and of other towns such as Widnes, is the defining feature of much of the C19 industrial expansion of S Lancashire. Further inland, N of the inhospitable Chat Moss, Leigh, Tyldesley and Atherton were new towns created by steam power, which transformed the coal industry and made possible the construction of large, multi-storey textile mills in flat central southern Lancashire. Like other settlements they were before the C19 semi-industrialised villages, with cottage textile and metal-working industries operating from workshops in basements, roofs and outriggers. The attractive, stone-built C16–C18 gentry halls and yeomen's houses in the rolling countryside of townships further N, like Orrell and Dalton, testify not only to agricultural prosperity but also to an early industrial base of mineral extraction, and textiles too.

The two principal towns of central S Lancashire, major components of that pre-steam economy, were Wigan and Warrington. Both have Roman origins; Wigan was a prosperous coal and textile town from the C16; Warrington was an ancient crossing point on the Mersey, and always the crossroads of S Lancashire. Contemporary Warrington is a reminder of just how much has changed in the last half-century. Around the remnants of the Georgian and Victorian town spread low-density late C20 housing, bland office blocks, massive distribution warehouses and shiny retail sheds – the very image of C21 Britain. Yet the title of George Orwell's *The Road to Wigan Pier* is enough, still, to evoke an image of the North that resonates profoundly, so ingrained is the idea of it as one great, sprawling industrial mass. The 'monstrous scenery of slag-heaps, chimneys, piled scrap-iron, foul canals' which Orwell describes was still much in evidence when Nikolaus Pevsner toured Lancashire in 1968, ably assisted in the southern parts by Edward Hubbard. But King Cotton was already dying, the catastrophic collapse of Liverpool's docks was only three years away, and redevelopment had begun to hollow out town and city centres, clearing swathes of C19 housing, and sending tens of thousands to new suburbs and to whole New Towns at Kirkby and Skelmersdale.

In the decades since the transformation has been profound. With the loss of entire industries much of their architecture has gone, and whole ways of life. Complete districts have been laid waste, and hundreds of thousands have emigrated from the Liverpool conurbation, urban depopulation on a scale without equal in Britain. In the last fifteen years, though, the revival that has emerged unevenly across the post-industrialised North has begun to gather momentum here. Wigan town centre has been spruced up and the once-grimy streets of terracotta and brick are now shining in smog-free air. Warrington New Town has swollen prosperously, fuelled by the motorway network. The core of Liverpool, a decade behind Manchester, is finally benefiting from sustained investment, transforming it on a wave – hopefully not a bubble – of optimism and confidence. But that is not to underestimate the scale or depth of deprivation still. A walk N from Lime Street Station will soon dispel any notion that Liverpool's thriving centre reflects a fully rejuvenated region.

Finally, a note on boundaries. This book covers the SW part of the historic county of Lancashire, and corresponds for the most part to the West Derby Hundred. The border to the W is of course the Irish Sea; to the S it is the River Mersey, except for a salient into old Cheshire to encompass that part of Warrington New Town S of the Manchester Ship Canal. (Since 1974 the whole area of Warrington Borough Council, which is mainly N of the Canal and comes within this guide, has in fact been part of Cheshire.) The E boundary up from the Mersey is that of Warrington Borough Council (but including Woolden), then that of Wigan Metropolitan Borough Council. This council's boundary is followed W, around Wigan itself, to the River Douglas and the Leeds and Liverpool Canal. From here the canal is followed W to Burscough, and thence the boundary is W across Halsall Moss to the coast N of Formby. Therefore the guide encompasses settlements in the area of West Lancashire District Council S of this line, and excludes that part of the West Derby Hundred N of it.*

GEOLOGY AND BUILDING STONES

BY FRED BROADHURST

The materials found directly beneath the soils over most of SW Lancashire consist mainly of unconsolidated clays, sands and peat, collectively known as Superficial Deposits. They are also frequently referred to as Drift because the material was once thought to be the debris from a great flood. The SUPERFICIAL DEPOSITS include material of glacial origin, formed mostly during the course of the last (Devensian) of the Pleistocene glaciations (2 million–10,000 years ago), and post-glacial material formed since, consisting of gravels in river terraces, windblown sands, peat, etc. The Superficial Deposits are of variable thickness up to about 260 ft (80 metres), but in some places are missing, owing either to non-deposition or to erosion, and here the underlying bedrock is exposed at the surface.

The BEDROCK (also known as 'Solid' rocks) consists mostly of stratified ancient sediments, some of which (the older) belong to the Carboniferous Period of geological time (360–290 million years ago), and the rest (younger) to the Permian and Triassic periods (290–210 million years ago). The Carboniferous rocks include many tough sandstones and so form the higher ground of the region, for instance in the Ramsbottom area (SE Lancashire). In contrast the Permian-Triassic rocks are generally much less resistant to erosion and form the lowlands of the Lancashire–Cheshire plain.

---

*The text of this volume covering the centre of Liverpool and its environs has been condensed and adapted from that of the Pevsner City Guide, *Liverpool* (2004).

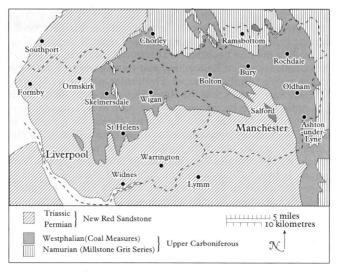

Sketch geological map of South Lancashire and surrounding area

The outcrop of the CARBONIFEROUS ROCKS in SW Lancashire includes the area of the Lancashire Coalfield, around
Skelmersdale, Wigan and St Helens, and adjacent areas of
outcrop of the Millstone Grit, notably in the higher ground
around Chorley (N Lancashire), N of the coalfield. These
Carboniferous rocks contain ancient sediments with evidence of
deposition from a vast river system carrying sediment from the
N into an enormous deltaic complex across northern England
and adjacent areas. The delta, far larger in extent than any
modern delta anywhere in the world, was associated with a region
of major subsidence. Evidence from the rocks indicates a
continuity of shallow water conditions showing that deposition
kept up with subsidence. On numerous occasions sediment was
built up to water level and plant growth led to the formation of
peat, which, on burial by later sediment, was transformed into
coal. The total thickness of Carboniferous sediment accumulated
in this way in SW Lancashire was probably about three miles. The
evidence of magnetism in the rocks (palaeomagnetism) indicates
formation at or close to the Equator, so the coal seams are
interpreted as tropical swamp deposits. The magnetic and other
evidence indicate that Britain and adjacent areas have drifted
from the Equator to their present latitudes over a period of about
300 million years, a conclusion consistent with the geological
concept of Plate Tectonics, involving drifting continents and
ocean floors.

The Carboniferous in SW Lancashire contains a number of
sandstones, many of them formed in braided river systems which
led to the development of individual sandstone strata over large
areas. Other sandstones were developed as channel deposits, so

have a limited distribution. The rocks of the Lancashire Coalfield (the Coal Measures or Westphalian) are rich in coal, whereas the underlying sequence (Namurian) is rich in sandstones and was formerly known as the Millstone Grit. Both the Coal Measures and the Millstone Grit contain tough and erosion-resistant sandstones suitable for building. They contain a silica cement which occupies a substantial part of the pore space within the rock. This silicification appears to be related to the depth to which the sandstones have been buried. When fresh the sandstones are white or light grey but on weathering develop an attractive, brownish colour due to oxidation and hydration of the small amount of iron minerals present. The Carboniferous rocks also contain clayrocks (or 'shales') from which bricks can be made.

Carboniferous sandstones have long been used as building stones, at first locally, but later over a wide area as the construction of canals and railways allowed transportation over significant distances at an acceptable cost. The stone was used for buildings, walling, dam construction and, in the form of thin slabs (flagstones), as material for roofing ('grey slates') and for paving. Many of the mills and workers' houses associated with the Industrial Revolution were constructed with these materials. In the case of flagstones a number of quarries were converted to mines as overburden cover became excessive. The Haslingden Flags around Ramsbottom were particularly important as a source of flagstones, good examples of which can be seen in the paving on the N side of William Brown Street, Liverpool. The Museum, Library and Art Gallery on William Brown Street 79, 77 together with St George's Hall, Lime Street, Liverpool, are good examples of the use of Carboniferous sandstone, though mostly not from Lancashire.

The close of the Carboniferous Period is associated with a major change in the tectonic setting of northern England. The subsidence, which had allowed the accumulation of the thick stack of Carboniferous sediment, was replaced by uplift, in a process described as inversion. The change in late Carboniferous tectonics is associated with collisions between continents elsewhere in the world. These collisions completed a process of continental aggregation to form a single supercontinent, to which the name of Pangaea has been given.

Inversion brought the Carboniferous deposits back up towards the surface, where they were subjected to weathering and erosion under the desert conditions of the Permian-Triassic. The erosion supplied the sediment for accumulation as the (Permian-Triassic) New Red Sandstone.

In SW Lancashire the Carboniferous strata are generally inclined downwards towards Cheshire and eventually disappear beneath the cover of the Permian-Triassic red rocks, the NEW RED SANDSTONES (which occur *above* the Carboniferous, as distinct from the Old Red Sandstones which occur *below* the Carboniferous). Some of these rocks indicate deposition in the form of sand dunes, others in stream channels, revealing that the region was a land area. The lower (older) strata are rich in sandstone (some suitable as building stone), the higher (younger) rich in clays and silts and with substantial deposits of salt. The highest and youngest strata of the Triassic have been removed by erosion in SW Lancashire. Magnetic evidence indicates deposition at about 10 degrees latitude during the Permian, but 30 degrees by the time of the Triassic. This is further evidence of the northward migration of SW Lancashire (and adjacent areas) from the Equator after the Carboniferous. By the Permian and Triassic the region had reached the latitudes characteristic of today's Sahara Desert. The fossil sand dunes even provide evidence of a prevailing north-easterly wind, the equivalent of today's Trade Winds in the northern hemisphere. The New Red Sandstone channel sediments have features characteristic of flood deposits, which can be recognised in modern deserts and which result from flash floods. The higher and younger strata in the New Red Sandstone sequence contain deposits of rocks rich in clay, silt and, notably, rock salt and gypsum. Such evaporite deposits are forming today in the playa lakes and saline lagoons of modern deserts.

Deposition of the Permian-Triassic (New Red Sandstones) in Britain took place in detached basins, each related to a fault system involving crustal extension and rifting. Deposition of sediment took place as the faulting developed. The Cheshire Basin is an excellent example of such a rift-basin, and contains sediment more than $1\frac{1}{2}$ m. in thickness. The crustal extension is related to the break-up of the supercontinent Pangaea, the fragments of which were gradually separated by the formation of new ocean floor, ultimately producing the geography of the world in which we live today.

In terms of building stones in the Permian-Triassic, the sandstones are of great interest. In general, they are much less resistant to erosion than the Carboniferous rocks. They have not been subjected to deep burial and lack the quantities of silica cement so characteristic of the Carboniferous sandstones. However, before the development of canals and railways these red rocks were the only building materials available locally at reasonable cost. The younger (but still Triassic) Helsby Sandstone is tougher than most of its Triassic associates and at outcrop is resistant enough to form low escarpments in Cheshire, such as Helsby Hill and Alderley Edge. The stone was worked extensively on the Wirral and at Runcorn and Lymm. The Anglican Cathedral in Liverpool is an excellent example of the use of this stone, which came from the Woolton Quarry, five miles away.

To the S of SW Lancashire, around Wem and Whitchurch, close to the Cheshire/Shropshire boundary, there is a small area underlain by JURASSIC rocks. These rocks contain marine fossils indicating deposition on a sea floor. Detail of the rock sequence can be matched with that of the main Jurassic outcrop in the Midlands and beyond. It is clear that the Cheshire Jurassic was once continuous with that of SE England but has been isolated by erosion. Research on detrital grains of apatite (a calcium phosphate mineral) in the Permian-Triassic of NW England has established the maximum temperatures to which the apatite grains have been exposed. These temperatures, in turn, provide evidence of the depth to which the apatite has been buried (in this case by a cover of Jurassic and younger sediments). It appears that in the s Lancashire region a cover of post-Triassic sediments up to about 1¼ m. is likely. The uplift required to bring about this erosion probably occurred at the end of the Cretaceous (about 70 million years ago) – at a time when the North Atlantic Ocean was opening, the ongoing process of the break-up of Pangaea. The evidence from the apatite grains indicates that the end-Cretaceous uplift was centred on the middle of the Irish Sea area, and maximum erosion occurred here. This uplift (probably associated with the ascent, underground, of molten rock, a potential volcano) was apparently responsible for the general south-easterly tilt seen in the rock strata from the Jurassic up to the early Tertiary in s and E England. Later, the elevated region of the Irish Sea area collapsed to form the marine basin seen today. Further volcanicity to the N developed in response to tension to form the volcanic centres of Antrim and the Western Isles of Scotland. However, this volcanic activity failed to develop into an extension of the North Atlantic and it was replaced by successful fracture w of Ireland. The final opening of the North Atlantic has been linked to a general tilting of the British Isles, up in the N and w, down to the s and E. Erosion in the uplifted N and w of Britain has exposed ancient tough rocks in contrast to the young and easily eroded rocks of the s and E. The great variety of landscape in the British Isles owes its existence to this tilting process, a process which still continues, though its effects are masked by the changes in sea and land levels caused by the melting of ice sheets at the close of the Devensian ice sheets 'only' some 10,000 years ago.

The post-Triassic rocks of the s of England have provided some of the C20 building stones to be seen in sw Lancashire. In particular, reference must be made to the Portland Stone of Dorset, a late Jurassic (about 150 million years old) white limestone, oolitic in nature and containing many fossils. An excellent example of its use is the Cunard Building on the waterfront at the Pierhead in Liverpool.

A worldwide cooling of the climate during the Tertiary Period, combined with continuing northwards migration, eventually brought Britain within range of ice sheets from the Arctic. The earliest glaciation is linked to the commencement of the Pleistocene Epoch (and the Quaternary Sub-Era) about 2 million years ago. Subsequent warmer intervals and further glaciations followed climatic changes which are linked to astronomical controls on the amount of radiation reaching Earth from the Sun. Such climatic cycles are known as Milankovitch Cycles (after the work of Milutin Milankovitch in the 1920s–30s). The last glaciation (Devensian, named after the Roman town of Deva, the modern Chester) ended about 10,000 years ago, and at present we are enjoying the warmer interval that followed. Future glaciations are certain (unless brought under human control).

The PLEISTOCENE DEPOSITS of SW Lancashire include layers of clay with boulders, the so-called boulder clay, or till, deposited directly from ice sheets. This material (together with the clayrocks of the Carboniferous) is a source of clay for brick manufacture. Sands generated from melt-waters associated with shrinking ice are common and include the Chelford Sands of Cheshire, used for the manufacture of glass. Postglacial deposits include river terrace materials, important for the production of gravel and also peat, which until recently was an important ingredient in compost and products used to improve soils.

Up to the time of the Industrial Revolution the construction of permanent buildings relied on stone for support and decoration. However, during the Industrial Revolution the frequency of fires in the mills seriously raised the cost of fire insurance and resort was made to the incorporation of CAST-IRON FRAMES in buildings to reduce the scale of damage in the event of fire. By the start of the C20 the price of STEEL had fallen to such a level that steel could be used in preference to cast iron. At this stage stone (or brick) was no longer needed for the main structural support in buildings. Buildings with a steel frame could now be clad with thin panels of natural stone, the purpose of which was limited to decoration and waterproofing. As the cost of this stone was now a smaller proportion of the total building cost, it was possible to utilise attractive materials from all parts of the world. This has produced a situation where the oldest buildings in any given town or village reflect the local geology, later buildings reflect the improvements in transport that have taken place and the youngest buildings, based on steel frames, are covered with cladding stone from all corners of the world. Architects are all selecting stone from the same high-quality worldwide sources, so the new buildings have a cosmopolitan aspect. Most towns in SW Lancashire contain examples of buildings clad with natural stone. Liverpool contains many such buildings; for example, No. 19 Water Street is faced with larvikite from S Norway, while State House, Dale Street, is faced with gabbro from South Africa.* In recent years the production of block stone for building has been replaced to some extent by production of aggregate for use in the preparation of concrete blocks, curbstones, etc., and referred to as reconstituted stone.

A good introduction to the geology of SW Lancashire is included in Aitkenhead et al., 2002 (*see* Further Reading). Especially useful are geological maps at the scale of 1:50,000 published by the British Geological Survey. Individual areas are covered by 'Drift', or 'Solid', or 'Solid and Drift' editions. The 'Solid' editions show the distribution of the bedrock formations as they would be seen if the Superficial Deposits were removed.

---

* *Rock around Liverpool: A Geological Guide to the Building Stones of the City Centre*, Liverpool Geological Society, 2001. Building stones used in the C18 and C19 are discussed in G.H. Morton, *The Geology of the Country around Liverpool, including the North of Flintshire*, 1891.

PREHISTORIC SOUTH-WEST LANCASHIRE

BY R.W. COWELL

The earliest recorded occupation of the area is after *c.* 10,000 years ago, at the end of the last Ice Age. After the final retreat of the ice the physical landscape of SW Lancashire was considerably different from that of today. The coast lay much further to the W, leaving a belt of land about six to nine miles wide which has been lost to subsequent sea-level rise, along with many archaeological occupation sites that no doubt once existed in this zone. By *c.* 9,500 years ago the landscape was clothed in open woodland of pine, birch and hazel, through which bands of mobile hunters and gatherers moved. This was the period known as the MESOLITHIC, which lasted until about 6,000 years ago.

Sites of the early prehistoric period are usually recognised by concentrations of stone tools found on ploughed farmland and other exposed surfaces. The earliest sites, probably over 9,000 years old, are found on the higher areas of the Wirral. These tell us that the early Mesolithic hunters spent part of their year in North Wales, where they found stone, specifically chert, which they brought back to the Wirral to make their tools. There may be one similar site in our region, at Little Crosby, where tools are made from the same kind of chert. Another possible site is known close to Simonswood Moss, and a small camp has been excavated in the uplands at Anglezarke, near Chorley (N Lancashire).

The next several thousand years represent a period of changing environment, involving a rise in sea level and an increase in precipitation. By about 7,500 years ago, when Britain had been an island for several hundred years, the sea level had risen significantly in SW Lancashire, and for short periods marine conditions even extended to the E of the present coastline. Inland of this new coastal zone waterlogging took place, with the spread of swamp and fen. A belt of former wetlands, now mainly farmland, existed along virtually the whole of the W Lancashire coast S of Martin Mere. Inland they also formed in poorly drained hollows from Kirkby, through Knowsley and Simonswood to Rainford, with a belt of wetlands skirting the W of Manchester and Bolton.

The greatest concentration of sites is in the coastal zone, particularly around the estuary of the River Alt, extending N through Halsall, with a large site at Banks near Southport. Here the wetlands provided rich environments for hunters and gatherers with seasonal, widespread availability of fish, wild birds and plants. Many later Mesolithic sites represent various kinds of small, short-stay activities associated with hunting and gathering expeditions, such as bivouacs, hunting stands, kill and butchering sites. These appear to be the main type of site inland. An important environment was provided by the major river valleys flowing through the region, with sites recorded in the Alt-Ditton valley near Widnes and the Douglas (chiefly in N Lancashire). Sometimes, as in the valleys of the Ditton, or Croxteth Brook, NE of

Liverpool, repeated short-stay visits were made to the same location. Sites here have been excavated and produced evidence of
small occupations, with between 200 and 500 pieces of struck
flint, based around natural hollows, probably formed by uprooted
trees. The tools include a few arrowheads and implements that
may have been used for piercing or scraping various materials.

Because of the need to be mobile, particularly where resources
were less predictable, hunter-gatherer groups are thought to have
spent part of their annual round in the uplands. The Pennines
have the greatest concentration of Mesolithic sites in the country.
They are found mainly between the 1,200 ft (366 metre) and
1,600 ft (488 metre) contours, probably at the upper level of the
forest edge, with the greatest concentration in a fairly restricted
area between Saddleworth and Marsden, where the uplands are
at their narrowest. A lowland site at Mawdsley, on the edge of a
former wetland about nine miles W of the Pennines, includes
about 400 stone tools or waste pieces, of which about three-
quarters are made from a dark chert similar to that used on
many later Mesolithic Pennine sites, suggesting that people were
frequenting both environments.

Agriculture was introduced into Britain about 6,000 years ago,
in the NEOLITHIC period. However, in this region there are no
great changes in the centuries during which agriculture became
established. Settlement sites are still small, and are found in many
of the same places as previously, and some of the stone tools
found on them differ little from those used by hunter-gatherers.
The landscape was also still heavily wooded with little sign of
extensive clearance for farming. However, new, specifically
Neolithic structures appear in Britain, associated with large
public and ritual sites, at about the same time. In the North West
they are found outside our area, an example being the damaged
communal burial long mound known as the Pikestones on
Anglezarke Moor, near Chorley.

Polished stone axes, the main recognisable new stone tool of
this period, are relatively common across the region, with concentrations of finds from N Wirral, Liverpool and Warrington, as
might be expected from areas with large-scale urban development. Axes are also found on the E fringes, along the Pennine
slopes. The polished axes are the easiest way to trace the networks of Neolithic exchange in this area. A number, such as those
from Little Crosby, are made from stone from so-called 'factory'
sites in Cumbria, while others originate in North Wales. A
particularly evocative illustration that farming changed lives little
in the early stages comes from prehistoric human and animal
footprints, including aurochs, red deer and roe deer in beach
sediments at Formby Point, which are testament to hunting
episodes in Mesolithic and early Neolithic intertidal environments. On the beach to the S, near Hightown, a length of wooden
trackway, about 4 ft 6 in. (1.4 metres) wide, has been traced
over a distance of c. 200 ft (60 metres). Radiocarbon dates show
that this was also of early Neolithic date. During the late
Neolithic period, after c. 4,800 years ago, the sea level was gen-

erally lower and bones of red deer, boar and cattle have been found close to the trackway on the present beach, in peat associated with the remains of a former forest of this date. By c. 4,000 years ago, the coastline had approximately stabilised in its present position.

The LATE NEOLITHIC period marks significant social changes, with intensification of settlement, land use and artefact production, long-distance networks in place, increased regional interaction, particularly in the realm of ritual and ceremony, and indications of the existence of social hierarchies. Recent aerial photography has potentially identified the first known communal ritual monument in the region, known as a henge, at Halsall. There was also an important burial site, known as the Calderstones, in Liverpool. The site was destroyed in the C19 but six stones survived and are now in an ornamental greenhouse in the adjacent Calderstones Park. The stones appear to have belonged to a structure known as a passage grave, and have spiral carvings on them that show stylistic links with surviving passage graves in Anglesey and Western Ireland. Such monuments are the best guide to the emergence of centres for social groupings based on defined territories.

After c. 4,500 years ago, the introduction of bronze metalwork and single burials under round mounds known as barrows, often with personal grave goods and associated with new styles of pottery, become the dominant feature. These changes suggest that the late Neolithic culminated in a different kind of society, with an emphasis on personal prestige and display: the EARLY BRONZE AGE.

The largest concentrations of these burials come from the Pennines, often being located above c. 820 ft (250 metres), although several do occur in the lower reaches of valleys, particularly around Bolton. In the lowlands identifiable burial sites are fewer, at least partly because of the greater pressure of agriculture and urban development. There are burial sites at Astley Hall, Chorley and at Ribchester (both in N Lancashire), both of which have produced multiple cremations with collared urns, although only fragmentary barrow structures were recovered, particularly at the latter site. A group of burials lies to the N of Warrington, around Winwick, with five barrows in an area of about one-and-a-half square miles. Several have been excavated, the most productive from NW of Southworth Hall Farm. This revealed a two-phase monument with concentric circles of stake holes beneath the mound and multiple cremations, mostly unassociated with pottery, except for one with a food vessel and two with collared urns and an accessory cup. The radiocarbon dates for the two phases spanned c. 400 years, between approximately the C18 and C14 B.C. Further along the Mersey valley, a site destroyed in the C19 at Wavertree, Liverpool, consisted of eight burial urns with burnt bones, of which only two collared urns have survived, with no record of an accompanying structure.

It is the coastal areas again which have the best evidence for settlement of this period. There are two localities, represented by

Liverpool, the Calderstones, before relocation.
Drawing by William Lathom, 1825

late Neolithic or early Bronze Age stone tools, at Hale on the
lower Mersey and at Little Crosby. They cover larger areas than
earlier settlements, and have a greater density of stone tools, of
a very different character. The nature of these sites suggests,
however, that rather than being permanent settlements, they may
have been formed by many repeated visits. There are also many
sites across sw Lancashire where only single finds of flint scra-
pers or knives occur. These two characteristics suggest that even
in the Bronze Age mobility was still an important element of land
use. The few excavated sites do not reveal evidence for large-scale
occupation. At Tarbock, E of Liverpool, Beaker pottery and fired
clay, possibly from an oven, was found in a deposit of burnt
stones in a short segment of excavated ditch, with a radiocarbon
date 4,070–3,630 years ago. At Kirkby, N of Liverpool, a small,
irregular structure was formed by two discontinuous stretches of
shallow gully, with fragments from a collared urn and radiocarbon dates 3,900–3,360 years ago. In a similar river valley location, overlooking the Ditton Brook in Tarbock, on the site of a
Mesolithic occupation, even less distinct traces of settlement
were located in the form of two small pits, with Bronze Age
pottery and a radiocarbon date of 3,570–3,080 years ago.

The nature of settlement and land use in the region in the LATE
BRONZE AGE (c. 3,000 years ago) is still largely unknown. From
this point until the appearance of the Roman army in the later
CI A.D., material culture, particularly the use of pottery, is sparse
everywhere in the region. It may have been that in this period
the movement began towards what, today, we might more readily
recognise as farmsteads, perhaps associated with changes in
social organisation. However, such patterns in the North West are
not easy to see, and the main evidence for the late Bronze Age
relates to scattered metalwork finds. They occur around the
mouth of the Mersey and are marginally more frequent in the
upland river valleys N of the Manchester embayment. The exceptions are two hoards just N of our area, at Portfield Camp

(Whalley), probably a smith's hoard, and at Winmarleigh, which has a proportion of weapons in it. Such a metalwork pattern has been interpreted as representing a low or unwealthy population, and the lack of weapon finds suggests that social stratification may not have been as marked as in other areas.

Hillforts, the most typical feature of the settlement pattern in a number of areas in the LATE BRONZE AGE/IRON AGE, *c.* 2,700 years ago, are rarely found in the North West, outside N Cheshire and North Wales. This may be a reflection of a different kind of social organisation in this area. The settlement pattern is now much better understood in the region than it was in the mid 1990s, with the recent excavation of six farmstead sites, three of which lie in SW Lancashire. They date from the period after *c.* 300 B.C., which nationally saw an expansion of settlement and woodland clearance and an intensification of land use. At Brook House Farm, Halewood, two concentric ditches, *c.* 115 ft (35 metres) apart, enclose a roughly D-shaped area of *c.* 4 acres (1.5 hectares). Incomplete structures relating to grain storage and ancillary buildings are known from the interior, along with short sections of boundary gullies, perhaps marking building or other activity plots, and pits that may have been used for storage and rubbish disposal. Most of these contained very fine debris from ironworking and a small amount of pottery, known as Cheshire VCP (Very Coarse Pottery), which is associated with the transport and use of salt, probably from central Cheshire, around Middlewich and Nantwich. The massive inner ditch, which probably had a large earthen bank fronting it, appears less like a

Lathom.
Reconstruction of a round-house excavated at Duttons Farm, *c.* C1–C2 B.C.

defensive feature than a social statement of prestige. The outer ditch was much less massive, and formed an enclosure that may have allowed cattle to be corralled between the two ditch circuits. A small assemblage of cattle and pig bones was found in the inner ditch, some with signs of butchering. The site overlooks a regularly flooded valley floor, which also implies that grazing for animals may have been important. Another farm of very similar form and setting lies about 15 miles to the E, at Great Woolden Hall, Woolden, which also has links to the Cheshire salt-producing areas.

The other main farmstead in the area, at Duttons Farm, Lathom, appears to have been a very different kind of settlement. It lies in good farmland, on a small area of well-drained sand, which probably included a spring. This is surrounded by heavier clayland and the former wetlands of Hoscar Moss. There are four adjacent roundhouses spanning the period from c. 200 B.C. to the early Romano-British period. The largest is 35 ft (10.5 metres) in diameter, with a double entrance, and adjoining small fields or paddocks of possible late Iron Age date. There are also two granary buildings, a number of storage pits, and a quernstone for grinding corn, made from stone from the central Pennines. There is no trace, however, of an enclosure ditch. Although cattle bones do not survive in the acid sand subsoil, it does appear as if arable farming may have been more important here than on other sites so far recognised in the region.

SOUTH-WEST LANCASHIRE FROM THE ROMAN CONQUEST TO THE MIDDLE AGES

BY ROBERT A. PHILPOTT

The Roman Period, A.D. 43–410

At the time of the Roman occupation, the North of England was occupied by a broad confederation of tribes called the Brigantes or 'upland people'. SW Lancashire may have been the home of a sub-tribe known as the Setantii from the name of their harbour, Portus Setantiorum, which appears to have been located near the mouth of the River Wyre at Fleetwood (N Lancashire). After the Roman conquest of southern Britain, the Brigantes became a client kingdom. The relationship was fraught and the Roman army had to intervene on several occasions to restore order. Evidence of their military activities is difficult to trace, but coin finds in the region dating from the reigns of the emperors Claudius (A.D. 41–54) and Nero (A.D. 54–68), are probably a legacy of these early Roman attempts to bring peace.

By the early 70s A.D. the Brigantes were finally brought into the province of Britannia, and within a few years SW Lancashire was ringed by a series of Roman FORTS. No certain fort is known within SW Lancashire itself. The legionary headquarters was established at Chester to the S, to the E a fort was constructed at

Manchester, while other forts were built at Ribchester to the N
and Northwich to the SE. Until recently it was considered that
Roman SW Lancashire was a virtually uninhabited area of woodland and marsh. However, evidence from pollen trapped in peat
deposits indicates that a good proportion of the land had been
cleared of trees, and recent archaeological work (*see* above) has
revealed a network of small farms across the region. The Roman
army also required good communications, and MILITARY ROADS
represent the backbone of the system. SW Lancashire was crossed
by a road linking the forts at Middlewich and Lancaster which
passed through settlements at Wilderspool and Wigan. From
Wilderspool a road ran SW to Chester while another road ran E
from Wigan to Manchester. Sections of the main N–S road have
been excavated at Newton-le-Willows and Winwick. They show
the road had a foundation of clean sand on which was laid a layer
of pebbles; on this in turn was set a layer of flattish sandstone
slabs and finally a thin surface layer of gravel. The road measured
about 15 ft (4.5 metres) wide and had side ditches to drain surface
water. By contrast the minor roads and trackways which linked
local communities with the wider world have proved much more
difficult to find. However, excavations at Duttons Farm, Lathom
(*see* also above) revealed an unsurfaced Roman trackway complete with deep wheel-ruts partly infilled with gravel, which was
probably a local track heading for a ford across the River Tawd.

In the late C1 substantial SETTLEMENTS grew up at Wigan and
at Wilderspool. The latter, on the main N–S road, owed its importance to its position at the lowest bridging point on the S bank
of the Mersey. There may have been an earlier fort on the opposite bank but the site has proved elusive. Numerous finds first
brought the settlement to attention in the mid C18. Excavations
in 1895–1905 on the Greenall's Brewery site located hearths, furnaces for iron, bronze and glass working, and remains of large
timber buildings marked by post-holes and slots for beams.
During the 1960s–70s and 1990s further excavations at the
Brewery and at Loushers Lane produced extensive traces of large
rectangular timber buildings, which had the appearance of workshops. More sophisticated stone buildings are indicated by a
Corinthian stone capital found in 1976 at Loushers Lane which
possibly adorned a temple, while quantities of roof tiles, the
classic Roman *tegulae* and *imbrices*, may have roofed other
substantial structures.

During the C2 pottery kilns at Stockton Heath near
Wilderspool were in production making *mortaria* (internally
gritted grinding bowls) as well as other vessels. The settlement
as a whole was industrial, producing pottery, glass, iron, bronze
and other metal items for the military market further N. The
goods were shipped via the Mersey though we need not expect
permanent harbour installations. The settlement flourished from
c. A.D. 90 through the C2, but by the C3 a reduction in military
demand brought about a sharp decline.

Roman Wigan is much less well known. A cremation burial,
together with finds of coins, pottery and other items in the C19,

suggested that Wigan was the site of the Roman *Coccium*, listed in the Antonine Itinerary, a Roman route-book compiled in the early C3. It was only when excavations took place in the Wiend in the 1980s that Roman timber buildings were revealed, dated by associated pottery to the late C1 or early C2, with several later phases of rebuilding. More recently a hypocaust was uncovered. The town was built on a coalfield and coal was exploited both in the Roman town and also in farmsteads outside. Wigan may have served as an industrial and manufacturing centre for the army, in common with Wilderspool, perhaps Walton-le-Dale at the Darwen–Ribble confluence (N Lancashire), and other Roman towns of the Cheshire plain, but further work is required to confirm this.

There is little doubt that the Roman plantation of towns, perhaps under military supervision, and the arrival of workers and artisans from outside the area, must have led to a rise in demand for food and raw materials. This would have been met in part from newly established farms in the countryside. Romano-British FARMSTEAD SITES are known across virtually the whole area, from Ince Blundell in the W to Ashton-in-Makerfield in the N with a particular concentration N and W of Warrington in the Mersey valley, especially in the area of Newton and Winwick. Most have been observed through aerial reconnaissance during dry conditions, when the enclosing ditches around the farms form distinctive marks in crops. Others have been identified from thin scatters of Roman pottery in the fields, or by chance in building developments. Over the last twenty years well over a dozen enclosed settlements have been found within the area, including a square enclosure at Southworth, near Winwick, where excavations revealed a farmstead occupied in the C2. Further N, at Lathom, an Iron Age farmstead remained in use into the Roman period, maintaining the traditional style of roundhouse.

The enclosed settlements took different forms in plan, with square, rectangular and oval examples all being noted. All types are associated with Romano-British pottery and finds when examined in detail. The forms may be related to the type of agricultural regime, square enclosures fitting better into a network of ploughed arable fields, while curvilinear boundaries may have been more suited to pastoral activity and stock rearing. One of the more unexpected sites is a hamlet at Court Farm, Halewood, where well over a dozen buildings were found dating from the C2–C4. The style of building is unusual, with houses of figure-of-eight plan, like two conjoined roundhouses, with a door in the middle of the long side. This type appears to be a local development and has been also found at Wilderspool and Tarbock. Settlements like Court Farm may have been more common than we realise, but the lack of enclosing ditches means they do not show up from the air.

Romano-British INDUSTRIAL PRODUCTION has also been found in the countryside. At Ochre Brook, Tarbock, what seemed at first to be a simple farmstead produced a large quantity of distorted roof tile, clearly the rejects from manufacturing, although the kilns were not located. Some of the tiles bore the stamp of the 20th Legion at Chester, including several examples of the only dated tile stamp from Roman Britain, corresponding to A.D. 167. The stamp also provides the name of a rare identifiable individual from the region, one Aulus Viducus, who worked as a contractor for the legion.

The period leading up to and beyond the collapse of Roman authority in A.D. 410 remains deeply obscure in this area. Wigan and Wilderspool declined in importance in the C3 and from then on the native population becomes increasingly difficult to identify as the use of datable objects such as pottery and coins diminishes. It is assumed that the native British population continued to farm much as before but that the rapid economic collapse meant that manufactured goods were no longer available.

The Early Medieval Period, 410–1066

Small KINGDOMS developed in the immediate post-Roman period but their names and extent are uncertain. Some have suggested that Makerfield (containing Ashton, Newton and Ince) was an early British lordship, and the place has a concentration of British (i.e. Celtic) place names such as Bryn, Penketh or Culcheth, which developed in the period before the Anglo-Saxon linguistic and social domination of the region. A regularly laid-out inhumation cemetery with over 800 grave pits over a mile from the parish church at Winwick probably began in this period. The cemetery, which was excavated in advance of quarrying in 1980, probably served a Christian community. A few place-names such as Eccleston in St Helens indicate the survival of other Christian communities in this obscure period, and early churches at the head of very large parishes such as Prescot, Childwall or Walton may represent some of the oldest post-Roman centres. Circular churchyards have been used as an indicator of Early Christian sites, with examples at Prescot, Winwick and Melling, though this is not an infallible rule.

ANGLO-SAXON involvement in the North West was late by comparison with the S and E of England. Rivalry between the Anglo-Saxon kingdoms of Mercia and Northumbria during the C7 was resolved with adoption of the Mersey as the southern boundary of Northumbria in 678. Anglo-Saxon place names ending in '-ing' or '-tun', such as Billinge, Atherton or Cronton, indicate the location of settlements, although the modern settlements may not always occupy the original site. Otherwise, archaeological evidence for this period is sparse. Durable metal objects were rare and were recycled when broken, pottery was probably not used at all, and the timber buildings have left little trace in the ground. Rare archaeological evidence of the early medieval period was recovered at Court Farm, Halewood, where a ditch and pits were dug across the disused Roman site. A radio-carbon determination from a pointed wooden stake in the base of a pit dated to the C9, but although the ditch probably formed an enclosure around a settlement, no recognisably Anglo-Saxon buildings were present.

From the late 860s the Danish conquest of York brought Northumbria and eastern Mercia under the Danelaw, the region of eastern England subject to Danish control. The Viking settlement of sw Lancashire and neighbouring Wirral probably also began in the C9. Viking place names are concentrated in the w part of the area in the coastal zone of Sefton. Physical traces are, however, harder to find. One of the most important Viking finds was a hoard of at least eighty coins found at Harkirk, Little Crosby, in 1611. The coins were subsequently lost, but study of drawings of them suggested that the hoard was buried c. 910. Elsewhere, two carved jet pieces for the game *hnefatafl* of Anglo-Scandinavian type were found beneath the Norman castle at Mote Hill, Warrington. The other main survivals from this period are carved stones which betray Viking influence in the design. Fragments of crosses are known from Aughton (C9 *p. 680* cross-head), Winwick (the C10 arm of a massive ring-headed cross) and Walton-on-the-Hill (a cross-shaft), significantly pointing to the pre-Conquest origin of the parish churches there.

Norse settlement left a legacy of place names and dialect words. Some indicate settlements with churches, as at Kirkby or Ormskirk; a number of '-by' names denote farms or larger settlements, such as West Derby, while minor place names such as The Scholes at Eccleston indicate a Viking 'shieling-hut', a seasonal shelter for pasturing animals. Two place names are of particular significance to the Viking settlers. Thingwall, from the Old Norse *thing-vollr*, meaning 'meeting mound' and identical in origin to the Manx Tynwald, may have stood on the low hill where the present Thingwall Hall now stands, while Roby, Old Norse for 'boundary village', may have marked the limit of an enclave of Viking settlers in sw Lancashire.

The Later Medieval Period, 1066–1500

After the Norman Conquest the powerful new landowners constructed motte-and-bailey CASTLES at the chief places in each Hundred to stamp their authority on the local population. A castle was constructed at Warrington near the crossing of the Roman road over the Mersey, on a site probably in use in the Anglo-Saxon period. At both West Derby and Newton-le-Willows, Roger de Poitou constructed a timber castle on an earthen mound (motte), with ancillary buildings within an outer enclosure (the bailey). The motte at Newton survives at Castle Hill while that at West Derby was levelled in 1817, only its name being preserved in Castlesite Road. Earlier C20 excavations across the West Derby moat revealed the footings of a timber bridge.

Newton-le-Willows, Castle Hill.
Drawing, 1843

The administrative functions and the population of West
Derby were soon transferred to the new royal borough of
LIVERPOOL, on a sandstone eminence beside the tidal inlet,
the Pool, which had been made a borough by King John in 1207.
Liverpool Castle was constructed *c.* 1235 by William de Ferrers.
The castle was surrounded by a moat and had turreted curtain
walls connecting four towers, and enclosing a courtyard. A document of 1347 enumerates the buildings: a hall, chapel, brew-
house, bakehouse and a covered well within the central courtyard.
A drawbridge and gatehouse formed the main entrance. The
remains were demolished in 1726 for the construction of St
George's church. Of medieval Liverpool nothing can now be seen
above ground, but the modern street plan preserves the medieval
core of seven streets in an H-plan beside the tidal Pool.

A number of other places were granted market or borough
CHARTERS. Borough charters are recorded at Wigan (1246),
Ormskirk (*c.* 1286) and Warrington (pre-1233), while other places
have the attributes of a medieval borough – such as burgage plots
and tenure – without the charter surviving (Prescot pre-1537,
West Derby by 1237, Newton by 1311, Hale by 1323, Widnes by
1355, and Farnworth by 1395). Some of these places, such as
Prescot, Warrington or Ormskirk, were located where people
already congregated to attend parish churches, and local lords
attempted to profit from the informal trading which was already
going on. Wigan received its charter as a royal borough in 1246
thanks to the efforts of John Mansell, rector and lord of the
manor. By the c16 Wigan had considerable local autonomy, with
a mayor and corporation. Other charters were granted as speculative ventures, to stimulate new trade and exchange, as at Newburgh and Hale. By no means all of these grew into successful
towns, and the harsh economic climate of the late medieval
period weeded out the weaker ones. The borough of Roby, for

example, was granted a charter in 1372 by Sir Thomas de
Lathom. Excavations showed medieval occupation and associated C14 and C15 pottery, as well as a series of large pits, possibly for tanning, but there is no pottery beyond the C15 on several
plots, and the earliest C18 maps suggest that the borough had
shrunk to a small village by the end of the medieval period. Some
other places of early importance fell into decline. West Derby was
rapidly overshadowed by Liverpool, its population fell, and by
1297 cattle were grazing on the site of the castle.

Within the boroughs plots of land were allocated to the
burgesses on payment of a fixed rent, usually of 12d. per annum.
These BURGAGE PLOTS were often regularly sized and set out,
and in some cases can be identified even today. At Prescot the
'reverse S' boundaries of the burgage plots suggest they were laid
out over existing fields. C16 documents indicate that the plots
contained gardens, orchards and livestock enclosures as well as
manufacturing or craft installations such as bake ovens and
pottery kilns. Rare archaeological evidence of medieval urban
industry comes from Prescot in the form of waste pottery from
a plot at Derby Street.

In SW Lancashire few secular medieval buildings survive for
investigation today. One notable exception is Aigburth Grange,
the monastic grange of the Cistercian Abbey of Stanlow,
Cheshire.

The upper social echelons were reflected in the MAJOR
HOUSES. At the apex in the region was Lathom House, which,
after its construction by Thomas Stanley in the later C15, was
termed the 'Northern Court'. This magnificent building is
reputed to have influenced Henry VII as a model for Richmond
Palace. It had nine towers, a gatehouse and two courts within the
encircling walls. It was demolished after its capture during the
Civil War. Excavations close to the surviving stable block have
recently uncovered the remains of a massive ditch and thick stone
walls, almost certainly from the late medieval building. Other
major houses with medieval origins include Speke Hall and
Knowsley Hall. They and others are discussed on pp. 29–36.

MOATED HOMESTEADS were established by landowners of differing status, as much as symbols of status as for defence. The
wealthier landowners erected large halls with ancillary buildings;
junior branches, or freemen somewhat lower in the social scale,
emulated their superiors with more modest moated houses. Moat
building nationally saw its heyday in the C13 and early C14. The
claylands of the region are well suited to moat building and in
West Derby Hundred alone Dr Jennifer Lewis has calculated that
there are about 120 moated sites or substantial ditched enclosures, while over half the medieval townships have at least one
moated site. The dating evidence for moats is poor, though at
least six existed by the time the Legh of Lyme survey was undertaken in 1466. Lewis postulates that many may be connected with
expansion into forests on the margins of townships. Excavations
have recently been carried out at a number of sites. At Eccleston
Hall the moat was confirmed and traces of stone buildings from
the late medieval period revealed. Timbers from a series of fish-

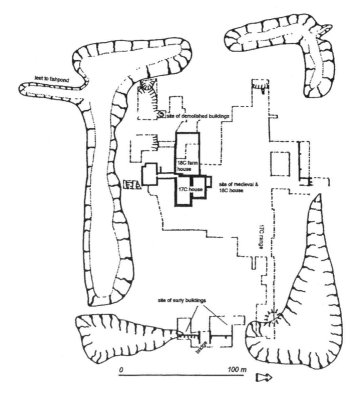

Warrington, Bewsey Old Hall.
Plan, showing moat

ponds or pits, probably from an earlier hall, were dated to the early C14, fifty years before the first surviving record. Excavations have taken place too at Micklehead Green, Sutton, Twiss Green, Barrow Old Hall (Warrington), the Boteler home at Bewsey Old Hall (Warrington), and Old Abbey Farm, Risley, which was probably founded in the mid C13. Some moat sites also retain associated features such as fishponds (Rainhill Old Hall, Speke Hall) or gatehouses (Bradlegy Old Hall).

Excavation has also proved the medieval origins of several FARMS which first appear in the documentary record somewhat later. C14–C15 pottery was found at Lea Green, Sutton, at a yeoman farm which is first recorded in the C17. Close to Daggers Bridge Farm, Tarbock dendrochronology showed that a plank had been made from a tree felled *c.* 1235, a date consistent with pottery discarded in nearby clay- or sandpits, showing that this too was a farm of medieval origin.

Little is known of the HOUSES of the ordinary people. Such evidence as we have indicates construction in timber and wattle-and-daub, with clay floors. A peasant cottage, probably of C13–C14 date and constructed with timber posts set in pits in the

ground, was excavated at Brunt Boggart, Tarbock. Another building, possibly a byre, was excavated at Fazakerley, and the clay
floor of a third structure, possibly a small cottage, was found at
West Derby.

Many medieval TOWNSHIPS in the area did not have a nucleated village but consisted of separate dispersed farms. The
method of open-field farming where tenants cultivated inter-
mixed strips in common fields, familiar from the classic Midlands
pattern, also took on a distinctive regional form here. Many fields
were enclosed early on and were farmed separately by single
tenants. Separate estates were often carved out of the extensive
woodland on the edge of townships. At other places villages are
thought to have developed after the Norman Conquest, as the
population was probably too low and dispersed to support communal agriculture in many places. However, between the C12 and
mid C14 the population rose dramatically, increasing demand for
food and taking into cultivation land considered marginal before.
A map of c. 1580 illustrates a small estate at Burtonhead, Sutton,
which may have been typical. It shows the hall, three named
houses and three other buildings grouped around an area of
hedged enclosures. At least one field was divided into strips, suggesting it was farmed by separate tenants.

Prominent landowners established hunting PARKS as a private
leisure pursuit. The parks were bounded by a bank and pale or
palisade to keep the deer in and wild animals out, and usually
contained a substantial area of woodland. Families such as the
Lathoms created large parks (Knowsley and Lathom); that at
Knowsley existed by 1292 but was expanded twice by the mid
C16 to include not only former arable land but possibly also a
settlement, indicated by a scatter of medieval pottery within the
later park boundary. More modest parks were created by lesser
landowners. Richard de Tarbock claimed to have two parks at
Tarbock in 1334–6, and a mid-C13 document records that the
boundary of Little Park began on the road in front of Sir Henry
de Tarbock's door. A park at Newton is first mentioned incidentally in 1322 in an accusation of theft from one Meyrick de
Wigan, while in 1337 John of Kirkby was granted a licence 'to
impark 500 acres of land, wood and moor' within his manor of
Kirkby. There was a royal park in SW Lancashire too, at Toxteth,
created at the beginning of the C13.

There are just three religious houses within the area, a reflection of its relative poverty and remoteness in the medieval period:
4 Burscough Priory, the Benedictine foundation at Up Holland,
and the Austin Friars in Warrington (discussed on p. 23.)

CHURCH ARCHITECTURE TO THE
SEVENTEENTH CENTURY

Earlier Medieval Churches

EARLY CHRISTIAN, ANGLO-SAXON and Norman remains in SW
Lancashire are very light. There are no structures and nothing

known *in situ* of pre-Conquest origin.* From the NORMAN period there is part of a corbel table at Grappenhall (Warrington, but historically in Cheshire), a simple blocked doorway and some walling at Aughton and Farnworth (Widnes), a restored window *p. 143* at Ormskirk, a scalloped capital in a wall at Childwall (Liverpool), and a waterleaf capital dug up at Sefton. But there are also four Norman tub FONTS carved with primitive power. Walton (Liverpool; reconstructed following war damage) has carved panels representing, amongst others, the Temptation, the Flight into Egypt, and St John Baptist, separated by foliate panels. The others have arcading: Grappenhall (Warrington), Huyton, with heads, and Kirkby, the most thrilling of all, with figures including saints, Adam and Eve and probably St Michael spearing the serpent, which has wrapped itself around the bottom like a roll moulding. All are battered and worn.

s Lancashire was notably lacking in MONASTIC HOUSES, so we are fortunate to have the remains of three in the area covered. At Up Holland is the early C14 Dec chancel of the priory church of the last Benedictine foundation in the country (1317–18), which became a parish church in the C17. The splendid arcade of tall and slender piers is in a class of its own in the area. The piers seem to presage Perp, because they are of four-shaft-and-four-hollow section, but the arch mouldings are firmly Dec. Evidently the church was truncated before completion, because the sturdy tower with its handsome but heavily weathered portal is probably early C15 and stands where the crossing was planned. Nothing else remains of the priory but ruined dormitory walls. Of the Augustinian Burscough Priory, founded in 1190 by Henry de Lathom, little more survives than the remains of the tower piers, probably of late C13 date, but a number of fittings and tombs at Ormskirk and Lathom Chapel are said to have come from here. Excavations in Warrington on the site of the Austin Friars founded in the late C13 revealed foundations of the N wall and column plinths for the nave, as well as an unusual later transept, broad and aisled, which was probably built by *c.* 1350, and evidence for a tower over the W bay of the chancel.

A characteristic of Lancashire is the great size of the ancient parishes, reflecting the scarcity of the population. In the part covered by this book there are only thirteen. So chapels of ease were built for the distant faithful. That at Maghull, now a fragment beside a C19 replacement, is the oldest Gothic building: C13, including an E window with intersecting tracery and round arcade piers. The only other C13 work is the bottom of the tower at Wigan and the arcade of the Derby Chapel at Ormskirk, which has octagonal piers of late C13 date. When it comes, however, to DECORATED work from the C14 there is a surprising amount to see, especially of towers and STEEPLES. A distinctive group are the four steeples of Ormskirk, Aughton, Halsall and Standish (the last replaced), all of which move from a square tower to a spire

* For Anglo-Saxon fragments *see* p. 18.

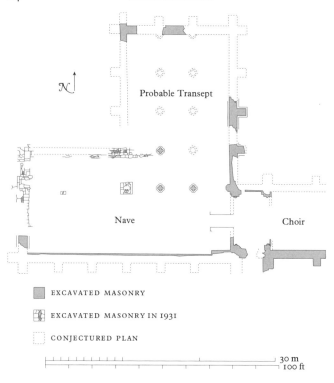

EXCAVATED MASONRY

EXCAVATED MASONRY IN 1931

CONJECTURED PLAN

Warrington Friary.
Plan after early C20 excavation

by means of a broached octagonal belfry stage. They appear to
be early to mid C14. Sefton is another C14 steeple, but the idiosyncratic corner pinnacles defy dating: possibly C17 or even C19
in their present, almost Mogul form. Winwick has a mid-C14
steeple too, a tremendous presence with huge buttresses and a
recessed spire. The S aisle here may be slightly earlier, because
the (renewed) piers are of quatrefoil section. A complete puzzle
is the N arcade, which has C16 arches but clumsy fat piers much
too wide, with attached shafts and hollows, and standing on
reused bases made of upside-down capitals carved with mitred
bishops' heads. An arcade at Halsall is a bit later, for it has octagonal piers, and arches with sunk quadrants; the S arcade piers at
Huyton are octagonal too, but the arches are now double-
chamfered. The N chapel there is of similar date. There are further
towers at Farnworth – another chapel of ease – and more modestly at Hale, and much-interfered-with Dec chancels at Childwall and at Warrington, where it is built over a vaulted crypt.
Windows and belfry openings at nearly all these churches have

reticulated tracery, most memorable at Warrington because of the curious twisting variety there.

Churches from the Fifteenth Century to 1600

The PERPENDICULAR STYLE appears first, it seems, at Halsall's extremely handsome chancel, in a transitional fashion without parallel in s Lancashire. The excellent sedilia and piscina, the best by far in s Lancashire, are firmly Dec in style, forming a cusped and richly moulded ogee arcade. Dec too is a doorway, and the door itself, which has blank reticulated tracery. Perp is certainly creeping into the tracery of the big two-pointed windows, though. Huyton w tower has fully Perp tracery, but that is almost it for what one might call classical Perp. Sir Thomas Gerard founded a chantry chapel c. 1453 at Windleshaw (St Helens). The ruins are small and plain, but the belfry opening is still reticulated. The little Lathom Park Chapel, founded by the 1st Earl of Derby and consecrated in 1509, is undoubtedly Perp, but much altered.

That leaves the large body of works undertaken in the C16 on Lancashire churches which are instantly recognisable from their bluntness, and most particularly their uncusped, round-headed tracery. The 1530s–40s must have been a period of exceptional prosperity in the sw of the county, for most of these projects date from then. They are probably the work of one community of masons, as the same masons' marks appear in different combinations, and the stylistic similarities are overwhelming. Two most handsome, large and superficially similar churches are Winwick and Sefton. An inscription of 1530 dates the new aisle walls and clerestory of Winwick. The big windows have almost round arches, and contain embattled super-transoms, those to the aisles with Tudor roses or plaques carved IHS. Sefton's reconstruction, over the first fifty years of the C16, extended to a new chancel under a continuous roof, floodlit by still more generous windows of more or less uniform design. Tracery is similar to Winwick's except that the lights are generally pointed and the window heads intersect. This apparent revival of a late C13 motif is characteristic also of Ormskirk, and of Aughton's N aisle, where the same masons' marks can be found. Here, as at the Sefton clerestory, the windows have fully round arches. At Ormskirk the tracery is in the twin belfry openings of the massive w tower, for which money was bequeathed c. 1542. Standing cheek-by-jowl with the smaller and sleeker C14 steeple, it gives the church its extraordinary appearance. At Wigan the tracery of the similar belfry openings is of the round-arched variety. The rest of the church is what its rebuilding architects *Sharpe & Paley* claimed was an accurate copy of the big Perp original, but drawings seem to show that the old aisle windows had multiple, stepped, round-headed lights, as survive in the N chapel, whilst the clerestory had intersecting windows of the Sefton kind. A ruined chapel at Lydiate is another member of the group. Another variation on the fat towers is that at Leigh, restored faithfully by *Austin & Paley*. Simple windows of the Wigan chapel type are in the vestry at Aughton and at Grappenhall, though the Perp of the chancel windows here is more developed. The arcades at these two more humble churches have octagonal piers and double-chamfered arches. Grappenhall's are dated to the 1530s. Sefton's altogether grander arcade piers, of the same date, have sections of four demi-shafts and four hollows in the diagonals. Almost identical are those at Wigan, but their form before the C19 restoration is unclear.

Standish, a rare Elizabethan church, is both the climax of the Gothic in our area, and an extraordinary glimpse into the future. All but the steeple (now a C19 replacement) was rebuilt *c.* 1582–9 with aisles and clerestory by a master mason called *Lawrence Shipway*. Today's windows are conventional Perp, but there is evidence that before the C19 the lights were uncusped. Inside, however, the Gothic form is diluted by some detailing in the roof (*see* below) and in the arcade arches, which rest on columns with
11 remarkably correct Tuscan bases and capitals. This is the earliest known large-scale use of the Tuscan in England, and it is quite unexpected to find it in backward Lancashire.

There are a number of Perp ROOFS, typically flat and panelled with heavy moulded beams. Those over the aisles at Winwick are quite rough, so too those at Leigh, which have saltire pattern. Farnworth has roofs with saltires too, but of much superior workmanship. The roof over the Legh Chapel at Winwick is also more refined, and it has big angels attached. Standish has superb roofs,
13 incorporating some post-Gothic elements: guilloche and arcade mouldings, and consoles supporting the tie-beams. Different are the nave and N aisle roofs of Aughton, which have arched braces to collar-beams, and wind-braces, those over the N aisle cusped to form elongated quatrefoils.

For FURNISHINGS Sefton has few rivals in the North West of England. Chief amongst its treasures is a glorious complex of
10 seven early C16 SCREENS. The earliest appear to be the parclose
p. 581 screens, with exquisitely fine Late Gothic tracery, which bear the initials of James Molyneux, rector 1489–1509. Most splendid is the great crested chancel screen, also with Molyneux's initials, which has tantalising Renaissance motifs in the form of friezes with crude cherubs, some holding horns and some holding medallions. If the screen really is the work of Molyneux, these are extraordinarily early. Other screens have idiosyncratic round-arched tracery, like the windows. Molyneux's stalls and bench ends have delightful carving. Elsewhere, there is a much-restored Perp chancel screen at Huyton, with fine Flamboyant tracery, and a simple mutilated example at Lathom Park Chapel, where there is also a stocky oaken eagle lectern. Both are said to have come from Burscough Priory. There are late C15 stalls at Halsall, with the only MISERICORDS in the area; also some bench ends, with poppyheads and tracery. FONTS are invariably simple and octagonal, sometimes with quatrefoils, as at Sefton. At the C19 Roman Catholic church of Our Lady, Lydiate are a series of excellent alabaster panels of the Nottingham school, which came from the C16 chapel of St Catherine.

For MONUMENTS, the earliest effigy may be the knight with crossed legs at Sefton, who is plausibly Sir William Molyneux, †1296/8. Of the C14 there are some bruised slabs, e.g. at Standish, very badly preserved effigies at Wigan and Warrington, a defaced alabaster priest at Huyton, and another cross-legged Knight at Sefton, of *c.* 1330. A C14 Purbeck marble effigy of a cleric at Standish was appropriated for a primitive tomb-chest at the end of the C16. The outstanding tomb is at Warrington, C15 *p. 603* and of alabaster. The effigies of Sir John Boteler (†1463) and

Winwick, St Oswald. Brass of Sir Peter Legh (†1527) and wife. Drawing.
(J.L. Thornely, *Monumental Brasses of Lancashire & Cheshire*, 1893)

his wife lie on a chest carved on three sides with statuettes of angels, saints etc., also the Crucifixion, Assumption, and Holy Trinity. These are framed by billowing banners or canopies supported by poles, a romantic alternative to the usual arches or tabernacles. A further four damaged alabaster effigies of the late C15 are in the Derby Chapel at Ormskirk, including, supposedly, the 1st Earl of Derby and his two wives, removed from Burscough Priory; also two C16 tomb-chests with indents for brasses (two similar at Sefton). So finally to the C16 and Halsall, which has the alabaster effigy of a priest, in a pinnacled and boldly cusped Dec recess, and an overpainted tomb-chest with effigies of a knight and his lady.

There are a few good BRASSES, including the impressive Piers Gerard (†1492) at Winwick, under a triple canopy, and Sir Peter Legh (†1527) and his wife at the same church, he wearing the vestment of a priest under his armour. At Ormskirk is a knight in armour of *c.* 1500, at Childwall a double brass, and at Sefton three of the C16, including Sir William Molyneux (†1548), unusually wearing antique armour, and Sir Richard Molyneux (†1568), with two wives and a brood of thirteen children.

STAINED GLASS has fared very badly, and fragmentary pieces are all that survive. Grappenhall (Warrington) has the most interesting, plenty of parts of figures with characteristic C14 green and yellow, including St Bartholomew carrying his skin over his arm. Halsall has some Dec fragments, and Up Holland and Sefton jumbled bits, the latter including C16 Passion emblems, elements of a Visitation and, unusually for the date, the martyrdom of Thomas à Becket. A few C15 or early C16 morsels from Garston chapel of ease were reinstalled at Speke Hall in the C19.

Seventeenth-century Churches

This is a very quiet century for church building. By far the most interesting is the broad Gothic Survival nave at Prescot, dated 1610, with thin octagonal arcade piers and single-chamfered arches. The clerestory has domestic-style three-light mullioned windows, over the chancel arch still with trefoil heads; but the
21 roof has alternate hammerbeam trusses, with Jacobean pendants and consoles. Wind-braces are quadrants, forming perfect uncusped circles, also quite unlike medieval designs. Huyton, a few miles away, has a very similar chancel roof of 1663. Winwick nave roof, from the very end of the C17, follows closely the panelled late Perp form of the aisles, but with some distinctly un-Gothic mouldings. This seems to be a case of Gothic Revival, not Survival.

Prescot also has a characteristic, transitional set of early C17 chancel FURNISHINGS. The stalls with strange poppyheads, dated 1636, are unmistakably Jacobean in detail – e.g. lozenge and arcade moulding – but in type continue the Gothic tradition. Also present are a communion rail and panelling with attached benches on turned legs. Jacobean fittings elsewhere are devoid of Gothic motifs, e.g. a communion table at Leigh with carved bulbous legs and inlaid chequer frieze, communion-rail balusters at Sefton with ball finials, and the good screens around the Derby Chapel at Ormskirk and under the tower arch at Farnworth, with balusters in the upper parts. Simple, shaped PEW ENDS can be found at Standish, Ormskirk, and Up Holland. PULPITS are at Standish and Sefton, the latter, dated 1635, 19 tremendously carved with dense arabesques. For contrast go to Eccleston (St Helens) where there is a late C17 pulpit, reputedly from St Saviour, Southwark, London, and certainly entirely typical of examples of the period in the City of London churches. The octagonal font at Ormskirk, dated 1661, has typically ele- 20 mentary symbolic motifs. Sefton has the only WALL PAINTING, Biblical texts in the arcade spandrels.

One of the more curious MONUMENTS is at Farnworth (Widnes), a knight, probably Richard Bold (†*c.* 1602), deliberately made to look like 1500. In the same chapel are standing alabaster effigies of Richard Bold (†1635) and wife, an unusual arrangement for the date if they were always thus. Sir John Ogle (†1612) at Prescot stands too, and looks as if he always has. Edward Wrightington (†1658) at Standish is another alabaster, 22 with recumbent effigy, and of excellent workmanship. The marble memorial at Winwick of Richard Legh (†1687), slightly stiffly 24 composed with its two free-standing busts under a baldacchino, looks forward to the C18. There are many little BRASS plaques, including at Culcheth an odd inscription to Elizabeth Egerton (†1646) signed *John Sale sculpsit*. The biggest monument is the Case MAUSOLEUM at Huyton, of *c.* 1681, a sandstone box with architectural detail of advanced form for the area.

NONCONFORMIST CHAPELS of course first appear in the later C17. St Helens meeting house is the oldest still in use in Lancashire, having been purchased in 1676, but the simple stone-built vernacular house could be as old as 1597. Park Lane Chapel, Bryn (Ashton-in-Makerfield), built by Presbyterians in 1697, has also been remodelled, but retains its original pulpit and preacher's hat peg.

DOMESTIC AND OTHER SECULAR ARCHITECTURE TO *c.* 1700

Medieval Domestic Building to c. 1500

Nothing survives of the fabric of the CASTLES built in SW Lancashire in the C11 and C12, nothing of Warrington, West Derby, Newton or Liverpool. The only substantial remnant is the motte at Newton, which stands beside the southbound carriageway of the M6. Dr Jennifer Lewis has identified further possible sites from documentary evidence, such as Up Holland and Widnes (*see* p. 18 for further discussion of this subject).

At Bradley Old Hall, Burtonwood, a ruined gatehouse does survive, with remnants of its vaulted passage, but the house

erected here by Sir Peter Legh in the 1460s was fortified probably as much for status as for military purposes. The same is true
of Lathom House, the pre-eminent medieval residence in the
area, indeed one of the greatest MEDIEVAL HOUSES in the North.
This massive structure was built by Thomas Stanley on his elevation as Earl of Derby at the end of the C15. Though the accuracy of known representations is open to doubt, it seems that the
structure had a curtain wall punctuated by seven towers and two
gatehouses, and contained two courts (*see* also p. 20). Lauded in
the C16, it survived two sieges during the Civil War before being
demolished in the early C18.

Lathom was stone; also of masonry was the Derbys' other
major house in SW Lancashire, at the great deer park of Knowsley
(*see* also p. 22 for parks). The core of the S wing of the present
mansion comprises all or part of a building of *c.* 1500, probably
a substantial hunting lodge. A single compact building, much
altered and refenestrated, it had two turrets, and was built on an
undefended site. Lodges were places of occasional retreat and
recreation and therefore required less comprehensive accommodation. Few other stone buildings are known. The gatehouse of
Bold Old Hall survived into the C19; fragments of Old Hutte
(Hale) into the 1950s.* Tantalising fragments have been uncovered from the Molyneux family's Sefton Old Hall. The sandstone
walls of The Granary, Aigburth (Liverpool) may be medieval,
because the building was part of the grange of the Cistercian
abbey of Stanlow, Cheshire. The ruins of Halsall Old Rectory
indicate an impressive C14–C15 house with fine traceried
windows to the hall. The massive ashlar blocks of The Scholes
(St Helens) are hard to date accurately. This modest, much-
modified hall could be C15, or later.

More common, as much in the rolling, higher E as the sodden
low-lying W, is TIMBER CONSTRUCTION. Archaeological investigation has produced evidence for a C12 timber hall at Bewsey
Old Hall (Warrington). Before Old Abbey Farm, Risley (near
Warrington) was demolished to make way for millions of tons of
Manchester refuse, analysis of wall-posts and reused timbers
hidden in the modest brick farmhouse revealed an aisled hall of
the late C13 or early C14. Such a plan form has only rarely been
found in Lancashire, but Gary Miller has also identified what
may be arcade posts at Johnson's Farm, Up Holland.

CRUCK FRAMING was a common system. Examples of cruck
trusses are still being uncovered within masonry reconstruction,
but in the absence of accurate dating, their sequencing is impre-
cise. Some of the earliest could be those at The Granary, Aigburth (Liverpool), where the grange is first mentioned in 1291.
p. 32 Two of the best-preserved are at Peel Hall, Ince-in-Makerfield,
where the blades are of impressively massive scantling. These
have been ascribed to the C15. The same applies to the truss
embedded in the neighbouring Kirkless Hall, Aspull.

---

*The last part of Old Hutte and its moat were swept away to create the Halewood
car plant (*see* p. 110).

Regardless of construction, the standard medieval PLAN was tripartite. The 'upper' end contained family accommodation, a parlour and above it a solar or great chamber, the centre was the hall, and the 'lower' end housed services: kitchen, buttery, dairy, brewhouse. The entrance was at the lower end of the hall, and in larger houses it opened into a transverse screens passage separating the hall from the service areas. In the largest houses, and indeed in many houses in SE England of lower status, this type incorporated two storeys at both ends. POST-AND-RAIL construction – walls of vertical posts and studs and horizontal sills and rails, with a structurally separate roof – was the easiest means to do this in timber. Evidence for both post-and-rail construction and two storeys in SW Lancashire is scanty before the C15, but from then we have a few examples, all now encased in brick. Great Woolden Hall, Woolden, has a number of doors in timber-framed walls with ogee-shaped heads, a very rare motif in Lancashire; the building may predate the C15. Aughton Old Hall appears C15; the part of the frame still exposed shows chunky timbers and the blocked former doorway into the screens passage. Bradley Hall, Standish has a hall and a two-storey service wing both of C15 date, but – as exposed framing inside demonstrates – of separate builds. In almost all cases surviving cross-wings are of different dates to the hall or house body; incremental improvement was the norm. At Peel Hall, Ince-in-Makerfield, the lower end was rebuilt in the late C15 or early C16 with roof trusses without known parallel, having kingposts with a forked base, like an upside-down Y.

Variety of ROOF structure, one of the intriguing features of the surviving medieval post-and-rail houses, supports the growing scepticism about clear and identifiable regional variations in timber-framed construction. Morley's Hall, Astley, dated to *c.* 1463 by Nigel Morgan, has a crown-post; other crown-posts have been identified in SE Lancashire too, though these have been considered in the past a southern characteristic. The hall wing of Bradley Hall has kingpost trusses with raked struts. Rainhill Old Hall is C15 or C16, and has a splendid roof of arch-braced collars and quatrefoil wind-braces. This is over a first-floor room, but in the position where one would anticipate the hall. This roof is plausibly either *ex situ*, recycled from the hall when the house was reduced in the C17, or that of the solar. Hurst Hall Barn, Glazebury, deserves to be better known. It is the remnant of a 12 hall roofed with quatrefoil wind-braces like Rainhill, and kingposts and raked trusses which, strikingly, are cusped, as at Stand Old Hall, Whitefield, SE Lancashire (demolished). Two wall-posts remain, massive timbers with spreading bases and a long splay. These and the remaining braces are of distinctively wide, flat scantling, reminiscent of the so-called plank-framed houses such as Baguley Hall, Wythenshawe (SE Lancashire). That house is C14, possibly a pointer to the age of Hurst. Both Hurst and Morley's appears to have SPERE trusses – a North-Western speciality in which fixed posts and partitions flank the screen at the lower end of the hall – with mortises to receive spere-posts.

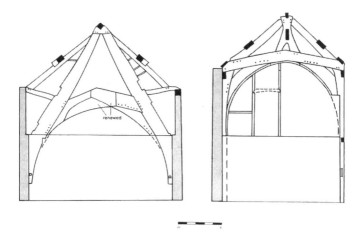

Ince-in-Makerfield, Peel Hall.
Sections through hall (left) and north wing.

Aughton Old Hall still has a spere-post, buried inside later alterations along with a spere truss, and kingpost trusses.

Morley's Hall is a rarity in this area: a medieval manor house
surrounded by a wet MOAT. Moats are difficult to date, and their
purposes have proved hard to pin down, as discussed on p. 20.
The majority of platforms are now abandoned, and most moats
are dry or infilled. Those still completely wet can be found in a
variety of circumstances: incongruously amidst post-war housing
estates (New Hall, Tyldesley), surrounding later farmhouses
(Bradley Old Hall, Burtonwood and Gidlow Hall, Aspull – a C16
fragment restored in the C19), or romantically incorporated into
the garden of a newer house (Rixton Old Hall).

Domestic Building from c. 1500 to c. 1700

14 The exceptional GREAT HOUSE is Speke Hall, a wonderfully
evocative timber-framed mansion, built over seven decades from
about 1530 by Sir William Norris and his son Edward. Its planning is typically medieval and Tudor, and the principal rooms are
p. 464 the best of their kind in the area. The house encloses a courtyard, which is entered via a gateway (not here the gatehouse of
the aristocracy) in one of the three ranges containing lodgings,
the kitchens and other services. In the fourth side, facing the
15 entrance, is the last surviving open hall in SW Lancashire (Hurst
Hall Barn aside). It was built with two innovations increasingly
common for gentry houses in the Tudor period: a chimneyed fireplace, and a ceiling; most halls had previously been lit by open

hearths (e.g. Hurst Hall Barn). When fireplaces were installed in older houses, the most common position was against the rear wall, e.g. at Kirkless Hall, Aspull, with its characteristically massive external chimneystack. At Speke it was placed against the screens passage, an arrangement found across the North, and in larger houses especially in the North West. Lydiate Hall (very ruined) was another. The huge, elaborate and quite bizarre brick overmantel of Speke has a close relative at Little Moreton Hall in Cheshire. Speke also has a dais fireplace in one of the two oriel bays at the high end of the hall.

Despite these efforts to make the great hall more comfortable, in the C16 many of its functions migrated, chiefly to the parlour. Increasingly devoid of any sleeping function, this was becoming the focus of family life and entertainment. The Great Parlour at Speke abuts the high end of the hall, next to the stairs to the family chambers. Its status is abundantly clear in the elaborate heraldic overmantel, panelled walls, and a splendid, though later, plaster ceiling. In the C17 the best room was sometimes to be found on the first floor, and was known as the great, or later, dining room. This was an evolution of the medieval solar and might occupy its position at the upper end of the hall. Lightshaw Hall, Golborne – plain brick to look at – is a timber-framed solar wing dated to the 1550s. Beams to its ground floor are as well-moulded as on the first floor, suggesting this was a parlour.

sw Lancashire has no other surviving houses of such status from this period. Bold Old Hall (demolished) appears to have been of similar scale, though not coherent, and to have had a stone gatehouse. By the early C19 it had three ranges, but may once have had a fourth. Standish Hall is another that may have had such a plan. We must wait for the C18 before great houses are built again. But the gentry and prosperous yeomanry (especially in and around the Douglas Valley) were busy in the C16 and C17, spending incomes from agriculture and, in many districts, from coal and textiles too. Older houses were modernised, with walls rebuilt, of which more below. Chimneys appear, as described above. Floors were inserted into open halls to create additional chambers; the declining ceremonial use of these halls may also have been a factor. Both Peel Hall and Kirkless Hall had floors inserted in the C16, and so too Morley Hall, Astley and Bradley Hall, Standish. Peel Hall illustrates how cruck-framed halls were adapted by attaching outriders from the cruck blades to the eaves to create a useable upper storey. Replacement parlour cross-wings are another common C16–C17 feature, e.g. at Aughton Old Hall and Ackhurst Hall, Orrell.

NEW GENTRY HOUSES were built to the traditional tripartite, cross-wing plan until the end of the C17. Light Oaks Hall, Glazebury, built in the 1620s with the profits of Derbyshire lead mining, has a single-storey hall, now lined with fine panelling from the chamber directly above. This was now a favoured location for a dining or great room, and the increasing prevalence and status of such first-floor rooms brought new importance to providing STAIRCASES of appropriate dignity. A stair-tower at the

rear of the hall was a showy solution. Those at Gidlow Hall,
p. 146 Aspull (dated 1574), Moor Hall, Aughton, and The Scholes, St
Helens, are in the most common position, at the upper end.
Increasingly, though, staircases are incorporated within the
fabric, normally in the upper cross-wing. Most until the late C16
were narrow and steep; the remnants in the attic of the first staircase at Speke, of c. 1531, testify to their meanness. It was replaced
within a few decades by a well stair with enclosed core – not
grand, but nevertheless comparatively early for a formal staircase
in a private house. It ascends to the upper of two superimposed
access corridors running along the inside of two courtyard
ranges, early examples of internal passages. The one known
example of that quintessential Tudor and Stuart room, the
GALLERY, was discovered only recently at Astley Hall (1650). It
is not the grand and gracious long gallery of popular
imagination, but its lesser relation, the 'passage gallery'. These
typically are short, in the roof space, and existed primarily
to provide access to chambers off them. Having few windows,
they were less for recreation and therefore often lack elaborate
plasterwork.

Recusancy was endemic amongst the aristocracy and gentry of
Lancashire, and PRIEST'S HOLES and secret CHAPELS are a distinctive feature, though not as common as you may be told. Speke
Hall has secret hiding places and an 'eavesdrop', a small hole in
the eaves from which approaching visitors could be observed
covertly. A chapel is recorded, but the location is unclear. The
quality of the kingpost roof in the attic of the 1618 cross-wing at
Ackhurst Hall (Orrell) is reason to suspect that this was a secret
chapel. Roger Anderton established an important mission and a
secret printing press at Birchley Hall, Billinge, after 1613. The
chapel here may have been in the attic of a prominent wing,
which was rebuilt in the early C18 with a less clandestine chapel
reached from an external staircase.

At the very beginning of the C17 new concepts of formal planning and architectural composition finally begin to appear in SW
Lancashire in the shape of SYMMETRICAL FAÇADES. The first
flickers may be observed at Speke, where the courtyard façade
of the hall range has compass bays at either end dating from after
1540; that to the l. is apparently primarily for balance, for it seems
never to have lit rooms of any significance. The N range, through
which landward visitors entered the house, was finished in 1598
and is notably more regular than the earlier parts.

Traditional linear U- or H-plans begin to stop expressing internal hierarchies externally. Ince Hall (Ince-in-Makerfield, demolished) was a timber-framed gentry house with a balanced façade,
built at about the beginning of the C17. At the same time an interesting and impressive group of stone houses was being erected,
mostly also within a few miles of Wigan. The progenitor was
17 Birchley Hall (Billinge), dated 1594; Bispham Hall (Billinge) is
least altered (though extensively rebuilt in the late C20). The
others are Winstanley Hall (Wigan), Hacking Hall (North Lancashire) and Staley Hall (Cheshire). All have tall symmetrical

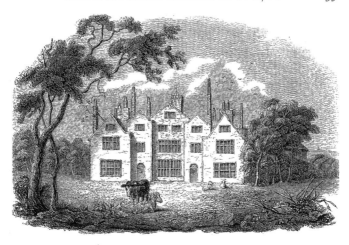

Wigan, Winstanley Hall, east front. Engraving.
(M. Gregson, *Portfolio of Fragments Relating to the History of the County Palatinate and Duchy of Lancaster*, 1869)

façades made of five gabled parts receding to the centre, filled with large windows. They are traditionally planned, which limits the attempt at symmetry, because the entrance remains at the lower end of the hall, in one of the re-entrant projections, and cannot be replicated in the other, which forms the hall oriel. Hacking, and presumably others of the group, had a great or dining chamber over the hall, like Light Oaks Hall, Glazebury, which also had a near symmetrical façade. However, symmetry was by no means universal, as demonstrated by the five unequal gables of Astley Hall (*c.* 1640).

This was a transitional period in MATERIALS too. Speke Hall has a TIMBER FRAME of the elaborately picturesque style that flourished here and in Cheshire in the C16. The basic frame, of the generic West of England square-panelled type, is densely filled with embellishment: herringbone, quatrefoils and concave-sided lozenges. A surviving fragment of the original façade of Worthington Hall, dated 1577, suggests that this was even more intricately framed. Demolished examples are far too many; notable among them are Standish Hall and Newton Hall, Newton-le-Willows. A much-restored but still splendid façade is that of The Barley Mow pub in the centre of Warrington, with jettied gables. This is a very rare survival in the area of a C16 urban building; there is also a single C17 gable in Prescot. Coved jetties occur quite frequently, for example at Worthington Hall, and also at the so-called Cromwell House in Warrington. The simpler framing of this and other buildings – large panels without embellishment – is emblematic of lower status and probably often of a later, i.e. C17, date too. Braces are straight, and frequently the only extravagance is a multitude of raked struts in the king-post trusses exposed in gable ends.

Of course the timber-framed buildings on which these observations are based make up only a fraction of the total built, because of demolitions and because the vast majority were rebuilt with stone and brick walls in the C16 and especially the C17. The latest timber-framed structures probably date from about the 1630s. STONE was favoured in and around the Douglas Valley and higher ground around Wigan. Along the Mersey valley and across the coastal plain, where there was no stone, BRICK was the new status symbol. It appears at the very end of the C16, possibly first in the oldest parts of Croxteth Hall (Liverpool) and Bewsey Old Hall (Warrington). By the mid C17 its use – laid in English Garden Wall bond – had percolated down to the yeomanry. Light Oaks Hall (1620s), with lozenge-pattern, is one of the most impressive examples. Piecemeal reconstructions of earlier timber frames include Garrett Hall Farmhouse (Tyldesley), Bradley Hall (Standish) and Peel Hall (Ince-in-Makerfield). Evidence for others, such as Giant's Hall, Standish, and Bedford Hall, Leigh, is equivocal, partly because timber-framed internal walls continued long after masonry was adopted for the external envelope.

p. 406

A quick word on WINDOWS. For this period they are almost always mullioned. Most of the survivors are of stone, though Club House Farmhouse, Shevington has a timber example of the kind that was built into timber-framed houses. The Manor House at Rainhill has examples of the two stone moulding types: on one side chamfered, and on the other ovolo, a later style which never entirely supplanted the former. Bewsey Old Hall (Warrington) and Alder House, Atherton were built at opposite ends of the C17 with stepped lights, a variation much more common in the West Riding. Wealth might be expressed by the amount of glass in a façade: Light Oaks Hall, built by the man described as the wealthiest in Leigh parish, has some of the biggest transomed windows, with king mullions.

The best FITTINGS are at Speke. Besides those already mentioned, there is some STAINED GLASS, including reused armorial pieces of *c.* 1490–1500 in the Great Hall. Lawson's Farmhouse in Golborne contains a splendid plasterwork wall panel, a bush bearing fruits, acorns etc., probably of the earlier C17.

Vernacular Architecture and Farm Buildings

The better HOUSES of the yeomanry are not always distinct from those of the lower gentry. Though miniaturised versions of the double cross-wing plan are found – for example Gantley House, Billinge – asymmetry is more common. Giant's Hall, Standish, Manor House, Rainhill and many more have a prominent parlour cross-wing at one end, often an addition. The most frequent plan is the baffle-entry type, with an entrance lobby against the side of a transverse fireplace heating the housebody; a variation has the entrance at the end. Smoke from these fireplaces was drawn

up a timber-framed smoke hood over the hearth. Most were subsequently replaced by brick chimneys, but Lawson's Farmhouse,
Golborne still has a back-to-back pair. The smoke hood was supported by posts – speres or heck-posts – with a big bressumer
spanning between, and this made the inglenook. Club House
Farmhouse, Shevington, dated 1663, has a fire window within the
inglenook, and moulded stone speres. Manor House, Worthington, has the more common timber speres. Another frequently
found status symbol is the two-storey porch. Guild Hall Farmhouse, Rainford, has one of 1629 with a four-centred entrance;
that at Prior's Wood Hall, Dalton, has the round-arched entrance
typical of the later C17. Some brick-built houses might be
enlivened with raised decoration, commonly in diamond patterns, and occasionally and very charmingly in hearts, as at
Brookside Farmhouse, Abram (1716). At Pennington Hall,
Aspull, it considerably spells out the date, 1653.

These houses may encase cruck frames, as at Worthington
Manor. Crucks were employed longer by the lower levels of

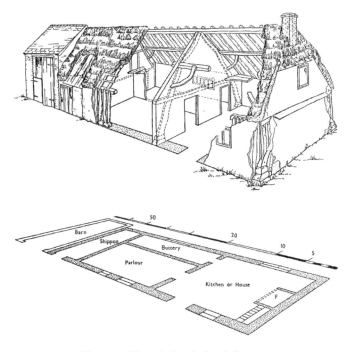

Haskayne (Downholland), Stock Cottage.
Plan and cutaway view

society, and in the coastal plain and much of the Mersey valley,
where good timber or masonry was hard to find, cruck blades,
normally of inferior quality, continue even into the C18. They
formed the structure of the characteristic but now rare vernacular building of these areas, the whitewashed and thatched,
timber-framed, single-storey LONGHOUSE. Thanks to the stew-
ardship of the last squire of Hale, the architectural historian
Peter Fleetwood-Hesketh, that village retains a number of
them. Others can be found in Formby, Newton-le-Willows and
Haskayne. The plan consists usually of housebody, parlour and
buttery, and a shippon, where livestock was housed. These are
not true longhouses, because livestock and humans had separate
entrances, rather than sharing a common cross-passage. Frequently the shippon was subsequently absorbed into the domestic accommodation. There were no chambers, only sleeping lofts
reached by ladders; in most cases a full upper floor was inserted
in the C18 or C19, e.g. at the Scotch Piper Inn, Lydiate, and at
Stock Cottage, Haskayne.

There is no great wealth of AGRICULTURAL BUILDINGS.
There are cruck-framed C16 BARNS at Cross Barn, Ince Blundell
(an unusual cruciform plan) and Speke Hall, and post-and-rail
survivors at Crosby Hall, Newton Park Farm, Newton-le-
Willows, and Martin Hall, Burscough – though none are
remotely pristine. Bickershaw Hall barn has thick, superbly made
trusses; a building at Tarbock Hall Farm has king-strut trusses
dated to the C16. Philip Powell has identified around
the Douglas Valley a variation on Dr Brunskill's combination
'Lancashire Barn', containing a shippon, but as an aisle attached
to one side, beside the cart entrance. An example can be seen at
Club House Farm, Shevington. The most polished agricultural
building of the C17, also in Shevington, is the GRANARY at Forest
Fold Farm, which incorporates ground-floor stables and is
embellished with quoins and diamond-shaped ventilation holes.
Another brick granary, with brick mullion windows, is at Sutton
Hall Cottages, St Helens. DOVECOTES are at Ashurst Hall,
Dalton (C17), and at Kirkby, the latter an odd Georgian thing
shaped like a stumpy industrial chimney.

Public Buildings

The few survivors of the C16 and C17 are modest. At West Derby,
now in Liverpool's suburbs, is the manorial court, a simple two-
bay, single-storey ashlar structure which may be Elizabethan. The
interior has been heavily restored, but the arrangement appears
C17 and the bench original. Derby House in Up Holland, dated
1633 and of stone too, may also have been a manorial court and
jail. Its plan is a rare pre-C18 survival in the area of a typical urban
form dictated by narrow medieval burgage plots – a single gabled
bay to the street, three storeys high. Many GRAMMAR SCHOOLS
date from the C16. Halsall, founded in 1593, was in an extension
to the church. Others are quite simple vernacular buildings,

stone with mullioned windows mainly, e.g. Walton (Liverpool), *c.* 1613, and Up Holland, *c.* 1661. Grandest is the Merchant Taylors' School, Great Crosby, established in 1620, with a two-storey porch and big transomed windows with king mullions.

THE EIGHTEENTH CENTURY

Churches and Chapels

More CHURCHES were built in Lancashire in the C18 than in any other county. Many of the finest, in booming Liverpool, were later destroyed. They began with *John Moffat*'s St Peter, Church Street, completed in 1704. St George, begun 1726, the chief architectural work of the dock engineer *Thomas Steers*, had a classical tower and spire. St Thomas, Park Lane, of similar arrangement, was built (if not designed) by *Henry Sephton*. The finest was the domed and centralised St Paul of 1763–9, by *Timothy Lightoler*, who also probably did the Gothic St John, finished in 1784. All these are gone. All that survives on the Anglican side is St James, Toxteth, built 1774–5 as part of an abortive suburban development, and Holy Trinity, Wavertree, 1794, by *John Hope* – but Wavertree was outside Liverpool then.

Sephton was the leading architect-mason in the area in the first half of the C18. He designed a tower and spire for Prescot church in 1729, combining pilasters and a triglyph frieze with Gothic motifs. Before that he designed the enjoyable little church of St Aidan, Billinge, completed in 1718 with a rustic Baroque façade, quite incorrect but full of enterprise, and with Tuscan arcades but reticulated tracery. The façades of Holy Trinity, Warrington's second parish church, consecrated in 1760, are by contrast

Liverpool, St Paul.
Engraving by E. Rooker after P.P. Burdett, 1773

entirely classical, with pilasters, Gibbs surrounds and masses of rustication. Twenty years later came Wigan's second church, St George, a simple brick box except for the W façade, which is a curious mixture of the modern – a triglyph frieze – and the old-fashioned – the elaborate shaped gable.

When adapting medieval churches, classical styles were some-times favoured earlier in the C18. The nave and aisles of Orm-skirk church, rebuilt in 1729, were entirely classical. However, the new nave of St Elphin, Warrington, built in the 1770s, was fash-ionably Gothick, with Y-tracery. Apart from St Paul, Liverpool, these churches were standard 'Georgian prattling boxes', as the Ecclesiologists would scornfully call them, a rectangle with two tiers of windows to light galleries on three sides. Smaller churches include chapels of ease built or rebuilt to serve remoter parts of the vast medieval parishes. Many are very simple: Burtonwood (1716 etc.), Golborne (1732 etc.), Hollins Green (1730s), Hale (1758–9, attached to a C14 tower), All Saints, Hindley (1767, probably by *John Eyes*, and retaining galleries), and Great Sankey (Warrington), 1767–9. St Peter, Formby (1746) has handsome pilastered window surrounds and intersecting Gothic glazing, and a little W tower supported on square Doric columns to form a porch.

p. 533

The chapels of ease differed little from NONCONFORMIST CHAPELS, not surprisingly at a time when some preachers and congregations still jumped in and out of the Anglican church. The best-preserved, Chowbent in Atherton, was built in 1721 by a Presbyterian society ejected from the Anglican chapel. It has a simple brick shell with two tiers of windows, a gallery around three sides, box pews and a triple-decker pulpit in the centre of the longer N wall. Gateacre Chapel, built in 1700, is a plain, altered sandstone box. Also Presbyterian is the very small Ancient Chapel of Toxteth, largely rebuilt in 1774. Tyldesley Chapel, erected by the Countess of Huntingdon's Connexion in 1789–90, was the first place of worship in the town. It has superimposed elementary Venetian windows. Larger, though altered, is the Uni-tarian Chapel in Warrington, of 1745.

The most interesting C18 ecclesiastical buildings, however, are the circumspect ROMAN CATHOLIC CHAPELS. Lancashire was a heartland of the old faith; and chapels were built even before the Catholic Relief Act of 1791 repealed restrictions on worship. Thereafter, cautiously, Jesuit and Benedictine missions and their patrons erected increasing numbers, still fearful of attracting attention and violent protest. An exceptionally early free-stand-ing chapel may survive at Little Crosby, but it became a school and the structural evidence is unclear. St Peter, Seel Street, in the centre of Liverpool, was erected in 1788 as a self-effacing brick box, no different from a modest Nonconformist chapel. Rural chapels were often carefully out of the way. The Portico Chapel (St Helens), built in 1790, was screened from the turn-pike by a barn, and has a blank N wall to appear like an agricul-tural building. It has the characteristic plan of these chapels, with a presbytery attached to the E end, here combined in a single simple, gabled rectangle. The presbytery has an unexpectedly polite façade, the gable pedimented. At St Benet, Netherton, 40 1793 (now in the care of the Historic Chapels Trust), the presbytery is an ordinary three-bay house facing a quiet lane, and the chapel is a plain brick rear wing. It retains the common internal arrangement: small w gallery only, and enrichment on the E only – here a grand double-pilastered aedicule, with drapes in the pediment held open by cherubs. Such a Baroque composition was thoroughly old-fashioned, but very Roman. At the Portico Chapel the E wall is divided into three by pilasters and the centre is a shallow, bowed chancel recess.

As for the FURNISHINGS of Anglican churches, Sefton has a reredos of *c.* 1730 with Ionic pilasters and originally a pediment, and rails with twisted balusters that may be a couple of decades earlier. There are a number of handsome COMMUNION TABLES: Standish (1703, octagonal, twisted legs), Winwick (1725, cabriole legs, inlaid), St Elphin, Warrington (also inlaid), and Holy Trinity, Warrington (a splendid bit of Rococo with marble top). Wonderfully out of place in the tiny late C19 Methodist chapel at Farnworth (Widnes) is part of an early C18 triple-decker PULPIT from Runcorn parish church, Cheshire. A later, more restrained pulpit is at Holy Trinity, Warrington. The beautiful alabaster FONT given to St Peter, Liverpool, in 1702 has found a new home in the suburbs at St David, Childwall. Prescot was given a new font in 1755, actually a very pretty Italian stoup with a shallow reeded basin. Box pews, mostly minus doors, remain at Holy Trinity, Warrington. Farnworth has dado panelling made up of C17 and C18 pews, and Georgian gallery fronts. Georgian ORGAN CASES are at Leigh, of 1777 by *Samuel Green* and still with Rococo detail, and St Paul Stoneycroft (Liverpool), from the demolished St Paul, Liverpool. Many churchyards have SUNDIALS, e.g. Ormskirk, Prescot and Lowton; best is the superb, stocky Baroque one at Farnworth from Bold Hall, with drapes hanging from the neck and *Giacomo Leoni*'s signature recessed corners.

There are surprisingly few MONUMENTS to mention. The best by *Daniel Sephton*, Henry's son, is an ambitious wall monument at Prescot, with Rococo cartouche and obelisk. A good example of the work of *B. Bromfield* of Liverpool, one of the most prolific late C18 carvers, is an aedicule with engaged columns at Winwick. Easily the best monument is a neglected interloper, *John Francis Moore*'s excellent marble statue of Catherine Macaulay, writer and historian. It was unveiled at St Stephen Walbrook, London, in 1778, and given to the Warrington library in 1872. The best churchyard monuments are at St Elphin, Warrington, e.g. a late C18 sarcophagus supported by detached corner volutes.

Domestic and Public Architecture

The movement away from the conservative plans and elevations of the C17 previously described can be traced from the last decades of that century. The earliest farmhouse yet identified which abandoned the baffle-entry plan for gable-end chimneys and a central entrance is Scythe Stone Delph Farm, Rainford, dated 1682, but this plan did not become standard until well into the C18. Double-pile houses do not appear until as late as *c.* 1700. Among the first are Alder House, Atherton, 1697, and the present Colliers Arms, Aspull. Alder House looks compact, but is by no means a fully formed double-pile house: the plan is in fact an end baffle-entry arrangement with rooms added either side of a rear staircase. The fenestration is irregular, and the roof-line is still packed with gables. Land was no longer the source of funding for all these houses: Alder House was built by an iron merchant in Atherton's thriving nail industry.

26
p. 164   At the Manor House, Crawford, dated 1718, finally the true COMPACT PLAN is achieved, with a symmetrical façade, entrance into the centre of the hall, and behind the hall and opening off it in the second pile the staircase. But it still has a full-height porch, and little classical decoration, banded quoins aside. Stone
25   Hall, Dalton, possibly a decade earlier, has a charmingly clumsy classical façade with giant pilaster strips, a big pediment, and a pedimented doorcase. But the plan is still awkward – a house part and parlour in the front, and two rear wings with the stair-case between – and the roof still has upper crucks. A few miles away is Woodcock Hall at Newburgh, dated 1719, with a sym-metrical façade, a fashionable semicircular doorhood, a double-pile plan, and cross-windows – but still three gables to top the façade. Astley Old Vicarage is another of this transitional group, with cross-windows to the front and mullioned windows at the sides and rear; mullioned windows remained common in the early C18. Sashes only slowly superseded cross- and mullioned windows; Moorcroft House, Newburgh (1741), has early sur-vivors. A frequently encountered feature is an up-to-date early C18 staircase with square-panelled newels. At Gathurst Fold, Orrell, it comes with bulbous balusters; at Byrom Hall, Lowton (1713), with twisted balusters. These two houses illustrate the change from low, linear, mullion-windowed homes to the compact three-bay house. With Manor House Farm, Astley (1731) and Walker's Higher Farm, Aspull (1755), we arrive at the fully formed C18 brick box of the wealthier farmer or tradesman.

Local inspiration for such developments was provided at the beginning of the C18 by a number of ambitious houses and public buildings with BAROQUE façades, clustered around Liverpool, which in turn derived from national trends. Remarkably, the houses are the first known in SW Lancashire to express the clas-sical orders. Despite stylistic linkages, the identities of most of their masons and architects remain frustratingly elusive. First
28   comes the s wing of Croxteth Hall (Liverpool), built in 1702 by the 4th Viscount Molyneux: a curious, but ambitious composi-tion raised up on a substantial brick terrace, with a super-sized portal and sash windows – amongst the first in s Lancashire – under alternating pediments. Inside (until a fire in the 1950s) was a formal plan consisting of a first-floor enfilade of panelled rooms with plaster ceilings centred on a grand saloon, then replacing

the hall and dining chamber as the most important room of fashionable houses.

The same designer and craftsmen were surely responsible for the sandstone N wing of Woolton Hall (Liverpool), built about two years later by Richard Molyneux, the Viscount's son. The charmingly unsophisticated carving of the pediment trophies echoes those above Croxteth's entrance, and both parapets feature unusual gadroons. The illiterate fenestration (an even number of bays) and inept proportions were caused by the need to shoe-horn a huge saloon and dining room into the ground floor, splendidly fitted up with bolection panelling. Of about the same date but more coherent is the delightful Manor House, 27 Hale, with giant rusticated pilasters and a Baroque frontispiece, but also parapet gadroons and the same pediment trophies. To this group might be added little Cronton Hall, which under the plaster and C19 alterations may have had a pilastered façade not unlike Hale, and a similar, now demolished house at Edge Hill (Liverpool).

Often mentioned with these houses, though in many details different, is the former Blue Coat School of 1716–18 in Liver- 29 pool, the grandest PUBLIC BUILDING to date, the oldest surviving building in the centre, and by any standard a big school for the time, expressing the growing wealth and sophistication of the town. The plan is three sides of a quadrangle, the style Wren-inspired provincial, with a central pediment, cupola, and round-arched windows in distinctive double surrounds. *Thomas Steers* has been suggested as the architect, or *Thomas Ripley*, who designed the stylistically similar Custom House shortly afterwards (now demolished). Other schools are naturally more modest. The old school at Newburgh, endowed in 1714, is memorable for its T-plan and odd mullioned-and-transomed windows, which have almost semicircular heads. We will pick up the story of C18 public architecture below.

A different level of sophistication and worldliness marks the façade of Ince Blundell Hall, begun *c.* 1720, which we now know 30 is by *Sephton*. This is in the mainstream of English provincial Baroque, a nine-bay façade derived ultimately from Buckingham House in London. Sephton was also the master mason of the grandest house of all, Knowsley Hall, which became the princi- 31 pal seat of the Earls of Derby on the succession of the 10th Earl. From the 1720s until 1737 he extended it with a brick E wing of enormous length but surprisingly little cohesion or architectural sophistication. The spare stylistic cues are from the English Baroque. Was Sephton the designer? It is hard to think so when it is compared with the erudition of Ince Blundell. John Martin Robinson suggests he was working under the Earl's direction. To add to the mystery the parapet is articulated by stumpy pilaster strips, panelled with flowers, just like at Croxteth. The rambling exterior reflected the planning, with discrete apartments for family members; most public rooms were in the exciting S wing.

At the S end of this new Knowsley wing we encounter PALLA-DIANISM, not in a conventional Burlingtonian or Campbell form, 31

Bold Hall, by Giacomo Leoni, *c.* 1732 (demolished).
Lithograph by G.C. Greenwood, after Isaac Shaw, *c.* 1845

but in the exceptional shape of a two-storeyed loggia of stone
columns. John Martin Robinson has identified its derivation from
Palladio's Palazzo Chiericati in Vincenza, as illustrated in Leoni's
edition of the *Quattro Libri*. *Giacomo Leoni*, a Venetian and a
Catholic, was working for two of Derby's neighbours in this
period, but only fragments remain of both of their houses, the
new Lathom House of the later 1720s, and Bold Hall, of *c.* 1732.*
Leoni, the first architect of national standing to enter our story,
was no orthodox Palladian; instead he attempted to adapt his
ideas to the English country house. Both houses had rusticated
basements, porticoes (attached at Bold), and a *piano nobile*. Bold
was a nine-bay box of simple grandeur; Lathom was one of the
p. 225 greatest Georgian houses in the North. The thirteen-bay mansion
was linked by quadrant loggias to service wings; the w of these –
32, 33 which housed the stables – survives, as apartments. At both places
giant and melodramatic gatepiers still stand.

Mention must be made of three other houses of the early C18.
The accretive Hindley Hall (1728 etc.) is brick, with a swept
p. 140 parapet. Atherton Hall (1723–43, mostly demolished 1825) was
the only known excursion outside Yorkshire by *William Wakefield*.
The surviving towers of the service wings, pedimented on all four
sides, are distinctly Palladian, but the tremendous surviving door
surround points to the fact that Wakefield's architecture was
overwhelmingly Baroque. Allerton Hall (Liverpool), started
in the 1730s but not finished for eighty years, demonstrates the

---

* Leoni was probably introduced to these clients by Peter Legh, who had extensive
estates in SW Lancashire, and for whom Leoni was remodelling Lyme Park,
Cheshire from 1725.

Palladian influence of Leoni. It was conceived on a scale comparable with Atherton, yet its builders were merchant brothers, a mark of the accelerating commercial wealth of the county.

Bank Hall, Warrington, now the Town Hall, is the outstanding 35 mid-C18 house of S Lancashire. Dating from 1749–50, it is by *James Gibbs* at the end of his career, and is finished inside with good Rococo plasterwork and excellent cantilevered staircases. 36 This compact house was neither country house nor villa, being built by Thomas Patten on the outskirts of the town where he could keep an eye on his copper and glass works across the fields. (The foundations and cellars are made up of blocks of copper slag.) The plan is stiflingly symmetrical, and still features private apartments on the *piano nobile*, quite an old-fashioned feature. There are earlier ROCOCO INTERIORS: the Stucco Room – extended in the 1890s – is amongst the fragments of the surviving 1730s interiors at Knowsley Hall, and two rooms with excellent stuccowork survive at Ince Blundell, which was completed by *Henry Blundell* from the 1760s. He was proud to be his own architect, designing a grand park gateway whose archaic Baroque character is explained by the fact that Blundell copied it from a painting in his collection. We will return to this avid collector.

Palladianism, simplified and astylar, informed the large number of houses of middling size built from the mid C18. Maghull Manor is bay-fronted and peculiarly far deeper than it is wide. Bickerstaffe Hall (1772), of only three bays, was almost certainly built by the Stanleys as a hunting lodge. Another lodge – bigger, more refined, and pedimented – is the derelict Newton Park Farmhouse (Newton-le-Willows), built in the same decade at the centre of a small park. A whole gaggle around Liverpool was built by merchants following, more humbly, in the footsteps of Allerton Hall, as primary residences, not weekly retreats. Survivors include Newsham House, Fairfield, and the ashlar-faced Olive Mount, Wavertree (1790s), built by a grocer and tea-dealer. The most striking is The Hazels, Huyton, 1764, a superior but unorthodox Palladian box with a taut five-bay façade, rising to a full-width pediment framing a three-bay pediment within it.

The greatest PUBLIC BUILDING of the C18 is Liverpool Town 34 Hall and Exchange of 1749–54 by *John Wood* of Bath. Wood had recently completed an exchange for Liverpool's arch-rival, Bristol. His appointment was secured with a favourable report from one of the town's most remarkable C18 residents, the businesswoman Sarah Clayton, who gathered opinions of him in Bath. Rich Palladian façades survive, with carved panels illustrating the sources of Liverpool's wealth, elephants, slaves and all. In 1788 *James Wyatt* designed, and later *John Foster Sen.* executed, a new dome raised on a lantern and a ballroom extension. After a fire in 1795 the same team created a new Neoclassical interior with a grand staircase up to a circuit of quite 56 superb rooms, far and away the best Georgian interiors in SW *p. 287* Lancashire, and with few comparisons amongst civic architecture of the period. Other Georgian TOWN HALLS are lost. Wigan's was of the market-hall model, with an open-arcaded ground-floor market, built 1720. Prescot had a masculine mid-C18 Palladian Court House, with a cupola at one end and a bow at the other. Its demolition after the Second World War still shames the town. Parish governance has left three Late Georgian stone LOCK-UPS of different shapes: Everton's (Liverpool) is round with a conical stone roof, Wavertree's (Liverpool) is octagonal, and Farnworth's (Widnes) is a simple rectangular shed.

One of the first expressions of NEOCLASSICISM in domestic architecture was Halsnead Park (Whiston) of 1789, *Soane*'s only Lancashire house, demolished in 1932. Another was Haydock Lodge, destroyed in the 1970s. The Doric gateway now re-erected at Newton-le-Willows was probably the best part. At Little Crosby, the Blundell family followed up the C18 makeover of Crosby Hall with a Greek Revival library containing superb mahogany bookshelves fitted out in 1815.

Of the C18 GOTHIC REVIVAL there is little. Most interesting is the undated folly or bathhouse near Ormskirk. The Receptacle at Haigh, two-storey almshouses built in 1772, has primitive pointed surrounds. On the domestic front there is only Formby Hall, with a castellated parapet, but this could just as easily be early C19 as C18.*

Two aspects of agricultural architecture emerging in the Late Georgian period must be mentioned. The tradition of combining agricultural and domestic accommodation continued in the form of the LAITHE HOUSE, consisting of a barn and residence with separate entrances. This has usually been viewed as an upland, Pennine species, but there are examples at Eccleston (St Helens), Worthington and Standish, and elsewhere. A once-common feature of farms was the paddy house or 'PADDY SHANT', basic accommodation for itinerant harvest labour which acquired its name after the Irish influx in the 1840s. At Light-shaw Hall, Golborne, it is a room in the basement. At Eltonhead Farm, St Helens, it is a single room on each of two floors, attached to an out-range. They never intercommunicate with the farmhouse, and are seldom heated.

Designed Landscapes

There are no outstanding intact examples of DESIGNED LAND-SCAPE. Elements, almost shadows, of formal Early Georgian landscapes survive at Allerton Hall and Atherton Hall, both now public parks. The park at Atherton was approached by an avenue from Leigh church, whose tower formed an eyecatcher. The grandest park is Knowsley, enclosed in the early C19 by a wall over ten miles long. Strong traces of the formal terraced gardens illustrated in the early C18 remain, and a sequence of lakes linked

---

*Adam's massive baronial scheme for Knowsley Hall was not executed. He did have one success in SW Lancashire, but his enlargement of Woolton Hall (Liverpool) is a minor, and disappointing, Neoclassical work. Uncertainty remains as to whether he was involved in its execution.

by a dell survive from the landscaping that accompanied the 10th Earl's building programme. All these features were later softened and remodelled in naturalistic *Capability Brown* fashion. He was paid for a plan in 1775, but whether it was acted upon is not known. Of the other big name there is only *Repton*'s park for Garswood New Hall, now a golf course, the house demolished, and possibly work at Lathom House. Of less lauded designers, there is strong evidence – in the form of a survey dated 1815 – that *John Webb* (*c.* 1754–1828) designed the small but well-formed and well-maintained park of Crosby Hall, Little Crosby. This is a high-walled island designed in informal style on the windswept coastal plain; seldom have shelter belts been more necessary. A similar park at neighbouring Ince Blundell is now given over to agriculture, though the structure of belts and clumps survives. Croxteth is kept up as a public country park, now encircled by Liverpool suburbia, and retains a sense of inclusion and composition. Haigh Hall's parkland is now a country park too, but there is no evidence of the formal late C17 gardens or their C19 successors. The ploughed-up park at Bold, once one of the biggest in Lancashire, now has the M62 running though the middle. The M6 has done the same at Winstanley.

Of LANDSCAPE STRUCTURES not already mentioned, the outstanding cases are the TEMPLES at Ince Blundell, built by Henry Blundell to house his celebrated collection of antique sculpture; they constitute one of the greatest expressions of the Neoclassical ideal in Britain. Inspired by visits to Rome with his fellow collector Charles Towneley of Towneley Hall, Burnley, he devised appropriately Roman settings in which his collection could be displayed, as he intended from the outset, for the public. *William Everard* designed the Garden Temple in the 1790s, with a Tuscan tetrastyle front. The Pantheon is altogether more splendid, an ashlar miniature of the original (substituting an Ionic portico for Corinthian). It was built *c.* 1800, and though Blundell probably had a hand in it, the professional designer is unknown. Sadly the interior was stripped of its statuary in the 1950s.* Also at Ince Blundell is the late C18 Priest's House, a striking round building with the cardinal faces flattened.

OBELISKS were erected in the C18 at Allerton Hall, and in Atherton and Leigh marketplaces. Another of the C18 was transplanted from Lyme Park, Cheshire, to Earlestown market square in the 1870s. Amongst vanished items were a Gothick banqueting house at Ince Blundell, and another at Haigh made of the hard, workable coal called cannel. Still standing at Knowsley is the summerhouse or eyecatcher of 1755, called for obvious reasons the Octagon. In the park is the barbican-like lodge by *William Burn* (1849), landscape ornament rather than practical barrier, and other lodges and a boat-house by him in a Loudonesque *ornée* manner. Otherwise in this part of Lancashire LODGES are generally minor; *Leoni* designed plain octagons at Lathom.

*It is now in the Liverpool Museum and the Walker Art Gallery, Liverpool.

STABLES – Lathom aside – are disappointing, but Croxteth's rambling late C17–early C18 ranges are informally handsome. A part of *Leoni*'s yard at Bold Hall survives, with a pilastered centre, and a Palladian brick range at Ince Blundell. Winstanley has a peculiar collection of ranges of different dates, dominated by the rearing horses of the Neptune fountain of *c.* 1830 by *William Spence*.

Urban Housing

By *c.* 1700, coal, trade and manufacturing had created a merchant class rich enough to erect fine new HOUSES in many towns. An early survival is a mid-C18 façade on Millgate Street, Wigan: five squat bays of sashes with the keyed lintels endemic at that date, and a pedimented doorcase. Of a number surviving in Prescot, the best now houses the Prescot Museum. Its pediment and proportions show the influx of Palladian ideas. Perhaps slightly earlier is No. 43 Burscough Street, Ormskirk, a more sophisticated version of the same 1–3–1 façade, with the first-floor windows of the centre recessed, and an excellent Ionic doorcase. Wigan's grandest C18 houses form an early suburb climbing N up Standishgate, their sequencing revealed in the changing styles of window surrounds. There are others in Warrington. All these are – or were – free-standing houses. A rung down are the first speculatively built TERRACED HOUSES, of which Warrington still has a few good examples. Winwick Street has a short run with lugged window surrounds typical of the early C18. Stanley Street was probably developed by the artist *Hamlet Winstanley*, and named in honour of his patron the Earl of Derby. Quoins and rusticated wedge lintels suggest the 1740s. Later in the C18 Bewsey Street was built up in short rows, a suburban extension.

But these are scraps compared with the building boom then beginning in LIVERPOOL, which was to make it one of the greatest, if possibly the least celebrated, of the Georgian townscapes of Britain. Despite the Corporation owning all the land, no systematic plan was employed, and new streets such as Duke Street and Seel Street followed the lines of existing lanes and field boundaries S or E of the centre. Lessees acting as property developers elsewhere introduced the formal model of squares pioneered in London a century earlier, of which four were laid out around the middle of the C18. Only scraps remain, and nothing at all of Sarah Clayton's Clayton Square, which introduced the first uniform façades. Other C18 streets, e.g. Duke Street, had irregular frontages developed individually or in small rows, and most merchants had attached or detached warehousing on their property. This (minus the warehousing) was true even of Rodney Street, laid out in 1783–4 by the lawyer and renaissance man William Roscoe, which began the colonisation of the high ground to the E. It is remarkably well preserved, and all the more enjoyable for the constant fidgeting of the building lines. A peculiarity of these Liverpool houses is that the staircase often rises parallel to the street front from the rear of the entrance hall, and not perpendicular to it.

Rodney Street succeeded in attracting mercantile families into a new suburb elevated above the noise and filth of the centre. *Cuthbert Bisbrown*, a builder, had earlier attempted to establish the first PLANNED SUBURB, a high-class area called Harrington for 'gentlemen not obliged by business to reside in the centre and bustle of the town'. Laid out on a grid plan from 1771, it failed miserably, possibly because of its very isolation. In Liverpool even some grander merchants did not stop 'living above the shop' until the C19, *see* p. 64. Nevertheless, the flight to the suburbs had begun. It would not be reversed for two hundred years.

IMPROVEMENT ACTS helped to mitigate the effects of the bustle on the centre, and bestow dignity appropriate to the growing reputation and prosperity of Liverpool. The first, in 1786, enabled the rebuilding of the w side of Castle Street with uniform classical façades probably by *Samuel Hope* of Manchester; fragments survive. Wigan too undertook some town planning five years later, when King Street was laid out. There are still a few of the early houses on this, the first straight street in the town.

SOUTH-WEST LANCASHIRE IN THE INDUSTRIAL REVOLUTION

The traditional jibe 'Manchester Men; Liverpool Gentlemen' has at its heart a truth that underlies the map of s Lancashire, the first industrial economy and society in the world. It implies that Manchester was all grubby manufacturing, while Liverpool was trade and finance. Liverpool has been Manchester's political and social rival since it emerged from obscurity in the C17, but in economic terms their relationship was until the mid C20 as much about mutual dependency and complementary specialisms as bitter competition.

Liverpool was the entrepôt, not only for industrial Lancashire but for most of the industrialising North and Midlands, where raw materials from the New World and Asia arrived and finished products left for markets overseas. It owed everything to the sea and the River Mersey. Ship-owning and overseas trading required sophisticated financial systems, and Liverpool developed into a banking and insurance centre second in the country only to London. Manufacturing was never a dominant part of the mature Liverpool economy, although processing the first significant imported commodities, tobacco and sugar, provided major industries for two hundred years.

Other towns developed varied economies. In the E, Leigh and Tyldesley looked to nearby Manchester, expanding as centres of linen and silk production before turning to cotton in the later C19. Wigan, a noted producer of woollen bedding textiles in the early modern period, grew as a major centre of metallurgical industries and coal mining from the C16. Further sw in the Lancashire coalfield, Prescot and the districts that would become St

Helens prospered in the C18 by supplying Liverpool with coal. These places were extensions of Liverpool's economy just as Leigh or Oldham were of Manchester's. Coal at St Helens was a primary reason for the development there of the glass industry at the end of the C18, which helped create the present town. Warrington prospered by its advantageous position on the navigable Mersey midway between the two great centres. It had copper, then cotton and metal-working industries, from which wire-working emerged as the town's great specialism. File-, nail- and watch-making and similar craft trades drove the economies of other smaller towns, such as Prescot and Atherton. The other important industry, chemicals, was a C19 creation which blossomed in St Helens and created Widnes.

Mining

Evidence discovered beneath Wigan suggests that the Lancashire Coalfield has been exploited since the Roman period. By the end of the C17 the extraction of COAL was firmly established in Prescot, around what became St Helens, and especially Wigan, where workings were opened right in the centre of the town. Here the much-prized cannel was mined, a hard coal that produced a brilliant smokeless light. To drain the workings under his estate, Sir Roger Bradshaigh of Haigh Hall in 1652 began construction of the Great Sough, a drainage tunnel that took seventeen years to excavate. This impressive piece of civil engineering is the only notable monument to this phase of the industry, for other operations were largely small-scale and ephemeral: drift mines where the seams outcropped, tiny shafts called bell-pits, and – later – deeper pits operated with cages driven by a horse gin. In the late C18 steam power made it possible to reach new depths and pump them clear of water. The first *Newcomen* engine in the area is recorded at Orrell in the 1770s. Equally vital was the proper ventilation of workings on this new scale, and the pilastered exhaust chimney of one such system of 1840 still stands on Aspull Common. It was built by the Earls of Balcarres, Bradshaigh's successors at Haigh. The 6th and 7th earls took an active and progressive interest in their mining concerns, and in 1839–41 on the Leeds and Liverpool Canal at Aspull the 7th Earl built an integrated workshop and barge depot. The cupola'd central pavilion of the courtyard-plan complex remains.

By the beginning of the C20 hundreds of mines from Prescot to St Helens and Wigan, and on to Leigh and Atherton, were in production, but the last pit closed in 1992, and nearly all have vanished. Here and there are some simple brick buildings or shabby entrance gates, though most of the pit-head buildings of Astley Green Colliery have been preserved as a museum. The steel headstock of 1912 is the last still standing in Lancashire, a noble and mournful monument to a vast industry. The greatest legacy is the coalfield landscape, which has been remodelled throughout. This is most complete between Wigan, Ince and

Leigh, where in addition to new hills – the spoil heaps – there are extensive lakes, called flashes, created by subsidence.

Transport and Communication

The rise of the port of Liverpool in the C17 was remarkable. It supplanted Chester as the River Dee silted, taking over Irish trade and the export of Cheshire salt. After it entered the triangular Atlantic trading system at the end of the century its fleet of ocean-going merchantmen grew rapidly, exposing the port's physical constraints. So the Corporation built the world's first enclosed mercantile DOCK, designed by *Thomas Steers* and *p. 260* opened in 1715. One new dock followed another to meet demand, until by the end of the C18 there were five, at a time when no other town could boast more than one. The first substantial remains are early C19, such as the red sandstone river wall at *John Foster Sen.* and *John Rennie*'s Prince's Dock, opened in 1821 for the blue-riband American trade. Cotton for Lancashire's mills was now the most important cargo. Foster was replaced by *Jesse Hartley*, one of the greatest engineers of the C19. As the Liverpool architect and historian J.A. Picton recalled, this former bridge-builder from Yorkshire, who took up his post as the world's first full-time dock engineer without ever having built a dock before, for thirty-six years

> guided with a despotic sway the construction of some of the mightiest works of the kind ever erected. Personally he was a man of large build and powerful frame, rough in manner, and occasionally even rude, using expletives which the Angel of Mercy would not like to record; sometimes capricious and tyrannical, but occasionally, when he was attached, a firm and unswerving friend. Professionally he had grand ideas, and carried them into execution with a strength, solidity and skill that have never been exceeded.

His ideas were sometimes innovative, his workmanship always superlative. In architectural matters he was remarkably assured, and highly idiosyncratic, whether operating in a massively Grecian or a fortress Gothic idiom. All these facets are present in his masterpiece, the Albert Dock and its associated ware- *96* houses, built 1843–7 principally for the Far East trade. The ware- *p. 265* house stacks are a peerless synthesis of the latest technology from textile-mill construction and ideas on warehouse planning, interpreted by Hartley with some unique and pioneering twists.

The Hartley era ended in 1861, and continued expansion of Liverpool's docks was entrusted to *G.F. Lyster* and then to his more competent son *A.G. Lyster*. They made use of technologies introduced by Hartley to handle the huge new iron steamships. Foremost of these were hydraulic power, and river locks. As ships grew bigger, so did the docks, which from the 1870s were made of mass concrete. The climax of these works were Alexandra

Dock (opened 1881) and the vast Gladstone Dock (begun 1910), the last new docks in Liverpool until 1971. Standardised transit sheds, from the 1880s two storeys high, and later made of reinforced concrete, lined the quays. Storage facilities evolved through ever more gargantuan single-commodity warehouses –
97   the elder *Lyster*'s Italianate Waterloo Grain Warehouses (1866–8), and the younger's towering Tobacco Warehouse (*c.* 1897–1901) – to silos for grain and petroleum. (For a fuller account *see* p. 262.) Meanwhile at Garston new docks for exporting coal opened in 1853, 1875 and 1910.

Without good COMMUNICATIONS Liverpool and its port were nothing, and from the C17 its business classes took the lead in enhancing them. They promoted TURNPIKES, which by the mid C18 connected the city with Prescot, Warrington, Wigan and beyond. But water transport was of much greater importance to internal trade. They backed the Irwell and Mersey Navigation, completed in 1736, to improve communications with Manchester, and the Douglas Navigation, begun in the 1730s, for the export of Wigan coal. It was they too who ushered in the CANAL AGE by promoting the Sankey Brook Navigation to ease the flow of coal from the mines around Parr (now St Helens) and Haydock. This sometimes overlooked project opened in 1757, so predating the celebrated Bridgewater Canal, yet it has the key features of the modern canal: an entirely new still-water channel, raised up by nine locks from the Mersey. *Henry Berry*, Steers' successor at Liverpool and a native of Parr, was the surveyor. Much has been infilled, but on the outskirts of St Helens are the remains of the Old Double Dock, the earliest staircase lock in Britain, and at Winwick Quay (Warrington) is a little boatyard and dry dock from 1841. Francis Egerton, 3rd Duke of Bridgewater, and his engineer *James Brindley* extended his canal to Runcorn on the Mersey in 1776 in order to reach Liverpool, thus connecting the port via the Grand Trunk Canal to the new industries of the Midlands. He also built the small Duke's Dock in the port for transhipment; its splendid warehouses, comparable to the best in Manchester, are demolished. Six years earlier the first sod of the Leeds and Liverpool Canal was cut amongst the meres
101   at Halsall. The first engineer was *John Longbotham*. When completed in 1816, the canal linked the East Coast and the mills of W Yorkshire with Lancashire manufacturing and with Liverpool, where locks down to the docks finally opened in 1846, allowing direct transhipment. The canal was built for barges of greater beam than narrowboat dimensions, and on the edge of Wigan they are carried up 200ft (61.5 metres) in a flight of twenty-three locks. The best surviving group of canal WAREHOUSES, just below at the basin in Wigan, was restored in the 1980s as Wigan Pier. They illustrate the evolution of the type from low stone-built structures of the 1770s, through the inclusion of twin barge-holes to allow barges to enter the building, to the taller proportions of a Victorian example with brick walls and cast-iron columns. Another contrasting pair is at Leigh, where branches of the Leeds and Liverpool and the Bridgewater canals met in 1820.

The development of EARLY RAILWAYS was also stimulated by the mining industry. Wagonways can still be traced in the Douglas Valley w of Wigan, where coal from the mines in Orrell and Winstanley was carried in trucks by horse and by gravity down to barges on the river and the Leeds and Liverpool Canal. *George Stephenson*'s Liverpool & Manchester Railway, promoted and *p. 414* financed by Liverpool men, ushered in railways as we understand them today when it opened in 1830, with passenger services running to regular timetables. Chat Moss was crossed on a bed of brushwood; Olive Mount (Liverpool) was conquered with a vertically sided cutting sliced 70 feet (21 metres) into the bedrock. The two greatest civil engineering structures followed precedents in canal construction: the world's first railway tunnel, spearing for two miles under Liverpool to the docks at Wapping, and the world's first railway viaducts, of which that crossing the Sankey valley, with its splayed and pilastered piers rising to a cor- 98 belled parapet, is the most celebrated. Skew-arch bridges such as that at Rainhill attracted much comment too, although they were not a new type either. These structures established with remarkable maturity forms that would be repeated thousands of times on railways throughout the world. How much of the credit we can assign to *Stephenson* – who was not a civil engineer – is unclear. *Jesse Hartley*, who was a bridge builder, was a consultant.

STATION DESIGN took longer to mature into a distinctive tradition. The Warrington terminus of the Warrington & Newton Railway, a branch of the L&MR opened in 1831, is a rare early example, now a pub: there is nothing to tell it from a simple brick house. Of similar date is a substantial and symmetrical brick villa near St Helens Junction Station, Sutton, probably built as a private venture to provide refreshment for travellers on the L&MR, in the manner of a roadside inn, before station refreshment rooms had been invented. By contrast, the monumental Neoclassical screen of the first Lime Street Station (1836) was designed by the Corporation Surveyor *John Foster Jun.*, reflecting the significance attached by the town to the project. The second station at Edge Hill, also of 1836, provides a glimpse of the Lime 99 Street terminus – ashlar carved into banded rustication and emphatic keystones. Its plan, with rectangular buildings on opposing platforms containing booking office, waiting rooms, etc., is recognisable, even if there are as yet no visible design elements specific to railways. One of these, the canopy, had appeared by the following decade at Earlestown, wrapped around a delightful little neo-Elizabethan gem encrusted with oversized chimneys. The Liverpool, Crosby & Southport Railway opened as far as Waterloo in 1848, an early commuter line. Of a similar date is the Southport & Manchester Railway route from Wigan to Southport, lined with picturesquely composed and substantially built Tudorbethan station buildings and gatekeeper's cottages.

By the mid C19 the network had spread to all the major towns, making the railway bridge, cutting and embankment a part of the everyday landscape. Lime Street Station was given two new gracefully curving train sheds, in 1867 (*William Baker* and *F. Stevenson*) and 1878–9 (*E. W. Ives*). The first had briefly the greatest span in the world – 200 ft (61.5 metres) – and they remain some of the finest in the country, memorable for the cigar-shaped struts of bound rods. The cavernous approach cuttings make a sublime entrance into the city. Of the two other major termini in the city, only the façade survives of the hotel and offices that fronted *Henry Shelmerdine*'s Exchange Station (1880s, for the Lancashire & Yorkshire Railway). Central Station opened in 1874 at the end of the last main line built in the area, that of the Cheshire Lines Committee. It is demolished as well, but the attractive intermediate stations are still standing, of eclectic cottagey design. Good examples are at Cressington Park (Liverpool suburbs) and Widnes.

As for VICTORIAN ENGINEERING, tunnels with handsome portals are at Edge Hill (1847, with associated engine house), and at Dingle for the Liverpool Overhead Railway. This elevated electric railway, begun in the 1880s, ran the length of the docks on an iron viaduct until 1956. One of the engineers, *Charles Douglas Fox,* also worked on the Mersey Railway, the under-river commuter line to Birkenhead, opened in 1886. The most outstanding BRIDGE of the period is the Britannia Railway (1864–8) spanning the Mersey at Widnes, designed by the London & North Western Railway's engineer *William Baker* to carry a new route from Crewe to Liverpool. Three 300-ft (92-metre) iron lattice-truss spans are clasped onto 75-ft (23-metre) stone pylons by crenellated iron clamps, and onto the approach viaducts by stone 'barbicans'. This achieved a dream of bridging the Runcorn Gap, which decades before had caused Telford to propose a suspension bridge with an unprecedented principal span of 1,000 ft (308 metres). A road crossing was finally realised with the Runcorn Transporter Bridge of 1905 (engineers *Webster & Wood*). This was demolished in the 1960s, but a smaller and later example of the type, built by the soap-makers Joseph Crosfield & Sons to link two parts of their works, still straddles the Mersey at Warrington.

Canals were not killed off by the railways, and in the form of the MANCHESTER SHIP CANAL (1887–1903) they took on a scale never equalled in Britain. The project was Manchester's attempt to bypass Liverpool by allowing ocean-going ships to travel directly to it. This meant heroic civil engineering, nowhere more so than at Warrington, where a cutting criss-crossed by massive iron and steel rail and road bridges and dammed by a lock complex makes a vista of thrilling industrial power. (Sir) *Edward Leader Williams* was the chief engineer.

Industries and Industrial Architecture to the early C20

Industrialisation of TEXTILE PRODUCTION began in Manchester and the surrounding valleys. Early mills were water-powered; they required riverside sites where a head of water could be produced, which at first ruled out sites in the lowland W of the county. Nevertheless many towns in SW Lancashire, at least in the E part, became important cotton-producing centres in the C19, building on long histories of HANDLOOM WEAVING. Wigan built a cloth hall in the 1780s; Warrington had a thriving fustian-cutting industry in the C19, based in well-lit top-floor workshops. Leigh too produced fustians, and muslins as well, until in the 1820s it became for half a century a centre of the Lancashire silk industry. A row of weavers' houses in Higginson Street illustrates what few architectural features these cottage industries required. The loom shops were on the ground floor, with an extra window to provide better light. In other houses, such as a row of 1825 in Bradshawgate, Leigh, weaving was done in the basement. Piecework was also supplied from isolated farms and cottages, and in proto-industrial villages such as Glazebury and Lowton households supported themselves by a combination of agriculture and domestic manufacture, in brick terraced housing often indistinguishable now from any early C19 workers' dwellings. There is a similar row of c. 1800 at Higher Green Lane, Astley Green. The cloth came into receiving houses, like that of the Leigh silk agent Robert Guest. His house is three-storeyed, with a taking-in door and a hoist and separate door and stairs, bypassing the domestic accommodation, to the open top floor. This housed warping mills and winding machines, and warehousing for the cloth pending its despatch to Manchester merchant-manufacturers.

A sort of halfway house to full-scale factory production was the gathering of handlooms in mill-like WORKSHOPS. A rare surviving example in Ormskirk, dating from c. 1800, has two low storeys of close-set windows. By this time steam power made possible the construction of SPINNING MILLS on the Lancashire Plain, incorporating the famous inventions: James Hargreaves' Spinning Jenny of 1764, Richard Arkwright's water frame of 1771 and Samuel Crompton's spinning mule of 1779. Wigan had eight such mills by 1818 and twenty-six in 1870. Peel's Cotton Works at Latchford in Warrington had a *Boulton & Watt* engine to power spinning mules in 1787, before even anything in Manchester. There are no survivors from the early phases, except a section of Victoria Mill, Wigan, of c. 1840. The mills that still stand belong to the later C19 and the early C20. Gidlow Mill in Wigan, of 1863–5 by *George Woodhouse*, illustrates many important developments: an integral boiler and engine house, and 'fireproof' construction of cast-iron columns supporting cast-iron beams and brick jack arches. Gidlow was an example of the increasingly common INTEGRATED MILLS, weaving as well as spinning with the aid of the recently introduced power-looms in single-storey weaving sheds with north lights.

Most other mills are vast deep-plan Late Victorian and Edwardian structures from the last phase of expansion. The biggest concentrations are in Wigan and in Leigh, which specialized in ring spinning, an American technique adopted in the later C19. Leigh has good specimens by two practices that specialised in mill design. Butts Mill, 1906–7, is typical of *Stott & Sons* of Oldham. The extravagant and distinctly Byzantine water tower, with copper dome and polychromatic terracotta banding, is characteristic of the dynasty under the helm of *Abraham Henthorn Stott Jun*. The mill has reinforced concrete floors on rolled-steel beams, a feature which began appearing from the later C19, but was never universal. Also in the town is the *Stott*'s delightful Alder Mill offices, of 1907. Leigh Mill, by the rival firm *Bradshaw, Gass & Hope* of Bolton, is a very complete example of the double mill. These consisted of two separate mills built end-to-end and powered from a central engine house, and so could be erected in two phases. The second half of Leigh Mill, opened in 1923, was one of the last Lancashire spinning mills to be built. Western Mills in Wigan, along with Atlas Mills, Bolton (SE Lancashire), are considered to have been the largest textile complex in the country. Of the five mills here, three by *Stott & Sons* from the late C19 still stand.

The Lancashire cotton industry had all but ended by the 1970s. (The single-storey Unit 1 at Howe Bridge Mills, Atherton, built in 1978, is therefore a freak, the only building to be built for cotton spinning in the county since the 1920s.) Many of the mills which have escaped demolition are, like Western Mills, used as warehousing or light industrial space. In revealing contrast to Manchester, the first conversion to apartments (also in Wigan) was announced only as this book was going to press.

Few towns can be more closely associated with a single industry than St Helens is with GLASS. There had been glass-

St Helens, British Plate Glass Company works, Ravenhead, with the
Great Casting Hall on the right. Engraving.
(*The Pictorial History of the County of Lancaster*, 1844)

furnace cones at Warrington in the late C17, and bottle making on Thatto Heath early in the following century, but the key development was the opening of the Sankey Brook Navigation. This persuaded investors to back a local colliery owner and found the British Plate Glass Company at Ravenhead in 1773. With French expertise and local coal and sand, the Company created a manufactory of impressive scale: the Great Casting Hall was one of the finest industrial buildings of the C18. The last parts were demolished in the 1970s, though stables, manager's house and a windmill still stand. In 1901 the company was bought out by Pilkington Brothers, the firm begun in 1826 that is still synonymous with the town. In the 1840s–50s Pilkingtons grew rapidly, producing blown sheet glass (a blown cylinder cut open, rather than a spun disc) and the cheaper, translucent rolled glass which was much in demand for factory and station roofs. Glass was made in batches in brick furnace cones, though none of these survive. However, the World of Glass museum preserves an early example of the regenerative tank furnace, introduced by Pilkingtons in 1873, which made possible continuous production of sheet glass. It is probably by *J. Medland Taylor*, who designed numerous buildings for Pilkingtons; the large plate-glass plant at Cowley Hill, opened 1876, may also be his. C20 advances in production cumulated in the 1950s in the revolutionary float tank process. The remaining plants, whose huge concrete chimneys dominate the skyline, employ this technique.

In the mid C19 the CHEMICAL INDUSTRY was as important to St Helens as glass. James Muspratt and Josiah Christopher Gamble established the town's first alkali works in 1828. Alkali (soda ash) was central to the manufacture of glass, and of soap and detergents, which were used in huge quantities in the textile industries. The industry began to desert St Helens from 1847 for the River Mersey, closer to the key raw material of Cheshire salt, effectively creating the modern town of Widnes. It rapidly evolved into one of the centres of the chemical industry, thereby acquiring a reputation as one of the most unpleasant places in Britain. The Catalyst museum occupies Italianate offices and laboratories of *c.* 1860. Soap-making was a related industry.

The industrial base of SW Lancashire was more diverse than in the SE of the county, being founded on local DOMESTIC CRAFT ENGINEERING. By the end of the C18 a high degree of specialisation was apparent. Warrington was famed for pins and files, trades transformed in the C19 into a huge wire-working industry requiring large but unremarkable plants. Ashton-in-Makerfield made locks and hinges; Chowbent, which became Atherton, prospered from the Middle Ages on nail- and chain-making, which evolved into bolt manufacture. Collier Brook Bolt Works is a mid-C19 survivor there. Prescot was from the mid C18 a centre for the production of clock and watch parts and tools. These craft industries required WORKSHOPS, little single- or two-storey buildings with a hearth and a chimney, in back yards or attached as outriggers to the craftsman's house. Only in Prescot do these survive in anything like a recognisable state. The clock-parts industry collapsed in the 1860s when assailed by cheap American and Swiss imports. A last-ditch attempt to compete was the Lancashire Watch Company, whose factory of 1890–2 by *Stott & Sons*, with an iron frame filled with rows of large windows and floored with concrete, was based on American practice.

Every town had at least one BREWERY. Leigh has two C19 examples of the once common, small-scale premises. The Lilford Brewery (1895) is of the sort built by landlords to supply their own business; the bigger Derby Brewery, with a tower, cooperage and stables, supplied a number of hostelries. The Wind Pump erected in 1845 to supply water to the Haigh Brewery stands in the middle of a field, like a giant peppermill. The delightful former Gateacre Brewery (Liverpool) of the 1860s, a compact three-storey block, sits happily in its villagey setting. These concerns and many others succumbed to the big brewers. One of the biggest was Greenall, Whitley & Co., whose large late C19 brew-house and malt-house at Warrington, designed by the brewery specialists *R. Davison, Son & Mackenzie* (later *Inskipp & Mac-kenzie*), have been converted into offices. The best brewery building is Cain's, Toxteth (Liverpool). The architect of the splendidly ornate Renaissance structure was perhaps Walter W. Thomas. For the excellent pubs built by Cain's and Greenall's, along with Walker's, *see* p. 83.

OTHER INDUSTRIES have had mixed survival rates. Of Liverpool's sugar-processing industry hardly a thing remains. Of its tobacco-processing industry there is Ogden's Tobacco Factory of 1900 in Everton, by *Henry Hartley*, with an office frontage sprouting a clock tower. Another tower, of more theatrical, middle-European form, is the signature of Beecham's Factory, St Helens' most manic building. It was built in 1884–7 by *H.V. Krolow* and *Harry May* (both of Liverpool) as a factory to produce Thomas Beecham's famous pills. Less licentious but somewhat bigger is the steepling façade of Wigan's Coop Suit Factory (now a business centre), established to employ Lancashire girls made redundant by the Lancashire cotton famine. It has four parts, the first of 1871 by *R. Todd* of Southport, united by cream and red brick and superimposed giant blank arcades. FOUNDRIES were significant businesses in many towns, including Liverpool, Warrington, Wigan and Ince. Two to mention are Francis Morton & Co.'s at Garston, which supplied prefabricated churches, stations, barracks and schools to the four corners of the Empire, and the Haigh Foundry near Wigan, established by the 6th Earl of Balcarres in 1788, which cast many components for Liverpool's Albert Dock in Liverpool. The oldest buildings here now are mid C19. Remains of C18 copper-smelting in War-rington and St Helens lie in the foundations and walls of buildings as lustrous blocks of slag. Lastly, GAS. The Wigan gasworks admired by Pevsner has disappeared, but there are good Victo-rian gasholders with cast-iron stanchions in the form of Tuscan columns at Bootle.

p. 626

p. 558

103

ARCHITECTURE IN THE EARLY
NINETEENTH CENTURY

Urbanisation, Housing and Domestic Architecture

Economic growth turned villages into towns and towns into cities. It drew in hundreds of thousands of migrants, especially from Ireland. Irish immigration had a powerful impact on Liverpool and towns such as St Helens, and the faith they brought with them resulted in striking numbers of Catholic churches. Except at Liverpool, this explosive growth was almost entirely unplanned. St Helens, a small roadside hamlet called Hardshaw before the canal arrived, spread like a spider as mines and manufactories opened up around it; Leigh was two separate settlements until the street of Bradshawgate was extended in the second half of the C19 to unite the medieval village with the mills to the E. Railways and

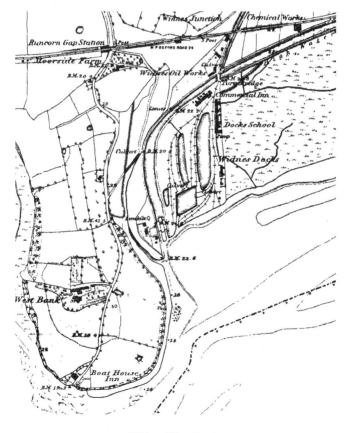

Widnes, West Bank.
(Ordnance Survey, 1849)

docks were a stimulus too. In 1830 George Stephenson co-established the Vulcan Foundry engine works near Newton-le-Willows, with workers' housing. A few miles away and a few years later Earlestown was founded, with a railway wagon works. Widnes developed in disjointed fashion after the rival St Helens & Runcorn Gap Railway and Sankey Brook Navigation canal arrived in 1833 on the salt marshes of the Mersey facing Runcorn, establishing small coal docks. Two decades later the railway company opened a new and larger dock downstream at Garston, creating another town. Villages such as Golborne and Astley acquired a semi-urban character, with simple rows of workers' cottages. New settlements established to a FORMAL PLAN number only one: Vulcan Village of 1833–8, and that is only a triangle of streets with a school, pub and green at the centre. But other employers did provide WORKERS' HOUSING. The British Plate Glass Co. built a terrace of back-to-back cottages beside its works at Ravenhead (St Helens) in the 1770s. Though no longer back-to-backs, these are the earliest survivors. At Haigh and Aspull the Earls of Balcarres erected occasional well-built stone rows, the earliest of which may be late C18. Now that the mines and works have gone, their locations appear almost random. Other Late Georgian workers' terraces are at Orrell and Up Holland.

LIVERPOOL in the early C19 assumed an architectural character very different from that of Manchester. Dedicated to commerce, it was free from utilitarian mill buildings and the smoke and clatter that went with them. Its new residential quarter was well planned, punctuated by classical churches and public buildings, and in its old, congested centre it was beginning to carve out spacious new thoroughfares. After a visit to Manchester in 1826 the artist John James Audubon returned with relief 'to bright Liverpool again', where the streets 'looked very wide, very clean, very well lined with very handsome buildings'. A few years later Alexis de Tocqueville made the same comparison, but saw beneath the surface: 'Liverpool is a beautiful town. Poverty is almost as great as it is at Manchester, but it is hidden.'

Housing conditions were worst in the larger towns. Both Warrington and Wigan had terribly insanitary COURT HOUSING, but the most extensive and notorious were built in the new suburbs of Liverpool, especially Vauxhall. They were entered via a passage through street-fronting terraces which opened onto a narrow yard flanked by back-to-backs, generally of a single room on three floors. Appallingly overcrowded, with minimal ventilation, no running water, and communal earth closets, they were a fearful source of disease. By the time construction was banned in 1864, they numbered 3,000 in the borough, housing 110,000. Cellar dwellings were equally infamous, generally consisting of a single room; some were inhabited as late as 1914. The last back-to-backs remaining in Liverpool, built off Duke Street in the 1840s, were restored in 2003. Most of SW Lancashire's surviving workers' housing belongs to the later part of the C19, and is discussed on p. 86.

MIDDLE-CLASS HOUSING was normally built away from polluted town centres, uphill and up-wind of industry. In Wigan the

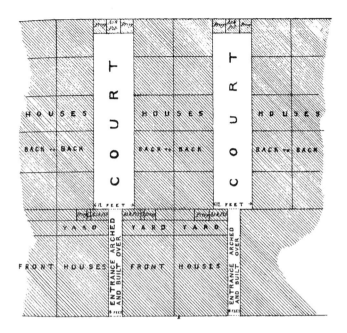

Liverpool, court housing.
Plan by W.H. Duncan, 1840

process began in the C18 to the N along Standishgate. In Warrington early C19 houses sprouted along the NW extension to Bewsey Street, itself a C18 suburban extension. Two houses in semi-rural areas built by colliery owners are The Mount, Orrell, a large ashlar Late Georgian villa erected by John Clarke, proprietor of the Orrell Colliery and banker, and the straightforward Blackbrook House (St Helens), built of good red brick before the 1840s. The new suburb of Liverpool above the town centre, begun at the end of the C18 by the laying out of Rodney Street (*see* p. 48), spread in the early C19 with dozens more spacious streets lined with generously proportioned terraces. Despite the incursions of the University and slum clearances, this remains a magnificent Georgian quarter, without compare in the North and Midlands. In contrast to the new industrial towns, this was formally planned, and the Corporation was the main planner. *John Foster Sen.*'s plan of 1800 established a grid centred on Abercromby Square, which, like Great George Square, laid out in 1803, had an enclosed garden after the London squares. Developers had to conform with an agreed elevation, imposing the uniform design absent from C18 residential streets. At Percy Street and Gambier Terrace, begun in the 1830s in stone not brick, the elevations reached a peak of sophistication. Wavertree became an extra-urban suburb with some buildings of urban type, e.g. the pedimented Sandown Terrace of *c.* 1840.

For those of a better station a range of private RESIDENTIAL PARK ESTATES was begun in the 1840s, gated developments mostly developed by local consortia, whose drives were lined with tree-fringed classical and Tudor Gothic villas. Of those in Liverpool, Sandfield Park (West Derby) was the grandest. There are three at Aigburth heading down to the riverfront. Others followed N of the city. A kind of precursor in Aigburth is St Michael's Hamlet, a little picturesque group by the foundry proprietor *John Cragg*, employing his cast-iron windows, verandas etc.* At Waterloo just N of Liverpool, a plainish hotel of 1818 started the development and established the name of a 'sea-bathing place' on the nearest seafront to the city. Beach-facing terraces followed from the 1820s, many with delightfully filigree iron verandas.

In Allerton the richest of Liverpool rich had been building MANSIONS since the C18 in extensive landscaped grounds. The first, Allerton Hall, was completed with its intended Palladian facade in the early 1810s by William Roscoe, lawyer, M.P. and man of letters, who built at the rear a grand Neoclassical library. Neoclassical also are Springwood (1839) with its tremendous staircase – begun by a plantation owner and completed by a ship-owner – and the remains of the house known as Allerton by *Thomas Harrison*, started in 1815. The best part of the stuccoed Kenyon Hall in Culcheth is another grand central hall with superimposed Ionic screens through which the staircase divides and returns. It was occupied in 1839. Childwall Hall (demolished) was a picturesque castellated pile by *John Nash*. Outside Warrington, (Sir) Gilbert Greenall, brewer and M.P., built Walton Hall in 1836–8 in an unsophisticated Elizabethan Gothic.

Neoclassicism prevailed for construction and refurbishment of the COUNTRY HOUSES of the old money, frequently made possible by money of decidedly new character. The *7th Earl of Balcarres* spent much of his colliery income from 1827 until the 1840s on the austerely impressive and superbly built Haigh Hall, which he may have designed himself. It certainly has ironwork supplied by his own foundry and ingenious doors of his own invention, and Neoclassical plasterwork supplied by *M. Stuber* of Paris. The Earl also designed numerous estate buildings and houses, in Loudonesque fashion except for the grand Neoclassical gateway on Wigan Lane (Wigan). The Winstanley Collieries paid for the sympathetic renovation of Winstanley Hall by *Lewis Wyatt*. Immense colliery incomes funded, too *John Foster Jun.*'s expansion of Garswood New Hall (demolished) for Sir John Gerard, with a palatial façade in the manner of Nash. Foster was also patronised by the Stanleys, for whom he extended the C15 part of Knowsley Hall in castellated fashion, creating the lantern-lit State Dining Room. The doors alone are 30 ft (9.2 metres) high. *William Burn* followed him and proposed complete reconstruction in elaborate castellated Gothic, but built only lodges, estate

53
p. 184
54
107

---

*The gorgeous two-storey veranda at the Rathbone family home, Greenbank House, Mossley Hill, is of the same date.

buildings (*see* p. 217), and two quite substantial houses. Designed landscapes are discussed on pp. 46–7.

Public and Commercial Buildings

For PUBLIC BUILDINGS Neoclassicism was the norm. Liverpool's Exchange was removed from the Town Hall to a new building of 1803–8 by *John Foster Sen.* immediately behind, containing news room, counting houses and warehouses. It has been replaced twice since. Of the town's dozens of civically or privately funded public works, there is room only for a quick list. *Thomas Harrison*'s distinguished Lyceum (1800–2), the Union News Room (1800), and *Foster Sen.*'s Athenaeum (1799, demolished) were news rooms and libraries. The Botanic Gardens (1802; removed to Edge Lane), and the Liverpool Royal Institution, converted by *Edmund Aikin* from a grand late C18 house in 1817 with lecture theatre and exhibition rooms, were both promoted by William Roscoe. Then there are Aikin's Wellington assembly rooms, and *Foster Jun.*'s colossal domed and porticoed Custom House, unnecessarily demolished after the Second World War. In 1837 both a Medical Institution and a Mechanics' Institution 59 opened. *Foster Jun.* converted a quarry into St James's Cemetery in 1827–9, a sublime landscape of walks and tunnels adorned by two jewels, the Oratory or chapel, and the circular Huskisson Mausoleum. A Jewish cemetery of 1837 in Kensington also survives, atmospherically abandoned behind a dignified entrance screen. Add to that an earlier Theatre Royal (demolished), and cemeteries, public baths, infirmaries and markets (to which we will return) and the widening and rebuilding of central streets from the 1820s, and the range and scale of civic and cultural investment in Liverpool become apparent.

Many of these works were products of the GREEK REVIVAL, which dominated Liverpool architecture *c.* 1815–*c.* 1840. The town at this period was often compared with the maritime cities of Antiquity, and the adoption of Greek architecture can be seen as symbolic, over and above mere fashion. The leading local figure in the Revival was the Corporation Surveyor *John Foster Jun.*, most of whose buildings have been demolished. We have encountered his father *John Foster Sen.* already; his son succeeded him as Surveyor until 1835, though the family had by then been tainted by allegations of corruption. His travels in Greece with C.R. Cockerell and the German archaeologists Haller and Linckh shaped the austere Grecian style he most commonly employed.

Cockerell was also the mentor to *Harvey Lonsdale Elmes*, the youthful architect of St George's Hall. This was the civic culmi- 77 nation of these decades, and the climax of the Grecian phase of p. 292 all English architecture, a building that can hold its own in comparison with any of these years in Europe. Elmes's Neoclassicism was innovative by any measure, certainly in a town littered with Foster's Greek orthodoxy. The axial planning that combined the

p. 323

briefs of two separate competitions – for a concert hall and for assize courts – is bold and decisive, if not entirely successful. The scale is overpowering, and the external use of massive square pillars was a stroke of genius. Elmes died of tuberculosis aged 78 only thirty-four, and eventually *Cockerell* saw the hall through to completion in 1856. To him are due the rich Roman interiors, especially the jewel-like Small Concert Room.

Only in the field of education does Gothic compete with the classical, for most SCHOOLS were religious foundations. Two minor schools of 1829, at Tyldesley and Standish, both altered, have two tiers of simple Gothick windows, but surviving schools of note are chiefly 1840s or later, and belong to a later part of the story.

Beyond Liverpool, this is a quiet period. St Helens built its first town hall and court house in 1839. It is demolished. There are 58 two DISPENSARIES: Warrington's, of 1819, quite big but entirely domestic in appearance, and Ormskirk's, 1830 and splendidly civic: a charming little ashlar façade with a pedimented Greek Doric portico.

In the field of COMMERCIAL ARCHITECTURE, early C19 Liverpool witnessed the decline of the centuries-old model of combining a merchant's home, counting house and warehouse in one premises (though a workshop and showroom on Duke Street was built as late as 1858 with the proprietor's house). The earliest surviving purpose-built commercial buildings are on North John Street, widened in the 1820s under John Foster Jun. These had shops on the ground floor; Barned's Buildings in Sweeting Street, of *c.* 1840, dispense with shops. In Prescot is what could be an extremely rare example of a purpose-built office from this period outside Liverpool. It looks like a single-storey gate lodge. BANKS, 38 for the first time, are purpose-built too. The building of Messrs Heywood on Brunswick Street, Liverpool – three ashlar storeys completed in 1800 – is an exceptionally early example by any standard. By the 1830s smaller towns could boast them too: Ormskirk has an ashlar one, and Warrington the pilastered Trustee Savings Bank (1829). WAREHOUSES in Liverpool, although now predominantly independent of housing, continued to be built according to the form established in the C18,* a brick envelope encompassing a building whose narrow frontage and deep plan 102 was determined by plot dimensions. Building high, normally about five or six storeys, was therefore necessary to maximise floor area.** This basic unit might be multiplied side-by-side. The introduction of bonded storage meant smaller windows.

Ecclesiastical Buildings

Church architecture of the early C19 in SW Lancashire is a rich seam. After many losses, the only surviving Neoclassical Anglican church is *Samuel Rowland*'s St Bride, Percy Street, Liverpool

---

* What may be the earliest surviving free-standing warehouses, on College Lane, seem to date from the late C18.
** The exceptional Goree Warehouses in the Strand, built by the Corporation, were reputedly thirteen stories high.

(1829–30), a prostyle temple with a monumental Ionic portico. The early C19 also saw GOTHIC re-emerge as an archaeologically serious and architecturally sophisticated style. The new steeple of Childwall church (Liverpool), erected in 1810–11, is still in the pretty Georgian Gothick fashion which would be revolutionised a few decades later. One important figure in the transformation was *Thomas Rickman*, an insurance clerk in Liverpool, who began to study old buildings whilst recovering from a breakdown. The results were published in 1817 as *An Attempt to Discriminate the Styles of English Architecture from the Conquest to the Reformation*, to which we owe the classification of medieval architecture under the terms Early English, Decorated and Perpendicular. Rickman's name is linked with three amazing Liverpool churches built in 1812–16 by the ironmaster *John Cragg*, of 45 which St George, Everton, and St Michael-in-the-Hamlet, Aigburth, still stand. But the extent of his involvement is obscure: Rickman was scathing of Cragg's Gothic detailing, and some components were cast before Rickman became involved. Nevertheless both are remarkable for their pioneering use of prefabricated cast iron. The interior of St George's is an unalloyed joy, the cast iron imparting poise and delicacy. Tracery, roof structure, columns and arches supporting the galleries are all iron. St Michael-in-the-Hamlet extends prefabrication to parapets, battlements and other external details, and a dado made according to Cragg's patent cladding system.

The Gothic of these churches is delightful, but the detailing is not yet archaeologically correct. They are part of a group in and around Liverpool in which Dec–Perp Gothic edges towards Ecclesiological levels of accuracy. *Thomas Harrison*'s steeple for Our Lady and St Nicholas, begun 1810, is the most Gothicky, with a delightfully delicate stone lantern. St Luke, St Luke's Place, is contemporary and attributed to the *Fosters*, and its Perp is more sophisticated. The deep chancel added in 1822 is exceptional for the period. Rickman's pupil *John Broadbent* designed a tower at St Mary, Walton, a few years later in which only a few details, e.g. quatrefoiled circular windows, clearly betray the date.*

These churches were locally funded; others were supported by the CHURCH BUILDING COMMISSION, which dispensed funds voted by Parliament in 1818 and 1825. The rapid population growth meant more Commissioners' churches were built in Lancashire than in any other county, though the SW part was not blessed with the numbers or the surprises of the SE. Two styles predominate, E.E. lancets and Perp; larger churches have thin W towers and galleries on three sides. The flat elevations and monotonous plans have contributed to their lasting unpopularity – but then the same could be said of many C18 preaching boxes. Perhaps we still live under the influence of Ecclesiological scorn.

The earliest example is also the best and the most ambitious. *Sir Robert Smirke*'s St George, Tyldesley, of 1821–4 stands promi-

---

*Not all was as advanced: *Rowland*'s St James, Latchford (Warrington), late 1820s, still has wooden intersecting tracery and, originally, galleries reaching across the chancel arch.

nently at the end of the main street. It is archaeologically careful, with a recessed spire connected by flying buttresses with the pinnacles, *à la* Louth. However, it also has unconvincing Geometric aisle windows, and squashed Y-tracery in the clerestory. Perp gets one other outing, at *Daniel Stewart*'s St John, Burscough (1829–32), with its uncouth pinnacled buttresses on the blank w front. Of the two works by *Edward Blore* – like Smirke, a London architect – only Christ Church, Croft (1832–3) remains. The stumpy sw steeple is of wholly incorrect but quite enterprising design. Christ Church has lancet windows, the original short chancel, and an interior typical of the smaller examples: simple and broad, with a w gallery only and with massive, elaborate roof trusses. *Thomas Rickman* himself designed two Commissioners' churches at the end of his partnership with *Henry Hutchinson.* At St John the Divine, Pemberton (Wigan), 1830–2, Rickman appears to have misplaced most of his medieval studies, but St David, Haigh (1830–3) at least has lancets shafted inside with shaft-rings. St Clement, Toxteth (Liverpool), of 1840–1 by *George & Arthur Yates Williams*, has a strange w end, with an octagonal w bell-turret on a projecting bay containing gallery stairs. Its showy roof is a fake hammerbeam. St Catharine (1839–41), serving Wigan's poor new suburb of Scholes, is an inept and ungainly church by *Edmund Sharpe* before he became expert on the Decorated style.

Other churches in sw Lancashire in the 'Commissioners' style', but not financed by them, are as follows. Towerless and aisleless boxes in the lancet-and-buttress manner include All Saints, Thelwall (Warrington), 1843 by *J. Mountford Allen*, tiny St Thomas (Melling) of 1834, and St Nicholas (Halewood), 1838–9 by *A. Y. & G. Williams* (later expanded, and given a tower). Holy Trinity, Seneley Green, Garswood (1837–8, by *John Palmer)*, has rudimentary w transepts containing gallery stairs. St Thomas, Lydiate (*A.H. Holme*, 1839–41), has a little w tower. Others have steeples: Emmanuel, Wargrave, which formed part of a formal group with lodges, rectory and school, all now demolished; Christ Church, Eccleston (St Helens), which may have been designed by its donor, a mill-owner called *Samuel Taylor*; and St John Evangelist, Knotty Ash (Liverpool), 1834–6, which has Perp windows between the usual thin buttresses, slender arcades and a ribbed nave roof. Stylistically apart, *Cunningham & Holme*'s St Anne, Aigburth (Liverpool), begun two years before, is Norman Revival, built ahead of the fashion which swept England in the 1840s.

The post-Relief Act tradition of timid ROMAN CATHOLIC chapels continued into the early C19, with isolated buildings like St Mary, Aughton (1823), and St John, Burscough. One half of St John's E façade is the presbytery, the other half, behind blank bays, the church. Two churches on Standishgate in Wigan, completed in 1818–19, demonstrate growing confidence. St John, classical and big, was originally set well back down an alley. It has a tremendously spacious interior with an ample apse embellished by giant Corinthian columns, and a beamed ceiling. A

Jesuit church, its architecture was that of a Roman order. St Mary, a secular foundation, is the earliest fully Gothic Catholic church in the area, with an attractive galleried interior and a tower- 41, 43 less Perp façade, with a large and handsome window, which seems remarkably accurate for its date. St Patrick, Park Place, Toxteth (Liverpool), by *John Slater* (1821–7) has an unusual cruciform plan in which the arms contain gallery stairs and porches, screened outside with Greek Doric columns. Like the Wigan churches, its presbytery was detached. A few years after the Emancipation Act of 1829, a watershed in Roman Catholic culture, came St Anthony, Vauxhall (Liverpool), by *John Broadbent*, a pupil of Rickman. Designed in the lancet manner, its impressive uninterrupted interior has three giant arched niches of equal height at the E end, containing the altars – a common R.C. arrangement at the time. Gothic too is St Austin, Aigburth (Liverpool), of 1838, with odd octagonal turrets like stumpy factory chimneys. The first really exceptional Catholic church in Lancashire was completed two years later. St Bartholomew, 49, 50 Rainhill, by the little-known *Joshua Dawson* of Preston, was assertively positioned in full view beside the turnpike. It was based not on Greek precedents, but on ancient Rome. A prostyle temple in superbly worked red sandstone, with a hexastyle portico, it has a superb basilican interior lined with Corinthian columns carrying a coffered tunnel vault. The Italianising campanile was erected a few years later.

Many NONCONFORMIST CHAPELS were built in Liverpool, but most have been demolished. Only part still stands of *John Foster Jun.*'s enterprising façade of the Scottish Presbyterian church of St Andrew, Rodney Street (1823–4). Occupying an acute corner is the vigorous Great George Street Congregational 48 Church (1840–1) by *Joseph Franklin*, a Corinthian interpretation of Nash's All Souls, Langham Place, London (interior destroyed). In every way more modest is the Friends' Meeting House at Warrington (1829–30), a plain sash-windowed box, with a characteristically planned interior of understated charm.

When it comes to FURNISHINGS, many early C19 churches retain GALLERIES, and a surprising number still have BOX PEWS, including St Catharine, Scholes (Wigan). The most remarkable survival is certainly St Clement, Toxteth, where even the two-decker pulpit with integral reading desk remains directly in front of the little communion table. This was a strongly Evangelical church from the outset. The vogue for second-hand CONTINENTAL WOODWORK is evident at Eccleston, where French or Flemish Rococo pieces are incorporated into the gallery front and communion rail. Of Catholic fittings, St Anthony, Scotland Road, has ambitious stone reredoses of the 1830s possibly by *Broadbent*. Quite unexpected is the baldacchino at St John, Wigan, by *J.J. Scoles* (1834–5), an extravagant domed tempietto.

The best series of MONUMENTS of this date is in the younger Foster's Oratory or chapel at St James's Cemetery, Liverpool, including Neoclassical pieces by *Francis Chantrey*, *John Gibson* and *Joseph Gott*. Gibson's include William Earle, †1839, seated

and wrapped in a cloak. Gott did a vividly informal statue of
William Ewart, †1823. Chantrey also carved monuments elsewhere, especially the kneeling figure of 1822 on Peter Patten
Bold's monument at Farnworth (Widnes). *Westmacott* is represented at Prescot (†1803). By *John Bacon Jun.*, 1806, and entirely
46 in the style of his father, is Richard Watt, merchant, at Standish,
with a medallion portrait on an urn, and a lively relief of the Liverpool riverfront. *R.J. Wyatt* in Rome did the beautiful relief at
Winwick to commemorate Mrs Legh (†1831), and as beautiful is
the anonymous relief for Thomas Wilson-Patten (†1819) at Warrington. At Farnworth is another large relief, by the later-to-be-
famous *Tenerani* of Rome for Princess Sapieha (†1824), the
daughter of Peter Patten Bold, who married a Lithuanian prince.

Public sculpture of the period is considered on p. 82, mid- to
late C19 churches and furnishings on p. 87.

VICTORIAN AND EDWARDIAN DEVELOPMENTS

Commercial Architecture

C19 Liverpool was overwhelmingly a place of trade. In 1844 the
German visitor J.G. Kohl wrote of it: 'Every house . . . is either a
counting-house, a warehouse, a shop, or a house that in one way
or other is either an instrument or the result of trade.' The *Building News* observed a few years later that whereas in Manchester
the warehouse was the most notable type, in Liverpool, 'piles of
"offices", or commercial buildings, have for some time past, given
the largest scope for architectural display'.

A speculative development, Brunswick Buildings, off Castle
Street (1840s, now demolished) pioneered a new direction for
this 'display': a lavish Italian Renaissance palazzo style redolent
of Renaissance merchant princes, which not surprisingly found
great favour in Liverpool's business community. Brunswick
Buildings' iron-and-glass central court, which helped light the

Albany Building, Old Hall Street, by J.K. Colling, 1856–8.
Lithograph from W. Herdman, *Views in Modern Liverpool*, 1864

offices, became a common, if not universal feature (at Albany Building, a very large speculative block of 1856–8 designed by *J.K. Colling*, the court is unroofed, and the offices are reached from internal corridors lit by light wells). The Classicism generally prevails, and the Ruskin-inspired Venetian Gothic so prominent in Manchester is almost absent, despite the obvious appeal of the Maritime Republic to a port city. A Gothic block worth singling out is Seel's Building of *c.* 1872, in Church Street, a rare commercial work by *E. W. Pugin*, with a curiously modelled façade.

Peter Ellis provoked the ire of critics by rejecting all historical 90 styles with his Oriel Chambers in Water Street, 1864. They were outraged by his novel use of materials, the *Building News* calling it 'a kind of greenhouse architecture run mad'. Pevsner and many others have seen its remarkable façades, with their great expanses of glass set in an iron frame, and the extremely early use of curtain-wall construction, as a precursor of the Modernist C20. Yet besides Oriel Chambers and No. 16 Cook Street, only a couple of very ordinary designs by him are known, and his immediate influence was seemingly negligible.

MIXED-USE COMMERCIAL BUILDINGS remained a distinctive part of the Victorian townscape of Liverpool, now in the form of buildings offering multiple occupancy, lettable offices, and storage facilities. For example, Granite Buildings of *c.* 1882 by *Grayson* have an impressive pedimented façade of granite – of a severe and original style which reminded Pevsner of Lethaby – which fronted a very large block of offices. At the back is a row of gabled fruit warehouses, faced with utilitarian white-glazed bricks.

Liverpool was by 1900 the third greatest shopping centre in Britain, after London and Glasgow, and it amassed quite a collection of DEPARTMENT STORES; a few examples still stand. Compton House on Church Street, designed and built by *p. 314* *Thomas Haigh & Co.* in 1866–7, is one of exceptionally early date, even by international standards. The huge façade with corner towers, which originally had pavilion roofs, bears a close resemblance to Les Magasins Réunis in Paris, a French Renaissance-style complex begun in 1865.

Alongside the speculative offices, mixed-use schemes and shops were prestigious flagship buildings. The pioneering sector was BANKING, and rival premises filled up Liverpool's streets, especially Castle Street, which was transformed into the premier business thoroughfare, and one of the most resplendent streets in Britain. Highlights include the former North and South Wales Bank, 1838–40, by *Edward Corbett* of Manchester, whose details, like *Cockerell*'s brilliant and characteristically inventive Liverpool 89 branch of the Bank of England, 1845–8, are massively scaled; these are buildings designed to inspire confidence in the financial institutions they house. Later, Grecian gave way to eclecticism. *W. D. Caröe*'s delightful Adelphi Bank, of *c.* 1891–2, is a Northern Renaissance jewel. The sequence ends with the handsome striped marble façade of *Norman Shaw*'s Parr's Bank, 1898–1901, English Baroque of an imaginatively Shavian kind.

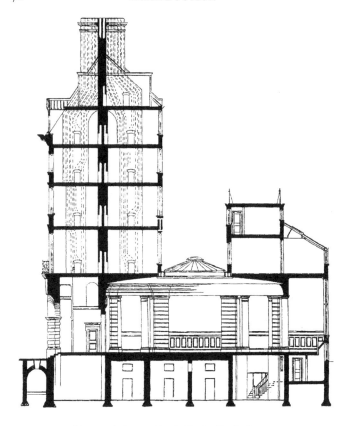

Liverpool, former Parr's Bank, Castle Street,
by Richard Norman Shaw, 1898–1901.
Section

These last three were by designers of national reputation, but
much of the commercial townscape is due to LOCAL ARCHI-
TECTS. *J.A. Picton*, later *Sir James*, began practising on his own
in 1835 (and became the town's unofficial historian). Busy
Grayson & Ould polychromatically transformed much of Castle
Street in the late C19. In the suburbs, the best secular buildings
are frequently bank branches by local firms, especially the
branches of the Bank of Liverpool from the turn of the century.
Willink & Thicknesse revealed a refined talent in two superb
Shaw-inspired buildings, at Walton and Aigburth Vale; *James
Rhind*'s unexpectedly masterful Kensington branch turns the
corner with Borrominesque verve.

102   PRIVATE WAREHOUSES abounded, particularly in a long strip
adjacent to the docks. Their general form had altered little since
the Georgian period, though regulations introduced in the wake
of a series of expensive fires required non-combustible external

features and thicker timber floors and posts to delay collapse. Typical examples can be seen in Argyle and Henry streets. Only occasionally were warehouses constructed with the more expensive cast-iron frames and brick jack-arch floors. Two fine survivors were part of the initial wave in the 1840s: a pedimented example at the corner of Vulcan Street and the dock road, and *S. & J. Holme*'s vast but remarkably plain complex for P.W. Brancker in Vauxhall. Decoration was rarely more than minimal, and though polychromy appears in the city centre in the 1860s, later C19 premises (e.g. on Parliament Street) are forbiddingly utilitarian; unlike the commercial warehouses of Manchester, which were intended to impress visiting clients. Liverpool warehouses were predominantly for storage.

The late C20 saw the destruction of the canyon-like townscape of the warehouse streets. Of RAILWAY WAREHOUSES, losses are even greater. The splendidly muscular but atypical Midland Railway warehouse in the middle of Liverpool is by *Culshaw & Sumners* (1872–4). A flavour of the dozen or so now vanished complexes built by rival railway companies adjacent to Liverpool docks is given by the warehouse built in Warrington in 1882 by the Cheshire Lines Committee. Warehouses built on the dock estate are described on p. 262.

James F. Doyle, a high-profile local, had a hand in two buildings which foreshadowed FRAMED CONSTRUCTION in the C20 city. He supervised construction of *Shaw*'s 1898 White Star Line building, a variant of Shaw's New Scotland Yard, which set new records for scale and height in Liverpool. At the same time he designed, with Shaw's assistance, the Royal Insurance Building, 91 sumptuous and imposingly Baroque, which employs one of the earliest steel frames in Britain to support the upper floors over a column-free General Office. Liverpool was at the forefront of introducing new construction techniques, and these made possible the unforgettable Pier Head trio, the Edwardian climax of the commercial core. The headquarters of the Mersey Docks and 1 Harbour Board by *Briggs & Wolstenholme* with *Hobbs & Thornely*, 1903–7, has a steel frame, this time encased in concrete; it does away with load-bearing mass walls – the swaggering Baroque exterior is only a facing of Portland stone. The colossal Royal Liver Building, of 1908–11, by *Walter Aubrey Thomas*, and the Cunard Building, a headquarters-cum-passenger terminal by *Willink & Thicknesse* with *Arthur J. Davis*, dispense with steel altogether, and the masonry hangs from entirely reinforced-concrete frames. These are buildings constructed to much the same principles as offices today. Thomas, a pupil of Doyle, was the leading local commercial architect of the early C20, and his Royal Liver Building is in spirit truly the country's first skyscraper. Far bigger than necessary for the Royal Liver Friendly Society's own accommodation, from the outset it offered abundant lettable office space. This was a widespread feature of flagship buildings in Liverpool; back in the 1850s, *Cockerell*'s Liverpool & London Insurance Co. building was designed as four blocks, all but the front one being let to tenants.

The Cunard Building shows the Baroque Revival giving way to a more restrained CLASSICISM, derived partly from the Ecole des Beaux Arts in Paris (where Davis had trained) and partly from American architects such as McKim, Mead & White. This transatlantic influence came directly through the charismatic *Charles Reilly*, Professor of Architecture at the University College from 1904, and against the background of the fascination of Liverpool businessmen with America. We will return to Reilly and his school after the First World War.

Such was the commercial power of the city that this has been an unashamedly Liverpudlian story. Beyond Liverpool the scale, scope, and very often the standard of commercial buildings falls dramatically. BANKS are often best. Parr's Bank began in Warrington; the dull façade of their branch there, of 1877, by the local *Thomas Beesley*, hides a splendid columned banking hall added to the rear. Its other branches embody a changing range of styles: St Helens', erected *c.* 1860, is High Victorian Gothic; Wigan's, by *William Owen*, of 1898, has a tall French Renaissance façade, the most refined in that town; Leigh's, by *J.C. Prestwich*, 1908, is banded Baroque, with a hint of Mannerism and a hint of France. Manchester-based banks employed Manchester men. In 1847 *Edward Walters*, then the city's leading commercial architect, designed a façade for the District Bank in Warrington with columns over pilasters; in 1866 the practice (then *Walters, Barker & Ellis*) turned out a little palazzo for the Wigan branch. *Mills & Murgatroyd*, working for the Manchester and County Bank in the 1890s in the same town, employed a pretty Loire style.

Most commercial premises were combined with warehousing, workshops, or with SHOPS. Warrington has one of the finest mid-Victorian commercial buildings, designed by *John Douglas* early in his career (1864) as the showrooms of the furniture-makers Robert Garrett & Sons (combined with their workshops behind), with a High Victorian Gothic façade of the most refined kind. When Warrington's Bridge Street was widened from the 1880s it was lined with new shops and pubs sporting terracotta and faience façades in an increasingly frothy mix of mainly Renaissance styles. In a 1908 competition for a circus at the town's focal cross-roads, Charles Reilly selected *J.E. Wright, Garnett & Wright*'s scheme, and its Neo-Georgian idiom established the aesthetic of redevelopment there until 1939. Wigan town centre was transformed in the late C19 and early C20 by mostly local practices in a variety of styles, harmonised by the use, predominantly, of red Ruabon brick and terracotta. *Heaton, Ralph & Heaton*, the most prolific of the Wigan firms, designed a building to front the Market Place in a part-stripy and part-timber-framed manner derived from John Douglas, to whom *William Chasen Ralph* had been assistant.

The CO-OPERATIVE MOVEMENT, born in Rochdale, had branches – often several – in every town. Warrington Co-operative Central Building by *Albert Warburton* (1909) has eccentric Wrenaissance detailing; above its two storeys of plate-glass shopfronts was a hall seating 700. Leigh Central Buildings (1897), another very large Co-operative premises with a big upstairs hall, is the grandest building on Bradshawgate, that town's principal commercial thoroughfare. The architect was *J.C. Prestwich*, who, with his son from 1907, is almost entirely responsible for the architectural character of the town. In one short walk along Bradshawgate, Prestwich's stylistic development over thirty years, from Gothic to Baroque, unfolds. Along the way are the practice's own offices, with continuous windows to light the drawing office.

Public and Civic Buildings

In contrast to SE Lancashire or Yorkshire or the Midlands, the best TOWN HALL in the region – Liverpool's – had already been built by 1840. Wigan, the next largest town, demolished its Georgian town hall in 1882 but never built a replacement, making do with conversions. Likewise in Warrington, where the town fathers acquired Bank Hall, *Gibbs's* splendid C18 mansion. The seaside dormitory of Waterloo built a modest villa-like town hall in 1862, by *F.S. Spencer Yates*. *Henry Sumners'* St Helens Town Hall of 1873–6 does at least face a public square, but the limp Gothic detailing is a disappointment. Widnes, a decade later by *F. & G. Holme*, is Northern Renaissance style, but wanting the planned tower. Earlestown Town Hall, 1892, by *Thomas Beesley*, does have a prominent clock tower, but infuriatingly it is not quite on the market square. Bootle's, by *John Johnson*, built a few years earlier, already shows signs of the Baroque Revival, which reached maturity in the shape of Leigh Town Hall, by *J.C.* 85 *Prestwich*, completed in 1907. With this, his *magnus opus*, Prestwich handles two contrasting but impressive façades with confidence and inventiveness. Prestwich also designed the offices of Atherton Urban District Council, 1898–1900, one of a number of modest offices built by the rural and urban district councils created in 1894. Three by *Heaton, Ralph & Heaton* opened in 1903 around Wigan, at Ince-in-Makerfield, Abram and Hindley.

St Helens Town Hall shows how a middle-sized town in the 1870s could still house most civic functions in one complex: council chamber and offices; public hall; fire house, police station and parade yard; police court. Bootle opted to erect individual buildings adjoining its Town Hall, to create a rudimentarily planned civic centre: library and museum, police station and court, post office, public baths and technical school (demolished). Unified by stone, styles were more Baroque or Northern Renaissance. Wigan built municipal offices in the 1860s; Liverpool Corporation built the huge, indeterminately styled Municipal Buildings in Dale Street, with its odd spire, begun by *John Weightman* in 1862 and completed under *E.R. Robson*, his successor as Corporation Surveyor. Further buildings sprang up around it, including in 1898 the City Education Offices by *Charles E. Deacon*, 1898, in French Renaissance style. A new central fire station followed in Hatton Garden by *Thomas Shelmerdine*, Robson's more talented successor, adept in an imaginative Jacobean style as here, but also comfortable, as in the former Tramway Offices of 1907 opposite, in classical mode.

Liverpool's suburban POLICE and FIRE STATIONS were often combined, e.g. at Edge Hill, behind a delightful mid-C19 Perp Gothic front. The New Bridewell at Kirkdale by *Shelmerdine*, 1885, is in a new style – a kind of Shavian Old English – with expanded accommodation for both services, including a parade hall. Ormskirk's police station, built after 1850 for the local force, has an elegant classical frontage. Half a century on, *R. Burns Dick* designed a large terracotta-trimmed complex for the Warrington constabulary sporting Mogulish turrets. The County Council built some quietly pleasant stations of *c.* 1900 with Tudor details for the County Constabulary, including Newton-le-Willows, by the County Architect *Henry Littler*.

LAW COURTS too were principally the responsibility of local authorities. Older courts were combined with other uses; St
p. 292 George's Hall is the grandest example of the traditional amalgamation of Assize Courts and great public room. As the C19 progressed, planning increased in sophistication to reflect the professionalisation of the legal process. The principal concern was – as it is today – the separation of judges, jurors, witnesses, public and defendants; the result was a labyrinth of separate entrances, circulation routes and service accommodation. The changes can be observed by comparing St George's Hall with the Liverpool County Sessions House by *F. & G. Holme*, a lavish Venetian Renaissance-style building of 1882–4. Both have interiors of outstanding quality, and are amongst the best-preserved C19 court houses anywhere. From the 1840s Police and Petty Sessions courts (the precursors of magistrates' courts) handled minor criminal cases, frequently in simple courtrooms combined with town halls, as at St Helens, or police stations, as at Liverpool, Newton-le-Willows and elsewhere. County Courts were introduced at the same time for low-level civil cases, for which Central Government was responsible. The C19 survivors in SW Lancashire are from the 1890s: Wigan's is an extension of *Littler*'s Elizabethan Magistrates' Court; Warrington's, now an arts centre, is one of a number by *(Sir) Henry Tanner* of the Office of Works which have much French Gothic amongst the details. They did not require secure circulation, and are planned and furnished less theatrically and intimidatingly.

Of PRISONS, we have two left to note. Military medieval architecture was the normal model in the early 1850s when *Charles*
86 *James Peirce* designed Walton Gaol (Liverpool), a big, now butchered complex dressed as a Norman castle and built on a linear variant of the radial plan. *Weightman* designed the Liverpool Central Bridewell in Cheapside a decade later – in the classical tradition, for a classical streetscape – as part of the police and courts complex noted earlier.

The POST OFFICE was another arm of Central Government. As the country's second port Liverpool got an enormous General Post Office in the 1890s by *Tanner*, like a Loire château. His earlier branch at Edge Hill, recently demolished, was Renaissance revival. Warrington's GPO, by Tanner's successor *W. Potts*, has some sophisticated Mannerist detailing.

The MARKET HALLS of SW Lancashire have suffered grievously. Only Warrington Fish Market survives, the mid-C19 iron frame refurbished as a shelter in the centre of a late C20 shopping centre. Undoubtedly the greatest loss was *John Foster Jun.*'s St John's Market, Liverpool of 1822, the precursor of all the iron indoor markets of the Victorian age.

Public Health and Welfare

Prince's Park, Liverpool was the first PUBLIC PARK in Lancashire (it was a private development, although some public access was always intended). It was *Joseph Paxton*'s first park design and was laid out with *James Pennethorne* in 1842, earlier than his influential Birkenhead Park across the Mersey. Following Nash's Regent's Park, part of the cost was to be met by selling plots around the edge. This financing device was also employed, with mixed success, for the chain of parks Liverpool Corporation established in the 1850s–60s around the town to provide recreation and air for the town's overcrowded residents. The greatest is Sefton Park, the largest in the country since Regent's Park, which was laid out by the French landscape gardener *Edouard André* to a Parisian plan of sweeping curved drives, with the local architect *Lewis Hornblower*. The excellently restored octagonal Palm House is of 1896, supplied by *Mackenzie & Moncur* of Edinburgh. Stanley Park and Newsham Park were Sefton's siblings, designed by Paxton's pupil *Edward Kemp* with architectural contributions by *Robson*, the City Architect. Stanley Park is outstanding too, a distillation of Kemp's gardening theory. Other municipalities followed. In the 1870s Wigan opened Mesnes Park in the heart of the town, designed by *John McClean*, with buildings by *W.H. Fletcher*. Widnes got a little promenade on the Mersey shore between the chemical factories; parks at Ormskirk, Atherton and Hindley are unremarkable. Others were private estates municipalised. Warrington got two this way, one of them from the gardens around Bank Hall when it became the Town Hall. Looking ahead into the C20, the acquisition of a number of mansion grounds created a green lung at Allerton and Woolton in S Liverpool, and C18 – designed landscapes became country parks at Croxteth in Liverpool, at Leigh, and at Haigh Hall near Wigan.

Legislation of the 1850s empowered local authorities to open CEMETERIES to supersede overcrowded urban graveyards, one of the greatest sanitary concerns of the age. The first in Liverpool opened on Smithdown Road, Toxteth, in 1856, with chapels and lodges by *Thomas D. Barry*. *William Gay* did the layout, inspired by his Undercliffe Cemetery, Bradford. He was 88 rewarded with the commission for the City of Liverpool Cemetery at Anfield, opened in 1863, but fell out with his employers and was replaced by *Edward Kemp*, who is probably responsible for the complex pattern of intersecting drives. With its ingenious and unconventional entrances by *Lucy & Littler* and careful attention to the status of the Nonconformist and Catholic sections, this is one of the finest municipal cemeteries of the North, though two of the three chapels have gone (a sadly common situation), and their catacombs are derelict. Other cemeteries followed, commissioned by suburban townships soon absorbed into the city – Everton (1880), Kirkdale (1881), West Derby (1884). Other towns were quick to implement the legislation too, though none excite greatly. *Thomas D. Barry* was the designer of many in the 1850s – Warrington, Wigan (at Ince), Atherton (which still has his typical Gothic chapels), and St Helens (incorporating a C17 Catholic burial ground around the remains of the chapel of St Thomas). Ince-in-Makerfield appointed the young *Alfred Waterhouse*, who deployed Romanesque for the Nonconformist cemetery chapel. The latest cemetery is Edwardian, built by Liverpool at Allerton, with formal planting in place of mid-C19 naturalism. It retains a full complement of buildings. Anfield Cemetery was the location for what was only the country's fourth CREMATORIUM, a private project headed by the shipping magnate Alfred Holt. *James Rhind*'s chapel (1894–6) is conventional Perp Gothic.

To provide a WATER SUPPLY for the growing population, Liverpool Corporation bought out private suppliers in 1847 and built reservoirs at Rivington (N Lancashire), from which water was piped to town-centre reservoirs designed by its water engineer, *Thomas Duncan*, in the 1850s. The now-empty covered cistern of his Park Hill Reservoir, Toxteth, is a tremendous forest of cast-iron columns and jack vaults. To supply the Everton ridge, Duncan built a magnificent circular water tower with a tank carried high on Piranesian arches. The other architecturally impressive complex is at Aughton, of 1880: an engine house and boiler room in Ruskinian Venetian Gothic.

Liverpool Corporation opened the country's first PUBLIC BATHS at the Pier Head in 1829 to designs by *Foster Jun.* (demolished). The Corporation embarked on an extensive programme of bath- and washhouse-building; the town pioneered the latter in 1842, though the earliest survivor, in Steble Street, Toxteth, dates from 1874. A later series of suburban public baths by the engineer *W.R. Court* benefited from architectural input by *Shelmerdine*. That at Lister Drive, Stanley (1901–4) has stripy, free English Renaissance façades and an interior lined with tiles designed by *Voysey*. Bootle added seawater baths to its new civic centre in 1888; the Jacobean Revival frontage by *George Heaton* remains. Warrington baths are a prosaic amalgam begun in 1866. All in all, SW Lancashire has nowhere near the variety nor the quality of baths still to be found in and around Manchester.

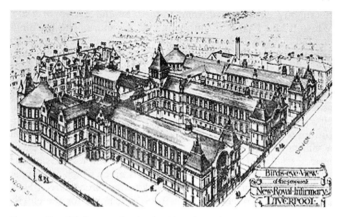

Former Royal Infirmary, Pembroke Place, by Alfred Waterhouse, 1887–90.
Engraving

For HOSPITALS, we must return to Liverpool. The first Infirmary there, erected in 1749 on the site now occupied by St George's Hall, was replaced on a fresh site by a building by *Foster Jun.*, itself replaced in 1887–90 by a now well-restored complex by *Waterhouse*. This adopted the prevailing pavilion ward concept, advocated by Florence Nightingale. Two ward blocks are circular, an early instance in Britain. The Northern and Southern Hospitals are demolished, but almost all of the city hospital at Fazakerley survives, with attractively detailed *Shelmerdine* buildings of *c.* 1906. At Old Swan the contemporary City Hospital East (now Rathbone Hospital) includes a beautifully composed Arts and Crafts lodge.

There is room here only for a list of the gaggle of SPECIALIST HEALTH BUILDINGS – built in as many different styles – which testify to Liverpool's leading role in medical practice and research in the C19: the Lying-In Hospital (*J.D. Jee*, 1861), the Eye and Ear Infirmary (*C.O. Ellison*, 1878–80), *Grayson & Ould*'s Consumption Hospital, the School of Tropical Medicine (1913–15 etc., by *Sidney W. Doyle*), and the Hahnemann Homeopathic Hospital (*F. & G. Holme*, dated 1887). The last two were built at the expense of private benefactors: Alfred Jones (shipping) and Henry Tate (sugar) respectively.

Many hospitals were dependent on public fundraising and private donations, like the former Bootle Borough Hospital, developed from 1870 in large part thanks to the Earls of Derby. Of other hospitals outside Liverpool, Wigan's Royal Albert Edward Infirmary opened in 1873 in Gothic buildings by *Thomas Worthington*, symmetrically planned about a tower over the administration block. Cottage hospitals were erected for smaller communities, as at Haydock in the 1890s.

Some hospitals evolved from WORKHOUSES. Warrington Hospital started out as the plain brick E-plan workhouse of 1851, and its slightly enriched infirmary added by the *Owens* in 1899. Whiston and Ormskirk hospitals are two more. The buildings erected by the West Derby Union which encompassed many Liverpool suburbs and satellites, illustrate the growing extent and specialisation of accommodation provided by a large, increasingly urban union.* Two were built for adult paupers, including one at Walton in 1864–5 by *William Culshaw*, twenty-three bays long and three storeys high with a clock tower. Another was built principally for children, but by the 1870s the efficacy of these institutions were being questioned, and in 1887–9 the Guardians built a 'village' at New Hall in Fazakerley, after the German and Swiss model. *Charles H. Lancaster*'s self-sufficient complex consisted of cottages arranged formally along a broad street, which terminates in a porticoed hall with a fancy clock tower. Broad Green Hospital, by *C.O. Ellison*, opened in 1906 as a home for the elderly poor. Just before the First World War the Union began a new Infirmary for 'chronic infirm paupers', designed by *Lancaster*, on the site of a house called Alder Hey. There was also a children's convalescent home and a home for 'mental defectives'. This extensive empire was run from a large brick headquarters on West Derby Road, built in 1901–2.

A number of other INSTITUTIONS for orphans and deprived children survive, including the Warrington Union's Padgate Cottage Homes of 1880–1. The Catholic Church, immensely powerful in S Lancashire, funded establishments whose architecture is as bleak and forbidding as their Dickensian names. *Pugin & Pugin* designed the Blackbrook House Industrial School, St Helens (1903–4) and the boys' home at Ditton Hall, Widnes (1911 etc.) run by the Sisters of Nazareth. Another practice with an extensive Catholic workload, *Edmund Kirby & Sons*, was responsible for the quadrangle-plan Liverpool Catholic Reformatory Association Nautical Schools, Rainhill Stoops (Widnes), begun in 1904. By contrast the Salford Union Cottage Homes at Culcheth of 1901, with their varied façades, are refreshingly informal.

LUNATIC ASYLUMS begin in earnest in SW Lancashire after the 1845 County Asylums Act. The largest, *Elmes* and *William Moseley*'s County Asylum at Rainhill, was opened in 1851, and demolished in 1990. A little remains of another, by *W.S. Skinner, Crisp & Oatley* of Bristol, built at Winwick 1897–1902.

Other PHILANTHROPIC VENTURES cared for deserving people whom other authorities could not or would not help. *Thomas Worthington*'s Liverpool Convalescent Institution, built in 1873 at Woolton, is cleverly planned and imposing, with splendid views from the broad terrace between the two Gothic ward blocks. *Alfred Waterhouse* designed the Turner Memorial Home, Toxteth, for 'chronic sufferers', erected in the 1880s. It has a dig-

---

* The site of Liverpool Workhouse, reputedly the largest in the country, is now occupied by the Catholic cathedral.

nified chapel. In 1880 the Parkhaven Trust was established at Maghull Manor House for epileptics, for whom a series of large detached homes was set out in the grounds from the end of the C19. BUILDINGS FOR THE BLIND included the first blind school in the country, established in Liverpool in 1791. Its second home, in Hardman Street, of 1849–51, by *Arthur Hill Holme*, has an impressive pedimented façade screening a utilitarian structure informed by contemporary workhouse design, with four radiating wings. The school moved to suburban premises by *H. & A.P. Fry* at Wavertree in 1899, the same year that a Catholic blind school, in Gothic style, opened at West Derby (Liverpool). In the city centre there was the octagonal-plan Adult Deaf and Dumb Institute, Princes Avenue, 1886–7, by *E.H. Banner*. The Workshops for the Outdoor Blind (1870, by *G.T. Redmayne* of Manchester) provided employment: basket-, brush- and mat-making.

The welfare of sailors and their dependants was another preoccupation for sections of Liverpool's middle class. Two SAILORS' HOMES were built providing respectable accommodation and sober entertainment, both now demolished, of which *John Cunningham*'s Sailors' Home in Canning Place (1846–8) had an extraordinary galleried court. Close to the site is the former home of the Mersey Mission to Seamen, polychromatic brick by *G.E. Grayson*, which opened in 1885 with a chapel and, rather hopefully, a Temperance pub. The Gordon Smith Institute for Seamen offered a library, reading room and a hall in a building of 1899 which still stands. The Seamen's Orphan Institution p. 425 (Fairfield), 1870–5, by *Alfred Waterhouse*, is a huge and irregular building in characteristically economical brick and terracotta Gothic, forming a tremendous backcloth behind Newsham Park.

For landlubbers there was the YMCA movement, for which *Briggs & Wolstenholme* designed a large building in St Helens (1902–3), in pinkish brick with lashings of terracotta. Boys' and girls' CLUBS were intended to provide improving recreation and education for working-class children. Handsome examples from the 1880s are on Stanley Road, Kirkdale (Liverpool). Another in Liverpool is the Florence Institute for Boys at Toxteth (1889, probably *H.W. Keef*). There are surprisingly few ALMSHOUSES in the area; most attractive are the Gothic range at Aughton of 1851.

Education and Cultural Improvement

For obvious reasons most CHURCH SCHOOLS continued in Gothic dress. The Collegiate Institution in Everton (Liverpool) 81 was Anglican, and *Elmes*'s towering building of 1840–3 is adamantly and massively Perpendicular, and planned to segregate the three ranks of pupils. Its large neighbour, the school for St Francis Xavier, by *Henry Clutton*, by contrast looks to French Gothic sources for inspiration. Smaller schools offered greater scope for picturesque charm. The former Ince Blundell school of

1843 by *J.J. Scoles* is wrapped in a bold scroll inscription. It was paid for by the local landowners – here the Blundells – like the attractive examples at Knowsley, Haigh (both 1845) and Lathom (1881). A good Catholic building of 1860, rock-faced and Puginian, is tucked behind St Austin in Aigburth (Liverpool). Huyton has one built a year later by the Congregationalists against their chapel at the expense of the brewer Sir Andrew Barclay Walker, with a miniature steeple. It was the Lancashire (later National) Public Schools Association, formed in 1847, that led the campaign for a locally controlled non-sectarian education system which culminated in the 1870 Education Act. This spawned BOARD SCHOOLS, in this area rarely of great individual excitement, though the survivors – of which there are fewer and fewer – are often local landmarks. Liverpool of course built the most, employing most frequently *T. Mellard Reade*. His first, of 1874, at Chatsworth Road, Edge Hill, has stone Gothic façades, but the majority have mixed revival details, in red brick with red terracotta dressings. He has two at Anfield from the 1880s, where there is also a third by *Charles Deacon* with a bobbin-like tower. Arnot Street School, Walton, is by *Edmund Kirby* and really quite eccentric. In the early C20 the classicism was purer, as at the demolished building on Lister Drive, Stanley.

GRAMMAR and FEE-PAYING SCHOOLS produced a number of handsome buildings. *Lockwood & Mawson*'s new Merchant Taylors' School for Boys at Great Crosby, 1878, is still Gothic, with a big central tower. After 1900 the Baroque Revival became a firmly entrenched scholastic style. One notable example is the large new premises of the Liverpool Blue Coat School at Wavertree, 1903–6, with another prominent clock tower. *Briggs, Wolstenholme & Thornely* skilfully managed the fall of land here to create two frontages of very different character and scale, and provided a domed Greek-cross-plan chapel. Ormskirk Grammar School and the Hindley and Abram Grammar School (Hindley) are Jacobethan exceptions from the 1900s.

Buildings for FURTHER EDUCATION include UNIVERSITY COLLEGE Liverpool, founded in 1881, for which *Waterhouse* designed the Victoria Building – Gothic of course, with a proud clock tower and some excellent interiors – as well as some lesser buildings, all in his familiar red brick and terracotta. The Wrenaissance style made a belated appearance in the form of *Briggs, Wolstenholme & Thornely*'s Ashton Building (Faculty of Arts) in 1912–14. MECHANICS' and TECHNICAL INSTITUTES were established to serve the workforce, often by industrialists themselves. Examples in SW Lancashire are almost exclusively from the 1890s–1900s. Outstanding is the Liverpool Central Technical School (and Museum extension) designed by *E. W. Mountford* in 1896, an imperious Baroque sandstone *massif* of metropolitan sophistication, with excellent carving, reliefs etc. by *F. W. Pomeroy*. There is a branch at Wavertree by *Shelmerdine* in a free C17 style. In other towns they are almost exclusively of red brick with terracotta dressings. One of the largest is at Leigh, by *J.C. Prestwich* and *J.H. Stephen*, free Renaissance with many shaped gables.

Woodhouse & Willoughby's building at Widnes has energetic asymmetry and profuse detailing; the Gamble Institute at St Helens by *Briggs & Wolstenholme* (1894–6) was named after the alkali baron who paid for it. After 1900 civic Baroque takes over, e.g. at Newton-le-Willows (*Henry Littler*) and at *Briggs & Wolstenholme*'s Wigan Mining and Technical College, the town's 83 grandest civic building (subsequently the Town Hall). William Lever paid for Warrington Technical School, by *William & Segar Owen* (1901), next to *William Owen*'s earlier public hall, Parr Hall, and near his School of Art (1883). The first part of Liverpool's Art School is of almost exactly the same date; the second, more accomplished phase (by *Willink & Thicknesse*) is of 1910.

In several towns (Atherton, Leigh, Widnes, St Helens) the science and art schools were combined with a PUBLIC LIBRARY. The Museums Act of 1845 and the Public Libraries Act of 1850 heralded the first few local authority library proper, and a rash of combined libraries and MUSEUMS. Liverpool held a competition in 1856 for such a building on a site facing St George's Hall. *John Weightman* gave the winning Italianate design of *Thomas Allom* a 79 severe Greco-Roman makeover. This initiated a group of magnificent classical buildings dedicated to art, culture, law and learning that would make William Brown Street – together with Elmes's masterpiece – an expression of enlightened civic investment without equal in the provinces. The Technical School and Sessions House already mentioned came later, after the Walker Art Gallery by *Cornelius Sherlock* and *H.H. Vale*, 1874–7, and the magnificent, echoing, domed rotunda of the Picton Reading 80 Room, by *Sherlock* alone, 1875–9. Much of this was made possible only by the generous patronage of Liverpool's mercantile elite, as the names of the buildings and the street recall.

Warrington was quick off the mark too, selecting *John Dobson*'s design for a free library and museum in 1853. But the borough flinched at the cost, and a simplified version by a local, *Thomas Stone*, was erected instead. The original museum galleries, refurbished in the late C19, are a delightful surprise, crowded with narrow mezzanines and mahogany specimen cabinets. Hindley went for a dual-purpose building too, quirky free Elizabethan by *Thomas Worthington*. Wigan employed *Waterhouse* to design a library only, and got of course an economical but highly accomplished Gothic building. After 1900 came a rash of libraries courtesy of Andrew Carnegie's millions. Baroque predominates, often with little domes or rotundas. Newton-le-Willows's (*J. Myrtle Smith*, 1909) is pretty; Ashton-in-Makerfield's and Pemberton's (Wigan), both by *J.B. & W. Thornely*, occupy prominent corner sites; Great Crosby's (1904–7, *Anderson & Crawford*), is stylistically eclectic. Many of the wonderful BRANCH LIBRARIES by *Thomas Shelmerdine* in the Liverpool suburbs were also funded by Carnegie. Everton, opened 1896, is the best, its warm orange brick and taut grid of stone dressings and windows set off by a trio of bold gables and an end tower. The series nears its end in the battered buttresses and rendered walls of the Arts and Crafts-style Garston (1908). Repoussé copper plaques by *J.A. Hodel* or

C.E. Thompson in Celtic Art Nouveau style commemorate the openings.

Nineteenth-Century and Edwardian Public Sculpture

Liverpool's exceptional PUBLIC SCULPTURE begins in 1813 with the Nelson Monument by *M.C. Wyatt* and *Richard Westmacott* at Exchange Flags, a superb bronze group including four life-size captives in chains. This was followed in 1822 by *Westmacott's* equestrian bronze of George III on London Road. The construction of St George's Hall created a focus and a further impetus for commemoration. Niches around the Great Hall are filled with statues of the great and good; artists include *Chantrey*, *John Gibson* and *G.G. Fontana*. The exterior was given New Sculpture relief panels from the 1880s mostly by *Thomas Stirling Lee*, whose naturalistic nude girls aroused controversy. Around the building many more works sprung up: in the 1860s equestrian bronzes of Albert and Victoria by *Thomas Thornycroft* and the big Wellington Column by *Andrew* and *George Anderson Lawson*, in 1879 the cast-iron Steble Fountain, one of a number of similar jobs worldwide by *Paul Liénard*, and in the 1880s Disraeli by *C.B. Birch*. On the w side, St John's Gardens (opened 1904) was conceived as the setting for more statues, some by *George Frampton*. At the same time the Pier Head was being laid out, and this was a natural location for subsequent hero-worship, e.g. *Frampton's* iconographically unusual Alfred Jones Memorial. *C.J. Allen* (1862–1936), who taught at the School of Architecture and Applied Arts, was the most important Liverpool sculptor around 1900 and his work can be found throughout the city centre, on buildings such as *Doyle's* Royal Insurance Building. His finest work (with *F.M. Simpson* and *Willink & Thicknesse*, 1902–6) is the vast domed monument to Queen Victoria in Derby Square.

The most memorable public art outside Liverpool is the profusely designed and dazzlingly gilded iron gates at Warrington Town Hall, made by the *Coalbrookdale Company* for the 1862 London Exhibition. The town also has a Cromwell Statue (1899, by *John Bell*) and a Boys' Own-style memorial to the Boer War hero Lt-Col. O'Leary by *Alfred Drury*. St Helens has a good seated bronze of the Queen, a copy by *Frampton* of a Calcutta commission. Another seated bronze is Sir Francis Sharpe Powell in Mesnes Park, Wigan, by *E.G. Gillick* (1910).

Leisure and Recreation

Social drinking was big business, and from the late C19 PUBS became much gaudier to attract new custom. Some were flagship outlets of smaller firms, such as the Bedford Brewery's Boar's Head of 1900 on Leigh Market Place, all frilly red terracotta ornament and protrusions. Much more sophisticated is the Red Lion Hotel in Litherland (1905), built by the Blezards Brewery, which has absorbed the influence of Shaw and Webb. Not far

p. 323
94

away, the Seaforth Arms Hotel is in the more usual blocky and stripy free English Renaissance style. Brewers' pubs are often the architectural high points in dreary districts. Foremost are those of Greenall, Whitley & Co., which enliven St Helens and Warrington (its home towns), Widnes, and places in between. *William & Segar Owen*, *J.E.Wright*, *Garnett & Wright* and other local practices designed them, in a range of Domestic Revival styles. Distressingly few retain original interiors, but the North West's two finest and most extravagant gin palaces are largely intact. The Vines and the Philharmonic Hotel in Liverpool were designed by 95 *Walter W. Thomas* for the brewer Robert Cain. The latter (*c.* 1898–1900) is one of the most celebrated pubs in the country, with an exuberant exterior, excellent Art Nouveau gates, and an interior as luxurious as one could imagine – mahogany, cut glass, mosaic floors, repoussé copper panels by *H. Bloomfield Bare* and *Thomas Huson*, and extravagant plasterwork by *C.J. Allen*. Middle-class fret about the dangers of alcohol gave rise to Temperance Hotels, such as the Grand Hotel in Wigan and the Coffee House, Wavertree (Liverpool), which was remodelled in 1904 by *Walter W. Thomas*, working shamelessly or in penitence between his Cain commissions.

The first purpose-built HOTEL in the area opened in 1816, at the new seaside resort of Waterloo. Its modest classicism has little in common with Liverpool's two great railway hotels: *Alfred Waterhouse*'s towering Gothic edifice on Lime Street for the 93 London & North Western Railway (1868–71), and the Midland Railway's smooth-skinned Adelphi Hotel by *Frank Atkinson* (1911–14), said to have been without equal outside London. Rooms such as its marble-lined Central Court and Empire-style Hypostyle Hall cry out for restoration to their former glory.

Mid-C19 party politics were the catalyst for MEMBERS' CLUBS. Leigh's Conservative Club, of 1879, by *J.J. Bradshaw*, was big enough to become later a cinema and nightclub. On Dale Street in Liverpool is another former Conservative Club (by *F. & G. Holme*, opened 1883), lavish outside and with an impressive staircase, and a contemporary former Junior Conservative Club, later Junior Reform Club by *Thomas E. Murray*, in the Gothic style rare in the city.

The earliest of surviving THEATRES in SW Lancashire is the tiny Theatre Royal (now The Citadel), St Helens, of 1861 by *E. Beattie Jun.* The oldest remnant in Liverpool is the stuccoed façade of the Playhouse, which may date from the reconstruction of 1895. *Frank Matcham* is represented by the former Olympia Theatre, Kensington (Liverpool), of 1905, a rare surviving variety theatre designed to host circuses. Wigan's entertainment district is King Street, though the remaining theatres now dispense liquid pleasures. The Royal Court Theatre (1886 and 1895 by *R.T. Johnson*, remodelled by *J.P. Briggs*, 1899) could seat a staggering 5,000. Former Edwardian variety theatres can be found in Warrington and St Helens, and on a much smaller scale at Haydock. Many became CINEMAS, of which one purpose-built example is the former Futurist on Lime Street, Liverpool, built in 1912 as the City Picture House (*Chadwick & Watson* of Leeds) with a classical terracotta façade.

SPECTACTOR SPORT, another growing mass entertainment, has left little by way of architecture. None of the substantial early C19 stands at the racecourses at Aintree and Newton-le-Willows survives. Likewise, there are no interesting football structures from before the late C20, but the rugby league ground at St Helens' Knowsley Road is an evocative reminder of the ramshackle past. Liverpool Cricket Club's ground at Aigburth, opened in 1881, has the most complete Victorian sporting arena, with a set of buildings by *Thomas Harnett Harrisson* in matching brick and half-timbering.

p. 123

Victorian and Edwardian Domestic Architecture

The aristocracy prospered from the rapid expansion of Liverpool and its environs across their extensive landholdings, and many enlarged their COUNTRY HOUSES to create grander public rooms, enhanced circulation and more extensive and sophisticated services. Ince Blundell was modernised in 1847–50, probably by *J. J. Scoles*, when the Pantheon was made into the entrance hall and a new dining room and picture gallery were created with Raphaelesque decorative schemes by *Crace*. The Earls of Sefton more than doubled Croxteth Hall into a full courtyard plan. In 1874–7 *Thomas Henry Wyatt* added wings inspired by the remaining fragment of *c.* 1600, and rebuilt accommodation behind the s range of 1702 in a style to match it. *J. Macvicar Anderson* completed reconstruction in 1902–4 in a continuation of Wyatt's '1702' idiom. (Before any of this *Eden Nesfield* and *John Douglas* had designed a number of pretty estate buildings, notably Nesfield's dairy.) Knowsley Hall got vast new service wings, and in 1908–12 what the architect *Romaine-Walker* called 'a restoration to what never existed'. He gave the house a Georgian grandeur that it had never possessed, creating public rooms from the apartments of the E wing, notably a lavish Carolean-style staircase. For designed landscapes, *see* pp. 46–7.

p. 205

105

p. 406

p. 218

The flight to the SUBURBS accelerated from the 1840s along railways and later tram lines. Palmyra Square, Warrington, built up from the 1850s, is the last gasp of new town-centre housing for the middle classes. In Wigan, Widnes and St Helens solid new houses were built on hilltops upwind of the foul industrial air; in Warrington it was across the Mersey into Cheshire; in Liverpool they spread s and w, around Sefton Park and old village centres like West Derby, Childwall and Woolton, and the private residential parks established from the 1840s (*see* p. 62). Railways meant that once-sleepy villages like Aughton and Huyton swelled with villas and houses, and a string of settlements appeared along the coast N of Liverpool.

Early Victorian HOUSES were normally stucco with Tudorbethan or Italianate details, as in Liverpool at Fulwood Park, Aigburth and in Wavertree. One of the finest Italianate villas is

Cowley House in St Helens (1850), designed by *Charles Reed*. It contains two frequently encountered status symbols, an impressive top-lit staircase and a prospect tower. Such towers also appear at country residences. West Tower, Aughton, is picturesque Tudor Gothic. The Tower, Rainhill, was enlarged for a St Helens chemical manufacturer by *Edmund Kirby* in 1879–80 with an extraordinarily large tower, topped by a fairytale corner cupola and vulgar, freely Jacobean interiors. Italianate lingered into the 1870s, when one of its biggest manifestations, the symmetrical Crofton, was built in Mossley Hill, Liverpool, for Alfred Holt, founder of the Blue Funnel shipping line, by *Rhind & Banner*.

DOMESTIC GOTHIC emerged from Regency superficiality in the mid 1840s at Oswaldcroft, Childwall, one of the few surviving houses by *A. W. N. Pugin*. The entrance façade best preserves Pugin's carefully crafted and sparse asymmetry; the plan is the Pugin 'pin-wheel' type that would be very influential. Houses in Mossley Hill, one of the most exclusive Liverpool suburbs, show the spread of Pugin's ideas. At the top is the most theatrical The Holmestead, part pre-Pugin Tudor Gothic, part High Victorian. Down the hill are large, austerely Gothic houses of polychromatic brick, one by *W. & G. Audsley*, and at the bottom another by *Waterhouse* (1869), which follows the compact plan developed by the architect for commercial clients. This first appeared at New *p. 390* Heys, a house in Allerton – still the premier address in the city – where Waterhouse also built the much larger Allerton Priory, 106 with a civic-looking tower, an elaborate arcaded stair and a highly unusual plan.

Waterhouse and Pugin aside, all the architects mentioned so far were local. That there are not more works by architects of national repute is partly because of losses in Allerton, including major houses by *Elmes*, *Scott*, and *Norman Shaw*. The other survivals are for churchmen. Wigan Hall by *G. E. Street* (1875–6), built by the Rector of Wigan, is one of the finest C19 houses in S Lancashire, with elevations – stone below, half-timbered above – of understated but masterly arrangement. An elaborate wooden staircase dominates the interior. Two Liverpool vicarages by two other greats remain: that of St Agnes, Sefton Park, by *Norman Shaw*, superbly composed of sparse brick walls, choice details and bay windows; and that of St John the Baptist, Tue Brook, by its designer, *G. F. Bodley*.

After 1880 major mansions are scarcer. At Rainford Hall, Col. Richard Pilkington employed the architect of his family's glassworks, *J. Medland Taylor*, for Jacobethan expansion and remodelling. A member of the beerocracy, Sir Andrew Barclay Walker commissioned the fashionable London practice of *Sir Ernest George & H. A. Peto* in the 1880s to extend Gateacre Grange (now Liverpool), a Jacobethan house of 1851, with interiors of metropolitan sophistication, in a rich C16–C17 manner tinged with Aestheticism. Such an appointment differentiated Barclay Walker as a man now moving in the highest echelons of national society. Once the merchant princes reached these heights, through money or marriage, they frequently withdrew to the country. Thomas Henry Ismay, owner of the White Star Line, left the Waterloo waterfront in the 1880s for a grand house by Norman Shaw on the Wirral.

The opening of a railway N of Liverpool in 1848 stimulated the development of almost continuous SEASIDE DORMITORIES for the middle classes along the coastal dunes to fashionable Southport (in N Lancashire). At Waterloo, where development of the coast had begun, the Regency façades of Adelaide Terrace, mainly of the 1850s, gave way to the restless stepped fronts of Beach
104 Lawn. The Blundells of Crosby Hall developed N from here, launching Blundellsands in the mid 1860s as a residential estate with a layout by *T. Mellard Reade* and *G.W. Goodison*. The principal features, as at their contemporary plan for Birkdale Park up the coast (in N Lancashire), were a serpentine drive and a park. Mellard Reade designed a lodge, some Gothic housing, including an aborted crescent, and probably the hotel as well. Surviving villas are large and often Italianate; the best is later, *Frank*
108 *Atkinson*'s dapper Redcot of 1909, for the builder of Atkinson's Adelphi Hotel. Beyond Formby, a fishing hamlet turned prosperous suburbia, the Blundells began a second, unimaginatively planned development at Hightown, with modest Edwardian homes in a roughcast Arts and Crafts style. A more interesting house is tucked in amongst the huge dunes at Formby, a semi-detached holiday cottage of 1882 with Japonaiserie half-timbering, designed for a Liverpool shipping executive by *A.H. Mackmurdo*.

Relentless population growth meant new suburbs of WORKERS' HOUSING marched in every direction. Legislation and BYE-LAWS were introduced from mid century in all towns and cities to regulate their construction and design. This brought improvement, but enforced a monotonous townscape. Those at Leigh, Atherton, Tyldesley and Wigan are generally earlier, plainer and less generous than in the surviving areas of Liverpool (e.g. Anfield and Edge Hill/Kensington) and Bootle, where façades are frequently broken by bay windows and simple decorative or polychromatic brick or terracotta details. Their development and construction were undertaken to a remarkable degree by tradesmen (and materials) from North Wales, as frequently memorialised in the street names. For a lucky few in Liverpool there was MUNICIPAL HOUSING. Possibly the first outside London were flats in Vauxhall, built after a competition in 1867. They have gone, as have projects of the 1880s and 1890s, but Vauxhall retains an example of 1910–12 of the Corporation's schemes to house those displaced by slum clearances after 1895. It features two-storey houses and three-storey blocks of flats with external stairs and access balconies and W.C.s in towers at the rear, all with cottagey details.

There are few MODEL SETTLEMENTS in this part of Lancashire. The leading Wigan mill-owners, the Eckersleys, built in the 1850s what they described rather incautiously as their own Saltaire at Poolstock (Wigan); most of it was pulled down in the late C20 as unfit. More interesting is the village created by the jam-maker Sir William Hartley at Fazakerley, now on the N edge of Liverpool. The factory, by *James F. Doyle*, opened in 1886 – parts, including the bizarre castellated entrance, survive – and the housing followed two years later to designs by *William Sugden & Son* of Leek, selected in competition. The settlement is small, the housing with some half-timbered gables amounts to little architecturally, and the layout of four streets facing outward from a court is unimaginative, but Hartley's operation was socially progressive. Women were paid four-fifths of the wages of men, health care was free, and profit-sharing began in 1889. The most accomplished ESTATE VILLAGE was built in the late C19 by a family of successful brewers, Greenalls, at Walton (Warrington).

PIT VILLAGES are the most frequent new settlements. When the Wigan Coal & Iron Co. (the Earls of Balcarres' operations renamed) sunk a new pit at Crawford *c.* 1850 it built a pretty village in stone along a single street, but most colliery villages have only dour brick terraces. Gin Pit (Astley) and Crooke (Shevington) are little more than a couple of short, parallel streets; where there were a number of pits, villages expanded haphazardly along existing roads into characteristic straggles of mean rows. Haydock, Ince and Abram have these and also small grids of streets. Clock Face (St Helens), also developed by the Wigan Coal & Iron Co., was at least formally planned around a generous recreation field, *c.* 1907. The exception is Howe Bridge, the creation of Ralph Fletcher of Fletcher, Burrows & Co. in the 1870s. He employed *J. Medland & Henry Taylor* to design characteristic schools and rows of brick cottages – punctuated by gables which incorporated baths, shops and a club, and *Paley & Austin* to create a beautiful church. Later settlements by the company are simpler, but in 1913 it erected the country's first pithead baths at the Gibfield Colliery, enabling miners to walk home clean and changed.

The GARDEN SUBURB movement had some success in SW Lancashire. Ebenezer Howard himself in 1907 inaugurated the first of two planned in Warrington, but it hardly got off the ground. The Liverpool version at Wavertree was much more successful, and remains popular. The simple leafy layout and low, roughcast cottages are attractive in understated, typical Garden Suburb fashion. *Raymond Unwin* did the first part, begun in 1910, and *G. L. Sutcliffe* the second. An institute and a little green were also provided. The styles of the movement clearly influenced the first housing erected along Liverpool's Queens Drive, the ambitious and very early orbital road designed by the City Engineer *J.A. Brodie* with arterial off-shoots, according to American parkway principles. It was begun in 1904, but most of the housing was put up after 1918.

Victorian and Edwardian Ecclesiastical Architecture

The 1840s revolutionised ecclesiastical architecture. A more accurate use of medieval styles, in buildings close to medieval plan, began to appear, though the decade continued to produce such archaeologically inaccurate churches as St James, West Derby, Liverpool (*E.Welch*, 1845–6). *A. W. N. Pugin* was one of the chief engines of the revolution, and in sw Lancashire he worked both for fellow Catholics and for Anglicans. One of his rare Church of England commissions is the new chancel of the medieval church of Winwick, in his academic and beautifully composed Dec style. Of his Catholic works, the private chapel at Childwall (Liverpool) was replaced by his son *E. W. Pugin*, and at Old Swan (Liverpool) only the steeple of his St Oswald (*c.* 1840–2) still stands, alongside his modest but interestingly planned Convent of Mercy. Pugin's approach was embraced at St Mary, Little Crosby, 1845–7, by *Weightman & Hadfield*, built by the Blundells of Crosby Hall with the style and position of an Anglican village church, with a solidity quite apart from the flimsiness of many contemporary buildings. Three equally good-looking commissions – St Bede, Appleton (Widnes), St Alban, Vauxhall (Liverpool), and St Anne, Ormskirk – were completed by the same practice in the 1840s, all with little trefoil clerestory windows. A mightier church from the decade is *Charles Hansom*'s St Anne, Edge Hill (Liverpool), with a big w tower and high and handsome nave with quatrefoil piers.

Pugin's ideas were first brought to Anglican church-building in the area by *Edmund Sharpe*, author of *Architectural Parallels* (1848), one of the important source-books of the Gothic Revival. His St Mary, Knowsley (1843–4), has stylised foliage capitals and a stone tower vault: quite a contrast to his archaeologically illiterate church at Scholes (Wigan) completed in 1841 (*see* p. 66). *W. Young*'s St Paul, Westleigh (Leigh), opened 1847, is also Ecclesiologically sound, with clearly expressed parts, especially a deep and separate chancel. The following year, Sharpe began St Nicholas, Sutton (St Helens), with *E. G. Paley*, an architect fully imbued with the new spirit, who continued the practice after Sharpe quit the profession in 1851. The partners' 'restoration' of Wigan parish church in 1845–50 resulted in an almost completely new building, but followed the Perp original with considerable sympathy. Paley's later churches, always highly competent, have well-executed details, such as the stiff-leaf capitals of St Thomas, Stockton Heath, and are handsomely large – like two completed in 1866, St Peter, Hindley and St James, Poolstock (Wigan) – but somehow they are quite lifeless (all that would change when Hubert Austin joined the practice, as we will see). St Elphin, Warrington's parish church, was substantially rebuilt from 1859 by *Frederick & Horace Francis*, possibly their finest work, with a memorable crossing and a thrillingly high steeple, visible for miles. An imposing crossing tower is the high point of St Mary, West Derby (Liverpool), the only significant work here by *George Gilbert Scott*, begun 1853, with an interior of a scale, height and nobility as yet unseen in the area. *The Ecclesiologist* called it 'a great improvement on any church now existing at Liverpool'. Other 1850s–60s Anglican churches have wide, aisle-less naves, broad transepts and shallow chancels, combined with more convincingly medieval details: St Mary, Grassendale (Liverpool), by *Arthur Hill Holme*, with innovative laminated timber trusses; St Luke, Great Crosby (1853–4, by *Holme* and his brother *George Holme*); Holy Trinity, St Helens, by *W. & J. Hay*; and *H. Gee*'s St Philip, Litherland (1861–3).

By these decades some architects had broken away from a rigid adherence to archaeology, and HIGH VICTORIAN GOTHIC was born. *E. W. Pugin* established an office in Liverpool and designed a number of churches in SW Lancashire, including an uncompleted Roman Catholic cathedral in the city (now demolished). His surviving churches, identifiable by an apsidal E end, a gabled w end surmounted by a bellcote, and frequent round windows, were often designed to meet the needs of large but poor urban congregations. He set out on his new road with Our Lady of Reconciliation, Vauxhall (Liverpool, 1859–60): a single space under one continuous roof, with narrow aisles and widely spaced arcades to give good sight-lines. In this feature it just predates J.L. Pearson's more famous St Peter, Vauxhall, in London.

CONTINENTAL INFLUENCES also begin to infuse designs. Medieval France was a significant source in the 1860s. St Ann, Warrington (1866–8) is a bold, severe and highly knowledgeable *p. 622* building by the great Chester architect *John Douglas*, with a plan of the type derived from Albi Cathedral and some Toulouse churches, that is with deep internal buttresses linked longitudinally by arches. *Henry Clutton* developed a distinctive style for his Catholic churches, based on Italian and French precedents. Our Lady of Compassion, Formby (1863–4) has a few bands of yellow brick, a simple example of the trend for polychromy. The plan is Italian Romanesque, with transepts and three parallel apses; the arcades are of two slender columns, paired in depth, with shaft-rings and naturalistic capitals. This quintessentially Cluttonian motif, derived from early French Gothic, is found on a tremendous scale at St Michael, Ditton (Widnes), built in the 1870s for Jesuits expelled by Bismarck from Germany with a huge and forthright w tower. *G.E. Street*'s unorthodox St Margaret of Antioch, Toxteth (Liverpool), paid for by Robert Horsfall of a family of prolific church builders, has non-native features such as brick, extensive internal polychromy, and a lack of structural division between nave and chancel. *Scoles* rebuilt the Catholic chapel of Ince Blundell Hall in 1858–60 as a large parish church – still attached to the mansion – in a simple but dignified Quattrocento style, enhanced by a decorative scheme possibly by *Crace* and large grisaille paintings by *Gebhard Flatz*. Another inspired by Italy is the remarkable Anglican church of St Bridget, Wavertree (Liverpool), of 1868–72 by *E.A. Heffer*, an Italianate basilica with a high campanile, heavily coffered ceiling, and a free-standing altar in the apse. The unconventional Liverpool practice of *W. & G. Audsley* also looked overseas: their big Christ Church, Kensington (Liverpool) is Lombardic Romanesque, of strongly polychromatic brick inside and out, with a clean-limbed campanile. *J.L. Pearson*'s St Agnes (1883–5) – paid for by the 68 stockbroker H. Douglas Horsfall, son of Robert – demonstrates

Liverpool (Wavertree), St Bridget, interior, engraving.
(*The Builder*, vol. 29, 1871)

that French-derived Gothic carried on beyond its peak in the
1860s without going stale. Pevsner thought it one of the three
most thrilling Victorian churches in Lancashire. Though St Agnes
is of early C13 style it has transepts at both E and W ends and a
pair of tall, spired turrets in its E re-entrant angles. Brick outside
gives way to stone for the magnificent, vaulted interior, which
reaches a climax in the wonderfully diversified apsidal E end.

Pevsner adopted Goodhart-Rendel's term ROGUES to describe
some architects. *J. Medland & Henry Taylor*, Manchester architects with a relish for the quirky and unorthodox, designed St
Peter, Parr (St Helens), 1864–5, with walling in copper slag and
red and buff stone, and an odd timber roof. Unusual roofs were
a speciality: another is at St Elizabeth, Aspull, consecrated in

1882, which is full of Taylorian motifs – polychromatic brick-work, a chancel arch on detached brick shafts, and some freely developed capitals. Ten years later and also in Aspull, St John Baptist, New Springs, bends the rules even further, with an unusual plan, pyramid roofs on the tower stacked one on top of another, and peculiar tracery combining stone and brick. *Joseph Hansom*, the other rogue at work, experimented like E.W. Pugin with plans that removed obstacles between the congregation and the Mass. At St Joseph, Leigh, opened in 1855, he attempted an aisle-less nave so wide that the hammerbeam roof failed during construction and had to be braced and propped by slender cast-iron columns. The result is bizarre and thrilling. Our Lady Immaculate, Prescot (1856–7) also has an aisle-less nave; little St Benedict, Hindley (1869) has narrow passage aisles behind arcade piers packed so closely together that there are two arches for every aisle window. One further roguish work is St Cyprian, Edge Hill (Liverpool), begun in 1879 after its architect *Henry Sumners* had died, which has a clerestory of big mullion-and-transom windows, each under a gable.

From these excursions we return to a purer Gothic. The way is led at the end of the 1860s by the work of *G.F. Bodley*, a Vic-torian master who turned from bold, Continentally inspired High Victorianism to graceful English C14 forms. His St John the Baptist, Tue Brook (Liverpool) is a pivotal work, where he first fully realised his mature English Dec style. It is large, but exter-nally very quiet, so that its great refinements and beauty only gradually act on you. Inside, carefully composed as it is, the lasting impression is of the gloriously complete decorative scheme, some of which was executed by *C.E. Kempe*. Bodley designed everything, including the reredos, pulpit, font and screens.

Then we come to *Hubert James Austin* (1841–1915), the only local church architect of real genius. He joined *Paley* in 1868 after a pupillage under his brother Thomas Austin in Newcastle and a period as assistant to Sir George Gilbert Scott, and transformed the firm into a practice which decorated Lancashire, and espe-cially SW Lancashire, with churches the equal of any in the country. Pevsner declared their work to be of the highest Euro-pean standard of their years. The sometimes confusing evolution of the practice is worth noting:

1836–45	Edmund Sharpe
1845–51	Sharpe & Paley
1851–68	E.G. Paley (Sharpe retires from architecture)
1868–86	Paley & Austin
1886–95	Paley, Austin & Paley (E.G. Paley's son Henry Anderson Paley joins the partnership)
1895–14	Austin & Paley (E.G. Paley dies)
1914–15	Austin, Paley & Austin (H.J. Austin's son H.A. Austin becomes a partner)
1915–	Austin & Paley (H.J. Austin dies)

H.J. Austin had a masterful command of balance and composition allied to an exquisite eye for detail, and handled masonry with compelling confidence and authority. He was also fortunate to have so many wealthy clients. There is not the space to describe all the highlights and variations, but one of the first churches begun after Austin joined the practice, St Matthew and St James in Mossley Hill, Liverpool, illustrates most of the best and most frequent characteristics. It has a magisterial tower, and is built of ashlar throughout, subtly striated, and marked by bands of carved text and outbursts of flushwork arcading (inspired by the East Anglian churches that he had studied). The lofty interior is graced by an immense crossing, and the tower is vaulted. Mossley Hill is Dec; the contemporary St Chad, Kirkby follows the same formula, but with lancets and some Norman details. Its tower has a saddleback roof. St Matthew, Highfield (Wigan), built in the 1890s, has lancets and a recessed spire, as does the crossing tower of the glorious Dec estate church of St John Evangelist, built for the brewer Sir Gilbert Greenall at Walton (Warrington). The latter has virtuoso tracery, another common trait. Yet another is a beautifully composed asymmetrical arrangement of chancel, chapel, transept and organ chamber, as at Christ Church, Waterloo, a church in a free Perp style with some distinctly Art Nouveau tracery details. The wooden sexpartite vault is unusual for a practice that favoured open roofs. Others in a similar style are St John Baptist, Atherton, and St Mary, West Bank (Widnes), which shows them still productive in 1907. St Peter, Westleigh (Leigh), consecrated in 1881, is almost wholly of brick, including the heavily buttressed central tower. St Michael and All Angels, Howe Bridge (Atherton), 1875–7, has a substantial flèche only and an unusually intimate interior of brilliant resourcefulness.

The *Austin & Paley* practice also carried out major RESTORATIONS; the bodies of Leigh and Ormskirk parish churches were all but rebuilt in handsome Perp fashion. Two other restorations deserve a citation: *Basil Champneys'* chancel at Up Holland, built over a basement vestry, and *W. D. Caröe's* loving and scholarly programme at Sefton, where he had been a choirboy; here, from 1907, he reordered the interior, restored the stunning Perp screens, and created a magnificent roof to match.

Other LOCAL ARCHITECTS were at work, of whom *John Douglas* of Chester was the only one to approach Austin's achievements; his St Ann, Warrington has already been described. Two of the small group of timber-framed churches designed are also in SW Lancashire: Great Altcar, 1878–9, a charming forest of timber, and St James the Great, Haydock, a project begun in 1889 in partnership with *D.P. Fordham*, where the technique offered protection against anticipated mining subsidence.* *G.E. Grayson's* All Hallows (Allerton, Liverpool), 1872–6,

---

* In the 1860s *J.J. Scoles* gave Holy Cross at St Helens a flat roof and a lacy wooden chancel arch for the same reason.

is notable for its date for the return to Perp, including a big tower. After Grayson was joined in practice by *Edward Ould*, a pupil and assistant to Douglas, the firm did the airy St Peter, Woolton (Liverpool), and St Faith, Waterloo (opened 1900), which shows great maturity and sophistication both externally and in the atmospheric, passage-aisled interior. *C.E. Deacon* was also alive to the spirit of a more progressive Gothic. St Dunstan, Edge Hill of 1886–9, designed with his then partner *Charles Aldridge*, is another impressively large Liverpool church, with an unusual but effective w front of angle turrets and a big overarch, and rich and roguish fittings. Deacon's St John Evangelist, Hindley Green, completed ten years later, is also inventive in details, plan and spatial manipulation. Two other Late Victorian Perp churches are St Peter, Newton-le-Willows, by the York practice of *Demaine & Brierley*, and St Thomas, Ashton-in-Makerfield, by *F. H. Oldham* of Manchester. Other late C19 architects working for Anglicans include *James F. Doyle* at Maghull, Widnes, Litherland and Mossley Hill (Liverpool), and *Henry Shelmerdine*, who shared Doyle's palette of stock brick, red brick and terracotta trim at St Paul, Widnes.

From their Liverpool office the *Pugin* dynasty continued churning out ROMAN CATHOLIC churches into the C20. St Mary, Warrington (1875–7), continues typical *E. W. Pugin* motifs 61 – twin w windows, elsewhere plenty of round windows, wide nave and arcades, heavy naturalistic capitals – but was finished after his death by his brother *Peter Paul Pugin*, of the successor practice *Pugin & Pugin*. Its churches are normally rock-faced, Dec and apsidal, often with gabled transeptal projections, e.g. Our Lady Immaculate, Bryn (Ashton-in-Makerfield, 1903), or crossgables over the aisles, e.g. St Francis de Sales, Walton (Liverpool, opened 1917). The eccentric exception of St Mary of the Angels, Everton (Liverpool), built by the White Star Line heiress Amy Elizabeth Imrie to introduce Italian religious art to the city's poor, has a basilican plan and imported Italian altars and other artefacts. Another prolific, if uneven, producer of Catholic churches was *Sinnott, Sinnott & Powell*. Typical of their better work is Our Lady Star of the Sea, Seaforth (1898–1901). More interesting is Sacred Heart, Warrington, of 1892–4, admired by Pevsner for its straightforward brick strength. *Edmund Kirby* was also an architect to the Catholic Church; his showpiece is the elaborately E.E. Sodality Chapel of St Francis Xavier, Everton (Liverpool), of 1885–7.

Towards the end of the C19 the influences of the Arts and Crafts Movement and the Free Style produced some churches of tremendous freedom. *Bodley & Garner* returned in the 1890s for St Luke, Warrington, one of their least-known but most extraordinary designs. The style is the trusted Dec, but with twin naves under a single roof; Bodley's attempt to fuse them with a single chancel is valiant, but imperfect. At *Leonard Stokes*'s St Clare, Sefton Park (Liverpool), Gothic is a stimulus, no longer an 69 authority. Sheer walls enclose an interior inspired by Bodley's St

Augustine, Pendlebury, but interpreted with Stokes's singular vision, e.g. the tear-drop section of the pier bases. The excellent fittings are outdone by those of the nearby Unitarian Church of 1896–9 and its library, designed around a little cloister with a church hall by *Thomas Worthington & Son* (perhaps especially the son, *Percy Worthington*). There are woodcarvings here by *C.J. Allen*, wonderful Art Nouveau metalwork by *Richard Llewellyn* 72 *Rathbone* and outstanding murals by *Gerald Moira*.

The movement away from strict historicism was taken up by *Giles Gilbert Scott*, who at the age of twenty-two won the com- 70, 71 petition to design an Anglican CATHEDRAL in Liverpool (1903). *p. 349* Bodley, one of the assessors, was appointed joint architect, and his imprint is evident in the first part to be built, the exquisite Lady Chapel. After Bodley's death in 1907 Scott radically revised the design, and a quite different expression of the Gothic emerged in a building of awe-inspiring dimensions and ambition. The plan, though, is a triumph of form over function. Scott designed most of the furnishings too, including a Spanish-inspired reredos as gargantuan as its surroundings. The cathedral combines areas of sheer walling with concentrations of intense ornament. At his superb St Paul, Stoneycroft (Liverpool), 1913–16, *Scott* stripped away the remaining decoration, leaving severe brick masses breaking back and forth, lit by tall lancets and crowned by another mighty tower. In the churches at Warrington and Catharine Street, Liverpool, designed by *Matthew Honan* there is a foretaste of the interwar Catholic fashion for the Neo-Byzantine.

Of the numerous small and simple NONCONFORMIST CHAPELS, the Sutton Oak Welsh Chapel (St Helens) of the 1850s stands apart for its building material, blocks of lustrous copper slag. Few grander Early Victorian chapels survive, but there are two ashlar boxes from the 1840s, one pedimented Neoclassical – Shaw Street Primitive Baptist Chapel, Everton (Liverpool) – and one lanceted Gothic – for the Congregationalists in Newton-le-Willows, by (*Sir*) *J.A. Picton*. Twenty years later, *J.A. Picton & Son* did a bigger box in Everton (Liverpool) for the charismatic Rev. Frederick Hall Robarts, mildly classical, with a gallery around all four sides. Italianate was still favoured in the 1880s by the Methodists of Nutgrove (St Helens), but most of the best surviving chapels from the second half of the C19 are Gothic. The scale of the Welsh Presbyterian church of 1868 near Prince's Park, Liverpool (derelict), designed by the *Audsleys* in Early French Gothic, reflected the prosperity of a community that once supported dozens of Welsh-speaking chapels. Other Presbyterian congregations followed, e.g. at Blundellsands (free Perp by *W.G. Fraser* and *A. Thornely*), and the Congregationalists too by the end of the century, e.g. at Huyton with *W.D. Caröe* in an early C13 English style with a sophisticated and imaginative interior as one expects of this architect, and at Great Crosby, where *Douglas & Fordham* interpreted a rare Nonconformist commission with customary flair in the 1890s. Methodists frequently built in Dec styles with steeples, as at Ormskirk (*Peter Balmer*, 1870s) and Sefton Park, Liverpool (*Hayley & Son* of Manchester, 1860s, with a pair framing the W end). Great Crosby Congregational Church and the Ullet Road Unitarian Church (see above) illustrate the growing stylistic liberalism evident by 1900. Two other buildings also bear witness to it: St John Methodist Church, Hindley (1900–1, by *William Waddington & Son* of Manchester) has the common plan of transepts and very shallow E end, but an original W front: Mossley Hill Baptist Church, Liverpool (1905–6), bizarrely (for Lancashire) faced in flint, is centrally planned, with wide thin arches made possible by iron and steel. Methodist activities were consolidated from the 1890s in central mission halls, a deliberate nationwide attempt to create a distinctive identity. Our three are all of red brick and yellow terracotta, including two by *Bradshaw & Gass* with big domes: in Renshaw Street, 73 Liverpool, and at Wigan (where only the frontage remains, to a Wrenaissance design). The third, at Linacre Road, Litherland, includes a big Children's Chapel and a three-storey Sunday School.

The unusual diversity of Victorian Liverpool's population is expressed in three tremendously un-English religious buildings. Princes Road Synagogue, Toxteth (opened 1874), *W. & G.* 76 *Audsley*'s best surviving work, combines Gothic and Moorish elements in a fine example of Orientalism. The richly polychromatic interior, with its pointed horseshoe arcades, is adorned by a sumptuous marble Ark, pulpit and Bimah. The Greek Orthodox church of St Nicholas, Toxteth (opened 1870) is Byzantine, 74 closely copied from the former church of St Theodore in Constantinople at the suggestion of *W. & J. Hay*, and built under the supervision of *Henry Sumners*. Domes and tunnel vaults roof a spatially effective but muted interior, planned as a cross in a rectangle. Sources from the North naturally informed the charming Gustav Adolfs Kyrka or Swedish Seamen's Church of 1883–4, a 75 compact Nordic *stavkirke* translated by *W.D. Caröe* into bright red brick, with a slender picturesque spire.

Of CHURCH FURNISHINGS not already described, the most spectacular are the CATHOLIC HIGH ALTARS and REREDOSES, towering Gothic confections of pinnacled niches, statues and tabernacles. Three from the early 1850s are at St Francis Xavier, Everton (Liverpool); excellent marble examples are at *Hansom*'s St Joseph, Leigh. *E. W. Pugin* and *Peter Paul Pugin* designed many elaborate ones, normally in collaboration with *Messrs Boulton* of Cheltenham, e.g. at St Mary, Warrington, and Sacred Heart, Everton (Liverpool). *J.F. Bentley* was responsible for the High Altar at the chapel of Bishop Eaton Monastery, Childwall (Liverpool), and also for a superb gold-leaf triptych there. Another excellent triptych, by Messrs *Salviati*, was installed at St Faith, Waterloo, in 1901. By them also is the mosaic Last Supper on the E wall of St Bridget, Wavertree; another, designed by *Henry*

Holiday, framed by beautiful Pre-Raphaelite angles and virtues in *opus sectile*, is at St Chad, Kirkby. Of PULPITS, the big and elaborate alabaster Gothic piece on dwarf piers at St Peter, Leigh, comes from Manchester Cathedral. The rich Italianate furnishings of Liverpool's School for the Blind, by *Philip Thicknesse* and *Frank Norbury*, *c.* 1900, are now at St Andrew, Clubmoor, Liverpool. The Paschal candlestick is astonishing. At St Thomas, Stockton Heath (Warrington) are excellent life-sized angels painted on the chancel roof by *Mary Farren* of Cambridge, installed in 1877 along with *Minton* tiles designed by *R. Reynolds Rowe*. Two architectural practices whose furnishings are easily recognisable are *J. Medland & Henry Taylor* and *Paley & Austin*. For the former, St Elizabeth, Aspull is a good case study, with its open, slender and curvy iron screens and massive podgy font on stumpy colonnettes. For the work of *Hubert Austin*, St Matthew and St James, Mossley Hill can stand for many, including an alabaster font and woodwork in characteristically intricate Flamboyant style. St Mary, West Derby has fittings and furnishings by *J. Oldrid Scott*, designed after the death of his father. Furnishings at the end of the period include those by *Giles Gilbert Scott* for his own St Paul, Stoneycroft, ranging from the Flamboyant pulpit to the strikingly abstract Gothic bronze altar rail.

There are vast quantities of Victorian and Edwardian STAINED GLASS in SW Lancashire. *A.W.N. Pugin* designed glass for Winwick made by *Hardman & Co.*, the Birmingham firm that the later Pugins continued to patronise, as in Warrington at St Mary, and at the chapel of Bishop Eaton Monastery, Childwall (Liverpool). George Gilbert Scott also employed *Hardman* for most of the glass of St Mary, West Derby (Liverpool), though the fine w window of 1856 is by *William Wailes*. Glass by Wailes can also be found at e.g. All Saints, Wigan, part of a diverse collection including *Heaton, Butler & Bayne, Burlison & Grylls* and *Clayton & Bell*. The last firm's best work in this part of Lancashire was for G.E. Street at St Margaret, Toxteth (Liverpool) at the end of the 1860s. Bodley's St John, Tue Brook (Liverpool) has an indifferently preserved *Morris & Co.* E window of 1868, and other more impressive windows with *Burne-Jones* figures. St Nicholas, Halewood has a bigger scheme, but little anywhere in the country compares with the *Morris & Co.* ensemble at All Hallows, Allerton (Liverpool), a church built by the shipping magnate John Bibby as a memorial to his wife. In them can be observed the firm's stylistic evolution from the mid 1870s through the 1880s, as Burne-Jones developed his pictorial style and took over the design of the backgrounds. Some other *Morris* windows are excellent, as at St Mary, Prescot, and the w windows of St Stephen, Gateacre (Liverpool) of 1883. Intense colouring is also a characteristic of the work of *Henry Holiday*, e.g. at St Michael, Huyton, and St Chad, Kirkby. Best is the superb E window of Up Holland parish church, of 1883–4 and 1903–4, full of movement and exquisitely modelled drapery. The Lancaster firm of *Shrigley & Hunt* are prolific, and can be excellent, e.g. the fine figures and rich colouring of 1883 at St James, West

Derby (Liverpool). Other local practices encountered include *Abbott & Co.*, also of Lancaster, and *H. Gustave Hiller* of Liverpool. The instantly recognisable figures of *C.E. Kempe* can be found in many windows, but in great assemblages only at St Michael and All Angels, Howe Bridge (Atherton) and St Peter, Woolton (Liverpool), both put together incrementally. The earliest glazing at Scott's Liverpool Cathedral was by *James Powell & Sons* (designer *John William Brown*), *Burlison & Grylls*, *Kempe* and *Morris & Co.*, but the bulk is inter-war and post-war.

Good CHURCH MONUMENTS are infrequent because public memorials became the C19 norm for commemoration of the great and the good. Some aristocrats were remembered by reviving the recumbent effigy, e.g. John Wilson-Patten, Lord Winmarleigh, †1892, at St Elphin, Warrington, by *H.H. Armstead*, and the 14th Earl of Derby at Knowsley by *Matthew Noble* (1872).* Founders and inaugural priests have some noteworthy memorials, like the granite obelisk to Richard Evans, †1864, outside the former Congregational church at Newton-le-Willows, and the BRASS by *Barkentin & Krall* at St Margaret, Toxteth (Liverpool), showing Robert Horsfall, †1881, holding a drawing of the church. Progression beyond the Gothic Revival is represented by the Arts and Crafts copper plaque to Nicholas and Agnes Blundell, †1894 and 1890, at Little Crosby, and a haunting headstone in the churchyard of St Austin, Aigburth (Liverpool) to Domingo de Ybarrondo, †1909.

THE INTER-WAR YEARS

Commercial, Civic and Public Architecture

In terms of style, inter-war architecture begins a few years before 1914, to an agenda set substantially in SW Lancashire by *Sir Charles Reilly* (1874–1948), the influential head of the Liverpool School of Architecture from 1904 to 1933. He rejected what he saw as the excessive individualism of much late C19 and early C20 architecture, favouring instead at first Regency and modern French architecture, and then a purer American-inspired CLASSICISM, after a visit to the United States in 1909. It was an approach particularly suited to a city with strong ties to North America. Reilly built little himself, though his Guild of Students for the University of Liverpool of 1910–13 and the chancel of Holy Trinity, Wavertree (Liverpool) are good illustrations of his manifesto. Instead, he set about propagating his view of a truly modern, international style through journalism and teaching. He sent his best students to gain experience in the offices of leading New York practices, of whom *Herbert J. Rowse* returned to become the outstanding Liverpool architect of his generation. Water Street, in the business heart of Liverpool, has today an extra-

---

* In 1929 the 16th Earl was also memorialised with a recumbent effigy, on a monument designed by *Sir Giles Gilbert Scott* in Liverpool Cathedral.

ordinarily North American character, in no small part due to Rowse's two great COMMERCIAL BUILDINGS. The first was India Buildings of 1923–30, designed in conjunction with *Arnold Thornely*, and complete with a tunnel-vaulted shopping arcade; Reilly wrote that it 'would not disgrace Fifth Avenue'. Two years after completion, it was outdone by Rowse's Martins Bank opposite, whose arcaded and Travertine-clad banking hall is the match of any in the country, and one of the sights of Liverpool. Other major commercial buildings in the new style, not all with direct links to Reilly, include West Africa House, *Briggs, Wolstenholme & Thornely*'s contribution to the transformation of Water Street, and *Frank Atkinson*'s Adelphi Hotel of 1911–14 (*see* p. 334). Its emergence just before the First World War can also be witnessed in the work of *Gerald de Courcy Fraser* by comparing his severe Premier Buildings with two looser department stores, the Bon Marché, and the vast Lewis's (largely destroyed in 1941).

By the early 1930s Reilly was switching his allegiance to the MODERN MOVEMENT. This is reflected in the Leverhulme Building of the School of Architecture at the University, opened in 1933, which he designed in conjunction with *L. B. Budden* and *J. E. Marshall*. Reilly's pupil *Harold Dod*, who had designed the Athenaeum Club, Liverpool (1924) in his master's earlier style, stripped the classicism of the façade of the University's Harold Cohen Library (1936–8) to almost nothing, and built in utilitarian Modernism at the back. *Rowse* followed a different path. For the Mersey road tunnel (1925–34) he designed a series of priapic ventilation towers in a smooth, cubic Art Deco style. Most are faced in Portland stone, and have evocative sculpture by *Edmund C. Thompson* and *George T. Capstick*. Later, an interest in the stripped brick Modernism of W.M. Dudok inspired his Philharmonic Hall, Liverpool (1936–9), and offices for Pilkington's Glass in St Helens (1937–40). Dudok was also the inspiration at a number of pithead baths of the late 1930s designed by *J. H. Bourne* and others for the Miners' Welfare Committee, such as at Clock Face colliery (St Helens). A design all of its own is Warrington's Masonic Hall by *Albert Warburton* (1932–3) with its unusually public Masonic iconography.

The influence of Dudok, American monumentalism and Art Deco detailing are combined in the most forward-looking TRANSPORTATION PROJECT of the era, the hangars, control tower and terminal of Liverpool's first airport, built 1935–40 at Speke and designed by *Edward Bloomfield* of the City Surveyor's Department. This is now among the best-preserved first-generation airports in the world. Expansion of the dock estate paused after the completion in 1928 of the giant Gladstone complex. Government aid underpinned investment in the road network: the Mersey tunnel, an outstanding civil-engineering achievement by *Basil Mott* and *J. A. Brodie*, and the East Lancashire Road from Liverpool to Manchester, built in 1929–34 (*W. H. Schofield*, County Surveyor, *Henry Swire*, engineer), one of the first entirely new trunk roads in the country. The 40 ft (12.3 metre) carriageway has gentle bends, but no lengthy level straights for fear that headlights would dazzle oncoming traffic; junctions were by roundabout.

For EDUCATION and HEALTH BUILDINGS in the period, Neo-Georgian was the default mode. Of the large number of SCHOOLS – normally with a long frontage and a central accent, perhaps some pilasters, almost certainly a cupola – the Wade Deacon Grammar School, Widnes (*Stephen Wilkinson*, County Architect), 1930–1, will suffice as an example. More ambitious is the unfinished quadrangle for the Liverpool College in Mossley Hill by *Leathart, Granger & Webber* (opened 1929), with giant pilasters and a loggia. Two teacher-training colleges on a grand scale are the former St Katharine's College at Childwall (Liverpool), 1930, by *Slater & Moberly*, with nods to Home Counties vernacular, and Edge Hill College at Ormskirk by *Wilkinson* (1931–3), which is Reilly-like. Also Neo-Georgian are Liverpool University's first halls of residence at Mossley Hill (*Willink & Dod*, 1937–9), and the most common health-building type, nurses' homes. Exceptions to this hegemony include the Health Centre, Widnes (1938–9), a new health initiative in a Moderne style; the former Mesnes High School, Wigan (1935–7, by *A.E. Munby*), an unresolved mixture of Moderne and Neo-Georgian; and an extension to Liverpool's School for the Blind by *Anthony Minoprio* and *Hugh Greville Spencely* (1930–2), stripped classical with excellent detailing, including carvings by *John Skeaping*.

THEATRE and CINEMA architecture followed, and bent, wider stylistic trends. From the 1920s there is the Empire Theatre, Liverpool (*W. & T.R. Milburn*), of Portland stone and with Ionic columns. Into the 1930s, Moderne or Art Deco appears, as in the sleek stone façade of Liverpool's Forum Cinema, Lime Street (*William R. Glen*, 1931), the brick Royal Court Theatre (*James B. Hutchins* of *Wainwright & Sons*), and the former Abbey Cinema, Wavertree (1939, *Alfred Shennan*). The auditorium of Rowse's already mentioned Philharmonic Hall is the best interior that survives in the area. Reilly's pupil *H.H. Davies* specialised in suburban PUBS: lovingly Neo-Georgian when gently inserted into Liverpool's early C19 townscape, e.g. the Blackburne Arms, Catherine Street; more assertive and infused with the new classicism and recent ideas about planning near the new estates, e.g. The Gardener's Arms, Old Swan. Road houses, often Tudorbethan, were established along the East Lancashire Road and elsewhere.

Public Art

FIRST WORLD WAR MEMORIALS vary in style and form. Gothic examples include a gatehouse by *Austin & Paley* at Standish parish churchyard (1927) and a superb octagonal pillar in front of Wigan parish church by *Sir Giles Gilbert Scott* (1925). Neo-classical monuments include those at Atherton (by *Bradshaw & Gass*) and at Leigh, where *J.C. Prestwich & Sons*' cenotaph forms the centrepiece of a memorial square. It is of Portland stone (after

112

Lutyens' Cenotaph in Whitehall). So too is Widnes' dignified obelisk, by *Harold E. Davies* and the sculptor *Herbert Tyson Smith*. Crosses, symbols of Christian sacrifice, are common, often, e.g. at Wigan Cemetery (Ince), copies of *Sir Reginald Blomfield*'s Cross of Sacrifice designed for overseas war cemeteries. Variations are at Woolton, an Art Nouveau-style Celtic cross, 113 and Wavertree, where *Tyson Smith* created a superb, arrestingly tapering form flanked by grieving women in stylised classical dress. The two most powerful pieces are in central Liverpool. 110 *William Goscombe John*'s Memorial to the Heroes of the Marine Engine Room at the Pier Head, unveiled in 1916, has strikingly naturalistic engineers flanking a granite obelisk: a notably early monument to working-class heroism. By contrast, 111 the Cenotaph, by *L.B. Budden* and *Tyson Smith* (unveiled 1930), is magnificently, unflinchingly unheroic. Either side of a simple altar-like block are continuous bronze reliefs showing mourners, endless gravestones and emotionless, marching solders. Others with figures are comparatively rare; that at Eccleston (*see* Prescot) is a dynamic bronze of a mother reaching up to an alert young officer.

Housing and Planning

Thousands and thousands of COUNCIL HOUSES were built from 1919 onwards with Government grants, under a series of Acts beginning with the 'Addison' Act. The uniformity of the estates in Widnes, St Helens and other places derives from the design manuals provided by the Ministry of Health, the first of which, largely written by *Raymond Unwin*, was underpinned by Garden City philosophy and design. Strict conditions were imposed on layout, density, and house sizes and plans.

Liverpool undertook the most ambitious and interesting schemes. A series of estates, with geometric street layouts characteristic of inter-war public housing, was built off *Brodie*'s orbital Queens Drive (*see* p. 87). Norris Green, begun 1926, was the largest. Under *(Sir) Lancelot Keay*, Director of Housing from 1925, the standard hipped-roof semis and foursomes were overlain with Georgian details or vernacular motifs, at least in the most visible streets. Much of this can no longer be discerned, so shabby are some estates (e.g. Norris Green), so defaced by 'home improvements' are many others. Churches, schools and elegant shopping parades integrated with public halls (e.g. Dovecot Estate, Knotty Ash) were provided, though pubs were banned. Keay's ideas culminated in Speke, a proto-New Town for 20,000, with an industrial estate and new airport. Construction began in *p. 460* 1937 to a symmetrical Beaux Arts plan with boulevards, but was interrupted by the Second World War, and the scheme was not completed until the 1960s. Public facilities were late and diluted, and the prosperous mixed community imagined by its creators never materialised. The worst of the city's slums were replaced by smaller numbers of FLATS by Keay and his department, bold

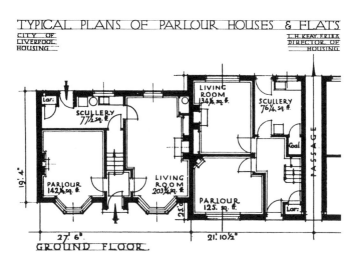

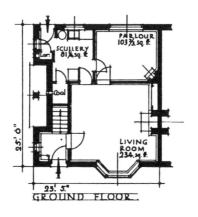

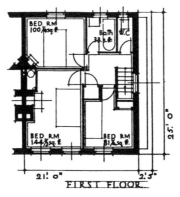

Liverpool Corporation, housing plans.
Ground- and first-floor plans by L.H. Keay, 1930s

blocks with strongly horizontal lines inspired by European Modernism. The best survives: St Andrew's Gardens (*John Hughes*,
completed 1935), with a semicircular plan lifted from the Horseshoe Estate in Berlin.

PRIVATE HOUSING consists overwhelmingly of thousands
of specimens of Osbert Lancaster's 'By-pass Variegated'. One
example, John Lennon's childhood home at Woolton (Liverpool),
has been evocatively restored by the National Trust. Notable
INDIVIDUAL COMMISSIONS are few. Blythe Hall, Lathom, was
rebuilt *c.* 1920 by the 3rd Earl of Lathom with bits inside from
Leoni's Lathom House, and a grandiose Greek Doric swimming
pool.

Religious Buildings

The biggest project of the time was still the ANGLICAN CATHE-
DRAL in Liverpool, slowly marching forward with great windows
of stained glass by *John William Brown* and *James H. Hogan* and
sculpture and monuments by *Edward Carter Preston*. The biggest
non-project was *Lutyens'* ROMAN CATHOLIC CATHEDRAL. It
was a conceit of staggering proportions to begin in 1933 at the
height of the Great Depression the construction of a church that
would have been bigger than St Peter's itself. It never progressed
p. 355 beyond the crypt, but that is enough to reveal the scale and the
potential of this extraordinary but flawed design. With its inventive combination of Roman, Byzantine and Renaissance sources,
it was certainly not a staid exercise in historicism.

Of PARISH CHURCHES, the extraordinary St Mary Lowe
House (R.C.) in St Helens, by *Charles B. Powell* of Dublin
(1920–9), uses a weird mixture of Byzantine and Continental
Romanesque, with a domed crossing. There are more churches
in this mainly Catholic revivalist fashion, whose signature is the
dome and whose progenitor is Bentley's Westminster Cathedral.
Pevsner was scathing about 'one of the deadest ends in mid-C20
ecclesiastical architecture', but visitors are filled with admiration
114 at the interiors of *J. Sydney Brocklesby*'s St Oswald and St Edmund
Arrowsmith, Ashton-in-Makerfield, and St Theresa, Sutton Manor
(St Helens). A curious figure, Brocklesby designed a sequence of
churches inspired by domed Romanesque models in the South
of France, and attempted to recreate the methods of the medieval
master mason. At St Oswald the result is an interior of spatial
115 delight, with exceptional stained glass by *Harry Clarke*, and
superb carved capitals, arches etc. by the *Howe* brothers.[*] They
struggled on alone at Sutton Manor after the money ran out, and
the church was completed with simplified upper parts in 1953.

Carved stone was costly, and in the new suburbs around Liverpool parish churches arose in cheaper brick with concrete and
steel framing. All Souls, Allerton (1927), by *D.A. Campbell &
E.H. Honeybourne*, is a large essay in Romanesque Revival whose

[*] There is more of Clarke's wonderful glass at St Mary, Warrington.

handsome campanile is the visual anchor for a Corporation estate. Other architects – all graduates of Reilly's School of Architecture – showed awareness of Continental developments. Pevsner identified a touch of 1920s Sweden in the lancets of *Quiggin & Gee's* Christ Church, Norris Green (1931–2). But the first real stirrings come with *Bernard A. Miller*, whose St Christopher, Norris Green, begun 1930, has a blocky brick exterior and parabolic arches inside. Miller's St Columba, Anfield, is pale and silvery, and has round arches instead, with a *Mary Adshead* triptych, and also her magnificent reredos from Miller's St Christopher, Withington (SE Lancashire, 1935, demolished). Still more important is *Francis Xavier Velarde*, who worked exclusively for the Roman Catholic Church. The Italian Romanesque of his St Matthew, Clubmoor, also begun in 1930, provides few clues of what was to come, but in 1936 he moved forward with the design of St Monica, Bootle, where the rhythm of tier above tier of round-arched openings – something, as Pevsner put it, between Henry VIII and Giorgio de Chirico – was inspired by the recent churches of Dominikus Böhm in Germany.

Elsewhere, the Church of England and the Nonconformists continued resolutely to build Gothic churches, e.g. Aigburth Methodist Church, Liverpool. *Austin & Paley* atrophied on the death of its creative powerhouse, Hubert Austin, in 1915, producing inert Perp repetitions of previous work at Orrell, Abram and Wigan. At St Helens parish church of 1920–6, *W.D. Caröe* kept alive the tradition of spatial and archaeological sophistication to which Hubert Austin had belonged. *C.E. Deacon & Sons'* Liverpool churches of the late 1930s, at Childwall and Knotty Ash, were still in a Late Victorian form, though stripped of Gothic detail.

Caröe's superb FITTINGS at St Helens are about the best of the period; many others, and much STAINED GLASS of the period, were First World War memorials. A good example is the refined Perp chancel screen by *Giles Gilbert Scott* at St Faith, Waterloo, of 1921. *Hardman & Co.* produced some good glass, e.g. at St Mary Lowe House, St Helens. Its conventionalism contrasts with a number of works by *Caroline Townshend* and *Joan Howson* in the area, and the outstanding *Harry Clarke* glass mentioned above.

Industrial Buildings

American ideas inspired several INDUSTRIAL INNOVATIONS. The Mersey Match Factory at Garston (Liverpool) of 1919–21 was the first building in Britain made of flat-slab concrete construction (i.e. with beamless floor-slabs). *Sven Bylander*, the engineer, had designed the steel frame of Selfridges in London for the factory's architects, *Mewès & Davis*. The functional, linear and highly glazed elevation derived from Albert Kahn's 'daylight factories' was screened by a Neo-Georgian range. By contrast, the Littlewoods Building of 1938 (probably by *Gerald de Courcy* 117

Fraser) on Edge Lane in Liverpool is a huge white Art Deco advertisement in the same vein as the celebrated factories on the Great West Road in London. It outdazzles any of the factories put up on the contemporary industrial estates, inspired by Slough and the Team Valley Estate in Gateshead, which were begun by Liverpool Corporation at Speke and Aintree to encourage investment in the wake of the Great Depression. Other industrial buildings were inspired by Dudok – *see* p. 98.

SOUTH-WEST LANCASHIRE FROM 1945

Post-war Planning and Housing

Liverpool's docks were a major target for the Luftwaffe, and Bootle and Liverpool were both badly bombed. A large part of Liverpool's business district was flattened, and some significant buildings suffered grievously. The Blue Coat School and the Liverpool Museum were rebuilt behind preserved façades, but *Foster Jun.*'s great Custom House was short-sightedly demolished to generate employment. Reconstruction in Liverpool in the lean 1950s was insipid, e.g. in Lord Street, but tempered by *Jacob Epstein*'s giant bronze striding out from *Gerald de Courcy Fraser*'s renewed Lewis's department store.

Liverpool, redevelopment proposals.
(*Liverpool City Centre Plan*, 1965)

Planning for COMPREHENSIVE REDEVELOPMENT in Liverpool was not finalised until the City Centre Plan of 1965 by *Graeme Shankland* (Planning Consultant) and *Walter Bor* (Chief Planning Officer). This headily up-beat document reflected the revived prosperity and confidence of a city basking in the glow of Beatlemania. Its authors declared that two-thirds of the centre was obsolete, and that projected rates of growth made wholesale renewal both necessary and feasible. A mere handful of buildings were earmarked for preservation, plus four conservation areas. New roads were central to the Plan, and required demolition on an enormous scale. Although this programme was scaled back, the city was nevertheless fragmented by multi-lane highways that cut off the centre from the waterfront and from the districts to the N and E. New high-rise buildings were to be grouped in clusters framing the old business centre (discussed below). More office blocks were erected along Stanley Road in Bootle under that borough's own town-centre renewal plans, drawn up 1958–65, which also proposed a civic quarter around the existing C19 buildings. In both Liverpool and Bootle, shopping-centre developments (*see* p. 110) were executed before the rest of the plan. Of the St Helens' area plan of 1969 only fragments were realised: a shopping centre and part of the road network.

In tandem with redevelopment came REHOUSING. In some smaller towns and villages the shortage immediately after the war was met with PREFABRICATED HOUSING, built to a variety of proprietary designs. Hale is one such village, and Hindley one such town, with examples of two common types: the *B.I.S.F* – British Iron and Steel Federation (steel frame, trusses and cladding) – and the *Orlit* house (concrete). Some of these replaced bomb damage, but the principal drive remained slum clearance, now at a pace and on a scale only dreamt of before. In the early 1950s the solution was low-rise housing and medium-rise apartment blocks, but later in the decade high-rise schemes were introduced. In Liverpool, under *Ronald Bradbury* (City Architect and Director of Housing from 1948) and *J.W. Boddy* (responsible for housing from 1963), DECK-ACCESS SCHEMES and TOWERS were built in great numbers, notably in Everton, sometimes as small groups, sometimes as part of mixed-height schemes. Towers were intended to replace C19 villas as part of a Corbusian transformation of Sefton Park, though only a few were erected. Prefabricated construction was adopted from 1963 when the Council accepted a tender for almost two-and-a-half thousand dwellings in towers built to the French *Camus* system; other industrialised systems were also used. In 1969 Pevsner foresaw the potential failure of these schemes. Design, management and social problems – and depopulation – have meant that all but a handful of the towers and slabs built have been demolished, the infamous 'Piggeries' of Everton lasting a mere twenty-two years. Beyond the Liverpool conurbation, Wigan was the only authority in SW Lancashire to build tower blocks, in Scholes, where they rise up a hill opposite the town centre, as part of a mixture of low, medium and high rise.

Tower clusters also appeared in the extensive SUBURBAN ESTATES built by Liverpool Corporation. Some of these estates were begun before 1939, notably in Speke; others were planned beyond the city boundaries. They spread from Allerton – where a house from 1952 in which Paul McCartney grew up has been opened to the public by the National Trust – to Halewood in the S and around the city, across Childwall, Croxteth and Huyton, which gained a scrappy little town centre. Bootle created nearly 10,000 mainly low-rise houses on land in Netherton and Sefton.

During the 1970s–80s the failures of post-war housing inspired CO-OPERATIVE HOUSING and COMMUNITY ARCHITECTURE movements on Merseyside which achieved worldwide recogni-
p. 586   tion. Liverpool City Council abandoned wholesale clearance for a policy of upgrading privately owned by-law housing. Long-established tenant communities wishing to remain together established co-operatives, acquiring properties and managing their refurbishment with loans from the Housing Corporation. The first was at Granby, Toxteth, in *c.* 1970. From 1977 co-ops undertook new-build schemes, a radical departure from the tra-ditions of local authority housing. For the first time future resi-dents – not housing professionals – took charge of the design process, selecting architects and working with them to develop plans that suited individual tastes and needs. The most famous and largest scheme is the Eldonian Village, begun 1987, where *Wilkinson Hindle Halsall Lloyd* helped develop an informal plan with cul-de-sacs lined by brick bungalows and houses with indi-vidual gardens. If the results in an inner-city location seem defi-antly suburban, that is exactly what people wanted. Elsewhere, inward-looking schemes by private developers shun the city's streets behind defensive walls.

Significant PRIVATE HOUSES are few. 1963 was a year of con-trasting schemes: *Claud Phillimore* drastically reduced the size of Knowsley Hall and built the quietly Neo-Georgian New House for the Stanley family; *Gerald R. Beech* completed his three calm and discreet Modernist houses in Woolton, Liverpool; and *Nelson & Parker*'s idiosyncratic Maeldune went up amidst the dunes of Blundellsands.

The New Towns

Redevelopment and housing were designed within the framework of REGIONAL PLANNING. Since the 1920s this had advocated new urban settlements, and green belts. Speke was begun before 1939; a similar development created by Liverpool Corporation at Kirkby to the NE, 1946–7, was effectively a municipally developed new town for a projected population of 50,000, incorporating a huge industrial estate. *Ronald Bradbury* and his team were
p. 214   responsible for the detailed planning. Three residential zones, featuring a mixture of housing types, were laid out informally according to existing features, in contrast to the Beaux Arts layout of Speke. But the architecture is poor, and Kirkby has suf-

fered many of the same social and economic problems which have afflicted other C20 estates.

The 1946 New Towns Act made the creation of NEW TOWNS national policy, through development corporations funded by the Exchequer. Skelmersdale was the first of three designated to house Liverpool overspill. *Sir Hugh Wilson*'s plan is typical of the so-called second-generation New Towns. Its compactness has its roots in Wilson's own Cumbernauld plan; the separation of pedestrian and vehicular routes derives from Radburn, the American 'Town for the Motor Age' created in 1929. (Radburn plans became an orthodoxy in 1960s Britain; the second stage of Bootle's Netherton/Sefton housing scheme has one too.) Landscaping is careful and generous, and where it makes use of natural denes, effective, but the town centre is a failure. The second New Town, Runcorn, lies in Cheshire; the third, designated in 1968, was at Warrington, one of only three to be grafted on to an existing town. By the time the Outline Plan was approved in 1973, adopting the proposals of *Austin-Smith:Lord*'s 1969 draft masterplan, the rationale had shifted from housing overspill to managing growth at the crossroads of the North West's mainline railways and motorway network. The Borough was responsible for developing the centre; the Development Corporation planned and managed three expansion areas. Radburn was the guiding principle at the outset, but the second chief architect and planner, *Hugh Canning*, reintroduced road-facing housing. He also wanted to blur distinctions between public and private housing. Two contrasting housing schemes by *Terry Farrell* and *Richard MacCormac* encapsulate these ambitions. In the long term, Warrington has proved a resounding success economically, but not in the main architecturally: housing built since the Development Corporation was wound up in 1989 is the usual private house-builders' fare.

Transport and Communications

The modernisation of TRANSPORT was central to regional planning. Liverpool's Dock Board collapsed in the early 1970s, but not before constructing the huge Royal Seaforth container-ship dock (opened in 1971). Two of Liverpool's three railway termini were demolished, and services concentrated at Lime Street. The old Central Station site was redeveloped as the focal point of an integrated commuter network, as proposed in the Liverpool City Centre Plan, with a new underground loop line and N–S tunnel. As the railways contracted the MOTORWAY SYSTEM expanded, with Warrington as its hub from 1963, when the M6 reached S Lancashire. Planning and construction was led by *Sir James Drake*, Lancashire County Surveyor and Bridgemaker 1945–72, a pioneer of motorways in the UK. A second Mersey tunnel opened in 1974 brought traffic from the M53 to the Liverpool Docks and city centre, with a witty ventilation tower in Vauxhall by *Bradshaw, Rowse & Harker*. BRIDGES on the M6 include the

intrusive Thelwall Viaducts and the surprisingly elegant viaduct
across the Douglas valley at Shevington. (*Mott, Hay & Anderson*'s
huge bowstring arch bridge of 1956–61, spanning 1,000 ft
(308 metres) across the Mersey at Widnes, is off the motorway
network.) At Burtonwood, the M62 has one of the few imagina-
124 tive SERVICE STATIONS, *Patrick Gwynne*'s twin octagonal pavilions (1972–4) with copper roofs that begged the nickname
'witches' hats'.

Public Buildings

Several new CIVIC CENTRES were planned in the 1960s. Kirkby
built an anonymous assemblage of wings at the base of a small
tower. Huyton's new offices have a similar dreary feel. The
Municipal Offices at Widnes by *M. Nevile Player* (1967) occupy
a more refined tower standing on pilotis; those at Warrington and
Wigan are brutish concrete blocks. St Helens' and Bootle's plans
were never realised.

LIBRARIES are among the better civic buildings. Crosby began
a new one in 1964 (actually at Waterloo) by *G. Ronald Mason*, a
horizontal brick design with a civic hall still rooted in the 1950s.
It contrasts with the glass and steel boxes that are *Ronald Bradbury*'s contemporary Liverpool libraries, erected in suburbs such
as Allerton and Clubmoor. Lancashire County Council provided
facilities in the overspill towns. Skelmersdale Library (1978), a
big cuboid of textured concrete modulated by vertical strips of
windows, is one of a thoughtful series by the County Architect
Roger Booth, and related to the neighbouring Police Station,
and another at Wigan. They employ the Council's proprietary
system of rib-finished, load-bearing, pre-cast panels. Several LAW
COURTS have been erected since the great country-wide modernisation programme began in the 1970s. The hulking Queen
Elizabeth Law Courts, Liverpool (*Farmer & Dark*, begun 1973)
was a pioneer of these new Crown Court complexes, and a foretaste of their generally dispiriting architecture. St Helens (1980
by *R.A. Mallett*), more modest in scale, has a kind of moat and
drawbridge. Warrington Combined Court of 1992 (*Howell,
Killick, Partridge & Amis*) is more welcoming, though it too has
vestigial turrets.

Most of the most noteworthy EDUCATIONAL BUILDINGS
were built by the UNIVERSITY OF LIVERPOOL. *William
Holford*'s expansion plan of 1946 formed the basis for its invasion
of the Late Georgian streets around Abercromby Square, and for
the decision to appoint a variety of architects. Pevsner was vexed
by the resulting 'zoo of buildings' and by the lack of respect for
the Georgian surroundings, particularly at the more assertive
buildings erected from the early 1960s onwards. *Yorke, Rosenberg
& Mardall*'s clinical Electrical Engineering and Electronics
building is one of the better animals, though not one of their best
in this white-tiled idiom. Another is the Arts and Law buildings
of 1961–6 by *Bryan & Norman Westwood, Piet & Partners*. *Denys
Lasdun & Partners*' Sports Centre (1963–6) attracted Pevsner's

ire, but its forceful and cohesive angled form now seems surprisingly sympathetic to the Georgian streetscape. Elsewhere in the city centre, Liverpool John Moores University occupies *Ronald Bradbury*'s 1950s–60s College of Technology. Of suburban halls of residence, both the best, Carnatic Halls by *Manning & Clamp* (1965 etc.), and the largest agglomeration, at Greenbank, are set in attractive landscapes made from the mature grounds of C19 merchants' houses in Mossley Hill. One of the best post-war buildings in SW Lancashire is *Gerald R. Beech*'s light-footed Wyncote university sports pavilion of 1961–2 at Allerton, a transparent box cantilevered out from a podium. *Weightman & Bullen*'s teacher-training college campus (1964–6, now Liverpool Hope University College) at Childwall, Liverpool, deserves a mention for its tight plan of disciplined blocks (for the chapel *see* below).

A similar concept was adopted by *Roger Booth* for the Glenburn High School and F.E. College at Skelmersdale, an integrated pavilion plan system built of the County's 'heavy concrete method'. This is the most interesting of the SCHOOLS in our area designed by the County Council. Much of the huge programme undertaken by Liverpool City Council under *Bradbury* has been demolished, or is now battered and worn. A well-maintained example from the 1950s is the New Heys Community Comprehensive, Allerton, designed in partnership with *Herbert Thearle & Partners* and much admired at the time. However, the most aesthetically successful post-war schools are two at Orrell by *Lyons, Israel, Ellis & Partners*, 1960–2: Up Holland High School (1958–60) and Abraham Guest High School (1960–2).

Adjoining Liverpool University is *Holford Associates*' Royal Liverpool University Hospital (planned 1963–5, opened 1978), the most interesting healthcare project. This massive concrete complex ignores the streets around it, but its towering bulk and sculptural boiler house can appear as a dramatic Brutalist hill town. A new building type was the LEISURE CENTRE. Heatwaves Leisure Centre, Stockbridge Village (1988), a little-known work by *Nicholas Grimshaw & Partners*, is a big shed built on a tight budget, but done with some verve, most memorably in the nautical shape of a tall, stayed mast.

Commercial and Industrial Buildings

One has to go to Bootle to see the commercial visions of the 1960s realised. Stanley Precinct is a Corbusian avenue of banal OFFICE TOWERS, many by *Gunton & Gunton*, begun in the mid 1960s. The *Hind Woodhouse Partnership*'s Triad Building, a Brutalist monster opened in 1974, is tallest. The relocation of Government departments kick-started the Precinct, but Bootle's largest and most successful complex, the *Ministry of Public Building and Works*' National Giro Centre (1966–8), is elsewhere. A few high-rise offices were built in Liverpool, under the City Centre Plan of 1965 (*see* p. 105), including *Tripe & Wakeham*'s Royal Insurance headquarters of 1972–6 (now Royal & Sun

Alliance), a massive, stepped brown pyramid above the riverfront. Pilkington's adopted the new American model of a landscaped campus for their headquarters in St Helens, planned in the 1950s and finished in 1965. *Fry, Drew & Partners'* tightly integrated plan of pavilions and courts on the edge of a lake included a twelve-storey tower for prestige.

SHOPPING CENTRES are an important post-war type. Those at Kirkby and Huyton of the 1950s and early 1960s are still open-air parades. Later examples demonstrate evolving approaches to integrating these ever more massive complexes into town centres. Enclosed structures planned on split levels, with services beneath the shops, first appear in 1960s–70s redevelopments. Both the New Strand Centre at Bootle (*T.P. Bennett & Son*) and St John's Precinct, Liverpool (*James A. Roberts*) were given vertical accents to offset their spreading bulk, at the one a residential tower, at the other a giant boiler chimney prettified with a revolving restaurant. The St John's centre entailed the demolition of *Foster Jun.*'s pioneering St John's Market, and it brutally crashes the setting of St George's Hall. By contrast St Helens' Church Square Centre, by *Kingham Knight Associates*, 1970–5, has street frontages, and a feeling for the scale of its surroundings. The Golden Square Centre, Warrington (*Ardin & Brookes & Partners*, 1973–83) retains the town's market square, refashioned as a lively pedestrian space surrounded by a mall. But historic streets and buildings were destroyed; most of those retained are little more than replicas. The Galleries by *Leach, Rhodes & Walker* replaced Wigan's old markets in the mid 1980s, after developments such as the Milburngate Centre at Durham had pioneered greater sensitivity in plan and roofscape. Its façades are integrated thoughtfully into the streetscape, and it has a variety of animated indoor and outdoor spaces. The architectural language will not be to everyone's taste, but the success of the planning should be recognised. More recent shopping-centre developments are discussed below.

INDUSTRIAL ARCHITECTURE to *c.* 1980 has few highlights. Kirkby's huge industrial estate includes one impressive factory by *Sir Percy Thomas & Son*, built *c.* 1950 for ICI Metals. Two plants for industries new to the area were of record-breaking size: Heinz's Wigan factory (1954–9, by *J. Douglass Mathews & Partners* with *Skidmore, Owings & Merrill*), and the Halewood car plant at Speke (Liverpool) built by Ford in the 1960s. The most imposing structure is Fiddler's Ferry Power Station at Cuerdley Cross, whose symmetrical grandeur dominates the flat Mersey valley for many miles. The most memorable is a product of one of the oldest industries: Tate & Lyle's Sugar Silo of 1955–7 on Liverpool's dock road, a gargantuan, ribbed, parabolic-arched concrete tunnel.

Religious Architecture

Early post-war ecclesiastical projects included making good war damage to Liverpool's churches. The empty shell of St Luke,

Bold Place, was conserved as an unofficial memorial. At Our Lady and St Nicholas, *Edward C. Butler* added a simple Perp building to the C19 steeple, in which orientation was reversed. *Quiggin & Gee* rebuilt the body of St Mary, Walton, in a reserved Gothic with concrete vaults on a steel frame. Parabolic concrete arches were used when *Adrian Gilbert Scott* replaced all but Pugin's steeple at St Oswald, Old Swan (though this was not due to bomb damage).

CATHOLIC CHURCHES in SW Lancashire at first followed traditional longitudinal plans with prominent campaniles, e.g. *Velarde*'s exquisitely crafted, Spanish-inspired St Teresa, Up Holland (designed 1952), and the Romanesque St Patrick, Earlestown, by *Felix A. Jones* of *Jones & Kelly*, Dublin. St Pius, Widnes (1960), is a clean, intimate church vaulted from floor level. These are the tail-end of historicism (for the time being), but not the end of longitudinalism – two examples with expressed concrete frames are St Teresa, St Helens (1964, *W. & J.B. Ellis*), with angled windows *à la* Coventry Cathedral above passage aisles, and Holy Name, Fazakerley (Liverpool), designed in 1962 by *Peter S. Gilby & Associates*, where the frames project on one side like the legs of a giant centipede.

CENTRALISED PLANS had by then begun to emerge, ahead of the Second Vatican Council (1962–5), which endorsed the Liturgical Movement's manifesto for bringing the congregation closer to the Mass. Two firms dominated their spread across SW Lancashire. *Weightman & Bullen* broke the mould first at St Catherine, Lowton, in 1957–9, with a hexagon. This is attached by a lobby to an openwork concrete belfry tower over the baptistery, an arrangement found, with variation, in other churches, including their St Ambrose, Speke (Liverpool), 1959–61. At St Margaret Mary, Knotty Ash, Liverpool (1962–4), the roof is made to appear to float, and is opened in the centre to a lantern like a folded spire. At the chapel of Christ's College of Education, Childwall (now Liverpool Hope University, Childwall), in 1965, the spire is expanded into a fractured pyramid roof, gashed with glass, over a Star of David plan. *L.A.G. Prichard & Son*, whilst not always abandoning 1950s models (e.g. St Oswald, Padgate, Warrington, 1965), explored more muscular solutions. St Jude, Wigan (1963–4) has concrete frames fanning out from a long E wall to meet canted walls, filled from floor to roof with superb abstract *dalle de verre* windows by *Robin Riley*. This auditorium plan was developed at St Agnes, Huyton, into a more fluid form as a pair of concrete vaults expanding to jutting prows, surely inspired by Jørn Utzon's designs for the Sydney Opera House. Christ the King, Wavertree (Liverpool, 1967), has laminated timber frames.

The outstanding centralised plan is Liverpool's ROMAN CATHOLIC CATHEDRAL. In 1959 *Lutyens*' scheme was finally abandoned and a new competition launched, won by *Frederick Gibberd*. He extended the unfinished crypt to create a podium for a great circular concrete tent with sixteen perimeter chapels and porches, making it the first cathedral to abandon the tradi-

118

p. 356

tional longitudinal plan. The massive lantern holds its own with
Scott's Anglican tower, and is filled with magnificent abstract
119 glass by *John Piper* and *Patrick Reyntiens*. Everything focuses on
the simple central altar beneath a suspended baldacchino. The
creation, at last, of ceremonial steps up to the W end has done
justice to a building of international importance.

CHURCHES OF OTHER DENOMINATIONS are as a rule much
less interesting, except perhaps St John Chrysostom, Everton
(Liverpool), where *Saunders Bell*'s *Robin Wolley* adopted the fan
plan for a corner site in 1975. Three Nonconformist designs illustrate different approaches to the integration of community
facilities: the Methodist church at Eccleston (St Helens), by
Penn-Smith & Weston, c. 1960, has a courtyard plan with church
hall and church around it; the *Mason Richards Partnership*'s
Methodist chapel on Palmyra Square in Warrington (1975) is a
large brick box with hall above chapel; and the United Reformed
Church, St Helens, by *Peter Bridges* and *Martin Purdy* of *APEC*
(1976), which externally is nearly all roof, is planned with offices,
lecture theatre, and a combinable church and hall. In the last
few decades facilities have been created within existing
churches, usually by means of a room or hall in the W end of the
nave. Rarely has this been done well. Sometimes, as at St
Cyprian, Edge Hill (Liverpool) or Our Lady of Lourdes and St
Bernard, Toxteth (Liverpool), it is appallingly destructive or
crude. At St Peter, Woolton (Liverpool), a stone-clad hall, by
Brock Carmichael Associates, 1989, was built against the W end
with mixed results.

Fire damage has offered greater creative scope. The E end of
St Luke, Great Crosby, was rebuilt after a fire in 1972 by *Saunders Boston* with attached vestries etc. like three Modernist
chapels. The new roof has steel tension rods, like the fine example
by *Peter Skinner* for the fire-gutted chancel of Paley & Austin's St
John, Atherton, 1996–7; here a glazed screen fills the chancel
arch above the Victorian screen, which now serves as a reredos
to a nave altar. The chancel is now a hall. Changing liturgical
practice has also caused REORDERING, if only to bring the altar
away from the E wall. A good comprehensive scheme is *Bartlett
& Purnell*'s work of 1979 at Clutton's huge St Michael, Ditton
(Widnes). Most of the Victorian fittings were removed; the spare
replacements emphasise the church's austere dignity.

The most ambitious STAINED GLASS is at the cathedrals.
Scott's masterpiece was completed with brightly coloured nave
windows by *Herbert Hendrie* and *William Wilson*, and especially
Carl Edwards, whose great W window (1978) is of an intensity and
fluidity unique in the building. The Catholic cathedral has
already been mentioned. *James Powell & Sons* also made the
dense, vibrant abstract glass designed by *Carl Edwards* for St
Matthew and St James, Mossley Hill (Liverpool). A primitivist
scheme of *dalle de verre* by *P. Fourmaintreaux* (1963) illuminates
the otherwise uninteresting church of St Barnabas, Warrington.
Powell & Sons were also responsible for the excellent abstract *dalle
de verre* which lights *H. Bannister*'s CREMATORIUM CHAPEL at

St Helens Borough Cemetery (1959–62). A Portland stone catafalque, the chapel is a component in a formal landscape that includes a drum-like Chapel of Remembrance.

Out-of-Town Development, Conservation and Regeneration since c. 1980

The last two decades or so have witnessed two trends, sometimes seemingly in opposition: urban expansion along new motorways and trunk roads, and increasingly successful attempts to reinvigorate town and city centres. The former include retail, distribution, and BUSINESS PARKS, mostly collections of big blank sheds and dull office buildings. At Warrington New Town *Nicholas Grimshaw* was commissioned in the late 1970s to design *p. 641* a flexible business unit to set a standard for future development. Its ingenious modularisation and aesthetic leanness proved a dead end, and only two industrial buildings of note have since been erected in Warrington: the Barclays cash store by *Don Collins* and the engineers *White, Young & Partners*, whose sweeping roof is a functional response to security requirements, and the excellent aluminium-skinned Royal Mail Terminal by *Austin-* 125 *Smith:Lord*, completed in 1997. The same practice designed the line of crisp steel boxes which form the Boulevard Industry Park, Speke (Liverpool). Warrington Science Park, envisaged along US lines as a campus with pavilions set in leafy parkland, was executed with higher-density mediocrity. Since *Chamberlin, Powell & Bon*'s contribution has been demolished, the most interesting building is British Nuclear Fuels' Hinton House, 1984, by *DEGW*, with tiered wings draped in planting. Buildings on *EDAW*'s Estuary Commerce Park, built across the disused Speke airfield in Liverpool from 1997, do not bode well for the future setting of the wonderful inter-war airport buildings, so well reused by *Falconer Chester Architects*. RETAIL PARKS have similar big sheds, but with giant fascias, and floundering in seas of car parking. They begin at Warrington with the first British store for IKEA, the brand synonymous with out-of-town shopping, designed in-house in association with *Kingham Knight Associates* and opened in 1987.

The economic threat to historic urban centres posed by out-of-town shops and offices has been countered by a revived appreciation of their C19 buildings and of the economic benefits of CONSERVATION AND REUSE. This came too late to save many fine buildings; Prescot's Georgian town hall, the homes of the Nonconformist Warrington Academy and John Cunningham's Sailors' Home in Liverpool are three of far too many examples. Campaigns like those which saved St Francis Xavier and *Harrison*'s Lyceum in Liverpool were perhaps a turning point *c.* 1980, though recent cases such as that of the remaining houses in Cleveland Square, Liverpool, illustrate that there is still too little appreciation or understanding of the area's magnificent architectural inheritance.

CULTURAL PROJECTS, backed by Government or European grants, have frequently been a key element of conservation-led regeneration. Catalyst, a museum of the chemical industry created by *Brock Carmichael Associates* from 1989 out of an 1860s office block, belongs with the landscaping of the derelict river-front of Widnes. In the 1990s the same practice adapted the former Mechanics' Institution to become the Liverpool Institute of Performing Arts; *Ken Martin*'s conversion of the Midland Railway goods warehouse into the Conservation Centre of National Museums Liverpool was another important scheme. More recently *Studio BAAD* of Leeds have made the redundant law courts in Warrington into the Pyramid Arts Centre, with impressive assurance. Many commercial centres have been pedestrianised, often under schemes including new PUBLIC ART, such as the large mosaic by *Sebastian Boyesen* in Wigan's Market Place and a set of robust furnishings in the centre of Warrington by *Landscape Design Associates* with the American artist *Howard Ben Tre*.

AREA REGENERATION includes the revival of the redundant dock estate s of Liverpool's Pier Head by the Merseyside Development Corporation, formed by Michael Heseltine in 1981, shortly before the Toxteth Riots. The focal project was the triumphant restoration from 1983 of the Albert Dock and warehouses, possibly the single largest conservation project ever undertaken in the United Kingdom. Thanks go to *Holford Associates*, *W.G. Curtin & Partners* and the *Franklin Stafford Partnership*, and to *Brock Carmichael* and *James Stirling* for their thoughtful contributions (the Merseyside Maritime Museum and Tate Liverpool art gallery respectively). There are other good warehouse conversions, but the standard of new docklands architecture is depressing; the diabolical Customs and Excise Building by *PSA Projects, Birmingham* is possibly the nadir. Highlights are *David Marks Julia Barfield Architects*' Liverpool Watersport Centre (1993–4) and *Eduard Ross*'s skeletal footbridge at Prince's Dock. Water has been important in other regeneration schemes. Cleaning up the canal in the centre of Wigan in the 1980s was essential to the restoration and reuse of canal-side mills and warehouses as offices, business units and a museum, a successful project marketed as Wigan Pier. St Helens has not learnt the lesson, despite building a museum of glass by *Geoffrey Reid Associates* which spans the Sankey Brook Navigation. Will Leigh?

Another major regeneration project in Liverpool was begun in the 1990s in an area of run-down streets of C18 houses and C19 warehouses s of the city centre now called Ropewalks. The pioneer here was the developer *Urban Splash*, responsible almost single-handedly for the revival of CITY-CENTRE LIVING in the North West. It invested when no-one else would, reusing redundant commercial buildings with wit and sophistication; good design is fundamental to the fashionable lifestyle it markets. The Concert Square scheme, completed in 1994, included the residential conversion of a Victorian factory – the first such venture in sw Lancashire outside the Liverpool docks. Dozens of similar schemes have followed since 2000, providing work for local architects such as *Union North* and *Brock Carmichael,* and increasing the city-centre population for the first time in a century (though trailing behind the transformation of Manchester city centre). More recent Urban Splash projects are by the spin-off practice *ShedKM*, with whom the developer has expanded outside the commercial core, converting *Elmes*'s burnt-out Collegiate Institution to apartments and the former match factory at Garston 127 to offices with Modernist intervention. As this book was going to press the first residential conversion of a mill in SW Lancashire – in Wigan – was announced.

SW Lancashire has suffered from dreadfully low standards of NEW ARCHITECTURE for decades. The massive expansion of universities in the 1990s produced only one really good building, Liverpool John Moores University's Aldham Robarts Learning Resource Centre by *Austin Smith:Lord*. Many Liverpool schools are being rebuilt at the time of writing under the Private Finance Initiative, on which one fears the verdict of future commentators. In this context *John McAslan & Parker*'s recent Centre for Arts at De la Salle School, Eccleston, St Helens is a beacon of precision and clarity. Much better are a number of railway stations on Merseyside rebuilt by *Brock Carmichael* in the 1990s with a common, clean and robust language, and the library at Huyton by *Mills Beaumont Leavey Channon*, 1997, with a glass façade, now interpreted through the prism of High-Tech architecture.

The transformation of central Liverpool continues, fuelled further by the award to the city of the title European Capital of Culture for 2008. This has encouraged a new wave of office and residential schemes, but whilst there has been much to praise amongst conversion projects, mediocre high-rise apartment blocks now threaten to overwhelm the famous Mersey riverfront. Prince's Dock, adjoining the Pier Head, is a worrying foretaste of what may come unless the city reacquires, as Manchester is beginning to, an appetite for higher design standards. There are some reasons for optimism. FACT, a gallery and cinema in the Ropewalks by *Austin-Smith:Lord* (2003), has an interior to be proud of, and the commissioning of architects of the calibre of *Wilkinson Eyre*, *Will Alsop* and the Danish practice *3XNielsen* for sites flanking Albert Dock shows a growing architectural ambition, even if only the first of these may ever be realised. The enormous *Grosvenor Group* retail development begun in 2004 in the historic core marks a decisive break, with discrete retail buildings designed by leading architects largely according to the historic street plan – an acknowledgement of the failure of the monolithic approach. *ShedKM*'s excellent Ash Grange, Knotty Ash, 2002–4, is a clarion call for more imagination in the suburbs; *Buttress Fuller Alsop Williams'* young people's centre in Warring- 126 ton, 1999–2001, sets an example to other towns. Wigan's new football and rugby stadium, by *Atherden Fuller Leng*, 1999, deserves praise too. However, if standards in the area's economic and cultural centre are still so low, can one expect a dramatic rise in the calibre of architecture and urban design in the post-industrial towns and depressed suburban estates? This is not a question unique to sw Lancashire: a sustained commitment to the best environments for home and for work should be intrinsic to the process of reinvention and revival everywhere.

FURTHER READING

The most useful GENERAL and COUNTY HISTORIES are W. Farrer and J. Brownbill's excellent *Victoria County History of Lancashire* (1906–14), especially vols 3, 4 and 5; Edward Baines, *History of the County Palatine and Duchy of Lancaster* (4 vols), 1831–6; and J. Aikin, *A History of the Country from Thirty to Forty Miles round Manchester*, 1795 (facsimile edn, 1968). For GEOLOGY see N. Aitkenhead *et al.*, *British Regional Geology: the Pennines and adjacent areas* (British Geological Survey), 4th edn, 2002. For ARCHAEOLOGY *see* Denise Kenyon, *The Origins of Lancashire*, 1991; Tim Strickland, *The Romans at Wilderspool: the story of the first industrial development on the Mersey*, 1995; R.W. Cowell and R.A. Philpott, *Prehistoric, Roman and Medieval Excavations in the Lowlands of North West England: excavations along the line of the A5300 in Tarbock and Halewood, Merseyside*, 2000; and J.M. Lewis and R.W. Cowell (eds), 'The Archaeology of a Changing Landscape: the last thousand years in Merseyside', *Journal of the Merseyside Archaeological Society* 11, 2002. Jen Lewis, *The Medieval Earthworks of the Hundred of West Derby*, British Archaeological Reports, British Series 310, 2000, is an exhaustive and invaluable survey of moated sites, with cogent introductory chapters.

The only overview for ARCHITECTURE in Lancashire as a whole is Peter Fleetwood-Hesketh's eloquent *Murray's Lancashire Architectural Guide*, 1955. An introduction to the medieval churches is given by S.R. Glynne, *Notes on the Churches of Lancashire* (Chetham Society), 1893. G. Miller, *Historic Houses in Lancashire: The Douglas Valley 1300–1770*, 2002, is a very impressive discussion and gazetteer with large amounts of new information on yeomanry and gentry houses in townships around Wigan. J. Martin Robinson, *A Guide to the Country Houses of the North West*, 1991, is a gazetteer encompassing even many of the smaller houses. H. Taylor, *The Old Halls in Lancashire and Cheshire*, 1884, is much more selective. A good source for the mid to late C20 is the journal *Architecture North West*, published between 1963 and 1970. Sources for individual towns are mentioned below. Studies for individual ARCHITECTS include Anthony J. Pass, *Thomas Worthington: Victorian architecture and social purpose*, 1988; and C. Cunningham and P. Waterhouse, *Alfred Waterhouse, 1830–1905: biography of a practice*, 1992. Roger N. Holden, *Stott and Sons*, 1998, considers a practice specializing in cotton mills.

For INDUSTRIAL ARCHAEOLOGY *see* P. Rees, *A Guide to Merseyside's Industrial Past*, 1991, and R. McNeil and M. Nevell, *A Guide to the Industrial Archaeology of Greater Manchester*, 2000. For COTTON MILLS in Wigan, Leigh and elsewhere the standard source is Mike Williams with D.A. Farnie, *Cotton Mills in Greater Manchester*, 1992. For CANALS and RAILWAYS see C. Hadfield and G. Biddle, *The Canals of North West England*, 2 vols, 1970; H. Malet, *Bridgewater: the canal duke, 1736–1803*, 1977; and Mike Clarke, *The Leeds and Liverpool Canal: a history and guide*, 1990. Of a number of studies of the Manchester Ship Canal, D. Owen, *The Manchester Ship Canal*, 1982, and P.M. Hodson (ed.), *The Manchester Ship Canal: a guide to historical sources*, 1985, stand out. For railways, *see* Geoffrey O. Hold, *Regional History of the Railways of Great Britain: the North West*, 1978. The most useful, and detailed, history of the L&MR is R.H.G. Thomas, *The Liverpool and Manchester Railway*, 1980. Dock literature is listed below under Liverpool.

For SCULPTURE, MONUMENTS and the DECORATIVE ARTS see T. Cavanagh, *Public Sculpture of Liverpool* (Public Monuments and Sculpture Association), 1997; P. Curtis (ed.), *Patronage & Practice: sculpture on Merseyside*, 1989; James L. Thornely, *Monumental Brasses of Lancashire and Cheshire*, 1893; P. Hebgin-Barnes, *The Medieval Glass of Cheshire and Lancashire* (*Corpus Vitrearum Medii Aevi Great Britain*, Summary Catalogue), forthcoming; and R. Bailey, *Corpus of Anglo-Saxon Stone Sculpture, Lancashire and Cheshire*, also forthcoming. Barrie and Wendy Armstrong, *The Arts and Crafts Movement in the North West of England: a handbook*, 2005, is excellent on SW Lancashire, and more inclusive than its title suggests.

LIVERPOOL has its own literature. Older histories include Ramsay Muir, *A History of Liverpool*, 1907. J. Touzeau, *The Rise and Progress of Liverpool from 1551 to 1835*, 1910, contains interesting information relating to building. G.H. Pumphrey, *The Story of Liverpool's Public Services*, 1940, and B.D. White, *A History of the Corporation of Liverpool 1835–1914* are useful studies. F.E. Hyde, *Liverpool and the Mersey*, 1971, is the standard economic history of the port. More recent publications include P. Aughton, *Liverpool: a people's history*, 2003 (2nd edn), and Tony Lane, *Liverpool: city of the sea*, 1997, a readable account focusing on the late C19 and C20 from a sociological viewpoint. A huge amount of detail is contained in the 'Annals of Liverpool', a cumulative, chronological list of key events published annually in Gore's street directories from 1813 until 1940, and reissued as *An Illustrated Everyday History of Liverpool and Merseyside*, 1996, with an introduction by Fritz Spiegl. Susan Nicholson, *The Changing Face of Liverpool 1207–1727*, 1981, enables the interested person to identify the location of early buildings. Detailed MAPS start with J. Chadwick's of 1725; other C18 surveys are by J. Eyes, 1765 and G. Perry, 1768. M.A. Gage's large-scale map of 1836 shows individual ground plans. J. Bennison's map of 1835 covers the rural outskirts as well as the urban centre.

Turning to LIVERPOOL ARCHITECTURE, J. Sharples, *Liverpool* (Pevsner Architectural Guides), 2004, an account of Liverpool city centre and selected inner suburbs, has been condensed into this volume. The classic older account is J.A. Picton's two-volume *Memorials of Liverpool*, 1873 (revised edns 1875, 1903), the first volume historical, the second a street-by-street account seen with an architect's eye. Also by Picton is *The Architectural History of Liverpool: a series of papers read before the Liverpool Architectural and Archaeological Society*, 1858. Thirteen articles by T. Mellard Reade, published as 'The Architecture of Liverpool' in the Liverpool journal *The Porcupine*, 1865–6, are bracingly forthright in their criticisms. C.H. Reilly, *Some Liverpool Streets and Buildings in 1921*, 1921, is entertaining and perceptive about buildings of all periods. The key C20 book is Quentin Hughes, *Seaport*, 1964. The outstanding black-and-white photographs of the original edition poignantly capture the rugged splendour of a townscape which has changed greatly. The same author's *Liverpool*, 1969, is very useful for buildings of the 1950s–60s; his *Liverpool: city of architecture*, 1999, brings the story up to the end of the C20. Also handy is *Buildings of Liverpool*, a guide issued by the Liverpool Heritage Bureau, 1978. J. Sharples, A. Powers and M. Shippobottom, *Charles Reilly and the Liverpool School of Architecture 1904–33*, 1996, looks at an important phase in the city's development, with brief biographies of important architects. Post-war reconstruction is documented in *Liverpool Builds, 1945–65*, issued by the Corporation's Public Relations Office, 1967, the planned redevelopment of the core in the visionary *Liverpool City Centre Plan*, 1965, produced under the direction of W. Bor and G. Shankland. Lionel Esher, *A Broken Wave*, 1981, has an excellent chapter on Liverpool, reassessing the post-war era.

For MAJOR BUILDINGS there are for St George's Hall, two detailed articles by J. Olley in *Architect's Journal* 183, 18 and 25 June 1986; for the Anglican Cathedral, V.E. Cotton, *The Book of Liverpool Cathedral*, 1964, and P. Kennerley, *The Building of Liverpool Cathedral*, 2nd edn, 2001; for the Pier Head, P. de Figueiredo, 'Symbols of Empire: the buildings of the Liverpool waterfront', *Architectural History* 46, 2003; for the Metropolitan Cathedral, an essay by John Summerson reprinted in his *The Unromantic Castle*, 1990, and an essential account by the architect, Frederick Gibberd, *Metropolitan Cathedral of Christ the King, Liverpool*, 1968. For churches, D. Lewis, *The Churches of Liverpool*, 2001, is valuable for illustrations. On HOUSING, C.W. Chalklin, *The Provincial Towns of Georgian England*, 1974, has useful coverage of Liverpool. J. Longmore's unpublished Ph.D. thesis for the University of Liverpool, 'The Development of the Liverpool Corporation Estate 1760–1835', 1982, is extremely interesting. I.C. Taylor, 'The Court and Cellar Dwelling: the eighteenth-century origin of the Liverpool slum,' *Transactions of the Historic Society of Lancashire and Cheshire* 122, 1971, and Alan McDonald, *The Weller Way: the story of the Weller Streets Housing Co-operative*, 1986, look at two very different manifestations of working-class housing. The city's warehouses are analysed in C. Giles and R. Hawkins, *Storehouses of Empire: Liverpool's historic warehouses* (English Heritage), 2004.

There is an extensive literature on the DOCKS. N. Ritchie-Noakes, *Liverpool's Historic Waterfront: the world's first mercantile dock system*, 1984, is indispensable, but only considers docks s of the Pier Head; A. Jarvis, *Liverpool Central Docks 1799–1905*, 1991, casts a perceptive eye over many of those to the N. His *The Liverpool Dock Engineers*, 1996, is an equally fascinating elucidation of dock design and construction. A. Jarvis and K. Smith (eds), *Albert Dock: trade and technology*, 1999, has a number of essays putting the complex in context. S. Mountfield, *Western Gateway*, 1964, recounts the history of the Dock Board. Books on LIVERPOOL SUBURBS include David Lewis, *The Illustrated History of Liverpool's Suburbs*, 2003; M. Chitty, *Wavertree: a guided walk*, 2000; and J.G. Cooper and A.D. Power, *A History of West Derby*, 1983.

Most of the TOWNS are not well served by historical literature. ST HELENS is fortunate to have T.C. Barker and J.R. Harris, *A Merseyside Town in the Industrial Revolution: St Helens 1750–1900*, 1954 (reprint 1993), a pioneering academic study. On the town's defining employer, there are two books by T.C. Barker, *Glassmakers: Pilkington, the rise of an international company, 1826–1976*, 1997, and *Pilkington – An Age of Glass: the illustrated history*, 1994. Mary Presland, *St Helens: a pictorial history*, 1995, has informative captions. For NEWTON-LE-WILLOWS *see* J.H. Lane, *Newton-in-Makerfield: its history*, 1914. The best introductions to WIGAN and LEIGH are Philip Powell, *Wigan Town Centre Trail*, 1998 (2nd edn) and Philip Powell and Jennifer Duggan, *Leigh Town Centre Trail*, 2000. These are much more than pamphlets, with excellent historical introductions and architectural guides. Also, for Wigan, A.S. Tindall, *Wigan: the development of the town* (*Greater Manchester Archaeological Journal* I), 1985, and for a history of mining in and around the town, Alan Davies, *The Wigan Coalfield*, 1999. Other publications on Leigh include a series by Norma Ackers for the Leigh History Society and John Lunn, a *History of Leigh*, 1960. Lunn also wrote *A History of Atherton*, 1971. A good new history of WARRINGTON is Alan Crosby, *A History of Warrington*, 2002. An older one is A.M. Crowe, *Warrington Ancient and Modern: a history of the town and neighbourhood*, 1947. For its archaeology, including medieval and industrial, *see The Archaeology of Warrington's Past*, 1976, produced by Archaeological Services Ltd; for Warrington New Town, *Warrington New Town Outline Plan*, 1972, produced by Warrington Development Corporation. About WIDNES there is Charles Poole, *Old Widnes and Its Neighbourhood*, 1908, and G.E. Diggle, *A History of Widnes*, 1994 (revised edn by Peter Riley). For ORMSKIRK *see* Mona Duggan, *Ormskirk: the making of a modern town*, 1998.

BIBLIOGRAPHIES include T. Wyke and N. Rudyard (eds), *Cotton: a select bibliography on cotton in North West England*, North Western Regional Library System, 1997. A Manchester region bibliography is published annually in the *Manchester Region History Review*, which started in 1987. For archaeology *see* M. Nevell, 'A Bibliography of North West Archaeology 1991–2000', *Archaeology North West* 5, 2000. An extremely useful cumulative INDEX was published in 2002 to the annual *Transactions of the Historic Society of Lancashire and Cheshire*.

More detailed information on individual buildings can be obtained from The Department of the Environment and DCMS

List of Buildings of Historic and Architectural Interest for the relevant area, now available on-line at *www.imagesofengland.org.uk*. The Liverpool Record Office at the Liverpool Central Library has extensive collections, including local journals. Collections may also be found at the local studies and archive centres of individual towns and boroughs, at the Greater Manchester County Record Office for the area of Wigan Borough Council, and at Cheshire County Record Office in Chester for Warrington and Widnes council areas, which are now within Cheshire. The Sites and Monuments Records for Merseyside and for Greater Manchester can be consulted, the latter at the Manchester University Field Archaeology Unit, as well as the archive on Greater Manchester cotton mills. Local architecture and architects are the subject of numerous theses and dissertations of the universities of Liverpool and Manchester.

Buildings of national importance are covered by GENERAL ARCHITECTURAL HISTORIES. Good starting points are John Summerson's *Architecture in Britain 1530–1830* (Pelican History of Art), last revised 1991 (and now partly counterbalanced by Giles Worsley, *Classical Architecture in Britain: the heroic age*, 1995); *Victorian Architecture* by R. Dixon and S. Muthesius, 1978; and *Edwardian Architecture* by A. Service, 1977. Elain Harwood, *England: a guide to post-war listed buildings*, 2000, features several examples in the area. Standard thematic works include J. Booker, *Temples of Mammon: the architecture of banking*, 1990; M. Girouard, *Victorian Pubs*, 1975, J. Earl and M. Sell, *Guide to British Theatres*, 1750–1950 (Theatres Trust), 2000; Clare Graham, *Ordering Architecture: the architecture and social history of the English law court to 1914*, 2003; Kathryn Morrison, *English Shops and Shopping*, 2003; and Harriet Richardson (ed.), *English Hospitals 1660–1848*, 1998.

For INDIVIDUAL ARCHITECTS the essential works are H.M. Colvin, *Biographical Dictionary of English Architects 1600–1840* (3rd edn), 1995; the *Directory of British Architects 1834–1914* (British Architectural Library) (2nd edn), 2003; and A.S. Gray, *Edwardian Architecture: a biographical dictionary*, 1985. For SCULPTURE, the standard accounts are Margaret Whinney, *Sculpture in Britain 1530–1830* (Pelican History of Art), revised by John Physick, 1988; R. Gunnis, *Dictionary of British Sculptors 1660–1851*, revised 1968 (3rd edn forthcoming), B. Read, *Victorian Sculpture*, 1982; and Susan Beattie, *The New Sculpture*, 1983. INDIVIDUAL BUILDINGS are often described in contemporary periodicals, *The Builder* and *Building News* (later *Architect and Building News*) for the C19, and the *Architectural Review*, *Architect's Journal* and *RIBA Journal* for the C20–C21. *Country Life* covers selected country houses. A database of periodical articles is available at the British Architectural Library (at the RIBA), and on-line at *www.architecture.com*.

A full bibliography of GENERAL WORKS, including much on individual architects and artists, can be found at the Reference Section of the Pevsner Architectural Guides' website, *www.lookingatbuildings.org.uk*.

GAZETTEER

ABRAM

with PLATT BRIDGE

Rural until coal mining began in earnest in the second half of the
C19. Now Abram and the adjoining Platt Bridge to the N are
large, run-down former colliery villages. Late C19 brick terraces
strung out along the old lanes, and in new streets in Platt Bridge,
with plenty of C20 housing too, but little else. Platt Bridge's
centre, such as it is, is mostly a bleak scattering of retail sheds.
The landscape all around is strangely fascinating: it has been
completely redrawn by the mining – built up by spoil, sunken
and flooded by subsidence (to form lakes called flashes), scarred,
barren or abandoned as scrub.

ST JOHN EVANGELIST, Warrington Road. By *Austin & Paley*,
1935–7, illustrating how atrophied the practice had become by
that date: it is very conservative, in the style of the firm *c.* 1910.
The first church, of 1838, was demolished because of subsidence (a plaque in the churchyard marks the site of its altar).
Quarry-faced Darley Dale stone (red dressings inside). The
broad squat W tower with saddleback roof is overwhelmed by
the rest of the church. Did mining below preclude anything
more substantial? The ancillary attachments rather square,
especially the aisles, which spells 1930s. Inside there are similarities with the practice's St Luke, Orrell (q.v.), built ten years
before. Masonry bare as Austin & Paley always did, and a
careful arrangement of E spaces, a typical Hubert Austin device
of fifty years before, though here a shadow of the former virtuosity. Nevertheless, the practice was still capable of producing a dignified interior. – Stone PULPIT and integrated low wall
at the vestigial chancel arch. – STAINED GLASS. W window. Cut
from the E window of the old church. 1856. – Five post-war
windows by *James Powell & Sons*. – MONUMENTS. A couple of
1830s tablets from the first church. – A CROSS in the churchyard to the seventy-five victims of the 1908 Maypole Colliery
disaster (*see* below).

ST NATHANIEL, Church Road, Platt Bridge. By *George Bradbury
& Sons*, 1903–5. Built largely at the expense of the industrialist, James Carlton Eckersley. Very red brick, and really quite
big, with a high S tower, prominent in the district. Its massiveness is tempered by the transparency of the tall belfry stage:
you can see right through the big traceried openings, with

constantly changing effect as you move around it. Griffins lean
out from the top of the stair turret. Mostly lancets, but the E
window is a big Dec affair. Interior with brick arches and white
walls, the tall four-bay nave and aisles split in half by a screen
in 2002–3 to create hall, kitchen, etc. at the W end. This was
done by the *Pickard Finlason Partnership*. The S chapel was
screened off in 1951. – REREDOS. First World War memorial.
Wooden, with triptych. – STAINED GLASS. E window by *Design
Lights*, 2003.

HOLY FAMILY (R.C.), Lily Lane, Platt Bridge. 1960, *Massey &
Massey*. Brick, SW tower and open W porch.

ABRAM DISTRICT COUNCIL OFFICES (former), Warrington
Road. Opposite the churchyard is this decent, Free Style building, dated 1903. By *Heaton, Ralph & Heaton*. Two storeys. Red
brick and lots of terracotta, with gables, oriels, fat-columned
door, Gibbs surrounds and heavy cornices to both floors.

VICTORIA HOTEL, Liverpool Road, Platt Bridge. A big, confident Edwardian pub of 1904 by *Heaton, Ralph & Heaton* for
the Airey Brewery, Wigan.

MAYPOLE COLLIERY (former), now Maypole Industrial Estate,
Park Lane. Here are some of the few surviving pit structures
in the Wigan coalfield. The colliery opened in 1895 and closed
sixty-four years later. In 1908 seventy-five lives were lost in the
coalfield's worst disaster (*see* St John Evangelist churchyard,
above). Chimney, shaft head and several utilitarian buildings,
all red brick, remain in a run-down state.

(WARRINGTON ROAD, No. 126. Philip Powell reports a farmhouse of C17, C18 and C19 phases. Splat-baluster staircase.)

BROOKSIDE FARMHOUSE, Bickershaw Lane, 1 m. E. Painted
brick, dated 1716. Raised brick decoration below the first-floor
windows, characteristic of SW Lancashire. Charmingly, the
pattern is hearts, not the more usual diamonds.

3090   AINTREE

Just outside Liverpool. C20 housing and industrial estates
forming the dreary edge of the conurbation, and of course the
racecourse. The Leeds and Liverpool Canal runs through it (*see*
p. 52).

ST GILES, Aintree Lane. 1955–6, by *J. G. R. Sheridon* of *Edmund
Kirby & Sons*. Brick. Rectangular aisle-less nave with pairs of
tall rectangular windows separated by buttresses, small chancel
with triangular-headed lancets, and NW tower with a triangular arrangement of six circular lights near the top of each face,
and a flèche encircled at the base by a ring of shafts united by
a ring beam – on the model of Nash's All Souls, Langham
Place, London. – SCULPTURE of the patron saint at the foot
of the tower.

HOLY ROSARY (R.C.), Altway Avenue 1956, by *Edmund Kirby
& Sons*. T-plan. Brick. The nave is lit only by continuous

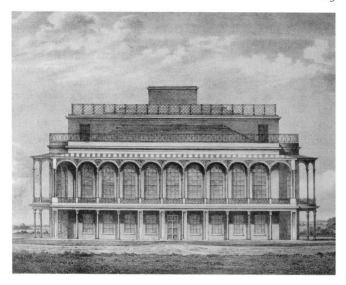

Aintree, Racecourse Grandstand, 1829 (demolished).
Elevation by John Foster Jun.

clerestory strips. Behind the broad, low, blank w front is a canted roof supported by rows of columns forming narrow aisles. The sw campanile is a tall slender concrete tripod from which the bell hangs. The base, containing the baptistery, is circular and, bizarrely, faced in cobbles.

AINTREE METHODIST CHAPEL *see* WALTON, p. 490.

RACECOURSE. It opened in 1829 with a grandstand by *John Foster Jun.* This burnt down and was replaced in 1885 by the structure now called the County Stand. Facing the course this has a terrace with cast-iron columns supporting tiered roof seating above. Brick, round-headed windows, but heavily altered, including with a neo-vernacular rear façade similar to the Queen Mother Stand, s, of 1990–1 by *Brotherton & Partners.* On the other side the big, modernist Princes Royal Stand (opened 1998). In 2005 construction began of two new stands and other facilities by *BDP.* They promise to be more interesting.

ASHTON-IN-MAKERFIELD

5090

Originally a small settlement at the crossroads of the Liverpool–Bolton and Wigan–Warrington roads. It made locks and hinges; from the second half of the c19, numerous pits were sunk. There was some cotton too. Now, of course, all this has gone. Along the staggered crossroads in the centre are large late c19 and early C20 pubs, shops etc., some, e.g. the Cross Keys on Bolton Road, with terracotta trimmings. Around this the usual late C19 and C20 housing, with a few more big pubs. Housing for the 'better sorts' is on Wigan Road to the NW, with one or two bigger villas, e.g. No. 90 (1893, heavy and bayed) and No. 161, 'Burnbrae' (1908, Arts and Crafts-ish). The town has swallowed up the hamlet of Bryn to the North. Many of the colliery sites are now industrial estates. In 1851 the population was 5,679; by 1901 it had risen to 18,697, and by the end of the C20 to over 27,000.

St Thomas, Warrington Road. A pretty good church by *F.H. Oldham* of Manchester, built in 1891–3 to replace a Georgian building (a chapel of ease is first recorded in 1515). Late Victorian Perp. Red sandstone, much of it recycled from its predecessor. The W tower is not really big enough to balance the long body of the church, and was apparently deliberately kept low (it did, until the 1960s, have a saddleback roof). On the N side is a transeptal projection, set diagonally so as to fit the site. In this projection a round window with entirely free tracery. The rest of the windows with Perp tracery, rectangular in the clerestory; the E window especially handsome. A small SE vestry was added by *Austin & Paley* in 1928. Inside are wide aisles and arcades of almost semicircular arches dying into the piers. The arches are very broad, at the request of the vicar, presumably to enhance sight lines from the aisles. The result has satisfying spatial qualities. Impressive roof, skeletal trusses of tie-beams and big braces forming a pointed arch beneath. Since 1961 the organ has occupied the former Lady Chapel, N. The vestry was extended into the original organ chamber, S of the chancel, behind a screen replaced in 1995. – Chancel PANELLING, 1908. Free Perp. – A pretty, Gothic ORGAN CASE of 1826, from the old church. – So too the CHANDELIER in the N aisle, and the William IV ROYAL ARMS now attached to the organ. – STAINED GLASS. Most is by *A.L. Moore* of London. The E window, 1897, marking Victoria's Diamond Jubilee, is excellent. – A number of wall MONUMENTS from the previous church, some C18, are hidden behind the organ.

Our Lady Immaculate (R.C.), Downall Green Road, Bryn, 1 m. NW (across the M6). A substantial, rock-faced red sandstone church of 1903 by *Pugin & Pugin* (which means *Peter Paul Pugin* at this time). Towerless; single roof containing both nave and aisles; twin-gabled transeptal projections. The tracery is essentially Dec and there is a typical Peter-Paul-designed round window in the E wall. A light and lofty, rendered interior with tall, slender arcade columns. These have delicate carved flowers draped below the neck. The chancel is square-ended, rather than Peter Paul's usual apsidal form, with the usual Lady (N) and Sacred Heart (S) altars either side. W organ loft between chapel and projecting SW baptistery (now chapel). – ALTARS. Three, all marble, by *Peter Paul Pugin*, 1903, with canopies, pinnacles etc. Good examples in excellent condition. – REORDERING by *Philip Johnston*, 1999. Sympathetic celebrant ALTAR incorporating second-hand elements on a platform beneath the chancel arch. Displaced pews and choir stalls were recycled to create SCREENS at the W end. – STAINED GLASS. E window. An attractive First World War memorial. Arts and Crafts style; blues, reds, lilies.

ST OSWALD AND ST EDMUND ARROWSMITH (R.C.), Liverpool Road. A remarkable Romanesque church of 1925–30 by *J. Sydney Brocklesby*, ambitious for its date, and designed with a confident and unabashed historicism. The cost was *c.* £30,000. It replaced a chapel of 1822, and was built to house the shrine of the Holy Hand of Edmund Arrowsmith, the English martyr (who was from Haydock). Brocklesby created a thoughtful and interesting plan, full of rich spatial experiences, complemented by the excellent carving of the *Howe* brothers and superb *Harry Clarke* glass. It is the culmination of a closely related sequence of Roman Catholic designs by Brocklesby inspired by the Romanesque churches of the South of France. The basic form – a domed nave and apsidal chancel with ambulatory – first appeared at St Augustine, Nottingham (1921–3); the W front is the mirror image of Sacred Heart, Tunstall, Staffordshire (1922–3). It has a SW tower with a pyramid roof and a NW round turret with a conical roof – a prickly pile of pointed stones (after Notre-Dame-la-Grande, Poitiers). In between is a giant arch of three orders enclosing a window above the W door with its tympanum of the Coronation of the Virgin. The nave has a clerestory with corbel table and triplets of windows under two saucer domes (cf. Cahors Cathedral);* between and E and W of these are pinnacled flying buttresses that delineate cross-passages inside. The buttresses rise above side chapels and confessionals which are arranged within continuous walls, so they appear like aisles. The chancel is apsidal, with an ambulatory. The windows are round-headed throughout, with enriched surrounds beautifully carved by the *Howes*. The stone is Darley Dale and Parbold, tooled in Neo-Norman fashion.

Even after the surprises of the exterior, the INTERIOR is a revelation. The plan is quite complex. There are three major units, the two domed bays of the nave and the apsidal chancel, and these units are separated from one another by narrow intermediate bays delineated by transverse arches. Wrapped around all of this is the ambulatory, a continuous, narrow aisle-cum-passageway extending to the W end of the church; the original shrine is set in a little apse at its E end, behind the chancel. The ambulatory is opened up to the chancel by a five-bay arcade in the apsidal end. Above this arcade is a clerestory of seven windows set into a stencilled hemispherical vault. In

114

---

*Though a pitched roof covering the domes is shown in an illustration in *The Builder* in 1926.

the chancel side walls are SEDILIA in the form of interlacing arches. Flanking the nave are chapels and confessionals. They are separated from it by the ambulatory, which here is formed of pairs of three-bay arcades with slender four-shaft columns, creating a richly layered, almost Arabic, spatial experience. To the N are the confessionals and St Joseph's Chapel and, to the S, St Theresa's Chapel and the Chapel of Our Lady and the English Martyrs. The two intermediate bays form cross-axes, which project beyond the ambulatory as the E and W bays of the St Joseph and Lady chapels; arcades screen off the W bays. The chapels are tunnel-vaulted and the Lady Chapel also has an E apse which, since Edmund Arrowsmith's canonisation in 1970, has housed the shrine. At the W end is an organ gallery carried on a screen of five stilted arches. The baptistery is in the base of the tower.

Throughout, the bare ashlar is sharply detailed by the *Howe* brothers' superb CARVING of corbels, arches etc. In particular, the columns and capitals of the nave arcades are beautifully carved, each one differently (cf. their work at St Theresa, Sutton Manor, St Helens, p. 568). Brocklesby provided very few detailed drawings; everything was set out full-size on site. He believed this method was as close to that of medieval craftsmen as was possible.

FITTINGS. The former SHRINE of the Holy Hand was designed by *F.X. Velarde*, in English (Pennycot) marble with bronze gates. The reredos contains a grilled niche for the relic. – ALTARS. Marble High Altar from Pietrasanta with frontal of five very squat blank arches containing the Lamb of God and representations of the Evangelists. – The Celebrant Altar is of 1822, from the earlier church. Mahogany. Of voluptuous, Baroque form (cf. that at St Benet (R.C.), Netherton, p. 521). – Our Lady and the English Martyrs Chapel altar, with arcaded frontal, from Pietrasanta too, and similar to the High Altar. St Edmund's hand is in a glass-fronted tabernacle on top. – St Joseph's Chapel altar, partly alabaster, from the 1820s building, but remodelled. Splendid painted wooden REREDOS with scenes from the life of St Joseph. 1935 by *William G. Simmonds*. The Christ figure is in low relief. – FONT. Octagonal with quatrefoil panels. Base with four attached colonnettes. – PULPIT, designed by *Brocklesby* and carved by the *Howes*, with a bowed front with a panel depicting peacocks drinking from the well of eternal life, derived from a relief at Ravenna. – SANCTUARY RAIL. Sienese marble, with bronze gates. – Holy water STOUPS by *Brocklesby* and the *Howes* again (W end of nave). Free-standing stone blocks, with reliefs of cowering devils. – Sacristy GATES. Good. Bronze. Art Deco geometric. They look like *Velarde* again. – STAINED GLASS. Magnificent Arts and Crafts glass by the *Harry Clarke Studio*, 1930–7, densely textured and intensely coloured, with a glowing, jewel-like quality. Clarke himself died in 1931, and of the nineteen windows the seven in the apse clerestory were installed before his death. Abstract designs or figures, e.g., Christ, King and Priest in the W window, Sir Thomas More in St Joseph's Chapel, and the remarkable emerald St Agnes in St Theresa's Chapel. Later glass similar but without the virtuosity and primal energy: three windows by the *Harry Clarke Studio* in the Chapel of Our Lady and the English Martyrs to Canon James O'Mera, †1970, one to mark the Millennium in the ambulatory, first from s, by *Design Lights*. – The cast-iron GATES and the GATEPIERS to the churchyard, *c.* 1822, are contemporary with the first chapel.

The PRESBYTERY, of three bays and brick, was a house formerly owned by the Gerards of Garswood New Hall (*see* p. 174) – the family on whose land the chapel was built – and therefore predates 1822. Perhaps late C18.

PARK LANE CHAPEL, Wigan Road (A49), Bryn, 1½ m. N. Of 1697, but all features Victorianized, making it a very peculiar creature. It was built Presbyterian and became Unitarian. The C17 brick is hidden by grey render and buttresses, and the fenestration has been renewed with round heads, but the original form with four unevenly spaced windows in the s side remains essentially intact. The alterations are principally of 1826 and 1871–2, though the present w extension (once a cottage, then a Sunday School) is of 1903–4. This has a bellcote. The interior is small, simple, and drunken as a result of mining subsidence; nothing is perpendicular. Much has been altered (roof rebuilt, w gallery removed), but the PULPIT with its iron hat peg is from 1697, formerly set centrally against the N wall, and around the walls is a DADO made of the doors of the original pews, with date and initials.

LIBRARY, Wigan Road. This Carnegie-funded edifice is by *J.B. & W. Thornely*, 1905–6. Red brick and stone. It occupies a good position, at a sharp angle between Wigan Road and Old Road, addressing it with a gable flanked by two corner turrets with lead caps. Also a cupola over a lantern in the centre.

HAYDOCK LODGE, Lodge Lane (A49 s). The large late C18 house was demolished in the 1970s; a hotel stands on the site. A former gateway is now at Newton-le-Willows (q.v.). The park, created in 1344, is now HAYDOCK PARK RACECOURSE.

ASPULL
and NEW SPRINGS

6000

The village lies under big skies across the crown of a broad bare hill, looking out sw over Wigan and the Lancashire Plain, and e across to Bolton and the Pennines. It is built up quite meanly around the large, spidery, now fractured Common (also called Aspull Moor). There was mining here for the valued cannel coal (*see* Haigh) from at least the C16, with, later, railways across it to the small-scale pits. A rare and monumental survivor of these is the brick VENTILATION CHIMNEY of 1840 from the Wall Hey Pit furnace, e of Haigh Road. Square; clasping pilasters. Before mechanical fans, mines were ventilated by heating air in furnaces beneath upcast shafts such as this, so drawing fresh air down another shaft and through the workings.

Scattered around the Moor are short terraces of miners' cottages. DUKE'S ROW, at right angles to Wigan Road, is an exceptionally early example, built by the 6th Earl of Balcarres of Haigh Hall (q.v.) in the late C18. Dressed Coal Measures stone; two storeys; two rooms deep, one bay wide (except No. 1). The windows are casements in unmoulded stone surrounds, of two lights, except for the three-light versions on the first floor of the S front. Were these just for bedrooms? The double garages along the backs, which partially screen the row from the Common, are aesthetically unfortunate if practicably desirable. Immediately E is a detached building, new house, once part of an early C19 colliery. Then, the shorter, early C19 MOSS PIT ROW, probably by the *7th Earl of Balcarres*, with the canted lintels found elsewhere in the parish. Also C20 housing, much of it built over the N part of the Common, which survives there in fragmentary greens. The most prominent alteration to the landscape is S of the village – the 'WOOCHIE', a spoil heap that is now a thickly wooded knoll.

ST ELIZABETH, Bolton Road, ½ m. SE. At the extremity of the Common. By *J. Medland & Henry Taylor*. Begun 1876, consecrated 1882. Largely paid for by Roger Leigh of Hindley Hall (*see* p. 130). The unusual dedication is to St Elizabeth of Hungary (his first wife was Elizabeth). Stock brick and red brick trim and quite stark, in part because a proposed N aisle and transept were never built, so this side and its buttresses are temporary-looking and utilitarian. No tower; petite octagonal bell-turret with spirelet over the nave E gable instead. W front with a typical Taylor motif: stepped-up lancets in the S aisle W wall following the roof-line. Lancets elsewhere too, and a wheel window in the W front. Beneath this is the baptistery under a lean-to roof, an odd and awkward arrangement, as if it were a later addition, though it is not. Gabled S projection for the organ loft.

The interior is full of Taylorian interest. Restlessly patterned polychromatic walls. Nave roof of original form, the principal kingpost trusses clamped between giant paired arch braces. Arcade with round piers continuing around the W end. There are also some diamond-section brick piers, e.g. between the aisle windows. Chancel arch rising from detached brick shafts. Pretty capitals edging into Arts and Crafts; along the arcade they have foliage and flowers in the corners, and a butterfly, and around the chancel, baptistery and aisles they are waterleaf, quite correct on the chancel arch, but elsewhere freely developed. Sedilia with granite colonnettes, and piscina. The FITTINGS are evidently by the architects. – REREDOS. Bold, stone. Central projecting flat canopy on shafts with waterleaf capitals housing a cross. – COMMUNION TABLE (S aisle). A simple affair from the demolished St Margaret, Pennington Green, which St Elizabeth was intended to replace. – ROOD SCREEN. Slender, wrought-iron. – PULPIT. Stone, pierced quatrefoil panels. Integrated with a low arcaded wall beneath the chancel arch. – FONT. Typically roguish. A fat bowl on a round pier, with four stumpy colonnettes around it connected to it by mini-buttresses, like a Dan Dare rocket. – SANCTUARY LAMPS. 1921. – STAINED GLASS. E and W windows presumably 1880s. Nave N, second from W, a crisp, fresh Annunciation by *H.M. Doyle* of Liverpool, 1954. Baptistery, two windows by *J.H. Stammers*, a memorial to John Hesketh, 1956. Little figures. S aisle, first from W, by *Rosemary Rutherford*, 1969. A glowing, swirling Transfiguration.

OUR LADY OF THE IMMACULATE CONCEPTION (R.C.), Haigh Road. 1855–8, by *J. Goodwin*. Small, with aisles, and quite pretty. Coursed rubble. Circular window of seven quatrefoils in the W gable. Quatrefoils for the clerestory also. Bellcote removed. Octagonal arcade piers. In the mid 1990s a new stone-clad N vestry was added, with stepped lancets, and a new E wall just beyond the chancel arch to replace a 'temporary' E wall erected in 1858 in anticipation of a chancel that was never built. In this new E wall is a rose window from *Peter Paul Pugin*'s demolished St Edmund, Collyhurst, Manchester, of 1894. High Altar cut down and bits used around the church. – STAINED GLASS. Some aisle windows by *Design Lights*, mid 1990s or later.

Aspull has a number of interesting non-industrial HOUSES too, including AINSCOW'S FARM, Bolton Road, across Hall Lane from St Elizabeth. C17 and later. Brick with stone plinth and quoins. Two storeys. The NE side, facing the Common, has three abutting, stepped and gabled projections, the l. one with raised diapering and a blocked mullioned window in the return.

Beyond the Common there are:

WALKER'S HIGHER FARM, Scot Lane, 1¼ m. NE. Dated 1755. A polite three-storey, three-bay S façade – Flemish bond, quoins and keystone lintels, a delightful Rococo cartouche datestone, and formerly with sashes – but the puff runs out after that: the other walls are of English Garden Wall bond with casement windows.

GIDLOW HALL, S off Dodds Farm Lane, 1 m. SE. A trim stone house standing within a wet moat. Dated 1574, and thus one of the oldest stone houses in the area. The present modest dimensions date from 1840, when an E range and a porch were demolished. Of *c.* 1574 some masonry in the S front, with its reset datestone containing Thomas Gidlow's initials; the E wall; a fireplace; and the sturdy stair-tower at the rear. Also, indications of a former screens passage aligned with a blocked entrance door to the l. of the modern one (thus the 'upper' end of the building was to the E, with the stair tower). The roof contains reused C15 trusses whose details and carpenter's marks, Gary Miller suggests, indicate that they once belonged to a structure of some size and quality. – The brick BARNS of the moat, now converted to a house, may be C16 at heart.

HINDLEY HALL, Hall Lane, 1½ m. SE. Now a golf clubhouse, and the garden and park lost to the course apart from a HA-HA and ICE HOUSE. The house is quite handsome: brick, seven bays, three storeys. The parapet sweeps up to the slightly projecting middle three bays. Six-bay l. return; extensions of different dates to the r. Obviously it is Georgian, but what date? – c. 1807 and 1767 have both been suggested, but rainwater heads with dates of 1728, 1730 and 1838 were described in 1904. The 1838 one had the initials of Robert Holt Leigh, †1843 (said to have been the greatest snuff-taker in England), whom a C19 source claimed rebuilt the house to his own designs. Perhaps then a house of c. 1728 (hence the swept parapet) was remodelled by Leigh (hence the tall, low-silled sashes and pilastered stone doorcase). Ground-floor interiors heavily altered, but there are some plaster friezes and cornices and a staircase with three turned balusters to each tread. – Vernacular STABLES, BARN etc., of c. 1800, to the N.

PENNINGTON HALL, Pennington Green, 1 m. SE. A brick yeoman's house. Emphatically dated 1653 in raised brickwork across the l. cross-wing, with diapering and other patterns. The r. cross-wing looks similarly venerable, but the brickwork of the central bay has been renewed. Stone window surrounds and mullions, those in the cross-wings square not chamfered. Formerly with a baffle-entry plan. – C17/C18 BARN alongside.

NEW SPRINGS

¾ m. SW of Aspull Common on Wigan Road. An industrial settlement on the banks of the Leeds and Liverpool Canal, now more or less an E extension of Wigan. Off Calf Lane are the brick-built former Kirkless workshops of the Wigan Iron & Coal Co.

ST JOHN BAPTIST, Chapel Street. 1896–7, by *J. Medland & Henry Taylor*, replacing an iron church. It cost £5,230. Two types of brown brick and very red brick trim. Typically inventive Taylorisms: small W tower with its upper part corbelled out slightly and finishing in a pyramid roof on a truncated pyramid, as if one had been stacked over the other; and deceptively simple windows full of odd combinations of brick and stone tracery, e.g. the W windows, round-arched with a thick brick mullion down the middle and unmoulded stone cusping in the quarter-circle heads either side. The chancel is higher and narrower than the nave and there is a big S chapel and a N vestry/organ loft, so that in total the E end is wider than the nave. This causes fun in the broad, aisle-less, exposed-brick interior. The problem: how to mediate between the nave, the narrower chancel and its flanking organ loft and chapel? Taylor's witty and effective solution was to throw out arches, angled in plan and filled lower down with screens, from the fat round stone piers carrying the chancel arch to the nave walls,

with the result that the E end seems to embrace the congregation, who sit beneath a stretched hammerbeam roof. Either
side of the chancel are arcades, filled N with the organ and S
by a bold and sinewy PARCLOSE SCREEN, which is surely the
work of *Taylor*. – The light and curvy IRONWORK must be
Taylor again: communion rail, and combined low railing and
slender, minimal arch forming a vestigial chancel screen. –
STAINED GLASS. E window, single panel of Christ's baptism by
Heaton, Butler & Bayne, 1897. E window, S chapel. *Jones &
Willis*, memorial to John Christopher, †1923.

HOLY FAMILY (R.C.), Cale Lane. Begun 1958. Brick. W tower.

ST JOHN BAPTIST PRIMARY SCHOOL, Wigan Road. 1880, by
J. Medland & Henry Taylor again. Single-storey, brick, with
cusped intersecting tracery in the gable ends. To the l. is the
old school house, dated 1877, brick with gables and mullions,
and the cipher of the Earls of Crawford and Balcarres of Haigh
Hall (q.v.) who paid for both.

LEEDS AND LIVERPOOL CANAL (*see also* Ince-in-Makerfield).
The Canal reached Wigan from the W in *c.* 1780 and the S
branch of the Lancaster Canal reached Haigh (q.v.) from the
N in the 1790s. Not until 1812–16 was the flight of twenty-three
locks built in Aspull, Ince and Wigan (q.v.) to join the two, 2½
m. and 200 ft (61 metres) in height apart. This was the last link
in the Leeds and Liverpool Canal. For details of the LOCKS *see*
p. 211. There are also a number of dated road BRIDGES and,
at Top Lock on Withington Lane, a pretty dressed-stone LOCK
KEEPER'S COTTAGE. Two bays and two storeys. Plain window
surrounds and replacement windows. Little brick TOLL HOUSE
to the r., with stables behind.

COLLIERS ARMS, Wigan Road. Of 1700. One of the earliest
double-pile houses in the area. Three storeys and two bays. The
windows are still mullioned (some replaced in the C20). Stone
under the plaster and fake timbering. (Moulded beams, staircase with twisted balusters, and pilastered fireplace on the first
floor. DCMS.) Built, presumably, as a farmhouse; the former
farm buildings to the SW include a Lancashire combination
BARN.

KIRKLESS HALL, Farm Lane, beside the canal. A two-storey,
seven-bay house, now subdivided, of complex evolution. The
exterior is brick, of various dates. Beneath are the remains of
a late medieval cruck-framed hall, with a late C15 post-and-
truss framed cross-wing, and stair-tower behind, attached to
the l. There were probably five cruck trusses; three remain, the
two that defined the service end (now second bay from r.), and
the upper part of the central truss over the hall. This has a yoke
decorated with a carved roundel and initials facing the dais
end. The truss is now supported by the roll-moulded beam
across the hall, put in possibly in the mid C16, when a floor
was inserted and a massive stone fireplace built against the rear
wall (the brick chimneystack has been rebuilt in much
simplified form). The fine internal timber framing of the cross-
wing has recently been exposed; it was externally re-clad in

brick in the mid C17 with the usual raised diapering, but also very odd segmental-headed windows with brick hoods, most of them now blocked and some replaced by mid-C19 sashes. The rest of the building appears to have been re-clad in brick piecemeal in the C18 (when the r. bay was added, and when the house may first have been subdivided) and the C19, and now has sashes. The porch is C19 and cement-rendered, replacing one elaborately timber-framed in the manner of the later C16.

OLD SCHOOL HOUSE, Withington Lane, ¾ m. E. Formerly Knowsley House; a school after 1845, and a house once more. Much altered, but the gabled central bay with its blocked mullioned-and-transomed window, of brick under the render, must be a C17 remnant.

SLAG HEAP, E of the Leeds and Liverpool Canal, ¼ m. S of Cale Lane. The Kirkless Iron and Steel Works, 1858–1930, was a vast belching complex on the side of the hill; the heap of blast-furnace slag remains as a prominent and violent scar, surreally littered with huge, dark, cork-stop-shaped blocks of slag.

STONE ROW, Wigan Road. 1830. Six single-bay, double-depth, two-storey cottages of Coal Measures sandstone. Built and probably designed by the *7th Earl of Balcarres*, possibly for workers at the Haigh Sawmills just to the W (*see* Haigh). The distinctive segmental lintels are also seen in cottages in Aspull village, and the first-floor three-light casements at the back recall those of the earlier Duke's Row (*see* p. 128).

ASTLEY
with GIN PIT
Tyldesley

7000

On the N edge of Chat Moss, straddling the Leigh branch of the Bridgewater Canal and the East Lancashire Road, and merging with Tyldesley to the N. A linear, post-medieval industrial settlement created by hand-weaving of muslin and later silk – see the large number of cottages of *c.* 1800 lining Higher Green Lane – and then mining. Also an unexpected number of interesting older houses spread across the landscape.

ASTLEY GREEN COLLIERY, Higher Green Lane. Parts of the colliery, which operated 1912–70, are preserved as a museum, notably the noble lattice-steel HEADSTOCK of 1912, the last survivor in Lancashire. It is 98 ft (30 metres) high, and was built by *Head Wrightson* of Stockton-on-Tees. The ENGINE HOUSE with huge 3,000 h.p. compound steam winding engine, MANAGER'S OFFICE, GARAGE and colliery GATES also survive.

ASTLEY HALL, Church Road. Also known as Dam House. A substantial but compact house built by Adam Mort in 1650. A hospital for most of the C20, now triumphantly restored as a community centre with teashop, community rooms, health centre and business accommodation. The restoration work in 1999–2000 uncovered the most interesting feature, a timber-framed LONG GALLERY running the length of the attic, which had been subdivided for centuries. Only 64 ft (19.7 metres) long, it is an instance of the 'short' long galleries found in the attics of some smaller houses, built by those who, despite more modest means, still aspired to this important symbol of gentility. It is also the only known example in the North West of the passage type of gallery, i.e. providing access to chambers and closets off it, as well as a space for exercise and recreation. Therefore it is not as well lit as the archetypal long gallery, with a window only at each end and one in the S front between the chambers. This façade is of five bays and three storeys, but not at all symmetrical, with irregular gables stepped back and forth. Lots of generous mullioned or mullioned-and-transomed windows, though some are C19. Replica datestone of 1650 above a C18 Doric doorcase with broken pediment. Extended in phases, all with mullioned-and-transomed windows to match, to form the present quadrangle: NW extension and two-storey E wing, early C19; N wing, a single-storey service range, also early C19, and C18 coach house; W wing, after 1845, single-storey services. All is built of brick – the newer wings are of machine brick, but the C17 house and the E wing are pebbledashed, the attractive result of which is quite Cumbrian in appearance. Inside, apart from the gallery, there is little of interest. The plan of the first phase has parlours and kitchen to the l. of the hall, and a service room to the r. Most of the limited decorative elements, including elaborate door frames, are Regency Gothic; the most impressive room is of that phase, the first-floor BILLIARD ROOM in the E wing with handsome exposed roof trusses (pendants, cusping etc.).

Now there is housing on the site of the hospital buildings which had been built across the grounds. Inflexibly and unimaginatively suburban as this is, it does not impinge too assertively on the setting of the Hall.

OLD VICARAGE, Church Road. A very attractive and interesting house from the period when new ideas of classicism and planning were being incorporated uncertainly into lesser Lancashire houses. Possibly of 1704 – though if it were in the South of England one would date it decades earlier. Brick. Double-pile plan, with a roof of two gables forward of the spine, and a transverse gable over the rear. Three-storey façade of five bays and the two gables. The upper windows are surviving wooden cross-casements; the ground floor has flush sashes and a handsome eared and pedimented doorcase, in stone. On the returns the evidence of surviving and blocked windows implies more cross-windows forward of the spine, and mullioned windows under the gabled rear. At the back of the house are later lean-to extensions. Simple interior, with an absence of cornices or other plasterwork. Ovolo-moulded beams. Dog-leg staircase with square newels and replica bulbous balusters. Doors on the ground floor are panelled in the early C18 fashion, but some still have elaborate fleur-de-lys hinges. The brickwork appears to be consistent all the way round, and the mullioned windows (cf. Moorcroft House, Newburgh, and Knight's Hall, Up Holland) and the hinges are probably manifestations of faraway Lancashire's architectural conservatism. The doorcase and sashes could be an early C18 makeover, just a few decades after the house was built.

The church of St Stephen was across the road; the large, mainly C18 building burnt down in 1961. The CHURCHYARD remains. The new church, sculpted masses of brick completed in 1968, is ¼ m. SW on Manchester Road. It has *dalle de verre* STAINED GLASS designed by *Hans Unger* and *Eberhard Schulze*.

CHADDOCK HALL, Chaddock Lane. A house of four bays. Now rendered with C18 and later windows, but with a datestone of 1698. Gabled l. bay, probably a Georgian addition, the next bay also gabled and, Philip Powell reports, containing timber framing quite probably of the C16, and a raised cruck truss. Gabled cross-wing to the r. (i.e. formerly an H-plan) now demolished. Mr Powell also describes good ceiling plaster-work, C17 panelling and a fine early C18 staircase. The house deserves further study. To the r., a brick BARN with stone dress-ings and some rear walling, and very badly worn but elaborate stone arms in a dentilled architrave. Later C17?

MANOR HOUSE FARM, Higher Green Lane. Standard double-pile Georgian house, of relatively early date for the area: 1730, according to a lost rainwater head. Brick, three storeys. Sashes, and casements. Three original bays, and a fourth with separate entrance to the l., added before *c.* 1764. Also an outshut at the back. Door surround with attached Ionic columns and over-sized entablature. The earliest fabric of the attached brick farm buildings (now housing) dates from the C17.

MORLEY'S HALL, Morley's Lane. An important house, only yards from the S side of the East Lancashire Road. It sits on a rectangular MOAT, still completely wet, and is reached by a par-tially rebuilt little bridge. The present building, now three dwellings, has an irregular U-plan around a little cobbled yard. The S range, and the S half of the W range, are early C19, plain and brick-built. The other half of the W range and the N range are largely brick too, with mainly C18–C20 windows. But the bricks on the N side are C17 or early C18, some of the walling is of big dressed stone blocks, some is rendered, and every-thing is wonky. This is the remnant of the house described in 1540 as having stone walls rising 6 ft (1.8 metres) above the moat and timber framing above that. Much of the latter sur-vives. The W part is the former hall, dendro-dated to *c.* 1460. A floor has been inserted, and a chimneystack at the S end, but the original tie-beams are visible upstairs. The S one has at its centre a boss carved with a lovely rose, so presumably this was the upper end of the hall. Both it and the middle tie-beam are cambered, and have empty mortises for arch braces. The N one, however, is horizontal and appears to be part of a spere truss, with evidence of mortises this time for spere posts, now removed. In the attic the roof is revealed as of crown-post construction, of single-rafter type; the former is unusual in the North West (there are others at Ordsall Hall, Smithill's Hall and Cheetham's College, all SE Lancashire); the latter is almost unknown. The crown-posts have massive longitudinal and transverse diagonal braces which are structurally redundant and surely for show – smoke-blackening is further evidence that the hall was open to the roof.* Abutting the hall range is the taller C16–C17 two-storey N range. Various parts of the frame are exposed inside, including wall-posts with shaped cheeks, and the wall-plate is visible outside. Beyond the moat on the E side are assorted C18–C19 FARM BUILDINGS.

PEEL HALL, Peel Lane. What secrets and surprises might a thorough study of this house reveal? Brick on a stone plinth. H-plan, with one limb on the N side extended in the C19. Philip Powell believes the core, including a dog-leg staircase with turned balusters, to be C17. A very odd later feature is the loggias between the cross-wings at both front and back, created by propping a bold parapet with two-storey cast-iron fluted Ionic columns. Farm buildings include a brick HAY BARN with pointed arches, a feature of Cheshire farms very rare in Lancashire. The site, apparently, has remnants of a MOAT.

(Philip Powell also reports two, altered, C17 yeomen's houses – SALES FARMHOUSE, Moss Road, and COLDALHURST FARM, Coldalhurst Lane – both of brick with segmental hood-moulds, and each accompanied by a combination barn.)

GIN PIT

At the end of the Ley Road is a little grid of terraces and the remains of Gin Pit Colliery, and a workshop of Manchester Collieries. The PIT BATHS, canteen etc. of Nook Colliery lie ¼ m. SE on North Lane, 1930s buildings in the Dudokesque style of the Miners' Welfare Committee (cf. Clock Face, p. 569).

ATHERTON
and HOWE BRIDGE

6000

A small town centred on a low ridge on the N edge of the Mersey plain. The historic core was the village of Chowbent, at the E end. Nail making was a prominent local industry there from the Middle Ages until the C19, when it evolved into bolt manufacture and the village developed into a cotton and coal town called Atherton. A local board was formed in 1858. The population was 4,600 in 1851, 16,000 in 1901 and about 21,500 today. Big mills near the centre, long C19 bylaw terraces S, and a large mid-C20 estate N. The main street, Market Street, is C19 and later and of little interest, except perhaps for the Wheatsheaf Hotel, one of

* Nigel Morgan, 2002, unpublished.

those big, brassy late C19 pubs. The best and the most interesting architecture is due to the owners of the Atherton Collieries, the Fletchers, who sunk the first shafts in 1768, – and especially to the progressive Ralph Fletcher, †1916. He was the force behind the reconstruction of the parish church, and provided for the miners of Fletcher, Burrows & Co., as the firm became in 1874, the model village at Howe Bridge and the country's first pithead baths.

63 St John Baptist, Market Place. Replacing a chapel dating back to the C17. By *Paley & Austin*, who had already designed Howe Bridge church for the chief benefactor, Ralph Fletcher (*see* p. 141). The style is Late Dec. The chancel and three bays of the nave were built first, 1878–9; the rest, including a sw tower completed to a modified design, was opened in 1892. Following a devastating fire in 1991 which destroyed much at the E end, the church was repaired and reordered by *Peter Skinner* in 1996–7.

The whole is monumental, one of Paley & Austin's best, and the tower is magnificently mighty. Dressed stone with red ashlar trimmings and plain tile roof. Five-bay nave and two-bay chancel under a continuous roof, the division expressed N by a chimney and S by the organ chamber and attached two-storey vestry. Aisles, the N with square-headed windows, the S with pointed. The tower has five stages and octagonal clasping buttresses, panelled higher up, and rising above the embattled parapet as turrets with little concave hats. Red ashlar is employed with increasing density up the tower until, at the parapet, it is all red. From 1899 mining subsidence pulled the tower away from the S aisle until it was stabilised, out of alignment and leaning, and a fillet inserted between the two. Elsewhere, the virtuoso tracery is of particular note, e.g. the square clerestory windows, two to a bay, and the grand six-light E window. Under this is a chequerboard pattern of emblematic shields, roses, foliage etc. Big seven-light W window too.

Enter the INTERIOR up steps through a vaulted chamber under the tower into the impressively scaled nave and aisles, with arcades of clustered columns, moulded capitals and double-chamfered arches. Over the nave is a carefully detailed hammerbeam roof, with modern steel ties. Skinner's post-fire reordering involved inserting a huge glazed screen of rigorous wooden mullions and transoms into the chancel arch above *Paley & Austin*'s intricately carved, Flamboyant CHANCEL SCREEN, which survived the fire. This now serves as a reredos to the altar on a platform in the E bay of the nave. Solid screens block the arches at the E end of the aisles either side. The unfortunate consequence of these changes, otherwise successful, is that the sophisticated visual relationship between the nave and aisles and the chancel, N chapel and organ chamber is severed. Visible through Skinner's screen is his excellent new roof, with delicate webs of steel ties, over the shell of the chancel, which was converted into a church hall (in 2005 unfinished, awaiting funds). – PULPIT. Stone, with good marble semi-relief panels in shallow niches (scenes from the Life of Christ). A memorial to Bishop Fraser, †1885. – BOX PEWS. Dated (e.g. 1728) doors etc. from the previous chapel, reused as dado panelling in the vestry. – Fine alabaster FONT. Octagonal with enriched panels. By *Paley & Austin*? – LAMPS (nave) by *Peter Skinner* in the manner of George Pace. – STAINED GLASS. E window by *C.E. Kempe*, 1896. The Passion and the Apostles. S aisle, *Ward & Hughes*, London, 1895. As part of the 1996–7 works all other windows were re-glazed in clear glass by *Design Lights* of Bolton with simple elegance, and organic shaping of the cames in the heads of the lights. Re-set in one S aisle window, excellent post-Gothic window panels of 1922 by *Edward Moore*, taken from the N chapel which was dedicated to Ralph Fletcher.

St Anne (former), Tyldesley Road (A577), Hindsford. 1891–1901, by *Austin & Paley*. Low NE tower with a stair-turret, and W of it a N transept. Aisles. Dec details, e.g. reticulated tracery in W, E and transept windows. Divided into flats in 2003–4, destroying the fine NE group of spaces. The W bay alone remains open from floor to rafters.

St Richard Chichester, Mayfield Street. Dated 1927. Small, brick. Perp windows.

Chowbent Unitarian Chapel, Bolton Old Road. 1721, enlarged 1901. It has the best-preserved C18 ecclesiastical interior in South Lancashire. Built by a Presbyterian society after it was ejected from the chapel of ease (since rebuilt as the parish church). Outside it is a stark, brick, gabled preaching box standing on a rubble plinth, with two tiers of identical round-headed windows on all sides, except where a vestibule and organ chamber were added on the S side in 1901. Dressings are stone. Above the W gable is a bellcote, a delicate cupola with ogee cap and very slender columns. The interior has GALLERIES on E, S and W sides, reconstructed in 1901, with bolection-panelled fronts and staircases in the S corners with turned balusters and pendant newels. The galleries stand on six timber Doric columns, four of which continue above in more slender form to support the flat plaster ceiling. This was renewed (and perhaps) embellished in 1901 (and remade in 1981). It is divided up by bands of fruit and nut decoration. A stately triple-decker PULPIT, with massive hinges, is set centrally against the N wall facing the complete set of BOX PEWS, which have fielded-panelled doors, intact both upstairs and down. – Another PULPIT, in the vestibule, came from Wharton Hall via Chorlton Road Unitarian Chapel, Manchester. Simple, possibly late C17; where from originally? – STAINED GLASS. Mid-C20 memorials in most lower windows. Some signed *Shrigley & Hunt*, others probably also by them. Vestibule. 1995 by *Jan Swiercynski*. One pane for each of the 350 years of the congregation. – MONUMENTS. Amongst the tablets: Rev. James Wood, †1759, minister when the chapel was built, above the pulpit; John Mort, †1788, by *B. Bromfield*,

topped by an urn; Thomas Sanderson, †1854, a sarcophagus
with fasces and urn, by *Pattersson* of Manchester. –
GATEPIERS. Bulgy and rusticated with urns, early C18. The
cast-iron gates are 1854.

SUNDAY SCHOOL. Part of the MINISTER'S HOUSE –
No. 49 Bolton Old Road – was used as a schoolroom from its
completion *c.* 1721. In the 1820s an extension for schooling
was added r. This was itself extended, at the rear, along Alder-
fold Street, in 1860 and again in 1890.

BAPTIST CHAPEL, Tyldesley Road. An unremarkable building
of 1988, but including good fittings from its demolished predecessor, and also a STAINED GLASS window by *Robert Anning
Bell*, of 1904.

CEMETERY, Leigh Road. 1855–7. A pair of little chapels and a
lodge by *Thomas D. Barry*. Rock-faced stone. The chapels, with
very deep and steeply pitched roofs and ivy growing wildly over
them, are very Hansel and Gretel.

FIRST WORLD WAR MEMORIAL, Leigh Road. By *Bradshaw &
Gass*. Handsomely Neoclassical, with bronze name plaques on
the four equal sides, between clasping pilasters. Urn on top.

COUNCIL OFFICES, Bolton Road. 1898–1900 by *J.C. Prestwich*.
Red brick and red stone dressings. Only six bays, with a corner
tower with cupola. Two stone doorways, one with a swag under
a flat hood, the other beneath a bay window emblazoned with
the town arms.

PUBLIC LIBRARY and SCIENCE AND ARTS SCHOOLS, York
Street. Next door to the Council Offices. By *Bradshaw & Gass*.
Put up 1904–5, paid for by Andrew Carnegie. Shiny red brick.
With gables, and mullioned-and-transomed windows on the
first floor and round-headed ones below.

In the tightly enclosed little MARKET PLACE in front of the
parish church is an OBELISK, erected in 1781 by Robert Vernon
Atherton. With sunken panels, like the one he put up in Leigh
(q.v.), though the shaft dates largely from an 1867 restoration.
Rusticated pedestal. Facing it is an attractive red brick and
terracotta former BANK in Northern Renaissance style, with
cupola'd corner oriel. It was built in the 1890s for the
Manchester & County Bank.

ALDER HOUSE, Alder Street, off High Street. A charming and
fascinating house, built for a man with pretensions. He was
Ralph Astley, an iron merchant in Atherton's thriving nail-
making industry. His initials, and those of his wife Ann and
the date 1697, are on the naïvely carved pitched canopy resting on big brackets. Hammer-dressed stone with stone slate
roofs. Compact: three bays by three, with three storeys and
three gables on each of three sides. In fact it is one of the
earliest examples of a double-pile plan in Lancashire, though
in almost every other respect very conservative, exhibiting no
Renaissance symmetry or proportion. The windows are still
mullioned-and-transomed; those in the gables have three
stepped round-arched lights and a stepped hoodmould over, a
motif of the West Riding and NE Lancashire from at least fifty

years earlier. Many windows and the s front were rebuilt in the
C19; the lower parts of the w (entrance) front apparently in the
C20. The peculiar, massive buttresses here are dated 1881, and
early photographs show a C19 prospect tower attached to the
l. corner.

The best way to understand the house is to look at the s
front, and think of it as a conventional single-depth, two-unit,
two-storey C17 farmhouse, with a fire window to the l., and
parlour to the r. Thus the entrance in an otherwise strangely
un-architectural w façade is understood as an end-baffle entry,
entering the housebody in the end wall alongside the firehood.
This is lost, and a later wall now partitions an entrance hall
from the housebody (see the beam mouldings). The staircase
is in the conventional place for such a farmhouse, against the
rear wall of the housebody. By creating a kitchen to the E of it,
sharing a chimneystack with the parlour, and an extra room to
the w, a primitive double-pile plan is created. The multiplicity
of gables and ridges allows the double-depth building to be
roofed with timbers of modest size and quality, requiring no
advanced roofing technology, and must in every sense have elevated Astley's home above those of his yeoman neighbours. But
it is something of a sham: three gables per elevation suggests
three rooms when there are only two, and the big windows in
the gables light only attics. Inside is a contemporary staircase,
partly destroyed but restored, and a fire-surround and overmantel (re-set) on the first floor.

CHANTERS, Chanters Avenue. Dated 1678 on the lintel, with the
initials probably of William Atherton, brother of John Atherton of Atherton Hall (*see* p. 140). Baffle-entry plan with
two-storey porch and cross-wing, in hammer-dressed stone.
Heavily restored at the beginning of the C20, when it was possibly cut back at the r. end. Multi-mullioned windows. Two
gables have oculi and the r. return has little single round-
headed lights. Cross-wing quoin dated 1732 (when this part
was raised?). Original studded door, inglenook and ovolo-
moulded beams.

INDUSTRIAL REMNANTS. COLLIER BROOK BOLT WORKS
(former), Bag Lane. A very rare survivor of the mid C19. The
forge has a characteristic row of chimneys sprouting through
the pitched roof.

PITHEAD BATHS (former), Coal Pit Lane off Wigan Road (A577).
Built in 1913 by Fletcher, Burrows & Co. (*see* p. 136) at their
Gibfield Colliery. Architecturally unremarkable and knocked
about, but of interest as the first purpose-built pithead baths
in the country. The architects may have been *J.C. Prestwich &
Sons*, who did the contemporary and similarly detailed miners'
HOUSING – uniform, of brick with pebbledashed uppers –
½ m. W on and off the A577 Wigan Road, and the branch
CO-OP at the corner of Lovers Lane.

MILLS. All closed. The finest is ENA MILL, Flapper Fold Lane,
1908, by *G. Temperley & Son*, Bolton. A very complete multi-
storey spinning mill – boiler and engine houses survive – with

Eloration of Atherton in the County of Lancaster the Seat of Richard Atherton Esq. *Design'd by Wm Wakefield Esq. 1723*

Atherton Hall, by William Wakefield,
1723–43 (demolished), elevation.
(*Vitruvius Britannicus*, vol. 3, 1725)

terracotta dressings and concrete floors. Now well cared for as
a business centre. Close by on Gloucester Street is HOWE
BRIDGE MILLS, developed *c.* 1870–1920 by Fletcher, Burrows
& Co. and once employing the wives and daughters of their
miners. Surviving elements date from 1892, 1914 and 1978.
The last, UNIT 1, the only building to have been constructed
for cotton-spinning in the North West since the 1920s. Single-
storey, with a blank two-tone panelled brick wall to the road,
rounded at the corners.

ATHERTON HALL, off Old Hall Mill Lane, 1¼ m. SSW. An odd
hotchpotch incorporating the service wings of *William Wakefield*'s handsome house of 1723–43, illustrated in *Vitruvius Britannicus* vol. 3. Wakefield was a Baroque architect – see the one
doorway with a very massively rusticated surround – but not
impermeable to the Palladian tide; also identifiable are his tall
square corner towers with brick pilaster-strips at the corners
and pediments on all sides. The mansion itself was demolished
in 1825; the site is an atmospheric grassy square, still recognisably the focal point of the landscape. Since then bits and
pieces have been added and adapted haphazardly as housing
to form the present three-sided court, including some tidying-
up by *Isaac Taylor* of Manchester in 1930. Wakefield's service
wings are the sides of this court. Converted into seven houses
from 1979.

Much of the PARK was given to the town of Leigh (q.v.) as
a public park and remains attractively wooded. The AVENUE,
the approach from Leigh parish church, survives as an arrow-

straight street of late C19 middle-class housing embedded in
that town, laid out with the church tower framed artfully at the
sw end. At the other end, until 1905, the drive crossed a lake
on *Wakefield*'s LION BRIDGE. A memorial incorporating one,
almost unrecognisably worn, lion and a few bits of masonry
was erected at the site in the 1990s.

HOWE BRIDGE

sw of Atherton on Leigh Road is this model mining village,
created in the 1870s by Fletcher, Burrows & Co. *J. Medland &
Henry Taylor* designed brick terraces of two-up, two-down
cottages. On Leigh Road itself these are articulated by gabled
projections, and also house shops, a village CLUB (dated 1875)
and former BATHS (dated 1873). The w terrace is raised up
above the road on a retaining wall, on top of which in front is
a path known as the Prom, and little gardens. The middle projection is bigger and higher and has a half-hipped roof, and
contained the original shop behind the three-bay ground-floor
arcade, which has stone piers and Gothic capitals (now filled
in). The baths were beneath, and entered under the Prom.
At the top end on the E side are SCHOOLS dated 1887 and
1901, extended in 1932. The roguish details of these – flèche,
bellcote, chimneys and gables – appear characteristically
J. Medland Taylor too. (Inside are original timber screens and
fireplaces with scriptural instructions. Philip Powell.) There
was also a cricket ground, bowling green and tennis courts for
physical and moral improvement. On the w side of Leigh Road
s of the church is one of many former branches of the Leigh
Friendly Cooperative Society designed by the *Prestwiches*,
which has in its side elevation a butcher's-shop window above
a basement clogger's shop.

ST MICHAEL AND ALL ANGELS, Leigh Road 1875–7. Though
Medland Taylor was an accomplished church architect, this is
by *Paley & Austin*. It is one of their most stimulating churches.
Coursed yellow stone with red ashlar dressings. Unified roof
for nave and chancel, the position of a substantial turret-like
octagonal two-stage flèche and 'transepts' apparently – but not
quite actually – indicating the line of demarcation. Single-bay
chapels attached w of the 'transepts'. Well-considered window
details; lancets, some in stepped groups, some cusped. w end
with two two-light windows separated by a massive central buttress, and three little lancets in the gable above. Matching
vestry of 1938 at the E end. A delightful contrast to the otherwise austere exterior is the gabled stair-turret against the
chancel N wall, which has blind ashlar arcading with attached
shafts and shaft-rings.

INTERIOR. The simple aisle-less nave has a characteristically
handsome open roof, with crown-strut principals. The E end
is masterfully modelled. Arcading with fat round and cluster
piers and double-chamfered arches. Two-bay chancel with

proper quadripartite vaulting springing from massively stumpy
clustered shafts sitting on corbels. The architects subtly subvert
assumptions based on conventional church planning. Thus,
what are understood externally as transepts and chapels read
internally the other way round, i.e. the lower w volumes form
transeptal spaces, and the higher gabled projections actually
lie E of the chancel arch and function as organ loft, s, and as
aisle-cum-chapel, N. Also, the bays of the N chapel are divided
by thick arches, like internal flying buttresses, the roofs
between them low then high then lower still; and above the
arcade is a kind of internal clerestory of open lancets, through
which in the gloom are the little lancets high in the gabled projections of the outer walls – an unexpected spatial delight. –
REREDOS. 1903. Marble. – CHOIR STALLS. 1919. Characteristic of *Austin & Paley*'s free-Perp church furniture. – PARCLOSE
SCREENS. Good, Dec style. – CHANCEL SCREEN and PULPIT.
1919. Elaborately wrought and cast iron. Excellent quality. The
screen is vestigial, only three feet high, the pulpit is formed of
cast-iron balusters. – FONT. Panelled marble drum. – STAINED
GLASS. Almost all bar the (good) E window is fine work by
C.E. Kempe, 1896 etc. Also a window by *Edward Moore*, 1922,
N transept. Most are memorials to members of the Fletcher
family. – Vicarage. 1904–5.

AUGHTON

An ancient parish, but not one of the jumbo-sized ones normal
in Lancashire. The village is on the s slope of the low sandstone
spur on which Ormskirk is also built, where it descends to the
(once) marshy River Alt. To the NE is AUGHTON PARK, a large
development for Liverpool commuters begun with the arrival of
the railway in 1849, which merges with Ormskirk (q.v.). It is leafy,
but with straight not curvy streets, and there are no houses of
particular interest. TOWN END, E, is built up around a railway
station too. There are a number of biggish houses, mainly C19.

ST MICHAEL, Church Lane. An interesting church, very varied
externally, and charming internally, which before Victorian
restoration seems to have had a C12/C14 nave, a C14 steeple,
and otherwise to have dated from the mid C16. Local pale grey-
brown sandstone; scraped inside. The oldest feature is a
Norman s doorway, blocked and with a buttress built against
it. The Norman wall extends to the w, see a lancet again hardly
visible from the outside, and a bit to the E. Inside it is clear
how the wall was later raised. Then, chronologically, follows
the N tower, and this is Dec. It becomes octagonal by plain
broaches. Bell-openings C14 too, in this top stage. On top is a
spire. All this is almost exactly like the steeple of Ormskirk
church next door. (Halsall is also similar, as was Standish,
qq.v.). Inside the tower, in the N wall is a boldly cusped TOMB
RECESS. To the nave and a N chapel there are chamfered

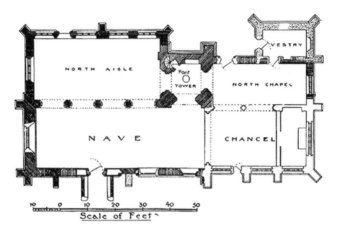

Aughton, St Michael, plan in 1907.
(*Victoria County History of Lancashire*, vol. 3, 1907)

arches. There is a crude and narrow one to the N aisle. This
may be later, after the present aisle was built. This appears to
date from *c*. 1545–8 and is as wide as the nave, but there was
apparently an earlier and narrower one, as indicated by a roof
scar on the W side of the tower. The arcade is Perp, with octagonal piers and double-chamfered arches. This may be mid-C16
too; the N aisle walls certainly are an early post-medieval job
with windows that are round-headed and that have uncusped
intersecting tracery, like at Ormskirk, and the clerestory of
Sefton, built at the same time not five miles away (and the
clerestory of Winwick, q.v.). Indeed the same mason's marks
can be found on Sefton s aisle.

The W windows of aisle and nave were rebuilt in a restoration of 1876 by *W. & J. Hay*, and are more elaborate than those
shown in a sketch of 1817, especially the reticulated nave one.
Victorian photographs show the chancel to have had more
of the distinctive Lancashire late Perp windows (i.e. with
uncusped round-headed lights) before the Hays completely
rebuilt it in 'correct' Perp. But the chancel N aisle or chapel
must again be a 1540s lengthening of a C13 original. The little
embattled N vestry – see its mullioned window with four
round-headed lights – looks mid-C16 too (though the VCH
says C17), but it is engulfed by a vestry and organ loft of
1913–14, mostly with similar windows and incorporating older
masonry in some lower walls and buttresses. As part of this
work the choir vestry was removed from the N chapel. The
(restored) three-light mullioned window high up in the nave s
wall was probably inserted in the C17 to light a pulpit. The
other windows in this wall, square-headed reticulated ones, are
entirely early C20. Nave and N aisle have good C16 roofs with

arched braces to collar-beams and with wind-braces. Those of
the N aisle are cusped, forming elongated quatrefoils. The old
chancel had one of these roofs too, with timber ANGELS, some
now preserved under the tower. The Hays' replacement has
stone angels. – COMMUNION TABLE, N chapel. Dated 1716. –
FONT. Dec. Octagonal with billeted rim, on a quatrefoil stem.
C19 cover. – COMMUNION RAILS. C18. Turned and fluted. –
PARCLOSE SCREEN. 1913–14, Free Flamboyant style, surely
the work of *Austin & Paley*. – CROSS-HEAD. Part of an Anglo-
Saxon cross-head in a recess in the N wall, with crude interlace. It has been dated *c.* 850 and compared with crosses
at Bolton (SE Lancashire) and Whalley (N Lancashire). –
Medieval SLAB with cross carved into it, found 1913. Under
the tower. – *Ex situ* NICHE, in the splay of a S window. Crude
and much damaged. Possibly C16. – MONUMENTS. A number
of Neoclassical plaques. Gothic chest tomb of 1856 in a recess
in the chancel inspired by the medieval example. By *J. S. Westmacott Sen.* – STAINED GLASS. N, first from W. A very few
medieval fragments. E window, and another in the N aisle, by
W. J. Medcalf, 1899, – SUNDIAL. 1736.

CHRIST CHURCH, Liverpool Road (A59T), Aughton Park,
1½ m. NE. *W. & J. Hay*, 1867–71. In a very prominent position
at the summit of the Aughton–Ormskirk ridge. Suitably big W
tower, visible for miles around. The church is big too, with
aisles. The stone is rock-faced, and the style is Dec. Five-bay
arcades with foliate capitals. Most effective is the tower arch
with stone arch thrown across it halfway up, a little gallery. –
Flouncy PULPIT, of 1886, and REREDOS, neither very good.

ST MARY (R.C.), Prescot Road, 1½ m. SE at Bowker's Green.
Another isolated, self-effacing pre-Emancipation chapel.
Opened 1823. Rather than the usual back-to-back arrangement, the PRESBYTERY is at right angles. It is three bays and
of brick. The chapel is now rendered, and has, as was customary, a blank N wall and three large round-headed windows
in the S side. A little porch in the otherwise almost entirely
blank W end facing the road. Inside, a gallery on cast-iron
columns fills the W bay and a large plaster sunburst the middle
of the ceiling. A plain round arch in the E wall reveals a shallow
chancel recess with a pretty oval saucer dome, which has at its
centre the Holy Dove. The pairs of giant attached Corinthian
columns and an entablature once framed an altar painting.
That, and the High Altar, altar rails and the pulpit were all
removed when the church was reordered *c.* 1985.

ALMSHOUSES and SCHOOLMASTER'S HOUSE, Church View, on
the E side of Church Lane. The nine almshouses are dated
1851. Dressed stone and Tudorbethan, with lots of gables. A
pretty composition – symmetrical except for the little turret
with steep pyramid roof in the front l. corner (the part seen
from the approach). To the N is the large schoolmaster's house.
Dated ten years later, but built in the same stone and in similar
style. One architect must be suspected for both. Compact and
high with steep roofs and gables and tall, Puginian chimneys.

Mullioned-and-transomed windows, apart from the N side, which has lancets and a pointed door.

On the little GREEN ¼ m. SE of the parish church are one or two Georgian houses and the former SCHOOL, in three phases dated 1856, 1880 and 1953. The 1856 building is a single storey of pale dressed stone, four bays with a hipped roof and parapet. Large windows; side door with – still – Y-tracery in the pointed surround above it.

AUGHTON OLD HALL, St Michael's Road, N of the parish church. A little house carefully restored to reveal an early C16 hall and a slightly later cross-wing. Walls are largely of early C18 brick, but stone – mainly dressed – is used for the plinth, quoins, the r. end wall, and the lower walls of rear of the cross-wing and another gabled extension on that side. Little two-light mullioned window in the r. end wall, otherwise wooden C18–C20 casements and horizontal sashes. Main range of three uneven, cottagey bays. In it, abutting the cross-wing, is a blocked doorway, made up of wall-posts and a timber lintel with a depressed pointed arch. Above this is a window and above that a fragment of the wall plate, a couple of feet below the present eaves. A third wall-post is immediately r. of the door. Behind the door, inserted into the screens passage, are two massive back-to-back stone fireplaces, that heating the cross-wing with a C17 segmental arch. Presumably a floor was inserted in the hall around that time. Upstairs a moulded spere post and truss are partly visible, and also further trusses over the hall part, with kingposts. Where the two wings abut the entirely separate framing of the two parts is exposed: the end truss of the hall, with canted tie-beam and raking struts, and the rectangular panels and straight braces of the cross-wing.

GERARD HALL, Prescot Road, opposite St Mary. Three uneven bays and r. extension. Mid-C19 door and window surrounds and quoins, and pebbledash. At the rear is exposed late C17 or early C18 brick on a stone plinth. Inside some intriguing, presumably reused, beams.

HIGH WRAY, Formby Lane. A brick house once called Elders-bury, of at least three phases. Now a nursing home. The first phase is at the back and much altered, but has two gables and some six-over-six sashes. Attached to the front of this is the principal façade, dated 1863. Jacobean Revival, with full-height bay windows. The two shaped gables appear to have been rebuilt and may date from the last phase, which added a low Domestic Revival extension to the r., of the early C20. This has half-timbered gables, mullioned windows and a big Carolean, bracketed door hood. It houses a large drawing room with an inglenook and full C17-style oak panelling. The rest of the interior appears to have been done over at the same time, partly in similar fashion and partly in Adamesque style. At the rear is an Arts-and-Craftsy CARRIAGE HOUSE with a deep porch on battered piers.

MOOR HALL, Prescot Road, 1½ m. E. In Stanley hands until 1850. The entrance front is at first glance largely C18 and C19

Aughton, Moor Hall.
Early C19 engraving .

– low, rendered, gabled and Picturesque. But above the door
is a long stone inscription bearing the date 1566 and the names
of Peter Stanley Esq. and his wife Cecely. In plan it is clearer
that their house is the l. seven bays, consisting of a hall flanked
by cross-wings. At the back are some mullioned windows. If
the current entrance is in the original position – and indeed in
1907 it led into a cross (screens) passage – then that would
imply the standard arrangement of kitchen and services in the
E wing, and great chamber or parlour in the W. Four-centred
fireplace in the N wall of the hall (DCMS). The E extensions
are C19, but a little two-storey protrusion on the W end appears
to be a garderobe. There is a separate stair-tower in the usual
position off the back of the hall. Some stone walling is visible
at the rear; the extent of timber framing is unclear (the DCMS
reports wall-posts in the E wing, and a roof with kingposts and
raked struts).

WEST TOWER, Mill Lane, ½ m. NW. On the edge of the ridge,
with fine views S and W to Liverpool and the sea, is this mid-
C19 house with 1909 alterations, now a hotel. A highly picturesque composition with striking similarities to Woolton Tower,
Woolton, of c. 1856–7 (see p. 513), i.e. many steep gables with
prominent eaves, neat groups of tall octagonal chimneys,
mullioned-and-transomed windows, and a slender prospect
tower, which has an identical machicolated top with shaped
battlements incorporating arrowslits. The 1909 work appears
largely to be internal. To the r. of the entrance is an excellent
Arts and Crafts inglenook. The doorcases in the hall and the
splat balusters of the staircase, and the early-C18-type ceiling
plasterwork and doorcases of the three S rooms (now knocked

into one) are surely of this time too. N of the house is a little yard facing the lane with picturesque STABLES, COTTAGES etc. on three sides. Mid-C19, stone, disparate.

WATERWORKS, Springfield Road, ½ m. SSW. Handsome brick buildings with stone dressings. The ENGINE HOUSE is dated 1880. In the sides on the ground floor, two triplets of round-headed windows under stripy round arches, and above, two groups of four lights, with Gothic columns between and similar arched lintels. These motifs reappear in the splendid portal in the end wall, and the arches in the former BOILER HOUSE. The RESIDENCES have fewer stone dressings but are also carefully detailed, and the 1941 block is in a quiet Moderne classical. Chimney demolished above the base.

BICKERSHAW   <small>6000</small>

A little straggling pit village NW of Leigh, once ringed by workings. The colliery closed in 1992, the last in Lancashire. The large lake or 'flash' caused by mining subsidence S of the pit is now a country park.

ST JAMES, Bickershaw Lane (B5237). 1905, by *F.R. Freeman*. Brown stone with red stone dressings. Nave and chancel, the bellcote on the E gable of the nave.

(BICKERSHAW HALL BARN. Philip Powell reports that beneath the asbestos covering are very fine chamfered trusses of no later than the C17. Stone walls.)

BICKERSTAFFE   <small>4000</small>

A very small village W of Skelmersdale, with the M57 cutting through it.

HOLY TRINITY, Church Road. 1843. By *Sydney Smirke* for the 13th Earl of Derby. The N aisle, with plate tracery, is probably the enlargement of 1860. The older part still has pairs of lancets and thickly pinnacled buttresses between, in the Commissioners' tradition. But in the W steeple is a portal with quite correct E.E. detail, though the tympanum with the three angels adds a happy touch of Victorian romanticism. Wide polygonal apse with shafted lancets outside and a blind arcade of engaged shafts inside. W gallery on timber posts. – FONT. Octagonal, with interlaced round arches. – First World War MEMORIAL outside the W end. Gothic. Slim diagonal buttresses with crocketed pinnacles. Between these a crocketed cross.

Behind the church is the former PARSONAGE, surely by *Smirke* too. Stone and asymmetrical, with gables, big chimneys etc., and a porch with shaped gables. Two-bay enlargement, l., possibly 1920s.

BICKERSTAFFE HALL, Hall Lane, S of the church. Now a farm-house. A pretty three-bay, two-and-half-storey brick house dated 1772 on the handsome rainwater heads, with a cupola bellcote on the M-pattern roof. The dog-leg staircase, with three balusters per tread, is consistent with that date. Nevertheless the door is not central, but between the l. and centre windows. Above it is a plaque carved with an eagle and child, the badge of the Stanleys. A re-set datestone of 1667 low in the façade, from the previous house, has the initials of Sir Edward Stanley, of a cadet branch of the family. His grandson became the 11th Earl of Derby and moved to Knowsley (q.v.), but afterwards built the present house at his childhood home, possibly as a hunting lodge. At the rear is a dairy and attached to that a charming open-sided room for the farmhands, with stone benches around the sides, and a massive timber reused as a lintel. The FARM BUILDINGS include, facing the house, a symmetrical brick range, possibly early C19, with a central cartway under a gable and carriage doors either side. Originally the road ran between the two. Also an ENGINE HOUSE and CHIMNEY, and on the present road, C19 COTTAGES in estate fashion.

THE OLD WINDMILL, Church Road, ½ m. NW. Without sails; now a pretty house with an oversailing conical slate roof. Rendered white, and with a significant batter.

BILLINGE

Including Billinge Chapel End and that part of Billinge-with-Winstanley W of the M6. A large village of suburban character; until the mid C20 it was small and widely scattered. The lack of an obvious centre is a legacy of this. There are a number of interesting C17 and C18 houses.

39 ST AIDAN, Main Street (A571). 1716–18 by *Henry Sephton*, enlarged by *Sir T.G. Jackson* in 1907–8. A chapel of ease first established in the early C16. Sephton's replacement is a charming little essay combining provincial Baroque ornament with Gothic survival (or revival, take your pick). The nave has four bays of large round-headed windows with reticulated tracery, separated by Doric pilasters. Castellated parapet, with urns above the pilasters. The W façade is a piece of remarkable originality. There are pairs of corner pilasters with a piece of triglyph frieze. The centre bay has a doorway with two detached Doric columns, and they support a very little tower which has Ionic corner pilasters and a small square-headed Gothic three-light window and original clock, and an open columnar rotunda on top. The nave roof rises up almost to the tower entablature. The interior has arcades of slender Doric columns on high square bases (which box pews of course would have hidden). Segmental barrel-vaulted ceiling between them, lit by that Gothic window in the W front.

At the E end was a little apse; Jackson dismantled and rebuilt it further E, inserting a S transept and a hipped-roofed N organ

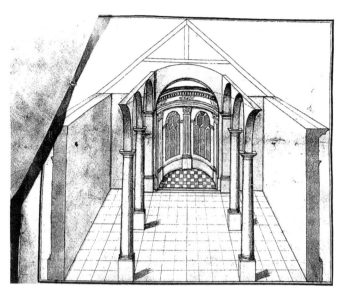

Billinge, St Aidan, cutaway view.
Contract drawing by Henry Sephton, 1716

chamber and vestry to create a Tractarian chancel. Sephton's
apse had only two windows (of the same pattern as the nave
ones) and paired Corinthian pilasters between. Jackson could
not resist 'correcting' this unorthodox arrangement, adding a
third window so that glass, rather than pilasters, is behind the
altar. In theory Jackson would seem excellently suited for handling the combination of Gothic and classical motifs with
understanding and agility; in practice his parts are externally
overbearing (was the jarring striated masonry necessary?) and
the truss at the E end of the nave odd and unsuccessful. His
Free Style FITTINGS are much more assured and of high
quality. He also removed the box pews and the side galleries
of 1823–4, but left the original W GALLERY. It stands on little
stone Doric columns that are jammed up behind the W arcade
columns, with which they share modified bases. Under it is a
glass SCREEN of 1993: for once, there is little to object to, as
its framing is minimised and hidden where it can be behind
the columns. – COMMUNION TABLE. In the S transept.
Handsome, early C18. – CHANDELIER. Brass, C18. – STAINED
GLASS. The chancel windows have good *Hardman* glass of
1913. – C18 brass TABLET. Against the S wall but originally
attached to the pew of James Scarisbricke, a leading Liverpool
merchant who initiated the C18 rebuilding of the chapel and
gave £200 towards the cost (as recorded on a BOARD on the
S wall). – MONUMENTS. Thomas Snape, †1801. With a small

group of Charity by *William Spence*. Meyrick Bankes, †1827. Signed by *Franceys & Spence* of Liverpool. – In the churchyard the tomb of George and Kitty Smith, †1720. In the form of a coffin with rings at the ends and low relief carving on the 'lid', including a curtain and a serpent encircling a winged skull.

St Mary (R.C.), Birchley Road (A571). 1828. Dressed stone, with a wide, decidedly non-Anglican three-bay front. This has arched windows, one either side of a porch of two pairs of baseless, unfluted Doric columns. Panels above all three parts. Bellcote at the apex of the pedimented gable. Sides with three similar windows each, all tied together by an impost band. Shallow apse and attached PRESBYTERY at the E end, both later C19. An almost featureless barn of an interior, with segmental vaulted ceiling. Shallow W gallery and round chancel arch to the apse, both later C19 too.

Billinge Hospital (former), Upholland Road, 1¼ m. N of St Aidan. At the time of writing the prominent slab block of 1964–7 by *A. Brocklehurst*, admired by Pevsner, is due to be demolished. The remnants of the Wigan Union Poorhouse, erected in 1855–7, by *W.M. Mangnall*, already have been.

Billinge Beacon, SW of Crank Road, ⅔ m. NW of St Aidan, at the summit of Billinge Hill (582 ft, 179 metres). It was originally a summer house of Winstanley Hall (*see* p. 677) and had a pyramid roof. There are spectacular views over the Mersey valley and beyond to the coast and Wales, but the hill is disfigured by four separate telecommunications masts. In more sensitive cultures these would be combined in one elegant structure.

Billinge Hall, Crank Road 1⅓ m. WNW of St Aidan. Low and small with cross-wings. C17 but quite a bit altered. Mullioned windows. Said to contain an unheated room in the centre.

Birchley Hall, Delph Meadow Gardens, off Birchley Road (A571) 1 m. SW of St Aidan. Dated 1594. Built during the ownership of James Anderton of Lostock, and bearing the initials of his younger brother Thurston alongside the date. The progenitor of a series of closely related gentry houses including Bispham, Winstanley, the old Haigh Hall and also Hacking Hall (Billington, N Lancashire). They are stone-built with half-H plans and dense, symmetrical five-gabled façades, having square projections in the re-entrant corners so that the front recesses in stages to the centre. Birchley is unique in having the entrance on the first floor, though there are contemporary houses in Lancashire with a *piano nobile* too, e.g. Gawthorpe Hall (N Lancashire) and Clegg Hall (SE Lancashire). The original entrance, in the l. re-entrant projection, is blocked and bereft of its external steps; the C19 replacement entrance is in the ground floor of the r. projection. Numerous other alterations, including the replacement of many of the mullioned windows by assorted sashes and more modern windows.

At the rear are extensions, but much more prominent is the largely plain wing to the l., projecting forward. Its first two floors could be of the same date as the house (surviving mullioned windows and a common plinth). The taller second floor is clearly an addition and houses a CHAPEL, with an external staircase, now altered. After 1613 Roger Anderton established here an important Catholic mission and a secret printing press. Nevertheless this chapel is far too prominent to be the one described as built in 1618, though that may have existed elsewhere in this wing. If the window surrounds in the l. return are anything to go by, an early C18 date seems more likely. The projection against this return contains a sacristy and confessional. In the house, which is now a care home, little of interest survives besides the occasional four-centred doorway. The massive external chimneystack still stands against the rear wall of the hall, but the room itself (and others) has been sub-divided. Abutting the stack, the staircase turret is now occupied by a lift. – MILL DAM behind the house, with a small watermill building, but no machinery.

BISPHAM HALL, Crank Road, 1¼ m. NNW of St Aidan. Of 17 c. 1600–10, with older and later fabric. One of the local group of houses begun with Birchley (see above). It follows the symmetrical half-H plan with square projections in the re-entrant angles, so that there are five staggered gables. Unlike at Birchley, the entrance is on the ground floor, in the r. re-entrant projection. Dressed stone, with a complete and regular set of large mullioned windows, on the ground and first floor with transoms. Some are chamfered, others ovolo-moulded; many are restorations. The l. return has a big chimneystack for the parlour, and a splendid canted bay rising through all two-and-a-half storeys. The r. return has a massive chimneystack, for the kitchen. The date appears to be c. 1600, or possibly after 1610 when the manor was inherited by William Bispham, a wealthy London grocer with extensive estates. However, the building seems to incorporate fabric from an earlier house, possibly built c. 1559: the masonry of the rear corner of the r. wing, including two windows in the rear wall, has been dated to the C16. The round-arched porch entrance is an alteration of the mid C17 (the inner doorway has a depressed four-centred arch); ditto the additions with mullioned window to the r. The interior was quite plain, with timber-framed walls, but the house was reduced to a roofless shell by fire and neglect, and restored internally and rebuilt externally in the 1990s. A small late C17 rear extension was demolished after the fire. – An OBELISK of c. 1815 with a ball on top faces the front of the Hall. As the inscription explains, a memorial to Wellington and the victors of Waterloo.

COSY COTTAGE, No. 19 Park Road, 1 m. N of St Aidan. A pretty little later C17 house. Rendered and whitewashed rubble, stone slate roof and low mullioned windows. Two bays with door to l., and beyond that a lower extension which may have been a shippon with chamber or granary over.

DERBYSHIRE HOUSE, Crank Road, 1⅓ m. WNW of St Aidan. Or Darbyshire House, because it was built by Thomas Darbyshire in 1716. Dressed stone. For the area and time a stylistically advanced yeoman's house, classical and symmetrical, of five bays and two storeys with stone cross-windows and quoins and bands. The big door surround has a bolection-moulded architrave, pilasters and pediment. Still single-depth, though, and with mullioned windows at the back. Restored in the 1990s with the addition, l., of a two-bay one-storey extension featuring simplified renditions of the 1716 windows.

FIR TREE HOUSE, Pimbo Road, 1¾ m. WNW of St Aidan. Dated 1704. Dressed stone. An early double-pile yeoman's house of four bays and a central door, but still with a baffle-entry plan and thus the odd profile of a single central stack. Originally cross-windows, now C20 sashes. The rear has mullioned windows as at Derbyshire House and other transitional houses. (Back-to-back stone fireplaces, one still with recessed four-centred arch. Some walls timber-framed. DCMS.)

GANTLEY HOUSE, Smethurst Lane, 1¼ m. NNW of St Aidan. Small stone C17 yeoman's house of standard three-bay, two-cross-wing plan. Most windows still mullioned.

LYME VALE FARMHOUSE, Birchley Road (A571), 1¼ m. SW of St Aidan. Double-pile house, dated 1733. Timber mullioned-and-transomed windows, entrance with segmental hood on scrolly brackets. A lower and older wing, l., projects from beneath the C18 roof.

WINSTANLEY HALL see Wigan, p. 677.

3090   BLUNDELLSANDS

Blundellsands, N of Waterloo (q.v.), was created from the 1850s as a suburb for wealthy Liverpudlian businessmen by the Blundells of Crosby Hall (see p. 240). William Blundell was the chairman of the nascent Liverpool, Crosby & Southport Railway and shrewdly offered the company land free of charge, provided the line passed through the empty coastal part of his estate, where the beach and rabbit-infested dunes, the healthy breezes and the magnificent prospect across the sea to Snowdonia had the makings of a profitable residential development – if it had a direct railway link to Liverpool. That duly opened in 1850. Commenting on the success of the enterprise in 1899, the *Crosby Herald* noted not only these advantages but also that 'setts are an anathema; . . . roads are wide and lined in many cases with fine trees . . . which impart a garden aspect to the whole neighbourhood'. Now it merges with both Waterloo to the S and Crosby inland, and though pleasant and prosperous, it is no longer the exclusive estate envisaged by its creator.

ST NICHOLAS, Bridge Road. 1873–4, by *Thomas D. Barry & Sons*. Yellowish quarry-faced sandstone. Dec, no tower or transepts, only aisles and a flèche; high polygonal apse with gables above the windows. The W front has two windows and a circular window above, all with attractive tracery, and beneath them a more interesting low polygonal baptistery projection open to the church by tripartite arcading. This is by *W.D. Caröe*, 1894. His parents were members of the congregation, and his is the memorial PLAQUE to them in the baptistery. – ORGAN CASE. By *Caröe*, 1920s. – STAINED GLASS. N aisle w, by *Kempe*, early. – Also a number by *Mayer* of Munich.

ST MICHAEL, Dowhills Road. *Quiggin & Gee*, 1929–31. A big brick church, of simple but effective boxy masses and minimal free Perp tracery (long mullions, no transoms). No tower.

ST JOSEPH (R.C.), Warren Road. 1885–6, by *A.E. Purdie*. In the E.E. style and reasonably large, with aisles but no transepts. Odd w front with a diagonal porch and attached apsed chapel to the r., and a turret on the l. The turret is octagonal with a tall pointed slate roof, and has a large portal at the bottom.

METHODIST CHURCH, Mersey Road *see* Great Crosby, p. 181.

UNITED REFORMED CHURCH, Warren Road. 1898–1905, by *W.G. Fraser* and *A. Thornely*, for a Presbyterian congregation. Large and of quarry-faced red sandstone. Big windows in free Perp forms. NW tower, transepts and flèche between.

CROSBY LEISURE CENTRE, Mariners Drive. Opened 2003. It has the dubious honour of being the first leisure centre to open that was built under the Private Finance Initiative. *Parkwood PFI Projects* are responsible. It tries hard to be interesting, but has absolutely no finesse. The seaward end is a large, rather brutal flying saucer: a big, spreading, ribbed metal roof rising gently to a small dome. Under the eaves is a single storey of tinted wrap-around glazing, raked inwards. Extending from the rear is a blank brick wing. The location on the edge of the dunes has great potential, but rather than the building jutting out romantically amongst them (cf. Maeldune, p. 154), a miserable tarmac cordon of car parking keeps the two apart.

STATION. The Liverpool, Crosby & Southport Railway opened southward as far as Waterloo in 1848. The original building is down steps from Mersey Road. It is in character a simple symmetrical cottage.

WEST LANCASHIRE GOLF CLUB, N of Hall Road West. A trim, boxy clubhouse by *Tripe & Wakeham*, 1961. Banded fenestration to the entrance side of the projecting first floor.

RESIDENTIAL DEVELOPMENT. The first lease was signed in 1854, and there were five properties by 1861. But it seems that the present plan, by *T. Mellard Reade* and *G.W. Goodison*, was not made until 1865. The layout was similar to their contemporary plan, never fully executed, for Birkdale Park (N Lancashire). The principal feature is the aptly named road, THE SERPENTINE. There is a PARK stretching from one side of its sweep across to the other. Exclusivity was ensured by the barrier of the railway to the E and the absence of a road S to Waterloo. The only ways in were by train, and by a gated lane from Crosby (now Blundellsands Road). *Mellard Reade* evidently designed a number of buildings, and himself lived in one until his death. His pretty LODGE of 1881 – upper parts half-timbered – is on West Blundellsands Road opposite the station. The former HOTEL across the road, brick, Tudorbethan and now flats, may not be his, but the big and odd Gothic terrace at Nos. 18–24 WARREN ROAD, dated 1867 on its own Gothic archway, surely is. According to the estate plan, this was to have been only the start of a gentle crescent, and the corner tower would have formed an apex with another crescent sweeping in from the E. There are still a number of the large detached villas shown spaciously arranged on early C20 maps, though many, especially towards the sea, have been replaced by blocks of flats and closes of little houses. Warren Road has fared better than most and still illustrates the evolution from mid-Victorian Italianate and classicism at the S end, e.g. SANDFORD, one of the pre-1865 houses, on the corner with Blundellsands Road West, through to Edwardian Domestic Revival further N, e.g.

108 No. 78, REDCOT, by *Frank Atkinson* for the builder of his Adelphi Hotel (*see* p. 334), William Morrison. This is of 1909, neo-William-and-Mary style, with a big hipped roof. Five bays; semicircular porch with a semi-dome. Next to it is No. 80, also dated 1909, in a white, suburbanised Arts and Crafts style.

Of more recent housing easily the most interesting is MAEL-DUNE on The Serpentine, set into the side of a dune by *Nelson & Parker* in 1963. Over a granite-block basement with garage, the house projects out on a floor of shallow reinforced concrete arches. There are two storeys largely clad in timber, but facing the sea the *piano nobile* is fully glazed. Counterbalancing this rectangularity is the r. return, which is a curved brick wall to buttress against the dune, and a copper-clad stair-turret which rises above the roof to form an asymmetrical observation tower for watching the comings and goings of Mersey shipping. It may not be the most elegant of houses, but it has conviction and a tremendous feeling for its bracing seaside site.

5090 # BOLD

Largely flat and uninteresting country S of St Helens, for much of the C20 blighted by coal mines and now split in two by the M62.

BOLD HALL. Not one but two of Lancashire's grandest and most interesting halls were at Bold, and hardly a trace remains of either. The OLD HALL, 1 m. NNW of Bold Heath, had more hearths, twenty-two, than any other building in Prescot parish in 1662. It had C16/C17 ranges on three sides of a court on a square moat platform. There were many gables, parts were stone and parts timber-framed, and parts probably much older; the site dates from the C12. The last remnant made it into the 1930s as a farmhouse, but Peter Bold had abandoned p. 44 it *c.* 1732 for his NEW HALL, designed by *Giacomo Leoni*, ⅔ m. N (the two sites are now separated by the M62, driven through the centre of the old PARK which was once one of the largest in Lancashire). This was one of the first instances of a

Palladian country house in sw Lancashire: big and bold, nine bays and three storeys of brick above a rusticated ground floor, with an attached Corinthian portico. It was demolished in 1899, and remnants now are limited. Bits and pieces were reused at Meols Hall (N Lancashire). The single-storey E range of *Leoni*'s once three-sided STABLES, w of the hall site, still stands. On the w (yard) side it is brick with stone dressings, but the E façade which faced the Hall is all stone: channelled rustication with a pediment over the central three bays on bulgy Tuscan columns. Also, his three-bay COACHMAN'S HOUSE on what was the axis of the stables. Similar details to the stable w side, but replacement windows and four emphatic chimneystacks in a square, possibly rebuilt in the C19. A few cottages, a fish pond and the walled garden as well. The former s drive approaches over the – now dry – Old Hall MOAT, on a little stone BRIDGE. Attached at the platform end are massive GATEPIERS, rusticated, with *Leoni*'s favoured recessed corners and very boldly projecting cornice.

MOATED SITES Besides the Old Hall, five more of these have been identified in Bold. Of these, only that at OLD MOAT HOUSE, s of Gorsey Lane is still wet.

CLOCK FACE *see* St Helens, p. 569.

BOOTLE

3090

Bootle was a bathing resort in the early C19; by the end of the century it was a gritty, seamless extension of Liverpool, though under the Earls of Derby, the dominant landowners, a stubbornly independent one. It was their estate office that prepared the town's grid layout. The population grew from 6,400 in 1860 to 58,500 in 1900. The stimulus to growth was at first the Leeds and Liverpool Canal, and then more importantly the extension of the Liverpool docks N beyond the city. Today, Liverpool's most important operating docks are all in Bootle. Post-war recovery from extensive bomb damage culminated in the 1960s with an ambitious town-centre redevelopment scheme. Bootle has lived in its Corbusian shadow ever since.

CHRIST CHURCH, Breeze Hill. By *Slater & Carpenter*, 1866. Prominent site, but an unimpressive, narrow-shouldered exterior with w tower with broach spire; odd quatrefoil-section pinnacles on the broaches. Red sandstone with pale stone stripes. Nave and aisles, twin lancets in the aisles, single lancets in the clerestory; apse. The interior looks polychrome brick and stone, but both the black and the red are merely painted on.

ST ANDREW, Linacre Road. 1903, by *Willink & Thicknesse*. Red brick and yellow terracotta details. No tower, but an elegant flèche-cum-cupola. Free Perp tracery. Altogether a Nonconformist type, but quite handsome. – STAINED GLASS. E window, *c.* 1920 after Burlison & Grylls.

ST MATTHEW, Stanley Road. 1890–1, by *Aldridge & Deacon*, serious and without any tricks, if not quite up to their best work. Starkly unadorned with few mouldings and no dressings. Warm red Ruabon brick. Lancets. The w façade to the street with five lancets under a relieving arch, a porch on the l. and a turret on the r. with a pointed roof. A sw porch too, and aisles and transepts. Quiet interior.

St James (R.C.), Chestnut Grove. 1884–6, by *Charles Hadfield*. Very large indeed, but placed out of the way in a side street, and since the demolition of surrounding terraces standing forlornly amongst shapeless grassed areas and replacement low-density housing. Red sandstone, Geometrical tracery. sw tower with porch, turning octagonal in the top stage. High nave, unfortunately proportioned. The tall arcades have alternate octagonal and round columns. Odd nave roof, with coves either side of narrow trusses. On Hadfield's death only the two-bay chancel had been completed; the commission was completed by his son, *M.E. Hadfield*. – Rich marble and alabaster FITTINGS, including an arcade around the chancel, altar rails and a handsome REREDOS of 1890 (but said to be by *Charles Hadfield*). Two tiers of five canopied statues. – STAINED GLASS. Two windows by *Mayer* of Munich in the n aisles (one dated 1913).

Attached PRESBYTERY, Old English style. Brick and sandstone dressings. Later?

St Monica (R.C.), Fernhill Road. By *F.X. Velarde*, 1935–6. An epoch-making church for England, though of course not for Europe. The inspiration came clearly from Dominikus Böhm's churches of 1928–30 (St Joseph, Hindenburg; Caritas Institute, Cologne-Hohenlind; St Camillus, Mönchen-Gladbach). Powerful rectilinear lines in pale brick, stripped down with almost no moulding, e.g. the eaves. Massive, broad w tower opening to the full width towards the high nave with a giant round arch. Tall internal buttresses or wall piers almost the full height of the nave – with only a very narrow clerestory above – form arcades by means of transverse tunnel vaults between each. Aisles are created by punching arches through these buttresses, the s as a full aisle, but the n only as a low narrow passage. The buttresses reach above the aisle roofs on the exterior and each is pierced there by an arch, like square-topped flying buttresses. Yet the nave has a flat ceiling, with thin steel ribs. The distinguished and unforgettable feature of the church is the windows, of mullions and transoms, and a stark round arch to every light. In the chancel n and s walls are seven-light windows with two transoms. The n aisle has one two-light window with two transoms per bay, and the tower w face has three particularly tall two-light ones with three transoms. This in particular is a Böhm motif. Above each of the three is a very tall, slender and extraordinary angel. These are by *H. Tyson Smith*.

The ALTAR WALL is a pale textured background with angels in low relief climbing up. The sculpture here is by *W.L. Stevenson*. Pevsner thought it too prettified. This is unfair, though it certainly contrasts with the otherwise sparse bare brick interior. Also part of the original scheme, the floating CANOPY, the surprisingly Art Deco ALTAR RAILS, and the fluted FONT and STOUPS. Reordered in 1984–5 with, on a platform, a quiet nave ALTAR and LECTERN and a new FONT. These, and a TABERNACLE, are made up from the old altar.

The careful composition and sparse rigour extends to the PRESBYTERY, though the windows have been replaced.

WELSH PRESBYTERIAN CHURCH (former), Stanley Road. By *Noel Woodall* of *R. Owen & Son*, 1951. Coursed yellow sandstone. Remarkably old-fashioned Gothic for the date, though quite an original design in elevation and arrangement of detail (is it a C19 building rebuilt after war damage?). NW tower with needle spire, the octagonal belfry stage looking as if it had been inserted into the square tower. Now offices, with an inserted floor destroying the interior. Hall, attached E, replaced by offices.

TOWN HALL, MUSEUM, POLICE STATION and POST OFFICE, Oriel Road. *See* below.

SWIMMING POOL (former), Balliol Road. *See* pp. 158–9.

BOOTLE LEISURE CENTRE, North Park. Opened 1997. Two brick boxes sandwich three parallel rows of giant Y-shaped steel members supporting gull-wing roofs. A glass wall runs across behind the outermost stanchions. The swimming pool is in this central section.

HUGH BAIRD COLLEGE OF FURTHER EDUCATION, Stanley and Balliol roads. *See* p. 159.

BOOTLE BOROUGH HOSPITAL (former), Derby Road. Now offices. Four phases, all brick, on either side of Seymour Street. The earliest two sections are to the N, and by *C. O. Ellison*. The lower part is the original, of 1870, the higher an extension of *c.* 1885, with a thin pinnacled water tower. Both mildly eclectic with shaped gables. By contrast the C20 parts S of Seymour Street are Wrenaissance (1915) and a more sober Neo-Georgian (1931).

MUNICIPAL OFFICES, Stanley Precinct. *See* p. 159.

INLAND REVENUE, Stanley Precinct. *See* pp. 159–60.

NATIONAL GIRO CENTRE, Netherton Road (A5038). 1966–8. The headquarters of the then new Post Office Giro, by the *Ministry of Public Building and Works*. Very large complex comprising six interlinked buildings, with a cruciform-plan, ten-storey block dominating the spreading other parts. An impressively lucid, well-proportioned composition, in part because of the elegance of the structural module.

WAR MEMORIAL, Stanley Road. Unveiled in 1922. By *Hubert E Bulmer*; figures modelled by *Hermon Cawthra* of London.

DOCKS. *See* Liverpool, p. 276.

PERAMBULATION

We begin on ORIEL ROAD where – yes – Bootle has a Victorian CIVIC CENTRE, even if it is not at all imaginatively planned: simply a block with public frontages on three sides. What is

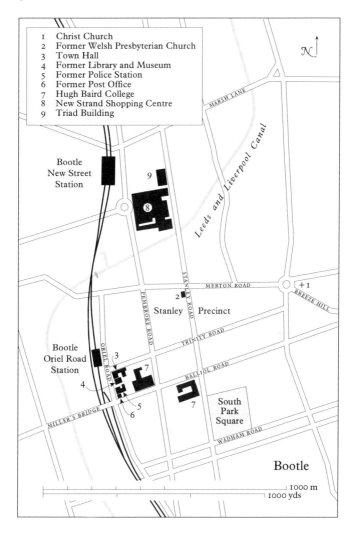

1 Christ Church
2 Former Welsh Presbyterian Church
3 Town Hall
4 Former Library and Museum
5 Former Police Station
6 Former Post Office
7 Hugh Baird College
8 New Strand Shopping Centre
9 Triad Building

Bootle New Street Station

Leeds and Liverpool Canal

MARSH LANE

MERTON ROAD

Stanley Precinct

BREEZE HILL

STANLEY ROAD

PEMBROKE ROAD

TRINITY ROAD

Bootle Oriel Road Station

ORIEL ROAD

BALLIOL ROAD

South Park Square

MILLER'S BRIDGE

WADHAM ROAD

Bootle

1000 m
1000 yds

more interesting is that almost all of it survives, the principal
exception being the Technical School. From the l., and all in
yellow sandstone, are: the TOWN HALL, 1880–2, by *John
Johnson* with a spire and loosely Baroque hall range, and an
extension on Trinity Road; then the former LIBRARY and
MUSEUM, 1887, also by *Johnson*, with a low five-bay façade, a
bit more mixed and Renaissancey, of big ground-floor windows
beneath blank panels; the former POLICE STATION, begun
1890, by *C.J. Anderson*, with a tall entrance tower topped by a

Bootle, Stanley Precinct.
Drawing of proposed development, 1960s

tent roof; and then the former POST OFFICE, a little more
Baroque, at the corner of BALLIOL ROAD. Round the corner
are the disused BATHS, 1888, by *George Heaton* in a Jacobean
Revival style. Across Balliol Road is the former SCHOOL
BOARD OFFICES, Northern Renaissance, but mainly red
brick. There is not much to say of the interiors of any of these;
the Library and Museum have been divided up as offices and
the Town Hall, which was damaged in the Second World War,
was extensively rebuilt internally in 1959–62 by *Briggs, Thornely & McLaughlin*. The Council Chamber, with heraldic glass,
is the sole public space still in its original form.

E of here up Balliol Road is Bootle's ambitious town-centre redevelopment, begun in the mid 1960s. The Corporation's planning consultants were *Gerald Eve & Co*. It takes as its backbone
the dead straight Stanley Road, made a declaration of modernity by lining it with slabs and towers. Though these plans were
realised to an extent not achieved by many towns, C19 houses
and shops still line the road in parts to interrupt and undermine the Corbusian vision. On the corner of Balliol Road and
Stanley Road is HUGH BAIRD COLLEGE, 1966–8, by *Thomas
Finlay*, Borough Architect. Then, N of Balliol Road, the
STANLEY PRECINCT, 20 acres (8 hectares) of slab offices
mainly by *Gunton & Gunton*, architects to the developer, the
Kenyon Construction Co. It was intended to diversify Bootle's
economy away from its dependence on the docks and related
industries, and was prompted by the decision to relocate
Inland Revenue offices, first to ST HUGH'S HOUSE (1964)
on the E side, and then to MAGDALEN HOUSE to its SE

(completed 1965). LINACRE HOUSE (opened *c.* 1966), by *E.R. Furber* of the *Ministry of Public Building and Works*, is the lower block s of St Hugh's House, and was built for the Ministry of Social Security. s of Linacre House, on the corner of Balliol Road, is the nine-storey BALLIOL HOUSE (completed by 1967), for the Revenue and the Bootle Corporation. E of this, fronting Balliol Road, ST PETER'S HOUSE and the adjoining ST ANNE'S HOUSE (completed by 1967) were for various Government departments. Then came the most northerly block on the E side, St John's House, a mammoth but little-loved complex with an eighteen-storey tower, designed by the *Ministry of Public Building and Works* for the Revenue, which was demolished in 2001 and replaced by a much smaller red brick building, set back. Buildings on the W side of Stanley Road, starting N of the former Welsh Presbyterian Church (*see* p. 157), were intended for commercial letting. First comes DANIEL HOUSE (at fourteen storeys the tallest still standing), then ST MARTIN'S HOUSE (by *W.H. Robbins & Associates*, completed 1968), and finally MERTON HOUSE (now council offices).

Across the LEEDS AND LIVERPOOL CANAL (*see* p. 485) is the NEW STRAND SHOPPING CENTRE, a low, grim concrete thing built from 1965. This was intended as the 'explosion point' from which urban renewal, including the Stanley Precinct, would flow. Conceptual design was by *Professor H. Myles Wright* and *A.E. Weddle*; detailed design by *T.P. Bennett & Son*. It was conceived with two levels of malls. At the rear on Jersey Street is a raised octagon with a folded roof; a twenty-storey residential tower, a bus station and a multi-storey car park are also incorporated on this side. Though it borders the canal, because of the date it ignores rather than embraces it. Lastly, to its N is the towering TRIAD BUILDING by the *Hind Woodhouse Partnership*, 1971–4. It cost £2.5m. Central service core with three radiating wings rising above a podium incorporating showrooms (now shops). Twenty-four floors in all, the core and wings of projecting, faceted concrete modules, *à la* Richard Seifert. Windows set back in each module. This is a texture strong enough to invigorate such big faces, and the endless repetition is powerful in steep foreshortening. But the concrete is dark and dull even on a sunny day, and the building aggressive and loveless.

THE OLD HALL, Nos. 1 and 3 Merton Road. Small, late C18 and altered. Rainwater head dated 1773 with the Derby arms on No. 3, which is brick and of four bays. No. 1 is of stone and has some early C19 Gothic casements. Said to have been a shooting lodge.

GASHOLDERS, Litherland Road. Two good later Victorian examples, big and with Tuscan columns for the stanchions of the cast-iron guide-frames.

HARLAND & WOLFF LTD. Two of the Belfast shipbuilder's former premises. On Grove Street, a FOUNDRY. The most complete and impressive structure in the industrial strip adjoining the docks. Big brick façade of gables, late C19. On Regent Road (part of the dock road) at the junction with Raleigh Street, the offices of the otherwise demolished SHIP-BUILDING & ENGINEERING WORKS, opened in 1913.

HEALTH AND SAFETY EXECUTIVE HEADQUARTERS, Pembroke Road. Under construction in 2005. By *Cartwright Pickard Architects*, under the Private Finance Initiative. To house 1,500 staff and covering 30,000 square metres. Four storeys. Offices arranged in blocks either side of an internal street. Orthogonal apart from a street-corner drum. An emphasis is placed on energy-efficient design.

BURSCOUGH

4010

A little rural town of industrial character in flat country NE of Ormskirk (q.v.), at the junction of the Leeds and Liverpool Canal with its Rufford Branch, and the railway lines from Wigan to Southport and Liverpool to Preston. These made possible the creation of industry here, allowing the importation of cotton and grain from the Liverpool docks, and coal from the coalfield. Along the canal there were small cotton MILLS and warehouses, some C19 examples surviving s of Burscough Bridge station, and later steam-powered flour mills. A big example of the last, still with its tall chimney, was in 2005 to be converted into apartments. This was Ainscough's Mill, built *c.* 1855 and extended 1885 and 1894 by *Hind & Lumb*. On the roads s and w are the villas of the Victorian middle class.

ST JOHN, Liverpool Road North (A59), Burscough Bridge. 1829–32, by *Daniel Stewart*, a Commissioners' church, costing £3,440. Red ashlar. Gabled façade with four buttresses finishing as uncouth octagonal and embattled pinnacles. A bell-turret at the apex. Most striking is that it is entirely blank, with three blank windows. The two-light windows of the sides have the same incorrect Perp tracery. The chancel is of 1887–9, by *William Waddington & Son*. Elaborately free Perp windows, including the big E window, with round-arched lights. s vestry *c.* 1932. The three galleries of 1857 have been retained.

ST JOHN (R.C.), Chapel Lane, ½ m. s. Of 1815–18. An L-plan variation on the normal pre-Emancipation arrangement. Brick on a sandstone plinth, the s side rendered. This s façade is of four bays, intended to disguise the church as a house: the l. two are the PRESBYTERY, the r. two, with blind windows, are the end of the church. On the N side the church sticks out as a wing with three large round-headed windows on the E side; the back of the presbytery has a door and round-headed stair window above it, with sashes either side. The little tower is of 1915. Inside the church a familiar plan: (liturgical) w gallery on cast-iron columns, round sanctuary arch, coved oval ceiling to the sanctuary and a REREDOS with four Corinthian semi-columns.

To the w is BURSCOUGH HALL FARMHOUSE, early C17, altered and extended and rebuilt after it was all but destroyed by fire in the 1990s. Here Catholic worship was practised before St John was built. This was possibly in the large first-floor room which had an arched roof truss. Two low storeys with four unequal gables. Brick, with assorted windows and doors.

BURSCOUGH PRIORY. *See* Lathom, p. 224.

CANAL, Wheat Lane. At the junction of the Leeds and Liverpool Canal and the Rufford Branch Canal is a basin and DRY DOCK. They are of *c.* 1781 and of coursed sandstone. The resident engineer was *Richard Owen*. Also two locks on the Branch Canal here.

RAILWAY BUILDINGS. The buildings on the Wigan–Southport line of the Southport & Manchester Railway are very attractive. They are of sandstone and Tudorbethan, and date from *c.* 1855–60. There is the BURSCOUGH BRIDGE STATION building, Red Cat Lane, and a number of CROSSING-KEEPERS' COTTAGES up and down the line.

SQUARE HOUSE, Square Lane. Two phases of two-storey Late Georgian. The l. three bays are brick, the r. two are coursed sandstone.

MARTIN HALL, w of New Lane, 1 m. w. The house is gone but there is a timber-framed BARN, probably later C16. Full-height porch. The square framing is not visible outside because of C17 dressed stone cladding, and an extension in brick. There is a four-light mullioned window in the e outshut. Inside, the remains of the frame has nogging below and, above, an unusual infill of horizontal staves coated in daub.

BURTONWOOD

An ugly, featureless C20 village; it was only a few cottages and farms until the collieries arrived in the C19. They, of course, have gone now.

ST MICHAEL, Chapel Lane. Founded in 1606, rebuilt in 1716 and again in 1939 by *Edwin J. Dod*. His is the s aisle with its arcade of Tuscan columns, the NW vestries and the present SW tower (though this is probably to the design of the previous one, which was situated axially to the nave). The church was rebuilt once more in 1984 following mining subsidence (see the poor brickwork). Thus you have to go round to the e and N to find any C18 bricks. Prior to 1939 the entrance was in the centre of s side. Arched C20 windows, probably to earlier pattern. Modest C19 hammerbeam roof. Reordered in 1988. – In the front of the choir stalls two remnants of a PEW with the date 1610 and the name of Sir Thomas Bold (of Bold Hall, q.v.), the founder of the chapel. Incorrect but infectiously exuberant provincial decoration, with the Bold griffin. – STAINED GLASS. Memorial to RAF Burtonwood (*see* Warrington, p. 639) by *Jan Swiercynski*, 1988. With photo-etched images. – Opposite is a little cemetery and a remarkably unattractive late C20 church hall.

BURTONWOOD MOTORWAY SERVICES. *See* p. 639.

BRADLEY OLD HALL, Bradley Lane, off Hall Lane, ½ m. N. There is a wet moat with, across the causeway, a ruined gatehouse of *c.* 1460–5 built by Sir Peter Legh, with a four-centred arch in yellow sandstone. Colonnettes remain, as well as, within, springers of the fallen vault. E side and inner arch collapsed. At the front corners are decayed, red sandstone canted mock turrets with diagonal buttresses, and the outer faces elsewhere appear to be red stone too. Is the yellow stone an early C19 restoration? In the middle of the platform is a three-bay house, with modern windows, and brick walls, some pebbledashed. The brick may be C18, but the front door with its ornately scrolling wrought-iron strap hinges, decayed, looks C16 or earlier. (Inside is an early C18 stair, and a part of an inscribed beam dated 1597 reused as a purlin, but formerly in the hall. DCMS.) The suspicion is that a timber frame lurks behind the brick, and possibly medieval fabric too. A site worthy of further investigation.

COLLINS GREEN, 1 m. N, is colliery terraces.

CLOCK FACE *see* ST HELENS p. 569.

CRAWFORD

Up Holland

5000

A pit village, but quite a pretty little one, built by the Wigan Coal & Iron Co., which sank a shaft here *c.* 1850. The colliery closed in 1938. The single street is lined with stone-built terraces.

MANOR HOUSE, Manor House Drive, off Crawford Road. Idiosyncratic transitional house dated 1718, built by a wealthy yeoman. The plan, double-pile, is advanced, but the symmetrical façade is curiously, if charmingly, old-fashioned. Five bays, two-and-a-half storeys, the central bay still a full-height gabled porch, with the flanking windows uncomfortably squeezed against it, and the outer bays with dormer windows in gables, which match the top stage of the porch. Thus they have corner quoin-pilaster strips, which on the porch continue to the ground. The same at the façade corners. The windows still have mullions and transoms (cross-type in the dormers), but 'modern' in as much as they are of square section and have architraves with crude keystones. The porch is still round-arched with impost mouldings, but the door has a semicircular fanlight and fielded panels. In common with other houses of the date, e.g. Knight's Hall, Up Holland (*see* p. 601), new-fangled ideas were limited to public façades; the triple-gabled rear elevation has mullioned windows with chamfered surrounds. Materials are unusual too: an exterior of limestone – extremely rare in SW Lancashire – but brick cross-walls with massive ridge chimneystacks. Three principal rooms across the front, staggered transverse corridor, with small rooms and two

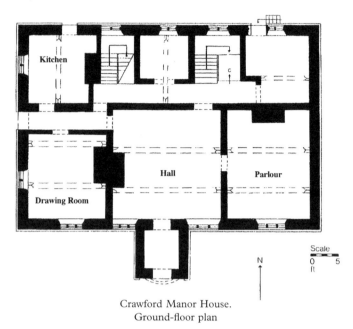

Crawford Manor House.
Ground-floor plan

dog-leg staircases beyond. Principal staircase with square, panelled newels and turned balusters. Restored from dereliction
in the 1990s when housing was built across the grounds,
though without destroying the vista up to the façade.

Panelled GATEPIERS with ball finials and fluted Doric
quarter-columns at the corners (cf. St Aidan, Billinge, and
Cronton Hall, qq.v.). They may be *ex situ* as their classicism is
more sophisticated than that of the house. OUTBUILDINGS,
SW, dated 1668, of stone and partially rebuilt, and SE, with 1727
datestone, largely of brick and now converted without much
feeling to housing.

CROFT

Croft was a dispersed village, a scattering of cottages and farms.
Now it is an uninteresting dormitory to Warrington, the cottages
and farms heavily modernised and housing estates erected. The
best surviving house is SPRINGFIELD FARMHOUSE, Spring
Lane, a standard late C18 brick three-bay box with pedimented
doorcase and fanlight.

CHRIST CHURCH, Lady Lane. 1832–3, by *Edward Blore*, a little
Commissioners' church that cost £1,457. Red sandstone with
a stumpy SW steeple of wholly incorrect but quite enterprising
design. Lancet windows and short chancel. The simple, broad

interior has a little W GALLERY, and massive cross-braced roof trusses. – Oak FURNISHINGS. – Creed, Decalogue and Lord's Prayer, in pointed painted panels. On either side three E lancets containing STAINED GLASS by *Mayer* of Munich, 1896. Very good figures: Christ flanked by Peter and James. Elsewhere, post-war glass by *Shrigley & Hunt*. The best is S fourth from W, quintessentially 1950s.

ST LEWIS (R.C.), Mustard Lane, Little Town. 1826–7, replacing a Jesuit mission in Southworth Hall (*see* below). Brick. To the E the church, to the W and back-to-back with it, within one envelope, the priest's house, in the usual manner. The latter has a chequered front and a doorway with engaged Doric columns, the former arched windows to N and S and a W front with gable pediment and pedimented porch. Inside, the E wall has four Corinthian pilasters with a shallow apse and flanking blank arches between them. The outer pilasters are cranked around the re-entrants. Under the N arch is the door to the vestry, under the S a Lady Altar. The flat ceiling has a coved and bracketed cornice and a rose of acanthus within garlands of husks.

SOUTHWORTH HALL, Southworth Lane, ½ m. W. A house is first mentioned in the C13. The current building – of brick and of five bays (the outer ones projecting under gables), with cross-windows and a massive chimneystack – is of 1932, by *Geoffrey Owen*, and a pretty faithful likeness of its C17 predecessor, albeit reduced by one storey to two. The back elevation was adapted for C20 living. From the old house there is a large segmental-arched fireplace in the single-storey hall, and the brick base of its chimney.[*] Also, the studded door and four-centred stone surround in Owen's porch. The door is – and was – central (i.e. creating a symmetrical façade). The current, C19, staircase was formerly the back stairs. C17 brick and stone reused in garden wall. The Southworth family's other medieval house, Samlesbury Old Hall, survives (N Lancashire).

A Bronze Age ROUND BARROW was excavated ½ m. WSW of the Hall in 1980. It displayed two phases: a small ditched sand mound associated with two cremations was succeeded by a larger turf mound covering a burnt timber structure and nine cremations, three in collared urns and two in globular vessels. The radiocarbon dates for the two phases spanned *c.* 400 years, between approximately the C18 and C14 B.C. The barrow was surrounded and overlain by a large Early Christian CEME-TERY. This comprised at least 800 graves covering an area of over 1,200 square metres. There were at least three phases of burial, but few bones survived in the acidic soil conditions. A possible church, 26 ft (8 metres) long and 13 ft (4 metres) wide, was suggested by the layout of the graves.[**]

[*] The C19 panelling in the hall is from Norton Priory, Runcorn, Cheshire, demolished in 1928.
[**] Information supplied by Adrian Tindall.

CRONTON

HOLY FAMILY (R.C.), Hall Lane. 1910. Quarry-faced red sandstone. Small. Lancets, small NW tower.

CRONTON HALL, Hall Lane. A handsome, almost square double-pile house with a hipped roof. The façade is of five bays and two storeys over a semi-basement, stuccoed, and unusually compartmentalised by strings, cornices and vestigial superimposed pilaster strips. These may once have been full pilasters, pared down when the front was altered in the C19 (is the roof of this date too?), because the house is essentially early C18. This is patent from the excellent staircase seen in 1969 running throughout from basement to the upper floor. It has twisted balusters, the twist starting only above an urn shape, and a handrail curving up to the newel posts. The W side is entirely blank, and in the basement either side of the front steps are low, five-bay mullioned windows, one unaltered and one altered (cf. Moorcroft House, Newburgh, p. 522). By contrast, the excellent GATEPIERS in front are sophisticated for the time. They have big urns, and paired Doric columns to the outside. To the house they have attached quarter-columns at the corners, a motif found on the gatepiers of the Blue Coat School, Liverpool (*see* p. 302), the Manor House, Crawford, and St Aidan, Billinge (qq.v.), all begun in 1716–18, which may date the house more precisely. Fine wrought-iron gates too, though somewhat rusted away. E of the Hall, FARM BUILDINGS dated 1816, now housing.

Cronton, even with lots of C20 infill, is small. On HALL LANE are a medieval CROSS BASE and one or two cottages and farmhouses, including SUNNYSIDE FARMHOUSE, just E of the Hall. It has inside a pair of crucks exposed (DCMS). Baffle-entry plan with cross-wing. Brick; cross-wing with sandstone plinth. Probably a C16 or early C17 cruck frame, encased in brick and given an upper floor in the C18.

CUERDLEY CROSS

Penketh

On the A562 is a little square green bounded by probably C18 cottages, and 1950s houses. ½ m. E is a farmhouse dated 1733. But dominating all, and indeed all for miles around, is FIDDLER'S FERRY POWER STATION, 1963–73 by the *Central Electricity Generating Board*. A truly sublime building overpowering a flat and featureless setting. Coal-powered, 2,000 megawatt capacity. Formally planned: orientated SW toward the Widnes bridges and rigorously symmetrical about the axis, with a massive 650 ft (198 metre) high chimney behind the 865 ft (264 metre) by 200 ft (61 metre) high face of the boiler house, and four cooling towers either side spread out in a lozenge pattern – a sort of gigantic, transmogrified *cour d'honneur*. Because of their immense presence in the landscape, by the 1960s a great deal of thought was invested in the design and landscaping of power stations.

CULCHETH

Culcheth is now a large characterless village, a scattering of cottages and farms developed into a sprawling suburban dormitory since 1946, initially to house the scientists of the Atomic Energy Research Establishment, Birchwood (*see* Warrington, p. 638). Dismal 1950s–70s shopping parades define the centre (with a little plain SUNDAY SCHOOL, dated 1821). More interesting are the flat-roofed semis at Fowley Common, built during the Second World War as accommodation for HMS *Ariel*, now Risley Remand Centre (identical houses in Warrington, p. 624). The streets here have deferentially patriotic names – Churchill, Eden, Bevin, Attlee, Beaverbrook.

HOLY TRINITY NEWCHURCH, Church Lane. 1904–5, by *Travers & Ramsden*, replacing a C17 chapel destroyed by fire. Incredibly retardataire. This brand of Neo-Norman might be 1850. W tower, aisles, quarry-faced stone. Dull interior, with parish room in W bay, behind a clashing wooden screen (1991). – REREDOS with the Adoration of the Magi on painted glass panels by *Kayll & Co.*, Leeds. – FONT. Marble, quatrefoil plan, on four stubby piers with merging capitals. Presumably 1905 too. – Two CHANDELIERS in the chancel. Brass, C18, four tiers; from Culcheth Hall (demolished *c.* 1958). – STAINED GLASS. More quantity than quality. Much by *A. Seward & Co.* of Lancaster, including an impressive Crucifixion in the five-light E window, a memorial to Charles Crofton Black, †1913. – BRASSES. In the parish room a brass inscription to Elizabeth Egerton, †1646, signed *John Sale sculpsit* – an oddity of the first order; also one to William Ratclyff, †1561, and family; a third brass is of three girls, hands clasped in prayer, the dead daughters mentioned on the Ratclyff brass. These two brasses are fragments of a larger memorial.

SALFORD UNION COTTAGE HOMES (former), Stonyhurst Crescent. Built in 1901 with an oval plan and varied treatment of the front elevations, though the rears of every cottage are identical. Now housing.

KENYON HALL, Broseley Lane, on the NW edge of Culcheth, is a classical mansion now serving as a golf clubhouse. It appears to be early C19 with alterations. Rendered, the ground floor with channelled rustication. The orientation is 90 degrees out from what one might expect: the N side has the entrance loggia; the E front is seven bays, the middle three projecting in a shallow segmental bay, with a grossly insensitive single-storey extension; and the S front is seven bays, the r. three slightly projecting with a later segmental ground-floor bay, and with a later blank W extension containing the billiard room (there were large conservatories attached here in 1886). Giant pilasters at most angles, hideously pink. The W side is definitely the back, with C20 extension and alterations.

Some good INTERIORS. Much of the plan is taken up by the top-lit central hall, which contains a very grand staircase rising around the sides via quarter-pace landings to a first-floor landing supported by two Ionic columns. The ceiling is supported by two more Ionic columns above these, now with a partition between. Lantern, once square, replaced by lenses set in a concrete disc. Off this on the ground floor are four rooms, knocked into two, with high-quality ceilings (in 1886 they were, clockwise, the library, drawing room, music room and dining room). The dining room in the centre of the s façade has a superb cornice, with a frieze of pomegranates and pears, unusual ceiling rose, and square engaged Corinthian columns that once flanked the buffet. All this decoration (and the stair balustrade) seems mid-C19. The billiard-room lantern is now hidden behind suspended ceiling tiles.

The LODGE is single-storeyed, stuccoed with pedimented gables and a Doric entrance porch in the re-entrant angle.

Across Broseley Lane is a really quite big VILLA of 1906, Stockbroker Tudor with half-timbering, turrets etc. It is the best of a number of early C20 houses built by the new money of Leigh in the northern part of Culcheth, which is called Twiss Green.

NEWCHURCH OLD RECTORY, ¼ m. s on the A574, is a generous two-storey, three-bay, red brick house of 1812 with pedimented Doric-columned doorcase. Steps up to it with wrought-iron balustrade.

HOLCROFT HALL, 1 m. w on the B5512. A rendered exterior, the proportions and massive chimney the clues to the late C15–early C16 date. It was enlarged in the C18, but in the late C20 it disgracefully had its cross- and mullioned windows replaced with uPVC frames, and gained a crude E extension. One can only hope that the interior features described by the DCMS – heavily moulded beams, massive roof timbers, a now internal Gothic window, a priest hole and sealed triangular openings – remain.

HOLE MILL FARM, ⅓ m. further s on the B5512 is, mercifully, a farmhouse that has so far escaped mauling. Brick, three bays, two phases – C18 and possibly C17. Inside is a charming provincial Chinese Chippendale staircase, presumably of the 1750s.

DALTON

Dalton is an attractive landscape of up-and-down country N of Skelmersdale and s of the River Douglas, rising to the peak of Ashurst's Hill, at 569 ft (175 metres). This is the last outpost of the high ground of E Lancashire before it falls away to the coastal plain, and from it there are stupendous panoramic views to Manchester and the Pennines, North Wales, Liverpool and the sea beyond, and round to Blackpool Tower and the Lakeland hills. There is no village, but there is a concentration of C17 farmhouses at Elmer's Green, which is now in Skelmersdale New Town (*see* p. 589). Dalton was part of Wigan parish until the 1870s.

ST MICHAEL, Higher Lane. 1875–7, by *T.H. Wyatt*. How did he come to the attention of the client, John Prescott of Dalton

Grange? The church is a strong job in coursed rubble, with a sw tower carrying a saddleback roof. No aisles, but transepts. Lower chancel with polygonal apse, s vestry. Lancet windows. Prominent statue of St Michael in a niche between two of them in the w front. Chancel and transept arches. A simple interior reordered after a fire in 1988 by *Anthony Grimshaw Associates*, with a new ALTAR under the chancel arch, and a lectern and SCREENS, by the architect. The unusual and not entirely successful decision was taken to relocate the organ pipes into the upper part of the chancel, where they are concealed by a flat latticework ceiling inserted just above the level of the lancets' heads, and by a matching latticework screen in the chancel arch. Attached to this is a copy after a C12 CRUCIFIX from the Basilica of St Clare, Assisi, painted by *Barbara Grimshaw*.

ASHURST HALL, Higher Lane. Next to the church. The house is C19 in C17 style, but of no special interest. However, in front is a picturesque detached GATEHOUSE, dated 1649 before the tablet above the arch was worn away. Though itself quite small, it implies there was a substantial house here. Typical archway for the date – moulded round arch with keystone, and moulded responds. Two-light mullioned window above this. Low one-bay wings with two-light mullioned windows. Also a C17 DOVECOTE. Square. Restored 1985. C19 FARM BUILDINGS, now converted.

BEACON TOWER, on top of Ashurst's Hill (N of Beacon Lane). Said to have been erected or re-erected here *c.* 1798–1800 in anticipation of Boney's invasion. The design is remarkably austere and quite sophisticated – a square block below, one step and then a pyramidal spire. The block has three blocked-up windows and a door with keyed lintels around the four sides, but there is no other moulding or decoration.

There are a good number of C16–C18 YEOMEN'S HOUSES scattered across Dalton, possibly because the manor was divided early. They are sandstone-walled and mainly mullion-windowed. One of the finest, BELLE VUE FARM, Scott's Fold (1683), is now a sad, vestigial ruin.*

HOLLAND'S HOUSE, Lees Lane, N side, 1 m. NE of the church. An uneven and wobbling six-bay, two-storey house. The stone case is, l., late C17 with mullioned-and-transomed windows, and, r., early C18 and symmetrical, with baffle entry to house-body and kitchen, and cross-windows. Inside, remnants of an early C17 timber frame and lots of quarter-round beams.

LOWER HOUSE, Lees Lane, N side, 1 m. NE of the church. Three-unit house including two cross-wings. The envelope of the E wing seems later (C18) than the rest (late C17). It contains two crucks (C16?). One of these is at right angles in the w wing – rare evidence of a cruck-framed cross-wing.

* Much of the information about the houses has been revealed by the investigations of Gary Miller, and all the houses – and others not mentioned here – are described in detail in his *Historic Houses in Lancashire: the Douglas Valley 1300–1770*, 2002.

PRIOR'S WOOD HALL, N of Lees Lane, I m. NNE of the church. In a lovely setting at the end of a winding drive lined with beeches. It is a picturesque combination of C17 house and grander C19 wing. From the approach, to the W is the back of the low, late C17 house. H-plan, the W wing a slightly later addition. This may have been for a separate household, since there is no intercommunication still. Haphazard windows, mostly multi-mullioned. More of these, but more regularly, on the N side, which is the entrance front with a little two-storey porch in the centre and a transomed stair window in the E wing. Big inglenook (baffle entry). Reused moulded timbers in the roof, hinting, Miller suggests, at a substantial late C15–early C16 house here. Attached to the E is the much taller three-storey C19 wing facing S, i.e. the other way. It is in no way hard, like some Victorian additions, and is carefully irregular in most parts. The details convincingly copy the earlier building, and the stone harmonizes. It is an excellent work.

25 STONE HALL, ¼ m. N of Crow Lane. A locally significant little house, an ambitious and charismatically rustic first flowering of classical architecture below the level of the gentry, still nestling in wonderful isolation. No exact date, but almost certainly of the first decade of the C18 – that is, contemporary with nearby Bispham Hall (see p. 151), with which it shares both similarities in the façade, and ownership at that time (the Ashursts of Ashurst Hall, see p. 169). Three bays only, but each bay separately flanked by rusticated giant pilasters (i.e. six in all). Rubble and extensive ashlar dressing. Fine doorway with swan-neck pediment. Above this a blank plaque – no window – and crowning the central bay a pediment, rather steep, with a slightly too large œil de bœuf that is a little low in the tympanum. The windows are of the cross-type, which was very up-to-date in Lancashire at a time when mullions were still the norm (employed here on the back and sides). The plan struggles awkwardly to follow that new fashion, a double pile: the front contains a traditional housebody, with the door into it, and a parlour (with double bolection-moulded door between the two); projecting from the rear are two gabled wings containing the services, and sandwiched between them under a catslide roof a dog-leg staircase, with panelled newels. Chimneystacks are not at the gable ends but inside, where the wings meet, and the roof even contains an upper cruck, very late for a building of such ambition. Lesser, mid-C18 extensions to rear. C18 BARN.

DOWNHOLLAND
with HASKAYNE

Flat and sparsely populated former moss country W of Ormskirk crossed by the Leeds and Liverpool Canal (see p. 485).

DOWNHOLLAND HALL, E off Black-a-Moor Lane. C16/C17. Three irregular bays with low multi-mullioned windows and one later sash. Mainly brick, but the ground floor on the r. is

stone and has a single drip-course over door and window. This
suggests a stone building rebuilt and possibly extended in the
C17.

COTTAGES, School Lane, Haskayne. The characteristic vernacular building type of W Lancashire was the low single-storey
whitewashed cottage, huddled in the windswept landscape
under a thatched roof. Most were cruck-framed, with livestock
accommodation at one end (*see* Introduction, p. 38). No. 107
SCHOOL LANE is one survivor, though extensively 'modernised'. C17, containing parts of four cruck trusses. The S end
may have been the shippon. STOCK COTTAGE, ½ m. N, at least   *p. 37*
retains a traditional appearance externally. Whitewashed walls
of brick and rubble, thatched roof. Eyebrow dormers to the
house half, r. Baffle entry. Inside is an inglenook and middle
crucks. The former agricultural part, l., has external stairs to
a chamber. Probably C17.

EARLESTOWN *see* NEWTON-LE-WILLOWS

ECCLESTON *see* ST HELENS

FARNWORTH *see* WIDNES

FORMBY   *2000*

In the early C17 'Formbie' was a port with nine ships; by 1718 it
had been removed from shipping lists and was no more than a
fishing hamlet. The old channel then silted up, and old Formby
is now two miles from the sea. Modern Formby was created by
the arrival of the railway in 1848 as a Liverpool dormitory.
Despite false starts, such as a stillborn scheme of 1875 to create
another Southport here, Formby is nevertheless now quite large,
leafy and prosperous, and suburban in character despite being in
the countryside. It is sheltered from the sea by big sand dunes
planted with pines to prevent erosion.

ST PETER, Green Lane. Dated 1746. Brick with stone plinth and
quoins. Three bays. On each side three big round-headed
windows, handsomely framed in Doric surrounds of pilasters
and triglyph friezes, and keystones and aprons. Intersecting
Gothick glazing. W front with small round windows and a
narrow tower supporting a stone belfry cupola. The tower
stands on square Doric columns which formed an open porch
until infilled *c.* 1830 with oddly bulging convex walls to house
a staircase to a new W gallery. This is carried on slender Doric
timber columns. A jarring contrast is the High Victorian ashlar
Gothic chancel, vestry and S chapel of 1873. The vestry,
however, has an extension aping the vocabulary of the C18 nave,
possibly of 1935 when N and S galleries were removed. Timber

and glass s porch, 1884. The roof of 1900 has handsome king-post trusses. – PULPIT. C17 style, with tester, originally from St Saviour, Upper Huskisson Street, Liverpool (demolished), and almost certainly *c.* 1900 by *Willink & Thicknesse*. – STAINED GLASS. E window by *Shrigley & Hunt*.

ST LUKE, St Luke's Church Road. The building, by *William Culshaw*, dates only from 1852–5, but stands close to the site of an ancient chapel. It was built in anticipation of the rapid expansion of the township towards the sea after the opening of the railway. In the end that took many decades and the church remained an isolated folly amongst the sand dunes into the C20. Aisle-less, with transepts and a bellcote, i.e. no tower. Rock-faced stone. Geometrical tracery. Somewhat dreary interior. – FONT. Norman, simple, with a rope moulding. – LEDGER with marginal inscription to Richard Formby †1407, from the old chapel.

HOLY TRINITY, Rosemary Lane. 1889–90, by *C.A. Atkinson*. Crazy-paving walling of sandstone rubble. Lancets. Shallow transepts and s vestry and organ loft. No tower; instead, a timber bell-turret with slate flèche rising from the vestry and organ projection. – REREDOS. By *Woolfall & Eccles*, *c.* 1920. PARISH HALL. 1908. Arts and Crafts-derived, with roughcast walls, hipped roof and gablets.

OUR LADY OF COMPASSION (R.C.), School Lane. 1863–4, by *Henry Clutton*. Brick, red with a few yellow bands; also stone trim. Robust. No tower. It is an interesting building in so far as it is inspired in plan by Italian Romanesque churches with transepts and three parallel apses. This E end is rib-vaulted solidly. The nave has Clutton's favourite arcades of two slender columns, paired in depth and provided with shaft-rings. Naturalistic capitals. The NW view is enlivened by a little round turret with a conical roof and the rounded projection of the baptistery. They date from 1923. Reordering, and meeting room, 1991 by *Richard O'Mahoney*.

PRESBYTERY, School Lane. Built, it is said, in 1688 (plaque) as a Roman Catholic chapel by the Blundells of Ince Blundell, but used as a barn until 1796, then a chapel until 1864, then cottages, and from 1930 for over sixty years a convent. Roughcast; three bays with extensions N and s to make a cruxiform plan. Possibly raised. Much altered internally.

OLD PARSONAGE, Green Lane. Three brick bays of 1772, with, r., a one-bay one-storey extension and, l., a later cross-wing.

CRUCK-FRAMED COTTAGES. Scattered through the suburban streets of Formby are a number of whitewashed cottages with cruck frames hidden behind later brick or stone walling. They include:

DEAN'S COTTAGE, Windsor Road. Single-storeyed. Thatched; brick walls. Possibly C16. Said to contain a central housebody open to the roof and exposing crucks, and to retain a sleeping chamber.

Nos. 53 and 62 GORE'S LANE. Both single-storeyed with thatched roofs and timber gutters. Possibly C16–C17 in origin.

No. 53 has sliding sashes and an eyebrow dormer; No. 62 may have been its barn and animal house.

MAY COTTAGE, No. 15a Green Lane. (Dated 1690 inside. DCMS.) Roughcast, and slate roof. Crucks truncated with collars and short kingposts. No. 21 is also whitewashed and thatched, but two-storeyed with gable-end chimneys and no crucks, and therefore probably C18.

No. 2 TIMMS LANE. Thatched and brick but not white-washed. Casements and sliding sashes. At least C18, but if it contains cruck parts then it is almost certainly older.

Little C19 and C20 HOUSING of note. Despite the hopes of many, including the Southport backers of the Formby Land & Building Co. launched in 1875 (and wound up in 1902 with only a few houses erected), development w of the railway did not proceed substantially until the C20. The most interesting building is SANDHILLS COTTAGES, out amongst the pines on the edge of the dunes, E of ALBERT ROAD. This is a pair by *A.H. Mackmurdo*, built in 1882 as a holiday cottage for Albert Crompton, who worked for the ship-owner Alfred Holt in Liverpool. He let the other half. Simple, as befits the purpose; now altered. Two storeys and six bays, with half-hipped tile roof and shaped wooden ground-floor veranda on the s side. Weatherboarding, roughcast and tile-hanging, with remnants on the rear of Japanese-pattern half-timbering to the upper floor.

The oddest houses are certainly TOWER HOUSE and TOWER GRANGE on Grange Lane, a fairytale vernacular fantasia of whitewashed brick gables and projections, wonky tile and thatched roofs and windows of all shapes and sizes. They are largely a creation from 1904 by *C.A. Atkinson*, which makes use of salvaged materials, and is said to include the remnants of a medieval grange of Whalley Abbey. Perhaps it is more likely that Atkinson's starting point was farm buildings of the C17 or so.

FORMBY HALL is outside Formby itself, some 1¾ m. NE on Southport Old Road. The house is ascribed to the early C17, and made of brick of this date. The three-bay façade has been altered, with all the characteristics of early C19 Neo-Tudor, i.e. big hoodmoulds over square-headed heavy mullioned windows with ogee lights, and in the l. and r. attachments curious doorways with truncated ogees. There are battlements too. But all this may be earlier, because John Formby, †1776, was a close friend of Horace Walpole's associate in Gothic Revival explorations, John Chute. The house was rebuilt from dereliction in the 1980s, after the floors and internal walls had collapsed.

GARSWOOD

5090

Seneley Green

Scattered farms, then collieries in the C19, and then a dormitory in the later C20.

HOLY TRINITY, Rectory Road, North Ashton. 1837–8, by *John Palmer*. Built as a chapel of ease to St Oswald Winwick (q.v.), which Palmer had repaired in 1836, it soon became Ashton-in-Makerfield's first parish church. Yellow ashlar. The sides have the familiar long lancets between buttresses, but the W front is unusual. It has rudimentary W transepts containing the stairs to the W gallery, with two lancets each, and a small tower of 1937–8 with an octagonal top stage which is un-Gothic despite lancet bell openings. This replaced a bellcote and shallow porch; its pointed door has been reused. The chancel, of 1914, has stepped triple lancets and a N organ chamber. The nave is broad and aisle-less with shallow spidery roof trusses. These have raked struts with bracing between forming sloping pointed arches. – W GALLERY on spindly cast-iron columns with Gothic-panelled front, original BOX PEWS and free BENCHES. – CHANCEL WOODWORK. 1914. Richly and thickly carved, but without much grace. It includes a couple of misericords. – CHANDELIERS. Two, C18, brass and handsome. From a demolished local house. – STAINED GLASS. Good *Shrigley & Hunt* work in the chancel, E window *c.* 1914, N and S lancets a few years earlier. Nave N, 1st E. The last surviving patterned window from the 1830s.

The OLD RECTORY next door is 1840, thought to be by *Palmer* too, and with a later S addition. Irregular, but not exactly picturesque. Jacobethan of sorts, with lots of gables. Tall octagonal chimneys taken down.

OUR LADY IMMACULATE (R.C.), Downall Green Road, Bryn. *See* Ashton-in-Makerfield.

SENELEY GREEN GRAMMAR SCHOOL (former), School Lane, Garswood. Now a library. On land gifted in 1589, and apparently built immediately. In 1728 it was rebuilt at a cost of £65. A simple stone rectangle of two storeys and three bays, with puzzling fenestration. The two-light mullioned windows, the larger ones with transoms, certainly look more C17 than C16, but might they actually form part of the 1728 works? Knight's Hall, Up Holland (q.v.), 6 m. N, dated 1716, has mullioned windows with the same distinctive hoodmoulds, simple monoliths with ends finished at 45 degrees. Yet even by the standards of the county, mullioned-and-transomed in the late 1720s would be very conservative. On the S side a low gabled extension, probably of the date of the plaque in the E gable – 1902. First floor removed and ceiling inserted.

MANOR HOUSE, Garswood Road, Garswood. Small, possibly C17 or earlier, but bookended improbably by two-bay Georgian extensions of different scale and character (i.e. vertical not horizontal). All now rendered. The door has a huge fanlight and bolection moulding, suggesting an earlyish C18 date.

GARSWOOD NEW HALL, SE of the village, was palatially expanded in the style of Nash by *John Foster Jun.*, *c.* 1828, and demolished in 1921. At the junction of Millfield Lane and Liverpool Road (the A58, 1 m. SSE) impressive Edwardian GATEPIERS and railings remain. Further S on the E side of the lane is what is known as the DOWER HOUSE, reputed to be of *c.* 1820s and by *Foster* too. It is one-storeyed, stuccoed, asymmetrical and very odd, with a doorway with thick, heavy Tuscan columns and broad windows with rectangular surrounds but round-arched lights – a combination of the French Revolution with Henry VIII. The cipher is of Sir John Gerard, the owner. Could it have been offices really, or the steward's house? The park, landscaped by *Humphry Repton* in 1796, is now a golf course.

HOLLIN HEY FARMHOUSE, N of Old Garswood Road, 1¼ m. SW. Stone ground floor with mullioned-and-transomed windows, dated 1680 with the initials TG (Thomas Gerard?). First floor rebuilt in polychromatic brick in 1875.

TITHE BARN FARM, Tithe Barn Road, ¼ m. SSW. Model Victorian farm with architectural embellishments.

GATHURST *see* ORRELL

GLAZEBROOK

Rixton-with-Glazebrook

6090

A linear village of little attraction along the B5212. Three CHAPELS date from the growth that followed the draining of the mosses in the 1870s: the Free Methodist, the Salvation Barracks and the Primitive Methodist. The latter, 1908, shiny red brick and buff terracotta, the least modest.

STATION. Of the same Cheshire Lines Committee design as Widnes (q.v.), with gables with divers patterns to the bargeboards. The water basin on the Liverpool platform with dock leaf in a pointed arch is dated 1872. A pretty row of COTTAGES as at Padgate Station, Warrington (q.v.).

GLAZEBURY

6090

Glazebury is quite a large village strung out along the A574 with numerous C19, C18 and a few C17 houses and weavers' cottages, virtually all 'modernised' in the later C20 with miserable visual consequences. Two plain C19 Methodist chapels. There was a cotton mill alongside the railway.

ALL SAINTS. 1851, by *E.H. Shellard*. A pretty coursed rubble exterior with reticulated tracery. Bellcote, aisle-less. No chancel arch. Elegant oak PEWS.

HURST HALL BARN, Hurst Lane. A fascinating, important and enigmatic fragment of a medieval timber-framed hall of rare construction. There is a reference to an estate in 1311, and from the C14 to the C18 at least it was held by a branch of the Holcroft family (*see* Holcroft Hall, Culcheth). Beyond that we know little. Adjoining the S gable of the present Late Victorian farmhouse is a barn with a spectacular roof, which appears to be the substantial part of a possibly C14 hall. The S side is largely open and the gable ends are modern brick. Between them are four bays, not all of the same length, with three tiers of quatrefoil wind-braces (some missing), ridge purlin and four trusses of three different designs. From the E, with suggested interpretation of their functional relationship to the possible plan of the former hall, these are: a cusped kingpost and raked struts with a tie-beam, moulded on the W side only with rolls and hollows (possibly a spere truss, with the screens passage to the E, hence the moulding on the W side only; however, there is little convincing evidence for spere posts). Next, an arch-braced collar (associated with an open hearth). Third, another kingpost and raked strut truss, the kingpost an uncusped replacement, this time with an arch-braced and cambered tie-beam. Finally, a similar truss, now missing its arch bracing (the W end of the hall, and the site of the dais). Or, in fact, was the dais at the E end, rather than the screens? The third truss is supported on massive posts, with broad arch braces (one lost) to the deep wall-plate running between the gable ends which supports the others. The posts are magnificent: T-section, 20 in. (50 cm.) wide with a splay rising from cheeks at the foot to the tie-beam, and all this fashioned from a single, monumental piece of timber. They stand on sandstone padstones, and there are remnants of an interrupted sill. The sandstone plinth is largely replaced by brick. Mortices in the wall-plate indicate the former position of intermediary posts. No corner posts or closed trusses survive; was the hall ever more than four bays long?

This type of kingpost roof is peculiar to the North West and the West Riding, but the nearest parallel for the combination with cusping and raked struts was Stand Old Hall, Whitefield, N of Manchester, which also became a barn and collapsed in the 1960s. Stand had speres and the same characteristically massive timbers as Hurst. These, especially the very broad posts and braces, are reminiscent of the so-called 'plank framing' tradition of Lancashire and N Cheshire (e.g. Baguley Hall, Wythenshawe, Manchester), where frame timbers are quite dramatically wider than they are deep – more like planks.

LIGHT OAKS HALL, Light Oaks Road. The hall was newly rebuilt when its owner, Henry Traves, died in 1626. Traves, with lead mining interests in the High Peak, was easily the wealthiest man in the extensive Leigh parish and his new house has an extremely fine E front, even after the S bay (which contained the parlour) was demolished *c.* 1947, leaving the centre bay and N bay. Two storeys. The old centre bay has ten-light mullioned-and-transomed windows with a king mullion, and the N bay a similar five-light window. All have hoodmoulds. Between is the original studded door, in a heavy chamfered surround with a four-centred arch. This is all sandstone (some replacement), but the building is brick, constructed in diaper pattern above the ground floor. A rear wing projects at the N end, where there is a massive chimneystack (there was a matching wing behind the demolished s bay). The house is only now double-pile because of a 1960s extension filling in the remaining L. The front door opens directly into the dining room (as described in a 1626 valuation) filling the centre bay, lined with immaculate early C17 oak panelling removed from the chamber above in the C20. The fire surround and overmantel have lozenges and attached colonnettes etc. as one would expect for the date, but are said to be a C20 creation. If so it is extremely convincing. A central armorial panel is attached. Two others flank it; a fourth, with combined arms and the date 1657, is above a door. They are all C17 and postdate the wainscoting. They relate to the family of Traves' nephew Sir Henry Slater, to whom the estate fell in 1655. Sir Henry's arms are the central panel. The doors have cocks-head hinges. There was no staircase in the surviving C17 building, but presumably one in the demolished part.

THE RAVEN INN, Warrington Road. Said to be of 1562, but under the C20 fake timber frame it is brick, and double-pile, and so unlikely to be any earlier than the early C18.

GOLBORNE

A few farms and weavers' cottages in the N of Winwick parish until a cotton mill opened in 1839 and a colliery c. 1870 (closed 1989). Now it has distribution warehousing. The PETER KANE MEMORIAL SQUARE of 2000 is the centre of the industrial township, ringed by four little chapels of the 1860s–70s of the usual denominations, and the Co-operative Central Buildings, police station, terraces etc. The square is an attempt at placemaking rather let down by gaps and scarred gables. On BRIDGE STREET, s, is some pre-industrial housing, altered, but still happily grouped. On GOLBORNE ROAD and ASHTON ROAD are many early C19 handloom-weavers' cottages. PARK ROAD has biggish villas, e.g. Nos. 51 and 53–55, gently Gothic with gables. No. 51 is particularly charming. Under C17 brick, No. 37 BARN LANE is partially timber-framed. The village now merges with Lowton to the E (q.v.).

ST THOMAS, Church Street. Chancel, nave, s aisle and w tower with low pyramidal roof are by *Joseph Clarke*, 1848–c. 1851. Next come the N organ loft, dated 1906, and two bays of a planned N aisle, now a chapel. *Heaton, Ralph & Heaton* supplied designs for such additions in 1897. Then, in 1924–7, the present s vestries were built and the chancel raised, to designs by *F.E. Howard*. The quarry-faced stone holds the disparate elements together; the tracery is mainly Dec or Perp. Finally, a two-storey parish hall opened in 1999 where the rest of the N aisle would have been. Stone-faced with Gothic windows and quite archaeological in its details, though the attempt to resolve the awkward roof lines of the w gable is unsatisfactory. Inside: stumpy, circular arcade columns, crocketed ogee doors to the s vestry, and an oriel window looking down into the N chapel from the new hall. – STAINED GLASS. E window, a memorial to the Rev. Charles Quick, †1885, by *Enfield & Schmidt*. N chapel, a memorial to the victims of a pit disaster, 1980. – FIRST WORLD WAR MEMORIAL, sited axially in front of the tower. In the form of an Anglo-Saxon Cross.

LAWSON'S FARMHOUSE, Bridge Street. Tucked behind TOWN FARMHOUSE, dated 1740, is this C17 brick building. Twin-gabled two-bay elevation. (The interior includes a large plasterwork panel, probably early C17, in the principal room – a bush bearing fruits, acorns etc. all in deep relief. Also, an inglenook with firehood, and a staircase with heavy turned balusters. Philip Powell.) There is a C17 garden wall.

GOLBORNE PARK. *See* Newton-le-Willows.

LIGHTSHAW HALL, Lightshaw Lane, 1½ m. N. Now a farm-house with fragments of a moat around it. Plain brick exterior of two storeys and three bays, with a little two-storey E wing, but with wall-plates and two replacement wall-posts in the almost completely blank W wall hinting at the magnificent timber frame inside. This has been dendro-dated to the mid 1550s (in 1554 the owner, Henry Kighley, died and left Light-shaw to his son, but reserved it for his widow); it appears to be that of an upper wing to a now vanished hall, containing a great chamber above a parlour.

The principal surviving elements of the timber frame are the trusses dividing the bays, and the wall-posts that support them. The s truss has a kingpost flanked by impressive pierced qua-trefoil panels. It appears to have been open on the first floor

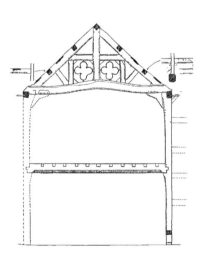

Golborne, Lightshaw Hall.
Section of the timber frame

to a solar or great chamber. A chimney was later built against the S side of the truss and the room divided and ceiled. The N truss is closed. It has queenposts, and a massive reused tie-beam, dendro-dated to the late C13 (the first mention of a hall at Lightshaw is C13). Three doors were inserted beneath it, one with a Tudor head. The ground floor appears to replicate the arrangement of a one-bay N room and a two-bay S room, subsequently divided. On this floor there are four excellently and identically moulded beams. Empty mortises in the wall-posts testify to the arrangement of external framing before this was replaced by the brick walls from the C17 onwards. A door leads to a 'paddy shant' for migrant labourers in the basement. The E wing is built of C17–C19 bricks. Windows are mainly modern copies of C18 originals.

There are still a great many unanswered questions about Lightshaw. How was the solar originally heated? Where were the stairs to it? What did the C13 tie-beam belong to? The building is clearly a fragment of a larger complex – pieces of timber and stone have been found beneath the ground around the farmhouse – but exactly where were the hall and service ranges? The blank W wall and C18 maps both suggest the hall may have abutted that side. Were the bits of cruck framing reused in a BARN SE of the house a part of it?

GREAT ALTCAR 3000

Straggling thinly along the crooked B5195 E of Formby, across flat reclaimed marshland.

ST MICHAEL. An utterly charming church of 1878–9 by *John Douglas*, built at the expense of the 4th Earl of Sefton to replace a little Georgian chapel, in a round churchyard. One of a small group by him that are timber-framed, inspired by the timber medieval churches of Cheshire, such as Lower Peover. Five-bay nave with a bell-turret over the W gable, a N passage aisle under the same roof and a lower chancel. Red tiled roof. The framing is mainly close studding and the windows are flat-headed with cusped ogee-headed lights. Most have three or four lights; the transomed, five-light W window is particularly handsome. The bell-turret with a low-fitting pyramid roof. The N vestry and organ chamber is a very careful composition of gables and roofs, and a brick porch. Inside is spacious and light, but cosy. The roof is a marvellous forest of timber, the nave with collared trusses, close-studded vertical struts, and wind-braces. The chancel roof is more elaborate. A braced timber arcade to the N passage aisle; in the W bay of the nave the timber structure supporting the bell-turret. Everywhere the wood has texts carved into it. The FITTINGS, chancel rails, pulpit etc., are carved timber designed by *Douglas* too, in his vernacular-cum-Gothic style (though the painted tiled panels of the REREDOS by *Heaton, Butler & Bayne* were destroyed). –

STAINED GLASS. In the W window one light by *Edward Frampton*, 1885. – LYCHGATE. Matching, and no doubt by *Douglas*.

Great Altcar is by and large an estate village, and most of the housing bears early C20 dates and the cross Moline of the Molyneuxs of Croxteth (*see* p. 406), lords of the manor since the C16.

HILL HOUSE FARMHOUSE, Causeway Lane, 1¼ m. ESE of the church. 1673. Sandstone rubble. C19 r. extension under three gables.

OLD GORE FARMHOUSE, Altcar Lane. *See* Lydiate.

₃₀₉₀   GREAT CROSBY

On the N edge of the Liverpool conurbation and for the most part comfortable leafy suburbia. The centre has been cut up by a little ring road. Home Farm on Cooks Road, which may have been C16, was cleared away for it and The Green has been reduced to a roundabout and supermarket car park. Great Crosby now merges with Blundellsands and Waterloo (qq.v.).

ST FAITH. *See* Waterloo, p. 642.
ST LUKE, Liverpool Road. 1853–4, by *A. & G. Holme*. Still the aisle-less early C19 type with transepts and apse, but more archaeologically correct in the Dec details. W tower with angle buttresses and broach spire. Pale quarry-faced sandstone. A fire in 1972 destroyed much of the E end. Repaired by *Saunders Boston* and reopened in 1975, with a new roof that has a web of steel tension rods and hangers, a new apse to which are attached vestries etc. like three Modernist chapels, and the architects' new CHANCEL FITTINGS. The box pews were replaced by PEWS from the demolished St Benedict, Everton, of 1886–7. – STAINED GLASS. Transept windows with glass of 1866–84 by *Capronnier*, restored after the fire.
ST MICHAEL, Downhills Road. *See* Blundellsands, p. 153.
ST PETER AND ST PAUL (R.C.), Liverpool Road. 1892–4, by *Sinnott, Sinnott & Powell*, replacing a classical box of 1826 with a top-heavy tower. Yellow quarry-faced sandstone and red sandstone ashlar dressings. The big W front and the presbytery form a good group set back from the road. Six-light W window with tracery of a Geometrical-cum-Perp variety. The interior, as so often with these architects, is quite unoriginal. It is the tried and tested combination of a tall nave, big arcades on muscular round piers, transepts and shallow apsidal chancel. No clerestory (the aisles are tall) and no chancel arch. There is the usual W gallery and small N and S chapels. – FITTINGS. Heavy, painted stone (and possibly marble). The REREDOS has niches and goes around three sides of the apse. – ALTAR. Reordered *c.* 1985 with a simple new altar W of the chancel, and the

removal of the High Altar. The tabernacle pedestal is presumably made up of fragments of it.

UNITED REFORMED CHURCH, Eshe Road and Mersey Road. 1897–8. A rare Nonconformist church by *Douglas & Fordham*, built for the Congregationalists. Substantial and good. Squared red sandstone, a flèche; grouped lancets except for Geometrical windows in the N transept and the W end. The latter, a splendid big free composition, is flanked by beefy corner buttresses topped by octagonal turrets. The whole is very satisfying. Inside, low arcades and unusual hammer beam roof. Connected to the r. by a link is a large gabled hall. This is *F & G. Homes'* school room of the mid 1880s. – REREDOS. A First World War memorial with gesso work by *Joseph Lawton*, 1920. – The STAINED GLASS of the E window, by *Shrigley & Hunt* (design attributed to *Carl Almquist*), also forms part of the memorial. – N aisle, two lancets by *Edward Frampton*.

WESLEYAN CHAPEL, Mersey Road. By *James F. Doyle*, opened 1891. Pale squared and coursed sandstone. Typical Methodist plan with transepts (here twin-gabled) and shallow E end. Dec-cum-Perp tracery. It had a NW steeple, but the W front was severely damaged by a bomb in 1941 and rebuilt without it. When reopened in 1958 it had new windows and a symmetrical arrangement of low, broad octagonal porch turrets to l. and r. The doors of these are now blocked and entry is into a new glazed narthex between the porches (where there had been a door until 1941). Various matching SCHOOLS at the rear.

NAZARETH HOUSE, Liverpool Road. The oldest part – nearest the road – is CROSBY HOUSE, a stuccoed five-bay, two-storey house with pediments over the outer bays and a Doric porch in the centre. Perhaps *c.* 1830–40. Next to it is a CHAPEL by *Pugin & Pugin*, opened 1911. Large, and characteristic of the practice, with accommodation for the sisters on the ground floor, beneath the chapel itself. More, undistinguished, buildings E and forward of the chapel; the principal part could conceivably be another work by Pugin & Pugin, but it is plain and the massive later roof structure is bizarre and ugly.

TOWN HALL. *See* Waterloo, p. 643.

LIBRARY and CIVIC HALL, Liverpool Road. *See* Waterloo, p. 644.

LIBRARY, College Road. 1904–5, by *Anderson & Crawford* of Liverpool. Andrew Carnegie paid for it. Hard red brick and stone with English Renaissance and Baroque touches. Asymmetrical. Big stone octagonal turret with copper cap; little dome over the porch.

THE MERCHANT TAYLORS' SCHOOL FOR BOYS, Liverpool Road. 1878, by *Lockwood & Mawson*. A picturesque range with tall central tower, of red brick and stone dressings. The centre is symmetrical, with classrooms flanking the tower, but the end pavilions differ: one has a hipped roof, the other is gabled with a massive mullioned-and-transomed bay window. Mostly this frontage is only a single storey, but a high one. The style of course is Gothic. The tower has the entrance portal at the base and the top has four thin tourelles with arcaded lancets between, and above the parapet a timber pyramid raised up on a stage of louvres and broken halfway by another. Pretty LODGE, and assorted residences and later teaching blocks. Thankfully these have yet to impinge on the setting of the 1878 façade, which in archetypal fashion looks out across the cricket pitch.

THE MERCHANT TAYLORS' SCHOOL FOR GIRLS, Liverpool Road. A jumble of late C19 and later blocks jammed against each other; but hidden behind them away from the road and facing W towards the sea is the original boys' school, founded in 1620 by John Harrison. The building, which may have been completed in 1622, is quite large for an early C17 school. Sandstone with a stone tile roof. Two-storeyed, with a two-storey porch. Mullioned-and-transomed windows with hollow-chamfered mullions. They are of eight lights on the ground floor and fourteen on the first floor (one each side of the porch), and have nicely profiled king mullions. Round-arched porch entrance. Pretty frieze of *paterae* on the façade string course. At the back a staircase projection with a six-light window on each floor and a late C18 doorway.

SACRED HEART SCHOOL, Liverpool Road. Set back from the E side. Opened 1908. Red brick, two-and-a-half storeys and eleven bays, the outer ones projecting forwards as shallow wings. In the centre a castellated tower with big two-centred portal; otherwise largely free Tudor style, with mullioned-and-transomed windows.

LIVERPOOL ROAD (A565), running N–S, has always been the principal thoroughfare of Great Crosby. In addition to the buildings listed above there are a few Late Georgian houses with enriched doorways of types familiar from Liverpool, and assorted C19 villas too. The N end is pedestrianised and has two good Tudorbethan PUBS. The best, now called The Village, is dated 1901. It is in fact a whole, curving corner block. The ground floor is red ashlar, above which the outer sections are rendered upper parts with splendid panels of pargetting, dormers and wooden mullioned windows. In the centre are three gabled bays of lavishly and very expertly detailed half-timbering, e.g. terms, pilasters, arcading, rinceau friezes and concave-sided lozenge panelling. On the opposite corner The George is of 1929 and Tudorbethan again, with a similar mix of materials. Handsomely and more freely composed. Well detailed too, but as one would expect for its date not as intricately as its earlier neighbour. Beyond it Liverpool Road is closed by the windowless side of a Sainsbury supermarket – advantageous for them, terrible for the townscape.

MOOR PARK. 1890s onwards. A group of leafy streets N of Moor Lane with attractive middle-class-sized semis in Garden Suburb style (pebbledash, wooden casements, tile roofs), and also some in Stockbroker Tudor. No. 35 ELM AVENUE stands out for its purer, Voyseyish Art and Crafts appearance.

GREAT SANKEY *see* WARRINGTON

HAIGH

Pronounced 'Hay'. On a high wooded hill dropping down into the leafy dene of the River Douglas, with fine views to the s and sw of Wigan and the Lancashire Plain beyond. The estate and park of Haigh Hall dominate. From the c14 this was the home of the Bradshaigh family and subsequently of the Lindsays, Earls of Balcarres and (from 1808) Crawford, until in 1947 Wigan Corporation bought it and opened the park to the public. It is now a beautiful, sylvan escape on the town's doorstep. Haigh was once famed for its cannel, a hard black coal that burns brilliantly without smoke, and could be carved into ornaments. The Bradshaighs were mining it from at least the c16 and it made them and then the Lindsays rich; the hill is dotted with old mine workings. The GREAT SOUGH is the most important early remnant, a tunnel built in 1653–70 to drain the Bradshaighs' Park Pit. At over a thousand yards it was a significant engineering achievement. It was quadrupled in length over subsequent centuries to an outfall into the Yellow Brook in the Lower Plantations.

ST DAVID, Copperas Lane. By *Thomas Rickman & Henry Hutchinson*, 1830–3. A Commissioners' church (cost £3,433). Nave with bellcote and chancel. Curious tooling – heavy and banded. Narrow repetitious bays of thin buttresses and long lancet windows, shafted inside with shaft-rings, which shows Rickman's antiquarian leanings. Wide interior, originally possibly with galleries. Broad flat ceiling flatly panelled with large spiked quatrefoils. The E end was extended in 1886 by *J. Medland Taylor*. It is tripartite and has a hammerbeam roof. Medland Taylor probably also did the tripartite stone W gallery. The baptistery is under its S arch. – FONT. A cube with corner pendants on a round pedestal. – STAINED GLASS. S, 3rd from E, by *Heaton, Butler & Bayne*. – The substantial stone LYCHGATE, 1909, has scary winged beasts bursting from the corners of the eaves.

OUR LADY OF THE IMMACULATE CONCEPTION (R.C.), Haigh Road. *See* Aspull.

Little of interest in the small village. 1 m. WNW is RED ROCK LANE with a number of c17 and c18 cottages and farms and an 1870s school with Tudor Gothic windows. At its W end, spanning the River Douglas, is a dye works, with two rows of housing called LAKESIDE COTTAGES. The earlier (N) group – dating from either side of 1860 – have label moulds and wide eaves.

HAIGH HALL AND ESTATE

HAIGH HALL was built 1827–*c.* 1844 by the *7th Earl of Balcarres*, almost certainly to his own designs and reputedly at a cost of

£100,000. The house is austerely impressive and so massively
built in superb Parbold grit ashlar that it seems indestructible.
This is just as well because the magnificent position is very
exposed, near the top of the hill looking out w over Wigan as
far as Snowdonia and the Isle of Man. Moreover, the previous
house (with medieval fragments and C17 and C18 wings) had
suffered from subsidence due to old mine workings.

The last male Bradshaigh died in 1770. The estate came to
Alexander Lindsay, the 6th Earl of Balcarres, through marriage. When he came to live here in 1802 he found the old
house ruinous and the furniture sold off, so he set about its
repair and refitting. This continued up to his death in 1825,
when his son James, the 7th Earl, almost immediately halted
work to build anew. James, an inventor, engineer and biblio-
phile, continued the modernisation of the estate's mines and
foundry begun by his father (*see* p. 187). He was also an enthu-
siastic architect, designing not only the Hall but a number of
estate buildings as well. Whether he took any professional
advice or assistance we do not know.

53   EXTERIOR. The house is a robust stand-alone square, of
three storeys, with a heavy modillion cornice and urns on the

Haigh Hall.
Ground-floor plan

parapet (now removed) all around, but no other decoration.*
Work began on the NE wing (services and bedrooms) in 1827,
and on the SW wing overlooking the park and view in 1828.
This was roofed and furnished by the end of 1832. It has seven
bays, three of them full-height canted bays, a curiously out-of-
time feature that may be a nod to the three bays of the early
C17 front it replaced. Along the first floor is a balcony with an
ornamental cast-iron balustrade, made at the *Haigh Foundry*.
The SE (entrance) front was not erected until 1836–40, the
1720s wing it replaced remaining occupied until then. The
centre seven bays (of eleven) may be the C18 brick front
refaced. In 1844 the Tuscan portico was added, with columns
arranged 2–1–1–2. It is built of a different stone after the
Parbold quarries used previously had been exhausted. Since
then the only addition to the exterior is the penthouse behind
the parapet on the NE side, with a rainwater head dated 1865,
built to house family offspring.

The INTERIOR is notable chiefly for a series of rich and
impressive plaster ceilings. *M. Stuber* of Paris was paid £237
for plaster ornament, cases of which arrived between 1828 and
1832. *Robert Hughes & Sons* of Manchester were paid much
more for plastering ceilings and walls, and another firm for
supplying moulds. So what belongs to whom, and who provided the overall design? Probably, the most elaborate elements
are Parisian, and the rest was made around them. So to the
plan. The ENTRANCE HALL is in the centre of the SE front,
with a beamed ceiling, anthemion frieze and two black marble
fireplaces, supplied by the *Esher Street Marble Works*, London,
for £78. The STAIRCASE HALL behind, oddly not on axis with   54
the entrance hall, is magnificently spacious and has a glorious
plaster pendentive vault, with a glazed central dome. The
superb plasterwork includes friezes with griffins and acanthus
scrolls – French? – and swags and masks. Beneath this rises the
grand flying imperial staircase, with an elaborate cast-iron
balustrade. Here and elsewhere the doors are oak, with pol-
larded panels. The BREAKFAST ROOM is to the l. in the S
corner. Across its end wall is a blind, finely carved oak arcade
with Composite pilasters, saved from the staircase hall of the
demolished 1720s wing. It was carved by *Timothy Rannigar* and
Peter Meredith. The breakfast room is now knocked into the
LONG LIBRARY, occupying most of the SW front. On the first
floor above these are the SALOON (?) in the S corner and then
an ANTE-ROOM, with a more delicately plastered apse with
niches, leading into the massive DRAWING ROOM. This has
rich and heavy ceiling plasterwork of overlapping lozenge compartments and lots of the Parisian Neoclassical griffins, torches

---

*Little card models survive of two alternative schemes for the Hall: one for new
three-storey additions to the existing C17 and C18 wings, and another for a new
building, basically U-plan, with embattled parapet.

etc., but employed in isolated groups, not as part of a convincingly integrated design. Behind this on the NW front is the original DINING ROOM, with another good ceiling – panels with symbols and the family arms, but English not French in design. The marble fireplace is one of a number from the old house adapted and reused (*see* also the saloon). The room also contains the base of an ornate bookcase. Remarkably, this is the only one left in the house, for James and especially his son Alexander, the 8th Earl, were passionate bibliophiles with one of the finest private libraries in Europe. By the mid C19 this dining room, the drawing room and another ground-floor room had all become additional libraries, with fitted bookcases all the way round; 'walls, tables, shelves, rooms, passages and finally floors were covered with books', recalled the 8th Earl's daughter. Was there any other house with so many public rooms given over to books? As a result, archaically, the entrance hall was pressed into service as the dining room.

The principal BEDROOMS were along the SE front. In the E corner is more of *Rannigar*'s excellent early C18 woodwork carefully reused: a STAIRCASE with three square columns on vase balusters to each tread, round column newels and carved tread ends. In 1873 the house was redecorated at a cost of £80,000 for the visit of the Prince and Princess of Wales, but nothing of this remains. The interiors are rather sadly empty now, not helped by the current choice of paints and carpets. There are none of the many Parisian pieces bought by the 7th Earl, nor any part of the excellent picture collection. Only one piece of furniture survived the 1947 sale; many of the books were gifted to the John Rylands Library, Manchester.

Throughout the building is evidence of the 7th Earl's inquisitive and ingenious mind: the ashlar was cut by a steam saw invented by him; most of the windows to the public rooms are to the Earl's 'combination' design (also found elsewhere on the estate), with a single sash above and inward-swinging casements in the lower part which opened automatically with pressure on the handle, and which drop when closed into a draught-proof metal channel; the roof trusses are strengthened by suspended iron tension rods; and central hot-air heating was supplied by seven basement stoves through flues to brass grilles in the skirting.

The STABLES, dated 1865, are by the *7th Earl* too. Though he studied a number of grand local examples, they are decidedly common in comparison with the house. Red brick with yellow brick trim. Italianate tower with pyramid roof over the entrance. SE wing converted to café and shop etc. in 1989, NW wing to a golf shop with tinted-glazed external lift tower under an aping pyramid roof in 2001 by *Wigan Metropolitan Council Architects Department*.

The PARK is spacious and in places wild and wooded and romantic, though less so since a golf course was laid out over part. Nothing remains of the formal gardens shown in Kip & Knyff's *Britannia Illustrata*, 1707, nor of a number of structures

(which included, later, a Gothic eyecatcher called the Obser-
vatory and a structure made entirely of cannel), and very little
of subsequent layouts. The LANCASHIRE CANAL South
Branch, excavated in the 1790s and now part of the Leeds and
Liverpool Canal (*see* Aspull), ambles through the park below
the house, crossed by a number of contemporary stone
bridges. The main drive winds down through the Upper and
Lower Plantations (with a network of paths laid out, it is said,
to provide employment during the 1860s Cotton Famine)
across the canal and the River Douglas to PLANTATION GATE,
on Wigan Lane, an impressive ensemble with a central stone
arch flanked by lodges, all in austere Neoclassical style. The
arch has paired Doric pilasters either side; the lodges have set-
back Tuscan columns, two to the outside and two to the park
side. This group is contemporary with the hall and is presumably by the *7th Earl* again. There is another good C19 LODGE
at the end of Hall Lane, U-plan with hipped roof, broad eaves
and round-headed windows.

Estate Buildings

There are a number of pleasant Loudonesque estate buildings,
many attributed to the *7th Earl*. Most are of brick with gables,
frilly bargeboards, label moulds and cast-iron casements; many
have iron porches of geometric design and good staircases.

ESTATE OFFICES, New Road. Now Latham House. Symmetrical, of two storeys, with Neo-Jacobean bits. 1892.

HAIGHLANDS, N of Copperas Lane. Despite the recycled 1720
datestone, built in the mid C19 for Colin Lindsay, a son of the
7th Earl, who complained it was too low and too small. The
architect was presumably the *7th Earl*; it has his 'combination'
windows (*see* Haigh Hall).

HAIGH COTTAGE, Hall Lane. Built in the 1820s and extended
in the 1840s. An incremental total of six bays. Stone.

HAIGH HOUSE, Haigh Road (in the village). Another of the
higher-status examples.

HAIGH FOUNDRY, Leyland Mill Lane. In 1788 the 6th Earl, with
his brother and a Wigan iron-founder, Corbett, established the
Haigh Foundry here, incorporating the Brock Mill forge into
the operation. In 1812 it built Lancashire's first steam locomotive. Other products included structural ironwork and
swing bridges for the Albert Dock, Liverpool (q.v.), and the
ironwork of Haigh Hall. The Foundry closed in 1885 and the
original foundry building is demolished, but the site remains
in manufacturing use. s of the lane are cast-iron gateposts and
a stone, four-storey, mid-C19 range beside the River Douglas;
N under the railway arch along the riverbank are two brick
ranges and a chimney of similar age. At Brock Mill, ½ m. N
along WINGATES ROAD, is a pretty row of three rubble COT-
TAGES dated 1821 (now two, blocked door r.) for Foundry

employees, with cusped Gothic cast-iron casements. Philip Powell reports that Nos. 14–15 WINGATES ROAD, with large windows, an elegant stone staircase and a stone floor supported by cast-iron columns, was the Foundry drawing office.

HAIGH SAWMILLS, ¼ m. NW of Wigan Road, N of the Leeds and Liverpool Canal. 1839–41. Despite the modern name, this was the integrated central workshops for the 7th Earl's mines and barges. Dressed stone. Three bays, two storeys, with a clock set in the parapet of bold plain ashlar. On the roof an octagonal cupola with spindly Tuscan columns. Now a house, with replacement windows, it was the central office pavilion of a big three-sided court facing the canal. A pity the rest is lost.

HOME FARM, School Lane. Presumably by the *7th Earl*. Farmhouse, *c.* 1853 with Gothic casements. Farm buildings, 1853, a quadrangle with rusticated archway entrance. Both of brick with stone dressings.

MOAT HOUSE, to the N off Copperas Lane. Another building seemingly by the *7th Earl*. A villa, *c.* 1840: brick, gables and chimneys, on a medieval moated platform, the moat partly dry and integrated into the garden design. Built for a land agent.

THE RECEPTACLE, S of Hall Lane. Almshouses erected in 1772 by Dorothy, Lady Bradshaigh in memory of her husband Sir Roger. *Richard Melling* (an engineer) and *Michael Baker* (stonemason) were paid £5 for 'rearing' the building; a Mr Gudgeon was paid £1 for an estimate. Two storeys, coursed and dressed stone, with crude pointed window and door surrounds. On the ground floor were five apartments, each of a housebody, bedroom and buttery. The whole of the first floor was a common room, reached by an external stair at the S end. Converted *c.* 1985 into three two-storey houses.

SCHOOL, Copperas Lane. 1845, probably by the *7th Earl*. Symmetrical, brick, with three gables – quite handsome. Twin doors under the central gable, for girls and boys. Charming octagonal stone chimneys, grouped in fours. 'Combination' windows (*see* Haigh Hall).

Nos. 1–4 SCHOOL LANE. A pretty row of four cottages dated 1854. On the other side of the lane is the DAIRY, now residential. More brick, bargeboards, gables and stone dressings outside, and still with its vaulted and tiled dairy room inside. All presumably by the *7th Earl*.

WIND PUMP, S of Copperas Lane. Erected in 1845 to supply well water to John Sumner & Co.'s Haigh Brewery. It looks like a small brick windmill or a giant peppermill, with a curious bullet-shaped cap topped by a finial. Restored 1975. The brewery stood in the village, behind the Balcarres Arms, until the 1950s.

HALE

Mrs Thomas Carlyle wrote to her husband in 1844 that Hale was 'the beautifulest village in all England'. That may seem an extraordinary claim now, but despite the advance of Liverpool to within a couple of miles and the inevitable ugly C20 village extensions and house improvements, its rural tranquillity is still quite startling. Around Church End, at least, the village retains its preindustrial character. Hale was an important, though treacherous, fording point on the Mersey from at least the C12, until the Manchester Ship Canal intervened and the Widnes bridges were built. The ford was at the end of Within Way.

ST MARY, Church End. Modest embattled C14 W tower, much smoothed over, with diagonal buttresses and two-light belfry openings, with quatrefoils. The rest of 1758–9, though nothing remains inside of that date, or of the 1874 and 1903 restorations: a fire in 1977 left only the walls standing and revealed the foundations of a narrower, timber-framed church. This is unlikely to have been the building replaced in 1758: the rebuilding contract with *William Hatton* of Prescot, mason, stipulates that ashlar from the old building be reused. The windows have keyed-in arches, except for the W wall, where there are two circular windows, one on top of the other, either side of the tower. The broad, strikingly unembellished E wall has a central Venetian window, with pilaster mullions and a cherub in the keystone. At the E end of the N wall is a small gabled projection, and to the W the (Gothic) vestry of 1874. On the S side is a small porch and plaque above, marking the rebuilding.

The present appearance of the INTERIOR is entirely the creation of *Buxeby & Evans*, 1979–80, a space both calmer and grander than before. The richly panelled roof follows neither the C18 form, low, flat and corniceless, nor its Edwardian replacement, pitched and open. Why the neo-C17 form for a mid-C18 church? Five compartments, deeply coved and heavily moulded. The wood is varnished chestnut. – FITTINGS. The ORGAN GALLERY, W, on Tuscan columns, is a replica of one of 1759 destroyed in the fire (the E recess that previously housed an instrument is now a chapel). Other fittings come from a variety of sources. – The FONT under the tower was returned after a century adorning a garden. The bowl, with cherubs, C18. – The delightful early C17 oak PULPIT, on tiny Tuscan columns, comes by way of York Minster. – PEWS, from Paley & Austin's superb St Mary, Ince-in-Makerfield (q.v., sadly demolished), but unremarkable. – In the churchyard, S, the TOMB of John Middleton, the 'Childe of Hale', †1623, who grew to 9 ft 3 in. (2.8 metres) and was exhibited at James I's court. The simple stone slab, with inscription inlaid in lead, is set in railings, and is curiously only 6 ft (1.8 metres) long. Across the lane is the HISTORY TREE, 1996, the Childe carved *in situ* from a dead beech, patinated with images of the village and its history.

MANOR HOUSE, Church End. C17, partially rebuilt at the beginning of the C18. Not originally the manor house: at the time the house was given its remarkably ambitious, grand and 27 mysterious features, it was the parsonage. The vicar from *c.* 1703 was the Rev. William Langford, and his lavish remodelling must date from soon after that. The façade is of five bays, red sandstone and brick, two storeys with dummy *œil de bœuf* windows at the top and a balustraded parapet, with peculiarly slim balusters. Giant rusticated Doric pilasters mark the ends, and superimposed rusticated quoin pilasters delineate the middle bay. This has a broad doorway with Langford's monogram in a cartouche above the door, fluted engaged Corinthian columns, and a scrolled pediment containing Langford's arms; superimposed is a window flanked by long pilasters on huge brackets, both of dubious correctness, rising above the columns below; and on top is a pediment, naïvely carved. Round the corner to the r. the scheme continues with a shallow giant-arched recess and the start of another pediment, cut off abruptly and left unfinished. What can the full intention have been? Now it makes for an odd but instructive contrast with the humbler unrebuilt rear section, which is early C17, lower, and three-storeyed. Indeed from the rear the original house is revealed as a two-gabled structure, the N higher, probably later and two-storeyed, and the W façade no more than a thin theatrical screen built up above the gable ends. (The best interiors date from Langford's remodelling, a fine panelled entrance hall with fluted pilasters subdivided by an arch from a staircase with twisted and columnar balusters and fluted columnar newels, and a secondary staircase with endearing splat balusters. DCMS.)

LODGE, Church End, dated 1876, sub-Norman Shaw, to Hale Hall, demolished in the C20. This was an idiosyncratic C17 house with a W front of 1806 by *John Nash* echoing the earlier work. The unremarkable late C19 service buildings and the walled garden survive.

A number of C17, C18 and C19 whitewashed COTTAGES in the village. The best group, on Church End opposite the Manor House, is C17, single-storey, brick and thatched. Crucks inside. To the r. is No. 14, traditionally the Childe's home, with crucks also and an apparently rare surviving sleeping loft with ladder access (the standard arrangement in such single-storey cottages till the C20). These, and other cottages on the High Street, owe their survival complete with thatch and e.g. horizontal sliding sashes to *Peter Fleetwood-Hesketh*, architectural historian and last lord of the manor, who sympathetically modernised them to preserve the character of the village. At the w end of the village on the High Street (beyond No. 22, 1665; thatch, timber frame, cruck trusses), the old SCHOOL HOUSE. The four l. bays, with porch and cupola, 1739; rebuilt (reconstructed?) 1876 and extended r. Further w on Hale Road are eighteen 1930s *cottages ornés*, of one or two storeys, whitewashed, thatched and with fake timbering: superior interwar suburban housing rather sweetly dressed up in keeping with the village. A thatched garage is particularly enjoyable. At the other end of the village on Town and Carr lanes is a small estate

of AIREY PREFABRICATED HOUSES, erected *c.* 1950. All concrete (including overlapping cladding like weatherboarding);
gabled roofs. 20,000 of these, designed in 1925 by the Leeds
builder *Sir Edwin Airey*, were built in the late 1940s.

LIGHTHOUSE, Hale Point, Church Road. Handsome, of 1906,
standing 45 ft (13.7 metres) high at the southernmost point in
Lancashire. Closed 1958. It replaced an earlier lighthouse of
1836.

DUCK DECOY, ½ m. E off Hale Gate Road. A rare and elaborate
construction, dating at least from 1730 and possibly from a
century before that. Covering 5 acres (2 hectares), it has a
hexagonal moat (to keep vermin and trespassers out) crossed
by a little swing bridge. Within that, set amongst trees, is a pool
with five curved and tapering radiating creeks called 'pipes'.
Ducks were driven by dogs into these, and trapped by netting
carried over them by hoops. Disused since the early C20, after
draining of the Lancashire mosses sent duck numbers into
drastic decline.

DUNGEON WHARF, 1½ m. W at the end of Dungeon Lane. C18
red sandstone remains of a wharf on the Mersey that served a
saltworks established by 1697, and later a shipbreaking yard,
closed 1912.

HALEWOOD   *4080*

A very little village swamped by the post-war suburban advance
of S Liverpool. The E of the parish, extending to the banks of the
Mersey, is still essentially rural.

ST NICHOLAS, Church Road. The original building is a chapel
of ease of 1838–9 by *A.Y. & G.Williams*. This was an exceedingly
simple aisle-less red sandstone box, with lancets and a bellcote
over the W gable.* Its form is most evident from the NW; the
side lancets were always hoodmoulded, unlike the W openings.
In 1847 the pre-Ecclesiological transepts and tiny polygonal
apse were added. These have triplets of lancets, each of equal
height, squeezed into each of the three faces of the apse, which
was rebuilt in 1894. The SW tower, by *Cornelius Sherlock*, was
erected in 1882–3 and is a bit more correct, though quite small
and slim. The lowest stage is treated as a porch, and arched
open on three sides. Inside, as so often, the transepts cause
some complicated timber arrangements in the roof, which is
hammerbeamed over the nave. – BOX PEWS. – The pride of the
church is its STAINED GLASS, by *Morris & Co.* The sequence
begins with the lancets of the nave S side, of 1874; all the rest
were made by 1882, except of the three lancets of the chancel
E end, which are of 1892. The side lights of this group, which

---

*Nevertheless it was praised by the Bishop of Chester at the consecration as 'such
an exercise of architectural taste that . . . it may be recommended as a model to
those who have a similar design in view.'

are by *Morris* himself, are the only two not credited to *Burne-Jones*. These, and the other apse windows, are large single figures. – Windows in the transept ends by *W.H. Sullivan* of Liverpool, 1871. Both are poor, compared with Burne-Jones and Morris. It is curious that one has (still) a large pictorial scene, though the other has small scenes in medallions.

To the E a nice group of simple little former SCHOOLS and SCHOOL HOUSE. The first school, on the r. with a lancet in the gable, is of 1842; the matching Boys' School – on the l. side of the school house, so making a small court – is apparently as late as 1874. Behind the church is the OLD RECTORY, of *c.* 1843. Red ashlar and three bays, the r. a slightly projecting gable. Good entrance.

IRON AGE FARMSTEAD, Brook House Farm, Lower Road. Excavated in the 1990s. Two concentric ditches, *c.* 115 ft (35 metres) apart, enclose a roughly D-shaped area of *c.* 4 acres (1.6 hectares). Dated to the period after *c.* 300 B.C. Evidence for grain-storage structures and ancillary buildings, and short sections of boundary gullies, perhaps marking building plots or other activities. The massive inner ditch appears more a statement of prestige than a defensive feature. The less substantial outer ditch possibly formed an enclosure for herding cattle.

ROMANO-BRITISH HAMLET, Court Farm, N of Church Road. Over a dozen buildings have been found, dating from the C2–C4. Houses have an unusual figure-of-eight plan, like two conjoined round-houses, with a door in the middle of the long side. This appears to be a uniquely local type (*see* Introduction, p. 16).

HALE BANK. *See* Widnes, p. 658.

HALEWOOD CAR FACTORY. *See* Speke, p. 462.

HALSALL

One of the large ancient parishes. The village is still very small and straggly, set on a low elongated island in the flat, coastal (formerly moss) country between Southport and Ormskirk.

ST CUTHBERT. A large and picturesque medieval church which, though the current patina of the sandstone helps disguise it, was much restored by *Paley & Austin*, first in 1873 E of the chancel arch and then in 1886 W of it. The earliest features are Dec, including the four-bay arcades with octagonal piers and arches with sunk quadrants. The inner surround of the S aisle E window goes with the arcades, and also possibly the W tower, one of a group that includes Ormskirk and Aughton, i.e., square, continuing by broaches to an octagonal belfry stage, and finished with a spire (rebuilt entirely in 1852). These towers are early C14; this one has been altered or is later – see the later C14 or early C15 straight-headed two-light bell openings and the W window. No clerestory. Perp S porch and S doorway rebuilt in 1886. Noble transitional late Dec/early Perp

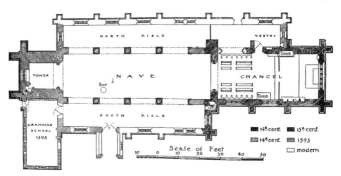

Halsall, St Cuthbert, plan.
(*Victoria County History of Lancashire*, vol. 3, 1907)

chancel with two rood turrets and big, tall, two-centred, three-light windows. Also crude pinnacles and worn gargoyles, including in the SE corner a man praying in a boat (the NE one is a C20 copy). The E window is of five lights. SEDILIA and PISCINA are more firmly Dec in style, forming a fine quadruple arcade, cusped and richly moulded. Also the N recess (*see* below), the pinnacled E statue recess and the wide and handsomely moulded, typically Dec doorway to the vestry. Rood stair S side only; access to N side via passage up and over the chancel arch. The window on the S side could be post-Reformation and hence meant to light a pulpit rather than rood. Attached to the S of the tower and the end of the S aisle is the former GRAMMAR SCHOOL, with formerly a 1593 datestone. It originally had two storeys. The present appearance, embattled with large two-light pointed windows, is C19 and like a chapel. The aisles were rebuilt in 1886 with straight-headed windows incorporating Paley & Austin's favourite Perp tracery. The wagon roof of the nave is a replacement of the same date. The chancel roof – of arch-braced collars – is original.

REREDOS. A painted triptych by *Shrigley & Hunt*, 1886. – FONT. C19 bowl, but the stem, of multiple shafts, is possibly early C14. – STALLS. Some parts late C15, with excellent MISERICORDS, e.g. two men wrestling. On the N side all but one are C19. – The ends with poppyheads and tracery. N aisle, remnants of the Ireland PEW, early C17, with arcading. – DOOR to the vestry, with reticulated, i.e. C14, tracery in the head. – STAINED GLASS. C14 fragments in the S aisle E window, with much ruby red, and N aisle W window, arranged by *Harry Harvey*, 1990. – *Hardman* glass in the chancel and tower window. 1850s–80s. – MONUMENTS. Boldly cusped recess in the N wall of the chancel, with crocketed gable and pinnacles. This is C14. The alabaster effigy of a priest within it may be early C16, but has been adapted to fit. It can plausibly be identified with Richard Halsall, rector 1513–63, who left instructions for a monument to be put in the recess on the N side of the chancel. – Overpainted tomb-chest with recumbent effigies of a knight and a lady. Sir Henry Halsall, †1523, and wife have been suggested. – Thomas Blundell, †1816. By *Crake* of London. Mourning woman by an urn with weeping willow. – BRASS by *John Hardman & Co.* to Lt William Astley Blundell, †1899. A scroll opened by kneeling angels with enamelled cartouche at the centre. – SUNDIAL in the churchyard, 1725. With big baluster stem.

FIRST WORLD WAR MEMORIAL, Halsall Road. By the church. Slender octagonal shaft with gabled head carved with the Crucifixion. It incorporates a cross base of possibly C15 date.

OLD RECTORIES. There are two. In the woods 200 yards N of the church are the remains of the medieval one – masonry discovered embedded in the rambling old rectory when it was demolished in the mid C19, and consolidated as a folly. It is the remnant of a wall with two-centred-arched doorways at either end. The jambs of two tall two-centred-arched windows are in the W part, with evidence of another door in the centre. There are stumps of assorted adjoining walls and other independent fragments, but the plan is not at all clear. It could be the N wall of a C14 or C15 hall range, the windows lighting the hall. A further ¼ m. NE on Halsall Road is *Sydney Smirke*'s large and dignified replacement of 1844–5, now called HALSALL HOUSE. Coursed, squared sandstone. Mainly Jacobethan. The entrance side is symmetrical, with a Gothic loggia of four-centred arches between gables to which tall octagonal chimneys are attached. Other elevations are more irregular, and in the SE corner is an octagonal turret with lancets and ogee cap. (Inside, a large Jacobean-style staircase and some good joinery and plasterwork. DCMS.)

HALSALL HALL, New Street, ¼ m. SW. This is a very odd building, low, long and brick. As restored for housing in the 1990s it has a symmetrical E façade of ten bays and two storeys. The two central bays have a gable with a small altered Venetian window and pilaster strips. The first-floor windows are sashes, now four-pane, but the ground floor has stone-mullioned windows regularly interspaced with five depressed-arched doorways. Quoins, string course and plinth. It was not as regular before restoration: the centre and the r. had tall ground-floor sashes and blank walls above, with a datestone of 1882. The W elevation has mullioned windows on both floors. Buried in the S cross-wall of the centre section is a blocked mullioned window. Attached to the ends of the W façade were farm buildings forming a yard.

So what is all this? The plan makes little sense for an C18 or C19 house: it is only single-depth. The bricks anyway are largely handmade and narrow – C17 or early C18. The buried mullioned window points to a C17 origin; the variety of mouldings in the external mullions may be evidence of phasing, or reuse. It was probably not even built as the Hall proper; there is archaeological evidence of a building to the NW. The key is perhaps the rainwater heads bearing the date 1769 and the initials of Charles Mordaunt. He was the first resident lord of the manor for a century and by 1779 had established a cotton mill at Halsall, which employed '160 poor children and women'. The enterprise, however, may not have survived the century. There is no evidence in the fabric that the Hall was the mill, but Mordaunt may have adapted and extended s an existing building as housing for employees, possibly using windows from elsewhere. One last puzzle is the stepped rock-cut 'tanks' under the s end of the building, connected to a channel. Their purpose remains obscure, but it has been posited that they predate the extension of the building over them in the C18.

LEEDS AND LIVERPOOL CANAL. On 5 November 1770 Halsall was the unlikely location for the first sod-cutting of this great enterprise, instigated in Leeds. The engineer of the first section was *John Longbotham*. There are a number of stone BRIDGES.

HASKAYNE *see* DOWNHOLLAND

HAYDOCK

5090

The archetypal colliery township: hard red brick C19 terraces, and C20 housing too, straggled out along a low ridge above the Sankey valley. There is no centre. To the w it merges with Blackbrook (*see* St Helens, p. 566). There was probably mining here in the C16, but it was with the arrival of the Sankey Brook Navigation (canal) in 1757 (*see* Introduction, p. 52) and then the nearby Liverpool & Manchester Railway in 1830 that exploitation got underway in earnest. The population rose from 734 in 1801 to 6,000 by the 1880s. The last pit closed in 1971. On the main street, CLIPSLEY LANE, are a couple of brick cottages, including No. 96, rendered, the little and exuberantly and freely Wrenaissance Conservative Club, built as the Tivoli Variety Theatre *c.* 1914, the former Cottage Hospital dated 1892 and 1896, and a couple each of simple C19 chapels and big pubs.

ST JAMES THE GREAT, Church Road (an extension of Clipsley Lane). This interesting church is actually three buildings. The first is the little former National School of 1837, with cusped lancets. Attached to its E is the first church proper, 1866 by *W. & J. Hay*. Tiny, brick, aisle-less. There were big doors between the two to accommodate overspill. The Hay building is now the N aisle of the second church. This is by *Douglas & Fordham*, 1889–91, and of unusual design – structural timber-framing with brick nogging, on a sandstone plinth. *John Douglas* had designed a series of timber churches twenty years earlier (e.g. St Michael, Great Altcar, q.v.). The technique was revived here because its flexibility offered protection against anticipated mining subsidence (and indeed the floor does now slide away to the s). The wooden windows are rectangular free Perp.

Originally there was a timber-framed E end too, crowned by a low tower and little spire, but this was taken down and rebuilt in brick and render (the framing on the interior is fake), without a tower, by *Edwin J. Dod* in 1931. Ironically, the old work was condemned not by subsidence, but rampant rot. The marvellously atmospheric INTERIOR, of dark-stained oak everywhere, is like an aisled timber hall, with queenpost trusses. ORGAN LOFTS to W (1986) and N, the latter with Perp-detailed posts. The church was reordered in 1990 with the removal of choir stalls, the bringing forward of the altar, etc. The hanging ROOD of 1952 was designed by *Edward Hines* of the Warham Guild, carved by *Jethro Harris*. The 1860s church, now the Lady Chapel, has a scissor-braced roof and a TRIP-TYCH of 1999 with icons from the Romanian monastery of Basana.

ST MARY, West End Road. 1908–10, by *E.H. Barker*. Towerless. Aisles. Quarry-faced red sandstone; glazed-brick interior. Reordered in 1993, and extended W with offices and café behind a loggia. A glazed arch, across which first-floor offices bridge, unites old and new. – Substantial C13-style PULPIT dedicated to Col. Pilkington, †1908.

CHRIST CHURCH UNITED REFORMED CHURCH, West End Road. 1891–2, by *T. W. Cubbon*. Hard, pinkish brick. Dec, with good NW steeple. Forming one well-balanced picturesque composition with a linked chapel-like hall.

GRANGE FARM, Grange Road. The five-bay front part is brick, early C19 and Georgian in character. The rear is supposedly earlier, but the stonework looks C19.

NCB TRAINING CENTRE (former), Kilbuck Lane, N of the A580. 1956, and typically a product of the Coal Board. A big brick tower with fins set into the cut-away corners. The SAINSBURYS' DISTRIBUTION CENTRE, a truly vast silvery shed immediately N, is a reasonably disciplined standing-seam aluminium box of the late 1990s.

HAYDOCK LODGE. *See* Ashton-in-Makerfield.

A commuters' HOUSING ESTATE created by the Blundells of Little Crosby (q.v.) on the coast N of Blundellsands. It is here because the railway from Liverpool to Southport passes through. There is a four-square Italianate Victorian PUB by the station, perhaps built as the Hightown Hotel in the 1870s. Development really got under way *c.* 1905 with Arts and Crafts-inspired detached and semi-detached houses along tree-lined streets. Many of these are straight, not sinuous like the contemporary Garden Suburb planning with which one associates such housing. The first surveyor was *T. Mellard Reade*, who had also laid out Blundellsands for the Blundells. His son *William Reade* succeeded him in 1909. The houses are attractive with white-painted roughcast and black-and-white painted timber casements. The most varied designs are on ST

GEORGE ROAD. SELCOTH, No. 27 Blundell Road, two-and-a-half storeys and three bays under one gable, also stands out. RATHBONE ROAD has a short painted brick terrace, Garden Suburb in style, on each side. Even the church of ST STEPHEN is roughcast; it looks like an Arts and Crafts village hall and only modest crucifixes on the gables hint at a religious purpose.

Between these streets and the foreshore is post-war development, initiated with a housing scheme by *Eric Thomson & Associates* begun in 1965 on and off THORNBECK AVENUE. 1,000 houses were planned, but the full scheme, with its school, library and shops, was never realised. Completed housing is low, of beige and brown brick and render, with pitched roofs.

BARN, Grange Farm, Grange Lane. Possibly C16. Brick walls on a stone plinth, with battered buttresses. Six bays. (Collar-and-strut trusses, some wind-braces. DCMS.)

HINDLEY
with HINDLEY GREEN

6000

A former colliery and cotton town, half on and half above the Lancashire Plain. It was well known for nail making for two centuries before mining and textiles came. The population rose from 2,332 in 1801 to stabilise at *c.* 25,000 by 1901. The centre, such as it is, is Market Street–Bridge Street, the St Helens–Bolton Road (A58) as it winds up off the plain. In the C19 it expanded out by workers' terraces and along Atherton Road to join up with the township of Hindley Green 1½ m. SE, and in the C20 spread N of it. The better sorts lived on Hall Lane up above the station.

ALL SAINTS, Chapel Fields Lane. This delightful brick chapel began as a chapel of ease to Wigan Parish Church, built in 1641. On and off from 1643 until 1698 it was Presbyterian. It then reverted to the Established Church and was taken down and rebuilt in 1766–7. This is the building we see. In 1765 the Trustees spent five shillings on ale whilst 'considering Mr Eye's alterations in the plan'. This is presumably *John Eyes*, of the dynasty of Liverpool surveyors. The chapel is of two by four bays, with a doorless W front with two large arched windows, a small lunette window over, and a gable with a fragile cupola bellcote on top. The arched windows have their wooden mullions as three stepped pointed lights. Large, ugly vestry added in 1933. The W gallery, on Doric cast-iron columns, is of 1767; a faculty for the N and S galleries, on quatrefoil cast-iron columns, was granted in 1790. The vestry was then moved further E and a NE staircase built too. In 1875 the *Wigan Observer* described the chapel as 'hideous. . . . many weaving sheds present a finer appearance', and in 1880–1 the box pews and triple-decker pulpit were removed. Reordered in 1989, with replica C18 chandeliers. – REREDOS. Late C19, from Holy Innocents, Liverpool, installed 1933 and now at the W end. – Dado PANELLING from the gallery pews, reset. – STAINED

GLASS. E window, 1953, by *Powell & Sons.* – MEMORIALS. A few tablets in the galleries. The best is Lt-Col. Nathaniel Eckersley, †1837. Suitably martial, with a fine pile of trophies etc.

ST JOHN EVANGELIST, Atherton Road, Hindley Green. 1898–9, by *C.E. Deacon.* It cost £4,750. Much more inventive than a cursory look might suggest. Stock bricks and red brick dressings. Strange windows, their lights round-headed and yet cusped. Vestry with chunky battered chimney. Elaborate bell-turret at the W end of the chancel and N organ loft, looking together like a crossing and transept. They aren't, but it is implied inside too by two braced trusses across the W bay of the chancel. The trusses span between unmoulded square piers which are narrower than the nave, so that the W one forms a kind of chancel arch. The nave has three-and-a-half bays with octagonal stone piers dying into brick arches, without capitals. – REREDOS, ALTAR and ALTAR RAILS. By *F.H. Crossley* of Chester, 1937–8. Gothic. – PULPIT. A heavily ornate piece of 1910. – STAINED GLASS. Lots, but not very good. E window a Te Deum by *Clayton & Bell,* 1920. A number of others signed *Abbott & Co.* with various dates.

VICARAGE, 1910, by *Heaton, Ralph & Heaton.* Attractive, mildly Arts and Crafts.

ST PETER, Atherton Street. 1863–6, by *E.G. Paley.* A good handsome size, in a prominent location set back from the main crossroads, with a SW tower with broach spire. Rock-faced stone. The tracery is Dec. Stone-faced C20 church hall with round-headed windows attached SW. The interior is well detailed, but has no excitements – it is very much a pre-Hubert Austin church (he joined Paley in partnership in 1868). Six-bay nave with good crocket capitals on the round arcade piers. Little corbelled detached shafts support a scissor-truss roof. Reordered with platform extending W of the chancel arch. – ORGAN (W end). Completed 1873. By *Edmund Schulze,* the celebrated German organ-maker, in very handsome twin oak cases – in the Germanic tradition – of 1879. Superb, elaborately free Dec pierced framing which looks distinctly *Paley & Austin.* Pipes splendidly stencilled. – Two good wrought-iron GASOLIERS. – STAINED GLASS. Late C19 and late C20. E window to Alfred Dunnings, †1870. Good. S aisle, 2nd from E, to Bernard Hasting, †1881, aged only nine. His photograph is incorporated twice in the unusual pictorial-style window, which is by *Duhamel Marrelle* of Evreux.

ST BENEDICT (R.C.), Market Street. 1869, by *Joseph Hansom.* If of no great size or architectural interest outside, it is surprising and original inside. No tower; W gable with relieving arch. Dec tracery. Quarry-faced stone with red ashlar dressings. Round apse. Very simple W gallery. Narrow passage aisles behind the incredibly closely spaced arcade piers, so that there are two arches to every aisle window. Each slender rectangular pier is much deeper than it is wide and has no mouldings except for an attached column that rises up to the clerestory, from where an equally thin roof-rib arches up. So the nave appears as a compressed series of thin, closely spaced ribs rising from the floor to the apex of the roof. The Lady Chapel was added by *F.X. Velarde* in 1954. It is a small circular room with a conical roof, connected to the S aisle by a rectangular space.* It has an altar with a TRIPTYCH. The re-glazing of the church, with strong shapes and opaque colourless and blue glass, must also be by *Velarde*. And are the hanging ROOD and suspended altar CANOPY in the chancel by him too?

ST JOHN METHODIST CHURCH, Market Street. 1900–1, by *William Waddington & Son* of Manchester, the Nonconformist specialists. A large church-style building (as opposed to a chapel 'box'), with transepts and apsidal chancel, and an original W front. This has a commandingly tall but rather too slender octagonal NW steeple rising above the porch, closing the view up Market Street. The steeple is mainly red ashlar; elsewhere this is used for dressings only and the rest is pale coursed stone. Round-headed windows, those to the W front with free, simple tracery in an unusual arrangement. The interior is complete with its original fittings unaltered. Small W gallery only. A curious roof, with kingposts rising up between coves. – Attractive, elaborate FONT. Round, with arcading and eight little attached marble shafts. – Pretty STAINED GLASS with geometric patterns and flowers and fruits.

UNITARIAN CHAPEL, Presbyterian Fold. The Presbyterians built a chapel here after they were ejected from All Saints in 1698. The present building is of 1788, but greatly altered in 1877, when the E end was lopped off to accommodate the large, hard and overwhelming SUNDAY SCHOOL. The chapel, of rendered brick, has three round-arched windows in the S wall, with 1877 frames. Only two windows on the N side, with plain frames. W gable blank, with vestry attached. The interior, with E gallery, is entirely of 1877.

CONGREGATIONAL CHAPEL (former), Chapel Street. Now retail premises. 1910, by *Herbert Wade* of Blackpool. A hard red brick box with Perp tracery and stubby tower.

CEMETERY, Hill Road. 1879–80. LODGE and CHAPEL by *George Heaton*. The usual three chapels were built; the single survivor is the Nonconformist one. Quarry-faced stone with thick red ashlar dressings. The chapel has an apse and some Geometric tracery; the lodge, gables and mullioned-and-transomed windows. Both have cusped lancets.

DISTRICT COUNCIL OFFICES (former), Wigan Road. 1903, by *Heaton, Ralph & Heaton*. Brick with some free Neo-C17 stone detailing. It stands in isolation in the fork of two roads, with the three-bay W entrance front facing the junction with an open pediment on banded pilasters flanked by segmental oriel windows. The odd thing is that this is facing away from the town centre.

---

*Pevsner thought that the windows were rather 1925- than 1955-looking; he consistently thought Velarde's work inexplicably old-fashioned.

POLICE STATION, Castle Hill. A pretty, little, and pretty convincing Neo-Elizabethan building, apparently of the 1840s and 1860s. Of quarry-faced stone, with three gables, mullioned windows and a four-pointed door surround. Patricroft (SE Lancashire) has a similar one.

LEYLAND FREE LIBRARY AND MUSEUM, Market Street. 1886, by *Thomas Worthington*. Free Elizabethan, asymmetrical, quirky but enjoyable. Brick and stone dressings. It pivots about the rather odd entrance and staircase hall on the corner of Cross Street and Market Street, a sort of tower crowned by a high pyramid roof with a glazed break in it, with arched porch attached. Continuing along Market Street r. of this are three two-storey mullioned-and-transomed bay windows with half-octagonal shafts capped by finials between. Behind the windows on the ground floor is the lending library and on the first floor the former reading room with arch-braced ceiling and grand bookcase with broken pediment. The open-well staircase has a wrought-iron balustrade.

BROOKFIELD HIGH SCHOOL, Park Road. Formerly the Hindley and Abram Grammar School. Three phases: the centre 1902, N wing 1909, and S wing 1929. The earliest has gables and mullioned-and-transomed windows, the latest is in an austere classicism, but they are all harmonised by the use of the same stone.

MARKET STREET and its extension BRIDGE STREET have a twisting townscape of some potential, but are now run down. The best of the commercial buildings are the BANKS: the Royal Bank of Scotland, terracotta Edwardian, and the inter-war Lloyds TSB, small but severely classical.

HOUSING ESTATE. A large, sprawling post-war council estate E of Bridge Street. There are many PREFABRICATED HOUSES, including the *B.I.S.F* (British Iron and Steel Federation) design with steel frame and roof trusses, and ribbed steel cladding to the upper floor, and the *Orlit* house, which is all concrete, with cladding like massive ashlar blocks. Also a Brutalist, and now desolately run-down, shopping parade.

Nos. 599–619 ATHERTON ROAD, early C19, were for muslin and silk weavers.

SOUTHWORTH HOUSE, No. 444 Atherton Road. The best of the small number of pre-industrial houses on Atherton Road. Early C18, brick (Flemish-bond front, English garden bond elsewhere, cf. Walker's Higher Farm, Aspull, q.v.). Stone quoins, bands and window keystones. Three storeys, two bays; small extension to r. The windows are C20, but their proportions would suggest they were always casements. Column balusters on the stairs (DCMS).

PROSPECT MILL, Platt Street. Now Hindley Business Centre. A 416-loom weaving mill of 1887 by *Stott & Sons*. It became the Prospect Mill in 1910, from when the banded water tower most likely dates.

HINDLEY HALL. Actually just inside Aspull (q.v.).

HOLLINS GREEN
Rixton-with-Glazebrook

A nondescript village, with only a few buildings predating the draining of the mosses in the 1870s.

St Helen, School Lane. A chapel of ease until 1874. The carcass and presumably the stone cupola are of *c.* 1735–8, but the brickwork has been extensively repaired and the detailing seems largely part of a charmless 1882 restoration. Scars of earlier openings visible. The cupola is a pretty octagonal ogee-capped turret with naïve little Ionic columns attached at the angles. The present E window is of 1921, inserted to allow for a high altar below; the previous one now in the chancel S wall. W GALLERY, C19, and a brass CHANDELIER, C18. Reordered 1972.

Mount Pleasant, set back from Glazebrook Lane, is a rather handsome farmhouse dated 1851 on the façade of good red brick. This projects beyond the return walls, a kind of polite screen to the common brickwork of the rest. Two storeys, three bays, the outer two slightly projecting. Doorcase recessed in an arched opening behind a lacy contemporary cast-iron porch. The façade has the vernacular high wall face above the upper windows that allowed for taller attics, sometimes for grain storage, though here it appears to have been used for servants' accommodation. Some good lively plaster cornices etc., especially in the stair hall. Now offices, the C19 farm buildings behind also converted.

HOWE BRIDGE *see* ATHERTON

HUYTON
with ROBY

St Michael, Huyton Lane. In appearance mostly C19, but in fact a medieval church. The material is red ashlar. The tower is Perp, but the obelisk pinnacles look C17 or early C18. To the NE, now attached as a choir vestry, is the Case MAUSOLEUM of *c.* 1681. Of heavily worn sandstone, with a round window and a doorway with open segmental pediment and bolection architrave. The very wide S aisle and the narrower N aisle were rebuilt in 1815–22, and the low N arcade dates from that time too. It is a facsimile of the S arcade, which is C14, with octagonal piers and double-chamfered arches. The S doorway is of the same time. Broad nave. The chancel is Perp, much interfered with; original priest's doorway. The hammerbeam roof in the chancel is probably mostly of 1663, cf. the nave roof of St Mary, Prescot (q.v.). The hammerbeam braces are consoles; the wind-braces are quarter-circles, forming perfect uncusped circles. A community room was created in the W bay of the S aisle in 2003 by *Robin Wolley* behind a glazed Gothic screen. Not that bad. – FONTS. One is Norman, the other Perp. The Norman one is tub-shaped and has primitive heads in primitive arcading, and a frieze of rosettes above. The base is modern. The Perp one has the usual pointed quatrefoils with shields. – SCREEN. A fine, typically Northern piece of *c.* 1500 with single-light divisions and dainty Flamboyant tracery. An inscription, no longer preserved, told of pulling the screen down 'in time of rebellion 1647' and repairing it and setting it up again in 1663. The Jacobean-style repairs are worth seeking out. – WOODWORK in the chancel, *c.* 1700 and probably Flemish. – STAINED GLASS. In the S aisle, two windows by *Henry Holiday*, 1883 and 1885. E window, an Ascension. Good colouring. – MONUMENT. Defaced effigy of a priest, alabaster; C14 or C15. He is probably John de Winwick, †1359.

ST AGNES (R.C.), Huyton Hey. 1964–5, by *L.A.G. Prichard & Son*. So hemmed in by neighbouring buildings that it is difficult to comprehend the plan until one has stepped inside. The concept is very effective: a pair of large, pointed concrete vaults fanning out from a long E wall, each finishing as a jutting prow filled with glass between close-set mullions. It results in a light and airy interior. Some details are good, e.g. the sweeping pier between the two prows which supports the vaults; some are fussy, e.g. the porch; and some are odd, e.g. the spire over the altar.

ST BARTHOLOMEW, Church Road, Roby. 1875, by *Ewan Christian*. Competent, conventional. W tower with broach spire, round apse, prominent clerestory. The style is of *c.* 1300. Dull interior, reordered by *Robin Wolley* in 1988 with a hall in the W end. – REREDOS and apse wall incorporate C17 Flemish panelling. – STAINED GLASS. S aisle W, by *Kempe*, 1899.

ST GABRIEL, Hall Lane. Begun 1894. Single vessel with no tower. Aisles of three gables, each filled with a large Perp window. Capital-less arcades. Wagon roof with tie-beams.

ST MARGARET MARY, Pilch Lane. *See* p. 437.

UNITED REFORMED CHURCH, Victoria Road. 1889–90, by *W.D. Carøe* for the Congregationalists. With a prominent steeple. C13 details. Interior with aisles, and arches thrown across the nave between each set of piers and across the aisles too: a typically inventive and spatially interesting exercise by Carøe. He was one of the few architects to span the Anglican–Nonconformist divide. – STAINED GLASS. First World War memorial by *Abbott & Co.*

Huyton has little historic form because the village was largely demolished to make way after 1945 for a town centre. Of the villagey past by the church is a pretty little GREEN with a tall CROSS. This dates from 1897, but replicates one by *Rickman* of 1820. The Green has very much an estate-village character with its cottages, and Huyton is indeed very close to Knowsley (q.v.). There are still Victorian VILLAS amid leafage on either side of Huyton Hey Road and at Huyton Park (begun in the 1850s), but any rural character and most of the village have been obliterated by contiguous inter-war housing estates built

by the Liverpool Corporation, and the disastrous and incoherent little TOWN CENTRE.

The HOUSING ESTATES are: the Huyton Farm and
Knowsley estates, of 1932 etc., Longview Farm, of 1937 etc.,
the Brookhouse Estate, of 1946 etc., and Stockbridge Village,
of the 1960s. The earlier ones are by (Sir) *Lancelot Keay*.
Longview Farm has his standard Neo-Georgian designs, e.g.
in Wastle Bridge Road, but also some with less common Vernacular Revival motifs, e.g. half-timbered bay windows with
nogging on Lyme Cross Road. Stockbridge Village is still
largely low-rise and low-density, with also two groups of three
towers, but far bleaker and more depressing, with lots of
scruffy grassy areas.

ROBY retains a bit more of a village character, with some cottages and villas along Roby Road (A5080). On the corner with
Station Road, pretty estate COTTAGES of the C19, some stone
with big chimneys and elaborate half-timbered bays, others in
chequered brick with delicately ornate cast-iron verandas. The
stump of a medieval CROSS in front of them.

SHOPPING CENTRE, Derby Road. 1962 by *Chapman, Taylor &*
Partners. Low parades, of exposed concrete framing with brick
or glazed panels. Pedestrianized. Built a few years before the
beginning of the age of enclosed malls.

LIBRARY, Poplar Bank. 1997, by *Mills Beaumont Leavey Channon*.
Steel frame and full-height glazing forming elevations which
are a little restless in detail. Open-plan interior.

NATIONAL WILDFLOWER CENTRE, Roby Road (A5080). Built
in Court Hey Park, formerly the estate of Robert Gladstone
(the house was demolished after the Second World War).
Modest C19 stables have been converted as part of a scheme
by *Hodder Associates*, selected by competition. Opened 2000;
funding from the Millennium Commission. The new construction is calm and reserved – a very long, low and narrow
concrete-and-glass link between walled garden and park. A
promenade deck runs all the way along the top. Long windows
with timber shutters that pivot up to form sunshades.

PARK HALL, Huyton Hey Road. Former Congregational chapel
of 1856, with attached at right angles a school of 1861. The
school is by *H.H. Vale* for Andrew Barclay Walker, the brewer
(*see* Liverpool, p. 299). Small, picturesque and Gothic. Rubble
with red sandstone dressings. The school entrance is in a little
turret with an extremely tall and slender splayed pyramid roof,
like a wizard's hat.

HEATWAVES LEISURE CENTRE, The Withens, Stockbridge
Village. *Nicholas Grimshaw & Partners*, 1988. In desperate surroundings, this is a simple building – a windowless industrial
shed – made memorable by two bright red, playfully nautical
touches: a pair of boisterously oversized ventilation cowls
flanking the ramped entrance in the centre, and the towering
central mast, supporting external trusses extending out above
the apex of the roof from the base of the mast to meet free-
standing columns at each end (cf. Grimshaw's Oxford ice rink,

1984). Stainless-steel rods brace the mast and stretch from mast to truss. This structure is lightweight, economic and internally column-free, and was later reinterpreted by the practice for their grandstand at Lord's Cricket Ground. Uplifting architecture does not have to be expensive architecture.

Bowring (golf course), Roby Road (A5080). The house of *c.* 1761 is demolished, but the surviving brick service wing points to its restrained demeanour.

Derby Lodge Hotel, Roby Road (A5080). The core is a house built as Edenhurst in the 1840s, for Richard Earle, manager of Lord Derby's estates from 1839. Of red ashlar in a Jacobethan style in the manner of *William Burn*, who was at this time designing numerous buildings for his lordship (*see* Knowsley), but rather plainer than one would expect of him. The lodge, however, is entirely characteristic. The house has been extensively and disastrously extended in bad pastiche for hotel use.

The Hazels, Kingswood Business Park, Liverpool Road (A57). A house of 1764 built of smooth red brickwork. Compact, but quite large, and with unusual façades. The front of three storeys and five bays is severe, with a three-bay pediment framed within a five-bay pediment. This fronts a simple gabled roof, with another full-width pediment across the back. Underneath this, the façade has on the *piano nobile* Venetian windows on either side of a canted bay. Another Venetian window on the side elevation lights the intermediate landing of the spacious staircase, which starts in one flight and returns in two. Cross-vaulted corridors run across on the ground floor and upper floor. The site was a college and is now being redeveloped as a business park, with bland blocks of tinted glass and white panelling.

Hurst House (Golf Clubhouse), Huyton Road. The house in its present form looks *c.* 1830. Of rendered red ashlar. Five bays and two storeys, with a porch of coupled Roman Doric columns. Interior gutted and opened up. Behind in the 1870s a huge red excrescence developed, with a high slender clock tower (with dome cap), a big broad tower dated 1877, and turrets on the stables as well. This work was done for Jacob Atherton. Most of it was demolished in the 1960s, leaving the scarred towers standing awkwardly alone and apart.

INCE BLUNDELL

Ince Blundell Hall. A splendid Georgian house, with attendant temples built by Henry Blundell to house his important collection of classical sculpture. This was one of the finest expressions of the Neoclassical ideal in the country, and the removal of most of the collection on its sale to Liverpool Corporation in 1959 is a matter of the deepest regret.*

* Now at the Liverpool Museum and Walker Art Gallery.

The Blundells settled here before the C14 on a low island (Innis in Celtic) amidst the meres and mosses near the coast N of Liverpool. A new house was built *c.* 1720 by Robert Blundell, Henry's father, on the site of the old mansion. *Henry Sephton* – the leading mason-architect in the area in the early C18 – is now identified from a signed elevation as the designer. Henry Blundell finished the house with enthusiasm after he took control in 1761. Later he wrote that by 1776, 'I had fitted up all the apartments [and] built a large body of offices without the help of a Wyat or any architect.' He enclosed the park and erected two splendid gateways, and built the Garden Temple to the l. of the mansion and then the Pantheon to the r. to house the antique sculpture which he collected voraciously. In the mid C19 Thomas Weld modernised the house after a disputed inheritance was finally settled in his favour, extending it up to the Pantheon, redecorating with *Messrs Crace*

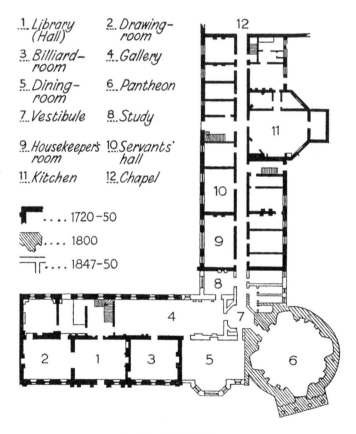

1. Library (Hall) 2. Drawing-room
3. Billiard-room 4. Gallery
5. Dining-room 6. Pantheon
7. Vestibule 8. Study
9. Housekeeper's room 10. Servants' hall
11. Kitchen 12. Chapel

■.... 1720–50
▨.... 1800
⊤⌐.... 1847–50

Ince Blundell Hall, plan.
(*Country Life*, vol. 123, 1958)

and building a huge new Italianate chapel. The few changes made since then have been undertaken by the Augustinian Sisters who have run the house as a nursing home since the 1950s.

30 So to the EXTERIOR. The traditional start date of *c.* 1720 is about right for the main, i.e. E, front. This is late English Baroque, and evidently inspired by Buckingham House, London. It is of brick with sandstone dressings, of 3–3–3 bays and two-and-a-half storeys including an attic above the cornice, and finished with a panelled parapet. The central three bays of the two principal floors are all of stone, with pairs of giant pilasters and two giant semi-columns, all Corinthian. There are also giant angle pilasters. Above all these on the attic storey are pilaster strips. Ground-floor windows l. and r. of the centre have pediments, those in the centre are segmental-headed and have giant keystones. The first-floor windows have apron panels and consoles. Weld, in 1847–50, had the chimneystacks rebuilt, plate glass installed, a bay window grafted onto the S return and a new dining room, in sympathetic detail, added to the N end. With this is a vestibule linking the Pantheon to the house so that the Pantheon could function as an entrance hall. The architect was probably *J.J. Scoles*, who is reported as carrying out work on the house in 1857, and who also designed a village school erected in 1843 (*see* p. 209), and the new chapel built in 1858–60.

INTERIOR. Inside the house at the S end are the MUSIC ROOM and the DRAWING ROOM (with the bay window), both with splendid Rococo stucco ceilings. Richard Wilson supplied landscapes for the Drawing Room (no longer present) in 1763–7, which may indicate the date of the stuccowork. Overlaid on ceiling and walls is Crace's delicately pretty Raphaelesque decoration. Unfortunately the excellent chimneypiece, and other superb C18 examples, were removed to Lulworth Castle, Dorset by the Welds when they sold the house in 1960. The STAIRCASE is much less ostentatious, with a chaste metal railing, and the staircase hall is not a grand space at all. The former ENTRANCE HALL behind the centre of the façade is small, simple and sober, with the back wall partitioned off by the Sisters as a corridor. This continues through the C18 dining room to the N to Weld's 1840s DINING ROOM, fitted with excellent full-height oak panelling designed to frame Belgian tapestries, but now bizarrely housing giant photographic prints. Good *Crace* ceiling. Beyond is Weld's octagonal VESTIBULE – the hub of the house – connecting the 1720s building to the Pantheon and the service wing. Off it, and behind the Dining Room, is the coved PICTURE GALLERY (now Chapel) created by Weld to house Henry Blundell's collection by knocking together and extending rooms N of the staircase. It has a complete and splendid *Crace* scheme.

Now outside to the two fascinating structures built by Henry Blundell to house sculpture. From 1776, when at the age of fifty-two he travelled to Rome for the first time with his friend

and fellow Lancastrian Catholic Charles Towneley, Henry's
great passion was collecting, and by the time he died he had
bought almost six hundred pieces of sculpture. Towneley, at
the time the greatest English collector of antique statuary, was
a great influence and source of advice. First Henry displayed
his acquisitions in the GREENHOUSES he built W of the hall.
Then he rebuilt part of one as a gallery. This, octagonal and
now derelict, lies on axis behind the GARDEN TEMPLE erected
c. 1790–2 to house the rapidly expanding collection. A portrait
of the minor Liverpool architect and surveyor *William Everard*
exhibited in 1869 represented him holding a model of this
temple, so the design is probably his. The small, mainly stucco
building has a tetrastyle Tuscan portico, and incorporates in its
fabric Roman reliefs, busts, and a huge and alarming mask in
the pediment. Some of the reliefs are replicas dating from the
thorough restoration of c. 2000 by *Philip Johnston* of *Cunliffe
Surveyors*. The Latin inscription is a wry reference to the
Lancastrian climate: 'In this place it is summer and spring all
year round' (because the building was heated, by ducting air
warmed over external fireplaces through hollow walls and
venting it out of the parapet urns). Inside, the roof is peculiar:
a shallow, panelled pyramid with the corner rafters visible. It
is, apparently, modified. Scuplture recesses around the walls,
including a blind 'Venetian window' in the centre of each side,
two of which also contain the entrances. More sculpture was
displayed on the floor. All that remains are Roman masks and
relief panels from sarcophagi and cinerary chests set in the
walls.

A flood of new statuary was acquired in 1800–2, and to
display it Blundell built the PANTHEON on the other side of
the house c. 1802–5. The architect is unknown, and though
Blundell probably had a hand in it, it is surely too sophisticated to be his alone. He does refer to a Mr Hope measuring
stonework in 1802, and *John Hope* or one of the Manchester
Hopes has been suggested as executant architect. It is a miniaturised version of the prototype, of which Henry Flitcroft had
built one for a similar purpose at Stourhead, and Towneley
commissioned Joseph Bonomi to design another. However,
Gerard Vaughan has suggested that the inspiration might as
easily have come from Simonetti's Sala Rotunda in the Museo
Pio-Clementino at the Vatican, opened to the public during
one of Blundell's visits. Blundell's version is an ashlar, domed
rotunda with an attached Ionic tetrastyle portico in place of
the Corinthian of the Pantheon. Antique reliefs are set in the
stonework. The portico does not face in quite the same direction as the Hall, probably because it was aligned with an eyecatcher in the park known as Blundell Tower. But that has been
demolished, and without a *raison d'être*, the orientation is now
a bit awkward. The interior is certainly not awkward: beautiful and impressively large, cool and lofty under a coffered
dome and a glazed oculus. As at the real thing, the oculus is
the only source of light. Giant pilasters around the walls are

interspersed with niches for statuary, four of which have marble columns of the 'Venetian window' type, so that visitors could walk around the statues they framed. Blundell was committed from the outset to public access to his collection, and the original separation of the galleries from the house may have been partly to preserve the privacy of the domestic accommodation.

This leaves the auxiliary parts of the house. Extending w off the vestibule to the Pantheon is *Henry Blundell*'s OFFICE WING, built at right angles to his father's mansion after 1766. This is a rather plodding Palladian affair, suggesting the limits of Blundell's architectural talents. A pedimented centre with cupola over, and at the E end a pavilion that, until new windows were opened up in the later C20, had only a Venetian window beneath a Diocletian window flanked by busts in blank round windows. A large, two-storey octagonal kitchen half-projects from the rear in the centre, into which a floor was inserted in the later C20.

The pavilion at the E end was probably matched by one at the W, but attached at this end now is the CHAPEL OF THE HOLY FAMILY (R.C.) by *J.J. Scoles*, built 1858–60. It is also the parish church. A large, tall, plain brick exterior, with clerestory windows only down the sides, and an apse. The detail outside and inside is a modest Quattrocento, but the interior is enlivened immeasurably by the splendid PAINTED DECORATION. The Renaissance arabesque style is similar to that in the house, and it may well be *Crace* again. Lining the nave in architectural frames are large grisaille PAINTINGS by *Gebhard Flatz*, in Quattrocento style too. Flat coffered ceiling. w gallery on Doric columns, with balustrade. – The big w window contains STAINED GLASS by *Forrest* of Liverpool, *c.* 1860–7. Under the gallery are four good inter-war *Hardman* windows. – Large BRASS to Charles Blundell, *c.* 1860, probably *Hardman* too. It has two angels carrying an inscription, with a cross above.

GARDENS and PARK. On the lawns are an early C19 marble COLUMN supporting an eagle, and a SUNDIAL dated 1743. Viewed across the HA-HA from the lawn the park retains much of its structure despite being tenanted, with mature belts and clumps. It was created in two phases by Henry Blundell, in the mid 1760s and then probably in the 1770s. The Gothick prospect tower is gone, but the KITCHEN GARDEN remains, with a colossal curving brick wall to keep out biting westerlies. Construction of the PARK WALL, two miles long, began in 1765 and continued into the 1770s. In it are three gateways, pre-eminent amongst them the LION GATE or Liverpool Gate on the A565, ⅔m. SSE of the house. This is a splendid sandstone thing by *Henry Blundell*, probably of the 1770s, but still Baroque. The style is explained by the fact that the structure is copied from a gateway in the background of a painting owned by Blundell, the *Marriage of Bacchus and Ariadne* by Sebastiano Ricci. The centre has Doric semi-columns flanking an arch carrying a full Doric entablature and a wide, open pediment with a wreathed urn. Rusticated pedestrian entrances l. and r., and above each a stately lion. A small lodge is on the park side. The EAST GATE, on Park Wall Road ⅔ m. ESE, is presumably also the work of *Henry Blundell*. Stone was purchased for it in 1777–8. It is another archway with flanking pedestrian entrances, but this time there are paired Ionic pilasters, festoons and rosettes across the frieze and an unbroken pediment, and the pedestrian entrances have tented caps. The other entrance is a GATEHOUSE on the A565, mid-Victorian and of brick, in a French Renaissance style. By *Scoles*?

STABLES, SW of the house. The single brick range has rainwater heads dated 1814, but is it earlier? Nine bays, the middle three under a wide pedimental gable. Keyed-in round windows above conventional sashes. In the centre, a giant brick arch and, set in the slightly recessed wall within this, the entrance with fanlight and above that a Diocletian window. The end bays have doorways similarly recessed.

Besides the stables is a puzzling building erroneously known as the OLD HALL. That building actually stood on the site of the present mansion. This building is a single three-storey brick range with irregular, low mullioned windows and a (renewed) gabled roof. Brick suggests a date probably no earlier than *c.* 1590; the massive depressed four-centred door lintels point to construction no later than the mid C17. But what exactly was it? The windows have been moved about, the interior altered substantially, there is now no chimneystack, and apparently there was only one fireplace fifty years ago (in the S gable end). The building was used for drying hops in the C19, and it seems most likely that it was built for some kind of agricultural use. But it is still baffling.

CROSS BARN, Cross Barn Lane, W of the Hall. Now a house. Two cruck trusses dendro-dated to *c.* 1540. Cruciform plan, brick walls, lots of alterations. It was a R.C. chapel in the C17 and C18.

Outside the park:

PRIEST'S HOUSE, A565, opposite the park wall. Very striking. It looks late C18. It reads as circular, partly because of the shallow conical roof rising to a tall, circular, central chimneystack. But in fact it has four curving faces alternating with four flat ones. There are two storeys, and the material is brick except where the ground-floor windows on the flat faces are set in ashlar within arched recesses. Might *Henry Blundell* be the architect? Because the Blundells were such unyielding recusants, should we expect the shape to be symbolic, perhaps of heaven?

SCHOOL (former), Back o'th' Town Lane. 1843, by *J.J. Scoles*. Sandstone. Asymmetrical, with mullioned windows and an inscription winding its way around the building on scrolls.

MOSS FARMHOUSE, North End Lane, 1⅓ m. W. The walls of limewashed brick contain three cruck frames of probably C17 date.

INCE-IN-MAKERFIELD

'The most diligent search all England over would scarce reveal such an uninviting spot as the Lancashire town of Ince.' So declared the *Illustrated Church News* at the end of the C19, when Ince was a chaotic township of mining, iron smelting, engineering and chemical works, criss-crossed by a bewildering network of railways. Development had been spurred by the completion of the Leeds and Liverpool Canal through it in 1816; before it was mostly mossland. One man above all was responsible: Thomas Knowles, who started as a pit boy aged nine and rose up to found the powerful Pearson & Knowles Coal & Iron Co.

Most of the industry and its railways have now gone, but the scrawny incoherent sprawl of brick terraces (the meanest demolished) and C20 housing remains. It is divided in two: Lower Ince along Warrington Road (A573) and Upper Ince along Manchester Road (A577). The landscape is heavily scarred by industry: to the S and W are a series of 'flashes', extensive lakes created by mining subsidence, now a haven for wildfowl.

CHRIST CHURCH, Ince Green Lane, Lower Ince. 1863–4, by *E.G. Paley*. An aisle-less church in rock-faced stone with Geometrical tracery, and with nothing of the vitality and subtlety that Hubert Austin would bring to Paley's practice a few years later. Polygonal apse and transepts with plate-traceried wheel windows. N transept turret; open three-bay W porch. Archbraced hammerbeam roof; chancel arch with clustered shafts. – STAINED GLASS. W window by *F. Holt*, 1893.

ST MARY, Warrington Road, Lower Ince. A simple 1978 conversion of a very plain 1870s school. It replaced *Austin & Paley*'s grand church of 1887, demolished owing to subsidence and rot. – Some STAINED GLASS from the old church, *c.* 1889 and 1923, re-set.

INCE CEMETERY, Warrington Road, Lower Ince. The dainty CHAPELS were won in competition by *Alfred Waterhouse* in 1855, and completed in 1857 – early for him. The Church of England example is simple Gothic with a bellcote, but the other, for Roman Catholics, is Norman with an apse, which is unexpected. Both were semi-derelict in 2005. The contemporary LODGE is also *Waterhouse*. All are of rock-faced stone with ashlar dressings.

WIGAN BOROUGH CEMETERY, Cemetery Road, Lower Ince. Across the railway from Ince Cemetery. Two lodges and three chapels were designed by *Thomas D. Barry* in 1855; of the chapels only the Nonconformist one remains. Gothic. Pale coursed stone. Bellcote and porch. It is all deep, steep-pitched roofs, so typical of cemetery chapels. In 1955 it was extended at the rear in matching style as a crematorium. The First World War MEMORIAL, 1925, is a reasonably accurate copy of *Sir Reginald Blomfield*'s standard Cross of Sacrifice design.

COUNCIL OFFICES, Ince Green Lane, Lower Ince. 1903, by *Heaton, Ralph & Heaton*, then Wigan's leading practice. Red brick and red terracotta. Cross-windows and balustrade parapet. The centre three bays break forward, with segmental oriels and fancy, fanciful gables. In the middle is a big frilly door surround, with the typical Edwardian motif of alternately blocked columns. There is also a little cupola. Inside is a top-lit staircase with wrought-iron balustrade, and a ground-floor hall projecting from the rear.

POLICE STATIONS, both by *Heaton, Ralph & Heaton, c.* 1900. The better is on County Police Street, Higher Ince. Brick and stone dressings, gables, mullioned-and-transomed windows. Now closed. The more modest is on Warrington Road at Spring View, ½ m. s of Lower Ince.

LEEDS AND LIVERPOOL CANAL. Wigan was reached from the w in *c.* 1780, and the s branch of the Lancaster Canal was completed to Haigh (q.v.) in the 1790s, leaving a gap of just 2½ miles to complete the 127-mile route between the two cities. A height difference of 200 ft required the construction of a flight of twenty-three LOCKS (a quarter of the total for the whole canal), built in 1812–16 just inside the boundary with Wigan (the top few, and Kirkless Hall alongside, are actually in Aspull, q.v.). Stone, with a mixture of timber and metal gates, overflow channels, footbridges etc. The dimensions of the Leeds and Liverpool's 'short boats' – 62 ft by 14 ft – determined those of the locks, because they had a much greater beam than the narrowboats used on most of the canal system. There are also a number of dated ROAD BRIDGES.

COACHING INN HOTEL, Warrington Road, Lower Ince. 1895. Big. Neo-Jacobean. Ruabon brick. Imposing in its isolation.

INCE HALL, Ince Hall Avenue, Higher Ince. Formerly a fine timber-framed house, possibly of 1601; burnt down in 1854 and completely rebuilt in its present, unremarkable, brick form.

PEEL HALL, Georges Lane, Higher Ince (on the w bank of the canal). The modest, wobbly C17 brick exterior conceals parts of a superb cruck frame of C15 or earlier date, which would make the hall one of the oldest houses in Lancashire. Gary Miller has pointed to similarities between the trusses and those of Taunton Hall, Ashton-under-Lyne. There are four bays, of two storeys, the outer ones projecting forward under gables. Also a gabled extension at the rear. Stone roof slates and C20 casements. The cruck building almost certainly consisted of a central two-bay open hall flanked by a solar or parlour bay, N, and a pantry and buttery s of a cross-passage (where the front door still is). Two trusses remain, the former central truss of the hall and that dividing it from the N rooms. The blades are magnificently massive and rise to 22 ft (6.7 metres) in height. The hall one has an arch-braced cranked collar (renewed where later pierced), the blades meeting at a saddle blackened by the former open hearth; the blades are also better finished on the N side, which faced the dais. The N truss was formerly closed; its tie-beam was removed to improve circulation when,

p. 32

probably in the C16, a floor was inserted into the N wing and the hall, where it is supported on a roll-moulded beam (cf. the example at Kirkless Hall, Aspull, close by). Upstairs it is clear how the eaves were raised by outriders attached to the cruck blades to create more headroom in the new first-floor rooms. Wind-braces are visible too. By this stage, however, the S service bay had already been replaced by the present, two-storey post-and-truss wing, dated to the late C15–early C16. This contains another fine truss, with an arch-braced canted tie-beam and an extremely unusual kingpost with a forked base, like an inverted Y. The truss dividing the wing from the hall part has a similar post, only the fork is much larger, extending very nearly to the apex. The wing appears originally to have been unheated. Next to be rebuilt was the N bay, as a gabled parlour cross-wing in the C17, by the addition of a projecting gabled block to the W side. Many reused timbers in its roof. The date of the fireplace in the hall, and its stack – axially positioned against the N cruck frame – is uncertain. Ceiling-in the room would have finished off the open hearth, but the initial replacement may have been a smoke-hood. In the late C17 or C18 the house was re-clad in brick in at least two phases. Then, the rear wing was added in the (mid?) C18, assorted chimneys were inserted and the present stairs, and at some stage too the house was split into two. A flooded moat survived into the C20.

WESTWOOD HALL, Westwood Lane, Lower Ince. Not to be confused with the demolished Westwood House. Rendered, with C18 and C19 windows. One three-storey bay, one two-storey bay with rear wing. (Philip Powell reports that the E wing contains an upper cruck frame and part of a C17 staircase.)

KENYON
Golborne

A hamlet 1¼ m. N of Croft on the B5207.

BARROW FARMHOUSE, Kenyon Lane. Brick, of three storeys. A newel post is dated 1763, but the two platbands and especially a brick label mould suggest a C17 or early C18 date. Perhaps then 1763 is the date of improvement. Do the scars in the return suggest the second storey was raised? The S front is rebuilt in stretcher bond. Replacement windows. The plan was originally baffle-entry (now altered to a door in the r. return). Inglenook with massive bressumer.

HIGH PEAK, Main Lane. A big Queen Anne-style villa dated 1891. Brick. Built by the Marsh family, who abandoned the C18 Westleigh Old Hall, Leigh (demolished). Hugely extended and drastically altered for a nursing home *c.* 1988, but behind the large mullioned-and-transomed window the staircase with splat balusters survives. Attached stable/coachhouse.

KENYON HALL. *See* Culcheth.

KIRKBY

In 1921 Kirkby's population was 1,116. Forty years later it was 52,000. Modern Kirkby was first conceived by Liverpool Corporation in the 1930s, but not created until 1946–7, when it purchased a Royal Ordnance Factory 6 m. NE of the city centre and 4,000 acres (1,600 hectares) of adjoining farmland from the 7th Earl of Sefton. The aim was to house people displaced by slum clearances in a 'complete community unit' – a quasi-New Town in the image of Speke (*see* p. 460), but larger still. The subsequent story is not one of unbroken decline – in the 1960s jobs were plentiful and residents were generally happy – but in following decades appalling levels of unemployment and endemic vandalism, the terrible deficiencies of some housing, the inability to establish a middle-class population, and the pervasive bleakness and isolation, made Kirkby a byword for the failure of post-war overspill estates. A significant problem from the outset was the division of responsibility between the Liverpool Corporation and Lancashire County Council. The formation of Kirkby Urban District Council in 1958 did little to alter this. Only in 1974, with the creation of Knowsley Metropolitan District Council, was governance unified. Efforts continue to tackle Kirkby's problems; the latest high-profile scheme is the first phase of the Merseytram, which it was hoped would link the town to Liverpool city centre in 2008. In 2005 however, construction was looking increasingly unlikely.

ST CHAD, Old Hall Lane. By *Paley & Austin*, 1869–71, replacing a Georgian chapel of 1766 which in turn replaced a much older chapel. One of Paley & Austin's most powerful churches, externally by virtue of its massive, high tower with the blunt saddleback roof of the type which Bodley had introduced in the 1860s, and internally by the superb excelsior of the tall high tower arches with their clustered shafts and the sexpartite vault inside it. All this is Gothic and the arches are pointed, but details are Norman, and the rich S doorway within a many-ordered porch is ornately so (also the N porch, now blocked). The church is large, and of red sandstone all over – dressed and coursed without and ashlar within. Windows are mostly lancets and the chancel is short and square-ended. The buttressing of the tower on the N and S sides deserves special attention. Low down it broadens sufficiently to form the E and W walls of small transeptal projections inserted between, like infilled flying buttresses.

The INTERIOR is magnificent, particularly the compelling use of ashlar. The nave, once entered, strikes one as long and very high. Open wagon roof, and a bit of scholarly fun with the arcade piers: N octagonal and S round. Every capital is different. Arches are pointed and double-chamfered, and above them the clerestory is of coupled lancets behind relieving arches which are joined up by narrower intermediary arches to form an arcade. Externally the tower reads as a crossing tower, and internally the details are of one too, but in actual fact it is over the choir, with steps and drum-like stone PULPIT under the w arch. To the N is the organ chamber, to the s the vestry. The short sanctuary is E of the tower, with arcading some way up the walls and impressive SEDILIA with a carved scene in the tympanum of the arch over. The shafts below each have a different capital. – FONT. Installed 1880; it had been a water cistern at the school. Early Norman, tub-shaped. On the bowl saints, Adam and Eve with the tree and the serpent, the Angel of the Expulsion, and St Michael spearing a serpent.* The serpent creeps round the underside of the bowl like a rope moulding, and the short shaft (modern) and the base have indeed fat roll mouldings. – MOSAIC. All of the E wall beneath the arcading is a Last Supper, framed by beautiful Pre-Raphaelite angels and Virtues in *opus sectile* designed by *Henry Holiday*, 1898. – STAINED GLASS. By *Henry Holiday*, from 1872 over a long period. The w windows, e.g., of 1897. He is recognisable everywhere, though the style and the intensity of the colouring change. The E windows, 1871, are badly faded.

KIRKBY TOWN. The Corporation envisioned a satellite, providing housing and employment for all social classes. However, as the site lay a mile or so beyond the municipal boundary, in this case the city was acting like a private developer. *Sir Lancelot Keay* prepared a plan in 1948, but this was opposed by Lan-

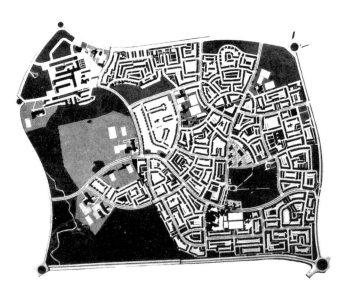

Kirkby, detail of town plan, showing the Southdene residential area, and, top left, the town centre

---

* Francis Bond, in *Fonts and Font Covers* (1908), interpreted it as 'with His staff He bruises the head of the dragon'.

cashire County Council, the planning authority, which wanted
to preserve a bigger green belt around the city and restrict suburban spread. In 1949 the *County Planning Officer* drew up a
new TOWN PLAN in cooperation with Keay's successor *Ronald
Bradbury*, intended to house 47,000 people by 1971. It was
divided into a town centre and three neighbourhood units,
given the insipid names Southdene, Westvale and Northwood
(as if it were some kind of exercise or model). Bradbury and
his team were responsible for detailed layout design, in co-
operation with the County, and for the design of housing. The
plan marked a departure from the geometric formality of
Keay's estates, especially the Beaux Arts layout of Speke. Bradbury frowned upon its long straight terraces and emphasised
how the road layout of Kirkby was made informal by founding it on existing roads, contours and natural features. Each
neighbourhood was given shops, schools, churches etc. Construction began in Southdene in 1950 and the first HOUSING
went up in 1952. This was to standard City Housing Department designs, typical of the date: little pitched-roof groups, in
brick, though most are now refenestrated and many reclad in
so many different ways. 1,000 were finished by 1954 and
10,000 by 1961 – all built by the *Unit Construction Ltd.* Nearly
60 per cent were two-storey houses, over 10 per cent two-storey
pensioners' flats, another 22 per cent flats in three-storey
blocks, and the rest four-storey maisonettes and eleven-storey
towers. The deeply unpopular three- and four-storey blocks
have been demolished. Six tower blocks remain, in Southdene,
out of a total of fourteen. Some open-market housing, built by
developers, was included from the outset. However, much of
the area reserved for it was in a future fourth neighbourhood
unit to the N – later called Tower Hill – which was instead used
from the 1960s for a second phase of municipal housing, built
this time by Kirkby UDC to house an estimated 10,000
second-generation residents (in 1961 a remarkable 48 per cent
of the population was under eighteen). In fact, as unemployment rose sharply the population of the town actually fell by
15 per cent in the decade from 1971, and Tower Hill's notorious seven-storey maisonette blocks, built in 1972, were demolished a decade later – over thirty years before the council was
due to finish paying loan charges on their construction.

The TOWN CENTRE is located between the three neighbourhood units close to St Chad's church, but not too close:
a 200-yard 'exclusion zone' was placed around it to preserve
its rural setting, apparently at the Earl of Sefton's insistence.
How much better the centre might have been if that magnificent building, rather than standing in splendid isolation, had
been made its focal point. Instead, the centre lies to the SE,
shapeless and very unambitious, and surrounded by roads and
car parks. It is insular, mostly low-rise and of no architectural
interest at all. The market opened in 1960. The shopping centre
– mostly pedestrianised parades – lacks coherence because it
developed piecemeal as three separate developments by differ-

ent developers. The Library, designed by the *Architect's Depart-ment* of *Lancashire County Council*, opened in 1964, and the first phase of the CIVIC CENTRE, by *Jackson & Edmonds*, is of 1966–9. This is a nine-storey tower. Later phases included the Swimming Pool, *c.* 1970, Council Chamber and Assembly Halls. These last two are planned as staggered wings extend-ing from the base of the tower.

The best architecture in the town is to be found at many of the SCHOOLS built from 1952 by the *Architect's Department* of *Lancashire County Council*. At any rate, at least the best archi-tectural detail: a signature water tower supported at one end halfway up a slim brick tower and at the other by splayed steel legs.

KIRKBY INDUSTRIAL PARK. In the late 1930s the Liverpool Corporation took tentative steps towards creating an industrial estate here, but on the outbreak of war a Royal Ordnance Factory was established. At its peak this employed 23,000 and supplied 10 per cent of all national ammunition. Some housing, semi-detached with monopitch roofs, survives on Spinney Road. The factory closed in 1946, and immediately parts of it were opened as an industrial estate; many of the one thousand buildings on its 750 acres (300 hectares) were con-verted and extended. The wartime grid plan remains essen-tially intact. A further 550 acres (220 hectares) s of the ordnance factory to the East Lancashire Road (A580) were also included in the scheme, and in the late 1960s an exten-sion, now called Knowsley Business Park, was begun s of the road. Easily the best buildings are the FACTORY built for ICI (Metals Division) on the East Lancashire Road, by *Sir Percy Thomas & Son*, *c.* 1950. The main structure is behind, but the most architecturally ambitious line the road. The façades are big blocks of brickwork separated by lower and slightly recessed upright grids of glazing, creating a powerful and dis-ciplined rhythm.

WHITEFIELD HOUSE, Ingoe Lane. A three-bay Georgian house with lower one-bay wings surrounded by the post-war housing. One is glad to see it has survived. Dated 1703 but clearly not; an internal datestone is said to have 1793 (DCMS), which is much more believable. Opposite is a highly curious Georgian DOVECOTE known as the Pigeon Hole. A short red stone tower with bracketed cornice, like a stumpy industrial chimney. Said to have had a pigsty in the base. And just s on Ingoe Lane is a C17 yeoman's house. Three bays including cross-wings, with mullioned windows throughout the façade. Baffle-entry plan. Dated 166? and 'rebuilt 1912'.

SIMONSWOOD HALL, on Hall Lane, 1½ m. NNW of the church, just outside the town. Dated 1687; thoughtfully restored in the 1880s. Sandstone, of three bays including a w cross-wing. Only in this gable there is a transomed window (an alteration?); those on the ground and first floors are long and low and have mullions only, and up to six lights. All have label moulds. Tall rebuilt stacks at the ends of the building. A door in the centre bay has a surround of ashlar with voussoirs and a shaped key-stone. This is the only classical element – is it an alteration too?

KNOWSLEY

The principal estate of the Stanleys, Earls of Derby and premier family of Lancashire, since 1702. They have owned the manor even longer, since the C14.

KNOWSLEY HALL. The device of the Stanleys, Earls of Derby, is *sans changer*. It has not prevented successive earls from changing Knowsley Hall more often and more drastically than most of their fellow noblemen have changed their mansions. The estate became Stanley property by marriage in 1385, and is Stanley property to this day.* The chief seat of the family was Lathom House (q.v.) until the death of the 9th Earl in 1702, when it was alienated from the male line. Knowsley grew from a medieval hunting lodge to a large spreading brick C18 house under the direction of the 10th Earl, to be extended yet further in medieval style in the early C19 by *John Foster Jun.* and others, then tidied up in Neo-Georgian in the early C20 for the 17th Earl by *W.H. Romaine-Walker*, before being drastically reduced by *Claud Phillimore* after the Second World War. The result is confusing and also confused, and whilst still undeniably on a very grand scale, it does not flow together into one coherent whole. It has always been thus, as successive rebuildings have been piecemeal on the old foundations, without regard for classical symmetry.** The hall is secreted away in a vast park enlivened by lodges and cottages designed by *William Burn*.

The house is roughly L-shaped. The older and more drasti- 31 cally altered wing runs E–W, i.e. with fronts to N and S, and is on the r. of the forecourt as the visitor approaches the house from the W. To its E, that is at the head of the forecourt, is the later, more unified wing and this runs N–S, i.e. has its fronts to E and W and projects a bit S beyond the end of the first wing. They are for convenience called the S wing and the E wing below. The S wing is of ashlar, the E wing of brick. The oldest part is about the centre of the S wing. It is known as the ROYAL LODGING and has two rounded turrets on the N (forecourt) side, one with a spiral stair and the other with a four-centred arch at ground level. These towers, with conical roofs, are clearly visible in C17 views of the house. This phase is conventionally ascribed to *c.* 1495, the year Henry VII stayed at Knowsley in a suite of rooms recently erected by the mason *Robert Rochdale*. At that time the house was a hunting lodge,

---

*Sir John Stanley married Isabel Lathom, the heir to the Lathom estates at Knowsley, Lathom (q.v.) and elsewhere.
**Robert Adam* and then *William Burn* both produced vast castellated schemes to unify and dignify the ramble, but neither was executed.

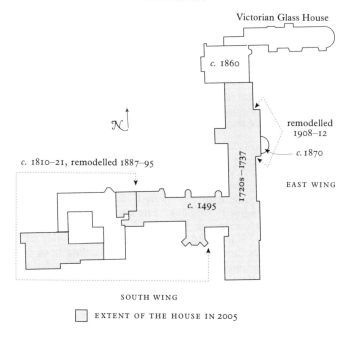

Knowsley Hall.
Block plan

but an important one, at the centre of a substantial park.* It
was regularised as part – possibly the first part – of the massive
rebuilding campaign undertaken by the 10th Earl after he
inherited in 1702. To the forecourt there are nine bays of tall
sash windows, divided into groups of three by the towers. In
the centre, double doors surmounted by a wide broken segmental pediment. Of *c.* 1495 are minor fragments of two piers,
one in the service courtyard, the other by the now isolated
Dynamo Tower at the w end. Otherwise all around here is C19
(*see* below), though much was demolished in the last Knowsley
change, effected by *Phillimore* in 1953–4.

The E WING was rebuilt in brick in phases by the 10th Earl
from the 1720s, apparently starting at the N end. Work seems
to have finished in 1737. Payments are recorded to *Henry
Sephton*, but John Martin Robinson argues that the Earl had a
personal involvement in the design. The w front, facing the
forecourt, is all of a piece in English Baroque with its 6–7–6
rhythm of fenestration. Two storeys over a basement, and an
attic storey as well over the centre section. When completed by

---

*The possible site of an earlier moated manor has been identified ½ m. SE of the
Hall.

the 10th Earl it had a terrace concealing the basement. A pediment over the central seven bays and a large cupola are shown in an early C18 painting by Mollineux, but it is not clear if these were ever executed. The quoins are original, as are the decorative parapets over the outer sections (with prominent central urns flanked by scrolls); the present matching central attic and parapet (with the Stanley eagle and child) and restored small-pane windows are by *Romaine-Walker*, *c.* 1908; the modest w porch, steps and the revealing of the basement are *Phillimore*'s.* Phillimore's changes were part of the creation of an iron-railed FORECOURT, inspired by that shown in the Mollineux view. The wrought-iron GATES closing it are of *c.* 1730 and were brought from elsewhere in the park. This whole remodelling is extremely successful, creating a convincing, handsome and dignified entrance.

The E side of the E wing is very long – in 1937 it was still a full 415 ft (126.5 metres), including a library extension of *c.* 1860 to the N end, and a huge glasshouse beyond that – and here it is clearly in several parts that do not correspond directly to the rhythm of the w façade. The r. part is of four bays and two storeys and plain, and – see the windows and quoins – clearly part of the early C18 block. Then follows the centre, which was completely rebuilt by *Romaine-Walker* in 1908–12 with 2–5–2 bays and two-and-a-half storeys, inspired by Gunby Hall, Lincolnshire, of 1700. Romaine-Walker described his work at Knowsley as 'more of a restoration to what never existed . . . than an old house'. Here his intention was to give some ordered vertical emphasis in the centre to counter the much-criticised rambling horizontality of the wing. The door has a big swan-neck pediment and on the parapet is a mighty, all-singing-and-dancing Derby arms based on that over the s portico (*see* below). This centre replaced a whacking big and pretty dreadful staircase tower of *c.* 1870 with a steep pyramid roof, as if it were a public building, possibly by *Paley & Austin*. This in turn replaced an C18 chapel (a predecessor is mentioned in the C16, and shown in a C17 drawing). After that a continuation of 5–6–5 bays, all two-and-a-half storeys high, but one storey lower because the land falls away to the s. Until *c.* 1895, however, there were only two storeys and a parapet. A painting by Peter Tillemans at the hall clearly shows the earlier wing on this site with a variety of gabled parts, some timber-framed, some stone, some brick.

The s END of the E wing is the climax of the 10th Earl's rebuilding, a handsome five-bay stone portico or loggia of two storeys. The rest of his new wing is mildly English Baroque, but John Martin Robinson has identified a Palladian source for this in the Palazzo Chiericati in Vicenza, as illustrated in Leoni's edition of Palladio's *Quattro Libri* (1715–20). Leoni was working next door at Bold for the Earl's friend Peter Bold in the 1730s (*see* p. 154), but there is no direct evidence pointing

* Phillimore created in the basement servants' accommodation on a scale not seen since in this country. He took down a *porte còchere* and outer hall by *Burn*.

to his involvement at Knowsley. The portico has paired Doric columns below, and paired fluted Ionic columns above. In the parapet balustrade is a large carved heraldic tablet dated 1732, and surmounting that is a splendid Derby arms against a backcloth of trophies. Behind the portico, the wall of the house has niches on both floors, and on the upper floor also pediments to the windows and much stucco decoration.

Continuing along the s front, the E wing jumps back with six bays facing w after the portico, then the s WING begins with a link of three bays. Attached on the ground floor is a colonnade of coupled Doric columns. At this point sandstone replaces brick and the building projects forward again. This is the medievalizing C19 part, i.e. that designed by *Foster*, who was paid from 1810. It was completed in 1821 and contained new services. However, its appearance on this s side is now as remodelled in 1887–95. The designs could well have been produced by the *Knowsley Estate Surveyor*. The State Dining Room lies behind the Royal Lodging, then it recedes again with a nine-bay arcade against it. Foster's work w of the Royal Lodging was largely single-storeyed; it was heightened and extended into a large castellated courtyard. Service and servants' facilities were notably extensive at Knowsley, and even included a staff library. Much of this is demolished; Foster's heightened and altered Flagstaff Tower now terminates the wing, leaving the Dynamo Tower of 1895 isolated beyond.

INTERIOR. There is not as much of the C18 inside as the exterior would make you expect. The 10th Earl's E WING was planned on old-fashioned lines to provide separate apartments for members of his family because the principal rooms in the old wing were retained. Though the new wing did contain a picture gallery, four 'Painting Rooms' and a 'Statue Room', a sequence of grand public rooms was only carved out, by knocking rooms together, from 1895, at first by the *Estate Surveyor* and then in 1908–12 by *Romaine-Walker*. Of the early C18 there is some but perhaps not all of the full panelling and fluted Ionic pilasters of LORD DERBY'S ROOM behind the portico on the ground floor. This was probably typical of the better rooms. A shell-headed niche may have been a buffet and the room used for summer dining. The MORNING ROOM and BREAKFAST ROOM on the principal floor above were created in 1908 from old sets; the coved ceilings and chimneypieces (and Rococo festoons?) date from then, but the panelling either incorporates or repeats the originals. Likewise the Ionic pilasters (fluted, with husk-garlands like those in Lord Derby's Room) and splendid and convincing Rococo plasterwork of the STUCCO ROOM linking old and new wings. This was described as richly embellished; its present form, double the original, was created in 1895. The doorcase between it and the PICTURE GALLERY in the E wing, dated 1733, is the best surviving internal feature of the C18, a gorgeous Borromini-inspired piece that hints at the Gallery's original decoration. This too was doubled in width in 1895 (by moving the w wall outwards), with new double doors in the N wall. In its present form it includes an Inigo Jones-esque chimneypiece by *Romaine-Walker* with a massive and lavish overmantel, conceived as a shrine to the beheaded Cavalier 7th Earl, and classical bookcases introduced when *Phillimore* converted it into a library.

N of here is a sequence of three rooms due in their present form to *Romaine-Walker*, an enlarged ENTRANCE HALL (original dimensions indicated by ceiling beams), with ante-rooms either side. The hall has rich Carolean-style oak panelling, the N ante-room Chippendale bookcases, and the S one apparently authentic *ex situ* Jacobean panelling. Behind these in the centre of the E façade is *Romaine-Walker*'s most magnificent space, a huge STAIRCASE in the lushest Carolean style, to replace the C19 tower. It is convincing, and has a superb oak acanthus-scroll balustrade (now painted white). Messrs *Litchfield* did the joinery for this phase. Finally, there is the large WALNUT DRAWING ROOM, in the SE corner on the principal floor, another space created from apartments in 1895 and decorated fashionably with Louis XIV-style *boiseries* of carved walnut. Some of these are original, others new to match, and were almost certainly supplied by the Parisian firm of *Carlhian* – John Harris has identified pictures of the room amongst their records. If correct, they could also have been responsible for the high-quality decoration of 1895 in the Stucco Room and elsewhere if, as it seems, these alterations were planned by the Estate Surveyor.

The S WING contains the one great room predating the Victorians, the vast STATE DINING ROOM created by *Foster* [107] *c.* 1810–21. Like a great hall, with doors 30 ft (9 metres) high. Two typical Gothic fireplaces and a decadent ormolu chandelier alone survive from this phase; everything else is part of a Brobdingnagian reworking of 1890, including the bay window, finely carved dado and magnificent roof. The last is a large rectangular lantern supported on console brackets, glazed with round-arched lights around the sides. All this woodwork superbly and elaborately carved. The other rooms on the first floor of this wing form the Queen's Rooms, a private apartment fitted out in Neo-Adam style by *Romaine-Walker*. Sadly, post-war sales have deprived Knowsley of its magnificent library, and the best paintings and furniture.

LANDSCAPE. The first reference to a park at Knowsley is in 1292; today it is one of the biggest in Britain, in parts really quite wild. It has been expanded at least three times, the last time in the first half of the C19 when it was enclosed in a wall over 10 m. long. The SE section was turned over in 1971 to a commercial SAFARI PARK. There is a chain of LAKES E and NE of the Hall. The top one, WHITE MAN'S DAM (or the Great Lake), is by far the biggest and is said to have been created by the 10th Earl *c.* 1720–30, and possibly extended later in the C18. On its E bank on top of Stand Hill is the WHITE MAN himself, a lead statue on a pedestal. Below White Man's Dam in an arc round to the S lawn of the Hall is a sequence of much smaller waters, partially descending within a dell. The largest is OCTAGON POND to the E of the Hall. On the opposite side

is the OCTAGON itself, a summer house of 1755 built also to
be an eyecatcher, of local buff stone. The wiggling HOME
POND is the last; it appears to have evolved from the square
pool shown in early C18 paintings at the foot of formal gardens
ascending on the E side of the hall. These are gone, though the
general form of TERRACING remains, Edwardian in current
design with balustrading and arcades. *Capability Brown* was
paid £100 in 1775 for 'A General Plan for alteration of the
Place' and more the following year for plans for a kitchen
garden and alterations to the grounds around the hall, but it
is unclear exactly what his proposals were or to what extent
they were implemented. Certainly there is some typical
naturalistic later C18 landscaping around the Hall, e.g. the
remodelling of the square pool. WALLED GARDENS behind the
stables.

Many SUBSIDIARY BUILDINGS. *Phillimore* designed the
NEW HOUSE in the Park ⅓ m. NE of the Hall for the 18th Earl
and his family, who vacated the Hall on its completion in 1963.
It is in a quiet Neo-Georgian style, but at ten by nine bays with
a bowed porch quite imposing, and contains some of the choic-
est fittings taken from the Hall, and a huge Imperial Staircase.

STABLES, N of the Hall. *William Burn* was engaged to design
them. Under construction in 1847. They are large and of red
brick with red sandstone rustic quoins and alternating surrounds to big ground-level arches, some containing windows,
some doors. The cupola was brought in after 1945.

A large number of COTTAGES scattered around.

BOATHOUSE, on White Man's Dam, ½ m. NE of the Hall. A
charming building by *William Burn* of 1837, with deep eaves
on pierced brackets and elaborate bargeboards with pendants.
Verandas around, some lost. It had accommodation for the
boatkeeper in a symmetrical cottage facing landward, to which
is attached a reception or banqueting room projecting out over
the water with almost continuous windows on three sides. This
sits on top of the boat dock by means of iron beams of interesting and complex form.

THE NEST, ¾ m. N of the Hall, to the E of the Home Farm
(*see* below). The entrance side is gabled and looks 1830s, the
garden side is Georgian with a bow window. The house was
the centre of the 13th Earl's menagerie and aviaries.

HOME FARM, ¾ m. NNW of the Hall. The very large model
C19 complex one would expect. In 2003–4 most of it was converted into business units. At the heart is a stockyard with a
tall and handsome octagonal BELLCOTE at its centre. It has
stone dressings and a cupola.

LODGES. There are quite a number, the best by *William
Burn*, mainly of *c.* 1837–40. The M57 was driven through his
finest, Liverpool Lodge, in 1972. BRIDGE LODGE, within the
park ¼ m. ENE of the Hall, is the most impressive survivor,
though roofless. 1849. Stone, picturesque and asymmetrical, a
castle-style composition incorporating a bridge over the dell
linking White Man's Dam and the Octagon Pond, a gateway

and a turreted residence. Burn's other lodges are in red sand-stone ashlar and are lively like the Boathouse, though all different, with jolly, very florid bargeboards, lots of gables, mullioned windows, label moulds, etc. They are ORCHARD LODGE, W of the Stables, LONGBOROUGH LODGE on the East Lancashire Road, 2 m. NNE of the Hall, HUYTON LODGE on the approach from Liverpool, ½ m. S of it, CROXTETH LODGE on Knowsley Lane 1 m. W and ORMSKIRK LODGE by the Home Farm, 1¾ m. NNW.

ST MARY, Knowsley Lane. A largish church with an intimate interior, the work of *Edmund Sharpe*, and then of *E.G. Paley*, his later partner, after Sharpe's death, then Paley and his new partner *Hubert Austin*. Entirely at the expense of successive Earls of Derby, Sharpe did the nave, aisles and the W tower in 1843–4, Paley the transepts in 1860, *Paley & Austin* the Derby Chapel (N) in 1871–2, and *Paley, Austin & Paley* an enlarged vestry on the S side in 1892–3 and a new E window. Sharpe was archaeologically correct and exhibits great dignity, both in the tower with its broach spire and in the long arcades of quatre-foil piers with stylised foliage capitals. No central aisle. The stone vault in the tower is unexpected and impressive. All this is notable for the date in SW Lancashire. Sharpe's church has lancet windows, his successors introduced bar tracery, especially in the Derby Chapel, and a little rose window over the chancel arch. In 1981–2 the church was reordered with a nave altar, and meeting and service facilities were installed in the base of the tower. The chapel in the N transept dedicated in 1978 was also screened-in.

REREDOS. 1866, by *Edwin Stirling*. – FONT. The stem with attached shafts is of the 1840s; the outsized marble basin of 1890. – PULPIT. 1945–6. – BENCH. From Knowsley Hall, dated 1646. Every inch is intricately carved with, e.g., the Nativity and devices. – TOWER SCREEN. Bottom half of 1904, Dec and probably by *Austin & Paley*. The upper part is of 1981–2. – Carved wooden ROYAL ARMS, dated 1567. Are they from the Hall? – WALL MOSAIC in the chancel. S wall, 1912–13, N wall, 1923. Fine *opus sectile* with scrolling inscriptions and the Annunciation, Nativity, the Three Kings and angels. – The plentiful STAINED GLASS includes the excellent E window by *Shrigley & Hunt*, of 1893, showing Christ in Glory and the four Archangels. A window in each transept by *Lavers & Barraud*, 1871. Chancel S, by *Powell & Sons*, 1923. – MONUMENT of 1872 to the 14th Earl of Derby, by *Matthew Noble*. In the Derby Chapel, which was built in the Earl's memory. Recumbent alabaster effigy, naturalistically carved, on a free Gothic chest. – Large wall-mounted BRASS to George Charles Hale, 1902 by *Jones & Willis Ltd*. With relief medallion.

There is a small, obviously estate-built VILLAGE around the church. C19 COTTAGES on KNOWSLEY LANE and TITHE-BARN LANE, some vernacular but most Victorian and Edwardian in a number of eclectic forms, and almost certainly designed in-house by successive *Estate Surveyors*, for the

Knowsley Estate had a tradition of designing its own buildings. The SCHOOL N of the church facing the small triangular GREEN is of 1845 and much less amateurish. Red sandstone, nicely symmetrical. Tudorbethan – prominent chimneys, Tudor-arch doorway, mullioned-and-transomed windows (with iron, diamond-pattern casements). Extended in similar fashion at either end with little pavilions. Across the green is the VILLAGE HALL, both bigger and uglier than one might expect. 1896–7, by *John Leslie*, Estate Surveyor. On the green is a First World War MEMORIAL CROSS by *T. Wickford Potter*, a later Estate Surveyor. DUMBREES HOUSE, the old vicarage on the W side of Ormskirk Road, is big, ashlar, asymmetric and Tudor Gothic. It is surely – with e.g. a pyramid-capped stair-turret – by *William Burn*, who did a lot of work for the 13th and 14th Earls (*see* above), and produced designs for a parsonage. Now hemmed-in by housing built tightly over the gardens.

STOCKBRIDGE VILLAGE and other HOUSING ESTATES. *see* Huyton, p. 203.

LATHOM

4000

A rural place NE of Ormskirk which was the principal seat of the mighty Stanleys, Earls of Derby, until the C18. There is no village to speak of.

BURSCOUGH PRIORY, Mill Dam Lane. On private land. Founded *c.* 1190 for Augustinian Canons; by 1296 there were six of them, and the prior. The church had transepts, a central tower and a later N aisle. The cloister was on the S side, and measured 67 ft (20.6 metres) square. All that survives above ground are the two piers between the N transept and crossing plus the semi-octagonal NE arcade respond and a stump of the chancel N wall. This must date from the late C13. A number of FITTINGS and TOMBS at Ormskirk church (q.v.) and Lathom Chapel (*see* below) are said to have come from Burscough, which was the burial place of the Stanleys until the Dissolution.

LATHOM PARK CHAPEL. *See* p. 226.

ST JAMES, Westhead. *See* Ormskirk, p. 536.

LATHOM PARK PRIMARY SCHOOL, Hall Lane. 1881, by *Thomas Kissack* for the 1st Earl of Lathom. Brick with stone dressings. T-plan, with gables (half-hipped to the main range) hood-moulded lancets and a bellcote. Pretty.

LATHOM HOUSE, ⅓ m. E of Hall Lane. The surviving building at Lathom has great presence, but it is only a fragment of one of the great C18 houses of Northern England, itself built on the site of one of the grandest medieval seats of the North. The fragment is the W SERVICE WING of *Giacomo Leoni*'s Palladian house for Sir Thomas Bootle, a building difficult to date precisely, but possibly begun *c.* 1725 and finished *c.* 1740. It had two service wings connected with the centre by quadrant links of unfluted Ionic columns (a fragment of wall from the W

32

quadrant is preserved as if it were a monastic ruin). The centre was of thirteen bays and two-and-a-half storeys, the middle three bays raised with an attic with oval windows (by *T.H.Wyatt* in 1862) and a pediment. The windows of the *piano nobile* were also pedimented. Perrons by Wyatt on both sides reached up to the main entrances. That splendid mansion was demolished in 1929, one of the worst C20 losses in the county. The E service wing stood until the 1950s; now only the W wing survives, in 2005 being restored from dereliction as housing. Its size is a reminder of the monumentality of the house, and the stables. It is of ashlar, one-and-a-half storeys high, seven by four bays in size and topped by an octagonal cupola with ogee cap. Ground-floor windows and doors (those on the S side of the C21) have Gibbs surrounds; there are projecting quoins. Three-bay pediment on the E side, i.e. facing the *cour d'honneur*, and beneath that an arched entrance leading through to a yard surrounded by C19 single-storey ranges, including a carriage house and stables. These have openings forming an arcade, now glazed as part of the residential conversion.

Recent archaeological investigation has revealed that the stable block and courtyard is built across an infilled moat, with sandstone revetments, some 42 ft (13 metres) wide, and the footings of walls and towers. This is the MOAT of the medieval home of the Stanleys, one of the greatest houses of the medieval North. Lathom had become their capital messuage by marriage in 1385. The house was probably reconstructed and improved by Thomas Stanley after his elevation following the Battle of Bosworth (1485). It was described in an early C16 poem as having 'nine towers on high and nine on the outer walls', but documentary and figurative evidence suggests an uncrenellated building with many external windows, i.e.

Lathom House, by Giacomi Leoni, *c.* 1725–40.
Engraving by R. Sears, after G. Pickering, 1832

despite moat, walls and towers, this was a house not a castle, built chiefly for pleasure, not defence. Damaged when twice besieged during the Civil War and partly dismantled afterwards, it was apparently partially rebuilt at the Restoration. The 9th Earl began a 'sumptuous and lofty new front', but this was unfinished on his death in 1702, when the house was alienated from the male line and Knowsley became the principal seat. Parts of this building – some Georgian sources claim – were included in Leoni's house. In the mid C19 possibly medieval fabric was discovered during repair work, something confirmed by the recent investigations.

LATHOM PARK. It was created *c.* 1250 or earlier; *Humphry Repton* produced a scheme in 1792. Remains of the landscape include a HA-HA partially following the line of the medieval moat. NE of the surviving buildings is a WALLED GARDEN. The park has been ploughed up. For the NEW PARK *see* below.

8   LATHOM PARK CHAPEL. Quite a distance – ⅓ m. – WNW of the house. Founded by the 1st Earl of Derby in 1500 as a chantry chapel with his almshouses (*see* below), and consecrated in 1509. A simple little rectangle of three bays with an octagonal stone bellcote corbelled out from the W gable, and otherwise no genuine external Perp features except for one doorway uncovered in the S wall. This may have led to the priest's house, demolished in the C18 and replaced by a SCHOOL (now a house). The Perp E window is apparently of 1898, but whether it follows the form of the original is not clear. Whitewashed inside and out, except for the outside of the E wall, where red sandstone rubble is exposed. The window tracery in the sides is of very pretty (and uninformed) early C19 Gothic forms. It dates from a restoration of *c.* 1817, from when also come the wagon roof with delicate rib-work (equally pretty and uninformed) and the little W organ GALLERY. The SE vestry would seem to be substantially of that date too, with label-moulded mullioned window and Tudor-arched door. It has a delightful ribbed parachute plaster vault. – FONT. In the vestry. Simple, worn octagonal bowl on octagonal stem. From Burscough Priory? – SANCTUARY SCREEN. Delicate, no tracery. Including Perp parts believed to have come from Burscough, but substantially altered and restored: after the siege of Lathom House in 1644 (supposed musket-ball holes still visible) and *c.* 1817, and in 1964 when *Ernest Gee* removed the early C19 additions. – LECTERN. A splendid oak eagle said also to be from Burscough, on a baluster stand of C17 or early C18 date. – HATCHMENT. A magnificent and unusual example carved in low relief. The cartouched arms themselves, probably of Robert Bootle, †1758, sit in an oval frame with drapes, gloves etc. – STAINED GLASS. Prevalently yellow heraldic glass of the early C19. In 1964 the date 1823 and name *William Seddon* were found on one of them. *Mary Charlotte Bootle Wilbraham*, daughter of the owner of the house, is said to have designed them. E window, 1898.

Simple ALMSHOUSES are attached to the W end of the chapel in an L-shape. Whitewashed and exposed rubble. Eleven dwellings, now nine. They have been altered, but the windows are set in blank arches and the doors on the E side have label moulds. Their history is unclear, but the 1st Earl founded a hospital for eight old men at the same time as the chapel. Are they therefore Tudor, and substantially changed, or possibly C17? On the W side is a former STABLE block, an arcade of eleven narrow arches with keystones. Early C18.

GATEPIER and LODGES, Hall Lane. By *Leoni*. The lodges are 33 simple two-storey octagons with a Gibbs door surround in the rusticated ground floor. They are hidden behind high quadrant screen walls, though the S one is now revealed by a large gap made when the house was extended, *c.* 1960s. The odd thing here is that the extension was made low as if to be hidden, only for the opening-up of the wall to defeat any attempted discretion. The surviving gatepier is stupendous, a sumptuous piece 20 ft (6.2 metres) high. The inside and outside faces are elongated aedicules framing niches with enormous keystones. Their Tuscan attached columns are blocked with bands of frosted rustication which wrap around the sides of the pier to unite the two faces. Heavy cornice.

½ m. N is the PRESTON LODGE entrance, by contrast chaste Late Georgian with single-storey, pyramid-roofed LODGES in the screen walls. Wrought-iron gate between.

BLYTHE HALL, Blythe Lane. Sandstone. The main range is an H-plan, low with mullioned windows and two ridge chimneys. It is probably an early C17 house, altered in the C19 and extensively remodelled by the theatrically obsessed 3rd Earl of Lathom *c.* 1920. He added – via a link – a wing to the rear of the r. end, of five symmetrical bays, the gabled outer ones with full-height canted bays, the centre with a ground-floor loggia and low mullioned windows over. An older range attached to the rear at the l. end, possibly C16, was demolished *c.* 1974. The interior of the C17 part is said to have been equally lavishly transformed for the 3rd Earl, with an open hall with impressive two-storey colonnaded Ionic screen occupying most of the rear wall, behind which is the staircase. Elsewhere is excellent panelling, apparently from Leoni's house. The most celebrated feature of the *c.* 1920 work is the swimming pool behind the new wing. In Greek Doric style, with coffered ceiling and semi-fluted, semi-mosaic columns, it is reminiscent of the pool at the RAC Club, Westminster, by Mewès & Davis.

CRANES HALL, Cranes Lane. Said to have been the Lathom Estate Manager's house. Façade of two storeys and five bays, the l. three of one build, with earlier C18 sashes and a door moved into to the r. bay. Two successive one-bay extensions to the r. are later Georgian. At the rear is a small C17 element and various additions. All this of roughcast render on stone, and probably some brick.

HALTON CASTLE, Ormskirk Golf Course, s of Cranes Lane. At the centre of the Stanleys' New Park, created 1470, is a square platform and a MOAT, wet on one side, which is conjectured to be C16. This is presumably the site of the house, sometimes called New Lodge, that was regularly occupied by the Earl of

Derby in the C16; it was not a castle. Buildings were demolished *c.* 1725; excavated remains have been dated to the C16.

PILKINGTON'S TECHNICAL CENTRE, E off Hall Lane. Pilkington's the glass-makers acquired the Lathom House estate in the C20 and in the 1950s built a large building by *Courtauld's Technical Services* S of the site of the house.

ANCIENT FARMSTEAD SITE, Duttons Farm, Hall Lane. Four round-houses dating from *c.* 200 to 5 B.C. were excavated in the 1990s. The largest is 35 ft (10.5 metres) in diameter. Two granaries, and a quernstone for grinding corn, made from stone from the central Pennines, also found. No evidence for an enclosure ditch. It appears that arable farming was more important here than at contemporary sites in the region, such as Brook House Farm, Halewood, *see* p. 192.

p. 13

LEIGH

The flat featureless topography of the Lancashire Plain does Leigh no favours; approaching from any direction, the town is still dominated by its remaining textile mills, all now closed. The big mills came relatively late, as did coal mining on a large scale. Before that there was a substantial silk industry, and before that muslin, fustians and linen in the C16. Industrialisation was stimulated by the arrival of branches of the Bridgewater Canal in 1799 and the Leeds and Liverpool in 1820 (from Wigan, to join the Bridgewater), and then by railways. The Bolton & Leigh Railway opened in 1828, two years before the Liverpool & Manchester. In 1841 the population was 11,000, and this had quadrupled by the end of the century; in 2001 it was 39,000. The industrial town emerged from three separate townships: Leigh itself with a medieval church and market, Bedford to the E, where most of the biggest mills were built, and Westleigh on the other side, with more weaving and spinning. The built-up areas did not merge until after 1850. Local governance united in 1875, when a Local Board was created. In 1894 an Urban District Council was formed and, finally, in 1899, Leigh was granted a borough charter.

The architectural highlight is the old market place with the church and town hall facing each other across the open space. There are the usual grids of bylaw housing, and beyond them C20 public and private semis. Any building of any merit that is not a church or mill is almost certainly by the local firm of *J.C. Prestwich & Sons*, capable – sometimes very capable – in a number of styles. *James Caldwell Prestwich* commenced practice in Leigh in 1875 and was joined by his son Harold in 1907; the firm was still in business in the 1980s.

CHURCHES

ST MARY, Market Place. 1869–73, by *Paley & Austin*, except the tower, which is probably early C16 and was refaced in 1910 by the same firm (by then *Austin & Paley*). The large church is red sandstone and built on the foundations of the old. Perp in all motifs, though the tracery is characteristic of Paley & Austin. The clerestory of square-headed windows runs through the nave and chancel and is embattled, as is the tower, where the design of the belfry stage compares with Wigan and Ormskirk parish churches (qq.v.). On the s side the division between nave and chancel is picturesquely expressed by a chapel doorway set diagonally. There is a s porch, and pointed-roofed octagonal turrets at the e corners. The choir vestry is a special n attachment, well done in 1909–10 by the same architects to suit the church. Six-bay interior with octagonal piers and double-chamfered arches; impressive in scale but none yet of the spatial thrills of which Paley & Austin were later capable. The tower arch and sloping w wall are evidently real Perp, and the roof-line and arcade imposts of the previous nave appear in the wall, illustrating how very much lower it was. The n aisle roof is real Perp too, reused from the old n aisle. Panelled, with moulded beams, bosses, and saltire pattern in the e bays. The nave roof, a peculiar hammerbeam with elongated braces alternating with tie-beams, is derived from the design of the old. Why don't the clerestory windows and roof bays align with the arcades? s chapel with PISCINA and REREDOS.

REREDOS and ALTAR. Both by *Paley & Austin*, 1870 and 1890 respectively. The wooden reredos in particular is extremely handsome in the practice's elaborate Free Flamboyant style. Both gorgeously painted by *Shrigley & Hunt* with lots of gold, red and green and good figures. – CHOIR STALLS, PARCLOSE SCREENS (1914), part of the ORGAN CASE (1910) etc. by the architects, in the same characteristic style. The fine case of the 1777 organ by *Samuel Green* of London – still with Rococo embellishment – is preserved on its vestry side. – The COMMUNION RAIL is iron. – COMMUNION TABLE. Now in the Lady Chapel. Good. Given 1705, but early C17. With carved bulbous legs and inlaid chequer frieze. Chapel panelled in 1915 in Jacobean style to match. – PEWS. Against the w wall, the canopies of the churchwardens' pews from the old church, dated 1686. – FONT. *Paley & Austin*. Stone. Octagonal on octagonal pier. Corner shafts; carved panels between, alternately with semi-relief scenes. – TOWER SCREEN. 1894. Neo-C17. – W DOOR. C16. Studded oak. – CHANDELIER. C18. Brass. A cut above the norm. – STAINED GLASS. w window by *Kempe*, c. 1905. e window, 1889, by *Shrigley & Hunt*. Some glass in the s aisle is signed by them too. But the best of the rest is in the Lady Chapel, †1891 etc. – MONUMENTS. A few tablets from the old church in the tower. – First World War memorial. Bronze tablet in wooden Free Perp frame (*Paley & Austin?*).

CHRIST CHURCH, St Helens Road, Pennington, ½ m. s. 1850–4, by *E.H. Shellard*. Big, rather lifeless church. Some Perp, some Dec tracery. Coursed stone and ashlar dressings. w tower, nave and aisles, chancel. The aisles have eaves, but everywhere else has parapets. Octagonal piers inside, but still a w gallery. This now has a glazed screen under it. – CHANCEL FITTINGS.

Made by the congregation after the Second World War. Oak. – STAINED GLASS. Including: N aisle, two *Morris & Co.* windows, part of a First World War memorial, pretty awful. Chancel S, S aisle 1st, 2nd and 4th from E, undistinguished interwar *Abbott & Co.* S aisle, 5th from E, James Hunter, †1917, by *Walter J. Pearce.* The best glass, S aisle E and 3rd from E, is *c.* 1900 and unmarked.

VICARAGE. Mid-C19, of brick, and still largely in the Georgian tradition.

ST PAUL, Westleigh Lane, Westleigh, 1 m. NNW. By *W. Young.* First designs 1845; opened 1847. Dec style, i.e. in cognisance of the Pugin–Scott revolution, and an early example for SW Lancs. Nave and broad S aisle, chancel and squat S tower outside the aisle. This looks unfinished; a belfry stage and broach spire were intended. The blank and unmoulded arcade flush in the N wall can only have been intended to allow for a future N aisle. The exterior is girdled by massive iron ties to counter subsidence. They criss-cross the interior too. This has correct octagonal piers, arch-braced trusses rising from crenellated corbels, and a chancel arch. The organ is under the tower. Vestries were inserted at the E end in 1964, behind a curved grey brick screen with a new ALTAR in front of it, an odd and not successful idea. – CHANCEL SCREEN and integrated PULPIT. Intricately Dec, and very like Austin & Paley. – Quite good C19 STAINED GLASS in the S aisle widows and especially the E window.

ST PETER, Firs Lane, Westleigh, ¾ m. W. By *Paley & Austin* and one of their most radical and thrilling churches. Rainwater head dated 1879; consecrated 1881. Cost, £7,000. Very ordinary brick with red sandstone dressings. Nave and chancel separated by a bold tower, with pyramidal roof, an ashlar frieze below the top, and heavy buttresses. These are flush with the E and W faces. N aisle and vestry. N and S windows are straightheaded. The details are Dec throughout. Reticulated tracery in the large E window, and unmistakably Paley & Austin tracery in the side windows. Inside, the nave and chancel impress by their big timbers – hammerbeams in the chancel; tie-beams, kingposts, and ranks of curvy wind-braces in the nave. Nave arcade of round sandstone piers with moulded capitals. Responds and arches without any capitals, built up entirely of moulded brick, support the central tower and its ribbed quadripartite vault, all in brick too. – REREDOS. A good sober rectangular stone job by the architects, with four niches and statues. – CHANCEL SCREEN. Wrought-iron and slender. The frieze is the same as the one on the tower. – PULPIT. Big, elaborate and alabaster, on dwarf piers, with blank ogee arcading and canopied statues at the corners. It is good quality, but out of place here, and indeed comes from Manchester Cathedral. The massive stairs, with angels on the newels but otherwise plain, were presumably concocted – or reworked – to fit its new home. – STAINED GLASS. E window by *Abbott & Co.,* Lancaster, 1949. Ascension. Decent. Nothing else.

FIRST WORLD WAR MEMORIAL in the churchyard. 1919. *Bratt* of Leigh, sculptor.

St Thomas, Chapel Street, Bedford. J.S. Crowther was given the commission before his death in 1893; his pupil *R.B. Preston* took over. A large church built in two phases. Chancel and the two E bays of the nave and aisles, 1902–3; the rest, including a SW tower detached from the nave, 1909–10. Very hard red brick. Lively Dec tracery. Five-bay arcades with a transeptal widening of the fourth and fifth bays. – Extensive chancel FITTINGS by *Sir Charles Nicholson*, 1932–3. – STAINED GLASS. A memorial to Ellen Higson by *Powell & Sons*. Others by *A.K. Nicholson* of London, 1911–38. – Second World War memorial LYCHGATE.

St Joseph (R.C.), Chapel Street, Bedford. 1855. An important work in *Joseph Hansom*'s oeuvre, with an original façade, and a startling interior that shows him experimenting with plan and form to suit the needs of his Jesuit clients. Hammer-dressed stone. Tight W façade set back a distance from the street, with a big W tower with angle buttresses with many set-offs. The top of the tower reads as a steep gable between the buttresses, which finish as large pinnacles, because the saddle-form of the roof is hidden. At the apex of the gable is a hefty statue of St Joseph. By contrast the sides of the church are simple, with three-light Geometric windows and buttresses and a massive pitched roof of slate. Inside one sees that this is because this is a big preaching box, a single, very wide room of nine bays, with a short apsidal chancel. Hansom was exceptional in the 1850s for his individual preference for wide, uncluttered interiors, but here he over-reached himself when it came to designing the roof. It seems that he began a hammerbeam roof, but that the hammerbeams were unable to take the weight transmitted through the huge arch-braced trusses, and the roof failed. Therefore, the hammerbeams were extended and rows of very tall cast-iron columns (with surprising palm capitals) were put in to support them, and braced – creating arcades when Hansom had sought to avoid them. Directly above the columns, iron arches were inserted on top of the hammerbeams, going longitudinally between them, i.e. W to E. The result is a whimsical web of braces and arches. The ceiling of the apse is gloriously painted. There is a W organ gallery and a little chapel through three little arches in the S wall, with a painted boarded ceiling, cusped in section. – ALTARS. Three, with excellent marble REREDOSES, all with canopied statues. The High Altar has a tall filigree canopy sheltering a crucifix surmounting the tabernacle. – Another reredos, with relief scenes, in the S chapel. – The church was reordered *c.* 1987 by the *Pozzoni Design Group*. A celebrant ALTAR and AMBO, made of marble recycled from the dismantled altar rails, is placed on a platform in the second bay. A glazed SCREEN was put under the W gallery at the same time. – C19 ROOD. – STATIONS OF THE CROSS. In timber ogee frames. – STAINED GLASS. The best is in the apse, S, 4th from W, and appears original. By *Mayer & Co.*, no date.

On Chapel Street to the r. of the church, forming one side of its approach, is St Joseph's Hall, an ambitious church

hall of 1925. The central recessed section of the street front is
stone, with a big gable with a window in it – both with bold
curvilinear tracery – and beneath that a triple-arch arcaded
entrance.

SACRED HEART (R.C.), Walmesley Road. 1929, brick, Dec. NW
tower, nave and narrow aisles, N transept and short chancel.
Quite big.

WIGAN ROAD METHODIST CHURCH, Wigan Road, Westleigh.
Foundation stone 1913. Shiny red brick and buff terracotta
dressings. W front, a little, loosely derived version of King's
College Chapel, with a big handsome window with terracotta
tracery.

UNITED METHODIST CHURCH (former), Plank Lane, Westleigh. Early C20 brick and terracotta dressing with a single
roof. Perp, including another handsome W window. Now a
nursery.

PUBLIC BUILDINGS

85 TOWN HALL, Market Street. 1904–7, by *J.C. Prestwich*. An
exceptionally good building, expressive yet not showy. Unlike
most of Leigh, which is red brick, it is of sandstone (from
Darley Dale). To the Market Place it has a front of seven bays
with a *piano nobile* of giant columns alternately blocked, and
tall windows, a very tall hipped roof, and a complex, beefy
cupola perched on top. The portal has a big, almost semicircular pediment. In addition there is a l. angle bay with rather
more Baroque decoration articulated separately, and this leads
to the Market Street frontage, which is longer, in itself symmetrical and, with shops to the street, less stately. It has a separate entrance for the sanitary department. Nothing unsanitary
need therefore enter through the main portal into the dimly lit
entrance hall, with its scagliola columns and beamed plaster
ceiling, and the rates office to the r. Up the stately flying imperial staircase opposite the portal, with square stone balusters
and broad handrail, are the Council Chamber and two smaller
committee rooms, across the Market Place front of the *piano
nobile*. The Council Chamber has a segmental plaster ceiling
with mouldings, and a shallow wooden gallery on columns at
one end. The planning here is quite clever: the rooms can be
combined by opening or even removing large doors between
them. This is an example of a trend *c.* 1900 to more flexible
planning that is also found at the town halls of Sheffield and
Lancaster. The doors are gathered in huge pilastered surrounds
with giant segmental pediments. Across the vestibule, on the
Market Street side, is the Mayor's Parlour. Throughout the
public spaces there are wainscot and doorcases in lavish,
largely Wrenaissance style supplied by *Garnett & Sons* of Warrington, but they are just slightly flimsy-looking. The windows
of the Council Chamber are filled with large STAINED GLASS
figures by *H. Gustave Hiller* of Liverpool, dated 1908, person-
ifying Weaving, Spinning, Commerce, Education, Engineering
and Mining. He also did the big, handsome coats of arms of

local families in the staircase windows and roof-light. The
geometric precision of the latter is especially attractive.

THE TURNPIKE CENTRE, Market Place. 1971, and still by *J.C.
Prestwich & Sons*. The building rather skulks. It houses a library
and art gallery in Brutalist concrete. The vertically textured
first-floor façades are blank except for the heavy projecting
slots, angled downwards, which would not look out of place
on Rommel's Atlantic Wall. Above the main entrance is a large
concrete panel, a deeply textured abstract relief SCULPTURE
by *William Mitchell*. A theatre was planned.

PUBLIC LIBRARY AND TECHNICAL SCHOOL (former), Railway
Road. Now Leigh College. 1894, by *J.C. Prestwich* and *J.H.
Stephen*. Big, red brick and asymmetrical. A big elaborate
Dutch gable on the r., three smaller dormer gables along the
centre and an ogee-capped corner tower on the l., and another
big gable on the return. Large cross-windows.

BEDFORD HIGH SCHOOL, Manchester Road (A572). The E
block, at right angles, is the former Grammar School of 1931.
Interwar scholastic classicism, with a central section of giant
pilasters and the inevitable square cupola. The other part, *E.
Brocklehurst*'s Manchester Road Secondary School of 1932, is
much plainer.

LEIGH CENTRAL PRIMARY SCHOOL, Windermere Road. Built
as the Girls Grammar School in 1915. Red brick. Queen Anne
meets English Baroque with no fewer than three cupolas on
the single range.

SCHOOL (former), King Street. Foundation stone laid in 1896.
Street façade in hard red brick with large Geometrical window
and, l., a stair-tower with pyramid roof. The sides, in stocks,
with two layers of large windows.

FIRST WORLD WAR MEMORIAL, Church Street. The centrepiece of a small formal square, a memorial garden. 1922,
by *J.C. Prestwich & Sons*. Ashlar Portland cenotaph. Bronze
plaques on either side framed by engaged columns. These have
capitals copied from the Tower of the Winds in Athens, i.e. with
one row of acanthus leaves and an upper row of palm leaves.

PERAMBULATION

A walk around the commercial centre of the town begins
at the old MARKET PLACE, the historic heart and townscape highlight – if indeed it can be described thus – of Leigh.
It is bound by the TOWN HALL, the TURNPIKE CENTRE
and PARISH CHURCH (*see* above), and on the E side by an
empty lot and a splendid pub called THE BOAR'S HEAD, the
flagship of the Bedford Brewery. 1900, with extravagant
and terracotta cupola, oriels, columns etc. and a double-
decker stable.* In the middle of the Market Place – which

* 100 yards N of The Boar's Head on Leigh Road is the GRAND THEATRE AND
HIPPODROME (former), by *J.C. Prestwich*. Opened 1908. Tall and crisp eclectic
façade of red brick and buff terracotta, spoilt by the gormless modern rearrange-
ment of the ground floor.

is paved in brick – is an OBELISK with sunk panels, erected
by Robert Atherton in 1762, and since moved and rebuilt
twice.

MARKET STREET leads S down the side of the Town Hall to the
crossroads at the centre of Leigh, where Market Street and
King Street – the old toll road – cross the principal shopping
thoroughfare, Bradshawgate, and its W extension, Railway
Street. The CROSSROADS were widened and redeveloped in
1898–1900. All the best stuff on these streets is by *Prestwich*,
e.g. the NATWEST BANK on the NW corner of the crossroads
built for Parr's Bank in 1908, in banded Portland ashlar with
emphatic first-floor window surrounds with giant keystones.
On the NE corner is a dire building of 1964 which replaced
Prestwich's exuberant Rope and Anchor Hotel (remnant to the
r.); on the SE corner a typical former BURTONS branch from
between the wars, with a giant Corinthian order; and on the
SW corner an Italianate BARCLAYS BANK in Coal Measures
sandstone with corner cupola, built for the Manchester Union
Bank *c.* 1870s.

The bank has a façade on BRADSHAWGATE, Leigh's best street,
whose present form owes much to the redevelopment of the
S side from 1888 to designs by *Prestwich*. His own former
OFFICES are Nos. 14–18. They have the initials JCP and a continuous row of tall windows on the first floor held tautly
together by Ionic pilasters and entablature, which lit the
drawing office. Beyond Ellesmere Street is a row of shops of
1889–90 by him, with Dutch gables over every bay, and further
on more with Jacobean gables, of 1899. Across Albion Street,
now the entrance to *Cullearn & Phillip*'s covered MARKET and
SPINNING GATE SHOPPING CENTRE of 1989, is the former
CO-OPERATIVE CENTRAL BUILDINGS, by *Prestwich*, the
grandest commercial building in Leigh. It cost £19,000 and
was built in 1897–9. Three big storeys, plus gables, of his
favoured Flemish Renaissance in Ruabon brick and terracotta.
Next, on the corner of Vernon Street on the N side, is the
HSBC BANK, built in 1906 as shops and the Leigh Club. An
eclectic mixture of Renaissance motifs mainly in red sandstone, with Art Nouveau corbels and an enriched corner. *Prestwich* was both architect and developer. Returning to the S side,
there are remnants of Bradshawgate's earlier, semi-industrial
character. Nos. 100–112 are a row of little shops that originated
before 1825 as weavers' cottages, with basement loom shops;
E of them, on the corner with Brown Street North, is a former
muslin- and silk-master's receiving house of *c.* 1800 (*see* Industrial Architecture, p. 237). Finally, on the opposite corner, the
former LILFORD HOTEL, one of *Prestwich*'s earliest works. Of
1876, it shows him starting his career in a conventional High
Victorian Gothic.

Returning to the crossroads, RAILWAY ROAD is Bradshawgate's
W extension. Alongside *Prestwich*'s NatWest Bank is a big handsome pub by him – now chambers – of 1899. Massive shaped
gable. Next door is one building not by Prestwich, the former
CONSERVATIVE CLUB, later a cinema and nightclub. Big,

gabled and eclectic, by *J.J. Bradshaw* of Bolton, 1879. But *Prest-wich* inevitably gets the last word, designing the former LEIGH BAZAAR opposite, which incorporates a former ropewalk on Cook Street of 1834. When the hardware store opened in 1880 it had more elaborate gables, and its 200 ft (61 metres) of coun-ters created quite a stir.

The final arm of the crossroads is KING STREET, once the turn-pike s to St Helens. The little, brick GEORGE AND DRAGON (a pub since at least 1698) is a rare C17 survivor. On the w side the flamboyant Flemish Renaissance YORKSHIRE BANK of *c.* 1900, and a five-bay stuccoed Police Station and Magistrates' Court of 1840 which was from 1875 Leigh's town hall. On the same side at the corner with TWIST LANE, a massive 1890s PUB, carved with the name Eagle and Child. It is more Flemish Renaissance with a ribbed corner chimneystack, and must be by *Prestwich*.

An extension of the walk continues s across the LEEDS AND LIV-ERPOOL CANAL (*see* p. 237) to PENNINGTON, where King Street becomes ST HELENS ROAD (A572), and is lined, beyond CHRIST CHURCH (*see* p. 230), with the best middle-class HOUSES. All are late C19 and early C20 and by *J.C. Prestwich (& Sons)*. Amongst them, THE GRANGE, 1897, Queen Anne Revival, red brick with shaped gables. The finest, TATRY of 1904, is a very good essay in the Arts and Crafts style. Rough-cast. The ground-floor windows are sashes in stone surrounds with stone mullions, and a stone transom hiding where the sashes meet. It has a good staircase. Also roughcast Arts and Crafts, but on a more modest scale, are Nos. 2, 4, 6–8, 7–9 and 10 HAND LANE and a series on BEECH GROVE, E off St Helens

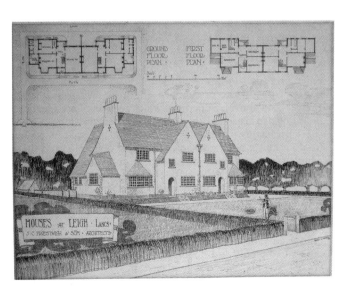

Leigh, houses on Beech Grove, by J.C. Prestwich & Son, *c.* 1914.
Contemporary elevation and plans drawn for the architect

Road. *Prestwich* was the developer as well as the architect. The Beech Grove houses have battered chimney stacks.

INDUSTRIAL ARCHITECTURE

BREWERIES. Two small (former) examples on BROWN STREET NORTH. On the W side, the LILFORD BREWERY of 1895, built by the landlord of the neighbouring Lilford Hotel (*see* Bradshawgate, p. 235); on the E side opposite, the DERBY BREWERY, a complex of *c.* 1871 with a narrow five-storey brewing tower, and stables and coopers' workshops. The much larger Leigh Brewery on Brewery Lane, and its brewing tower of *c.* 1900 with an early steel frame, has been demolished.

CANAL WAREHOUSES. On the Leeds and Liverpool W of King Street bridge there are two, adjoining, now a restaurant and offices. One is of *c.* 1820, the date the branch opened, two storeys, stone, with broad-arched loading doors and, l., a canted two-storey bay window (the agent's house?). Inside are timber floors and posts. The other is of 1894, three storeys of machine-made brick, with covered external hoists and cast-iron columns inside. An instructive comparison between two generations of the same building type.

SILK INDUSTRY BUILDINGS. In 1827 silk weaving began to replace fustian and muslin manufacture as the town's principal business. Within a decade Leigh was one of the centres of the Lancashire industry, only for it all to collapse after the duty on French silk was lifted in 1870. Little evidence remains. In HIGGINSON STREET is a brick terrace built *c.* 1840 for handloom weavers. These are two-up, two-down cottages with a specialist feature, an enlarged ground-floor window or two in the S-facing rear wall, which lit the loom shop. Piece work was 'put out' to them by local agents of the Manchester merchant-manufacturers. One of the few surviving RECEIVING HOUSES, No. 5 WILD'S PASSAGE off King Street, is that of Robert Guest, the muslin-master turned silk agent whom the Higginson Street weavers supplied (he also owned the Leigh Brewery, *see* above). Superficially a large, brick Late Georgian house of two bays and three storeys, it contains a number of specialist features: a separate entrance and staircase, a 'taking-in' door and a hoist giving access to the open-plan top floor, where would have been warping mills and winding machines, and warehousing for the cloth before it was sent on to Manchester. This floor required massive trusses. There is another example on the corner of BRADSHAWGATE and BROWN STREET, *c.* 1830, with the top-floor taking-in door clearly visible, and behind, on the corner of GAS STREET, a different type – an independent warehouse. It has few windows, but others had plenty and doubled as loom shops.*

COTTON MILLS. Silk was replaced by an expanded cotton industry. At its height in the early C20 Leigh was the fifth-

---

* Information on the buildings of the silk industry was supplied by Philip Powell.

largest spinning centre in Greater Manchester measured by the number of spindles. The industry here developed relatively late, from the mid C19, and was concentrated in large multi-storey mills that still command the skyline. Only five remain, none still spinning. The two of most note, excellent examples of the last generation of Lancashire mill construction, are of the 'planned double' type, designed from the outset for expansion. BUTTS MILL, Butts Street, of 1905 or 1907, is by *Stott & Sons* of Oldham, mill specialists. Only one half was built. Reinforced concrete floors and cast-iron columns clad in brick with buff terracotta dressings. Six storeys. The distinctly Byzantine SW stair tower, with copper dome on scalloped top stage, buttresses, little domed corner turrets and terracotta banding, is typical of Stotts under *Abraham Henthorn Stott Jun.*, and surely influenced by Westminster Cathedral. The LEIGH MILL, Park Lane, by comparison, is by another leading mill designer of the period, *Bradshaw, Gass & Hope* of Bolton. It is one of the few planned doubles that were actually doubled: the E block with cupola'd tower, the chimney and the boiler house are 1913, the W block is 1923 (and one of the very last Lancashire spinning mills to be built). Monumental, but more prosaically detailed. Six storeys again. Red brick with buff brick banding and dressings, on a metal frame. It had over 200,000 mule spindles at its peak, and is now, with one steam engine intact, one of the most complete survivors of its type in Greater Manchester.

One other notable mill building is the ALDER MILL OFFICE, Clyde Street, 1907. The mill itself is demolished, but this little building, with its attached entrance gates, is a delight. It is distinctively *Abraham Henthorn Stott Jun.* again, only one storey high, in red and yellow banded brick with yellow terracotta dressings and a characteristic Stott parapet of terracotta swinging between posts, of a sort, with flat finials. Projecting slightly from the corner is an octagonal tower with a similar terracotta parapet and a copper dome. The elaborate iron gates are hung from iron piers with moulded Art Nouveau decoration.

OUTLYING BUILDINGS

BEDFORD HALL, Hooten Lane, 1 m. ESE. The exterior is that of a mid-C17 yeoman's or minor gentry house. Brick, three bays and two storeys, including two cross-wings, with multi-mullioned windows. The W side is remarkably symmetrical, with simple doors in each wing. These must date from the subsequent subdivision into two cottages. The two chimneystacks against each wing correspond too. The window surrounds are not chamfered, as is normal in Lancashire, but are convex. On the E side is a two-storey porch, against the S re-entrant angle, and another stack adjoining it for the hall. Inside, however, is unmistakable evidence that the brick is a later encasing of a timber-framed structure. In the W wing wall-posts rise through both floors, with brackets to support the moulded beams of the ground-floor ceiling. This section was therefore built as a two-storey structure. On the first floor the posts begin to splay, and the bottom of arched bracing is visible below the ceiling, which was only inserted in the last fifty years. The W wing appears to be the higher end, for the mouldings on the beams are better. There is also a blocked door frame on this floor between the S wing and the central section, with a two-centred arch. This is a puzzle because one would expect the hall before to be open to the roof. Perhaps the door frame was moved here from elsewhere during the C17 or earlier, when the floor was put in the hall. This C17 floor is supported on crude ovolo-moulded beams. The windows of the hall bay, alone, have transoms, both upstairs and down. That could be because this first-floor room was a parlour, or dining chamber. To the NW is a small brick building containing the remnants of the Bedford MILL.

BICKERSHAW, Plank Lane, 1½ m. WSW. The massive colliery closed in 1992. Surviving where Plank Lane meets the Leeds and Liverpool Canal are two large former PUBS probably by *Prestwich*: one of 1901, with gabled and ribbed chimneys, and across the road the Britannia Hotel, dated 1903, which is the usual exuberant brewery mishmash, pivoting the corner not by a turret or tower, but by a handsome chimney (cf. the former Eagle and Child pub, King Street).

LIGHT OAKS HALL. *See* Glazebury.

SANDY POOL FARMHOUSE, Dunham Grove, 1 m. ESE. A little, potentially interesting building with the combined arms of Richard Shuttleworth and Frances Urmston, who married *c.* 1640, on a stone plaque in the front. A Shuttleworth is first recorded here in 1301.

YEW TREE FARMHOUSE, Carr Lane, off Hand Lane 1 m. S. Of *c.* 1700–10. Brick. Much altered, but retaining raised-heart decoration, and an early (for Lancashire) double-pile plan. (Good contemporary staircase. DCMS.)

LITHERLAND

It begins as a northern continuation of C19 industrial Bootle, indistinguishable from it, and becomes, further N and E, anonymous C20 suburban sprawl.

ST ANDREW, Linacre Road. *See* Bootle, p. 155.

ST JOHN AND ST JAMES, Monfa Road. 1910–11, by *James F. Doyle*. A brown brick church with red Ruabon brick and terracotta dressings. Eclectically Gothic. Nave and low aisles, transepts and chancel. SW tower and porch, square and buttressed for the bottom half and octagonal above that, with tall lancet belfry openings and then little pinnacles rising above the pierced parapet. Square staircase turret set against the SE face. Big interior of exposed brickwork with red sandstone quatrefoil piers. Kingpost trusses to the nave, panelled and ribbed roof over the chancel.

ST PHILIP, Church Road. 1861–3, by *H. Gee*. Of small quarry-faced yellow sandstone blocks. Geometrical tracery. Still unaisled and with transepts – the tradition of the pre-archaeological decades of the early C19. The detail also is often ignorant. The way the spire starts as low as the ridge of the nave roof is but one example. Hammerbeam roofs. – STAINED GLASS. Good five-light E window by *Shrigley & Hunt*.

ENGLISH MARTYRS (R.C.), School Lane. 1934–5, by *L.A.G. Prichard*. Brick, Romanesque, with a SW campanile.

LINACRE METHODIST MISSION HALL and SCHOOLS, Linacre Road. A strikingly large complex by *W.J. Morley & Sons* of Bradford, which cost *c*. £35,000. Ruabon brick and copious buff terracotta dressings. Eclectic style. The Mission Hall is of 1904–5. Its façade has big round-headed windows. Centre demarcated by two little turrets, with between them twin round-arched entrances, a big tripartite window above, and a pediment above that. (Inside, the hall – reordered in 1967 – has five-bay round-arched arcades and a segmental-vaulted ceiling, all with elaborate plasterwork, and no galleries). The Hartwell Street elevation (i.e. the r. flank) has six bays of two levels of windows and gables, and attached to the r. a second hall – the CHILDREN'S HALL – of 1908–9, with a big five-bay façade to the street, the middle three under a pediment. It housed the senior school. Across Hartwell Street is the former SUNDAY SCHOOL of 1914–15, equally large at five by nine bays, with three floors of windows and gablets projecting above the parapet. Whilst lavish use is made of decorative terracotta, the façades of all the buildings are pretty flat. At the peak, about 3,000 children attended Sunday School here every week.

PUBS. Two big examples. On the corner of LINACRE ROAD and Hapsford Road is MA KENTS, three storeys of brick and sandstone dressings, slightly baronial in style, with a circular corner turret with conical roof. Late C19. Much better is the RED LION HOTEL on Church Road beside the Leeds and Liverpool Canal (*see* p. 52). Dated 1905 and built by the Blezards Brewery. A handsome building showing the influence of Shaw and Philip Webb. Eleven bays, three storeys. Brick, except for roughcast facing to the second storey on most of the front. Tall, simple chimneystacks. Two bays at each end project, the l. two as a tower with pyramid roof, the r. pair with a pediment and Venetian window. Mostly sash windows, with mullions on the top floor and keystones elsewhere. Running above the ground floor is a broad stone frieze carved with strapwork incorporating the name of the pub and various badges.

LITHERLAND PARK, off Sefton Road. A mid-C19 residential estate, but of little interest, and largely with C20 housing. U-plan layout.

LITTLE CROSBY

A wooded island in flat former moss-and-mere country N of Liverpool. The Blundells of Crosby have been lords of the manor since the Middle Ages. They were no relation of the Blundells of Ince Blundell, though the two houses are only a mile apart.

ST MARY (R.C.), 1845–7, by *Weightman & Hadfield*. Just like an Anglican parish church – a sign of the strength of Catholicism in this part of the country. It is very much an estate church, though, and was built just outside the park of Crosby Hall by the Blundell family, proud recusants. A simple, straightforward building, and already archaeologically accurate. The architects had been quick in learning the Pugin lesson. W tower with broach spire. Nave and aisle. Dec tracery. SEDILIA. – ALTAR brought forward. – S, family, chapel behind a PARCLOSE SCREEN. – Another S chapel, transept-like, added in 1883. WALL PAINTINGS here by *Arthur Tomlinson*, 1935. – MONUMENTS. William Blundell, the builder, †1854. With recumbent stone effigy in a tomb recess in the chancel. Nicholas and Agnes Blundell, †1894 and 1890. Repoussé copper plaque in the Arts and Crafts style; in the porch.

The PRESBYTERY is two-faced. To the road it is a Tudorbethan house of 1850; to the rear is attached a block with a 1719 datestone. It has indeed been the home of a priest since the C18. If the attached former CHAPEL (now a house) is of the same date, as is claimed, then it is exceptionally early for a purpose-built free-standing Catholic place of worship. The normal form of the pre-Emancipation chapel is much clearer at the rear – a simple brick structure with three tall roundheaded windows. Presumably the road side was originally blank (cf. Portico Chapel, St Helens, p. 570); its present appearance dates from 1859 (indicated by a datestone), when it became a convent and village school.

CROSBY HALL. Home of the Blundells of Crosby since the Middle Ages. The house was reduced in the mid C20 and is now back to the five-gabled C16–C17 core more or less as it was made to look in 1784–6 (when a Tudor gatehouse was also demolished). Stone, three storeys and five bays. The entrance front has a pediment and beneath this is a lunette and beneath this a Venetian window. The front also has clues to the true age of the building: the irregularities of the ashlar, the three parallel roofs and a reset datestone of 1576. But the peculiar little corner turrets, though at odds with classical precepts, are apparently C18; they do not appear on a drawing of 1738. Neither are the ground-floor windows to the r. of the entrance shown out of alignment in the drawing, as they curiously are now. The turrets, which contained closets, may have been created to manage the transition to an older service wing to the l. and an extension of the early C19 to the r., which projected slightly. They were demolished in the 1950s and the present N and S façades created; the tetrastyle Ionic portico on the S side was brought in from Claughton Hall near Garstang

(N Lancashire), built 1816–17. On the garden (E) side is a wide canted bay l. of the door. This dates from 1815 and corresponds to the handsome library inside, with its Neoclassical plaster-work and splendid built-in mahogany bookcases. The open-well staircase is walnut, of the 1780s. The ground floor is otherwise notably low-ceilinged; the first floor is much higher. Early C17 panelling in some of the upper floor rooms, possibly *ex situ*.

The drive from BACK LANE passes between farm buildings and cottages. On the N side are the STABLES, and attached at right angles, a BARN, both converted by *Martin Perry Architects* in 1989–91 as a residential centre along with the other build-ings around the yard. The stone, single-range stables are shown in the 1738 drawing and have a datestone of 1637, and a mullioned window in the gable end (a recent copy of the worn original). The present appearance is Georgian: of 1784–6? The barn, however, is probably C16 and originally timber-framed, but clad in stone and shortened at the N end in the C17. The S end was subsequently converted into a coachhouse. A C19 GIN-HOUSE, now a meeting room, is attached.

There is a survey of the small PARK by *John Webb* dated 1815, so the present design could be his. In it, SSE of the house, is the chapel known as HARKIRK. Present building of 1889. In it a decorated STOUP dated 1668. It stands in a Roman Catholic burial ground first used in 1611. Some C17 and C18 headstones are incorporated into the walls of the chapel. No trace of the gardens laid out S of the house in 1721–2, and tan-talisingly recorded in the 1738 drawing. *Robert Lugar* designed a Bailiff's Cottage in 1828. This is probably the Tudor Gothic LODGE on Back Lane on the E side of the park. Frilly bargeboards, label moulds etc. Another LODGE on Little Crosby Road at the S end of the village inside the rusticated GATEPIERS topped with lions. Refined Late Classical excellent ashlar, with pediments, banded quoins, recessed, round-arched windows, and a round-arched porch. There is one other lodge, on the N side of Back Lane, to Ince Blundell (q.v.).

The VILLAGE is a single pretty street along the W wall of the park, with little cottages and farms attractively irregular in design and building line. Some are brick, some are stone; some are C19 Estate-style, most are earlier, e.g. Nos. 18–22 on the E side. These are whitewashed, but underneath is stone and brick of a number of phases. Nos. 18–20 are apparently the oldest part, with mullioned windows and two cruck frames inside. The envelope is C17 and the crucks possibly earlier. Opposite is another stone cottage with mullioned windows, dated 1669.

LIVERPOOL

BY JOSEPH SHARPLES
AND RICHARD POLLARD

Introduction	243
The Docks	259
South Docks	263
North Docks	276
Central Liverpool	280
Religious Buildings	280
Public Buildings	286
Streets	306
The Cathedrals Area and the	
University of Liverpool	344
Anglican Cathedral	344
Metropolitan Cathedral	353
Other Religious Buildings	360
University of Liverpool	362
Other Public Buildings	371
Streets	373
Liverpool Suburbs	380
Aigburth, with St Michael's Hamlet, and Fulwood,	
Grassendale and Cressington parks	380
Allerton	386
Anfield	392
Childwall	397
Clubmoor	402
Croxteth	405
Edge Hill, and Kensington	409
Everton, with London Road and	
Royal Liverpool University Hospital	417
Fairfield	424
Fazakerley	427
Garston	429
Gateacre	431
Hunt's Cross	434
Kirkdale	435
Knotty Ash	436
Mossley Hill	439
Norris Green	445
Sefton Park, Prince's Park and surroundings	447
Speke	456
Toxteth	469
Tue Brook, Old Swan, Stanley and Stoneycroft	477
Vauxhall	484
Walton	487
Wavertree	492
West Derby	501
Woolton	506

INTRODUCTION

The great seaport of Liverpool has the most splendid setting of any English city. It lies on the E bank of the broad River Mersey, rising gently to a ridge crowned by the two cathedrals. Its shape is roughly a semicircle, the straight side formed by the water-front, with the Pier Head at its centre. The combination of hills and water shows many buildings to advantage, and the higher ground to the E gives spectacular views across the city to the river, the open sea, and the distant mountains of North Wales. Liverpool inherited virtually nothing from its humble medieval origins, and in the boom years from the C18 to the early C20, older structures were regularly swept away regardless of histori-cal interest.* Consequently, in the historic centre Late Georgian, Victorian and Edwardian buildings predominate.

The Growth of Liverpool, to c. 1800

Before the later C17 Liverpool was a very modest settlement, occupying the peninsula between the river and the tidal creek known as the Pool (now obliterated, but following the course of Canning Place, Paradise Street, Whitechapel and Old Haymarket). It is first mentioned c. 1192, and in 1207 it was made a borough. The H-pattern of the seven MEDIEVAL STREETS is still visible: they are Chapel Street, Tithebarn Street, Dale Street and Water Street, with Old Hall Street, High Street and Castle Street forming the extended crossbar. A castle was built in the early C13 on the site of what is now Derby Square (*see* p. 320), and the small chapel of St Mary del Key near the water's edge is first mentioned in 1257. Close to it, the church of Our Lady and St Nicholas was built c. 1360, though the present building is entirely C19 and C20. In 1406 Sir John Stanley obtained permission to fortify his house at the foot of Water Street, known as the Tower. All these have dis-appeared, and only in what are now the suburbs does anything pre-C18 remain: parts of All Saints, Childwall, a fragment of Crox-teth Hall of c. 1600, the early C17 Ancient Chapel of Toxteth, and a few more minor C17 survivals; and one timber-framed Tudor house of exceptional importance, Speke Hall.

Liverpool's development as a great commercial PORT began properly in the mid C17, when trade with the colonies in America and the West Indies was added to established European, Irish and coastal trade. Liverpool's position was ideal for transatlantic trade, importing tobacco and sugar from the New World and exporting goods from the nascent industries of the Midlands and the North. The first recorded American cargo – tobacco – arrived in 1648, and the refining of West Indies sugar began c. 1667. In 1672 the Corporation took a thousand-year lease of the lordship from the 3rd Lord Molyneux, so obtaining control over a very

*For the prehistoric CALDERSTONES, *see* p. 389.

Liverpool, detail from a panorama of the city.
(*Illustrated London News*, 29 April 1865)

large area immediately E of the medieval core. Celia Fiennes
described Liverpool in 1698 as having twenty-four streets, with
'mostly new built houses of brick and stone after the London
fashion . . . built high and even.'

Spectacular growth came with the C18. In 1715 Liverpool
opened the first commercial enclosed wet DOCK in the world (*see* *p. 260*
Docks, Introduction p. 260), constructed within the mouth of the
Pool, and this was the focus for rapid development E of the historic centre. New streets radiated from it, including Duke Street
and Hanover Street, lined with merchants' dwellings and associated warehouses and counting houses. Daniel Defoe visited soon
after 1715 and marvelled: 'Liverpoole is one of the wonders of
Britain . . . What it may grow to in time, I know not.' But the
early C18 town was effectively landlocked by mosses and meres,
and growth depended on improving INLAND COMMUNICA-
TIONS. In the 1730s the River Weaver was made navigable into
Cheshire, and the Mersey and Irwell Navigation scheme made it
possible to convey goods by water to Manchester. Canals followed: the Sankey Canal from the St Helens coalfield to the
Mersey in 1755–7, followed by the Bridgewater Canal, linking the
Duke of Bridgewater's collieries at Worsley with the Mersey at
Runcorn. In 1770 the great Leeds and Liverpool Canal was
begun, eventually connecting the port with the manufacturing
towns of NE Lancashire and Yorkshire when completed in 1816.
By the end of the C18 four more wet docks had been built, and
by 1792 Liverpool was handling about a sixth of the tonnage from
all English ports, whereas in 1716 her share had been one twenty-
fourth. A large measure of this prosperity was due to the slave
trade, for which Liverpool was by 1740 the chief port in Europe.

Of the EARLY C18 TOWN the only survival is the large former
Blue Coat School (now Bluecoat Chambers) of 1716–18, which 29
stood originally beside the new stone parish church of St Peter.
This, along with every other C18 Anglican church in the centre,
has vanished. The handsome Royal Infirmary of 1745–9 has gone
too. However, the most splendid public building of the mid C18,
the Town Hall and Exchange of 1749–54 by *John Wood* of Bath, 34
still stands in somewhat altered form. From 1788 *James Wyatt* *p. 287*
extended it, and when the building was gutted by fire in 1795 he
redesigned its interior, providing reception rooms of exceptional 56
splendour. Among English civic buildings of its date, it is probably second only to London's Mansion House in richness. Away
from the medieval core, RESIDENTIAL SQUARES such as the
mid-C18 Clayton Square and Williamson Square were laid out,
but no overall plan was imposed, and streets tended to follow the
lines of existing lanes and fields. The first attempt at a formally
planned SUBURB was the abortive Harrington scheme, laid out
from 1771 by the builder *Cuthbert Bisbrown*, but it resulted only
in the church of St James, 1774–5, notable for its Gothic cast-
iron gallery columns. The only other C18 church surviving in the
centre is St Peter, Seel Street (R.C.), of 1788; Holy Trinity,

Wavertree, of 1794 by *John Hope*, was built well outside the town. In the 1780s–90s houses spread steadily SE, the grandest survivor 37 being Thomas Parr's of *c.* 1799 in Colquitt Street, with its attached office and warehouse. In 1783–4 Rodney Street was laid out, with parallel service roads behind the houses, beginning the more spacious residential development of the high ground to the E. Further out, in what was in the C18 the country and is now the suburbs, are a number of houses. From the early C18 there is the ambitious but curiously restless and crowded S façade of 28, Croxteth Hall, added 1702, and the unexpectedly splendid public p. 406 rooms of Woolton Hall. Allerton Hall, begun in the 1730s, introduced Palladianism. From the second half of the century there are *Robert Adam*'s unexceptional alterations to Woolton Hall, and Olive Mount, Wavertree, of the 1790s. This is a now all but unique survivor of the extra-urban VILLAS built by the wealthiest merchants.

The Nineteenth Century

The slave trade was abolished in 1807, but expansion continued, and in architecture and planning a Neoclassical orderliness became widespread. In the centre the most significant work was p. 323 the new Exchange of 1803–8 (demolished), by the elder *Foster*, perhaps with the involvement of *Wyatt*. It enclosed the Exchange Flags, where in 1813 the Nelson monument by *M.C. Wyatt* and *Richard Westmacott* was unveiled, followed in 1822 by *Westmacott*'s equestrian bronze of George III in Monument Place. These marked the beginning of a taste for ambitious PUBLIC SCULPTURE which lasted into the C20. The very early purpose-built 38 bank of Messrs Heywood in Brunswick Street, 1798–1800, is the first of the showpiece financial buildings that lined Castle Street and its tributaries during the C19.

It was not until *c.* 1800 that serious CULTURAL INTERESTS found architectural expression. *Thomas Harrison*'s distinguished Lyceum in Bold Street, 1800–2, and the elder *Foster*'s Union News Room of 1800 in Duke Street, both included libraries. The leading figure in Liverpool's emergence as a cultural centre was William Roscoe (1753–1831), lawyer, poet, M.P., anti-slavery campaigner, historian, botanist and art collector, who was active in promoting the Botanic Gardens (founded in 1802), the Liverpool Academy (founded in 1810), and the Liverpool Royal Institution (opened 1817). The latter occupied the former Parr house in Colquitt Street, converted by *Edmund Aikin*, who was also responsible for the Wellington Rooms of 1814–16 in Mount Pleasant. These were later joined by *Clark Rampling*'s Medical 59 Institution and *A.H. Holme*'s Mechanics' Institution in nearby Mount Street, both opened 1837. All are products of the GREEK REVIVAL, which dominated Liverpool architecture *c.* 1815–*c.* 1840. The leading local exponent was *John Foster Jun.*, who had travelled in Greece as a young man with C.R. Cockerell and who served as Corporation Surveyor in succession to his father, *John*

Foster Sen. Most of his buildings have been demolished, including the colossal Custom House on the site of the infilled Old Dock, and the pioneering St John's Market of 1820–2. His St James's Cemetery survives, spectacularly sited in a disused quarry, with its Oratory in the form of a Doric temple. This contains excellent Neoclassical funerary sculpture, including important monuments by *John Gibson*, who began his career in Liverpool before settling in Rome.

The greatest monument of the new Liverpool of these years, classically inspired and culturally aspiring, is *Harvey Lonsdale Elmes*'s ST GEORGE'S HALL, which came about through combining separate projects for assize courts and a concert hall. The executed design of 1841–54, with an interior completed by *C.R. Cockerell*, is exceptionally inventive, and quite unlike the conventional adaptations of temple architecture in the younger Foster's buildings. Pevsner in 1969 called it 'the freest neo-Grecian building in England and one of the finest in the world', though part of Elmes' originality lay in his use of Roman sources as well as Greek. 77, p. 292 78

Of the many classical CHURCHES AND CHAPELS built in the first four decades of the C19 shockingly few remain. Apart from Foster's St Andrew, Rodney Street and Oratory, the only survivors are *Samuel Rowland*'s St Bride, Percy Street, *John Slater*'s St Patrick (R.C.), Park Place, and *Joseph Franklin*'s Great George Street Congregational Church. The last shows a move away from Greek austerity towards Roman – and indeed Victorian – richness. Some extremely interesting early Gothic Revival churches survive. The tower and spire of Our Lady and St Nicholas, begun 1811, are by the arch-Grecian *Thomas Harrison*. St Luke, Bold Place, of 1811–31, nominally designed by the *Fosters*, has a surprisingly prominent chancel. St Mary, Edge Hill, is a preaching box of 1812–13. The influential system of classifying medieval architecture under the terms Early English, Decorated, etc., was invented in Liverpool by the Quaker *Thomas Rickman*, whose name is linked with three extraordinary churches built 1812–16 by the ironmaster *John Cragg*, of which St George, Everton, and St Michael-in-the-Hamlet still stand. Rickman made drawings for Cragg, but to what extent he influenced the appearance of these churches is unclear – he said of Cragg: 'His ironwork is too stiff in his head to bend to any beauty' – and they are chiefly remarkable for their pioneering use of cast-iron prefabricated parts. Rickman's pupil *John Broadbent* did the impressive Dec-cum-Perp w tower of Walton of 1829–32, and St Anthony (R.C.), Scotland Road, of 1832–3, in a plain lancet style. St Clement, Toxteth, 1840–1, by *Arthur & George Yates Williams*, is also in a Commissioners' lancet style and has a remarkably little-altered box-pewed interior. St John Knotty Ash of 1834–6 is Perp, but St Anne Aigburth, built 1836–7 and designed by *Cunningham & Holme*, is an early example of the Norman Revival. Of secular Gothic in this period there is *Elmes*' Collegiate Institution School in Shaw Street, Everton, 1840–3, and among Gothic houses Cragg's picturesque group at St Michael's Hamlet, Greenbank at Mossley Hill, and Walton rectory. 48 44 45 81

In RESIDENTIAL ARCHITECTURE and PLANNING the start of the C19 saw important new developments. Great George Square was larger than any C18 predecessor, with an enclosed garden, and terraces of uniform design. *John Foster Sen.*'s residential grid plan for the Mosslake Fields area, centred on Abercromby Square, was approved in 1800. From 1827, the adjoining area between Falkner Street and Upper Parliament Street was similarly laid out, with Falkner Square in the middle, so that by the 1840s Liverpool had a very extensive area of high-class terraced housing. Only part of this survives today. In Percy Street and

57 Gambier Terrace in the 1830s stone was used instead of brick, and a more imaginative approach to terrace design adopted. At the same time places such as Wavertree and Edge Hill were rapidly developing as detached suburbs; Clare Terrace, Edge Hill, is an impressive example of the urban form of much of the resultant architecture. By contrast at Allerton the ranks of semi-rural villas swelled with Neoclassical arrivals such as *Harrison*'s Allerton (now only a fragment), Calderstones, and Springwood, possibly by *John Cunningham*, and dated 1839.

The Victorian period was a golden age for Liverpool during which the population rose from 286,000 in 1841 to 518,000 in 1891. The increasing complexity of the DOCK ESTATE in the mid C19 is reflected in the range and scale of its buildings. *Jesse Hartley*'s stand out, superbly crafted in granite and often start-lingly original (*see* Docks, Introduction, p. 260); his sublime mas-

96, p. 265 terpiece of utilitarian classicism, Albert Dock, was erected in the 1840s. Later warehouses for single commodities include the

97 massive Italianate grain warehouses by *G.F. Lyster*, 1866–8, at Waterloo Dock. Hundreds more warehouses, privately owned,

102 lined the streets inland from the dock road. This distinctive townscape is all but destroyed, though the huge Clarence Warehouses, Vauxhall, built *c.* 1844 by *S. & J. Holme* for P.W. Brancker, are notable survivors. The dock system was served by an expanding RAILWAY NETWORK, begun as early as 1830 with the opening of the pioneering Liverpool & Manchester Railway. At Edge Hill

99 there is its Neoclassical station of 1836, not the original, but still remarkably early to remain in use.

OFFICE BLOCKS (*see* also pp. 68–70) dominated Victorian Liverpool's commercial heart. Barned's Buildings in Sweeting Street, apparently of *c.* 1840, are a sober, dignified terrace of repetitive bays. A new approach was introduced soon after at Brunswick Buildings (demolished), an Italian Renaissance palazzo, and one of the earliest instances anywhere of a speculative office building treated in so self-important a manner. Florentine palaces had an obvious symbolic appeal for Liverpool's merchant princes, as did those of Venice. The need to admit ample light was vital, and the glass-roofed central light well became a standard feature, for example at *C.R. Cockerell*'s great quadrangle for the Liverpool & London Insurance Co. of 1856–8, and at Imperial Chambers,

90 Dale Street, of *c.* 1873. *Peter Ellis*' Oriel Chambers in Water Street, 1864, represents perhaps the most extreme solution to the problem of lighting: exterior stonework is pared down to but-

tress-like strips, between which identical iron-framed oriel windows project like faceted glass bubbles. The courtyard elevation is even more extraordinary: a very early instance of curtain-wall construction. Also distinctive are mixed-use buildings, combining office accommodation and storage facilities for several businesses. Good examples are Fowler's Building, Victoria Street, designed by *Picton* in 1865, and Granite Buildings in Stanley Street, of *c.* 1882, by *G. E. Grayson*. Parallel with the growth of speculative offices runs the development of the prestigious flag-ship building, though often with lettable spaces too. BANKS led the way here, and two Early Victorian examples survive, the former North and South Wales Bank in Derby Square, 1838–40, by *Edward Corbett* of Manchester, and the former Royal Bank in Dale Street, *c.* 1837–8, by *Samuel Rowland*. The Liverpool branch of the Bank of England, 1845–8, is the last and arguably the best 89 of three provincial branches designed by *Cockerell*, colossal in its individual parts, and giving the impression of unshakeable strength and solidity. Towards the end of the C19 offices became larger, with Northern Renaissance and subsequently English Baroque styles more in evidence. Much of Castle Street was rebuilt by the busy practice of *Grayson & Ould*, and with the construction of the striped marble façade of *Norman Shaw*'s Parr's Bank in 1898–1901, the street's transformation into one of the *p. 69* most opulent Victorian commercial thoroughfares in the country was complete. *Shaw*'s 1895–8 building for the White Star Line in James Street was the first of a new generation of giant office blocks, establishing an enlarged scale for the centre. The local architect *James F. Doyle*, who supervised its construction, also won the competition (judged by Shaw) for the even bigger Royal Insurance Building of 1896–1903 in North John Street. Behind 91 Baroque façades it hides a very early example of a virtually self-sufficient steel frame. Some of the best suburban buildings are banks put up at this time, e.g. *Willink & Thicknesse*'s polished, Shaw-inspired branches of the Bank of Liverpool at Walton and Aigburth Vale.

The wealth generated in offices and warehouses is reflected in PUBLIC BUILDINGS. St George's Hall became the focal point for an exceptional group of grand classical edifices dedicated to art, culture, law and learning. First came *John Weightman*'s Museum 79 and Library, 1857–60, borrowing Elmes' Graeco-Roman manner. The Walker Art Gallery by *Cornelius Sherlock* and *H.H. Vale*, 1874–7, and the Picton Reading Room by *Sherlock* alone, 1875–9, 80 are still Neoclassical, though *F. & G. Holme*'s County Sessions House, 1882–4, opts for a degree of High Renaissance swagger. By contrast, the Municipal Buildings of 1862–8 in Dale Street, by *Weightman* and *E.R. Robson*, successive Corporation Surveyors, have French pavilion roofs, foliate capitals, and a tower with an unclassifiable spire, and the Walton Gaol of *c.* 1850–4, where Weightman may have assisted *Charles James Peirce*, is a Norman castle. A later Corporation Surveyor, 86 *Thomas Shelmerdine*, used Baroque when the occasion called for grandeur (e.g. in the Hornby Library of 1906), but the most characteristic works from his office are free Jacobean, for instance Hatton Garden Fire Station of 1895–8 and an exemplary series of lively and varied libraries such as Kensington, 1890, and Everton, 1896. Wealth was also expressed in the proliferation of SHOPS, e.g. Messrs Cripps at Nos. 14–16 Bold Street, with its huge expanses of plate glass, and *Lewis Hornblower's* premises for Elkington's in Church Street. In a class apart, the magnificent and exceptionally early department store Compton House, by *Thomas Haigh & Co.*, 1866–7, also survives in Church Street.

p. 314

Beyond the city centre, wealth was lavished on MANSIONS in affluent suburbs such as Allerton, Aigburth, Mossley Hill, West Derby and Woolton. Gothic of course was very popular: Holmestead, Mossley Hill – *c.* 1845 by *A.H. Holme*, extended *c.* 1869–70 – is particularly exuberant. *Alfred Waterhouse* built a number of characteristically sombre houses in his home city, Allerton Priory, 1866–71, being the most ambitious. Italianate is also common, e.g. Crofton, built in the 1870s in Mossley Hill for Alfred Holt, engineer and ship-owner. *Sherlock's* Jacobethan Gateacre Grange was carefully extended, and internally fitted out with a tinge of Aestheticism, by *Sir Ernest George & H.A. Peto* in 1883–4 for the brewer Sir Andrew Barclay Walker. Too many other houses have been destroyed, including works by both *Scott* and *Shaw* in Allerton. For those a rung or two below the wealthiest there were private PARK ESTATES, leafy gated communities of polite villas: Fulwood Park, Grassendale Park, Cressington Park, Sandown Park and Sandfield Park, the grandest. All were begun in the 1840s, the first three on the banks of the Mersey.

106

An outstanding innovation of the mid C19 in housing and planning was the creation of PUBLIC PARKS as the focus of residential suburbs. The earliest was Prince's Park, paid for privately and laid out from 1842 by *Joseph Paxton* and *James Pennethorne*. As with Regent's Park in London, the idea was that plots round the edges would be developed with high-class houses, and the rental income would pay for the park's upkeep. The earliest houses are classical, stuccoed, and mostly arranged in pairs or short terraces backing on to the park. From the 1850s the Council followed this example, aiming to surround the town with a belt of parks: Wavertree Park and Sheil Park, opened in 1856 and 1862 respectively; then, under the Liverpool Improvement Act of 1865, Stanley Park to the N, Newsham Park to the E, and Sefton Park to the S. Sefton Park was the most ambitious, the largest public park anywhere in the country since London's Regent's Park. The design competition was won in 1867 by the Parisian landscape gardener *Edouard André* and the local architect *Lewis Hornblower*, and the layout follows the naturalistic style of the Paris parks (which in turn derived from Paxton and Loudon in England). The fringes were sold off as building plots to recoup the costs, but the resulting large villas are mostly rather dull. Exceptions are The Towers of 1874 by *G.A. Audsley*, and *James F. Doyle's* Gledhill of 1881. Stanley Park and Newsham Park were designed by *Edward Kemp*, a protégé of Paxton, who was also substantially

responsible for the landscaping of the excellent City of Liverpool 88
Cemetery, Anfield, completed in 1863.

For RELIGIOUS BUILDINGS, St Margaret Princes Road,
1868–9, by the great *George Edmund Street*, was the centre of the
High Church movement in Liverpool, and has an interior rich
with mural painting and glass by *Clayton & Bell*. It belongs to an
extraordinary cluster of religious buildings in this street, which
illustrate the cultural diversity of C19 Liverpool: *Henry Sumners*'s
Greek Orthodox church of St Nicholas, 1870; the ruinous Welsh 74
Presbyterian church by the brothers *W. & G. Audsley*, 1868;
and the synagogue of 1874, by the *Audsleys* again, which fuses 76
Moorish and Gothic to sumptuous effect. Near Sefton Park is a
cluster of outstanding late C19 churches. *J.L. Pearson*'s St Agnes, 68
1883–5, is in the style of the C13, red brick on the outside but
stone within, and vaulted throughout. It was the gift of Douglas
Horsfall, one of a munificent family of Liverpool church builders.
A short distance away is the R.C. church of St Clare, 1889–90, 69
by the young *Leonard Stokes*, using Gothic motifs in a looser
manner. For Arts and Crafts furnishings, the nearby Unitarian
Church of 1896–9 by *Thomas Worthington & Son* of Manchester
has woodcarving by *C.J. Allen*, metalwork by *Richard Llewellyn
Rathbone*, stained glass by *Morris & Co.*, and outstanding murals
by *Gerald Moira* in the vestry and attached library. Elsewhere in 72
the new suburbs further terrific churches were erected at the
expense of benefactors made wealthy by Liverpool: in West Derby,
George Gilbert Scott's imposing St Mary, 1853–6, in all but name
the estate church of the Molyneux's of Croxteth; in Tue Brook
G.F. Bodley's St John, 1867–70, a seminal work that marks the 62
beginning of his mature C14 style; at Mossley Hill, St Matthew
and St James, 1870–5, *Paley & Austin* at their most imposing, with 64, 65
one of their most monumental towers; and at Allerton, All
Hallows by *G.E. Grayson*, with one of the best ensembles anywhere of *Morris & Co.* stained glass, largely by *Burne-Jones*. 67

Mass immigration from famine-stricken Ireland in the 1840s
swelled Liverpool's already large Roman Catholic population,
and CATHOLIC CHURCHES survive in greater numbers than
those of other denominations. Only the steeple remains from
A.W.N. Pugin's St Oswald, Old Swan, 1842, next to his tiny
Convent of Mercy. (His other building in the city is a rare surviving house, Oswaldcroft, Childwall.) St Francis Xavier,
Everton, by *J.J. Scoles*, opened in 1848, is enriched with highly
decorated altars and other original furnishings, and by the spectacular Sodality Chapel added in 1885–7 by *Edmund Kirby*.
A.W.N. Pugin's son *E.W. Pugin* built several Liverpool churches,
among them St Vincent de Paul in St James Street, 1856–7, and
Our Lady of Reconciliation in Eldon Street, 1859–60, plainer, but
more innovative in plan. The survival of NONCONFORMIST
BUILDINGS is so patchy that it is impossible to draw conclusions
about the stylistic preferences of different denominations.
Notable examples are the late Greek Revival Baptist Chapel of
1847 in Shaw Street, and *W.I. Mason*'s Toxteth Tabernacle of
1870–1, for the Baptists, in a bizarre mix of Italianate and Gothic.

It is surprising that the Arts and Crafts Movement did not flourish more in Liverpool, especially after a School of Architecture and Applied Arts was founded at University College in the 1890s. Robert Anning Bell, R.L. Rathbone and C.J. Allen all taught there. Sculpture by *Allen* and copper panels by a student, *H. Bloomfield Bare*, form part of the decoration of *Walter W.* 95 *Thomas*' remarkable Philharmonic Hotel, *c.* 1898–1900, but apart from this the practical results of Liverpool's experiment in architectural education are not easy to find. More tangible is the wealth of ARCHITECTURAL SCULPTURE AND PUBLIC MONUMENTS commissioned *c.* 1880–1915 from practitioners of the New Sculpture, notably for the exterior of St George's Hall, St 110, 111 John's Gardens and the Pier Head.

Splendid public and commercial buildings represent only one side of Victorian Liverpool. Insanitary court housing continued *p. 61* to be built (*see* p. 60), and standards of construction remained low, even after the 1842 Liverpool Building Act, which introduced elementary controls on the design of new housing, and the 1846 Liverpool Sanitary Act. In 1867 the Council held a competition for the design of LABOURERS' DWELLINGS, and as a result built St Martin's Cottages (demolished) in Ashfield Street, Vauxhall. These rather bleak flats, with lavatories on the half-landings of their open staircases, were perhaps the first municipal housing in England outside London. From 1895 the Corporation undertook to replace demolished slums with housing for those dispossessed. The only survivals from this period belong to the Bevington Street Area scheme, opened 1912: terraced houses in a friendly cottage style, and three-storey flats in Eldon Grove with bay windows and half-timbering. Nevertheless, the vast majority of new working-class housing continued to be provided privately. More stringent bylaws created in the late C19 and early C20 whole districts of monotonous if often quite generous terraced houses, most commonly of six rooms including a parlour and three bedrooms. Their development was dominated to an extraordinary degree by speculative Welsh builders and allied tradesmen using Welsh materials and capital raised largely within the Welsh community, frequently through building societies. The Dingle, Earle Road and Anfield are good remaining areas, each traversed by arterial routes lined with three-storey rows containing shops, a characteristic element of the Liverpool townscape. Anfield is unique in retaining all of the schools provided there by the Liverpool School Board, for whom *T. Mellard Reade* was the most prolific architect.

Such SUBURBS were a great advance on the squalid courts, but housing reformers nevertheless continued to seek further improvements. These were, for a privileged few, realised at the 109 Wavertree Garden Suburb, begun in 1910 with a layout and housing by *Raymond Unwin* himself. The Garden City movement would have a much greater impact after the First World War by informing the design of the vast new council estates.

In the 1850s SANITATION was improved by the provision of a new water supply from Rivington, 25 m. to the NE. The associated reservoirs at High Park Street in Toxteth and Margaret Street in Everton were designed by *Thomas Duncan*, water engineer to the Corporation, whose Everton water tower is one of the city's most powerful monuments. Liverpool pioneered the provision of public washhouses from 1842: the earliest remaining seems to be the former Steble Street Baths and Washhouse of 1874. A programme of public baths followed, the best surviving being those at Lister Drive, Stanley of 1901–4, designed by *Shelmerdine* with the engineer *W.R. Court*.

Edwardian and Inter-war Liverpool

Liverpool became an Anglican diocese in 1880, but not until 1904 did work start on building a CATHEDRAL. Even in a city where classicism was so deeply rooted, there was a prejudice in favour of Gothic as proper for a church, and *Giles Gilbert Scott*'s competition-winning design of 1903 was chosen from an entirely Gothic shortlist. Scott's cathedral is both a culmination of the C19 Gothic Revival and a highly individual, unhistorical work of imagination. Vast in scale, it carries forward into the C20 that taste for the gigantic and sublime which is so typical of C19 Liverpool. Functionally the plan is not entirely convincing, but in emotional terms, by generating awe and wonder through the enclosure of vast spaces, the building is an overwhelming triumph. His St Paul Stoneycroft, another early work in the city, is in its way as magisterial and inventive.

70, 71,
p. 349

In SECULAR ARCHITECTURE, the most individual Liverpool architect of the early C20 was *Walter Aubrey Thomas*.* Specialising in commercial buildings, his work shows notable inventiveness and stylistic variety, as well as ambition matched by technological resourcefulness. His greatest undertaking was the colossal concrete-framed Royal Liver Building of 1908–11, one of the famous early C20 trio at the Pier Head. Its neighbours are the headquarters of the Mersey Docks and Harbour Board by *Briggs & Wolstenholme* with *Hobbs & Thornely*, 1903–7, and the Cunard Building of 1914–16, by *Willink & Thicknesse* with *Arthur J. Davis*. These three signify the high-water mark of Liverpool's prosperity, and together give the city its unique waterfront silhouette. A match for them in scale and ostentation was the Cotton Exchange in Old Hall Street, 1905–6, by *Matear & Simon*, the magnificent façade of which has been demolished. In the suburbs such Edwardian swagger found expression in *Briggs, Wolstenholme & Thornely*'s new Blue Coat School, Wavertree, of 1903–6.

92

1

82

The Cunard Building, the latest of the Pier Head group, shows a decisive shift away from Baroque exuberance towards a cooler, more restrained classicism. The source of this was partly France and partly the classicism of American architects such as McKim,

---

* 1859–1934; not to be confused with Walter W. Thomas (*c.* 1850–1912) of Philharmonic Hotel fame.

Mead & White. TRANSATLANTIC INFLUENCE found fertile soil in early C20 Liverpool through the influence of *Charles Reilly*, head of the Liverpool School of Architecture from 1904. He himself built little, but his Guild of Students of 1910–13 and the chancel of Holy Trinity, Wavertree, illustrate his tastes. Reilly's pupil *Herbert J. Rowse* was the outstanding architect of the inter-war years, and American-influenced classicism reached its peak in his India Buildings of 1923–30 (in conjunction with *Arnold Thornely*), and Martins Bank headquarters of 1927–32. Liverpool's tradition of high-quality ARCHITECTURAL SCULPTURE continued, the dominant sculptor of these years being *Herbert Tyson Smith*, whose flat, linear style suited both classical and modern architecture. His are the powerful reliefs on the Cenotaph, one of the most arresting First World War memorials anywhere.

During the 1930s classicism seemed to have run its course, and architects explored alternatives. *Rowse* adopted a streamlined Art Deco style in his ventilating stations and entrance features for the first Mersey road tunnel (1931–4), while for the Philharmonic Hall of 1936–9 he was influenced by the boxy brick architecture of W.M. Dudok. *Minoprio & Spencely*'s 1930–2 extension to the School for the Blind is severely simplified classical, while *Harold Dod*'s Harold Cohen Library of 1936–8 is a Jekyll and Hyde design, stripped classical in front and functional brick at the rear. But it was in PUBLIC HOUSING of the 1930s that European Mod-ernism made its boldest appearance in Liverpool, in large blocks of multi-storey flats built under the direction of *(Sir) Lancelot Keay*, Director of Housing from 1925 and later City Architect. Most have been demolished, but the best, St Andrew's Gardens, survives. It was designed by *John Hughes*, another Reilly student, and has sweeping balconies and windows in long bands. Envelop-ing the city, Keay planned and built huge estates of normally Neo-Georgian houses, with occasional vernacular motifs. The backbone for this expansion was a pioneering orbital road, Queens Drive, and a series of arterial routes conceived by the City Engineer *J.A. Brodie* and begun as early as 1904. They were designed according to the American parkway concept, broad and tree-lined with central reservations for tram lines. Keay housing can be seen along and either side of Queens Drive and the East Prescot Road, and at Speke where he laid out from 1936 a 'self-contained community unit' – a proto-New Town in conception, a giant suburban estate in execution. Speke is the site of Liver-pool Airport, where the terminal building and hangars of 1935–40 by *Edward Bloomfield* are a celebration of high-speed travel as eloquent as Rowse's tunnel structures.

It is in Keay's new suburbs that the most enterprising CHURCHES of the 1920s–30s are to be found. Two are in an Italian Romanesque style with landmark campaniles: All Souls Allerton by *D.A. Campbell & E.H. Honeybourne* and *F.X.Velarde*'s less conventional St Matthew Clubmoor of 1930, his first church. *Bernard A. Miller* too displayed some awareness of Con-tinental trends in his two blocky churches opened in 1932, St

Christopher Norris Green, and St Columba Anfield, adorned now by a magnificent reredos by *Mary Adshead* from his demolished St Christopher Withington (SE Lancashire). In contrast to such Modernist ventures stands the greatest single inter-war project, the Roman Catholic Cathedral designed by *Lutyens* and begun with amazing confidence in 1933. The crypt – the only part *p. 355* to be carried out – gives a sense of the stupendous scale intended, and also of the style. Lutyens' design drew on ideas from Ancient Rome, Byzantium and Renaissance Italy, but was not a backward-looking piece of historicism. Like Scott's Anglican Cathedral, it was a deeply imaginative development from traditional themes, and unmistakably a C20 work.

Post-war Liverpool

Its strategic importance made Liverpool a key target in the Second World War. Bombing reduced to rubble a large part of the business district S of Lord Street and Derby Square, and many other important buildings were destroyed or severely damaged. Reconstruction was patchy in quality. The S side of Lord Street was drearily rebuilt, while elsewhere, prestigious sites were filled with respectfully traditional buildings, harking back to before the war. The freshest early post-war office building is *H. Hinchliffe Davies'* Corn Exchange of 1953–9, while adjoining the docks, Tate & Lyle's parabolic Sugar Silo of 1955–7 is the most exciting continuation of the functional warehouse tradition.

In 1959 there was a decisive break with the past, when Lutyens' ROMAN CATHOLIC CATHEDRAL scheme was abandoned for a new design competition. *Frederick Gibberd*'s winning proposal, 118, completed in 1967, is Liverpool's most important building from *p. 356* the second half of the C20, and the only one of international significance. The centralised plan is expressed externally in the great conical roof, the radiating buttresses with chapels between, and the circular lantern tower with its crown of pinnacles. Leading artists provided the furnishings, notably *John Piper* and *Patrick Reyntiens*, whose abstract stained glass floods the interior with 119 intensely coloured light. Centralised plans also form the basis of the best post-war churches, a series of Roman Catholic commissions by local practices *Weightman & Bullen* and *L.A.G. Prichard*, completed in the 1960s: St Ambrose, Speke; Christ the King, Queen's Drive; St Margaret Mary, Knotty Ash; and the chapel of a teacher-training college in Childwall. Campaniles and fractured or folded lanterns figure prominently.

The UNIVERSITY OF LIVERPOOL was quick to plan its expansion after the War, commissioning *William Holford* as early as 1946 to draw up proposals. These formed the basis for the takeover and gradual demolition of the Georgian streets around Abercromby Square, and for the decision to employ a variety of architects rather than just one. The earliest buildings are rather timid, except *Basil Spence*'s Chadwick Laboratory of 1957–9. Those put up from the early 1960s onwards, as expansion gathered pace and public funding increased, are more assertive, including the Arts and Law buildings by *Bryan & Norman West-wood*, *Piet & Partners*, the aggressive Sports Centre by *Denys Lasdun & Partners*, and *Yorke, Rosenberg & Mardall*'s clinical white-tiled Electrical Engineering and Electronics building. Sub-urban sites were developed too, producing *Gerald R. Beech*'s

120 exquisite Wyncote sports pavilion of 1961–2 – a transparent box – and a series of halls of residence carefully planned within exist-ing garden landscapes, such as Carnatic Halls by *Manning & Clamp*, begun in 1965. Adjoining the university is *Holford Associ-ates*' giant Royal Liverpool University Hospital, planned 1963–5 but not opened until 1978. Its towering ward block and highly sculptural boiler house are powerful Brutalist works.

Wartime bomb damage was less destructive than the subse-quent efforts of architects and planners. Under *Ronald Bradbury* (appointed City Architect and Director of Housing, 1948) and *J. W. Boddy* (who took over responsibility for housing in 1963), a huge programme of slum clearance saw SLAB BLOCKS AND TOWERS built in great numbers, notably in Everton, and the dis-placement of tens of thousands of residents to the Corporation-developed satellite of Kirkby and the new towns of Skelmersdale and Runcorn. The failure, in social terms, of much of the high-rise housing led to its demolition in the 1980s–90s, along with most of Keay's inner-city flats. In 1965 construction of *James A. Roberts*' giant but controversial St John's Precinct began, erasing Foster's 1820–2 market hall and the surrounding street pattern, and injuring the setting of St George's Hall. Reconstruction received further encouragement in 1965 when the LIVERPOOL

p. 104 CITY CENTRE PLAN by *Graeme Shankland* and *Walter Bor* was published, providing a framework for comprehensive redevelop-ment. Its proposals were eventually scaled back, but not before widespread demolition, new roads and rebuilding had obliterated large areas. Of the big office blocks built around Old Hall Street at this time, *Tripe & Wakeham*'s Royal Insurance headquarters of 1972–6 (now Royal & Sun Alliance) is the only notable one. Commercial buildings in the centre are mostly forgettable, except *Bradshaw, Rowse & Harker*'s extraordinary bank of *c.* 1971, with its angular glass façade in sober C19 Dale Street. More appeal-ing is *Hall, O'Donahue & Wilson*'s lively 1968 extension to the Playhouse.

The confidence that gave rise to the City Centre Plan was short-lived. The collapse of British manufacturing in general, and of the Lancashire textile industry in particular, deprived the port of its core business, while the decline of Imperial links and the emergence of Europe as Britain's main trading partner meant Liverpool lost out to the ports of the SE. At the same time con-tainerisation reduced the need for manpower. The consequences were disastrous: soaring unemployment, poverty, and a dramatic fall in population from 746,000 in 1961 to 510,000 in 1981, when riots in Toxteth brought widespread destruction.

Central government responded with various initiatives. The MERSEYSIDE DEVELOPMENT CORPORATION was established in 1981 (before the riots) to bring about regeneration. It was responsible for the Liverpool International Garden Festival of 1984, which left a legacy of reclaimed industrial land s of the centre, and the elegant Festival Hall by *Arup Associates* (now disused). Around the South Docks, closed to shipping in 1972, housing, small businesses and leisure uses were established. Architecturally, the MDC's greatest achievement was the restoration of the long-derelict Albert Dock warehouses, a landmark in the rehabilitation of the city's redundant C19 buildings. The conversion of part of one block by *James Stirling* to house a Liverpool outpost of the Tate Gallery set a very high standard for future reuse schemes. The preservation of the Albert Dock was a victory for conservationists, and in the late 1970s and early 1980s successful campaigns were also waged to retain the Lyceum and St Francis Xavier's church. Like other post-industrial cities, Liverpool has since come to see 'heritage' as the key to a lucrative tourist trade. A sense of nostalgia for the ravaged C19 city, and a loss of confidence in contemporary design, seems to be reflected in the adoption of 'Victorian' polychrome brickwork and other decorative details in some large developments of the 1980s, for instance the Clayton Square Shopping Centre by the *Seymour Harris Partnership*. Council housing built in the 1980s also shows a return to C19 materials and scale. At the same time, disenchantment with failed municipal housing schemes of the past fuelled collaboration with commercial housebuilders, the rise of housing co-operatives and COMMUNITY ARCHITECTURE: national movements in which Liverpool played a leading role during the 1970s and 1980s (*see* p. 487). Visually, the result of these trends is that large areas of the inner city now have the informal, spacious, low-rise character previously associated with suburbs.

Much of the best work of recent years, including the Albert Dock scheme, has involved CREATIVE ADAPTATION AND REUSE. In the 1990s the former girls' school, Blackburne House, was sensitively transformed into a women's training centre by *Pickles Martinez Architects*, while *Brock Carmichael Associates* adapted and extended the neighbouring former Mechanics' Institution to become the Liverpool Institute of Performing Arts. Of the same period are *Dave King* and *Rod McAllister*'s interesting High-Tech additions to the 1930s School of Architecture and the 1960s wing of the Guild of Students, both at the University of Liverpool. But the leading exponents of reuse have been the developers *Urban Splash*, originally with their in-house designers *Design Shed*, latterly with *ShedKM*. Their pioneering Concert Square scheme, completed 1994, included the residential conversion of a former C19 chemical factory. It was the first such venture in Liverpool (other than the Albert Dock and Wapping warehouses), and it triggered the regeneration of this run-down area. More recently Urban Splash has moved out into the suburbs, collaborating again with *ShedKM* on the confident, cocky restoration as offices of the Mersey Match Factory, Garston, of 1921 (the first building in the United Kingdom to be built of flat-slab concrete construction). Close by, the derelict

1930s hangars and terminal of Speke Airport have also been restored, as hotel, offices and leisure centre, by *Falconer Chester Architects* – a praiseworthy job on awkward buildings.

It is a measure of the city's lack of prosperity and confidence that so few architecturally significant buildings have been erected in the last thirty years. The most enlightened client has been the Liverpool John Moores University, which commissioned the Aldham Robarts Learning Resource Centre of 1992–3 from *Austin-Smith:Lord*, followed by the Peter Jost Enterprise Centre and Avril Robarts Learning Resource Centre. The same architects' recent FACT building is disappointing outside, though the interior is spatially intriguing. *David Marks Julia Barfield Architects*' elegant Watersport Centre in Queen's Dock, 1993–4, is excellent. In the suburbs Ash Grange, Knotty Ash, sheltered housing of 2002–4 by *ShedKM*, is a bright star of innovative design amidst so much residential and commercial development that is numbingly third-rate.

Of all British cities, Liverpool rose most spectacularly in the C18 and C19, and collapsed most dramatically in the second half of the C20. After decades of decline the economic tide may now have turned, but although there is much construction under way or planned in the centre, it remains to be seen whether the results will live up to the best architecture of the past, and depressed suburbs have yet to witness significant change. There is some hope in the employment of architects of the calibre of *Wilkinson Eyre* and *Page & Park* on some current schemes. A project that will have a huge impact entails reconstructing 42 largely derelict acres (17 hectares) W of the traditional shopping district as a gigantic exercise in 'retail-led regeneration'. As well as department stores and smaller shops, the Paradise Street Development Area – masterplanned by *BDP* for the developers Grosvenor – will have apartments, hotels, a new bus station and extensive underground car parking below a public garden. The scale is vast, though unlike the monolithic shopping developments of the 1960s it aims to respect the historic street pattern, and will have separate buildings designed by a range of architects. Work started on site late in 2004. Elsewhere, a steady stream of new-build and conversion schemes is already catering to the fashion for city-centre living and the boom in student housing, but the standard of design is often depressingly poor. The visual primacy on the riverfront of the Pier Head trio is being assailed by mediocre towers behind and at Prince's Dock to the N, and by a proposed new museum to the S raising the possibility that the city will destroy its defining image in an inadequately considered lust for development. Confidence was boosted in 2003 when it was announced that Liverpool will hold the title European Capital of Culture in 2008, and further recognition came in 2004, when much of the waterfront and commercial centre was designated a World Heritage Site by UNESCO. The key question over the coming years will be whether Liverpool can rediscover a commitment to the best in architecture and urban design, as it is transformed under the potentially conflicting pressures of economic investment and conservation.

The docks are described first – because they belong neither to the centre nor to the suburbs exclusively. Then comes the centre, with religious and public buildings followed by the streets in alphabetical order. The adjoining cathedrals area is next, including a perambulation around the University. Inner and outer suburbs are listed together in alphabetical order; *see* the map on p. 381 for their geographical relationship.

THE DOCKS

INTRODUCTION

Liverpool emerged from insignificance in the C17 to become the country's third port by 1700. A century later it was second only to London, and the foremost transatlantic port in Europe. Its strategic advantages – proximity to Ireland, easy Atlantic access and excellent communications with a booming industrial hinterland – outweighed its substantial natural limitations. Overcoming these to meet the ever-increasing demands for expansion required the development of the largest single system of enclosed docks in the world, one of Britain's greatest engineering achievements. By 1700 the small silting Pool was totally inadequate for the growing merchant fleet; the strong currents, stiff westerlies, shifting sandbanks and huge tidal range meant that expensive ENCLOSED DOCKS were the only means of providing safe, deep berths. Moreover, high ground inland forced expansion into a ribbon of foreshore up and down the river, 7 m. long but seldom more than ½ m. wide, on ground reclaimed from within the tidal margins: a truly heroic undertaking. The huge cost necessitated corporate action and thus, unlike London and its private wharves, from the outset Liverpool's docks were a unified public enterprise, owned and managed until 1858 by the Dock Trustees (the Corporation by another name) and thereafter by the independent Mersey Docks and Harbour Board (MDHB). This enabled the town to expand the dock system on a scale that only London would better, and with a technological and stylistic coherence none could match. The zenith was the beginning of the C20, when Liverpool's tonnage surpassed those of the next six ports put together. Decline was presaged by the emergence of new rivals, especially Manchester, which built the Ship Canal (opened in 1894) specifically to bypass Liverpool, and Southampton. The Second World War, in which the port was the county's principal gateway for men and *matériel*, left widespread destruction. A surge of post-war prosperity ended abruptly in 1971 when the MDHB collapsed under spiralling debt and crippling labour disputes. All docks s of the Pier Head were closed in 1972, joined sixteen years later by the oldest to its N. In the early C21, the successor Mersey Docks and Harbour Co. has begun to post record cargo figures, though

Liverpool, Old Dock and Dry Dock, by Thomas Steers, by 1710–16.
Detail from J. Chadwick's map, 1725

the port today handles a far smaller percentage of the country's
maritime trade.

In 1708–9 *Henry Huss* and *George Sorocold* surveyed and
designed schemes to improve the Pool, though it was *Thomas
Steers* who was commissioned to build a 'wet' dock, that is one
enclosed behind gates, within it. This, the 3.5 acre (1.4 hectare)
OLD DOCK of 1710–16, set the pattern for the sail era: roughly
rectangular, and approached through gates from a tidal basin.
Earlier docks, e.g. London's Blackwall Dock of *c.* 1650, were for
laying up and repairing ships, so Steers' was the world's first commercial enclosed dock, designed for loading and unloading at any
state of tide. By the time four more had been constructed under
Steers' successors *Henry Berry* (1750–89) and *Thomas Morris*
(1789–99), Liverpool's docks covered some 25.7 acres (10.4
hectares); no other port had more than one. Very little pre-1840
fabric survives; the best remaining c18 walls line Duke's Dock
(1773), the only survivor of a number of small private docks and
basins.

The delays and allegations of corruption that dogged the construction of Prince's Dock brought about the resignation of the
next engineer, *John Foster Sen.*, in 1824 and the appointment of
Jesse Hartley (1780–1860), a bridge builder from Pontefract,
trained as a mason, but with no previous experience of dock
building. Hartley nevertheless became the world's first full-time
professional dock engineer and within months had presented
plans for expanding the docks into a fully integrated system.

From 1846 he relied increasingly on his son and assistant *J.B. Hartley*, who succeeded him for a year after his death. By then he had built or rebuilt twenty-six docks, increasing their acreage from 46 to 212 (18.6 to 85.8 hectares). Hartley's achievements, which mark him out as one of the greatest C19 engineers, were based on experience, attention to detail, openness to new ideas, a fearsome capacity for work and sound management. His docks were superbly built, relatively cheap and of conventional layout, and only his last, Canada Dock (1859), was at 17.4 acres (7 hectares) substantially larger than Prince's. Nevertheless, there were innovations. From Waterloo (1834), docks were interconnected, without separate river entrances, reducing operating costs. Tidal basins were replaced by half-tide docks, with gates onto the river, allowing access at more states of the tide. He built specialised docks: Clarence (1830), exclusively for steamers; three, beginning at Brunswick (1832), for unloading timber onto sloping quays; three warehouse docks for bonded goods (*see* p. 262), starting at Albert (1843–7); and Stanley (1844–8) as an interchange with rail – the first of its kind – and canal. All his work is distinguished by outstanding masonry, nowhere more so than in the twelve docks built in his distinctive cyclopean granite, a combination of massive headers and small irregular pieces of rubble knitted together like a jigsaw puzzle. *Hartley* also raised the standard of design on the Dock Estate to ARCHITECTURE of the highest calibre. His earlier Greek Revival structures – e.g. the massive 1830s gatepiers in the dock wall and the utilitarian classicism of the Albert warehouses – were, Pevsner declared, endowed with 'a sense of the cyclopean, the primeval, which is unparalleled'. The Gothic castle idiom that emerged in the 1840s was more overtly emblematic of security (e.g. the accumulator towers at Stanley and Wapping) and often arrestingly whimsical (e.g. the Wapping Policeman's Lodge). Hartley's architectural talent was not matched by his successors.

The emergence in the mid C19 of iron-hulled steamships, of a previously unimaginable size, stimulated the first radical change in dock design. They cost huge sums to build and operate and ran to regular timetables, making rapid turn-arounds imperative. The solution to this, and to the unrelenting demand for more berths, was three building programmes by *G.F. Lyster* and his more talented son *A.G. Lyster*, Dock Engineers 1861–97 and 1897–1913 respectively, characterised by three developments: the branch-dock plan, with fingers off a vestibule; two-storey transit sheds for more rapid goods handling; and river locks to eliminate delays associated with half-tide docks. Concrete quay walls adopted from the 1870s made them possible. The principal new docks of unprecedented size, built downstream where the channel was deeper and the foreshore wider, culminated in the Gladstone Dock of 1910–27. Selected older docks were comprehensively rebuilt along similar lines, e.g. King's, *c.* 1898–1906. But in the 1960s a revolution spread through shipping, replacing loose mixed cargoes with standardised, pre-packed containers which required large open quays for rapid transfer and storage.

The layout of the Royal Seaforth Dock was revised during design and it opened in 1971 with the key new characteristics: specialist (container and bulk) berths around a single polygonal dock with massive gantry cranes and vast areas of hardstanding for storage of containers and timber.

The first WAREHOUSE on the Dock Estate was at King's Dock (1793, demolished), erected by the Corporation to store tobacco. More followed in the wake of the 1803 Warehousing Act, which extended the privilege to hold goods in bond – that is in a secure warehouse without paying duty – to a variety of commodities provided that the closed-dock system was adopted: an integrated walled complex of dock and warehouses, as pioneered in London at the West India Dock (1799–1809). Vested interests, e.g. carters, private warehouse-owners and unscrupulous merchants, blocked full implementation in Liverpool until *Hartley*'s magnificent Albert Dock was erected in the 1840s. With the destruction of most of the equivalent London warehouses, Albert is now the best location to evoke the ambition and monumentality of the system. Similar fireproof (i.e. iron and brick) warehouses followed at Wapping and Stanley docks. Subsequent warehouses were for particular goods, e.g. the vast Waterloo grain warehouses by *G.F. Lyster*, 1866–8. *A.G. Lyster* built the even larger Tobacco Warehouse at Stanley Dock, *c.* 1897–1901, introducing steel and concrete. Like many Lyster buildings, it was enlivened by free Renaissance detail in terracotta, probably by the architectural draughtsman *John Arthur Berrington*. The ultimate development was bulk storage, beginning in 1881 with rock-cut casemates at Herculaneum Dock for petroleum and followed in the C20 by oil-tank farms, grain silos and Tate & Lyle's sublime parabolic sugar silo of 1955–7.

TRANSIT SHEDS, for the temporary shelter of goods on the quayside, were always more widespread, though rarely of architectural pretension. Only a rebuilt gable at Salthouse Dock (1855) survives of Hartley's. The *Lysters*' steamship docks had standard enclosed brick and iron or steel designs; C20 developments included electric cranes and concrete construction. With the onset of containerisation, generic single-storey portal-frame structures designed around articulated lorries, containers, pallets and forklift trucks have been erected at the Royal Seaforth Dock.

Most goods have always left the docks by road. For this, BRIDGES were provided across passages. Beginning with an order in 1809, a standard cast-iron swing bridge was introduced based on a *John Rennie* design; an 1840s example survives at Albert Dock. Later, wider passages for steamships were spanned by hydraulically powered swing bridges, or lifting bridges, e.g. Stanley Dock. The first link to the canal network was indirect, the Duke of Bridgewater's Duke's Dock of 1773. A direct connection opened in 1848 to the Leeds and Liverpool Canal at Stanley Dock. The Liverpool & Manchester Railway opened in 1830 with a goods station serving the docks, and by the end of the C19 an internal RAILWAY extended the length of the docks. For workers, the elevated electric Liverpool Overhead

Railway operated along the length of the docks from 1893 to 1956.

After closure the semi-derelict South Docks, upstream of the Pier Head, were colonised by small business. Debate about REDEVELOPMENT ended in 1981, when the Merseyside Development Corporation (one of the first Urban Development Corporations) was created to assume ownership and lead regeneration. In 1988 its remit was extended to the obsolete docks N from the Pier Head to Stanley Dock, and it was wound up in 1998. The MDC undertook environmental and infrastructure improvements, demolition and selective restoration. Central to its approach was the exploitation of water as an attractive backdrop, and many docks were restored to working order. Development was zoned for both business and industry and leisure and housing, though in execution the emphasis switched to the latter (e.g. Brunswick Dock). An early priority was the restoration of Albert Dock as a flagship mixed-use development: the first phase was completed in 1984. By 2004 most sites S of the Pier Head had been developed, the glaring exception being King's Dock. N of the Pier Head, progress to 2004 was limited to Prince's and Waterloo docks.

Regeneration has been economically successful, but the architecture is extremely disappointing. There has been a widespread failure to rise to the potential of the extraordinary location. The best by far is conservation: the magnificent repair and conversion of Albert Dock, but also the residential conversion of Wapping Warehouse by *Kingham Knight Associates*. The best new building is *David Marks Julia Barfield Architects'* Liverpool Watersport Centre, 1993–4, at Queen's Dock. *Eduard Ross's* bridge at Prince's Dock (2001) is noteworthy too. Otherwise a lack of commitment to good design is sorely evident in banal office and housing schemes. Unlike London's Docklands, standards have yet to improve significantly.

The docks are described, alphabetically, in two sections divided by the Pier Head: the South Docks and the North Docks. *See* p. 276 for the dock wall and the Liverpool Landing Stage. The Pier Head itself is discussed on pp. 330–3.

SOUTH DOCKS

These developed in broadly chronological fashion S from the Pier Head for 2½ m. along the reclaimed foreshore to Dingle, where rock outcropping prevented further expansion upstream. By 1900 they were already struggling to cope with the growing size of steamships; the subsequent slow decline ended abruptly in 1972 with complete closure. Mixed-use regeneration from 1981 was headed by the restoration of Albert Dock, a self-conscious symbol of rebirth.

ALBERT DOCK. *Jesse Hartley's* peerless masterpiece, one of the   96
great monuments of C19 engineering, is unquestionably the
architectural climax of the Liverpool docks. In 1969 Pevsner

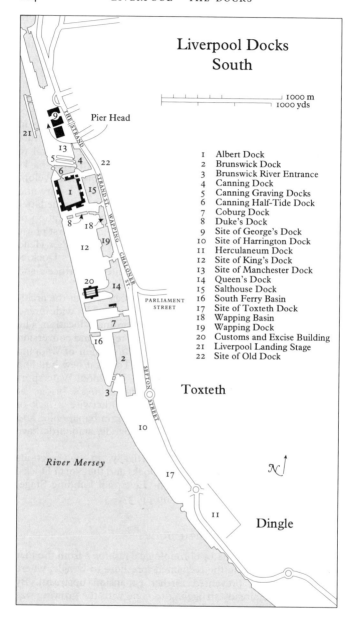

Liverpool Docks
South

1000 m
1000 yds

Pier Head

River Mersey

Toxteth

Dingle

PARLIAMENT
STREET

1	Albert Dock
2	Brunswick Dock
3	Brunswick River Entrance
4	Canning Dock
5	Canning Graving Docks
6	Canning Half-Tide Dock
7	Coburg Dock
8	Duke's Dock
9	Site of George's Dock
10	Site of Harrington Dock
11	Herculaneum Dock
12	Site of King's Dock
13	Site of Manchester Dock
14	Queen's Dock
15	Salthouse Dock
16	South Ferry Basin
17	Site of Toxteth Dock
18	Wapping Basin
19	Wapping Dock
20	Customs and Excise Building
21	Liverpool Landing Stage
22	Site of Old Dock

wrote that 'For sheer punch there is little in the early commercial architecture of Europe to emulate it.' In its bare bones it is an integrated warehouse–dock complex, built in 1843–7 without any combustible material, for the secure storage of

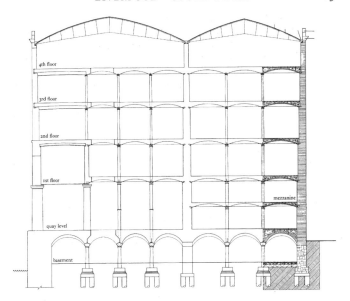

4th floor
3rd floor
2nd floor
1st floor
mezzanine
quay level
basement

Liverpool, Albert Dock warehouses, by Jesse Hartley, 1843–7.
Transverse section

high-value bonded goods. At the centre is a 7.75 acre (3.1 hectare) dock, with 40 ft (12.2 metre) walls constructed in Hartley's habitual cyclopean granite. Grouped around this – and standing on almost 5,300 beech piles – are five 60 ft (18.3 metre) high warehouse stacks, with vaults below, each constructed of a brick skin wrapped around a cast-iron frame. They contain over one million sq. ft (92,900 sq. m.) of floor-space. Ancillary buildings and a perimeter wall erected to prevent theft surround the warehouses. But what solicits admiration now, apart of course from the scale, is the monumental solemnity of the warehouses, which are pared down to a synthesis of austere classicism and technological functionalism.

HISTORY. In 1841 local opposition to the creation of a 'closed-dock system' in Liverpool, in pursuance of the 1803 Warehousing Act (*see* p. 262), was finally overcome. The site chosen was constricted by docks to its N, S, E and by the Mersey to the W. Work began immediately when Canning and Salt-house docks were run dry. Excavation began in 1843, the first warehouse stacks came into operation at the opening by Prince Albert in 1846, and the last were finished the following year. The complex cost in excess of £700,000.

The dock was initially a great success, specialising in the Far East trade, and extensions were added to the S stack in 1853–5, but within two decades its entrances were too small and awkward for the latest ocean-going steamships. The presence of the warehouses made rebuilding impractical (making Albert one of the very few Liverpool docks to remain in its original form) and by 1914 hardly any ships unloaded here. Nevertheless Hartley's warehouses continued to store e.g. bonded tobacco, wines and spirits until 1972. By that time they were far from pristine: the N stack was converted into a cold store as early as 1899, the SE stack had not been repaired since a bomb in 1941 had blown a corner off, and other parts were derelict.

A myriad of sometimes wildly unrealistic proposals came and went until 1983, when the newly created Merseyside Development Corporation (MDC), in partnership with the Arrowcroft Group, embarked on an ambitious restoration programme, a task that to 1997 had cost £177 million. The first phase opened in 1984, but in 2004 a few sections still remained undeveloped. It is arguably the largest single conservation project ever undertaken in the United Kingdom, and fundamentally a great success. New uses include hotels and bars, shops, offices and apartments, many by the *Franklin Stafford Partnership*, the Merseyside Maritime Museum by *Brock Carmichael Associates*, and *James Stirling*'s Tate Liverpool art gallery. The dock has become Merseyside's premier tourist attraction, but an isolated one: the windswept dock road remains a hostile barrier to the hoped-for extension of the city centre into the dock and on to the riverfront.

96   Hartley's WAREHOUSE design married the traditions of warehouse planning and of fireproof textile-mill construction. A deputation was sent to study the most recent closed-dock system in London, the St Katharine Docks, where *Philip Hardwick* had designed warehouses in 1826–7, and these formed the basis of Hartley's design. As Hartley had no previous experience in the field, Hardwick himself was also consulted, along with his successor at St Katharine, George Aitchison Sen., and others. Hartley laid out five separate warehouse STACKS, each five storeys high on basement vaults. No two stacks are identical because of the irregular plan of the basin and interruptions for the passages. Each has large yards for carts cut out of the rear, an idea taken from the St Katharine Docks. The massive load-bearing brick walls are over 3 ft (0.9 metres) thick at ground level, diminishing to 1 ft 7 in. (0.48 metres). On the quayside is a COLONNADE of hollow cast-iron columns 15 ft (4.6 metres) high, filled with masonry.* These are unfluted Greek Doric of the most Primitivist kind, with powerfully squat proportions. The colonnade was the key concept borrowed from Hardwick's warehouses; its principal advantage was that on a constricted site warehouse accommodation could be maximized whilst still providing quayside space for unloading, inspecting, weighing and sorting

---

*In the infill of 1855 in the SE corner the ground-floor columns are granite, from which spring brick groin vaults.

cargo. Goods, once landed, could be taken in by means of internal hoists and external cranes, or put onto carts for onward distribution. The broad elliptical arches that break the colonnade and bite into the floor above were Hartley's innovation, allowing cranes and ships' tackle to swing goods over the quay. Above the colonnades the massive façades are stripped bare, relying solely on function for proportion and articulation. The crane arches create the principal stresses, the slightly recessed hoist doors the secondary. The one, slightly incongruous, concession was the cupola'd clock tower, designed by *Hardwick*, above the NE stack (removed *c.* 1960). Note everywhere Hartley's fastidious attention to detail: granite replaces brick or sandstone where quoins or other elements were susceptible to damage by carts, and the corners of the E stacks flanking the Salthouse passage are rounded so as not to foul ships' rigging. Where windows were not required initially he provided blanks, not bonded-in.

So to the INTERIORS. The basic plan followed St Katharine, with five storeys plus vaults and a mezzanine floor behind the colonnade. Hartley developed the mezzanine concept further by merely providing footings (in the form of flared capitals) halfway up the internal columns, leaving future users to determine if and when to insert a floor. Prompted by a series of warehouse fires, for the STRUCTURE Hartley looked to contemporary textile-mill construction (a decision reinforced in 1842 by the Great Fire of Hamburg and another devastating blaze in Liverpool). Between 1841 and 1843 he drew up six alternative designs to consider degrees and types of fireproofing. Full-scale mock-ups of two of these were then tested to destruction before a system of cast-iron columns and beams supporting brick-('jack'-)arch floors was chosen (the St Katharine stacks had wooden floors and roofs). This was already established as best practice in textile-mill design. The *Haigh Foundry*, Wigan (*see* p. 187), and the *Gospel Oak Iron Works*, Staffordshire, supplied the structural ironwork.

This frame was built up above magnificent sandstone and brick vaults, which spring from elegant, cambered cast-iron beams spanning cast-iron columns. Arching in two directions, they swell rhythmically like the barrels they once stored. Above, the cast-iron frame rises on a module of 18 by 12 ft (5.5 by 3.7 metres), the columns supporting beams of inverted Y- and V-profile. From these spring the shallow jack arches, covered with ash and aggregate and laid with tiles. Hartley arranged the arches in the outer bays at right angles to the walls and provided plenty of iron tie-rods to restrain the lateral thrusts that had caused notorious mill collapses, but what makes his frame stand apart is the outstanding aesthetic quality of the ironwork: muscular and elegant, fluid and sculptural, beautifully detailed. And to cap it, he invented a remarkable stressed-skin roof, made of wrought-iron plates riveted together and tied across the eaves by slender wrought-iron rods suspended on hangers from ribs attached to the underside. Though of an undeniable delicate beauty, it suffered problems with thermal expansion and, after the Stanley Dock warehouses (1852–4, *see* p. 279), the concept was abandoned until revived by C20 engineers. Cast-iron window frames, stone parapets and staircases, lateral and spine brick fire-break walls and wrought-iron fire-doors completed the fireproof construction. The best place to examine the internal structure is the Merseyside Maritime Museum in the N stack (*see* below).

Lifts and hoists were initially manually powered, but in 1848–9 the warehouses became the world's first to be fitted with hydraulic cranes and hoists, ordered from *William Armstrong* in Newcastle. The hydraulic jiggers of *c.* 1878 in the colonnade were part of a later expansion of the system.

RESTORATION was a mammoth undertaking. The MDC restored docks, locks and bridges, installed services and landscaped the site, and undertook repair and restoration of the warehouses. Arrowcroft and leaseholders converted the interiors. To ensure continuity *Holford Associates* and *W.G. Curtin & Partners* were retained throughout as consultant architects and engineers respectively. They did the N stack and the N end of the W stack (the Tate) in 1983–6. The rest was undertaken by the *Franklin Stafford Partnership* with *Ward, Ashcroft & Parkman* as engineers. Around the basin existing window frames were replaced in aluminium to the original pattern. The new glazing fitted to most rear elevations attracted criticism, though the recessed angled glazing installed in place of loading doors did create welcome shadow and depth. All blank windows were opened up.

CONVERSIONS. Beginning, clockwise, with the N stack and the MERSEYSIDE MARITIME MUSEUM. Chiefly 1984–6, by *Brock Carmichael Associates*. A museum had been considered as early as 1884, and Albert's N stack emerged as the preferred home in 1978. Brock Carmichael's scheme is generally a success. The fully glazed wall behind the colonnade is sympathetic and confident, and removing the mezzanine has created a lofty foyer. Throughout, columns, beams, arches and walls (and Hartley's iron roof) are exposed. So too, unashamedly, are the services, although some bulky exhibition designs have masked the structure. However, the staircase is a triumph. It slices through the structure in flights staggered sideways by one bay per storey, opening up views right through the building. It has an appropriately nautical flavour, like companionways ascending from deep inside a ship's hull, and by making Hartley's structure instantly comprehensible, it also succeeds in turning the building itself into a major exhibit.

Next, the NE, SE and S stacks, and S end of the W stack. *Franklin Stafford* have done most, beginning with SHOPS and OFFICES on the ground floor and mezzanine, in phases, clockwise, 1983–8. Some of this has been lost to later fit-outs with generally frameless glazed façades, but where it survives it is undoubtedly the least successful element. Intrusive, clumsy concrete mezzanines, wooden-framed glazed partitions. In the upper floors the practice created offices in the SE stack, 1992–3, and the NE stack, 2001, and apartments in the S end of the W stack, 1987–96. In the W end of the S stack is a hotel, by the American *Hausman Group*, 1998.

Lastly, TATE LIVERPOOL, in the N end of the W stack. 1984–8, by *James Stirling* of *Stirling, Wilford & Associates*. The gallery selected the dock for its first regional outpost in 1981. Stirling, who was working on the development of the gallery's London home, was asked in 1984 to convert Albert and produced an admirably simple and clear plan. Running along the back of the spine wall is a core one structural bay wide, containing a staircase and other services. Flanking this are the galleries and secondary spaces stacked straightforwardly within Hartley's structural system. The spaces are clean, calm and elegant. As at the Maritime Museum the structure is celebrated, though the screens for picture-hanging and controlling natural light necessarily interfere, forming a new inner wall. Services and lighting are gathered in hefty, angular ducts slung beneath the jack arches. The museum's façade was a panelled blue and orange screen (much of it replaced by glazing in 1997–8) with portholes and bold and elegant signage, self-effacingly set back behind the colonnade. Behind this is the foyer, originally spanned by a mezzanine café in the form of a swelling blue balcony (nicknamed the 'blue bum' by Stirling), and lofty ground-floor galleries created by removing the mezzanine. As part of the controversial phase two works, 1997–8, *Michael Wilford & Partners** relocated the balconies to create a more spacious foyer. The ground-floor galleries to the l. became a bookshop and a new, larger café, into which the balcony was re-inserted, folded back on itself above an island bar. The vacant top floor was fitted out as galleries for temporary exhibitions, retaining Hartley's stressed-skin roof E of the spine and creating a new north-light roof W of it.

This was an intensely personal commission for Stirling – his only project in his home town – and throughout his response is notable for its restraint. Both Hartley and Stirling had famously powerful personalities, but at Liverpool Stirling put aside his usual exuberance in deference to Hartley's masterpiece.

RELATED STRUCTURES. An imposing foil to the warehouses in the NE corner is the DOCK TRAFFIC OFFICE, completed in 1848 to a slightly hunched design of two storeys over a basement by *Philip Hardwick.*** The pedimented Tuscan portico is a *tour de force* in cast iron; each column is made of two sections over 17 ft (5.2 metres) high, and the architrave is a single casting. A year later *Hartley* introduced some hauteur by adding a second storey containing a flat for the principal clerk. With that came the splendid tapering chimneystacks and prob-

---

*Stirling died in 1992.
**He was preferred by the Dock Committee over Hartley here (and for the clock tower) possibly because for Architecture it wanted an Architect.

ably the first-floor cornice, which is far bolder than that proposed by Hardwick. The core is a large galleried hall, a double cube with coved ceiling. Converted by the *Building Design Partnership* as Granada Television news studios in 1984–5.

The SWING BRIDGE of 1843 across the Canning–Albert passage in the dock's NW corner is a cast-iron two-leaf structure supplied by the *Haigh Foundry*, Wigan. The last surviving example of a pattern, once common in the docks, which was derived via Hull from *John Rennie*'s pioneering design for the London Dock (1803–4). The N railings could be pivoted flat so as not to foul ships' ropes when swung open. Restored 1984.

PERIMETER WALL. Security against theft was a fundamental to the closed-dock system and so the warehouses were enclosed by a 12 ft (3.7 metre) wall, erected across the cart bays on the N, E and S sides, but free-standing along the riverfront (intended as a public promenade; magnificent views of the W stack from here). It was pierced by gates, whose massive GATEPIERS, with wild rustication and characteristic slots for sliding gates, can be seen W of the swing bridge and in the SE and SW corners. POLICE LODGES are built alongside the gates against the inside of the wall.

Other ancillary buildings included a simple, two-storey COOPERAGE (1846) inside the wall in the NW corner and, beyond on the pierhead, residences for key employees. Only one remains (the last of over forty on the Dock Estate), the three-storey PIERMASTER'S HOUSE of 1852–3 with dogtooth eaves corbelling; to the l. is the Piermaster's Office. Restored from dereliction by *Brock Carmichael Associates* to their appearance *c.* 1910, for the Merseyside Maritime Museum, 1983–4. Outside the walls is the ALBERT HYDRAULIC POWER CENTRE, by *G.F. Lyster*, 1878. Tall chimney. Uncultured restoration as the Pumphouse Inn in 1986.

BRUNSWICK DOCK. First suggested in 1809; built by *Hartley* 1827–32 for timber imports. Present form: 1905 rebuild and S extension in concrete, with river lock, by *A.G. Lyster*. As redeveloped since the 1980s it succeeds because the quayside housing creates a sense of enclosure, and because the expanses of water are alive with boats in the LIVERPOOL MARINA. This is despite the weakness of the architecture. The illiterate 1980s Marina and Harbourside Club stands in a key location requiring something far more accomplished. In the SE corner HMS EAGLET, the Royal Naval Headquarters, Merseyside, by *Bannister Storr Associates*, 1996–8. Heavy-footed public architecture. Clustered roofs, banded walls. Feeble HOUSING on the E quay: too suburban, lost above the massive quay walls. On the W quay it is at least of an appropriate scale and density. One lock of the RIVER ENTRANCE reopened for small craft in 1987, with a *Brock Carmichael Associates* control room meant to evoke the form of a ship. E of it the preserved top rail of a lock gate – superlative joinery – and the only surviving TRANSIT SHED, of *c.* 1908, converted in 1982 in appropriately robust, industrial fashion (see N elevation) into a business centre.

SOUTH FERRY ISLAND between Brunswick Dock and the river has more bad apartment blocks. They are built on the site of the DOCKYARD, established by *Hartley* with responsibility for the construction and maintenance of the docks, and around Hartley's now infilled Brunswick Half-Tide Dock of *c.* 1832. Two of his characteristic GATEMEN'S SHELTERS (cf. Canning Half-Tide Dock, below) survive on the river wall, flanking the old entrance. N of these are his magnificent sweeping RIVER STEPS, each step a massive block laid at a dramatically acute angle, like uprooted bedrock.

CANNING DOCK was created in 1829 by locking the Dry Dock, the tidal entrance basin to the Old Dock (*see* p. 260) which lay inland across what is now Strand Street on the site of Canning Place until *c.* 1826. The largest blocks of the NW quay wall are thought to be of *c.* 1737, making them the oldest surviving stonework in the docks. Canning Nos. 1 and 2 GRAVING DOCKS, built 1765–9, were subsequently lengthened, and finally deepened by *Hartley* in the 1840s. Alongside, mid-C19 railway offices attached to a GREAT WESTERN RAILWAY WAREHOUSE of *c.* 1891. Brick. In the GWR's house style. Spanning the Canning passage is a delightful iron rodstay FOOTBRIDGE, a two-leaf swing bridge of *c.* 1845, probably by *Hartley*. All this restored as part of the Albert Dock scheme from 1983.

CANNING HALF-TIDE DOCK. The entrance to the Albert system, created in 1842–4 by *Hartley* out of the Gut, the narrow entrance to the Dry Dock (*see* Canning Dock). The LAMP STANDARDS are replicas of Hartley's elegant tapering design. The RIVER ENTRANCE is a typical Hartley design of two 45 ft (13.7 metre) passages divided by a masonry island. N passage sealed; gate and stayed swing bridge of 1983–4 across the s passage. Note the quality of Hartley's granite masonry and the attention to detail, e.g. the upward sweep of the island coping, making a warning of the edge and a foothold when handling hawsers in wet weather. The octagonal GATEMEN'S SHELTERS flanking the entrance and the LIGHTHOUSE on the island are excellent *Hartley* architecture. Superb stonework, with highly original detailing: e.g. the roofs of massive overlapping granite slabs, the finials, and the tapering sides and oriental eaves brackets of the lighthouse. In appearance and function they echo entrance lodges to a country estate.

On the pierhead s is *Tony Cragg*'s SCULPTURE *Raleigh*, 1986, evoking the working docks in reclaimed granite and recast iron. On the pierhead N, the three-storey PILOTAGE BUILDING of 1883, with projecting pedimented, cupola'd centre and Renaissance detail, probably by *John Arthur Berrington*. Converted in 1980 by the *Building Design Partnership*, along with sheds to the N, for museum use (currently the MUSEUM OF LIVERPOOL LIFE). On the river wall outside stands a memorial to Irish emigration by *Mark de Graffenried*, 2001. Bronze. A heroic (but lifeless) young family.

COBURG DOCK. A complex history, beginning with construction *c.* 1817–23 as Union Half-Tide Dock (the first in Liverpool) and Brunswick Basin, is reflected in the materials of the QUAY WALLS: sandstone, limestone, granite and concrete. Redeveloped in conjunction with Brunswick Dock as a marina, with some feeble housing. Bolder, however, is MARINER'S WHARF on the N quay, 1989–97 by *David Backhouse*. The first housing in the South Docks. A terrace treated as pavilions dominated by gabled projections over fat columns, intended to evoke warehouses, in the vein of Troughton McAslan and Jeremy Dixon in London's Docklands.

DUKE'S DOCK runs behind Albert Dock's s stack through car parks. Named after Francis Egerton, 3rd Duke of Bridgewater, who completed a private transhipment dock in 1773 for goods carried by barge to Manchester via his Bridgewater Canal. This forms the central section today. Its narrow dimensions are unlike any other surviving dock; in conception it is much more a canal basin.* Although much patched, the best remaining example of C18 dock-wall construction. The E section is a 1790s extension, the W is *Hartley*'s half-tide dock of 1843–5. None of the 166 buildings noted in 1899 survives.

(GEORGE'S DOCK. 1762–71. The city's third, infilled 1900 and the buildings of the Pier Head erected on the site (*see* pp. 330–3). Parts of its walls are preserved in the lower basement of the Cunard Building.)

HARRINGTON DOCK. *See* Toxteth Dock.

HERCULANEUM DOCK. The furthest upstream. Built following a failed private scheme; named after the pottery that had occupied the site. *G.F. Lyster*'s first major work. Graving docks and a coaling dock, opened 1866 and expanded in stages until 1902, cut deep into outcropping rock. Infilled by the MDC for access to the 1984 International Garden Festival (*see* p. 383) and redeveloped with insipid offices and housing. On the old entrance island is the CHUNG KU RESTAURANT, 2000 by *DTR Sheard Walshaw*. A two-storey drum, with fully glazed riverside dining rooms. Rear service wedge, finishing in a sharp prow sheltering the entrance. Around the s and e perimeter, sixty-one curious CASEMATES cut into the rock, faced in concrete with pilasters between. By *G.F. Lyster*, 1881–2, for the storage of petroleum. Above, the noble entrance to the DINGLE TUNNEL of the Liverpool Overhead Railway, 1896.

KING'S DOCK. Now a vast temporary car park. From 1906 remodelled as one body of water with Wapping Dock, with two branches. It was originally constructed in 1785–8. The MDC filled the branches in 1986, but a series of ambitious propos-

---

*Nancy Ritchie-Noakes, in *Liverpool's Historic Waterfront* (1984), gives *John Gilbert*, the Duke's resident engineer, as the probable designer.

als for retail and leisure development came to nothing until 2005, when construction began of a conference centre and indoor arena by *Wilkinson Eyre*. Its form, according to the architects, is inspired by the design of a mobile phone. The rest of the site will be developed with hotels, offices, apartments and shops.

(MANCHESTER DOCK. Built before 1785 for barges and flats and filled with spoil from the Mersey Tunnel excavations in 1928–36.)

MUSEUM OF LIVERPOOL LIFE. *See* Canning Half-Tide Dock.

(OLD DOCK. *See* p. 260)

QUEEN'S DOCK. Completed 1795–6 by *Thomas Morris* under the same programme as King's Dock. Doubled in size 1810–16; rebuilt for steamships 1898–1906, with two branches and a graving dock. Redevelopment has been aesthetically the least successful here. A few truly feeble buildings occupy the E side, including a casino (2003), with a glass façade leaning out over the dock. The N branch has been partially infilled as a car park, an appropriately dreary setting for the CUSTOMS AND EXCISE BUILDING, 1991–3, by *PSA Projects, Birmingham*. This has the scale but none of the quality that a major public commission on such a prominent site demands. A five-storey quadrangle, the E and W wings bridging the flooded graving dock in exposed steel frames, the mean N and S wings in buff concrete blocks. Beige, faceless, remote, it is a sadly apposite home for the taxman. Outside the W façade, SCULPTURE: Time and Tide, 1993, by *Philip Bews*. Two bronze figures raised on columns and a frieze (made by *Diane Gorvin*). These face the RIVERSIDE WALK, created by the MDC in the 1980s between the Pier Head and Dingle, opening up over three miles of river-front to the public. In the dock's SE corner is the LIVERPOOL WATERSPORT CENTRE of 1993–4, the best new building completed under the MDC. An early work by *David Marks Julia Barfield Architects*, designers of the London Eye. A pavilion visually 'floating' in the dock (though actually built on piles), so emphasizing its purpose. Exposed steel frame cleanly articulated. Clear vertical separation between 'wet' and 'dry' areas, the latter a deck above, supported on steel trees.

SALTHOUSE DOCK. Begun, as the South Dock, by *Thomas Steers* in 1739 and finished by *Henry Berry* in 1754, in part to serve a salt works. Remodelled and enlarged by *Hartley* 1841–2 as Albert's export dock. This was part of a one-way system: ships entered at Canning Half-Tide, discharged in Albert, and proceeded to take on cargo in Salthouse before leaving via Canning and Canning Half-Tide. All that remains of the encompassing TRANSIT SHEDS is the gable dated 1855 in Hartley granite in the SE corner, reconstructed in 1980. The removal of sheds has opened up views of the Albert warehouses unknown before closure.

SOUTH FERRY BASIN. Constructed *c.* 1817–23 for ferries and fishermen. Small, but remarkably little altered. *See* Brunswick Dock for South Ferry Island.

TOXTETH DOCK and HARRINGTON DOCK. By *G.F. Lyster*, built
1882–8 and 1875–83 respectively, obliterating four small C19
predecessors. The MDC infilled the docks and in 1986–94
converted *Lyster*'s four brick and iron TRANSIT SHEDS into
offices and industrial units for the BRUNSWICK BUSINESS
PARK. The landward two are import sheds of 1883–9, the first
two-storey transit sheds in Liverpool and the world's first
designed to work on both levels simultaneously, by ships' tackle
below and travelling hydraulic roof cranes above. Best-preserved is the N one (now Century Building), with a clock tower
pleasantly enriched in *John Arthur Berrington* fashion. Single-
storey export sheds, typical of many built by the MDHB, were
erected on the W quays. West Harrington Shed, *c.* 1884–8 (now
Glacier Building), has had the most architectural makeover, by
the *Owen Ellis Partnership*, 1993–4. Porthole windows, and
cable-stay masts supporting a canopy. Also, in the NW corner,
the lively TOXTETH HYDRAULIC POWER CENTRE, 1889,
extended 1911, and alongside, CUSTOMS DEPOT of 1890. Crisp
Berrington Renaissance detailing.

WAPPING DOCK. Built by *Hartley* together with WAPPING
BASIN to the N in 1851–5 to unite the docks N and S of Duke's
Dock. Later effectively merged with King's Dock. On the E
quay is WAPPING WAREHOUSE, completed in 1856 by *Hartley*.
Like its siblings at Stanley Dock, a simplified, more utilitarian
version of the Albert design: unbroken rear elevation (note the
fantastically shaped quoins of the cart arches) to incorporate
railway sidings, no mezzanine, simpler vaults, a conventional
roof, and quayside columns of concave, not convex, section (a
more satisfactory structural form for hollow cast-iron shafts).
Sensitively converted into apartments by *Kingham Knight Associates*, 1986–9, when the bomb-damaged S end was demolished
(the quayside columns are preserved) and a new well-matched
S wall built.

   S of the warehouse two of *Hartley*'s architectural flights of
fancy. The accumulator tower of the WAPPING HYDRAULIC
POWER CENTRE, 1855–6, restored 1988, is an embattled
octagonal brick folly, the turret on top the boiler chimney.
Adjoining boiler and engine house in granite with Tudor
arches. The extraordinary POLICEMAN'S LODGE is the central
pier of a demolished double gate in the dock wall. Oval, with
a blank, snaking arrow-slit motif and a bizarre conical roof of
overlapping masonry bands terminating in a flattened finial-
cum-chimney. The granite masonry is itself a thing of great
beauty. A fragment of the DOCK WALL (*see* p. 276), lowered,
stands alongside the warehouse.

   KING'S WATERFRONT, Wapping Basin W quay, seven- and
eight-storey apartment blocks by *Patrick Davies Architecture*,
2000–2. White and tritely Deco-nautical.

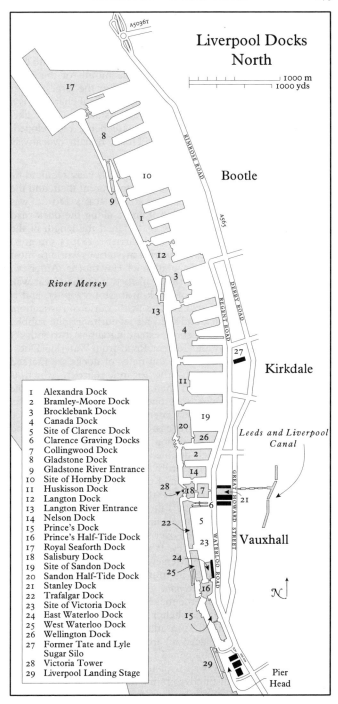

Liverpool Docks
North

1000 m
1000 yds

River Mersey

Bootle

Kirkdale

Leeds and Liverpool
Canal

Vauxhall

Pier
Head

1   Alexandra Dock
2   Bramley-Moore Dock
3   Brocklebank Dock
4   Canada Dock
5   Site of Clarence Dock
6   Clarence Graving Docks
7   Collingwood Dock
8   Gladstone Dock
9   Gladstone River Entrance
10 Site of Hornby Dock
11 Huskisson Dock
12 Langton Dock
13 Langton River Entrance
14 Nelson Dock
15 Prince's Dock
16 Prince's Half-Tide Dock
17 Royal Seaforth Dock
18 Salisbury Dock
19 Site of Sandon Dock
20 Sandon Half-Tide Dock
21 Stanley Dock
22 Trafalgar Dock
23 Site of Victoria Dock
24 East Waterloo Dock
25 West Waterloo Dock
26 Wellington Dock
27 Former Tate and Lyle
    Sugar Silo
28 Victoria Tower
29 Liverpool Landing Stage

NORTH DOCKS

In 1796 this shore was a sandy beach lined with bathing machines; over the next two hundred years these gave way to ever bigger docks stretching eventually to the mouth of the river. Today the operational port is consolidated in the largest, most northerly docks, an area whose bustling industrial character is a reminder of what the whole of the Dock Estate was once like. The oldest docks, nearest the centre, are being redeveloped, though a number, notably Stanley Dock, remain evocatively semi-derelict.

A highlight is the DOCK WALL. Perimeter walls were required by the 1803 Warehousing Act (*see* p. 262) to prevent theft, and the first section, by *John Foster Sen.* at PRINCE'S DOCK, was begun in 1816. It was extended N and S along the dock road by *Hartley* and the *Lysters* until it stretched the length of the docks, a physical and psychological barrier *c.* 18 ft (5.5 metres) high, behind which the docks were a mysterious world to most Liverpudlians. The novelist Nathaniel Hawthorne, American consul in Liverpool in the 1850s, likened it to the Great Wall of China. Foster's part is of brick, with stone coping, and is interrupted by stone GATEPIERS with curious rustication. *Hartley* employed brick and then his favourite granite rubble. The longest remaining section, extending almost two miles N along Waterloo Road and Regent Road from Waterloo Dock, is a remarkable sight. Names and dates of docks are marked by stone plaques set into the gigantic barrier, which is punctuated every now and then by Hartley's colossal triple gatepiers. The earlier (i.e. S) ones are Greek Revival style, *c.* 1834, but the extraordinary later examples (N from Clarence Graving Dock) are peculiarly castle-like – fat, massively round turrets with vestigial castellation, and slots for sliding gates. The central piers, which doubled as a policeman's hut, have slit windows and a door. Hardly any of the wall S of the Pier Head still stands (*see* p. 270 and p. 274).

Another significant structure is the LIVERPOOL LANDING STAGE and MERSEY FERRY TERMINAL at the Pier Head. By the 1980s rail and road tunnels had reduced the Mersey ferry service – which once carried over sixteen million people a year – to the verge of bankruptcy. It was relaunched as a tourist attraction, for which the Mersey FERRY TERMINAL on the river wall was refurbished in 1991. The building, and adjoining restaurant, are by *Ronald Bradbury*, mid-1960s. *Brock Carmichael Architects* did the make-over, with tented roof. The motif is continued for the shelter on the Liverpool LANDING STAGE, once the berth of Transatlantic liners. The current 1975 concrete pontoon replaced an iron structure first floated in 1847 and eventually lengthened to over 2,500 ft (760 metres). The narrow masonry well N of the Pier Head, built by *G.F. Lyster* in *Hartley*'s distinctive granite in 1873–6, housed a floating roadway down to it. Inland are the drum piers that flanked the approach, and one of a chain of 1990s Neo-Hartley sewer-interceptor stations.

ALEXANDRA DOCK. 1874–82, by *G.F. Lyster*. At 44 acres (17.8 hectares) the largest to that date. Still operational.

BRAMLEY-MOORE DOCK. By *Hartley*. Operational. One of the 1848 group (*see* Stanley Dock, p. 279). From 1856 it had a high-level railway link for the export of coal. A derelict *Lyster* ACCU-MULATOR TOWER survives.

BROCKLEBANK DOCK. Opened for timber in 1862, rebuilt 1904–8, and again with the construction of the second Langton River Entrance in 1949–62. Operational.

CANADA DOCK. *Hartley*'s last, opened 1859 for the North American timber trade. A reminder, a statue of a moustachioed lumberjack leaning on his axe, crowns the gable of the former Canada Dock Hotel, *c.* 1860, on the corner of Bankfield Street opposite. Rebuilt with branches and a GRAVING DOCK around the turn of the C20. Operational.

CLARENCE DOCK. Liverpool's first steamship dock, proposed 1821 and completed by *Hartley* in 1830 at a distance N of the existing docks for fear of fire. Closed in 1928 when a power station (demolished 1994) was erected on the site. Immediately N, CLARENCE GRAVING DOCKS, *c.* 1830, by *Hartley*, with magnificent masonry. Subsequently lengthened. GATEPIERS of the castellated type (*see* Dock Wall, p. 276).

COLLINGWOOD DOCK. 1848, by *Hartley*. The 'vestibule' part of the Stanley Dock system. Derelict gates and barge locks at either end.

GLADSTONE DOCK. Operational. The massive – 49-acre (19.8-hectare) – culmination of the *Lysters*' building programmes. Enormous GRAVING DOCK (now wet) begun 1910, the river entrance (i.e. lock) and two branch docks completed 1927. Impressive three-storey concrete transit sheds demolished. The river entrance is still the principal entrance to the dock system.

(HORNBY DOCK. *G.F. Lyster*, 1880–3, with concrete quay walls. For timber. Now infilled.)

HUSKISSON DOCK. Opened in 1852 for the timber trade, and *c.* 1900–2 extended s with branches by *A.G. Lyster*. Central branch destroyed in 1941 and replaced by two TRANSIT SHEDS, presumably by the Dock Engineer *Adrian J. Porter*, completed 1957 and *c.* 1960. Two storeys, entirely reinforced concrete, including vaulting roofs.

LANGTON DOCK. *G.F. Lyster*, opened 1879. Today partly filled with industrial plant. The present Langton RIVER ENTRANCE dates from 1949–62.

NELSON DOCK. One of the five docks opened by *Hartley* in 1848. Castellated gatepiers in the dock wall (*see* p. 276).

PRINCE'S DOCK. Both *William Jessop* and *John Rennie* were consulted over plans for a new dock here, before construction to Rennie's outline designs began under *John Foster Sen.*, *c.* 1810. Work was still not finished when it opened in 1821. The first C19 dock, at 11.4 acres (4.6 hectares) it was substantially larger than the C18 projects. The North Atlantic trade migrated to newer, larger docks, and by the C20 the dock was home to coastal and Irish traffic, for which quays were modernised early in the century.

In 1988 the dock passed to the Merseyside Development Corporation, since when the utilitarian buildings have been cleared, the E quay widened and commercial redevelopment begun to a masterplan by *Taylor Young*. The results so far, though, are shot through with mediocrity. The architecture is both bland and fussy, the planning and urban design soulless; adjoining the Pier Head, this is one of the finest urban locations in Britain, yet it could be a business park anywhere. So far three OFFICES: in the SW corner, No. 8 by *Kingham Knight Associates*, 1996–7, next to it No. 10 by *Austin-Smith:Lord*, 1999–2000, and then No. 12 by *Atherden Fuller Leng*, 2002–3. All instantly forgettable corporate architecture. Across the dock, the CROWNE PLAZA LIVERPOOL HOTEL, 1997–8, by *Kingham Knight* also. Messy entrance court to The Strand. At least the more recent buildings stand up to the quayside. Most interesting is the FOOTBRIDGE, 2001, designed by *Eduard Ross* whilst still a student. *Ian Wroot*, his senior lecturer at Liverpool John Moores University, was project architect. A white steel carcass linking jutting quays to divide the dock, visually, in two. In 2005 a new wave of development was under way, including more hotels, a multi-storey car park and residential towers. Quality appears not to have improved, but heights have grown dramatically: the first on site are two TOWERS at the N end by *Atherden Fuller Leng*, of twenty and ten storeys. Even higher structures are planned.

Of the dock's archaeology, note at the S end the blocked passage to George's Basin (subsequently a graving, then a branch dock) and the original coursed red Runcorn sandstone quay wall. Along the riverside walk where derelict river steps survive it is possible to glimpse the original RIVER WALL. At the N end the remains of PRINCE'S PIER, marking the end of the Liverpool Landing Stage until 1975. The wharf, of 1899–1900, was the first reinforced concrete structure in the docks, and is one of the earliest surviving British examples of the *Hennebique* system. Designed by the French company's agent *Louis Gustave Mouchel*, with *A. G. Lyster*. Its success led Lyster to adopt concrete swiftly and extensively, which may have encouraged its early use elsewhere in the city.

PRINCE'S HALF-TIDE DOCK. Derelict at the time of writing. Built as a tidal basin to Prince's Dock and rebuilt in 1868 by *G. F. Lyster*, in Hartley fashion: e.g. a triple entrance based on Salisbury Dock, and granite walls.

ROYAL SEAFORTH DOCK. The latest, most northerly, and largest, and the centrepiece of the thriving operational docks. Opened 1971. Purpose-built for container shipping, bulk grain, and timber, but at a cost (£54 m) that helped to bankrupt the MDHB. 85 acres (34.4 hectares) of water, and many more of hardstanding, transit sheds and a huge grain SILO complex.

SALISBURY DOCK. By *Hartley*, opened 1848. The entrance to the Stanley Dock system. On the island between the river gates stands Hartley's VICTORIA TOWER, an idiosyncratic Gothic clock tower in his usual granite. Built 1847–8; based on a *Philip Hardwick* drawing dated 1846. Round below, hexagonal above. Clock faces on all sides and an elongated belfry stage. Projecting castellated parapet. As Pevsner concluded, 'It is all ham, but it tells of the commercial pride of the decades.' On the river wall S is *Hartley*'s DOCK MASTER'S OFFICE, 1848. Rectangular and embattled medievalism.

SANDON DOCK. *Hartley* again. Opened 1851, with six graving docks. Infilled in 1989 for a sewerage treatment works, with Postmodern trim, by *Athanassios Migos* for *Kingham Knight Associates*. On the river side, SANDON HALF-TIDE DOCK of 1901–2, replacing the original basin.

STANLEY DOCK. The most evocatively derelict dock in Liverpool in 2005, opened with four others on 4 August 1848. By *Hartley*. Exceptionally, built inland of the dock road. Granite quays and PERIMETER WALL, with the castle-style GATEPIERS. Conceived as an integrated interchange with rail and the Leeds and Liverpool Canal (*see* p. 485). A flight of four LOCKS by *J.B. Hartley* rising E of Great Howard Street connects the latter, but subsidiary railway and barge docks were never built (the blocked passages remain in the N and E quays respectively). Instead, two WAREHOUSES were erected in 1852–4 (E end of N stack demolished following war damage). Like the near-identical Wapping Warehouse, these are a simplified version of the Albert Dock warehouses. They were also the first dock warehouses designed for rail and hydraulic power, the latter provided by the picturesque STANLEY HYDRAULIC POWER CENTRE, 1854, N of the 1930s rolling-bascule lifting ROAD BRIDGE. Embattled accumulator tower with turret chimney (cf. Wapping Dock). Extended in brick with another chimney, 1913.

A twin hydraulic power centre, S, was demolished for the gargantuan TOBACCO WAREHOUSE, built on land reclaimed from the dock in front of Hartley's S stack, *c.* 1897–1901, by *A.G. Lyster*. Free Renaissance detailing, probably by *John Arthur Berrington*, is concentrated in a heavy cornice – what Osbert Lancaster once called 'above the snow line'. Rising 125 ft (38 metres) through thirteen storeys over a basement, with a floor area of 36 acres (14.6 hectares) and constructed of 27 million bricks, it was claimed to be the largest single brick building in the world. Fireproof construction: steel and concrete floors; cast-iron columns. Since closure in 1980 its size and deep plan have not been the only barriers to reuse: the floors are only 7 ft 2 in. (2.2 metres) high because the 77,000 casks were stored in single tiers to avoid breakage. In the dock's SE corner is the KING'S PIPE, the chimney of the *c.* 1900 furnace in which tobacco scraps were destroyed.

TATE & LYLE SUGAR SILO (former). An unmissable and titanic 121 structure on Regent Road opposite Huskisson Dock, designed to house 100,000 tons of raw sugar. 1955–7 by the *Tate & Lyle Engineering Dept.* A reinforced concrete parabolic tunnel, 528 ft long by 87 ft high inside (161 by 26.5 metres), believed to be the largest such structure in Europe. The pre-stressed concrete floor acts as the tie of the arch. Richly sculptural surface of deep, closely spaced ribs. Sugar was delivered to the crown on conveyor belts from ships in Huskisson Dock; the clear span simplified removal by bulldozer.

TRAFALGAR DOCK and VICTORIA DOCK. Opened in 1836 as part of the same programme as Waterloo Dock, to a similar design by *Hartley*. Little has survived modernisation, except the perimeter wall with its tremendous Greek Revival GATEPIERS (*see* p. 276).

WATERLOO DOCK, by *Hartley*, opened to general traffic in 1834 orientated E–W, but was rebuilt as a specialist grain dock with two branches aligned N–S by *G.F. Lyster* in 1863–8. With the repeal of the Corn Laws, the MDHB reconstructed Waterloo as the world's first bulk-grain dock, to handle imported North America grain. The mighty surviving WAREHOUSE, of 1866–8 and also by *Lyster*, was the E of three: the N stack was demolished after war damage, the W stack in 1969. In their place now stand hipped-roofed apartment blocks completed in 2001. These cannot match the warehouse's massiveness or quality of detailing but, being built right up to the quayside, they maintain a sense of ordered enclosure. The warehouse was converted into apartments by *Kingham Knight Associates*, 1989–98. With five storeys of brick above a mightily rock-faced granite ground-floor arcade, it has as much floor-space as all the Albert stacks combined. The arcade, originally open, functioned like a transit shed. Above rise windows gathered regularly in round-arched pairs, and pilaster strips flanking the five hoist bays, two of which climb high above the bold parapet to house machinery. The structure is fireproof: cast-iron columns and beams, brick arches and cement floors. The chief novelty was an innovative system of hydraulic elevators and conveyor belts, to move the grain about. It never worked properly, however, and the dock rapidly became obsolete.

WELLINGTON DOCK. 1850. By *Hartley*. Operational.

CENTRAL LIVERPOOL

The centre here is demarcated by the following: on the W, the Dock Road and King Edward Street; on the N, Leeds Street; on the E, Scotland Place, Byrom Street, Hunter Street, Commutation Row, Lime Street, Renshaw Street, Berry Street and Great George Street; and on the S, Parliament Street.

RELIGIOUS BUILDINGS

For the ANGLICAN CATHEDRAL *see* p. 344, for the R.C. CATHEDRAL *see* p. 353.

St Luke, St Luke's Place. A proud building with a high, grace-   44
ful tower, rising impressively from a steep flight of steps and
dominating the view up Bold Street. Burned out in the Second
World War and now a roofless shell. It was built by the Corporation, whose Surveyor, *John Foster Sen.*, made plans as early
as 1802. The foundation stone was not laid until 1811, and work
dragged on for a further twenty years, so it is unclear what,
if anything, can be traced back to the 1802 design. In 1811
Thomas Rickman was shown what seem to have been new
drawings, made by a 'young man' in Foster's office, to which
he suggested amendments; Picton later wrote of St Luke
that 'rumour ascribed the design to [Foster's] assistant, *Mr
Edwards*'. For its date it is an unusually rich and ambitious
Gothic Revival design in the Perpendicular style. Three-stage
tower, the top richly panelled, with ogee hoodmoulds over the
belfry windows. Octagonal clasping buttresses rise above the
pierced and battlemented parapet to become tall turrets.
Tucked into the angles between tower and aisles are single-
storey porches. The aisles have very large windows, separated
by buttresses carrying big pinnacles. In 1822 it was decided to
add a chancel. One of the most striking features of the building, this is based (fairly loosely) on the C15 Beauchamp Chapel
at Warwick. Such a large chancel, distinguished from the body
of the church by its richer architectural treatment, is exceptional before the propaganda of the Ecclesiological Society.
The elder Foster was succeeded as Corporation Surveyor by
his son, *John Foster Jun.*, who completed the church, having in
1827 sought permission to make internal and external changes.
The interior does not survive, but nave and aisles were of
nearly identical height, with plaster vaults and a gallery at the
w end only. A FONT (damaged), designed by the *Audsleys* in
the early 1870s and carved by *Norbury*, survived in 2001.
In the tower, a cast-iron BELL FRAME of 1828 by *George
Gillebrand*. Around the site, Gothic cast-iron RAILINGS by
Foster & Griffin, and octagonal stone PIERS with lushly crocketed tops. This enclosure, never used for burials, was laid out
as a garden in 1885. The church ruins were earmarked for demolition in the 1950s and 1960s, but have come to be regarded
as a war memorial.

Our Lady and St Nicholas, Chapel Street. The parish
church of Liverpool, occupying a venerable site. It was originally built *c.* 1360 as a chapel of ease to Walton. Before that
there was another chapel, called St Mary del Key (i.e. Quay),
first mentioned 1257, which Chapel Street was named after. It
stood at the bottom, overlooking the river. Nothing is left of
it, nor is there anything left of the St Nicholas of the C14. The
oldest part of the present church is the steeple, for which the
Greek Revivalist *Thomas Harrison* of Chester made a Gothic
design in 1810, after the previous spire and tower collapsed.
The foundation stone was laid in 1811. It has panelled buttresses, which become octagonal higher up. In 1814 Harrison
designed 'an elegant and appropriate Lantern' for the top. This

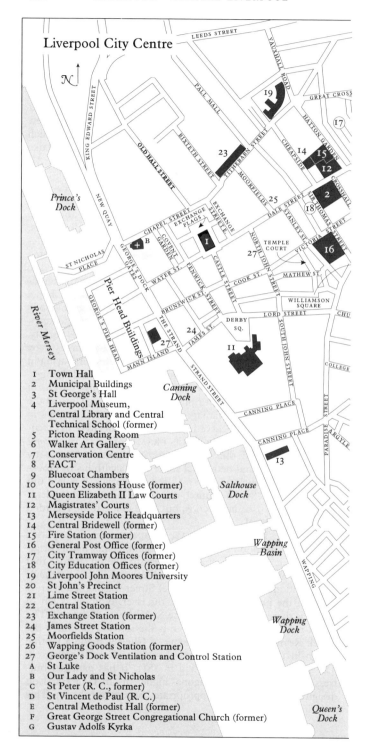

Liverpool City Centre

1   Town Hall
2   Municipal Buildings
3   St George's Hall
4   Liverpool Museum,
    Central Library and Central
    Technical School (former)
5   Picton Reading Room
6   Walker Art Gallery
7   Conservation Centre
8   FACT
9   Bluecoat Chambers
10 County Sessions House (former)
11 Queen Elizabeth II Law Courts
12 Magistrates' Courts
13 Merseyside Police Headquarters
14 Central Bridewell (former)
15 Fire Station (former)
16 General Post Office (former)
17 City Tramway Offices (former)
18 City Education Offices (former)
19 Liverpool John Moores University
20 St John's Precinct
21 Lime Street Station
22 Central Station
23 Exchange Station (former)
24 James Street Station
25 Moorfields Station
26 Wapping Goods Station (former)
27 George's Dock Ventilation and Control Station
A   St Luke
B   Our Lady and St Nicholas
C   St Peter (R. C., former)
D   St Vincent de Paul (R. C.)
E   Central Methodist Hall (former)
F   Great George Street Congregational Church (former)
G   Gustav Adolfs Kyrka

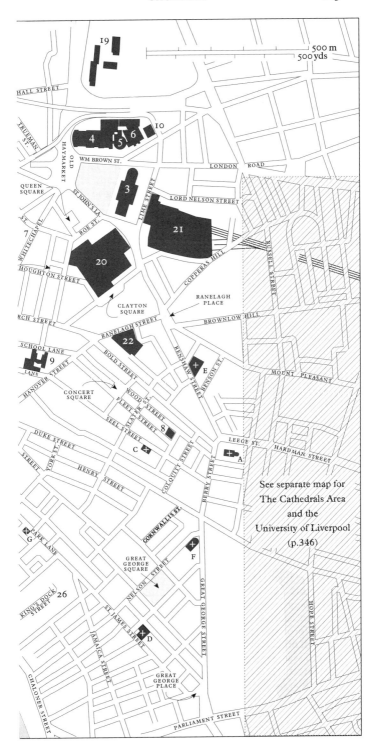

delightful structure is a delicate cage of stone tracery, consisting of a spire on a recessed octagon. Flying buttresses connect to the corner pinnacles. The WEATHERVANE in the form of a ship is probably the original one made by *John Sutherland*. The rest, except for the vestries which flank the tower (presumably Harrison's), was bombed in 1940. A simple Gothic building by *Edward C. Butler*, completed 1952, replaced it. Flat elevations without buttresses, Perp windows. Narthex, three-bay nave with aisles, sanctuary with flanking chapels. Open timber roof with tie-beams. The orientation was reversed in the rebuilding, so the altar is against the tower wall.

FITTINGS. SCREENS with etched glass by *David Peace*, 1984 – STATUE, in chapel r. of the altar, Our Lady of the Key, by *Arthur Dooley*, 1993: a stark figure standing in the prow of a ship. – STAINED GLASS. S aisle, Our Lady and St Nicholas, 1951, by *Harcourt M. Doyle* of Liverpool. – The only MONU-MENT from the old church, in the vestry in the base of the tower, commemorates the Rev. R. Roughsedge, †1829, and is by *William Spence*. A bust against a tablet with Greek cresting, with a fine relief of Faith, Hope and Charity on the base.

The CHURCHYARD was laid out as a garden in 1891. On the W side, a MONUMENT to those who died in the Liverpool Blitz, bronze, by *Tom Murphy*, 2000: mother and children on a spiral stair. On the N side of the church, overlooking Chapel Street, a STATUE, Christ upon an Ass, early 1970s, by *Brian Burgess*. In the exterior of the churchyard wall, at the corner of Chapel Street and George's Dock Gates, the WILLIAM SIMPSON MEMORIAL FOUNTAIN, dated 1885, by *Thomas Cox*. Gothic, with bronze portrait medallion by *Joseph Rogerson*. Gothic archway at the SW entrance, probably 1880s, but apparently a replica of an earlier one that stood at the corner of Chapel Street.

ST PETER (R.C., former), Seel Street. The oldest surviving church in the centre. As constructed in 1788 – three years before the Catholic Relief Act – it was a simple brick box with a pedimented gable, five bays long, with round-arched windows above and segmental ones below. It would have been virtually indistinguishable from a Methodist chapel. The exterior brickwork was later covered with render, scored to resemble masonry. In 1817 *John Slater* was paid £1,060 for extending the W end. He added an extra bay and transept-like projections, N and S, containing stairs up to the galleries. In the one facing the street is the main entrance, with fluted Doric columns and a frieze displaying the date of foundation (*Thomas Rickman* may have supplied the drawing for this). A large, square sanctuary, hidden behind the adjoining house on the E, was formed *c.* 1845 by 'Mr Picton' – presumably *J.A. Picton*. Much of the interior, with its three galleries on timber columns with, was obscured by conversion to a bar in 2005. The flat ceiling has been removed, revealing the kingpost roof. The sanctuary, with Corinthian pilasters and a pedimented aedicule that once framed an altarpiece, still has its segmental plaster ceiling. To the l. of the church is the former school of 1831, distinguished by its pediment. St Peter's Square, opposite, is one of several landscaped spaces formed in 2002–3 to improve pedestrian movement through the Bold Street–Duke Street area. It gives the church a prominence it would not originally have had.

ST VINCENT DE PAUL (R.C.), St James Street. 1856–7, by *Edward Welby Pugin*. Gothic, with Geometric tracery. The most striking feature outside is the high, delicate timber bellcote on the w gable. Inside, five-bay nave with octagonal piers, with deeply carved foliage capitals. An additional bay at the w end contains a choir loft with porch below. The sanctuary has a rich alabaster REREDOS with statues in niches, designed by *E. W. Pugin* in 1867, with carving by *Farmer*. Marble front of high altar added 1927. Above the reredos, a nine-light window with STAINED GLASS of 1925 completely fills the E wall. Chapels l. and r., separated from the sanctuary by twin-arched openings, have statues in canopied niches, apparently 1890s. The Lady Altar of 1899, l., is particularly striking: standing Virgin under a lofty canopy, against a relief of the Annunciation in a circular field. The PRESBYTERY, also by *Pugin* and contemporary with the church, adjoins on the N. It is large, of red brick with stone dressings, and all the windows have trefoil heads.

CENTRAL HALL of the Liverpool Wesleyan Mission (former), Renshaw Street. By *Bradshaw & Gass* of Bolton, opened 1905. Red brick and yellow terracotta, with a domed tower over the corner entrance, a big dome over the main space, and further subsidiary domes, some pointed. The style promiscuously mingles classical, Byzantine, Gothic and Jacobean, and much of the terracotta has a swirly Art Nouveau character. It all looks thoroughly un-churchlike, and might just as well have been a theatre or department store (the large ground-floor windows were in fact designed for lettable shop units). The Hall belongs to a national movement by the Methodists to build such complexes around this time, centralising their activities and creating an identity distinct from the Church of England. Now a nightclub, with ground-floor windows and decorative details playing up the Art Nouveau aspects of the original design. The horseshoe-shaped main auditorium seated 2,500. 73

GREAT GEORGE STREET CONGREGATIONAL CHURCH (former). 1840–1, an outstandingly good building by *Joseph Franklin*, replacing a chapel of 1811–12 which burned down. Oblong in plan, it turns the sharp corner of Nelson Street and Great George Street with a semicircular portico of fluted Corinthian columns enclosing a round inset tower – comparable to Nash's All Souls, Langham Place, in London, but more massive and imposing. The columns are monoliths, said to have come from a quarry in Park Road, Toxteth. The tower has a band of guilloche incorporating little wheel windows, and a shallow dome, now missing its finial. The sides have giant unfluted Corinthian pilasters and two tiers of windows, 48 round-arched above, square-headed below. Minister's house attached at the back on the Great George Street side. Good classical cast-iron RAILINGS. In 1975 work began on conversion to an arts centre, resulting in horizontal subdivision of the galleried interior and the loss of all its fittings. The architects were *Kingham Knight Associates*. The ungainly new roof makes an unwelcome appearance above the parapet. The only part of Franklin's interior that survives is the circular vestibule under the dome, with two stone staircases that gave access to the gallery.

75 GUSTAV ADOLFS KYRKA, Park Lane. The Swedish Seamen's Church, 1883–4, an early work by *W.D. Caröe*. He obtained the commission through his father, then Danish Consul in Liverpool. A fancifully picturesque building in red brick, roughly square in plan, but rising to a higher octagonal centre under a pyramid roof. Scandinavian features include stepped gables and the concave-sided lead-covered timber spire over the entrance. Octagonal interior with pointed wooden vault, now horizontally divided at gallery level. Polychrome plaster reliefs by *R. Anning Bell*, *c.* 1899, originally part of an altar-piece, relocated to the stairs. The pastor's house, l., is integrated.

PUBLIC BUILDINGS

Municipal, Cultural and Legal Buildings

TOWN HALL, High Street. The Town Hall has a complicated history. Built in the mid C18 by *John Wood*, it was modified, extended and reconstructed in the late C18–early C19 by *John Foster Sen.* under the direction of *James Wyatt*. Further changes in the late C19 and C20 will be noted as we come to them.

34 HISTORY AND EXTERIOR. The building stands near the ancient centre of Liverpool, on a commanding site at the junction of High Street, Dale Street, Castle Street and Water Street. Its immediate predecessor of 1673 stood just to the S, 'placed on pillars and arches of hewen stone', with the Public Exchange for merchants below. In 1747 the Council began negotiations to purchase the present site for a new building, and in 1749 a design by *John Wood* of Bath was approved. Six years earlier Wood had completed the Bristol Exchange, publishing the plans and a description in 1745. It is hardly surprising that Liverpool, with its considerable wealth and limited architectural talent, should have bought in the services of one of the outstanding architects of the day.

The first stone of WOOD'S BUILDING was laid on 14 September 1749, and it opened in 1754. Like its C17 predecessor, it consisted of a ground-floor exchange with a council room and other public offices above. Older buildings abutted the W and N sides, so it had only two elevations, S and E, which survive in altered form. Each is nine bays long, with a rusticated ground floor, Corinthian pilasters to the *piano nobile*, and

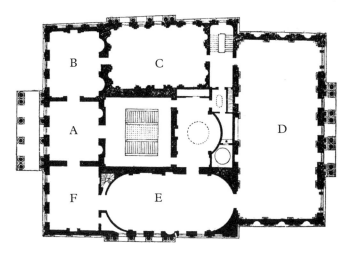

Liverpool, Town Hall, first-floor plan from the *Kaleidoscope*, c. 1820.
(A, Central Reception Room; B, West Reception Room; C, Dining Room;
D, Large Ballroom; E, Small Ballroom; F, East Reception Room)

round-arched windows with square Corinthian piers between
the pilasters. The middle three bays on the E side break forward
slightly under a pediment, and here the pilasters give way to
attached Corinthian columns, arranged 2–1–1–2. Originally
the middle of the principal (s) side was the same, but with
sculpture in the pediment; the portico here is a later addition.
Between the capitals on both fronts are panels of vigorous
carving in high relief, mostly illustrating the foreign trade
which was the source of Liverpool's wealth. On the E these
include, in the words of John Prestwich (probably writing in
the 1780s), 'Busts of Blackamoors & Elephants with the Teeth
of the Latter, with such like emblematical Figures, representing
the African Trade & Commerce'. *Thomas Johnson*, *William
Mercer* and *Edward Rigby*, who appear in the accounts as
carvers, may have been responsible.* Tripartite central
entrances on each side originally gave access to the Exchange
courtyard in the middle, Doric colonnades making covered
walks on all four sides. According to contemporary descriptions it was dark and confined, and the merchants preferred to
transact business in the street outside. Another account says
the building had a 'noble cupola', and a large, square, lead-
covered dome with a lantern appears above the centre of the
s range on John Eyes' map of 1765. Was this inelegant structure part of Wood's design? Inside, Wood's building had a
grand stair off the E walk, and principal rooms on all four sides

---

*The s pediment sculpture – an allegory of Liverpool's maritime commerce – was
by *William Stephenson*.

of the first floor, including the Town Hall (s range), Council Room and assembly rooms.

A campaign of ALTERATIONS began in 1785 when the Exchange Committee resolved that adjoining buildings be removed. By 1786 orders were given for the newly exposed w front to be plastered and painted, but it was not until 1792 that *John Foster Sen.* prepared a new design for this façade, closely following Wood's s and E fronts. (Orders for altering the ground floor of the E elevation were given in 1796, when the original square-headed windows were presumably replaced with the present round-headed ones.) The carved panels on the w continue the theme of maritime commerce but make no direct reference to the slave trade – a more controversial subject by the end of the c18. The square dome was taken down in 1786, and the ambitious idea of erecting a new dome over the central court was conceived. In 1787 instructions were given to demolish the houses on the N side, with the intention of erecting a large extension for the mayor's office and court, with a new assembly room above, and the following year *Foster* was ordered to show survey plans to *James Wyatt*. Wyatt's designs for a new dome and N block were adopted, and thereafter Foster supervised the building under his instructions.

Wyatt's N ADDITION follows the earlier parts in having a rusticated basement with round-arched windows, but is distinguished by its higher roof and sparer, more refined ornament. The portico with its four pairs of Corinthian columns did not originally project so far. It was rebuilt using the original columns in 1899–1900, in connection with the reconstruction of the Council Chamber (*see* Interior, below). The badly weathered statues above were ordered from *Richard Westmacott Sen.* in 1792. The three-bay end elevations have paired pilasters framing niches, and oval windows under garlands.

In 1795 the Exchange was devastated by fire. Wyatt and Foster's unfinished N addition escaped unscathed, but Wood's building was gutted. The Council at once decided to rebuild within the external walls. Wyatt's DOME was completed in 1802. It rests on a high drum with tall pedimented Corinthian aedicules at the angles (perhaps derived from Gandon's Dublin Custom House, and ultimately from Wren at Greenwich), and large tripartite windows between, divided by further pairs of columns. At the cardinal points of the springing of the dome are four clock faces, each supported by a lion and a unicorn, and crowning the whole a *Coade*-stone STATUE of a seated female figure, variously identified as Minerva or Britannia, by *J.C. Rossi*. Today it is overshadowed by taller neighbours, but when built Wyatt's noble dome was a dominant feature of the skyline. The PORTICO in the middle of the s front, completed in 1811, replaced Wood's centrepiece; at the same time the attic windows on this side were replaced by panels carved with swags and garlands, probably by *Frederick Legé*. The space underneath the portico (intended for election hustings) encloses two ramps, ingeniously introduced by *Donald W.*

Insall & Associates in the early 1990s to improve access. At both ends are arched openings with luscious wrought ironwork in C18 style by *George Wragge*, probably introduced in 1913 by *Romaine-Walker & Jenkins*. Sturdy early C19 cast-iron RAIL-INGS incorporating Greek Revival lamp standards, made by *William Bennett* of Liverpool, surround the building.

INTERIOR. The main entrance leads into the VESTIBULE, something of a surprise after the Neoclassical exterior. Encaustic tile floor of 1848, incorporating the arms of Liverpool. Sumptuous wooden fireplace, made up from C17 Flemish carvings, presented in 1893; in 1898 the oak panelling was added by *Frederick Moore Simpson* (with door handles and fingerplates by *R.L. Rathbone*) and the groin-vaulted ceiling was plastered. Lunettes with poor murals by *J.H. Amschewitz*, completed 1909: King John Creating Liverpool a Free Port (w), Industry and Peace (N), Liverpool the Centre of Commerce (E), and Education and Progress (S). In the post-1795 reconstruction the ground floor on the E SIDE was intended to house the Surveyor, Town Clerk and Treasurer, whose rooms appear to survive in altered form. They have groined vaults (ordered in 1802) and one now contains a good *ex situ* C18 marble fireplace. At the back in Wyatt's N addition is the COUNCIL CHAMBER, enlarged in 1899–1900 to fill the ground floor. The centre was extended out, creating a recess for the Lord Mayor's dais and resulting in the external changes to the N portico noted above. *Thomas Shelmerdine*, Corporation Surveyor, was architect. Mahogany-panelled walls, with each round-arched window framed by unfluted columns and a serpentine entablature. Elaborate light fittings, vaguely Art Nouveau, by *Singer* of Frome. Charles Reilly in 1927 described the overall effect as 'in the best saloon-bar style'. Tucked between the Council Chamber and the main stairs is the HALL OF REMEMBRANCE, where the names of Liverpool's First World War dead are inscribed. MURALS by *Frank O. Salisbury*, with titles including Duty's Call, Sacrifice, Immortality and Triumph, completed 1923. From here stairs lead to the basement, with cloakrooms round a vaulted foyer, formed in 1913 by *Romaine-Walker & Jenkins*. (On the w side, off the sunken area, is a brick-vaulted ice house.)

Wyatt's STAIRCASE HALL, occupying the site of the central open court of Wood's Exchange, is one of the great architectural spaces of Liverpool. The staircase rises in a single broad flight between two pairs of unfluted Corinthian columns (which support the upper landing) to a half-landing. From here two narrower flights, not attached to the walls, return towards the upper landing, which takes the form of a broad gallery running round three sides. The walls here have segmental heads with Diocletian windows. Pendentives carry the soaring drum with its large expanses of glazing, and high over all is the coffered interior of the dome. In 1913 *Romaine-Walker & Jenkins* laid a new marble floor and added extensions supported on Tuscan columns to both ends of the half-landing;

the motto of the city round the base of the drum was redone in raised letters, and cherubs' heads and swags in relief added between the windows. Four impressive PAINTINGS by *Charles Wellington Furse* were installed in the pendentives in 1902. The subjects – energetic scenes of dock labour – are striking in this ceremonial setting. In niches at the foot of the stairs are two extraordinary cast-iron STOVES, each in the form of a Greek Doric column surmounted by a trident head. These and other stoves were apparently supplied by *Moser & Co.*, and possibly designed by *J.M. Gandy*, who received payments for unspecified designs, 1811–13. On the half-landing a marble STATUE of George Canning, 1832, by *Francis Chantrey*.

The FIRST FLOOR is entirely occupied by entertaining rooms, designed by *Wyatt* and executed under Foster's supervision (designs apparently approved 1805). They have interconnecting doors, so the visitor makes a complete circuit. The roughly square CENTRAL RECEPTION ROOM, behind the s portico, has a circular ceiling with fluted pendentives, and beautiful Neoclassical plasterwork by *Francesco Bernasconi*, who was responsible for most of the stucco throughout. Stoves in niches on either side of the central door, with cylindrical bases and elaborate superstructures incorporating winged female herms. Doors on the r. lead into the WEST RECEPTION ROOM, of similar shape but with a segmental-vaulted ceiling. White marble chimneypiece with rich fittings of brass and cast iron. The DINING ROOM, entered from here, occupies the w side. The most sumptuous room in the building, with Corinthian pilasters of yellow Carniola marble (an artificial material), a coved ceiling divided into moulded compartments, and an elaborate plaster frieze with scrolls, urns and crouching dogs. Between the pilaster capitals are roundels painted with pairs of cupids, possibly by *Matthew Cotes Wyatt*, James Wyatt's son, who devised a much more ambitious scheme of allegorical decoration in 1811. Built into pairs of niches at either end are mahogany cabinets with brass fittings (for warming plates), supporting candelabra in the form of red scagliola vases, ordered from *Joseph Brown* in 1813. Between the windows, another pair of extraordinary Neoclassical STOVES: the grate is in the square base, with elaborate perforated doors and slender candelabra at each corner, on top of which is a sturdy column with a swirling skirt of fleshy acanthus. A door at the NE corner leads to a top-lit room running w–e above the Hall of Remembrance, given its present form and its elegant plaster decoration in 1913 by *Romaine-Walker & Jenkins*. The central N door of the Dining Room leads to the top of the secondary stairs, also rebuilt 1913.

From here the LARGE BALLROOM is entered, occupying the whole upper floor of Wyatt's N extension. The decoration, with giant Corinthian pilasters of yellow Carniola, was not completed until 1820. Opposite the windows, a balconied niche with a coffered semi-dome, for the musicians, between white marble chimneypieces carved by *William Hetherington*. From the segmental-vaulted ceiling, with stucco work by *James Queen*, hang three spectacular chandeliers, supplied by *Thomas Hawkes & Co.* in 1820. The huge mirrors at either end seem to be later C19. Doors at the SE corner open into the SMALL BALLROOM, filling the E side, with red Carniola pilasters and a segmental vault with shallow end apses; in the N apse, two niches for musicians – the same arrangement as Wyatt's saloon at Heveningham Hall, Suffolk. It opens into the EAST RECEPTION ROOM, which balances the West Reception Room and completes the circuit. Most of the FURNITURE in these rooms was designed and made for the Town Hall *c.* 1817–*c.* 1820, and is of superb quality.

The combination of richly decorated apartments for entertaining and more functional spaces for civic administration, council meetings, etc., is found in other late C18 public buildings, but not on the magnificent scale seen here. This is probably the grandest such suite of civic rooms in the country, an outstanding and complete example of Late Georgian decoration and a powerful demonstration of the wealth of Liverpool at the opening of the C19.

MUNICIPAL BUILDINGS, Dale Street. Designed 1862 by the Corporation Surveyor *John Weightman*, modified by his successor *E. R. Robson*, and completed 1867–8. The aim was to unite the scattered offices of the expanding Corporation. Large rectangular block with giant attached columns and pilasters, corner pavilions, and a clock tower in the middle of the Dale Street front, its curious pyramid spire strongly reminiscent of Charles Barry's slightly earlier Halifax Town Hall. Statues representing Industry, Commerce, Navigation, etc., decorate the attic. The style is hard to pin down – *The Builder* could do no better than 'Corinthianesque, treated very freely'. The columns do indeed have Corinthian capitals (carved by *Earp* of London), but with English ferns rather than acanthus, and each one different: a Gothic rather than a classical feature. At the same time there is a fashionably French character to the whole, especially the big, curved roofs of the corner pavilions. Inside, offices and committee rooms surround the central, top-lit Treasurer's Public Office. Stairs and corridors have unusual ceramic-tiled dados resembling parquetry, probably made by a technique of printing from the grain of natural wood, patented by *William Scarratt* and *William Dean* in 1865.

MILLENNIUM HOUSE. *See* Victoria Street, p. 340.

ST GEORGE'S HALL, Lime Street. Early C19 Liverpool lacked a suitable venue for its triennial music festivals and other large assemblies. Following a public meeting in 1836, a company was formed to raise subscriptions for a hall, and early in 1839 a competition was announced for a building dedicated to meetings, festivals, dinners and concerts, to be called St George's Hall. The winner was a twenty-five-year-old London architect, *Harvey Lonsdale Elmes*. New assize courts became necessary at about the same time, Liverpool having become an assize town in 1835. A second competition was held, and this too was won

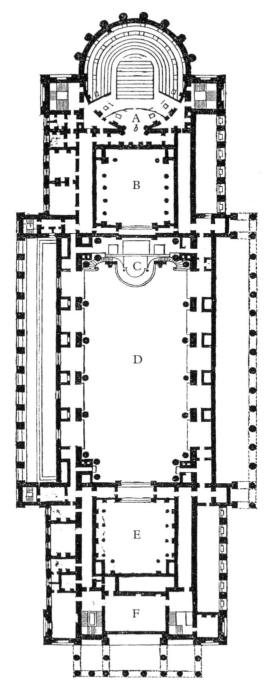

Liverpool, St George's Hall, plan from *The Builder*, vol. 13, 1855.
(A, Small Concert Room; B, Civil Court; C, Organ; D, Concert Hall;
E, Crown Court; F, Grand Jury Room)

by *Elmes*. The planning of Elmes' court building was heavily criticized in the press, and the Corporation Surveyor, *Joseph Franklin*, was asked to make new designs. Elmes protested, however, and, given the chance to revise his proposals, he was ultimately awarded the commission.

The chosen site was extremely prominent, elevated above the town and adjoining the newly built Lime Street Station (*see* p. 304). The initial idea was to set the buildings at right angles, the courts on the w side of Lime Street (previously occupied by the Infirmary of 1749) and the hall just s of where the Wellington Column now stands. They would have enclosed two sides of a formal *place*, with the façade of the station (1835–6, by *John Foster Jun.*, demolished) making a third. In 1840, however, Elmes was asked to explore alternatives, and his suggestion to combine hall and courts in one exceptionally large building on the w side was adopted.

Size was important if St George's Hall was to express adequately the pride and confidence of the thriving town. Elmes made a drawing in which the cross-section was superimposed on other great buildings, drawn to scale: Westminster Hall, St Paul's Cathedral, and most significantly the new Birmingham Town Hall (begun 1832) were all to be surpassed. The inscription over the s portico, *Artibus, Legibus, Consiliis* (To Arts, Laws and Counsels), proclaimed unequivocally that this huge edifice was a monument to civilized values, in a town where the previous largest buildings had been dedicated to commerce. Construction began in 1841 and the building opened in 1854 (the Small Concert Room in 1856). When Elmes died, in 1847, the interior was not far advanced. Work continued under *Robert Rawlinson*, the Corporation Surveyor *John Weightman*, and (from 1849) *C.R. Cockerell*, who was appointed architect in 1851. The decoration of the interiors is largely due to him. Elmes' former assistant, *W.H. Wordley* was retained. As many as 299 men laboured on the site at its busiest, and the cost was almost £290,000.*

Elmes' competition designs were conventional Greek Revival, but the combined building designed in 1840–1 is altogether more inventive, drawing on Roman sources as well as Greek. Certain features of the competition designs are retained: the long lateral portico and pedimented s end from the first St George's Hall, and the long windowless attic of the Assize Courts. But the unifying feature – the giant Corinthian order – is not present in either design, and is thoroughly Roman in derivation. The s portico is pushed beyond the original edge of the site where the ground falls away. Towering above St John's Lane, it recalls visionary C19 reconstructions of the temples in the Roman Forum. That Elmes relished such magnificent effects is clear from his perspective drawings.

---

*This compares with over £700,000 for the Albert Dock and its warehouses, built at the same time.

To explain the novelty of Elmes' classicism the influence of the great Prussian architect K.F. Schinkel has sometimes been cited. Elmes did not visit Germany until 1842, after the external design was largely finalised, but he may have known Schinkel's work through illustrations. Square pillars of the sort used by Elmes are found in Schinkel, but also in William Wilkins' The Grange, Hampshire (begun 1809), which Elmes probably knew. Whatever influences he was exposed to, however, Elmes' design seems to have grown out of the unusual requirements of the brief, coupled with deep archaeological knowledge and an experimental attitude to antiquity. As Elmes wrote to his collaborator Rawlinson: 'How frequently I observe the great & true end & aim of Art entirely lost sight of in the discussion of some insignificant detail or quaint Antiquarianism. Bold and original conceptions never can find favour while so much stress is laid upon precedent.'

94   EXTERIOR. The Concert Hall is placed lengthways in the centre (indicated by the great windowless attic), with the Crown Court to the s and the Civil Court to the N. At the N end is an apsidal entrance hall with the elliptical Small Concert Room above. All four elevations are different, and expressive of the various spaces within, but tied together by the unbroken horizontal of the entablature. The s front has an eight-columned portico, two columns deep, raised on steps above a rusticated podium. Sculpture for the pediment, designed by *Cockerell* and executed by *W.G. Nicholl*, became unsafe and was taken down in 1950. The substructure of the portico is not as Elmes intended. The steps surrounding it are due to *Cockerell* and date from after 1849. Cockerell also introduced paired flights of steps in front of the podium, replaced in the late 1850s by the rusticated wall facing St John's Lane. In 2004 this was pierced by a new central doorway. The main entrance front is on the E, facing the station. It has a portico of sixteen columns, corresponding to the Concert Hall inside. On either side, corresponding with the courts, the order continues in square, unfluted pillars. Their lower parts are embedded and read as pilasters, but their upper parts are free-standing. Between the pilasters are RELIEFS, added 1882–1901, by *Thomas Stirling Lee*, *C.J. Allen* and *Conrad Dressler* (the first two at the s end, by Lee, aroused controversy through the inclusion of naturalistic nudes). The outer bays are blank and solid. The W side now overlooks St John's Gardens (*see* p. 335), but until 1899 faced the church of the same name. Smaller rooms for court purposes occupy the ground and first floors here, lit by large windows. The projecting central part has the same square pillars as the ends of the E front, but here they support only a massive entablature and no roof, so admitting light to the Concert Hall behind. The N front has a semicircular apse with three-quarter columns, and three doorways. These are flanked by STATUES of nereids and tritons bearing lamps, by *Nicholl*, matching statues under the s and E porticoes.

INTERIOR. The main entrance, central behind the E portico, is the least satisfactory part of Elmes' plan. Instead of a spacious and dignified vestibule, it leads into a corridor running N–S to the courts at each end. A matching corridor runs along the W side. Crossing the corridor and entering the CONCERT HALL 78 brings further disappointment, because the entrance is on the short rather than the long axis. The space is so magnificent, however, that disappointment is quickly forgotten. This is one of the greatest Victorian interiors, and perhaps more expressive of C19 civic pride and aspiration than any other. It is 169 feet long and 77 feet wide, and roofed with a mighty tunnel vault 82 feet high to the crown. This vault was planned by Elmes before his death but constructed under *Rawlinson*'s supervision. To lessen the weight Rawlinson used hollow bricks throughout; when the centring was struck in 1849 the vault settled by just three-eighths of an inch (1 cm.) at its crown. Elmes' inspiration for this vaulted space seems to have been Blouet's reconstruction of the frigidarium of the Baths of Caracalla in Rome, published in 1828. The vault is carried on columns of polished red granite, placed in front of massive piers, and there are arches between the piers – five on each side – with transverse tunnel vaults running to the outer walls. Within these arches are balconies, positioned above the outer corridors. On the W side the arches also contain windows. The projecting balcony fronts with balustrades of coloured marbles, and the three-dimensional, polychrome treatment of the lower walls with niches for sculpture, are due to *Cockerell*. So is the richly panelled plasterwork of the vault, with its allegorical spandrel figures of Virtues, Science and Arts (Elmes' intentions were more restrained). Also by *Cockerell* is the *Minton* tile FLOOR, with its pattern of interlocking circles against a diapered background, in shades of buff, brown and blue. *Ludwig Grüner* (Prince Albert's mentor in art) is said to have advised on its design, and *Alfred Stevens* has been credited with the figure panels of tritons, sea nymphs and boys on dolphins. The sunken central area is usually hidden under a removable floor.

By *Cockerell*, too, are the fantastically rich bronze DOORS, and the GASOLIERS, converted to electricity in 1896. The doors have openwork panels of foliage, incorporating tridents and the letters SPQL (the Senate and the People of Liverpool), boastfully adapting the SPQR badge of ancient Rome. The gasoliers hang from brackets in the form of ships' prows. *Cockerell* placed the massive ORGAN at the N end, on a circular platform carried by short columns. Heroically muscled atlantes, carved by *E.B. Stephens* to *Cockerell*'s design, support the pipes on either side. Installing the organ entailed removing two of Elmes' red granite columns, eventually reused in the entrance gates to Sefton Park (*see* p. 453). The organ blocks the axial view from Crown Court to Civil Court. It was a view to which Elmes attached great importance, echoing the vistas in Blouet's restoration of the Baths of Caracalla. The S end of the Concert Hall is as Elmes intended, with a great round arch enclosing a screen of two columns supporting an entablature. Gates between the columns open directly into the Crown Court.

The niches round the walls contain twelve STATUES of C19 worthies. They are, anticlockwise from the N end of the W side: William Roscoe by *Chantrey*, 1841 (transferred from the Liverpool Royal Institution); Sir William Brown by *Patrick MacDowell*, 1860; Peel by *Matthew Noble*, 1853; George Stephenson by *John Gibson*, 1851 (in classical dress: Gibson, the arch-Grecian, said his aim was to make the railway engineer look like Archimedes); Rev. Hugh McNeile by *G.G. Adams*, 1870; E. Whitley by *A. Bruce Joy*, 1895; S.R. Graves by *G.G. Fontana*, 1875; Rev. Jonathan Brooks by *B.E. Spence*, 1858; Gladstone by *John Adams-Acton*, 1868; the 14th Earl of Derby by *William Theed the Younger*, 1869; the 16th Earl of Derby by *F.W. Pomeroy*, 1911; Joseph Mayer by *Fontana*, 1869.

Strongly coloured pictorial STAINED GLASS was added to the semicircular windows at each end in 1883–4 by *Forrest & Son* of Liverpool: St George and the Dragon s, the Arms of Liverpool N. The present painted decoration on walls and vault, of 1974–5, is based on redecoration carried out in 1875.

The CROWN COURT has a tunnel vault on red granite columns, the CIVIL COURT a coved ceiling and a greater number of grey granite columns. Beyond the courts are two entrance halls. The SOUTH HALL is a disappointment, being relatively low and leading from the temple portico of the s front dead against a blank wall. It has Ionic columns in the corners. (Underneath is an impressive vaulted space, originally intended by Elmes as an entrance hall, but subsequently abandoned as the design of the s end evolved. It was adapted to serve its original purpose by *Purcell Miller Tritton*, 2003–5, as part of a programme of repairs and alterations aimed at improving access, much of the building having been disused since the courts moved out in 1984.) Above is the GRAND JURY ROOM, with a rich marble chimneypiece designed by *Wordley*. Only the NORTH HALL makes an appropriately dignified impression. It has Greek Doric columns on the landing and a Greek Doric ambulatory in the semicircle of the apse. A copy of part of the Parthenon frieze runs round the walls, and there are splendid lamp standards by *Cockerell*. On the axis is a STATUE of Henry Booth, 1874, by *Theed the Younger*, placed here 1877. Booth was an engineer and the chief promoter of the Liverpool & Manchester Railway. His l. hand rests on a screw coupling of his own invention, beneath which is a scroll with a drawing of Stephenson's locomotive *Rocket*, designed with Booth's assistance.

The most beautiful interior is the SMALL CONCERT ROOM, reached from the North Hall by stairs W and E. It is virtually circular in plan, half projecting to form the external apse, another echo of the Baths of Caracalla. Its shape is due to *Elmes*, but *Cockerell* was responsible for the lavish and sensuous decoration, completed in 1856. A balcony runs round, supported on caryatids which are more Baroque than Greek in their lively naturalism. They are cast in an artificial material, and are said to have been modelled by *M. Joyon*. The balcony front of cast-iron latticework swells outwards between each support, creating an undulating effect. Behind the platform are attached columns, the lower third decorated with arabesques. They support a frieze with griffins, and the space between is filled with mirrors. The griffin frieze continues round the auditorium on pilasters, with wood panelling between, elaborately grained. The ceiling has a flat central area divided into radial panels, with grilles for ventilation.

Below, the cavernous BASEMENT is a Piranesian region of soaring brick piers and arches, as Roman in its way as the building above. Here was the steam engine that powered the extremely elaborate heating and ventilation system devised by *Dr Boswell Reid*. Along the W side are cells for prisoners awaiting trial, served by a roadway with arched entrances in William Brown Street and St John's Lane.

THE PLATEAU is the flat open space between the Hall and Lime Street. Cockerell designed the four lions, carved by *Nicholl* and set up from 1856 (moved to their present positions by 1864), and the cast-iron lamp standards with dolphin bases. This forum-like space became the location for important public MONUMENTS. An equestrian bronze of Prince Albert by *Thomas Thornycroft*, 1866, is balanced by one of Queen Victoria, 1869, also by *Thornycroft*. In 1883 Disraeli, by *C.B. Birch* (now on the Hall steps) joined them. All three are suitably dignified. In 1887 a far too animated Major-General William Earle, by *Birch* again, was installed at the S end of the Hall's E front. Between the two equestrian statues, where Disraeli once stood, is the CENOTAPH, unveiled 1930. Architect *L.B. Budden*, sculptor *H. Tyson Smith*. A simple horizontal block suggesting an altar or a tomb, with a continuous bronze relief over 31 ft (9.4 metres) long on each side. The relief facing Lime Street shows mourners of all ages in everyday dress, against a military cemetery with gravestones receding to infinity. The other side has marching soldiers, barely individualized, moving collectively like automata. It is one of the most remarkable war memorials in the country, unflinching in its depiction of the scale of loss and grief, and in its refusal of allegory or heroic idealization.

THE WILLIAM BROWN STREET GROUP. Until the mid C19 William Brown Street was Shaw's Brow, a steep hill with a ragged collection of buildings on the N side, and the C18 Infirmary and St John's church on the S. In 1843, as St George's Hall began to rise on the Infirmary site, Samuel Holme hoped it would become the focus of a sort of forum, 'round which should be clustered our handsomest edifices, and within the area of which our public monuments ought to be placed'. This is exactly what came to pass over the next sixty years. However, instead of combining to enclose a formal space, the new public

buildings were strung out in an irregular line along the slope.
Their effect is therefore not that of a forum so much as a splendid architectural backdrop to the Hall. Individually they are
not in the same league as Elmes' masterpiece, but taken
together as a piece of romantic classical urban scenery, they
have no equal in England. In the late C20 the street was closed
to through traffic and partly paved over.

79   MUSEUM and LIBRARY were first to be built. The Free
Public Library, established in 1850, was temporarily housed
from 1852 in the old Union News Room in Duke Street
(*see* p. 321), along with important natural history collections
bequeathed by the 13th Earl of Derby. Then the Shaw's Brow
site was acquired, and in 1856 an architectural competition was
held. The terms noted that it would 'form one side of an open
space at right angles with St George's Hall', so it seems a
formal *place* was still under consideration. *Thomas Allom*'s
winning scheme was too costly, so the Corporation Surveyor
John Weightman produced a revised design, built 1857–60. The
merchant and banker William Brown offered to meet the cost,
and the street was renamed in his honour. Allom had proposed an Italianate façade, with much sculpture. Weightman
produced a broadly similar composition – a six-column
Corinthian portico with attic, flanked by five-bay wings and
projecting end bays – but in a severely Graeco-Roman style,
in the mould of St George's Hall. The great flight of steps in
front was not formed until *c.* 1902, taking the place of a broad,
elevated terrace here. Bombed in 1941, the Library was rebuilt
1957–60 and the Museum 1963–9 by *Ronald Bradbury*, behind
Weightman's preserved façade. The C19 skyline was wrecked
in the process by a rooftop addition. Rear extension to the
Library, 1978.

The former MUSEUM EXTENSION AND CENTRAL TECH-
NICAL SCHOOL (now given over entirely to museum use)
adjoins the Museum on the l. Won in competition by *E. W.
Mountford*, 1896, opened 1901. Baroque, with Mannerist
touches: notice how the rustication wraps round the first-floor
window jambs, leaving only the capitals and bases of the hypo-
thetical columns exposed. The original main entrance is
in the convex w façade to Byrom Street (a feature echoed in
Mountford's Old Bailey, London, 1900–7), which has giant
Ionic columns in pairs above. At each end of the William
Brown Street elevation are advancing pedimented bays, with
extravagantly blocked columns flanking big, deep niches lined
with windows. Allegorical sculpture in pediments and above
windows is by *F. W. Pomeroy*; also the beautiful bronze lamp
standards by the Byrom Street entrance. The lower floors,
entered from Byrom Street, were for the Technical School: a
lofty entrance hall, followed by the long, low, marble-lined
vestibule, leads to the former lecture room and examination
hall. These spaces have plaster reliefs by *Pomeroy*, some
coloured by *Robert Anning Bell*. The upper floors, entered from
the neighbouring Museum, are U-shaped galleries. In 2000–1

Law & Dunbar-Nasmith transformed one of two central open courts into an atrium, bridged by high-level walkways. The space is impressive, though the curved glass roof unfortunately compounds the damage done to the skyline by Bradbury's earlier Museum addition. At the same time a new entrance from William Brown Street was formed.

The PICTON READING ROOM on the E side of the Museum 80 and Library is by *Cornelius Sherlock*, 1875–9. Circular plan, after the British Museum Reading Room (1854–7). The semicircular façade with Corinthian colonnade nicely accommodates the street's change of direction, and echoes the apsidal N end of St George's Hall opposite. The roof is a shallow dome covered with zinc on a framework of iron, with a glazed oculus. Niches behind the colonnade contain weathered plaster statues by *Benjamin Edward Spence*: Jeanie Deans, The Lady of the Lake, Highland Mary. Inside, the 100 ft- (30 metre-)diameter reading room retains its bookcases and cast-iron gallery (a second, higher gallery was added later). It was lit with electricity from the start by three arc lamps in the glazed dish that still stands on an octagonal wooden structure in the centre. The basement was originally a lecture theatre, kept free of obtrusive columns by supporting the floor of the reading room on arched wrought-iron girders (engineer *James N. Shoolbred*), now boxed in. Attached to the rear is the HORNBY LIBRARY by *Thomas Shelmerdine*, opened 1906, funded by Hugh Frederick Hornby to house his bequest of books and prints. Impressive stone-faced Edwardian Baroque interior, a five-bay aisled hall under a plaster barrel vault. Halfway up the columns a balustraded gallery runs all round. Outside the door, an Art Nouveau copper plaque of 1907 by *C.E. Thompson* commemorates Hornby's gift.

The WALKER ART GALLERY is next, by *Sherlock* and *H.H. Vale*, 1874–7. It was paid for by the Mayor, the brewer Andrew Barclay Walker. It served originally for exhibitions of contemporary art, but rapidly acquired a permanent collection. With the decision to site it where the street veers away from St George's Hall, any thought of creating a forum-like enclosure seems to have been abandoned. More decorative than the Museum and Library, it is still chastely Neoclassical for its date. Corinthian portico of six columns with pediment. Extensive sculpture by *John Warrington Wood*: on either side of the steps, weathered seated figures of Raphael and Michelangelo; above the portico, Liverpool (a copy, *c.* 1996). Over the windows, four long reliefs, l. to r.: The Laying of the Foundation Stone of the Walker Art Gallery by the Duke of Edinburgh, 1874; The Visit of Queen Victoria, 1851; King John Granting Liverpool's First Charter, 1207; The Embarkation of King William III at Hoylake, 1690. Extended at the back by Sherlock, 1882–4, doubling its size. In 1931–3 an even larger rear extension was added by *Arnold Thornely*. At the same time he remodelled the entrance, creating a spacious Travertine-lined hall with flanking staircases, lit from above through a circular opening in the landing. It is a good example of the American-influenced classicism so ably handled by Liverpool architects between the wars. In 2001–2 the wedge-shaped gap between Thornely's extension and the C19 building was partly filled in by *Law & Dunbar-Nasmith*, creating a new first-floor foyer for the exhibition rooms at the rear. It is top-lit and paved in pale stone.

The former COUNTY SESSIONS HOUSE stands detached on the E of the Walker Art Gallery (actually in Islington, but visually part of William Brown Street). 1882–4, by *F. & G. Holme*. Exuberantly Late Victorian, its style derived from Renaissance Venice rather than ancient Greece and Rome. Portico with coupled columns. The front is lavishly decorated but the sides and rear are mostly bare brick (the NE side was originally hidden by buildings). Complex internal layout, largely preserved, with separate circulation for prisoners, public, solicitors and witnesses, and barristers and magistrates. Staircase hall, rich with marble, mosaic and *sgraffito* decoration, under little saucer-domes. Magistrates' room with panelling and C17-style plaster ceiling. Two courtrooms, the larger with dado of *Burmantofts'* tiles.

The WELLINGTON MONUMENT in front of the Sessions House was erected 1861–3: a very late example of a column-monument for Britain. The Duke died in 1852, but funds were slow to come in, and a design competition in 1856, won by *Andrew Lawson* of Edinburgh, was followed by further delays while a site was secured. It is a Roman Doric column supporting a bronze statue of the Duke (the subject of a second competition in 1861) by *George Anderson Lawson*, 132 ft (40 metres) high overall. Bronze plaques on the pedestal display the names of Wellington's victories, and on the S face is a relief of Waterloo by *G.A. Lawson*, installed 1865. The form was no doubt intended to echo Nelson's column in Trafalgar Square, but also complements its very Roman setting near St George's Hall. W of the Wellington Monument is the cast-iron STEBLE FOUNTAIN, unveiled 1879. Neptune, Amphitrite, Acis and Galatea are seated round the base. Designed by *Paul Liénard*; other versions in Boston, Geneva, Launceston (Tasmania) and elsewhere.

QUEEN ELIZABETH II LAW COURTS, Derby Square. By *Farmer & Dark*. Design work began in 1973 but the courts did not open until 1984. Ten storeys, containing twenty-eight courtrooms in the core. Faced with vertically ribbed pre-cast panels of dark, pinkish concrete, with brown ceramic tiles used e.g. in strips between the stair windows, and lead-covered mansard roofs. On the N side the stair-towers of different heights dominate. On the S, some of the uprights stand clear, creating strong contrasts of light and shadow. Richly sculptural from most angles, though rather oppressive in bulk and colouring. Royal arms over the entrance by *Richard Kindersley*, cast in concrete.

MAGISTRATES' COURTS, Dale Street. Part of a group of 1857–9, designed by *John Weightman* and supervised by his assistant *G.H. Rollett*, that also included the main Bridewell, offices and quarters for the police, and a fire station (later replaced). The classical Courts have a simple but dignified ashlar façade. The BRIDEWELL, facing Cheapside, is a grim and surprisingly large prison, of red brick with stone dressings, set behind a high screen wall with rusticated piers. Front block with central pediment and small, barred window openings. By this date castellated medieval was the usual prison style, but classicism still held sway in Liverpool.

COUNTY SESSIONS HOUSE (former), Islington. *See* William Brown Street group, p. 300.

FACT (for Film, Art, Creative Technology), Wood Street. Completed 2003, by *Austin-Smith:Lord*, containing cinemas and galleries for electronic media. The façade to Wood Street and Back Colquitt Street is a rather depressing grid of identical square zinc panels, sweeping unbroken round the corner above a blue brick plinth. Small windows take the place of a few panels, and there is a large, curved area of glazing over the corner entrance, but the overall impression is of a metallic screen, as regular as graph paper. By contrast the elevation to Fleet Street is mostly glass, and jutting through it at divergent angles above the ground floor are the blank end walls of two cinema auditoriums. Inside is a multi-level foyer, complex and exciting, defined by the curved undersides and walls of the auditoriums, which seem suspended overhead. A curving staircase rises behind the big window on the corner of Wood Street.

PLAYHOUSE, Williamson Square. Built 1865 and reconstructed 1895, which may be the date of the unexciting stuccoed façade. In 1911 auditorium and basement foyer were redesigned in an impressive Neoclassical manner by *Stanley D. Adshead*, Professor of Civic Design at the Liverpool School of Architecture. In 1968 a startling EXTENSION by *Hall, O'Donahue & Wilson* was completed, comparable with Patrick Gwynne's exactly contemporary addition to the York Theatre Royal. The rear part houses dressing rooms and a large workshop, the front, foyer spaces and bars. It is a spectacular composition based around three cylinders. The largest starts at the first floor and is two storeys high. It is fully glazed and cantilevers from a central column over the pavement. To the l., a smaller cylinder, also cantilevered from a central column but only partly glazed, interlocks with the first. The third element is inside: a hollow column, originally containing the box office, around which stairs climb to the floors above. The interior creates an atmosphere of excitement and anticipation, exactly right for a theatre foyer, and at night the exterior is equally thrilling.

EMPIRE THEATRE, Lime Street. *See* p. 326.

ROYAL COURT THEATRE, Roe Street. *See* p. 335.

BLUECOAT CHAMBERS. *See* Education Buildings, p. 302.

Police and Utilities Headquarters

MERSEYSIDE POLICE HEADQUARTERS, Canning Place. 1980s, by the *City Architect*. High and impressively forbidding, and brick-clad in deference to nearby Albert Dock.

FIRE STATION (former), Hatton Garden. Rebuilt 1895–8, officially by *Thomas Shelmerdine*, the Corporation Surveyor, but possibly designed in his office by *James Bain Hikins*. Red brick with generous stone dressings, long and low, in a free and imaginative Jacobean style. Watch-tower with serpentine balconies. Being converted to flats, 2005.

GENERAL POST OFFICE (former). *See* Victoria Street, p. 340.

TELEPHONE EXCHANGE (Lancaster House), Old Hall Street. 1936, incorporating training facilities for telephone engineers. Seven storeys, brick, with rounded corners, subdivided by bold fins from first to fourth floor.

CITY TRAMWAY OFFICES (former), Hatton Garden. 1905–7, by *Shelmerdine*, classical and symmetrical. Imposing four-storey façade dominated by three projecting bays, those l. and r. having allegorical sculpture.

Education Buildings

CITY EDUCATION OFFICES (former), Sir Thomas Street. *See* p. 336.

LIVERPOOL JOHN MOORES UNIVERSITY, Byrom Street. The JAMES PARSONS BUILDING (originally College of Technology) by *Ronald Bradbury* was put up in phases: brick-faced s part 1956–9, curtain-walled N section opened 1965, followed by further additions. The result is large and dull. Not so the PETER JOST ENTERPRISE CENTRE just behind, 1994–5 by *Austin-Smith:Lord*. Three floors reducing to two across the sloping site. Lower floors and projecting rounded stair towers sleekly clad in silver-coloured aluminium panels. Top floor completely glazed, with a curved monopitch roof. This has a lattice of tubular beams on its underside, and continues beyond the glass walls to be supported externally on angled struts, leaving the interior column-free. At the N end of the site, SECURITY CONTROL CENTRE, by *Cass Associates*, completed 1997. Triangular, with a boldly oversailing roof. (For the Avril Roberts Learning Resource Centre, *see* p. 338; for other buildings of the University *see* pp. 372–3, 377, 379–80 and 442.)

29 BLUECOAT CHAMBERS, School Lane. Begun 1716, this is the oldest surviving building in central Liverpool and, at the time it was erected, by far the largest secular building in the town. Now a centre for the arts, it was built by Bryan Blundell, a sea captain, as a residential charity school. The original purpose is recorded in Latin across the façade, with the date 1717. The school opened in 1718, though building continued for a few years. It had fifty children by 1719, with room for a hundred more. Despite alterations, extensions and reconstructions, the EXTERIOR retains its early C18 appearance to a considerable

degree. It is of brick with painted stone dressings and encloses three sides of a quadrangle, separated from School Lane by a low wall with railings and gatepiers. Two-storey central block with round-arched windows, the middle three bays breaking forward slightly under a pediment crowned with a pretty timber cupola. Two wings, just one bay wide and not quite parallel, extend forward on each side. They have three storeys rather than two, creating a discordant effect at the inner corners where the different levels collide. The ground- and first-floor windows of the wings are square-headed, those on the top floor oval, while the end elevations have arched windows that match the central block. All the large windows have keystones carved with cherubs' heads, presumably alluding to the building's function. The arched windows have unusual double surrounds: a moulding round the opening, and a separate, outer frame with pilasters supporting an arch. The main door has Ionic columns and a broken segmental pediment, apparently copied from the demolished St Peter's church, completed 1704, which stood opposite. The wings have three square-headed doors, each charmingly approached by ziggurat-like flights of steps.

The INTERIOR has been much altered, but vaulted cellars survive under the E wing and the original ground-floor plan can be traced in parts. When William Enfield described the school in 1773, the upper floor of the main block contained 'a large room, employed as a chapel and for other purposes'. This may have been the original arrangement, and is the same as the early C18 Grey Coat Hospital school, Westminster. Access would have been by the open newel staircase in the SE corner, extensively repaired but apparently incorporating early C18 work.

Who was the architect of this ambitious building? *Thomas Ripley* has been suggested, largely on the grounds that he is known to have designed the stylistically similar Custom House (demolished) shortly afterwards. Another candidate is *Thomas Steers*, the dock engineer, whose name appears in Blundell's account book. However, there is no conclusive evidence that either was involved.

Originally the school appeared less severe: there were statues at the corners of the pediment, and the brick parapet was interspersed with lengths of balustrade and had urns at the corners – details removed during major early C19 repairs and enlargements with which *John Foster* (Sen. or Jun.?) and the builder *Bartin Haigh* were involved. The biggest change was at the back. In *c.* 1723 thirty-six almshouses for rent to the parish had been added here, in the form of wings enclosing a quadrangle, open towards College Lane. The rear of the central block originally resembled the front, but in 1821 it was rebuilt by Haigh in its present convex form. It is not clear when the almshouses were removed, but the utilitarian buildings now enclosing the rear courtyard look early C19. A new wing on the E side by *BIQ Architecten* of Rotterdam is under construction, 2005.

The school moved to Wavertree in 1906 (*see* p. 495), and the future Lord Leverhulme bought the building and saved it from demolition. After bombing in 1941, a sensitive restoration by *Shepheard & Bower* was completed in 1951. This is commemorated by a tablet in the NE corner of the front courtyard, flanked by reliefs of a Blue Coat girl and boy by *Herbert Tyson Smith*. In the 1990s the central steps were replaced with a ramp. The craft shop at the back of the rear courtyard has metal and glass screens towards College Lane, by *Helen Brown* and *Gareth Roberts*, completed 1999.

Transport Buildings

93 LIME STREET STATION, Lime Street. The monumental building in front is by *Alfred Waterhouse*, 1868–71. Originally the station HOTEL, it reopened in 1996 following conversion into a student hall of residence. Symmetrical, except for the differing oriels in the end pavilions. Five storeys plus dormers, with pavilion-roofed corner towers, and two further towers with short spires flanking the central entrance: the splendid skyline is visible from far away. Windows mostly round-arched or with straight tops on quadrant curves. Statues over the main entrance by *Farmer & Brindley*, perhaps representing Europe and America. Waterhouse's competition-winning design was for a brick building with stone dressings, but presumably because of its proximity to St George's Hall the façade was carried out entirely in stone. Inside, a majestic staircase with open well and wrought- and cast-iron handrail leads visibly right up to the top floor.

The original passenger terminus of the Liverpool & Manchester Railway was E of the centre, in Crown Street, but in 1832–5 the line was extended from Edge Hill to Lime Street. The present station is the third on the site. The first, opened 1836, had a timber roof by *Cunningham & Holme*, and a Neo-classical screen in front by *John Foster Jun.*; in 1846–50 it was rebuilt, with offices by *William Tite* and a single-span iron roof more than 153 ft (47 metres) wide by *Richard Turner*. The 100 present iron and glass train shed behind the former hotel was begun in 1867 by *William Baker* and *F. Stevenson* and had then the largest span in the world, though it was almost at once outstripped by London's St Pancras. The span is 200 ft (61 metres), carried by sickle-shaped beams on massive Doric columns. The shed curves in plan. A second shed to the S, parallel and virtually identical, was added in 1878–9 (supervising engineer *E.W. Ives*). Restoration and re-glazing of the entire roof, completed in 2001, has revealed it as a thing of spectacular beauty. Incorporated into the cast-iron colonnade on platform 1 is a group of four columns, more closely spaced than the rest. Designed by *Edward Woods*, they date from the 1846–50 rebuilding, and are all that remains of a bridge which carried Hotham Street over the tracks. Enclosing platforms

1–6, a two-storey L-shaped building of black glass, containing booking office, restaurants, etc. Designed by *British Rail London Midland Region* architects, completed by 1984. Of the same date, a long glass screen dividing platforms 7–9 from the concourse, with an etched mural by *Dianne Redford, Lindsey Ball, Andrew Cooper* and *Clifford Rainey*, now sadly neglected. The design alludes to the early history of the station and of the tunnel linking it with Edge Hill. Trains now approach Lime Street through a mixture of tunnels and cuttings. The latter, created when the number of tracks was doubled in the 1870s, slice verlically through the striated bedrock. The whole experience is thrillingly sublime.

CENTRAL STATION, Ranelagh Street. Top-lit concourse, linked by escalators to the underground platforms, all designed by *British Rail London Midland Region* architects and opened 1977. The same surface finishes are used throughout the Merseyrail underground system: white ceramic tiles for concourses, yellow melamine cladding for corridors and escalators, and on the platforms modular units of dark brown fibreglass incorporating signage, seating and litter bins. The effect is dreary, to say the least. What is now the Northern Line platform was opened in 1892 as the terminus of an eastward extension of the Mersey Railway connecting Liverpool with Birkenhead (*see* James Street Station, below). The engineers were *James Brunlees* and *Douglas Fox*, with *C.A. Rowlandson* and *J. Fright*. Here, partly obscured by the 1977 redesign, the sheer walls cut into solid sandstone can still be seen, roofed over with brick jack arches. Behind the present concourse and reached via Fairclough Street is the site of the previous Central Station, a ground-level facility built for the Cheshire Lines Committee and opened in 1874. Its massive stone walls now enclose a car park. Abutments of the demolished glass and iron roof can be seen on the w side.

EXCHANGE STATION (former), Tithebarn Street. *See* p. 338.

JAMES STREET STATION, James Street. The original Liverpool terminus of the Mersey Railway, the under-river line to Birkenhead, opened 1886. *James Brunlees* and *Charles Douglas Fox* were the engineers. The surface building, bombed in the Second World War, was replaced with a dull 1960s office block, MOOR HOUSE, by *Gotch & Partners*. The tracks and platforms, excavated in the rock 92 ft (28 metres) below the pavement, survive more or less unaltered under a single, broad, brick-lined vault. Platform seating, etc., in the 1977 Merseyrail house style (*see* Central Station, above); mural SCULPTURE, Dream Passage, on platform 2 by *Tim Chalk* and *Paul Grime*, 1992.

MOORFIELDS STATION. *See* p. 319.

WAPPING GOODS STATION (former), King's Dock Street. The station opened in 1830 as part of the Liverpool & Manchester Railway for the transhipment of goods to shipping in the docks, from which initially the railway was barred. The site is now an industrial estate, but in the retaining wall at the E end is the blocked entrance to the WAPPING TUNNEL, of 1826–9, up which wagons were rope-hauled to Edge Hill Station (*see* p. 413). This was the first substantial railway tunnel in the world.

BUS STATION, Canning Place. By *Wilkinson Eyre*, 2005. A pair of long, thin, glazed shelters, facing each other across Canning Place. Their roofs are flat at the end nearest the river, curving upwards and twisting through forty-five degrees as they converge towards Paradise Street. Adjoining, a CAR PARK by the same architects. The ramps between the floors emerge from the main block, sweeping out at one end and in at the other. On the w they are screened, on the E boldly exposed. At each end, a slim, sheer, stair-tower, angled to the main block. Part of the Paradise Street Development area (*see* p. 258)

MERSEY ROAD TUNNEL (QUEENSWAY). The tunnel was con-structed 1925–34 by the engineers *Basil Mott* and *J.A. Brodie*, with *Bertram Hewett* as engineer-in-charge. It was one of the great engineering feats of its day, being at just over two miles – or nearly three including its branches – the longest under-water road tunnel in the world. Main entrance in OLD HAY-MARKET by *Herbert J. Rowse*, appointed architect in 1931. Curved retaining walls of Portland stone – sleek and sheer, suggesting speed and efficiency – flank the semicircular arched entrance, with a relief of two winged bulls above, 'symbolic of swift and heavy traffic'. Art Deco carved decoration by *Edmund C. Thompson* and *George T. Capstick*. The walls end in sturdy arched lodges with fluted column-like buttresses. Overlooking the traffic from either side, bronze STATUES of George V and Queen Mary by *W. Goscombe John*, 1939, originally behind the tunnel entrance, facing w. The layout in front has also changed, the most significant loss being the great lighting column faced with black granite opposite the entrance.

Rowse also designed a second ENTRANCE near the docks in New Quay, with an associated ventilation station (*see* p. 335); other VENTILATION STATIONS in North John Street and at the Pier Head (*see* p. 332); plus corresponding structures on the Birkenhead (Cheshire) side. All are characterised by cubic shapes and square towers. Rowse was also responsible for the tunnel interior, now altered, which had a black glass dado framed in stainless steel. (For the second Mersey road tunnel, Kingsway, *see* p. 486.)

STREETS

ARGYLE STREET. Two warehouses, probably from the first half of the C19, recently converted into flats. One, adjoining the Bridewell (*see* p. 310) is of six storeys; the other, further SE on the same side, of five.

BERRY STREET. On the w side between Wood Street and Seel Street are the premises of the mason and builder *John Walmsley*, designed and erected by himself *c.* 1798. They formed a U-shaped block open to Berry Street, but the central yard was later filled in. The much-altered stucco façades of the wings, with pediments and pilasters, can still be traced. On the side facing Seel Street, a good doorway with Composite columns and open pediment.

BIXTETH STREET. BEREY'S BUILDINGS (entrance in George Street) is a big, muscular office block of 1864. *W. Culshaw* signed the drawings, but the design is likely to be by his future partner *Henry Sumners*. Ten bays by six, of red brick with sandstone bands above a grey stone basement. Square-headed windows under segmental arches; some other details, such as the pointed arches to the end bays, are Gothic. Recently converted into flats, with a floor set back above the cornice. Next door, LOMBARD CHAMBERS, Venetian Gothic in polychrome brick, presumably 1860s.

For the Cotton Exchange *see* Old Hall Street, p. 329; for Orleans House, *see* Edmund Street, p. 322.

BOLD PLACE. Early C19 houses overlooking St Luke's church (*see* p. 281).

BOLD STREET. Laid out by 1785 and mostly built up by 1796, it occupies the site of Joseph and Jonathan Brooks' rope walk. It was originally residential (above ground-floor level many Late Georgian house fronts of brick or stucco remain) but soon the houses gave way to high-class shops, and it remained a byword for exclusive shopping until the Second World War. Its fortunes have since declined steeply, but architectural evidence of its former character survives throughout.

At the lower end, the former LYCEUM of 1800–2, designed by *Thomas Harrison* and built by *William Slater*. Chaste Greek Revival in ashlar, and one of the finest early buildings of Liverpool. The principal façade faces NW: four demi-columns with windows between, and a pedimented window on either side. Above the central windows, reliefs of Geography, Apollo and Commerce, by *F.A. Legé*. The Bold Street façade has a recessed Ionic portico of six columns, flanked by tripartite windows under segmental arches. Now converted to a variety of uses, it was designed to house two separate institutions, the Liverpool Library (a private subscription library founded in 1758, one of the oldest in the country) and a news room. The library occupied the galleried rotunda in the centre, lit by a glazed opening in the dome. The plaster and woodwork here are probably by *Slater* rather than Harrison. The former news room at the NW end, commanding the view down Church Street, has a segmental-vaulted ceiling and a wide arched recess opposite the windows, with friezes painted rather naïvely in grisaille to imitate classical relief sculpture. They are mostly adapted from the Parthenon and the Temple of Apollo Epicurius at Bassae.* The present ceiling is a restoration, part of a refurbishment by *Edmund Percey Scherrer Hicks*, completed 1990. The room had been subdivided horizontally in 1903,

---

*The temple at Bassae was excavated in 1812 by the Liverpool architect John Foster Jun., in the company of C.R. Cockerell; casts of both the Parthenon and Bassae friezes were in the collection of the Liverpool Royal Institution by 1823.

resulting in the loss of Harrison's original ceiling. The basement, entered from the NW end, has Edwardian-looking plasterwork and woodwork. Threatened with demolition for a shopping development in the 1970s, the Lyceum was only saved after a vigorous battle by conservationists.

On the opposite corner a former branch of the North and South Wales Bank (now HSBC), 1903, by *James F. Doyle*. Edwardian Baroque in brick and stone, with attached columns above the corner entrance. Ground floor altered. Nos. 14–16 have an impressive shopfront with large areas of plate glass rising through two floors, carefully restored 1981. Built for John Cripps, Shawl Merchant and Manufacturer, who moved to these premises in 1848, the front was certainly in existence by 1861, and is therefore an exceptionally early survival of its type. Such lavishly glazed fronts were made possible by new technology which facilitated the production of glass in larger sheets. Next door at Nos. 18–26 is the former RADIANT HOUSE, by *Ernest Gee* of *Quiggin & Gee*, opened in 1938 as offices and showrooms for the Liverpool Gas Co. Faced in quartzite, with fluted columns of Swedish green marble to the ground floor, the sheer façade is broken only by a bronze first-floor balcony. It dwarfs its neighbours, but is nevertheless a stylish job. On the same side, at the SE corner of Concert Street, the former MUSIC HALL, 1852–3, by *Arthur H. Holme*, ornate Italianate in brick and stone, now painted. It replaced a Music Hall of 1785–6 by *Charles Eyes*, burned down in 1852. The auditorium of the present building was on the first floor, with shops below, but within a few years it was entirely given over to retail use. Entrance remodelled with paired columns, 1990s. At the back in Wood Street, a colonnade, probably part of Eyes' building.

No. 58 has an Arts and Crafts façade and is of 1906, by *T. Myddelton Shallcross*. Leaded glazing across the first floor breaks forward into three shallow oriels; eaves cornice on deep brackets. The large Italianate block at Nos. 43–47, by *G.E. Grayson*, was completed in 1885 as a branch of the Union Bank of Liverpool. The ground floor had shops flanking a lofty central doorway leading to the banking hall. Now it is shops right across, though the segmental pediment of the doorway survives, with nice carving. Opposite, on the corner of Slater Street, a former branch of LLOYDS BANK, late 1920s, by *George Hastwell Grayson* (G.E. Grayson's son) in partnership with *Leonard Barnish*. Large flat expanses of Portland stone, subtly relieved with crisp carving, perhaps by *H. Tyson Smith*. Back on the opposite side, Nos. 75–79 are of stucco, probably *c.* 1833 by *Joseph Franklin*. They form a Greek Revival composition of five bays, with a pediment supported by Ionic columns set in, and smaller pediments at each end on pairs of very thin pilasters.

No. 92 has an exceptional Graeco-Egyptian façade of *c.* 1879, strikingly similar to Alexander 'Greek' Thompson's work in Glasgow of twenty years earlier. The first-floor glazing runs unbroken behind the masonry, and the top floor is an open loggia. Who designed this curiosity? The most likely candidates seem to be the brothers *W. & G. Audsley*. At No. 100, the Queen Anne style makes its only appearance in the street, in a façade of finely jointed small red bricks, dating from *c.* 1879. This is followed by an open space, Ropewalks Square, created in 2002 to provide a way through to FACT (*see* Public Buildings, p. 301). Opposite, at the corner of Roscoe Place, the former head office of the LIVERPOOL SAVINGS BANK, a six-bay palazzo by *William Culshaw*, 1861. The National Debt Commissioners, acting in the interests of depositors, at first stipulated it should be 'free from all useless ornament', but were persuaded to allow greater expenditure (the total was *c.* £9,000) because the site had been acquired cheaply. Stone was used throughout, rather than the intended brick-and-stone. The unarchaeological capitals of the ground-floor windows seem to be adapted from Cockerell's recently completed Liverpool & London Insurance Co. (*see* Dale Street, p. 318). On the opposite side at the top, turning the corner into Berry Street, HAVELOCK BUILDINGS, *c.* 1858, by *Horace Field Sen.* of London. Four-storey stuccoed shops with showrooms and living accommodation above, now missing its pierced parapet and chimneys. On the top floor, a photographer's glass house 55 ft (16.8 metres) long was in existence by 1861. Still partly glazed, it can be seen from the back.

BRIDGEWATER STREET. *See* PARLIAMENT STREET.

BRUNSWICK STREET. Created in the 1780s. On the S side, between Fenwick Street and Lower Castle Street, the former private BANK of Arthur Heywood, Sons & Co., simple and dignified ashlar of 1798–1800, possibly to a design of 1789 by *John Foster Sen.* Five bays, three storeys, the ground floor with channelled rustication and round-arched windows. Doorcase with pilasters, clearly later. Attached, on Fenwick Street, a matching house of three narrow bays, stuccoed, the stone ground floor presumably once with a doorway. This is an exceptionally early purpose-built bank, and though it combines office and living accommodation in the traditional way, the house is an appendage to the business part, rather than the other way around. On the N side, opposite, the former UNION BANK head office, *c.* 1870, probably by *John Cunningham* (replacing premises by *Cunningham & Holme*, 1840). A well-detailed five-bay palazzo with rounded, inset corners, surprisingly correct and restrained for its date. Doric pilasters to the ground floor, Corinthian aedicules framing first-floor windows. At the back, along Fenwick Street, an extension by *G.E. Grayson*. Inside, noble banking hall with polished red granite columns, glazed dome, and rich plasterwork.

For the Corn Exchange, *see* Fenwick Street, p. 323; for India Buildings, *see* Water Street, p. 341.

BUTTON STREET. The block bounded by Button Street, Rainford Square and Rainford Gardens has polychrome brick warehouses built for Edward Graham, beginning with a group

38

dated 1863 in Rainford Square and ending in Rainford Gardens in 1880.

BYROM STREET. E side mostly occupied by the Liverpool John Moores University (*see* Public Buildings, p. 302). Crossed at its S end by two FLYOVERS with pedestrian walkways, 1967–71, designed by the city engineer *N.H. Stockley* in conjunction with *Shankland Cox & Associates*, with *W.S. Atkins & Partners* as consulting engineers. The aim was to separate city-centre traffic from traffic using the first Mersey Tunnel. On the W side between the two flyovers (actually in Fontenoy Street) a SCULPTURE, Palanzana, by *Stephen Cox*. Made for the Liverpool International Garden Festival, 1984, relocated 1998. A tree-like form wrapped around a large sphere, carved from volcanic stone quarried at Palanzana, near Viterbo in Italy.

CAMPBELL SQUARE. Created as part of a regeneration project, begun in 2000 and ongoing, embracing Campbell, Henry, York, Argyle and Duke streets. The architects for the whole scheme are *Brock Carmichael Associates*. Old buildings are being adapted, and in some cases entirely rebuilt. Gaps are being filled with new buildings, generally complementary in scale and materials. The former BRIDEWELL, 1861, built as police cells and offices with a forbidding perimeter wall, is now a restaurant. Italianate, asymmetrical, with two towers of different heights, the taller one for ventilation. In the square a SCULPTURE, The Seed, 2002, by *Stephen Broadbent*: an egg-shaped pod, silvery outside, copper-coloured inside.

CANNING PLACE. The site of the Old Dock, the first commercial wet dock in the world, infilled in the 1820s to create a spacious *place* where *John Foster Jun.* built his vast Greek Revival Custom House, 1828–39, demolished following Second World War damage. A late 1960s office scheme has in turn been demolished. Canning Place is a focus of the huge Paradise Street Development Area (*see* p. 258), and will be the site of a new department store for the John Lewis Partnership (by *John McAslan*), facing the new bus station (*see* p. 306). A sliver of the Old Dock is to be exposed. To the N will be a public garden, concealing two thousand underground parking spaces.

CASTLE STREET. One of the seven ancient streets of Liverpool, named from the castle on the site of Derby Square. Very narrow until 1786, when the W side was rebuilt on its present line, opening up the view N to the Town Hall. *Samuel Hope* of Manchester was paid 20 guineas by Liverpool Corporation for designs for the new elevations, though whether these were followed is not clear, since *John Foster Sen.* was also asked to make designs. The buildings were brick with stone dressings, subsequently stuccoed. From the 1840s Castle Street became the chief financial street, and was almost entirely rebuilt by banks and insurance companies, vying with each other in the splendour of their offices. Classical styles predominate.

E SIDE. At the corner of Dale Street, the former premises of the art dealers AGNEW'S (now part of the HSBC building, Dale Street), 1877, by *Salomons, Wornum & Ely*. Very similar to their contemporary building for Agnew's in Bond Street, London: Queen Anne style, red brick, carved decoration rather than moulded terracotta. After this, the former BRITISH & FOREIGN MARINE INSURANCE CO., 1888–90, by *Grayson & Ould*. Red brick with red sandstone and terracotta, Renaissance with Gothic touches. Mosaic frieze above the first floor with shipping scenes, designed by *Frank Murray* and made by *Salviati*. Next door, the same architects' QUEEN INSURANCE BUILDING and ARCADE, 1887–8, with lively terracotta decoration. Shops on the ground floor, and an archway leading through to Queen Avenue, with attractive offices in cream glazed brick and red sandstone (for the remainder of Queen Avenue, *see* Dale Street). Next, the former SCOTTISH EQUITABLE CHAMBERS, *c.* 1878, classical with bands of polished granite, and the former SCOTTISH PROVIDENT BUILDING, 1874, both by *G.E. Grayson* before his partnership with Ould. No. 27 is a three-bay building of 1846 with Corinthian columns and pediment. Built by the lawyer and developer Ambrose Lace for his own offices, originally entered from Union Court, with ground-floor shops facing Castle Street. Convincingly ascribed to *Arthur H. Holme*.

Between Union Court and Cook Street is the former Liverpool branch of the BANK OF ENGLAND by *C.R. Cockerell*, 1846–8. One of the masterpieces of Victorian commercial architecture, and among Cockerell's greatest works, combining Greek, Roman and Renaissance in a remarkably vigorous and inventive way. Only three bays wide, but overwhelmingly massive and powerful. Ground and first floors are tied together by attached Roman Doric columns, framed by rusticated angle pilasters. Second floor recessed, with a central Ionic aedicule window set in a round arch that pushes up into the open pediment. This impressive composition is developed from Cockerell's Manchester branch of the Bank and his earlier Westminster Insurance office. Seven bays to Cook Street, with three great tripartite windows under rusticated arches (the middle one originally lit the tunnel-vaulted banking hall). The huge crowning cornice on pairs of curved brackets is more prominent here. The front contained the residence of the Bank's Liverpool agent, entered from Union Court, with the sub-agent's house at the opposite end, entered from Cook Street. The first-floor windows to these residential parts have curved balconies with graceful ironwork.

On the other corner of Cook Street, No. 43, CASTLE CHAMBERS, 1955–9, by *Felix Holt*. A very large Portland stone block, its upper floors set back in the middle of the long Cook Street elevation. Next door, on the corner of Harrington Street, the former EQUITY & LAW BUILDING, 1970, by *Quiggin & Gee*. The projecting windows echo Peter Ellis' Oriel Chambers of 1864 (*see* Water Street), by this date regarded as admirably proto-modern.

W SIDE. On the corner of Derby Square, and making the most of its prominent site, No. 62, the exuberant TRIALS

HOTEL, built as the Alliance Bank by *Lucy & Littler*, 1868. 'Italian, of the Venetian type', according to *The Builder*, with high chimneys, balconies, and much carving. Domed banking hall with paired Corinthian columns. The two bays on the r. are a matching addition by *G.E. Grayson*. At Nos. 48–50, a tall, narrow building four bays wide, 1864, by *J.A. Picton*, originally the Mercantile and Exchange Bank. Polished red granite columns frame the ground-floor windows, and the first-floor lunettes have carved heads in roundels. T. Mellard Reade wrote in 1866 that it had 'the not uncommon defect of appearing as though made in lengths and sawn off to suit consumers'. Was it conceived as part of a larger block to be erected in stages? It is sandwiched between altered fragments of the 1786 rebuilding, with ends of a pediment visible on either side. No. 44 has an 1880s faience façade with foliage in the gable. At No. 42, the former VICTORIA CHAMBERS, dated 1893, by *Grayson & Ould* again. Renaissance style, large and straggling, with three gables incorporating sculptures of mermen. Ground floor altered.

Next door, at the corner of Brunswick Street, the former ADELPHI BANK by *W.D. Caröe*, *c*. 1891–2, colourful and exotic. Northern Renaissance with much decorative carving, including figures in niches by *Charles E. Whiffen* to Caröe's designs. Alternate bands of red and white stone, with green copper for the onion domes and finials that add a touch of fantasy to the roof-line. The corner entrance has exceptionally beautiful bronze doors of 1892 by *Thomas Stirling Lee*, with scenes of brotherly love (Adelphi means 'brothers' in Greek) in sensuous low relief. On the other corner of Brunswick Street, the former LEYLAND & BULLINS BANK (now Bank of Scotland), dated 1895, with an extension dated 1900 in Brunswick Street. *Grayson & Ould* in Renaissance mode again. The gable to Brunswick Street is framed by domed angle turrets, echoing Shaw's contemporary White Star Line building (*see* James Street). *Shaw* himself, in association with *Willink & Thicknesse*, was responsible for the NATWEST BANK (originally Parr's), 1898–1901. Classical, of five bays. Basement of smooth grey granite with round-arched entrance, richly rusticated. Above, bands of grey-green and cream marble, the window surrounds and cornice red terracotta. Circular, domed banking hall, with offices stacked above, ingeniously supported by steel trusses. The remainder of this side is all *Grayson*: No. 14 of *c*. 1885, classical, with a splendid cast-iron staircase rising through the centre; the former EDINBURGH LIFE ASSURANCE, dated 1897 (and therefore done in partnership with *Ould*?), coarser and rather flabby; and finally, on the corner of Water Street, an exquisite François I-style block erected in 1882 for the jewellers Robert Jones & Sons. Ground floor with very elegant projecting display windows. Office floors subtly polychromed, with bands of contrasting stone.

p. 69

Delicate carving around the windows, and good wrought-iron balconies.

CHAPEL STREET. One of the seven ancient streets. Starting near the E end, YORKSHIRE HOUSE, at the corner of Rumford Place, is by *T. Wainwright & Sons* (*J.B. Hutchins*), 1929. Classical, in Portland stone. Giant square piers extend from first to third floor, enclosing expanses of metal-framed glazing. Immediately W, UNITY, a mixed-use development by *Allford Hall Monaghan Morris*, is under construction in 2005: two towers – one residential (twenty-seven storeys), one offices (fifteen storeys). The fine five-bay HARGREAVES BUILDINGS opposite, dated 1859, is by *J.A. Picton* in Venetian palazzo style. Carved heads of Cortez, Columbus, etc., in roundels between the ground-floor windows, commemorate exploration of the Americas. On the N side, at the bottom, the THISTLE HOTEL, 1970–3, by *Victor Basil* and *Keith McTavish* of *William Holford & Associates*. Eleven-storey tower – a convex-sided triangle in plan – on a two-storey podium. Concrete cladding, windows in bands. Constructed using the British Lift Slab method, each complete floor being jacked up and fixed around the core.

CHEAPSIDE. On the W side towards Tithebarn Street, CABLE-HOUSE, a 1960s electronics factory imaginatively converted into flats and live-work spaces by *Union North*, *c.* 2000. Much external cedar panelling, and a zinc-clad penthouse floor with pod-like projections containing windows. On the same side, a couple of robust polychrome brick warehouses, one dated 1884. For the Bridewell, *see* p. 301.

CHURCH ALLEY. The ATHENAEUM, a private club by *Harold Dod*, 1924. This institution, the only one of Liverpool's sub-scription libraries and news rooms to survive into the C21, dates back to 1797; it originally occupied a building in Church Street by *John Foster Sen.*, demolished for street widening. Chaste American classicism, with a strong French accent. The club occupies three floors above ground-floor shops. The simple, segment-headed entrance, its keystone carved with the head of Athena, said to be by *H. Tyson Smith*, leads via a broad corridor to an elegant elliptical staircase. The best interior is the second-floor Library. Shallow segmental vaulted ceiling with Greek Revival decoration, and three subsidiary bays, separated by paired columns. Three large paintings by *Edward Halliday*, part of the original decoration, show The Contest between Athena and Poseidon, The Story of Marsyas, and Athena and Arachne. Their restrained classicism, without strong shadows or violent action, is a good match for the architecture.

CHURCH STREET. Named after the demolished parish church of St Peter, 1699–1704. No. 2 on the corner of Paradise Street is the former SEEL'S BUILDING, completed by 1872. A rare essay in commercial architecture by *Edward Welby Pugin*, best known for his R.C. churches. Gothic, rock-faced stone with ashlar dressings, with second-floor balconies and an angled corner entrance. The piers separating the two-light windows break forward to support the balconies, then recede, only to be corbelled out again on the third floor, creating an oddly undulating façade. The initial letter s of the Seel family is worked into the balcony tracery. Ground floor altered. Next door, the former COOPER'S store (now W.H. Smith), *c.* 1920 by *Gerald de Courcy Fraser*. The principal, E elevation overlooking St Peter's churchyard was obliterated by an extension to the neighbouring store. The elevation to Church Street has a square tower and Mannerist details. Between here and Church Alley, occupying the site of St Peter and its churchyard, is the sprawling bulk of the former WOOLWORTHS, 1923, by the firm's house architect *William Priddle* (now HMV, Top Shop, etc.). Coarse classical, with a large glazed area in the middle. Portland stone, rather than Woolworths usual white faience.

On the opposite side, at the corner of Williamson Street, a former branch of LLOYDS BANK in red brick with a green copper roof. By *Herbert James Rowse*, 1930–1. Carved decoration in Portland stone, now unfortunately painted, by *Herbert Tyson Smith* and *Edmund C. Thompson*. The round-arched windows and parapet are Neo-Romanesque, but much of the ornament is Art Deco. After this, the Italianate shop now occupied by CLARKS was designed by *Lewis Hornblower*, *c.* 1858, for the art metalworkers and electroplaters Elkington's. *The Builder* disliked the thin columns to the upper floors, 'which suggest rain-water pipes without being so'. They are polished granite, sadly painted.

Filling the block between Tarleton Street and Basnett Street is the majestic COMPTON HOUSE (now Marks & Spencer). Built for the retailer J.R. Jeffery, whose premises on the same

Liverpool, Compton House, Church Street,
by Thomas Haigh & Co., 1866–7. Engraving, *c.* 1867

site burned down in December 1865. The replacement was designed within two weeks by *Thomas Haigh & Co.*, builders, and opened just eighteen months later. It is of international significance as an exceptionally early purpose-built department store, finished five years before the Bon Marché in Paris. J.A. Kilpin, President of the Liverpool Architectural Society, described it in 1867 as a building 'which neither London, nor Paris, nor Genoa, nor Venice, nor Rotterdam, nor any other city . . . can excel in richness of architectural decoration, I mean as built for business purposes by a single firm'. The show front is a very elaborate affair in stone, eleven bays and four storeys with a big square tower at each end. These originally had high pavilion roofs, giving a distinctly French Renaissance look. In fact the façade bears a close resemblance to Les Magasins Réunis, a Parisian shop complex by *Gabriel Davioud*, begun in 1865. Much carved decoration (by *Messrs Williams*), including a figure of Commerce over the entrance. The interior, now altered, was thoroughly fireproofed. On the upper floors were extensive workshops, as well as sleeping accommodation and recreational facilities for live-in staff. Side elevations largely of brick, reduced in length.

On the other corner of Basnett Street, the former BON MARCHÉ (now part of John Lewis), 1912–18, by *Gerald de Courcy Fraser*. Portland stone on a steel frame, decorated with an odd mix of French Renaissance trophies (one on Basnett Street includes a First World War tank) and ancient Egyptian motifs. Upper floors added *c.* 1922–3. Next door, a simpler Portland stone block of 1928 by *Hillier, Parker, May & Rowden* sweeps round into Parker Street. Facing these on the S side at the corner of Church Alley, SPINNEY HOUSE, 1951–5, by *Alfred Shennan* for Littlewoods Mail Order Stores. One of the city's earliest large-scale post-war efforts, it is hardly a forward-looking landmark: faced in Portland stone with Art Deco-classical details, it might have been designed twenty years earlier. Carved decoration by *Herbert Tyson Smith*. Church Street entrance remodelled in the form of a tunnel by *OMI Architects*, *c.* 2003. Outside, a bronze STATUE of Sir John Moores, founder of Littlewoods, and his brother Cecil, by *Tom Murphy*, unveiled 1996. Nos. 14–18, on the same side, are a good former branch of the Bank of Liverpool (now Alliance & Leicester), 1913–15. Baroque, the ground floor mutilated for a large window. Finally, at the Hanover Street corner, the best of *Gerald de Courcy Fraser*'s big classical blocks, PREMIER BUILDINGS (now Lloyds TSB), 1912–14. It is tall – eight storeys – and the narrow proportions are emphasised by thin vertical corner strips against channelled rustication. First-floor windows round-arched; those on the two floors below the main cornice recessed between square piers with quirky Mannerist capitals.

Marking the E end of Church Street, a bronze SCULPTURE, The Great Escape, by *Edward Cronshaw*, the result of a competition in 1994: a man restraining a rearing horse made of unravelled rope.

CLAYTON SQUARE. This irregular space is all that remains of one of central Liverpool's few attempts at formal Georgian planning, a residential square built up slowly from 1751 on land leased by Sarah Clayton. In the 1920s the NW half was built over with a single block (now TESCO METRO, etc.) by *Walter Aubrey Thomas*, originally for a hotel. With the plans amended by *Stewart McLauchlan*, it opened in 1925 as a department store. Portland stone, with giant three-storey pilasters turning into piers at the top. More recently, the SE half of the square was rebuilt by the *Seymour Harris Partnership* as the CLAYTON SQUARE SHOPPING CENTRE, opened 1988. Round-arched windows and Postmodern gables, the walls faced with blue and red brick and artificial stone, in imitation of High Victorian polychromy. Shops on two levels, round a cruciform arcade under glazed barrel vaults, with a glazed dome over the crossing. The inspiration no doubt came from Victorian precedents such as Manchester's Barton Arcade, but the steelwork here is comparatively clumsy. Originally, the shorter arm was open from pavement to roof, but the first-floor shops have been extended across.

COLLEGE LANE. Two four-storey brick warehouses, apparently in existence by 1803 and, if so, among the earliest surviving in the city. They have central loading bays, the doors more or less flush with the façade. This, and adjoining derelict streets, are to be transformed as part of the Paradise Street Development Area (*see* p. 258). A pedestrian arcade by *Dixon Jones* will link with School Lane.

COLQUITT STREET. Nos. 14–18, are part of a terrace of houses of the 1790s, described by Picton as 'commodious and respectable', now partly converted to commercial uses. No. 24 is the former LIVERPOOL ROYAL INSTITUTION, built *c.* 1799 as the combined residence and business premises of Thomas Parr, and in Picton's words 'one of the best examples extant of the establishment of a first-class Liverpool merchant of the period'. Lower pavilion blocks on either side of the five-bay house are connected to it by single-storey screen walls with niches. That on the r. was the carriage house, on the l. the counting house. Behind the latter is Parr's five-storey warehouse, a dignified structure with pediments on three sides, unsympathetically converted into flats in the 1990s. From 1815 the buildings were adapted as the Liverpool Royal Institution, dedicated to the promotion of literature, science and the arts. *Edmund Aikin* was architect for the remodelling, and the porch is his, an early and influential use of Greek Doric in Liverpool (*Thomas Rickman* helped with the drawings); the ubiquitous *John Foster Jun.* was also involved from 1822. The most prominent addition is the large, windowless block behind, built to contain a lecture theatre with top-lit exhibition rooms above.

COMMUTATION ROW. Occupying – but failing – a key site opposite the William Brown Street group and St George's Hall (*see* p. 291) is COMMUTATION PLAZA, offices and apartments completed 2002, by *Geoffrey Reid Associates*. Artificial stone,

symmetrical, with round corner pavilions and a portico of
copper-clad columns. Insubstantial and crude by comparison
with its grand C19 neighbours.

CONCERT SQUARE. A lively informal space overlooked by refurbished industrial buildings. These include HOLME'S BUILD-
INGS, polychrome brick warehouses dated 1867 and 1869, and
on the opposite side a former chemical factory, now bars,
restaurants and a gallery, with flats above. The earliest part of
this, a boldly modelled four-storey red brick range with segmental-arched windows facing Wood Street, dates from
c. 1896. It is a fragment of a block designed by *Aston Webb*. The
conversion was completed in 1994 by the developers Urban
Splash and designed by their in-house architects *Design Shed*,
who also laid out the square. Apart from the docks, this was
the first residential refurbishment of an industrial building in
the city centre, and a catalyst for subsequent developments in
the area. At one corner of the square, The Tango, a painted
steel SCULPTURE by *Allen Jones*, commissioned for the 1984
Liverpool International Garden Festival and relocated.

CONCERT STREET. A cast-iron SCULPTURE, Reconciliation,
1989, by *Stephen Broadbent*: two embracing figures.

COOK STREET. No. 16, described as 'newly erected' in 1868, is
by *Peter Ellis*. Tall, narrow front divided into three great arches,
rising through five storeys from pavement to gable. The middle
arch is wider and higher, and pushes the cornice up to form a
curving gable with a little obelisk crowning the keystone. The
proportions are those of a warehouse (the central arch recalls
a loading bay) but the building was designed as offices. As with
Ellis' Oriel Chambers (*see* Water Street, p. 342), there is an
amazing amount of plate glass to stonework, so that the façade
resembles one huge mullioned window. The offices facing the
rear courtyard have large areas of glazing too, and a remarkable spiral staircase, cantilevered and expressed externally, and
now entirely glazed. Externally completely utilitarian, the
staircase ironwork inside is quite decorative, with a Gothic
balustrade, and mullions in the form of slender spiral columns.
The shallow vaulted ceilings are lath and plaster, it seems, not
brick. No. 14, almost contemporary, could not be more different. It was built as the NATIONAL BANK. The drawings, dated
1863, are signed by *William Culshaw*, but the designer was
probably *Henry Sumners*. Five bays, Italianate. The Queen
Anne windows between the ground-floor columns are later.

CORNWALLIS STREET. On the NW side, the former WORK-
SHOPS FOR THE OUTDOOR BLIND (i.e. blind people living
in their own homes), yellow brick Gothic of 1870, by *G.T.
Redmayne* of Manchester. They contained large rooms for
making baskets, brushes and matting, and space for lectures
and social gatherings. Upper part reconstructed after wartime
bomb damage.

CROSSHALL STREET. On the E side, N of Victoria Street,
CROSSHALL BUILDINGS, by *F. & G. Holme*, put up in two
phases *c.* 1878–80. Offices combined with warehouses, the

latter entered at the rear. Fireproof construction, façades of red brick and terracotta. Next door, the former VICTORIA CHAPEL of the Welsh Calvinists, 1878–80, by *W.H. Picton*. Surprisingly late for a new place of worship in the commercial centre. Early Gothic, with round-arched windows and stiff-leaf capitals. After this, and with a façade to Dale Street, WESTMINSTER BUILDINGS, 1879–80, by *Richard Owens*. A well-detailed Gothic block with carving by *Joseph Rogerson*. Originally there was a spire over the main entrance. A good example of a building combining shops and offices with ware-housing at the rear, very characteristic of later C19 Liverpool. Being converted to flats, 2005.

DALE STREET. One of the seven ancient streets. Lanes and narrow streets run off N and S, echoes of medieval burgage plots.

Beginning at the W end: No. 1, beside the Town Hall, is *C.R. Cockerell*'s great office complex for the LIVERPOOL & LONDON INSURANCE CO., 1856–8. He was assisted by his son *F.P. Cockerell* and by *Christopher F. Hayward* (resident architect *Joseph Boult*). Four linked buildings filling an entire block, the richest one (now Royal Bank of Scotland) facing Dale Street, the other three a little plainer and intended as lettable offices. The Dale Street building is a Venetian-looking palazzo with attached columns between the second-floor windows, and a memorable central entrance: a Doric doorcase of polished red granite with open pediment, in a rusticated niche carved with heavy garlands. Originally there were similar garlands between the attic windows of the frieze (a strong echo of St Mark's Library, Venice) and over the side entrances facing the Town Hall. Carving mostly by *Edwin Stirling*, with some by Cock-erell's favourite sculptor, *W.G. Nicholl*. Towards the Town Hall the NW stairs are expressed externally, as at the Château de Chambord, the balustrades and treads both visible, here framed by expanses of plate glass. The buildings originally enclosed a glass-roofed court, faced with glazed white tiles and lined with access galleries. The court became wider as the upper galleries stepped back, to maximise daylight. Interior of fireproof construction, some of the cast-iron columns originally serving as flues.

Opposite, HSBC, *c.* 1971, by *Bradshaw, Rowse & Harker*, a startlingly aggressive façade of twenty-eight identical, faceted windows of reflective glass, framed in stainless steel – a Space Age descendant of Oriel Chambers (*see* Water Street). Next door a large, stone classical building with giant attached Corinthian columns, much carved decoration (wreaths, fleshy acanthus scrolls) and a big sculptured royal arms on the parapet. It is part of a group of offices by *Samuel Rowland*, *c.* 1837–8, originally for the Royal Bank. On the r. an archway leads into Queen Avenue, with simpler offices on each side and the former bank itself at the end, an exquisite Greek Revival design. Five bays, the centre breaking forward under a pediment, with Doric columns below Ionic. Superb masonry.

The detail here is much more refined and correct, and it is difficult to believe it is by the same architect as the street front. Main hall with four Corinthian columns near the corners and sumptuous plasterwork, recently spoiled when a mezzanine was introduced.

No. 14 is the former STATE INSURANCE, 1903–5, by *Walter Aubrey Thomas*. Wiry, sinuous Gothic. Originally symmetrical, with a balancing gable l. of the slim octagonal tower. Ground-floor restaurant (now a nightclub) at the back – part of the original scheme – with sumptuous multicoloured marble decoration, incorporating circular reliefs by *Alfred R. Martin*. This was top-lit, with offices above arranged round a glass-roofed court. Next door, at the corner of North John Street, STATE HOUSE, a bleak seven-storey tower above a podium, by *Edmund Kirby & Sons, c.* 1962. No. 11 at the corner of Hackins Hey, for the Queen Insurance Co., 1859, by *J.A. Picton*. Perhaps his best surviving office block: Italian Renaissance and Gothic details, with upper balconies and a bold machicolated parapet. Nos. 21–25 are RIGBY'S BUILDINGS, re-fronted in stucco, 1865, with offices and a warehouse grouped round an inner courtyard. On the same side, No. 31 is the former REFORM CLUB, an impressive red brick palazzo of 1879 by *Edmund Kirby*. Rather sombre, except for the continuous first-floor balcony with its delicate wrought-iron balustrade. The façade of the neighbouring GUARDIAN ASSURANCE BUILDINGS, 1893, probably by *Grayson & Ould*, has pretty carved decoration. It was absorbed *c.* 1990 into a coarse Postmodern office block.

Back on the s side, for the former Royal Insurance building, *see* North John Street. Next door, THE TEMPLE, by *J.A. Picton*, begun 1863, with a central domed tower. One of several office buildings by Picton for the banker Sir William Brown. Two long brick ranges with huge windows extended behind, but only the w one survives, converted to flats 2005. The other was replaced with an addition by *Falconer Chester*, completed 2001, tall and thin and curved in plan, with aluminium cladding. Then the Gothic PRUDENTIAL ASSURANCE building by *Alfred Waterhouse*, dated 1886, in the same red brick and terracotta as the company's London headquarters. Extension, including tower, added by *Paul Waterhouse*, 1904–6, closing the view down Moorfields. Vaguely Art Nouveau details. On the N side, facing down Stanley Street, a stucco façade with two giant Corinthian columns, probably 1820s, incorporated into a dull red brick office block by *Bradshaw, Rowse & Harker*, completed 1985. (Behind is Moorfields underground station, part of the Merseyrail system opened in 1977. The station concourse at first-floor level was intended to be reached by elevated walkways in neighbouring buildings, but these were never constructed.) Opposite, on the corner of Stanley Street, the red sandstone MUSKER'S BUILDINGS, 1881–2, by *Thomas E. Murray*, in 'a coarse and florid sort of "Manchester Gothic"' (*The Builder*). Originally intended as shops and offices, it seems to have been adapted as the Junior Conservative Club during construction, then used as the Junior Reform Club. Next door, IMPERIAL CHAMBERS, *c.* 1873. Gothic details but mostly square-headed windows. Central entrance leading to a glass-roofed court surrounded by offices (now flats). Then, at the corner of Sir Thomas Street, the former CONSERVATIVE CLUB, won in competition by *F. & G. Holme*, 1880, and opened 1883. Lavish French Renaissance, with a balcony, and cherubs in the first-floor spandrels in the manner of Sansovino. Impressive staircase inside. Being converted to a hotel, 2005.

Opposite, between Hockenhall Alley and Cheapside, PRINCES BUILDINGS, 1882, by *Henry Shelmerdine*: shops, offices and leather works. A rather ungainly red brick pile, with giant granite pilasters and sandstone and terracotta details. Large mullioned-and-transomed windows in the mansard, with pedimented gables. Absorbed into the HOCKENHALL ALLEY elevation, l., an extraordinary survival: a three-storey house of the meanest kind, just one bay wide, probably early C19. Back on the s side, the Municipal Buildings (*see* p. 291) and Westminster Buildings (*see* Crosshall Street, p. 318) are followed by the TRAVELODGE, a hotel by *ShedKM*, completed 2002. Two distinct blocks, raised above a set-back ground floor. That facing Dale Street is cubic, faced in blue render, and punched with square windows. The other, set at an angle, faces Manchester Street. It is mostly of glass, an all-over grid of squares, masking the division into bedrooms. Adjoining in PRESTON STREET is PRESTON POINT, two C19 warehouses converted into flats by *ShedKM*, with balconies behind horizontally slatted timber screens.

At this point the s side comes to an end above the entrance to the Mersey Tunnel. On the N side, No. 127 is the offices of NATIONAL MUSEUMS LIVERPOOL, a seven-storey tower of 1964–5 by *Ormrod & Partners* (*D.H. Mills*). Polished granite facing. Nos. 135–139 are a terrace of three brick houses of *c.* 1788, including, at the corner of TRUEMAN STREET, the grandest surviving Georgian house in the business district, built for the distiller John Houghton, whose works adjoined. The houses were set back from the old building line, allowing Dale Street to be widened. The Trueman Street elevation has a three-bay pediment and a Venetian window over the tripartite doorway. Finally, at the corner of Fontenoy Street, No. 151, built for the Blackburn Assurance Co. by *William P. Horsburgh*, *c.* 1932. Classical, with iron-framed glazing between giant pilasters. The corner entrance leads to a very impressive Travertine-lined spiral staircase, rising to a stained-glass dome.

DERBY SQUARE. A historic nodal point, site of the C13 castle, and later of St George's church (1726–34, by *Thomas Steers*, reconstructed 1819–25 by *John Foster Jun.*; demolished 1897). From here, Castle Street leads N to the Town Hall, and from opposite, South Castle Street formerly led to the Custom House in Canning Place. The E side was rebuilt by *John Foster Jun.*, 1826, with two quadrants flanking Lord Street, forming

St George's Crescent. In the Second World War the area was severely damaged, and in the rebuilding South Castle Street was obliterated and the Queen Elizabeth II Law Courts (*see* p. 300) built across its path.

QUEEN VICTORIA MONUMENT, 1902–6, by *F.M. Simpson*, with *Willink & Thicknesse*; bronze sculpture by *C.J. Allen*. Domed baldacchino on clusters of diagonally set columns, raised on a stepped podium enclosed by four concave walls with balustrades. Standing figure of the Queen under the dome, with Fame on the summit. The groups above the columns are Justice, Wisdom, Charity and Peace, and on the enclosing walls Agriculture, Industry, Education and Commerce. This was Allen's *magnum opus* and is one of the most ambitious British monuments to the Queen.

No. 2, PEARL ASSURANCE HOUSE, *c.* 1954–5, by *Alfred Shennan & Partners*. A big Portland stone block, curved like the N half of Foster's crescent that it replaced. Pediments over the first-floor windows, and other Neo-Georgian touches. CASTLE MOAT HOUSE, 1838–40, by *Edward Corbett* of Manchester for the North and South Wales Bank, is tall and narrow on an island site, with giant Corinthian pilasters on the Fenwick Street side and a pedimented front. The front originally had a portico *in antis*, later filled in. The temple effect is undermined by three tiers of domestic-looking windows between the pilasters. The site lies partly over the castle moat, so the bank was given a deep, vaulted basement, used as bonded warehousing.

DUKE STREET. In the C18 Duke Street was affluent, with grand merchants' houses having attached warehouses and counting houses at the rear. A fashionable, tree-lined 'Ladies' Walk' extended for much of its length. In the C19 business activity shifted to the streets round the Exchange, and the rich moved up the hill to the spacious residential quarter building there. The Duke Street area was increasingly taken over by warehousing and by the small industries which had always operated close to the docks, and the respectable houses began their inevitable decline.

Starting at the w end: HUMYAK HOUSE, a tall warehouse on the l. dated 1864, is followed by five late C18 houses with columned and pedimented doorways. In DUKE STREET LANE, opposite, a three-storey warehouse of 1863. The adjoining red brick building with a short cylindrical tower at the corner of Campbell Street is part of a wider regeneration scheme by *Brock Carmichael Associates* (*see* Campbell Square, p. 310). No. 64 is an ornate five-bay palazzo by *John Elliott Reeve*, 1876, built as offices and stores for the brewer Peter Walker, with an attached warehouse at the back in Henry Street. On the opposite side at the corner of Slater Street is the severe but well-proportioned ashlar UNION NEWS ROOM of 1800 by *John Foster Sen.* The main entrance was in the centre of the five-bay Duke Street façade, and had a large carving of the royal arms crowning the parapet above. The elevation to

Slater Street breaks forward slightly under a central pediment and has a tripartite window on the first floor. It was adapted as Liverpool's first public library in 1852, when the utilitarian brick extension at the rear was built to house the natural history collections presented to the town by the Earl of Derby. Later it became offices: *R.T. Beckett* designed the three-bay Jacobean extension, l., 1896, and further additions followed. The whole block was rebuilt behind the façades, *c.* 1990, by *Kingham Knight Associates*.

Above Slater Street, more Late Georgian houses, including some once-grand five-bay examples, now mostly very decayed. At the corner of Colquitt Street, a Neo-Georgian block by *Wilkinson Hindle Halsall Lloyd*, completed 2003. A rather crude replica of part of a longer mid-C18 terrace on this site, the derelict remains of which were demolished in the 1990s. Behind and at right angles, and originally reached by a base-ment passage from Duke Street, a short terrace of smaller dwellings was built between 1836 and 1848. Remarkably this has survived (renovation completed 2003), and is the only example of back-to-back housing remaining in Liverpool. At a later date doors were punched through the spine wall, con-verting eighteen houses with one room to each floor into nine of twice the size with windows front and back. Bizarrely resited in the car park, 2005, is *John Gibson*'s monumental Neoclassi-cal bronze STATUE of a toga-clad William Huskisson, made in 1847 for the steps of the Custom House. Lastly, on the corner of Nelson Street, an elaborately stuccoed classical building of *c.* 1858 by *Henry Sumners*. It housed a furniture workshop and showrooms, and incorporated the proprietor's dwelling at the Duke Street end.

EDMUND STREET. ORLEANS HOUSE, 1907, a large E-plan office block with its long elevation facing Bixteth Street. By *Matear & Simon*, using the same cast-iron cladding panels as their Cotton Exchange opposite (*see* Old Hall Street). STANLEY HALL, built as the headquarters of R. Silock & Sons, animal-feed producers, opened in 1938. By *Medcalf & Medcalf*. Frieze in the entrance with scenes of animal husbandry. Extended w in the 1950s by *Fraser, Son & Geary*. This part has an overdoor relief of a cow being fed; the style suggests *Herbert Tyson Smith*.

EXCHANGE FLAGS. Laid out in 1803 as a meeting place for mer-chants, this square was the centre around which Liverpool's office district developed, and remained its commercial heart for over a century. The present EXCHANGE BUILDINGS, enclosing three sides of the Flags, are by *Gunton & Gunton*.* First phase opened 1939; completed 1955. Artificial stone on

---

* They occupy the site of two earlier Exchanges. The first – of 1803–8 by *John Foster Sen.*, possibly with *James Wyatt* – echoed the N portico of Wyatt's Town Hall exten-sion, forming a noble Neoclassical quadrangle. It was replaced, 1863–70, with a florid French Renaissance building by *T.H. Wyatt*.

Liverpool, Exchange Buildings (demolished), and Nelson's Monument.
Early C19 lithograph by W. Crane, after Robert Barrow

a steel frame, stripped classical, lumpish and ill-proportioned.
Reliefs by *Edmund C. Thompson* and *George T. Capstick* over
entrances. In the centre of the N side, bronze WAR MEMORIAL,
1924, by *Joseph Phillips*. Moved here from the old Exchange
News Room, 1953, and placed between piers supporting stone
sculptures by *Siegfried Charoux*.

In the middle, the imposing and dramatic NELSON MON-
UMENT, designed 1807–8 by *Matthew Cotes Wyatt*, executed in
bronze by *Richard Westmacott*, and unveiled 1813. Cylindrical
plinth with four battle reliefs, separated by life-size nude male
captives in chains – memorable works of Romanticism. Above,
the apotheosis of the hero of Trafalgar, with a skeletal figure of
Death emerging from under a captured flag. The contributions
of Wyatt and Westmacott are difficult to disentangle. Wyatt
claimed that his design was no 'embryo brought to maturity
by another', but conceded that his ideas for the reliefs, at least,
were very sketchy.

EXCHANGE STREET EAST. No. 26, former Royal Exchange
Assurance, by *Willink & Dod*, 1927. Portland stone, restrainedly
classical. Converted into flats, with a penthouse added, 1990s.
Next door, MASON'S BUILDING, offices, by *John Cunningham*, c. 1866. Renaissance style, with much carving. The *Building News* was not impressed: 'a great deal of showy but
commonplace ornament . . . the whole having rather the effect
of the regulation cement front of a gin-palace translated into
stone'.

FENWICK STREET. The CORN EXCHANGE, 1953–9, by *H.
Hinchliffe Davies*, succeeds earlier corn exchanges on the site
by *John Foster Sen.* and *James A. Picton*. Probably the most
imaginative of Liverpool's early post-war office buildings. A
podium – three storeys in Drury Lane, reducing to two in
Fenwick Street because of the sloping site – housed the news

room and trading floor. Set back above is a seven-storey block, I-plan, with cylindrical tank rooms on the roof. It was intended to be higher. Ends subtly canted, with windows in a central, vertical panel. Stair windows correspond with the half landings, making a chequerboard pattern. Cladding of Portland stone, with grey-green faience panels between windows. Window frames recently replaced with uPVC.

FLEET STREET. Near the NW end, opposite Roe Alley, an early C19 warehouse (now flats); on the opposite side, just above Concert Square, Vanilla Factory: glass-fronted new-build offices by *ShedKM*, 2003–5. Next door, the BAA BAR, an industrial building of 1897, converted in 1991 by *Design Shed*. Steel supports of a type used in motorway construction hold up the façade at ground-floor level.

FONTENOY STREET. *See* pp. 310 and 320.

GREAT CROSSHALL STREET. Near the E end, N side, the former ST JOHN'S NATIONAL SCHOOL, 1850, by *John Hay*. First floor with trefoil-headed arcade enclosing paired lancets. Ground floor originally arcaded, filled in by *William Culshaw*, 1854. Infants', boys' and girls' classrooms were on separate floors, reached by a spiral stair in a (demolished) rear turret.

GREAT GEORGE PLACE. Former NORTH AND SOUTH WALES BANK, Gothic, *c.* 1878. Could it be by *J.P. Seddon*, who designed the bank's Birkenhead branch around the same time? Tall and narrow, it looks even more so now all its neighbours have been demolished. Square- and trefoil-headed windows.

GREAT GEORGE SQUARE. Laid out *c.* 1800 with the active involvement of the Council, built up by 1836. Once the grandest of Liverpool's residential squares, it was bombed in the Second World War and only a handful of C19 houses survive. Originally each side was a unified terrace with central pediment.

HANOVER STREET. In the C18 Hanover Street was lined with the substantial houses of merchants. The Hanover Hotel at the corner of Fleet Street is apparently a much-altered survival from this period. Opposite, the former CRANE BUILDING (now Hanover House), 1913–15, by *Walter Aubrey Thomas*. Built as a store selling musical instruments, it is one of the most striking structures of its date in the city. Buff-coloured terracotta is used for the richly decorated lower floors, the capitals of the giant pilasters, and the massive cornice. These areas of decoration are separated by large expanses of plain wall, following American precedents for the treatment of tall buildings. On Hanover Street, the red brick pilasters emerge in their upper parts to become piers, a motif derived from St George's Hall. Inside, a theatre with Neoclassical auditorium. CHURCH HOUSE, corner of Paradise Street, is by *George Enoch Grayson*, 1885. The r. half was originally an institute for the Mersey Mission to Seamen, the l. half a temperance pub. Blue, yellow and red brick under a red-tiled roof, with round-arched windows to the second floor and much moulded brick decoration. Opposite, No. 12, a splendid curved block by

Edmund Kirby in hot red brick and terracotta from the *Ruabon Terracotta Works*. Built 1889–90 for Eills & Co., shipowners and merchants, with ground-floor offices and warehousing above; an earlier warehouse of 1863 is incorporated round the corner in Argyle Street. Big round-arched windows to the ground floor, three-light windows to the first and second floors, and four-light windows on top. The detail is somewhere between Gothic and Early Renaissance. The piers between the windows extend above the openwork parapet as tall chimneys. A sensitive refurbishment in the 1990s moved the entrance to the inner courtyard, reached via the former cartway in Duke Street. On the other corner of Duke Street a reconstruction, 2005, of an 1840s stuccoed classical block, curved in plan, with pilasters to the upper floors.

Hanover Street falls within the Paradise Street Development Area (*see* p. 258), and will be the scene of much new building from 2005. Architects at work or due to be employed are *Austin-Smith:Lord*, *BDP*, *Brock Carmichael*, *CZWG* (at the corner of School Lane), *Page & Park* and *Haworth Tompkins*.

HATTON GARDEN. KINGSWAY HOUSE, 1965–7, by *Derek Stephenson & Partners*, a large office block incorporating first-floor elevated walkways, as favoured by the 1965 Liverpool City Centre Plan. On the opposite side, the former PARCEL SORTING OFFICE, 1933–4, worked on by a succession of Office of Works architects, *C.P. Wilkinson*, *C.J. Mole* and finally *J. Bradley*. Large, handsome Neo-Georgian in red brick, with a screen of sturdy Greek Doric columns in grey granite. Recently converted into flats by *Falconer Chester*, who added the glazed penthouse.

HOUGHTON STREET. The JOHN LEWIS PARTNERSHIP, formerly George Henry Lee's, occupies a disparate group of buildings. The block on the corner with Basnett Street, dated 1897, was apparently reconstructed in 1908 to designs by *Henry Hartley*, with marble pilasters framing the display windows. Attractive plasterwork survives inside. In 1910 the façade was doubled along Basnett Street as far as Leigh Street, and in 1928 a more ambitious addition by *Gunton & Gunton* of London was built on the corner of Houghton Lane. Of Portland stone with giant Ionic columns, it is adapted from Selfridge's in London, which took over Lee's in 1919. It was intended that more of the store would be rebuilt to this pattern. For John Lewis' building on the corner of Basnett Street and Church Street, *see* Church Street.

JAMES STREET. The former NATIONAL BANK, *T. Arnold Ashworth & Sons*, *c.* 1920. Big, American-influenced classical, in Portland stone, coarser than the work of other Liverpool exponents of this style. Columned banking hall now a bar, upper floors now flats. No. 30, Albion House, was built as the WHITE STAR LINE, 1895–8, by *Norman Shaw*, with *James F. Doyle* superintending construction. This mighty eight-storey block brought a new scale to Liverpool's commercial architecture. The *Architectural Review* thought it made 'everything round it look little and mean', and it still holds its own among its big neighbours. The composition is a development of Shaw's New Scotland Yard, London (1888–90), but the Strand elevation also echoes the tall gabled warehouses then typical of this dockside street. Granite ashlar lower floors, rustication round the basement windows. The upper floors, as at New Scotland Yard, are banded with red brick and Portland stone. Colour aside, the absence of ornament is notable: apart from wrought-iron balconies to the second floor and a continuous fifth-floor balcony, there are few projections from the cliff-like walls. The gable was crowned with a complicated aedicule, not rebuilt after war damage; a large clock projecting from the SW turret was removed at the same time. Entrance in James Street, with blocked surround and broken pediment. Inside, Shaw's ground-floor general office was severely functional: exposed cast-iron stanchions and girders, boldly riveted, supported a fireproof ceiling of terracotta panels made by *J.C. Edwards* of Ruabon. This remarkable interior survives, obscured by partitions and suspended ceilings. For James Street Station, *see* p. 305.

LIME STREET. Starting at the N end, the EMPIRE THEATRE in its present form is by *W. & T.R. Milburn, c.* 1925. Portland stone façade with paired giant Ionic columns. Auditorium with graceful classical plasterwork. Rounding the corner into London Road, a thoroughly feeble glazed extension, 2002. On the S side of the station (*see* p. 304), CONCOURSE HOUSE, a thirteen-storey tower of 1967–8 by *R. Seifert & Partners*, with a curved row of single-storey shops serving as a podium. In 2005 there are plans for a twenty-nine-storey, oval-plan tower by *Glenn Howells Architects* to replace it. On the corner of Skelhorne Street, the CROWN HOTEL, probably remodelled *c.* 1905. Interior with lush plaster ceiling and beaten-copper bar front. Opposite, rounding the corner into Elliot Street, the disused former FORUM CINEMA by *William R. Glen*, opened 1931. Sleek Portland stone façade with almost no decoration, subtly modelled in advancing and receding planes. Back on the E side, the former FUTURIST CINEMA, now also disused. Built as the City Picture House, 1912, by *Chadwick & Watson* of Leeds, subsequently altered. At the corner of Copperas Hill, THE VINES, a large and riotously Baroque pub of 1907 by *Walter W. Thomas*, for the brewer Robert Cain. Ground floor of polished red granite with bow windows (the brilliant-cut panes mostly replaced with etched copies) and monstrously elongated keystones above the doors. Three big Dutch-looking gables and a high cylindrical corner tower, capped with a dome and a squat little obelisk. Inside, the sumptuous fittings include plaster reliefs by the *Bromsgrove Guild* and *Gustave Hiller*.

LORD STREET. Laid out in 1668 by the 3rd Lord Molyneux. The S side, largely destroyed in the Second World War, was rebuilt in the 1950s with steel-framed, mostly Portland stone-faced blocks, none very exciting. At the corners of South John Street these are giving way, 2005, to new shops in connection with the

Paradise Street Development Area (*see* p. 258). MERCHANTS COURT, 1957–60, by *Quiggin & Gee*, has green marble columns on the ground floor and a wavy balcony to Derby Square. On the N side, some older survivors. At the corner of Dorans Lane, the former VENICE CHAMBERS, with a Gothic parapet and yellow and white glazed brickwork in lozenge patterns *à la* Doge's Palace, 1882, by *Edmund Kirby*. The Dorans Lane elevation has projecting windows between glazed brick piers. At Nos. 81–89 a more ambitious Italian Gothic building of 1901 by *Walter Aubrey Thomas*. Striped façade of red and white stone, composed of three giant round arches, with a band of small pointed windows above. It resembles three bays of the arcade and triforium of a church, with the middle bay slightly wider. Above, however, each bay has its own gable. The arches enclose full-width mullioned-and-transomed windows, recessed in the centre to form a giant niche. This originally led to a shopping arcade.

MATHEW STREET. Dominated by CAVERN WALKS, a large shopping centre with offices above, 1982–4, by *David Backhouse*. The façades use Victorian-derived materials and motifs, and have terracotta decoration round the entrances by *Cynthia Lennon*. Side elevations more original, with large areas of glazing sloping outwards towards the bottom. Inside, an atrium, octagonal at ground level, narrowing and becoming square as it rises through seven floors: an unusual and exciting space, let down by pseudo-Victorian decorative touches. The present Cavern Club in the basement is a rebuilding of the demolished original, made famous in the early 1960s by The Beatles. The dreadful life-size bronze SCULPTURE of them in the atrium, *c.* 1984, is by *John Doubleday*. Mathew Street has more SCULPTURES on the same theme: From Us to You, 1984, by *David Hughes*, above the doorway of No. 31; Carl Gustav Jung (whose 1927 description of Liverpool as 'the pool of life' has been taken as a prediction of the city's role in 1960s pop culture) by *Johnathon Drabkin*, set into the wall of No. 18; Four Lads Who Shook the World, 1974, by *Arthur Dooley* high up at the N end; and, close to the last named, John Lennon, *c.* 1996, by *David Webster*. These are striking as evidence of a cult.

Here and in adjoining streets was a centre of the fruit and provision trade, and there is a cluster of warehouses from the first half of the C19. No. 18 on the corner of Rainford Square, now a pub, was apparently in existence by 1836. Opposite, a smaller but more handsome warehouse, with a pediment to Mathew Street and a curved façade to Temple Court, with good ashlar doorcases and large office windows. Perhaps *c.* 1840. Another similar warehouse at No. 23 (and two more in Temple Court, perhaps 1830s). Nos. 20–22, a warehouse with blind Gothic tracery in the gable, and attached offices, is late C19 by *Grayson & Ould*.

NELSON STREET. Early C19 houses on the NW side. The very large CHINESE ARCH, completed 2000, was designed and made in China by the *Shanghai Linyi Garden Building Co. Ltd* and erected here by Chinese craftspeople. It marks the long association of this area with the Chinese, who began to settle here at least a century ago.

NORTH JOHN STREET. At the corner of Dale Street, the former
91 ROYAL INSURANCE head office, 1896–1903, won in competition by *James F. Doyle*. The assessor was *Norman Shaw*, subsequently retained as 'advisory architect', though his contribution is unclear. Sumptuous Neo-Baroque on the grandest scale. Long façade to North John Street, with off-centre entrance under a gold-domed tower. High and narrow gabled façade with angle turrets to Dale Street – a composition derived from Shaw's White Star Line building and New Scotland Yard. Second-floor frieze by *C.J. Allen*, illustrating the theme of insurance. Despite appearances, the massive Portland stone walls (above an impressive basement of rugged grey granite) are not load-bearing: floors and chimneys are carried by a virtually self-supporting steel frame, one of the earliest in Britain. This allows the former General Office, which fills most of the ground floor, to be completely free of columns. This, and the tunnel-vaulted Board Room (on the first floor, overlooking Dale Street) have neo-late C17 stucco decoration. Opposite, the windowless cliff of a VENTILATING STATION for the Mersey Tunnel, 1931–4, by *Herbert J. Rowse* (*see* p. 306). Nos. 37–45, E side, are CENTRAL BUILDINGS, 1884, a huge office block by *Thomas C. Clarke*. Twenty-bay front, the lower part a giant Doric colonnade of polished granite. Ground floor and basement, recessed behind, are completely glazed. Corner towers were intended, and a roof incorporating further floors, but as it stands the façade ends abruptly at the main cornice.

The W side of North John Street from Cook Street to Lord Street is representative of the commercial street architecture of 1820s–40s Liverpool. More such blocks – four storeys, usually stuccoed, with rounded corners – survived in the central area until the Second World War. The one at the corner of Cook Street has a rainwater head dated 1828; Nos. 24–26, HARRINGTON CHAMBERS, complete this block, with giant pilasters and shopfronts below. Nos. 28–40 form a single, almost symmetrical composition, elaborately stuccoed. Central attached Corinthian portico, with pilasters in the middle of each wing. An inscription inside the r. part, Marldon Chambers, says this was built in 1841 – a likely date for the entire façade – and remodelled in 1884. The attractive doorway with Renaissance carving must belong to the remodelling.

OLD CHURCH YARD. MERSEY CHAMBERS is by *G.E. Grayson*, *c*. 1880. Italianate, with round-arched windows and a higher central feature. More individual rear elevation to Covent Garden, with projecting windows partly of cast iron, set between yellow glazed-brick piers. Inside, glass-roofed court and fine cast-iron staircase. Board Room of *c*. 1920, classical in the Liverpool manner of this period, with oak panelling incorporating a First World War memorial.

OLD HALL STREET. One of the seven ancient streets. Near the S end, E side, the ALBANY BUILDING, 1856–8, an exceptionally large speculative office block by *J.K. Colling*, for the banker R.C. Naylor; converted to flats 2004–5. Imposing palazzo of red brick, dressed with sandstone and polished granite, and with much stylised foliage carving, a speciality of the architect. *The Builder* summed up: 'a very free treatment of the Renaissance, with Arabesque variations'. Side elevations plainer, with cast-iron hoists serving basement storage areas. Splendid gates on Old Hall Street, designed to look like wrought iron, but cast locally by *Rankin's Union Foundry*. They lead via a tunnel-vaulted passage with granite columns and elaborate plasterwork to a central courtyard. Within the long side blocks the former offices are ranged on either side of broad spine corridors, pierced at intervals by light wells. Next door, the former COTTON EXCHANGE by *Matear & Simon*, 1905–6. The front was demolished in 1967, an unforgivable act of vandalism. It was a magnificent classical design with Baroque angle towers, the architectural embodiment of the cotton trade, central to Liverpool's prosperity. Its replacement is a thoroughly unremarkable block of 1967–9 by *Newton-Dawson, Forbes & Tate*. The sides and rear of Matear & Simon's building, largely offices let to cotton traders, survive more or less unaltered. The six-storey façade to Edmund Street is notable, composed of classically detailed cast-iron panels decorated with wreaths, made by *Macfarlane's* of Glasgow. They incorporate very large windows designed to admit the maximum of N light, necessary for examining cotton samples. Bixteth Street elevation of Portland stone, and more conventional; that to Ormond Street of brick. Immediately behind the front was the main exchange hall. This too was demolished in 1967, creating an open courtyard, but much of the colonnade that originally surrounded the trading floor survives behind the new elevations. The columns are superb monoliths of beautiful larvikite, quarried in Norway and polished in Aberdeen before being shipped to Liverpool. On the pavement at the corner of Old Hall Street and Edmund Street, a colossal STATUE representing the Mersey, by *William Birnie Rhind*, from the top of one of Matear & Simon's towers. In the courtyard, statues of Navigation and Commerce by *Rhind*, also from the façade, and the Liverpool Cotton Association WAR MEMORIAL, an advancing infantryman in bronze by *Derwent Wood*, 1921, originally on a tall pedestal in front of the building.

Nos. 21–23 are CITY BUILDINGS, remodelled by *Frederick G. Fraser, c.* 1908. He inserted large iron-framed windows to suit cotton traders attracted by the new Exchange. Nos. 25–31, between Fazackerley Street and Union Street, a former Midland Bank, by *Woolfall & Eccles*, 1925. Portland stone, classical, with round inset corners. (In UNION STREET itself, No. 7, a two-bay brick house of *c.* 1760, a survivor from before mid-C19 commercial redevelopment.) On the opposite corner of Union Street, CITY EXCHANGE, by *KKA*, completed 2001. A large glass-walled concourse with a space-frame roof and split-level interior, giving access to two earlier buildings, the Royal Insurance headquarters, now ROYAL & SUN ALLIANCE, by

Tripe & Wakeham, 1972–6, and the LIVERPOOL DAILY POST AND ECHO, by *Farmer & Dark*, 1970–4. The former is a massive irregular stepped pyramid, thirteen storeys with three car-parking levels below, faced with ribbed panels of yellow-brown concrete. Narrow slit windows give it a fortress-like air. At pavement level its blank walls give little pleasure, but from a distance – and especially from the river – its rugged bulk and distinctive silhouette contribute greatly to the skyline. As the monumentally self-important head office of a local insurance company, it follows worthily in the tradition of the Royal Liver Building. Inside, open-plan offices surround a central lift core. Impressive spaces for staff dining, recreation, etc., including a double-height sports hall entirely lined with wych-elm. Panelling in various woods designed by *Lyle Ellard*, some removed during refurbishment. The Post and Echo is more conventional, a speculative office tower on a podium containing newspaper accommodation. Both buildings were designed with elevated walkways, in accordance with the 1965 City Centre Plan (*see* p. 256).

No. 100 is the SIR JOHN MOORES BUILDING for Littlewoods, designed by *Littlewoods Department of Architecture & Planning (W.L. Stevenson)* and put up in two phases from 1962. Then Liverpool's highest multi-storey office block, it set the scale for much of the surrounding rebuilding. In front, a large aluminium sculpture by *Patrick Glyn Heesom*, the 1965 winner of a competition held by Littlewood's. Opposite, No. 105, completed 2004, a twenty-eight-storey apartment tower, plus hotel and health club, designed by *Abbey Holford Rowe*; the hotel has an impressive balconied atrium at its core. No. 101, by the same, is offices, and a further office tower is planned to complete the scheme. Part of the site was occupied from *c.* 1790 by a basin of the Leeds & Liverpool Canal, and a brick canal building of *c.* 1800 remains (reconstructed) in front of the new hotel. It was originally one of a pair, flanking the entrance to Mr Clark's wharfside coalyard.

PARADISE STREET. CHANCERY HOUSE, 1899, by *James Strong* of Walker & Strong, was built as the Gordon Smith Institute for Seamen, with library, reading room and assembly hall for sailors ashore. Red brick and terracotta, with red sandstone dressings. Blind Gothic tracery above the windows, and three big stepped gables. Converted into offices by *Brock Carmichael Associates*, 1980–2. (SE of here, just the plan of C18 Cleveland Square survives.) N of Hanover Street, Paradise Street is due to be largely rebuilt as a pedestrianised boulevard at the heart of the Paradise Street Development Area (*see* p. 258).

PARLIAMENT STREET. Here is the most impressive surviving range of late C19 warehouses in the central area. They are huge and very plain, seven storeys high, of red brick, with blue brick around the small windows and the towering loading bays. To the N in WATKINSON STREET and BRIDGEWATER STREET, further huge brick warehouses of the 1870s, etc.

ı PIER HEAD. The buildings at the Pier Head (more properly George's Pier Head) occupy the site of George's Dock, opened in 1771 and obsolete by the end of the C19. In 1899 the Corporation drained it and extended Water Street and Brunswick Street across it, creating three superb sites for new buildings fronting the river. The sites varied in shape, and no restrictions were imposed to ensure the buildings formed a coherent group: the result is an amazingly disparate trio. In the early C20 the Pier Head was a bustling interchange for trains, trams, ferries and ocean liners, and the buildings were conceived as landmarks, symbols of maritime Liverpool at the height of its prosperity and self-confidence. As Pevsner wrote in 1969, 'They represent the great Edwardian Imperial optimism and might indeed stand at Durban or Hong Kong just as naturally as at Liverpool.'

First came the offices of the MERSEY DOCKS AND HARBOUR BOARD (MDHB, now the Port of Liverpool Building) at the S end, 1903–7. *Briggs & Wolstenholme*, with *Hobbs & Thornely*, won a local competition in 1900, then radically reworked their design. Steel encased in concrete, with a facing of Portland stone. A very large rectangular block, proudly Baroque, with polygonal corner turrets crowned by stone cupolas. These originally had lanterns on top. In the centre, a much bigger, copper-covered dome, on a high drum with coupled columns and pedimented aedicules. It was added at the last minute to make the design more imposing, and gives a look of Brumwell Thomas' Belfast City Hall. The riverside front has a rounded pediment at each end and a triangular one over the entrance. The top floor above the cornice, a later alteration, injures the proportions. Above and around the entrance, sculptures by *C.J. Allen*, including weathered statues of Commerce and Industry. Corridors from here and the NE and SE corners form a Y-plan, meeting in a lofty octagonal hall, overlooked by galleries on each floor. This is directly under the great central dome, hidden by a lower domed ceiling. In what is effectively a secular cathedral of commerce, this hall takes the place of the crossing, and the quasi-ecclesiastical impression is reinforced by the words of Psalm 107, 'They that go down to the Sea in ships . . .', inscribed within the lowest tier of arches. Off the E side, a semicircular staircase, open to the hall. Stained glass on the stairs and landings, by *George Wragge* of Salford, displays the arms of British colonies and dominions. The same firm supplied the decorative metalwork inside and out.

In 1906 the site at the N end was acquired by the Royal Liver Friendly Society for its new headquarters. The ROYAL LIVER BUILDING, 1908–11, by *Walter Aubrey Thomas*, is perhaps the most extraordinary office block of its date in the country. It is almost certainly also the tallest, and was referred to as a skyscraper in the contemporary press. Far bigger than was necessary for the Society's accommodation, it provided abundant lettable space, as well as being an advertisement to a worldwide public. It consists of an oblong block orientated W–E, eight storeys high to the main cornice. Piled on top are two further storeys with corner domes, and two extravagant clock towers w and e that reach 295 ft (90 metres) above the pavement. The structure is of reinforced concrete faced with granite cladding. The style is impossible to label. The round-arched windows and the short columns below the main cornice recall Louis Sullivan's Auditorium Building of 1886–9 in Chicago. Pevsner detected faintly Byzantine motifs in the towers, which also seem to have echoes of Hawksmoor's London churches, while the semicircular porch facing the river is more straightforwardly Baroque. A n–s corridor divides the building, with light wells on each side. Originally lined with white glazed brick, these were refaced with curtain glazing during refurbishment in 1977–82 by *Arup Associates*. The two giant Liver birds, symbols of the Friendly Society which add a surreal flourish to the clock towers, are of sheet copper (originally gilded) on steel armatures. They were made by the *Bromsgrove Guild*.

The middle site was acquired in 1914 by the Cunard Steamship Co. for its head office. The CUNARD BUILDING, completed 1916, has generally been described as the work of the local firm *Willink & Thicknesse*, with *Arthur J. Davis* of *Mewès & Davis* as consultant. However, recently discovered drawings, apparently by Davis, show that the design had been brought close to its final form well before the contract with Willink & Thicknesse was signed. The palazzo shape and broadly Italian Renaissance style – comparable with the work of Americans such as McKim, Mead & White – were chosen to contrast with the discordant buildings on either side, rather than attempt to reconcile them. The structure is again of reinforced concrete, clad in Portland stone. The stonework, particularly the rustication, was designed to be enhanced by the inevitable accumulation of soot, but cleaning has evened out the intended contrast of light and dark. Frieze with shields of First World War allies, carved by *E.O. Griffith*; models for the corner eagles supplied by *C.J. Allen*. Those parts occupied by Cunard served both as headquarters and as a passenger terminal. The w entrance led to the top-lit public office, with first-class passengers' lounge adjoining. Other classes were accommodated in the basement along with baggage handling and storage. A stately marble-lined corridor with Doric columns links the n and s entrances, giving access to lifts and stairs.

e of the former MDHB offices is the GEORGE'S DOCK VENTILATION AND CONTROL STATION, the most ambitious of the buildings for the first Mersey road tunnel by *Herbert J. Rowse* (see p. 306). The design, approved in 1932, shares the streamlined, Art Deco character of the other tunnel structures. Reconstructed in 1951–2 by *Rowse* after war damage. It contains offices, and huge fans that extract foul air and force clean air in. Portland stone-faced, with notable sculptures by *Edmund C. Thompson*, assisted by *George T. Capstick*. On the w front, a figure with helmet and goggles represents Speed, and black basalt statues of Night and Day in niches allude to the ever-open tunnel; on the n and s fronts, four panels illustrate

Civil Engineering, Construction, Architecture and Decoration.
s across Mann Island (once an island amidst docks) is the brick
pump house of the Mersey Railway tunnel, *c.* 1885, by *Grayson
& Ould.*

The Pier Head became a favoured location for public MON-
UMENTS. At the N end in St Nicholas Place, the MEMORIAL
TO THE HEROES OF THE MARINE ENGINE ROOM, by   110
William Goscombe John, unveiled 1916. Conceived as a monument to the engineers of the *Titanic,* it is a granite obelisk
topped by a gilded flame. At the corners, nude figures sym-
bolizing Earth, Air, Fire and Water emerge from a background
of stylized waves. By contrast, on the W and E sides, two pairs
of engineers are portrayed with striking naturalism. In British
public sculpture this is an exceptionally early monument to the
heroic working man. Equestrian bronze STATUE of Edward
VII in the middle of the Pier Head, also by *John,* placed here
in 1921. Directly in front of the Cunard Building, the CUNARD
WAR MEMORIAL, a rostral column by *Arthur J. Davis* with
a nude Victory in bronze by *Henry Pegram,* unveiled 1921. W
of the former MDHB offices, the bronze ALFRED JONES
MEMORIAL, by *George Frampton,* unveiled 1913. Jones was a
shipowner and founder of the Liverpool School of Tropical
Medicine. His likeness is confined to a medallion on the plinth,
while flanking statues of Research and the Fruits of Industry
represent his achievements allegorically. On top, a female
figure in medieval dress carrying a ship symbolises Liverpool.
SW, the MERCHANT NAVY WAR MEMORIAL, unveiled 1952;
a column like a lighthouse, in a semicircular enclosure.
Designed by *Stanley H. Smith* and *Charles F. Blythin,* with
sculpture by *H. Tyson Smith.*

The present landscaping of the open space between the Pier
Head buildings and the river is by *Allies & Morrison,* 1995. The
shabby restaurant overlooking the Mersey belongs to an earlier
remodelling of the area carried out from 1963 by the City
Architect, *Ronald Bradbury.* For the Mersey Ferry Terminal, *see*
p. 276.

THE PLATEAU. *See* St George's Hall, p. 297.

QUEEN SQUARE. The original square no longer exists but its
name survives, attached to the wide, busy road lined with bus
shelters, and to the recent buildings on the N side. The bus shelters and the QUEEN SQUARE CENTRE on the S side, with
conical roof and clock turret, are by *Brock Carmichael Associates,* *c.* 1995. The buildings on the N side were put up from
c. 1995. The MARRIOTT HOTEL by *Falconer Chester,* a round
tower with three wings, is linked to a multi-storey car park by
the same architects, faced with brown and blue brick like a Victorian warehouse. Between is a paved square with a SCULP-
TURE, Unknown Landscape 3, by *Nicholas Pope,* made for the
Liverpool International Garden Festival 1983–4 and re-erected
here 1998. Other new buildings fringing the square are depressingly tawdry.

RAINFORD SQUARE and RAINFORD GARDENS. *See* Button
Street and Mathew Street.

RANELAGH PLACE. The ADELPHI HOTEL (now the Britannia Adelphi) is the successor to two earlier Adelphi hotels, of 1826 and 1876. The latter was bought in 1892 by the Midland Railway Co., who replaced it in 1911–14 with the present building by *Frank Atkinson*. Then regarded as the country's most luxurious hotel outside London, its French-influenced classicism invited comparison with the most sophisticated Continental establishments. Its size and splendour reflect Liverpool's key position in transatlantic travel in the early C20. Unfinished at the outbreak of the First World War, the original plan was never completed. The windows are set almost flush in the smooth, cliff-like walls of Portland stone, with restrained decorative carving by *H.H. Martyn & Co.* This flatness hints at the hidden steel frame. Inside, the main spaces of Atkinson's broadly symmetrical plan survive, but his refined decoration has been much altered. Top-lit CENTRAL COURT lined with pink marble pilasters, glazed screens with French doors opening into large restaurants on either side. Beyond is the HYPOSTYLE HALL, a square space with impressive Empire-style decoration and four massive Ionic columns supporting the ceiling; beyond this originally lay the open-air Fountain Court, surrounded on three sides by terraces under vaulted ceilings. The Fountain Court was to have been enclosed on its fourth side by a ballroom block, but this was never built.

RANELAGH STREET. Next to the Lyceum, LIVERPOOL CENTRAL, a complex of shops above an underground station of the Merseyrail network (*see* p. 305). Designed by *Edmund Percy Scherrer & Hicks* and completed *c.* 1984; refaced 2001 by the *Owen Ellis Partnership*, who also redesigned the glazed roof. Street elevations rendered and painted white, with large areas of glass framed by steelwork. Opposite, No. 19 is a tall, narrow, polychrome Gothic shop dated 1868. Next door to this, turning the corner of Cases Street, a handsome classical stucco block with giant pilasters, 1843, by *William Culshaw*. The MIDLAND HOTEL on the other corner looks mid-C19, but has a rich pub front of *c.* 1900. Next door, the CENTRAL HOTEL bears the date 1675, for which there seems no justification, though its origins go back further than 1887, the other date on the façade. Probably converted from pub to hotel in response to the opening of Central Station in 1874. Interior 1970s Neo-Victorian, incorporating genuine C19 woodwork and brilliant-cut mirrors.

On the corner of Renshaw Street is LEWIS'S department store. The present building, designed 1947 by *Gerald de Courcy Fraser* and carried out by *Fraser, Sons & Geary*, replaced Lewis's previous store, also by *Fraser* and put up in stages 1910–23, which was bombed in 1941. Part of the earlier façade survives at the E end of the Renshaw Street elevation: Portland stone, eight storeys, with slim red granite columns dividing the windows. The post-war rebuilding is also Portland stone, and to the same height. The divisions echo those of the older build-ing, but the style is a stripped-down classicism. Above the former main entrance at the corner, a giant bronze STATUE by *Jacob Epstein*. A nude male figure, striding forward purposefully on the jutting prow of a ship, it dates from 1954–6 and symbolizes Liverpool's resurgence after the war years. Below, three lively relief panels in *ciment fondu*, also by Epstein and made in 1955, show scenes of childhood. Inside, the former cafeteria on the fifth floor (no longer accessible) has a huge tile mural in Festival of Britain style by *Carter's* of Poole, showing food and crockery.

ROE STREET. ROYAL COURT THEATRE, red brick Art Deco by *James B. Hutchins* of *T. Wainwright & Sons*, 1938.

RUMFORD PLACE. On the E side, RUMFORD COURT, a unique survival of mid-C19 offices in Late Georgian domestic style, arranged round two linked courtyards. The main court may be as early as the 1830s, but the E sides of this and the smaller court are 1869 by *Henry Sumners*, with big bipartite windows under cast-iron lintels. Near the N end, a VENTILATING STATION for the New Quay spur of the Mersey tunnel, by *Herbert J. Rowse*, 1931–4 (*see* p. 306). Two square towers. Alone of the tunnel structures on the Liverpool side it is of brick, with geometrical ornament.

ST JOHN'S GARDENS. The C18 Gothic Revival church of St John, 1775–84, possibly by *Timothy Lightoler*, was demolished in 1899, and its extensive churchyard laid out as St John's Gardens by *Thomas Shelmerdine*. Opened in 1904, they at last provided the long-envisaged formal public space adjacent to St George's Hall. Shelmerdine's surrounding walls in debased classical style (now missing their railings) contrast unhappily with the Hall and the buildings in William Brown Street, but the Late Victorian and Edwardian SCULPTURE within is of exceptional interest. Here leading sculptors were employed to create 'Liverpool's al fresco Valhalla'. At the NE corner is William Rathbone, by *George Frampton*, 1899–1900, with reliefs illustrating his philanthropic work. Frampton designed the plinth incorporating a bench. Continuing clockwise: Sir Arthur Bower Forwood, 1903, also *Frampton*; Monsignor James Nugent, 1905, by *F. W. Pomeroy*; Canon T. Major Lester, 1907, *Frampton* again; and Alexander Balfour, by *A. Bruce Joy*, 1889 (erected in St John's churchyard before the gardens were formed). The unremarkable grey granite plinth is by *Alfred Waterhouse*. In the middle are the Gladstone Memorial, by *Thomas Brock*, unveiled 1904, and the lively King's Liverpool Regiment Memorial, by *W. Goscombe John*, 1905: Britannia presides, with soldiers in C17 and early C20 dress below, and a vigorous figure of an C18 drummer boy.

ST JOHN'S PRECINCT. By *James A. Roberts* of Birmingham, but much altered. Permission was given in 1962 and it opened in stages from 1970. It combines a covered market, shops on two levels, a hotel and a multi-storey car park, and covers *c.* 6.2 acres (2.5 hectares). The sloping site was previously occupied by small streets surrounding the old St John's Market, a very large and severely functional building by *John Foster Jun.*, opened in 1822. The precinct is a bleak and brutal affair, monolithic, inward-looking, and awkwardly related to the different levels of adjoining streets. The side facing Lime Street and St George's Place is truly disastrous, failing to establish any coherent relationship with the s portico of St George's Hall, and presenting an off-putting barrier in the form of access ramps and a sunken roadway. The dominant feature – also dominating much of the city centre – is the so-called Beacon, over 450 ft (137 metres) high, really a giant chimney for the boilers. It was apparently modelled on the Euromast at Rotterdam. The revolving restaurant near the top was converted into a radio station *c.* 1999, and the metal structure above, triangular in plan, added to carry advertising. Earlier 1990s alterations, by *Bradshaw, Rowse & Harker*, aimed to give a friendlier look: clumsy external staircases and a ballroom on top of the car park were demolished, and large parts clad in decorative brick and reflective glass. The strong horizontals were broken up by little gables, and brightly coloured metal pediments introduced above the entrances. Whatever interest Roberts' design may have had as an example of heroically scaled Modernism was lost through this prettification.

St John's Lane. The former Pearl Life Assurance, 1896–8, by *Alfred Waterhouse*. Stone, with an octagonal corner tower and spire, adapted from the architect's National Liberal Club in London. Part of the ground-floor interior survives, with colourful *Burmantofts* faience.

Seel Street. Fragmented terraces of the 1790s and *c.* 1800, some with pedimented doorcases, many derelict. On the corner of Slater Street, midway along the s side, a derelict building occupied by watchmakers in the second half of the C19, with generous windows to the former workshops. Further e on the opposite side, at the corner of Back Colquitt Street, a C19 industrial range, imaginatively transformed and extended at the rear by *Austin-Smith:Lord*, 2004–5, to enclose two sides of Art House Square. The new parts are variously faced with glass, brick and render, in planes that overlap or collide at unexpected angles; a slender belvedere rises at one corner. On the corner of Colquitt Street, the former Royal Telephone Exchange, 1939, by the *Office of Works*, of thin Roman bricks with recessed pointing. A well-mannered Modernist design which takes account of its Georgian neighbours. For the former St Peter's church *see* p. 284.

Sir Thomas Street. No. 14, the former City Education Offices, 1897–8, by *Charles E. Deacon*. High, narrow façade in a French late Gothic–early Renaissance style, with much carving. Impressive central staircase enclosing a lift – the original arrangement. Board Room with elaborate Renaissance plasterwork, and a delicately carved chimneypiece (stolen, 2005). No. 20, Minerva Chambers, *c.* 1885. A striking design: a sort of palazzo, but with a very irregular window rhythm. Thin columns rise one above the other from basement to first floor, their proportions more like cast iron than stone. Transoms cut across where the first- and second-floor window arches spring.

SLATER STREET. At the corner of Fleet Street, the former ST ANDREW'S SCHOOLS, a stuccoed classical block of 1818, paid for by the merchant John Gladstone. It provided places for 150 boys and 130 girls. Next door, the simple, pedimented CHARITABLE INSTITUTION, funded by Gladstone and others, which provided free accommodation for Liverpool charities. No. 13, opposite, is a former combined house and warehouse, early C19.

SOUTH JOHN STREET. A main artery of the Paradise Street Development Area (*see* p. 258). Spanned by pedestrian bridges, it will have multi-level shops linked by stairs and escalators.

STANLEY STREET. Nos. 6–20, GRANITE BUILDINGS, *c.* 1882, by *G.E. Grayson*. Built as offices and warehousing for the fruit and provision trade. The façade had three gables, the middle one now lacking. It is entirely of granite, polished, rough, or fitted together in an irregular jigsaw, reminiscent of Jesse Hartley's dock buildings (*see* p. 261). Tripartite windows divided by cylindrical columns. The style is a sort of simplified classicism, perhaps determined by the intractability of the granite. The rear is a complete contrast: the N end has office-type windows but the rest comprises a row of gabled warehouses. Utilitarian white glazed-brick facing.

THE STRAND. As the name indicates, here was the shoreline of the Mersey before land was reclaimed for dock construction. The traffic island in the middle marks the site of the Goree Warehouses, a mighty early C19 arcaded range, demolished following Second World War bomb damage. No. 7, WELLINGTON BUILDINGS, a twelve-storey classical block of *c.* 1923 by *Colin S. Brothers*. BEETHAM PLAZA, built as offices in 1965–7 by *Gotch & Partners*, was converted into apartments by *Brock Carmichael Associates*, completed 2000. Facing the courtyard opening to DRURY LANE, ground-floor restaurant with wavy glass wall. Also an ingenious fountain by *Richard Huws*, completed 1966. Pivoted cups of various sizes, mounted on posts, fill with water until they overbalance, producing random cascades.

SWEETING STREET. BARNED'S BUILDINGS, *c.* 1840, an early purpose-built office block, now flats. Three storeys, with a pedimented centre and classical details. It looks like a terrace of houses, except for the cast-iron hoists indicating the basement was used for warehousing.

TEMPEST HEY. One isolated C19 survivor on the E side, a block with narrow round-arched windows to the ground floor, 1849, by *William Culshaw*. Originally ground-floor offices, with a sales room and storage above. Facing the S end of Tempest Hey, the five-bay, palazzo-style PERCY BUILDINGS, *c.* 1879. The long Eberle Street elevation has huge windows with central cast-iron mullions. Here are the premises of the Liverpool Artists' Club, containing a bronze war memorial of 1919 by *C.J. Allen*.

TEMPLE COURT. *See* Mathew Street and Victoria Street.

TITHEBARN STREET. One of the seven ancient streets. Nos.
7–17, SILKHOUSE COURT, by *Quiggin & Gee*. Designed by
1964, built 1967–70. Fifteen-storey tower with three-storey
corner blocks. Glazing and concrete cladding in alternate
bands. Next door, MERCURY COURT: façadism on a monumental scale. This was originally a hotel and offices above
ground-floor shops fronting Exchange Station, the terminus of
the Lancashire & Yorkshire Railway (closed 1977). The first
station, raised above Tithebarn Street, opened in 1850. In 1882
it was decided to rebuild on a larger scale, level with the street,
and *Henry Shelmerdine* was appointed architect. The two
phases were completed in 1886 and 1888. Shelmerdine's façade
is stone, classical, eighteen bays long, with a higher central
section marking the twin-arched main entrance. (This incorporates a memorial to John Pearson, chairman of the L&YR:
a bronze relief portrait by *F.J. Williamson*, 1890.) Office
complex behind *c.* 1985, by *Kingham Knight Associates*. Opposite, at the corner of Moorfields, two good Victorian pubs: THE
RAILWAY, with stained glass illustrating the 1886 Exchange
Station and its forerunner, and THE LION, mid-C19 with a rich
and well-preserved interior of *c.* 1900. On the N side, at the
corner of Pall Mall, the former BRADFORD HOTEL. Begun
1880s and extended. Italianate, with a little domed corner
turret. (On the E side of Pall Mall, near the junction with Leeds
Street, a very large apartment block by *Falconer Chester*, 2003;
for Pall Mall N of Leeds Street, *see* pp. 485–6.) Nos. 59–61,
dated 1871, were built as a printing and bookbinding factory
with integrated warehousing. Yellow brick; large windows with
cast-iron mullions.
    Further E at the corner of Smithfield Street, a good classi-
cal building, the former COLLEGE OF COMMERCE, 1928–31,
by the City Surveyor, *Albert D. Jenkins*. Brick and Portland
stone. Corner crowned with a sculpture of Neptune in a ship's
prow; reliefs of shipping by *Hooper & Webb*. Extension along
Tithebarn Street by *Ronald Bradbury* completed 1953, another
at the back begun 1965. Attached, and united internally, is the
AVRIL ROBARTS LEARNING RESOURCE CENTRE of Liverpool John Moores University, by *Austin-Smith:Lord*, opened
1998. Curved plan, following the street line. Façade of brick at
each end, glazed in the centre, with a clerestory right across.
Impressive full-height entrance space, with an elegant but
vertiginous steel staircase, lit by deep, circular skylights. The
top-floor reading room has more of these skylights. It is a
mezzanine or deep gallery, overlooking the floor below under
the sweep of the monopitch roof.
TRUEMAN STREET. *See* p. 320.
VICTORIA STREET. Cut through a congested area of narrow
streets and opened in 1868. The W part became the heart of
the fruit and provision trade. Despite losses it remains one
of the best-preserved Victorian streets in the city. The start is
at the W end.

North John Street to Stanley Street: No. 1, N side, Italianate, 1881, by *Cornelius Sherlock*. Next door, FOWLER'S BUILD-INGS, a nine-bay stone palazzo with polychrome brick ware-housing behind, by *J.A. Picton*, 1865–9. Granite columns to the principal floor and curvy, almost Baroque window surrounds above. An odd segmental pediment supporting an urn sits on top of the cornice. After this, Nos. 11–13, built 1926–8 as Lloyds Bank by *Grayson & Barnish*. Handsome five-bay palazzo in grey brick and Portland stone. The former banking hall has giant Ionic columns. Next, VICTORIA BUILDINGS, 1870s, a quiet palazzo with the centre curiously recessed, then No. 21, UNION HOUSE, dated 1882, possibly by *Thomas C. Clarke*. Classical façade with ground-floor colonnade of red granite; contrasting side elevation to Progress Place, with large areas of glazing and exposed cast iron. Entrance vestibule with a plaster frieze illustrating tea shipping, etc., leads to an impressive cast-iron staircase. No. 25, next door, by *W.H. Picton*, 1881. Front block with rusticated granite ground floor, simpler rear part with warehousing.

The S side starts at the corner of North John Street with CENTURY BUILDINGS, 1901, by *Henry Hartley*. Red sand-stone, with a polygonal turret and Renaissance details. Then No. 8, PRODUCE EXCHANGE BUILDING, 1902, by *Henry Shelmerdine*. Big, loosely Baroque, with a little turret in the form of a tempietto. The ground floor of grey granite was a Lancashire & Yorkshire Railway goods depot, and a goods entrance survives at the back in Mathew Street. In the foyer a First World War memorial by *Edward Carter Preston*, a bronze plaque with classical figures. Next door, the former FRUIT EXCHANGE, *c.* 1888, also built as a goods depot, this time for the London & North Western Railway. Converted into an exchange by *J.B. Hutchins*, 1923. Thirteen-bay façade in Flemish Renaissance style with an oriel at each end. After this, a domestic-scaled building with rainwater head dated 1831, a survivor from before the creation of Victoria Street, rounds the corner into Temple Court. Between Temple Court and Stanley Street, COMMERCIAL SALEROOM BUILDINGS, by *James F. Doyle*, opened 1879. It cost £15,000. Queen Anne style, red brick with stone dressings above granite. Three principal storeys, crowned by a frieze carved with swags and a pretty balustraded parapet, and decked out with attractive wrought-iron gates and balconies. The ground floor contained a sale-room for fruit, connected by lifts with basement storerooms.

Stanley Street to Crosshall Street. The N side starts with LISBON BUILDINGS, 1882, and ASHCROFT BUILDINGS, 1883, the latter by *Hoult & Wise*, two exuberant red brick piles with plenty of carved stone decoration. Ashcroft Buildings was put up by James Ashcroft, cabinet-maker and manufacturer of billiard tables, for his showrooms and workshops. The flat roof was used for seasoning timber. Next, between Cumberland Street and Sir Thomas Street, the comparatively sedate former

BANK OF LIVERPOOL, 1881–2, by *George Enoch Grayson*. Classical, stone, with a central pediment and attached columns of polished grey granite. On the s side, between Stanley Street and Sir Thomas Street, are the remains of the former GENERAL POST OFFICE, 1894–9 by *Henry Tanner*, with sculpture by *Edward O. Griffith*. The original design – livelier than Tanner's slightly earlier London GPO in St Martin's le Grand – resembled a Loire château with an eventful skyline of shaped gables, chimneys and pavilion roofs, but the top two floors were removed following war damage. The surviving façades are being incorporated into a shopping centre, 2005 (*see* Whitechapel, p. 343). Against the Stanley Street elevation a SCULPTURE, Eleanor Rigby, a poignant seated female figure in bronze, by *Tommy Steele*, 1982. For the Conservation Centre *see* p. 343.

Crosshall Street to Manchester Street and Whitechapel: The N side begins with the former printing works of Tinling & Co., 1961–3 by *Morter & Dobie*, with a jagged sawtooth arrangement of windows to Crosshall Street. Then CROWN BUILDINGS, 1886, Gothic, with a corner turret, followed by the more characterful JEROME BUILDINGS, 1883, and CARLISLE BUILDINGS, 1885, both by *John Clarke* for H. Rankin, whose Union Foundry close by supplied structural ironwork. Identical above the ground floor, they form a single composition. Red Ruabon brick, with red Runcorn stone dressings and red roof tiles. The most prominent feature is the row of six dormer windows, each with a pyramid-shaped roof. Next, Nos. 75–77, ABBEY BUILDINGS, 1885, Tudor Gothic, with three gables and an oriel over the entrance. All these have warehouse-type rear elevations with loading bays. Finally, a restrained classical block by *F. & G. Holme*, turning the corner into Manchester Street. With Abbey Buildings it was converted into apartments by *Urban Splash Projects*, 1990s. They substituted a minimalist top floor for the original decorative chimneys and dormers.

On the s side the triangular block bounded by Victoria Street, Crosshall Street and Whitechapel was transformed into City Council offices, MILLENNIUM HOUSE, by *Falconer Chester*, 1990s. Some older buildings were replaced, the façades of others retained. The new parts are rather plain and mostly faced with green and buff brick, with a sweeping metal roof at the Crosshall Street end. The C19 frontages are a brick palazzo by *John Clarke*, 1878–9, with matching elevations in Victoria Street and Whitechapel, and the classical IMPERIAL BUILDINGS, 1879, by *E. & H. Shelmerdine*, impressively sited at the sharp corner of these two streets. It is faced with cream terracotta by *Gibbs & Canning*. Female figures representing Commerce and Industry stand sentinel below the corner dome.

WAPPING. A section of the dock road. The mid-C19 stuccoed BALTIC FLEET is a survivor of the dozens of pubs along the dock road that once served the famously thirsty dockers.

WATER STREET. One of the seven ancient streets. It slopes dramatically down to the Pier Head, with tall buildings framing the river view.

Starting next to the Town Hall, the former headquarters of MARTINS BANK (now Barclays), 1927–32, is the masterpiece of *Herbert J. Rowse*, and among the very best inter-war classical buildings in the country. Won in a competition judged by Charles Reilly, the design perfectly expresses the American classicism promoted through Reilly's Liverpool School of Architecture, where Rowse studied before travelling in Canada and the United States. Portland stone on a steel frame, ten storeys, the upper ones set back. Ornament is judiciously concentrated at top and bottom, more emphasis being placed on beauty of proportion than on surface decoration. Interior more opulent. The central entrance leads to a majestic top-lit banking hall, with island counter and vaulted arcades on four sides. Travertine walls, floor and columns (the latter hollow, threaded on to the frame), relieved with gilding, bronze and coloured marbles. Every detail, down to the stationery holders, was overseen by Rowse. Circular corner lobbies, those at the SW and NE giving access to lettable offices on the upper floors. These cantilever out over the banking hall, up to the skylight edges. The eighth-floor board room is like the hall of a Renaissance palace, with large chimneypiece and painted, beamed ceiling. On the roof, penthouses for lift machinery and a flat for the manager, linked by colonnades enclosing a roof garden. Interior and exterior SCULPTURE, illustrating themes of money and the sea, is by *Herbert Tyson Smith*, assisted by *Edmund C. Thomson* and *George Capstick*. The flat, linear style is influenced by the Paris Exhibition of 1925. The main bronze doors are specially notable.

No. 3, a mid-C19 palazzo at the corner of Lower Castle Street, follows the old line of the S side, before 1920s street widening. No. 7, all in grey granite, is of two phases. The Fenwick Street elevation, *c.* 1896 by *Grayson & Ould*, has Celtic interlace ornament in the lunettes. The front block to Water Street was demolished and rebuilt further back *c.* 1933–4 by *Palmer & Holden*, for the National and Provincial Bank. It seems to be modelled on Sanmicheli's Palazzo Pompei, Verona. Of the same date the splendid bronze doors with ferocious lions' heads, and the barrel-vaulted banking hall with Art Deco reliefs. Palmer & Holden's façade follows the building line established by its giant neighbour, INDIA BUILDINGS. *Arnold Thornely* and *Herbert J. Rowse* won the competition for this in 1923 (assessor Giles Gilbert Scott). Completed 1930; extensively damaged by bombing in 1941, and reconstructed under Rowse's supervision. Built for the shipping firm Alfred Holt & Co., it has nine storeys and occupies an entire block, containing offices, shops, a bank (formerly), a post office, and access to the James Street underground station. In scale, combination of functions, and architectural treatment it emulates the most ambitious early C20 American commercial buildings. Steel-framed, cliff-like Portland stone walls, Italian Renaissance detail. Arched entrances in Brunswick Street and Water Street (bronze lamps by the *Bromsgrove Guild*, modelled on those of the Palazzo Strozzi, Florence) open into spacious elevator halls, vaulted and lined with Travertine, linked by a noble tunnel-vaulted arcade of shops through the centre (not part of the competition-winning design). Corner entrances, NE and SE, lead to polygonal lobbies. On the ground floor between them, the former bank (now offices), with an impressive coffered ceiling. Sculpture of Neptune above the Water Street entrance by *Edmund C. Thompson*.

90 No. 14, at the corner of Covent Garden, is ORIEL CHAMBERS, 1864, by *Peter Ellis*. Liverpool's most celebrated Victorian office block, reviled in its day, but elevated to the status of a Modernist icon after bomb damage in 1941 exposed its cast-iron frame and attracted the attention of historians. In 1969 Pevsner described it as 'one of the most remarkable buildings of its date in Europe'. Its façades (basement and three-and-a-half storeys) are mostly of glass. The tall oriel windows with their extremely slender cast-iron frames are individually boxed out ('suggesting the idea that they are trying to escape from the building', according to the *Building News*, 1868) and separated by narrow stone piers with nailhead decoration. The piers end in ungainly pinnacles, and the parapet has battlements and an elaborate central gable, but otherwise few details are based on historical precedent. The dominant motif is the relentlessly repeated oriel, expressing the modular cast-iron frame and leading Charles Reilly to call the building 'a cellular habitation for the human insect'. Desks positioned in these projecting windows received light from top and sides as well as in front. The elevation to Covent Garden was originally almost twice as long: the bomb-damaged N part was replaced in 1959–61 with a sensitive addition by *James & Bywaters*. The C19 offices are arranged on each side of a corridor, aligned with the off-centre entrance on Water Street. The exposed utilitarian H-section stanchions of the frame support fireproof floors of shallow brick vaulting. On the W the offices overlook a courtyard, reached via a passage on the l. of the Water Street façade. The elevations here are even more startling: the glazing is cantilevered out in front of the stanchions in horizontal bands – a pioneering instance of curtain walling.

Next door, NEW ZEALAND HOUSE, c. 1893, by *Walter Aubrey Thomas*, and surprisingly restrained for him. Then RELIANCE HOUSE, 1954–6, by *Morter & Dobie*, tasteful Neo-Georgian. Flanking the side entrance in Tower Gardens are two mosaic panels of shipping, salvaged from the Edwardian Baroque predecessor, bombed 1941. Finally on this side, 92 No. 22, TOWER BUILDINGS, by *Thomas* again, designed 1906, completed by 1910. Steel-framed, clad in white glazed terracotta by *Doultons* above grey granite, with a bizarre mix of Baroque and medieval motifs. Main elevation facing George's Dock Gates symmetrical, with three short towers having square, crenellated angle turrets. The medieval tower of the Stanley family, fortified 1406 and demolished 1819, was here.

Opposite, WEST AFRICA HOUSE, by *Briggs, Wolstenholme & Thornely*, complete by 1920. Another good, American-influenced Portland stone block, this time with Greek rather than Italian Renaissance details.

WATKINSON STREET. *See* Parliament Street.

WHITECHAPEL. At the corner of St John's Lane, the OBSER-VATORY, offices by *Falconer Chester* completed in 2000. Curved, fully glazed façade. For Millennium House, *see* Victoria Street. The CONSERVATION CENTRE was built as the Midland Railway goods warehouse, 1872–4, by *Culshaw & Sumners*, with a matching addition of 1878 facing Peter Street. Converted for the conservation studios of National Museums Liverpool by *Ken Martin, c.* 1995, with minimal changes to the polychrome brick and stone exterior. More decorative than the average warehouse, it nevertheless gives an impression of great strength and solidity. Main façade concave, following Cross-hall Street, with windows in giant round arches. Immense doorways to Whitechapel, Peter Street and Victoria Street, high enough to admit the largest loads. Adjoining, a building with incised Greek ornament, probably 1870s. On the other corner of Peter Street, BENNETT'S BUILDINGS, Tudor Gothic offices (now flats) in red brick with yellow sandstone, 1881–2, by *John Clarke*. On the same side between Sir Thomas Street and Stanley Street, the MET QUARTER, a shopping centre by *Edmund Kirby & Sons* (interiors, *The Design Studio*), due to open in 2006. Part will occupy the shell of the former GPO in Victoria Street (*see* p. 340). The new part is a mostly stone-clad box, with a full height splayed entrance from Whitechapel to the central atrium. Opposite, at the corner of Richmond Street, a large Gothic block of *c.* 1875 by *H.H. Vale*, of stone-dressed white brick, originally with black pointing.

WILLIAMSON SQUARE. The W side was built up by 1765; some C18 houses survive here, considerably altered. Repaving of 2005 incorporates a fountain. For the Playhouse, *see* p. 301.

WOLSTENHOLME SQUARE. The S side was built up by 1765; two altered houses survive at the SW corner. In 2004 a huge ARTWORK, Penelope, by the Cuban-born *Jorge Pardo*, was installed among the central trees: ten illuminated spheres rise high above the square on a tangle of sinuous, brightly coloured stems.

WOOD STREET. Near the NW end, at the corner of Roe Alley, the former premises of the *Liverpool Mercury*, dated 1879. The Italianate yellow brick front part contained offices, the factory-like block at the rear housed the presses. (For Nos. 24–28, *see* Concert Square.) Higher up, above Slater Street, the TEA FACTORY, a former warehouse, the earlier part (adjoining FACT, *see* p. 301) by *Gerald de Courcy Fraser, c.* 1930. Converted into loft apartments and offices over ground-floor bars by *Urban Splash Architects*, 2002. Next to FACT, at the corner of Back Colquitt Street, a fireproof brick warehouse with giant arches enclosing the ground- and first-floor windows, all that remains of the Apothecaries Hall, rebuilt after a fire in 1846. Unsympathetically extended and converted into flats,

2004. At the corner of Colquitt Street, ROYAL HOUSE, a telephone exchange by *Building Design Partnership*, completed 1974.

YORK STREET. At the Duke Street end, altered C18 houses on both sides, some with warehousing. At the SW corner of Henry Street, a large block of late C19 four-storey warehouses in polychrome brick. Adjoining these, at the corner of Argyle Street, a more austere block of particularly impressive warehouses of 1884, by *David Walker*. The strip of wall containing each vertical row of windows is recessed slightly, then corbelled out near the top to bring it flush with the parapet, giving an almost fortified look. Both these blocks were being converted to residential use in 2005.

THE CATHEDRALS AREA AND THE UNIVERSITY OF LIVERPOOL

From the late C18, and especially after 1816, the high ground E of the old town centre was laid out with regular streets and developed as a favoured residential quarter. Much has been destroyed, but enough remains to make this one of the best areas of Late Georgian to Early Victorian terraced housing in any English city. It also acquired churches (mostly demolished) and institutions, many associated with education and medicine. In the late C19 the new University College made its home here, hastening the destruction of the surrounding streets as it expanded after the Second World War, but adding at least some new buildings of value. Liverpool's two C20 cathedrals are a dominant presence, visual anchors that give coherence to a large and architecturally diverse district.

The area is bounded on the N by Copperas Hill, Seymour Street, Monument Place, Pembroke Place and West Derby Street; on the E by Grove Street; on the S by Upper Parliament Street; and on the W by Great George Street, Berry Street and Renshaw Street.

ANGLICAN CATHEDRAL
Upper Duke Street

70   Liverpool Cathedral, the life's work of *Sir Giles Gilbert Scott*, represents the final flowering of the Gothic Revival as a vital, creative movement, and is one of the great buildings of the C20. Construction began in 1904 at the height of the city's prosperity, and finished in 1978 as her long economic decline reached its lowest point. Funded to a large extent by the city's merchant class, it marks the climax of the private patronage of public architecture that flourished in C19 Liverpool.

The diocese was established in 1880. At first, St Peter in Church Street (since demolished) served as pro-cathedral, then in 1884–6 a competition was held for a new building on the site of St John, next to St George's Hall. It was won by *William Emerson* with a domed Gothic design, but the project lapsed in 1888. In 1901 the present magnificent site was selected, a rocky ridge elevated above the city, ensuring that the cathedral dominates the skyline seen from the river. The ridge determines the building's N–S orientation, compass N being ritual W (in the following description N means ritual N, etc.). On the landward side the former quarry of St James's Cemetery (*see* p. 361) adds further drama. A two-stage competition was held, in which architects were asked initially to submit portfolios, including cathedral designs if they wished. At first Gothic was stipulated, but this aroused objections and the condition was dropped. The assessors were G.F. Bodley and Norman Shaw, and out of the 103 entrants they shortlisted five: *Austin & Paley*, *C.A. Nicholson*, *Malcolm Stark*, *W.J. Tapper* and *Scott*, all of whom had submitted Gothic drawings. Among those rejected were *Beresford Pite* (Byzantine), *C.H. Reilly* (classical) and a team effort by *W.R. Lethaby* and others (a strange, organic design, apparently to be built in concrete). Scott – a Roman Catholic – was chosen as winner in 1903, but since he was only twenty-two, the aged *Bodley* was nominated joint architect. Not surprisingly it was an unhappy collaboration. When Bodley died in 1907, Scott became sole architect.

The winning design was for a cruciform cathedral with a six-bay nave and three-bay choir, and a pair of towers over the transepts. There were also subsidiary transepts not projecting beyond the aisles, three to the nave and one to the choir. After the competition the plan was modified, and the Lady Chapel moved from behind the high altar to the SE corner. It was built first and opened in 1910. Amazingly, in 1909–10 Scott decided to redesign the cathedral completely. Work had begun on the choir, so he did not have an entirely free hand, but he made such sweeping changes that virtually nothing of the competition-winning design is recognisable. His governing aim was to replace the twin towers with a bigger, central tower. The crossing of the original transept was too narrow for this, so Scott positioned it further W, with a second transept matching the original one to frame it. This produced a very broad, uninterrupted central space, something which the terms of the competition had called for, and which Scott's winning design failed to provide. He placed the main porches N and S between the transepts. All this left the nave reduced to three bays, the same as the choir. The result is a plan symmetrical about both axes, shaped as much by aesthetics as by function. According to the new scheme construction progressed from E to W over seven decades, though Scott continued to revise and refine the design until his death in 1960: choir and E transepts were consecrated in 1924; under-tower and W transepts were opened in 1941; the final pinnacle of the tower was set in place in 1942; and constructing the nave took from 1948 to 1978.

PUBLIC BUILDINGS

1   Postal Sorting Office
2   Philharmonic Hall
3   Aldham Robarts Learning Resource Centre
    (Liverpool John Moores University)
4   Liverpool John Moores University
    (formerly Notre Dame Convent and
    Teacher Training College)
5   Liverpool Art School
6   Liverpool Institute of Performing Arts (LIPA)
7   Liverpool Community College Arts Centre
8   Blackburne House
9   School for the Blind (former)
10   Royal Infirmary (former)
11   Liverpool Women's Hospital

UNIVERSITY OF LIVERPOOL, SELECTED BUILDINGS

12   Victoria Building
13   Walker Engineering Laboratories
14   Ashton Building
15   Civil Engineering
16   Proudman Oceanographic Laboratory
17   Harold Cohen Library
18   Electrical Engineering and Electronics
19   Biological Sciences
20   Guild of Students
21   Sports Centre
22   Senate House
23   Department of Education and
    Department of Corporate Communications
24   School of Architecture and Building Engineering
25   Department of Civic Design
26   Rendall Building, Roxby Building,
    Modern Languages and the Law School
27   Sydney Jones Library
28   Chatham Buildings and Management School
29   Chadwick Laboratory
30   Chemistry
31   Science Lecture Rooms
32   Mathematics and Oceanography

RELIGIOUS BUILDINGS

A   Liverpool Cathedral
B   Metropolitan Cathedral (R. C.)
C   St Bride
D   St Andrew (former)
E   St Philip Neri (R. C.)
F   Synagogue (former, now Unity Theatre)
G   Third Church of Christ Scientist

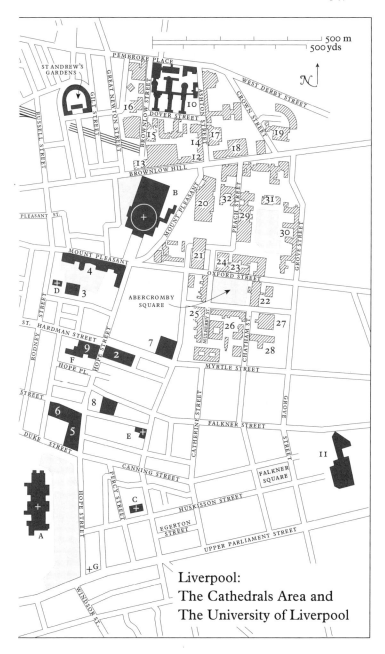

Liverpool:
The Cathedrals Area and
The University of Liverpool

Exterior

70 The overall impression is of massive, brooding bulk, and a certain sombreness due to the colour of the stone (red sandstone, mostly quarried at Woolton, in the suburbs SE of the centre, *see* p. 506; brick and concrete are used where they cannot be seen). The total external length is 619 ft (189 metres). We begin at the E end and work W, following the course of construction. The earliest part is the LADY CHAPEL, tall and narrow with a polygonal apse, in style akin to late Bodley. Closely spaced buttresses with numerous slight weatherings, pierced top and bottom by galleries with openwork balustrades. Dec tracery, varying from window to window. Porch with a lofty two-arched balcony above, with Quattrocentro-style sculptures of children by *Lillie Reed*. The CHAPTER HOUSE is connected with the choir by a passage which continues as an ambulatory behind the sanctuary. In Scott's 1904 scheme it was to have been rectangular, balancing the Lady Chapel, but instead an octagonal plan was adopted. This better exploits the picturesque possibilities of its location by the cemetery, from the edge of which, in distant views, it appears to grow like the tower of a fantasy medieval castle. It has a higher stair-turret on one side and, like the Lady Chapel, an arcaded balcony near the top, linked to the choir by a bridge high up.

The E elevation of the CHOIR is dominated by a very large Dec window, divided by a mullion with statues in niches. This is flanked by buttresses and corner turrets with short spires. By contrast the N and S elevations are in a more personal, 'modern' Gothic, adopted with the redesign of 1909–10. This style, used for the rest of the cathedral, is characterized by large, unbroken expanses of wall, with knots of intricate decoration concentrated towards the top. The choir side windows have quadrant jambs into which the arch mouldings die, a motif used throughout and derived from advanced late C19 Gothicists (among them Scott's father). They also have simpler tracery than the E window, a rather bald late C13 Geometrical consisting of two lights with a sexfoil above. Widely spaced buttresses separate them, and a gallery of small arches runs above. The carved ornament often seems influenced by Spanish late Gothic examples, and indeed Scott visited Spain soon after construction began.

The composition of the two TRANSEPTS flanking the tower and the S porch – the RANKIN PORCH – is impressive in the extreme, and unlike anything in medieval church architecture. Although generally kept shut, this, and not the W end, is the main entrance front (the interior tells a different story, as will be seen). The transept ends are sheer cliffs of masonry, each with a long, narrow two-light window, between which the cavernous porch is recessed in deep shadow under a broad segmental arch. Scott's enthusiasm for Spanish detail is again evident from the grille that closes the arch, and from the three doorways within, their heads merging into the tracery of a single large window above. The flat roof is reinforced concrete.

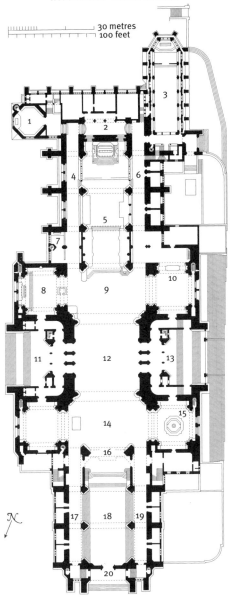

ANGLICAN CATHEDRAL

30 metres
100 feet

N

1 Chapter House	11 Welsford Porch
2 Ambulatory	12 Under Tower
3 Lady Chapel	13 Rankin Porch
4 North Choir Aisle	14 Western Transept
5 Choir	15 Baptistery
6 South Choir Aisle	16 Nave Bridge
7 Chapel of the Holy Spirit	17 North Nave Aisle
8 War Memorial Chapel	18 Nave
9 Eastern Transept	19 South Nave Aisle
10 Derby Memorial	20 West Porch

Liverpool, Anglican Cathedral.
Plan

Low, arched entrances projecting l. and r. of the transepts lead
to the undercroft. The whole composition, minus the undercroft entrances, is repeated for the sake of symmetry on the N
side in the WELSFORD PORCH. This has little functional justification since it opens straight into the abyss of the cemetery.
Both porches have SCULPTURE by *Edward Carter Preston*,
columnar statues strongly influenced by C13 French portal
figures at, e.g., Chartres. Those in the Welsford Porch depict
Old Testament prophets and New Testament writers, linked by
the theme of the Resurrection. Those in the Rankin Porch represent the Active Life, with figures from Christ's parables.

The TOWER (paid for by the Vestey family, Liverpool meat
importers) is a magnificent landmark. Its design was repeat-
edly revised by Scott, resulting in greater height (331 ft; 101
metres) and a more subtly tapered outline. The lower part is
square, with large windows N and S, of three lancets with a rose
above. The eight-sided upper stage has tapering octagonal
turrets at the angles, ending in delicate lanterns.

The NAVE follows the choir, but is more simply detailed: the
buttresses have fewer weatherings and neither they nor the
window mullions have figure sculpture. Scott redesigned
the W FRONT in 1942, with a projecting porte cochère, but by
the time building reached this point costs had risen so much that
a simpler design by *F.G. Thomas* and *Roger Pinckney*, finalized in
1968, was adopted. It has a giant arched recess flanked by pairs
of buttresses. The W window fills the recess and consists of three
lancets under a decorative horizontal cresting (a composition
adapted from the tower windows), above which the tympanum
of the arch is fully glazed. Over the ceremonial central door, a
bronze STATUE of Christ by *Elisabeth Frink*, installed 1993.

Interior

71 Internally, Scott's version of Gothic is characterised not by
columns and arcades, but by solid walls and vaults. Nave and
choir derive from medieval churches such as Albi in SW France:
short walls projecting from the outer walls support the main
rib vault and are pierced at the bottom to form aisle passages.
Cross-vaults roof the spaces between these piers and support
a triforium, but no clerestory. Looking from W to E, the side
windows are mostly hidden from view, and masonry predominates. The spatial effects are awe-inspiring, but on a practical
level the plan is less convincing. The nave feels detached, and
the huge transepts, out of sight of the sanctuary, seem redundant (the NW one has been adapted as a shop). The N and S
porches, so dominant externally, seem poorly related to the
interior, bringing one in at the mid-point of what is, internally,
an emphatically longitudinal building. In the end, however,
practical considerations seem less important than emotional
responses. As Goodhart-Rendel wrote of the unfinished cathedral in 1953: '. . . it stands aloof from architectural reality,
having neither the functional nor the constructional inevitabil-
ity of the ancient buildings whence its forms are ultimately
derived – it is either a great engine of emotion or nothing.'

Entered at the W end, the cathedral unfolds in reverse chronological order. The distance from W door to E window is 457 ft (139 metres). The sunken floor of the NAVE – 4 ft (1.2 metres) lower than the aisles – was planned by Scott in 1942, with the probable intention of making a semi-independent space for less formal events. A highly theatrical round-arched BRIDGE across the E end, supporting a balcony reached by long flights of stairs, sets it apart even more. Originally meant to carry an organ, this serves also to frame the distant view of the altar and delay the moment at which the full height of the central space is revealed. The rib vault has two quadripartite bays for each of the three bays below. Sadly, to reduce costs, the two westernmost vault bays were constructed from moulded glass-fibre rather than stone.

The TRANSEPTS and the immensely high UNDER-TOWER are sublimely impressive, the octagonal rib vault of the latter rising to 175 ft (53.3 metres). Foundations for the choir and E transept had already been laid before Scott's redesign of 1909–10. This explains the massive NE and SE transept piers, originally planned to carry the twin towers, and the curious vaulting devised to overcome the difficulty of the central space being wider than the choir. For the sake of balance these were repeated westward, but with variations in detail. The doors of the Rankin Porch are generally closed, but the identically planned Welsford Porch, N, is accessible. Approached from outside, its three external doors open into a vaulted vestibule, now used as a café. A turn l. or r. leads by a curving passage to one or other of the transepts, while straight ahead are three inner doors opening into the under-tower. Seen from inside the cathedral, these have the same Spanish-influenced decoration as the outer doors, and similar sculpture by *Carter Preston*, matching the doors of the Rankin Porch opposite. The figures on the N side represent Virtues and Vices, those on the S side the Liberal Arts and Sciences. The interior of the CHOIR, like its exterior, has more decorative carving than the nave. Bishop's Throne in the middle bay on the S. The aisles are connected behind the altar by the vaulted AMBULATORY. Off the NE corner is the CHAPTER HOUSE, with a circular balcony just below its concrete domed ceiling.

The LADY CHAPEL is reached from the S choir aisle. The first part of the cathedral to be completed, it is a good deal richer than what followed, possibly reflecting the early involvement of *Bodley*. The slope of the site means its floor lies below choir level, and it is reached by stairs at the W end. These pass behind an arcaded W gallery, with a striking view down into the chapel. Like the choir and nave it has wall piers, but here they are not so deep and the windows are proportionally bigger, so the effect is brighter and less ponderous. The piers are pierced with narrow passage aisles, and linked by arches supporting a balcony. This is screened by arcading, with a floridly carved foliage cresting and an elaborate inscription below. The stone-carving here, as in the choir, seems to have been directed by *Joseph Phillips*. Its rough naturalism contrasts with the later, more precise work of Carter Preston. The vault has sinuously curving ribs of a kind which occur in Spain (and Bohemia), but hardly in England. The floor is asymmetrically patterned in black and white marble. The DOOR in the second N bay has a marvellous lock and wrought-iron hinges.

FURNISHINGS. Most of the furnishings and monuments were designed by Scott or executed under his close supervision, giving a remarkable stylistic unity. Main REREDOS of distinctly Spanish appearance, the composition apparently derived from the gateway of the College of St Gregory, Valladolid. Stone, partly gilt, with sculpture conceived by *Walter Gilbert*, modelled by *Louis Weingartner*, and carved by *Arthur Turner* and others at *H.H. Martyn*'s of Cheltenham. – COMMUNION RAIL, with figures representing the Ten Commandments, by *Gilbert* and *Weingartner*. – Bronze GATES from sanctuary to choir aisles by the *Bromsgrove Guild*. – STALLS by *Waring & Gillow*; in 1996 two PAINTINGS by *Christopher Le Brun* were incorporated, The Good Samaritan and The Prodigal Son. – ORGAN CASE, on both sides above the stalls, designed by *Scott*. – Chapel of the Holy Spirit, N choir aisle, REREDOS with an alabaster relief of Christ praying, by *William Gough*. – War Memorial Chapel, NE transept, REREDOS with sculpture by *Gilbert* and *Weingartner*. – FONT, SW transept, marble, with relief figures by *Carter Preston*; CANOPY, designed by *Scott*, square with Flamboyant top. – Near the NW transept arch, a STATUE of the Holy Family, by *Josefina de Vasconcellos*. A fibreglass moulding, installed by 1965. – Lady Chapel ALTARPIECE, carved and painted wood with elaborately crested top, German- or Flemish-looking. Designed by *Bodley* and *Scott* and made by *Rattee & Kett*, the reliefs from models by *G.W.Wilson*. – ORGAN CASE by *Scott*. – Kneeling STATUE of the Virgin, glazed terracotta, late C15–early C16 Florentine, ascribed to *Giovanni della Robbia*. – Gilded wrought-iron ELECTROLIERS by *W. Bainbridge Reynolds*.

STAINED GLASS. Much of the glass was made by *James Powell & Sons* (*Whitefriars*). Their earliest surviving is in the E and N windows of the choir, designed by *John William Brown* and made 1911–21. Sombre in colouring, it is decidedly subordinate to the architecture. The N window in the NE transept, 1921–2, brighter and more translucent, is by *Brown* and *James H. Hogan*. Hogan developed this approach further in the huge under-tower windows, designed 1933, and particularly in his replacements for bomb-damaged windows on the choir S side, SE transept, and Lady Chapel S side, begun 1941. The damaged windows of the Lady Chapel apse and N side were replaced from *c.* 1948 to designs by *Carl Edwards*. The large windows in the NW and SW transepts with their chunky figure style are by *Herbert Hendrie*. The nave windows are much more brightly coloured towards the W, probably because they were made after Scott's death and without his controlling influence. The most easterly on the S side is by *William Wilson*; all the rest are by *Edwards*, culminating in the great W, or Benedicite window, installed for the dedication of the finished building in 1978. Its intense colour and fluid design, and the colossal scale of the Christ figure at the top, mark a radical departure from all previous glass in the cathedral. *Burlison & Grylls* did the ambulatory windows and *C.E. Kempe & Co.* the window on the Chapter House stairs, all completed in 1916. *Morris & Co.* produced the Chapter House windows from 1915 onwards.

MONUMENTS. In the Lady Chapel, Helen Swift Neilson, †1945, by *Carter Preston*, with a relief of musicians; also First World War Nurses by *David Evans*, 1928, with an austere relief of a nurse bandaging a soldier's head. – s choir aisle, forming the back of the Bishop's Throne, Bishop Chavasse, †1928, carved by *P. Induni* and *J. Phillips* from a model by *Evans*, incorporating a representation of the E part of the cathedral. Also three monuments by *Carter Preston*: Sir Robert Jones, †1933; Bishop Ryle, †1900, an impressive recumbent effigy, carved 1930–1; and Dean Dwelly, †1957. – N choir aisle, E end, A.J.M. Melly, †1936, by *Carter Preston*. – SE transept, the 16th Earl of Derby, †1908, unveiled 1929. Designed by *Scott*, the figure apparently modelled by *Thomas Tyrrell* and a Mr *Wilson*. Recumbent bronze effigy on a classical marble tomb-chest. At the head a model of the cathedral, its w end tantalisingly veiled. – E of the Derby monument, Sir Max Horton, by *Carter Preston*, 1957. – SE transept, above the arch on the w side, memorial of the 55th (West Lancashire) Division, with sculpture designed by *Gilbert* and *Weingartner*.

CATHEDRAL PRECINCT. The land sloping down to Great George Street was originally occupied by early C19 terraced houses. Scott prepared speculative designs for new housing here, but nothing resulted. In 1982 a redevelopment competition was won by *Brock Carmichael Associates* with the landscape architects *Derek Lovejoy & Partners*. The resulting three-storey brick housing is grouped into oval courts, enclosing car parking and private gardens. The level open space in front of the cathedral, known as QUEEN'S WALK, is part of the scheme. An intended grand processional route from the corner of Upper Duke Street and Great George Street to the Rankin Porch has not materialised. In 2005 a footbridge across St James's Cemetery was being planned (*see* p. 362).

METROPOLITAN CATHEDRAL (R.C.)
Mount Pleasant

Liverpool's Metropolitan Cathedral, designed by *Frederick Gibberd* and built 1962–7, was the greatest Roman Catholic post-war architectural commission in Britain. It was also the first cathedral to break with longitudinal planning (a tradition upheld by Basil Spence in his design of 1951 for Coventry Cathedral) in favour of a centralised arrangement, as encouraged by the Liturgical Movement. Gibberd's revolutionary plan was realised with modern materials – the building belongs in the mainstream of 1960s monumental concrete design – and was complemented by mainly abstract furnishings. It stands on top of the beginnings of an earlier, profoundly different, and hugely ambitious cathedral, designed by *Edwin Lutyens*.

The size of Liverpool's Catholic population, even before the immigration that followed the Irish famine of the 1840s, is clear from such ambitious churches as St Peter (*see* p. 284), St Patrick (*see* p. 472) and St Anthony (*see* p. 484). In 1845 *A. W.N. Pugin* was reported to have made designs for a cathedral in Liverpool, and after the formation of the Catholic diocese of Liverpool (1850) a cathedral was actually begun to the designs of his son *E. W. Pugin* in 1856 in St Domingo Road, Everton. Building progressed no further than the eastern chapels, which served as part of the parish church of Our Lady Immaculate until demolition in the 1980s. The rôle of pro-cathedral was filled by the church of St Nicholas in Hawke Street, an early C19 Gothic Revival building, demolished in 1972.

The Lutyens Cathedral

In 1928 the dynamic Richard Downey was appointed archbishop and made it his aim to build 'a cathedral in our time'. The magnificent site at the top of Mount Pleasant and Brownlow Hill, formerly occupied by the workhouse, was bought in 1930. This ensured that the building would be seen in relation to the Anglican Cathedral, rising half a mile to the s, and that the two great churches would crown the skyline. The commission was given to *Edwin Lutyens* – no competition was held – and his design was exhibited at the Royal Academy in 1932.

Lutyens' vision of the cathedral is preserved in numerous working drawings, in watercolour perspectives by Cyril Farey, and above all in the gigantic wooden model now in the care of the Walker Art Gallery. Though classical in detail, it was a design of remarkable inventiveness, described by John Summerson as 'perhaps . . . the latest and supreme attempt to embrace Rome, Byzantium, the Romanesque and the Renaissance in one triumphal and triumphant synthesis'. The building would have been colossal, 680 ft long by 400 ft wide (207 by 122 metres), with a dome 168 ft (51 metres) in diameter and rising to 510 ft (155 metres) externally, dwarfing the tower of the Anglican Cathedral and outstripping St Peter's in Rome. The plan was longitudinal but compact: a short nave with double aisles, transepts also with double aisles, the dome as wide as the nave and inner aisles, and a short chancel with apse and circular chapter house behind. Before the nave there was to be a great narthex, the transept ends were to have angle chapels, and the apse was to be flanked by large apsed chapels and sacristies. The materials were to be buff brick with grey granite dressings. The design of interior and exterior, excluding the dome, was a development – on a stupendous scale – of the three-dimensional triumphal-arch motif Lutyens used for the Memorial to the Missing of the Somme at Thiepval.

Work began in 1933, but only the CRYPT was completed. It stands partly above, partly below ground, at the N end, beneath where the choir and chapter house would have been. The grey granite exterior should be understood as no more than the

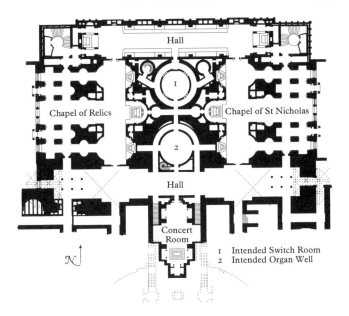

Hall

Chapel of Relics

Chapel of St Nicholas

Hall

Concert
Room

1 Intended Switch Room
2 Intended Organ Well

Liverpool, Metropolitan Cathedral (R.C.).
Plan of crypt

plinth from which the cliff-like walls of the ritual E end would
have soared (the cathedral was – and is – not orientated; ritual
E equals compass N, ritual W equals S, etc.). The entrance is
from a sunken court on the ritual S side. Pevsner was shocked
by what he called the 'exasperating whimsy' of Lutyens' unconventional detailing here: the tapering pillars that flank the
doors, partly free-standing and partly absorbed, and the
transom of the great semicircular window, seemingly forced
into a downward curve by the keystone above. But such details
are surely personal and expressive distortions of the classical
language, in the tradition of Michelangelo or Giulio Romano.

The doors lead straight into the CHAPEL OF ST NICHOLAS,
with nave and aisles terminating in three apses. The piers are
so massive that the space seems hollowed out of the earth
rather than built. Granite dressings are used, but walls and
vaults are of brick (left bare, not plastered as Lutyens
intended). An identical space (now the CONCERT ROOM)
occupies the corresponding area on the ritual N side, and on
the central axis, between the chapel apses, are two great circular chambers, directly below what would have been chapter
house and choir. One was intended to contain the organ, the
sound of which would have risen through a grille; the other
was to be the electrical switch room. On each side of the
chapels, two immense vaulted halls run the full width of the
building. The one on the ritual E side, originally intended as
the lower sacristy, is lit by five semicircular windows and has

stairs at either end. These are cantilevered around a circular
well, and each flight starts with convex and ends with concave
steps. The hall on the opposite side has groups of columns at
each end, creating shadowy three-naved fragments. Opening
off its ritual w side is the CHAPEL OF THE RELICS – the burial
place of the archbishops – directly under what would have been
Lutyens' High Altar. The remarkable gate is a circular slab of
Travertine that rolls open and shut, fretted with carving in the
form of a cross. Inside, the chapel is faced with marble and
Travertine and has pairs of Doric columns in recesses. Deep
semicircular arches above these columns enclose sculpted sarcophagi. It is a solemnly impressive interior.

The Gibberd Cathedral

Work on the crypt ceased during the Second World War; Lutyens
died in 1944, Archbishop Downey in 1953. By now it was clear
that Lutyens' scheme was impossibly large and costly. A scaled-
down version by *Adrian Gilbert Scott*, published in 1955, was
not pursued. Finally, in 1959 a competition was held for an
entirely new design.

The terms reflected the liturgical trend of the late 1950s and
beyond, which favoured the closer involvement of the faithful in
the Mass. Architects were required to provide for a congregation of 3,000 (later reduced to 2,000), all within sight of the
altar. In a letter sent to competitors, Archbishop Heenan
impressed upon them that 'the high altar is not an ornament to
embellish the cathedral building. The cathedral, on the contrary,
is built to enshrine the altar of sacrifice. The attention of all who
enter should be arrested and held by the altar.' The winner was
Frederick Gibberd, whose circular plan with central altar met this
requirement in the simplest and most obvious way. Another stipulation was that the Lutyens crypt be incorporated, and this
Gibberd achieved with notable success. He transformed the
crypt roof into an elevated piazza (already proposed by *Scott* in
1955), extending this level platform across the rest of the site to
form a podium. The cathedral stands at one end, raised high
above the uneven contours of the site, and set apart in a way
appropriate for a sacred building. At the other end, the crypt

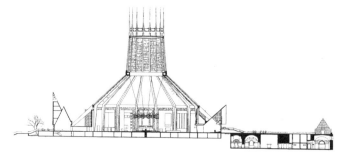

Liverpool, Metropolitan Cathedral (R.C.).
Section, showing the Lutyens crypt, right

stairs are nicely finished off with a pair of stone-faced pyramids. An outdoor altar is set against the ritual E end of the new cathedral. Within the podium are a car park, sacristies, and other offices, linked internally with both crypt and cathedral.

The plan of Gibberd's building can be read from the EXTE- [118] RIOR. It is a circle 195 ft (59.4 metres) in diameter surrounded by thirteen chapels, the main entrance and two side porches. The structural elements are exposed. Sixteen boomerang-shaped concrete trusses rise vertically from the podium then slant inwards, supporting the conical roof of the central space. They are tied together by a ring beam at the height of the bend of the boomerangs and again at the top. The boomerangs are helped in their work by flying buttresses from the lower ring down to the ground, continuing unbroken the diagonal line of the roof, so that they resemble the poles of a tepee or the taut guy ropes of a tent. These buttresses – the most striking exterior feature – were not part of Gibberd's original conception, but were suggested by the engineer *James Lowe*. They give a superficial similarity to Oscar Niemeyer's Brasilia cathedral, 1958, but Niemeyer's graceful, organic curves are very different from Gibberd's jutting, angular shapes. From the upper ring the trusses extend upwards to form the glazed lantern tower, ending in a spiky crown of pinnacles (the cathedral is dedicated to Christ the King) with cobwebby stainless steel between. Gibberd's cylindrical tower with its pinnacles responds to the tower of the Anglican Cathedral, and in views both near and distant the two buildings appear linked. He intended that his cathedral should have a ceremonial approach from Hope Street, but a pre-existing building in Mount Pleasant prevented this. Eventually in 2003 a broad, axial flight of STEPS was provided by *Falconer Chester*, rising from a new SQUARE at pavement level flanked by buildings by the same architects: to the E, the single-storey VISITOR CENTRE, with a garden above incorporating ramped access, and a curved façade of coursed slate to Mount Pleasant; to the W, a new university building, 2004, stone-faced, with windows in horizontal strips.*

Speed and economy were important factors in construction, and the use of new materials and techniques led before long to leaks and other chronic problems with the fabric. A campaign of repairs from the 1990s has changed the external appearance significantly. The concrete frame was originally faced with off-white mosaic, which became unsound and proved impossible to repair. It has now been clad in glass-reinforced plastic. This makes the members slightly thicker, and the joints in the new material give a misleading impression of masonry construction rather than poured concrete. The conical roof, originally clad in aluminium, has been renewed in stainless steel, and the podium has been repaved with concrete flags, replacing the original random slate. The restoration of the Gibberd cathedral

---

* In the garden, an artwork by *Susanna Heron* is under construction, 2005: a low, circular plinth of stone.

was carried out by *Vis Williams Prichard*, the repair of the Lutyens crypt and piazza by *O'Mahony Fozzard*.

Gibberd's chapels and entrance porches, positioned between the flying buttresses, are of varied shapes and have different arrangements of windows. However, their consistently tall, narrow proportions and Portland stone facing helps unify them. The main doors are at the base of the great wedge-shaped BELL-TOWER that closes the view N along Hope Street. The bells hang in openings punched through the thin apex of the tower (recalling Marcel Breuer's St John, Collegeville, Minnesota, 1953–61), and the surface below is carved with an angular, geometric relief designed by *William Mitchell*, incorporating three crosses. The discipline of this contrasts with the huge sliding DOORS below, also by *Mitchell*. They feature the symbols of the Evangelists, treated in an expressionist style that made Pevsner think of 'the introduction to some cruel Mexican ritual'. They look like bronze, but are fibreglass.

119   INTERIOR. The entrance leads through a low porch directly into nave and sanctuary. The first uplifting impression is of vast height and space, and of intense colour from the stained glass, contrasting with the darkness of the roof. The disappointment is that almost everything can be taken in at once: the building does not reveal itself gradually or hold many surprises in store. The boomerang-shaped trusses (here of exposed concrete poured into smooth shuttering) appear in full clarity. That the chapels and porches are treated as independent buildings, unconnected with the main structural frame, is made wonderfully clear, because each is bordered l., r. and top by strips of intense blue glass with flecks of red (by *John Piper* and *Patrick Reyntiens*).

The focus of everything is the central ALTAR, a single block of pure white marble, 10 ft (3 metres) long, quarried at Skopje in Macedonia. Raised on a stepped platform, the eye is led towards it by the radial-patterned grey and white marble FLOOR, designed by *David Atkins*, and by the luminous TOWER directly above.* This is a cylinder of abstract stained glass by *Piper* and *Reyntiens*, with three great bursts of colour (yellow, blue and red) symbolising the Trinity. The design, which has echoes of the artists' earlier work in the baptistery at Coventry Cathedral, spreads right round, taking no account of the ribs, and changing continuously as one makes a circuit. The individual pieces of glass, 1 in. (2.5 cm.) thick, are bonded with epoxy resin (visible as a network of fine black lines) and set in concrete frames. The result is that glass predominates over concrete, which was not the case in Gibberd's original tower design. The same technique is used for the blue glass framing the chapels.

Of the surrounding CHAPELS, some are open to the nave, others present a largely blank wall, others still are horizontally divided, with a low, enclosed space below a balcony. Most prominent is the BLESSED SACRAMENT CHAPEL, directly

---

*The circular plan brings with it functional difficulties – when the cathedral is full the celebrant has his back to a large part of the congregation – and there are acoustic problems too.

opposite the main door, and the axis this creates between ritual
w and e is reinforced by the position of the organ and the symmetry of the two flanking chapels. The entrance is low under
the organ, beyond which the side walls diverge, radiating from
the centre point of the Cathedral. The roof slopes steeply
upwards to the altar wall, faced with pitted stone. Next but
one in an anticlockwise direction is the LADY CHAPEL. It has
the same divergent walls, but is smaller, with a triangular sanctuary, tall, narrow windows, and a flat roof with exposed concrete beams making a lattice pattern. To its l., the CHAPEL OF
ST JOSEPH has wood panelling, and a funnel-like pyramid
ceiling. Immediately r. of the main entrance is the cylindrical
BAPTISTERY, its skylight hidden by a suspended cone which
diffuses the light.

FURNISHINGS. Gibberd's preference for abstract, allusive
art was not always in step with the Cathedral Committee's
taste, and the harmony he achieved between architecture, furnishings, sculpture and glass is therefore all the more remarkable. Since the building opened it has acquired a good deal of
more conventional religious art – figurative, narrative or overtly
symbolic – some of which sits uncomfortably in the context of
Gibberd's Modernism. In the following description, furnishings are contemporary with the Gibberd building unless other
dates are given.

On the central altar, CANDLESTICKS by *R.Y. Goodden*, and
an ethereal CRUCIFIX of pale gilt bronze – just a figure, without
a cross – by *Elisabeth Frink*. – Suspended above, *Gibberd's* BAL-
DACCHINO, a crown-like canopy of aluminium rods incorporating lights and loudspeakers. – Concentric curved BENCHES
by *Frank Knight*. – Expressionist STATIONS OF THE CROSS in
cast and welded metal, 1993–5, by *Sean Rice*, who also designed
the LECTERN near the High Altar with two intertwining eagles.
– The vivid red STAINED GLASS in the Chapel of St Paul of the
Cross (now Chapel of Reconciliation) is by *Margaret Traherne*.
– In the Chapel of St Joseph, the PANELLING of the rear wall
was carved and painted by *Stephen Foster*, 1983, with scenes
from the life of St Joseph in a folk-art style; the side walls were
similarly carved in 1995. – In the Lady Chapel, a terracotta
STATUE of the Virgin and Child by *Robert Brumby*, and
STAINED GLASS in subdued browns by *Margaret Traherne*. – In
the recess r. of here (not strictly speaking a chapel), a STATUE
of Abraham in various metals, cast and welded, by *Rice* again,
1990s. – In the Blessed Sacrament Chapel, the abstract painted
REREDOS and STAINED GLASS by *Ceri Richards* were conceived
as a single composition – a triptych – 'suggesting a mysterious
infinity of cool space' in Gibberd's words. TABERNACLE DOORS
also by *Richards*, with more straightforward eucharistic
imagery. Small STATUE of the Risen Christ by *Arthur Dooley*,
presented 1986. – In the Chapel of St Thomas Aquinas (now
Chapel of Unity), bronze holy-water STOUP by *Virginio Ciminaghi*; MOSAIC of Pentecost by *George Mayer Marton*, 1957,
brought in 1989 from the demolished church of the Holy
Ghost, Netherton. – Baptistery GATES by *David Atkins*. In the

crypt, another set of STATIONS OF THE CROSS, designed by *Howard Faulkner*, 1930s, and carved in oak by *Frederick G. Pugh* and *James Barnett*, in a style recalling Eric Gill's for Westminster Cathedral.

E of the cathedral, but linked, are CATHEDRAL HOUSE and the (former) CONVENT OF CHRIST THE KING, and just N of these, the CATHOLIC CHAPLAINCY of the University of Liverpool. All were designed by *Gibberd*, and all are faced with Portland stone. Relatively small in scale, of two storeys: a good foil for the main building. Convent and Cathedral House have narrow vertical windows to the ground floor, and there is an enclosed garden between Cathedral House and the podium. The Chaplaincy has more blank walling, and arched windows facing the Lutyens crypt.

OTHER RELIGIOUS BUILDINGS

ST BRIDE, Percy Street. 1829–30, by *Samuel Rowland*. The best surviving Neoclassical church in the city. Set in a railed enclosure, with pedimented gatepiers of cast iron. A temple-like rectangular box, towerless, with a monumental portico of six unfluted Ionic columns across the W end. Under the portico, two imposing doorways and a large central window, all with inward-sloping sides. The side elevations have six tall windows also with inward-sloping sides, with fine architraves on brackets. Bays one and six have giant pilasters with bands of anthemion at the top. Slightly projecting chancel, E, with large tripartite and pedimented window, flanked by lower vestries. Inside, three galleries on slender cast-iron columns, connected by sweeping quadrant curves (the space underneath partitioned off in the 1980s). Chancel framed by massive square piers with anthemion decoration; E window with unfluted Ionic columns. – STAINED GLASS: E window, *c.* 1905, Renaissance style. – MONUMENTS. Rev. J.H. Stewart, †1854, by *Patteson* of Manchester, tablet with veiled urn. – Tablet by *William Spence* to W.M. Forster, his wife and servant, †1831. Carved and gilded ROYAL ARMS, dated 1817, from St John, Old Haymarket (demolished, *see* p. 335).

ST PHILIP NERI (R.C.), Catharine Street. *Matthew Honan* exhibited drawings in 1912, simplified in execution after his death by *M.J. Worthy* and *Alfred Rigby*. The church opened in 1920. Neo-Byzantine, red brick with stone dressings, with a vault of reinforced concrete. Round-arched door flanked by baptistery and chapel, forming a single-storey projection across the front. Doorway carvings of Christ and the Virgin and Child, and a life-size Last Supper above, completed by *Tom Murphy* after 1945. Broad nave of six bays with passage aisles (the l. one added later) and arcades of square piers with chunky capitals, some carved. A segmental vault over the first three bays, a dome over the other three, and a semi-dome over the apsidal sanctuary. The nave vaults look like stone, but the surface is cork, applied to the concrete by *F.X. Velarde* to remedy damp. Above the arcades and in the apse, mosaics and

coloured marbles create an atmosphere of Byzantine splendour. – ALTAR GATES said to have been designed by *Peter
Kavanagh*. – In the r. aisle, attractive MURALS of biblical scenes
(part of an uncompleted scheme), *c.* 1954 by *Robin McGhie*,
who also designed the reliefs under the gallery.

ST ANDREW, Rodney Street. Built for the Scottish Presbyterians, 1823–4, burned out in 1983, and now a ruin. The body,
simple rendered brick with tiers of round-arched windows, was
designed by the church's Committee of Management and their
surveyor, *Daniel Stewart*. The once-imposing Greek Revival
façade of blackened ashlar is by *John Foster Jun*. Picton considered it one of Foster's most successful efforts, and Schinkel
sketched it during his 1826 visit to Liverpool. Recessed portico
with Ionic columns, originally flanked by square towers with
pedimented aedicules to each face, and small domes. N tower
demolished. In the churchyard, single-storey SCHOOLS, 1872,
by *H.H. Vale*. Italianate with a Venetian window, and like the
church ruinous. Also a notable MONUMENT to William
Mackenzie, railway contractor, †1851. A large, plain granite
pyramid, 1868.

SYNAGOGUE (former), Hope Place. *See* Unity Theatre, p. 373.

THIRD CHURCH OF CHRIST SCIENTIST, Upper Parliament
Street. 1914, designed by *W.H. Ansell* as a Temple of Human-
ity for the Positivist Church. A stark brick building, notable for
having few historicist details. Windowless canted apse to Upper
Parliament Street, Diocletian clerestory windows above the
blank side aisles.

ST JAMES'S CEMETERY, Upper Duke Street. An exceptionally
ambitious early cemetery, laid out 1827–9 to the designs of
John Foster Jun. For sheer drama its only rival is the Glasgow
Necropolis, but whereas the Necropolis climbs a hill, the
Liverpool cemetery lies in the sombre depths of a former
quarry, a perfect foil for the Cathedral above. The N, W and S
faces are rough and wooded. The long E face was shaped by
Foster into monumental terraces lined with catacombs and
ramps. The catacombs have round-arched entrances with rusticated surrounds. The scale is colossal – was Foster influenced
by ancient sites such as Palestrina? Regrettably, *c.* 1969–71 the
cemetery floor was cleared of most of its gravestones for a
public garden. In the middle is the HUSKISSON MAU-
SOLEUM, a circular domed temple of 1833–4 by *Foster*, based
on the Choragic Monument of Lysicrates. It marks the grave
of William Huskisson, the Liverpool M.P. fatally injured at the
opening of the Liverpool & Manchester Railway. Originally it
contained a marble statue by *Gibson*. – Overlooking the cemetery from the NW is the ORATORY, or chapel, *Foster*'s best surviving building. It is a perfect Greek Doric temple with a
six-column portico at each end. The walls are windowless, the
interior lit from above. Ionic columns support the coffered
plaster ceiling. Rich collection of MONUMENTS, mostly Neoclassical reliefs, some brought in the 1980s from demolished
buildings. They include: the Nicholson family, 1834, by *Francis*

Chantrey, with mourners over an urn; William Earle, †1839, by *John Gibson*, seated in profile, wrapped in a cloak and musing over a book; Dr William Stevenson, †1853, by *J.A.P. Macbride*, a sickbed scene with the doctor in attendance (originally in St Mary, Birkenhead, where its Gothic frame would have seemed less alien); William Hammerton, †1832, by *Gibson*, a fine relief of mother and children receiving charity, in classical dress; William Ewart, †1823, by *Joseph Gott*, a vivid, informal statue sitting with legs crossed, amiably expounding something; Emily Robinson, †1829, by *Gibson*, seated in profile, modelled on a Greek stele; Agnes Jones, †1868, by *Pietro Tenerani*, a free-standing Angel of the Resurrection with trumpet (originally in the chapel of the Brownlow Hill Workhouse). A red granite slab r. of the entrance commemorates Foster, who 'on his return from long and arduous travels in the pursuit of his art . . . enriched his native town with the fruits of his genius, industry and integrity'. At the SW corner, a splendid rusticated entrance ARCH, and a small Greek Revival LODGE.

In 2005 *Buro Happold* and *Hales Associates* were appointed engineer and architect for a planned pedestrian bridge across the cemetery. The design, of complex twisting form, has a glass deck and balustrading.

UNIVERSITY OF LIVERPOOL

The University started as University College in 1881, became a member of the federal Victoria University (along with Owens College, Manchester) in 1884, and has been the University of Liverpool since 1903. The earliest buildings, erected between the 1880s and the Second World War, are concentrated around Brownlow Hill, Ashton Street and Brownlow Street. Immediately after the war, *William Holford* was commissioned to plan for expansion. His report was published in 1949, and in 1950 the new Precinct was designated, stretching S and E of the earlier buildings; later enlarged, it now measures approximately 880 by 440 yds (800 by 400 metres). Holford offered a framework for growth rather than rigid proposals, but a good deal of what we see today can be traced back to him. Most importantly, he did not envisage a formal layout, nor did he favour employing a single architect. The resulting visual diversity is partly due to this, partly to changes in funding, student numbers and land ownership. In 1969 Pevsner said of the Precinct: 'The whole is not a whole but a zoo, with species after species represented.' What makes the variety more striking is that the buildings occupy an area laid out in the early C19 with uniform terraces and a regular grid of streets (*see* Abercromby Square, p. 368). Most of the Precinct is now pedestrianised and much planting has been carried out, obscuring the former thoroughfares. However, the university buildings are mostly aligned with these streets, and the Late Georgian pattern provides a counterpoint to the clamouring individualism of their architecture. In the 1960s the University built its main halls of residence in the suburb of Mossley Hill (*see* pp. 441–2) and very little student housing was provided in the

Precinct. Recently, a good deal of accommodation has been built on the fringes, much by private developers, and of little architectural interest.

The following route covers the whole Precinct, beginning with the older buildings on Brownlow Hill, just N of the Roman Catholic Cathedral.

VICTORIA BUILDING, Brownlow Hill. 1889–92, by *Alfred Water-* 84 *house*. The main teaching and administrative building of the fledgling University College. Stridently red and assertively Gothic, faced with fiery Ruabon brick and terracotta, offset by common brick. Under this resilient skin the construction is fireproof, with iron frame and concrete floors; steel was apparently used in the Jubilee clock tower. This tower (terracotta modelling by *Farmer & Brindley*), with its lead-covered spire, marks the main entrance. To the l., the former library with gabled dormers; to the r., the principal staircase and a semi-circular lecture theatre, both expressed externally. Double-height apsidal entrance hall faced in *Burmantofts* terracotta, glazed and unglazed, mostly browns with touches of pale blue. An arcaded first-floor landing runs round the S side and the apse. The stately staircase is also arcaded, allowing glimpses through to the hall. Corresponding with the apse is the stage of the lecture theatre above, an impressive space. The former library – now the Tate Hall – was stripped of fittings in 1938, and the tie-beams removed from Waterhouse's open roof. The former librarian's room at the W end has C17 panelling installed in 1948, from the demolished Worden Hall at Leyland, Lancashire. – SCULPTURE: in the apse of the entrance hall (designed to receive it), life-size marble statue of Christopher Bushell, *c.* 1884, by *Albert Bruce Joy*; opposite the main entrance, the University War Memorial, 1926–7, by *Gordon Hemm*, carving by *C.J. Allen*; on the stairs, plaques to Charles W. Jones, 1910, *Allen* again, and George Holt, 1897, a fine bronze relief portrait by *George Frampton*.

Adjoining, and facing Brownlow Hill, the WALKER ENGINEERING LABORATORIES, 1887–9. Also by *Waterhouse* and of brick and terracotta, but simpler. In the entrance hall a statue of Leopold, Duke of Albany, by *Count Victor Gleichen*, 1886. W extension, 1963–6, by *Courtaulds Technical Services Ltd*, including a seven-storey tower. (It is intended, in 2005, to demolish the tower, and place a long, stainless steel-clad teaching block by *Sheppard Robson Architects* on top of the remaining 1960s building.) A rib-vaulted passage between the Victoria Building and the laboratories leads to a quadrangle, enclosed on the S by the rear of the Victoria Building, and on the W and N by buildings more or less complementary in materials and styles, but comparatively dull. The HARRISON-HUGHES ENGINEERING LABORATORIES, opened 1912 (W), by *Briggs, Wolstenholme & Thornely*, are Gothic in brick and sandstone. The THOMPSON YATES BUILDING, 1894–8, by *Alfred Water-house* (N), is brick and terracotta, with a terracotta plaque of

1896 by *C.J. Allen* showing female personifications of Physiology and Pathology. To its l. is the WHELAN BUILDING (originally Anatomy), 1899–1904, by *Alfred & Paul Waterhouse*, with the former semicircular lecture theatres expressed externally, and to its r., the JOHNSTON BUILDING and the GEORGE HOLT PHYSICS LABORATORY, completed 1904, by *Willink & Thicknesse* with *F.M. Simpson*.

The E side of the quadrangle is a complete contrast. The ASHTON BUILDING, erected for the Faculty of Arts 1912–14, is by *Briggs, Wolstenholme & Thornely* and *Frank W. Simon* (Simon was responsible for the exterior, according to Charles Reilly). Here the University at last abandoned the Gothic agenda set by Waterhouse, turning instead to classicism of a type derived from Wren. Main block of four storeys and seven bays, with a bold cornice. Outer bays largely brick, the middle three of Portland stone with giant pilasters. Big pedimented window with Michelangelesque figure sculpture by *William Birnie Rhind*. A tunnel-vaulted passage, l., leads to Ashton Street where the façade is more conventional, with six giant pilasters supporting a pediment. On the parapet to either side, pairs of sphinxes by *Rhind*.

Returning through the quadrangle, W of the Whelan Building is CIVIL ENGINEERING, 1958–9, by *E. Maxwell Fry*. A T-plan tower, rising from a podium. The E face of the tower is windowless and slightly concave, and bears the names of great engineers in large raised concrete letters. In the entrance hall a mural by *Peter Lanyon*, The Conflict of Man with the Tides and the Sands, 1959–60. Enamel on ceramic tiles. Across Brownlow Street is the large and ungainly former ZOOLOGY BUILDING (now School of Biological Sciences) by *Willink & Thicknesse*, opened 1905. Off-centre entrance under a stubby square tower. The doors had metal roundels sculpted with delicate representations of animals, recently removed. Adjoining this on the S is the DERBY BUILDING (originally Electrotechnics), of the same date and by the same architects, but Georgian in style, and on the N the HARTLEY BUILDING (originally for Botany), opened in 1901, by *F.W. Dixon*. At the corner of Brownlow Street and Dover Street is the former MUSPRATT BUILDING, 1905–6, by *Willink & Thicknesse*, with corner domes. E of this in Dover Street, the MUSEUM of the demolished Royal Infirmary Medical School, a small ashlar classical block of 1872–3, by *Thomas Cook*. Back in Brownlow Street, on the W side further N are the PROUDMAN OCEANOGRAPHIC LABORATORY by *Architects Design Partnership*, 2003 (reusing the steel frame of a 1920s Neo-Georgian building by *Arnold Thornely*), and the elegant JANE HERDMAN LABORATORIES of 1927–9, by *Briggs & Thornely*. Brick, with stone dressings, in a Neoclassical style reminiscent of American campus buildings. A rear extension by *Weightman & Bullen*, set diagonally and linked by a glazed stair, was completed 1985. After this, with its main front in Pembroke Place to the N, is the SCHOOL OF TROPICAL MEDICINE. The central,

Liverpool, The Pier Head. Left, the Royal Liver Building, by Walter Aubrey Thomas, 1908–11, centre, the Cunard Building, by Arthur J. Davis (Mewès & Davis), and Willink & Thicknesse, completed 1916, and, right, the Mersey Docks and Harbour Board building, by Briggs & Wolstenholme, with Hobbs & Thornely, 1903–7 (pp. 330–2)

Near the River Alt, south-west of Great Altcar (p. 142)

3. Kirkby, St Chad, font, C12 (p. 214)
4. Up Holland, St Thomas, nave arcades earlier C14, chancel by Basil Champneys, 1882–6 (p. 597)
5. Halsall, St Cuthbert, door, C14 (p. 193)
6. Winwick, St Oswald, north arcade, piers, possibly C16, arches, possibly late C16 (p. 679)

3	5
4	6

7. Ormskirk, St Pete
    and St Paul,
    south-west steeple
    C13–C14, and west
    tower, *c.* 1540s
    (p. 531)
8. Lathom, Lathom
    Park Chapel, and
    almshouses
    beyond, founded
    1500 (p. 226)
9. Sefton, St Helen,
    mainly earlier C16
    steeple C14
    (p. 580)
10. Sefton, St Helen,
    parclose screen,
    early C16 (p. 581)

7	9
8	10

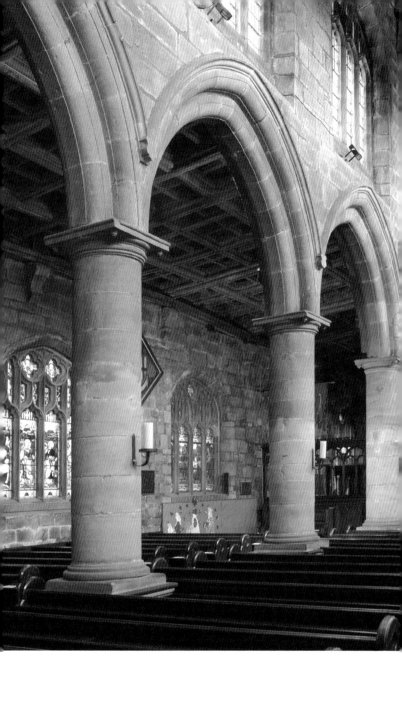

11. Standish, St Wilfrid, nave, c. 1582–9 (p. 591)
12. Glazebury, Hurst Hall (barn), roof and timber frame, C14–C15 (p. 175)
13. Standish, St Wilfrid, nave roof, 1580s (p. 591)

11 | 12
   | 13

14. Liverpool (Speke), Speke Hall, north range, completed 1598, and, left, the dairy by W. H. Picton, *c.* 1864 (p. 463)
15. Liverpool (Speke), Speke Hall, the Great Hall, *c.* 1530 (p. 467)
16. Liverpool (Speke), Great Parlour ceiling, possibly 1612 (p. 467)
17. Billinge, Bispham Hall, largely *c.* 1600–10 (p. 151)
18. Up Holland, Douglas Bank Farmhouse, 1656 (p. 600)

14	17
15	18
16	

19. Sefton, St Helen,
    pulpit, 1635
    (p. 582)
20. Ormskirk, St Peter
    and St Paul, font,
    1661 (p. 533)
21. Prescot, St Mary,
    nave roof, 1610
    (p. 541)

22. Standish, St Wilfrid, monument to Edward Wrightington, †1658 (p. 592)
23. Standish, St Wilfrid, monument to Edward Chisnall, †1653 (p. 592)
24. Winwick, St Oswald, monument to Richard Legh, †1687, bust possibly by John Nost (p. 682)

25. Dalton, Stone Hall, *c.* 1700–10 (p. 170)
26. Crawford, Manor House, 1718 (p. 163)
27. Hale, Manor House, frontage *c.* 1703–10 (p. 189)
28. Liverpool (Croxteth), Croxteth Hall, south front, 1702 (p. 406)
29. Liverpool, School Lane, Blue Coat School
    (now Bluecoat Chambers), begun 1716 (p. 302)

25	28
26	29
27	

30. Ince Blundell Hall, by Henry Sephton, *c.* 1720, with, right, Dining Room, 1847–50, probably by J.J. Scoles (p. 206)

31. Knowsley Hall, east wing, *c.* 1720s–1737, partly remodelled by W. H. Romaine-Walker, 1908–12 (p. 217)

32. Lathom House, stables by Giacomo Leoni, *c.* 1725–40 (p. 225)

33. Lathom House, gatepier by Giacomo Leoni, *c.* 1725–40 (p. 227)

34. Liverpool Town Hall, by John Wood, 1749–54. Dome completed 1802 and portico completed 1811 by James Wyatt (p. 286)

30	33
31	
32	34

35. Warrington Town Hall, built as Bank Hall, by James Gibbs, 1749–50 (p. 611)

36. Warrington Town Hall, built as Bank Hall, by James Gibbs, 1749–50, principal staircase (p. 612)

37. Liverpool, Colquitt Street, house and warehouse of Thomas Parr, *c.* 1799, adapted as the Liverpool Royal Institution (p. 316)

38. Liverpool, Brunswick Street, Heywood's Bank (former), 1798–1800 (p. 309)

| 35 | 37 |
| 36 | 38 |

39. Billinge, St
    Aidan, by Henry
    Sephton, 1716–18
    (p. 148)
40. Netherton, St
    Benet (R.C.),
    1793 (p. 521)
41. Wigan,
    Standishgate, St
    Mary (R.C.),
    1818 (p. 665)
42. Wigan,
    Standishgate, St
    John (R.C.),
    1818–19, interior
    (p. 664)
43. Wigan,
    Standishgate, St
    Mary (R.C.),
    interior (p. 666)

    39 | 42
    40 | 43
    41

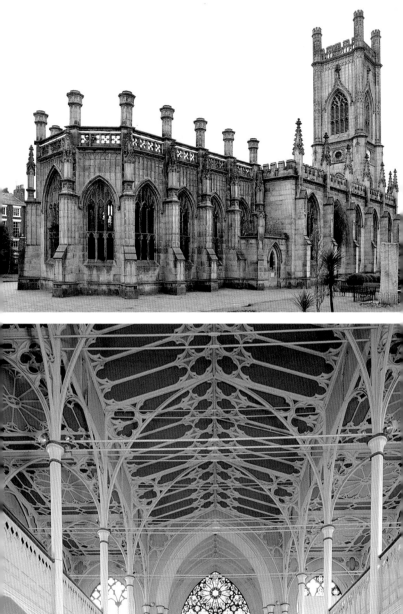

44. Liverpool, St Luke, begun 1811 (p. 281)
45. Liverpool (Everton), St George, built by John Cragg, 1813–14 (p. 418)
46. Standish, St Wilfrid, monument to Richard Watt, by John Bacon Jun., 1806, detail (p. 592)
47. Winwick, St Oswald, monument to Ellen Legh, †1831, by R. J. Wyatt, detail (p. 682)

44 | 46
45 | 47

48. Liverpool, Great George Street Congregational Church (former), by Joseph Franklin, 1840–1 (p. 285)
49. Rainhill, St Bartholomew (R.C.), by Joshua Dawson, 1838–40 (p. 547)
50. Rainhill, St Bartholomew (R.C.), by Joshua Dawson, interior (p. 547)

48
49 | 50

51. Ince Blundell Hall, the Pantheon, c. 1802–5 (p. 207)
52. Ince Blundell Hall, the Pantheon, interior (p. 207)
53. Haigh Hall, probably by the 7th Earl of Balcarres, 1827–c. 1844 (p. 185)
54. Haigh Hall, probably by the 7th Earl of Balcarres, staircase hall ceiling
    (p. 185)

51	53
52	54

55. Liverpool (Mossley Hill), Greenbank, south front, *c.* 1812–16 (p. 442)
56. Liverpool Town Hall, Dining Room by James Wyatt, design approved 1805 (p. 290)
57. Liverpool, Hope Street, Gambier Terrace, begun early 1830s (p. 376)
58. Ormskirk, Burscough Street, Dispensary (former), 1830 (p. 536)
59. Liverpool, Mount Street, Mechanics' Institution, by A.H. Holme, 1835–7, converted and extended as LIPA by Brock Carmichael Associates, 1992–6 (p. 372)

55	58
56	59
57	

60. Leigh, St
Joseph (R.C.
by Joseph
Hansom,
1855, interi-
(p. 232)
61. Warrington
St Mary
(R.C.), by
E.W. Pugin
and Peter
Paul Pugin
1875–7,
interior
(p. 609)
62. Liverpool
(Tue Brook
St John the
Baptist,
G. F. Bodle
1867–70,
interior
(p. 478)

63. Atherton, St John
    Baptist, by Paley
    & Austin, 1878–92
    (p. 136)
64. Liverpool
    (Mossley Hill),
    St Matthew and
    St James, by Paley
    & Austin, 1870–5
    (p. 439)
65. Liverpool
    (Mossley Hill), St
    Matthew and St
    James, by Paley &
    Austin, interior
    (p. 439)

63
64 | 65

66. Great Altcar, St Michael, by John Douglas, 1878–9, interior (p. 179)

67. Liverpool (Allerton), All Hallows, east window, figures designed by Edward Burne-Jones, 1875–6 (p. 386)

68. Liverpool (Sefton Park), St Agnes, by J.L. Pearson, 1883–5, interior (p. 447)

69. Liverpool (Sefton Park), St Clare, by Leonard Stokes, 1889–90, interior (p. 449)

66	68
67	69

70. Liverpool, Anglican Cathedral, by Sir Giles Gilbert Scott, 1904–78 (p. 344)
71. Liverpool, Anglican Cathedral, by Sir Giles Gilbert Scott, interior looking east from the nave (p. 350)
72. Liverpool (Sefton Park), Ullet Road Unitarian Church, detail of library ceiling painted by Gerald Moira, completed 1902 (p. 450)
73. Liverpool, Methodist Central Hall (former), by Bradshaw & Gass, opened 1905 (p. 285)

| 70 | 72 |
| 71 | 73 |

74. Liverpool (Toxteth), Greek Orthodox Church of St Nicholas, by Henry Sumners, opened 1870 (p. 472)
75. Liverpool, Gustav Adolfs Kyrka, by W. D. Caröe, 1883–4 (p. 286)
76. Liverpool (Toxteth), Synagogue, by W. & G. Audsley, 1871–4, interior (p. 474)

74
—
75   76

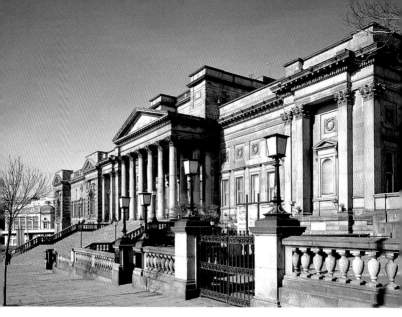

77. Liverpool, St George's Hall, by Harvey Lonsdale Elmes, 1841–54 (p. 291)
78. Liverpool, St George's Hall, the Concert Hall, by Harvey Lonsdale Elmes with C.R. Cockerell (p. 295)
79. Liverpool Museum and Library, by John Weightman, 1857–60, and, left, the Museum Extension and Central Technical School, by E.W. Mountford, opened 1901 (p. 298)
80. Liverpool, Picton Reading Room, by Cornelius Sherlock, 1875–9 (p. 299)

77 │ 79
78 │ 80

81. Liverpool
    (Everton),
    former
    Collegiate
    Institution,
    by Harvey
    Lonsdale
    Elmes,
    1840–3
    (p. 421)
82. Liverpool
    (Wavertree)
    Blue Coat
    School, by
    Briggs,
    Wolstenholm
    & Thornely,
    1903–6
    (p. 495)

83. Wigan, Town
    Hall (built as
    the Mining
    and Technical
    College), by
    Briggs &
    Wolstenholme,
    1900–3
    (p. 666)
84. Liverpool,
    Victoria
    Building,
    University of
    Liverpool,
    by Alfred
    Waterhouse,
    1889–92
    (p. 363)

    81 | 83
    82 | 84

85. Leigh, Town Hall, by J.C. Prestwich, 1904–7 (p. 232)
86. Liverpool (Walton), Walton Prison, by Charles James Peirce, possibly with John Weightman, *c.* 1850–4 (p. 490)
87. Liverpool (Sefton Park), Sefton Park, Palm House, by Mackenzie & Moncur, opened 1896 (p. 454)
88. Liverpool (Anfield), City of Liverpool Cemetery, gates, clock tower and lodges, by Lucy & Littler, *c.* 1861–4 (p. 394)

| 85 | 87 |
| 86 | 88 |

89. Liverpool, Castle Street, Bank of England (former), by C.R. Cockerell, 1846–8 (p. 311)
90. Liverpool, Water Street, Oriel Chambers, by Peter Ellis, 1864, detail (p. 342)
91. Liverpool, North John Street, Royal Insurance building (former), by James F. Doyle, 1896–1903 (p. 328)
92. Liverpool, Tower Buildings, Water Street, by Walter Aubrey Thomas, completed by 1910 (p. 342)

| 89 | 91 |
| 90 | 92 |

93. Liverpool, Lime Street, Lime Street Station Hotel (former), by Alfred Waterhouse, 1868–71 (p. 304)

94. Warrington, Town Hall, gates by the Coalbrookdale Company, designed by Kershaw and Crook, exhibited 1862 (p. 612)

95. Liverpool, Hope Street, Philharmonic Hotel, by Walter W. Thomas, c. 1898–1900 (p. 375)

96. Liverpool, Albert Dock, by Jesse Hartley, 1843–7, west warehouse (p. 263)

97. Liverpool, Waterloo East Dock, Waterloo Grain Warehouse, by G.F. Lyster, 1866–8 (p. 280)

93	96
94	
95	97

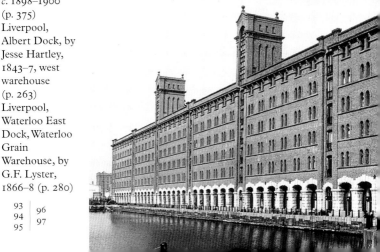

98. Newton-le-
    Willows, Sankey
    Viaduct, by
    George
    Stephenson and
    Jesse Hartley,
    1828–30 (p. 526)
99. Liverpool (Edge
    Hill), Edge Hill
    Station, 1836,
    westbound
    platform
    building (p. 99)
100. Liverpool, Lime
    Street Station,
    train shed roof
    by William Baker
    and F. Steven-
    son, begun 1867,
    detail (p. 304)
101. Wigan, Leeds
    and Liverpool
    Canal, and
    Western Mills,
    No. 1 Mill, by
    Stott & Sons,
    1884 (pp. 673,
    675)
102. Liverpool, Argyle
    Street, warehouse,
    earlier c19, and,
    right, the
    Bridewell, 1861
    (pp. 301, 306)

    98 | 101
    99 | 102
    100 |

103. Wigan, Coop's Suit Factory, centre section, by Issitt & Verity, 1888 (p. 671)
104. Waterloo, Beach Lawn, 1860s–70s (p. 645)
105. Ince Blundell Hall, Picture Gallery (now chapel), ceiling decoration by J.G. Crace, c. 1850 (p. 206)

103 | 104
     | 105

106. Liverpool (Allerton), Allerton Priory, by Alfred Waterhouse, 1866–71, staircase hall (p. 391)

107. Knowsley Hall, State Dining Room, by John Foster Jun., c. 1810–21, remodelled 1890 (p. 221)

108. Blundellsands, Warren Road, Redcot, by Frank Atkinson, 1909 (p. 154).

109. Liverpool (Wavertree), Fieldway Green, Wavertree Garden Suburb, by G. L. Sutcliffe, c. 1913 (p. 500)

106 | 108
107 | 109

110. Liverpool, Pier
Head, Memorial
to the Heroes of
the Marine
Engine Room,
by William
Goscombe John,
1916, detail (p. 333)

111. Liverpool, St
George's Plateau,
The Cenotaph,
1930, detail of
relief by H. Tyson
Smith (p. 297)

112. Wigan, All Saints
churchyard, First
World War
Memorial, by Sir
Giles Gilbert
Scott, 1925 (p. 493)

113. Liverpool
(Wavertree), Holy
Trinity church-
yard, First World
War Memorial, by
H. Tyson Smith,
c. 1920 (p. 493)

114. Ashton-in-Makerfield, St Oswald and St Edmund Arrowsmith
    (R.C.), by J. Sydney Brocklesby, 1925–30, north arcade (p. 125)
115. Ashton-in-Makerfield, St Oswald and St Edmund Arrowsmith
    (R.C.), stained glass by the Harry Clarke Studio, c. 1933–7, detail
    (p. 126)
116. Liverpool (Speke), Airport (former), terminal and control tower, by
    Edward Bloomfield, 1937–9 (p. 458)
117. Liverpool (Edge Hill), Littlewoods Building, probably by Gerald de
    Courcy Fraser, opened 1938 (p. 416)

118. Liverpool, Metropolitan Cathedral (R.C.), by Frederick Gibberd,
  1962–7, steps by Falconer Chester, 2003 (p. 356)
119. Liverpool, Metropolitan Cathedral (R.C.), by Frederick Gibberd,
  interior (p. 358)
120. Liverpool (Allerton), Wyncote Sports Pavilion, by Gerald R. Beech,
  1961–2 (p. 388)
121. Liverpool, North Docks, Tate & Lyle Sugar Silo (former), by the Tate &
  Lyle Engineering Dept, 1955–7 (p. 279)

118 | 120
119 | 121

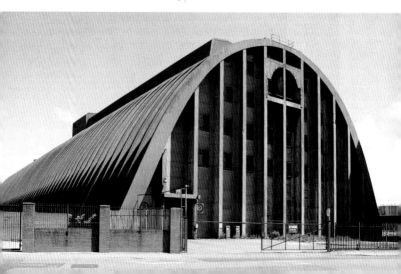

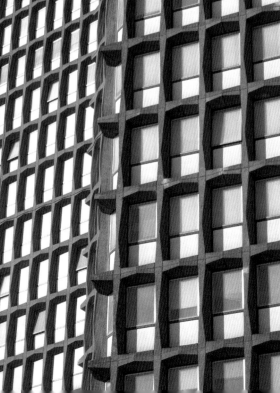

122. St Helens
 (Ravenhead),
 Pilkington Glass
 Headquarters,
 by Fry, Drew &
 Partners,
 completed
 1964–5, tower
 and lakeside
 range (p. 572)
123. Bootle, Triad
 Building, by the
 Hind Woodhouse
 Partnership,
 1971–4, detail
 (p. 160)
124. Warrington
 (Westbrook), the
 Burtonwood
 Motorway
 Services, by
 Patrick Gwynne,
 1972–4,
 westbound
 pavilion (p. 639)
125. Warrington,
 Royal Mail Rail
 Terminal, by
 Austin-
 Smith:Lord,
 completed 1997
 (p. 624)

122 | 124
123 | 125

126. Warrington, Tim Parry Johnathan Ball Young People's Centre, by
    Buttress Fuller Alsop Williams, 1999–2001 (p. 633)
127. Liverpool (Garston), Mersey Match Factory, by Mewès & Davis and
    Sven Bylander, 1919–21, south elevation, with service pods, part of the
    office conversion by ShedKM, 2001 (p. 431)

uninspired Baroque part by *Sidney W. Doyle* was built in phases, 1913–15 and 1939–40, and flanked by dull extensions in 1966 and 1978.

Filling most of the E side of Brownlow Street is the former ROYAL INFIRMARY. It is by *Alfred Waterhouse* and dates from p. 77 1887–90. It was Liverpool's third purpose-built infirmary. In 1978 it was superseded by the new hospital in Prescot Street (*see* p. 421). After years of dereliction, it was admirably refurbished in the 1990s by the University's Estates Department, and externally now appears more or less as designed. Common brick with red terracotta dressings, very plain, with some Romanesque and Gothic touches, and round arches used extensively. Administration block with Gothic gables and porte cochère facing Pembroke Place. Behind, six ward blocks branch N and S from a spine corridor running from W to E (the link between administration block and wards has been demolished). The S ward blocks end at Dover Street with external arcaded balconies flanked by towers. Typical pavilion plan, except that the NW and NE blocks are circular, the earliest use of this plan-form for a large-scale new hospital in England. Circular wards had recently been used at the Antwerp Civil Hospital which Waterhouse had visited, but they did not win the approval of Florence Nightingale when he consulted her over his Liverpool designs. They were nevertheless adopted because pre-existing buildings constricted the site at these two corners. In Ashton Street, at the E end of the spine corridor, are the mortuary and boiler house, the latter with a Gothic chimney. At the W end of the spine corridor, in the middle of the Brownlow Street front, is the former CHAPEL. It has nave and aisles, and beautiful turquoise tilework by *Burmantofts*.

In the early C20 the corners of the site became available for expansion. At the corner of Pembroke Place and Brownlow Street, a new outpatients' department (now the FORESIGHT CENTRE) was added by *James F. Doyle*, 1909–11. Waterhousian Gothic in red brick and terracotta, with octagonal angle turrets. Inside, it had a full-height central waiting room lined with cream and green tiles, only the ends of which survive. At the corner of Pembroke Place and Ashton Street a new nurses' home (now CEDAR HOUSE) by *Edmund Kirby & Sons* was begun in 1923. This alone among the Infirmary buildings is classical.

On the E side of Ashton Street are the SHERRINGTON BUILDINGS of the Faculty of Medicine. Long, dull block fronting the street, 1951–7, by *Weightman & Bullen*. Inside on the first floor, excellent relocated memorial to Sir Robert William Boyce, by *C.J. Allen*, 1913. A frieze of figures alludes to Boyce's work on tropical medicine, and mosquitoes decorate the border of his portrait. A rear wing, at right angles and raised on stilts, was added by *Weightman & Bullen*, 1965–7. In 2001–2 the same architects rebuilt the N end of the front block. Further S, facing the Ashton Building, the HAROLD

COHEN LIBRARY, 1936–8, by *Harold Dod*. Symmetrical, Portland stone-faced, and vestigially classical. The wings, lower than the central block containing the reading room, were extended upwards and given curved roofs by the *Gilling Dod Partnership*, 1997. Sculpture over the main entrance by *Eric Kennington*, a female figure superimposed on an open book, representing Learning. The brick-faced bookstack block at the rear is entirely different: uncompromisingly functional, with windows in continuous bands.

Facing the Victoria Building across Ashton Street is ELEC-TRICAL ENGINEERING AND ELECTRONICS, 1962–5, by *Yorke, Rosenberg & Mardall*. Six-storey block with lower blocks grouped behind, all faced in the horizontal white-glazed tiles that were the practice's trademark at this time. The tiles are vertically aligned, not staggered like bricks, to emphasise their status as cladding; they also correspond to the module of the building, covering the surface entirely without a single tile having to be cut. Windows mostly in bands, but the ground floor of the high block is fully glazed behind the uprights of the frame, to form a transparent foyer around the lecture theatres. The impression of purity and aloofness is underlined by the surrounding 'moat', across which the main entrance is reached by a footbridge. *Yorke, Rosenberg & Mardall* added the COMPUTER LABORATORY at the rear in 1967–9, and extended it 1973–4. This time the tiles have their long sides upright. Further E, across Crown Street is BIOLOGICAL SCIENCES. The original building, 1965–9, by *R. R. Young*, was reduced in height in 2003. A recent very large extension by *David Morley Architects* is curved in plan.

Returning to the corner of Brownlow Hill and Mount Pleasant brings us to the GUILD OF STUDENTS. The earliest part (N end) dates from 1910–13. It is the major work of *Charles Reilly*, Roscoe Professor of Architecture, and illustrates his enthusiasm for a hybrid classicism combining Regency, Greek, and French Beaux Arts elements. Markedly different W and E elevations are meant to reflect that the former was for women, the latter for men. This division is also evident in the plan. The women's side, facing Mount Pleasant, is composed like a Regency house and has squat Doric columns to the ground floor which continue round the bow window. The upper floor of the bow has slender baluster-like columns in pairs. The men's side, of six bays, has a massive Beaux Arts balcony and bluntly pedimented windows to the first floor, and round windows over. N elevation largely windowless (it originally overlooked a railway cutting), with two bowed staircase pro-jections and a pedimented portion with brick columns high up in the middle. The best interior is the former GILMOUR HALL, designed as a debating chamber, now unhappily converted into a bar with split-level floor. Ponderous Doric columns in the corners and a richly compartmented ceiling. The two spiral staircases are also impressive, especially the men's with cast-iron latticework balustrade. Some rooms have classical reliefs by *Ethel Frimston*. Sensitive extension, s, by *Reilly*, *L.B. Budden* and *J.E. Marshall*, 1932–5. In 1962–5 a further large southward extension by *Bridgwater, Shepheard & Epstein* was added. Dark brick with bands of grey mosaic round the windows, and two opposing monopitch roofs. This was imaginatively adapted in the mid 1990s by *King McAllister*. They subdivided former restaurant spaces, inserting free-standing mezzanines of meticulously detailed steelwork. The courtyard was roofed with a huge wedge-shaped skylight, echoing the Metropolitan Cathedral's sloping roof and framing a view of its tower from within. (Across Mount Pleasant, on the opposite corner with Brownlow Hill, a large office building by *Falconer Chester* with a curved glass façade to Mount Pleasant was nearing completion in 2005.)

sw from here is No. 126 Mount Pleasant, built as the SCHOOL OF HYGIENE and CITY LABORATORIES, dated 1914. Begun under *Thomas Shelmerdine* and completed under *A.D. Jenkins*, successive Corporation Surveyors. Classical, in red brick with much stone. Big and lumpish and unworthy of its splendid site. Turning into Oxford Street, Nos. 14–30 are a terrace of *c.* 1820. Brick, two-and-a-half storeys above a basement, with recessed doorways under arches, flanked by Doric columns. Typical of the housing that covered this area before the university. On the N side, MULBERRY COURT, student housing of two phases round a landscaped quadrangle. Block fronting the street by *Manning Clamp & Partners*, 1978–81, with shops recessed behind a colonnade; a similar block at right angles behind. The other two sides are hostels of 1967–70 by *Gerald Beech*. Also by *Beech*, the glass-faced BEDFORD HOUSE on the s side of Oxford Street, 1965–6, originally a club for non-academic staff.

Opposite Bedford House stands the most startling and assertive of all the university's post-war buildings, the SPORTS CENTRE by *Denys Lasdun & Partners*, 1963–6, extended 2003–4 by *Austin-Smith:Lord*. The plan of the Lasdun part is lucid and practical: sports hall and swimming pool balance each other on the N and s sides, with stairs, changing rooms, squash courts, etc., stacked between. As for the raw concrete and glass exterior with its dominant slanting lines, Pevsner considered it a calculated insult to the Late Georgian rectangularity of nearby Abercromby Square. Pool and sports hall have tilted roofs that slope down towards the spine. The s elevation leans inwards and is entirely glazed, the roof carried by slender raking columns passing just in front of the glass. Ground floor recessed behind this angled colonnade (the N elevation was identical before the recent extension). W and E ends almost windowless above the ground floor, with only a sliver of glazing just below the roof. Each is crowned by an overhanging water tank which seems to weigh down the two roofs at the point where they meet. Inside the sports hall a splendid brick climbing wall devised by *Donald Mill*, with concrete projections, like a piece of abstract sculpture. N extension, equal in size to Lasdun's building, which it crashes into destructively. It has a catenary roof, suspended between A-frames, and much silvery cladding.

So to ABERCROMBY SQUARE, now entirely occupied by the university. This is the most complete survival of the housing built all over the area in the early C19. Before 1800 this elevated tract was a heath known as Mosslake Fields. In that year the Select Improvement Committee recommended the adoption of plans made by the Corporation Surveyor, *John Foster Sen.*, for laying out the area between Crabtree Lane to the s (now Falkner Street) and Brownlow Hill to the N. Foster's plan was a straightforward grid running N–S and W–E, with a large and prestigious square, Abercromby Square, at its centre. Little progress was made until the lessees surrendered their interests in 1816. In 1819 *Foster* produced an elevation for a terrace on one side of the square. This was adopted for the w side with slight modifications, but those taking out leases were allowed more flexibility on the other sides. The centre of the E side was occupied by the Ionic portico of St Catherine's church, 1829–31, by *John Foster Jun.*, bombed in the Second World War and demolished for the Senate House (*see* p. 369). Building on the three sides which survive was largely complete by 1830. The houses are brick, of three storeys plus basement, with a Greek Doric porch in the middle of each side, the other doorways having Doric pilasters. In the middle of the communal garden is a pretty circular domed building, surrounded by a cast-iron trellis, designed by the elder *Foster* in 1822 for storing garden tools.

No. 19 on the N side, now the DEPARTMENT OF EDUCA-TION and DEPARTMENT OF CORPORATE COMMUNICA-TIONS, is of seven bays and higher than its neighbours. Designed 1862–3 by *William Culshaw* for C.K. Prioleau, a South Carolina-born businessman; early in the 1880s it was altered to become the Bishop's Palace. Perhaps the grandest surviving C19 house in the city centre, with a fine top-lit hall with circular balustraded openings on the first and second floors. Some ground-floor rooms have 1860s painted ceilings, the best being the former dining room, with figures in classical dress seen through a *trompe l'œil* oculus. The vestibule ceiling has a palmetto tree – as featured on the flag adopted by South Carolina in 1861, when it seceded from the Union. On the same side, No. 23 and adjoining houses were given lavish late C17-style interiors for the School of Education *c.* 1921, by *Ronald P. Jones*. No. 25 at the w end of the terrace is the SCHOOL OF ARCHITECTURE AND BUILDING ENGI-NEERING, with a rear extension (the Leverhulme Building) by *Reilly, Budden & Marshall*, opened 1933. It aims to harmonise with the square and yet be Modernist of a kind still rare in England by this date. Note the horizontal window band. Pro-jecting glazed stair between new and old, added by *Gerald Beech*, 1970s. The 1930s extension was itself extended –

inwards and upwards – by *Dave King* and *Rod McAllister* (with the *Gerald Beech Partnership*), 1987–8. They added a three-storey open-plan studio and gallery space, partly occupying the central courtyard, partly rising above the old roof level. It is a lightweight steel and glass structure with exposed constructional details, services, etc., intended as an object lesson for students.

The E side is filled by SENATE HOUSE, by *Tom Mellor & Partners*, 1966–8. Proportions and materials respond sensitively to the neighbouring terraces, but the lack of a central entrance is keenly felt, especially since the portico of St Catherine was demolished to make way for it. Instead, there is an off-centre projecting platform, designed for a bronze sculpture, Squares with Two Circles, by *Barbara Hepworth*. The main entrance, perversely, is tucked away in the short return at the N end, facing Oxford Street. The Senate Room, a circular drum surrounded by a square colonnade, forms a pavilion at the back.

Leaving the square at the SW corner, Bedford Street South begins with the DEPARTMENT OF CIVIC DESIGN, 1950–1, by *Gordon Stephenson*. Red brick, with a band of glazing to the first-floor library. The first new building in the Precinct to be completed after the war, it has the slightly undernourished look that marks that period of austerity. In the rear courtyard, a Portland stone sculpture, The Quickening, 1951, by *Mitzi Cunliffe*: a bird resting in the palm of a large hand. On the same side, a few early C19 stuccoed houses behind front gardens, now university departments. Across the end of the street, and defining the S edge of the Precinct, the ELEANOR RATHBONE BUILDING, 1970–3, a lacklustre affair in blue-grey brick by *Yorke, Rosenberg & Mardall*, not a patch on their earlier work for the University.

Spreading E from Bedford Street South is a group of four blocks by *Bryan & Norman Westwood, Piet & Partners*, 1961–6. They constitute the most coherent and satisfying part of the Precinct, partly because their architecture is consistent and partly because the spaces between are planned with as much care as the buildings themselves. The RENDALL BUILDING (originally Arts Library and lecture rooms) is a hollow square. Brick below, concrete above, much of the upper storey faced with slabs which deviate slightly from the vertical, creating a kind of seasick feeling. Inside, large areas of glass overlook the quiet, cloister-like court. The upper floor, originally a reading room, has been subdivided, and the abstract stained glass by *Gillian Rees-Thomas* is now difficult to see. On the E side the court is open at ground-floor level to a pleasant, irregular area of grass and trees, formed from the back gardens of houses in Abercromby Square, an idea proposed by *Holford* in 1949. It is enclosed by two taller slabs, the ROXBY BUILDING and MODERN LANGUAGES. Just behind these, the last and most interesting of the group, the LAW SCHOOL. Square in plan and very restrained externally, with slender vertical fins of concrete (recently painted) to the upper floors. The roof hints at the intricate internal planning, with the library, lecture theatre, moot room and various circulation spaces interlocking like pieces of an ingenious puzzle.

On the opposite, E side of Chatham Street is the CHATHAM BUILDING, 1860–1, originally a Welsh Presbyterian Chapel, by *Oliver & Lamb* of Newcastle. Brick and painted stone, coarse Italianate, with giant pilasters and a grotesque bellcote crowning the pediment. Large rear extension for the MANAGEMENT SCHOOL by *McCormick Architecture*, completed 2002. L-shaped, with glazing between brick piers. Clerestory above a heavy projecting course of artificial stone. Immediately N, the three-storey brick and concrete SYDNEY JONES LIBRARY, by *Basil Spence, Glover & Ferguson*, completed 1976. Set back from Chatham Street behind a sloping, brick-paved forecourt. A pair of stair-towers marks the central entrance. Down both sides projecting brick boxes contain individual work spaces, like the partly open drawers of a row of filing cabinets. On the forecourt a red-painted abstract sculpture in steel, Red Between, 1971–3, by *Phillip King*, installed 1977.

Chatham Street leads back to the E side of Abercromby Square, past a hexagonal pillar box of the type designed by *J. W. Penfold*, introduced in 1866. Passing Senate House and crossing Oxford Street we reach the OLIVER LODGE PHYSICS LABORATORY, 1966–8, by *Tom Mellor & Partners* with the *United Kingdom Atomic Energy Authority* as executive architects. The same dark brick as Senate House (to which it is linked by a bridge over Oxford Street) with copper cladding above the windows.

A passage leads to THE GREEN, an open space created in 1960 by clearing C19 housing. Along the W side is the CHADWICK LABORATORY, 1957–9, by *Basil Spence*. An eight-storey tower on stilts, from which a spine corridor runs N with single-storey laboratories branching off symmetrically. At the opposite end from the tower are lecture theatres, again symmetrical, with the raked auditoria cantilevered from the centre. Inside, the plan is admirably clear, but from outside the building is mostly too low to have much impact, and the painted concrete and grey mosaic cladding to the tower have not aged well. Near the tower entrance, a cast aluminium sculpture, Three Uprights, by *Hubert Dalwood*, won in competition 1959. In the entrance hall leading to the lecture theatres, an impressive mosaic MURAL of the same date by *Geoffrey Clarke* (a cast-aluminium relief, also by *Clarke* and now in the entrance under the tower, was made originally for the Oliver Lodge Physics Laboratory, 1966–8). The E side of The Green is all CHEMISTRY, by *Stephenson, Young & Partners*, in several phases. The red brick parts are 1951–4 and 1956–8, the curtain-walled ROBERT ROBINSON LABORATORIES at the S end 1960–2, and a small extension at the N end 1973–4. Closing the N side, the SCIENCE LECTURE ROOMS, 1965–7, by *Robert Gardner-Medwin* with *Saunders, Boston & Brock*. The N-facing entrance front is a strong, jaggedly Brutalist composition, mostly in raw concrete. A frieze of abstract sculpture by *David Le Marchant*

Brock and *Frederick Bushe* on the ground floor, above which two of the auditoria jut out, one sideways, one head on. On the other three sides, panels of brick predominate. First-floor foyer with big windows overlooking The Green.

N of the Science Lecture Rooms, across the line of an E–W railway cutting covered over during the 1960s, is VETERINARY SCIENCE, 1958–60, by the Liverpool-trained *E. Maxwell Fry*. Fry was a pioneer of Modernism in Britain, but this is sadly unremarkable. The E and W ends of the rear elevation facing Brownlow Hill have reliefs of a horse and a bull carved into the brickwork by *Eric Peskett*. Attached to the main building on the E, the SMALL ANIMAL HOSPITAL, 1976–7, by *Ormrod & Partners*. W of Veterinary Science is the ALSOP BUILDING, containing shops, a pub, a bank, etc., 1965–8, by *Tom Mellor & Partners*, and S of this are MATHEMATICS and OCEANOGRAPHY, 1959–61, by *Bryan Westwood*. Two parallel blocks, of six storeys and two storeys, linked by single-storey labs and a covered walkway, with a grassed courtyard in the middle. The cladding originally included large pyramidal panels on the ends of the higher block, intended to create chiaroscuro effects as they became stained with soot. They have been replaced with brick, but panels with smaller geometrical relief patterns survive on the long elevations. At the S end of the two-storey block, the university's original computer room, with copper-covered hyperbolic paraboloid roof. The penthouse on the higher block had a roof of similar form, for which a grossly inappropriate replacement has been substituted. The main entrance on the W has an iron SCREEN by *John McCarthy* incorporating mathematical symbols, and the same artist made the five-panel MURAL in the entrance hall of the higher block, illustrating the growth of mathematical ideas.

OTHER PUBLIC BUILDINGS

POSTAL SORTING OFFICE, Copperas Hill. 1973–7, by *IDC Ltd* from a design by *Twist & Whitley*. A huge oblong block clad in concrete panels, with a cluster of brown brick towers marking the N entrance. Approached from Skelhorne Street it looks impressively fortress-like. Resited in the enclosure l. of the entrance, a rare early PILLAR BOX of 1863, one of the unusually large 'Liverpool Special' boxes, with rope mouldings and a crown on top.

PHILHARMONIC HALL, Hope Street. 1936–9, by *Herbert J. Rowse* (its predecessor of 1846–9 by *John Cunningham* burned down in 1933). It owes something to Rowse's assistant *A.E. Rice*, who made a similar concert-hall design 1932–3, while at the Liverpool School of Architecture. Of brick, and starkly cubic except for two rounded stair-towers in front: the influence of the Dutch architect W.M. Dudok is clear. Rear extension by *Brock Carmichael Associates*, completed 1992. The main doors and first-floor windows of the Rowse building have etched glass by *Hector Whistler*. Just inside the entrance, a

MEMORIAL to the musicians of the *Titanic* in repoussé copper, by *J.A. Hodel*. On the landings, gilded reliefs of Apollo by *Edmund C. Thompson*. In contrast to the blocky exterior, the auditorium is sensuously curved. Walls and ceiling form a continuous shell, broken into gentle, overlapping folds. Originally of fibrous plaster, this was entirely rebuilt in concrete by *Brock Carmichael*, working with acoustic consultants *Lawrence Kirkegaard Associates* (completed 1995). New recessed lights and other changes now mar the smoothness of Rowse's design. Incised Art Deco female figures on the walls by *Thompson*, representing 'musical moods', were reinstated. Above the platform, a kinetic sculpture, Adagio, by *Marianne Forrest*, 1995.

LIVERPOOL ART SCHOOL, Hope Street. The earliest part faces Mount Street. It is dated 1882, by *Thomas Cook*. Classical details, but no particular style. N-facing studio windows. The main entrance is in Hope Street, in a wing by *Willink & Thicknesse* dated 1910. This is one of Liverpool's best buildings in the refined classical style of the early c20 promoted by Charles Reilly. *Cook*'s return elevation is not parallel with Hope Street, and Willink & Thicknesse mirror this at the other end, so the Hope Street façade is gently concave. Square central porch, flanked by segmental bows with giant panelled pilasters. In 1961 a further extension along Hope Street was opened, designed by the City Architect's Department (*Ronald Bradbury*). Mostly curtain-walled, with brick at the s end.

ALDHAM ROBARTS LEARNING RESOURCE CENTRE, Maryland Street. This white-rendered library for Liverpool John Moores University, 1992–3, by *Austin-Smith:Lord*, is the most notable 1990s building in Liverpool. It combines computer facilities with bookstacks, and was intended to link physically with the restored St Andrew's church next door, forming a gateway to the university campus from Rodney Street. Square plan, divided into four subsidiary squares by internal 'streets' that cut across each floor N–S and W–E. Shallow curved roofs identify these externally, and to N and s they end in glazed stairtowers. The main entrance is in the NE quarter, a three-storey atrium behind a wavy glass wall, set back under the oversailing space-frame roof. This unites the building with its attractively landscaped grounds, and helps knit its uncompromisingly modern design into a largely c19 setting (for the university buildings to the N, *see* Mount Pleasant, p. 377).

59 LIPA (Liverpool Institute of Performing Arts), Mount Street. Built 1835–7 as the Mechanics' Institution (the date 1825 on the façade refers to its inception). The competition was won by *Arthur Hill Holme*; *James Picton* was executant architect. Ashlar façade, restrained but imposing, with pairs of giant unfluted Ionic columns at the entrance, and no pediment. Converted to its present use by *Brock Carmichael Associates*, 1992–6. They rebuilt the rear parts (creating a new main entrance), added a ramped approach to Holme's entrance, and designed a new block to the r., with elevations to Mount Street and Pilgrim Street. This is mostly stone-faced, but the curved

corner is glazed, enclosing a helical staircase. On the Pilgrim Street front, windows in vertical strips project at an angle. Between new and old, a glazed atrium. The C19 entrance hall has cast-iron gates between Ionic columns. Straight ahead is the U-shaped former lecture hall (now a theatre), with a gallery on slender iron columns, reached by two graceful open staircases outside the door.

BLACKBURNE HOUSE, facing Hope Street. The S part, built as a private house *c.* 1800, has a portico of four columns towards Blackburne Place, and a central staircase hall under a domed skylight. In 1844 it became the girls' school of the Mechanics' Institution (*see* LIPA, above), latterly the Liverpool Institute High School for Girls. In 1874–6 *W.I. Mason* added the central tower with French pavilion roof, and the N wing that balances the original house, which was partly refaced to match. In 1994 *Pickles Martinez Architects* completed a sensitive adaptation as a women's training centre.

LIVERPOOL COMMUNITY COLLEGE ARTS CENTRE, Myrtle Street. By *Austin-Smith:Lord*, 1999. Red brick, with an oversailing aluminium roof supported on a slender column at the corner. An extension along Mulberry Street, by *Ellis Williams Architects*, is under construction 2005.

SCHOOL FOR THE BLIND (former). *See* Hardman Street, p. 375.

UNITY THEATRE. Built as a synagogue, 1856–7, by *Thomas Wylie*. Yellow brick with stone dressings and touches of polychromy, in what *The Builder* called 'a modification of the Byzantine or Cinque-cento style'. The original vestry and Reader's house formed advancing wings, with an arcaded portico between. A high hemispherical dome with windows round the base, distinctly Byzantine, soon proved defective and was replaced with a shallower dome. Rebuilding as a theatre *c.* 1997, by *Mills Beaumont Leavey Channon* of Manchester, did away with the dome and incorporated the portico into a projecting glazed foyer (painted top-floor window by *Terry Duffy*), with two performance spaces stacked behind. Joining of new and old is awkward. Next door, the JOE H. MAKIN DRAMA CENTRE of Liverpool John Moores University was formerly the Hebrew Schools by Messrs *Hay*, begun 1852, extended to the r. 1870s, and upwards 1880. Brick with stone dressings, Gothic.

Former ROYAL INFIRMARY. *See* p. 365.

LIVERPOOL WOMEN'S HOSPITAL, Crown Street. 1992–5, by the *Percy Thomas Partnership* from a conceptual design by *HLM*: red brick and white cladding with light blue metal roofs. SCULPTURE outside the main entrance, E: Mother and Child, 1999 by *Terry McDonald*.

STREETS

ABERCROMBY SQUARE. *See* p. 368.

BENSON STREET. Nos. 8 and 10, *c.* 1842, were the offices (combined with a dwelling) of Samuel & James Holme, leading mid-C19 building contractors. A handsome Greek Revival composition in ashlar, crowned by a pediment filled with acanthus scrolls, no doubt intended to advertise the firm's skills. *Arthur Hill Holme* (brother of Samuel and James) probably designed it, possibly with *John Cunningham*.

BLACKBURNE PLACE. Set back behind a carriage drive is BLACKBURNE TERRACE, six houses, dated 1826, the middle four with paired Doric porches. Opposite, an impressive railway VENTILATION TOWER, 1890s.

BROWNLOW HILL. *See* pp. 363 and 366.

CANNING STREET. One of the longest and best-preserved C19 residential streets in the area. The E continuation of Duke Street, it was laid out in the late 1820s–early 1830s to link up with the town centre. Red brick three-bay terraced houses, of three storeys above a basement, with columned doorcases. Nos. 1–43 were mostly complete by 1836. Nos. 4–16, unusually, are stone-faced. Nos. 18–50, *c.* 1845, form a terrace with two pediments and cast-iron balconies of lush acanthus; opposite them, a stuccoed Italianate terrace, probably 1850s.

CATHARINE STREET. Houses of the first half of the C19. Nos. 44–50 are stuccoed with columned porches, *c.* 1840. AGNES JONES HOUSE was formerly the Women's Hospital, 1932, Neo-Georgian by *Edmund Kirby & Sons*. Recently converted into student accommodation by *Brock Carmichael*. Opposite (w side), PHILHARMONIC COURT, student housing begun 1973 by *Saunders & Boston*. The BLACKBURNE ARMS at the corner of Falkner Street is an elegant Neo-Georgian pub by *Harold E. Davies & Son* (i.e. *Harold Hinchliffe Davies*), 1927.

EGERTON STREET. Modest two-storey houses of *c.* 1844 tucked behind the larger terraces of the main streets. No. 2, PETER KAVANAGH'S, a pub with murals of *c.* 1929 by *Eric Robertson* inside.

FALKNER SQUARE. The central garden is shown on a map of 1831, but the stuccoed houses did not begin to appear until the mid 1840s. The E side is a unified composition with a central pediment. The rest are looser, and several houses have canted bay windows, and balustraded balconies and parapets. Drawings for No. 29 are signed by *William Culshaw*, 1845. Was he responsible for the elevation of the whole s side and therefore probably the N and W sides too, or did his drawings conform to an overall elevation by another?

GAMBIER TERRACE *see* HOPE STREET.

GROVE STREET. No. 117 is THE OCTAGON, an unusual house with Gothic details. Built in 1867 by Dr. J.W. Hayward, to demonstrate his ideas on domestic heating and ventilation. His system required a tall chimney, visible at the rear, in which were combined the smoke flue from the kitchen and a shaft for expelling foul air, extracted from all the rooms by a system of ducts. Hayward's colleague, Dr Drysdale, built a similarly equipped house at Waterloo (*see* p. 645).

HARDMAN STREET. On the corner of Baltimore Street, a shopfront of 1888 in Queen Anne style, for the bakers Kirkland Bros. Immediately E stood St Philip, 1815–16, one of

John Cragg's cast-iron churches (*see* pp. 381 and 417). Some ironwork fragments survive inside the later block built on the site. On the s side, the long Grecian frontage of the former SCHOOL FOR THE BLIND (now the Merseyside Trade Union, Community and Unemployed Resource Centre), 1849–51, by *Arthur Hill Holme*, built when the school's original site in London Road was taken to extend Lime Street Station. The pedimented central section originally had single-storey three-bay wings, later extended and raised to two storeys. Here was the committee room and a shop selling items made by pupils. Behind this show front of Bath stone the buildings are of brick, and more utilitarian. Four wings radiate from a domed rotunda, a plan reminiscent of mid-C19 workhouses. The s wing contained a concert room for performances by pupils. A longer wing at the back, at right angles to this, was for rope-making. The entrance hall (originally the shop) has pilasters and classical plasterwork, and the rotunda a cast-iron balcony with classical details. Dome painted in Socialist Realist style by *Mike Jones*, 1986, reflecting the present use. On the Hope Street corner, l., an extension by *Anthony Minoprio* and *Hugh Greville Spencely*, 1930–2: stripped classicism in Portland stone, the fluted pilasters echoing the vanished portico of *John Foster Jun.*'s Greek Doric chapel, 1818–19, moved here from the London Road site in 1850–1.* Carvings by *John Skeaping* show activities at the school: brush-making, knitting, basket work, piano tuning and reading Braille.**

HOPE STREET. Straightened in the 1790s and built up thereafter; early C19 houses survive at intervals. Near the N end, the MASONIC HALL, a palazzo of 1872 by Mr *Danson* of *Danson & Davies*; additional entrance bay and interior by *Gilbert Fraser* and *W.P. Horsburgh*, 1927–31. At the corner of Hardman Street, the most richly decorated of Liverpool's Victorian pubs, the PHILHARMONIC HOTEL, *c.* 1898–1900, by *Walter W. Thomas*. It is of exceptional quality in national terms. Like The Vines in Lime Street, built for the brewer Robert Cain. Jauntily eclectic exterior with stepped gables, ogee domes, windows in many shapes and styles, and a serpentine balcony over the door. Superb Art Nouveau gates of wrought iron and beaten copper, sometimes ascribed to *H. Bloomfield Bare*. Sumptuous interior, divided by mahogany and glass partitions. Music is a recurrent 95 decorative theme, a reflection of the name and of the nearby concert hall. The designers and craftsmen were supervised by *G. Hall Neale* and *Arthur Stratton* (of the School of Architecture and Applied Arts at University College). Repoussé copper panels by *Bare* in the panelling flanking the fireplace. More copper panels by *Bare* and *Thomas Huson* in the former billiard room; also plasterwork by *C.J. Allen* – a

---

* Dismantled columns from the portico now lie abandoned at Camp Hill, School Lane, Woolton.
** Excellent bronze doors by *James Woodford* are now at the School's Wavertree premises; *see* p. 496.

frieze and two figure groups, The Murmur of the Sea (over the fireplace) and attendants crowning a bust of Apollo (over the door). The decorative richness even extends to the lavatories.

On the N corner of Hope Place, a former carriage works of *c.* 1867, converted to a hotel 2003. Buff brick with round-arched first-floor windows – a sort of pared-down Venetian palazzo, surprisingly grand. On the S corner, the majestic former HAHNEMANN HOMEOPATHIC HOSPITAL, Loire-château-style in red Ruabon brick and stone, by *F. & G. Holme*, dated 1887. HOPE PLACE itself has early C19 terraces. Opposite, FEDERATION HOUSE, 1965–6, by *Gilling Dod & Partners* for the Building Trades Employers. Curtain walling; ground floor with an aggressive concrete relief by *William Mitchell*. Where Hope Street widens at the top of Mount Street there is a curious SCULPTURE, A Case History, by *John King*, completed 1998. Items of luggage, cast in fine-surfaced concrete, are piled on the pavement. Their labels refer to individuals and institutions linked with the area. At the S end, facing the Anglican Cathedral, is GAMBIER TERRACE. Open views to the W made this a most desirable residential site, and in 1828 the developer Ambrose Lace obtained approval for a terrace here. Six houses were built in the early 1830s, four more in the late 1830s–early 1840s, but the terrace was not completed until the early 1870s, to a very different design. The architect of the original (N) part is unknown. It is of ashlar and stucco, and extremely grand. The first seven bays have giant attached Ionic columns above, and a Greek Doric porch (also an enclosed Doric porch at the side, in Canning Street); then come twenty-one recessed bays with a Doric colonnade in front of the ground floor, supporting a continuous first-floor balcony (the same motif as Nos. 3–17 Percy Street, *see* below); then six bays with giant Doric pilasters, suggesting the start of a centrepiece. No. 10, though it matches, in fact dates from the early 1870s. The rest of the 1870s section is of yellow brick, symmetrical in itself, with pavilion-roofed end blocks.

MOUNT PLEASANT. At the bottom, rounding the corner of Renshaw Street, the red brick and stone former UNIVERSITY CLUB, 1903–5, by *Willink & Thicknesse* (perhaps with *F.M. Simpson*). Jacobean-cum-classical, with mullioned-and-transomed bow windows running through the upper floors. ROSCOE GARDENS, higher up on the same side, marks the site of the graveyard of the demolished Renshaw Street Unitarian Chapel, commemorated by a pretty octagonal domed monument with Tuscan columns, 1905, by *Ronald P. Jones*. Nos. 50–52 are two five-bay houses, probably 1780s, with later additions. No. 50 has an unusual doorway, with an open pediment projecting on brackets turned outwards. After these, the YMCA, 1874–7, by *H.H. Vale* (supervised by *W. & G. Audsley* after Vale's death in 1875). C13 Gothic, in brick with red sandstone dressings. Asymmetrically placed tower.

No. 62, next door, is of 1767, making it the oldest house in the street. Five bays and two storeys. A modest, rather rustic-looking building. No. 68, grander, was built *c.* 1788 for the merchant and future mayor, George Dunbar. Three storeys and five bays, the centre framed by a giant blind arch and breaking forward under a pediment. Charming doorway, carved with musical instruments and a frieze incorporating cherubs with globe and compasses. No. 70 is the former Consumption Hospital, 1903–4, by *Grayson & Ould*. Harsh red brick and terracotta, with central pediment and advancing wings. On the N side, small early C19 terraced houses, becoming grander beyond CLARENCE STREET. There are more early C19 houses in Clarence Street itself, N.

The S side from Rodney Street to Hope Street is a confusing agglomeration of buildings, formerly the NOTRE DAME CONVENT and TEACHER TRAINING COLLEGE, now occupied by Liverpool John Moores University. The core is No. 96, a five-bay late C18 house. Inside, a fine imperial stair-case, possibly 1830s, with a beautiful cast-iron balustrade of lushest acanthus. Four bays were added to the r., apparently 1850s, for the convent school. To the l., a training college for female teachers by *J. & C. Hansom*, 1856–7. H-plan, with a stair-tower in the middle, and a forbidding screen wall across the front. Italianate touches. To the r. of the school, a block of 1865–7 by *M.E. Hadfield & Son*. Here, eventually, the nuns went Gothic. Uneventful street elevation, but the CHAPEL wing at the rear, the slender flèche of which is visible, is more impressive. Round apse and buttresses with many set-offs, in polychrome brick and stone. In the apse wall, a carving of the Virgin Mary with two kneeling nuns, in severe medieval style by *Theodore Phyffers*. Chapel interior with quadripartite vault of brick and stone (now painted) carried by clustered shafts on corbels. Plate tracery in side windows; lancets in sanctuary, three with good early C20 stained glass said to be by *Early* of Dublin. Subsequent additions to the convent are all more or less Gothic. Facing Mount Pleasant, r. of the chapel block, two ranges by *Edmund Kirby*, 1870s–90s. To the l. of the training college, and turning the corner into Hope Street, further build-ings by *James O'Byrne*, 1880s, and *Pugin & Pugin*, 1900s.

Opposite, the former WELLINGTON ROOMS, 1814–16, won in competition by *Edmund Aikin* of London, who then moved to Liverpool. Assembly rooms paid for by public subscription. Single-storey ashlar façade combining Greek and some Roman elements. The ends break forward and have pairs of Corinthian pilasters, and the central door is in a semicircular projection recalling the Monument of Lysicrates (originally an open colonnade, infilled in the 1820s because it gave insufficient shelter; porches on the W for sedan chairs and on the E for car-riages have also been enclosed). Capitals after the Temple of Vesta at Tivoli, admired by Soane. In the blank walls to either side two fine panels of sculpture, sometimes ascribed to the young *John Gibson*: pairs of winged female figures bearing gar-lands, adding a touch of gaiety to what is otherwise a rather solemn-looking place of entertainment. Inside, the plan largely survives. At the back is the ballroom with plaster decoration of various dates. The frieze with dancing maidens may be Aikin's, but the garlands and wall panels look later. *See* p. 353 for the Roman Catholic Cathedral, and p. 357 for the buildings flanking the square at the bottom of the ceremonial steps.

On the s side, on the curved corner with Hope Street, the MEDICAL INSTITUTION, 1835–7, by *Clark Rampling*. Convex façade, with a central portico of six Ionic columns set in, and solid end blocks with pilasters. The plan is well adapted to the wedge-shaped site: library and committee room flank the central hall and stairs, which lead to the double-height lecture theatre in the angle at the back. Council room remodelled by *Edmund Rathbone*, 1907, with panelling in the style of *c.* 1700 and an elaborate chimneypiece of beaten copper. In the entrance hall a memorial tablet (a sarcophagus with garlands) to the founder, Dr John Rutter, †1838, brought from the demolished St Peter, Church Street. Facing Oxford Street, a weak extension in artificial stone by *Robertson Young & Partners*, opened 1966.

For the last section of Mount Pleasant, NE from here, *see* the University perambulation, pp. 366–7.

MOUNT STREET. Nos. 7–33, stepping down the hill opposite LIPA (*see* Public Buildings, p. 372), are small houses probably of *c.* 1820.

MYRTLE STREET. N side, W end, the former LYING-IN HOSPITAL, 1861, by *J.D. Jee*. Stone, Tudor, with a little oriel below the central gable. Tall Neo-Georgian rear addition by *Rees & Holt*, 1931, the first stage of a planned rebuilding for the Cancer Hospital. Next door, the former EYE AND EAR INFIRMARY, 1878–80 by *C.O. Ellison*. Old English à la Norman Shaw. Red brick with red sandstone and moulded terracotta, timber-framed gables, and splendid chimneys. Converted to flats, 2003. After this, the Gothic ST LUKE'S ART WORKSHOPS, 1880, by *Henry Sumners*. Built for *Norbury, Upton & Paterson*, architectural carvers, whose work it features. Façade divided by an off-centre buttress with a statue in a niche. On the opposite, s side, the former SHELTERING HOME FOR DESTITUTE CHILDREN, 1888–9, *Ellison* again, this time on a tight budget: red and brown brick, rather grim. At the corner of Sugnall Street, facing the back of the Philharmonic Hall, it incorporates an 1840s house with nice ashlar details. Further E on the N side, MINSTER COURT, a complex of 1930s municipal flats, converted to private housing from 1982 by *Barratt*; *Kingham Knight Associates* were architectural consultants. Access decks were turned into private balconies, and glazed stair-towers added.

OXFORD STREET. *See* p. 367.

PERCY STREET. The grandest street in the area, with stone-faced houses, mostly in terraces of markedly original design. Nos. 2 and 4, Tudor Gothic, are dated 1835. The rest are Grecian, and seem to be mostly of *c.* 1830–6. Nos. 3–17, E side, form a tripartite composition, with a projecting pedimented centre and ends with giant pilasters. Doric colonnades support balconies in front of the recessed parts. No. 6, w side, has four bays and first-floor pilasters. Nos. 8–18 have giant Corinthian pilasters and pediments framing the end houses, and porches with square columns. Nos. 20–32, simpler, have Soanian incised decoration round the doors. Who designed these houses, so unlike those in neighbouring streets? *John Foster Jun.* has been suggested, but his buildings show none of their inventiveness. Other possibilities are *Samuel Rowland*, architect of St Bride, and *John Cunningham*, an Edinburgh-trained architect brought to Liverpool by the builder Samuel Holme, one of the Percy Street lessees.

PLEASANT STREET. The former PLEASANT STREET BOARD SCHOOL, built as the Hibernian Schools, 1818. Originally a two-storey brick rectangle with classrooms and master's house under the same roof. Extended and altered from 1851, but the domestic part, w, survives more or less unaltered, with a columned doorway to May Street.

RODNEY STREET. Laid out 1783–4 by William Roscoe and others. Its length, width and straightness were unprecedented in Liverpool, as was the provision of parallel service streets at the rear. It was developed piecemeal up to the 1820s with houses for the affluent. A few have five bays with central doors, but most are three bays, erected in pairs or short runs and not always to a consistent building line. All are of brick. Many handsome doorcases, mostly recessed with columns, slender Ionic or slender Greek Doric, or Tuscan columns with pediments. In the longer s part, Nos. 51a–75 form a terrace with central pediment. No. 62, built for John Gladstone 1792–3, was probably designed by *John Whiteside Casson*. It was the birthplace of W.E. Gladstone. No. 29, one of the five-bay houses, has a massive Greek Doric porch, almost certainly an addition by *Edmund Aikin*, 1817.

ST ANDREW'S GARDENS. This and the former Myrtle Gardens (now Minster Court – *see* Myrtle Street), are almost all that remains of several ambitious estates of walk-up flats built by the City between the wars under its Director of Housing, *Lancelot Keay*. St Andrew's Gardens, completed 1935, is by Keay's assistant *John Hughes*. The main element is a five-storey, D-shaped block (the model was Bruno Taut and Martin Wagner's Horseshoe Estate, Berlin), faced in buff brick, with continuous balconies overlooking a central court. Arched entrances, semicircular on N and S, parabolic on W and E. This block was refurbished in the 1990s; the rectilinear blocks that made up the rest of the estate were reduced in height or demolished.

SEYMOUR STREET. Nos. 11–53 are a long terrace, begun *c.* 1810, rebuilt behind preserved façades 1992. *John Foster Sen.* was one of the developers, and probably the architect. On the grassy area in the middle of the road, a bronze SCULPTURE, Sea Circle, 1984 by *Charlotte Mayer*.

UPPER DUKE STREET. On the N side, MORNINGTON TERRACE, *c.* 1839–40, with a central pediment. Opposite, at the corner of Cathedral Gate, the DEAN WALTERS

BUILDING of Liverpool John Moores University, *c.* 1990, by *Building Design Partnership*. Postmodern Neo-Georgian, out of respect for nearby Rodney Street, with a domed corner tower.

UPPER PARLIAMENT STREET. The extension of Parliament Street made in 1807, it marked the boundary between Liverpool and Toxteth Park until 1835. Some good early C19 houses survive. Nos. 96–98, s side, have at their core an ambitious five-bay house of *c.* 1840. Porch with paired Ionic columns, decorative window surrounds in ashlar, elaborate cast-iron balconies. Further E on the opposite side, FALKNER TERRACE (Nos. 155–177), stuccoed, with first-floor pilasters. Mostly in existence by 1831, restored 1980s. (For the Florence Nightingale Memorial *see* Toxteth, p. 475.)

LIVERPOOL SUBURBS

AIGBURTH

with ST MICHAEL'S HAMLET, and FULWOOD, GRASSENDALE and CRESSINGTON PARKS

The semi-rural Mersey shore s of what is now Sefton Park and Mossley Hill was already popular with those who could afford to build a house and run a carriage well before 1871, when the arrival of the railway and the tram accelerated suburbanisation. The process was complete by the mid C20.

ST ANNE, Aigburth Road. An interesting example of the early C19 Norman Revival, built 1836–7 in red ashlar and designed by *Cunningham & Holme*. Similar to their roughly contemporary Holy Trinity, Price Street, Birkenhead (demolished). Much extended; but first the original church. This was a six-bay, aisle-less preaching box with galleries on three sides and pulpit under the centre of the chancel arch. This is the w end today, with a confident w tower ('laughable' said *The Ecclesiologist*), round-arched lancets and flat buttresses and everywhere Norman details, e.g. the beakheads around the w door and the striking number of corbel heads and headstops inside and out. Even the GATEPIERS are Norman. The tower clock is surrounded by round-headed mouldings, making it look like a giant flower, but many other features are more convincing.

In 1853–4 broad transepts were added in precisely matching style, and the chancel extended too, then in 1913–14 it was lengthened again to its present three bays, with three lancets and a rose window in the E wall. The w GALLERY remains, and the 1850s galleries in the transepts (screened in below in 1913–14 to create vestry and Sunday School), but the N and s galleries were removed in 1893–4, leaving as a peculiar survival the E columns supporting an arched roof truss. The surviving gallery fronts have interlacing arcading with headstops.

ST MARY, Aigburth Road, Grassendale. 1852–3, by *A.H. Holme* for the residents of Grassendale Park and Cressington Park

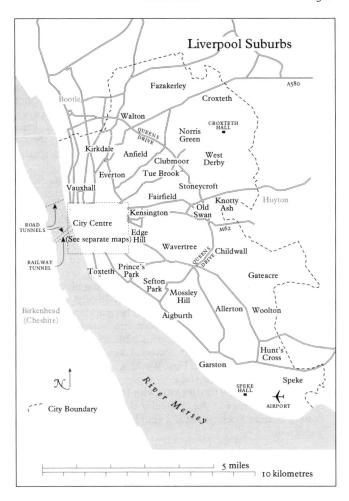

Liverpool Suburbs

(see pp. 384–5). Liverpool's Early Victorian Anglican churches were often remarkably reactionary. This has a broad aisle-less nave, wide transepts, and a short apsidal chancel. Dec, with a broached NW steeple. *The Ecclesiologist*, though critical, noted progress evident in the absence of galleries, and externally the church is more archaeologically correct than Holme's St Paul, Prince's Park (1847–8, demolished). Inside, the most interesting thing is the laminated beams of the timber roof, forming a flying cross over the crossing between the transepts. – STAINED GLASS. A mixed bag, including three windows in the chancel by *Evans*, 1884, and a W window of 1953, by *Joseph E. Nuttgens*.

ST MICHAEL-IN-THE-HAMLET, St Michael's Church Road. Built by *John Cragg*, 1813–15. Cragg was a fanatic of cast iron for all purposes, and used it very extensively here (*see* p. 384 for the houses he built around the church). Like his earlier St George, Everton (*see* p. 417), it may reflect the involvement of *J.M. Gandy*, and especially *Thomas Rickman*. Many cast-iron components used at St George recur, but at St Michael iron is also used for parapets, battlements, pinnacles, hoodmoulds and other details of the brick exterior. As at St George, ceiling and roof are of slate slabs held in a cast-iron framework. Cragg's new method for cladding the exteriors of brick churches with iron and slate, patented 1813, is used for the dado (except on the rebuilt N side); the slate was originally 'sanded' to resemble stone. The clerestory walls consist of a slim core of brickwork sandwiched between slate slabs: Rickman complained of the 'extreme thinness'. The church has a W tower, six-bay nave with clerestory and aisles, and chancel. In 1900 the N aisle was seamlessly doubled in width, bearing out Cragg's claim that his modular, prefabricated buildings could easily be enlarged. The internal structure is entirely cast-iron, the nave arcade consisting of slender clustered shafts supporting spandrels of openwork tracery. The windows are cast-iron too, the tracery of the E window being identical with that of St George. According to Goodhart-Rendel, St Michael was restored in 1875 by the *Audsleys*. The marble FONT is presumably theirs. – The E window has strongly coloured STAINED GLASS, 1858 or after, with biblical scenes in quatrefoils against vine scrolls and flowers. Lady Chapel E window, 1916, by *Shrigley & Hunt*; First World War memorial window in the porch by *Gustave Hiller*.

Well-preserved CHURCHYARD with many C19 monuments. Near the NE corner of the chancel is that of the Herculaneum Pottery Benefit Society, 1824, a simple slab with an appealing inscription:

> Here peaceful rest the POTTERS turn'd to Clay
> Tir'd with their lab'ring life's long tedious day
> Surviving friends their Clay to earth consign
> To be re-moulded by a Hand Divine!

The Herculaneum Pottery was to the NW, on the Mersey shore.

ST AUSTIN (R.C.), Aigburth Road. 1838. Plain, Gothic rectangle. Red ashlar W façade with small steep-gabled W porch, and above, a large rose window and two lancets. Most peculiar are the tall octagonal W turrets at the corners, almost like stumpy factory chimneys. The sides have more lancets, and buttresses, but are brick. Abutting the E end is a three-storey PRESBYTERY, with label-moulded sash windows and a good cantilevered staircase. In other words, a fairly conventional pre-Pugin R.C. church, but a bit grander than the norm. The S porch, not Gothic, is mid-1980s. Inside is the shallowest chancel, no more than a recess, flanked by a tiny N chapel and a blocked S doorway. Both are set in Gothic arches with gables over, and over them blank arches to match the chancel arch. W GALLERY. Reordered in 2000 with simple wooden ALTAR, and LECTERN and FONT incorporating bits of reused C19 fittings. – GRAVESTONE. Amongst the usual slabs and crucifixes in the churchyard is a remarkable memorial to Domingo de Ybarrondo, †1909. An organic shape, upright, and semicircular in plan, the upper part rounded and carved out on the face like a hood, and containing a cross which melts into it. From where does it derive?

The former SCHOOLS, now parish hall, at the rear beyond the presbytery, are by contrast to the church clearly post-Pugin, and pretty. Dated 1860. Single-storeyed, lancets, gables and octagonal gable chimneys. At the l. end a porch becoming a bellcote and a chimney above.

ST CHARLES BORROMEO (R.C.), Aigburth Road. 1899–1900, by *Pugin & Pugin* (i.e. *Peter Paul Pugin*). Dec Gothic in yellow rock-faced stone with red ashlar dressings. (Ritual) W tower with statues in niches. Aisle-less nave with open timber roof, polygonal chancel with a pair of smaller flanking chapels. Some early C20 STAINED GLASS.

AIGBURTH METHODIST CHURCH, Aigburth Road, opposite St Anne. Brick with stone dressings, a NW tower, and the typical free Perp motifs of the Edwardian Methodists, such as the handsome W window. Yet the date is 1926–7. The architect is *A. Brocklehurst* of Manchester.

CRESSINGTON STATION, Knowsley Road, Cressington Park. 1871. A good-looking variation on the standard design built by the Cheshire Lines Committee on their Liverpool–Manchester line. Two-and-a-half storeys, set in a cutting, so the street entrance and booking hall is actually the first floor, with an external door on the platform side directly onto a footbridge. Brick. The roof a mass of pretty bargeboards, half-hipped roofs and chimneys. Only small cast-iron canopies on the platforms.

LIVERPOOL CRICKET CLUB, Aigburth Road. It is not hard to see why this remarkably little-altered Victorian cricket ground of *c.* 1880–2 has appeared in television costume dramas. The architect was *Thomas Harnett Harrisson*. There is a three-storey pavilion, a groundsman's lodge, a scoreboard and a later Ladies' Pavilion, all in brick with lots of green- and white-painted half-timbered gables, many half-hipped. The pavilion is altered inside, though, and extended to the r. and rear.

LIVERPOOL INTERNATIONAL GARDEN FESTIVAL SITE, Riverside Drive, SW of St Michael's Hamlet. The 1984 Festival was the first of several held in the UK to bring about urban regeneration. It involved the reclamation and landscaping of 130 acres (53 hectares) of derelict and polluted industrial land. Houses have been built on part of the site, as was always the intention, but much of the remainder has reverted to wilderness. The FESTIVAL HALL survives, a serenely elegant structure by *Arup Associates*, won in competition in 1982. A gently curving vault with slightly lower semi-domes at each end, tied together by a lantern along the crest of the vault. The form is reminiscent of the Palm House at Kew. The steel framework of the central section has a skin of polycarbonate sheeting, while the ends are sleekly clad in ribbed aluminium. Column-free interior, designed for possible conversion to a sports and leisure centre after the Festival.

St Michael's Hamlet. The creation of *John Cragg*, proprietor of the Mersey Iron Foundry. It originally comprised the church of St Michael-in-the-Hamlet (*see* p. 381) and five villas. This little cluster made up a secluded semi-rural settlement near the river, just the sort of man-made incident in the landscape admired by writers on the Picturesque. From *c.* 1840 further villas were added, then in the 1880s a tide of terraced houses engulfed the Hamlet, changing its character completely. Cragg's five VILLAS are all stuccoed and painted, with Tudor Gothic details, and cast-iron windows, hoodmoulds and internal features. GLEBELANDS stands immediately s of the church, with THE HERMITAGE opposite (it has a pretty cast-iron veranda). HOLLYBANK adjoins the churchyard on the e, and has good openwork cast-iron gatepiers. The round building in the garden was originally a summerhouse. CARFAX is at the corner of St Michael's Road and St Michael's Church Road. THE CLOISTERS, further sw along St Michael's Road, has a veranda at the back, and an elliptical cast-iron stair inside.

C19 RESIDENTIAL ESTATES. There are three, all still today owned and managed collectively by the individual plot proprietors through a trust, or company. Each has an entrance on Aigburth Road and is planned with drives leading at right angles down towards the river.

FULWOOD PARK. This is the earliest of the three estates – the articles of agreement are dated 1840 – and the most upmarket: density was no more than one house per acre (compared with four per acre for the later two) and the minimum outlay on each house and grounds was £1,500. All buildings were to be of stone or rendered brick, and attics could only be lit from above, presumably to prevent the servants prying on neighbours. The developers, the merchant brothers William and Alexander Smith, provided a single, slightly serpentine road with GATES and LODGE at the entrance. These are of red ashlar, the lodge with gables and label moulds. Grand detached houses are set back in big, now mature, gardens. Almost all the initial residents were merchants. Quite a lot of late C20 infill, but still mostly large stuccoed villas, some Italianate, of the 1840s–50s, and two or three Gothic houses of the *c.* 1860s (there were eighteen houses by 1871). *S. & J. Holme* acquired the plots on the s side at the river end. Nos. 15–21 (odd) are theirs, varying in shape but sharing details such as mutule cornices, window mouldings and square-columned porches. At the end, the pair Nos. 23–25 with bargeboards and label moulds is probably theirs too.

GRASSENDALE PARK, 1½ m. SE of Fulwood Park, at the end of Grassendale Road. The Aigburth Land Company was formed in 1845 by a consortium of five businessmen who had purchased over 20 acres (8 hectares) for £10,500. Its fifty-four subscribers agreed the following year to erect 'moderate sized villas for their own residences' (in contrast to Fulwood these could cost as little as £400). The plan is a modified grid, with two parallel roads terminating at the Promenade along the Mersey shore, with glorious views. There were eleven houses by 1851 and thirty-five by 1891. NORTH ROAD and the PROM-ENADE developed more quickly; they have handsome stuccoed houses with good window surrounds, cast-iron balconies etc., in a variety of gentle styles. SOUTH ROAD is predominantly of later, less interesting brick houses. Quite a lot of infill too. Generous planting and mature trees. GATEPIERS and a little stucco LODGE.

CRESSINGTON PARK, abutting Grassendale Park to the s, is the last and easily the largest of the three Aigburth estates. The Second Aigburth Land Company was formed in 1846; a number of the key figures behind it were also promoters of Grassendale Park, and it appears to have been a more specu-lative development. Ninety purchasers acquired the 172 lots between 1851 and 1870. *Henry Sumners* won a competition to provide the PLAN in 1847, but this was amended by a *Mr Gray* before construction began in 1851. As at Grassendale there is a Promenade, but here there are three principal streets as against two, and an intermediate cross-street. Beside the GATES is the church of St Mary, erected to serve residents (*see* p. 380) and the LODGE of 1852. Single-storeyed and of three bays. Channelled rustication, central porch *in antis* with square Tuscan columns, Vitruvian scroll frieze. It is grander and more interesting than the houses turned out to be. By 1861 eight of these were occupied, twenty years later fifty, and more than double that by the 1920s. Most are not very big. An assort-ment of bricks and motifs; unusual for Liverpool are a few in white brick, with castellated parapets, e.g. No. 21 SALISBURY ROAD. On Knowsley Road is Cressington Station (*see* p. 383), built when the Cheshire Lines Committee railway was driven through in a cutting in 1868–71.

OTHER BUILDINGS. On Aigburth Road at Aigburth Vale, one of *Willink & Thicknesse*'s excellent BANK OF LIVERPOOL branches, now a bar. This one is of 1902. Red brick with stone dressings, free C17, with rather playful details including big smooth voussoirs to the ground-floor windows, shaped gables, and a corbelled-out octagonal corner turret with a top stage of swagged oculi and little corner columns, and a copper cap above that.

At the corner of Aigburth Road and AIGBURTH HALL ROAD is a pleasant example of Edwardian suburbanised Arts and Crafts, a roughcast and symmetrical house with shaped gables. A little E, where Aigburth Hall Avenue forks off, is a long low old red stone building with plenty of unsympathetic recent windows and doors, but also one three-light mullioned window and external stairs. The l. part is called THE GRANARY, and is thought to be a fragment of a grange of the Cistercian abbey of Stanlow in Cheshire. The grange is first mentioned in 1291. Inside three, possibly four pairs of crucks. Until the 1900s attached to the r. was the so-called Monk's Lodging, with massive sandstone masonry and depressed-arched lintels, and barns projected at both ends to form a three-sided yard. The barns may have been late C15–early C16, and one suggestion is that the building now known as the Granary was converted to that use when these new barns were built, having previously been a cruck-framed barn. However, until the cruck timbers are dendro-dated, the age of the building remains a mystery.

A number of big mid-C19 houses on streets either side of Aigburth Road, e.g. on Aigburth Hall Road, a handsome Italianate pair, and Nos. 17–19, a large, accretive house of red ashlar, with mullioned windows and elaborately bargeboarded gables. Also, THE GRANGE restaurant on Holmefield Road, smaller and stuccoed with a melange of motifs including carved wooden dragons at the ends of even frillier bargeboards. For buildings on or near LARK LANE, see p. 455.

ALLERTON

When they did not decamp across the Mersey to the Wirral, the city's most magnificent merchant princes built the city's finest mansions at Allerton 5 m. to the S E. Though too many have been destroyed, a number remain. Today Allerton is prosperous suburbia, in no small part due to the Corporation's acquisition from 1902 of a series of these mansions and their grounds, which became a chain of parks and public open spaces amounting to over 500 almost uninterrupted acres (200 hectares). The process began with the purchase of Calderstones (see p. 389) for £43,000, and also spread into Woolton . As a result Allerton is remarkably and sumptuously green and leafy, with magnificent beeches especially, and a vivid impression is retained of a continuous landscape of large adjoining grounds – small landscaped parks in fact – that characterised this wealthiest of Victorian suburbs.

ALL HALLOWS, Allerton Road. Built for John Bibby of Hart Hill (see p. 389) in memory of his first wife Fanny, daughter of Jesse Hartley – hence the size and the care taken. The architect is *G.E. Grayson*, the date 1872–6. Red sandstone. Mighty Perp tower of the Somerset type. Perp also the rest, an early case of the return to Perp. Ashlar-faced interior. The arcade of alternating pier shapes. – STAINED GLASS. All by *Morris & Co.* (except the N transept E, by *Heaton, Butler & Bayne*) and all their figure work by *Burne-Jones*. Altogether an outstanding ensemble. The best are the W and E, the latter the Adoration of the Lamb, done in 1875–6. They are in an exceptional and exquisite colouring of predominantly white and brown. The E window is an early example of Burne-Jones' late, pictorial style, employing a single continuous composition that spread across all the lights, regardless of the mullions. These two windows as well as the transept windows (of 1879, S, and 1880, N, with rich foliate backgrounds by *Morris*) incorporate small predella panels with stories, all remarkably easily readable – more so, undeniably, than C13 glass. The chancel N windows (angels) followed in 1881, the aisles in 1882–6. The colours are now stronger and darker, and also unusual: deep rose and pink, pale mauve, much dark blue, etc., the latter chiefly in small pieces in the backgrounds. By the time these were commissioned Burne-Jones had taken over from Morris the design of the backgrounds, and probably had more influence over the colouring, previously Morris' preserve too. – MONUMENTS. John Bibby, †1811. By *William Spence*. Portrait medallion at the foot. Standing figure of Hope above. Brought from St Thomas, Seaforth (q.v.) in 1978. – Mrs Bibby by *Frederigo Fabiani*, who did several of the monuments in the Staglieno Cemetery outside Genoa. Free-standing figures. She is rising heavenward and an angel with spread wings hovers over her.

ALL SOULS, Mather Avenue. 1927, by *D.A. Campbell & E.H. Honeybourne*. An impressively big, pale brick Italian Romanesque church with a campanile towering over the contemporary suburban streets. The brick changes remarkably with varying light, from silvery grey to orange-red. Spacious interior, of brick and plaster. Vaulted crossing. – Superb FONT and PULPIT, carved by *H. Tyson Smith*.

ST BERNADETTE (R.C.), Mather Avenue. 1935–6, by *F. Reynolds* of *Hill, Sandy & Norris*. Moderne Romanesque. Brick with campanile.

CEMETERY, Woolton Road. When, in 1905–6, the Liverpool Corporation assumed the responsibilities of the township burial boards in what had become the suburbs, it identified a need for a large new cemetery to serve the S area of the city. Part of the Allerton Hall estate S of Springwood Avenue was acquired and work was sufficiently advanced for the cemetery to open in 1909. The red sandstone LODGE, GATES, SUPER-INTENDENT'S HOUSE and three CHAPELS were well on the way to completion two years later. The chapels are Gothic, mainly with lancets and Geometrical tracery, the Anglican one predominantly with the latter. All have steeples. The Anglican steeple, at the head of the entrance drive, forms the focal point of the plan. With allowances for the curve of the site, this is symmetrical. The extent, density and formality of planting is in contrast to that of Victorian cemeteries in Liverpool, such as Anfield (*see* p. 394). It creates discrete compartments, breaking down the scale of the site. The cemetery was subsequently extended to a site N of the Avenue, where a CRE-MATORIUM CHAPEL opened in 1975.

LIBRARY, junction of Mather Avenue and Allerton Road. 1964–5, by *Ronald Bradbury*, City Architect. Good and straightforward on a prominent island site, a single tall storey with expressed steel frame, glass walls and a flat roof. The frame is exposed in the large unobstructed interior. Pevsner was irritated by 'the coarse, restless all-over concrete pattern' of the faceted walls on the N side and S aisle. The water tower, rounded and timber-clad and cantilevered from a concrete mast, is a delight.

CALDERSTONES SCHOOL. *See* below, p. 388.

NEW HEYS COMMUNITY COMPREHENSIVE SCHOOL, Heath Road and Allerton Road. Much admired when completed in 1956. By *Herbert Thearle & Partners* in collaboration with *Ronald Bradbury*, City Architect. Construction begun in 1953, as a grammar school. Three-storey teaching block, and at right angles a wing containing assembly hall, dining room and gym.

120 WYNCOTE SPORTS PAVILION, Geoffrey Hughes Memorial Ground, Mather Avenue, ¼ m. w of All Hallows church. By *Gerald R. Beech* for the University of Liverpool. 1961–2. A superb building, excellent in plan, details and spirit. The centre is the all-glass pavilion, all poise, elegance and transparency. It is a glass box, the first and second floors cantilevered out over the blank white ground floor, the top floor with a terrace in the round under an oversailing roof. A corridor through the first floor continues axially as an open-sided bridge to the changing rooms on one side, and a very long viewing platform on the other, running out between the running track and cricket pitch. The changing rooms are mostly blank walling. Everything about the composition is beautifully balanced, and with the contrast between the pure rationalist geometry of the white and glass boxes and the grass and trees of the sports fields, this is a model of Modernist theory, like a student prize design untroubled by the compromises of more complex projects.

SPRINGWOOD HOUSING ESTATE, s end of Mather Avenue. 1920s. Some three-storey blocks of flats with Neo-Georgian, and Reillyesque motifs (e.g. the metal Neoclassical balconies).

OAK FARM, Springwood Avenue. A derelict C17 farmhouse restored and extended to award-winning effect by *ShedKM*, 2003–5. With the demolition of minor C18 and C19 parts the farmhouse was reduced to a gabled block of red sandstone, of two bays, with mullioned windows on three sides, transomed to the first floor. Attached to the fourth side by means of a glazed entrance hall is a new two-storey wing. To the old farmyard it is a blank sandstone wall; to the garden it is fully glazed, revealing the ground floor to be one long open-plan living space. An assured, if hardly ground-breaking, commission. The Late Georgian farm buildings were in 2005 being restored and extended as more housing.

Merchants' Houses and the Parks

The surviving mansions and grounds cover a large swathe running for two miles S E from Harthill Road. Given the distances a car is advisable to investigate them all. When all this began in the C18, of course Allerton was not a suburb, and the mansions were in the country.

At the S W end of HARTHILL ROAD is BEECHLEY, now a nursing home. A large stucco villa in existence by 1835, with top-lit central staircase hall. N, on the w side, is CALDERSTONES COMPREHENSIVE SCHOOL, built up with many blocks around two C19 houses. HARTFIELD is the older. Stuccoed Italianate, probably late 1840s, extended in the 1880s with sandstone prospect tower, window surrounds and Composite-columned porch, and cast-iron veranda. Other later additions. To the S is QUARRY BANK, of 1866–7, by *Culshaw & Sumners* for James Bland, timber merchant. Muscular Gothic entrance with stocky, polished granite columns. Bizarre, tall chimney with an elaborate wrought-iron crown. Rich Gothic interior with top-lit, galleried entrance hall, and stained-glass stair window. Pretty, steep-roofed LODGE.

Where Harthill Road meets Calderstones Road is a sumptuous GATEWAY to CALDERSTONES PARK by *H. W. Pritchard* of the Surveyor's office. It has two gigantic atlantes and low quadrant walls with statues of the Four Seasons, brought from the demolished Brown's Buildings in the city centre (1861–3, by *J.A. Picton*) in the 1920s. The sculptor was *Edwin Stirling*. Also a stucco LODGE with big bargeboards in Harthill Road, the entrance to John Bibby's Hart Hill (demolished). The grounds were incorporated into Calderstones Park in 1913. The combined LANDSCAPE is a curious mix of Edwardian municipal – boating lakes, dells, botanic gardens, elaborate floral displays, bowling greens etc. – and the mature avenues, grasslands and ha-has of the early C19 landscaped parks. The MANSION HOUSE of Calderstones, now council offices, is of *c.* 1828. Painted ashlar with a Greek Doric four-column porch in front of the slightly recessed central bay. Round the corner is a segmental bay and round the back is an extraordinary attachment, an Art Deco outdoor theatre by *Lancelot Keay*, 1945–7. The stage is under an upswept roof that projects as a canopy for the orchestra pit too. The sides curve at the corners, like the canopy. No longer in use; the stage glazed in. The single-range STABLES and COACHHOUSE – extensive for a suburban mansion – are of red sandstone with lunette windows above segmental arches, but also rectangular windows. There is a separate three-bay block with lunettes as well.

The six CALDERSTONES themselves are in one of the Hart Hill greenhouses W of the Mansion House. They were moved here 1964, and came from a site N of the park which appears to have been a megalithic passage grave. Carved with cup-and-ring *p. 12* motifs, spirals and representations of human feet, similar to the Boyne passage graves in Western Ireland, and others in Anglesey. Also in the park are excellent Neo-Georgian wrought-iron GATES. These came in 1974 from Bidston Court, Birkenhead (Cheshire), a house of 1891 by *Grayson & Ould*.

ALLERTON ROAD marks the SW boundary of Calderstones Park and all the surviving leafy acres of Allerton. It is a document of destruction. At the N end on the W side were ALLERTON BEECHES and GREENHILL, built in 1884 by *Norman Shaw* for members of the Tate family of sugar refiners. Only the rather flat tile-hung COTTAGE and STABLES to the former remain, opposite the N entrance to Calderstones Park. ½ m. further along, CLEVELEY was by *Sir George Gilbert Scott* for

Joseph Leather, a cotton merchant, 1865. The houses of Cleveley Road occupy the site, but a LODGE, now called Hoarwithy, and COTTAGE and STABLES survive on Allerton Road. Coursed stone, ashlar dressings, gables and mullioned windows. The cottage retains cast-iron 'Chinese' glazing bars.

ALLERTON, a house by *Thomas Harrison* on the E side, was built in 1815 for Jacob Fletcher, son of a highly successful privateer. The grounds have been a municipal golf course since 1921. At the entrance is a pretty little Neoclassical LODGE. Greek Doric porch, with frieze and a little pediment. Also, delightful GATEPIERS with delicate paired Doric pilasters, and a triglyph frieze. The clubhouse occupies the much knocked-about STABLES. U-plan, red sandstone. A few yards s are the remains of the house. Just enough stands to mourn over the fire which gutted it in 1944 – a handsome colonnade of eight Greek Doric columns facing s, and round the corner a w front with a broad shallow bow and attached Greek Doric columns and one tripartite window r., one l., and another in a projecting bay l. And that is it. The upper walls have gone and around the back there is nothing but bare brick, revealing the pale sandstone to be for facings only. The ruins are in a poor condition, shrubs forcing apart the parapet masonry. Out in front of the s colonnade is an OBELISK, an C18 eyecatcher on a now-lost avenue from Allerton Hall (*see* p. 392).

SE from here the news is better. NEW HEYS, on the w side of Allerton Road, is an early suburban mansion by *Alfred Waterhouse*, now apartments. 1861–5, for the lawyer W.G. Bateson. A large but compact asymmetrical block in polychromatic brick, with steep roofs and mainly square-headed windows. The entrance front has a porch with Geometric tracery in pointed

Allerton (Liverpool), New Heys.
Drawing by Alfred Waterhouse, 1862

windows and a V-plan oriel and a gable over, a three-light Gothic window lighting the half-landing of the stairs to the r., and end gables, one with a corbelled chimney. There is a veranda on the w, garden, front, and a conservatory. The principal rooms are laid out in an L around the hall and staircase. Many of these features became standard elements of the designs Waterhouse offered his mercantile clients, scaled up or down and adjusted to the specifics of site (e.g. Mossley House, p. 441).

ALLERTON PRIORY, on the other side of the road, is a *Waterhouse* mansion of altogether greater ambition, now also apartments. Designed 1866 for John Grant Morris, a colliery owner; structure complete 1871. It cost over £16,500. A large asymmetrical house, rather dour in brown brick laced with blue brick bands and sandstone dressings. Entrance front with Gothic vaulted porch and a dominant, typical and rather civic Waterhouse tower. The upper stage has tourelles and on top is a steep truncated pyramid roof. Gothic colonnade to the garden. The leading motifs are C13, but Waterhouse was sensible in using motifs from other phases of Gothic or other periods as well, where usefulness pointed to them. The plan was very unusual, and unusual for Waterhouse. An entrance hall opens into a gallery running towards the s front, but not reaching it because it is blocked at that end by a link with sliding screens between the public rooms on either side. The 106 staircase opens directly off the l. of the gallery, with the service wing beyond it. It is a complex open-well design, rising through, around and over Gothic arcades. Scrolly wrought-iron balustrade.

The house is approached up the side of the grounds by a long woodland drive winding between imported rock. Morris was mayor while Sefton Park was being laid out by Edouard André with similar rockwork. A bridge over the drive has been demolished. At the bottom is a LODGE, with elaborately bracketed gabled parts emanating from a big central chimneystack. Facing the drive is an open-sided porch of turned posts supporting a timber-framed projection.

ALLERTON TOWER lay E of Allerton Priory, with a drive off WOOLTON ROAD. The house was completed in 1849, two years after the death of its architect *Harvey Lonsdale Elmes*. That it was not one of his best works is clear from the LODGE, a painful mixture of debased Early Victorian and classical motifs. The STABLES and the long ORANGERY still stand as well. The now glassless orangery is of fourteen bays with Tuscan columns. The house was demolished after the Corporation bought it and the grounds in 1924.

SPRINGWOOD, on Woolton Road s of the junction with Allerton Road, could be a work of *John Cunningham*. It is dated 1839, handsome, and eminently characteristic of that date, i.e. wholly classical, but very heavy in such motifs as balustrades, volutes etc. Five-bay entrance front with broad giant angle pilasters and an enclosed porch. SW garden front with two full-height

bow windows, and extending NW a matching stone conservatory, or orangery. N service wing of three storeys, the
top windows (with pedimented surrounds) interrupting the
cornice. Inside is a lot of good chunky Neoclassical plasterwork and coffered ceilings, and 9 ft- (2.7 metre-) high
mahogany doors. The centre is a noble top-lit staircase hall.
The most memorable feature is the bottom newel, around
which the handrail is wrapped like a snake's tail, narrowing to
a tip towards the floor. The attribution to Cunningham is
founded partly on features shared with his Lodge to the
Botanic Gardens on Edge Lane (*see* p. 413) – particularly giant
pilasters. These stylistic similarities are most apparent at the
charming LODGE, N of the house. Square plan, single storey.
All these buildings are of pale sandstone ashlar. The STABLES
are red and presumably later than the house. Springwood was
begun by William Shand, plantation owner, but completed by
the ship-owner Sir Thomas Brocklebank.

WOOLTON ROAD must be one of the most beautiful dual car-
riageways in the country. It winds gloriously between mature
beeches, many on the central reservation. On it, opposite
Springwood Lodge, are the GATES to Allerton Hall, now closed
to vehicles. Massive square piers of banded rustication.

ALLERTON HALL, Clarke's Gardens, Springwood Avenue, is the
last but also the earliest of these merchants' mansions. The
manor was held by the Lathoms in the C14, but the Palladian
house one sees now was almost certainly begun by John
Hardman, a merchant from Rochdale, who bought the estate
in 1736 with his brother James. Standing outside the red sandstone, three-storey entrance front, his is the centre including
the upper giant portico of unfluted Ionic columns and pediment and the four bays to the r., the last two projecting a little.
The ground floor is rusticated. It also includes the return of
course, where the windows have surrounds of stones of alternating size, like quoins. The house was completed faithfully by
William Roscoe (*see* p. 246) *c*. 1810–12, but he had to sell it in
1816 after he was bankrupted. Around the back are a number
of C19 additions. The interior, very severely damaged by fires
in 1994 and 1995, reopened as 'The Pub in the Park' with an
open-plan ersatz interior in the manner of contemporary pubs.
What survives is a room at the W end with panelled walls,
Kentian overdoors and a stucco ceiling with thin Rococo
decoration (called the Breakfast Room in 1824), and parts of
Roscoe's grand library attached to the rear towards the other
end of the house, with a back screen of fluted Ionic columns.
Adjoining it, his masonry-walled 'hot house'. – Good SUNDIAL
of 1750. The park was opened to the public in 1926.

ANFIELD

The success of Liverpool Football Club has made the name of
Anfield world-famous. Until the mid C19 this was semi-rural villa

land 2½ m. NE of the city centre, and there are some survivors of this period on Anfield Road. As Liverpool expanded it was rapidly overrun by dense streets of bylaw terraces, mainly for white-collar households. Much of this remains today, and with its Board Schools, churches and chapels, pubs and excellent park and cemetery, Anfield is a microcosm of the townscape of working-class Victorian suburbia.

HOLY TRINITY, Breck Road. 1845–7, by *John Hay*. Cost £5,000. Gothic, and typical of its date in several ways. The W steeple in its details, with an octagonal bell-stage rising into eight steep gables behind coupled pinnacles, and in its spire, is far from archaeologically justifiable, and the body of the church is still smooth, with tall windows. Also there are still broad transepts. Low apse. The basement windows lit a school. Aisle-less interior still, too, which recalls the eccentricities of E.B. Lamb, without the whimsy. Choir vestry, 1902. – REREDOS. 1883. – STAINED GLASS. The S transept windows by *Ballantine & Allan* of Edinburgh were in the chancel in 1849.

ST COLUMBA, Pinehurst Road. 1931–2, by *Bernard A. Miller*. Pale silvery grey brick (from Gloucestershire), impressively blocky, rising from nave to chancel and from chancel to sanctuary (though not as big as this may make it sound). Small round-headed windows, tall only in the sanctuary. No tower, but a bellcote on the chancel facing N. Parish centre in similar brick built against the W end in 1998. Interior in painted textured plaster, with arcades of three low bays, completely unmoulded. Chancel with big W and E arches. Reordered by *Paul W. Gregory* in 1984. He kept the original jazzy geometrical patterns of the panelled roof, but replaced Miller's cool blues, greys and silvers with warm red decoration. – Hanging ROOD by *Bainbridge Copnall*. – REREDOSES. *Mary Adshead* painted a triptych for the S chapel (1934, side panels 1936). Another *Adshead* reredos, from the demolished Miller church of St Christopher, Withington (SE Lancashire), was installed against the E wall *c*. 2001. It is very large, of Christ transfigured, in Byzantine style. In its own right remarkable, it fits the E wall without adaptation, but it upsets Miller's conception of the E end. He intended the rood, framed by the chancel arch, to dominate and hung a dark curtain at the E end as a neutral backdrop; the reredos is disruptive competition. – FONT. Portland stone. A drum, subtly tapering with wavy patterns around it. Lacquered cover.

ST MARGARET, Belmont Road and West Derby Road. By *Bruxby & Evans,* opened 1965. On a corner site; square building with a folding roof. Inside, laminated timber trusses and the seating radiate from a sanctuary in a set-back corner. Pevsner derided the building as modish, and, whilst conceding the trusses were interesting, thought the place too restless for worship. – Over the altar a bronze Crucifix by *Sean Rice*. – SCULPTURE. Outside, a statue of St Margaret from the previous church, a powerful building of 1871–3 by *W. & G. Audsley* destroyed by fire in 1961. It was in a fully convincing High Victorian Gothic and with structural polychromy outside. – Next to the church, the SCHOOL of 1877.

ALL SAINTS (R.C.), Oakfield. 1910, by *J. & B. Sinnott*. Rock-faced red sandstone. Without a tower; Dec details. Quite varied in the exterior. Interior with a rose window high up above the altar.

OAKFIELD METHODIST CHURCH, Oakfield Road. Red brick, with typically playful 1900-Gothic details. No tower.

CITY OF LIVERPOOL CEMETERY, Walton Lane, adjoining Stanley Park (*see* below). Also known as Anfield Cemetery. 1861–4. One of the best provincial cemeteries to be built after the 1852 Burial Act all but banned burials in ancient town-centre graveyards, then horrendously overcrowded and con-sidered dangerously unsanitary. Toxteth Park Cemetery (*see* p. 474) was the first in greater Liverpool, but this was the first to serve the parish of Liverpool itself. The inventive, symmet-rical LAYOUT has a complex genesis. A design competition was held in 1860, won by *Thomas D. Barry*. But the commission was awarded instead to *William Gay* who had designed Toxteth Park Cemetery and the splendid Undercliffe Cemetery in Bradford. He resigned the following year, and was replaced by *Edward Kemp* (soon to design Stanley Park). The two axial car-riageways and the position of the chapels are probably Gay's, but the distinctive feature, the elaborate intersecting arrange-ment of curving and circular secondary drives, is probably Kemp's. To him also is probably due the central sunken section. Under the turf of this part, and the terrace to its NE, are nearly 3,000 brick graves, built in order to create a plat-form for the chapels level with the main entrance. The plant-ing was initially informal clumps around intersections and the boundary, subsequently overlaid with formal avenues. The plan was carefully divided into three, with Roman Catholic and Nonconformist sections either side of the Anglican zone given prominence, a reflection of the size of these communities in Victorian Liverpool. Each part was anchored by a large E.E.-style CHAPEL by *Lucy & Littler*, who won the separate archi-tectural competition with amazingly ambitious Gothic designs of red sandstone, resourceful in plan and detail. Only the Non-conformist chapel remains, with a steeple over the porch, a N aisle for the coffins, and an apse. The Anglican chapel, at the head of the principal carriageway, was flanked by CATACOMBS, which survive in a derelict state. They have buttressed memorial arcades above ground; coffins descended by silent hydraulic lift from stone catafalques at either end. There are other *Lucy & Littler*-designed buildings around the perimeter, including the registrar's and clerk's OFFICE on Priory Road, and two ingenious GATEWAYS. The principal entrance, on Walton Lane, has lodges and an entrance screen with two car-riageways with outstanding iron gates. Between them the gatepier is enlarged as a clock tower of original Gothic design. The entrance to Cherry Lane doubles as a bridge under a railway, with castellated portals each with one tourelle, and heavy Gothic arches to the carriageway and its flanking footways, which are open to one another by arcades. Again excellent iron gates.

Headstones and MONUMENTS are impressive in sheer number, and noticeably varied in form. Perhaps the best collection is in front of the N columbarium, with e.g. a Celtic cross to John Highmett, 1890, a granite sarcophagus to Mary Ann Barker, 1892, and a granite baldacchino to Robert Daglish, 1904. Also of note, an Egyptian pylon to Alexander McLennan and his wife, 1893, NW of the crossing of the axial drives, and the large pinnacled Gothic canopy to William Bottomley Bairstow, †1868, by *W. Wortley*, NE of the registrar and clerk's office. In the sunken area is a First World War memorial consisting of the standard elements of an Imperial War Graves Commission cemetery, namely *Sir Edwin Lutyens*' Stone of Remembrance and *Sir Reginald Blomfield*'s Cross of Sacrifice (both in Portland stone) facing each other across a small lawn. The names of the fallen are engraved on two low Portland stone walls, one on either side of the lawn. S of the southern catacomb is a memorial designed by *Ronald Bradbury* in 1952, and carved by *H. Tyson Smith*, to the victims of the Liverpool blitz in 1941.

With a separate entrance on Priory Road is a CREMATORIUM CHAPEL, erected by the Liverpool Crematorium Co. in 1894–6 to free Perp designs by *James Rhind*. It was only the fourth in the country. Red sandstone, T-plan, the narrow 'bell' tower a decorous chimney for the furnace. The interior of the chapel was re-orientated in 1953 to face the long N wall. To the SE a COLUMBARIUM of 1951 by the *City Architect's Department*. A gently curving stone loggia with pergola attached.

STANLEY PARK. One of the best mid-Victorian parks not only of Liverpool but of the whole North, despite the steady accumulation of insensitive alterations and the best efforts of vandals. Designed by *Edward Kemp*, with architectural features by *E.R. Robson*, then Corporation Surveyor, it was laid out in 1867–71 at a cost, including land purchase, of £155,000. Stanley is the northern park in a chain of three created by the Corporation around the town outskirts in the 1860s. The others were Newsham and Sefton (*see* pp. 426 and 453). It was designed according to the principles espoused in Kemp's treatise, *How to Lay Out a Small Garden* (1850) with three complementary zones – a formal landscape, an informal landscape or Middle Ground intended as a neutral foil, and a Picturesque landscape. The formal landscape of TERRACES and walks was constructed at the top of the site (that is along the S boundary) to make the most of the magnificent panoramic views as far as Snowdon, the Isle of Man and the Lake District, now mostly lost behind the spread of Liverpool and Bootle and mature planting. Here architecture and landscape are superbly integrated. Robson designed a TOP WALK, with a very long red sandstone screen wall with Gothic pinnacles and blank arches, canted into three sections (behind it are building plots sold off to help finance the project), and closed at each end by two stone lodges (the E one destroyed by enemy bombing). Along the central section are five Gothic PAVILIONS with open arcades. The outer ones are free-standing and octagonal, brilliantly managing the change of axis and artfully framing views of the park and country beyond. Below this section is a lower terrace with a pierced and occasionally projecting balustrade.

From the terraces there were originally uninterrupted views across the Middle Ground falling away below, a grass swathe bordered by a serpentine path and naturalistic clumps and mounds (Kemp's particular style of 'Gardenesque'), and beyond that to the Picturesque landscape at the bottom of the hill along the Walton Lane boundary. These views are now heavily obscured by later tennis courts, bowling greens and straight tree-lined paths. The Picturesque landscape had a lake divided visually into four by islands and five BRIDGES, four of iron on stone abutments, and a Gothic one of five stone arches (parapet damaged). These connected a circuit of paths that wound around the undulating wooded banks, built up as mounds. The eastern sections of the lake were filled in the early C20, leaving the remnants of a BOAT HOUSE and the iron bridges landlocked and half buried, but despite the deterioration it is still possible to experience a sequence of carefully constructed and framed views. The pretty Gothic GAZEBO (once housing a drinking fountain) at the S end of the stone bridge features in many. The park is intensely composed, no more so than in this section which packs an amazing amount into quite a small area.

Arguably the only positive alterations to Kemp's design are on the W side of the Middle Ground: a derelict cast-iron BAND-STAND of 1899, and facing it a CONSERVATORY, once all glass and iron, and now also abandoned and only iron. This is still in the Paxton tradition but dates from 1900. Like the grander Palm House in Sefton Park (see p. 454), with which it shares many standardised components, it was paid for by Henry Yates Thompson, a banking heir, and supplied by *Mackenzie & Moncur* of Edinburgh. The excellent, naturalistic wrought-iron panels of the terrace running the length of the N side look like an addition.

The E part of the park is in a much lower key – a simple extension of the Middle Ground grassland. Much has been lost to a very large car park on the E edge and the unredeemingly ugly VERNON SANGSTER SPORTS CENTRE of 1970. Of block-work and profiled cladding, it doesn't appear to have a single window. In 2004 Liverpool Football Club were granted permission to construct a massive 60,000-seater STADIUM by *AFL* of Manchester, which will occupy the entire E section of the park. Construction is to be tied to the restoration of the rest. This stipulation must be adhered to, because its present condition is a disgrace. In the affluent southern suburbs, parks, notably Calderstones (see p. 389), are well maintained. By contrast Stanley seems almost abandoned. Yet it serves a severely deprived area whose need for attractive and safe green space is as great now as 150 years ago.*

RAWDON READING ROOM, Breck Road, next to Holy Trinity. Of *c.* 1906. In the style of Shelmerdine's branch libraries.

BOARD SCHOOLS. Anfield is unique in 2005 in retaining all three of its schools built by the Liverpool and the Walton-on-the-Hill school boards (the area spanned both in the 1880s). All are of two storeys and in common brick with red brick dressings, with names, dates and Liver Birds in relief panels. Two were designed by *T. Mellard Reade*: GRANTON ROAD (1880) and VENICE STREET (1885). The largest is ANFIELD ROAD, the first part a range of 1885 by *Charles Deacon* along Feltwell Road with lots of gables. Attached to the Anfield Road return, an extremely odd tower, turning circular in the top parts, behaving as if it were a bobbin, and ending in a broad conical spire broken by an open stage. Attached to the mid-point of the range, and parallel to Anfield Road, a long wing added before 1906.

LIVERPOOL F.C. STADIUM, Anfield Road. Opened in 1884 for Everton, Liverpool F.C.'s great rivals, who played here until in 1892 they moved across Stanley Park to their present home, Goodison Park, and Liverpool F.C. was formed. Unremarkable recent stands, but the massive skeletal roof trusses are a brooding presence on the skyline. Due to be replaced by a huge new stadium in Stanley Park (*see* p. 395). The site of the present stadium will become a public square. The FLAGPOLE inside the Anfield Road entrance is a topmast of Brunel's S.S. *Great Eastern*, which was broken up on the Mersey. Bought for 20 guineas in 1906, it is one of the very few surviving fragments of this celebrated behemoth.

ST DOMINGO VALE and ST DOMINGO GROVE. *See* Everton, p. 424.

CHILDWALL

Childwall was a large ancient parish mentioned in Domesday. It is now the only suburb of Liverpool which has kept a rural character, and that is only in its centre. The church hangs on the reverse slope of the ridge of high land extending s from Everton to Allerton, and the view is now spoilt by post-war City Council housing (*see* p. 434), which covers most of the wide shallow valley below. The historic centre is described first, then the cluster of religious and educational buildings on Woolton Road, and finally any other churches.

ALL SAINTS, Childwall Lane. The only remaining medieval church in the metropolitan area (Sefton is just outside, *see*

---

* It was always thus. In the 1870s the satirical local paper, *The Porcupine*, lampooned Sefton Park as a 'luxurious pleasure-ground for the currant-jelly lot'. It noted with disgust that Sefton cost twice as much as Stanley, and wondered if this had anything to do with the fact that, of Liverpool's sixty-four councillors, only five lived in the northern half of the town.

p. 580). It is red sandstone, and has C14 masonry and simple straight-headed two-light windows in the chancel and Perp masonry and equally simple features in the s aisle wall and s porch. The Salisbury pew (built as Isaac Green's Chapel) protruding E of the porch, on the other hand, is of 1739–40 (and had a Venetian window until 1912), the W steeple of 1810–11, the chancel E wall, chancel aisle and intersecting window of 1851–6 by *W. Raffles Brown*, and the N wall, aisle and vestry by *James F. Doyle* of 1905–6. The spire is recessed behind a typical Gothick openwork parapet, and the tower has a large window with Y-tracery. The spire replaced an earlier and similar one.

First impressions of the low INTERIOR are threefold. First is how very wide it is, because not only are there a nave and aisles, but also *Doyle*'s wide N extension, like an extra aisle, which runs through an arch into a transept-like N chapel (Plumb's Chapel of 1716).★ Thus there are three arcades. Second, because of a chancel N aisle, the church appears to have two chancels as well as two naves. The chancel N aisle was created by *Raffles Brown* from the C18 vestry, and joined up to the N aisle through an arch by *Doyle*. Aisle and chancel are divided by two unequal arches, and between them is a square-headed, C14 two-light window. Third, the chancel floor is lower than the nave (the church is on an E-facing slope), and everything W of the chancel arch slopes down to it quite significantly. The chancel sloped too, until it was raised on the level in the C19. Nave arcades are of plain octagonal piers with double-chamfered arches, but they are interrupted on both sides by a depressed round arch of double the size. This is due to the removal of one pier in 1747 to clear the view from the Salisbury pew (now screened in). The N arcade rebuilt twice since 1800, most recently by Doyle to match the S. W, organ, gallery. Low chancel arch. Roofs C19. Mutilated Dec PISCINA, at floor level because the chancel floor has been raised.

Re-set ARCHITECTURAL FRAGMENTS show the pre-C14 origins of the site. Attached to the porch W wall, a fragment of a Saxon CROSS SHAFT with basket ornament. Inside in the chancel E wall is a Norman multi-scalloped CAPITAL, set horizontally. Used as a gallery support is part of a C13 SHAFT with base.

FURNISHINGS. Fine early C20 CHOIR STALLS intended for the Lady Chapel of Liverpool Cathedral, by *Bodley* and *Scott.* Carving of rough naturalism in keeping with the other decoration of that chapel. – BENCH END. Attached to the s wall in a display case. Exuberantly coarse carving and poppyhead. The arms on it are of Norris and Harrington and it was probably commissioned by Edward Norris, †1606, of Speke Hall (*see*, p. 463; also monuments, below). – BOX PEWS. From the restoration by *Raffles Brown*, when three galleries were taken out. This was in 1851–3, and yet, in spite of the late date, still

---

★ Doyle's N extension replaced a smaller one of 1833 by *Stewart & Picton*.

box pews. – CHANDELIER. In the nave. Of brass, dated 1737, rich and elaborate, also in the ironwork of the support. Two copies of 1892 in the chancel. – HATCHMENTS. An unusually large collection, twelve in total. – Assorted BENEFACTOR and CHARITY BOARDS, from 1702 onwards. – SCULPTURE. Wooden Stanley eagle and child, of unknown provenance. – STAINED GLASS. E window, 1856, by *William Warrington*; also N chapel, 1857 (badly restored), N chancel aisle N, and chancel S, 1854. – S aisle E. *Kempe*, 1906. St Andrew and St George. By *Heaton, Butler & Bayne*, N aisle 1st from W, 1911, and 3rd from W, 1908. By *Percy Bacon*, chancel aisle E, 1906, good, N aisle 2nd from W, Susan Abbott, †1911, and eight clerestory windows, 1906, with good figures. N chancel aisle E, by *Mary Lowndes*, 1915. Best of all is the undated N aisle window, 1st from E. I Am The Vine. Excellent. Figures amongst a vine whose stylised leaves are treated individually, as if dappling the window. S aisle 2nd from E, Susanne Mary Harrison, †1964, by *Whitefriars Glass*. – MONUMENTS. In the S aisle, two round-arched funerary recesses. This was the chapel of the Norris family of Speke. – In one of them is now set a BRASS to Henry Norris, †1524 and Wife (?). 31 in. (79 cm.) figures. Later brasses: notably Major W. Pitcairn Campbell, †1855, by *Warrington*, more like a large panel, all Gothic with lots of red and blue enamelled leaf decorations etc. and small figures; to Charles Okill, †1847, *Sullivan & Sweetman*, Liverpool. In the churchyard, against the S wall, an elaborate Renaissance-style pedimented arch with mosaic decoration, a memorial to Eliza, wife of Sir Andrew Barclay Walker, †1882, and to Walker himself. Possibly by *Sir Ernest George & Peto*, who redid Walker's house, Gateacre Grange, at this time (*see* p. 433). A castellated HEARSE HOUSE, once dated 1811.

S of the churchyard, ELM HOUSE, a red sandstone, early C19 three-bay building with battlements. On the corner of CHILDWALL LANE opposite the church, the CHILDWALL ABBEY HOTEL, a Late Georgian Gothick inn of worn red sandstone with embattled parapet and nearly all its windows ogee-headed. On the ground floor each of these has a very primitive mask at its peak, and over the door is a primitive Ionic capital, of late C16–early C17 type. Where are these from? John Bibby was proprietor in 1778, but the present building could be later. It has two façades: E with two canted bays and a tri-partite doorway between with a tripartite window above (the side windows with plainly pointed arches); and S, of seven bays. This façade faces the brick, interwar PARISH HALL, built on the site of the vicarage. Behind this are the grounds of CHILDWALL HALL, a castellated mansion by *John Nash* demolished in 1949. A LODGE of *c.* 1835–45 survives ¼ m. W on CHILDWALL ABBEY ROAD. This is two-storeyed, a boxy red ashlar fortress with battlements, a few tiny lancets, and sash windows. It is at the head of a DRIVE of wonderful, high-pitched Roman-ticism, undoubtedly created at the same time. It meanders amongst beech woods, through a cutting hewn vertically from

the bedrock. The hall has been replaced by a Further Education College of depressingly undistinguished appearance,
1951–4, by *Ronald Bradbury*, comically refaced with disparate
set fronts as television sets. Alongside, on Childwall Lane, is
ASHFIELD SCHOOL, 1965–7 by *Herbert Thearle & Partners*,
extensive, with plenty of monopitch and some V-section roofs.
Amidst post-war suburban Childwall, ½ m. SW from the church
in WOOLTON ROAD, is an interesting group of Catholic
institutions:

BISHOP ETON MONASTERY (Redemptorists). In 1843 two
cousins bought Eton House, dated 1776 over the S door. One
cousin, Fr (later Bishop) James Sharples, together with
Fr George Brown, Vicar-Apostolic (later Bishop) of Liverpool,
made the house their official residence and in 1845 erected a
chapel, to modest designs by the great *A. W.N. Pugin*. In 1851
the Redemptorists took up residence and in 1857–8 they
demolished and replaced the chapel with the present CHURCH
OF OUR LADY OF THE ANNUNCIATION by A.W.N.'s son
E. W. Pugin. It has a simple exterior, now missing a little octagonal turret and spirelet, with features of *c.* 1300, an apsidal
chancel and transeptal projections. The N one of these contains
a chapel separated from the chancel by a tall, two-bay arcade
with slender columns; the S, a monks' aisle separated from the
chancel by a three-bay arcade, and above that the Abbot's pew
with three Dec windows. Three-bay nave arcade of round piers
with high-quality naturalistic foliate capitals. A shame about
the poor organ gallery, W, and glass screen underneath it. –
Alabaster and marble HIGH ALTAR of 1865, by *J. F. Bentley*.
Also his, the copper-gilt TABERNACLE, 1866. – Another ALTAR,
N chapel, 1866. Probably *Bentley* too. – He certainly designed
its superb gold-leaf TRIPTYCH, 1889, in which a copy of the
C15 Our Lady of Perpetual Succour in the Redemptorist
S. Alfonso, Rome, is now set. – Impressive celebrant ALTAR.
Veined marble. – Chunky marble PULPIT, with open-arcaded
sides. *Bentley* again? – Salvaged from the first chapel, the characteristic *A. W.N. Pugin* PANELLING around the chancel, and
STAINED GLASS by *Hardman*, including Our Lady of the
Annunciation (the former E window) in the N chapel N, also N
and S aisles 1st E, and N aisle 1st W. Large W window of 1919
by *Kempe*.
    The GATEWAY to the street is by *A. W.N. Pugin* too, with the
initials of the two bishops. A little LODGE next to this also
appears much more father Pugin than son. The C18 HOUSE,
its simple nine-bay brick form still clear (was it always nine?),
was rebuilt, presumably by *E. W. Pugin*, at the same time as the
church, with a new roof including dormers, a new N façade,
and a NW tower with a pyramid roof broken by a stage of
louvres. Extended in severe dormitory fashion: W in 1862, E in
1889–90 by *Sinnott, Sinnott & Powell*, and S from the end of
the 1862 wing in 1912.
To the W of this is ST JOSEPH'S HOME, built as a house called
Oswaldcroft, by the other Sharples cousin, Henry, in 1844/5–7

(*see* above). *A. W.N. Pugin* was again the architect. It has an expertly economical entrance elevation, with blank, chimneyed cross-gables at either end, and in between an off-centre porch and large square traceried stair window, and an ever-so-carefully-placed assortment of little windows. Embattled chimneystacks. The garden front is more elaborate, largely because the l. side was altered by *E. W. Pugin* in 1866, the date on the buttressed oriel. Inside, despite some hefty interventions (e.g. a lift), are remains of typical *A. W.N. Pugin* decoration: e.g. excellent floor tiles in the hall, stencilled ceiling by *Crace* in the drawing room and STAINED GLASS by *Wailes*. The kitchen, with arched recesses either side of the fireplace, is delightful. Later work is presumably *E. W. Pugin*'s of 1866, and includes an elaborate fireplace in the dining room. Timothy Brittain-Catlin has identified the plan as an important stage in the evolution of Victorian house design. It is developed from the 'pinwheel' plan of Pugin's The Grange, Ramsgate, in which the three major rooms are arranged around a central stair hall such that the principal axis of each is at right angles to the adjacent one. It was extremely influential.

To the r. of the entrance front is a detached COACHHOUSE, converted into a chapel or mortuary, now a kitchen. Attached to the other side is a large 1960s wing by *Weightman & Bullen* with a monopitch roof. Though the beige brick hardly complements the red ashlar, it is sufficiently self-effacing not to be a calamity. It could in any case easily be knocked down. The LODGE is characteristic of *A. W.N. Pugin*. It is, in fact, the only A.W.N.-designed lodge at an A.W.N. house.

LIVERPOOL HOPE UNIVERSITY COLLEGE, opposite the two former. By *Weightman & Bullen*, 1964–6, when the establishment was Christ's College Catholic teacher-training college. There are six four-storey blocks of student accommodation and a staff house grouped around a central hall and teaching block and – the most interesting part – the CHAPEL of 1965, which is a counterpoint to the disciplined and orthogonal alignment both in plan and elevation. The plan is a diamond overlaid by a square. In the corners created by this overlay are chapels screened by walls. The roof is a fractured pyramid, with the two halves rising in unequal pitches so that a slit of glazing is contrived where they meet, throwing light onto the altar (like Aarno Ruusuvuori's church at Hyvinkää, Finland). Interior with low ambulatory and timber-boarded roof rising to the cleft of light. – Brightly coloured abstract STAINED GLASS.

The campus now includes, across Taggart Avenue, ST KATHARINE'S COLLEGE (formerly Church of England), by *Slater & Moberly*, opened 1930. This is a large and handsome complex. The principal elevation has a big, two-and-a-half-storey centre with mullioned-and-transomed windows, a hipped roof, and tall, elegantly battered copper cupola. Lower accommodation wings extend from the sides and then project forward to create a big three-sided court. All this is in good narrow bricks, and the wings especially, with their unshaped brick mullions and regimented rows of chimneystacks each with a V-section rib running on down the wall to a brick corbel, are reminiscent of Lutyens' Home Counties Tudor.

From the rear of the central range projects the first-floor CHAPEL. A two-centred vault springs from low down. Cut out of it are tall, round-headed windows, one to a bay. Each has set into it a single C19 stained-glass female saint of excellent quality; these, presumably, came from the College's previous premises at Warrington, now demolished. The chapel forms one side of a much smaller court at the back, treated as a cloister with big semicircular windows around it at ground level. It was three-sided until closed in 1997 by a new LIBRARY wing by *Brock Carmichael Associates*. The brick is a reasonable match, and many of the 1930s details are taken up. But the result steers away – just – from pastiche. This is the best of a number of additions (some from 1966) which are partly responsible for hiding away the great court of 1930 and making its discovery so unexpected. There are now no vistas into it; there really ought to be.

ST DAVID, junction of Queens Drive and Rocky Lane. Opened 1940. By *C.E. Deacon & Sons*. With its sister Holy Spirit, Dovecot (*see* p. 437) it derives from the practice's St Dunstan, Earle Road of the 1880s (*see* p. 411). Brick in and out, with round-arched, capital-less arcades, and wagon roof. No tower, but impressive scale. Windows are square-headed and untraceried, grouped in threes in the aisles and clerestory, with five large ones under a retaining arch in the W front. – FONT. Superb alabaster stem and bowl, with cherubim, and well-carved ogee cap cover with Queen Anne's arms. Given in 1702 to St Peter, Church Street (*see* p. 313), demolished 1922.

ST PASCHAL BAYLON (R.C.), Childwall Valley. 1964, by *Sidney Bolland*. The priest wanted a traditional rectangular plan, with an E altar. There is a tall thin SW tower, but the building is of such chunky brick elements and so few windows are visible from the road that it appears almost industrial. Nevertheless, it is handsome in its way. The S wall consists of turrets with narrow, full-height windows set back between them, invisible from an angle. Usual complex around a little yard with hall, presbytery etc.

CHILDWALL COMPREHENSIVE SCHOOL, Queens Drive. *See* Wavertree.

CLUBMOOR

Clubmoor, 3 m. NE of the city centre, is almost entirely an interwar creation of Liverpool City's Housing and Architect's Departments. The quiet suburban architecture for residents of the overcrowded city-centre slums today hides deep-rooted social and economic problems.

ST ANDREW, Queens Drive and Muirhead Avenue. 1928–9, by *Pelham Morter* and *Glen Dobie*. Dull-coloured brick, nave and aisles, chancel, S chapel and N organ chamber. No tower.

Lancets. Little of interest except the splendid FURNISHINGS, acquired from the chapel of the School for the Blind in Hardman Street (demolished 1930, *see* p. 403). The chapel was enriched *c.* 1900 with a suite of Italianate marble and alabaster furniture by *Philip Thicknesse* and *Frank Norbury*.* Preserved here are the ALTAR, REREDOS, COMMUNION RAILS, FONT and monumental PULPIT and BISHOP'S CHAIR. But most extraordinary is undoubtedly the giant PASCHAL CANDLE-STICK, its ascending decoration representing the process of evolution from primeval vegetation through prehistoric creatures to the joyous sons and daughters of God. – COMMUNION TABLE, in the S chapel, separated from the chancel by delicate wooden SCREENS, from St Chad with Christ Church, Everton (demolished).

ST MATTHEW (R.C.), Queens Drive and Adshead Road. *F.X. Velarde*'s first church, opened 1930. A local landmark. The exterior, built of brick with a green pantiled roof, is not up to the reputation of the building. The NE campanile is very high, but the top stage with its stubby Romanesque angle columns beneath a copper cupola is decidedly awkward, and the body of the church with a pair of small round-arched windows to each bay is without distinction. But inside, the very low five-bay arcades to the passage aisles, the arches rising from the ground, are impressive, and so are the short chancel and short sanctuary, the segmental ceiling, and the pair of transverse brick arches separating the S transeptal chapel, one recessed behind the other. The distance between them corresponds to the width of the passage aisle which they continue. W gallery. – FURNISHINGS by *Velarde*, notably good and coherent: ALTAR, TABERNACLE and majestic BALDACCHINO, FONT, BENCHES with fluted-arched ends, and an excellent marble ALTAR in the S chapel with gilded triptych. – *H. Tyson Smith* did the relief sculpture, including altar front, CRUCIFIX and STATIONS OF THE CROSS, to Velarde's designs. Sadly, the altar rails and pulpit are lost. – Excellent SCULPTURE of St Michael overcoming the Devil, possibly designed as a side altar. – Later MOSAIC on the chancel walls, of uncertain authorship.

LIBRARY, Queens Drive. By *Ronald Bradbury*, City Architect. Completed 1964. One-storey glass-sided pavilion, with a baffle wall of ornamental concrete. It served as a prototype for other branch libraries, e.g. Allerton (*see* above). It is a pleasing building, but how could Liverpool for its sake pull down Larkhill House, a good C18 mansion of five bays with wings and colonnades?

CLUBMOOR HOTEL, Townsend Lane. One of the Neo-Georgian pubs in the city by *Harold E. Davies & Son* (i.e. *Harold Hinchliffe Davies*), built in the 1920s (cf. The Gardener's Arms, Tue Brook p. 483).

---

* Italianate mosaics by *James Edie Reid* of Gateshead were not brought to St Andrew.

HOUSING. QUEENS DRIVE is *Brodie*'s pioneering ring road, begun in 1904 (*see* p. 254) partly to be a spine along which the Corporation would build new housing for the masses of the city's slums. The serpentine MUIRHEAD AVENUE is one of Brodie's radial roads, though a minor one, with a central reservation originally hedged off for trams. This is exceptionally wide because it incorporates an existing mature avenue; indeed it is more linear park than highway engineering. From the S end to Queen's Drive it is lined largely with three storey blocks of walk-up FLATS, which illustrate the stylistic evolution of the Corporation's early C20 housing programme. The earliest are the large Arts and Crafts-inspired blocks which were being erected in 1925, of brick, pebbledash and bits of half-timbering, with gables, oriels, and outside steps to the upper flats against the ends. On the W side are some of the most ambitious examples of the Neo-Georgian style promoted by Lancelot Keay from the mid 1920s: long two- and three-storey blocks with details such as sash windows, gatepiers with ball finials, iron balustrades and Doric porches. These, though, are by *Quiggin & Gee*, an unusual instance of the Housing Department commissioning outside architects. Either side of these are blocks typical of *Keay*'s 1930s style, characterised by pale bricks and a distinctive combination of vernacular-inspired motifs (weatherboarded balconies) and Moderne metal-framed windows, including tall and narrow stair windows that project as a V-plan. A block at the S end on the E side demonstrates how this phase ran in parallel with Dudok-inspired Modernism, normally reserved for city centre sites. Opposite, at the junction with Alison Road, is a badly refaced example of a standard *Keay* design of the mid 1920s for corner sites, a pair of brick parlour houses with a two-bay loggia, complete with Tuscan column, in each swept-down return.

Muirhead Avenue runs through the middle of the LARKHILL ESTATE, 1921–3, one of Liverpool's first housing developments after the First World War. It spans Queens Drive between Townsend Lane in the N and West Derby Lane in the S and was designed by *F.E.G. Badger*, Director of Housing prior to Keay, and an engineer not an architect. His brick semis and groups of four are monotonous, and lack both careful detailing (in fact any detailing) or thoughtful planning and grouping. The principal thoroughfares are possible exceptions to this: on Queens Drive, for example, the houses are gabled, and faced with red sandstone recycled from old walls on the site. Nevertheless, they were amongst the best produced under the 1919 Addison Act, built to the maximum recommended dimensions and equipped with electricity, hot water systems and gas fires and cookers. Abutting to the NW is the WALTON-CLUBMOOR ESTATE of the mid 1920s, bound by railways to E (now closed) and W and by Walton Hall Lane (A580 East Lancashire Road) to the N. This, one of *Keay*'s first, illustrates that the bulk of his estates were no better detailed and little more interestingly laid out than Badger's, though on the main roads architectural standards rose to the levels for which he is renowned. Moreover, with less subsidy available, the houses were smaller.

CROXTETH

Hardly anything was here, 5 m. NE of the city centre, until the C20 apart from the Seftons' grand Croxteth Hall and its park. Now this is almost completely surrounded by housing estates.

GOOD SHEPHERD, Carr Lane. 1902–3 by *J. Oldrid Scott*, left unfinished and completed in 1931–7. Of the later date the whole w part of the aisle-less nave, and the top of the big central tower, since taken down. The capitals of the E parts remain uncarved. Scott's work is very conventional, with a polygonal apse and all lancets except for the big w window. The buff stone is dressed and coursed, with red sandstone dressings. Scott got the commission because he was designing fittings for the mother church of St Mary, West Derby (*see* p. 501), designed by his father.

OUR LADY QUEEN OF MARTYRS (R.C.), Stonebridge Lane. 1966–7 by *L.A.G. Prichard & Son*. Brick, square with a pyramid roof rising in the centre – a pauper's version of Christ the King, Queens Drive (*see* p. 494).

ST SWITHIN (R.C., former), Gillmoss Lane. There has been a Catholic chapel on and off in Gillmoss since the Reformation: the Molyneuxs of Croxteth Hall were prominent recusants. The present church is by *L.A.G. Prichard & Son* and opened in 1958, before the firm went Modernist (*see* Our Lady, above). A largish, brick, gabled box with triplets of triangle-headed lancets, and a tall SW campanile. The church was closed in 2004.

WEST DERBY CEMETERY, Lower House Lane. Opened by the West Derby Burial Board in 1884. The layout is by *William Wortley*, who had been clerk of works at Anfield Cemetery (*see* p. 394) and was subsequently the designer of Kirkdale Cemetery (*see* p. 427). Buildings were by *F. Bartram Payton* of Bradford. The site is flat and the formal symmetrical plan of little interest. Following Anfield Cemetery, brick graves were constructed to level the ground where it fell away in the NE corner. Inside the Gothic main entrance – one of its piers larger, with niches and a stumpy, miniature steeple for a cap – are a LODGE and substantial former REGISTRAR'S OFFICE and RESIDENCE. To the entrance drive this has a large oriel thrown up into a gable end and lighting the board room. To its l. are the staircase lancets and then a tall buttressed clock tower, with lancets as well, and a belfry stage of a continuous open Gothic arcade, like a belvedere, and a pyramid roof immediately above this. Otherwise, mullioned-and-transomed windows, and for the lodge too. Pale coursed sandstone. Neither the original mortuary chapels, nor *Ronald Bradbury*'s 1965 replacement, survive.

CROXTETH HALL. A very big, accretive quadrangle of a house. Croxteth Park was the property of the Molyneuxs, later Earls of Sefton, from *c.* 1475 to 1972. Since then it has been owned by the City Council, the rooms available for functions, the grounds a country park.

Sir Richard Molyneux built a hall, *c.* 1575–1600. Of that house, which was possibly E-plan, no more is visible externally than two much-restored gables with six-light mullioned windows on the E side, s of the gatehouse, and no more internally than one four-centred doorway with heavily studded door, once external. It seems this house once extended further s. If the date is right and the surviving old brick is original, this would be one of the very earliest known brick buildings in Lancashire. In 1702 Richard Molyneux, the 4th Viscount, built the fine s (actually sw) front, when Sefton Hall was demolished (*see* below) and Croxteth became the principal seat. A w wing was put up *c.* 1760. Then, for the 4th Earl, in 1874–7 *Thomas Henry Wyatt* added the N range and the E range as far as the gatehouse in one style – Jacobethan – and rebuilt and extended the existing range along the back of the 1702 wing in another, which carefully matched the 2nd Viscount's front. Finally, in 1902–4 *J. Macvicar Anderson* replaced the C18 w wing with something much larger, in a continuation of Wyatt's '1702' architecture.

28 The s FRONT of 1702, the showpiece of the house, is eleven bays wide, of brick with bright white-painted stone dressings such as quoins to the angles and the angles of the middle bays. The front has a very curious composition, restlessly and

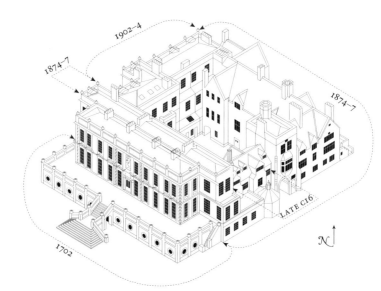

Croxteth Hall (Liverpool).
Axonometric view

uncomfortably disjointed because the rhythm of each of the three superimposed elements – the terrace, the windows and the parapet – is different, and they rarely align. The main floor stands on the big terrace (extended by Wyatt), which has big circular and oval windows and in the centre a broad perron. The windows of the main floor have pediments alternately triangular and segmental, but they are not evenly spaced. It is unclear why. The great central portal is too big for all this if one wants to apply correct criteria, but at the same time undeniably splendid. It has pairs of attached Corinthian columns, a carved frieze, and an open segmental pediment with trophies and the cross Moline (the Molyneux emblem). Above is an enriched architrave in place of the middle first-floor window, and of the same size, framing a panel with lots more trophies carved in charmingly provincial fashion. Above this the parapet is very nearly evenly spaced. There are urns along it, and under each of these is a stumpy pilaster strip, carved with plants or flowers, and one cheerful figure in contemporary dress on the l. return. There are strikingly similar features 2 m. away on the parapet of the E wing of 1737 at Knowsley Hall (*see* p. 217), where *Henry Sephton* was master mason and possibly architect. Could he have worked here too?

The later wings are of three storeys too. *Wyatt*'s 1870s work, beginning N of the C16 part on the E side and going round to the NW corner, is gabled Jacobethan and no doubt inspired by the C16 architecture, though on a much grander scale of course. It is tactful and scholarly and carefully composed to break up the mass, but nevertheless quite dull.* However, when at the same time Wyatt rebuilt the range running behind the S wing he choose the 1702 work as his pattern, but rationalised. It projects from behind it at either end, housing a dining room in the E part and a staircase hall in the W. *Macvicar Anderson* incorporated the W end into his new W wing, which matches Wyatt's details precisely and consists of two parts: to the r., ten taller bays in a 3–4–3 rhythm, of which the r. three are Wyatt's 1870s work; and to the l., six lower ones. He also apparently recycled Wyatt's Tuscan porch by shifting it N a few bays and sticking on it a segmental pediment.

INTERIOR. The house, for all its size, is a bit of a disappointment inside, principally because the 1702 wing was severely damaged by fire in 1952 and its enfilade of fully panelled and richly ceiled rooms largely destroyed. Indeed the upper parts are still mostly an empty carcass, and the roof a 'temporary' steel-framed structure. A couple of rooms have been rebuilt in simplified fashion, and one or two simple fireplaces look early C18. The one much more impressive surround may have been brought in. It is later C18. The once splendid central saloon has been subdivided, creating a corridor to the entrance on to the terrace. The two best spaces now are Wyatt's grand DINING ROOM with Carolean-style panelled walls and

---

* In the courtyard, reset above the archway, is a massive, bizarrely carved stone LINTEL from a fireplace at Sefton Hall, demolished in the C18.

stucco ceiling, and the yet grander STAIRCASE as remodelled by *Macvicar Anderson*. The unsatisfactory approach to this from the low, columned entrance hall on the W side is explained by the fact that the entrance hall is an alteration of 1902. As built by Wyatt, the entrance was further S on the W side, directly into the lower staircase hall, on axis with its single flight of stairs. These stairs rise up to the main floor, with a florid wrought-iron balustrade. Here there is a spacious landing all around, part of the principal circulation at the junction of the S and W wings. Around it are round-headed arches, in places open and in places blank as required. Through these on the N side a flight of stairs rises to the second floor, where a landing runs around on three sides behind an open arcade, with more wrought-iron balustrades across the openings. The whole thing is topped off by a big rectangular skylight set in a coved ceiling. In the SE corner the 1870s kitchens are as extensive as one would expect of a house of this size at that date, with an externally expressed polygonal game larder, impressively large confectionary kitchen etc.

The old STABLES, coachhouse, grooms' cottages etc., now mainly residential, form a large crooked L to the S of the house. They are reported to contain a cockpit with a small gallery. Brick, two-storeyed, with stone plinth and quoins. Datestones suggest that the S range is of 1669 and the S part of the W range of 1706. However, the N section of the W range, with cupola, is possibly of 1676 and has a couple of mullioned windows. Otherwise wooden casements, horizontal sashes, cross-windows and doors are inserted higgledy-piggledy, and with various additions and alterations the result is charming. In the yard a C19 COACH WASH, like a little iron Dutch barn, but with pump, trough and drain-away. N of this are single-storey C19 horse boxes and the utterly utilitarian, cloister-like C20 EXERCISE YARD, considerably altered as a restaurant. In the wall closing the yard on the N side are fine rusticated GATEPIERS that look contemporary with the 1702–6 works.

S of the stables is the HOME FARM, a large model complex (1849 and 1904 datestones). There is a straightforwardly attractive BULL-BOX in the paddock, square with a pyramid roof. Also, the single-storey brick DAIRY by *Eden Nesfield*, of *c*. 1861–70. A whimsical version of High Victorian Gothic: the dairy itself (there are two little wings S and E) with deep eaves on outsized timber brackets, louvre at the apex, and the walls nicely tiled inside. The ceiling beams retain their painted decoration but sadly the painted panels by *Albert Moore* between, of daffodils and cross Molines, have vanished, as have the tiled floor and a fountain. Eastlake called the dairy 'admirably conceived and executed with great refinement and artistic skill'. This is better appreciated from the S, yard, side. Here, in the re-entrant angle where the dairy and wings meet, is a porch with a single column with cushion capital. The adjoining C18 FARMHOUSE has an extension by *Nesfield* too, with a two-light Gothic window and round chimneystack. He also did the LAUNDRY and attached cottage of 1864–5, ¼ m. SE, which by contrast is in his Old English style, and a relatively early example of it. It is brick and rather plain and sadly boarded-up, but has characteristic ribbed chimneystacks, and pargetting, especially to the deep cove of a bay window. He must also surely have designed the KEEPERS' COTTAGES and the KENNELS ½ m. N of the Hall, the one in the same style as the farmhouse extension, the other in exactly the style of the laundry. (In addition Nesfield drew up plans, never executed, to reface the C18 W wing of the house in the style of the 1702 wing.) *John Douglas* also designed kennels, in High Victorian Gothic, *c.* 1861–70. They are ¾ m. NE of the Hall, and now outside the park on Old Kennel Close.

Other estate buildings include the plain early C19 ESTATE OFFICE, N of the Hall on the corner of the walled KITCHEN GARDEN, and a number of modest LODGES. *See* below for Mill Lodge, and West Derby, p. 503, for the much grander example at what was the principal entrance. The drive up from there passes under Croxteth Hall Lane via a handsome sandstone BRIDGE dated 1845. This is one of the most impressive features of the PARK, which retains a sense of space, seclusion and composition despite extensive late C20 housing development on it to within a mile of the house both N and S. W of the house on the edge of the lawns are two CANALS, Statue Pond and N of that the bent Long Pond. There is also an informal LAKE beyond the ornamental woodland N of the house. These are C19: none appears on earlier estate maps.

CROXTETH HOUSING ESTATE, on the S side of the East Lancashire Road (A580). Begun in 1950 and consisting of almost 2,500 units by 1965. Designed by *Ronald Bradbury* and his staff in the City Architect's and Housing Departments. Now entirely low- and medium-rise after a number of tower blocks were demolished, and depressingly bleak. Usual dismal shopping parade, incorporating a taller community centre with Festival of Britain-style cupola. On the E side of BETHERICK LANE is MILL LODGE. One of Croxteth Hall's, and small and quite simple but with thoughtful details, including an external stone bench integral with the small timber porch. Is it by *Nesfield*, who was paid £114 in 1859 for designing four lodges?

EDGE HILL

and KENSINGTON

This is very much inner-city Liverpool now, and poor and troubled too. Until the early C19 it was rural. Edge Hill, up above the city on the ridge, like Everton to its N, then came into favour for its good air and excellent views, and was built up with a better class of housing. A surprising amount of this survives. The arrival of the Liverpool & Manchester Railway in 1830 and the continued expansion of the city brought about the inevitable descent, and by 1914 the area was dense bylaw housing. Despite extensive clearances, quite large chunks remained in 2005, though hundreds more demolitions are planned as part of a ten-year programme to tackle the area's severe economic and social problems. Edge Hill's early railway structures are particularly interesting.

Churches

CHRIST CHURCH, Kensington (former). 1870, by *W. & G. Audsley*. An invigorating North Italian Romanesque building, in common brick with much structural polychromy in red and blue brick and stone, both inside and out. Extremely tall, almost detached NW tower, formerly with a steep pyramid roof, very prominent on Kensington at the top of the rise. The W door in it has crisp free Romanesque carving. The bell-stage is very tall, with in each face a twin round-headed opening under a relieving arch, with attached shaft between. All windows round-headed. Large round window with plate tracery in the W end.

In 2005 the big empty interior was all but derelict, but with an extraordinary church-within-a-church under the arches of the S aisle, patched together flimsily on stilts like something from the *favelas*. The arcades have round arches and polished granite shafts. Imaginative and chunky Byzantine capitals, all different of course, and similar ornament elsewhere. Nave roof with kingpost and arch-braced principals and scissor-braced intermediaries. Transepts, the S with an organ loft, and short chancel. – REREDOS. An arcade. All other fittings removed. – Remnants of Audsley STAINED GLASS.

ST CATHERINE (former), Tunnel Road, Edge Hill. By *John Denison Jee*. Erected on farmland, in 1862–3. Rather poverty-stricken in appearance, and now roughcast. The features are of *c*. 1300. Flèche on the E gable of the nave. Used as a storage lock-up.

ST CYPRIAN, Durning Road, on the corner with Edge Lane. 1879–81, by *Henry Sumners* (who died the year before construction began). A very remarkable church, quite roguish, and highly original in its details, such as the windows. The tracery is of no period at all. Rock-faced with a prominent W tower with higher stair-turret. Clerestory of big mullioned-and-transomed windows with segmental heads, each under a gablet. The continuous row of six of these on the Edge Lane elevation is the most strikingly original element of the exterior. Vestries of 1916 added to the E end. Broad nave with narrow passage aisles. N transept of three gabled bays, i.e. the axis is parallel, not at right angles, to the nave. Round-arched arcades, the capitals in a free Romanesque style with Arts and Crafts touches. This carving is of 1897 and designed by *Willink & Thicknesse*. The roof was also boarded in at this time, and the clock put in the tower. The W half of the nave was walled off rudely *c*. 1982 and divided up into ground-floor rooms and an upper hall. – STAINED GLASS. A window in the N transept by *G.J. Baguley & Son*, 1939.

St Deniol (former), Upper Parliament Street. *See* Toxteth, p. 470.

St Dunstan, Earle Road, Edge Hill. 1886–9, by *Aldridge & Deacon*. Very similar to their St Benedict, Everton, now gone. Pinkish-red Ruabon brick. Impressive if rather curious W front dominated by a big group of five stepped lancets flanked by two angle turrets. Above the lancets under the strong overarch are nicely brick-carved Evangelist symbols and a figure of Christ. Below, a low baptistery, opening into the nave in three arches, and a porch, l. A copper-clad flèche sits just E of the W front (apparently a NW tower was planned). The side windows are all lancets, small stepped triplets in the aisles, singles in the clerestory.

The interior impresses with gloomy atmosphere: big and broad, with round stone piers, but otherwise entirely brick. A frieze runs along the arcade arches and also round three sides of the chancel. E window of three stepped lancets high up. Reordered with a nave altar in 1967. The N chapel was glazed in at the same time. – REREDOS. A pile of alabaster with gabled tabernacle, but still hopelessly undersized for the space. Designed by *C.E. Deacon*. – LECTERN. Very rich wrought iron, with a small figure between the uprights of the shaft. By *Deacon* again. – Fine iron SCREEN. – STAINED GLASS. W window by *Burlison & Grylls*. A dozen or so brass PLAQUES to members of the Earle family.

St Mary, Irving Street, Edge Hill. 1812–13. Brick preaching box, with a slender square W tower with attached vestry, a broad aisle-less nave with pointed windows in two tiers with intersecting tracery, and a very short, never lengthened, chancel. Nave and chancel are thinly embattled. The nave was initially five bays long; in 1824–5 it was extended by the addition of a sixth enveloping the base of the tower, and including porches and gallery stairs. Little single-storey chapels were also built on either side of the chancel. Three windows, including the E window, have mid-C19 Perp tracery. Untouched inner-city CHURCHYARD, now a rarity.

The interior still has its three wooden galleries on very thin quatrefoil cast-iron columns and with pretty Gothic decoration on the fronts. They are of 1824–5; what was there before is uncertain. A late C20 wall under the W gallery created a parish room, but this is set back a whole bay, so is not intrusive. The plain ceiling is post-war; those of the stairwells, with cornices and roses, and the apse, with sunburst, reflect the character of the original. – FONT and PULPIT, moved from under the centre of the chancel arch *c.* 1913, when CHOIR STALLS were introduced. Box pews, see the height of the column bases, were replaced in the early C20. The galleries retain their original raked PEWS. Reordered again in 1958–60, with a platform mounting a nave ALTAR, and reduction of the altar. – REREDOS. 1908. The Last Supper. – STAINED GLASS. In the N wall two *Morris* windows, one 1873, the other 1879. E window, 1863. N, 1st from E, *Percy Bacon & Bros*, †1915. N chapel. *Hardman*, 1949. – MONUMENTS. Edward Mason, †1814. Tablet with winged genius on clouds. Drapery cascades down and is spread by two putti below to reveal the inscription written on it. Edward's daughter, Ellen Mason, †1842. *William Spence*. An archaeologically correct Gothic niche, missing its statue. – A number of wall PLAQUES.

SACRED HEART (R.C.), Hall Lane. *See* p. 420.

ST ANNE (R.C.), Overbury Street, Edge Hill. By *Charles Hansom*, 1843–6, in early Dec style, enlarged by *Pugin & Pugin* with chancel, apse and two transepts, 1888–9, and by *Peter Paul Pugin* with baptistery, 1893. A big church, reflecting the size of the local population in the C19, but now the surrounding terraces have been redeveloped St Anne stands in melancholy isolation. The Hansom work is pure Ecclesiology, in contrast to contemporary churches by local architects. Red sandstone very crudely tooled. Prominent w tower. The top appears sliced off because it is incomplete – Hansom intended a spire, omitted for fear of subsidence. At the foot the entrance has spandrels well carved with foliate designs.

A tall handsome nave with clerestory of quatrefoil lights. The arcades have quatrefoil piers. Open arch-braced roof. The Pugin & Pugin part has a good crossing and the chancel open in arcades of columns paired in depth to the organ chamber on the l., and to one of two chapels side-by-side, on the r. Superimposed above the arcades and continuing around the apse is another arcade, filled with lancets. Reordered by the removal of a baldacchino and altar rails, and the introduction in 1969 of a wooden ALTAR in the E bay of the nave. – The chunky marble and alabaster ALTAR RAIL remains. – Very big PRESBYTERY attached, NW, by *Peter Paul Pugin*, 1893.

ST HUGH (R.C.), Earle Road, Edge Hill. By *Pugin & Pugin*, opened 1904. Quarry-faced red sandstone. Dec tracery. No tower. – Hanging ROOD by *Bainbridge Copnall* (cf. St Columba, Anfield, p. 393).

KENSINGTON BAPTIST CHURCH (former), Jubilee Drive. 1889. Disused. Large, brick and Italianate.

Public, Commercial and Residential Buildings

LIBRARY, Kensington. The first purpose-built branch library in Liverpool. By *Thomas Shelmerdine*, 1890, enlarged 1897. Very pretty, and asymmetrical. *The Builder* called the style 'Germanic Renaissance'. Red brick and stone dressings. Entrance porch with a little semicircular pediment, and Ionic columns. Octagonal white-painted timber and glass lantern topped by a cupola. The design is full of little inventions; one of the most prominent is the arcaded parapets.

POST OFFICE at the corner of Hall Lane and Kensington. 1883, by *Henry Tanner*. Renaissance revival. Demolished 2005.

FIRE and POLICE STATION (former), Durning Road. A charming little mid-C19 Tudor Gothic façade. Ashlar. Mullioned windows, the upper lights quatrefoils. Tudor arches, battlements, elaborate chimneys etc.

CHATSWORTH SCHOOL, Chatsworth Drive. Opened 1874. By *T. Mellard Reade*. His first, of many, for the School Board. A big building with two façades at right angles. These, unusually for the Board's schools, are faced in sandstone. This is pale and quarry-finished, with red ashlar dressings. End and middle bays project slightly under tall gables. Gothic details.

ROYAL LIVERPOOL UNIVERSITY HOSPITAL, Prescot Street. *See* p. 421.

WEST DERBY UNION OFFICES, West Derby Road. A large brick office building of 1901–2, in all probability by *C.O. Ellison*. He was architect to the Guardians, and the vocabulary compares with that of the Broad Green POORHOUSE he designed for them (*see* p. 437).

BOTANIC GARDENS and WAVERTREE PARK, Edge Lane. The Botanic Gardens were founded in 1802 by William Roscoe in Mosslake Fields, moving to Edge Lane and opening there in 1836, and were acquired by the Corporation in 1846. In 1856 the Corporation laid out Wavertree Park on land immediately s which had been purchased for a jail, never built. It was later extended to surround the Botanic Gardens. Little of interest now; the conservatories were destroyed in the Second World War. The exception is the substantial and fine Curator's LODGE of 1836–7, Greek Revival with a front jammed against Edge Lane. Ashlar, unhappily altered. *John Cunningham*'s obituary in the *Liverpool Mercury* describes him as the architect. He was in partnership with *Arthur Hill Holme* at the time. Square plan. Flanked on the road side by short screen walls punctured by doorways and terminating with big panelled and battered piers, and with canted bays on the garden side.

JEWISH CEMETERY, Deane Road. The third built by Liverpool's Jewish community; opened in 1837 and closed to burials in 1904. Decaying rendered screen to the street, finished as channelled rustication. Ends projecting slightly with pilasters, the centre a large round-arched entranceway with pediment, Greek Doric half-columns and triglyph entablature.

EDGE HILL STATION, Tunnel Road. Edge Hill was from the outset the nerve centre at the Liverpool end of the Liverpool & Manchester Railway (*see* p. 53), the place where locomotives took over from the rope haulage used to bring trains up the inclined tunnels from the city termini at Crown Street, Wapping, and later Lime Street. The first station was ready for the opening in 1830, in the sandstone cutting ¼ m. w of the present station, beyond Chatsworth Street. It was at the entrance to the original tunnels, and was embellished with *John Foster Jun.*'s famous Moorish Arch, which contained the engines powering the rope systems. Sadly, nothing survives but the tunnel mouths and only the most archaeological of other remnants.

Edge Hill (Liverpool), the Moorish Arch, by John Foster Jun.
(demolished), on the Liverpool & Manchester Railway.
Engraving by A.B. Clayton, 1831

99   The present STATION dates from 1836 and was built at the
entrance to the tunnel to the new terminus at Lime Street. The
architect is unknown, but Foster and John Cunningham both
designed elements of the first Lime Street station (*see* p. 304).
It is low down and approached by setted ramps carried on
red sandstone arches with voussoirs, and rusticated ashlar
between. Between these the similar TUNNEL entrance of 1836.
Outer tunnel entrances of 1881–5. Two platforms, until 1881
with tracks on the inner sides only. Later additions were
stripped away *c.* 1978–80, leaving mainly the original structures. There are two matching ranges, classical, low, of two
storeys and six bays – some of the earliest station buildings in
the world still in use. Channelled rustication, with emphatic
keystones to the ground-floor openings. These have been
altered. The blocks originally contained a booking hall, waiting
room and two residences, and until 1870 they extended E with
engine houses for the rope haulage. In their place now stand
similar single-storey extensions probably containing fabric
recycled from them.

Rising up behind the N range is a splendid brick ENGINE
HOUSE of 1849, with relieving arches and round-arched
windows, and, in sandstone, a bold cornice and a plinth of vermiculated rustication. It powered the ropes through the new
WATERLOO TUNNEL to the N docks, the handsome entrance
to which, N of the station, is dated 1847 and has vermiculated
rustication too. Adjoining the engine house to the E is an ashlar
boiler house and a brick ACCUMULATOR TOWER built to

provide hydraulic power for the once-famous Edge Hill Grid-iron, a state-of-the-art marshalling yard opened in 1882.

⅓ m. E of the station is a SIGNAL BOX, typical of the often effectively composed examples built as part of the West Coast electrification of the 1960s to designs by the *Architect's Department* of *British Railways London Midland Region*. A common design grammar of simple boxy masses was conceived to be comprehensible against the clutter of the railwayscape when viewed from a speeding train. This is the mature type, with corner windows only and a heavy overhanging slab roof.

VENTILATION SHAFT, Crown Street. In the same idiom as an octagonal factory chimney, but shorter and broader, and handsome in its way. The shaft was sunk in the 1890s to ventilate the Liverpool & Manchester Railway tunnel to its Wapping goods station (*see* p. 305) when it was converted to steam haulage. The L&MR's original passenger terminal was on Crown Street too; no trace of it remains.

WILLIAMSON'S TUNNELS, Smithdown Lane. This is a true oddity, a labyrinthine network of largely uncharted multi-level tunnels, caverns, vaults, passageways and stairs cut into the sandstone bedrock under Edge Hill. They were the personal whim, obsession in fact, of Joseph Williamson, a successful if eccentric tobacco merchant who moved to MASON STREET *c.* 1805. The HOUSE, extensively altered, survives. First he put up some houses. These had cellars and vaulted platforms to create extended level gardens at the rear. From these he appears to have developed a fascination with tunneling, and until his death brought a halt in 1840 he devoted his wealth to creating the bizarre underground complex. Williamson was so secretive – few people were allowed in, no plans survive – that the purpose remains obscure. In part it may have been philanthropic, providing labour in the depression that followed the Napoleonic Wars. The refuge from the Apocalypse for a millennial cult is one more exotic theory. But in the main it seems to have been created for nothing more than personal amusement. This may explain the bafflingly chaotic plan. Their known extent is from Smithdown Lane in the W to Highgate Street in the E and from Edge Lane to the N to Grinfield Street to the S.

The tunnels were quickly filled in and bricked up after his death, but for the last decade or so an intrepid local group has gradually explored and cleared parts of the network. In 2002 a VISITORS' CENTRE opened off Smithdown Lane in the former Corporation Stables of 1867. By *Bryan Young & Associates*, it is a *c.* 30 ft (9 metre) high box with a full-height frameless glass façade erected in front of the entrance to Williamson's DOUBLE TUNNEL. This is a *c.* 20 ft (6 metre) high barrel vault lined in brick with a brick arch within it, springing from the same point as the vault but rising only halfway to the crown, and extending the full length of the tunnel. A Triple Tunnel, 180 ft (55 metres) long, has also been discovered, but has yet to be excavated. Also uncovered are the 'goblin' or banqueting hall, 70 ft (21.5 metres) long and 25 ft (7.7 metres) high. Other elements are said to have included two four-bedroom houses and Williamson's own accommodation.

OLYMPIA THEATRE, West Derby Road. 1903, by *Frank Matcham*. A large corner building, rather bald – not as opulent as Matcham can be and balder still now that the gable has been simplified. The big broad auditorium remains largely intact, with two galleries, boxes and ceilings dripping with plaster ornamentation. It was built as a variety theatre capable of hosting circuses – hence the elephants in the decoration, with a stage that could originally be lowered and filled with water.

BANK OF LIVERPOOL, former branches. On KENSINGTON at the corner of Deane Road is one of the best, an excellent building of 1898 by *James Rhind*. Riotously Neo-Baroque in brick and Portland stone. The composition comes together masterfully at the Borrominesque corner. It is cut out as a concave curve, with a convex oriel adorned by Ionic columns projecting above the entrance. Above the parapet the concave face continues as one of the identical sides of the grandly architectural triangular chimney, with entablature, pediments, and columns at the corners. The other branch is on a very prominent triangular site at the junction of SMITHDOWN ROAD and Earle Road. By *Willink & Thicknesse*, drawings dated 1903. Red sandstone ashlar, the corner a three-and-a-half-storey drum with attached pairs of superimposed columns rising correctly through the orders, capped by a stone saucer dome. (Opposite it THE BOUNDARY, a stripy, frilly and freely Jacobean revival pub of 1902, still has some decent joinery and decorative finishes inside, and has yet to be entirely gutted – an increasing rarity locally.)

117 LITTLEWOODS BUILDING, Edge Lane. 1938. Almost certainly by *Gerald de Courcy Fraser*. Looking down over Wavertree Park, a monumental symmetrical Art Deco building, still classically committed. All white render and simply detailed, relying on its scale, massing and clean uncluttered elevations for its commanding presence. This was as explicit a piece of advertising as the contemporary factories along the Great Western Road in London. The principal w elevation is very long with vertical glazing strips linking the two floors. They are closely set, with pilaster strips between. High central clock tower set back behind the entrance bays. Bookended by pavilions with very Baroque concave returns. The N return facing Edge Lane is one of a pair; the other terminates the parallel rear wing, which otherwise is only one-storeyed and functional.

GEORGIAN HOUSING. A little circuit of pleasant Late Georgian domestic architecture encircling St Mary's church. In IRVINE STREET, W, a terrace of brick, three-storey houses, some of three bays, with nice doorways with recessed columns of the type of the Rodney Street neighbourhood (*see* p. 379). A picturesque variety on NORTH VIEW N of the church. Some three-storey, but others two storeys high, like the terraces in HOLLAND PLACE (1830s) and houses in CHURCH MOUNT opposite the E end of St Mary. These have enriched doorways, though. E of them in MARMADUKE STREET (laid out *c.* 1806) is another brick row, early C19, and the handsome CLARE TERRACE of *c.* 1830, long and stuccoed (the ground floor channelled) with pedimented accents, originally three, but now missing the N end one. The elevations are slightly unusual: two floors of deep windows, and a row of narrow panels above. In OVERTON STREET S of Marmaduke Street is one more short brick terrace.

A separate fragment is Nos. 8–10 BROUGHAM TERRACE, on the S side of West Derby Road, the remains of a row of *c.* 1830 by *J.A. Picton*. No. 8 served from 1889 as the Muslim Institute, containing a lecture hall and mosque. Internal alterations in 'Saracenic' style, made by *J.H. McGovern* in 1895, have all but vanished.

EVERTON

with LONDON ROAD and ROYAL LIVERPOOL
UNIVERSITY HOSPITAL

John Housman wrote in 1800: 'Everton is a remarkably pleasant village, finely situated on an agreeable eminence . . . and commands many fine prospects: it has of late years become a favourite residence for gentlemen of independent fortune.' From the mid C19 this semi-rural suburb on the highest part of the ridge E of the city centre was overtaken by the expanding town and covered with closely packed terraced streets. In the 1960s these were largely replaced with tower blocks, and since the 1980s most of the towers have been replaced with low-rise, low-density housing. Much of the hill's W slope is again open land, reopening the spectacular views across the city to the river and beyond.

Religious Buildings

ST GEORGE, Heyworth Street. 1813–14. This was the first of three churches erected by *John Cragg*, employing cast-iron parts manufactured at his Mersey Iron Foundry (the others were St Philip, *see* p. 374, and St Michael-in-the-Hamlet, *see* p. 381). Cragg had been planning a church for Toxteth Park. *J.M. Gandy* produced designs in 1809, and in 1812 Cragg met *Thomas Rickman* and had him make new drawings. Then the opportunity to build in Everton arose, and the church went ahead on the present site. It is impossible to disentangle Cragg's, Gandy's and Rickman's contributions. Some cast-iron elements shown in Gandy's drawings are very close to the executed building, but these could have been designed by Cragg before Gandy's involvement. Certainly Cragg had already cast some components before Rickman appeared on the scene.

The exterior is largely of stone, the style Perp. High W tower with pierced battlements (original?). Large Perp three-light windows along the sides, with cast-iron tracery. The buttresses

between had cast-iron pinnacles, now removed. Six-light E
window in a short embattled chancel. The galleried interior is
a delightful surprise, extraordinarily light and delicate owing
to the use of cast iron throughout. Slender clustered columns
divide nave from aisles. Traceried arches span between the
columns to support the nave ceiling, and between the columns
and the outer wall to carry the flat ceilings over the aisles (the
tie-rods are a C20 insertion). Further traceried arches support
the galleries, which cut across the windows. The ceilings are of
slate slabs slotted between the cast-iron rafters, with cast-iron
tracery on the underside. Thicker slabs of slate attached to the
upper edge of the rafters form the roof – a system patented by
Cragg in 1809. – STAINED GLASS mostly destroyed in the war.
The only complete survivor is N, 3rd from W, 1863, by *A. Gibbs*.
E window, 1952, by *Shrigley & Hunt*. – MONUMENTS. Under
the tower, John Rackham, †1815, a tablet with an ambitious
Dec Gothic surround, designed by *Rickman* and carved by *S.
& J. Franceys*. S gallery, Thomas W. Wainwright (a surgeon),
†1841, with a relief of the Good Samaritan by *W. Spence*. N
gallery, Walter Fergus MacGregor, †1863, an elaborate Gothic
tabernacle incorporating a portrait roundel, by *E.E. Geflowski*.

ST JOHN CHRYSOSTOM, Queens Road. *W. Raffles Brown*'s
church of 1852–4, which displeased *The Ecclesiologist*, was
demolished in 1970 and replaced by *Saunders Bell*'s building,
opened in 1975. Square, spirelet rising from the centre of a
pyramid roof.

ST MARGARET, Belmont Road and West Derby Road. *See*
Anfield, p. 393.

ST POLYCARP (former), Netherfield Road North. 1886 by *George
Bradbury*. Common brick and red brick, Gothic, with Geometrical tracery in the five-light window to the main street.
Odd S aisle incorporating a gabled door. Interior said to be
faced with white glazed bricks.

ST FRANCIS XAVIER (R.C.), Salisbury Street. With its schools
and college, this made up C19 Liverpool's most extensive group
of religious buildings. The foundation stone of the church was
laid in 1842. *J.J. Scoles* was appointed architect, his drawings
are dated 1845, and the building opened in 1848. Rock-faced
stone, with Geometrical tracery. Nave and aisles under separate gabled roofs, with low confessionals down the ritual N side
forming a sort of subsidiary aisle. The tower ('below criticism'
according to *The Ecclesiologist*, 1853) stands outside the
opposite aisle. Recessed spire planned from the outset but
not added until 1883. For the Sodality Chapel on this side, *see*
below. Inside, eight-bay nave of very slender columns, with
huge bases and foliage capitals. The thinness of the columns
suggests cast iron, but they are Drogheda limestone (now
unfortunately painted, like much of the interior stonework).
They minimise the division between aisles and nave, allowing
a clear view of sanctuary and pulpit. Polygonal apse with high
altar, flanked by Sacred Heart Chapel, l., and Rosary Chapel,
r. The three very elaborate ALTARS with REREDOSES are early

1850s. The drawings for the Sacred Heart altar, dated 1852–3, are by Scoles' pupil *S.J. Nicholl*. Next to it, and of the same date, a life-size RELIEF of Christ with the Afflicted, after a painting by *Ary Scheffer*. – Above the sanctuary, carved and painted ROOD by *Early* of Dublin, installed 1866. – STAINED GLASS above the organ gallery, Christ the King, 1930, by *Hardman & Powell*; window l. of this, unveiled 1999, by *Linda Walton*. – An arch r. of the Rosary Chapel, now glazed, opens into the SODALITY CHAPEL, 1885–7, a showpiece by *Edmund Kirby*. Virtually an independent building. The exterior shows it to have a polygonal centre with lower, asymmetrical ends. The two-light windows are gabled, with pinnacles between. Inside, the style is E.E., with soaring Purbeck marble shafts. The elongated octagonal centre has a high plaster rib-vault, and a two-bay apsidal chancel with clerestory. Behind this is an ambulatory, and at the opposite end another, lower apse. The chapel houses the highly decorated altars of a number of sodalities (pious lay associations) and is richly evocative of the spiritual life of late C19 Liverpool Catholics. The chancel contains the ALTAR OF THE ANNUNCIATION, with marble reliefs carved by Messrs *Boulton* of Cheltenham, and a tabernacle door by *Conrad Dressler*; wrought-iron screens l. and r. incorporate electrotype RELIEFS of the Holy Family and The Presentation of the Virgin by *Dressler*, with *cloisonné* on the reverse. Opposite is the BONA MORS ALTAR, with a marble triptych; STAINED GLASS above designed by *Kirby*, made by *Burlison & Grylls*. The CHAPEL OF ST JOSEPH, richly panelled in wood, opens off the ambulatory.

Behind the church is the former COLLEGE, 1876–7, converted from 1999 into the Cornerstone building of Liverpool Hope University College. It was designed by *Henry Clutton*, to a plan by *Fr Richard Vaughan SJ*; architects for the conversion were *Downs Variava*. Red brick and terracotta. A strongly modelled classroom range faces Salisbury Street, with windows in threes between deep buttresses, and gabled dormers above a pierced parapet. (Simpler N addition, 1908, by *Matthew Honan*.) Behind, and parallel, is a huge assembly and examination hall under a pointed timber roof with dormers. The long sides have internal buttresses in the manner of Albi, linked by lateral arches creating an arcade. The buttresses are pierced to form aisles and again for a first-floor gallery, but later infilling has obscured this. The N end survives to full height, the rest now has a mezzanine; large windows between allow the space to be read as a whole. Abutting the E side of the College in Haigh Street are altered remnants of the former SCHOOLS. Rock-faced red sandstone, simple trefoil-headed windows. These appear to be the school buildings begun in 1853 to designs by *Joseph Spencer*, and extended by him in 1857.

ST MARY OF THE ANGELS (R.C.), Fox Street. 1910, by *Pugin & Pugin*. No longer in use. Brick and red sandstone, basilican plan, with round-arched arcades. The foundress was Amy Elizabeth Imrie, a Liverpool heiress and convert to Catholicism, who aimed to bring the religious art and architecture of Italy to this poor district. The church was apparently based on that of the Aracoeli in Rome, and Miss Imrie furnished it with altars and other artefacts acquired in Bologna, Rome and elsewhere. The HIGH ALTAR is said to have come from one of the chapels of Bologna Cathedral. – STATUE above the Lady Altar by *Zaccagnini*. – Good STAINED GLASS in the W rose window by *Earley & Co.* of Dublin, 1929.

ST MICHAEL (R.C.), West Derby Road. 1864–5, by *E. W. Pugin*. Brick, stone dressings. W front with a big rose window, but no tower. No aisle windows, only clerestory. Quatrefoil piers and above them large stops as if they were corbels for vaulting shafts. They have plenty of naturalistic foliage, *à la* Exeter. Polygonal apse with lancets high up. Big PRESBYTERY attached to the E end, thoughtfully detailed.

SACRED HEART (R.C.), Hall Lane. 1885–6, by *Goldie, Child & Goldie*. Dec Gothic, the polychromy of yellow and red stone obscured by dirt. W end approached by steps, with porch, and corner spirelet. Polygonal apse. Nave with octagonal piers of polished red granite. The HIGH ALTAR with its spectacular Benediction throne and the gorgeous alabaster REREDOS were added in 1891 by *Pugin & Pugin*; carving by *Norbury, Paterson & Co.*, statues by *Boulton* of Cheltenham. – White marble LADY ALTAR with *opus sectile* panels of the Annunciation, *c.* 1908, by *Edmund Kirby & Sons*. – Outside the E end, FIRST WORLD WAR MEMORIAL: a Calvary.

RICHMOND BAPTIST CHURCH, Breck Road. By *J.A. Picton & Son*, built 1864–5 for the congregation of the wildly popular Rev. Frederick Hall Robarts. Described at the time as 'a chapel of the dog kennel type'. Plain exterior in brick with stone dressings. Gabled façade, round-headed windows. Interior with gallery around on all four sides, standing on cast-iron Composite columns. Flat coffered ceiling. The BAPTISTERY, now in front and beneath the PULPIT, was until the mid C20 behind it. Original high-sided PEWS. Aesthetically awful partitioning at the W end: late C20 walls to separate off both the gallery and the space beneath it. Vestries of 1877, SUNDAY SCHOOL of 1931.

PARTICULAR BAPTIST CHAPEL (former), Shaw Street. Opened 1847, divided up into flats 2004. Red brick and red sandstone, with a pediment and two Ionic columns *in antis*.

Public Buildings

EVERTON LIBRARY (former), St Domingo Road. Opened 1896, perhaps the best of several branch libraries by *Thomas Shelmerdine*. Red brick and stone, with large mullioned-and-transomed windows and other Jacobean touches. Three identical gables reflect the original plan (reading rooms flanking central lending departments), but the arrangement of windows below each is different. Octagonal corner tower, with stubby Tuscan columns making a porch, and a short lead-covered spire.

POST OFFICE (former), Everton Valley. Edwardian. Of brick and stone dressings. Freely Wrenaissance. It turns a gentle corner with the entrance at the apex, having giant attached Ionic columns above it supporting a steep open pediment.

HOPE UNIVERSITY COLLEGE. *See* St Francis Xavier, p. 418.

COLLEGIATE INSTITUTION (former), Shaw Street. Built as an educational foundation comprising three distinct schools. A competition in 1840 was won by *Harvey Lonsdale Elmes*, fresh from his success in the St George's Hall and Assize Courts contests. The building opened in 1843. Elmes supervised only the construction of the façade, the rest being in the hands of the surveyor *Edward Argent*. Tudor Gothic in red sandstone, as stipulated in the terms of the competition. No doubt Gothic was chosen to signal its Anglican affiliation, a response to the secular (and Greek Revival) Mechanics' Institution (*see* p. 372). Thirteen-bay battlemented façade, with oriels at each end and a gatehouse-like feature – a tall, gabled arch flanked by octagonal buttresses – in the middle. Windows run through first and second floors, separated by buttresses that originally had high finials above the parapet. At the back, virtually free-standing, is the octagonal lecture hall. Students in the three schools came from different social classes, and the building was subdivided to ensure segregation. Gutted by fire in 1994, the shell was imaginatively converted into flats in the late 1990s by the developers Urban Splash and their architects *ShedKM*. At the front, new windows are tactfully recessed behind Elmes' tracery, but the rendered rear is uncompromisingly of today. The roofless lecture theatre is now a walled garden. Inside, the original main staircase survives opposite the entrance, with a carved overmantel from the headmaster's room relocated to the landing.

VENICE STREET SCHOOL. *See* ANFIELD.

ROYAL LIVERPOOL UNIVERSITY HOSPITAL, Prescot Street. Probably the biggest single 1960s public project in the city, a monumental, massed complex of exposed concrete. The architects were *Holford Associates*. Planned 1963–5, opened 1978. A general teaching hospital with over 800 beds, it replaced the Royal Infirmary (*see* p. 365) and three other C19 hospitals. It followed the model of contemporary American hospitals in having a high (twelve-storey) ward block raised above a podium containing outpatient services, etc. Two wings containing teaching accommodation project forward, and a long, lower block in front houses the University of Liverpool's clinical departments behind a façade consisting of a dense concrete grid. Entrance remodelled 2003. Seen from the back (s), the ward block is undeniably impressive, if intimidating. Horizontal and vertical concrete members divide it into a grid of windows on a much larger module. The verticals are detached, and die into an outward-leaning parapet. The block is framed by two great ventilation ducts serving the podium, and in the space between these and the ends of the wards are external emergency stairs. Inside, wards are of the deep-plan 'racetrack' type adopted from America, with bed spaces round the edges and services in a central core. In front of the main hospital building is the bizarre CHAPEL, a big windowless brick cube on a raked brick plinth.

W towards Daulby Street is the grim DUNCAN BUILDING, housing clinical sciences, with a sheer, windowless tower at the NW corner. At the SW corner of the site in Pembroke Place is the DENTAL HOSPITAL, 1965–9, by the *Anthony Clark Partnership* but forming part of the Holford Associates complex. To the E of the site, attached to the main building, a smaller block with similar leaning parapet runs N–S. Originally a training college, it was extended and converted to become the LINDA MCCARTNEY CENTRE in 2001. S of this is a residential tower block. The powerful, rugged BOILER HOUSE overlooks the site from the NE corner. The high chimney has water tanks cantilevered from its base, and looks like a giant upended hammer.

ROY CASTLE INTERNATIONAL CENTRE FOR LUNG CANCER RESEARCH, London Road. By the *Franklin Stafford Partnership*, completed 1997. Walls of rock-faced cast stone, glass above. The peculiar tower, a pointed oval in plan, swoops up at the corner like the prow of a boat.

EVERTON PARK, between Netherfield Road and Heyworth Street. This huge public park, half a mile from N to S, was conceived in the 1960s, though construction, to a new plan, did not begin until the mid 1980s. The idea is admirable, though the design, with terraces, pergolas and grand flights of steps, is over-elaborate for such a rough, windswept site.

WATER WORKS, Margaret Street. By *Thomas Duncan*, water engineer to the Corporation. A covered reservoir was built first, 1854, but only the retaining walls remain. It was followed in 1857 by the round WATER TOWER, 85 ft (26 metres) high to the tank, and one of the most impressive monuments of C19 Liverpool. Mighty rusticated arches support an upper tier of taller arches. Concentric with these are further piers linked by radial brick arches, the whole colossal structure recalling the prints of Piranesi. To the S are two PUMP HOUSES. The first, attached, has a square Italianate tower, now missing its top part. The second was added in the 1860s.

Perambulation

We begin at the W end of LONDON ROAD, where it joins Lime Street. Historically, London Road was the main route into town from the S and E, and also an important shopping street. After years of decline there has been much new building and refurbishment, following the setting up of the London Road Development Agency in 1992. For Commutation Plaza, N, *see* p. 316; for the Empire Theatre, S, *see* p. 326.

Heading E up London Road, on the N side, flanking Norton Street, are two large residential blocks with commercial uses on the lower floors; recent, by *Falconer Chester*. On the S, at the corner of Seymour Street, a former branch of the UNION BANK, dated 1890. Loire château style in stone, with a round corner tower. Possibly by *G.E. Grayson*, who did the bank's Bold Street branch a few years earlier. (For the adjoining terrace in Seymour Street, *see* p. 379.) On the same side, the NATWEST BANK at the corner of Hart Street occupies a building of 1899 by *W. Hesketh & Co.*, for the Liverpool Furnishing Co. Fancy Northern Renaissance with octagonal domed clock turret and elaborate gables, in fiery red terracotta supplied by *Jabez Thompson* of Northwich.

Here the two sides of London Road diverge, the resulting triangular open space presided over by an impressive equestrian MONUMENT to George III. Fine bronze statue of the king by *Sir Richard Westmacott*, 1818–22, closely modelled on that of Marcus Aurelius in Rome. On the N side, filling the block between Stafford and Audley streets, is AUDLEY HOUSE, a shop built in phases for the retailer Owen Owen and completed *c*. 1910; now T.J. Hughes. The architect seems to have been *Walter W. Thomas*. Yellow brick, with much stone. Pedimented windows, octagonal corner turrets with pointed roofs, and a tower in Stafford Street, W. On the same side of London Road, No. 129 looks late C19 and has exuberant Renaissance decoration all over. After this, at the corner of Gildart Street, a former DEPARTMENT STORE opened in 1937, an enterprisingly modern design by *Robert Threadgold* who worked in the office of *A.E. Shennan*. A big rectangular block faced in smooth buff terracotta, with windows in horizontal strips. The corner has a glazed stair-tower. Converted to student accommodation in the 1990s. London Road ends at Moss Street, where, at the corner of Prescot Street, there is an excellent former branch of the BANK OF LIVERPOOL, begun 1904, by *James F. Doyle*. Edwardian Baroque in Portland stone and grey granite, with an imaginatively detailed octagonal tower over the corner entrance. Convex balustraded balconies project between its columns, while each face of the entablature above is concave. For the Roy Castle Centre, diagonally opposite, *see* p. 422.

Moss Street leads N to ISLINGTON SQUARE, now merely a widening on the N side of the dual carriageway. Here are two attractive buildings, apparently of the early 1830s. The l. one is stuccoed, with slightly projecting end bays and a central porch. It was a music academy, and the first-floor cast-iron balconies incorporate lyres in their design. The other is a fine house of excellent brick, with a pediment across five of its six bays, and a handsome Greek Doric porch.

Turn N into SHAW STREET. (For St Francis Xavier and its college buildings, and the former Baptist Chapel, *see* pp. 418 and 420; for the Collegiate Institution, *see* p. 421.) From 1826 the W side was built up with high-class three-storey brick terraces. After years of dereliction a few survivors have recently been restored; others have been reconstructed behind preserved façades or rebuilt entirely using salvaged materials.

Gardens were laid out on the E side in the 1840s. Here stands a MEMORIAL to members of the Eighth (King's) Regiment killed in the Indian Mutiny, a Celtic cross in white marble by *H.S. Leifchild*, with weathered reliefs. First erected at Portsmouth in 1863, removed to Chelsea 1877, and finally to Liverpool 1911. Beyond on the same side is Everton Park (*see* p. 422); at the junction with Brow Side is the LOCK-UP of 1787, a round stone building with a conical roof, a relic of Everton's village centre.

Other Buildings

Everton acquired many public-housing TOWER BLOCKS in the 1960s, but few remain. The twenty-two-storey CORINTH TOWER on Netherfield Road North used the *Camus* system of prefabrication; it was recently demolished. Immediately W in Conway Street, two sixteen-storey tower blocks, converted to private housing 2003.

ST DOMINGO GROVE and the parallel – and less well preserved – ST DOMINGO VALE, are off Breckfield Road North, bordering Anfield (*see* above). Two long straight streets built as a private venture (with their own lodges, now gone), the Grove from 1845, the Vale from 1860. The mainly semi-detached houses are quite large and plain, mostly gabled, often bargeboarded, though some are Italianate. Most are altered.

THE MERE BANK pub, Heyworth Street, immediately E of St George's church. Dated 1881. Lively, with moulded terracotta panels, half-timbering and pargeting.

HOUSES, further S in Everton Road, between Plumpton Street and Lytton Street. 1830s survivors from Everton's period as a select middle-class suburb. No. 71 has a Doric porch; Nos. 47–65 form a terrace.

GRANT GARDENS, on Everton Road at the junction with West Derby Road, occupies the site of the Necropolis, an early non-denominational cemetery opened in 1825.

OGDENS TOBACCO FACTORY (former), Boundary Lane, on the corner with West Derby Road. 1900, by *Henry Hartley*. The staggered office range fronting Boundary Lane has a central clock tower with the entrance at its base. Entrance hall with mosaic floor and Jacobean style staircase.

(For Brougham Terrace and the Olympia Theatre, *see* Edge Hill and Kensington, pp. 416–17.)

FAIRFIELD

In the mid C19 this was a new and fashionable suburb across fields E of the town. Though it is a long time since it was last a smart address, many of the stuccoed semis and small villas survive.

ST JOHN THE DIVINE, Holly Road. 1851–3, by *W. Raffles Brown*. Pale coursed rubble sandstone. Dec, with a SW steeple and flowing tracery. The aisle windows curious in that they are traceried nearly all over. This, the last remaining work by Raffles Brown in the city, was damaged *c.* 1980 when all but the steeple, s aisle wall and lower parts of the w wall were replaced by *Robert Gardner-Medwin* with a new combined church and hall under awkward shallow-pitched roofs. The result is, externally, ham-fisted.

JEWISH CEMETERY, Deane Road. *See* Edge Hill and Kensington, p. 413.

LUNDIE MEMORIAL HALL (former), Beech Road. The hall to a demolished Presbyterian church (1863–4, *W.I. Mason*, Dec), now a gymnasium. Symmetrical, of painted brick, with a central flèche; the whole like a school. Illiterate Tudor Gothic-ish.

ROYAL LIVERPOOL SEAMEN'S ORPHAN INSTITUTION (former), Orphan Drive, Newsham Park. Built in 1871–5 by *Alfred Waterhouse* in the NE corner of Newsham Park (*see* below). The Institution provided housing and education, and in 1899 was home to 321 children. It became a hospital after 1949, and was empty in 2005. Large and handsome. Brick with stone dressings, in Waterhouse's economical Gothic. The plan pivots about a bold sw angle tower with steep pavilion roof. The w front looking out across the park is quite irregular with tall roofs, the s range (for girls originally) is plain and regular. A dining hall is the principal feature of the w front, with straight-topped, cusped three-light mullioned-and-transomed windows, a stumpy flèche, and inside, a heavy wooden minstrels' gallery. The chapel was at the N end (beyond the boys' range), but has been pulled down. Sanatorium 1878–9; chaplain's residence 1881. A swimming pool by *Alfred Culshaw* opened in 1900.

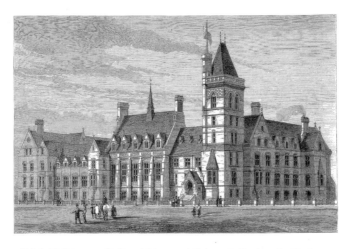

Fairfield (Liverpool), Royal Liverpool Seamen's Orphan Institution,
Newsham Park, by Alfred Waterhouse, 1871–5.
Engraving from *The Builder*, vol. 30, 1872

NEWSHAM PARK was laid out on an estate purchased from
Thomas Molyneux in 1846. His NEWSHAM HOUSE survives
within the park. Late C18, of five bays and two-and-a-half
storeys, with a three-bay pediment. Some discreet stone decoration emphasising the middle window. A plan to demolish it
was abandoned in favour of refurbishment as the Judges' Lodgings (which it remains) in 1866–7. *E.R. Robson* was responsible, and the porch is part of this. – STABLE BLOCK.

The park was one of a chain created by the Corporation in
the 1860s on the then outskirts of the town. Stanley and Sefton
parks were the others (*see* pp. 395 and 453). Like Stanley Park,
Newsham was designed by *Edward Kemp*, who was commissioned to produce a plan in 1864. Work began the following year.
It is, however, very much the poor relation. Like Stanley, it has
a picturesque component of lakes and wooded mounds (E edge),
and a Middle Ground of grassland (W), but there is no comparable formal landscape and few architectural elements. Beside
the Sheil Road entrance is a LODGE, of 1898, half-timbered vernacular style. Part of the cost of construction, as with the other
parks, was to be recouped from selling HOUSING plots along
drives around the perimeter. Most on the N and S sides were
built up in the 1870s–90s, mainly large brick semis with cata-
logue-bought embellishments; undeveloped plots in the SE were
later incorporated into the park. The ambitious ST FRANCIS
OF ASSISI ACADEMY by *Capita Percy Thomas* opened in 2005
in the park near the Shiel Road entrance.

s of Newsham Park is an area of stucco Early Victorian VILLAS,
many of the 1840s, in the usual variety of styles: Italianate and
bargeboarded Tudor Gothic. They were built on part of
the Newsham estate before the park was laid out. Some are in
ELM VALE, some on PRESCOT ROAD, some in FAIRFIELD
CRECENT and PROSPECT VALE. Good examples are Nos.
6–16 Prospect Vale and No. 30 Fairfield Crescent.

s of Prescot Road there are more, developed from *c.* 1830
on the estate of C18 Fairfield Hall (demolished): in HOLLY
ROAD, e.g. No. 12, Italianate, No. 14, Gothic, both larger; in
BEECH STREET, some short Italianate terraces set back –
Beech Mount (dated 1861), Oak Terrace and Elm Terrace;
in DEANE ROAD, e.g. Nos. 13 and 15, the former symmetrical Tudor Gothic with pinnacles and battlements; and in
LOCKERBY ROAD, Nos. 11–13 and 17 (Italianate). Two bigger
survivals on EDGE LANE have contrasting extensions. No. 311
on the corner with Laurel Road is classical and stuccoed, but
the four bays are not quite even – a frequent quirk in Liverpool at this time. External stairs of the 1960s, attached r., are
rigorously Modernist; the discipline and rhythm mean they are
surprisingly harmonious. DEVONSHIRE HOUSE on the corner
with Beech Street is an attractively unscholarly and picturesque Jacobean Revival house dated 1846. Stucco, with Gothic
bits too, including a giant blank arrow slit. Now a hotel, with
low sprawling extensions of speechless ugliness.

FAZAKERLEY

The flat northern extremity of the city. Mostly housing estates of between the wars and after.

EMMANUEL, Longmoor Lane. Brick, large, by *W.H. Ward & W.G. Cogswell*. Consecrated 1908. Lancets, no tower. – STAINED GLASS. E window by *Caroline Townshend* and *Joan Howson*, 1929. Large, for them.

ST PAUL, Formosa Drive. 1932, by *F.W. Nicholson*. Very modest, brick, round-arched windows. At the heart of one of *Lancelot Keay*'s less interesting estates, begun in 1926.

HOLY NAME (R.C.), Longmoor Lane. By *Peter S. Gilby & Associates*. Designed 1962, opened 1966. An unusual design that Pevsner thought mannered. The plan reflects the views of the Second Vatican Council, but is traditional in so much as it is rectangular, with nave facing sanctuary. SW campanile reduced to a concrete frame, shaped like slimmed colliery headgear, with a crucifix in the top. On S side of the nave the frames are exposed: massive roof beams project out to meet posts, tapering to the ground, that rise up outside a low, windowless aisle. The effect is like the legs of some giant centipede. By contrast the S wall of the sanctuary is a single window from aisle to roof, of eleven narrow lights divided by concrete mullions. Interior calmer and well lit, but suffering from restlessness in the multitude of surfaces. Between the roof beams are shallow transverse vaults. Integrated HALL and PRESBYTERY too. – STATIONS OF THE CROSS. By *Roger Smith*. Bold and symbolic. – STAINED GLASS. Five S windows by *Philip Brown*. Abstract *dalle de verre* inspired by the Holy Name.

METHODIST CHURCH (former), Longmoor Lane. Yellow sandstone. A Jacobean façade, dated 1891.

EVERTON CEMETERY, Long Lane. By the Everton Burial Board 1877–80. Layout and buildings by *Thomas D. Barry & Son*. Grid plan, roughly square, and a flat site. Well-detailed structures: the former REGISTRAR'S OFFICE, GATEPIERS and wrought-iron GATES, charming LODGES at the Higher Lane entrance, and a large and impressive R.C. mortuary CHAPEL survive. All are Gothic, in quarry-faced yellow sandstone, with red sandstone dressings. The chapel has Geometric tracery and a NW tower with broach spire. Two other chapels are demolished. There is an adjoining but separate JEWISH CEMETERY.

KIRKDALE CEMETERY, Longmoor Lane. Opened by the Kirkdale Burial Board in 1881. *Duckworth & Medcalf* of Liverpool were architects, the layout was by *William Wortley*, the Clerk of Works at Anfield Cemetery (*see* p. 394). Small, on a grid plan. The three chapels are demolished, but two brick, freely Tudorbethan LODGES remain.

AINTREE INSTITUTE, Longmoor Lane. Built by William Hartley for the workers at his jam factory (*see* p. 428), but on a site ¼ m. N of the complex. By *F.W. Dixon*, opened 1896. Tall brick building with gabled ends and stone dressings. That facing Longmoor Lane has free Perp details, including a large five-light window. The name attractively carved in stone in a panel beneath this.

UNIVERSITY HOSPITAL AINTREE, Longmoor Lane. The older part on the Longmoor Lane end of the site is *Thomas Shelmerdine*'s City Hospital North, opened in 1906. Virtually intact axial complex of single-storey pavilion wards etc. Flanking the entrance are residences; at the centre is the combined administration block and nurses' home. As one would expect of Shelmerdine most are thoughtfully designed and attractively proportioned, in two types of brick, with hints of Queen Anne and free English Baroque in the stone detailing. A number of large post-war blocks on Lower Lane, including *Studio BAAD*'s low-rise Accident and Emergency Department, 1991–3, between earlier frame-and-brick slabs.

NEW HALL, Longmoor Lane. An impressive and almost complete complex designed by *Charles H. Lancaster* for the West Derby Union as cottage homes for the upbringing of deprived children. Built 1887–9. The whole colony was to be independent as regards day-to-day provisions. A formal layout: asymmetrical superintendent's house and probationary ward flank the entrance to a broad straight street lined with ranks of identical two-storey gabled 'cottages' with five-bay fronts and H-plans, each of which housed a dozen or so children. Near the end the street opens out into a square, which is filled by the hall, with baths and other service buildings around it. The hall is a large building with tall round-arched windows and balustrade parapet. The end elevation, terminating the vista up the street, has a pediment on paired giant Corinthian pilasters, and above this a clock tower with fancy top, three ogee caps of reducing size stacked on top of one another. The hall is predominantly red brick with sandstone dressings; other buildings are largely brown brick. The farm and a couple of blocks gone, a couple of others are derelict. The survivors are now council and NHS offices.

HARTLEY'S FACTORY and VILLAGE, Long Lane. A model complex created by William Hartley for making his jam, but now sadly bashed about and partially destroyed. Low-rise remains of the brick factory of 1886 by *James F. Doyle*. It still has its elegant octagonal chimney. The detached entrance, despite extensive abuse, is the principal curiosity: a Baroque arch between machicolated turrets, flanked by projecting wings with all manner of motifs – round-arched windows, more machicolation, parapet urns and strange pilasters. A Dining Hall was added in 1895, lit by three large round-arched windows under linked shaped gablets. In 1888 Doyle judged a competition to design a workers' village adjoining to the S, which was won by *William Sugden & Son* of Leek. Gardens and mortgages were provided, and only a 3 per cent return was taken. Very small (was more intended?) – principally four short streets facing outwards from a central court. The gabled brick

houses are semi-detached, or four or six together. Others have
applied half-timbering above, with bargeboarded gables.
It does not add up to much, but is socially notable (*see* also
Introduction p. 87).

GARSTON

Forty-four species of fish were caught on the Mersey at Garston,
upstream from Liverpool, in 1774, but within twenty years John
Ashton's salt works had brought the Industrial Revolution to the
little village. The present port was created by the St Helens &
Runcorn Railway in 1853 when it opened a dock for the export
of coal. This was expanded by its successor, the London & North
Western Railway, to handle Wigan coal too, and a new town was
laid out on a grid plan. In 1904 Garston was incorporated into
Liverpool, though the port remained in railway ownership as a
successful specialist rival to the mighty Mersey Docks and
Harbour Board. The port is still open, though the coal and much
of the industry have gone, and Garston in 2005 is sad and run
down.

ST MICHAEL, Earp Street. 1875–7, by *Thomas D. Barry & Son.*
A large sandstone church wedged between gasholders and the
railway, next to the site of an C18 chapel,* itself a replacement
of one of the C13. NW tower and porch, outside the aisle, and
transepts, chapels and an apse. Buff quarry-faced stone with
red ashlar dressings. Dec, with fine large windows in the w end
and transept ends. The tower might have been a bit bigger but
the belfry openings are nicely treated with clustered shafts.
– Good REREDOSES, that in the chancel with opus sectile and
mosaic panels. – STATIONS OF THE CROSS, painted as a frieze
by *May L.G. Cooksey.* – STAINED GLASS. Three lancets in the
chancel by *Shrigley & Hunt*, 1886. – In the churchyard a
SHAFT, perhaps C17 and perhaps for a sundial.
ST FRANCIS OF ASSISI (R.C.), Chapel Road. 1904–5, by *David
Powell.* Red sandstone. Aisles and transepts and a NW tower.
Triplets of lancets. The tower is more sophisticated than the
rest. It recedes, and the angle buttresses become clasping and
polygonal at the belfry stage. Above this the shallow top stage
is octagonal and set back. – To the r. are SCHOOLS, which
incorporate the simple former Wesleyan CHAPEL of 1837. This
is rendered with crude lancets.
LIBRARY, St Mary's Road. 1908, by *Thomas Shelmerdine.* This is
one of the last of his charming branch libraries and unmistakably shows the influence of the Arts and Crafts Movement. It
is symmetrical and has a big central gable with a window, and
little half-timbered gablets l. and r. breaking through a low-
stooping roof. Canted bays rise up through the eaves beneath
the gablets. There is another of these to each side elevation.

---

* Fragments of stained glass from the chapel are now in the Great Hall at Speke
Hall (*see* p. 468).

The walls are rendered except for the red ashlar centre, which breaks forward slightly. The most striking motif is the battered buttresses at the corners and the corners of the ashlar projection. Inside are three parallel spaces with segmental-vaulted ceilings, separated by arcades. The central space is taller with narrow galleries around it. The beaten copper plaque by *C.E. Thompson* commemorating the opening is a lovely thing.

SIR ALFRED JONES HOSPITAL, Church Road. 1914–15, by *C.J. Anderson & R.S. Crawford*. A handsome nine-bay Neo-Queen Anne house with hipped roof and four prominent chimneys in a row. Brick. The outer two bays and the central one project slightly, the latter with half-circular pediment. Gibbs surrounds to ground-floor windows. Three-bay l. extension.

THE MERSEY MATCH FACTORY (former), Speke Road. 1919–21. Now offices, called THE MATCHWORKS. The first building in the United Kingdom to be built of flat-slab concrete construction (i.e. beamless floor slabs). Conventionally attributed to *Mewès & Davis*, but the important hand was that of the engineer, *Sven Bylander*, who had worked with them on the Ritz (he also designed the steel frame of Selfridges). Closed 1994, when it was the last British match factory; built for Maguire, Paterson and Palmer Ltd., but owned for most of its life by Bryant & May. The Speke Road façade is the manufacturing block, and almost all structure and function: a striking, long grid two storeys high and thirty-five bays long, but only three deep, all frame and glass, and set off by the cylindrical roof-top water tower with its pointed cap. The model is Albert Kahn's American 'daylight factories', such as Packard Motor Works No. 10 Building, Detroit, 1907. But not the decorative touches: Lancashire roses on the columns (which were originally faced in brick) and first-floor aprons of coloured tiles. A similarly tiled parapet is lost. These may be due to the influence of *Arthur Davis*, though the façade does not correspond to the drawing by him reproduced in *The Builder*; all surviving drawings are signed by Bylander. Inside, the flat-slab construction of the floor and roof is exposed, shutter-finished and carried on mushroom-capped columns via square bearing pads. The technique, conceived in the US by *H.T. Eddy* in 1890 and first applied by *C.A. Turner* in Chicago, was an important step in the development of reinforced concrete construction in the C20. Bylander was thwarted in London in his attempts to introduce it by the capital's Building Regulations.

w wing to the manufacturing block for services. Other, later, ranges mostly demolished when the factory was converted into offices by *ShedKM* for the developers Urban Splash, 1999–2001 with the appropriately robust industrial chic detailing typical of this collaboration. A mezzanine was inserted into the subdivided ground floor, but either side of the central circulation core the upper floor remains open and unaltered, revealing the pioneering construction. Giant free-standing steel door frames and formal landscaping complete the restored entrance front. The rear s elevation has been animated

by six silvery, fat and corrugated cylindrical service pods with 127
sinister slot windows – very retro sci-fi. This is a conversion
that successfully plays to the building's original aesthetic
strengths with alterations largely of wit and confidence. In
2005 *ShedKM* were converting a 1948 wing behind, and adding
the MATCHBOX, a strict three-storey fully glazed Modernist
pavilion.

When built, the factory's immodesty was hidden behind a
brick Neo-Georgian screen facing Speke Road – two pavilions
(the l. one never built) flanking a sprawling single-storey
welfare block. The latter was only demolished *c.* 1998, thus
revealing the manufacturing wing in a manner never intended.
This explains the now illogical siting (off-centre, in front) and
the incongruous design of the surviving pavilion, the ADMIN-
ISTRATION BLOCK. Portland-dressed with modillion cornice
and hefty projecting pedimented doorcase. This is surely the
work of *Davis*, as must also be the octagonal LODGE.

There is little else of note. Garston is split in two by the railway
and a bypass. S of this are the three DOCKS, of 1853, 1875 (N)
and 1910 (S, Stalbridge Dock), and the compact rectangular
grid of streets laid out from the 1850s. There is an industrial
sector nearest the river with remnants of the once extensive
copper works, tanneries (including DRYING SHEDS on Vulcan
Street) etc. The rest is residential, both C19 bylaw housing and
C20 replacements, including some concrete-block houses of
the 1920s. It may be of interest to the urban historian, but it
is a terribly depressing place, terraces boarded up or knocked
down, litter blown everywhere.

Public and commercial buildings lie N of the railway along St
Mary's Road and beyond, where the pre-industrial village was
centred. On ST MARY'S ROAD are three former BANKS in different classical styles. On WELLINGTON STREET is a former
three-storey brick TECHNICAL SCHOOL of 1909 with giant
corner pilasters and minor Baroque details, and the Gothic
former READING ROOM of 1861, like a little chapel.

GATEACRE

5m. ESE of the city centre.

GATEACRE CHAPEL (Unitarian), Gateacre Brow. 1700. A plain
sandstone rectangle, pitched roof with a cupola (both renewed
in 1885), segment-headed windows except for the round-
headed one above the round-headed doorway. Walls raised in
the early C18 when a W GALLERY was inserted. Three windows
to the S, two deeper ones on the N side flanking the original
position of the pulpit. Vestry 1872. Reseated in the C19. –
PULPIT, early C18 and panelled.

OUR LADY OF THE ASSUMPTION (R.C.), Hedgefield Road. By
L.A.G. Prichard & Son. Designed in 1949.

ST STEPHEN, Belle Vale Road. 1872–4, by *Cornelius Sherlock.*
Rock-faced red sandstone, in the style of *c.* 1300, with a NW

steeple. Nave, aisles and chancel. Five-bay arcades, the arches wide, with vine trailing around them. The w two are blocked. – STAINED GLASS. w window by *Morris & Co.*, 1883. Impressive scale. Four large figures topped and tailed by roundels, set against a pale green foliate background. Angels in the tracery. E window by *Frederick Preedy*, 1880.

Also by *Sherlock*, the pleasant CHURCH COTTAGES of 1872 to the N. Brick with half-timbered gables and tall diagonal Tudor chimneys.

GATEACRE SCHOOL, Grange Lane. First phase three-storeyed, 1958; main four-storey range and ancillary parts completed 1964. By *Ronald Bradbury*, City Architect. In a sorry condition in 2005.

Centre

The centre of Gateacre is a pretty little triangular GREEN, the gift of Sir Andrew Barclay Walker in 1887. On it is the handsome WILSON MEMORIAL DRINKING FOUNTAIN of 1883 under a heavy hexagonal sandstone canopy; the type of ancient market crosses but with Renaissance carving; and the JUBILEE MEMORIAL, with a bronze bust of Victoria, by *Count Victor G. Gleichen*, 1887, on a red granite pedestal. Some pleasant early-to-mid-C19 cottages and houses are gathered near it, some brick and some red ashlar. On the s side is the delightful former GATEACRE BREWERY of *c.* 1867, a compact three-storey building, with a louvre topped by ornate cresting, and a chimney. To its w is No. 28 GATEACRE BROW, 1889–91, by *W. Aubrey Thomas*. Lively: red sandstone below, half-timbering above, with a corner turret with ogee cap. Plenty of pargeting, apparently moulded from Flemish C17 panels illustrating scenes from the Bible.

GATEACRE BROW, rising w of the Green. Opposite No. 28 is a doctor's surgery, the former Midland BANK by *Weightman & Bullen*, *c.* 1965. A little cuboid built into the garden wall of Gateacre Grange (*see* p. 433). Pevsner admired it. Lit by a floor-to-ceiling window filling one side, and a continuous clerestory, both with closely and irregularly spaced mullions. On the s side, the Chapel (*see* p. 431) and then some little three-bay Georgian houses, mostly in red sandstone. Only No. 4 is unaltered.

GRANGE LANE, leading N from the Green. w side: set back, YORK COTTAGES, two little brick rows of *c.* 1840. In front of them, former STABLES of 1895 by *R. T. Beckett* for the polo ponies of William Hall Walker (later Lord Wavertree of Gateacre Grange, *see* p. 433). Half half-timbered. Converted to housing with a new range inside by *Rosario Zammit* in 1982. Then PARADISE ROW, which could be early C18: part three-storey and part two-storey, rough sandstone, platbands, horizontal-sliding sashes, and studded doors with fleur-de-lys hinges. Apparently a two-bay house with one-bay cottages on both sides. Next, SOARER COTTAGES of 1896, by *Beckett* again for William Hall Walker. On the E side behind a high wall is GRANGE LODGE, formerly Lower Grange. This was the site of a grange of Stanlow Abbey (*see* also p. 385). Recent analysis of the garden front suggests that the l. part, with mullioned windows, is of *c.* 1653, the centre, with finely panelled dining room, is of *c.* 1720, and that the r. section is of the 1820s. The roadside wing was rebuilt in 1867 and extended in half-timbered fashion in the 1890s. The modern garage has a reset datestone of 158?.

GRANGE MANOR, Grange Lane, ½ m. further NW past Gateacre School (*see* p. 432) is a pub built as a house called Gorsey Cop, *c.* 1850s. Big and square, with four prominent chimneystacks arranged in a square. Rendered, but the porch of paired Doric columns is red ashlar, so the house may be too underneath. The big ground-floor rooms have been knocked into one another, with a bar crudely jammed under the cantilevered staircase rising around the big, central, top-lit hall. Reasonable cornices.

In HALEWOOD ROAD, ¼ m. SE of the Green, a GATEWAY on the road probably of the early C18, broad, with a pediment on pilasters with alternate blocking. It stood here in the garden of a house demolished in 2004. No. 19 Halewood Road is early C19, with chequered brick.

ROSE BROW, heading N from the W end of Gateacre Brow. On the E side is GATEACRE GRANGE, being converted into apartments in 2005. A very substantial house in red sandstone built for the millionaire brewer Sir Andrew Barclay Walker. Gables, mullioned-and-transomed windows, tall octagonal chimneys: Jacobethan. The first phase is 1866 by *Cornelius Sherlock*. Additions by *Sir Ernest George & H.A. Peto* in 1883 differ only in a few details (e.g. ovolo-moulded mullions). Theirs is the N, service, end (two gables' worth as seen from the garden front), also the two full-height square bays attached to the garden front, and the stone conservatory on the entrance side. These have Norman Shaw-derived 'Sparrowe's House' windows.

The inside is spacious and oozes money. There are a few *Sherlock* ceilings with thin geometric plaster ribs, and a heavier panelled timber ceiling in the dining room. But mostly it is Ernest George, in his richly C16–C17 manner tinged with Aestheticism, with fittings of outstanding quality. Lobby fully fitted, some of it Cairene-style. The centrepiece of the hall is a superbly executed (by *James Forsyth*) veined-marble fireplace. Staircase running around three sides, with a half-landing on the second leading through an opening to the back stairs, and on to a landing on the fourth side overlooking the hall through three arches. The landing continues through the third of the arches, cantilevered out above the lowest flight of the stairs. The best room, presumably the drawing room, is r. of the entrance with good panelling, built-in shelving and fireplace. Conservatory off. To the l. of the entrance is the library, with glass-fronted cases. Dining room with big finely carved fireplace. Service extension planned around a four-storey light well, with delightful painted glass in the windows with pale flowers etc. (*James Powell & Sons* were paid £59 1 *s.* for glass.) A state-of-the-art kitchen of fireproof jack-arch construction was provided, hygienically tiled on floor, walls and ceiling.

There are two TERRACES in the garden, the lower with a seat, but below that the once extensive grounds that fell away E down to the village are now built over. N of the house, beyond the good *Ernest George* wrought-iron GATES, are the LODGE and the STABLE BLOCK against the street. This is U-shaped around a little yard and appears to be by *Sherlock.* Adjoining it to the N is a red sandstone house dated 1787, but much altered. Then come Nos. 1–5 ROSE BROW, and a pretty forge by Sherlock in stone, on the corner. (For houses in Acrefield Road, *see* Woolton, p. 512.)

CHILDWALL VALLEY ESTATE. A typical post-war estate by the Liverpool Corporation under the City Architect *Ronald Bradbury*, built 1958–64. A mixture of low- and medium-rise houses and maisonettes (and towers now demolished). Now dishearteningly featureless. The BELLE VALE SHOPPING CENTRE of *c.* 1973 is a big, brick, windowless fortress of a building.[*]

The LEE PARK ESTATE, encircled by Caldway Drive, ¾ m. ENE, was built in the grounds of Lee Hall, called by Peter Fleetwood-Hesketh 'one of the most perfect smaller Georgian houses in Lancashire'. It was demolished in 1956; the estate's high slab blocks have gone the same way. SE of it, another estate of the 1970s, shorn of its towers as well.

HUNT'S CROSS

6 m. SE of the city centre.

ST HILDA, Speke Road. Built in 1898. Very small, brick with terracotta tracery, mostly Perp. Dormers. – REREDOS. With repoussé copper panels. – STAINED GLASS. E window by *Caroline Townshend* and *Joan Howson,* 1921.

By the church the former STATION of the Cheshire Lines Committee *c.* 1873. Typical of those built on its Liverpool extension in details (brick, bargeboards etc.), and in its unusual plan closest to Cressington Station (*see* p. 383). On the side of a cutting, with the station-master's house in the dormered upper floor above the street-level entrance. Stairs descend to the principal rooms, which open through a door onto a cast-iron balcony overlooking the platforms, which are a further level down still. Thus the rail side is three-and-a-half storeys high. Opposite the church in KINGSMEAD DRIVE is a row of semis

---

[*] Pevsner was interested by Hartsbourne Walk, Hartsbourne Avenue, a scheme of pedestrian shopping with flats and maisonettes by *Gerald R. Beech,* emulating Habitat at the 1967 Montreal Expo: '1960s housing at its wildest. It is tricky, it is intricate, but is it competitive in cost, and it is practical in use? Also, is it an attractive environment? The young must decide.' They did. They knocked it down.

with half-timbered gables, built for middle-class commuters after the station opened.

KENSINGTON *see* EDGE HILL, p. 409

KIRKDALE

N of the city centre. Once the heart of industry and shipping; now derelict and desperate in many parts. Even the parish church (St Mary, of 1835) has been demolished.

ST ATHANASIUS, Fountains Road. 1956–7, by *Herbert Thearle*. Pevsner was dismissive: 'really a disastrous design, with the joke roof of the tower and the mean cast-concrete side windows so totally different in spirit'. This is a little harsh; the budget was very limited and the parish wanted a flexible building. The offending W tower, which was reminiscent of the campanili of Basil Spence's Coventry churches, has been replaced by a new porch. Inside, a MURAL, E, in Festival of Britain style behind rippled glass panels. – FONT and PULPIT carved by *H. Tyson Smith*.

ST JOHN EVANGELIST (R.C.), Fountains Road. 1885, by *J. & B. Sinnott*. Similar to a number of other churches by them, competent but dull. A big bold building in rock-faced buff sandstone with red sandstone dressings under a long slate roof. No tower, and no structural division between nave and chancel, though it is alluded to with transeptal bays interrupting the roof-line of the aisles and vestries. Stair-turret in the SE corner with a belfry with a little octagonal pyramid roof. Big Geometric seven-light E window and five-light W window. N chapel added 1927. – ALTAR by *Peter Paul Pugin*, 1898. – Large PRESBYTERY opposite, of 1892.

STANLEY PARK CHURCH, Walton Lane, opposite the Park (for which *see* p. 395). Built as a Baptist church in 1902, but sold to an Evangelical congregation in 1926. Quite large, red brick, T-shaped, with two levels of windows. The W façade has a big round-arched window and a shaped gable.

POLICE AND FIRE STATION (former), Westminster Road. A work of 1885 by *Thomas Shelmerdine*, the City Surveyor, and as so often with him an attractive one too. Brick. Picturesquely composed on a corner site. Old English style, with mullioned windows and big chimneys and roofs. Good details on the corner, especially the two moulded Gothic arches for the fire engines. Yard with a wing topped with a tiled spire interrupted by an open stage halfway. The Parade Room is like a large drill hall.

GORDON WORKING LADS' INSTITUTE (former), Stanley Road. Dated 1886, by *David Walker*. Like a nine-bay brick school with two floors of big windows. Freely Northern Renaissance Revival with, also, above the flat lintels in round blank arches, very free blank tracery. Elaborate gables with e.g. lots of scrolls. A handsome building (which would be more so if it had not lost finials and a cupola), it provided continued technical and physical education for the sons of the working class, and contained classrooms, a gymnasium and a concert hall.

BANKHALL GIRLS' INSTITUTE (former), Stanley Road. Dated 1889. A project to assist working-class girls, to complement the Gordon Institute (*see* above) only a hundred yards away. At five bays, smaller than the boys' building. Trim, dressed in a free Jacobean style: shaped gables, mullioned-and-transomed windows. Brick and stone dressings. Conventional paired pilasters flank the entrance, but superimposed on the first floor are scrolled strips with fruit and flowers hanging down them.

INDUSTRIAL ARCHAEOLOGY. The area between the LEEDS AND LIVERPOOL CANAL (*see* p. 52) and the docks was dense with warehouses, railway goods depots, timber yards etc. Though it is still industrial, almost all these have gone and mainly only mysterious fragments remain. The most complete vignette is beside the BANKHALL STREET BRIDGE over the canal, including a four-storey brick canal-side WAREHOUSE dated 1874, with barge hole (now blocked), and the former Caledonian Foundry and Engine Works N of it on Syren Street. For the Docks and the Tate & Lyle sugar silo *see* pp. 80 and 259; for the Harland & Wolff Shipbuilding & Engineeering Works, Regent Road, *see* p. 161.

KNOTTY ASH

On Liverpool's eastern municipal boundary, and now interwar suburbia merging into Huyton. Two mansions survive from more exclusive, and rural, days.

ST JOHN EVANGELIST, Brookside Avenue. 1834–6, by an unknown architect. The builders were *Richard & Paul Barker* of Huyton. Red ashlar. Narrow W tower with a recessed spire and thin polygonal buttresses. The sides of the church are tall, with three-light Perp windows and thin buttresses, whose crocketed pinnacles are lying in the churchyard. The taller chancel with S chapel is an addition of 1890 by *Aldridge & Deacon* in sympathetic Perp, though naturally much more 'correct'. Nave arcade of very slender columns and four-centred arches. Ribbed nave roof of shallow four-pointed profile. W GALLERY. – Timber REREDOS and open timber SCREEN. *H. Hems*, 1890. – STAINED GLASS. Centre window on the N side by *Morris & Co.* Lower lights 1872, including a representation of Absalom, upper lights 1890. *Burne-Jones* wrote in his account book of the 1872 scheme: 'a perfect type and ensample of what design should be – in the annals of ill-paid genius what withering homily may not this page afford!' N aisle 1st from E, chancel N, Lady Chapel E and S, various dates, by *H. W. Lonsdale*, made by *Heaton, Butler & Bayne*. – A collection of ceramic MEMORIAL PLAQUES by the *Della Robbia Pottery, c.* 1900, in the N aisle. – MONUMENTS in the churchyard include an excellent late C19 Celtic cross, archaeological in its fine carving. – Across the road from the w end is the small SCHOOL, dated 1837. Brick and sandstone dressings.

HOLY SPIRIT, junction of East Prescot Lane and Dovecot Lane. By *C.E. Deacon & Sons*, 1936–8. A sister church to the architects' St David, Childwall (*see* p. 402). Big, tall brick church in a severe, very reduced Gothic, e.g. the lancets are square-headed and have no surrounds. E end with three of these under an arch flanked by two square turrets that poke above the gable parapet.

ST MARGARET MARY (R.C.), Pilch Lane. By *Weightman & Bullen*, 1962–4. One of the best post-war churches in Liverpool. Its ancestry at the architects' St Ambrose, Speke (*see* p. 457) is evident in the tall campanile with its open concrete fretwork and baptistery in the base, and in its square plan. Low flat ceiling, except where the light floods in onto the altar from the square hole above it. This is a lantern, octagonal in plan, rising up with a folded spire. The walls are solid brick below, of stone above, with continuous glazing from gabled windows at eaves level. This and the narrow round columns (forming narrow aisles) combine to give the impression that the roof is floating free of the walls.

CALVARY CHURCH, East Prescot Road (A57). Independent Baptists. A 1930s church with a façade more like a small cinema. Brick, with a stepped gable in the centre, and below that a concrete rectangular grid of windows, and below that a simple concrete rectangular porch, broader than the window.

VILLAGE HALL, East Prescot Road (A57). *Aldridge & Deacon*, 1890 (parish room 1894). Big.

CHRISTOPHER GRANGE, Youens Way. A centre for the adult blind, with stained glass by *Patrick Reyntiens*, of 1970.

BROAD GREEN HOSPITAL, Thomas Drive. Designed by *C.O. Ellison* and completed in 1906 by the West Derby Union as a home for the elderly poor. After the First World War it became a TB sanatorium. Brick with brick dressings, including mullioned-and-transomed windows. Many later buildings, added without any architectural coherence, including structures of the 1980s by *Weightman & Bullen* (cardiology unit) and the *Percy Thomas Partnership*.

ASH GRANGE SHELTERED HOUSING, Brookside Avenue opposite St John. One of the few good residential schemes built recently in Liverpool's suburbs. By *ShedKM*, 2002–4. It consists of two refurbished eleven-storey tower blocks of the 1960s and a new, low-rise apartment block for the elderly. Following the upward sweep of the road, the low-rise section is a staggered terrace of big concrete cubes, which read to the street as 'picture frames' enclosing, recessed, two storeys of floor-to-ceiling glazing, balconies, and fillets of grey-painted wall. The arrangement of these and the staggering of the units is gently and rhythmically varied. Each unit has a grass roof. There is a similar row on the other side of an internal street, which has a bridge along it to provide access to the first-floor apartments.

At the N end of the street is a communal hall which wraps around the base of the nearer tower with a curved façade.

DOVECOT ESTATE, flanking the East Prescot Road, was developed in the grounds of the demolished Dovecot House from 1931 onwards to the designs of *(Sir) Lancelot Keay* and his Housing Department. The HOUSING is standard (*see* p. 254). In 1933 came the centrepiece, a SHOPPING PARADE with a library and public hall on Dovecot Place, nicely done on a convex curve. Three deep hipped and tiled roofs, each with a cupola, with link sections between. The central part is of five bays and breaks forward, with a ground-floor arcade leading to an axial passage through into the estate; above the central three bays are large round-headed library windows, and above them is an urn-topped parapet. The shops on either side have a rather thin continuous canopy on paired columns.

THINGWALL HALL, Thingwall Lane. An C18 house remodelled by *Harvey Lonsdale Elmes c.* 1846–7, with disjointed external results. Since 1903 owned by the Brothers of Charity. The C18 house, called Summer Hill on Yates' 1768 map, was probably a five-bay, two-and-a-half-storey box, and its upswept gable is visible two bays in from the E end of the S front. It was apparently extended *c.* 1790 with a new W-facing entrance wing attached to the W end. Its round-arched, fan-lit entrance is still recognizable. The staircase with chaste iron balustrade is part of this phase too. The present exterior appearance, though, is largely due to Elmes – painted ashlar, Roman Doric porch, bay windows (S one with attached, unfluted columns) and a S window with a recessed mullion derived from the Monument of Thrasyllus, Athens. It seems Elmes added one or more bays to the l. of the W front and pushed most of the S front outwards by several feet – leaving the rest awkwardly unaltered – to create a large drawing room with limited but good plaster-work. The other principal interior is Elmes' dining room l. of the entrance, containing more good plasterwork and a bay with corner pilasters with exquisite capitals of slender lotus leaves. Also an excellent fireplace, severely Neoclassical in black marble with fluted columns derived from the Ionic. The Brothers of Charity are probably responsible for the two bays on the E end of the house; they certainly built the utterly plain brick CHAPEL behind it, as well as large, now demolished, dormitories for the orphans under their care.

THINGWALL HOUSE, Thomas Lane. Built as Ashfield, *c.* 1869–72; the house was demolished after a fire in 2004. It was of brick with sparse stone dressings. Substantial, asymmetric Jacobethan. Large mullioned-and-transomed stair window, others plate-glass sashes. Not very exciting. Henry Arthur Bright, who died here in 1884, wrote a book about the garden. The surviving LODGE is of 1893 in Shaw–Nesfield fashion, with tile-hung walls. The house replaced an earlier residence, built by James Clemens. He was Mayor of Liverpool in 1776, the date inscribed, along with his initials, on the delightful stone LAMP STANDARD on the road outside. Battered and square in section, with distances to neighbouring villages carved on. Clemens' STABLES survive on Thingwall Lane. Rendered brick. Eight bays, the middle two with a pediment. Gothick Y-tracery in four-centred windows, some blank, the rest crude modern replacements.

MOSSLEY HILL

An exclusive C19 suburb on the eponymous hill between Sefton Park and Allerton, with superb views S across the Mersey to the Wirral and, beyond, to Wales. Despite demolitions, insensitive infill and suburban sprawl, there are still a number of big houses. Many now have institutional uses, and these are described under Public Buildings.

Religious Buildings

ST MATTHEW AND ST JAMES, Rose Lane. At the very crown of the hill is one of the best Victorian churches in Liverpool. It is by *Paley & Austin* and was built in 1870–5, and restored by *Alfred Shennan* in 1950–2 after war damage. It is uncommonly large, of red sandstone, and has a truly monumental crossing tower, as Paley & Austin liked. The style is late C13. Attached to the E end on the S is a polygonal vestry (a miniature chapter house), and attached to the W end, i.e. projecting N from the W bay of the N aisle, is the porch. This unusual device results in an asymmetrical W façade. Flushwork arcading across the E and W fronts is a legacy of Hubert Austin's study tour of East Anglian churches. Linked to the N porch is a parish room by *Donald Buttress*, 1975, self-effacing but still obtrusive. 64

Equally impressive interior with tall six-bay nave and two-light clerestory. Piers alternate between octagonal and eight shafts. The crossing is magnificent: mighty capital-less piers of eight stepped chamfers splitting into four and four chamfers around the soaring arches, and above them the open interior of the tower with a narrow wall passage behind transomed two-light openings. The choir is under the tower (a typical Paley & Austin feature, cf. Kirkby), with a low wall and integrated PULPIT beneath the W arch. Triangular-headed arcade around the sanctuary. S chapel begun in 1922. Two little bays but one huge hammerbeam. – FONT. Good, arcaded alabaster tub, presumably by the architects. – Little REREDOS. With a painted panel of the Last Supper. – COMMUNION RAIL. Brass. Excellent, Aesthetic style. Pierced foliate panels. – STALLS. Though they are *Paley & Austin*'s, it looks as if part of the back stalls may be Perp. Nothing is known of their provenance. – PARCLOSE SCREEN and fine ORGAN CASE typical of the practice, the latter in their intricate freely Flamboyant style. – STAINED GLASS. All the glass, including work by *Morris* and by *Holiday*, was destroyed in the Second World War. Now clear 65 glazing apart from the impressive E and W windows designed by *Carl Edwards* and executed by *James Powell & Sons*. Paradise Lost, W, has vibrant colouring and dense and dynamic design. The Apostles' Creed, E, less rich in colouring and more static. – In the passage to the church hall, two *Morris & Co.* windows brought from Cheadle Congregational Church (demolished 1970). – SOUTH AFRICAN WAR MEMORIAL. In the vestry porch. Copper; Art Nouveau. The oak saplings and roots are lovely. – Two BRASSES, Arthur Tydall Bright, †1879 and Guy Hugh Patterson, †1914. Gothic crosses with swords hung around them, the earlier much the finer.

The large and equally good VICARAGE, immediately E of the church, is dated 1873 and presumably by *Paley & Austin* too. A very free design. L-shaped, with large tower with pyramid roof, traceried staircase windows, and a hint of Philip Webb in the simple domesticity of the left-hand wing and the dormer of the garden front.

ST ANTHONY OF PADUA (R.C.), Queens Drive. Very big brick basilica, with a campanile, by *Anthony Ellis*, 1931–2.

ST BARNABAS, Allerton Road. By *James F. Doyle*, 1900–14. The exterior brick-faced, in a very odd pattern: of three or more sizes laid to look like squared dressed stone. Perp style, with a massive, handsome W tower, aisles and transepts. Cool, dignified interior, ashlar-faced. The arcade between chancel and S chapel finer and more ornate than the nave arcades. It is a serious, sober piece of work. – STAINED GLASS. E window by *H.G. Hiller*: a First World War memorial.

ELM HALL DRIVE METHODIST CHURCH. 1927. Quite modest. Bright red brick with Portland stone dressings. NW tower, with porch. Free Perp motifs.

MOSSLEY HILL BAPTIST CHURCH, Dovedale Road. 1905–6. Exceptionally ambitious and in the free forms then favoured by the Nonconformists. Bizarrely for Liverpool the walls are faced in flint. Dressings are red brick and terracotta. High SW tower, now missing its fancy top. Perp details, handled with a roguish touch. The plan is centralised. There are broad transepts, as broad as the wide nave, so that the interior is dominated by a vast crossing made up of the sort of dramatically wide and thin arches made possible by iron and steel structures. These arches rest on slender quatrefoil columns; they and the other arches are four-centred. Each arm of the cross is of one narrow bay except the W, which extends with a gallery and vestibule underneath. The square is made by pushing out bays in the angles of the cross. Thus, excepting the W extension, the interior reads as either a cross within a square, or a square (the crossing arches) within a square. – PULPIT set centrally in the E bay, with immersion FONT in front of it, and then the semicircular fan of BENCHES radiating outwards. – ORGAN behind the pulpit filling the E arch. – Windows with Art Nouveau drops of coloured GLASS. – Matching HALLS behind the E end.

Public Buildings

MOSSLEY HILL HOSPITAL, Park Avenue. Built over the grounds of MOSSLEY HOUSE, a mansion by *Alfred Waterhouse*. A design is dated 1869 and the client, Lloyd Rayner, was living there by 1872. It is typical of the plan developed by Waterhouse for his merchant clientèle. Gothic. Big and square. Dullish polychromatic brick. The w façade is symmetrical; the entrance front, with gabled porch, massive gable-end chimneystack and three-light staircase window, is not. Interior with top-lit central hall, with balconies running around on the first and second floors; at present filled in between ground and first floor with a translucent glazed ceiling. Big Gothic fireplace in the hall. The staircase ascends behind Gothic arcading then returns with a wrought-iron balustrade through more arches to the first-floor landing. Best of the details are the play-fighting cubs carved in stone at the top of the staircase arcade. Their tails extend as mouldings the length of the arcade plinth.

CARNATIC HALLS, Elmswood Road and North Mossley Hill Road. Halls of residence of the University of Liverpool. The maturely wooded parkland site of a house the name of which commemorated one of Liverpool's greatest prizes of privateering: the French East Indiaman *Carnatic*, brought into Liverpool in 1778, laden with spices and diamonds. The C20 architects are *Manning & Clamp*. The first phase was built in 1965–7, the second by 1977. The first phase halls, in purple brick and mainly three storeys, descend down the s side of the large sloping grounds in staggered, informal plan. They have an unusual rhythm of windows, rectangular ones with a thin slit window above each sticking out on one floor to the l., on the next to the r. The external spiral staircases, rising within a ring of concrete fins, are a nice detail. At the top of the slope and on the site of the original house, is CARNATIC HOUSE, containing bars and canteens. It is covered with one of those flat concrete roofs of big, projecting transverse tunnel vaults, with the arches fully glazed, which Sir Basil Spence's University of Sussex made fashionable. (He had them from Le Corbusier's Maisons Jaoul.) The building is L-shaped and the longer arm has a terrace and a reflecting pool at its foot and looks out w over the lawns. The concrete shuttering is exposed in the rude way popularized by Le Corbusier. Next door, on the s side of Elmswood Road, is DALE HALL by *Rolf Helberg*, 1958–9, Scandinavian style.

GREENBANK and HALLS OF RESIDENCE, Greenbank Lane and Greenbank Road. This was the property of the Rathbones. Since the 1930s the extensive landscaped grounds have been developed by the University of Liverpool as halls of residence. The HOUSE was first leased by the fourth William Rathbone in 1788, but was in existence by 1744. This may be the brick E wing, subsequently worked over. There is also a heavy Victorian extension in ashlar set back on the w side and

containing a billiards room. The centre, though, is delightful
Gothick of *c.* 1812–16, built by Hannah Rathbone. Rickman,
unsurprisingly, was sniffy: 'a curious mess of confusion as to
style and the attempt at Gothic as barbarous as most we have
about'. Painted a mustard colour. On the E side, three bays, the
outer ones with castellated ground-floor bay windows. The
centre is a tripartite porch and tripartite loggia above, both
vaulted. Round the corner on the S front is the most charming
two-storey iron veranda of delicate tracery across all four bays.
Hannah was the granddaughter of Abraham Darby, the famous
Coalbrookdale ironmaster, and her father a director. So it could
be by the *Coalbrookdale Company*. Or it could be by the local
foundry of *Joseph Rathbone & William Fawcett*. Incidentally,
whereas the former side is of painted ashlar, the latter is stuccoed. It is all painted. Inside, a plaster-vaulted entrance passage
with a large boss traceried as a mouchette wheel, a Gothic staircase and chimneypieces, and good cornices.

The landscaping of the whole precinct is excellent, moulding the existing formal pond outside the E front of the house
and the huge lawn to its S. The university halls, gathered
around the edges, are, on the E side: DERBY HALL, 1937–9,
by *Willink & Dod*, Neo-Georgian in red brick with high-
pitched roof and high archway through; RATHBONE HALL,
1958–9, by *Gilling, Dod & Partners* (the successor partnership),
architecturally the least successful; and the better utilitarian
extensions in yellow brick to both, 1960–1, by *M.G. Gilling of
Gilling, Dod & Partners*. And then W of Greenbank House
GLADSTONE HALL and ROSCOE HALL, 1962–4, by *David
Roberts*, good and unruffled, a staggered pair of four-storey
courtyards in deep red brick, articulated by paired full-height
recesses containing balconies.

I.M. MARSH CAMPUS, LIVERPOOL JOHN MOORES UNIVER-
SITY, Mossley Hill Road. At the top of the site in the centre
is a five-bay stuccoed VILLA, Bark Hill, of *c.* 1830. To the
garden (possibly the original entrance front) it has a porch of
pairs of Greek Doric columns, to the entrance a full-height
semicircular bow, which includes a pretty circular porch. The
bow has Doric pilasters. Decent staircase hall. To this house
additions were made: first l. and r., also stuccoed, then a Neo-
Georgian range of 1954 (by the then County Architect) projecting forward from the r. end, and finally in the 1960s a hall,
a twelve-storey block (demolished), the delightful EGG
DANCE STUDIO – a little free-standing, clear-span, glass-
walled oval – and a SPORTS HALL of hangar construction. This
is by *Roger Booth*, the County Architect. Refurbished in the
1990s with two masts at each end supporting internal roof
trusses. It is close to Holmefield Road and another 1830s villa,
HOLMEFIELD, this time with an Ionic portico, which also
forms part of the campus. 1870s billiard room extension, also
stucco.

LIVERPOOL COLLEGE, North Mossley Hill Road. The Junior
School moved here from Lodge Lane into buildings designed

by *Leathart, Granger & Webber* of London opened in 1929. These are scholastic Georgian with giant pilasters in stone and brick quoins. The N side has a full-length ground-floor arcade. The little CHAPEL, separate in the grounds, is by *Leathart*, 1934. They are only part of an intended quadrangle. After the war the rest of the school arrived, and existing C19 houses were occupied, two on each side of the road. One is Gothic brick, the others stucco and classical. Mossley Vale, 1858, by *William Culshaw* (now the music and art departments) has the highest-quality interior; Beechlands incorporates an earlier and smaller structure. Extensions and later blocks.

Houses

Many have become institutions and are described above. Of the rest:

NORTH MOSSLEY HILL ROAD, rising up to the church, has by far the most complete sequence. Houses in the lower reaches are mainly stucco and *c.* 1840s. Higher up on the W side is LINWOOD, a big polychromatic brick house apparently by *W. & G. Audsley* of 1869. Austerely Gothic with, on the gatepiers, decorative motifs so typical of the brothers. On the E side is ELMSWOOD, now a residential home, Tudor Gothic in pale ashlar, with barge-boarded gables, oriel and a huge square-headed, traceried stair window. This window apparently part of an extension, dated 1878 with the initials of Nicholas Duckworth (a cotton merchant) on the porch to the r. The first phase may be by *Cornelius Sherlock*. Further extensions and subdivisions for its present role. At the top on the same side of the road is HOLMESTEAD, the most theatrical house. Early Victorian Tudor with a High Victorian addition. The first part – mainly on the garden side – at least partly by *A.H. Holme*, *c.* 1845. The latter, of 1869–70 and possibly by *Culshaw & Sumners*, includes the entrance tower with oriel and steep pavilion roof, huge lantern-topped billiard room, and the large cast-iron conservatory. Good interiors of both periods, including *Morris* glass. Ugly inter-war extensions on the N side, now severed, date from a period as a convent. Two LODGES and outbuildings from the earliest phase; florid iron GATES from a later one.

CROFTON, North Sudley Road. Of *c.* 1876–8, for Alfred Holt, engineer and ship-owner, whose brother George remodelled neighbouring Sudley (*see* p. 444). It is very substantial, stuccoed and symmetrically Italianate, by *Rhind & Banner* (James Rhind did quite a bit for the Holts). Little altered externally, still with its ancillary buildings including lodges, stables etc. and a good but derelict cast-iron conservatory. Inside is a staircase hall with top-lit saucer dome. Despite development over the lower parts of the gardens, this is a rare survival of a large suburban villa complete with all its attendant outbuildings.

DELFIELD, Bark Hill Road. By *Arthur Hill Holme* for himself. 1850. Sandstone, Gothic. Good staircase.

DOVEDALE TOWERS, Dovedale Road. Now a pub. It was called Grove House and owned by A.G. Kurtz, an alkali manufacturer and art collector. A house was standing in 1836; the oddly tall wings at the rear, with pedimented gables, may be part of that. Kurtz had it extended in 1870–1 by *Charles Z. Hermann.* This is the bizarre 'debased' frontage with the most peculiar central tower, originally higher and wilder. Even before the work was finished poor Kurtz wrote in his diary that the tower looked 'quite out of proportion & the marble columns outside the upper storey appear unnecessary and pretentious . . . I feel rather sorry that I have had it altered . . . but everything [Hermann] takes in hand has a look of being overdone.' It is all stuccoed. Inside remnants of lavish fittings and finishes. The music room-cum-picture gallery has been demolished.

KELTON, Woodlands Road. The original house is an early C19 stuccoed villa with an Ionic porch of paired columns. Towering over this is a large Victorian Gothic extension of *c.* 1864–5 in yellow brick. Gables etc. It could not be more contrasting. The house became a convent, and the former CHAPEL dated 1925, of brick with lancets and Perp tracery, is attached to the other side. In the sanctuary STAINED GLASS by *Paul Woodroffe*, 1925. Now it is a care home, with single-storey blocks built over the gardens. The LODGE matches the Gothic wing.

SUDLEY HOUSE, Mossley Hill Road. A C19 house (known then as Sudley) last lived in by Emma Holt, who left it and her father's superb picture collection to the City. Two storeys, ashlar-built and austere. Of *c.* 1820, probably by *John Whiteside Casson,* altered and extended *c.* 1882–4 for George Holt, by *James Rhind.* The Georgian house has five bays on the s façade and its entrance with Tuscan porch on the E side. Of the 1880s are the square bays flanking this entrance, a new principal entrance and porch on the N side, and the w office wing, which includes a two-bay extension to the s front and a parapeted prospect tower set back behind.

The principal internal survival from the first phase is the fine staircase, with fluted Doric columns around the landing and a dome with glazed oculus above. It was clearly altered when the main entrance was moved from the E to the N. The result is a bit of a mess. From the 1880s entrance it is approached through a screen of Tuscan columns where the lower part of its w wall presumably was. The E wall has been opened up, leaving a section in the middle backing the fireplace warming the old entrance hall. The staircase is left exposed untidily in both the E and w holes. Most of the other rooms are a mixture of elements from both phases, and the house is gradually being redecorated in the Aesthetic style introduced by Holt in the 1880s. The library has excellent inlaid built-in bookcases and fireplace supplied by *J. O'Neill* of Church Street, the drawing room a fine C18 marble fireplace. Upstairs the tension is evident between the desire to preserve the house as a house (though all the furniture was sold in 1947) and the need to make the best of it as a gallery, for walls have been opened up to improved visitor circulation. In one room is a collection of outstanding Glasgow School furniture designed by *Herbert MacNair*, from his house in Oxford Street, Liverpool, demolished in the 1960s. MacNair taught at the University of Liverpool from 1899 to 1908.

The LODGE is an odd mixture of dormers and kneelers, and a segmental bay with a Doric colonnade around it which continues to the l. to form the entrance. It was altered by Holt in 1885: are the bay and colonnade part of a Georgian building?

NORRIS GREEN

A vast inter-war housing estate – which had a population the size of Shrewsbury – on the flat NE fringe of the city, now notorious for its chronic social and economic problems.

CHRIST CHURCH, Sedgmoor Lane. Of 1931–2 by *Ernest Gee* of *Quiggin & Gee*. Local brick with sparingly used shaped-headed lancets. Just a touch of the Sweden of the 1920s in these. Tall and narrow: a single-vessel nave and chancel with low aisles, high clerestory and apsidal E end. SW baptistery; Gee intended a tower over it. Interior with a coffered barrel vault in pine and details in blue Hornton stone, including the heavy round arcade piers, FONT, LECTERN and PULPIT. – Chancel E wall lined with BENCHES for bishop and clergy.
VICARAGE, S, 1937. – CHURCH HALL, N, 1929. Matching, with round-headed windows.
ST CHRISTOPHER, Lorenzo Drive. 1930–2. *Bernard A. Miller's* most original church, though simpler than first conceived. Hand-made brick, cross plan, with a broad, low, blocky crossing tower. No aisles. The main windows and the W portal are hyperbolic, quite an enterprising thing to do in 1930. But overall the stocky exterior is a little lumpen and awkward. The hyperbolic form is continued inside in the vaulting and the crossing arches. Chancel arch decorated with relief of dove between two angels. Original UPLIGHTERS at the angles of the crossing. The original colouring was dramatic: the E wall was deep violet blue behind the stainless-steel altar CROSS and its mounting of emerald green, the STALLS were grey, red and black with bands of stainless steel, and the metal casements were red, standing out from the cream-coloured plaster of the vaults and the oyster-grey ribs. But since 1964 it has been an unpardonable pale Wedgwood blue and cream. – Curving LECTERN and PULPIT are an integral part of the choir enclosure. – The FONT is extraordinary, an eight-pointed star in plan, straight in elevation, and all faced with mirror glass. 'Chichi', sniffed Pevsner. He thought the same of the wavy concentric parabolic arches of the E wall. – Incongruous C19 ORGAN in the S transept, saved from the bombed church of St Albans, Vauxhall. – Small CLOISTER attached to the E, including against the E wall an open-air PULPIT with sculpture by

Bainbridge Copnall. It is Byzantine in style with a canopy on columns. The N walk links the church with the CHURCH HALL of 1930. This is of brick on a steel frame, like the church, with a lower wing. Four cast cement PLAQUES by *H. Tyson Smith* of angels blowing pipes in each of the long walls.

ST TERESA (R.C.), Utting Avenue East. 1937, by *F.E.G. Badger*. It is a high and long and imposing church of brick with two shortish and narrow towers at the W end, longer than they are wide. But rarely has there been such a haphazard assortment of styles in one church. The columns are Romanesque, the arches Perp, the tall clerestory windows a 1920s Moderne, the fluted pilaster strips between them classical anyway, and on top of the whole is a Gothic timber rib-vault.

RANKIN PRESBYTERIAN CHURCH, Lorenzo Drive. A large Italian Romanesque church of 1930–1 by *George Downie*. The campanile is demolished.

HAIG MEMORIAL HOMES, Muirhead Avenue. By *Grey Wornum & Louis de Soissons* with the local firm of *Harris & Hobson*, 1929. For ex-servicemen and war widows. Three sides of a lawned quadrangle, brick, Neo-Georgian and much like *Keay*'s surrounding housing. (For Muirhead Avenue S of Queens Drive *see* p. 404.)

The NORRIS GREEN ESTATE was begun in 1926. It is an enormous thing, 650 acres (260 hectares), and by 1932 housed 37,500 people. The plan and housing were by *Keay*. The layout is as geometric as the vagaries of the site would allow and looks most impressive on a map or from the air. On the ground, however, it is monotonous and disorientating. The main thoroughfares, e.g. UTTING AVENUE EAST, are impressive enough, broad and tree-lined. The houses N of this road are Keay's normal cottagey Neo-Georgian (sashes – mostly replaced – pedimented doorcases and weatherboarded bays), in groups of two, four, six or eight. Away from the main roads they are plainer. To the S they are plainer still and pebble-dashed, and made of reinforced concrete, and the streets are very bleak indeed. To the anger of early residents, the BROADWAY SHOPPING CENTRE was not completed until 1929. It is low, long and two-storeyed, on a curve, and punctuated with gabled projections. Not nearly as ambitious or attractive as the slightly later example on the Dovecot Estate (*see* p. 438). A public hall built opposite it is now demolished. The LIBRARY on Utting Avenue East, by *Keay*, 1937–8 is squared, but with a three-bay entrance which shows that this is only a paring off of decoration and mouldings from a basically Neo-Georgian composition. Smaller shopping parades on either side of SCARGREEN AVENUE at the junction with Utting Avenue East. None of the schools is of architectural interest. The problems of crime, unemployment and poor services have been exacerbated by the structural failure of the concrete-built houses, and in 2005 the demolition of 1,500 of them was under way as part of a comprehensive redevelopment programme.

OLD SWAN, *see* TUE BROOK ETC., p. 483

PRINCE'S PARK *see* below

ST MICHAEL'S HAMLET *see* AIGBURTH ETC., p. 384

SANDFIELD PARK *see* WEST DERBY ETC., p. 505

SEFTON PARK, PRINCE'S PARK
and SURROUNDINGS

Prince's Park and Sefton Park, begun in 1842 and 1867 respectively, became the focus of an affluent residential area, spacious and leafy, and comfortably distant from the insalubrious city centre, 2½ m. to the NW.

Religious Buildings

ST AGNES, Ullet Road. 1883–5, by *John Loughborough Pearson*. It cost £28,000 and was paid for by the stockbroker H. Douglas Horsfall (son of Robert, who built St Margaret, Princes Road, *see* p. 470; and nephew of George, who built Christ Church, Linnet Lane, *see* below). In 1969 Pevsner described it as 'by far the most beautiful Victorian church of Liverpool . . . an epitome of Late Victorian nobility in church design'. Externally it is of red pressed brick with red sandstone dressings, the same materials as the surrounding houses. The C13 style, combining English and French elements, is typical of Pearson. It is a high, compact building, with aisles and clerestory, polygonal apse, and transepts at both the (ritual) E and W ends. The apse has blank arcading high up, and there are two turrets with short spires in the angles of the E transept and the chancel. No tower, but a lead-covered flèche marks the E crossing. Windows are lancets or have plate tracery, and those in the end walls of the transepts differ from each other. Two open, vaulted porches flank the short bay W of the W transept, and lead into a low, vaulted space below a gallery, which serves as a lobby. The visitor emerges from this shadowy area through a tripartite arcade into the soaring height of the W transept. The interior is ashlar-faced and stone-vaulted throughout with quadripartite rib vaults, and though not particularly large it conveys an impression of cathedral-like dignity. The four-bay nave arcades have round piers with continuous balconies of trefoil-headed tracery above, and a clerestory of high lancets over all. The E end is much richer, both in decoration and spatial complexity. A narrow ambulatory runs round the apse, divided from the sanctuary by an arcade with angel musicians in the spandrels. Above these is a continuous frieze in high relief representing the Adoration of the Lamb, and higher still, between the clerestory windows, statues of angels under canopies. All this SCULPTURE, along with the REREDOS, dates from 1893–5 and was carried out to Pearson's designs by *Nathaniel Hitch*, who had worked for him on the reredos of Truro Cathedral. S of the chancel is the LADY CHAPEL, one bay long with aisles, the N aisle continuous with the ambulatory. The wooden ORCHESTRA LOFT was designed by Pearson in 1893. – Dividing chapel from transept, a wrought-iron SCREEN of quatrefoil pattern, 1903; along with the REREDOS of 1904, designed by *G.F. Bodley* after Pearson's death. – The NE transept is completely filled by the ORGAN, raised up high on an extraordinary polygonal platform, vaulted underneath and supported by a central column of black marble with ten more columns round the edges. The view of the chancel through this shadowy forest of columns is thrilling. (What was Pearson's inspiration for such a structure? In form, though not in style, it recalls the great pulpits by the Pisani in Siena, Pisa and Pistoia.) – Some playful corbel heads and grotesques in the transepts carved *c.* 1910 by a Mr *Thomson*, including a falling horse (a rebus for Horsfall) just l. of the organ. – STAINED GLASS. Several windows by *Kempe*, the latest in the SW transept commemorating the founder's mother (†1902). Two in the Lady Chapel by *Bryans*.

Just behind the church in Buckingham Avenue is the VICARAGE, 1885–7, by *Richard Norman Shaw*, paid for by Douglas Horsfall's mother. Red brick with stone dressings, the mullioned windows unmoulded and asymmetrically arranged, the general effect severe. On the street elevation the only projection is a shallow canted oriel with tracery, indicating the chapel on the first floor. Towards the church the composition is more complicated, with a pointed-arched doorway, the flat chimney-breast to the r., its l. angle caught on a stone corbel, and canted oriels at each end, the one on the r. running through both floors. Also by *Shaw* the simple PARISH HALL behind.

CHRIST CHURCH, Linnet Lane. 1867–71, by *Culshaw & Sumners*. It was paid for by George Horsfall. A lively Dec Gothic design in stone, with quirky and original touches. The E elevation facing Linnet Lane has an apse flanked on the S by vestries and on the N by an open porch, and a tower with tall broach spire, the broaches convex in outline. The W end, facing East Albert Road, has diagonally set corner porches. The aisles are cross-vaulted, each window having its own gable, and the clerestory windows are merely arched heads filled with tracery. Inside, the six-bay nave has a hammerbeam roof and slender quatrefoil piers with foliage capitals. Sanctuary FLOOR and REREDOS by *Bernard Miller*, 1930. – STAINED GLASS in the apse seems contemporary with the building and may be by *Hardman*. Two early C20 windows, S aisle, by *Gustave Hiller* of Liverpool, one including a representation of the recently completed E end of the Anglican Cathedral. *Shrigley & Hunt* also supplied two windows.

ST CLARE (R.C.), Arundel Avenue. 1889–90, by *Leonard Stokes*. One of the most imaginative churches of its date in the country. It was paid for by the brothers Francis and James Reynolds, cotton brokers (Stokes was the godson of Francis Reynolds), and cost £7,834. The style is Gothic, but more loosely tied to historical precedent than Pearson's St Agnes of just four years earlier. Exterior of buff-coloured brick with stone dressings, the walls high and sheer, the window tracery late Decorated. No tower, only a turret with a spire in the angle of N transept and nave. The window in the cliff-like E wall is broad and high up and partly filled with blind tracery, and the hoodmould over it seems to hang down in a loop on either side – a foretaste of further unhistorical details within. Small statues of St Clare and St Francis in niches over N and W porches, possibly by *George Frampton*. The interior follows the example of Bodley's 69 St Augustine, Pendlebury, 1874 (and ultimately of Albi, etc.) in having internal buttresses, or wall piers. These are pierced to form narrow passage aisles, and linked by semicircular arches to create a low arcade supporting a continuous balcony on each side of the nave. The bases of the piers are teardrop-shaped in plan – rounded towards the aisles and triangular towards the nave – and the front parts are carried up as triangular shafts till they meet a chamfered horizontal band at the top of the wall. The chamfering is exactly one side of the triangle, so each bay seems bordered l., r. and top by a bevelled frame. Stokes wanted stone throughout, but unfortunately almost everything above the springing of the arches is painted plaster.

REREDOS over the High Altar, a large triptych combining painting and relief sculpture by *Robert Anning Bell* and *George Frampton*, 1890. It draws freely on Northern and Italian Renaissance sources, and provides a sumptuous focus for the whole interior. – *Stokes'* PULPIT is remarkable: four sides of a hexagon, stone, with panels of openwork tracery, the sides sloping inwards towards the top. – FONT. Chalice-shaped, of gorgeous alabaster with a copper cover. – Present HIGH ALTAR 1920s, ALTAR RAILS 1933. – To the l. a niche prettily painted in 1959 by an Italian Capuchin, *Fr Ugolino*, with angels drawing back curtains to reveal a view of Assisi. Hinges and other door furniture demonstrate Stokes' Arts and Crafts credentials.

The PRESBYTERY, attached to the NE corner and forming a single composition with the church, is simpler than Stokes intended. It should have had bay windows on the r., softening the junction. The hoodmould stops over the pointed-arched door incorporate the letters s and c, in a curvilinear style that strikingly anticipates Art Nouveau.

UNITARIAN CHURCH, Ullet Road. By *Thomas Worthington & Son* of Manchester (the influence of the son, *Percy Worthington*, may have been to the fore). The church, vestry and library (on the l. as viewed from Ullet Road) date from 1896–9; the hall on the r. and the linking cloister were added *c.* 1901. Unitarianism was a powerful force in C19 Liverpool, as such names as Roscoe, Rathbone, Holt, Booth, Brunner and Tate show. The congregation moved here from Renshaw Street in the city centre, and the ambitious new buildings demonstrate the wealth and confidence both of the Liverpool Unitarians and of the residential area around Sefton Park.

The buildings, of red pressed brick with red sandstone dressings, are attractively grouped round three sides of a central garden, giving a collegiate feel. The church is Gothic, with Decorated window tracery. No tower, but the (ritual) w gable has a prominent squared-off projection with three arched openings, like a bellcote but without any bells. The statue of Christ in the gable niche is after Thorwaldsen. Three magnificent DOORS of beaten copper with Art Nouveau foliate designs, by *Richard Llewellyn Rathbone*, lead into the spacious lobby. The interior was also to have been of brick, but happily ashlar was used instead, paid for by Mrs George Holt. The arrangement is more church-like than early C19 Nonconformist chapels, with nave and aisles and a separate chancel. – CHOIR STALLS by Messrs *Hatch* of Lancaster, the canopy above those on the r. by *C.J. Allen*. – REREDOS. Last Supper by *H.H. Martyn* of Cheltenham. – Good Art Nouveau LIGHT FITTINGS by the *Artificers' Guild*, London. – FONT of wood, 1906, designed by *Ronald P. Jones* and carved by *Allen*. – STAINED GLASS mostly by *Morris & Co.*, after designs by *Edward Burne-Jones*, that in the chancel dating from the opening of the church and better than the later windows. – The VESTRY, r. of the chancel, has PAINTINGS by *Gerald Moira*, completed in 1902. Four roundels on the ceiling represent Justice, Prudence, Temperance and Charity. Above the fireplace, a shallow-relief panel in painted plaster of the rising sun, a powerful Symbolist work.

Adjoining the vestry is the LIBRARY, with even more splendid painted decoration of the same date by *Moira* on the vaulted ceiling. The subject is the Triumph of Truth. A winged figure representing Time raises the victorious youthful female figure of Truth who scatters her enemies, Envy, Calumny, Intolerance and Ignorance. She is accompanied by artists, scientists, religious leaders and other seekers after truth, ancient and modern, ranging from Moses to Newton. The figures are linked by serpentine golden rays, issuing from the lamp held by Truth.

The HALL and CLOISTER were given by Sir John Brunner and Henry Tate. The exterior of the hall is picturesquely composed, with a canted bay window to Ullet Road, a smaller semicircular bay to York Avenue, and a little roof lantern with an ogee cupola. Inside, it has an impressive open-timber roof, an aisle down one side, and an attractively contrived inglenook with the arms of the donors above. In the cloister are two recessed bays with MONUMENTS from the earlier chapel in Renshaw Street. These include: a bust of William Roscoe, by *John Gibson*; Edward Roscoe, †1834, by *Gibson*, an angel in profile looking up, representing Hope; William Rathbone, †1868, by *J.H. Foley*, 1874, a large relief with the deceased on a sarcophagus and groups of mourners l. and r.; Charles Beard,

†1888, with profile-portrait medallion by *J.E. Boehm*; and William Rathbone, †1902, with profile-portrait by *C.J. Allen*.

INDEPENDENT BAPTIST CHURCH, Belvidere Road. Built as St John's Wesleyan Methodist Chapel, 1861–3, by *Hayley & Son* of Manchester. Decorated Gothic, rock-faced. The octagonal towers framing the W end originally had tall spires. Attached at the back is a school. The whole strong and rugged group looks as if it had strayed from a Pennine mill town.

ST COLUMBA (former), Smithdown Road. 1896–7, by *Woolfall & Eccles*. Originally Presbyterian. Only the large red brick and terracotta tower with saddleback roof remains. The nave, etc., was replaced in the 1990s by an old people's home, the shape of which echoes the vanished building.

PRESBYTERIAN CHURCH, Belvidere Road. Begun 1856, by Messrs *Hay*. Small, Gothic, rock-faced, with a rose window in the gable and a truncated square spire in the angle of the porch.

SYNAGOGUE, Greenbank Drive. 1936–7, by *Alfred E. Shennan*. Of buff brick, with faint echoes of Stockholm City Hall in the details. The galleried interior has Art Deco woodwork.

Other Buildings, and Parks

POLICE STATION (former), Lark Lane. *See* p. 455.

SEFTON PARK LIBRARY, Aigburth Road. Opened 1911, the last of the branch libraries designed by the Corporation Surveyor, *Thomas Shelmerdine*. Ashlar and roughcast on the ground floor with half-timbering above, and tall, diagonally set brick chimneys – like a Neo-Tudor village hall. In the entrance porch, a repoussé copper panel commemorating the opening by Andrew Carnegie, Celtic Art Nouveau style, by *J.A. Hodel*.

MARY CLARK HOME, Ullet Road. Brick and terracotta, 1892, with prominent chimneystacks and a porch balcony with Renaissance ironwork. Designed by *Arthur P. Fry* as accommodation for elderly single ladies.

LATHBURY HOUSE, Ullet Road. An old people's home by *Bradshaw, Rowse & Harker*, 1965. Its most striking feature is a glazed-in concrete external stair, wrapped around a square central column which rises above the roof-line to support a cubic concrete water tank.

PRINCE'S PARK was the first public, or at least semi-public, park to be provided for the citizens of Liverpool. It was the creation of Richard Vaughan Yates (1785–1856), iron merchant and philanthropic Dissenter. He bought the site for £50,000 from the Earl of Sefton and in 1842 employed *Joseph Paxton* to lay it out, working with *James Pennethorne*. The name commemorates the birth of Edward, Prince of Wales, the previous year. This was Paxton's first park design and a precursor to his much larger and more influential Birkenhead Park across the Mersey. It follows the model of Nash's Regent's Park in London, with sites for housing around the edges. The sale of building plots was intended to offset the cost of laying out the park, with a proportion of rental income paying for its upkeep. However, the take-up was slow, and in 1843 it was decided to establish a company to carry forward the work. Within the Park stood the principal church of the new suburb, St Paul's, a Gothic building of 1846–8 by *A.H. Holme*, demolished in 1974.

The MAIN ENTRANCE faces the Princes Road–Princes Avenue boulevard. The square gatepiers with curved flanking walls may be by *Pennethorne*; the handsome gates of a radial pattern are replicas of *c.* 1960. The plan has a curving drive round the edge, with the houses mostly outside this, facing the surrounding roads. The main landscape feature is Paxton's LAKE. It has an island, and at the s end a BOATHOUSE in the style of a Swiss chalet, possibly by *John Robertson*, now ruinous. The banks were laid out with gardens and winding paths. Aligned with the entrance, a red granite OBELISK, 1858, to the memory of Richard Vaughan Yates.

The HOUSES do not follow Paxton's original layout, which envisaged more terraces and fewer detached and semi-detached villas. In 1843 a national design competition was held, won by *Wyatt Papworth* and *Henry Currey*, but except for one block by Papworth their proposals were not carried out. Progress was slow: some sites were not developed until the 1860s, and others were never built on. Some of the earliest houses are on choice sites overlooking the lake. WINDERMERE TERRACE is stuccoed, with two bows facing the park. Next to it is WINDERMERE HOUSE, a handsome three-bay house with a porch of four Ionic columns, aligned with the E entrance to the park. (Next to this entrance, in Sefton Park Road, is PARK LODGE. Unremarkable externally, it is supposed to incorporate masonry from one of the lodges of the former royal hunting ground of Toxteth Park, *see* p. 469.) Also overlooking the lake is PRINCE'S PARK MANSIONS, a stuccoed terrace of eight houses by *Wyatt Papworth*, the only result of the 1843 competition. It was converted into flats from 1912.

In DEVONSHIRE ROAD, next to the main entrance, a brick and stone Gothic house of 1862–4 with later additions, by *Alfred Waterhouse* for the dock engineer George Fosbery Lyster. A little further along Devonshire Road on the NW side is a long, low, brick range with classical stucco ornaments and a central entrance. These were livery stables, probably 1850s; recently converted to residential use with clumsily inappropriate windows. Further along facing the park, at the corner of Sunnyside, is CAVENDISH GARDENS, of before 1848. Stuccoed, of nine bays and three storeys, with giant Corinthian pilasters to the end elevations and a pediment with giant Corinthian columns facing the park. In SUNNYSIDE itself, a row of attractive stuccoed, semi-detached houses with Italianate details, 1850s. The rest of this side of Devonshire Road has large detached houses backing on to the park, none earlier than the late 1850s. On the opposite side, at the end, an eighteen-bay terrace with projecting ends and centre, and cast-iron balconies in the recessed parts. It belongs to the earliest phase of development, and was complete by 1848. BELVIDERE ROAD has mostly houses of the 1860s on the park side. On the other side, near the Ullet Road end, is WELLESLEY TERRACE, probably early 1850s: red brick with stucco dressings, symmetrical and quite impressive (for the Presbyterian Church, *see* p. 451).

SEFTON PARK. Occupying 269 acres (109 hectares) bought mostly from the Earl of Sefton, this was by far the biggest public park laid out anywhere in the country since Regent's Park in London at the beginning of the C19. As with Prince's Park, the cost was to be recouped from the sale of building plots around the edges. In 1867 a design competition was won by *Lewis Hornblower* and *Edouard André*. It is not clear how the two came to work together. Hornblower, a Liverpool architect, had taken part in the 1843 competition for housing in connection with Prince's Park and had designed the main entrance lodge of Paxton's Birkenhead Park. André, aged just twenty-six, was chief gardener to the City of Paris, where he had been involved in the creation of such public parks as the Bois de Boulogne and the Parc des Buttes-Chaumont.

Spiralling costs meant that the winning design was not carried out in full. Despite this, Sefton Park is a magnificent achievement of mid-Victorian suburban planning and municipal enterprise. It should be remembered that the landscape was created from a featureless agricultural tract: there were no groups of trees, and no lake. Now, in its maturity, the park largely fulfils André's promise that its forest trees would in time appear 'as if planted by nature'. The layout embodies principles practised by André in Paris. The *Gardener's Chronicle* huffily summed it up as a 'Gallicised version of the Jardin Anglais', and the informality is indeed derived from the English parks of Paxton and Loudon. Instead of Paxton's serpentine paths, André favoured long sweeping curves which meet tangentially rather than intersecting, inducing the visitor to follow a roundabout route and so making the park seem even larger. Two streams that crossed the site were used to create a lake.

The MAIN ENTRANCE on Ullet Road, 1875, has Gothic gatepiers with a short central tower, its E.E. details debased with relish. The chunkily buttressed base supports two short, fat red granite columns with a thin sandstone one squeezed in between, all three holding up a steep little roof. There is a second Gothic gate at the Aigburth Vale entrance. (The granite columns are sections from much larger ones, removed from the interior of St George's Hall in the 1850s: *see* p. 295.) To the r. of the Ullet Road gate, a pretty LODGE of 1874 in *cottage orné* style, of red brick and sandstone with half-timbering. Similar LODGES at the entrances from Aigburth Vale, 1874, and Smithdown Road, 1878. Gates and lodges are by *Thomas Shelmerdine*, Corporation Surveyor. Gothic GATEPIERS at the entrance from Lark Lane may be earlier. A cast-iron BRIDGE carries

Mossley Hill Drive over one of the streams feeding the lake: a workaday structure of lattice girders on octagonal columns. ROCKWORK bordering the water features is by *M. Combaz*, who had worked with Edouard André on the Paris parks.

The chief building within the Park is the PALM HOUSE, a splendid iron and glass conservatory by *Mackenzie & Moncur* of Edinburgh, opened 1896. It was the gift of Henry Yates Thompson, whose great-uncle Richard Vaughan Yates created Prince's Park fifty years earlier. An octagonal domed structure on a plinth of polished red granite, which breaks forward at the angles to support eight statues (some marble, some bronze) by *Léon-Joseph Chavalliaud*. Their subjects illustrate horticulture and exploration, ensuring in a thoroughly Victorian way that the Palm House would give instruction as well as pleasure. They represent Le Nôtre, James Cook, Mercator, Linnaeus, Darwin, Columbus, Henry the Navigator, and John Parkinson (Apothecary to James I). Inside, more marble sculptures: The Angel's Whisper, 1850s, by *Benjamin Edward Spence*; a version of the same artist's Highland Mary; Two Goats, by *Giovita Lombardi*; and a classical bench with an inscription commemorating Thompson's gift. In 2001 a full restoration of the Palm House and its sculptures was completed. Facilities that allow its use for functions and performances have been constructed below ground level. Near the Palm House, bronze STATUE of Peter Pan by George Frampton, presented 1928, a replica of the original in Kensington Gardens, London.

On the E side of the lake, marble STATUE of William Rathbone V, unveiled 1877, begun by *J.H. Foley* and completed by *Thomas Brock*. Brock's reliefs on the base have been removed. – FOUNTAIN, a cast of the famous Shaftesbury Memorial in Piccadilly Circus, London, by *Alfred Gilbert*; unveiled 1932. The crowning aluminium figure of Eros has been removed to the Conservation Centre (*see* p. 343). – OBELISK of 1909 to Samuel Smith M.P., by *Willink & Thicknesse*. The plinth had bronze relief sculptures by *C.J. Allen*.

The fringes of the park, divided into villa plots, were sold off from 1872. The resulting HOUSES are generally more remarkable for size than architectural quality. Some of the more interesting lie NE of the entrance gates on Ullet Road. Rankin Hall, originally THE TOWERS, 1874, is a gigantic Gothic pile by *G.A. Audsley*. Red brick with red sandstone dressings. Arched entrance at the base of a high, square tower with a higher turret at one corner. Typical Audsley stained glass and stencilled decoration inside. SEFTON COURT, at the corner of Croxteth Gate, is Italianate and stuccoed, probably by *C.Z. Hermann*. Part of the interior was refurbished *c.* 1901 by the Liverpool Arts and Crafts architect *Edmund Rathbone*, with woodwork, metalwork and painting by the *Bromsgrove Guild*. HOLT HOUSE, 1874–8, by *Banner & Rhind*, is a large and austere classical building in red brick, for the cotton merchant and future Lord Mayor, Robert Durning Holt. In Mossley Hill Drive is GLEDHILL, 1881, by *James F. Doyle*. Old English in the manner of Shaw: picturesque asymmetry in red brick and sandstone, with tile-hanging, pargeting, half-timbered gables, mullioned windows and very tall chimneys. (For Greenbank Lane *see* Mossley Hill, p. 441.) In 1958 the City Architect and Director of Housing, *Ronald Bradbury*, and the City Engineer and Surveyor, *Henry T. Hough*, proposed replacing all the park-side villas with much denser housing, mostly in the form of slab and tower blocks. This plan was partly carried out, and Ullet Road E of Croxteth Gate shows the results: a Corbusian vision of high residential towers in a sylvan setting, with low-rise schools and other institutional buildings between. The five fifteen-storey TOWERS, clad in buff-coloured brick, were completed by 1965 (penthouses added to some, 2003). The views from the upper floors must be spectacular, but seen from within the park they undermine the illusion of open country-side. For the area E of Mossley Hill Drive and S of Greenbank Lane, *see* Mossley Hill.

GROVE PARK, leading off the S end of Lodge Lane, is a cul-de-sac of semi-detached villas, Classical, stuccoed, of the 1840s or early 1850s, some with nice cast-iron balconies. The development of Prince's Park, just to the S, was no doubt the catalyst.

LARK LANE, between Sefton Park and Aigburth Road, acquired a handful of interesting commercial and institutional buildings, following the creation of the park. At the corner of Sefton Grove, the former POLICE STATION of 1885 by *F.U. Holme*, red brick and stone with Gothic details. The ALBERT HOTEL at the corner of Pelham Grove is a large Gothic pub of 1873, an early demonstration of the architectural ambitions of Robert Cain, the brewer who later built the Philharmonic Hotel and The Vines (*see* pp. 375 and 326). No. 63 is the former CHRIST CHURCH INSTITUTE, 1884, with a gabled and half-timbered upper storey, the central part jettied out. Bickerton Street leads SE from Lark Lane to NEWLAND COURT, *c.* 1984, one of the earliest co-operative housing schemes in the city. Terraced houses round a quadrangle, designed by *Innes Wilkin Ainsley Gommon* for the Hesketh Street Co-operative. Also off the SE side of Lark Lane is HADASSAH GROVE, a delightful surprise: an L-shaped cul-de-sac lined with small but elegant houses, probably *c.* 1840, mostly brick, with stone dressings and classical doorcases. The area NW of Lark Lane, bounded by Linnet Lane, Ullet Road and Aigburth Road, began to be developed with substantial houses a few years earlier than Sefton Park. The biggest are on PARKFIELD ROAD and ALEXANDRA DRIVE.

SPEKE

In 1921 Speke was a quiet, decidedly rural parish with a population of 381, lying just outside the city boundary. In that year the last owner of Speke Hall, Adelaide Watt, died. Seven years later 1,800 acres (730 hectares) of the estate were acquired by the Corporation, which envisaged an industrial estate, along the lines of Trafford Park in Manchester or the Slough Trading Estate, to attract new manufacturers to Liverpool to alleviate unemployment. The airport established to the w of Speke Hall in 1930 was part of this scheme, and from 1936 the e part was developed under *Lancelot Keay*, Director of Housing, as a 'self-contained community unit'. In reality it was an isolated industrial suburb. By 1955 it had a population of *c.* 21,000, but as manufacturing jobs were lost, it subsequently became one of the most deprived wards in the country. Several attempts have been made to address this. The latest, spearheaded by the Speke Garston Partnership and the Speke Garston Development Company, has as its centrepiece the Estuary Commerce Park, a redevelopment of the 1930s airport including the exemplary reuse of its original structures. This, and other highly visible elements, are also intended to improve the image of the city to visitors arriving at the new airport, the expansion of which will dominate the future of Speke.

Churches

ALL SAINTS, Speke Church Road. By *J.L. Pearson*, 1872–5, but not on a par with St Agnes, Sefton Park (*see* p. 447). All Saints is simple, reasonable and serious, but devoid of Pearson's great enthusiasms. Red stone with a deep roof and a robust s steeple with broach spire. Dec details, five-light Geometrical e window. n aisle and n transept only. The arch between chancel and organ chamber is treated as a two-light opening with geometrical tracery, as the mid C19 liked it. The roof is a false hammerbeam.

ST AIDAN, South Parade. In 1953 *Bernard A. Miller* prepared a scheme for a church, hall and rectory around a cloister, on a pivotal site in the town centre.* The hall was built then, the church in 1956–7, the cloister never. The church is brick. A copper-clad barrel roof is set between full-height aisles under shallow concrete arches. n façade balanced: orientation is not immediately evident. Slight but elegant s e tower when there should be a landmark at the n end engaging the shopping precinct opposite, as Keay's plan envisaged. Instead of an entrance, the church shoulders a defensive n wall, and has a desultory plaza. Spacious nave, tall narrow aisles with tunnel vaults (extensions of the clerestory arches) w gallery. The roof is of the Lamella type. Chapel of St Thomas, at the e end, carefully framed in an arch behind the altar. Perspective deceives one into thinking it is a painted reredos. A glass SCREEN, etched with saints, beneath the w gallery and the colour scheme are part of a restoration by *J.M. Wilson & Son* (*D.G. Broome*, project architect), 1983–90. Fittings by *Miller*, including a jolly FONT, a big jar covered in tesserae. – STAINED GLASS. Richly coloured abstract panels set in clerestory windows.

---

*In 1939 A.C. Gladstone offered £15,000 towards the cost of a new parish church. He selected *Sir Herbert Baker*, but the war finished the project.

St Ambrose (R.C.), Heathgate Avenue. By *Alfred Bullen* of *Weightman & Bullen*, 1959–61. The best building on the Speke estate, though it is unshakeably redolent of a sports hall and boiler chimney. Disciplined rectangle of ten by seven bays; expressed concrete structure, brick infilling, and a clerestory on all sides under shallow concrete arches. On the entrance side is the elegant central tower, with tall, open belfry. 86 ft (26.5 metres) high, topped by an 11 ft (3.4 metres) cross. It doubles as a baptistery, and is separated from the body of the church by a three-bay narthex, so as to form an eyecatcher on Heathgate Avenue. Its quarry-faced stone cladding is not a success. The church interior is good: broad, light and lofty. On three sides a tall ambulatory of tunnel vaults (extensions of the outside arches), carried on thin, flat columns (cf. the aisles of St Aidan, Speke). These also support the flat roof, a grid panelled with large perforated nailheads (for the acoustics). Organ above the W entrance, chapels and confessionals recessed in the N wall, and a three-bay chapel, set back under tunnel vaults, in the E wall. Advanced liturgical arrangements, intended to enable full congregational participation: a processional way all around, no choir, and the altar brought forward of the E wall so that the celebrant faces the congregation. The two-tone brown ceiling was originally blue, the beige walls unpainted blockwork. The addition of lurid paintings along the E wall has lost the interior some of its coolness. – FURNISHINGS designed by *Weightman & Bullen*. – HIGH ALTAR, a bold broad slab of Cornish granite on a narrow pedestal, and matching TABERNACLE in a marble-floored sanctuary enclosed by the COMMUNION RAILS. – Now joined by a LECTERN and the tub-like FONT, moved from the baptistery. – STATIONS OF THE CROSS. Ceramic, by *A. Kossowski*.

Liverpool Airport

LIVERPOOL SPEKE AIRPORT (former), Speke Boulevard. An important group of buildings of 1935–40 by *Edward Bloomfield* of the city's Public Buildings Department, embodying the most advanced thinking of the time, and now the most coherent example of an early purpose-built airport surviving in Europe.

From the late 1920s, driven by the air-minded Councillor Sir Thomas White, Liverpool Corporation strove to establish itself as the premier 'air junction' in the North of England. The W part of the Speke Estate was identified as an ideal airport location: flat and free from fog.* It opened in 1933 at first using farm buildings as hangars and terminals. Purpose-built facilities were not begun until 1935, after a deputation toured Continental airports. It was the Fuhlsbüttel, the airport of

---

*In 1930 Sir Alan Cobham, with the architect *Sir John Burnet*, prepared an unexecuted scheme for a sleek US-influenced terminal.

Liverpool's great rival Hamburg, that most impressed. Speke is closely modelled on this 1929 design. The advent of jet airliners saw it gradually supplanted by Manchester Airport, which was more centrally located and easier to expand, although a jet runway was opened E of Speke Hall in 1966. The original terminal was superseded in 1986. In 1997 redevelopment of the pre-war airfield as the Estuary Commerce Park was begun by English Partnerships. In parallel, in 1998–2001, the airport buildings were successfully converted for new uses. However, when the business park is completed and the airfield built over the context of the buildings will be lost.

The terminal and hangars are *Edward Bloomfield*'s major work. He was project architect, working under the Surveyor, *Albert D. Jenkins*. The plan is clearly based on the Fuhlsbüttel: matching hangars flanking a gently curving terminal, with tiered observation decks and a central control tower. The integrated plan reflected current European thinking on airport design, the diluted brick Modernism shows the influence of Dudok, already apparent in Corporation housing schemes, whilst the monumentalism, particularly of the octagonal control tower, owes something to American airport design. The result was an ensemble without parallel in Britain before the Second World War. In the first phase, 1935–7, the w hangar (No. 1 HANGAR), and CONTROL TOWER. The hangar was the largest yet built for aeroplanes (as opposed to airships) in Britain. It measures 400 by 212 feet (123 by 65 metres), with folding wooden doors on the E and S sides and clerestory and side windows. Twin piers flanking the airside (E) elevation are decorated with stone relief eagles. The glazing between evokes the technology of flight: the transom lights like ribbed wings, the centre, the ribs of an airship. In 1998–2000 *Falconer Chester Architects* converted the building into a leisure centre with considerable success. The exterior was restored with the airside doors folded open and a glazed wall inserted between. Tinted and recessed, during the day it suggests the void it once was; at night the new windows light up to reveal the floors inserted for its new function. Working within the tripartite division of the side windows, these new floors extend back one-third the length of the building; the remainder remains undivided, for indoor tennis courts. A crisp extension against the rear elevation, partially timber-clad, houses squash and badminton courts. To the r. of the airside elevation is a small, single-storey bow-fronted wing which served as the first booking hall.

116   The permanent TERMINAL, gathered around the control tower, was built in 1937–9. Steel frame, brick walls. The gently curving airside (s) façade is 400 ft (123 metres) long. The viewing balconies, staggered like a grandstand, reflect the revenue-earning importance of air pageants between the wars. Principal passenger and baggage handling spaces were on the ground floor; a 200 ft (61.5 metre) long restaurant, reached by two circular staircases, occupied the centre of the first floor.

The 1998–2001 conversion into the LIVERPOOL MARRIOTT HOTEL SOUTH is another successful job by *Falconer Chester Architects*. To create a viable number of rooms, two new wings were constructed on the road (N) side, on either side of the originally projecting five-storey entrance tower, gently curving in a reflection of the 1930s plan. These ape the original detail: two tones of brick, strongly horizontal glazing. Interior in Neo-Art Deco. Sadly, the panoramic views across the Mersey will be lost when the business park is completed. The entrance GATEPIERS are actually two pairs of 1940, restored and re-sited as one in 1998. By *H. Tyson Smith*. Limestone; streamlined. The more elaborate inner pair, designed for the terminal, are capped with abstract winged motifs.

NO. 2 HANGAR, E of the terminal, was built with Air Ministry finance in 1939–40 to a simplified design. It is wider and shorter, with less elaborate glazing and a barrel-profiled roof constructed of the Lamella system of laminated steel trusses (ironically developed by Junkers, the German manufacturer better known for its bombers). The bas-reliefs decorating the airside piers are this time of a Modernist winged man. Refurbished undivided for use as a call centre by *Falconer Chester Architects* 1999–2001, also with a glass wall thrown up between the folded doors.

No. 2 Hangar is part of the ESTUARY COMMERCE PARK, begun in 1997, that will eventually cover all of the 1930s airfield. Masterplanning and landscaping by *EDAW*. Standard business park layout: pompous entrance on Speke Road, spacious roads, unrelated buildings isolated by car parking. Generous landscaping, with ponds and canals, robust but elegant street furniture. The plan should be censured for ignoring the pattern of the runways and taxiways, which should have been retained to create an original and contextual layout. The best single building is the security LODGE off Speke Hall Avenue, a small clerestoried box with a fully glazed bay, all angles like a shard. Other architecture so far, mostly white, curved-roof boxes. ESTUARY HOUSE, another call centre, in the NE corner on Speke Boulevard is a possible exception. By *McCormick Architecture*, 1998–9. A silver grid of steel pillars, eaves and brise-soleil with recessed black panels and windows between. Outside the N front, a substantial SCULPTURE, Coming Together, three embracing pylons-cum-figures, by *Stephen Broadbent*, 1999. Further phases planned.

LIVERPOOL JOHN LENNON AIRPORT, Speke Hall Avenue. A new terminal opened in 1986, alongside the 1966 runway E of Speke Hall. Present terminal building, 2000–2, by *Leach Rhodes Walker Architects*, incorporating elements of the first. A provincial example of the dominant airport style of the 1990s: the glass wall and big exposed roof rediscovered and popularized by Norman Foster at Stansted and Renzo Piano at Kansai. The roof, a sweeping curve, is of the Kansai aerofoil variety. In the departure concourse, a bronze STATUE of John Lennon by *Tom Murphy*, 2002.

For SCHOOLS and SWIMMING POOL *see* p. 461.

Housing Development

In 1930 the South West Lancashire Joint Town Planning Advisory
Committee proposed a 'satellite town' of 30,000, part dormitory, part industrial new town, bordered by green belts. The
Corporation's first plan, of 1932, recast this as an industrial
suburb with a projected population of 55,000. This was superseded by a scheme drawn up in 1936 by the City Surveyor
(revised 1937), with a new Liverpool–Widnes Road, based on
American parkway principles. s of this *Lancelot Keay*, Director
of Housing, designed the residential zone. Slightly amended,
this layout was adopted for construction. Keay's 'self-contained
community unit' was meant to include housing for *c*. 20,000 of
all classes, along with exceptional community facilities. The flat
featureless site suggested a formal PLAN, and the directional
confusion caused by the lack of a clear plan on earlier estates
(e.g. Norris Green, *see* p. 446) resulted in arterial avenues. Two
of these, Western Avenue and Eastern Avenue, form the principal entries from Speke Boulevard, and intersect the spine,
Central Avenue–Central Way. This divides through the town
centre (a 1946 amendment). The centre extends N as Speke
Park; a boulevard s to a promenade, sports stadium and lido
on the banks of the Mersey was not built. The seven schools
were formally arranged in zones flanking the centre and at the
E and W ends of Central Avenue–Central Way. Housing was
arranged in semi-detached pairs and short terraces along
straight streets and enclosed greens and closes. Curvilinear
planning is restricted to the edges where dictated by the site
shape.

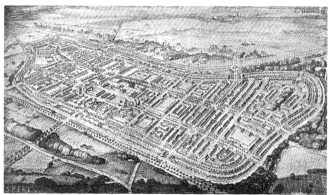

Speke (Liverpool), housing development, as planned in 1936.
Bird's-eye view

Construction of the first 500 houses began on the W edge in 1938. By the end of the war a further 900 had been erected; the last of the 5,700 went up *c.* 1953. But by the 1960s it was clear that Keay's 'adventure' had failed. Although he claimed Speke as a prototype New Town, in reality, it was an isolated, working-class suburb. There was no private housing, no trams (prohibited across runway approaches), the railway station never opened, and even the scaled-down shopping and public amenities were not completed until the 1960s. These problems were compounded from the 1970s by job losses. In 2005 the chronic deprivation was being tackled with investment in refurbished housing, new schools and community buildings, and possibly also new shopping facilities.

Perambulation

Speke is a vast housing estate of great monotony, so exploration is only for the committed. The salient points can be taken in starting on SPEKE CHURCH ROAD, the centre of the old village, where construction began. Gathered around All Saints' church are the tiny Gothic stone SCHOOL, *c.* 1875, probably by *Pearson* too, and one remaining row of three pedimented brick cottages, C18. E of the cottages on the S side of HALE ROAD, not actually in the estate, is THE FOX pub.* The streets around here, built up before 1948, illustrate the two styles intended for the whole development. On Church Road, at the N end is THE CRESCENT shopping parade, 1948, by the same department, but this time in Dudok-inspired brick. Thin concrete canopy, rounded projecting wings. A circular library was intended in front.

Further N, down WOODEND LANE and r. into BRAY ROAD, the HOUSING is representative of standard *City Housing Department* designs, mainly of non-parlour plan, in hipped-roofed semis and short terraces with, originally, Neo-Georgian touches. Variation came in house type, building line, finish (brick or render) and details such as bay windows and pediments. The aesthetic harmony visible in early photographs has been destroyed by alterations, e.g. hardly any sash windows survive. Crossing WESTERN AVENUE, to the l. is an example of the pairs of three-storey blocks of flats for childless couples that defined the ends of the transverse avenues. Continuing E on TARBOCK ROAD shows drearier, cheaper post-war construction: meaner, less emphatic chimneys and roofs, fewer bay windows and changes in building line. The tree planting, vital to softening the vistas, disintegrates too.

S down CONLEACH ROAD to the town centre. On the l., first the massive SPEKE FORWARD LEARNING CENTRE, 2001–2, on the site of Speke Park. A sprawling education and community complex by *Dane Ashworth Cottam*, replacing a

---

* There are no pubs in the earlier parts of the scheme because the Corporation initially banned licensed premises from its housing estates. At Speke, as elsewhere, the breweries simply erected them across the road.

number of schools and other facilities. Expanses of vivid blue or orange enliven basic breeze block walls. The blue demarcates the full-height spine corridor. Then the AUSTIN RAWLINSON SWIMMING POOL on North Parade. 1962–5, by the *City Architect's Department*, refurbished 2001–2 in matching orange. On the r., the cut-down remains, identifiable by shallow-pitch roofs and deep windows, of the three-storey four-bedroom terraced houses, 1947, designed by *Keay* for the middle classes. These were rather remarkable, the noble elevations and unusual planning (first-floor sitting rooms) inspired by Liverpool's Georgian terraces. However, their intended occupants never materialised and they were remodelled *c.* 1980. Ahead is the wretched TOWN CENTRE, a far cry from the confidence of Keay's 1946 masterplan. A curiosity, between the shops on CENTRAL PARADE, is a lamp standard of 1953 given by the Unit Construction Company to mark the Coronation. E from the centre, the estate is more monotonous still, lit up only by St Ambrose on HEATHGATE AVENUE (*see* p. 457).

SPEKE BOULEVARD, part of the A561, separates the housing from industry to the N. Construction began in 1938, based on the US parkway concept. At 350 ft (108 metres), including service roads, cycle ways and plantations, it was promoted as the widest in the country, but was eventually completed in 1966 as a more conventional dual carriageway. Landscaped with formal tree planting by *EDAW*, 2000–1. At the E end the massive SCULPTURE called Mersey Wave forms a gateway. 2003, by *Igor Marko* with the lighting artist *Peter Fink*. Two fans of 100 ft (31 metre) high lattice-work aluminium needles, one either side of the road.

Industrial Development

The industrial development N of the Boulevard illustrates the efforts of three generations to attract investment to Merseyside. An INDUSTRIAL ZONE was planned from the outset, set aside to the N. The first factory, begun in 1934 for Goodlass Wall, paint manufacturers, still stands at the end of GOODLASS ROAD, off Speke Hall Road, with a modish streamlined office block. By the mid 1950s nearly all the industrial zone had been haphazardly developed, without the architectural pretensions of its inspiration, the Slough Trading Estate, or the generous formal layout of contemporary Government-funded trading estates such as Team Valley, Gateshead.

E along the Boulevard (actually beyond the Speke Estate and the city boundary) is the HALEWOOD CAR PLANT, built by Ford in 1960–3 here, rather than in SE England, as a result of interventionist industrial policy. Consultant engineers *Posford, Pavry & Partners*. One of a new generation of integrated plants on greenfield sites that drew on the latest American thinking to maximise efficiency. The steel-framed structure is notable for sheer size: the roof covers 50 acres (20 hectares); it was claimed as the largest car factory in Western Europe when completed. To the E, a transmission plant completed in 1964. The 150 ft (45 metre) concrete mushroom WATER TOWER is a landmark.

From 1997 the BOULEVARD INDUSTRY PARK was laid out adjoining to the w to house component suppliers. They occupy units by *Austin-Smith:Lord*, 1998–2000, with landscaping by *EDAW*. An ordered line-up of clean steel boxes, with crisp office units – steel-framed with glass and terracotta cladding tailored to individual requirements – clipped to the corners. An attractive environment created without fuss or extravagance.

Speke Hall

When Christopher Hussey wrote about SPEKE HALL in 1922, [14] he could still grow lyrical over the 'windswept firs', the 'broad grassy glade', the 'fairy arabesque of leaves', the 'sweet scent', the stillness and distance from the 'ever-growing city'. Now behind the trees between the house and river is a taxiway of Liverpool Airport, the air reverberates to the howl of planes, and the hinterland has become all housing and commerce. But the approach remains magical: leaving behind the suburban sprawl, the Hall appears suddenly down an avenue, sunken and part-hidden across fields, nestled between coppices.

The house itself is one of the finest examples of timber framing in the county. It was built by the Norris family. John and Nicholaa de Norreys were recorded as living here in 1314. Elements of a cruck frame embedded in the SE corner are probably the oldest part, but otherwise it is almost completely C16, and quite lightly touched by Victorian restoration. It is laid out around a shady courtyard, and surrounded on three sides by a moat, now dry. William Norris II (1501–68) is the key figure: knighted in 1530 and elected M.P. for Liverpool in 1544, he rebuilt his home on a scale to reflect his rising status. His is the Great Hall, *c.* 1530, and the Great Parlour in the s range, erected immediately afterwards. The w range followed in the mid 1540s. His son Edward (1540–1606) completed the quadrangle in 1598 with the N range and gatehouse and E, kitchen, wing.

In 1795 the estate was purchased by Richard Watt, a merchant and plantation owner (his handsome memorial is in Standish church, q.v.), but over a century of neglect and tenancy was not arrested until Richard Watt V reached his majority in 1856. He restored and refurnished the house in a heavily Baronial fashion before dying tragically young in 1865. The estate was inherited by his eight-year-old daughter Adelaide, and so the Liverpool shipping tycoon, Frederick Leyland, leased Speke for ten years from 1867. Leyland was a

N

1 Vestibule
2 Lamp Room
   (ticket office)
3 Courtyard
4 Corridors
5 Small Dining Room
6 Billiard Room
7 Library

8 Gun Room
9 Great Parlour
10 Great Hall
11 Screens Passage
12 Blue Drawing Room
13 Servants' Hall
14 Kitchen
15 Scullery

Speke Hall (Liverpool).
Ground-floor plan

passionate art collector and patron; Whistler, who spectacularly fell out with him over his decoration of the Peacock Room
in Leyland's London house, stayed at Speke for long periods.
Leyland carried out considerable work on the interior with a
more thoughtful, Aesthetic Movement-tinged antiquarianism.
In 1878 Adelaide moved into Speke and remained there until
her death in 1921. The estate was subsequently sold to the Corporation, which built its new airport and town on the land (*see*
above), and the house passed to the National Trust in 1943.

EXTERIOR. The elevations are quintessentially picturesque,
black-and-white timber framing on a red sandstone plinth with
massive stone chimneys and lots of finialled gables. Mostly
there is big, bold herringbone bracing, but in selected places
are decorative designs, mostly quatrefoils. All around is a coved
and billeted eaves cornice. The uniformity is deceptive: a delib-

erate exercise in continuity which hides a complex building history that is still not fully understood.

A more or less chronological circuit begins on the S lawn, where there is no moat and no certainty that there ever was. The E end of the SOUTH FRONT, lower and set back, is a false-timbered laundry of *c.* 1860, but in it are buried probably the oldest surviving elements, two quite scanty crucks, one scorched by an open hearth. Wind-braces indicate that this extended at least one bay further E and W. A previous hall, or a kitchen? The two bays to the E of the central archway (to the screens passage) are entirely separate builds, as inspection of the join between, the mouldings and quatrefoils will reveal. The W one of the two also predates the present hall. The sandstone ARCHWAY is dated 1605 on the inner face, with sunflowers, the initials of Edward Norris and his wife Margaret and flanking Ionic columns. Open strapwork parapet. One would expect this to face outwards. Perhaps it was turned as part of later landscaping. To the W is the HALL itself, of *c.* 1530 but altered: the only windows originally were probably the upper row; infilled mullions remain. The great sandstone chimney is a puzzle; it is out of alignment and the projecting plinth has no parallels elsewhere in the building, but it has the universal bil-leted cornice. The best explanation is that the base predates the present hall. It is attached to a gabled bay with the only surviving C16 carved bargeboard; all others are restorations. Lastly, the projecting W end bay, the Great Parlour range of *c.* 1531, with a stone porch dated 1612. Its roof was shoddily built, with trusses out of alignment with wall-posts. As the SW corner was exposed to prevailing salt-laden winds, the framing is largely C19 replacement.

The WEST RANGE of *c.* 1544 has weatherboarding and C19 nogging, which are probably a response to the same environ-mental conditions. It is no surprise that this side of the house suffered most decay, being described as a 'complete wreck' in the mid C19. The wing extends N across the line of an earlier moat to terminate as the W bay of the NORTH RANGE. This is more complex than it appears: it seems to be of three phases. After the completion of the W range, one bay was added to the E of the end of the wing, indicated by non-alignment of the herringbone, and a break in the plinth under the second gable. The rest was built by Edward Norris, and commemo-rated by the inscription across the gatehouse – THIS WORKE 25 YARDS LONG, WAS WHOLLY BUILT BY EDW:N:ESQ:ANO1598. The gateway is emphasised with enriched framing – square panels with four spurs to create the effect of diagonally placed quatrefoils and the familiar Elizabethan concave-sided lozenges. The broad moulded arch is flanked by (later?) stone screens, crowned by typically Jacobean heavy cresting, which extend out to a sandstone BRIDGE across the moat. A large timber pointed-arch window occupies the bay to the E of this, with mullions and a transom. It looks an uncomfortable later insertion, but seems improbably prominent to have lit a recusant chapel, as has been suggested (two chapels are mentioned in a 1624 inventory). Projecting from the E end is a single-storey dairy of *c.* 1864 by *W.H. Picton*, Sir James Picton's son.

The EAST RANGE is not fully understood either. The section at the N end now occupied by the kitchen is of *c.* 1598–1602, though its two powerful sandstone chimneys may be later. The window between of seven lights with transom and crude uncusped round heads to the lights, is surely *ex situ*. The whole window is smaller than it sounds here and is typical of a kind lighting the best rooms of Lancashire yeomen's houses of the mid C16. It and the little gables above may be C19 insertions. Ruins of a stone DOVECOTE stand in the corner of a little E courtyard against the revetment of the moat, which is crossed by a stone BRIDGE, possibly of *c.* 1713. Across the bridge are the small STABLES, converted in 1868 from the remnants of a much larger cruck-framed barn. The poor quality of the surviving cruck blades suggests a C16 or later date. Beyond are some altered C17 or earlier COTTAGES.

Through the N porch is the intimate cobbled COURTYARD, deeply shaded by two big yews. Around it, the ranges are densely framed and richly textured by hundreds of protruding pegs, with quatrefoils panels sandwiched between almost continuous windows. These light passages or corridors on both floors on the W and N sides. As the main trusses of the W range roof only extend across the rooms, it seems likely that the passages on this, earlier, side were added during construction. The impression of order and symmetry stems from Edward Norris' decision to ape the form and detail of his father's façades, such as the unusual carved scroll motif rippling down the wall-posts. In each of the S corners is a canted bay added after that range was built. The E one is presumably primarily there to balance the W one, which lights the hall, because behind it are insignificant rooms. One puzzle is a small area of panelling completely unlike anything else at Speke, in the NE corner, part of the building we know is *c.* 1600. The doorway to the S range, into the screens passage, was the principal entrance. It has pilasters either side and urns on the cornice. A sandstone piscina may come from Childwall church (q.v.).

INTERIOR. This description follows the National Trust route. It begins in Edward Norris' N GATEHOUSE, the N and W CORRIDORS and the adjoining four rooms, restored and furnished by Leyland from 1867 with new panelling, door lintels copied from the screens passage, and *Morris* paper. Much of the furniture is Richard Watt's heavy Baronial stuff, reusing Continental carvings.[*] The SMALL DINING ROOM was created out of two smaller rooms. Overmantel with Dutch tiles illustrating Elsenburg, a house near Utrecht. Stone fire surround, with

---

[*] Speke's previous furniture was sold in 1812. It was described in the sales particulars as 'quite new . . . and . . . never used'.

carved stylised plants including sunflowers, copied from an early C17 example in a now demolished local house. Identical example in the BILLIARD ROOM. This had been a kitchen. The LIBRARY has a little fireplace with etiolated columns modelled on those in the Great Hall.

Now on to the SW corner and the mid-C16 STAIRCASE, quite modest to look at now, but relatively ambitious for the date (as is evident from a comparison with the remnants of the simple first staircase of *c.* 1531, out of public view in the attic). Beyond is the GREAT PARLOUR, also dated to *c.* 1531. Described as 'quite ruinous' in 1855. Some of the panelling is replacement, the rest is C16. The very ambitious overmantel is of *c.* 1567. Here are represented three generations of Norrises, Henry (†1534) on the l., Sir William, with two wives and their nineteen children in the middle, and Edward on the r. The prostrate figure at the bottom would seem to be Henry's older brother, killed at the Battle of Pinkie in 1547. Pevsner described the carving as 'ludicrous'; naïve would be kinder. The ceiling PLASTERWORK, however, is extremely accomplished: large panels of pomegranates, lilies, vines and roses between finely moulded beams with hops and honeysuckle trails. This is later, possibly of 1612, the date on the porch leading to the garden, a dating which bears out the comparison with work at Gawthorpe (N Lancashire), a house of 1600–5. The bay-window ceiling is a little later. C17 Continental and C19 armorial STAINED GLASS. Furnished by Richard Watt in overwrought antiquarian fashion. The massive buffet made up of numerous bits of older carving, e.g. a Flemish panel of *c.* 1580, was intended for the GREAT HALL next door. This room contains a number of puzzles. We know the date is *c.* 1530, which must be the origin of the panelled ceiling and the matching wall-posts (tops just visible). The wainscot is clearly of different dates and sources; the fine panelling across the upper end with bas-relief busts and elaborate coving, and the naïve colonnettes all around, are later C16 and obviously *ex situ*. Edward Norris' wife Margaret was from a family of merchants in the Low Countries, a likely source. The bays on both sides of the upper end, and the fireplace in the S bay, have already been discussed. The principal hall fireplace, at the low end, and its massive overmantel, are probably original (although the overmantel cuts into the ceiling panelling). Comparable examples in the same location against the screens wall were at Lydiate Hall (q.v.) and Denton Hall, Cheshire (both demolished). Little Moreton Hall in Cheshire has a similar elaborate overmantel of crenellations and pinnacles decorated with masks. That one is brick, and so is this, in herringbone pattern, beneath the plaster. The bressumer, with cable and vine decoration, is original but the red marble fire surround is by *George Bullock*, who restored the hall in 1808. He also repaired the chequered Swedish limestone paving, which is possibly C17. In the upper windows is STAINED GLASS of *c.* 1490–1500 with the initials of William Norris, †1506, and the Norris raven. This was presumably in the previous hall. In the N windows there are also some C15–early C16 fragments of saints, a devil, etc. from the chapel of St Michael, Garston (q.v.), demolished in the C19, and mid-C16 armorial glass. Two C16 Dutch roundels in the S bay. The SCREENS PASSAGE has richly moulded ceiling beams, befitting the principal entrance until the C19. Behind it is the BLUE DRAWING ROOM, which was surely the room described in 1624 as the Little Parlour. A family room on this side of the screens at that date is quite unusual. More of the armorial STAINED GLASS of *c.* 1530–50 and C15 fragments from Garston chapel. Some decorative elements, e.g. the sunflowers in the fire grate and door surround, are a further reminder of Leyland's interest in Aesthetic design.

Return to the stairs previously seen in the W wing, and climb to the FIRST-FLOOR GALLERY and bedrooms off it. The BLUE BEDROOM, OAK BEDROOM and GREEN BEDROOM are fully panelled in simple Jacobean fashion. The TAPESTRY BEDROOM has one of the few surviving original fire surrounds, with simple pargetting of probably early C17 date over. A special attraction of Speke is the HIDING PLACES and observation holes. The Norrises, like so many of the Lancashire gentry, were recusant Catholic. The Green Bedroom is one of several rooms with concealed access. Here there is a ladder behind the panelling, now exposed by a glass panel in the gallery. Above the courtyard entrance to the screens is a small hole in the eaves – an original 'eavesdrop' – with a concealed room behind.

At the end of the N wing a modern staircase descends to the SERVANTS' HALL. It was possibly once a family chapel (*see* above), but was described as the laundry in 1848 and fitted out in its present form thirty years later. Past the C19 DAIRY is the KITCHEN and SCULLERY.

The GARDEN is being restored by the National Trust as it was laid out by the last Richard Watt in 1855–65. He completed the draining of the moat, in the process formalising its line and creating the tiered embankment on the W side. Until 1967 the grounds extended S through the ancient shelter belt known as the Clough down to the Mersey, but then a taxiway was built when the airport was extended and a bund raised to protect the house from the sight and sound.

HOME FARM. Built by Adelaide Watt, 1885–8. *George Northcroft* of Warminster supervised the works until 1886 and prepared drawings for some of the complex. A Colonel Yeatman-Biggs was also consulted by Adelaide, who took a very close interest in the project. E-plan, with separate engine house. Quarryfaced red sandstone exterior. Gablet roofs. The E yard was covered (cast-iron columns remain, roof lost). A good example of the most advanced agricultural practice of the time, containing stables, shippon, pigsties, cart sheds, slaughterhouse, smithy and storage space, and a ventilation system. Converted by *Brock Carmichael Architects* in 2000–1 into shop, café etc.

NORTH LODGE. 1867–8, by *Thomas Shelmerdine*. Gabled and falsely timber-framed, as one would expect. Extended 1963.

STANLEY *see* TUE BROOK etc.

STONEYCROFT *see* TUE BROOK etc.

TOXTETH

This area bordering the city centre to the SE comprises a large part of Toxteth Park, a former royal hunting ground acquired by Sir Richard Molyneux in 1605. It remained undeveloped until 1771, when the land W of Mill Street, between Parliament Street and Northumberland Street, was laid out in a grid of broad streets. The intention was to form a new town, to be called Harrington, promoted by the builder *Cuthbert Bisbrown*. Apart from St James' church (*see* p. 470) little was achieved. When these streets were eventually built up during the early C19, the large blocks were subdivided and filled with insanitary housing. During the second half of the C19, virtually the whole area W and E of Park Road (with the notable exception of the boulevard leading to Prince's Park, and the hinterland of the Park itself) was densely covered with terraced housing, and dotted with churches and institutions serving a predominantly poor population. In parts this pattern survives, interspersed with cleared sites and the less formal housing layouts of the late C20.

For Prince's Park, Sefton Park and related housing, *see* pp. 451–5.

Religious Buildings

ST BEDE, Hartington Road. An illustration in *The Builder* of 1883 shows a church by *J.E.K. Cutts* and *A.H. Mackmurdo* of red sandstone with a huge SE tower, an E apse to the street and low transepts. The present building is of stock brick and stone dressings, with a gabled E front containing a pair of big Dec windows separated by a niched statue and surmounted by a circular window, flanked by gabled porches. In 1924 *R. Stubbs* rebuilt the church after a fierce fire. The roof, including the fancy but impressive flèche-cum-turret, is certainly his. Was in fact the church completely rebuilt by Stubbs to a new design, or was Cutts and Mackmurdo's design significantly revised, or even abandoned? Of the brilliance and daring of Mackmurdo nothing is noticeable.
  Adjoining l. is a lanceted CHURCH HALL with a little bell-tower, to all appearances a church in itself; adjoining r. is the big VICARAGE, dated 1891.
ST CLEMENT, Beaumont Street. 1840–1, by *Arthur & George Yates Williams* with minor later alterations. Ashlar, simple and rectangular with lancet windows, but there is one weird feature: an octagonal W bell-turret with pointed stone lid, placed over a bay projecting from the W end which is narrower, higher and with a steeper roof than the rest. This contains the gallery stairs, and N and S doors; the W porch is a later addition. Inside, the altar is placed in a shallow polygonal recess. GALLERIES on three sides, carried on cast-iron

columns. 'Hammerbeam' roof with the hammerbeams supported by a further set of iron columns superimposed on the lower ones (and behind the gallery fronts). Braces in both directions and collars with pendants and pierced tracery infill above. SCREEN of 1984 under the W gallery to create parish room. Otherwise the original arrangement and furnishings remain nearly intact, even the two-decker PULPIT with integral reading desk, in front of and obscuring the little communion table – this was a strongly Evangelical church from inception. The pulpit is quite ungainly and rendered asymmetrical by its stairs. Top deck on four iron columns, approached by a separate spiral stair (of 1892, replacing the original straight flight). Classical iron balusters, but Gothic trefoils here and on other furnishings and fittings. – BOX PEWS. Some removed around the pulpit.

This is a rare survival of an all but complete pre-Ecclesiological Victorian church, by luck or design little harmed since Pevsner called for it to be safeguarded.

ST DENIOL (former), Upper Parliament Street. Small brick chapel by *R. Owens & Sons*, opened in 1894 to serve a Welsh-speaking Anglican congregation. Now a furniture shop, and pretty battered about.

ST GABRIEL, Beaufort Street. 1883–4, by *H. & A.P. Fry*. Brick and terracotta.

ST JAMES, St James's Place. 1774–5, built and perhaps designed by *Cuthbert Bisbrown*. Now vested in the Redundant Churches Fund. Red brick with stone dressings. Battlemented W tower with pairs of round-arched belfry openings – was it intended to look Norman? Round-arched side windows in two tiers. Chancel 1899–1900, by *H. Havelock Sutton*. Conventionally Georgian interior, with N, S and W galleries on slender cast-iron columns, an early structural use. The columns are Gothic, quatrefoil in section (octagonal below, where originally hidden by pews), and perhaps derived from the published designs of Batty Langley. Open timber roof with Norman arches, introduced by *William Culshaw*, 1846. – STAINED GLASS. E window by *Henry Holiday*, 1881, presumably re-set when the chancel was built. – MONUMENTS. George Pemberton, †1795, with kneeling figure by an urn; Moses Benson, †1806, with mourning figure by a sarcophagus; and J.E. Irving, †1817(?), with seated figure.

ST MARGARET OF ANTIOCH, Princes Road. 1868–9, by *George Edmund Street*. Paid for by the Anglo-Catholic stockbroker Robert Horsfall, this was the centre of ritualism in C19 Liverpool. *The Architect* wrote in 1869: 'Perhaps, indeed, Mr Street has seldom produced a more thoroughly natural and simple work . . . possessing architectural qualities which will hold their own when fast-Gothic and fast-Art of all kinds have given way to increasing knowledge.' Simple but dignified Dec Gothic exterior of common brick with red stone dressings – the style more English-looking than French, unusually for Street. A timber bellcote marks the division between nave and chancel. In the centre of the W front a buttress with a statue of St Margaret in a niche, flanked by three-light windows and doors straight into each aisle.

Interior much richer, though dilapidated (repairs under way 2005). Five-bay nave without clerestory. Piers with clustered shafts of Irish marbles, laid in bands of alternating colours. Raised chancel, with sedilia and piscina, enclosed by a low marble wall. Divided from the E end of the S aisle by a two-bay arcade is a shallow, transept-like space (the corresponding N arches have been filled, and behind them the separate Jesus Chapel replaces the former 'transept'). Much C19 PAINTED DECORATION on walls and roof: saints, angels, biblical scenes, and Stations of the Cross, with stencilled borders. Particularly beautiful is the Marriage Feast at Cana, W wall. *Maddox & Pearce* appear to have been chiefly responsible, with some earlier work by *Clayton & Bell*; redecoration by *Campbell Smith*, 1967. – Wrought-iron sanctuary GATES by *Skidmore* (also the FONT COVER?). – PULPIT with busts of Doctors of the Church in gilded wood. – HIGH ALTAR with *opus sectile* reredos, post-war. – In the chancel floor, BRASS to Robert Horsfall, †1881, by *Barkentin & Krall*. Horsfall sits at the foot, holding a drawing of the church. – Good STAINED GLASS, mostly *Clayton & Bell*. The scene of Christ blessing the little children, in the N window of the W end, includes another likeness of Horsfall. S aisle W window in German Renaissance style by *Percy Bacon Bros*. – Two large E windows are post-war replacements, designed by *Gerald E.R. Smith* and *H.L. Pawle*, made by the *A.K. Nicholson Studio*. – The JESUS CHAPEL, added on the N by *Hubert B. Adderley*, 1924–6, has C19 stained glass re-set, and an elaborate polychrome Gothic reredos.

The VICARAGE, connected and set at an angle, makes an attractive group with the church.

OUR LADY OF LOURDES AND ST BERNARD (R.C.), Kingsley Road. By *Pugin & Pugin*, opened 1901. Brick with stone dressings. Perp, without a tower, but with a successful W front widened by placing outside the aisles the two porches, which open to the W. There are low-level windows and above, two three-light Perp ones with a niched statue between, and a round window above in the gable. The E window is an odd feature, really just a large traceried window head. Hideously reordered in 1980. The two-bay chancel was abandoned behind a curtain and a worship area created in the E part of the nave orientated diagonally to the SW. Partitioned off behind a screen of old pew parts, the two W bays of the nave and the area under the W gallery now form a hall. All this happens beneath a suspended ceiling.

OUR LADY OF MOUNT CARMEL (R.C.), High Park Street. 1876–8, by *James O'Byrne*. Plain exterior of red brick and red sandstone. Nave with clerestory and aisles, and a narthex across the (ritual) W end. Geometric tracery. Pevsner noted the doorways' 'quadrant jambs and arches dying into them, a motif typical of the most progressive work during the last quarter of the C19'. Inside, arcades with cylindrical polished granite columns, and foliage capitals carved by Mr *Hanley* of Chester. Virtually no division between nave and sanctuary. – Elaborate ALTARS, REREDOSES and ALTAR RAILS of alabaster, added later. – STAINED GLASS in the six-light E window, apparently 1880s. – STATIONS OF THE CROSS, oil paintings by *May Greville Cooksey*, 1928, etc.

PRESBYTERY, l. of the church, added by *O'Byrne*, 1880–1.

ST PATRICK (R.C.), Park Place. 1821–7, by *John Slater*. Brick with stone dressings, and an unusual cruciform plan. The body resembles a Nonconformist chapel, with two tiers of windows and a pedimented gable. The original entrances (disused) are in the W sides of a pair of short, two-storey transepts. These contain stairs up to the galleries, an arrangement used by Slater in his 1817 additions to St Peter, Seel Street (*see* p. 284). Four Greek Doric columns form a porch in front of each entrance. Prominent on the W front is a STATUE of St Patrick, from the St Patrick Insurance Co. building, Dublin. Inside are W, N and S galleries on cast-iron columns (the space under the W one partitioned off). Segmental plaster ceiling. At the E end, framed by giant Corinthian columns, a huge ALTAR PAINTING of the Crucifixion by *Nicaise de Keyser* of Antwerp, *c.* 1834. Said to have been commissioned for a church in Manchester and moved here after a fire; previously wider. In niches, high up to l. and r., Neoclassical STATUES of St Matthew and St Mark. Sanctuary reordered: the present ALTAR may incorporate parts of the 1867 High Altar by *J.F. Bentley*. To the l., a marble RELIEF of the Holy Family, probably from the 1891 altar of St Joseph by Messrs *Boulton* of Cheltenham.

74 GREEK ORTHODOX CHURCH OF ST NICHOLAS, Berkley Street. A close copy, considerably enlarged, of the former church of St Theodore in Constantinople, as illustrated in James Fergusson's *Handbook of Architecture* (1855). The idea of adopting this Byzantine model was due to *W. & J. Hay*, who won a competition in 1864, but building was carried out under *Henry Sumners*, and authorship was disputed when it opened in 1870. Red brick, with much stone. Three domes over the front, a fourth over the nave. They are raised on polygonal drums with round-arched windows on each face. *The Builder* described the stilted round-arched apse windows as 'an ugly and disproportioned feature to which no considerations of archaeology can reconcile us'. Interior spatially impressive, but without the richly coloured decoration that the exterior and the style lead one to expect. Under the W domes a narthex, with gallery overlooking the nave. The plan of nave and aisles is a cross within a rectangle. White marble columns with Byzantine capitals carry the central dome. The four arms have tunnel vaults. E end screened by the richly carved ICONOSTASIS.

ANCIENT CHAPEL OF TOXTETH, Park Road. So called since the 1830s. Associated with Nonconformity from its earliest years, it was licensed as a Presbyterian meeting house in 1672, and is now Unitarian. Built some time between 1604 and 1618 to serve what was then an isolated rural area, it was altered and largely rebuilt in 1774, when the walls were heightened. Some C17 masonry may have been reused. Externally it is a simple box of coursed stone with superimposed pairs of round-arched windows in the SW and NE walls. A little louvred bell-turret on the SE gable; doorway below, enclosed by a porch dated 1906. The present entrance is at the opposite end, through a porch with organ loft above, added in 1841 on the site of a school-house formerly attached to the chapel. Inside, a large arch opens into the chapel. The pulpit – the focus – is placed centrally against the SW wall, framed by the windows. The other walls have GALLERIES on wooden columns: those on the SE and NW seem to predate the 1774 rebuilding (the latter has a pew door dated 1700); the cross gallery only became practicable after the roof was raised. – BOX PEWS throughout; one l. of the pulpit has a door with the date 1650. – BRASS to Edward Aspinwall, †1656, originally set in the floor, now on the SW wall. Just an inscription. – MONUMENTS. Several late C18 and early C19 tablets.

Early C20 MEETING ROOM, etc., NW of the chapel. – Attractive GRAVEYARD, with a mid-C19 classical arcade on the NE side.

WELSH PRESBYTERIAN CHURCH, Princes Road. By *W. & G. Audsley*, opened 1868. Now derelict, but a proud and ambitious design, reflecting the success of Liverpool's C19 Welsh community. Early French Gothic in rock-faced stone. Nave and transepts form a T-plan, with an impressive NW steeple, the spire surrounded by pinnacles. Mostly plate tracery. W gable and crossing roof recently taken down. Brick lecture rooms and vestries behind.

PRINCES AVENUE METHODIST CHURCH. *See* p. 476.

ST PETER'S METHODIST CHURCH, High Park Street. 1877–8, by *C.O. Ellison*. A quirky 'rogue' Gothic design in polychrome brick. Over the door, a big window with plate tracery. A peculiar octagonal turret to its l. grows out of a buttress dividing nave and aisle, supported on the l. by a short flying buttress.

TOXTETH TABERNACLE, Park Road. Large Baptist chapel of 1870–1, by *W.I. Mason*. A bizarre patchwork of styles in polychrome brick and stone. The front has a pediment, above pointed arches springing from pilasters with approximately Corinthian capitals. Between these are three round-arched doorways with foliage capitals.

SYNAGOGUE, Princes Road. The most memorable surviving work of *W. & G. Audsley*, and one of the finest examples of Orientalism in British synagogue architecture. The Audsleys won the competition in 1871, and the building opened in 1874 (replacing one of 1807 in Seel Street, by *John Harrison*). Common brick, with red brick, red sandstone and polished red granite, combining Gothic and Moorish elements. Façade with high, gabled centre and lower wings, reflecting the division into nave and aisles. Centre framed by octagonal turrets. These, and the outer square turrets, had arcaded and domed finials like minarets (removed in 1961, a sad loss). The W door and rose window above are Gothic, but incorporate Moorish lobed

₇₆ arches. Interior dazzlingly rich with polychrome stencilled decoration, restored, but said to follow the original. Pointed horseshoe arcades spring from tapering octagonal columns of cast iron. Plaster tunnel vault over the nave, with transverse vaults. Seats in the aisles and galleries face inwards. The E end is divided off by a giant lobed horseshoe arch, framing the E rose window. Below this is the gleaming focus, the ARK, carved by *Alfred Norbury*, of multi-coloured marbles with five richly painted domes, like something out of the Arabian Nights. In front, the equally rich PULPIT and, further W in the central space, the sumptuous BIMAH, or reading platform (presented in 1875 by David Lewis, founder of Lewis's department store), both also carved by *Norbury*. – STAINED GLASS with abstract and floral patterns, by *R.B. Edmundson & Son* to the Audsleys' designs.

TOXTETH PARK CEMETERY, Smithdown Road. 1855–6, for the Toxteth Park Burial Board. The buildings are by *Thomas D. Barry* and the layout by *William Gay*. This was the first cemetery in the Liverpool conglomeration to be created under the terms of the Burial Acts. One of two CHAPELS survives, the modest and quirkily Dec Anglican one, and two Gothic LODGES on Smithdown Lane. The chapel is stone with a little bell-tower missing its spirelet; the lodges are red brick with stone dressings and spindly chimneys, and there are lovely wrought-iron GATES with Gothic piers between the pair. Gay's LAYOUT is simple but very successful: he exploited the natural dip down the centre of the site by elevating the chapels on terraces levelled from the slopes on either side. From the Smithdown Road entrance one drive runs straight ahead along the bottom of the dip, and two others curve up to the terraces to the l. and r. Gay had used terraces at his earlier cemetery, Undercliffe in Bradford, and almost certainly took the idea from Hamilton & Medland's Leicester General Cemetery, 1847, of which he was the first superintendent.

The terraces face each other across an atmospheric sea of C19 MONUMENTS and headstones. Amongst them are: on the main drive, the classical Pennington memorial, dated 1886, with a medallion above an angel holding a memorial scroll; *c.* 40 yards (35 metres) E of the main entrance, *E.A. Heffer*'s memorial of 1876 to John Perris, librarian of the Liverpool Library – an open book on a square plinth; *c.* 90 yards, (80 metres) SW of the main entrance, Samuel and Elizabeth Mylcrist, †1849 and †1858, a Gothic spire designed by *W. & G. Audsley* and carved by *C. Stirling*; and, on the terrace N of the chapel, a group of four Gothic obelisks and by contrast a large Celtic cross (Samuel Graves M.P., †1873).

Public Buildings

DOCKS. *See* pp. 274.

TOXTETH PUBLIC OFFICES, High Park Street. 1865–6, by *Thomas Layland*. Red sandstone, heavily Italianate, with channelled rustication. Single-storey wings; higher, pedimented centre with round-arched windows. Central room with C17-style garlands in plaster.

TOXTETH LIBRARY, Windsor Street. 1900–2, by the Corporation Surveyor, *Thomas Shelmerdine*. Red brick and stone trim. Symmetrical to Windsor Street, with two big Venetian windows under gables with obelisks, the main entrance with a far-projecting hood. Small cupola above. Two more Venetian windows to Upper Parliament Street. The former reading room (N side) contains a mural by *W. Alison Martin* and *Clinton Balmer*, an allegory with Knowledge enthroned; also a copper plaque in Celtic Art Nouveau style by *C.E. Thompson*, commemorating the opening by Andrew Carnegie.

PARK ROAD SPORTS CENTRE, Steble Street. The older part opened in 1874 as public baths and washhouse. White brick with red sandstone dressings, stepped gables, minimally Gothic.

FLORENCE INSTITUTE FOR BOYS, Mill Street. 1889, probably by *H.W. Keef*. A really good building, now ruinous. Bright red brick with delicate terracotta ornament, with three shaped gables, canted bay windows, and a polygonal turret. Founded by the former mayor Bernard Hall, for the recreation and education of poor working boys.

ADULT DEAF AND DUMB INSTITUTE (former), Princes Avenue. 1886–7, by *E.H. Banner*. Gothic, red brick and terracotta. Basically octagonal, with four short two-storey wings, and single-storey projections between. The form recalls Caröe's Swedish Seamen's Church in Park Lane (*see* p. 286). The ground floor originally contained rooms for recreation, education, etc. The chapel above had tiered seating so the congregation could see the minister's sign language.

GRANBY STREET SCHOOLS. By *T. Mellard Reade*. 1880, with extensions of *c.* 1897–9.

FLORENCE NIGHTINGALE MEMORIAL, Princes Road and Upper Parliament Street. 1913, by *Willink & Thicknesse*, with sculpture by *C.J. Allen*. Subtly detailed Ionic aedicule, framing a relief of her ministering to two men. It is built into the boundary wall of the former LIVERPOOL QUEEN VICTORIA DISTRICT NURSING ASSOCIATION, a nurses' home of 1900 by *James F. Doyle*, incorporating an earlier house on the l. Good Art Nouveau stained glass on the stairs.

TURNER NURSING HOME, Dingle Lane. 1882–5, by *Alfred Waterhouse*. Formerly the Turner Memorial Home (a 'home of rest for chronic sufferers'), erected by Mrs Charles Turner in memory of her husband, M.P. and chairman of the Dock Board, and their son. Picturesquely asymmetrical Gothic in red ashlar. Projecting timber porch, with an elaborate clock and the Perp E window of the chapel to the r., a conical-roofed turret to the l. In the entrance hall, marble STATUE of the Turners, father and son, 1885, by *Hamo Thornycroft*. They are seated, studying what are presumably plans of the Home (though it was designed after their deaths). The CHAPEL is dignified inside, all ashlar, with a N aisle behind an arcade of octagonal columns, and clerestory above. Open timber roof. W gallery with organ. – Alabaster REREDOS with reliefs of Christ healing the sick. – STAINED GLASS. E window, Life of Christ with Ascension, by *Heaton, Butler & Bayne* – Boards with the Ten Commandments, Creed and Lord's Prayer on either side, an old-fashioned arrangement by this date. – SE of the Waterhouse building, a 1990s extension in brick – Attractive LODGE on Dingle Lane, dated 1884.

PARK HILL RESERVOIR, High Park Street. 1853, by *Thomas Duncan*. A steeply battered stone retaining wall encloses the cistern, which has a brick-vaulted roof on a forest of cast-iron columns. Corner tower, originally with conical roof.

BRUNSWICK STATION, Sefton Street. A new station for the redeveloped docks, by *Brock Carmichael Architects*, built 1997–8. Despite a tight budget, robust but elegant, thoughtful and well detailed. A number of other stations in Merseyside have been redeveloped by the practice with the same common design vocabulary. Just s is an INCLINE to the Horsfall Street bridge over the line, erected 1866. Channelled ashlar and rustication, with urinals and a horse trough.

HOLYOAKE HALL (former), Smithdown Road. A Co-operative hall dated 1914, red terracotta with buff dressings, including the legends 'Co-operation' and 'Unity'. Free Style.

Perambulations

An important focus is the wide, straight boulevard made up of PRINCES ROAD, 'in the course of formation' in 1843, and PRINCES AVENUE, which runs parallel and dates from the 1870s. This is a unique example of formal planning on a large scale in C19 Liverpool, lined with three-storey terraced houses of the 1870s–80s, with some late C20 infill on a sadly reduced scale. Earlier houses are mostly of yellow brick and minimally Gothic; later ones, closer to the park, of red brick with columned porches and classical details in moulded terracotta. Behind, there is a sudden change of scale to the simplest of two-storey houses, in streets mostly laid out and built up during the 1860s–70s. Halfway down on the NE side, PRINCES AVENUE METHODIST CHURCH, *c.* 1965, with a metal SCULPTURE of Christ by *Arthur Dooley* attached. The pose suggests both Crucifixion and Resurrection. At the Upper Parliament Street end of Princes Road, next to the Synagogue (*see* p. 473), STREATLAMTOWER, 1871, by *W. & G. Audsley*, a large Gothic house of common brick and red sandstone, with a conical-roofed tower. Built for the wool broker James L. Bowes and his collection of Japanese art. Opposite, the KUUMBA IMANI MILLENNIUM CENTRE, by *Brock Carmichael*, 2004. A glazed stair projection with a bold, stone-faced fin signals the entrance. Further NW, next to the Greek Orthodox church (*see* p. 472), a drive-in NATWEST BANK, *c.* 1982, by *Gerald*

Beech. Brick, with rounded corners clad in stainless steel, and a mansard roof. sw of here, in Windsor Street, interesting buildings for Toxteth TV by *Union North*, 2003. One block is polychrome brick, one timber-clad.

For GROVE PARK, *see* p. 455.

A few buildings of interest are scattered along or near the busy main road made up of St James's Place, Park Place and Park Road. At the corner of Stanhope Street and Grafton Street (reached via Parliament Street), the BREWERY of Robert Cain. *James Redford* designed the rear part, completed 1887. The splendid five-storey red brick façade dated 1902 may be by Walter W. Thomas. It has elaborate Renaissance decoration in terracotta. The height drops at the corner for THE GRAPES, the brewery tap. The brewery was taken over in the 1920s by Higson's, who inserted their name into the decoration, but Cain's monogram and gazelle symbol are everywhere. On Park Road at the corner of Northumberland Street, the four-storey brick warehouse of COLEMAN'S FIREPROOF DEPOSITORY, a landmark on account of the red and white ceramic lettering emblazoned across it. The topmost inscription says it was rebuilt in 1900. Further along Park Road, s of Upper Park Street, the former LIVERPOOL SAVINGS BANK, South Branch, *c.* 1882, by *G.E. Grayson*. Stone, Renaissance, with mullioned-and-transomed windows. Near the SE end of Park Road, bounded by Byles Street and Miles Street, is the earliest of Liverpool's new-build co-operative housing schemes, WELLER STREETS, opened 1982. The leading role of tenants in designing their new houses was pioneered here; the architect was *Bill Halsall* of *Wilkinson, Hindle & Partners*. The simple red brick houses are grouped into L-shaped blocks enclosing landscaped courts, branching off a cul-de-sac.

TUEBROOK, OLD SWAN,
STANLEY and STONEYCROFT

3 m. ENE of the city centre. Lots of dense Late Victorian and early Edwardian bylaw streets, but some outstanding buildings too.

Churches

ST JOHN THE BAPTIST, West Derby Road, Tuebrook. 1867–70, by *G.F. Bodley*. A large, unshowy, but dignified and sensitive building, lying back and parallel to the road, and a key work in Bodley's *oeuvre*. For this was the first time he achieved fully his mature style, abandoning Continental models to embrace C14 English church architecture. The entire £25,000 cost was met by the wife of the Rev. J.C. Reade.* Red and buff stone, irregularly banded, an unusual feature for the 1860s. w steeple, long nave and aisles, a clerestory, and a lower chancel. The

* Her mother had done the same for St James, West Derby (*see* p. 501).

unadorned spire is bluntly recessed with flying buttresses from
pinnacles, Lincolnshire fashion. Only to the s, by the e end, is
there more liveliness, with the little forecourt of the vestry.
The features are a restrained and refined Dec; this turn to
simplicity is one aspect of the turn from High to Late
Victorian. The interior big but architecturally very simple too
– in fact it would hardly be notable if it were not for the
resplendent array of Bodley fittings and the vibrant decoration,
restored by *S.E. Dykes Bower* in 1968–71. The whole is
glorious. High nave of five bays with octagonal piers. The
clerestory windows are over the spandrels not the apexes of
the arcade arches. Eastlake in 1872 wrote as follows: 'For
correctness of design, refined workmanship, and artistic
decoration, this church may take the foremost rank among
examples of the Revival.'

DECORATION and FURNISHINGS. Glorious, richly coloured
STENCILLING of all the walls and all the roofs, including the
arch-braced trusses of the nave. Dykes Bower's restoration,
whilst undoubtedly magnificent in its overall and overwhelming results, is not straightforward. He followed not Bodley's
original scheme but the redecoration of 1910, designed by
Bodley and implemented by his partner *H.T. Hare* (Bodley
died in 1907), which introduced a different design to parts of
the aisle walls.* Dykes Bower also redecorated the clerestory
walls with a simpler pattern; the original was closer to that of
the arcade spandrels, which are Bodley's. – WALL PAINTING
by *C.E. Kempe* on the e wall of the nave: a superb Tree of the
Cross, with low-relief figures, over the chancel arch. Dykes
Bower overpainted the Jesse Tree on the w wall with his
clerestory stencil design (why?). – REREDOS. 1871. High and
gilt, with the e window high up above it, as Bodley liked but
not as he originally intended. The first, an early C16 Antwerp
altarpiece with wings (now in St Michael and All Angels,
Brighton) so offended the Bishop of Chester with its 'Popish'
carved tableaux of the Passion that he refused to consecrate
the church until it was removed. The present panels are painted
by *Kempe*, but have been crudely restored (not Dykes Bower).
The TABERNACLE and RETABLE date from 1942, the work
of a parishioner. – Under the tower is a chapel with another
gilt REREDOS, made up in 1978 from a *Bodley* screen from
Dunstable Priory Church in Bedfordshire. – NAVE ALTAR.
2003, also constructed out of bits from the Dunstable screen.
– ALTAR of 1948 in s aisle, with frontal made up of discarded
choir stalls. – PULPIT and FONT. *Bodley*. Font octagonal on
Purbeck marble shafts, with pyramidal cover. – SCREENS.
Bodley, obviously. Superb chancel screen with coving and a loft
parapet richly painted with flower panels and scenes. The
panels are by *Kempe* again. Screens also to the n chapel and

---

* The original wall painting was coming away from the walls by 1905. The vicar in
1905 commented ruefully, 'It costs a good deal to live up to Mr Bodley.'

to the S ORGAN, which is one composition with its case. –
PAINTINGS. Eight early C20 copies of Old Masters. Frames
with shutters and Gothic cresting. – STAINED GLASS. E
window of 1868 by *Morris & Co.*, not too well preserved. Also
theirs, the more impressive chancel S window with musicians
in two tiers on blue clouds, and the chancel N and S aisle W
windows by *Burne-Jones.* – Excellent BRASS designed by *Hare*,
1926. A life-size figure of the Rev. Ralph Brockman. – WAR
MEMORIALS. Unusually these are both statues. The First
World War one is a bad Mary by *Hare*, that to the 1939–45 conflict a much better John the Baptist by *Sir Ninian Comper*, from
1952. – The big VICARAGE, completed in 1890, is *Bodley* too.
Brick with mullioned-and-transomed windows and some
charming Queen Anne Revival interiors, especially the staircase hall. – PARISH HALL. By *Alfred Shennan.* 1931, rebuilt by
him in 1949.

ALL SAINTS, Broad Green Road, Old Swan. By *Thomas D. Barry
& Son.* Begun 1871, consecrated 1875. Rock-faced, in the Dec
style with large windows; without a tower, but with transepts.
A reasonable exterior, but the interior is unimpressive. –
REREDOS, *c.* 1910, possibly by *James F. Doyle.* – SANCTUARY,
including ALTAR RAILS and flooring, 1910 and definitely by
Doyle.

ST ANNE, Cheadle Avenue, Stanley. 1889–90, by *Aldridge &
Deacon*, replacing a preaching box of 1831. Solid, but they
were capable of designing with much greater imagination (e.g.
St Dunstan, Earle Road, *see* p. 411). Rock-faced, with a strong,
square S tower. Lancet windows and windows with plate
tracery. Nave, aisles, clerestory. Spacious interior, ashlar-faced,
with quatrefoil piers. The clerestory has detached arcading of
chamfered shafts without capitals and pointed arches towards
the inside. W screen of columns for a shallow (too shallow) and
low former baptistery now in a parish hall, created at the W
end of the church *c.* 1969. This was completely redone by
Anthony Grimshaw Associates in 1999 with an M section ceiling
to re-open views from the body of the church to the W window
and the baptistery. – Good-quality alabaster REREDOS by
Charles Aldridge, *c.* 1893. Three-bay arcade containing a relief
Last Supper. – Fine wrought-iron S chapel screen by *Joseph
Hodel*, 1909, replaced in 1972 by glazed DOORS. – STAINED
GLASS. E window and S chapel E window, by *Walter Lonsdale*,
executed by *Heaton, Butler & Bayne*, 1890. – Churchyard
cleared on the S side with the exception of the TOMB of the
Harrison family. Thomas Fenwick Harrison erected the
present church as a memorial to his father Thomas, who
founded the family shipping line.

ST PAUL, Derby Lane, Stoneycroft. By *Giles Gilbert Scott*,
1913–16, i.e. an early work, and outstandingly inventive and
good, as Giles Scott's early churches can be. It was paid for by
H. Douglas Horsfall, of the exceptional Liverpool family of
church builders (*see* p. 447). The EXTERIOR is entirely original. Severe, faced in pale grey brick, with a mighty central

tower crowned by a pyramid roof. This rises between the middle pair of three sets of bold transeptal projections, each with in its end wall a group of three very tall lancets recessed within a blank arch, and each with (of all things) a half-hipped roof. More arched recesses on the tower, two on each face, contain the belfry openings. Such details set off the great expanses of plain wall. The whole thing is terrifically sculptural and it all comes off beautifully. On the (ritual) s side between the three projections are tiny doorways in low masonry blocks. The structure is unusual, and is causing severe headaches – a brick sandwich containing a mass concrete filling. Inside, the three 'crossings' are three high and square groin-vaulted bays, separated from each other, and framed on the N and S sides (i.e. in the transepts) by short, pointed tunnel vaults. These vaults spring from massive square internal piers attached to the walls and pierced by low passages (themselves groin-vaulted), the motif of St Front at Perigueux and other churches in SW France that inspired English architects from the 1840s on. The chancel is up steps under the E 'crossing' with a chapel in its S transeptal projection and the organ loft and choir vestry in the N. – Interior DECORATION is very chaste. Plain white plasterwork with brick exposed only as dressings, and simple joinery, sparsely but carefully detailed. – WAINSCOT, altar CANOPY, SEDILIA, STALLS, PEWS, etc. – ALTAR RAIL. Bronze. Elegantly simple, with striking abstract Gothic detailing. – Low PULPIT, built into the low chancel wall. The most lavishly Gothic element, with blank Flamboyant tracery. – The ORGAN CASE incorporates a fine C18 front from the instrument of St Paul, St Paul's Square, Liverpool (1769), which closed in 1901 (*see* p. 39).

ST CECILIA (R.C.), Green Lane, Tuebrook. *Sandy & Norris* of Stafford, 1930. Detailed in a kind of Italian Romanesque. No tower, but gabled projections N and S at both ends. The W end has two corner turrets flanking a tall round arch in which the three-light W window and W entrance are deeply recessed. Brick with concrete dressing.

ST OSWALD (R.C.), St Oswald's Street, Old Swan. Of the church of *c.* 1840–2 by *A.W.N. Pugin* only the W steeple remains. It is Dec, of red sandstone, and has a broach spire and fine carved detail. The church itself was totally rebuilt in 1951–7 by *Adrian Gilbert Scott*. Exterior, of brick apart from the W front, conventional if boxy, with four-light Perp windows in the aisles. Not so the large, broad interior, where red ashlar gives way at head height to painted concrete. From little square arcade piers spring big hyperbolic concrete arches in four directions, that is across the nave, the aisles, and between the piers. The effect is certainly unusual, but not very successful. – High ALTAR with multi-marble BALDACCHINO. – Nave altar and LECTERN on a platform. – PRESBYTERY by *E.W. Pugin*, 1857.

The picturesque group of buildings gathered around courts and cloisters under the shadow of the spire s of the church evokes Pugin's ideal of a medieval Christian community. All are in red sandstone. There are two buildings with gable ends to the road. On the l. is a single-storey former SCHOOL, dated by Kelly to 1855 but appearing on an 1849 Ordnance Survey map. *A. W.N. Pugin* appears to have added a school by 1844, but is this it? It is very simple with plain mullioned windows. To the r. is a screen wall and at the end of this is another former school, of two storeys and T-plan, with paired trefoil-headed lancets and a little three-light Dec window in the street end. Stylistically this could be Pugin, but it is not on the 1849 map. In the wall between the two schools is the doorway to the tiny CONVENT OF MERCY, almost certainly by *Pugin*. The door opens into one of Pugin's long cloisters and at the end of this, attached to the rear of the smaller school, is the little convent building, L-shaped with M-pattern roofs and the same windows as the second school. The traceried window at the back lights the little first-floor chapel. There are only eight cells. Construction of the convent was not quite complete when the nuns moved in in 1845 (though, confusingly, it does not appear on the map either).* – S of this group is the PARISH HALL, a former Methodist chapel of 1845. A little brick box with round-headed windows and a stuccoed façade with scrolled attic and antefixa on the parapet.

STONEYCROFT WESLEYAN CHAPEL, Greenfield Road, Old Swan. By *Green & Parslow* of Liverpool. Foundation stone 1867. Rock-faced red sandstone, no tower. Barn interior with only a W GALLERY. – STAINED GLASS. W window with a bold and bright pattern. – Attached HALL at the rear.

Public Buildings

LISTER DRIVE, Stanley, was laid out by the Corporation from the late 1890s with a very generously spaced row of municipal buildings along its s side. Perhaps more than anywhere else this embodied the city's commitment to municipal improvement at the turn of the C20. *Thomas Shelmerdine*, City Surveyor, almost certainly had a hand in all. At the W end was a large power station of *c.* 1902 generating electricity for the trams (a common arrangement at the time), with a fine *Shelmerdine* front, now demolished.

Next, the former LISTER DRIVE BATHS of 1901–4. *W.R. Court*, the Corporation's Baths Engineer, planned the building, and executed elevations from 'sketch designs' provided by *Shelmerdine*. They are indeed instantly recognisable as his, in an asymmetric and stripy free English Renaissance style. Shaped gables, assorted C17- and C18-inspired windows and entrances. The L-plan building provided men's first-class and second-class plunge baths, first- to third-class private baths, and women's private baths. Women were able to use the first-class plunge bath on allotted days. The building is remarkably

---

* Information kindly supplied by Timothy Brittain-Catlin.

well preserved in its current use as a pet shop. The interior is lined with colourful glazed tile and brick supplied by *Pilkington & Co.* The best, not surprisingly, are in the first-class baths, with their little ceramic balcony, and pool subdivided by breeze-block walls into pens full of Koi carp! Tiled arcades, the piers with charming fish and leaf designs by *C.F.A. Voysey.** There are variations on the leaf pattern elsewhere in the building. The other plunge bath is plainer, and has a wooden floor inserted. Both are entered from a tiled entrance hall, small but still with room for a grand little staircase.

Then, until 2005, was a very large SCHOOL with some classical detailing. Finally, the LIBRARY on the corner with Green Lane. 1904–5. Another in the series of lively, well-detailed branch libraries by *Shelmerdine*. A corner composition with a pretty fat turret and C17 windows and other, more Wrenaissance details. Red brick and stone dressings.

SLAUGHTERHOUSE (former), Prescot Road, Stanley. 1929–31, by the architects of the office of the City Surveyor *A.D. Jenkins*. Very large and brick, with some Wrenaissance stone detailing and a thin central tower. Unexpectedly outshone by the altogether more accomplished ashlar LODGES, refined Neoclassical cuboids with, on each face, Tuscan pilasters *in antis* framing architraves, and a dentilled cornice entablature all around. The removal of the Liverpool cattle market to Stanley in 1830 was a key stimulant of development in the area.

WEST DERBY COMPREHENSIVE SCHOOL, Queens Drive. 1956–7, by *H.E. Davies & Son* with the City Architect. The layout was driven by the desire to retain the maximum number of trees. Immediately N is the former BLESSED AMBROSE BARLOW SCHOOL. A satisfyingly crisp design completed in 1961, though in 2005 in need of some care and attention. The architects were *Weightman & Bullen*.

RATHBONE HOSPITAL, Mill Lane, Old Swan. Built *c.* 1901–10 in more than one phase as the City Hospital East, presumably by the City Surveyor, who designed the City Hospital North at this time (*see* p. 428). But for the most part it is not up to the standard one expects of *Shelmerdine*. The fine exception is the delightful Arts and Crafts building r. of the entrance. It is not big, of two storeys, and on a staggered plan that pivots about a pretty octagonal turret with pyramidal roof. Brick, with attractive details including flush unmoulded mullioned windows and boxy, rendered oriels, three in a neat row on the street side.

Perambulations

But very short ones. At TUE BROOK, at the extreme E end of WEST DERBY ROAD is No. 695, TUE BROOK HOUSE, dated

* Thanks to Penny Beckett for this information.

1615 and thus the oldest dated house in Liverpool. It is a yeoman's house now closely set between suburban semis. Limewashed stone with red sandstone dressings and stone-flagged roof. Centre bay and two cross-wings. All front windows low and mullioned, of five lights, symmetrically arranged, except in the centre, where the plain, unmoulded doorway is set to the r. to allow for the five-light house-part window. The mullions are perfectly plain too. Further w on the s side, No. 354 may be as old, or older, but is heavily altered. Probably a single-storey stone and thatch cottage with an end baffle-entry plan (blocked door with massive lintel, r.), subsequently raised in brick and given a slate roof. w of GREEN LANE, with its villagey row of cottages and houses, Nos. 340–352 are an early C19 terrace of seven three-bay houses in chequered brick, the end ones pedimented. (For MUIRHEAD AVENUE, *see* p. 404). Finally, opposite St John's church, a former branch of the Bank of Liverpool of *c.* 1910, possibly by *James F. Doyle*. Corner site; French classicism. Banded ashlar ground floor, brick upper, mansard roof. Entrance in the cut-back corner, with attached Doric columns supporting a convex entablature. Above this a projecting Liver Bird and swags, and a wreathed *œil de bœuf* in the roof.

The district of OLD SWAN is so called after no fewer than three INNS on PRESCOT ROAD bearing variations of that name. One survives, C18 and C19 and altered. Opposite, two banks side by side make an entertaining comparison. Rising to the occasion at the junction of five streets is BARCLAYS, formerly the Bank of Liverpool, by *Grayson & Ould* – vigorously eclectic and stripy, with a cupola'd turret, Dutch gables, oriels, Gibbs surround around the door, and more; probably of *c.* 1905. The HSBC is straightforward inter-war Neo-Georgian of one storey, but has a later top storey, boldly – but disastrously – put on in an unmistakably 1960s style. The Edwardian bank forms a splendid termination to BROAD GREEN ROAD, heading SE. On it MAY PLACE, shown on Perry's Map of 1768. One of a tiny number of merchants' villas built in the countryside around Georgian Liverpool to survive (*see also* Olive Mount, Wavertree, p. 498). Red brick, of five bays, with a three-bay pediment and some sparing decoration of the middle window, and a Doric porch. The roof is as new as the large wings – the house was heightened by a storey, and extensions thrown out, when it was a convent. The crude new wings, though 'respectfully' lower and set back, are blithely and ignorantly at odds with the house's elegant proportions. Further s, CUNNINGHAM ROAD, typical 1920s municipal semis and short terraces, but made of concrete blocks. Off the road to the sw, OAK HILL PARK, said to have been begun in 1865 by Richard Radcliffe (*see* below). By 1904 there were some twenty-five villas; only half a dozen survive, none of great interest. Finally, at the end of the street, the GARDENER's ARMS, by *Harold E. Davies & Son*, opened 1924. One of their refined classical pubs, this one very much in the tradition of the Reilly school.

STONEYCROFT as an urban settlement is the creation of a lawyer, Richard Radcliffe, son of another developer of the same name (*see* p. 504). His development E of GREEN LANE includes the plain mid-Victorian stucco terraces in DERWENT ROAD WEST, later and larger brick houses in DERWENT SQUARE, and terraced sandstone cottages in SANDSTONE ROAD and HIGHFIELD ROAD. The cottages are not mean, with front gardens, some in set-backs, some with Doric-pilastered doorcases and big ground-floor windows. The plan, it is claimed, is derived from Bloomsbury. It does not look much like Bloomsbury. Construction began *c.* 1851 (the date on MERCERS TERRACE in Sandstone Road) and came to a halt in 1867 when the money ran out. Presumably the similar houses in neighbouring streets such as DERBY LANE, WOBURN HILL and ALBANY ROAD are Radcliffe's work too?

VAUXHALL

The square mile N of the centre. Development began with the construction of the Leeds and Liverpool Canal at the end of the C18. During the C19 the town advanced northward, shadowing the inexorable progress of the docks. The growth of industry round the canal, and the arrival of the railways with their goods yards from the 1840s, were accompanied by a tide of notorious slum housing. Construction of the approach roads to the second Mersey Tunnel, Kingsway (completed 1974), entailed much demolition, and economic decline in the late C20 erased more of the historic fabric. When Pevsner wrote in the 1960s, streets close to the river were still ravines of multi-storey brick warehouses. Sadly few survive; in their stead low-rise sheds. In housing the changes have been even more marked. Early C20 and post-war council flats have largely been replaced by informally grouped co-operative housing, and private developers have built in the same style. Elsewhere, large tracts of cleared land await reuse.

ST ANTHONY (R.C.), Scotland Road. 1832–3, by *John Broadbent*, a pupil of Rickman. When built it lay right at the N end of the town. Gothic, with lancet windows throughout. W front of ashlar, with gabled and pinnacled centre breaking forward. Stuccoed, battlemented side elevations with pairs of lancets between buttresses. The interior is exceptionally impressive: a broad, lofty space under a flat, panelled ceiling, uninterrupted by columns or side galleries. E end filled with three giant-arched niches of equal height, the wider central one containing the High Altar, with subsidiary altars l. and r.; statues in canopied niches flank the big arches. The altars have high and elaborate REREDOSES by *Broadbent*, the central one, perhaps designed in 1837, with three steep gables separated by pinnacled buttresses, like a cathedral façade in miniature. They are of carved stone, painted. On the rear wall of the W gallery, two carved PANELS of the Nativity and Epiphany, believed to be C17 Spanish or Portuguese. – STAINED GLASS of 1933 in the window over the High Altar. Under the church, a brick-vaulted crypt with over six hundred burial spaces.

ST ALBAN (R.C., former), Athol Street. 1849, by *Weightman & Hadfield*. Gothic, in the irregular, squared masonry that A.W.N. Pugin approved of. Impressively sturdy looking, especially the side away from the river, which has big buttresses linked by a continuous plinth. Square, battlemented tower. Interior converted into a rock-climbing centre and largely obscured. High pointed arches on round columns. Very tall, narrow nave with open timber roof.

OUR LADY OF RECONCILIATION (R.C.), Eldon Street. 1859–60, by *E.W. Pugin*. The church lies along the street. Clerestoried nave and aisles in rock-faced stone, with w rose window and a little bell-turret on the steep w gable. The clerestory windows are sexfoils. The impressive round E apse hints at the more interesting interior. Apse and nave form a single lofty space under one continuous roof. The relatively narrow aisles have arcades with widely spaced round columns, giving good sight-lines for a congregation of 1,800. This practical but dignified arrangement was Pugin's response to the need for large but economical urban churches. It is a very early example of the type, just predating J.L. Pearson's more famous St Peter, Vauxhall, in London. Interior brutally reordered, with a suspended ceiling over part, and the altar moved against the s wall.

ST SYLVESTER (R.C.), Silvester Street, by *Pugin & Pugin*, opened 1889. Quite a large church (and yet close to St Anthony), in red Ruabon brick with red sandstone. Main entrance through the prominent pyramid-roofed tower that stands close to the street, connected to the church by a passage. Elaborate HIGH ALTAR and REREDOS, 1906.

LIVERPOOL COMMUNITY COLLEGE, Vauxhall Road and Pumpfields Road. By *Ellis Williams Architects*, completed 2002. Red brick, with silver-coloured cladding.

DOCKS. *See* pp. 276–80.

LEEDS AND LIVERPOOL CANAL. The canal runs N–S through the area. Begun 1770, the section from Liverpool to Wigan opened in 1774 and immediately became the principal route for coal into Liverpool. The full length opened in 1816, linking the growing port with the manufacturing towns of E Lancashire and Yorkshire. The terminus was in Old Hall Street (*see* p. 330), and there were branches E of what is now Pall Mall. Manufacturing, including gas and chemical works, was drawn to the canal by the transport opportunities it offered, and by the ready availability of coal. These industries have all but disappeared, and the whole canal s of Burlington Street is now filled in, but evidence of its route can still be seen. On the E side of PALL MALL, N of Leeds Street, WAREHOUSES with cast-iron arched entrances, mostly single-storey. Some are late C19, others perhaps early C20. They were built on the w bank, with direct access to the wharf. Just N of these, in CHISEN-HALE STREET, a former canal BRIDGE, with pedimented abutments and Gothic cast-iron railings. Further N, where the waterway survives with newly landscaped banks, LEIGH BRIDGE (1861) and BOUNDARY BRIDGE (1836, widened 1861). In 1848 the canal was connected to the dock system and the Mersey by a sequence of four locks designed by *J.B. Hartley*, linked with Stanley Dock (*see* p. 279).

RAILWAY VIADUCT. W of the canal and parallel with the river, built 1846–8 by *William McCormick* and *S. & J. Holme*; chief engineer *James Thomson*. Red brick with stone dressings, originally over a mile long, with 117 arches. It was built for the Liverpool & Bury Railway, which after mergers during construction became the Lancashire & Yorkshire Railway; the terminus was Exchange Station in Tithebarn Street (*see* p. 338). Now linked to the Merseyrail underground system. The L&YR was carried over the London & North Western Railway line by a tremendous ARCH with a span of *c.* 100 ft (30 metres). The arch can be entered from the car park on the W side of Pall Mall, between Chadwick Street and Leeds Street. An oval plaque on each face, dated 1849, bears a Liver Bird and the names of the engineer *John Hawkshaw* and the contractors *McCormick* and *Holmes* (sic). In the 1970s the line was cut back to this point, where the tracks now plunge below ground. In the 1880s an additional stretch of viaduct was built in connection with the enlargement of Exchange Station. Some of its blue-brick arches survive along the W side of Love Lane, N of Chadwick Street and E of the original viaduct.

The second MERSEY ROAD TUNNEL, called KINGSWAY. First stage opened 1971; completed 1974. On Waterloo Road is the imposingly sculptural VENTILATION TOWER by *Bradshaw, Rowse & Harker*. Like a concrete rocket on its launch pad.

WAREHOUSING. The most impressive survivors are the enormous CLARENCE WAREHOUSES, Great Howard Street, easily the largest group of private warehouses left in the city, and when designed and built *c.* 1844 by *S. & J. Holme* for P.W. Brancker, the largest to date. Eleven separate stacks of six storeys within one shell relieved by only the most meagre embellishment. They were among the first fireproof warehouses (i.e. with iron columns supporting floors of iron beams and brick jack arches) in the town and were probably intended for multiple letting. Together with the nearby Stanley Dock warehouses (*see* p. 279) they make up the last large-scale remnant of a distinctive Liverpool townscape. At the other end of the scale is a group on WATERLOO ROAD, the dock road, flanking the bottom of Vulcan Street. They include a handsome mid-C19 pedimented fireproof warehouse (including iron lintels) and around the corner in Porter Street – a gulley of cut-down warehouses – a non-fireproof warehouse (iron columns but wooden floors) dated 1884 on the lively gable. *See* p. 485 for canal-side warehouses.

SCOTLAND ROAD, the main artery of a once teeming neighbourhood, was largely demolished in the later C20 and is now just a wide, busy highway. One of the few C19 survivors is immediately N of St Anthony, a former branch of the LIVERPOOL SAVINGS BANK, 1882, by *G.E. Grayson*. Stone, with a round corner tower.

HOUSING. The streets around Our Lady of Reconciliation had some of Liverpool's earliest municipal housing, but little remains. In ELDON GROVE are three blocks of three-storey flats, currently derelict, built in 1910–12 as part of a slum-clearance scheme. They have access balconies across the front, reached by open stairs, and are surprisingly decorative with bay windows and half-timbered gables. Projecting towers at the rear, triangular in plan and originally open-sided, provided each flat with an outdoor yard, WC and access to a refuse chute. The blocks face S onto an open space, originally with separate playgrounds for boys and girls, with a bandstand in the middle. In BEVINGTON STREET and SUMMER SEAT, S, are two-storey terraced houses forming part of the same scheme, dated 1911. They are cottagey-looking in brick and render, some with gables, set back slightly to break up the line of the terrace.

Between Vauxhall Road and Love Lane is the ELDONIAN VILLAGE, occupying the site of a demolished sugar refinery. The first phase, S of Burlington Street, was built 1987–90; phase two, N, was finished in 1995. Nationally, it was one of the biggest community-architecture schemes of the 1980s. Housing and layout were designed with the participation of future residents, who formed a co-operative for the purpose. Their architects were *Wilkinson Hindle Halsall Lloyd*. The Village has a mix of bungalows and houses, in pairs and short terraces. All have gardens, and are arranged round culs-de-sac called courts, branching off a winding spine road. To avoid the uniformity seen as typical of municipal housing, planning is informal and materials – mostly brick and stained wood – differ in colour from court to court. Internal layouts are varied to suit tenants' individual requirements. The architecture may not be aesthetically adventurous, but in its complete transforma-tion of an industrial wasteland and its preservation of an estab-lished community the Village is a remarkable achievement. A village hall and other community buildings, also by *Wilkinson Hindle Halsall Lloyd*, are on Vauxhall Road.

WALTON

Until 1699 Liverpool was a part of Walton-on-the-Hill parish. Since the late C19 Walton has been a nondescript suburb to the NE of the city centre.

ST MARY, County Road. Red ashlar. The parish church of Walton. An ancient foundation, though no ancient architec-tural features survive. The impressive W tower is of 1829–32, by *John Broadbent*. Dec-cum-Perp. For the date, quite archae-ologically correct – Broadbent was Rickman's pupil – though the quatrefoiled-circle windows are a giveaway. The N side was

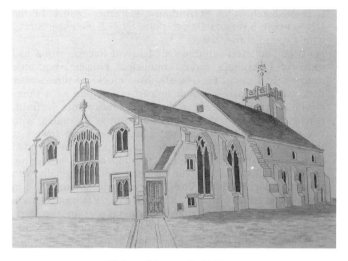

Walton (Liverpool), St Mary.
Drawing of 1811, before rebuilding

remodelled in 1840 and the close buttresses and perhaps
the windows suit that date. Chancel rebuilt in 1843; S aisle
(a chapel), ambulatory and vestry 1911, by *Nagington &
Shennan*. Rebuilt 1947–53 by *Quiggin & Gee* after being completely burnt out by incendiary bombs. Externally as before,
but the interior is all new, concrete vaults on a steel frame, in
a discreet Gothic. The nave vault springs low down, from the
level of the window sills. W GALLERY (intended for the choir)
of stone, on three arches with pierced tracery between and
above: like a (stone) minstrels' gallery above a screens passage.
– REREDOS, Lady Chapel. Including a copy by *Vincenzo Corsi*,
1860, of the Deposition by Fra Angelico. Once at Haigh Hall
(q.v.) – FONT. Norman, but cruelly hacked about. Red sandstone, massive and circular. The top moulding is now a coarse
egg-and-dart, and below are six carved panels representing,
amongst others, the Temptation, the Flight into Egypt and the
Annunciation. These are separated by foliate panels. Broken
into pieces in 1941 and restored by *E. Carter Preston*. – CROSS
SHAFT, Anglo-Saxon fragment, with interlace panels and a
panel with a running scroll. – STAINED GLASS by *E. Carter
Preston*.

Atmospherically leafy CHURCHYARD with gnarled trees, and
a fat early C18 baluster SUNDIAL. In the Walton Village section
of the boundary wall are side-by-side a HEARSE HOUSE and
MORTUARY. Both derelict, red sandstone and earlier C19. The
mortuary has a crude pediment and crude, and odd, rustica-

tion; the hearse house has a two-centred arch and, formerly, had castellation. – OLD RECTORY. *See* Alsop High School, p. 491.

ST JOHN EVANGELIST, Rice Lane. First part 1876–8, by *Aldridge & Deacon*; completed by *Deacon* with addition of the W end in 1897. Quarry-faced red sandstone, with lancet windows and, in the aisles, plate tracery. Thoughtfully unconventional in detail. Good W front with square turrets flanking the nave, topped by tall pyramid roofs (or thick pinnacles), and an ashlar porch open to the W at the W end of the S aisle. Turrets attached to the transepts have almost Moorish pinnacles. Stripped-down flèche close to the W end; a SW tower may have been the original intention (cf. the practice's St Dunstan, Earle Road, p. 411). – Nave ALTAR. Part of a reordering, of *c.* 1975–9. – REREDOS. Signed by *Thomas Woolner*. Marble panel. Crucifixus and kneeling Virgin and St John, richly sentimental. Said to be designed by *G.E. Street* (Kelly), though this seems unlikely. – STAINED GLASS, nave S. Two, possibly three, windows by *Henry Holiday*, *c.* 1879.

ST LUKE, Goodison Road. By *James F. Doyle*, 1898–1901. Little, of stock and red brick, all windows round-arched. No tower. Adjoining church hall. Towered over by the stands of Goodison Park, the home of Everton F.C., which is so close that the chancel seems to bless the stadium.

ST NATHANIEL, Fazakerley Road. 1909, by *Frank Rimmington*. Small, brick and half-timbered, with a stumpy flèche-cum-bellcote.

BLESSED SACRAMENT (R.C.), Walton Vale. 1876–8, by *Edmund Kirby*. A plain rectangle in plan, utterly simple externally. No tower, nor any break in the roof-line or aisle roofs. Just rows of lancets. Buff quarry-faced sandstone. At the W end big lancets, at the E end – which was rebuilt after Second World War bomb damage – a rose window high up. Interior with tall arcades and the usual N and S side altars, in no way remarkable. S extension, separated from the aisle by artless columns. School, or more seating? One could hardly call the reordering, or the chunky new ALTARS, elegant. – REREDOS. Superimposed Gothic arcades. The lower one contains painted panels of angels, the upper statues. – STAINED GLASS. Chapel E windows, *Hardman*, 1949. S aisle W by the *Early Studio*; probably also the E window.

ST FRANCIS DE SALES (R.C.), Hale Road. 1917, by *Pugin & Pugin*. Heavy quarry-faced red sandstone; Dec; no tower. Round window at W end, blank canted apse at the E. The odd arcade and its odd external consequence are the distinguishing feature. They are highly original. The arcade consists of normal low arches alternating with three wide and high arches. To these correspond outside three hipped cross-gables rising above the arcade parapet. Each has a little gablet filled with tracery. The principle is really that of de Keyser's Amsterdam churches, but translated into a rather lifeless Gothic. – Big

REREDOS with pinnacled niches and lots of arcading. – Behind, big brick SCHOOLS (1894), and across the road, the PRESBYTERY (1903).

STUART ROAD BAPTIST CHURCH. Built by a United Methodist congregation in 1904. Large; two storeys of windows all the way round. Hard, dark red brick. Plain sides. Façade livelier: two stair-towers with a Dutch gable between them and buff terracotta detailing, including banding, blocked architraves and a big Venetian window in the centre. Original interior furnishings and gallery.

AINTREE METHODIST CHAPEL, Walton Vale. A pretty Jacobean façade in pale sandstone, dated 1891. Not large.

HOLY TRINITY (UNITED REFORMED), Rice Lane. Formerly Presbyterian, of 1897–8. No tower, but the w porch with a flying spire *à la* Edinburgh and Newcastle cathedrals, though a very short one. The church itself is equally low-slung, the w end dominated by a large round window containing quatre-foiled circles. Pale quarry-faced sandstone, red ashlar dressings. A single roof.

86 WALTON PRISON, Hornby Road. Designed by *Charles James Peirce*, and possibly *John Weightman*, the Borough Surveyor, who supervised construction *c.* 1850–4. A long range aligned E–W (for adult male prisoners) with a series of ancillary wings projecting N and S – a linear variant of the radial plan. The main range is five storeys high – the highest of the radial prisons. Inside, the atria with their layers of galleries are yet more impressive because at the end of the C19 the floor was cut away and the basement converted into additional cells.

The central wing on the S side is for administration, with the chapel in the upper part. It is a huge Neo-Norman fortress, brick with much stone trim, e.g. cruciform gun-ports. A similarly styled gatehouse, 'grossly colossal' as Pevsner described it, and two late classical villas (governor's and chaplain's houses) have been demolished. The modern gatehouse, *c.* 1974, in the massive brick perimeter wall, rather unnecessarily continues to evoke the medieval form, e.g. faux machicolations. But the vehicle entrance is to one side. Most other ancillary buildings destroyed or rebuilt in the C20.

Contemporary TERRACES for the warders on Hornby Road next door. Two storeys, book-ended with three-storey bays. With segmental-headed windows, and bay windows and porches under a narrow, continuous catslide roof between the book-ends.

LIBRARY, Rice Lane. 1910–11, by *Briggs, Wolstenholme & Thornely*. Brick and stone dressings. Neoclassical in the Reilly manner. Two reading rooms and a lending room. The latter has a big shallow dome; the larger of the reading rooms has a segmental vault and cornice. Another of those attractive opening plaques by *J.A. Hodel*.

OLD GRAMMAR SCHOOL, County Road. At the entrance to St Mary's churchyard. A humble schoolhouse, C17, with mullioned windows (C19 renewals, some C19 additions) and a four-centred lintel over the door. The school was re-founded under Edward VI; the building presumably dates from shortly after 1613, when Thomas Harrison donated £120 'to be used for the maintenance of a free school'. There is a probably early C18 extension at the rear; its flank to the churchyard simply doubles the gable end of the main range. Altered inside.

ALSOP HIGH SCHOOL, Queens Drive. The main building is of 1923–6, by the City Surveyor *A.D. Jenkins* and his architects. An odd concoction with Gothic bits and a central tower, and canted in three sections. In the grounds facing Walton Village is the OLD RECTORY. Early C19 symmetrical Gothick. Red ashlar. Large, battlements and pinnacles, and a porte cochère.

ARNOT STREET SCHOOLS. *Edmund Kirby*. A long range of assorted parts, in bright red brick with sometimes eccentric detailing. The part on the corner with County Road has an angle turret with a pointed hat. The tallest section, rising up to a stumpy flèche, is of 1884; other parts are of 1894.

WALTON HOSPITAL. *See* Workhouse, below.

WORKHOUSE (former), Rice Lane. 1864–8, by *William Culshaw* of *Culshaw & Sumners* for the West Derby Union. Later part of WALTON HOSPITAL; in 2005 being converted into apartments. A large, long, symmetrical block of brick with stone dressings. Three storeys. Twenty-three bays plus pedimented four-bay wings projecting at each end. Standing in front of the centre is a massive CLOCK TOWER with a steep pavilion roof. Other hospital buildings include an H-plan 1930s NURSES' HOME and a large, low two-storey wing of the mid 1970s by the *Department of Health and Social Security Architects*. Rigorous expressed concrete frame, independent glazed walls set well back behind.

CEMETERY (former), Rice Lane. Consecrated in 1851 as the churchyard of the parish church of Liverpool, the first, quite small-scale, response to the closure of the town-centre burial grounds. Since the 1970s it has been a city farm, mostly cleared of gravestones and turned over to grazing. Two LODGES, with label moulds and gables, and a little lanceted CHAPEL of 1852 survive. All three are of red ashlar.

EVERTON FOOTBALL CLUB, Goodison Park, Goodison Road. Everton F.C. moved to a new ground on Goodison Road in 1892, from their old home, Anfield (*see* p. 397). By 1938 it had four double-decker stands, the first in the country so equipped. Only one of these, heavily altered, survives: the Bullens Road stand, of 1926, designed by the pre-eminent stadium architect of the era, *Archibald Leitch*. Other stands individually of no merit, but collectively and atmospherically tightly drawn around the pitch.

QUEENS DRIVE WALTON (A5058) *J.A. Brodie*'s pioneering ring road (*see* p. 254) was begun here at the N end in 1904. The Walton section was completed in 1909 and there are terraces of cottages that go with that date. Travelling E, these give way to Neo-Georgian municipal housing, characteristic of *Sir Lancelot*

Keay's interwar regime. Brodie also proposed radial arteries, and WALTON HALL AVENUE is one of them.

BANK OF LIVERPOOL (former), Rice Lane. Now, inevitably, a pub. By *Willink & Thicknesse*, 1898. One of the finest of the suburban branches built by the bank around 1900. Brick with ashlar details. Directly inspired by Norman Shaw, with its big Dutch gables with obelisks, stripes of ashlar, and its circular tourelles. The upper windows are set in deep-sunk, heavily splayed surrounds, like gun-ports. This is typical of the beautiful detailing and balance.

WAVERTREE

Wavertree was still not quite overrun by Liverpool when J.A. Picton, who was a resident, published his *Memorials of Liverpool* in 1873. But the ancient township, mentioned in Domesday, had been developing as a polite dormitory for a century, and in 1895 it was absorbed into the city. By the mid C20 the last vestiges of rural life had been snuffed out by relentless residential development, which included the Liverpool Garden Suburb.

Churches

HOLY TRINITY, Church Road. The Wavertree parish church, built as a chapel of ease to Childwall (q.v.). 1794, by *John Hope*, reordered and given a new E end by *(Sir) Charles Reilly*, 1911. Ashlar-faced with a W tower, alas deprived in the 1950s of its upper stages of superimposed cupolas, stone and then timber. The buttressing of odd obelisk shape is Reilly's. The body of the church is five bays long with two tiers of windows, the smaller, lower ones segment-headed, the large upper ones round-headed. Entries with pediments on brackets in the W bays. At the top a balustrade. Reilly added the E bay and the apse with three very close-set and slender round-headed windows, with straight architraves on brackets. To the l. and the r. of the apse, low attachments. But where Reilly's work is truly remarkable is inside. A chancel is created by massive, closely spaced square pillars which stand free above low enclosed aisle spaces, containing vestibules, vestry and organ chamber. The pillars down here of course appear as free Composite pilasters. This, it will be noticed, is a St George's Hall motif. The W entrances to the low enclosed spaces have pediments on brackets, and above them are, again free-standing, urns. The apse has a kind of white trellis in its vault. The old nave has a broad flat ceiling with an elegant rose. Reilly removed N and S galleries and embellished the newly revealed walls with drapery swags between the upper and lower windows. These are copied from one that had adorned the old E wall of the nave. A W GALLERY survives, on thin quatrefoil-section cast-iron columns. Under the tower Reilly created a circular vaulted baptistery. – The marble FONT, with a shallow bowl, is of a characteristically Reilly Neoclassicism. – PULPIT.

Square and typical of the late C18. Neoclassical and panelled, with dentilled cornice. – LECTERN. Also late C18. The shaft is a fluted Greek Doric column. Ormolu medallions. – STALLS. The two main seats are again characteristic of *Reilly*. In contrast to the varnished natural finish of the pulpit and lectern, his stalls and PEWS are painted black. – Many TABLETS. Most charming is that to James Worthington, †1799, and his wife Jane, †1815. Surmounted by a large urn flanked by drooping palm fronds.

FIRST WORLD WAR MEMORIAL, in the churchyard. A 113 large, superb design by *H. Tyson Smith*, in Portland stone. Memorable cross of rectangular section with extremely stubby arms, softened by gentle convex tapering and with round edges in place of sharp arrises. Standing guard with their backs against either side of the shaft are two grieving women wrapped in long, heavily folded classical drapery. All this stands on a large but crude rendered pyramidal base. It was covered in ivy. What was the original intention?

ST BRIDGET, Bagot Street. 1868–72. By *E.A. Heffer*, fabric, fit- p. 90 tings and all. This is an exceptional conceit for its date: a real basilica (even if the exterior is of common brick with red and purple brick); i.e. nave and aisles with an apse, and a high, thin NW campanile. Big, too. The design was adopted over Gothic to accommodate the most worshippers on the tight site. All windows of course are round-headed. The W entrance alone is freer, a broad round arch under a gable breaking out into a medallion of Christ. Inside a free-standing altar in the apse. The nave arcades of nine bays have round arches, and return on the W wall as a three-bay blank arcade. Foliated capitals of varied design; the columns of red, and the bases of black, Irish marble. Similar columns support the chancel arch. Tall clerestory lights. Heavily coffered and enriched nave ceiling. – REREDOS, a mosaic Last Supper, 1886, by *Salviati*. – PULPIT. Big and rectangular, but pretty vulgar. Polychromatic stone and marble with balustrade of stumpy Corinthian columns. – LECTERN. On a simple marble column. – FONT. Square and very stout, and carried by a colonnette at each corner. Marble, luridly polychromatic. Mosaic medallion in each face. – STAINED GLASS. Clerestory windows by *Charles A. Gibbs*. Big saints, badly faded. First World War memorial glass by *H.G. Hiller* in the tripartite baptistery window at W end, between nave and vestibule.

ST MARY, North Drive, Victoria Park. The original church, by *W. & J. Hay* in Sandown Park (*see* p. 499), was destroyed by bombing. The present building is a former Methodist chapel of 1872–3. Quite imposing, with a SW tower with broach spire (erected in the 1880s) and, typically, very shallow transeptal projections and apsidal E end. No aisles either. Dec tracery, quarry-faced yellow sandstone, and red sandstone dressings.

ST THOMAS, Ashfield. 1909, by *R. Wynn Owen*. Common brick and red brick with a tall and thin octagonal turret at the SE corner of the nave. It has a little needle spire. The fenestration of the church is by lancet windows. Continuous roof over nave and chancel; pitched roof over the aisles, that wraps around the W end over a narthex. This idea is echoed inside by the arcades of stumpy round stone columns standing on dado-height octagonal bases, which continue around the W end. Double-chamfered pointed brick arches. S aisle partitioned off with chipboard. Little gallery above the baptistery in the narthex. – STAINED GLASS. E window by *Williams & Watkins*, 1954. Dense and bright colouring.

CHRIST THE KING (R.C.), Queens Drive. By *L.A.G. Prichard & Son*, 1966–7. It is possibly their best work, more forceful than most others. With centralised plan, a pyramid roof and brick walls. These are convex in the quadrants, between square projections at the cardinal points. The interior is dominated by the laminated 'crucks'. Two rise in parallel from each side to meet the corners of the square beam which carries the pyramid. The W GALLERY is awkward in such a low space. Lighting is mainly indirect from windows behind and above the W and E ends, and in the N and S projections, which house chapels. – ALTAR, N chapel. Elegant table of polished black marble, with a REREDOS of a single statue in a Gothic niche. By *Giles Gilbert Scott*; made 1936, installed here 1993. Beautifully made, if incongruous.

OUR LADY OF GOOD HELP (R.C.), Chestnut Grove. 1885–7, by *J. & B. Sinnott*. Buff coursed and quarry-faced stone, with red sandstone dressings. Intersecting tracery. The porch was meant to carry a steeple. Vestries apparently later. Five-bay arcade with quatrefoil piers. Reordered with a nave altar only, and none in the chancel. – PULPIT. A heavy marble thing with lots of colonnettes and a pierced arcade.

ST HUGH (R.C.), Earle Road. *See* Edge Hill, p. 412.

CONGREGATIONAL CHURCH, Hunters Lane. 1830s, altered and enlarged in the 1850s and again in the 1860s–70s.

METHODIST CHURCH (former), Lawrence Road. 1902–3. Red brick. English Renaissance. Low SW tower with ogee cap. Raised up on a high basement containing school rooms.

HEATHFIELD ROAD WELSH PRESBYTERIAN CHURCH, Smithdown Place. There were once forty Welsh Presbyterian churches in the city. In 2005 there were only two, a mark of the assimilation and dispersal of the city's once-prominent Welsh population. The building was designed by *R. Owen & Son* and erected in 1924–7. Behind the imposing classical façade is a simple interior, with shallow transeptal E bays. The oak DAIS FURNITURE is of high quality. In 2005 the congregation intended to sell the chapel and SCHOOL for redevelopment and build a small new chapel and community centre.

ST STEPHEN UNITED REFORMED CHURCH, Woolton Road. By *Medcalf & Medcalf*, and opened in 1929.

Public Buildings

TOWN HALL (former), High Street. *See* Village Centre, p. 498.

GREGSON INSTITUTE, Garmoyle Road. *A.P. Fry* exhibited designs at the Liverpool Autumn Exhibition of 1895. Built at private expense to house a library and museum, now dispersed. Six-bay façade, the centre four of only one storey, in two types of brick with stone dressings. Hints of the English Baroque, e.g. in the emphatic keystones and the end gables treated as broken pediments, on giant pilaster strips. Extensive glazed tiling inside, including a peacock frieze.

LIBRARY, Picton Road. 1902–3, by *Thomas Shelmerdine*. Red brick and much stone. One of three public buildings on Picton Road built by Liverpool Corporation with Shelmerdine façades after Wavertree was absorbed into the city. This one is symmetrical, the details C17 to C18 as usual. Gabled wings with big windows, tripartite with a tripartite lunette above. The lower part has alternately blocked Ionic pilasters for mullions. Single-storey porch with segmental hood in the centre, with a balustrade above it and a recessed semicircular gable behind that. A very enjoyable little building.

CHILDWALL BRANCH LIBRARY, Childwall Road. Opened 1968. Part of the series of single-storey glass-walled branch libraries begun at Clubmoor (*see* p. 403) by the *City Architect's Department*. This one is larger and plainer.

TECHNICAL INSTITUTE (former), Picton Road. 1898–9, also by *Shelmerdine*. In a free C17 style, but plain by Shelmerdine's standards. Red brick with pale stone dressings. With mullioned-and-transomed windows and l. of the entrance a wide, shallow canted bay window. The doorway has alternately blocked Ionic columns supporting a big segmental pediment. Now offices.

PUBLIC BATHS, Picton Road. 1904–6. Like the other baths built by the Corporation at this time, this was designed by *W.R. Court*, Baths Engineer, with *Shelmerdine* supplying sketches for the façades. These are obviously his, with C17 motifs deployed in a freer Arts and Crafts-influenced manner. Compact street façade: red brick and sandstone cross-wings with shaped gables and large unmoulded mullioned-and-transomed windows. Between them, all in stone, the entrance recessed behind a big, keyed round arch, and above this a similarly recessed low six-bay mullioned window. A pity, though, that the ashlar of the upper parts has been painted white.

BLUE COAT SCHOOL, Church Road. This is without doubt the most impressive building in Wavertree and one of the most impressive half-dozen of its date in Lancashire. It is by *Briggs, Wolstenholme & Thornely* and dates from 1903–6. It is of red brick with stone dressings, less or more conspicuous. Towards Church Road the effect is rousing. To the r. is the entrance range with its clock tower, to the l. the chapel. The entrance range is one-storeyed, of nine bays with C18 Baroque details including cherubs, inspired by those adorning the old school buildings in School Lane (*see* p. 302). The tower is *c.* 105 ft (32 metres) high and sheer, and the whole top stage, with four aedicules and an ogee cap, is of stone. It was given by Sir Charles Nall-Cain in 1915. To the l. is the Board Room with a segmental-vaulted ceiling. Under the tower one enters the spine corridor, and straight ahead is the hall, with barrel-vaulted ceiling. Beneath was the dining hall, and on either side are very nearly symmetrically arranged courtyards. The ranges around these are of two-and-a-half storeys because of the fall of the land. Those, with cupolas, which are parallel to the hall project to the w to book-end a long w façade overlooking the Wavertree Playground (*see* p. 497) which is articulated by segmental pediments. The w end of the hall block, with another cupola, forms the centrepiece of this.

The CHAPEL, paid for by Thomas Fenwick Harrison as a memorial to his wife, is entered by a narthex and has a Greek-cross plan with short arms and an ample though low domed centre. To Church Road is the apse. In the diagonals are smaller apses, not visible outside. The cross-arms have Venetian windows, there are pilasters everywhere, the lantern has columns set inside. – MONUMENTS, brought from the old school. John Horrocks, †1823. Tablet with an urn on a pillar and two mourners l. and r. – Richard Dobson, †1835. Very Grecian and rather too ornate.

A large EXTENSION was built on the N side of the Edwardian school in 2002–3. *Aquila Consultancy Services*' design was revised by the *Derek Hicks & Thew Partnership* of Liverpool. On its own terms this is not a bad building at all, and certainly a lot more interesting than many recent school projects. Rectilinear and irregular, respectfully low, some parts of blue-glazed brick, others red brick or oxidised copper cladding, or bleached timber. To the street is a new entrance: a two-storey rectangular box, rendered white, with floor-to-ceiling windows variously recessed from the walls and roof, which thus form a frame. Sometimes uncompromising modernity is the best form of contextualism, but however much you wish this building well, it does not sit comfortably cheek-by-jowl with Briggs, Wolstenholme & Thornely's Edwardian Baroque.

CHILDWALL COMMUNITY COMPREHENSIVE SCHOOL, Queen's Drive and Childwall Road. Built 1935–7 as the Holt Grammar School. By *Albert D. Jenkins*, the City Surveyor. Neo-Georgian scholastic, with the inevitable long front and central cupola. A reasonable amount of stone dressing, including a three-bay porch of paired columns.

KING DAVID HIGH SCHOOL, Childwall Road. By *Sir Alfred Shennan & Partners*. Completed 1956–8. The PRIMARY SCHOOL on Beauclair Drive, with its windows individually treated in thin stone surrounds in the brick façades, though of 1963, looks earlier than the senior school, which has continuous bands of glazing.

ROYAL SCHOOL FOR THE BLIND, Church Road. Built on the site of Wavertree Hall. C18 GATEPIERS on Church Road, with replica C18 ironwork of 1986. The building is of 1898–9, by *H. & A.P. Fry* and of little individual merit. The original school was the first of its kind in Britain, founded in 1791. Some earlier city-centre buildings survive (*see* p. 375), but single and double bronze DOORS of 1931 by *James Woodford* from the

Hardman Street building are now inside at Wavertree. They have low-relief scenes: Christ Healing the Blind, The Cured Giving Thanks, and various scenes of the industry and products of the pupils – reed baskets, knitting and weaving, wicker and leather work.

WAVERTREE PARK. *See* Edge Hill, p. 413.

WAVERTREE PLAYGROUND, Prince Alfred Road. A large, featureless and largely treeless public park created in 1895 from the grounds of THE GRANGE, an C18 house demolished at the same time. Massive rusticated GATE PIERS of 1895 with equally massive ball finials.

TOXTETH PARK CEMETERY, Smithdown Road. *See* Toxteth, p. 474.

OLIVE MOUNT CUTTING, Mill Lane. A sandstone chasm on the Liverpool & Manchester Railway which was one of the wonders of the age when it opened in 1830. Nearly 2 m. long and cut sheer down to 70 ft (21.5 metres) into the bedrock, it is still impressive, though not as dramatic as it was before widening later in the C19.

Village Centre

A short perambulation beginning at the unmistakable centre of Wavertree. The PICTON CLOCK TOWER at the E end of the HIGH STREET was designed by *J.A. Picton* as a memorial to his wife and erected as a gift to Wavertree in 1884. An eclectic Renaissance curiosity in brick and stone with four clock faces under a dome topped by a tall finial. To the S on CHURCH ROAD NORTH is THE COFFEE HOUSE, possibly Wavertree's oldest pub. The C18 building has been heavily altered, notably in 1904 by *Walter W. Thomas*. Though not nearly as impressive as his spectacular Philharmonic and Vines pubs (*see* pp. 375 and 326), especially after the recent attentions of the brewers, it retains early C20 plasterwork and joinery. Opposite is the former ABBEY CINEMA of 1939 by *Alfred Shennan*. Detached corner building in brick with a convex glazed 'bastion' at the angle and vertical details to break up the bulk. It looks N across Childwall Road onto the remnants of the VILLAGE GREEN. On it the LOCK-UP of 1796, a stone octagon with blank windows on all sides on two levels, the lower ones in blank arches, and four gables. It is the work of a *Mr Hind*. The steep roof was added by *Picton* in 1869 after he intervened to prevent demolition. A short distance further N on MILL LANE is the spring water conduit called the MONK'S WELL. The lower stonework including the arch is undoubtedly medieval; the upper works, bearing the date 1414, are C19.

Returning to the HIGH STREET, on the S side are some Late Georgian buildings, including No. 102 with an excellent early C19 shopfront. On the N side is the big, handsome LAMB HOTEL, of the 1850s but still basically Georgian. 3–3–3 bays. Three-storey centre with Doric porch; projecting and pedimented two-storey outer parts. A few yards w is No. 95, claimant to the crown of smallest house in England, at 6 ft by 14 ft (1.8 by 4.3 metres) and two storeys. Now absorbed into the adjoining pub. Then the former TOWN HALL, built in 1872 as both the headquarters of the Wavertree Board of Health and a ballroom. The architect was *John Elliott Reeve*, of Wavertree. Very conservative for its date. Ashlar-faced, Latish Classical. Two storeys, five bays, with rusticated ground floor and pilasters above. A porch projects, with balcony over, flanked by two tiers of paired columns and topped with a pediment. Now a pub, restaurant etc. Then back to the s side for the big bulk of the Wavertree Gardens flats (*see* p. 500). High Street continues w with a number of c18–early c19 cottages and houses, e.g. Nos. 38–42, treated as one five-bay stuccoed house with panelled pilasters, and No. 26, with a doorcase with Adam columns. Finally the former Bank of Liverpool, Wavertree Branch, now a pub and Post Office, and looking like a big Late Victorian pub anyway. Red brick, gables and mullioned-and-transomed windows. For the public buildings that come after it, *see* above.

THE BROOK HOUSE, Smithdown Road, is also worth a mention. A lively, expansive pub of *c.* 1881 by *John Elliott Reeve*, with matching additions at each end, probably by *Walter W. Thomas*. Red brick and red sandstone (now painted) with timber-framed gables and mullioned windows.

Housing

Wavertree developed as a – largely genteel – suburb from the c18 and good examples remain of housing from all phases. Their disposition does not allow for an easy perambulation, so treatment is roughly chronological.

No. 28 CHURCH ROAD NORTH. In the c18 a number of Liverpool merchants built substantial homes in the fields around Wavertree village. This is mid-c18 and probably one of the first. Five bays, two storeys, red brick, with flanking wings. Keystone lintels, and a good doorcase with pediment on consoles. Hotchpotch garden front. Uninteresting post-war SYNAGOGUE in the garden.

OLIVE MOUNT, Mill Lane. A grander example of the above type: a fine house thought to have been built in the 1790s for James Swan, grocer and tea dealer. Five bays and two storeys. Unequal U-plan – the E side eight bays long – around a little service yard. Public faces in pale ashlar. The windows have no mouldings at all. Central porch with Adam-style columns, and a cast-iron honeysuckle parapet. This is a balcony to the large tripartite first-floor window, which has a stone bat's-wing motif above it. The other first-floor windows have garlands in recessed panels above them. Parapet. Heavy Victorian plaster-work in the hall and on the staircase, which is lit from above by a coved oval roof-light. But there are also remnants of the very austere 1790s scheme, including the simple wrought-iron balustrade, and plasterwork elsewhere.

At the turn of the C20 the house and grounds were developed as orphans' cottage homes, which later evolved into a hospital. Extensions to the rear of the house remain; most of the other buildings erected have now been demolished and replaced by housing, and this is promised also for the three thirteen-storey tower blocks built in 1963 with unabashed and ill-considered effrontery bang in front. *ECD Architects* have designed a low-rise residential scheme to replace them, around a new park.

SANDOWN LANE. In the C19 Wavertree began to attract the more modestly middling classes. Sandown Lane was a new street and is lined with their houses. Nos. 3–7 are among the oldest, put up before 1837. The stuccoed SANDOWN TERRACE, *c.* 1837–45, is by far the most ambitious, a unified design with a pediment containing the three wheat sheaves of Cheshire. The developer, William Bennett, later Mayor of Liverpool, was from Chester. Nos. 35–37 and 47–49 are brick semis of *c.* 1840, still resolutely Georgian. Greek Doric doorcases and one surviving fanlight. ALMA TERRACE, two linked pairs of semis, was built in 1855, the date of the Crimean battle of that name.

ORFORD STREET, largely 1848–52. An attractive street, with terraces of similar houses differing in detail, e.g. doorcases either Greek Doric, consoled or pedimented. Residents included joiners, a plasterer and a gardener – i.e. down a notch from the developments above, and part of the economy that emerged to service them. The cottage scale reflects this.

SANDOWN PARK. A small residential estate laid out in the late 1840s by the architect *Cornelius Sherlock* in Picturesque fashion, with winding drives, in the grounds of SANDOWN HALL (*c.* 1810, scandalously demolished only in 2000). A very few typically Early Victorian villas remain, mainly semis and stuccoed and quite modest. But mostly now it is little C20 houses. A church of the 1850s, St Mary, was destroyed by bombing. There is a LODGE on Sandown Road.

SANDY KNOWE, Mill Lane. Dated 1847. Designed by *(Sir) J.A. Picton* for himself. Red sandstone Jacobean, with shaped gables, a turret, finials, mullioned windows, etc. The curious polygonal addition is his library. The composition is totally asymmetrical and still quite impressive, despite being extended in many directions as sheltered flats in 1975 with abominable crassness and insensitivity. It beggars belief that Liverpool could do this to the home of one its most devoted sons. The library was almost completely blank until it was butchered by the insertion of crude windows in 1975.

Various stuccoed Early Victorian VILLAS on the heights N of the High Street, in Olive Lane, Olive Grove and Mill Lane, and Old Mill Lane. NEWSTEAD, Old Mill Lane, is quite substantial and Italianate, except for a castellated octagonal prospect

turret, and has attached a two-storey iron veranda and a conservatory. The others are large semis, mostly classical with
bracketed eaves cornices, but one or two have label-moulded
windows or vaguely Gothic. More stuccoed mid-C19 villas on
CHILDWALL ROAD near the junction with Thingwall Road.
MOSSFIELD between the two roads is heavily classical in a typically 1850s way.

VICTORIA PARK. Another residential estate, with its origins in a
scheme called Olive Park that appears to have ground to a halt
after only five houses were built. Nos. 1–3 NORTH DRIVE,
c. 1840, are the survivors. Stuccoed, Gothic doorways, fish-
scale slates. In the 1860s development was revived under the
name Victoria Park. Semi-detached and detached villas were
built up to the end of the C19 on lots along NORTH DRIVE
and SOUTH DRIVE, which *William Webb* laid out in 1862.
Unlike the earlier Sandown Park (*see* p. 499) it was not, in
today's parlance, a gated estate. It is attractively leafy, but the
houses are individually of no great merit.

CHURCH ROAD, opposite the Blue Coat School. A handsome
terrace of three big houses treated as one and dated 1904. In
a Shavian style. Brick, each of the outer houses with two two-
storey bay windows, pargetted on the upper floor, and a single
big half-timbered gable over them. Nice details to the returns.

WAVERTREE GARDEN SUBURB. Established as the Liverpool
Garden Suburb by Henry Vivian. The first section was begun
in 1910. *Raymond Unwin* designed the layout and housing. The
second phase, started three years later, was the work of *G.L.
Sutcliffe*, who probably designed many of the houses in the first
too. When construction ceased in 1915, 360 houses out of a
planned 1,800 had been completed. WAVERTREE NOOK
ROAD marks the divide between the phases, with Unwin's
work on the w side and Sutcliffe's on the E. The housing in
both, roughcast and gabled and built of bricks made by a co-
operative in Letchworth Garden City, is very characteristic of
the most advanced type of the Garden City movement. So too
is the planning, i.e. the self-conscious retention of the meandering form of THINGWALL ROAD and its broad verges, the
culs-de-sac off NOOK RISE, and at the centre of the second
phase, FIELDWAY GREEN. The foundation stone of a substantial INSTITUTE was laid in 1914, but the building was
never erected and the pair of probably early C19 stone cottages
on Thingwall Road, converted in 1912 as its temporary home,
still house it today. They are of unusual design, each two rooms
deep and only one wide, with a symmetrical gabled front of
two-over-two mullioned windows with labels and an oculus in
the apex, and no doors in the returns.

WAVERTREE GARDENS, High Street. This is just about the only
one of *(Sir) Lancelot Keay*'s 1930s Neo-Georgian blocks of
Corporation flats to survive. The style was considered appropriate for suburban sites; in the city centre he built similar
estates in a Modernist idiom (*see* St Andrew's Gardens, p. 379).
Now private apartments going by the name of ABBEYGATE.

West Derby has an ancient identity. It is a Hundred, and there was a modest motte and bailey castle in the late C12 and C13 (*see* p. 18). This was ruinous in 1327, by which time interest had shifted decisively to Liverpool. Nothing remains of it, or of anything in the village prior to the C16.

St Mary, West Derby Village. The parish church, but in scale and lavishness and uniformity wholly an estate church. The building lies indeed just inside the Croxteth Estate (*see* p. 409), facing the w lodge. Lord Sefton chose *George Gilbert Scott* to be his architect. Work began in 1853 and was completed in 1856. The preceding chapel had been built in 1793. Scott's church is of red stone, and it has a massive, proud crossing tower, crowned by rugged pinnacles at the corners, which was paid for by the banker John Pemberton Heywood. *The Ecclesiologist* called it 'a great improvement on any church now existing at Liverpool', though it did not like the tower. The nave has clerestory and aisles, there are high transepts, the fenestration of their end walls deliberately different one from the other, a s chapel and a n organ chamber, and a polygonal apse. The style is Scott's beloved Second Pointed, i.e. late C13 to early C14. SUNDIAL of 1795 from the previous chapel, on the s transept. The interior inspires awe at once by its height and nobility. Its climax is the massive crossing piers and arches. Capitals are elaborately carved with naturalistic foliage. Unfortunate C20 flooring.

FITTINGS. Many by *J. Oldrid Scott*. They include the STALLS, PARCLOSE SCREEN and wrought-iron ALTAR RAILS (all *c.* 1889), PULPIT (1892) and TESTER (1902), the s chapel furnishings (1897), and alterations to the REREDOS (with a Last Supper in inlaid marble), the tall FONT COVER and sanctuary PANELLING (all 1906). – SANCTUARY LAMP by *G.G. Scott Jun.*, 1873–4. A striking wrought-iron piece from which seven lamps drop down in an upside-down V formation. – STAINED GLASS. Fine w window by *William Wailes*, 1856. Much by *Hardman*, *c.* 1860–70, e.g. e windows, s chapel and both transepts. Also, some windows by *Percy Bacon*: n and s aisles, w, 1906, good figures, and s aisle 1st w, †1908. s aisle 3rd from w by *Charles Gibbs*, †1838. Poor. – BRASS. A good Gothic plaque on chancel floor by *Jones & Willis* to the Rev. John Stewart, †1889.

CHURCH HALL, offices etc. attached to the n side. By *Buttress Fuller Alsop Williams*, 2000. With a glazed corridor – an all-weather cloister – around three sides of a court. Some light and elegant interiors, but the plain brick exterior sits awkwardly with the church: it just looks a little bit cheap.

Good Shepherd, Carr Lane. *See* Croxteth, p. 405.

St James, Mill Lane. Rock-faced red sandstone. By *E. Welch*, 1845–6, and still pre-archaeological, i.e. with a w tower (its bell-stage battered, and now with a low pyramid roof in place of the original thin broach spire), and a nave with lancets –

with attached shafts – between buttresses, transepts, and originally a short chancel. The present chancel, s organ chamber
and N chapel are by *W. & J. Hay*, of 1875–6. Also by them the
semicircular attachment to the s side of the tower, which
housed an additional entrance and new gallery stairs. Interior
with broad aisle-less nave bridged by complex trusses employing iron tensioning rods and longitudinal bracing. Quite an
impressive web where they cross over the 'crossing'. Chancel
arch and chancel arcades with polished red marble columns.
E wall with five lancets with polished shafts and shaft-rings. In
1994 de-pewed, and the four W bays separated off by a solid
wall into a parish hall. Four back-lit stained-glass lancets are
re-set in this. *In situ* in the hall is the narrow W gallery. –
STAINED GLASS. *Shrigley & Hunt* at their best, in e.g. the
excellent N and S windows of the transepts, 1883, with
fine figures and, for them, very rich colouring and unusual
composition. E lancets by *William Wailes*, 1876. Some of the
original patterned glass survives in the N window of the W end.
– First World WAR MEMORIAL. Large glass mosaic composition, including a glass painting of the Lusitania.

ST PAUL (R.C.), Town Row. By *Pugin & Pugin*, 1914–15. Rock-
faced, with a shortish SW tower with a steep, slated pyramid
roof rising from projecting eaves. The aisles each have a row of
four cross-gables, and each of these has a three-light window
under it. There is an apse too. Usual Sacred Heart and Lady
altars l. and r. of the chancel. – Marble and alabaster FITTINGS
by *Pugin & Pugin*. During reordering in 1973–5 the REREDOS
was cut down, the ALTAR (with mosaic inlays in the frontal)
brought forward, and the PULPIT cut up to make lecterns. –
Sanctuary PANELLING, with low-relief saints, mid-C20.

WEST DERBY METHODIST CHURCH, Crosby Green. 1905 by
Green, Russell & Knowles. Four-light window in the street (W)
façade. Common brick back and sides. Flèche.

WEST DERBY CEMETERY, Lower House Lane. *See* Croxteth,
p. 405.

COURT HOUSE. *See* The Village Centre, p. 503.

LIBRARY, Queens Drive. *See* Clubmoor, p 403.

CARDINAL HEENAN HIGH SCHOOL; HOLLY LODGE
SCHOOL; ST EDWARD'S COLLEGE: *See* pp. 504–6.

WEST DERBY COMPREHENSIVE SCHOOL, Queens Drive. *see*
Tue Brook, p. 482.

ST VINCENT'S SCHOOL FOR THE BLIND, Yew Tree Lane.
Purpose-built in 1899, with a chapel of 1911 and a boys' wing
added in 1927. The 1899 block is long with a spine corridor.
Brick, pointed windows, gables, flèche over the entrance.

ALDER HEY CHILDREN'S HOSPITAL, Alder Road. T.C.
Molyneux had Alder Hey House rebuilt by *William Culshaw* in
1866. The Alder Road LODGE is presumably part of that
scheme. The house itself was demolished to make way for the
West Derby Poorhouse Infirmary, erected in 1911–15 to the
designs of *Charles H. Lancaster*. It became a specialist children's
hospital in the 1920s. Built with simple ward blocks in five parallel ranges, interrupted by an administration block. Sixth

range of 1932 fronting Eaton Road, slightly enriched. Assorted demolitions and later wings.

The Village Centre

The parish church is by the well-detailed Tudorbethan LODGE, *c.* 1860, and the park GATES. They are probably all by *W. Eden Nesfield*, who was paid £114 in 1859 for designing four lodges. Stone lions sejant holding iron pennants top the piers. In *c.* 1861–70 *Nesfield* also designed the brick COTTAGES on the corner outside N of the gates. The VILLAGE HALL lies S of the gates on TOWN ROW. Large, Domestic Revival, by *Alfred Shennan*, 1913. In front of the gates, in the centre of the road where it broadens (more car park now than informal square) is a stone DRINKING FOUNTAIN of 1894 by *A.P. Fry*, now missing its ornate iron lamp. A few yards NW, also in the road is the CROSS on the site of the old chapel of ease (to Walton, *see* above). Very Gothic, with a massive central shaft surrounded by four slender detached shafts supporting a seated figure of Christ at the top, in the C13 style, and too large for its tabernacle. The cross is by *Nesfield*, *c.* 1861–70, the carving by *Forsyth*. A little to the N is No. 10 ALMOND'S GREEN, C17 and of baffle-entry plan, with flattened four-pointed doorway. Two five-light windows below and two three-light windows above. Opposite is the COURT HOUSE, a tiny single-storey ashlar building with just a flattened four-pointed doorway and one mullioned window to the front, but of special interest as a rare example of a purpose-built manorial court largely complete with its fittings. A warrant was issued in 1585 to pull down and rebuild at a cost of £40. The fittings seem later – C17 and C18 – and the present table is a recent introduction. To the r. is the entrance to CHURCH VIEW, a sheltered housing scheme by the *Owen Ellis Partnership*, 1994, canted in five parts to embrace the entrance court. Low and horizontal, with monopitch roofs and generous glazing. Then, back on the street, the HARE AND HOUNDS, post-1885 despite its early C19 appearance. Stuccoed, with a pediment and a fanlight either side of an unpedimented centre.

NW of the church in MEADOW LANE is the PRIMARY SCHOOL, including most of the (part demolished) church school of 1860–1 by *H.P. Horner*. Quite odd: Gothic, of sandstone rubble, with a short tower with stumpy stone pyramid roof, and Dec windows. Some COTTAGES survive amongst suburbia on Town Row and Almond's Green. On the latter, Nos. 97–103 are a Tudorbethan group in ashlar erected by the Croxteth Estate, and dated 1863.

Houses

West Derby was a desirable commuting address in the C19 – in the country but close enough to Liverpool – but many of the mansions and villas that ringed the village have been swept aside by C20 suburbia. One of the grandest was DEYSBROOK,

where in 1847 three rooms were decorated by *Alfred Stevens.**
But others survive.

Plots on MILL LANE were developed from *c.* 1830. HOLLY
LODGE, a school since 1912, has an entrance on Queens Drive.
Built in the early 1830s by Isaac Cooke, Quaker banker and
cotton broker who purchased all of the N side of the lane. A
three-bay stucco house, extended N by two bays *c.* 1860 by
William Culshaw & Sumners, with a prospect tower, and a billiard room behind a colonnaded bay window on the garden
front. Inside are finishes of both periods, and coarse late C19
plasterwork and staircase. The centre bay of the W front (which
was the side of the house before the construction of Queens
Drive) projects slightly and is bowed. It originally contained
both principal stairs and, sandwiched between these and the
outer wall, the back stairs. Further alterations for the school,
and additions, most excitingly by *Nelson & Parker* in collaboration with *Ronald Bradbury*, 1965. Mannerist Modernism,
with e.g. concrete beams projecting boldly from the wall; other
pre-cast concrete elements expressed less dramatically. Load-
bearing blue brick. In the corner a white-glazed brick stair-
tower with slit windows.

Two other houses are also now part of the school. FREMONT is
an unremarkable stucco box with an Ionic porch. SANDHEYS,
to the E, more refined. Of *c.* 1833–6. Stuccoed too, and of three
bays, but much more generous and elegant. Panelled pilasters
at either end, and a mid-C19 porch with paired Ionic columns.
Deep canted bays projecting from either flank. Good plasterwork and a chaste mid-C19 staircase (the original arrangement
was like Holly Lodge). Extended twice at the rear, most
recently with a largish block *c.* 2002, reasonably crisp
Modernism. Further E on Mill Lane are two short TERRACES
of small two-storey houses with fanlights, entirely Georgian,
built in the 1820s.

HAYMAN'S GREEN was developed by Richard Radcliffe and laid
out *c.* 1840. A number of mid-C19 villas survive, stuccoed and
Italianate or label-moulded. A cut above is LOWLANDS, apparently by *Thomas Haigh*, architect and builder, for himself. A
house is shown here on the Ordnance Survey map of 1849, but
that does not appear to be the one now standing – unless it
was rebuilt. Conventional stuccoed Italianate outside – some
round-headed windows, wide eaves-cornices, etc. – but inside
like a dolls' house with a ludicrously pretentious, but enjoyable
hall at the core rising up to a lantern, with an imperial staircase and two levels of landings. It is so compressed in plan,
e.g. the entrance steps are inside rather than outside, that the
effect is quite vertiginous. Similarly sized is EDDESBURY, on
the corner with Almond's Green. Latterly the Margaret Beavan
School. 1884–5, designed by *James F. Doyle* for James Lathom,
broker. Freely and asymmetrically Jacobean, with shaped

---

* Part of this work was saved and is in store at the Walker Art Gallery.

gables, some mullioned-and-transomed windows and big chimneystacks. Nevertheless quite bland, and mainly in a harsh red brick.

SANDFIELD PARK, ½ m. s of St Mary's. The most upmarket of the city's Victorian residential estates, developed by T.C. Molyneux from *c.* 1845, with a Picturesque layout, behind its own walls and lodges. The houses were big and few, in fine spacious grounds, but a number have been demolished and extensive, sometimes kitsch infill has destroyed much of the exclusivity and seclusion. Nevertheless, some undeveloped parkland remains. The estate was created from the park of SANDFIELD HOUSE, which survives on the E side of SOUTH DRIVE as Old House. Brick façade, of five bays, reputedly concealing C17 fabric, though entirely transmogrified. U-plan STABLES too, of C17–C18 date. There are two LODGES to the estate, one on ALDER ROAD (with another opposite for Alder Hey House, now Hospital, *see* p. 502), and a grander one at the entrance on QUEENS DRIVE, of *c.* 1845, with pedimented gables and a little iron porch. Next to it the PARK ENTRANCE has six square pillars, but gates no longer, and a sign declaring the toll to be a penny per wheel. Immediately N of the lodge is BASIL GRANGE. It was one of the first houses to go up, but the present building is a replacement of 1880 with matching additions of 1890. Red sandstone. Irregular Jacobethan: tall chimneys, gables, mullioned-and-transomed windows. In 2005 being converted into apartments, with a new NE wing. s of the entrance is the earliest known survivor, GWALIA, *c.* 1845. Italianate, sandstone, with four-storey tower. Now a shell.

ST IVES, 1853, at the junction of South Drive and CENTRAL DRIVE, is Italianate too, with bargeboarded gables. At the N end of Central Drive is KILN HEY, a smallish house of the 1860s ineptly extended by *C. W. Blease*, for the bachelor Edward H. Cookson in 1885, when he entered local politics and needed a place to entertain. Later it was a nurses' home (e.g. the separate inter-war Neo-Georgian block) then a nursing home. Externally of little merit, but some good interiors of 1888 (when he became Mayor) survive, including a couple of panelled rooms, an Adamesque ceiling, and a grand staircase under a handsome coffered barrel vault, lit by a large Venetian window (glass by *Shrigley & Hunt*). A pity about the lift inserted blithely into the well of the staircase, disappearing into the ceiling.

ST EDWARD'S COLLEGE is on the s side of the NORTH DRIVE. The infants' school is in RUNNYMEDE, a big brick box of *c.* 1870 with typical stone dressings of the date. The hall and staircase, with good bold glass, were redone *c.* 1884–7 by *F. & G. Holme*, who also added the billiard room. The sixth form occupies ST CLARE, built in the mid 1860s in quarry-faced stone, and bigger, gabled and slightly Gothic. Inside are a number of rooms excellently redecorated in an Aesthetic style, notably a library and drawing room. Some of the fittings, of superb quality, are marked *Gillow*. They almost certainly date from *c.* 1881, when *G.E. Grayson* was employed. Also added then was a billiard room, now subdivided as a vestibule to the C20 CHAPEL. The back stairs and some ceilings are witnesses to the earlier, Gothic, interior. Between the two houses is a brick QUADRANGLE of the late 1930s designed for the school by *Edmund Kirby & Sons*. It contains some fine mahogany doors salvaged from St Domingo House when that outstanding C18 mansion in Everton was demolished. On the N side of North Drive is BISHOP'S COURT, looking of the 1840s. Three bays and two-and-a-half storeys, upright and stuccoed. SANDFORTH ROAD is the N edge of the Park. On it CLAREMONT, also 1840s. Built as two houses with the entrances in the returns. Big, handsome and stuccoed, and symmetrically Italianate.

1 m. SE from St Mary's are two more houses. LEYFIELD HOUSE in Green Lane is of *c.* 1830–40, of three bays, stuccoed, with a Doric porch. Now part of the Cardinal Heenan High School. BROUGHTON HALL, in Yew Tree Lane, is much bigger and more interesting. By *Walter Scott* for G.C. Schwabe, 1858–9. Now a convent. High Victorian Gothic, but idiosyncratically detailed inside and out, with workmanship of high quality. Rock-faced sandstone. A flattened E-plan with the details of the wings significantly differing, the l. with an oriel on elongated bracket. Lots of tall octagonal chimneys too. Attached l., a conservatory, not apparently the first one, of marvellously ornate iron, much of it foliate. The garden front less symmetrical and less successful. Entrance vestibule like an implied screens passage to the fully panelled (single-storey) Gothic hall. Dining room (now chapel) with odd trellis panelling; what must have been the drawing room with eccentric but virtuoso ceiling plasterwork, like an intricate doily. Also, a matching LODGE. Sprawling school blocks impinge to the r. of the house; to the l. is an altogether better building of 1968–9, built for the convent, and carefully placed in the landscape. Brick parts, mainly of four storeys with pilotis, arranged around a courtyard.

GORSE HEY, Queens Drive. One of the prettiest groups of *Lancelot Keay*'s inter-war municipal housing. On three sides of a grassy square, Neo-Georgian of his cottagey type with weatherboarded bay windows, but in the centre a more formal façade with parapet urns. The three central bays are a two-storey arcade of spindly Tuscan columns, within which the wall with its windows and doors is slightly recessed.

WOOLTON

Woolton was historically part of Childwall parish (*see* p. 397), and became part of the city of Liverpool in 1913. Its great contribution to the city's architecture is the red sandstone that lies under Woolton Hill. The quarries, latterly between Quarry Street and

Church Road, brought prosperity in the C19 and the character of a pretty industrial village, with little rows of houses stacked up on the sides of the hill around them. They were worked up until their greatest monument, the Anglican Cathedral, was completed in 1978, by which time the village was surrounded by big C19 houses in Woolton Park to the N, and C20 suburbia. An example of the latter, John Lennon's childhood home MENDIPS, Menlove Avenue, has been evocatively restored by the National Trust. It is an archetypal privately developed semi of 1933.

ST PETER, Church Road. 1886–7, by *Grayson & Ould*, replacing a classical church of 1826. Red sandstone, large, Perp, with a SE tower. Substantial interior with a five-bay arcade and wide aisles. Modest hammerbeam to the nave. S organ loft and vestry, and N chapel with stencilled, canted ceiling. A W extension by *Brock Carmichael Associates*, completed in 1989, houses a large eight-sided hall. It has diagonal buttresses with large rings at their tops. The old and the new are separated by a glass screen set between pairs of big round columns carrying shallow arches. The top-lighting arrangement that illuminates both the hall and the W window of the church is perhaps over-complex. – Very complete FURNISHINGS. REREDOS with five niches painted by *Sigismund Goetze*, 1905. – Alabaster FONT. Fat and octagonal, with tall, traceried cover. – Excellent alabaster PULPIT, with a lovely frieze of angels. – Very good iron SCREENS. Those encaging the N chapel are wonderfully swirly. – STAINED GLASS. Nearly all by *Kempe*. Various late C19 dates. Consistently good, the best the splendid W window of the Worship of the Angelic Host. Also two *Morris & Co.* windows, S aisle SE, 1874, and baptistery S, 1876. Not the firm at its best. N aisle, first from W, First World War memorial by *Heaton, Butler & Bayne*. – Splendidly ornate and massive timber-framed LYCHGATE, typical of *Edward Ould* (a former assistant to John Douglas). – FIRST WORLD WAR MEMORIAL. An atypical and powerful design, an Art Nouveau Celtic cross with stylised foliation winding up it. Inscribed simply PEACE. II NOVEMBER 1918, it is unusually and explicitly a commemoration of the coming of peace, and not of the sacrifice of the fallen.

ST MARY (R.C.), Church Road, tucked behind St Peter. 1859–60, by *R. W. Hughes* of Preston. Red sandstone, and quite big, but unadorned. Large transepts, but no aisles or tower. Geometric tracery; four-light S transept window, N transept rose window. Redecorated in 1981–2, including a stencilled lily-pattern sanctuary ceiling. – HIGH ALTAR and REREDOS. 1865. Probably *E. W. Pugin*. In 1948–50 *Weightman & Bullen* separated the two, putting the reredos back against the E wall. – STAINED GLASS. The E window typical *Capronnier*, dated 1878.

Big symmetrical Gothic PRESBYTERY by *E. W. Pugin*, 1864, connected to the church by a single-storey link. – Also a big red sandstone SCHOOL of 1869 with trefoil-headed lancets. It is actually in St Mary's Court, which is at a lower level, and there is now a footbridge from the churchyard to the first floor. CHURCH HALL on Quarry Street. Quarry-faced stone.

CONGREGATIONAL CHURCH (former), Church Road South. *See* Perambulation, p. 511.

ST JAMES METHODIST CHURCH, High Street. 1866, by *C. O. Ellison*. Quarry-faced red sandstone. Dec NW turret with open-work parapet. – CHURCH HALL on the opposite side of Church Road South. Same materials. Flèche, and oriel over the entrance.

OUTHOUSE, a SCULPTURE off Menlore Avenue. *Vong Phao-phanit* and *Claire Oboussier*, 2005. Based on two-storey houses by the *Owen Ellis Partnership* on a neighbouring site, but two-thirds the size and made of glass, with the 'windows' opaque. Intended to be used by local residents for meetings.

POLICE STATION AND COURT (former), Quarry Street. *See* Perambulation, p. 511.

LIBRARY, Allerton Road. *See* Perambulation, p. 511.

The OLD SCHOOL, School Lane. The most miserable of ancient schools. An almost featureless cottage that may be earlier, or later, than the erroneous date 1610 that it bears. A single storey. The tiny mullioned windows, one either side of the central door, are late C20. Before, there were only the Gothic windows in the gable ends, with simple Y-tracery. Are these C17? Another riddle is the masonry: only a single thickness, yet well made and with some blocks more than 4 ft (1.2 metres) long.

ST JULIE'S CATHOLIC HIGH SCHOOL, Speke Road. By *Weight-man & Bullen*, mid-1970s. Large and sprawling on three sides of Woolton Hall (*see* p. 509). Bare concrete block walls. Quite impressively composed, but the damage it has done to the setting of the Hall cannot be forgiven.

ST PETER'S VILLAGE SCHOOL (former). *See* Perambulation, p. 512.

LIVERPOOL CONVALESCENT INSTITUTION (former), Allerton Road. A large High Gothic institution by *Thomas Worthington*, opened in 1873 in spacious landscaped grounds amongst mature beeches. It was built with the surplus of the Liverpool Cotton District Relief Fund* for recuperating patients from the City's hospitals. With a generous fund at his disposal and an ambitious committee behind him, Worthington produced one of the best-planned and equipped buildings of its type, providing a variety of accommodation to suite varied types and stages of recuperation, and generous space for exercise and recreation. Polychromatic brick, gables and steep roofs. The site on a W-facing slope is superb, with views across Allerton to the Mersey, Wirral and Wales, and was chosen for its air and its then isolation. The E-plan makes good use of it. Two tall three-storey ward blocks (one male, one female) project out

---

*Established to assist those made unemployed during the Cotton Famine caused by the American Civil War.

from the slope, each housing eighty to a hundred patients in small wards of three to six beds. They also housed day rooms, and workrooms on the ground floor. Linking the rear of the ward blocks at first-floor level (but actually at ground floor behind because of the rise of the land) is a corridor with the service areas behind it. A w-facing terrace stretches between the ward blocks in front of the corridor, and in the middle projects a central wing (but not as far as the wards), which housed the dining hall and a public hall above. It has a tall hipped roof, buttresses and lancets, those to the public hall on the w front in an arcade of attached columns. It once had a flèche too. The public hall was an amendment to the original plan, paid for as a testimonial to W.E. Gladstone by public subscription. The corridor was a crucial aspect of the design, intended not only for circulation, but also as the sitting-out space for patients: to this end the wooden sides could slide open to admit the prevailing sea breezes. Entry is at the circulation level on the N side in an extension by *C.O. Ellison & Son*, built in 1883. It mostly matches the rest in detail, and has a clock tower over the door. The complex is now Woolton Manor Nursing Home.

WOOLTON HALL, Speke Road, may seem at first sight a disappointment if one visited knowing that one limb of the L-plan building is of *c.* 1709–14 and erected by Richard Molyneux, son of the builder of Croxteth Hall's w wing (*see* p. 406), and that the other part is an extensive remodelling of a C17 or earlier wing by *Robert Adam* (*c.* 1774–80), for a new owner, Nicholas Ashton. It is not helped by the contemptuous and contemptible erection in the 1970s of a convent and St Julie's High School (*see* p. 508) on three sides, so close that there are only a few feet between the old and new on two sides. So the house is severed from its grounds, except for the E lawn outside the Carriage Front. Therefore it is impossible to see Molyneux's N WING except in extreme close-up. This wing is an oddity. It has a pediment with trophies and the cross Moline. If original, the triglyph frieze is noteworthy: just one triglyph at the top of the angle quoins and just one metope in the middle. The fenestration is very awkward. First, there are two windows under the pediment, not three: apparently original illiteracy, not alteration. Second, the first-floor windows are squashed up into the frieze, leaving an uncomfortably deep area of blank ashlar between them and the ground-floor windows. It is tempting to link the wing to the equally unattributed 1702 w front of Croxteth, and also to Hale Manor (q.v.) of after 1703, which has similar pediment trophies. On the parapets of all three houses there are gadroons, a very unusual motif outside funeral monuments at this time. The single-storey two-bay addition to the r. is also early C18, probably after 1718 when Richard succeeded as 5th Viscount Molyneux. The apsidal end is of *c.* 1865 for the then new owner, J.R. Jeffery. He was the proprietor of the contemporary Compton House department store in Church Street (*see* p. 314), by *Thomas Haigh & Co.* Did they design this too, and the reglazing with plate glass? All this is red sandstone, except the s side which is brick.

Adam's E or CARRIAGE FRONT is not much more externally satisfying. He had to graft a new three-storey wing onto the existing two-storey one, but did not manage it with the élan associated with his normally ingenious remodellings. Indeed the extent of Adam's oversight of the implementation of his designs has been questioned. Seven bays, with two two-bay pediments at either end (the r. is the Molyneux wing altered). These outer parts are two storeys with medallions between lower and upper windows; the centre of three storeys with *paterae* in the top frieze. The small semi-circular porch was replaced by a big porte cochère *c.* 1865.

INSIDE, the reason for the oddities of the fenestration of the N front is gloriously apparent: a suite of rooms of quite unexpectedly ambitious proportions. They are the three-bay SALON and two-bay TAPESTRY ROOM, and the NEW DRAWING ROOM in the extension. The leftover window in the first phase is between its two rooms, and hid a vestibule and a privy stair. The rooms are lined with excellent contemporary bolection-moulded oak panelling, with fire surrounds and fine fluted pilasters: Composite in the Tapestry Room, and Corinthian elsewhere. All three rooms measure over 17ft (5.2 metres) to the flat ceilings; originally there were still higher, coved ceilings. The wall between the Tapestry Room and the New Drawing Room was taken down before the Second World War to make one combined room; the panelling in the New Drawing Room has been altered, and the doors in the N wall were inserted when a conservatory was added. The wall separating the Molyneux from the Adam work, and parts of the Adam structure elsewhere, are C17 or earlier, the last fragments of the earlier building. In the *Adam* part is a lovely little OCTAGON ROOM on the ground floor, and the FRONT PARLOUR, and another room on the first floor. They have characteristic but not outstanding stucco ceilings. The cantilevered STAIRCASE is also Adam, with a wrought-iron balustrade. But there is none of the virtuoso planning for which Adam is celebrated.

From 1898 the house was a hydropathic hotel, military hospital and then school, and until the early 1970s there were large and largely three-storey extensions to the S and the W.

ASHTON SQUARE is a row of C18 estate cottages off SCHOOL LANE. Gothick – that is pointed – window and door surrounds.

Village Perambulation

The village centre of medieval Woolton, properly Much Woolton, is still recognisable, with the steps and part of the shaft of the VILLAGE CROSS (the top is of 1913) and a pretty row of Early Georgian brick cottages and houses in winding WOOLTON STREET outside the N wall of the Hall. Woolton Street is intersected by HIGH STREET, which did not exist in 1845; despite their early C19 appearance, e.g. arched fanlights, the chequer-brickwork houses on the N side must post-date them. In the mid-C20 High Street was turned into a dual carriageway, severing the medieval centre from the modern one to the N, and, to the W, marooning the former LODGE to Woolton Hall, called Woodleigh, on a broad central reservation. This is 1840s, with unfluted Greek Doric columns; the upper storey with a frieze with swags and urns, may be *c.* 1865. The GATEWAY has been re-sited on the S side of the road. Two more lodges are trapped this way, WOOLTON WOOD LODGE, brick, shaped gables (the house is demolished), and HEATON LODGE beyond, to the Convalescent Institution (*see* p. 508). Flanking Church Road South on the N side are the St James Methodist Church and Church Hall (*see* p. 508), and to the W the former CONGREGATIONAL CHURCH of 1865 by *W. & J. Hay.* Not good. Rock-faced sandstone, round-arched nave windows and weak NW steeple. With its SCHOOL, intensively and insensitively converted into a care home. It is on the corner of QUARRY STREET. Where this meets ALLERTON ROAD is the little PUBLIC BATHS on the corner, built at the turn of the C20. To the N on Allerton Road can be seen the LIBRARY, built as a Methodist chapel in 1834. A simple Georgian box with sash windows. It had a front door in the street façade.

QUARRY STREET and the little streets off it are lined with short rows of mainly early C19 cottages for quarrymen and carters, some brick, some stone and some both. Nos. 2–8 Quarry Street have thick half-round window and door surrounds. There are more in ST MARY'S COURT, PIT PLACE, ROSE STREET and CASTLE STREET. There is also on the E side of Quarry Street the CHURCH HALL of St Mary's (R.C.), which is up on the hill behind (*see* p. 507). The quarries themselves come next, now packed with the – brick – noddy houses of THE OLD QUARRY and CLAY CROSS ROAD. The sight of these little houses in their resolutely suburban layout squashed up against the bottom of the sheer quarry faces, which rise over 100 ft (31 metres) high, is very peculiar indeed. On GREENOUGH STREET are Victorian former quarry STABLES, now housing; beyond them is the former POLICE STATION AND COURT dated 1873; no doubt, then, who were the troublemakers in Victorian Woolton. Brick. Asymmetrical, with a canted bay and arched door surrounds. The VILLAGE INN opposite is pedimented and dated 1854. The initials are those of the builder, *J.M. Fleetwood.*

MILL STILE is a narrow and dramatic footpath rising E from Quarry Street between the two quarries, with the faces falling vertically away on both sides. CHURCH ROAD is at the E end, and on the E side of it are VILLAS. CHURCHFIELD, formerly the parsonage, is ashlar, of three bays, and *c.* 1830. To the r. is ARCHBISHOP'S HOUSE, 1830s, with elongated Greek key incised into corner pilasters, and a Greek Doric porch. Later matching extensions, and bay windows, and a grand

Elizabethan billiard room on the garden side. It was built (as Beechwood) by the corn miller and developer *James Rose* for himself. Further down Church Road on the r. is ROSEMONT, another *Rose* villa of the 1820s with similar motifs, the porch *in antis* this time. Later bay windows. Finally, opposite ST PETER'S CHURCH (*see* p. 507), YEWFIELD. Similar date, but stuccoed, with an iron veranda to the ground floor. A pediment too, and label moulds. Gatepiers with vermiculated rustication. Next to it is the former ST PETER'S NATIONAL SCHOOL, dated 1823, single storey and brick. Behind is a much larger, eclectic, Late Victorian block. Below this Church Road falls away with rows of two- and three-bay early-to-mid-C19 cottages and houses, some with fanlights. A pretty stretch.

Turn l. into MASON STREET, with another three-bay Late Georgian house, with a fanlight, and then back into WOOLTON STREET and the FAMOUS ELEPHANT pub. Despite the 1772 datestone this is an early C19 structure rebuilt by *Harold E. Davies & Son c.* 1930. S of it is the modern centre of Woolton, an informal square at the corner of Woolton Street and ALLERTON ROAD. The sunken car park was a pond; it ought to be restored as the focal point of the village. Overlooking it is the VILLAGE CLUB of 1885. Brick, mullioned-and-transomed windows and a projecting central bay with half-timbering over the entrance. Also BARCLAYS BANK on the corner with Church Road South, one of *Willink & Thicknesse*'s Bank of Liverpool branches. 1901–2. Quieter than most, but the segmental bay with an ashlar hemispherical roof is a charming detail.

Houses on Woolton Hill

Most of the big C19 houses built by the 'carriage folk' – commuting Liverpool merchants – were erected N of Much Woolton village, on the crown and sides of Woolton Hill, to take advantage of the fine prospects to E and W. The best survivors are on the following streets, among later C20 infill:

ACREFIELD ROAD, from the S. On the W side is WOOLTON MOUNT, a development of five villas (two in a semi-detached pair) from the early 1840s. A short straight road paved with sandstone, flanked by four stuccoed buildings, one on either side at the bottom, and one on either side at the top. Some have label moulds and bargeboards, others classical details. S of Woolton Mount is BANKSIDE, a stuccoed Gothic villa. Further N on the same side, but actually on GLENROSE ROAD, are STRAWBERRY HOUSE, MOSSDENE and CRAWSFORDS-BURN. A long stuccoed façade with two little pediments, quoins etc. Unsightly bay windows added. On the other side of Acrefield Road is AYMESTREY COURT, now the Redbourne Hotel. Apparently by *H.B. Bare* for Sir Henry Tate, and largely of *c.* 1881–2 with additions and alterations. Big, and sub-Shaw in style. Red brick, with tall chimneys and some half-timbered gables, and cluttered by clumsy additions on the garden front. Most peculiar is the large gable projecting way out on corbelled brackets over the large mullioned-and-transomed stairwindow. The LODGE, dated 1884, and COACHHOUSE, dated 1887, could be by *F. & G. Holme*, who exhibited designs in 1885. They are similar, but also with tile-hung parts. The lodge is the best bit, and has painted parget panels of roses and sunflowers above the adage 'East or west home is best.'

WOOLTON PARK was laid out as a private road *c.* 1856–8. Beginning at the w end, RIFFEL LODGE, dated 1859. Quite substantial, with half-timbered and elaborately bargeboarded gables. RIFFEL HOUSE (now two) beyond, *c.* 1860–1, is large but not as good as the lodge. Gabled, vaguely Gothic. WOOLTON TOWER is on the E side, on TOWER WAY. Of *c.* 1856–7. Red sandstone. Eclectic, with lots of gables and a narrow and embattled prospect tower. The ballroom wing was added in the 1870s. A LODGE too. Then on the w side, BISHOP'S LODGE, 1869–71, by *Henry A. Bradley*. It was called Baycliff then. Big and largely brick. REYNOLDS PARK lies w of Woolton Park. Created a public park in 1929, the house destroyed by fire *c.* 1975. One LODGE is on WOOLTON HILL ROAD. *F. & G. Holme*, 1888. The influence of the Domestic Revival is evident in the hearth lights. Another more substantial Domestic Revival lodge is on CHURCH ROAD, dated 1888 too, but apparently not by the Holmes. Composed about a central chimneystack, with tile-hung and half-timbered gables, pargeting etc. Very Shavian. Of the grounds, note the YEW GARDEN and outside dining room, designed by *Leila Reynolds* and *Sir Charles Reilly* in the 1930s.

BEACONSFIELD ROAD, starting at the E end with KNOLLE PARK, now St Gabriel's Convent, at the junction with Church Road. A building of conundrums. A house is shown in the area on C18 maps. Henry William Ross, Italian merchant, was living here in the 1820s, and from 1829 Thomas Foster, brother of John Foster Jun., the architect. But how to relate the building to all this? Inside the GATES is a little pedimented LODGE with Greek Doric columns *in antis*, a miniature temple. Is this the work of *John Foster Jun.* for his brother? The house itself is of painted ashlar, with an entrance front of six generous bays, with a slight middle projection and broad giant pilasters. The first-floor windows have eared architraves, like the lodge. A slim four-column porch of crude Corinthian columns *in antis* is surely an addition, and there are other alterations which explain some of the peculiarities. There were iron verandas, and parts of these are re-set in front of the ground-floor windows, which is why these have no architraves. The cornice and panels over the upper windows are missing from the central bays. Most odd is the door, off centre to the r. Yet if it has been moved, why is there a curved masonry wall inside behind the centre (now a niche) where one might expect it to have been? The large institutional extensions to the s have been added since 1909, when the house became a convent and a school, and, subsequently, when a care home was attached.

The delightful entrance hall is on axis with the door, not the house. However, the plan reveals no obvious clues as to how it may have been altered if the front door had indeed previously been elsewhere. The hall is only single-storeyed, with four columns (much better than the portico) and a little dome. Good rich stucco, which is surely Early Victorian, and no fewer than eleven doors, with pairs in the corners. Many are false. To the l., the staircase with an apsidal landing. The arches are clearly later, but the iron balustrade may be 1820s–30s. At some point the staircase was extended down into the basement, presumably to give access to the GROTTO created against the N side of the house, which leads through into the gardens. There are rooms with Early Victorian cornices to the l. and r. in the entrance front, and one behind the hall and stairs in the E front. This, presumably the saloon, with a (later) segmental bay, is now the chapel.

Good sandstone STABLES front Church Road. The slightly projecting centre has a big voussoired arch and giant panelled pilaster strips. The ends are two-storeyed and project. Between the projections and the centre the walls were hideously raised, with doors inserted, when the building was converted to housing.

On the N side of Beaconsfield Road was BEACONSFIELD HOUSE (demolished), built in the 1830s by Ambrose Lace, solicitor (*see* p. 311). No. 84 survives, the COACHMAN'S HOUSE and STABLES of *c.* 1833. A pretty sandstone building with two steep gables to the road and three down the flank, tall chimneys, mullioned windows with label moulds and a door with ogee lintel. Further W is Nos. 35–37 Beaconsfield Road, the LODGE, a pre-existing building made over in similar Jacobethan style after 1848. On the s side is CEDARWOOD, the *Woman's Journal* House of the Year 1960, by *Dewi Prys Thomas* and *Gerald R. Beech*. Cantilevered timber upper storey with very shallow pyramid roof. Calmly unshowy, and carefully detailed and composed. Several other houses by *Beech* in this neighbourhood, e.g. COURT HOUSE, Beaconsfield Road, 1961, and THE GREY BUNGALOW, Quarry Street, 1963. Also on the s side, STONELEIGH, *c.* 1858–9, red sandstone. A disciplined classical villa of outstanding workmanship, with a Doric porch *in antis* on the entrance front. On the E side is a Late Victorian extension containing a fine panelled billiard room with inglenook. To the road is a service wing and yard.

Then down a lane on the l. NEWSTEAD, a much more modest house of three bays. Of *c.* 1820? The label moulds have carved stops, and the building has tentatively been identified as one of *Thomas Rickman*'s 'cottages'. Back on Beaconsfield Road are more mansions. On the r., BEACON HILL, *c.* 1868, stuccoed Italianate, and now part of Abbot's Lea School. ABBOTS LEA itself is set back behind. Of 1862, by *William Culshaw*, red sandstone, big and Gothic, with an early C20 extension. On the l.,

Woodcroft, built as Streatlam Cottage *c.* 1867 for James L. Bowes. He was a wool broker and noted collector of Japanese art (for his grand town house, Streatlam Tower, *see* Toxteth, p. 476). The house is of brick with stone dressings, and a gable and bargeboards on the entrance side and bay windows on the garden front.*

Finally, the site of Druids Cross House, Druids Cross Road. A villa of 1847 by *Harvey Lonsdale Elmes* in Italianate mode, demolished in 1978. The sandstone stables, with typical Italianate tower, survive buried in Druids Park, an estate of houses built over the site.

LOWTON
Golborne

6090

Once a scattered township of farms and weavers' cottages, across flat uninteresting landscape in the NE corner of the ancient parish of Winwick. Now split into two by the East Lancashire Road (A580): the S is still rural, but the N is heavily built up with late C19 and C20 housing which merges into Golborne (q.v.).

St Luke, Slag Lane. Nave, 1732, N transept, 1771, S transept, *c.* 1813. Brick with quoins and keyed-in round-arched windows with Y-tracery. Two superimposed lunette windows in the S transept too. The W tower is 1862 and turns the Georgian round arches to a Norman purpose with Norman enrichment. It replaced a cupola, and within it is the original pedimented door surround. The chancel is probably 1856, with triple round-headed windows and a round chancel arch, also with Norman detailing. A C20 NW vestry. The roof is C19. Only the W gallery, on slender cast-iron columns, survives of the C18 fittings – including transept galleries, box pews and font – *in situ* in 1968. They went in the unfortunate reordering of 1972, which introduced the crude Neo-Jacobean altar rails pushed forward of the chancel arch, and a blundering partition in the N transept. – The studded doors must be original. – Brass name plaques from the box pews mounted on the S wall. – stained glass. Not very good. The E window, commemorating Victoria's Diamond Jubilee, is by *Campbell, Smith & Co.* – monument. Crisp Neoclassical tablet to Ann Prescott, †1918, and her son. – sundial. Outside the W end. C18. Enriched (but damaged) baluster pedestal, missing the dial.

St Mary, Newton Road, Newton Common. 1860–1, by *E.G. Paley.* Modest and aisle-less. The best feature is the W front, which closes the view down Sandy Lane. Three-light window framed by buttresses united above by an arch to carry a double bellcote at the apex. A First World War memorial is axially aligned in front.

---

*A number of other villas are demolished, including Strawberry Field. Yes, that one.

ST CATHERINE (R.C.), Lane Head. By *Weightman & Bullen*, 1957–9. The first centrally planned Roman Catholic church in SW Lancashire, its design contains elements that would re-appear in modified form at subsequent churches such as St Ambrose, Speke (*see* p. 457). Hexagon plus detached open-framed concrete belfry tower over the baptistery, the two joined by a lobby.

OAKLANDS, No. 196 Newton Road. A big villa dated 1883. Pressed red brick, turret and bays, with some Gothic details (e.g. vine-scroll), and wooden panelling and panelled ceilings. The staircase is lit by a painted-glass window with Pre-Raphaelite women.

BYROM HALL, 1 m. NE of St Luke on Slag Lane. A gaunt three-bay, three-storey house with a date of 1713. Rendered brick. String courses, modillion cornice, and a barrel-shaped canopy on nice scrolled brackets over the door. Late C20 windows. Inside is a handsome staircase with twisted balusters and sunken-panelled rectangular newels. One door is still marked 'Cheese Room', a reminder that the area was once famed nationally for its cheeses.

FAIR HOUSE FARMHOUSE, Pocket Nook Lane. Probably early C17. Four bays with cross-wing to the l. Though encased in rendered brick and with replacement C20 stone mullions, it is timber-framed, as revealed in the r. gable end. Here is a king-post truss with raked struts arranged in herringbone pattern, typical of Lancashire. Below the tie-beam the wall is set back slightly, there are braces and a rare (though rebuilt) wooden five-light mullioned window. Lobby-entrance plan; behind the C20 porch is a well-preserved pair of back-to-back inglenooks (including smokehoods. Philip Powell).

HOLLY HOUSE, Newton Road, S of the A580, S side. A red brick Late Georgian box, of three bays and two storeys, with a pyra-midal roof and Doric door surround. It faces E – to shelter from prevailing westerlies? Fanlight and all sashes modern.

LIME HOUSE, Newton Road, S of the A580, N side. A villa built by William Eckersley, director of a Tyldesley mill, in 1903. His cipher abounds. Sprawling, brick and unhappy. Large unsym-pathetic late C20 additions. Inside, an Art Nouveau-detailed staircase, and stained-glass portraits of Crompton, Arkwright and Watt – the men whose inventions made the Eckersley wealth possible. Now a nursing home.

SANDFIELD HALL, Newton Road, S of the A580, S side. Built for George Airey, a Wigan brewer, in 1898. Brick, asymmet-rical with ogee-capped turrets.

LYDIATE

3000

The S part is now all but an extension of the C20 suburbia of Maghull (q.v.). N of the Leeds and Liverpool Canal (*see* p. 52) it is still rural, spread out sparsely along the A5147.

St Thomas, Church Lane. 1839–41, probably by *A.H. Holme* (*S. Holme & Son* were the builders). Simple little four-bay nave with lancets and a little w tower. The chancel, n vestry, s chapel etc. of 1912 by *Austin & Paley* of course much more varied and archaeologically correct. It is evident outside and particularly inside that this was just the first phase of a complete rebuilding which got no further than the chancel arch and the w arcade responds. The 1841 nave, making a curiously enjoyable contrast, is aisle-less, with a flat ceiling supported by unmoulded tie-beams, and a deep w GALLERY on spindly cast-iron columns, – as one would expect for the date. – STAINED GLASS. Good glass of 1913 in the chancel s window. – The rendered VICARAGE looks about contemporary with the nave and tower.

Our Lady (R.C.), Southport Road (A5147). 1854–5, by *J.J. Scoles*. Rock-faced stone. Late Dec/early Perp tracery including a reticulated e window; short nw tower, aisles with arcades of octagonal piers, and a w gallery. Scissor-brace trusses. – Rich REREDOS by *Edmund Kirby*, erected in 1878, with relief scenes and canopied statues. – SCULPTURE. A series of uncommonly fine Nottingham alabaster reliefs from the life of St Catherine. In addition a Visitation, and a St Cuthbert attached to the pulpit. They are all of *c.* 1420–40. The iconography of course is standard. The panels come from the old chapel of St Catherine (*see* below). – In the churchyard, the upper part of a medieval CROSS, on a base and lower shaft of the 1870s.

St Catherine (ruins), sw of Our Lady across the A5147. A little Perp chapel, five bays, no aisles, with a short w tower with a big arch for a w window. Pinnacles and battlements are now missing. Much of the stone appears to be recycled. Considerable debate about the age, but A. d'Arcy has persuasively argued for *c.* 1540–3. The windows are similar to those of Sefton church (q.v.), which is dated *c.* 1520–45, though with round-arched lights. Moreover, the same masons' marks can be seen at Sefton. That would make the patrons the same couple who built Lydiate Hall (*see* below) – Lawrence and Eleanor Ireland – and their initials and arms could once be seen carved into the masonry. Eleanor was also the sister of the rector of Sefton. The most peculiar feature is that there are no n windows at all. Here d'Arcy postulates an interruption in construction and the dispersal of skilled labour, giving as further evidence changes in the masons' marks in the upper parts of the walls, the crudity of the door lintels and the absence of a piscina. The chapel was probably built as a chapel of ease (to Halsall, q.v.) and was possibly conceived as a chantry too. It was roofless by the early c18.

Lydiate Hall, w of Southport Road (A5147), n of St Catherine. Much could still be written on Lydiate Hall when the VCH was published in 1907, and quite a lot photographed by the RCHM in 1953. Now there are only fragments closely hemmed in by trees. It was of courtyard plan, timber-framed on three sides, with a stone range on the e side (demolished in the C18) that may have been medieval. The other parts came from the C16, with important elements almost certainly put up by Lawrence and Eleanor Ireland in the 1540s. Amongst the evidence are drawings of panelling and door which have identical motifs to the screens of the S chapel at Sefton church, and lettering similar to that on the bench ends there (*see* p. 582). The door came from a first-floor room and was part of scheme supposedly depicting Henry VIII, five of his wives and Edward VI. Like that of Speke Hall (the Irelands were related to the Norrises of Speke), the hall had a cove at the upper end, a flat panelled ceiling and a fireplace built against the screens passage. Only the great, stone, Tudor-arched fireplace survives. To the S is a C19 mullioned-and-transomed window and the remains of a similar fireplace, destroyed by a falling tree in 2000. On the other side are the remnants of the N wing as rebuilt *c.* 1895 in pressed brick, but including a number of C16 fireplaces. – A FARM to the N with barn dated 1741.

OLD GORE FARMHOUSE, at the S end of Altcar Lane. A yeoman's house of brick on a stone plinth, with a plaque dated 1596. The suspicion must be that this is *ex situ* because the 1590s would be remarkably early for the use of brick by this level of society – the Lancastrian aristocracy was then only just beginning to adopt it. Also, it is set into a two-storey porch with round archway forming part of a baffle-entry plan, and this date would be equally early for such an archway and such an arrangement. Otherwise, of four bays with a complete set of low mullioned windows in the front. These have label moulds formed simply of a single course of raised bricks. These look mid- to late C17, probably the true age of the building.

SCOTCH PIPER INN, Southport Road (A5147). A pretty whitewashed and thatched pub, propped with a series of battered brick buttresses. The building has probably been an inn since the C17. Though not as old as the date of 1320 claimed on the sign, it contains parts of cruck frames dated to the mid to late C16. They are in the two single-storey bays, l., which were encased in brick in the C17. The later r. bay, which is half a storey higher, was possibly a shippon, and was rebuilt in the C18 using some stone and timber from the E range of Lydiate Hall. For once the simple interior has escaped the relentless march of pub refurbishment, and contains a tiny bar, and worn benches around another cosy room. How much longer can it survive?

SEAFORD CLOSE. Housing of 1965 between the canal and the A5147. By *Harding & Horsman*. A close of small houses with zigzag monopitch roofs and timber trim. 'Bright and up-to-the-minute', wrote Pevsner in 1969.

MAGHULL

N of Liverpool, an anonymous C20 dormitory with parades of shops and the remnants of an old village spanning the Leeds and

Liverpool Canal (*see* p. 52). Suburbanisation began with villas erected after the railway arrived in 1849.

St Andrew, Damfield Lane. 1878–80, by *James F. Doyle*. Sizeable, rock-faced, with a w tower, aisles, chancel etc. Late C13 style (lancets). Not of special merit. The interior in particular lacks interest. – STAINED GLASS. All by *A.L. Moore (& Son)*, 1890s–*c*. 1920. Best is the last, a First World War memorial under the tower. – MONUMENTS. Anne Jaret, †1885. An octagonal brass plaque in a foliated marble Star-of-David-shaped surround.

In the CHURCHYARD, a truncated pyramid to members of the Harrison family. The first burial, †1835, marks the date (see the heavy Grecian palmettes at the top). – Close by, a place of pilgrimage for boys of all ages, the grave of the model manufacturer Frank Hornby, †1936, marked on the tomb of his daughter Patricia, †1919. Gothic, a marble tabernacle sheltering a tombstone. – VICARAGE. Three-bay brick early C19 house, with ugly additions on the s front (by *Doyle*, or a bit later?).

Old St Andrew. Of the church only the chancel and the N chapel are left standing in the churchyard, a tiny but pretty fragment dwarfed by Doyle's w tower. They were part of a C13 chapel of ease to Halsall church (q.v.). The medieval fabric is mainly in the N half of the building; the SW corner dates from 1883, when the nave and large s extension of 1830 were demolished. The joins between old and new are evident in the s and w walls. C13 intersecting tracery in the chapel E window; the tracery of the chancel E window is C19. On the s side the little square-headed C14 window to the E is original; that to the w is a copy. The picturesquely placed turret is the reused and re-sited bell-turret of the former nave, which dated from 1755. The w doorway is clearly reused C13 material; the porch is 1883. Inside, a low arcade of two bays, with round piers and double-chamfered arches. Some nailhead moulding on the w respond. This and the moulding of the capitals (a hollow between two rolls) point to an earlier C13 date. C19 roofs. In the s wall, mutilated PISCINA and SEDILIA. – FONT. C14, octagonal. C19 base and COVER. – WALL PAINTING. Traces of probably medieval wall painting on the E wall s of the window. An angel's shoulder is just about visible. – MONUMENTS. Some C19 wall plaques.

Chapel House, NE of the church in Deyes Lane. Stone, four bays, with low mullioned windows and a two-storey porch with a mullioned-and-transomed window. Probably mid to late C17 (but not earlier, because the porch has a round-arched entrance, not four-pointed). Baffle-entry plan, presumably with parlour l. and housebody and kitchen, r. The plan is unusual in not having at least one cross-wing, and the large first-floor window in the l. return is clearly C19–C20; it is hard to imagine the original was as large.

Manor House, Sefton Lane, ½ m. w. A handsome late C18 house, possibly of 1780. Now a care home, with nothing of interest left inside. Brick. The façade is of a basement and

two storeys, with two full-height canted bay windows. These
windows have surrounds with attached Tuscan columns and
entablatures. Nice doorcase reached by an outer stair, with the
same attached columns, which have fluted necks, and a pediment with festoons across the frieze. The brick of this façade
is different from the sides: refacing, or was the best stuff limited
to the front? The house is considerably deeper than wide. The
brickwork and parapet suggest that the s side is an original
wing extending back, but that the N side is of two phases. The
1849 Ordnance Survey map seems to support the thesis of an
earlier L-plan. If this was so, the w section of the N side cannot
be very much later because it has hornless twelve-pane sashes
of thoroughly Georgian character. Below the parapet a cornice
unites all parts. A c19 prospect tower has been demolished. At
the end of the s front is an ARCH from the old church (*see*
above) re-erected here in 1885. Round c13 piers, double-chamfered arches; similar to the surviving arcade in the old chapel.
It was part of an arcade of at least three bays.

There is also a datestone of 1638 re-set over a doorway.
This probably came from an earlier house NE of the present
building, where the now-dry arms of its MOAT survive on the
N and E sides of a large platform. On the inner edge of the E
arm are the derelict remains of a small stone building, with a
fallen lintel dated 1667. This may have been the 'outcast' listed
in 1709. The grounds were extended to incorporate the various
big homes erected by the PARKHAVEN TRUST, established
1888 at the Manor House as the Maghull Homes to provide
residential care for epileptics. The best is HARRISON HOUSE,
opened in of 1902 for first-class patients. A slightly asymmetric, Shavian L-plan building, roughcast above the ground floor
of its two-and-a-half storeys. It is just inside the entrance from
Liverpool Road South, with c18 rusticated GATEPIERS, and a
LODGE set into the wall.

MELLING

³⁰⁹⁰ Still a small village, on a gentle little hill amidst farmland just
beyond the suburban sprawl of N Liverpool, and set in the angle
between the M 57 and the M 58.

ST THOMAS, Rock Lane. *c.* 1830–4, by *J. W. Casson*, replacing a
medieval chapel of ease. Additions of 1873 are the chancel, N
organ loft and s vestry – and the w tower too? (it is not on
Casson's plans). Simple little church of Commissioners' type.
Pink sandstone, crudely tooled. Lancet windows, feeble buttresses. The w tower has giant arches on the w and N sides containing windows and the door. Deep w GALLERY on cast-iron
columns. – STAINED GLASS. Three-light E window by *Holiday*,
1907. – MONUMENTS. Wall memorials including R. Bootle,
†1758, and a tablet to Margaret Hoskings, †1838, by *W. Spence*.
– SUNDIAL. In the churchyard. An c18 fluted Tuscan column

on a possibly medieval cross base. – LYCHGATE. A war memorial of 1921 with handsome framing.

OLD VICARAGE, Tithebarn Lane E of the church. Probably early 1830s. Tudor style, of ashlar, with mullioned windows and low-pitched roofs. Three symmetrical bays with two gables. A r. extension of 1849 demolished.

SCHOOL (former), School Lane, ¼ m. NE. Dated 1844. Tudor Gothic. Single-storey, dressed stone.

BARNES FARMHOUSE, No. 166 Tithebarn Lane, ½ m. E. Dated 1654. Low and humble, with low mullioned windows. Dressed stone, four bays, the r. one an addition. As is common in this part of the world the doorway still has a depressed pointed arch.

WOOD HALL, W of Brewery Lane, ⅔ m. WNW. Now a farmhouse. Three bays, brick with stone dressings. C17, with an C18 front including a doorcase with pulvinated frieze and a pediment on consoles. Above this a stone carved with royal arms and the initials IR. Is this an indication of the date of the building, or does it commemorate a visit by James II, as folklore would have it? The house was owned until the 1750s by the Molyneux family (not the Sefton and Croxteth branch). They were recusants, and the hall was certainly the location of secret Masses.

NETHERTON

A dreary post-war suburb built by Bootle Borough Council, which swamped a tiny hamlet in the flat landscape N of Bootle and Liverpool. Two parts: S of the meandering Leeds and Liverpool Canal (see p. 52), 4,500 dwellings of 1950–8; N of the canal, the Sefton estate begun in the mid 1960s according to Radburn principles; 3,000 housing units were envisaged. Some four-storey blocks were built in the Sefton estate scheme; otherwise both parts are low-rise.

ST BENET (former; R.C.), Chapel Lane. 1793, replacing a cottage and barn used by Benedictine priests sponsored by the Earls of Sefton. One of the best-preserved examples of a pre-Emancipation Catholic chapel in the North West, made redundant in 1975 but thankfully now in the loving ownership of the Historic Chapels Trust. Typically, a very modest and cautious brick exterior. To the road a standard three-bay house – the presbytery – with a pretty doorway that has a broken pediment and a fanlight. Attached discreetly to the rear is the chapel, with large, round-headed sash windows in the plain side walls. These have intersecting glazing bars in the heads. The bellcote on the W gable must be an addition. Inside, a W GALLERY with stick balustrade, panelled dado and a cornice. The E wall has a plaster aedicule of paired fluted Corinthian pilasters, an entablature with urns and garlands, and an open pediment. From the pediment hang swagged curtains revealing a Gloria and cherubs, beneath which an altar painting. Paint analysis has revealed a typically restrained C18 decorative scheme of

light stone, off white, and gilding of capitals, angels and rays.
The dado panelling was grained. – Marbled sarcophagus
ALTAR, possibly 1830s.

ORCHARD FARMHOUSE, Buckley Hill Lane (B5422). C17 with
additions. The oldest part is the r. bay with mullioned window.
Partly of dressed stone, partly of brick.

NEW SPRINGS *see* ASPULL

NEWBURGH

A pretty village in pretty country, on elevated ground sloping
down to the s bank of the River Douglas. Granted a charter in
1304; a restored C17 MARKET CROSS is on the Green.

CHRIST CHURCH, Back Lane. Built in 1851 on the site of a coal
pit. A little aisle-less single-vessel church with lancets, unconvincing buttresses and a bellcote over the junction of nave and
chancel. Sandstone. w gallery. A new, lower chancel with Geometrical tracery, and N vestries, added later.

OLD SCHOOL, Course Lane. Now two houses. The school was
endowed by Thomas Crane in 1714. That appears a plausible
date for this surprisingly large and curious-looking building.
Coursed sandstone with a stone slate roof; one-and-a-half
storeys forming a T-plan. The principal façade faces N: four
bays, the centre two cramped-up together with segmental-
headed mullioned-and-transomed windows on the ground
floor and mullioned windows above, rising into a little gable.
The outer bays – presumably to the classrooms – are much
wider, and each has a large mullioned-and-transomed window
on the ground floor only. These have almost semicircular heads
and are the distinctive motif of the building: there is another
in the E gable end facing the lane, another in the s end of the
wing projecting from the s side, and another in the w bay of
the s side. A number of other mullioned windows scattered
around. Finials formerly on the gables. A stone porch with
segmental-headed door is attached awkwardly at the w end of
the N façade. Has it been moved from the centre of the front?

PRIMARY SCHOOL, Back Lane. Next to the church. A girls'
school of 1860, with additions of 1890 (and low post-war
extensions too). The two Victorian phases are small and pretty,
of coursed sandstone with lancets and big steep gabled roofs.
They are joined by a short timber-framed link.

The little sloping GREEN has some attractive buildings around
it. The most interesting are on the SE side, which is COBB'S
BROW LANE. Nos. 1–3 are a brick baffle-entry farmhouse, subsequently divided, dated 1691 on the cross-wing. Some surviving mullioned windows and a corbelled platband. Possibly
a rebuild of an earlier structure. Next to them is handsome
MOORCROFT HOUSE, dated 1741 on the rainwater head. The

symmetrical, formal classicism of its brick, three-bay front is an enormous contrast with its vernacular neighbour built only fifty years before. Flush sashes, keystones and a high 'forehead' housing a big attic storey. Fine timber semicircular canopy on elaborate brackets. The cellar windows at the rear are still mullioned, though. Former barn attached to the r. Then the baffle-entry plan ROSE COTTAGE, which has a rubble façade with sliding sashes under big hoodmoulded lintels, but timber framing, including raked struts and a kingpost, exposed in the l. gable. This could be late C16–early C17; the rebuilding possibly early C18. Further s on the w side, LOWE'S FARMHOUSE is an early double-pile house, possibly of *c.* 1700, with a later Gibbs door surround. Three bays, three storeys. Hipped roof with coupled upper cruck trusses over the front range, twin gables at the rear. Staircase with newels composed of clusters of turned balusters.

DOE HOUSE, Tabby's Nook. C17 and altered and enlarged. The unusual feature is the porch which also includes the staircase, lit by a small two-light window up and to the l. of the segmental-headed doorway.

WHITE COTTAGES, Back Lane, ¼ m. NW. A cruck-framed longhouse, whitewashed and single-storeyed with lofts; now two cottages. C17 or earlier. The r. half was the shippon.

WOODCOCK HALL, E off Cobb's Brow Lane, ¼ m. S. An attractive brick house, dated 1719 on the splendid rainwater heads, illustrating the transition amongst the upper yeomanry to classicism. A symmetrical front of two-and-a-half storeys with a complete set of timber cross-windows and a semicircular door hood (cf. Moorcroft House above). The plan is double pile. Gary Miller describes a hall flanked by what was probably the parlour and dining room, and at the rear, but not on axis, a dog-leg stair with turned balusters and square newels. However, the façade still has three gables rather than a parapet, and there are four windows on the ground and first floors set against the three gables. Also there are no external classical mouldings other than the consoled door hood.

LEEDS AND LIVERPOOL CANAL. AQUEDUCT over the River Douglas, ⅓ m. ENE, by *John Longbotham*, 1771–2. Semi-elliptical sandstone arch with voussoirs. Also little semicircular aqueducts over Culvert Lane and Deans Lane, *c.* 1771–4. *James Brindley* succeeded Longbotham as resident engineer *c.* 1771–2, so they may be his.

RAILWAY. On Culvert Lane and Deans Lane, attractive GATE-KEEPERS' COTTAGES of *c.* 1860 of the type at Burscough (*see* p. 162).

NEWTON-LE-WILLOWS
with EARLESTOWN

5090

Newton-le-Willows (or Newton in Makerfield), formerly the head of a Hundred, is a town of two parts: the C13 borough and market established along the old London–Carlisle road where it crossed the dene of the Newton Brook, its historic form still alive, just, as the High Street; and the mean industrial extensions that now dwarf it to the w, Earlestown and Wargrave, born out of the opening of the Liverpool & Manchester Railway through Newton in 1830. This rapidly brought foundries, soda and vitriol works. The population was 1,643 in 1825; today it is *c.* 20,000. The Leghs were the dominant influence after the family acquired the barony in 1660. With that came Newton Hall, a marvellously picturesque early C17 house shamefully demolished in 1964.

CHURCHES

ST PETER, Church Street. 1892–1901, by *Demaine & Brierley* of York, on the site of a C17 chapel (the earliest reference is 1284). Newton was made a separate parish from Winwick in 1841, and a new church was built at Wargrave (*see* p. 525). St Peter's was largely paid for by the printer George McCorquodale and his family, and the vicar of the time. Handsome, red stone, with a satisfyingly massive w tower to terminate the High Street and turn the corner down Church Street into the wooded dene of Newton Brook. The style is a free Perp reminiscent of Paley & Austin, though the tracery details are more directly Art Nouveau and in place of Paley & Austin's greater spatial and material subtlety is a different pleasure in the play of chunky orthogonal masses. The interior however would benefit from that subtlety, being a bland space, with aisles (too broad) but no chancel arch. The roof is a visually weak arch-braced collar.

FITTINGS. POLYPTYCH and ALTAR FRONTAL, *Shrigley & Hunt*, 1910. Seven panels with elaborate Perp-panelled heads. A good clean would transform it. – PULPIT. A handsome Perp piece in alabaster by *A. W. Smith* of Manchester, 1907. With statuettes. – COMMUNION RAIL. Wrought-iron; Georgian. From the earlier chapel? – STAINED GLASS. *Shrigley & Hunt* did almost all of it. The E window, seven lights of the Ascension flanked by the Evangelists, is more interesting than their norm: a warmer palette and without the usual densely pinnacled backdrop. – SCULPTURE. Marble bust of George McCorquodale, N aisle. – MONUMENT. By the porch outside, a gravestone to Peers Naylor, †1842, with a locomotive in relief. The inscription reads:

> My engine now is cold and still,
> No water does my boiler fill;
> My coke affords its flame no more,
> My days of usefulness are o'er.
> My wheels deny their noted speed,
> No more my guiding hand they heed.
> My whistle, too, has lost its tone,
> Its shrill and thrilling sounds are gone.
> My valves are now thrown wide open,

My flanges all refuse to glide.
My clacks, also, though once so strong,
Refuse to aid the busy throng.
No more I feel each urging breath,
My steam is now condensed to death.
Life's railway's o'er, each station past,
In death I'm stopped, and rest at last.
Farewell, dear Friends, and cease to weep,
In Christ I'm safe; in Him I sleep.

ALL SAINTS, Crow Lane. 1913–14, by *William & Segar Owen*. Minor Perp, without the intended w tower, or transepts. The architects also designed the HIGH ALTAR. – STAINED GLASS. E window, *Shrigley & Hunt*, 1929.

EMMANUEL, Church Drive, Wargrave. Built here as Newton's first parish church in 1840–1, to serve its new industrial community (*see* Vulcan Village, p. 530).* The curious w steeple must be modelled on St Oswald, a mile away at Winwick (q.v.), from which the parish was carved – e.g. diagonal buttresses and undersized spire, set back – but not the bell-openings, three stepped lancets with lively Somerset tracery. The utterly simple church body has unmoulded lancets starkly recessed, and unmoulded lancets projecting. All is red sandstone. The original shallow chancel was incongruously replaced in 1925–6 by *Brierley & Rutherford* (appointed on the strength of Brierley's St Peter), part of a scheme to replace the whole church. Thus the roof pitches and masonry clash terribly, there is a blocked s arch to an intended Lady Chapel, and the junction with the nave is raw and of permanently temporary brick. Inside, the first church is broad and gallery-less, with big decorative trusses with pendants. A 1980s reordering created vestries under a new w gallery and filled in the chancel arch of 1926 (which shows the beginnings of the planned 1920s nave arcade) to form a parish hall to the E. The STAINED GLASS of 1943 remains in the three E lancets.

ST JOHN BAPTIST, Market Street, Earlestown. 1875–8, by *C. T. Whitley & Fry* of Dover (Whitley was the rector's son). A big church that would have been far more imposing if the w tower, which was not begun until the 1920s, had been completed. With a low concrete 1970s annexe attached to the unfinished tower, the w end is very untidy. Otherwise, lancets and Geometrical tracery, gabled N and S projections (now vestries) and apsidal chancel. Yellow quarry-faced stone and red stone dressing. Three-and-a-half bay nave of impressive scale, with alternating round and octagonal piers. Crown-post roof. Reordered: choir stalls and pews gone, platform extended w of the chancel arch. – Matching FONT and PULPIT. Stone with alabaster shafts. – STAINED GLASS. E windows, average *Shrigley & Hunt* work.

---

*An axial pair of lodges, Tudorbethan rectory and school, all 1840s, are demolished.

St Mary and St John (R.C.), Crow Lane. 1864, by *Gilbert Blount*. Rock-faced stone. C13 in style – lancets – with an ambitious NW spire (completed 1880), aisles and a polygonal apse. The W window is unusual: a large convex-sided triangle with three cinquefoil circles gathered inside. Reordered with ROOD. – The TRIPTYCH over the altar by *F.X. Velarde*, of *c.* 1958, has been removed. – SCULPTURE. Stations of the Cross by *David John*.

St Patrick (R.C.), Common Road, Earlestown. By *Felix A. Jones* of *Jones & Kelly*, Dublin, 1957–8. Italian Romanesque style, in brick and pebbledash, with a W loggia, S campanile and blank apsidal chancel with N and S chapels, each with a copper semi-domed roof. This makes the E end, in a sculptural way, the most interesting aspect. Interior with vaulted ceiling and narrow low aisles.

United Reformed Church (former), Crow Lane. Formerly Congregational. 1842, by *J.A. Picton*. A solid red ashlar box, with plain lancets, and a wheel window and twin porches in the gable end facing the road. Austere is the word for it. The interior had no galleries, and a flat ceiling divided by ribs into squares, with saltire-pattern ribs in each. In 2005 the church was closed, and residential conversion, entailing internal subdivision, was anticipated. Richard Evans, †1864, left enough money to build a second, bigger church (by *W. & J. Hay*, 1888), but that was demolished in the late 1960s. – The tall red granite OBELISK commemorating Evans remains.

Cemetery, Park Road South, Wargrave. The chapel is a brick octagon within a square, with porch, and lancets. 1884, by *R. Brierley*, Surveyor to the Newton Improvement Commissioners. He did the LODGE too.

TRANSPORT STRUCTURES

Liverpool & Manchester Railway. Newton was almost the halfway point on the L&MR, which was the first modern railway when it opened in 1830 (*see* Introduction, p. 53). It is the site of some its most impressive and influential engineering, and its most infamous incident. First, the engineering. To span the valleys of the Newton and Sankey brooks *George Stephenson* designed two RAILWAY VIADUCTS. They are undoubtedly handsome, but otherwise unremarkable until one grasps that they are in fact the world's first and thus the prototype for thousands that followed. There had been railway bridges before (e.g. on Stephenson's Darlington & Stockton Railway), but nothing of multiple large span. Of course, railway viaducts were decended from canal aqueducts, where the structural challenges had already been mastered. The SANKEY VIADUCT spanning Bradley Lane, N, 1828–30, being the longer at nine arches, has always been the more renowned; on opening, the L&MR organised five-shilling excursions from Liverpool to view it. Stephenson first proposed curious interlacing arches, which suggests he had little knowledge of aqueduct design. This prompted the directors to consult *Jesse Hartley*, the Liverpool Docks engineer, and a bridge builder by training (*see* p. 260). He favoured elliptical arches, but it was Stephenson's revised design, with 50-ft (15.4-metre) semi-circular arches, that was built. The faces are rusticated ashlar, but the structure is brick (revealed in the arch jambs). A cor-belled pilaster on each battered pier carries the cornice. The height is 60 ft (18.5 metres) to the crown of the arches. The builders were *Allcard* and *Fyfe* and the cost was £45,208, almost half the total for bridges for the whole line. The NEWTON VIADUCT, 1 m. E at Newton-le-Willows station, completed in 1828, has only four arches. Stone is largely restricted to voussoirs and pilasters.

And so to the infamy. E of the Parkside Road overbridge on the S side of the tracks,* a MEMORIAL – a severe stucco Neo-classical pavilion open on the rail side to reveal a wreathed aedicule containing a tablet – marks the spot where, during the opening celebrations on 15 September 1830, the Liberal M.P. for Liverpool, William Huskisson, was fatally injured by the *Rocket* (*see* p. 546) whilst attempting to climb to safety into the Duke of Wellington's carriage. Gripped by panic he grabbed the door, but it only swung open into the path of the locomotive. The tablet itself was probably erected not long after, the pavilion in the early C20. Restored from dereliction in 2000. The tablet is a replica (the original is at the National Railway Museum, York).

Finally, STATIONS. Between the two viaducts is EARLESTOWN STATION. On the island platform is a charming building of *c.* 1845, Tudor Gothic and monumental *en miniature* with lovely detailing. Stone, with handsome concave-sided chimneystacks and an embattled and panelled bay facing Liverpool. The pitch of the roof was lowered in 1903, when the canopy was replaced with the present timber structure, of chamfered posts and a forest of curved brackets. NEWTON-LE-WILLOWS STATION, 1845, is plainer, and largely of brick. E wing and present canopy later. The L&MR did not provide accommodation at most intermediary stations until the 1840s, though entrepreneurs provided refreshment buildings (*see* the Legh Arms, p. 528). Earlestown is finer than the norm because when built it was the junction for the line to Birmingham and London.

SANKEY BROOK NAVIGATION (Canal). Newton is the spot where the world's first modern railway spanned the country's first modern canal, and the meeting was a popular subject for artists and engravers. The canal (*see* p. 52), opened in 1757, is now disused and partially filled in. Off Bradlegh Road in the Sankey Valley Country Park are the last surviving iron SWING BRIDGE, *c.* 1857 (when the canal was repaired and moder-

*No public access – sit on the S side of a Liverpool–Manchester train to glimpse it.

nised) and, N, the remains of an original LOCK, with much-patched red sandstone retaining walls.

THE CENTRE

The historic centre of Newton proper is the HIGH STREET along the old Carlisle road. Despite the heavy traffic, relentless building 'improvements' and the few buildings of individual merit, this still manages to be a pleasantly modest market street – leafy, very gently winding, low-rise and wide. Beginning at the E end by the church are the C18 STOCKS. Opposite, the KIRK-FIELD ARMS (the principal inn at the turn of the C19), with illiterate modern Doric doorcases, and an adjoining apartment block, which is enough to make you grimace, particularly when you know it replaced the early C19 Town Hall and Assembly Room, demolished as recently as 1994. On the N side are Nos. 10–18, a terrace of three-storey, single-bay houses with a plaque – TL 1825 – and one or two cottages that have survived mauling (e.g. No. 26 with heavily rusticated render); further along, the big Neo-C17 PIED BULL HOTEL of the 1930s, a roadhouse reminder of Newton's trunk-route days. Then a handsome red sandstone ARCHWAY, built in the late C18 a mile further N as the gateway to Haydock Lodge (*see* Ashton-in-Makerfield), a Legh estate. Re-erected here in 1840 as the Market House; in 2002–3 restored by *Anthony Grimshaw Associates* as a restaurant, with rear extension. The archway is framed by a giant Doric aedicule crowned by the Leghs' ram, and is flanked by little wings of attached Doric colonnades with lunettes in between (the sills to the r. dropped to form sash windows). These terminate with slightly projecting bays of contrasting pattern. Further W are Nos. 158 and 160, little brick COTTAGES. No. 158 had a cruck and other fragments of a timber frame behind the later walls, which dendrochronology suggested dated from the late C16, and possibly from more than one phase. Floored *c.* 1615, dormer reconstructed half a century later. No. 160 was essentially C18. Such was their condition that restoration in 2002–3 became all but replication. Opposite, the former POLICE STATION, 1898–9, by *Henry Littler*, County Architect, converted into flats in 2002–3. T-plan (police court formerly in the stem), red brick, bays and a gable, with buff terracotta mullioned-and-transomed windows.

This is the end of the High Street. A few other cottages survive beyond, amongst C19 and C20 housing: On Ashton Road, N, one with a platband, and W on CROW LANE (the road to Earlestown) Nos. 159–163: a short row of three thatched C16 or C17 cottages, with timber frames beneath the brick. A cruck frame exposed in the E gable end. Nos. 159 and 161 have inserted first floors. No. 163 is probably later – note the break in the wall, the different arrangement of windows and chimneys, and the post-and-rail framing exposed in the W gable.

Also worth a mention is the substantial LEGH ARMS at the foot of Mill Lane beside the railway station. Built in 1854 by *Thomas*

Stone (initials on the datestone), the architect of Warrington Library and Museum (*see* p. 613), to replace an ambitious but now demolished building opened in 1830 beside the railway as a refreshment stop – a business which quickly failed. The rusticated wedge lintels, a pattern of the C18 hereabouts (cf. Newton Park Farm, p. 530), seem remarkably old-fashioned for the date.

EARLESTOWN

Earlestown has sadly little to recommend it, being bylaw housing encased in the usual C20 spread. It is named in honour of (Sir) Hardman Earle, the London & North Western Railway director principally responsible for the company transforming the small Viaduct Foundry into a large WAGON WORKS from 1853 (*see* below), which was the stimulus for a township.

TOWN HALL, Market Street, i.e. at the centre. 1892, by *Thomas Beesley*. Red brick, in a style ranging happily from plate tracery to shaped gables. Prominent clock tower – like a church tower with a variation on the upper stage of Big Ben stuck on top. Inside, a first-floor hall with pilasters. Outside, a BOER WAR MEMORIAL of 1904 with a crude soldier figure, adapted for subsequent conflicts.

TECHNICAL SCHOOL (former), Crow Lane East. Now the Newton campus of St Helens College. Designed by *Henry Littler*, County Architect, and built 1910–11. Red brick and stone, symmetrical, mildly Baroque. Against it is the little Carnegie LIBRARY, designed by *J. Myrtle Smith* in a slightly fuller, and prettier, Baroque to harmonise – though it was actually completed first, in 1909. Nice little top-lit octagonal entrance hall.

The location of the Town Hall illustrates how the centre of gravity shifted to the new industrial areas after the arrival of the railway. But inexplicably it doesn't stand on the MARKET PLACE, but just off it. This is a great pity, for that asphalted area is desperately sad, in spite of an C18 OBELISK, brought here in 1870 from the Leghs' Lyme Park quarries after fifty years in St Peter's churchyard. Even more indefensible are the squalid late C20 supermarkets on opposite sides, the NETTO a shed without even the manners to stand right up to the edge, but skulking behind car parking. If ever a place needed enlightened, imaginative placemaking, it is here.

THE SWAN INN, Swan Lane. Probably C18, principally serving visitors to the racing on Newton Common, which slopes away to the SW. This was first mentioned in 1680s, but the course with its large stands was abandoned in 1898 for a new one at Haydock Park (*see* Ashton-in-Makerfield).

WAGON WORKS (former), Earle Street. Some unremarkable C19 buildings remain after closure, as part of the Deacon Industrial Estate. The big GRIFFIN INN opposite the entrance, dated 1891, has elaborate Dutch gables and other early C17 style features.

WARGRAVE

WARGRAVE, s of Earlestown, was in fact the earlier industrial township, begun in 1830 when the VULCAN FOUNDRY was established by Charles Tayleur, a director of the Liverpool & Manchester Railway. It produced locomotives from 1832, when Robert Stephenson became a partner, until 1970. Some later parts of the once extensive engineering shops survive on Wargrave Road. Immediately s is VULCAN VILLAGE, uniform company terraces built between 1833 and 1838, now heavily improved and altered in appearance. Attractively arranged around a triangular space. In the centre, the pub and the former school, now divided as houses. The huge stone PLAQUE with the company seal featuring Vulcan and dated 1907, attached to the s end of the Manchester Street terrace, is from the pediment of the demolished Vulcan Institute. Cast-iron company NOTICES of 1835 bar from the village, amongst other undesirables, ballad singers.

OUTER NEWTON

p. 19 CASTLE HILL, immediately N of the M6, E of Rob Lane. The remains of a motte, believed to have been a castle built before the C13 and abandoned by 1341, though evidence both archaeological and documentary is slight (*see* Introduction, p. 18).

DEAN SCHOOL COTTAGE, Rob Lane, under the motorway bridge and l. into the woods. Built as a school in 1677 by John Stirrup, according to the plaque in the gable of the C17 part. Weathered coursed sandstone and mullioned windows. The w wing was built, *c.* 1973, when the by then roofless structure was extended and modernised.

GOLBORNE PARK, E of Newton Lane, N of the M6. Now a golf clubhouse. The fragmentary remains of a largely C18 house, now mostly demolished. What is left appears to be a later C19 rebuilding, not of great interest.

NEWTON PARK FARM, Newton Park Drive, off Mill Lane. A polite and handsome brick house, dated 1774 on a now-lost datestone. Built when the enclosed medieval park was owned by the Bankeses of Winstanley (*see* p. 677). Three storeys and five bays, the middle three projecting slightly under a pediment. Later, low extensions l. and r. So badly neglected that the back has collapsed, revealing that the W-profile roof is perpendicular to the façade, not parallel. Why such a refined farmhouse? It may well have been a lodge, i.e. a shooting box, for the use of the Bankes family. The first-floor plan may support this: two rooms across the front, interconnected by a folding panelled partition. Such a grand space would surely be more than even a prosperous yeoman might require, but ideal for entertaining hunting parties.

Behind is a probably C16 or early C17 BARN, with lots of later brick walling, add-ons and alterations, but actually timber-framed. Square-panelled framing here combined with the interrupted sill characteristic of the Northern Counties. Seven bays, central porches and queenpost roof.

WOODHEAD FARMHOUSE, W of Parkside Road (the A573), just S of the M6, 1½ m. SE. Probably early C18. A S front of three symmetrical bays, three storeys high, with a two-storey extension, r. stone plinth and quoins, otherwise brick. The frontage in prestigious Flemish bond, the others in the usual English Garden Wall. Mullioned-and-transomed windows still – three, two, three lights to the main block – but an elliptical Gibbs surround added to the door (inside a flimsy C20 porch). The surround may be an addition. The rear windows are scattered in contrast to the formality of the S front. C18 BARN behind.

ST OSWALD'S WELL, ½ m. S of Woodhead Farmhouse. Sunk and partially stone-lined. Reputedly the site of St Oswald's death (a claim disputed by Oswestry, Shropshire). The inscription IHS marks it as pre-Reformation; the letters M H are possibly the initials of the donor of the masonry.

ORMSKIRK

4000

with WESTHEAD

Ormskirk stands on a low sandstone spur in the coastal mosslands, along a Roman road from Chester to Lancaster. The small medieval market town was made prosperous in the C18 by industries such as clock- and rope-making, but C19 industrialisation and C20 indifference have left little of great interest in the centre apart from the church and the medieval street plan.

ST PETER AND ST PAUL, Church Street. In an irregular, probably oval, hilltop enclosure, and therefore probably a pre-Conquest foundation. From a distance this big, mainly Perp-looking church is more odd than attractive, owing to the immediate proximity of a broad, squat W tower and a thin SW steeple a little higher than the tower. There are of course historical reasons for this oddity, and they take some deciphering. The story begins with the one Norman chancel N window visible inside, whose surround, however, is not genuine. The two-bay arcade (octagonal pier) of the S (Derby) chapel comes next, for the responds belong to the late C13. By 1400 the nave probably had a S aisle, or at least the curious SW steeple indicates that a S aisle existed when it was built. The date of the tower is controversial; about 1435 is given by the VCH, but the forms are almost identical with those of the tower of Aughton church (q.v.) – which is also a S steeple – and that is assigned to the C14. Anyway, the bell-openings are Dec, even if minimum. The tower is square, but the bell-stage by means of broaches is octagonal; the spire on top was rebuilt in 1790 and again in 1832. The arches to the church are boldly chamfered, and against the aisle W wall is the former lower roof-line. Next comes the Scarisbrick Chapel, of a conventional Perp (late

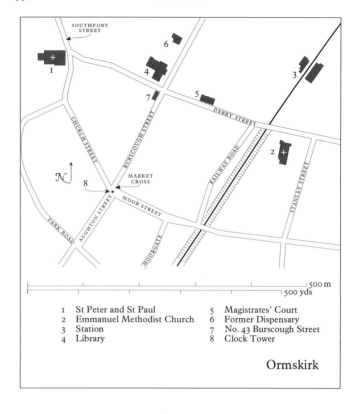

1   St Peter and St Paul
2   Emmanuel Methodist Church
3   Station
4   Library
5   Magistrates' Court
6   Former Dispensary
7   No. 43 Burscough Street
8   Clock Tower

Ormskirk

C15?), restored in 1868 by *E. W. Pugin*, then working at Scarisbrick Hall (N Lancashire). Then comes the massively fat w tower, for the building of which money was bequeathed in 1542. It housed four bells taken from Burscough Priory (*see* p. 225) after the Dissolution, which were hung in the 1570s. The tower has diagonal buttresses, and pairs of three-light bell-openings with uncusped intersecting tracery – the revival of a late C13 motif characteristic of local C16 Gothic (cf. Aughton and Sefton). The last Gothic phase is the Derby Chapel, whose simplified Perp windows go well with the date 1572 which is given by Glynne. It was restored in the 1840s.

In 1729 the body of the church was reconstructed classically, but the only evidence of this today is the classical mouldings of the parapet, the sundial, and the aprons and plinth of the three bays of the s aisle. The Gothic tracery here is due to *Paley & Austin*, who restored (i.e. rebuilt) the church in 1877–91 despite the protests of William Morris and the SPAB. To them

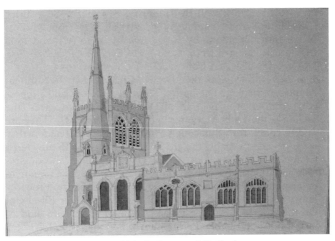

Ormskirk, St Peter and St Paul.
Drawing, 1811

are due many of the external features and the five-bay capital-
less arcades, which replaced classical columns, and which take
no notice of the SW tower. They may not be an invention of
the restorers, who may have had evidence for what they did.
Because they are tall and slender, because there is no clerestory
and because the aisles are broad and high, the interior is in
spirit a hall church, and a dignified one. The nave has an
evolved hammerbeam roof.

FURNISHINGS. FONT. 1661. Hexagonal, on six clustered
shafts. With the small simple motifs typical of Restoration
fonts, in this case a pelican, a cross, an hourglass, and also CR
and a crown. Given by the Countess of Derby, hence also the   20
Stanley emblem of eagle and child. – COVER, a typical *George
Pace* piece, 1973 (his also the wooden CHANDELIERS). –
SCREEN to the Derby Chapel. A good C17 example, with high
balusters. Another screen, of 1979, closes the tower to create a
parish room. – BENCHES. A few late C16 bench ends with scroll
tops. – SHELVES, made up in 1879 from old pews, with handsomely carved woodwork including owners' names (one dated
1682). – WOODWORK. Other benches, the pulpit, stalls, organ
case, etc. by *Paley & Austin*. – SCULPTURE. Small panel with
two men (St Paul and the commandment of the Jerusalem
cohort?), quite possibly Anglo-Saxon (E wall outside). Also a
saint with a book; Flemish (?), C18 (?). Also a stooping marble
statue of a maiden with a pitcher, the Israelite girl taken as a
slave by Naaman to be maidservant to his wife. By *J.
Warrington Wood*, 1873. Nothing seems to be known about its
origin. – STAINED GLASS. In the vestry the re-sited E window

of 1859 by *E.G. Paley*. By *Hardman*, two in the Scarisbrick Chapel, 1868, the E window, 1886, and S aisle, 1st from W, 1891. In the tower, windows by *Henry Holiday*, 1880 (W), and 1892 (N). N aisle, 1st–3rd from W, post-war by *James Powell & Son*. Not good. S aisle, 1st from W, *Patrick Nuttgens*, 1953.

MONUMENTS. In the Derby Chapel, two recumbent couples, of damaged alabaster. Three are late C15 and supposedly represent the 1st Earl of Derby and his two wives (the second is the Lady Margaret, mother of Henry VII). They are said to come from Burscough Priory (*see* p. 225). The fourth is later C16 and probably the 3rd Earl, †1572. – Also in the Derby Chapel two TOMB-CHESTS, C16. They have shields in quatrefoils and indents for brasses on top. On one they are for a man in armour, a lady and daughter, and inscription. Probably James and Margaret Scarisbrick and their daughter Elizabeth. On the other they are for a man in armour and a wife (and an inscription), probably Peter Stanley and his wife Elizabeth Stanley, the daughter in the first. – In the Scarisbrick Chapel on the wall a good BRASS. The style of armour is *c.* 1500, which points to James Scarisbrick, †*c.* 1494–1501. A 5 ft 5 in. (1.65 metre) figure.

In the churchyard a splendid fat C18 SUNDIAL. Elaborate vase pedestal with four consoles to the foot, a globe and fluted collar. – Also a good C19 cast-iron LAVATORY. – CHURCH HALL by *Alan Snape*, 1993. High roof, low sandstone façade, with porch and triangular-headed windows. Neither one thing nor the other.

ST ANNE (R.C.), Prescot Road. *Weightman & Hadfield*. 1850. A big church, and typical of them. Dressed rubble, crazy-paving fashion. Nave, aisles, chancel and N and S chapels, the former much bigger and more prominent. A big W tower, handsome and simple, with a pyramid roof. Low five-bay arcades. A panelled wagon roof in the chancel. The organ is under the tower, with a little wooden gallery projecting from the tower arch into the nave. – HIGH ALTAR by *Edmund Kirby*, 1874. – DATE-STONE. Set in a wall inside: 1668. I E D / R B FECIT. From where? – STAINED GLASS. Several early C20 windows in the aisles, one signed *Hardman*, the rest surely by the same. – A couple of pleasant HOUSES s of the churchyard.

EMMANUEL METHODIST CHURCH, Derby Street. 1878 by *Peter Balmer*. Large, with SW tower and Geometrical tracery. Three-sided gallery.

PUBLIC BUILDINGS

ORMSKIRK HOSPITAL, Wigan Road (A577). Incorporating the former WORKHOUSE of 1851–3 by *William Culshaw*, which is of brick, with the usual octagonal centre and three arms, one ending in a cross-wing fronting the street.

EDGE HILL COLLEGE OF FURTHER EDUCATION, St Helens Road (A570T), ¾ m. SE. Built as a new campus for the then

Edge Hill Teacher Training College, which was founded in Liverpool in 1885. Big and handsomely Neo-Georgian, 1931–3, by the County Architect *Stephen Wilkinson*. Brick and stone dressings, including a centrepiece of paired giant Corinthian columns flanking a giant arch; above, a square copper cupola. At the end of the central range wings project. Numerous later buildings, including a disciplined steel-framed former library of 1977, and a development begun in 2003 by the *Owen Ellis Partnership* which is like a business park: glass-fronted pavilions around a landscaped pond. In 2005 new blocks beside St Helens Road were rising, by *David Cook Architects*. SCULPTURE in the grounds includes pieces by *Robert Scriven* and *Don Manning*, commissioned since 1985.

ORMSKIRK GRAMMAR SCHOOL (former), Ruff Lane. Various elements, of quarry-faced stone and mostly mullioned-and-transomed windows, including a schoolmaster's house and classroom by *Sydney Smirke*, 1849–50 (extended 1864), and a larger block dated 1904, by *Frank Rimmington*.

STATION, Railway Approach. Two buildings. The older (now offices) is on the W side and dates from the opening of the line, to Liverpool, in 1849. Single-storeyed, of quarry-faced stone, with assorted square-profile mullioned and cross-windows, and corbelled eaves. On the E platform, a brick booking hall of the 1860s.

WATER TOWER, Tower Hill. 1853–4. Coursed sandstone, square plan, two tall Romanesque arches to each side. Grotesques, machicolated corbelling. Tank dismantled.

THE CENTRE

The centre of the town is the sorry Gothic CLOCK TOWER of 1876, on the site of the old market cross. A limestone STATUE of Disraeli, 1884, demarcates the other end of the market place. The four ancient streets that converge on it are now quite sad; most of the best Georgian buildings have been demolished (e.g. The Wheatsheaf Hotel), or butchered. Facing the clock tower some altered C18 buildings on the N side of MOOR STREET. Nos. 29 & 31 are a pair of shops with dwellings over, astride a common wagon-entry, with two gables to the street. CHURCH STREET goes W from the clock tower; No. 2 was built in 1779–80 as the Town Hall, with butchers' shops on the ground floor. Like the pedimented central two bays of a plain terrace; missing its cupola. BURSCOUGH STREET goes N. On the W side, the BUCK I' THE VINE INN, possibly late C17 but altered and extended; two small brick wings around a little yard. Then, on the corner with Derby Street, No. 43, the finest surviving Georgian town house. Mid-to-late C18. Red brick, three-storey 1–3–1 façade, the centre projecting slightly under a pediment, with the first-floor windows recessed in arches to the plane of the outer bays. Good, stone, pedimented Ionic doorcase. N of Derby Street, some more Georgian houses and the splendid DISPENSARY of 1830, now an agricultural club.

58 A three-bay, single-storey Greek Revival façade in ashlar, at the top of a flight of steps. The centre is a pedimented tetrastyle Doric portico. Inside, a central hall with pilastered walls, coved ceiling and skylight.

The best remaining group is on DERBY STREET, developed in the mid C19. Starting at Burscough Street on the N side are a series of ashlar buildings. First an enchanting SURGERY, purpose-built, or originally offices. One storey, three bays. Brick. The oversized stone dressings, especially the doorway which is enjoyably too big for the little façade, matching the details of the neighbouring MAGISTRATES' COURT. Built in 1850, for the police. Six elegant classical bays, the second and fifth projecting slightly with shallow pediments and entrances of blocked Tuscan columns and pilasters. Next the former ORMSKIRK SAVINGS BANK, dated 1832, with above the modern fascia three round-headed windows set in deep splayed reveals, and above that lion masks on the parapet. Then the stepped symmetrical façade of the former GIRLS' AND INFANTS' NATIONAL SCHOOL, with Elizabethan elements. On the S side at this end some houses of brick, and a PUB on the corner with Railway Street entirely in the Georgian tradition, with radiating fanlights and twelve-pane sashes.

Also of note:

No. 58 MOOR STREET. Built as a handloom weaving shop c. 1800, one range of two low storeys with close-set windows. In 1808 there were 181 cast-iron and seventy-seven wooden looms. Next to it, and presumably associated with it, a short terrace of little-altered cottages. All the buildings have small-paned horizontal sliding sashes.

CHAPEL HOUSE, Chapel Street. Later C17, altered. Occupied as a Dissenters' meeting house from 1662. Three irregular bays and three storeys. Rendered brick, with sashes.

GOD'S PROVIDENCE COTTAGE, Tower Hill. Red sandstone. Late C17, remodelled. With a peculiar stone door surround: a big raised roll moulding with an addition above the door around a large plaque. The plaque has sunken corners and the inscription 'God's Providence is our heritage G.H.A. 1690'.

AUGHTON HALL, Asmall Lane, ¾ m. NW. Datestone of 1670, but probably with origins of c. 1600; substantially restored in the late C20. Small, of brick on a sandstone plinth. L-plan. (Rear wing timber-framed, with stop-chamfered wall-posts and beams, a kingpost roof with raked struts and wind-braces, and a fine Tudor-arched fireplace on each floor. DCMS.)

BATH HOUSE, NW of Dark Lane, 1 m. NE. C18, brick, and intriguing. Perhaps a cold water plunge bath, at a site possibly developed as a spa from the late C17. Embattled Gothick. Some blank intersecting and curvilinear tracery. Derelict, the details all but hidden beneath ivy.

WESTHEAD

ST JAMES, Vicarage Lane, Westhead, ½ m. SW of the village in a peaceful tree-ringed churchyard. 1851, by *Sydney Smirke* for the 13th Earl of Derby. Greyish ashlar. sw steeple with broach spire, and a s aisle; the windows in the early C14 style. Yet in general impression not yet free of the Commissioners' past. Two-storey insertion in the two w bays, for parish room etc., 1997, by *Alan Snape*. – STAINED GLASS. Good e window by *Shrigley & Hunt*. – e of the church is the old VICARAGE, asymmetrically square with gables, mullioned windows and a Gothic stair window. Big, in the same stone as the church, and by *Smirke* too?

SCHOOL, School Lane. Dated 1889. With master's house attached. Crazy-paving walling. The school has Gothic windows etc.; the house is plainer.

DARBYSHIRE'S FARMHOUSE, School Lane, ⅓ m. s. (Dated 1677 inside. DCMS.) Baffle-entry plan. Brick on rubble plinth. The chimneys have decorative brickwork – sunk panels, lozenges etc. Adjoining barn, now a house.

ORRELL

5000

On land w of Wigan, rising up from the pretty little wooded Douglas valley in the N onto the lower slopes of Billinge Hill in the S. An important early coalfield, exhausted by the mid C19, with nail making too. There was no nucleated village. It is now C19 terraces and C20 housing, a Wigan dormitory. The earlier terraced miners' COTTAGES are tiny and of stone, e.g. the e side of MOOR ROAD, at the N end, and Nos. 65–71 SANDY LANE, dated 1825.

ST LUKE, Lodge Road. By *Austin & Paley*, the three w bays built 1926–7, the rest not until 1938. A planned sw tower never started. By and large, Perp. Polygonal apse. The arcade arches die into octagonal piers. Low wall beneath chancel arch with integrated PULPIT. Typical Austin & Paley spatial arrangement at the e, but without the vitality of earlier decades. – SEDILIA. – FITTINGS, by the architects, including an elegant, tapering octagonal FONT.

   CHURCH HALL. Completed 1983, by *Anthony Grimshaw Associates*, of stone reused from the 1874 church-cum-school.

ST JAMES (R.C.), St James Road. 1805, doubled in length in 1841 (the old work now rendered), w tower 1870 or 1882. The original building is a plain, decently built stone box with arched windows, and with the presbytery under the same roof at the gabled e end in the usual manner for a pre-Emancipation chapel. Its door has a fanlight and attached columns. The narrow Italianate tower is grander, with its ogee cap. The doorway with Tuscan pilasters and pediment looks reused, but is supposed to be original and *in situ*. Broad interior; plain, except for the Ionic e end where pilasters flank N and s altars and attached columns frame flock wallpaper and the High Altar. The present marble ALTARS are *c.* 1965. – W GALLERY on thin cast-iron columns. – NW chapel, a First World War memorial of 1922. Its decent STAINED GLASS looks older.

Most of the best buildings, and most public buildings included, are on ORRELL ROAD, the A577. From E to W:

ABRAHAM GUEST HIGH SCHOOL (S side). By *Lyons, Israel, Ellis & Partners*, 1960–2. Good, disciplined, carefully composed. Concrete framing and brick panels. The assembly and dining halls rise above with elegant concrete-mullioned clerestories. *See also* Up Holland High School, p. 539.

ORRELL LODGE (N side). Pilastered and rendered. Early C19. A LODGE also.

No. 126 ORRELL ROAD (N side). Perhaps 1830s? A little two-storey stuccoed Tudor Gothic villa, with cast-iron casements with reticulated heads under label moulds. What is remarkable is the full-height cast-iron veranda (some timber replacement), rising to the 2½-ft-wide (75 cm.) eaves on three sides. It has spindly quatrefoil columns with cusped arches between, some narrow, some broader and four-centred. The spandrels are cusped and have quatrefoils. Quite extraordinary. The round chimneys have crenellated crowns.

Then W, beyond the M6:

THE MOUNT (N side). Now a pub. Quite a grand Late Georgian house of slightly peculiar design. The earliest it is likely to be is the 1790s, the latest, 1816, when the owner, John Clarke, banker and proprietor of Orrell Colliery, was declared bankrupt. It is all ashlar. Facing S to the road, the centre is of three storeys and three bays, with a later porch, and attached are bowed two-storey wings which project front and back. But the only pediment is on the E wing, which also has a Tuscan porch: the original entrance front? Later extension, W. Beyond the little entrance vestibule with its sail vault is an impressive stair hall with an enriched plaster barrel vault. An open staircase with cast-iron balustrade rises to a balcony on three sides. Other interiors altered.

THE NUNNERY (N side). Two big stone houses under one roof, looking Late Georgian. The fenestration is not quite regular. It would be odd if it had been built as houses. So called because of its association with exiled French Benedictine nuns, who came here in 1821 and opened a school. This, presumably, is the origin of the Tuscan cupola over the r. gable end, and the clock below. But was it built as the nunnery, and school?

NUNNERY COTTAGE and MOUNT FARM COTTAGE (N side, W of the Nunnery). Two cottages, once one farmhouse. Date-stone of 1652 in the garden wall. All kinds of windows: mullioned, sashes and casements.

COUNCIL OFFICES (S side). By *R. Pennington*. Built for the Urban District Council in 1907–8. Only three bays and not very attractive. Red brick, stone dressing, Baroque doorcase.

ORRELL POST (N side), in front of the inter-war brick and half-timbered STAG INN at the crossroads with Moor Road and Gathurst Road. A C17 or C18 Tuscan column with rusticated band and a ball finial. A post at this crossroads is recorded in 1607.

No. 321 ORRELL ROAD (S side). Ashlar, dated 1820.

Nos. 274–276 ORRELL ROAD (N side). Almost in Up Holland (q.v.) A real oddball. Conventional bourgeois Victorian semis, apart from the bizarre stone façade, almost every inch carved with peculiar motifs, mostly in bands. Only the first-floor window surrounds approach plainness.

Elsewhere:

UP HOLLAND HIGH SCHOOL, Sandbrook Road. 1958–60. The first of *Lyons, Israel, Ellis & Partners*' two good schools in Orrell. Like the Abraham Guest High School (*see* above) it is concrete framed with brick and glass infill, but composed with more nervous energy, units jumping back and forth in a low, spreading and dynamic composition.

ACKHURST HALL, Ackhurst Lane, 1½ m. N. Minor C17 gentry house with lots of mullioned-and-transomed windows, the hall marked by a larger one (three-plus-four lights). Two gables, not of identical size. The smaller belongs to the two-storey porch, with a round-headed doorway. The larger is a cross-wing, which contains a parlour with a very good four-centred fireplace inscribed 1618 and a spiral staircase leading to the attic. Here there is a fine turned kingpost and moulded principals, most likely because it was a secret Catholic chapel – the parlour fireplace is marked with a cross and the initials of Fr Alexander Leigh. The wing, and the hall, were probably timber-framed originally (there are timber partition walls) and the date 1686 on the porch may commemorate the cladding of them in sandstone. – C17 baluster SUNDIAL.

BISPHAM HALL. *See* Billinge.

GATHURST FOLD, Gathurst Road (B5206), 1½ m. N. Dated 1708 and yet still entirely in the early C17 tradition. Recessed centre and projecting gabled wings, but no front door. The r. wing is earlier by a few decades, and was a parlour and staircase wing (blocked stair light), demoted to service use when the 1708 elements, the l. wing and the house body, were completed. The phases can be differentiated by the two styles of label moulds over the two- and five-light mullioned windows. Ovolo-moulded beams and a good early C18 staircase with turned balusters and panelled square newels.

GATHURST STATION, Gathurst Road (B5206), 1½ m. N. 1855, for the Lancashire & Yorkshire Railway. Handsomely Jacobethan, with good-quality detailing. Next to it, a contemporary UNDER-BRIDGE with two arches: one for Gathurst Road, and a much smaller one for a colliery tramway down to the Leeds and Liverpool Canal (*see* p. 485).

ORRELL HALL, Spring Road, ½ m. N. C17 (title deeds date back to 1640), but altered. Dressed stone, two-and-a-half-storeys. Mullioned-and-transomed windows survive at the rear; the front is two not quite equal gabled bays, with a round-headed entrance which looks right for the C17, and C18 sashes. But the whole is a little odd, neither a conventional three-unit house, such as Gathurst Fold, nor like its grander, symmetrical brethren (e.g. Bispham Hall, Billinge). It could be an example of a compact, early double-pile plan. And what to make of the decorative carving on the severed ends of the purlins peeking out under the front eaves? Rear courtyard of 1987–9, built when it became a nursing home.

ORRELL HOUSE, Gathurst Road, 1½ m. N. Rambling and incoherent. A 1737 datestone is now in the garden, but the stone building ranges across the C17, C18 and C19. Numerous gables and types of window, including a four-light mullion and a sash with rusticated lintel and consoled sill. The datestone has the name of John Jackson, a colliery owner and an original shareholder of the Leeds and Liverpool Canal.

ST JOHN RIGBY SIXTH FORM COLLEGE, Gathurst Road, 1 m. N. A large mid-C19 house built for the commercial manager of the Blundell Colliery.

PADGATE see WARRINGTON, p. 621

PARR see St HELENS, p. 566

PENKETH see WARRINGTON, p. 631

PLATT BRIDGE see ABRAM

PRESCOT

Prescot was the centre of an ancient, very large parish that stretched from Rainford in the N to the Mersey in the S. The old market town on its hill grew prosperous in the C17 and C18 by supplying Liverpool with coal and, especially, from the mid C18, by clock-, watch- and tool-making. Coal was transported along a turnpike opened in 1726. This was extended to Wigan, Warrington and beyond in the mid C18. In the C20 cable manufacture filled the void left by the collapse of the horological industry. Now Prescot has all but merged with Whiston and Rainhill (qq.v.), and lies only just beyond the suburbs of Liverpool.

ST MARY, Church Street. The site – note the circular churchyard – is possibly pre-Conquest; the building is interesting. Bits of masonry (chancel S, N vestry) are medieval (C15?); the nave and arcades are 1610; the steeple is 1729; the aisles are 1817–19, by *John Bird,* and the S vestry 1900. All of red sandstone. The overall impression is of a classical C18 W tower, broad aisles with battlements and windows of intersecting tracery, and a little fabric to indicate an earlier building. The rebuilt chancel is a puzzle. Though the side windows are like those of the aisles, the surrounds are not quite the same, and the E window is late uncusped Perp in form, though the tracery is thin and sharp like the rest. 1610, 1819, or some other date? The tower and

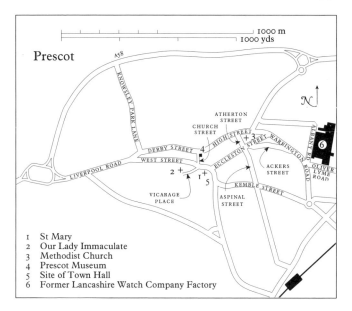

Prescot

1 St Mary
2 Our Lady Immaculate
3 Methodist Church
4 Prescot Museum
5 Site of Town Hall
6 Former Lancashire Watch Company Factory

spire are by *Henry Sephton*, who also designed Ince Blundell Hall, St Aidan, Billinge and St Thomas, Liverpool (demolished). Spire rebuilt after a lightning strike. Bell-stage with corner pilasters and a triglyph frieze. The twin belfry openings are round-headed; so too, lower down, is the triple light with two little circular lights above, all under a semicircular hoodmould. At the base, the door surround has a four-centred head containing blank uncusped tracery. It is possibly C16, and it also has a hoodmould.

The inside is wide and airy. Five-bay arcades with thin octagonal piers and single-chamfered arches of 1610. In the spandrels and re-set on the aisle walls are a series of lovely dated stone plaques with the arms and sometimes initials of the benefactors of the 1610 rebuilding. Narrow clerestory of three-light mullioned windows. Over the chancel arch are little trefoil-headed lights, three to the l. and r., and five up over the apex. The marvellous nave roof is very characteristic work of 1610. 21 It is dated too, and carved with the name of Thomas Bold, knight. Alternate tie-beam and hammerbeam trusses, braces and pendants. The arched wind-bracing is quite different from that of medieval roofs, being uncusped so that they form circular patterns. Though the chancel roof is in keeping, it is a copy, a part of the restoration of 1876 by *W. & G. Audsley*. They rebuilt the chancel arch and designed the Perp stucco panelling of the nave w wall, to make it good after they removed a gallery.

The chancel has an interesting set of early C17 FURNISHINGS. The STALLS with their strange poppyheads are dated 1636. They are unmistakably C17 (with e.g. lozenge and arcade moulding), but continue the Gothic tradition. The matching choirboys' desks are by the *Audsleys*. – The COMMUNION RAIL, partly projecting w to allow more communicants to kneel, is a Laudian speciality. – Dado PANELLING with characteristic frieze moulding around the E end with attached BENCHES supported by many baluster-like turned legs. – FONTS. One Norman, round, strikingly simple and therefore quite modern in appearance. The base is indeed modern. At Roby (q.v.) from 1755 to 1936. The other, given in 1755, in fact an Italian marble STOUP. A very pretty piece with a foot with concave sides and leaves and shells. Shallow reeded basin. – REREDOS. Designed by *Kempe*, 1891. Panelled timber. Hardly Gothic at all. – PULPIT and READING DESK. By the *Audsleys*. – CHANCEL SCREEN. 1921. Open, and freely Gothic. – STAINED GLASS. Some good late C19 glass in the s aisle. Also s aisle E by *Morris & Co.*, 1880. It is unusual in that most of the window is filled by pale, dainty flower quarries, and there are only three smallish figures near the top: Christ ascending and two angels. It is quite beautiful. Chancel side windows. Varied, patterned quarries designed by the *Audsleys*. Also, three interwar windows by *Edward Woore*.[*] – MONUMENTS. Sir John Ogle, †1612. Effigy in hose and with skull-cap. Has it always been upright? – A number of good Georgian tablets, including: Thomas Barron, †1751. By *Daniel Sephton*, Henry's son, with a fine Rococo cartouche against an obelisk; John Hodgkinson, †1798, and others, by *C.B. Robinson* of Liverpool, naturalistic drape drawn back over an urn; Sir William Atherton, †1803, by *Sir Richard Westmacott*, with a standing angel comforting a kneeling female figure, her hair down; Sophia Sherbourne, †1812, with urn, by *S. & T. Franceys*. – BRASS. George Case. 1836, designed by *A.W.N. Pugin*, made by *Hardman*. Floriated cross. – In the churchyard, which has been cleared and landscaped, a SUNDIAL dated 1741.

OUR LADY IMMACULATE AND ST JOSEPH (R.C.), Vicarage Place, behind St Mary. 1856–7, by *Joseph Hansom*. Typically roguish Hansom of that decade. Plate tracery. W end with two windows and a big central buttress supporting a Gothic cupola. Wide, aisle-less nave as he liked them, extremely shallow transepts divided from the nave by stepped tripartite arcading. Narrow chancel. W organ gallery. Reordered in 1995, with a simple NAVE ALTAR on a platform projecting from the chancel. Also a free-standing, almost styleless SCREEN at the W end. Timber frame and etched glass. – STAINED GLASS. Chancel and transept windows. 1857, by the *Crown Glass Company* of St Helens. Large figures, rich colouring, especially blues and reds. They also did nave glass, but it has gone. N, 2nd from W. By *Paul Woodroffe*, 1903. Two sparingly modelled figures in muted tones.

---

[*] The glass of 1840 from the E window, with its large classical figures and strong and sombre colours, was removed in 1985.

OUR LADY HELP OF CHRISTIANS (R.C.), Portico Lane. *See* St Helens, p. 570.

METHODIST CHURCH, Atherton Street. 1909. Shiny Accrington brick. Baroque features in sandstone, e.g. the porch. Not unhandsome.

PRESCOT MUSEUM. *See* Church Street, below.

WAR MEMORIAL, St Helens Road (A58), ¾ m. ENE. At the junction with Burrows Lane is a good memorial to the dead of the West Derby Hundred in the First World War. Bronze, sculpted by *Walter Gilbert* and *Louis Weingartner*. Tall Portland stone pedestal with (bronze) friezes. Steadfast young officer on top. At the base a mother in a splendid Edwardian outfit reaches, offering a palm of victory.

Prescot still had an attractive Georgian TOWN CENTRE fifty years ago; what remains now is fragmentary, and much of the sense of a continuous townscape has been ruined by the highways department. Widened roads and poorly designed new buildings, frequently set back, have seen to it. The historic form of the enclosed medieval MARKET PLACE on the hill below the s side of the church has been destroyed by pulling down the town's best Georgian buildings. They were the Court House or Town Hall of 1755 and Nos. 36–38 Market Place of about the same date, replaced by the present very mundane four-storey apartments in the 1960s. Surviving town-centre buildings of interest are listed by street:

ATHERTON STREET. *see* Buildings of the Watch-Making Industry, p. 544.

CHURCH STREET. No. 11, THE PRESCOT MUSEUM, is a conventionally handsome house of 1776. Five bays, the three middle breaking forward slightly under a pediment. Good brick. Pedimented doorcase. It contains a reconstructed watch-maker's workshop.

DERBY STREET. No. 2 is clearly early C19, and looks to all intents and purposes like a lodge – stuccoed, one storey, three bays, the middle a broad shallow bow, with pilasters. The entrance is recessed to the r. and has an eared architrave. But it is in all likelihood a rare example of a purpose-built Georgian office, still occupied by the same firm of solicitors that it was built for. If there was any domestic accommodation, it surely cannot have been for the solicitor himself. No. 3 is of five bays, with Doric porch. Further W is the CLOCK FACE pub, associated with the Knowsley Estate (q.v.). The principal face, at right angles to the road, is of red sandstone ashlar, *c.* 1830, and of five uneven bays. Panelled corner pilasters, parapet with wreaths and acroteria. Ground floor with bay window to the l., porch with Ionic columns, and tripartite sashes. The bays are uneven, probably because it is a refacing of an earlier C19 house, No. 54, which forms the street elevation. Brick, three irregular bays. Inset Doric doorcase with a big fanlight. No. 52 has a similar door, but the house is smaller. The adjoining cottages were rebuilt in 1985.

ECCLESTON STREET. No. 30: the r. gable is a genuine early C17, or possibly slightly earlier, timber-framed structure. The date on it, 1614, is not to be trusted. The l. gable is a C20 copy. Decorative framing includes elements like splat balusters running under the window and the more familiar concave-sided lozenges, which are very similar to the wind-bracing of St Mary's 1610 roof. Said to contain more C17 fabric, behind the modern shopfronts. Nos. 21–23 also have a timber frame, set back behind a Victorian extension. For No. 74, *see* Buildings of the Watch-Making Industry, below.

HIGH STREET. No. 11 – the Conservative Club – is another later C18 three-bay, three-storey house. It has a Doric pedimented doorcase.

VICARAGE PLACE, along the N side of the churchyard, has a varied terrace. The best is No. 10, four bays, standing alone. It is earlier, perhaps 1740s, and has nice curly brick lintels to the first-floor windows, segmental lintels to the ground-floor windows, and sash boxes almost flush with the wall. The glazing bars are a very rare survival in this part of Lancashire of the thick, early C18 type. Pedimented doorcase, probably later. Attractive square cast-iron gatepiers in the low garden wall in front. No. 8 next door is a late C20 fake, and not that good, but the arms in an elaborate Rococo cartouche set into the façade are those of King's College, Cambridge, Lords of the Manor, and were rescued from the Court House of 1755.

WARRINGTON ROAD. The HOPE AND ANCHOR is the town's best pub: a big eclectic job with ashlar ground floor and brick elsewhere. Dated 1906 on a rainwater hopper. A shaped gable, pilasters, various types of window (some cusped), and a corner turret with ogee cap.

Buildings of the Watch-Making Industry

For about a hundred years from the mid C18, Prescot was the country's – and one of Europe's – leading centre for the production of clock and watch parts and tools. It was a domestic craft industry, masters 'putting out' work to craftsman working at home in WORKSHOPS. These were typically two-storey wings or 'outriggers' attached to the rear of the craftsman's home, where coarser metalworking was done on the ground floor and more delicate tasks in the better light of the upper floor. The latter required the characteristic continuous first-floor windows. They compare with workshops in Birmingham's Jewellery Quarter and in Sheffield. The last workshop closed in 1952 and only a few altered examples remain, e.g. attached to the rear of the w side of ATHERTON STREET, a three-storey terrace of *c.* 1790; and at the rear of No. 74 ECCLESTON STREET, visibly in ACKERS STREET. It is C19, with windows on both floors, inevitably now uPVC. Also No. 132 PORTICO LANE.

The industry collapsed in the face of cheap American and Swiss imports from the 1860s. The LANCASHIRE WATCH

COMPANY was founded in 1889 as a last effort to save it by taking on the US manufacturers at their own game. But the enterprise folded in 1910 because the promoters did not fully understand the nature of modern factory production, or cater sufficiently for the mass market. Nevertheless they did build a large FACTORY on ALBANY ROAD in 1889–90, designed by *Stott & Sons*, which was unique in Britain, and informed by the Elgin National Watch Co. factory in Illinois. Now a business park, it consists of three iron-framed buildings, the most impressive being the narrow, three-storey, 300 ft (92 metres) long manufacturing block. The frame is exposed, and filled with brick aprons and continuous glazing on each floor to light the work benches. The floors are concrete. A fourth range was intended across the s front, with typical Stotts decorative treatment.

LODGE to Knowsley Park (*see* p. 223), N end of Knowsley Park Lane. Now cut off from the park by the A58 Prescot bypass. C19. Red sandstone. Simple Jacobethan.

ECCLESTON PARK. *See* St Helens, p. 575.

THE HAZELS. *See* Huyton, p. 204.

RAINFORD

4000

A large village N of St Helens with a quite a bit of dormitory development. There were a number of collieries around it.

ALL SAINTS, Church Road. 1878, by *Aldridge & Deacon*, near the site of a chapel in existence in 1541. Large, in buff sandstone with red ashlar dressings. Lancets. The NE tower is an addition of 1903 (by *Deacon?*) and is the best part of the church. Lively top and a charming oriel-like upper ending of the round staircase, only halfway up the tower. s chapel, 1928. The interior is not of great interest. – FONT. Gadrooned bowl on fluted Tuscan column. Dated 1723. – MONUMENT. Dulcibella Brownbill, †1813. With a small allegorical figure. By *S. & T. Franceys* of Liverpool.

VILLAGE HALL and offices, Church Road. The former Rainford Urban District Council offices, opened 1907. Shiny red brick and buff sandstone dressings. Free Jacobean revival. Asymmetrical, with the hall to the r.

GOLDEN LION, Church Road. A big pub next to the churchyard. The main part is rendered and of two-and-a-half storeys with keyed lintels and a broken pediment and pilasters around the door: later C18. The wing to the l. has similar details; the long low brick wing to the r. is C18 vernacular, altered.

GUILD HALL FARMHOUSE, Gore's Lane (B5205), 2 m. E. A handsome yeoman's house of 1629. Three large bays of multi-mullioned windows, including a cross-wing, r., with parlour and buttery. Baffle entry, with fire window in the housebody firehood. The stone porch with cross-window is dated 1688. The ball finials are probably 1688 too. Also largely of that date a rear extension to the cross-wing with a good dog-leg stair (DCMS). However, its w wall is timber-framed: a fragment of an earlier house?

MOSSBOROUGH HALL, Mossborough Hall Lane, 1½ m. SW. This was the medieval manor, but the present grey stone house, whilst quite large, is unremarkable Victorian Jacobethan. Set into one gable is a datestone, 1703, from the previous house. More impressive is the MODEL FARM complex, industrial in scale, dated 1852. The Derby Estate built all this.

RAINFORD HALL, Crank Road, 1½ m. SE. 1885–6, by *J. Medland Taylor* for Col. Richard Pilkington (Taylor had designed Pilkington's offices in 1880). A red brick house with sandstone dressings in a Jacobethan style, believed to incorporate a much earlier stone farmhouse which was clad in tiles and refenestrated to match the new wing. LODGE, STABLES, COTTAGES (including those on the Crank Road, S): *Taylor* too?

SCYTHE STONE DELPH FARM, Maggot's Nook Road. A little stone yeoman's house dated 1682. It has mullioned windows in an almost symmetrical façade of three bays, the centre projecting as a two-storey porch. Garry Miller has identified it as the earliest known yeoman's house in this part of Lancashire to abandon the baffle-entry plan for gable-end fireplaces. The porch leads into the housebody, with the staircase rising in it directly ahead; parlour l. The kitchen and buttery were in the rear outshut, and the roof incorporates reused upper crucks.

RAINHILL

Famous as the location of the trials of 1829 at which Stephenson's *Rocket* proved that locomotive engines could reliably haul trains along the new Liverpool & Manchester Railway, but already then an important coaching stop on the turnpike between Liverpool and Warrington. The once separate settlements of Rainhill and Rainhill Stoops are now merged as a commuters' dormitory. The huge WEST DERBY COUNTY ASYLUM, the first part by *H.L. Elmes*, 1847–51, the massive extensions of 1886 by *G.E. Grayson*, has been demolished.

ST ANNE, Warrington Road (A57). Red sandstone ashlar. The first, aisle-less church was of 1837–8 by *Edward Welch*. He began practice again in Liverpool in 1837 after he was made bankrupt by standing surety on the construction of Birmingham Town Hall, which he designed with Joseph Hansom. Of that date only the bottom part of the w tower survives. In 1843 Welch rebuilt the church, adding transepts and remodelling the tower in rather thin and starved Norman fashion but with a spire too. It was enlarged for a second time in 1868–9 by *G.H. Ridsdale* with a N aisle and Perp tracery, including unorthodox, low, rectangular clerestory windows. Only Welch's tower (minus the spire, dismantled in the mid C20), lower parts of the w wall and s transept were retained, and inside only the

Neo-Norman balustrade of his 1843 w gallery, reset on the w
wall, survives. sw vestries of 1961.

NATIONAL SCHOOL (former), on Warrington Road (A57) w of
the churchyard, was also begun by *Welch*. This is the centre and
w part, of 1840; the E side is the infants' school added by him
in 1848. Extended to the rear in 1875, and the front taken down
and rebuilt one bay forward in 1884. This is all one-storeyed
and ashlar and all well matched, following Welch's original part
with round-arched lancets and thin buttresses, which itself ape
his first church. Nice symmetrical façade to the road, with
triplets of lancets in gabled ends; attached to the centre was
a little porch now on the E side. Across the road are some
mid-C19 SEMIS.

ST BARTHOLOMEW (R.C.), Warrington Road (A57), Rainhill
Stoops. By *Joshua Dawson* of Preston, his only major recorded   49
work, but the 'idea' is said to have been due to Mr Carter,
a painter and glass-stainer also of Preston, who did the
first decorative painting. Erected 1838–40 and paid for by
Bartholomew Bretherton, stagecoach proprietor. Though not
at all large, this is the noblest Catholic church in South
Lancashire. It is aligned with a straight stretch of road skirting
the grounds of Bretherton's residence, now Loyola House (*see*
p. 548). This terminates in a grand classical triple archway of
the 1850s. The church is a prostyle temple in superbly worked
red sandstone, the façade a hexastyle portico of fluted Ionic
columns. The sides and the E apse have closely set giant Doric
pilasters and no windows at all. Attached by a short link wing
to the NE is an Italianate campanile with low-pitched pyramid
roof, added in 1849. Basilican interior with a six-bay nave, separated from narrow aisles by giant Corinthian columns. These   50
continue as fluted pilasters around the little apse, which is separated from the nave by a round arch carried on similar fluted
columns. St Bartholomew's is one of a number of Roman
Catholic churches ultimately of C18 French derivation (of
which the chapel at Prior Park, Bath, is another), whose defining features are coffered barrel vaults and continuous entablatures. Here, the vault has semicircular windows set into it,
which are hidden from outside by the parapet. These provide
the only source of light.

   For many years the interior had a highly polychromatic
Late Victorian decorative scheme. Now it is closer to the
subdued colouring described in accounts of the opening. The
columns are palely marbled, but the capitals remain gilded,
the entablature elaborately stencilled, and the apse painted
with three large saints on gold backgrounds. A reordering in
1984 has left only the ALTAR, brought forward and trimmed
down, of the original furnishings. The organ went, and the w
gallery front was given, bizarrely, pediments hanging from it.
Beneath this, inevitably, a clumsy glazed screen. – BRASSES.
Three large Bretherton family memorials, with Crucifixion
or similar scenes in upper part. They are: Bartholomew
and Jane Bretherton, 1869; Gilbert and Mary Stapleton, 1883;

Frederick Annesley and Isabella Stapleton-Bretherton, 1919, by *Hayes & Finch* of Liverpool. – Another, to the Rev. Thomas Kierman, †1885. With figure, by *Herbert & Co.* of Liverpool.

CONVENT OF THE SISTERS OF CHARITY, E of St Bartholomew on Chapel Lane. Opened 1856. Simple but pretty symmetrical three-bay sandstone façade with two-light mullioned windows and porch with pointed arch. Contemporary, single-storey school house in the same language attached to the rear.

LOYOLA HALL, Warrington Road (A57), Rainhill Stoops, by St Bartholomew. Built as Rainhill House by the Brethertons and supposed to be of *c.* 1824. Plain, ashlar, five bays. The windows have Regency proportions and Tudor hoodmoulds. The large porch with six columns and iron balustrade must be more recent. – CHAPEL, postwar, lit by large abstract STAINED GLASS windows by *Jonah Jones*, *c.* 1960.

TOWER COLLEGE. *See* The Tower, below.

LIVERPOOL CATHOLIC REFORMATORY NAUTICAL SCHOOLS (former), Norlands Lane, Rainhill Stoops. *see* Widnes, p. 656.

RAILWAY BRIDGE, Warrington Road (A57). 1828–9. There were sixteen skew bridges on the Liverpool & Manchester Railway. This example alone has always been famed, partly because it carried the turnpike and therefore the soon-to-be-outmoded stagecoaches (an epochal meeting no engraver could resist), and partly because, as the most acute, it represented the greatest engineering challenge. Muscular and handsome. Constructed of red sandstone in courses of banded rustication which corkscrew around the soffit and radiate from the arch to the abutments and parapet on each face as a spray of elongated voussoirs. The angle is 34 degrees, the span is 54 ft (16.6 metres) and the width 34 ft (10.5 metres), following the addition of 4 ft (1.2 metres) to the SW side in 1963. It seems that a full-size wooden mock-up was erected in a neighbouring field, a template for each and every block. Who was chiefly responsible? *George Stephenson* is emphatically named as the engineer on a parapet panel, but Stephenson was not a bridge builder; *Jesse Hartley*, one of the Company's consulting engineers, was a professional, so perhaps he made a more significant contribution.

The bridge is at the end of the platforms of RAINHILL STATION. The station building was put up by the London & North Western Railway *c.* 1860–70. One brick storey, low hipped roof and classical details including modillion eaves.

Along MILL LANE and VIEW ROAD, amongst C20 infill, are spacious C19 mansions built by businessmen of Liverpool and St Helens to take in the magnificent views S from this escarpment over the Mersey valley to Runcorn, Cheshire and the Welsh mountains. Earlier ones are smaller and often stuccoed. Later builds are of red sandstone, e.g. on Mill Lane the large Neo-Elizabethan L-plan RANNLEA, and next to each other further E two remarkably sumptuous examples. Of these THE TOWER, now Tower College School, was a house presumably not long built when purchased by Henry Baxter, a St Helens chemical manufacturer, and extended in 1879–80 for him by *Edmund Kirby*. The earlier part is rambling, free but debased Jacobethan, and of two storeys. Kirby's changes are much more capably detailed. Chief amongst them, in matching quarry-faced stone, is the extraordinary tower. Massive, of four storeys, with pairs of two-storey oriels, diagonal buttresses, and battlements, from which rise tall chimneys and in one corner a turret surmounted by a fairytale cupola. This is elaborate, wooden and octagonal, with an ogee finial – entirely fanciful. On the ground floor the tower has a library, fully panelled in a dense, free style. Kirby also added more, and more correct, mullioned-and-transomed windows to the existing house to light remodelled interiors: on the garden side two to his dining room, and on the entrance side a tall bay housing a staircase. These freely Jacobean interiors impress, not with any quality, but with their wonderful bourgeois vulgarity, e.g. the overmantel and built-in buffet in the dining room (Kirby also designed furniture). The fireplaces do have *de Morgan* tiles, though. Baxter's initials and invented arms are everywhere, e.g. in the stair-window stained glass. Much of the service wing demolished for largely undistinguished late C20 school buildings. Also a LODGE.

BRIARS HEY, 1868–70, adjoins to the w. Designed by *W.H. Brakspear* for John Crossley, a St Helens industrialist with interests in both glass and alkali manufacturing. Rock-faced sandstone. Roguish Gothic, with all kinds of unexpected motifs. At the E end the slate roof rises as a pyramid with a glazed timber stage to form a prospect tower. A large service range, incorporating stables and lodge, forms the E side of the entrance court and has a particularly fanciful roof. Impressive aracaded staircase hall, with fine tiled floor.

MANOR HOUSE, Mill Lane. Now the Manor Farm pub. A sandstone building of a typically C17 plan with a single cross-wing, of minor gentry scale, and with the cross-wing notably broad. Mullioned windows almost throughout, of seven lights on the s side of the wing, where there are four storeys of windows altogether, including a little one squeezed under the apex. Modern door on the s side; on the N side, a two-and-a-half-storey porch dated 1662 with rosettes and the initials of Alexander Chorley, and a studded door. This appears to be an addition. Its mullioned windows are ovolo-moulded, as are the others of the N side; those on the s and E sides are chamfered. One-and-a-half-storey w extension, also no later than *c.* 1710, i.e. with low mullioned windows. The house became a farmhouse, then a pub restaurant, now opened up appallingly inside in typical late C20 'ye olde inn' style. There is an inglenook and a fine four-centred corner fireplace, now *ex situ*. Cellars, with mullioned windows now below ground level.

RAINHILL OLD HALL, s of Blundell's Lane, ¾ m. sw of St Anne. Derelict but notable. An irregular L-plan. w wing of uncertain age (see the E side), stone, substantially remodelled in the C19, two-storeyed and of lesser interest. Not so the two-storey N wing, which has big sandstone blocks to the ground floor, a moulded string course and then C17 brick with stone dressings above that. N façade of three bays with a two-storey gabled porch in the centre. The round archway of the porch, with an impost moulding, suggests a mid-C17 or slightly later date, though the porch itself may be later than the brickwork of the rest of the wing. To the r. of the porch are mullioned windows. That on the first floor is of seven lights with a transom. Similar five-light examples in the E gable end (blocked) and the E end of the S side light an upper room with a splendid roof of arch-braced collars and quatrefoil windbraces. The E truss is exposed in the gable end. The mid-C14 date traditionally ascribed to the roof may be too early; if the roof is *in situ* it would seem to be that of a solar or great chamber (cf. Lightshaw Hall, p. 178); if *ex situ*, it may be that of the hall. Fragments of a timber frame to the first floor within the brickwork support the proposition that this is a late medieval building with lower masonry walls supporting an upper timber frame encased in brick in the C17. The staircase is later but its location is plausible for the medieval point of access to the first floor. In the S wall are the remnants of a blocked doorway that may have been the medieval entrance.

The two wings are joined by a link not shown in a map of 1843. A detached SE wing, possibly C17, and a cruck-framed barn are both demolished. Two limbs of a MOAT still visible. For five hundred years from the early C14 the manor was the possession and home of the Lancaster family. They were recusants and may have used the upper room as a chapel, by which name it has long been known. How they could have afforded to modernise the Hall in the C17 when they were crippled by successive fines is unclear.

SMITHY COTTAGE, Warrington Road (A57), Rainhill Stoops. Pretty sandstone cottage, C17 and altered. Mullioned windows, some modified with casements or horizontal sashes. Two storeys and three irregular bays. Baffle-entry plan. This may have been of the 'end' variety, because the r. bay, separated by a straight joint in the wall, and with a blocked doorway in the return, appears to be a separate, additional dwelling.

WOOD'S HOUSE FARM, School Lane (the part E of the A570), Rainhill Stoops, ½ m. ENE of St Bartholomew. Dated 1664 and 1707, but following a complete rebuild in 1983 more a pastiche of a house. Two storeys. Three-bay façade, with two gables with gablet between. The r. gable was the C17 wing – red sandstone, a six-light mullioned window on each floor and a stepped three-light window in the gable. The l. two bays were the early C18 bit, now in modern brick, with a keyed door surround and modern windows.

RIXTON

ST MICHAEL (former; R.C.), Moss Side Lane. Since 1975 a private house. Dated 1831 in the W gable. No architect is known. A simple example of the plan favoured by Roman Catholics before Emancipation, with the chapel with three tall sash windows and a two-storey presbytery back-to-back within a single gabled brick shell. There is a gallery above the now blocked w door. Awful c20 N porch.

RIXTON OLD HALL, s of Manchester Road. The manor of Rixton was held by the Mascys and then the Pattens (*see* St Anne's Chapel, St Elphin, Warrington). The moat is still wet, but the ancient house within was demolished about 1800 and a new one built immediately s. Modest, brick, three phases. The central three bays are probably the earliest, possibly late c18, with later extensions, r. one bay, and then l. two bays. Rear fenestration a jumble. Now offices. No interest inside.

ROAD BRIDGE over the Manchester Ship Canal, Warburton Bridge Road. 1903, of metal cantilevered pattern identical to one at Warrington (*see* p. 616). (Sir) *Edward Leader Williams* was the chief engineer. A slightly bizarre sight in such a flat rural landscape.

ROBY *see* HUYTON

ST HELENS

5090

The first sight comes as something as a surprise in our post-industrial age: before anything else of the town can be seen, a cluster of massive chimneys rises tall above the landscape, some of them still actually belching steam. For St Helens is a town, entirely the product of the Industrial Revolution, whose centre is still dominated by industry. The chimneys of course belong to the glass industry, for which St Helens has become world-famous. This is, however, a comparatively recent elevation: in the c19 chemicals were as important, as too were metal smelting and founding, and coal. Indeed it was the extraction of coal, allied to a pioneering waterway, that created a town here from nothing two hundred years ago.

Coal was being mined at Sutton Heath by 1540, but up until the mid c18 what is now St Helens was a sparsely populated corner of the parish of Prescot. The town centre lies in a wide flat hollow drained by the Sankey Brook, where a small chapel of ease dedicated to St Helen, first mentioned in 1552, stood on the road from Warrington to Ormskirk. Mining expanded through the c18 to supply booming Liverpool and the Cheshire salt refiners. The defining moment came in 1755 when the Liverpool Corporation successfully promoted a bill to make navigable the Sankey Brook down to the Mersey. The motive was to release the city and its salt merchants from their reliance for the supply of coal on the costly and often impassable turnpike. The SANKEY BROOK NAVIGATION, later the St Helens Canal, opened in 1757, i.e. preceding the Bridgewater Canal as the first modern canal in England (*see* p. 52).

The combination of coal, canal and from 1833 the St Helens & Runcorn Gap Railway lured industry: first copper smelting, then in 1828 the alkali industry, which thrived in the C19. There were foundries too, and brickworks, and by 1900 thirty-five collieries within the borough boundary. All of this has now gone. Chemicals went to Widnes and Runcorn. The last pit closed in 1968. Now only glass-making remains. In 1968 it employed *c.* 17,000; today the total is only *c.* 3,500, almost all with Pilkingtons. There was bottle-making from the beginning of the C18, but the key date was 1773, when the colliery owner John Mackay persuaded his fellow investors in the British Plate Glass Co. of the advantages of building their manufactory at Ravenhead (now part of St Helens) near the canal and his mines. The enterprise struggled initially, but within a few decades the canal was lined with the furnace cones of competing glass-makers. One of these, founded in 1826 as the St Helens Crown Glass Co., became Pilkington Bros in 1849. By consistent technological innovation, the firm evolved into a world leader. Most significant was the invention of the float-glass process, which, when launched at the Cowley Hill plant in 1959, did away simultaneously with both plate and sheet glass. Today, it is the vast integrated plants needed to produce float glass that dominate the town.

The settlement created by these scattered industries developed only slowly and untidily into a recognisable town. The population of the area in 1801 was *c.* 7,500. A commercial centre emerged along the old highway, now Church Street and Bridge Street, but a sizeable urban area only developed after 1850. The population of the district expanded to *c.* 45,000 in 1870, 84,000 in 1901. Municipal government came late too; until 1845, when an Improvement Commission was created, local government was divided between four townships. Incorporation came in 1868, but by that time the location and land requirements of industry had already determined St Helens' straggling, spidery form. By 2001 the population was 115,000 (in the area covered here) and housing had spread to engulf the village of Eccleston and all but merge the town with Haydock to the E and Prescot to the W.

Architecturally, there is too little of quality in St Helens. An oligarchy of industrialists sponsored C19 municipal improvement and public building: David Gamble (chemicals), Peter Greenall (brewing and much else) and the Pilkingtons. But they were not aesthetically discerning. From the C20, though, there are good Pilkington office buildings, and some interesting churches too. The town centre is one of the drabbest in Lancashire, an untidy and unhappy mix of, mainly, mediocre C19 survivors and second-rate post-war development. A redevelopment plan of 1965 was only partially realised, and there were the usual slum clearances, a pedestrian shopping precinct and an inner ring road. Derelict industrial areas have been redeveloped with little imagination. Throughout the borough, the substantial early C20 pubs of Greenall's family brewery, Greenall, Whitley & Co., in a range of Revival styles, are often the best buildings. One distinctive local feature is the use of blocks of copper slag for construction. In the

C19 its sale was a perk allowed to managers of the various copper works. It has a marvellously inky black lustre and a fantastical texture – contorted, blistered, pressed and pitted.

The centre is described first, with its churches, public buildings and a short perambulation. Outer areas are divided thus: NW and N, NE and E, S and SE, SW, and W.

THE CENTRE

CHURCHES

ST HELEN, Church Street. Still the focal point of the town and a prominent landmark. 1920–6 by *W.D. Caröe*. On the site of St Mary, the previous parish church, burnt down in 1916. This began as a chapel of ease called St Helen; a building was mentioned in 1552. Caröe's church is large, and of brick with very sparing red sandstone dressings (as originally conceived it was larger, grander and of stone). The style is developed from Dec and Perp but the whole is no longer historicist. Massive, freely Gothic NE tower. Impressively detailed and beautifully composed with pared-down buttresses at the diagonals and halfway along the sides providing a strong vertical emphasis, which is counterbalanced by shallow segmental relieving arches beneath the belfry stage. Nave roof with eaves, aisles with parapets. Aisle walls rather too flat. The E end is slightly canted; the W has a low sandstone narthex flanked by little towers, like open arms; a welcoming entrance.

The interior rewards study: spatially masterful, and subtle everywhere and in every detail. Broad five-bay nave and aisles. The narrow arcade piers, thoughtfully moulded and without capitals, continue as attached shafts in blank arches framing the clerestory windows, of a shape different from that of the arcade arches. Outside the aisles a second set of lower arcades forms passages, creating depth and framing marvellous vistas. E of the chancel arch, further arcade passages separate the chancel from a N chapel and S vestry vestibule. These passages are in line with the nave arcades. Careful composition is again evident above these passages: the organ gallery, N, balanced by minstrel gallery, S. Good sedilia too. The roof is a wooden tunnel vault, enriched in the chancel. The otherwise pristine interior has been spoiled by a screen and offices inserted in 1994 in the nave W bay, closing off the narthex and destroying the spatial rhythms of the W end. From here the parish hall in the Church Square development (*see* p. 560) is reached via an apartment bridging the street.

The C20 FURNISHINGS are designed by *Caröe*, in styles ranging across the Gothic and into the Renaissance, all of outstanding quality. – REREDOS. Erected in 1940 after Caröe's death, and allegedly created from one tree. Twenty-five statues in niches, and coving with tall filigree cresting. N chapel REREDOS too. – FONTS. Caröe's has a towering, theatrical

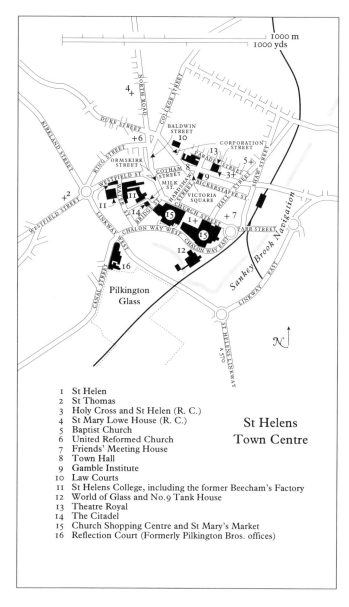

1000 m
1000 yds

Pilkington
Glass

N

St Helens
Town Centre

1   St Helen
2   St Thomas
3   Holy Cross and St Helen (R. C.)
4   St Mary Lowe House (R. C.)
5   Baptist Church
6   United Reformed Church
7   Friends' Meeting House
8   Town Hall
9   Gamble Institute
10 Law Courts
11 St Helens College, including the former Beecham's Factory
12 World of Glass and No. 9 Tank House
13 Theatre Royal
14 The Citadel
15 Church Shopping Centre and St Mary's Market
16 Reflection Court (Formerly Pilkington Bros. offices)

cover mixing Renaissance, northern European and Gothic.
Alongside is that of the previous church, dated 1731. – PULPIT.
On little legs, with Caröe's favourite lozenge motif. Tester. –
PARCLOSE SCREENS. Exquisitely carved and richly detailed,
heavily pierced. Gothic form, but often far from Gothic detail.
Surely inspired by the screens at Sefton (q.v.), which Caröe

had restored. – CHOIR STALLS. Beautifully carved too but more abstract, in a rectilinear way. – PEWS are by contrast simple but elegant, with lovely hand-carved seats. – ORGAN CASE. Full-blown Renaissance, intricately detailed. – PLAQUE. S aisle. 1670, from a schoolhouse built and endowed by John Lyon. Large, stone. – STAINED GLASS. Superb E window. Te Deum. Crowded with figures. N chapel E window. First World War memorial by *Horace Wilkinson*, 1927. Four good figures. S aisle, 3rd from w. Mountbatten memorial, 1983.

HOLY CROSS AND ST HELEN (R.C.), Corporation Street. 1860–2, by *J.J. Scoles*. Quarry-faced sandstone, with red ashlar dressings. A single-vessel nave and chancel, aisles and transepts, without tower. Dec. Inside, slender octagonal piers; the oversized STATUES of apostles in the spandrels are later. The flat roof with moulded beams and the curious wooden chancel arch, pierced and lacy and with ROOD, were late changes to the design, forced upon Scoles by concerns about the stability of the undermined ground. W GALLERY, now glazed beneath. Reordered with a nave altar. – Impressive REREDOSES with canopies etc. That in the Sacred Heart Chapel, N transept, behind an equally elaborate and heavy stone SCREEN of 1886, is from Munich, *c.* 1888. – ORGAN CASE of 1867. – STAINED GLASS. N transept window and E rose, 1862, by *Thomas Unsworth*. S transept windows by *M. Casolani*. In the aisles and in the screen to the w vestibule (now office) a full complement of richly and colourfully patterned glass of 1862. – Alongside, a slightly Gothic PRESBYTERY of 1862 and a former C19 SCHOOL.

ST MARY LOWE HOUSE (R.C.), North Road. A very large and very ambitious oddity of 1920–9, by *Charles B. Powell* of Dublin. It replaced a church, much enlarged, of 1793. The architect described the plan as based on 'the early type of Christian architecture' and the style as a development of Romanesque. The result is a confused building with a split personality. With a high, slender w tower and copper dome at the crossing. It is unfortunate that the two never agree, and that it looks like a giant, but friendly, snail. The w end has a strongly vertical emphasis and rectilinear lines and is Gothic, see the flying buttresses, embattled pinnacles and clustered turrets, and the impressive shape and details of the tower. The octagonal crossing tower is Gothic too and castellated, though it would have been better if the dome had not been put on. But everywhere the elongated windows are round-headed, and the transepts and E end, in contrast to the w, are all curves: the dome and the many apses are a cluster of cylinders. And there are MOSAICS in w and s entrance tympana. Almost no mouldings, except the windows of the SW memorial chapel, begun before the rest in 1920, and completed 1923 in a more conventional Romanesque. The craggy grey millstone grit, unusual in St Helens, was chosen for durability. Powell intended his church to embody the 'sturdy and tenacious' spirit of the Lancashire faith.

In the Bath-stone-lined INTERIOR, of almost cathedral proportions, the impression is more Mediterranean, in spite of the Gothic rib-vaulting (of hollow brick) of nave and aisles. But there is no doubt of the sheer scale. Four-bay arcade, with pink granite columns with capitals in no way period, carved with assorted emblems. Apsidal E end with ambulatory, the aspe with foliate frieze. Reordered with a raised apse floor, celebrant ALTAR under the dome, and Modernist FONT in a sunken area. – HIGH ALTAR by *Powell*, executed by *Boulton*. – SCREEN, *c.* 1979. – W DOORS, with luxuriant curvy strapping. – Very good pre-war STAINED GLASS by *John Hardman & Co.* The memorial chapel windows are best: delicate, with lots of grisaille; the aisle windows are pictoral, and more dynamic. The N aisle windows are saints. Lush apse windows. – In the N transept, two memorial TABLETS from the old church. One is the founder, Winifred Eccleston, †1793. – Along Crab Street a large PRESBYTERY and a cluster of late C19 and Edwardian SCHOOL buildings, the last dated 1903.

BAPTIST CHURCH, Hall Street. A simple brick box of 1888–9, dressed up in 1904 with a new E end by *John Willis & Sons* of Derby. This is pleasant, but not much more ambitious; of glazed brick, with a Perp window and NE turret with a little spire. A simpler hall of the same year and the same hand alongside.

(PRESBYTERIAN CHURCH, Tolver Street. The amateurish Gothic building of 1867–8 by *Corson & Aitken* of Manchester burnt down in 2004.)

UNITED REFORMED CHURCH, King Street. 1976, by *Peter Bridges* and *Martin Purdy* of *APEC*. Crucifix apart, completely un-churchlike. Nearly square in plan, low and mostly roof. Almost despite the roof, which is steeply pitched, reaches low, deeply overhanging and made of zinc (originally lead), and could be very sinister, the building is quite human. The interior is spacious and cleverly planned. The church itself is broader than it is long, and lit principally by a clerestory across the W end. Triptych RETABLE of stained-glass panels from the demolished Congregational church of 1883 on Ormskirk Street. Beneath a W gallery a screen of doors divides the church from a hall. Also a lecture theatre and extensive offices, linked by a staircase free-standing in a glazed stairwell. The offices are lit by rows of windows on two levels set into the roof.

FRIENDS' MEETING HOUSE, Church Street. The oldest still in use in Lancashire. The building was purchased in 1676 by a horse-collar maker, George Shaw, for his fellow Quakers. But how much older is it? It looks C17, though a building here was for sale in 1597. Low, two-storeyed, of stone (probably not local), with mostly low three- and five-light mullioned windows. Presumably built as a house, but its plan has been destroyed. The W gable has a big, now hidden, fireplace and bread oven (not tied in), the E gable the grandest window, of seven lights with a transom. The W room may therefore have been the housebody, and the E room a parlour. However, there is the lintel of a blocked doorway at ground level in the N façade, and part of the original floor clearly visible some 3 ft (2.7 metres) below the current one in a lean-to at the W end. The ground-floor windows relate to present floor levels and are therefore either not original, or were re-set when the floor was raised. There is no record of such work being done by the meeting. There is no upper floor now to go with the matching upper windows, though there is evidence for joists at the W end. SUNDIAL over the S door, dated 1753 now, but once 177? (a sundial is first mentioned in 1691–2). The stonework of all the S windows is replacement. The STAND is mid-C18, the roof late C19. Other fittings are early C20, including a sliding partition. At the back is an unobjectionable extension of 1965–6.

PUBLIC BUILDINGS

TOWN HALL, Victoria Square. 1873–6, by *Henry Sumners* of Liverpool. Not one of the great Victorian town halls of the North. It replaced a building by *A. Y. & G. Williams* of Liverpool, erected in 1839 close to Bridge Street.* Gothic, in a drab brick with much stone, with a thin asymmetrically placed tower. The composition sorely misses the lift given it by the spire burnt down in 1913. The details, e.g. the canopy over the entrance, are very odd. It originally housed the full gamut of Victorian public services: courts, police, library, the fire brigade beneath an assembly room, as well as Council Chamber and offices. Assembly room with arch-braced trusses rising from corbels. The end one frames a semicircle of Gothic plasterwork behind the stage, partially fitted with mirrors. Council Chamber impressively top-lit. Enriched panelling. The Members' Retiring Room is a matching addition. The fireplaces and sort-of-Tudorbethan ceiling plasterwork suggest it followed quite quickly.

GAMBLE INSTITUTE, Victoria Square. 1894–6, by *Briggs & Wolstenholme*, in their pressed brick and terracotta Free Style. The alkali baron David Gamble offered the Corporation a plot of land and £25,000 to erect a free public library and technical school, 'assisting our people to make themselves equal or superior to those countries where technical education has been an institution for a great many years'. £25,000 did not prove enough to complete the building, and it opened without a fourth storey or too much enlivening embellishment. So it is a shame it has since lost its ball finials too. A top-lit arcaded lending room with tall cast-iron columns is the focus of the interior.

LAW COURTS, Corporation Street. 1980, by *R. A. Mallett* (St Helens Metropolitan Borough Council). Low and brick and rectangular, and set back in soft landscaping from the street. Entrance via bridge to a *piano nobile*. Hints, therefore, of a

---

* There could have been a third, but a replacement civic centre proposed in 1969 was never built.

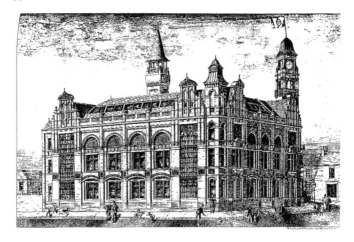

St Helens, Beecham's Factory (now St Helens College).
(*Building News*, vol. 49, 1886)

moated manor house. It contains three top-lit courtrooms,
wrapped in ancillary accommodation to insulate proceedings
from street noise. The scheme included a police station, but
this was not built.

ST HELENS COLLEGE, Water Street. The college occupies parts
of the former BEECHAM'S FACTORY, including refaced post-
war blocks and the original building on the corner of Westfield
Street. Built in two phases in 1884–7, with *H.V. Krolow* and
Harry May (both of Liverpool) as joint architects, as a factory
for Thomas Beecham's famous pills – 'worth a guinea a box,
largest sale in the world', as visitors are reminded above the
door. It is the town's most manic building and its signature is
the spindly and theatrical corner tower, of Central European
character. The style is eclectic, though with the elaborate
Northern Renaissance gables now reduced and finials gone,
the façades have lost much of their vigour (a turret has also
disappeared). Entrance beneath the tower, with keystone
incorporating an unsettling bust of the founder. The entrance
hall and staircase are richly finished in marble, mahogany and
mosaic. The college built the bowed glass link wing that closes
the courtyard in the 1990s. It is by *Ormrod & Partners*.

VOLUNTEERS' DRILL HALL, Mill Street. 1861, probably by the
local builder and architect *George Harris*. Asymmetrical and
classical, with pediments and round-headed windows.

WORLD OF GLASS, Chalon Way. Opened 2000. *Geoffrey Reid
Associates* (job architect *Paul Warner*). Proposals for a 'Celebration of Glass' emerged as part of the strategy to regenerate
derelict industrial land s of the town centre in the late 1980s.
In 1991 *BDP* prepared drawings for a glass exhibition and
museum on the N bank of the St Helens Canal (*see* p. 551) to

house the Pilkington and Borough Museum collections, to be linked by glazed bridge to the restored Pilkington's No. 9 Tank House on the S. This concept was eventually realized by *Geoffrey Reid Associates*, though the idea of reviving glass-making in the tank house was abandoned. The galleries on the N bank are disappointing. Two blank industrialesque brick boxes with battered faces are linked by a glass curtain-walled circulation box. Visitors enter through a replica conical glass furnace of brick. All in all competent, but not enough. Gollifer Architects' National Glass Centre in Sunderland (1998) does interesting things with the material, so it is disappointing that, in the home of British glass-making, a project part paid for by one of the world's leading glass-makers does not. No blame should be attached to the architects, whose ambitions were thwarted. They wanted, e.g., glass walls that changed colour and opacity at the flick of a switch.

Across a basic steel-and-glass footbridge, the No. 9 TANK HOUSE of 1887 has been well conserved. It is the earliest remaining gas-fired continuous tank furnace in Europe, and used Siemens's regenerative technology, which was imported by Pilkingtons in 1873. This made continuous production of blown cylinder-glass possible for the first time, by the constant feeding of raw materials through a labyrinth of flues. This brought vast economies, and glass-blowers worked shifts round the clock. The architect of the robust brick building, with massive buttresses, may have been *J. Medland Taylor*. Both he and then *Isaac Taylor* worked extensively for Pilkingtons after Col. William Pilkington brought in Medland Taylor to rebuild Rainford Hall (*see* Rainford, p. 546). Inside, the remnants of the flue system are revealed like ancient archaeological remains; above them four iron columns and beams support a massive, central free-standing chimney that rises through the pitched roof.

ST HELENS HOSPITAL, Marshall's Cross Road. An accumulation of extensions of little merit. Begun in 1873 in a villa – the asymmetrical block with beheaded tower – it was extended first in 1884, then by *Briggs & Wolstenholme* in 1902–4, which is most of what we see from the road. The best building is behind, *Biram & Fletcher*'s substantial Neo-Georgian nurses' home of 1935–8. There is also a breezy sub-High Tech late C20 service wing.

VICTORIA PARK. *See* p. 564.

STATION, Shaw Street. 1960–1, by *W.R. Headley*, architect to BR Midland Region. Clerestoried booking hall with roof of V-section on Y-supports. Crimpled concreted platform canopies. Now sadly shabby; in 2005 the 1960s buildings were due to be replaced.

PERAMBULATION

Start in VICTORIA SQUARE, one of St Helens' few public spaces of pretension. The Town Hall and the Gamble Institute (*see*

p. 557) are on two sides and *Briggs & Wolstenholme*'s typically Free Style brick and terracotta Prudential Chambers of 1902 on another. This has corner turrets. The square was replanned in 2000 when much of the traffic was taken out of it. In the process the fine STATUE of the enthroned Victoria, by *Sir George Frampton*, 1904 (a copy of one erected in Calcutta), was removed from outside the Town Hall to the edge of the square, facing neither here nor there. The First World War MEMORIAL, an obelisk by *Biram & Fletcher*, remains *in situ*. NE of the square on PARADE STREET is the Tudorbethan HARDSHAW HALL of 1840, freed now of most of the extensions added to it from 1884, when it became the Providence Free Hospital. Now social housing. E of the square in CORPORATION STREET are two theatres. The present THEATRE ROYAL, originally by *Frank Matcham*, 1890, was rebuilt in 1900–1 after a fire and reconstructed in 1962–3 by *B. & N. Westwood, Piet & Partners*. The new façade, 2003–4, is by *Ellis Williams Architects*. The centre is glazed for the roof, but not with refinement, e.g. the thick cross-bracing. Further E is the former HIPPODROME of 1903. A thin bit of stagey frippery, but with street presence, by *J.A. Baron* of St Helens. It replaced a wooden variety theatre of 1893.

Extending from the SE corner of the square is HARDSHAW STREET with CENTURY HOUSE, the town centre's only high-rise block (nine storeys only), and then the High Gothic former PARR'S BANK of *c.* 1860, extended l. and remodelled 1878, and now a pub. Ashlar, trefoil-headed window surrounds, attached shafts etc. The naturalistic foliate carving in the spandrels of the extension's upper windows is excellent. At the bottom, on the corner with Church Street, is BARCLAYS BANK of *c.* 1973, an unusual and attractive five-storey building with an expressed concrete frame, all white-painted. The upper three storeys consist of serrated rows of large windows, each set at an angle to the façade.

CHURCH STREET has always been the town's principal thoroughfare. To the l. on the N side opposite St Helen's church (*see* p. 553) is the Wrenaissance MARKS & SPENCER. All the brick of the principal three bays, including the big segmental pediment, is excellent carved work – cartouches, fruits and flowers, etc. This was the White Hart Hotel of 1905 by *J.M. Wilson*, built for the Greenall, Whitley & Co. brewery (cipher in the pediment) which stood behind on Hall Street (demolished and replaced by the present Hardshaw Shopping Centre in the 1970s). At the E end of Church Street is the early C19 RAVEN INN, one of the few pre-1850 survivors, and, on GEORGE STREET off HALL STREET, the former CONSERVATIVE AND UNIONIST BUILDING (now offices and dance club) by *Frank S. Biram*, 1907–8, with Baroque moments and a corner tower.

Return to St Helens church, still the focal point of the town and now the pivot of the CHURCH SQUARE shopping centre, *Kingham Knight Associates*, 1970–5. Though this is only a fraction of the redevelopment envisaged in the 1960s, it still occupies the whole of the s side of the street. Happily, it is human and urban in scale and materials. On its s side St Mary's Market was extended in 1999 with a glass wall with fussy brise-soleil by *Leslie Jones Associates*. This faces the World of Glass (*see* p. 558), which straddles a stretch of the Ravenhead branch of the Sankey Brook Navigation canal of *c.* 1772 (known as the Hotties after the boiling coolant water once discharged into it from the glass works). There are examples of the stone railway sleeper-blocks of *c.* 1830 reused as coping when the canal banks, corroded by industrial effluent, were rebuilt in the 1850s. They have distinctive rectangular impressions containing two holes, and can be seen elsewhere along the canal too. Canalside redevelopment here is scruffy and uncoordinated, and fails as urbanism because car parks and service roads sever it from the rest of the centre. Facing the cars across the canal are the harshly angular and mirror-glazed former Chalon Court (now Hilton) hotel of 1993 by *Alan Williams & Partners* and a characteristic late 1980s Safeway supermarket. There is no sense of civic spirit in any of this.

Bridge Street is nw from here across the car park. It has a couple of big early c20 pubs: the Nelson Hotel, with terracotta details, is dated 1902; the Market Place is Wrenaissance, with giant Ionic pilasters and a steep pediment with carved brickwork. On the l., up short Milk Street, is The Citadel. 1861. Designed by *E. Beattie Jun.* as the second Theatre Royal (the first was a simple wooden building of 1847). Rusticated ground floor, relieving arch across the principal façade and pilasters down the flank. The majority of windows are later insertions. After closure in 1890 it became the Salvation Army Citadel, but is now a performance venue once more. In 2000 a new entrance by *TACP Design* was created at the stage end, with double-height glazed bay above. The intimate auditorium retains the lower of two U-shaped circles, raised on cast-iron columns.

Back in Bridge Street, at the top, terminating the view, is the Palladian-revival Manchester and County Bank, now Yorkshire Bank, on Ormskirk Street. Dated 1914 in the pediment. To its r. is a building with full-height plate-glass windows on the first floor; to the l. are some Moderne showrooms, the best of the unremarkable retail buildings. Continue n up Baldwin Street to the roundabout. Here, at the bottom of North Road, is *Briggs & Wolstenholme*'s YMCA Building of 1902–3, one of St Helens' brightest buildings: pinkish Ruabon brick with lashings of terracotta details of various c17 types and a turret over the former entrance with terracotta dome. Weak later c20 extensions, that to the l. top-heavy and poorly proportioned. Opposite is the former Capitol Cinema of 1929, by *Gray & Evans* of Liverpool, now a fitness club, and the United Reformed Church (*see* p. 556), and on the roundabout a memorial to miners. Return to Victoria Square via Corporation Street, with the Law Courts (*see* p. 557) and a typical mid-c19 brick terrace.

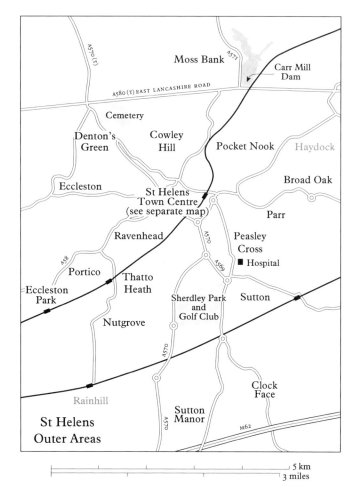

Map showing locations including Moss Bank, Carr Mill Dam, Cemetery, Cowley Hill, Denton's Green, Pocket Nook, Haydock, Eccleston, Broad Oak, St Helens Town Centre (see separate map), Parr, Ravenhead, Peasley Cross, Hospital, Portico, Thatto Heath, Eccleston Park, Sherdley Park and Golf Club, Sutton, Nutgrove, Rainhill, Sutton Manor, Clock Face. Roads labelled A570(T), A571, A580(T) East Lancashire Road, A58, A570, A569, M62. Scale: 5 km / 3 miles.

St Helens
Outer Areas

OUTER ST HELENS

North West and North: Windle, Cowley Hill, Denton's Green and Moss Bank

The township of WINDLE extended N and NW from the town centre. In the C18 there were small collieries, and little else. It is now bylaw terraces, some middle-class housing, then beyond that inter-war municipal housing (*see* p. 564), which was continued, largely after the war, N of the East Lancashire Road to Carr Mill and Moss Bank.

ST DAVID, Eskdale Avenue, Moss Bank. 1956–7, by *J.M.Wilson*. A well-balanced front with a prominent, square campanile on the l., low arcades in front of it, and a bare wall on the r.

with a pitched roof and one large arched window. Brick and concrete. The church is grouped with vicarage and hall round a courtyard.

St Mark, North Road. On the crest of Cowley Hill, a prominent termination to the dead-straight North Road rising from the town centre. 1883–5, by *James Gandy* of St Helens, paid for by the alkali baron David Gamble. It is a serious, competent building, and the w front is very well composed. Red brick, with lancet windows, deep roofs and a sw broach steeple. Apse at the e end. The brickwork is exposed inside. Round stone piers in the arcades and supporting the chancel arch. Hammerbeam roof, the trusses gathered in pairs. – stained glass. Chancel windows by *Shrigley & Hunt*, 1906. More of their glass in the s aisle. – First World War memorial. An ornate Gothic wooden surround to the n door. With statues.

St Patrick (R.C.), Loughrigg Avenue, Moss Bank. By the *F.X. Velarde Partnership*, 1963–4. Complex of hall, presbytery etc. forming a picturesque Modernist group of asymmetrically pitched roofs. They culminate in the impressive church, with two monopitch roofs rising towards each other, one of low pitch, the other extremely steep, and separated by a cleft. From here to the ridge of the steeper pitch is all glass, creating a dramatic light effect inside.

St Thomas (R.C.), Dentons Green Lane. A modest *Pugin & Pugin* church of 1892–3. Quarry-faced red sandstone, with an undersized w tower modelled on that of the Chapel of St Thomas (*see* below).

Borough Cemetery and Crematorium, Rainford Road. The root of this attractively mature landscape is the remains of the Chapel of St Thomas of Canterbury, known as Windleshaw Abbey, on Abbey Road at the w edge. Founded as a chantry by Sir Thomas Gerard *c.* 1453. Very small, plain w tower with arch towards the former nave and the roof-line. Worn stone. Fragments of reticulated window tracery remain. Low courses of masonry, largely re-erected, indicate the nave and chancel walls. To the s aisle only of a cross, on a battered square base on later steps. The inscribed date 1627 is graffiti. From the C17 this was a Roman Catholic burial ground, enclosed in 1778 and extended to its current boundaries in 1835, when Sir John Gerard gave it to the local congregations. Of that date are the cottagey lodges with label moulds. e of the tower, a tomb-chest to J.B.F. Graux de la Bruyère, †1787, the first manager of the Ravenhead glass works (*see* p. 572). The R.C. cemetery was absorbed into the non-denominational Borough Cemetery laid out in 1856–8 by *Thomas D. Barry*. This had three chapels, of which only the Anglican chapel remains, a typical *cottage orné* thing, with a curious chimney-like w tower. His asymmetric and eclectically Gothic lodges are on Hard Lane. The cemetery was further extended, and in 1959–62 the Crematorium Chapel and Chapel of Remembrance were erected in formal gardens to the w on Rainford Road. *H. Bannister*'s dignified Crematorium Chapel is like a Portland-stone-clad catafalque, rising from a wide platform which is colonnaded across the w approach (the disfiguring chimney was demanded by 1990s legislation). Entry from the n is via a covered carriageway, in the shadow of Death; exit to the s is through a glass screen to the Garden of Remembrance, into the light of Life. The interior is equally dignified, with a crimpled ceiling above a lofty clerestory. Excellent abstract *dalle de verre* STAINED GLASS of 1960 by *Powell & Sons* of Whitefriars, mirroring the circulation with, n, a tree in midwinter and, s, a tree in full bloom. The w window has eleven predominantly yellow lights representing the (good) Apostles. The Chapel of Remembrance, aligned diagonally at some distance, is a Portland-stone-clad drum on a broad shallow podium, calmly lit by a grid of green glass blocks on the e side but otherwise blank.

COWLEY HIGH SCHOOL, Hard Lane. Boys' School of 1930 with some classical-Moderne details. The girls arrived in 1992, on completion of the generous brick blocks, from *Biram & Fletcher*'s 1911–12 Edwardian Baroque building at the old site on Cowley Hill Lane (where the adjacent Boys' School of 1875–82 by *Henry Sumner*, with its raked lecture theatre, burnt down in 1993).

COWLEY HOUSE and VICTORIA PARK, City Road and Bishop Road. A better class of house colonized Cowley Hill in the C19, the grandest being Mr Ansdell's stately Italianate villa, of 1850 by *Charles Reed*. The style is typical of the date. Prospect tower with low-pitched roof. All façades are asymmetrical and rendered. Planned around a central staircase lit by an octagonal lantern, the stair cantilevered with cast-iron balustrade rising to a cantilevered landing. Good plasterwork. Well-preserved and attractive tiled floor. The building was converted for use by Age Concern in 1992–3, and in the process the entrance vestibule, framed by a columned arch, was blocked by a lift. Two other ground-floor rooms with plasterwork, one with a good cornice including flowers drooping down from the frieze. e of the house is the stable range, of brick with pitching eyes, now converted and linked to late C20 pastiche buildings. The house is composed perfectly in its landscape, which became a public PARK on Ansdell's death in 1886. Now much denuded, with a square Italianate LODGE of 1887 on North Road currently boarded up, an empty terracotta FOUNTAIN, given by Sir Henry Doulton in 1897, in the sunken garden s of the house, and a much-reduced GROTTO on the lakeshore, a relic of pre-Ansdell landscaping. It has reused carved stone, e.g. coats of arms, a mermaid, etc.; it had, until recently, a miniature tower with grotesque gargoyles on it.

BOROUGH HOUSING, Rivington Avenue and roads off it. Begun in 1921 under the aegis of the 1919 Housing and Planning Act. The first phase was designed by a committee of local architects led by *Frank S. Biram*. They got the job over the head of the Borough Engineer *Arthur W. Bradley* by agreeing to work well below the RIBA fee rate. The councillors were swayed by a belief that 'other things being equal the architect usually does it cheaper', and by the prospect of 'beauty, variety and everything that people want'. Sadly, despite being described as a 'garden city' development, the results are bleakly without merit, and *Bradley* took over for the second phase. His brick semis with hipped roofs appeared, with variations, throughout the borough. Aside from their brick quoins, they, and their layout, are entirely typical of the many thousands of houses produced in accordance with the official manual drawn up by *Raymond Unwin* that accompanied the 1919 Act.

INDUSTRIAL ARCHAEOLOGY. C19 industry in Windle (chemicals and a glass works) was concentrated along the GERARD'S BRIDGE branch of the SANKEY BROOK NAVIGATION (canal), of *c*. 1775. A nature park now flourishes where recently was derelict works and industrial waste. Along the heavily silted canal w of Merton Bank Road, however, is the NEW DOUBLE LOCK, *c*. 1775, for lifting barges to the Ravenhead and Burtonhead branches. Probably by *Henry Berry*, the Liverpool dock engineer (*see* p. 260), who was surveyor to the canal. Massive sandstone blocks and brick repairs. Restored 1991. To the N are the massive grassed (but once bare) TERRACES called 'burgy' banks, composed of the mixture of ground glass, sand and soda produced during the grinding and polishing of plate glass. The waste came from Pilkington's COWLEY HILL PLATE GLASS WORKS of 1876, a vast complex laid out E of City Road, where the float-glass process was pioneered in 1957. The plant is still operational.

THE ABBEY, Hard Lane. Very big Tudorbethan pub dated 1892. Three gables and little embattled tower. Brick and stone dressings.

THE CARR MILL pub, East Lancashire Road, A580 (*see* p. 98). A solidly handsome 1930s roadhouse. Tudorbethan motifs and classical arrangement (i.e. symmetrical centre and wings), with big stacks and hipped roofs.

MOSS BANK ROAD, the present N frontier of St Helens sprawl. There are some C19 COTTAGES, a single-storey terrace called YEOMANRY COTTAGES, recently and improbably dated 1725, and, set back N, the U-plan BIRCHLEY COTTAGES, with 1779 and 1909 datestones and in appearance essentially of the latter date.

RAINFORD ROAD. WINDLE GRANGE, E side. 1792, and Neo-Jacobean of 1849; outbuildings possibly C17. Opposite, No. 57, with a handsome shell-hood over the door, dated 1742. Carved brackets. Brick; altered and subdivided.

WINDLE HALL, Abbey Road, N of the A580. A home of the Pilkington family 1826–2000. Three storeys and three bays. Mullioned windows. Under the mid-C19 stucco skin is an C18, and possibly earlier, house. W and N wings now much reduced.

East and North East: Parr, Pocket Nook, Broad Oak and Blackbrook

PARR was well established as a colliery district when the first stage of the SANKEY BROOK NAVIGATION (*see* p. 52) penetrated the township in 1757 as far as the OLD DOUBLE DOCK, ¼ mile s of Blackbrook Road. This was the first staircase lock (that is a lock of two or more chambers, rising in height) in England, built 1756–7 (rebuilt 1885), almost certainly by *Henry Berry*. The gates have gone, but the masonry of the barrel-plan chambers is partially preserved as a cascade. With the canal came new industries, and by the end of the C19 POCKET NOOK, bordering St Helens town centre on the E bank of the canal, was home to at least five alkali works. Now that the mining and chemical works have gone Parr is a scrappy landscape of dreary C19 and C20 housing, light industry, and reclaimed green spaces such as ASHTON'S GREEN PARK, created in the 1990s by landscaping a long-closed colliery at the centre of the bleak mid-C20 borough housing of DERBYSHIRE HILL. A SCULPTURE, Poet Trees by *Thompson W. Dagnall* – a stand of carved tree trunks – is a focus.

E across the Blackbrook branch of the canal, opened *c.* 1757, is BLACKBROOK proper, rising up West End Road to merge with Haydock (q.v.). It is a ribbon of C19 terraces on two parallel streets, with later C20 housing spreading progressively s.

HOLY TRINITY, Traverse Street. 1857, by *W. & J. Hay*. They were among the last to hold out for aisle-less naves and long, wide transepts, i.e. a non-Ecclesiological theme. Startling crazy-paved walls of copper slag. No tower. Style of *c.* 1300 with intersecting tracery. The apsidal chancel is by *James Gandy*, 1883–4. NW extension, 1990s, to the right scale but with woeful materials and details. Church reordered and pews removed at the same time. W gallery walled in above and below. Spindly roof trusses which meet elegantly at the crossing as flying arches. – Good STAINED GLASS in the chancel. E, to the Rev. Flaherty, †1893, by *Kayll & Co*. Two s lancets by *S. Evans & Sons*, Liverpool. To Jane Hibbert, †1895.

ST MARK, West End Road. *See* Haydock.

ST PETER, Broad Oak Road, Parr. 1864–5, by *J. Medland Taylor*. Walling in three different materials: copper slag, red stone, buff stone. The result is very busy. SW broach spire; plate tracery. The double s transept leads to odd timber quirks inside. Squat piers, tall arches, cross-braced roof. An early work by Medland Taylor, and though the exterior and interior are typical of his idiosyncratic performances, by no means his best.

ST MARY IMMACULATE (R.C.), Blackbrook Road. A Catholic mission was established in 1674 and the first chapel erected *c.* 1752. The current little church is of 1844–5 by *Weightman & Hadfield*. Aisle-less and towerless. Dec. Later narthex with Tudor door. Bellcote on the nave E gable. Simple interior with Orrell Chapel, s, and ugly C20 W gallery. – ALTAR. 1931, by *Pugin & Pugin*. Carrara and Siena marble with canopies and two sculptural panels.

CHRIST CHURCH UNITED REFORMED CHURCH, West End
Road, Blackbrook. *See* Haydock.

BLACKBROOK HOUSE, Blackbrook Road, beside St Mary's
church. A villa of good red brick with a porch of paired Doric
columns to the l. Built for the Orrells, colliery owners. It must
predate the early 1840s when the last of their mines closed and
the family all but died out. It became a convent for the Sisters
of Mercy, who built the BLACKBROOK HOUSE INDUSTRIAL
SCHOOL attached to the l. By *Pugin & Pugin*, 1903–4, gloomy
and forbidding. Brick, three storeys, on a modified H-plan,
with first-floor chapel.

*South and South East: Peasley Cross, Sutton, Sutton Manor and
Clock Face*

The ST HELENS LINKWAY (A570) now speeds traffic rapidly
s from the town centre to the M62 through a heroically
reclaimed landscape. One roundabout has a large MONUMENT
of 1964 by *Arthur Fleischmann*, The Miner, commissioned for
the NCB's former regional headquarters at Lowton. A huge
bronze bust and arms clasping a lump of coal, on a pedestal
of cutting equipment. In the C19 and C20 this area was heavily
industrialized with mines and copper, alkali and glass works.
All that remains are: on Burtonhead Road, the modest buildings of the former RAVENHEAD SANITARY TILE & BRICK
COMPANY (emblazoned across a gable) and Ravenhead Colliery (closed 1968); and, marooned w of the Linkway, Can-
nington Shaw & Co.'s No. 7 BOTTLE MAKING SHOP, *c.* 1886,
apsidal and derelict. Now it is nature parks (successful) and
the ubiquitous retail parks (depressing).

w of the Linkway is PEASLEY CROSS and s of that SUTTON,
home in the C19 to glass (later chemical) and copper works.
Copper-slag boundary walls on Lancots Lane. Nondescript
and straggling C19 and C20 housing. s of Sutton are colliery
villages (*see* p. 569).

ALL SAINTS, Ellamsbridge Road, Sutton. 1891–3, by *Paley,
Austin & Paley*. Sizeable, and in the best tradition of the firm.
A central tower was unfortunately not built. Unfortunate too
are the replacement cement roof tiles. Red sandstone, the
details and especially the tracery already free of archaeological
correctness. The preference is for round arches inside Perp
windows. Impressive w window, most correct; e window with
staggered transoms; s transept window almost Art Nouveau.
sw porch, open to the w. Impressive, dignified interior.
Massive crossing piers for the unbuilt tower with crude ceiling
in its place. Parish hall of 1986, created behind a glazed screen
in the two w nave bays. This has weak detailing, but an
interesting spatial impact: it centralises the plan under the
crossing. – STAINED GLASS. e window. A Pilkington family
memorial, 1905, by *Shrigley & Hunt*.

ST NICHOLAS, New Street, Sutton. 1848–9, by *Sharpe & Paley*.
The convincingly squat w tower is of 1897. A 1960s vestry is
clamped discordantly around its base. The church has early

C14 detail. Typical small clerestory windows with three foiled circles and similar motifs. Typical also the angel corbels and hefty shafts to the roof of the intimate and friendly interior. – STAINED GLASS. E window, to Emily Blinkhorn, †1879. By *Henry Holiday*. Faith, Hope and Charity.

ST ANNE (R.C.), Monastery Road, Sutton. 1973. Octagonal, with attached octagonal chapel. Deep roof. The Passionist Monastery of 1910 was recently demolished.

ST THERESA (R.C.), Cannon Street, Sutton Manor. Begun 1930. *J. Sydney Brocklesby* prepared sketch designs based on his St Oswald at Ashton-in-Makerfield (q.v.), but it was built without him, possibly because he left his wife for another woman – not something to endear him to the Catholic Church. His master mason at Ashton, *Percy Howe*, persuaded the priest that he and his brother could realise his design without him. However, the scheme was far too ambitious for a poor mining community and in 1932 construction all but ceased. After the war the idea of a dome was abandoned and the building was completed in 1953 with a cheap clerestory raised in brick. The change can be seen in the W end stonework. Round-arched, free Romanesque, with a distinctly Italian feel to the impro-vised W front. The unusual plan, an apsidal E end with ambu-latory, and chapels separated from the nave by narrow aisles, passages really, is clearly derived from St Oswald. The interior sparkles with the talents that the Howes displayed first there: magnificently carved piers, capitals and arcades. Nave piers cir-cular with cushion capitals. Chapel of St Theresa, S, behind a beautifully carved screen. – Substantial attached PRESBY-TERY.

SUTTON OAK WELSH CHAPEL, Sutton Road. *c.* 1855. Built as a Methodist chapel, but home to a Welsh-speaking congrega-tion since 1893. Very modest. Polite W end in brick, with a typical St Helens doorcase of the date under alternate voussoirs. Of greater interest are the other walls, in gorgeous squared copper slag. N windows with C19 lattice iron glazing. Tiny residence attached to the rear.

HOSPITAL, Marshall's Cross Road. *See* Public Buildings, p. 559.

ST HELENS JUNCTION STATION, Station Road, Sutton. Where the Liverpool & Manchester Railway met the St Helens & Runcorn Gap Railway of 1833. The present buildings date from *c.* 1860s. The former PUB, now flats, of *c.* 1832 in Lionel Street was probably built to provide refreshment to travellers on the L&MR (there was a similar establishment at Newton-le-Willows, q.v.). A substantial symmetrical brick villa with broad eaves. Slightly projecting and gabled central bay with pointed arches to entrance and first-floor window. ¼ m. W along the line, near the St Helens & Runcorn Gap Railway overbridge, is that railway's large ENGINE SHED of 1859. Now part of the Penlake Industrial Estate, Reginald Road. Large round-headed windows; moulded base of vanished chimney.

SHERDLEY HALL FARMHOUSE, E of Sherdley Road, across the A570 St Helens Linkway. Dated 1671 on the lintel, though a hall was bought by Thomas Roughley in 1610. Stone. Three bays, with, l., a gabled porch forming an end baffle-entry and, r., a cross-wing, presumably with parlour. Low mullioned windows. It was supplanted in 1806 by Sherdley Hall, designed by *John Harrison*, the nephew of Thomas. St Helen's best house, it was demolished in 1949 after the borough purchased the estate and turned it into SHERDLEY PARK and golf course (in which the farmhouse sits).

SUTTON HALL COTTAGES, Eltonhead Road, just E of the A570. The partially rebuilt outbuildings to Sutton Hall, demolished 1935. L-plan. Brick. The projecting wing, the former granary, has three-light mullioned windows with label moulds all in brick too, indicating the C17.

COLLIERY VILLAGES. The land S of Sutton was agricultural until the 1870s, and from then colliery country: Clock Face, Lea Green, Sutton Manor, Bold. The last, SUTTON MANOR, closed in 1991. It was the last pit in England to be powered by steam. The gates on Jubits Lane remain, opening onto the landscaped site. Across the road, the village is archetypal. Built on a grid with examples of colliery housing from almost every decade since *c.* 1910, it is urban in design but feels terribly isolated. Many of the system-built 1960s terraces are boarded up. At CLOCK FACE, opened 1907 (just outside St Helens), the village on Clock Face Road (A569) was planned around generous public sports fields by the Wigan Coal & Iron Co. The spoil heaps have been landscaped into a country park. On Gorsey Lane are Dudok-style PITHEAD BATHS (now offices), 1939, by *J.H. Bourne* for the Miners' Welfare Committee. With strong horizontals, contrasting towers, and quadrant wings. Of the same date and architect are those at LEA GREEN, on Lowfield Lane (now a fitness centre). BOLD's are on Bold Lane (just outside St Helens), a boxier version of 1956 for the NCB, now offices too.

South West: Ravenhead, Thatto Heath, Nutgrove, Eccleston Park and Portico

The development of RAVENHEAD, a busy colliery district since the C17, is dominated by glass-making, and particularly by Pilkington Brothers (*see* p. 571). ST ANNS, W of Prescot Road, was popular for middle-class VILLAS and terraces from the later C19. The best is the crisp WYNBOURNE, 1905, on KINGS ROAD. Domestic Revival with Baroque bits and swaggering stained glass in the staircase window. C20 housing further out on Prescot Road at PORTICO, including a 1930s borough housing estate at GRANGE PARK, at the centre of which is the BROADWAY COMMUNITY HIGH SCHOOL, Neo-Georgian of 1938. S of Ravenhead are THATTO HEATH, NUTGROVE and SUTTON HEATH. The first recorded mining activity in the St Helens area was on Sutton Heath in the mid C16; the first glass-making at Thatto Heath 150 years later. It was a colliery district until the mid C20, which has left an incoherent legacy of C19 and C20 housing and waste industrial land, increasingly colonised by housing estates.

St John Evangelist, Crossley Road, Ravenhead. 1869–70, by *J. Medland & H. Taylor*. Lancets. Typically odd Taylorian difference between the clerestoried chancel and the roofs running down to low outer windows in the nave. Also, those low windows and a break in the roof slope imply aisles, but there are none. Rubble of various sandstones and, predominantly, the wonderful copper slag, with extensive brick dressings. Result: attractively mottled, like a fruitcake. Inside is utterly Taylor, with exposed brick, a broad and spidery hammerbeam roof and a typical wrought-iron chancel SCREEN. Typical FONT too, a squat tub with shafts at the corners. The chancel is narrow and separated from a N chapel and S organ chamber by three-bay arcades. W bay screened in beneath the four-light window. – STAINED GLASS. E window. To the Rev. Evans, †1884. Former baptistery window at W end. To Clara Evans, †1900 at Bloemfontein whilst serving as a nurse in the Boer War.

On the S side is a Neo-Elizabethan HALL of 1920 and a much bigger extension behind it by *Edmund Kirby*, 2003–4, housing another hall, kitchens etc.

St Thomas, Westfield Street. Harsh red brick, with a prominent NW tower. The chancel is by *Aldridge & Deacon*, 1890–1, with an E wall and internal details typical of them. The successful Free Gothic tower and the nave are of 1908–10, by *Frank S. Biram*. They replaced a Gothic church erected by the local brewer and town father Peter Greenall in 1839–40, as the focus of his Westfield estate. Following a fire in 1960, the nave was reconstructed with industrial-looking rectangular dormers in a new steel roof, and the church reordered. But Biram's tall paired lancets and slender arcade create a simple but broad and airy space. – Square FONT on squat piers, with Art Nouveau touches.

Our Lady Help of Christians (R.C.), Portico Lane, Portico. A fascinating Catholic chapel, because it was built just as soon as the Relief Acts would allow, in 1789–90. It is almost certainly by *George Marsh*, joiner and builder, of Liverpool. A Jesuit mission had been established at the Scholes (*see* p. 575) since at least 1716. The sixth priest, Fr Nicholas Sewell, built Our Lady. It conforms to the normal design of pre-Emancipation chapels in the North, i.e. one simple range, in brick, containing presbytery and chapel back to back, conceived to be anonymous, without outward ecclesiastical form or Catholic ornament. Set back, originally, behind high walls. The E end is the presbytery, with a polite pedimented façade. Round-headed sashes in relieving arches. The W two-thirds, without change in walls or roof-line, is the church, lit by three large pointed Gothick S windows. The N wall, with corresponding blank arches, is a more discreet façade to the Liverpool Turnpike. Likewise a barn stood to the N until the C20 to screen the chapel (or 'farm' as it was sometimes referred to). W gable with a cross on the stub of a C19 bellcote and two pointed windows. Below extends towards the lane the curious low porch or 'portico' with pointed doorways and windows (former schoolroom, r.), perhaps again to disguise the building.

The INTERIOR is a very simple box, enriched only by a shallow elliptical-plan alcove on the E wall, and pilasters with curious capitals flanking doors either side. There was originally a painting of the Ascension above the High Altar. W gallery removed. The ALTARS are late C19 German (introduced by exiled German Jesuit priests resident 1876–95). Reordered by *William Burrows* of the *Ellis Williams Partnership c.* 1981, when altar rails were removed and reused as the LECTERN and kneelers and the Lady Chapel altar repositioned as a CELEBRANT ALTAR on an extended platform. – Neoclassical TABLET, Rev. John Hughes, †1828. – A CROSS, missing the bottom of its shaft, stands outside the W door. Inscribed Frances Howard, dated 1652 on the reverse, and enriched with vines, flowers and abstract patterns. It stood on Eccleston Hill outside Seddon's Cottage (*see* p. 575) until 1822.

ST AUSTIN (R.C.), Heath Street, Thatto Heath. 1895, by *Sinnott, Sinnott & Powell*, in brick, with paired lancets. Red stone NW tower and W front added by *E. Quirke* in 1905.

METHODIST CHURCH, Nutgrove Road, Nutgrove. 1883. Italianate box with pediment, large twin round-headed windows, and Doric porch under. Soft red brick and extensive red stone dressings.

PILKINGTON GLASS. Immediately S of the town centre, the inner ring road, LINKWAY WEST (A58), occupies much of the historic site of Pilkington Brothers, established here alongside the canal in 1826 as the St Helens Crown Glass Company. For over a hundred years this was the centre of their empire. Today, N of the Linkway only No. 6 Tank House survives as part of the World of Glass (*see* Public Buildings, p. 558); to the S the works remain in use along Canal Street (which is built over the Ravenhead branch of the canal), although the main focus of production has shifted S of Burtonhead Road to the float plant that dominates the town.

The former OFFICES on Grove Street are by far the best architecture. 1937–40, by *Herbert J. Rowse*. Now flats called Reflection Court, standing rather forlornly on the edge of the Linkway. They were an extension to offices by *J. Medland Taylor* of 1888, demolished in 1997, and housed senior management. Two other *Rowse* buildings were completed in 1938, a canteen (with a 60 ft (18.5 metre) clear span in reinforced concrete) and a laboratory, both demolished in 1997 too. A Neo-Georgian scheme by *Arnold Thornely* (who had designed premises in 1924 which still stand attached to the rear of the Rowse building) was rejected in 1934, and *Rowse* was asked to submit proposals, probably on the advice of *Kenneth Cheesman*, head of the firm's Architect's Department. In the 1930s Pilkingtons showcased their products through advertising, showrooms and exhibition stands that were some of the very best examples of contemporary design, aimed at architects, and Modern Movement architects in particular. Thornely's Neo-Georgian did not fit this campaign image; Rowse's Dudokian Modernism did. His offices are on a horseshoe plan, in handmade brick, the same as his contemporary Liverpool Philharmonic Hall (*see* p. 371). The thrusting round prow with its bands of windows is balanced by the Odeonesque pylon (now mirrored without irony on *BDP*'s CINEMA, 2000, across the road). Good detailing. Only fragments of the originally extensive and diverse use of Pilkington's products remain inside, and in the courtyard garage, vaulted in concrete with inset glass lenses.

p. 56 Pilkingtons expanded SW up the hill into RAVENHEAD, acquiring the BRITISH PLATE GLASS COMPANY WORKS there in 1901. This enterprise was established with French expertise in 1773, beginning the industrial production of flat glass in St Helens (*see* St Helens Introduction, p. 552). The works' Great Casting Hall (1773–6) was one of the great industrial buildings of the C18, a gloomy cathedral 340 ft (109 metres) long and 150 ft (46 metres) wide. Six of the pointed-arched bays survived until the 1970s. Now all that remains, off STAFFORD ROAD, are the much-abused row of STABLES, with former clock tower and cupola and circular windows, MANAGER'S HOUSE with pediment and porch, and a former FARMHOUSE, partly of stone, which predates the factory (the date 1712 was inscribed). Immediately SE is FACTORY ROW, company housing. The ten cottages at the W end are contemporary with the factory, and amongst the oldest surviving industrial terraced housing in the North West. Eight of them were originally (sixteen) back-to-backs, with access to the rear row through the passage between the fifth and sixth house. The remaining cottages are dated 1854. No original windows or doors survive, and the roof is later. Further E on Ravenhead Road is the tapering tower of a WINDMILL, probably late C18, that may have powered the glass grinders. Now partially enclosed in a pre-1850 company SCHOOL HOUSE, extended and refurbished in 1916, when the early C19 NEW ROW cottages were absorbed.

122 ALEXANDRA PARK, the Pilkington head office, rises immediately W of the Ravenhead works, off Prescot Road. By *Fry, Drew & Partners*. Maxwell Fry had an association the firm stretching back to the 1930s, and had been commissioned by the Chairman Sir Alan Hudson Davies to design a house in Liverpool. Design work started in 1956; completion was in 1964–5, partially delayed by encountering long-forgotten mineshafts. The buildings are approached by a winding drive which allows them to be seen all the time at varying angles. The group consists of two parts: the office complex, made up of a quadrangle, tower, and a lakeside range attached by N and S bridge wings to form a second adjoining courtyard; and the narrow formalised lake (created by extending the works reservoir), with the canteen at its N end and a footbridge across the middle, to connect the offices to the works. A museum of glass (now closed; collections at the World of Glass, *see* p. 558) and

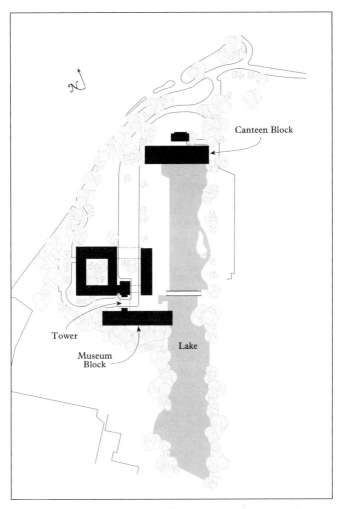

St Helens, Alexandra Park (Pilkington Glass headquarters).
Block plan

garage, low and long, runs from below the s end of the tower out into the lake s of the bridge, tying the office complex into the lake part.

The twelve-storey TOWER, 170 ft (52 metres) high, dominates. It was not part of the original scheme but added as a matter of prestige: without it the complex would be inconspicuous because of the fall of the land. It bridges the approach, with its short side to the second courtyard (nearest the lake) and subtly to one side of its axis, so that to its E the courtyard is open, beneath the s bridging wing, to the footbridge and the lower-level museum. The lakeside range and the quadrangle are four-storeyed. The module of the concrete framework chosen is generous. The framework itself is clad with black slate, and the bridging wings have white sill panels. Return wall surfaces have deep blue glass facing, in four tones. Under the tower is a surprisingly cramped entrance with a large back-lit abstract glass panel of thick relief and many mottled colours. This is by *Avinash Chandra*, and represents the interior of a glass furnace. As one enters it is above, and seen reflected in a mirror. The tower's pergola hides services, but the two identical tanks stand up above it as an integral part of the composition.

By means of an enclosed walkway along the w shore of the lake, the office complex is connected to the CANTEEN. This long, low, but deceptively large two-storey building closes the N end of the lake. Designed to serve almost 1,600 employees, now it is redundant and stripped. Inside are partly dismantled abstract murals by *Victor Pasmore*, the largest of which was 60 ft (18.5 metres) long. Additional light is drawn into the heart of the building from two garden courts. Each of these has a free-standing tapering cruciform pier, spreading into four arms at the top, a structurally redundant but wonderfully unexpected and dramatic feature. Pilkington products are used, as Fry said, extensively but not extravagantly throughout, though much of the pre-open-plan interior has subsequently succumbed to changing fads about working practices.

The rigour and clarity of the design have stood up well to changing tastes. The parts of the group are extremely well interlocked and grouped and the setting on the lake is very successful; there is far more subtlety at work here than the casual visitor may observe. Alexandra Park is one of the best of the first generation of UK company headquarters inspired by the American 'campus' concept developed by practices such as Eero Saarinen and SOM. Nevertheless, the project took so long to complete that by the time it was finished in 1965 it was made to look dated by the precision simplicity of SOM's trend-setting headquarters for Heinz at Hayes Park, which opened in the same year.

ELTONHEAD FARM, S of Eltonhead Road, 3 m. SSW of St Helens town centre. The farmhouse, now rendered, appears to be a two-cell, two-storey building probably of the early C17, to which a third bay, at the N end, has been added. But it is uncertain whether the elaborate datestone of 1663 (with achievement and initials) discovered abandoned nearby relates to either phase, or to something else. There are later outshuts. The range of farm buildings N of the house includes probably C17 fabric and, at the far N end, a C19 'paddy shant' (*see* p. 46) consisting of a single small room on each of two floors.

NUTGROVE HOUSE, Nutgrove Road, Nutgrove. 1810. A simple Georgian box in soft brick with an elegant Doric porch, built for the Liverpool printer Jonas Nuttall. Converted to apartments in 1997. Setting destroyed by housing development, leaving the house on the most miserly plot.

PRESCOT ROAD (A58). On the N side 1½ m. SW of the town

centre is a former schoolhouse or schoolmaster's house, now SEDDON's COTTAGE. The worn plaque once dated the building of the school to 1684. On the S side is ECCLESTON GRANGE, c. 1860.

ECCLESTON PARK. A private development of middle-class villas S of ST HELENS ROAD (A58), 2½ m. SW of the town centre, adjoining Prescot (q.v.). The earliest ones are at the N end of CENTRAL AVENUE and on PARK AVENUE. Late C19, none outstanding. Two substantial and very typical early C20 Greenall Whitley PUBS (*see* p. 552) on St Helens Road. Tudor-bethan.

THE SCHOLES, Scholes Lane. The core of this ashlar sandstone house could be C15, which would make it one of the few medieval houses in SW Lancashire built of masonry (*see* p. •• for others). But this is not certain. This part – probably the hall – is behind the two two-storey porches and the single W bay. The porches themselves appear Elizabethan. The E one now leads into a hallway, containing the (C19?) stairs, partitioned from the hall. The W one is probably in front of the original entry; directly inside it is a blocked transverse passage and covered-up inglenook. On the far side of this a former stair-tower, looking Elizabethan too, projects from the rear. So it appears that a fireplace was built against the screens passage, the hall floored across and a staircase built to the new first floor, probably all in the later C16. The house also had two cross-wings, giving it an H-plan, with a kitchen in the E wing. The W wing has been demolished, but evidence of its existence remains in the W wall, including a blocked first-floor door now obscured by the single-storey 1970s extension. The E wing was refaced in the earlier C18 and given flush-fitting sashes. Much of the house was refenestrated around this time, though three old mullioned windows remain in the NW corner, and there are a couple of C19 mullioned windows on the front. Beside the stair-tower are two small brick extensions, each containing only a little room on each floor, and each seemingly late C17–early C18. The W appears to be slightly older, and has a shaped gable; the N one has a castellated parapet. Both have sashes.

The best piece of decorative work is the entrance of the W porch with its fine Elizabethan mouldings and its four-centred arch. Inside little is visible, but there is a four-centred doorway into the E wing and a number of cruder versions on the upper floor between the older fabric and the N additions. The ground-floor Panelled Parlour in the gabled C17–C18 extension was fitted up with bolection-moulded wainscot, now crudely replicated as kitchen units. But a ceiling beam with carved rose remains. There are a number of boarded or panelled doors, ranging in style from the late C16 to C18. Upstairs in the older part is a datestone of 1681, with the initials of John and Elizabeth Hurst.

Outside the S front is a stumpy Doric PILLAR with an image niche at the top, carved out of an entablature, probably from a wayside shrine. This is assigned to the early C18, i.e. the time after 1704 when the 7th Viscount Molyneux of Croxteth had rented The Scholes and was made Rector of the Lancashire District of the Society of Jesus. A range of C17–C18 farm buildings to the SE was replaced in the 1970s by a nondescript office block.

West: Eccleston

The few scattered houses and farms of Eccleston were attached to St Helens by borough and private housing spreading W in the 1930s, and absorbed by post-war suburban sprawl.

CHRIST CHURCH, Church Road. 1836–8. Paid for by *Samuel Taylor*, the Lord of the Manor, to whom Peter Fleetwood-Hesketh also attributed the design. He was a cotton manufacturer. The dominant note is the rock-faced red stone. Lancets. W tower with needle spire, short transepts, and a short chancel. Hammerbeam roof with cast-iron braces. – FONT. Alabaster, Arts and Crafts taste, *c.* 1900. – The best woodwork is from elsewhere, though the BOX PEWS must be original. – COM-MUNION TABLE of bits and pieces, some C17? – PULPIT. Late C17, reputedly from St Saviour, Southwark. Certainly entirely typical of examples in the post-Great Fire London churches. – The WEST GALLERY and the COMMUNION RAIL have Rococo decoration and religious reliefs and are, it looks, Flemish or French C18 work. The Doric columns supporting the gallery came from St Peter, Liverpool (1699–1704) when that church was demolished in 1922. – STAINED GLASS. The best are S, 2nd and 3rd from the W to members of the Herman family, by *Shrigley & Hunt*. Also, S transept, to Samuel Taylor, †1880, the benefactor and probable architect, and N transept, John Penketh, †1887, his likely builder (*see* Eccleston Hall, p. 577).

ST LUKE, Knowsley Road. Building, 1929–31, was delayed until St Helens parish church was completed. *Biram & Fletcher* must have been busy making notes, for the weighty SE tower described by strong buttresses, the thin nave flanks with Perp windows under tile lintels, the thin brown bricks and red stone dressings are all very reminiscent of Caröe's church. Elegant waterspouts. A squat interior under a wooden wagon roof has a Domestic Revival feel. Oak-panelled chancel.

ST JULIE (R.C.), Howard's Lane. Completed 1969. By *L.A.G. Prichard & Son*. Cost £70,000. A red brick box with attached hall and presbytery. Large concrete-mullioned W window, triangular-headed windows elsewhere. Reputedly the world's first church dedicated to Julie Billiart, 1751–1816, Foundress and first Superior-General of the Congregation of the Sisters of Notre Dame of Namur. She was canonised in the year the church opened.

ST TERESA OF AVILA (R.C.), Devon Street. 1964, by *W. & J.B. Ellis*. Expressed concrete frame, brown brick panels. Apsidal E end, blank, narrow clerestory, and angled projecting windows on the N and S façades *à la* Coventry Cathedral. The entire W gable is glazed, from floor to ridge, particularly impressive from within. The interior is tall, articulated by the elegant canted framing, which is formed of concrete 'jointed crucks'. At the E end these are free-standing, creating a vestigial ambulatory; along the nave, aisle passages are created behind them beneath the zigzagging window bays. S chapel. – FONT and PEWS from the previous church (now church hall) across Devon Street. – Good STAINED GLASS of 1971–2 in the lowest panels of the W window.

METHODIST CHURCH, Burrows Lane. Opened 1966. By *Penn-Smith & Weston*. An alien form. Square in plan with the gables on all four sides extending almost to the ground, so it appears taller than wide. All roofs steeply pitched, and dense grids of chequered glass panels in the gables. Boxy brick porch. Lofty interior, with yellow crosses in the STAINED GLASS of the E and W gables. Usual ancillary buildings attached around a small courtyard.

WAR MEMORIAL. *See* Prescot.

DE LA SALLE SCHOOL, Mill Brow. At the entrance the excellent CENTRE FOR THE PERFORMING ARTS by *John McAslan & Partners*, 2003–4. An impressively lucid and beautifully proportioned composition precisely expressing the component parts: three identical cubes, each containing a classroom on the ground floor and a performance space above, with glazed stairwells between the classrooms. These are fully glazed; the performance spaces are clad in timber (and top-lit). The quality of this building only serves to highlight the poverty of so much contemporary school construction.

BLACK BULL, Knowsley Road. Built by Greenall's *c.* 1932 to quench the thirst of Eccleston's new suburban population. It is one of their largest, in a Tudor Gothic roadhouse style. Elegant garden front, roofs and chimneys tumbling down to the full length, fully glazed garden rooms overlooking a bowling green.

CLAY LANE FARMHOUSE, Gillar's Lane. Dated 1690 over the inner doorway.

ECCLESTON HALL, Prestbury Drive, is the best house in St Helens, an elegant ashlar villa of *c.* 1829–34, probably, like Christ Church, to the designs of the owner *Samuel Taylor*. His cash books don't appear to mention a professional, though there are frequent payments to *John Penketh*, builder and timber merchant, who seems to have been clerk of works. It is of five bays by three, the central three of the principal façade broken forward in a shallow bow in which the slightly recessed ground floor is articulated by engaged Greek Doric columns. Tripartite windows. The entrance façade, E, has a recessed central bay and flush Greek Doric columns carrying a first-floor balcony. A hipped roof with broad eaves all round gives it a slightly hunched appearance. Inside is a central top-lit staircase with simple cast-iron balustrade. Not all is straightforward, though. The tooling, mouldings and building line of the NW of the mansion reveal it to be of a different phase, and the more Italianate façade of the W wing (orangery, or billiards?) conceals lower service wings behind, lit by a menagerie of windows including labelled horizontal sashes and two- and three-light mullions with shouldered depressed arch lintels. This is a bit of a conundrum. The masonry looks older; the windows, despite their convincing irregularity, are probably of the 1830s or reused. Samuel Taylor inherited an earlier Hall (*c.* 1567, altered) from his father in 1820 before starting on his new house, but it stood SE and so it is unlikely that the present service wings are a part of it. But they could incorporate stonework from it.

The Hall became a sanatorium and then, in 1997, was converted into apartments. A poor pastiche range now closes the service yard, and the house is ruthlessly hemmed in with housing and left with only a remnant of lawn, S, in which to breathe.

ECCLESTON PARK. *See* p. 575.

GARDEN VILLAGE. Though fewer than a hundred houses were actually built, Pilkingtons began planning for the Eccleston Hall Estate in 1909 with grand ambitions. In 1919 a scheme of 4,000 houses to rival Port Sunlight was unveiled, planned by *Frederick Hopkinson* with advice from *Patrick Abercrombie* (who was in parallel planning another scheme for the firm in Yorkshire). Hopkinson was dismissed after only eight houses had been completed, and the project was continued sporadically to 1924 under Abercrombie's guidance. The purpose was to attract skilled staff; the economics of post-war house building killed it. The first fifty houses are in ECCLESTON GARDENS and SEDDON ROAD on Prescot Road. In 1923 thirty-one more were built on WILLOW ROAD in a simplified Lancelot Keay Georgian. Thankfully, R.A. Pilkington had an aversion to Accrington bricks.

HOME FARM, Old Eccleston Lane. A polite laithe house. Possibly C18, with the domestic end refaced in C19 Tudor Revival. Barn end with splayed pent porch. Stone.

ST HELENS RUGBY LEAGUE FOOTBALL CLUB, Knowsley Road. A ramshackle of undistinguished C20 stands and terraces, but collectively of an evocative kind increasingly uncommon in an age of one-piece all-seater stadia.

SEAFORTH

3090

The name comes from Seaforth House, built for John Gladstone, merchant and politician, in the early C19 to take advantage of the fine sea views and sandy beaches. It became a fashionable place for villa building, though not for long: the Liverpool docks were extended N towards the mouth of the Mersey in the later C19, and the villas gave way to bylaw terraces. Only fragments survive, on the E side of Crosby Road South, with pretty Gothic verandas of iron. Seaforth House was demolished *c.* 1880 and replaced by Seafield House, a large hydropathic hotel, which itself was knocked down *c.* 1970 to make way for the Royal Seaforth Dock (*see* p. 278). Much of the bylaw housing has been cleared too, and today Seaforth is a nondescript N extension of Bootle (q.v.).

OUR LADY STAR OF THE SEA (R.C.), Church Road. By *Sinnott, Sinnott & Powell*. 1898–1901. Big and serious-looking, deliberately so because it was built opposite the now demolished Anglican church of St Thomas (1815, of a 'lovable naïvety' according to Pevsner). Pale Parbold sandstone and red stone detailing. A strong building, but it sorely misses the splendid SW tower and spire planned. Instead, lower stages capped in copper. Conventional plan: nave with aisles to pack them in and a very short, broad apsidal chancel so all can be clearly observed. Hammerbeam roof. N and S chapels, W choir and organ gallery. Lifted by the quality of detailing and carving and the rich colouring. The carving is by local mason *Patrick Honan*; the luxuriantly naturalistic capitals are particularly fine. They crown polished granite piers. Unusually, the interior was restored in the 1990s after destructive reordering. – HIGH ALTAR. Tall, with pinnacles and TABERNACLE. Sicilian and Sienese marble. By *Dan Sinnott*, carved by *Boultons*. – Rich wooden ALTARS in N and S chapels. – STATIONS OF THE CROSS. Painted as blank traceried windows. – Vigorous PAINTINGS around the apse, scenes from the Life of Christ, by *May L. G. Cooksey*, *c.* 1909. Also N aisle. – STAINED GLASS. By *Hardman*, E and W windows. Muted colours. Aisle windows by *Atkinson Bros* of Newcastle upon Tyne.

ROYAL SEAFORTH DOCK. *See* Liverpool, p. 278.

THE PALLADIAN (former), Seaforth Road. A purpose-built cinema dated 1913, with classically detailed façade.

Three big PUBS. On Crosby Road South (A565) is a rock-faced Gothic pile, marooned now that the surrounding streets have been cleared. Further S at the acute junction with Knowsley Road is ST WINIFRED'S HOTEL. Wedge-shaped, with flanks of two gables each and a curved apex topped by a miniature arcade of stubby little semicircular openings, and above that by a conical roof. The SEAFORTH ARMS HOTEL on Seaforth Road is later, *c.* 1900–10. Handsome free English Renaissance. Channelled rustication to the ground floor, brick above, with gables and lots of elaborate stone dressings including blocked Ionic columns. In the re-entrant angle is a canted porch rising up to an octagonal copper dome.

POTTER'S BARN, Crosby Road South. Erected in 1841 as the coachhouse and gateway to the grounds – now a public park – of a house that was never built, because the business of William Potter, a China trade merchant, collapsed. Sandstone ashlar. A four-centred archway (now blocked) joins two buildings at right angles to each other. Mullioned windows and arrow slits.

SEFTON
with LUNT

3000

Sefton was a large ancient parish on the windswept, waterlogged coastal plain N of the Mersey. Its church is a prominent landmark in this flat landscape. Even today there is hardly a village to speak of.

9 ST HELEN. A large, very fine church, mostly late Perp and with a marvellous wealth of fitments – especially the gorgeous display of screens. It was lovingly restored in 1907–22 by *W.D. Caröe*, who was born and brought up locally and sang in the choir as a boy. There was a late C12 church; fragments, including a waterleaf capital, are displayed inside. The oldest parts of the standing fabric are C14 – the E bay of the N chapel, with Dec windows and a Dec PISCINA, and the W steeple with Dec windows too. Except for the chapel E window, all these windows are of the simplest reticulated kind. The chapel N window, first from E, is straight-headed. Inside in the tower E wall are the scars of the C14 nave roof, much lower than now, above the triple-chamfered arch dying into the imposts. There was a C14 N aisle – its outline and a lintel can clearly be seen in the W wall of the present aisle. This is C15; the second bay from E is early C15, the rest is late, with uncusped three-light windows and a plain double-chamfered doorway. (The buttresses vary in date from C14 to C19). The very curious pinnacles at the base of the spire are a problem. They are reminiscent of bee skips with finials – quite eastern in profile and quite unique. They can't be C14, nor can they be early C16. Perhaps C17? No work is recorded, though. The tops appear to be more recent. Are they of 1802, when the spire was damaged by a gale and the top portion rebuilt?

Almost everything else dates from a building campaign undertaken by three successive rectors, all cadet members of the Molyneux family of Sefton Hall and later Croxteth Hall (*see* p. 406) which held the advowson. Work was probably begun by James Molyneux, rector 1489–1509, and continued by Edward, and then Anthony, incumbent from 1536 to 1557, but it is uncertain when it started. Anthony's will stated that he had made 'so great coste of ye chauncell and revestre'. The Molyneux parts consist of: the S aisle, with large four-light transomed windows; the embattled clerestory with round-headed windows with intersecting tracery; the two-storeyed S porch with Molyneux arms, leaf spandrels to the four-centred arch and plain mullioned upper window; and the one-bay chancel with two-transomed N and S windows. Almost all windows of this phase are uncusped. Inscriptions (some lost) in the windows indicate that the S aisle was completed by 1540 and the E window by 1545. The present five-light E window is 1875, 'corrected' with cusping. Attached to the N end of Anthony Molyneux's revestry is a choir vestry added by *Caröe* in 1915–16 and extended in 1990.

Inside, the six-bay arcades are the doing of the Molyneuxs too. They are perfectly even on both sides and have piers with a section of four demi-shafts and four hollows in the diagonals. There is no chancel arch. The SEDILIA and PISCINA formed of one four-arch arcade (probably re-set and re-cut) and an ogee-arched AUMBRY go with the date of the rest of the chancel. The present internal arrangements are due to *Caröe*, but largely follow recommendations made by his mentor, *J.L. Pearson*, in 1892. The roofs, by *Caröe*, are out-standing, utterly convincing Perp with moulded beams and elaborate bosses, superbly carved by *Cornish & Gaymer* of Norfolk. The nave and chancel roof is particularly magnificent. The N chapel probably housed the chantry established by Edward Molyneux in 1535. It is now the Lady Chapel. The S chapel was the Chantry of St Mary, founded in 1528 by Margaret Bulcley. It is now known as the Molyneux Chapel.

SCREENS. The great glory of the church is the complex of seven screens, more and of greater variety than any other in the county. All are early to mid-C16, and were sensitively restored by *Caröe*. There are a number of problems, though. Stylistically the earliest appear to be the parclose screens, with exquisitely fine late Gothic tracery. On the chapel sides these bear the initials IM, presumably for James Molyneux, giving a date of 1489–1509. The only problem is that Anthony Molyneux claims to have built the chancel, which therefore can be no earlier than 1536. The CHANCEL SCREEN is the magnificent centrepiece of the whole church. It was carefully reconstructed by Caröe with the help of detailed drawings made before it was mutilated in the C19. Thus, though much of it is his, we can be reasonably confident about its fidelity. It is of noble height – Caroe raised it by 3 ft (90 cm.) – and richly carved, and has a ribbed coving and splendid broad cresting

Sefton, St Helen, chancel, looking west. Engraving.
(Richard Bridgens, *Sefton Church with part of the interior decorations*, 1822)

to the nave, and a massive canted canopy to the chancel with carved bosses, re-created by Caröe. It too has James Molyneux's initials and, intriguingly, Renaissance motifs in the form of friezes with putti, some holding horns and some holding medallions. They are remarkable if they really are so early. The screens across the N and S aisles are simpler, and though different, share a similar, and peculiar, debased round-arched Gothic. The S screen has motifs identical to some panelling at the demolished Lydiate Hall (q.v.) which has been credibly dated to *c.* 1540–50, when Anthony Molyneux's sister was married to its owner. E of it are screens enclosing the *ex situ* Sefton Pew, again highly ornate with idiosyncratic carving identical to the Lydiate panelling. E of the N screen is another similar to it, and between, the U-shaped Blundell Pew. The panelling here looks a little later and is no longer Gothic, and the pew ends have a Tudor rose and a Blundell squirrel.

OTHER FURNISHINGS. The chancel has its early C16 STALLS complete. The fronts have shallow recesses with seats for the choirboys, the ends have poppyheads and much carving, including more of James Molyneux's initials and a mobbed owl and hares, both Molyneux emblems. The choirboys' desks are by *Caröe*, but include some C16 fragments of *c.* 1500. – The contemporary BENCH ENDS have poppyheads too, and charming carved motifs including instruments of the Passion, the letters of the alphabet (minus W, X and Z), vines, pomegranates, roses and lilies, and a humpless camel ridden by a moor. – PEWS in the aisles by *Caröe*, inspired by the distinctive C16 bench ends of the Blundell Pew. – They replaced BOX PEWS and galleries (a remnant of these over the S door), though a couple of C18 examples survive at the W end of the N aisle, incorporating one, r., dated 1680. They were later occupied by the Mock Corporation, a social club for C18 Liverpool gentlemen. – REREDOS, with fluted Ionic pilasters and chancel dado panelling, given by Anne Molyneux, *c.* 1730. A pediment is lost. The sunburst is an addition of 1820. – HIGH ALTAR, now brought forward, by *Caröe*, with C17 shield of the Passion from Rouen in the frontal. – LADY ALTAR, and furniture, in the N chapel by *Caröe*. Retable/reredos with relief carving. – COMMUNION RAIL and TOWER RAIL. With twisted balusters, *c.* 1690–1700. The communion rail in the S chapel is Jacobean, with closely set balusters, each with a finial, like an elaborate picket fence. – PULPIT. Dated 1635. Complete with backplate and sounding-board. Dazzling, every surface covered in marvellous, close arabesque decoration like the finest embroidered dress in a Jacobean portrait. Once fixed to the middle pier of the N arcade. The Molyneuxs were ardent Royalists; around the sounding-board is carved, 'My sonne feare thou the Lorde and the Kinge and medle not with them that are given to change.' The snaking Gothic iron and timber stairs are *c.* 1819, cut down. – FONT. Plain, octagonal, Perp, with quatrefoils. COVER dated 1688 but still Jacobean in type, i.e. simple octagonal pyramid. – ORGAN CASE. *Caröe*. Intricately carved Gothic.

– LECTERN. A rare ecclesiastical work by *Herbert J. Rowse*, 1937. – DOORS. C15 N door and C16 S door. Studded; fleur-de-lys strap hinges. – Massive, battered C14 MUNIMENT CHEST. – HATCHMENTS. Four Blundells, the earliest to the diarist Nicholas Blundell, †1737. – CHANDELIERS. Three large ones, of brass, given in 1773. – WALL PAINTINGS. C17 biblical texts uncovered in the arcade spandrels. – STAINED GLASS. Fragments of early-to-mid-C16 glass in the chancel N and S windows and windows of the S aisle. The largest collection was brought together *c.* 1916 from the chancel and S aisle windows into the S chapel, 1st from E. This includes Passion emblems and elements of the Visitation, the Trinity and, unusually for the C16, the martyrdom of Thomas à Becket. The modern inscription is erroneous: the original came from the S chapel E window and bore Sir William Molyneux's name and the date 1542. S aisle, W window. Upper lights by *Henry Holiday*, 1864. Amongst his first designs for *Powell & Sons*. E window by *Clayton & Bell*, 1875. S chapel E window, to the Hon. Cecil Molyneux, †1916. S chapel, a series by *H.G. Hiller* of Liverpool, 1936 (the window W of this appears to be Hiller too). N aisle 2nd from W, *Walter Wilkinson*, 1927.

MONUMENTS. N chapel, early C14 tomb recess. In it an effigy of a knight, for which it was not intended, wearing chain mail and with his legs crossed. Quite plausibly he is Sir William Molyneux, †1296/8. – Another knight, *c.* 1330, also cross-legged, but bearded and placing his feet against a crouching figure with l. foot back and r. foot forward (and upper body missing). – Between chancel and chapels, two plain tomb-chests with coarse quatrefoils and shields. On the N one the defaced alabaster slab of Johanna, wife of Sir Richard Molyneux, †1439. – On the S one now the BRASSES of Sir Richard Molyneux, †1568, and two wives and thirteen children (22–23 in. (56–58 cm.) figures of the parents). In the Sefton Pew, brass of Lady Margaret Bulcley, †1528, daughter of an earlier Sir Richard (30½ in. (77 cm.) figure). In the S chapel, brass to Sir William Molyneux, †1548, and two wives (2 ft (160 cm.) figures). Highly unusually Sir William wears not contemporary garb, but armour, chain-mail tunic and hood in the style of the C13 or C14. In the chancel until 1989. Palimpsests on the reverse, one to Thomas Hay, a London goldsmith, †1405. – Henry Blundell, the collector (*see* Ince Blundell). 1813, by *S. & T. Franceys* of Liverpool, but designed and made by their apprentice *John Gibson*. Seated figure with allegorical groups, quite small, but as if it were the model for a major monument in Westminster Abbey. – Richard Rothwell, †1844. Wide sarcophagus with inscriptions. Urn on top. By *Franceys & Spence* of Liverpool. – Lots of ledger slabs laid in the floor, though the best two are raised, in the S chapel: marble slabs to the 3rd Viscount Sefton, †1699 (with descendants added), carved with superbly anatomical skull, and to the 4th Viscount's wife, Bridget, †1713. – First World War memorial in Gothic frame, presumably by *Caröe*.

The medieval hall, C16 mill and a grand Georgian rectory have all been destroyed. The hall, ancient home of the Molyneux, was one hundred yards s of the church. The dry MOAT was cut in two in 1964 when the B5422, Brickwall Lane, was diverted across it. Immediately s of it, Old Hall Farm was developed in the 1980s as a suburban cul-de-sac and the large brick BARN of *c.* 1700 badly converted (a garage projects from beneath a cart arch under a catslide roof!). On Sefton Mill Lane at the E end of the church is MILL HOUSE. Brick on a stone plinth, with 1753 datestone bearing the cross Moline, a Molyneux emblem. Now two houses.

½ m. NW of Sefton is LUNT, a few brick cottages, one Georgian house with pedimented doorcase, a mid-C20 housing estate, and a good brick TITHE BARN on LUNT LANE dated 1693. It has strong similarities to the Sefton barn and has also been crudely converted to housing. At the top of a flight of stone steps at the s end is a doorway with a very odd stone surround, the lintel of a bizarre kind of embattled form.

5000

SHEVINGTON

The parish rises up from the N side of the pretty wooded valley of the River Douglas NW of Wigan. There was coal mining. Shevington itself, Shevington Vale and Shevington Moor are mainly now C20 dormitories; CROOKE on the Leeds and Liverpool Canal is a little C19 industrial hamlet, with terraces etc. and formerly coal wharves. A MARINA has been created there from the lower end of the early C19 branch canal that formerly extended as a tunnel direct into the coal seams. A BARN, now a house, previously clad in C17 brick, has a cruck frame.*

ST ANNE, Church Lane. 1887. Brick with stone dressings. Aisle-less. Chancel and w bellcote. Lancets.

PRIMARY SCHOOL, Miles Lane, w. of the M6. Central stone block built as a school in 1814.

GATHURST STATION. *See* Orrell, p. 539.

CALICO WOOD FARM, Houghton Lane, N off Miles Lane. Beside the M6. The upper parts of a cruck truss survive inside the early C18 rebuild. (A wooden mullioned window from the old house remains in what is now an internal wall. Gary Miller.)

COACH HOUSE FARMHOUSE, Shevington Lane. Heavily modernised, but upper parts of a cruck truss – at least C16 – and a C17 timber-framed wing survive inside (Miller).

CLUB HOUSE FARMHOUSE, Church Lane. Timber-framed baffle-entry plan early C17 yeoman's house, with a parlour cross-wing. Clad in stone and extended, probably in 1663: that date and the initials of Seth and Frances Prescott and their

---

* It was associated with the timber-framed Crooke Hall, demolished in 1937. An elaborate carved panel bearing the date 1608 and the initials of the owners and the master carpenters is displayed at the Wigan History Shop (*see* p. 667).

son Thomas are on a delightful painted quarry in the five-light mullioned-and-transomed house-part window. A wooden diamond-mullioned window frame in the firehood wall is evidence that the house was originally timber-framed (and also that the r. bay is an addition). The timber-framed partition walls are not necessarily corroboration: around Wigan, masonry houses were frequently built with such internal walls in the C17. The firehood has a moulded stone spere; the stairs and corridors are modern. Stone BARN of a local variation of Dr Brunskill's 'Lancashire' combination type identified by Philip Powell: with shippon to one side of the threshing doors, in an aisle on one side of the barn attached. Dated 1660 – sensible Prescott invested in his business before turning to home improvements.

(FOREST FOLD FARM, ½ m. s of Miles Lane (B5375), w of the M6. Philip Powell reports a large yeoman's FARMHOUSE. Early C17, brick, C20 windows. Baffle-entry plan, with huge back-to-back inglenooks. Timber-framed internal walls. Stair-tower with barley-sugar balusters, later. Late C17, L-plan GRANARY and STABLE. Brick, with stone dressings, including quoins. Stables with mullioned windows, doors with keyed lintels, and ovolo-moulded beams. External stairs to first-floor granary, which has concave diamond ventilation holes. Few decent granaries survive in s Lancashire. – Also, an early C18 BARN, with good trusses.)

GATHURST FOLD. See Orrell.

GATHURST HALL, Gathurst Lane (B5206). Down in the Douglas valley. Very modest despite the name. Baffle-entry plan. The three-bay painted brick exterior encases remnants of an early C17 timber frame. (Ovolo-moulded beams. DCMS).

LEEDS AND LIVERPOOL CANAL. 250 years of transport history at DEAN LOCKS, ¼ m. w of Gathurst Bridge, Gathurst Lane (B5206). It is the site of a destroyed lock of c. 1740 on the River Douglas Navigation (see p. 52). On the canal itself is a blocked lock of 1774 into the river, and two operational locks: the first (and a cottage), c. 1781, the second mid-C19, to cope with increased coal traffic. Bridging canal and river is the Southport & Manchester Railway, opened in 1855, on a later, steel-decked structure; and oversailing everything, the M6 motorway on the massive GATHURST VIADUCT of 1959–63. *Sir James Drake*, County Surveyor and Bridgemaster. Round concrete piers, steel deck. From the valley floor its trabeated simplicity is surprisingly elegant.

SIMONSWOOD *see* KIRKBY p. 216

SKELMERSDALE 4000

Until the 1960s Skelmersdale was a large mining village in undulating farmland beneath Ashurst Beacon, 13 m. NE of Liverpool and 6 m. w of Wigan. In 1961 it was designated a New Town, to

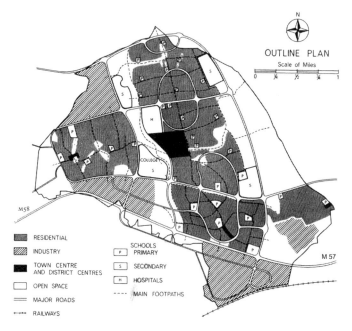

N

OUTLINE PLAN
Scale of Miles
0   ¼   ½   ¾   1

RESIDENTIAL

INDUSTRY

TOWN CENTRE
AND DISTRICT CENTRES

OPEN SPACE

MAJOR ROADS

RAILWAYS

SCHOOLS
P PRIMARY

S SECONDARY

H HOSPITALS

---- MAIN FOOTPATHS

M58

M 57

Skelmersdale New Town.
Plan

house overspill from Merseyside slum clearance, the first New
Town to be designated for eleven years and the first in Lancashire.* The master plan was made in 1963 by *Sir Hugh Wilson*
(of Cumbernauld fame) and is typical of the second generation
of New Towns. No longer spreading out by means of single,
semi-detached or short-terraced houses with plenty of garden
and plenty of road width, no longer a 'pretty' town centre.
Instead, the first parts consist of compact, longer terraces, a close
centre, and, architecturally speaking, instead of smooth rectangular shapes, single-pitch roofs and much Brutalist-inspired
cubic projection and recession.

The town was intended to accommodate about 80,000, of
whom some 8,500 lived in the area at the time of designation.
The site of just over 4,000 acres (1,620 hectares) is within the
catchment area of the little River Tawd, which rises in the s and
flows N to join the Douglas. The river runs down a steep-sided
clough through the middle of the town and forms the centrepiece
of the naturalistic Tawd Valley Park, the broad green backbone
of the LANDSCAPE PLAN. It is fed by small streams flowing down
gullies which, with mature trees, have been made a landscape
feature of the central development area E of the Tawd. Shelter
planting is also extensively employed, because the site is an

* A New Town was first proposed in 1956 in the County Development Plan.

exposed one. W of the river, around Old Skelmersdale where the topography is much flatter, landscaping is less extensive and bleaker; but the overwhelming impression, at least in the summer, is of the generosity of landscape and greenery. From the distributor roads the buildings are hidden amongst the trees and shrubs.

The principle underlying Wilson's PLAN was of a compact, truly urban town, with surrounding recreation areas. Because of the small size of the designated area, the neighbourhood plan employed, for example, at Cumbernauld was abandoned, and instead Skelmersdale was designed so that a large proportion of the population would be within easy walking distance of the centre, and all would also have access on foot to areas of open space. So, typically of second generation New Towns, there is a Radburn-derived hierarchy of roads and segregation of car and pedestrian. Main roads, including the M58 along the S boundary, and a secondary network of distributor roads, are intended to take traffic around rather than through residential areas; they are bewildering to the outsider. A separate radial footpath system links houses with shops, schools and community facilities and the centre and other parts of town, using underpasses and footbridges to avoid roads. This system was described later as 'the framework around which community sense would develop'. Public transport was subordinated to the car, and the town is extremely poorly served by rail; Upholland Station is on the very edge, two miles from the centre.

The principal concentration of development is an area up to 1 m. wide and 3 m. long from N to S, immediately to the E of the Tawd. It was intended that this would contain the town centre and 60,000 of the population. The other housing areas are at Old Skelmersdale to the W, where some bylaw terraces were retained and modernised, and a smaller development of the village of Up Holland to the E (see p. 597). Today the population is c. 40,000, still only half that projected in the 1960s. Industry is zoned in three areas, to the N and S of Old Skelmersdale and to the S, at Pimbo. Almost 3.5 million sq. ft of factory space were completed by the end of 1971.

The description dispenses with the usual order of buildings, and instead begins with the centre, followed by schools, then housing, and finally pre-New Town sites.

The CENTRAL AREA adjoining the River Tawd, which forms a linear, sunken park along its W perimeter, was not begun until 1971, seven years after the first housing. Different layouts were considered, including a compact, decked megastructure à la Cumbernauld. The implemented scheme, partly one-level and partly vertically separated, is not a success. Set in landscaped isolation and bordered on three sides by roads, it is disconnected from the surrounding residential areas, despite pedestrian links and bridges. There is also, today at least, no coherence to the plan for the pedestrian. To the E is the CON-COURSE SHOPPING CENTRE, an introspective structure with vertical separation of services and malls. First phase, 1971–3, with a long blank S side; second phase grafted to the N in the 1990s, with a big glazed zigzagging façade.* Attached to the N is a BUS STATION and a low multi-storey CAR PARK. On the W side, and feeling very much on the back side, are two desolate and half-hearted interconnected spaces which fail to knit together the public buildings around them.** On the S side are two well-proportioned buildings designed by *Roger Booth*, County Architect: the LIBRARY, opened 1978, and the POLICE STATION, completed 1976. Both are constructed of the County Council-devised Lancashire Rationalised Building Method, a system of lightweight pre-cast concrete panels whose appearance was intended to reflect the bluff character of the county. Pale cuboid pavilions of four and five storeys respectively, modulated by narrow vertical strips containing tinted windows, some of which project as boxy oriels. The concrete is textured like fabric. Ground floors smooth with continuous full-height glazing, often set back from the frame, e.g. forming a colonnade for the police station entrance. This was the last police station to be built before the County Council abandoned system-building as uneconomic. Typical of the subsequent architecture are the buildings to the N: the SWIMMING POOL and, W, SKELMERSDALE COLLEGE OF FURTHER EDUCATION, both low and predominantly brick; the College, late 1970s, quite disciplined. To the E of the centre is the brutal CO-OPERATIVE BANK BUILDING, 1981, by the *Skelmersdale Development Corporation Architects Department*.

SCHOOLS. The 1963 plan concentrated secondary education in four large comprehensives; primary schools were built as necessary throughout the residential areas. The first two comprehensive schools formed a single compact campus by *Roger Booth* on the SW fringe of the town centre, across the Tawd Valley Park: GLENBURN HIGH SCHOOL and Westbank School, now part of Skelmersdale College, built 1966–9 to serve 2,100 pupils. They follow a standard design first implemented at Castle School, Lancaster (N Lancashire), employing another of the County Council's proprietary systems, the 'heavy concrete method': load-bearing pre-cast concrete panels with a ribbed finish, large regular pre-installed windows, and a shallow modified V-profile roof. Precast columns, beams and floor plates too. All this could be erected without scaffolding. The schools are laid out almost identically, with three classroom pavilions, boxy and of three or four storeys, and a main building, of lightweight steel frame and north-light roofs, housing arts, crafts and shared sports facilities. They form a single plan staggered about a central counterpoint: a youth centre – with a hexagonal core from which sprout timber-clad points on the first floor, forming a floating star. Community use of site and facilities was central to the design. The other

*As originally conceived the second phase was to have been attached to the NE.
**The E one was a site intended for a Magistrates' Court.

two comprehensive schools were built, on independent sites, in 1972–6.

HOUSING, by the *Skelmersdale Development Corporation* architects, was intended, for the major part, to be at the relatively high density for New Towns of 60–70 persons per acre (148–172 per hectare). Areas of higher density towards the centre, with tower blocks possibly, were abandoned in line with contemporary thinking, decreasing family size and residents' changing aspirations. More than a dozen standard house types were developed by the SDC.

The first district, built 1964–7, was at NEW CHURCH FARM, E of Old Skelmersdale. The houses, of red brick with dark-tiled roofs, are grouped in terraces of one to three storeys around interrelated pedestrian courts. Footpaths link these courts to the main footpath network. For the most part the houses face away from cul-de-sacs, which branch off the periphery road. The net density is about 18–20 houses per acre. LITTLE DINGMOOR, 3,000 houses SE of the town centre, was completed at the same date to a similar plan, though some of the buildings here are system-built (and pebbledashed). Pedestrian ways open out in both places into squares with shops, meeting rooms, playgrounds, churches and primary schools. None of these are of any great merit, but, also typical of the New Towns, the generosity of the landscaping and planting, now maturing, is pleasant – at least when in leaf.

Subsequent districts, completed largely by the late 1970s, continued the theme of the first phases, with variations. Picturesqueness gave way to bleaker, uniform, system-built terraces and blocks off long parallel branch roads at places like TANHOUSE and BIRCH GREEN, E of the town centre. The concept of houses facing pathways and courts was maintained. The last Development Corporation housing was erected in 1984–5, at Tanhouse, by which time the balance between rented accommodation and housing for sale was swinging dramatically towards the latter. Later phases have consisted almost exclusively of developer-built private housing, and layouts have changed radically. The most recent scheme, at ASHURST in the N, 1990s, is all curved roads. The houses are little brick terraces, or detached.

ST PAUL, Church Road, Old Skelmersdale. 1903–4, by *Austin & Paley*. In free Gothic, Perp, but with many rounded forms in the tracery, as Austin & Paley did in those days – surely inspired by Winwick, Sefton and other local churches. A dignified ensemble. Five-bay nave and aisles. W baptistery. On the N side of the chancel, a big buttressed projection with a handsome window. This was to have been one of the firm's signature towers, but it never got above eaves level. – STAINED GLASS. E window by *Shrigley & Hunt*.

ELMERS GREEN. In connection with the construction of the New Town, Digmoor Hall and Dial Hall were pulled down. Neither was grand, but was this necessary? On Elmer's Green Lane, a hamlet of former farms on the edge of the development restored for the middle classes, amidst more recent suburban housing. They include, from N to S, and all on the E side: STANNANOUGHT FARMHOUSE, dated 1714, but still with a cross-wing plan. The wooden cross-windows, horizontally sliding sashes and good dog-leg staircase are more typical of the date. Then YEW TREE HOUSE, now two houses. Three bays including two cross-wings, one dated 1679, the other part dated 1710 and attempting to impose symmetry. Next, WIDDOWS FARMHOUSE, dated 1680 on the l. cross-wing (with mullioned window); the r. bay is an C18 replacement. HARSNIPS is a three-unit, baffle-entry plan yeoman's house dated 1667, but containing an older cruck truss (Gary Miller). The datestone may therefore refer to the cladding and raising of an earlier structure. Cross-wing. Finally, FELTON'S FARMHOUSE, the fragment of a post-and-truss structure of the late C16 or early C17 subsequently clad in sandstone and rendered. (The timber frame is visible inside. Upstairs are depressed, four-pointed doorways, wooden, and a fireplace, stone. Gary Miller.) An adjacent stone BARN, with two cruck trusses, probably of similar date, and subsequently clad.

UP HOLLAND. *See* p. 597.

5000

STANDISH
and LANGTREE

A sprawling towny village of C19 terraces and C20 semis on the Roman road N from Wigan (A49) where it crests a hill, swollen first by the now vanished mining industry and then by Wigan commuters.

ST WILFRID, Market Place. One of the most interesting churches of Lancashire. It is large and as a general impression entirely Perp – except for the hard W steeple with its octagonal top stage, made of a deathly coloured stone. This dates from 1867 or 1872 and replaced a C14 tower and C19 spire, which were equally undersized. Perp are the aisle windows and the large clerestory windows (though it seems that until C19 restoration the S aisle windows at least had lower sills, and were uncusped like the clerestory). Perp too is the two-stage S porch, the crenellation and the short chancel. But what of all this is actually late medieval? In 1543 the church was 'in grete ruyne', and it appears rebuilding was not begun until 1582. This is the date on the porch, and on an agreement signed by *Robert Charnock*, who appears to have been what in today's jargon is a project manager. *Lawrence Shipway* was the master mason. The dates 1585 and 1589, carved into the roof timbers, give an indication of progress. A document of 1603 shows that the new work kept to the footprint of the old, except where the N aisle was widened by a yard. However, the heads of the N aisle and clerestory windows are not as depressed as the others, and the N and S sanctuary windows have been altered apparently when the N and S chapels were extended and part of the chancel widened, suggesting two phases of activity. Also, the chancel-arch piers (which rise above the parapet externally and have ogee caps) contain rood stairs and sockets for the rood which suggests old parts kept. The old steeple was certainly retained, and apparently some walling, e.g. in the chancel with very basic C13–C14 PISCINA and AUMBRY. Much other masonry reused.

Whatever they may be, the works of the 1580s must be considered Gothic Survival, not Revival. Therefore the INTERIOR comes as a great surprise; for the arcades of the five bays and those of the two bays of the chancel have Tuscan columns on high pedestals. That one expects in the early C17 in the South (Salisbury Chapel Hatfield, St Katherine Cree London, etc.), but to find it in the 1580s, and in Lancashire, is remarkable. Yet a plaque with the date 1584 is right above the N chapel arcade. This in fact is one of the earliest known full-scale uses of Tuscan columns in the country. The details are correctly observed, even if the proportions are not right. There is a link with another not too distant example, Robert Dudley, Earl of Leicester's unfinished church at Denbigh, begun 1578: the 4th Earl of Derby, who was a signatory of the agreement to rebuild Standish and had been the ward of its patron Edward Standish, was a frequent correspondent with Dudley on his missions. The arches of the nave arcades have two orders of quarter-round mouldings, very slightly sunk; the chancel arcades have two orders of cyma reversa. Nave, aisles and E chapels have excellent panelled roofs. The nave and S aisle roofs have saltire-pattern ribs, and the N aisle has ovolo mouldings. The massive tie-beams of the nave and chancel are carved with the names and devices of major benefactors, e.g. Edward Standish with his owl and rat, on the nave E beam. Elsewhere are the names of carpenters. Though some motifs are un-Elizabethan, e.g. the fine but strange nave bosses, there is some guilloche and arcade moulding and the tie-beams rest on consoles. The S chapel is the Standish Chapel. It has a tablet stating that Edward Standish built it in 1589. It was reordered by *George Pace* in the 1960s. Pace went on to reorder the chancel in 1971. The low embattled E vestries are of 1913, by *Austin & Paley*, and make good use of the fall of the land not to impose on the church. Elaborate GATEHOUSE into the churchyard by the same, completed 1927 as a First World War memorial. It has an oriel and an octagonal stair-turret. Broken SARCOPH-AGUS, beside the S porch.

FURNISHINGS. REREDOS. 1886, by *H.C. Charlewood*. The mosaics with good glass-enamel figures are by *Powell & Sons*. – COMMUNION TABLE. Hexagonal marble top, 1693; charming octagonal gate-leg table with twisted legs, 1703. – COMMUNION RAILS. Oak staircase balusters from a (demolished) later C17 house in Wigan. Installed 1934. – SCREENS. Chancel and aisles. 1886, by *H.C. Charlewood*. Perp. Elaborate upper parts with shields, *Austin & Paley*, c. 1925. Tower screen. Intricately Dec, mid-C20. Presumably *Austin & Paley* again. –

PULPIT. Typically Elizabethan in style, but dated 1616. Elaborately carved. – A number of identical BENCHES with, e.g., Standish initials and devices. Some have 1620s dates. – FONT. Base C19, bowl C16, stem of unknown date. – ORGAN CASE in front of the tower arch. By *George Pace*, 1971, and elegantly typical of him. – At the same time, as part of his reordering, *Pace* moved the CHOIR STALLS of *c.* 1859 to the W end in front of the organ and stained them to match. – STAINED GLASS. A lot, including: E window by *J.H. Stammers*, 1964, mildly Expressionist, filling the window with glowing colour. Chancel N and S, 1878, by *C. Champigneulle*. Standish Chapel, 1st from E, by *H.G. Hiller & Co.*, Liverpool, 1926; 2nd from E, 1934, by *Shrigley & Hunt* with re-set fragment bearing the arms of Edward Standish dated 1589. S aisle, 1st from W, by *Ward & Hughes*, 1889. S aisle W, †1863. Remarkably blue. N aisle W, *J.B. Capronnier* of Brussels, 1877. N aisle, 3rd from W, 1886, by *Alfred O. Hemming*. N aisle, 5th from W (Duxbury Chapel), *Pendle Glass*, 2001. Porch, *Collier & Co.* Beautifully painterly. Clerestory, abstract drops of colour by *Ronald Sims*, from the 1980s onwards.

MONUMENTS. Behind the Rector's pew a crude and worn C14 slab of Maud, wife of Robert de Chisnall. Incised image. – Purbeck marble effigy of a clerk or cleric, C14. Appropriated by an inscription along the rim and by a primitive tomb-chest to Richard Moodie, †1586. The tomb-chest has in the middle a motif of short, coarse pilasters, two angels, and a garland. All this has nothing of the accomplishments of the church building. – Edward Wrightington, †1658. Recumbent effigy of alabaster; very good. On a tomb-chest. – Edward Chisnall, †1653. Extremely fine tablet with trophies (he was a Royalist hero of the Civil War), books and quill, graceful cartouches, excellent drapery and, at the foot, putto heads. It looks late, not mid-C17. Advanced for ultra-conservative Lancashire if it isn't. – Edward Dicconson, †1752, Catholic Bishop. Signed *D. Sephton*. – Cecilia Towneley, †1807. Tablet, a sarcophagus, by *Nollekens*. – Richard Watt, Liverpool merchant and purchaser of Speke Hall (q.v.). By *John Bacon Jun.*, 1806, entirely in the style of his father. Two amply draped women by an urn on a pedestal. On the urn a portrait medallion, and on the pedestal a lively, intricate, slightly fanciful relief of the Liverpool riverfront. – Rev. Richard Perrin, †1825. A tablet, wholly Adamish, i.e. very conservative. – A number of other tablets, and three small C17–C18 BRASSES in the chancel.

ST MARIE OF THE ANNUNCIATION (R.C.), Brook Road. 1883–4, by *J. O'Byrne*. Bright red brick with lancets, bellcote and aisles. A typical Catholic plan, i.e. an organ gallery over a vestibule at the W end, a broad nave, and a very short canted chancel flanked by altars at the end of the aisles. The arcades have big polished granite piers. Marble REREDOS with mosaics and tabernacle, from the 1930s. – Attached PRESBYTERY and HALL of 1908.

Little of interest in the village. The very small MARKET PLACE at the centre is unremarkable – in fact unbeautiful – except for the church. On the W side is a rendered house with C17 origins. The MARKET CROSS is Late Georgian on a C14 base (*see* p. 594), with C18 STOCKS at its foot; the WELL HOUSE, a slate roof supported on six columns covering the ancient well, is a 1998 replica of an C18 structure. On RECTORY LANE across from the church is a former SCHOOL, dated 1829. Dressed stone, two storeys. Crude pointed windows with Y-tracery. Converted into apartments in 2003, together with dreadful new-build housing. WIGAN ROAD is really an early C20 middle-class suburb of Wigan, though the grandest house off it, ASHFIELD HOUSE on Ashfield Park Road, is actually later C19. It has an imperial staircase.

THE BOAR'S HEAD, Wigan Road (A49), 1½ m. SE. Altered and rendered, but probably C17. Carved Standish arms on l. gable. Seated inglenook.

BRADLEY HALL, Bradley Lane, 1 m. NW. Now offices, marooned in an ugly trading estate (once a Second World War munitions factory). The exterior is that of a mid-C19 villa – brick, gables on three sides with ornate bargeboards, cusped mullioned windows – more so since the spindly diamond chimneystacks were cut down. The brick is probably C19, but it is a mixture and some may be C18. Moreover, the SW bay is a fake, a late C20 addition, and a surprisingly convincing one at that if it were not for the stretcher bond. But step through the front door and you find yourself in the skeletal screens passage of a timber-framed manor house. Upstairs and down, infill has been removed revealing two entirely separate frames, and quite a gap has opened up between them. The screens and the narrow three-bay hall to the r. are possibly late C15. The original upper wing has gone. A floor on heavy moulded beams was inserted in the later C16, at which time a stair-tower was added at the end of the screens as well (the present staircase is C19 Gothic). A parlour with fireplace was built off the hall around the same time. Upstairs the frame is revealed – king-post and strut roof trusses, wall-plates, wall-posts and braces. To the l. of the screens is the second frame, a two-storey service wing with a depressed ogee-arched doorway into it. The wing, extending back at right angles to the hall, seems to be a remodelling of an earlier structure *c.* 1600, with some massive ovolo-moulded beams and wall-posts, the latter with carved capitals.

LANGTREE HALL, E of Preston Road (A49), ¾ m. N. Medieval MOAT, late C20 house.

LODGES. On Wigan Road and the N end of Beech Walk. Similar but not identical. Single-storey, stone with pyramidal roofs rising to a central stack. Early C19. They served the rambling, part timber-framed Standish Hall, progressively demolished in the C20.

LODGE, Rectory Lane, ½ m. E. To the substantial, now demolished rectory. Two storeys, stone. Remodelling of an earlier building with C19 pointed, mullioned-and-transomed and bay windows.

MILE POSTS. On the A49. One N, and one S at the Boar's Head railway bridge. Delightful cast-iron signs on stumpy flat fluted posts cast by the *Haigh Foundry* (*see* p. 187) in 1837 for the turnpikes.

Standish has a great wealth of C16 and C17 YEOMEN'S HOUSES.* The best-preserved and most impressive is GIANT'S HALL FARMHOUSE, Standish Wood Lane, 1½ m. S. Stone exterior dated 1675, with long mullioned windows. Three bays including parlour cross-wing. A lower W bay post-dates 1675, but not by much. The interior is more puzzling: wind-braces and vacant mortises for a wall-post in some roof trusses suggest an earlier timber frame recased. On the other hand the truss with cruck blades reused as principals and the evidently recycled elements of the internal timber-framed walls point to the 1675 house being built with timber salvaged from an earlier building, probably on the same site. Firehood with timber spere post. Fine four-centred corner fireplace in the parlour cross-wing (and possibly more hidden). Is this 1675 or earlier?

WAYSIDE CROSSES. A sequence of four medieval wayside crosses between Standish and Wigan, route markers and potent providers of spiritual reassurance. All but Mab's Cross on Standishgate, Wigan (*see* p. 670), are in Standish parish, in STANDISH WOOD LANE and GREEN LANE and in the MARKET PLACE, surviving as gritstone bases. The last also has steps, and a C19 cross (*see* p. 593) (Norman Redhead).

SUTTON *see* ST HELENS

TARBOCK

A little hamlet and little else.

TARBOCK HALL FARMHOUSE, Ox Lane, N off Netherley Road. A moated site, the moat infilled in the C20. Licences for oratories are recorded in 1251 and the C14. The farmhouse is on the S side of the former platform, a long, low, two-storey brick building with an irregular façade and wooden casements. The brick and casements appear C18, but the position, the stone courses at the W end and the massive, now demolished chimneystack shown in Victorian photographs one bay in from the E end, suggest that the house has older bones. The farm buildings include a much altered SHIPPON (possibly developed from an earlier C18 barn), a late C18–early C19 THRESHING BARN, and the so-called CHAPEL. This cart shed, though radically remodelled, has some brick walling and a fine king-strut roof dated by Richard Morris to the late C16. This would make the brick some of the oldest in Lancashire. The building's purpose remains obscure: though the first floor appears to have been a single space, it is unlikely to have been the rec-

---

*For details *see* Gary Miller, *Historic Houses in Lancashire: the Douglas Valley 1300–1770*, 2002.

usant chapel alluded to in an inventory of 1608, because it stood outside the moat. That it was only part of an earlier hall cannot be ruled out, but seems unlikely too for the same reason.

ROSE COTTAGE, Greensbridge Lane. A single-storey brick building with dormers and still its thatched roof. It contains cruck blades, so probably C17 or earlier.

TYLDESLEY

(for ASTLEY *see* p. 132)

6000

A small industrial town of parallel brick streets along the same ridge as Atherton to the W (q.v.), with Chat Moss to the S and old pit country all around. In 1931, 63 per cent of male employment in the town was mining-related. The collieries have gone of course and the mills have all been demolished too. Extensive C20 housing spreads down the escarpment to merge with Astley (q.v.).

ST GEORGE, Elliot Street. 1821–4, by *Sir Robert Smirke*. A Commissioners' church prominently sited on the top of the ridge at the W end of the main street. Built for £9,646. An interesting building; for though it nowhere abandoned the Commissioners' principles, it is yet archaeologically much more careful than many. For example, the W tower has a recessed spire connected by flying buttresses with the pinnacles – *à la* Louth. Aisles and a clerestory, the tall, close-set arcade piers octagonal, and arches double-chamfered, even if the chamfers are too slight for the Perp period, and the capitals are wrong. The windows also have Y-tracery, though in the aisles they are cusped, and have a quatrefoil. The chancel was extended by a bay in 1886–7 in ashlar that matches well the creamy original. That accounts for the Geometrical tracery of its windows. Simple canted boarded ceiling and timber chancel arch: of 1887? There were N and S galleries and two, superimposed, at the W end; only the lower W example survives. – SCREENS. Late C19–early C20. Dec style and handsome. – Either side of the E window, large PANELS of 1914 showing two Evangelists each. Are they painted tiles or enamelled glass? – STAINED GLASS. Some good undated late C19 glass in the N aisle. Chancel N and S windows with good C19 saints from the Bishop of Manchester's palace, Bishopscourt, re-set here *c.* 1958. E window. By *William Pointer* of Manchester, 1956. – MONUMENTS. A couple of Neoclassical plaques and one to James Mort, †1855, with a grieving woman slumped over an urn. By *Garner* of Manchester. Rev. John Lund, †1924. Bronze plaque, with raised and enamelled cross.

SCHOOL (former, now flats), opposite the E end. Built 1829 and enlarged 1868, according to a plaque. Flat, two-storey front in lovely dressed sandstone, the windows with Y-tracery, the two r. bays presumably the extension. A further extension of this end removed in the 1990s when the building was converted.

TYLDESLEY CHAPEL, The Square. The first place of worship in the town. Built 1789–90 for the Countess of Huntingdon's Connexion. Brick, with two entrances from the square, and between and above, two very elementary Venetian windows, one on top of the other and too small for the façade. A C19 bellcote caps the gable. The side windows appear to have been adapted from Venetian to a round-headed type. But the blank E elevation has blind windows with Y-tracery, just to be contrary. Interior much altered, with galleries of various dates on three sides. – The PULPIT is said originally to have been on the W side with the communion table opposite.

ST JOHN, Mosley Common Road, Mosley Common, 1½ m. ESE. 1886. Yorkshire freestone. In easily the largest of a number of former pit villages around the town.

SACRED HEART (R.C.), Tyldesley Road, ⅓ m. NW. 1869, by *Edmund Kirby*. A pretty church with nave, chancel and aisles under one slate roof, and paired lancets. W end composed of a NW steeple, in form like the medieval examples at Halsall and Ormskirk (qq.v.), a large circular window with quatrefoil plate tracery, and below this a porch and baptistery. Buff quarry-faced sandstone with red ashlar dressings, including sparing bands. Picturesque, mullion-windowed PRESBYTERY attached at right angles to SE corner.

There is little of interest in the town itself. The main thoroughfare is MANCHESTER ROAD–ELLIOTT STREET. The best building on it is the handsome former Union Bank of Manchester, *c.* 1900 and probably by *F.W. Morton*. Single storey, three bays, corner site. Grandly Doric, ashlar, with continuous plinth, attached columns, full entablature. Channelled rustication above the plinth, and impressive carved arms above the door. (Art Nouveau stained-glass top-light hidden by a false ceiling. DCMS.) Opposite, a town house of *c.* 1800. On the corner with Johnson Street is the former Miners' Hall *c.* 1900. Midway along the street is the small SQUARE, which despite the chapel amounts to very little, thanks in no small part to the atrocious single-storey CO-OP on the opposite side. Off the Square in Stanley Street is the compact LIBRARY by *Bradshaw & Gass*, opened 1909. Brick and red sandstone. Charmless free English Renaissance with giant pilaster strips and aprons.

GARRETT HALL FARMHOUSE, Garrett Lane, 1 m. ESE. A low four-bay house of numerous phases, with cross-wing, that has C18 and C19 brick and render. But wall-posts are visible at the rear. There is also an external, brick, lateral chimneystack against this side. If this is an addition the timber frame could be C16 or earlier. (Internal timber-framed cross-walls. DCMS.)

NEW HALL, Whimbrel Road, ¾ m. SE, amidst a large post-war housing estate. A good wet MOAT, but the house is quite new and of no interest.

SHAKERLEY OLD HALL, Cumbermere Lane, ½ m. NE. Now a little wonky farmhouse of double-depth plan under an M-roof with cross-axial stacks. Rendered brick and modern windows conceal extensive timber framing of possibly early C17 date (Philip Powell).

SALE LANE. Two small later C17 houses. No. 7 with stone and mullioned-windowed cross-wing; No. 109 brick, with end baffle-entry plan.

UP HOLLAND   5000
including PIMBO and ROBY MILL

The w section of the parish, including the village, was designated part of Skelmersdale New Town in 1961 (*see* p. 585), but the rest is still largely rural and prettily so, especially the N where it dips into the Douglas valley. From the C17 at least there were collieries and quarries, and later brickworks – still operating – and the landscape is pocked by abandoned workings large and small. The flagstones of Liverpool traditionally came from Up Holland.

ST THOMAS, School Lane. The magnificent scale of the nave is explained by the fact that this was the E end of a Benedictine priory. The priory was founded in 1319 by Walter de Langton, Bishop of Lichfield, the last such medieval foundation in the country.* Of the priory buildings on the s side hardly anything remains (*see* below). The present chancel is an addition of 1882–6 by *Basil Champneys*, making the monastic choir now the nave. This is earlier C14. The tower is probably C15 and stands where the crossing tower was intended to be. The priory church was apparently never finished, and the C15 tower represents a scaling back of C14 ambitions. The outside of the w end shows where work halted: exposed in the w walls of the aisles are the arches, now filled with renewed late Perp windows, intended to separate the chapels of the medieval choir from the planned transepts, and, in the angles with the tower, the clustered E crossing piers. The tower has broad diagonal buttresses, a C19 reticulated w window and a quite sumptuous but very heavily worn portal with now defaced heads, figures and fleurons. The belfry openings are a puzzle. They appear C14, but the VCH says that they are grooved to receive glazing and may have been robbed from elsewhere in the priory. There is more C19 reticulated tracery in the big aisle windows, apparently copies of the original. If a drawing of 1727 can be trusted the medieval E window had Geometrical tracery.

The exposed crossing piers herald the splendour of the nave INTERIOR, which is unforgettable with its tall and slender 4 piers. The section is of four shafts and four hollows, more usually Perp than Dec, but the arches have a typically Dec section. Simple flat plaster ceiling of 1752 over the nave, with rosette; aisle ceilings are of hideous C20 tiles. Trefoil-headed

---

*Ten or eleven years before Sir Robert de Holland had founded a collegiate establishment in an existing church; this didn't flourish, and so Holland asked the bishop to re-found it as Benedictine.

PISCINA, with twin basins, in the s aisle. Champneys' chancel has a projection on the N side containing the staircase to the crypt (cf. the medieval precedent at St Elphin, Warrington, p. 604). This is actually the vestry and there is nothing remarkable down there, but the entrance from the chancel and the top of the newel stair is beautifully modelled. Champneys also removed three C18 galleries from the nave. – COMMUNION RAIL. With twisted balusters; late C17 or early C18. – BENCH ENDS. – A few in the aisles, mainly 1635. They have shaped tops (cf. Standish). – CHURCHWARDENS' PEW. A fine example dated 1679 with muntin-and-rail panelling. – CHANDELIER. C18. Brass. – STAINED GLASS. Medieval bits in s window, 2nd from E, assembled here as a pleasing great jumble. Superb E window by *Henry Holiday*, 1884 and 1903–4. Full of movement, excellent colouring, good figures and masterly drapery. Chancel N and s similar if not quite as good. *Holiday* too, designed at the same time. A further N chancel window, of *c.* 1904, illustrates developments in Holiday's style. s window, 1st from E, *Ballantine & Gardiner* of Edinburgh, 1902. s window, 3rd from E, by *Ward & Hughes*, given by Jane Wheelton, †1900. Good, with attractively muted colouring. s window, 4th from E, by *Curtis, Ward & Hughes*, 1916.

PRIORY REMAINS are few, and there has been no excavation. The complex was to the s of the church, and there appears to have been access into it from the W RANGE via an opening high up in the s aisle wall at the w end, now filled with a crude, broad lancet. s of this are the only standing remains, a rubble sandstone wall running N–S and turning E at the end. It has two partially buried doorways, with depressed arches, and seven bricked-up lancets above but few other recognisable features. SE is THE PRIORY, a house whose five-bay mid-C18 façade belies earlier origins. Is the fabric part of or robbed from the priory? The DCMS records elements of a C17 staircase and evidence that the E bays are an addition. Doorway with pilasters.

The CONSERVATIVE CLUB, on Church Street up above the w end, is the old parsonage. Three bays, dated 1822. Stone doorcase with attached Doric columns and broken pediment.

ST TERESA (R.C.), College Road. Designed by *F.X. Velarde*, 1952, built 1955–7. Carved and cast work inside and out by *H. Tyson Smith*. An excellent building, informed by the architect's study of early Spanish churches. Plain brick surfaces carefully and calmly modulated with e.g. small round-arched lights gathered in pairs or triplets, or triangles of three on the N side. These all have mullions cast in relief with angels or the Holy Dove. Also statues of the Four Evangelists standing on buttresses against the single, s, aisle. s campanile with pyramid roof and the only ashlar element, a belfry stage of three tiers of round-arched openings (cf. the windows of Velarde's St Monica, Bootle, p. 156). In the base the baptistery, with a square FONT. Faces carved in relief. Low arcade of round arches on round piers finished in gold mosaic. Canted roof with lozenge panels. Two round chancel arches, the E one smaller than the W, with between them the organ loft, N, and a chapel, S. E wall blank and gently curved. – From the nave the arches frame exquisitely the REREDOS, a big triptych with more relief carving of Christ and two angels. – ALTAR, now brought forward, beautifully carved with a low-relief angel on each of the rounded piers. – Metal ALTAR RAIL and wooden PEWS, both characteristic of the architect.

ST JOSEPH'S COLLEGE (former), W off Stoney Brow, 1 m. NNW. Secreted away up a winding drive through wooded, landscaped grounds is this vast R.C. school and seminary. It has 472 rooms. The plan is collegiate, a three- and four-storey quadrangle with one arm extended as a chapel. The first part, of 1880–3, by *James O'Byrne*, cannot be seen from the approach. It is the W range, of quarry-faced sandstone and with buttresses, a centre slightly projecting and gabled, and topped by a cupola. Also some ancillary wings at the back. The other three sides are *Powell & Powell*, 1921–8. They are of quarry-faced red sandstone and stylistically still in the C19. Huge crenellated towers at the corners, and another in the middle of the S, entrance, range with gabled porte cochère attached. Interiors largely unaltered in 2004, down to the industrial-scale heated drying racks, but individually of no great interest. Attic dormitories, though, are an evocative vista of braced trusses and panelled partitions. Endless corridors. Main 1920s staircase timber and fiddly.

Adjoining the W end of the S range is the huge CHAPEL, by *Purcell* of Powell & Powell. Full-blown Victorian Gothic in character, despite the date, with a mixture of Dec and Perp tracery. Unfinished SW tower. Lofty interior with impressive double-hammerbeam roof. A single vessel: ten-bay choir with Gothic STALLS all along the walls, separated by a Gothic SCREEN with hammerbeamed arch from a very short three-bay nave, more like an antechapel. This has short transeptal chapels, so creating a T-plan. Little chapels at the E end behind the High Altar too. Assorted large, mostly high-quality marble or wood ALTARS and REREDOSES.

In 2004 *AEW Architects* began converting the complex into ninety-two apartments.

UP HOLLAND HIGH SCHOOL *see* p. 539.

SCHOOL LANE winds down the hill from the church, tightly lined with stone houses and cottages of C17–C19 date. DERBY HOUSE on the S side is said to have been built as the manor court, and jail, by the Earls of Derby. A datestone of 1633 with the Stanleys' eagle and child crest is in the single gabled bay. Coursed rubble with a six-light mullioned window on the first floor, a sash window on the ground floor replacing a similar mullioned window, and below that a blocked, half-buried doorway with massive depressed-arch lintel. The rear has more mullioned windows and a plaque carved with the Stanleys' Legs-of-Man emblem. Further down on the same side THE OWL INN has a stone façade (C18?), but the S gable end has exposed timber framing, squared-panelled with angle braces. On the N side of the street, set back in a yard behind Nos. 8–14, the OLD GRAMMAR SCHOOL. The site was donated in 1659. Two storeys, mullioned windows. The full-height porch may be an addition. Doorway with depressed four-pointed arch Altered for workshops, with a range abutting l. of the porch.

On PARLIAMENT STREET NW of the church, some late C17/early C18 cottages with mullioned windows, and No. 30 which has three gables to the road, the centre projecting, and two more gables on each flank, and mullion-and-transom windows. Said to be C19, but is it not at least partly C17? Up the hill W from the church the village has C19 workers' terraces, but is now, as part of Skelmersdale, quite suburban (*see* pp. 585–7 for the development and plan of the New Town). For Moss Farmhouse, *see* below.

HALLS, FARMS AND HAMLETS

On ORMSKIRK STREET at Garnett Lees, 1 m. W, is an attractive collection of farms and cottages. MOSS FARMHOUSE is C17 with mullioned windows and an unusual two-bay cross-wing.

ASPINALL'S FARMHOUSE, Appley Lane South, Holland Lees, 2 m. N. A double-depth, double-fronted house facing S, having mullioned windows with label moulds in the W part. Datestones of 1663 and 1756. Such a plan is improbable for the 1660s, but the form before the mid-C18 rebuilding is unclear: possibly an L-plan with W cross-wing (is that a scar in the S front?) Sloping site, the E end having a basement with a depressed four-centred doorway at the rear. – BARN with 1663 datestone across the lane.

DOUGLAS BANK FARMHOUSE, Lees Lane, Holland Lees, 2 m. N. Close to Aspinall's. An attractive, superior three-unit yeoman's house dated 1656 and basically all of one piece. Unusually for Up Holland it is of brick except for the sandstone façade. This is of four bays, with two cross-wings and a gabled two-storey porch attached to the E wing forming a baffle-entry. The porch has a mullioned-and-transomed window on the first floor; all others are mullioned, of up to five lights. Rear stair-tower. (Firehood. DCMS.)

HALLIWELL'S FARMHOUSE, Lees Lane, 2 m. NNW. Complex. The full-height porch appears to be of 1671, and possibly also the E bay forming a large cross-wing with a parlour, buttery and stair. Big mullioned-and-transomed windows. The bay W of the porch is C18, replacing an earlier hall range, but now with crude late C20 mullioned windows. Put together, these two phases created a double-pile centralised plan. The ersatz W bay, extending out the back, is entirely late C20. Next to the house, a Lancashire combination BARN dated 1633, converted to a house.

HOLLAND HALL HOTEL, Lafford Lane, ⅓ m. NNE. Abysmal late C20 additions almost obscure a U-plan house dated 1654

on the W gable. It was remodelled in the C18, and hidden by 18
the extensions is a good pedimented doorway with flanking
windows of this time. Upstairs a section of timber-framed
internal wall has been revealed and next to it a moulded stone
rectangular fire-surround.

JOHNSON'S FARMHOUSE, Lafford Lane, 1 m. N. From the
outside a modest three-bay yeoman's house, with two cross-
wings. Rubble, covered in sickly coloured render. Low mullioned windows or later casements. The centre, i.e. the hall, is
only one-storeyed and Gary Miller reports that inside it has
two moulded posts at the W end. These are either spere posts,
or, possibly, the arcade posts of an aisled hall (though these
are rare in Lancashire, see p. 30); C15? The hall was probably
rebuilt in stone when the present upper (E) wing was built in
1647; the lower wing is later C17 and may be on the site of the
W end of the medieval hall range.

PIMBO. Most of Pimbo has disappeared under Skelmersdale (see
p. 587), but some buildings remain on PIMBO LANE. They are
C18–C19 farms, and also the derelict BOUNTY FARMHOUSE.
With a cruck truss. Rebuilt in the C17 and C19 (a single datestone states 1869 and 1667).

ROBY MILL, 1½ m. NNW, is a little hamlet of rubble miners' and
quarrymen's cottages and houses. KNIGHT'S HALL is the
most interesting. It has a sandstone façade of three parts: the
outer two bays on both sides are early C19, but not quite
matching; the middle three project slightly and are dated 1716
and have keyed window surrounds. These now contain C19
sashes, but if they have housed sashes from the outset then that
would be very early for Lancashire, where mullioned windows
were not at all uncommon at the beginning of the C18. For evidence of this one need go no further than the rear elevation of
the Hall, where there are five-light examples. A timber-framed
wall inside is evidence that the 1716 work is a rebuilding of an
earlier structure. Gary Miller has posited a date c. 1600 for
that.

CRAWFORD. *See* p. 163.

WARRINGTON

6080

Warrington is a natural crossroads. It lies halfway between
Liverpool and Manchester on what was until 1866 the lowest
bridging point on the River Mersey. It is where the main N–S
communications W of the Pennines meet E–W routes along the
Mersey valley. This has been the touchstone of its history and
development for at least two thousand years.

There is evidence of prehistoric settlement, and then of an
important ROMAN industrial centre in C1–C2 at Wilderspool on
the S bank of the Mersey, where it was crossed by the road
from Chester to Wigan. Evidence has been excavated for iron,
bronze and lead working, the production of pottery and glass,

and enamelling. Most of the products were shipped N to the military via the Mersey (*see* p. 15). At the Conquest Warrington was the head of a Hundred, administered from Mote Hill close to the ancient ford at Latchford.* There was a church here by the end of the C12. Today it and the then principal street, Church Street, lie well to the E of the town centre because the site chosen in the C13 for the first bridge was ½ m. downstream. The commercial focus of the town moved to the crossroads above the bridge, Market Gate, where it has been ever since.

p. 24

By 1292 Warrington was a borough, and also home to an Augustinian friary.** It also had one of the most important markets in the region (until the C19), and by 1600 there was linen and sail manufacture. In 1643 the town was set on fire by the Earl of Derby's troops under attack from besieging Parliamentary forces.

From the late C17 onwards industrial expansion was stimulated by waterways and road improvements. In the 1690s the Mersey was made navigable down to Liverpool, and by 1736 onwards up to Manchester by locks and cuts, as the Mersey and Irwell Navigation. The Sankey Brook Navigation of 1759, the country's first modern canal (*see* p. 52), carried coal from St Helens to the Mersey at Sankey Bridge, just below the town. The last and greatest waterway, the Manchester Ship Canal, opened in 1893. It was a dramatic intervention into the landscape, creating a new southern edge to the town. By 1820 seven turnpikes converged on the town bridge, making Warrington a major coaching and post centre. The RAILWAY arrived in 1831, linking Warrington to Manchester and Liverpool, and from 1837, to Birmingham and London.

These developments stimulated a far more diverse range of INDUSTRIES than most Lancashire towns: glass-blowing (from 1695), copper (from 1717), file and pin making, fustian cutting, some cotton, and, well into the C20, a lot of brewing, tanning, soap manufacture (from 1815) and iron works (from 1840). But above all there was wire working, synonymous with the town by 1900. The population rose from *c.* 2,000 in the mid C17 to perhaps 8,000 in the 1770s, 21,000 in 1851 and 65,000 in 1901. An Improvement Act was passed in 1813, the town became a municipal borough in 1847, and a county borough in 1900. In 1882 *The British Architect* reported courts and alleys off Bridge Street as bad as it had ever seen. The middle classes moved out from C18 suburbs such as Bewsey Street and mid-C19 developments such as Palmyra Square to escape industrial pollution, especially to Grappenhall, Appleton and Stockton Heath across the Ship Canal.

---

*MOTE HILL, immediately NE of the parish church, was a defensive site, possibly a ringwork modified by the Normans, occupied until the C13.
**The FRIARY was immediately s of Friars Gate. The plan of the church was found by excavation. It is unusual, consisting of a narrow nave and chancel built possibly in the 1260s, and a broad-aisled N transept of four wide bays, probably built by *c.* 1350. There was a rectangular tower over the W bay of the chancel. After the Dissolution parts of the church remained in use for the townspeople, but first the tower and later the nave were demolished.

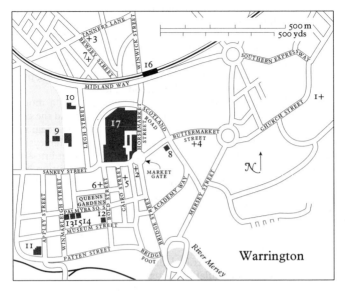

1	St Elphin
2	Holy Trinity
3	St Alban (R.C.)
4	St Mary (R.C.)
5	Unitarian Chapel
6	Wesleyan Chapel
7	Wycliffe Congregational Chapel
8	Friends' Meeting House
9	Town Hall
10	Law Courts
11	Police Station
12	Museum and Library
13	Pyramid Arts Centre
14	Parr Hall
15	Technical School (former)
16	Central Station
17	Golden Square Shopping Centre

There was cultural advancement too. The Warrington Academy (1757–83) provided university-standard education for Dissenters, who were debarred from the universities. Joseph Priestley was one of the tutors. The Warrington Museum and Library was established in 1848; its 1857 Bold Street building was one of Britain's first purpose-built rate-supported library.

In 1968 Warrington was designated a NEW TOWN. This was conceived to accommodate overspill Manchester slum clearance, but implemented to manage motorway-fuelled growth (*see* New Town, p. 634). The population of the designated area was 130,000 in 1968; in 2001 it was 192,000. The Borough was responsible for redeveloping the town centre to cope with this increase, with inner-relief roads and new shopping centre. This has been at the expense of much of the older ARCHITECTURE of the town: over half of the fifty-two buildings listed by 1968 have been demolished, and others exist only as façades. This has done much to destroy the pleasant Georgian character noted by Peter Fleetwood-Hesketh as recently as 1955. Much of the remaining architectural character is due to two local firms which dominated the profession here at the end of the C19 and beginning of the C20,

J.E. Wright, Garnett & Wright and *William Owen* (from 1898 in practice with his son *Segar*). Both were very competent in a range of styles. Owen carried out work at William Lever's Warrington soap factory, and became the first architect to be employed at his model settlement, Port Sunlight, Cheshire. Both practices were employed by the brewer Greenall, Whitley & Co., whose big pubs are frequently handsome neighbourhood landmarks.

Since the 1960s Warrington has been reinvented as a motorway town *par excellence*. It is still a natural crossroads and the convergence of the M6, M56 and M62 has made it a thriving regional centre, ideally placed between the conurbations of Merseyside, Greater Manchester and central Lancashire, for the quintessentially C21 activities of out-of-town retailing, distribution and warehousing.* Prosperous motorway Warrington is blighted by a general poverty of urban design and architecture; the retail shed, distribution warehouse and suburban estate are its defining characteristics. But the earlier phases of the New Town do have excellent landscaping and some interesting buildings, and a couple of recent works are very good.

The town centre is described first, with its churches, public buildings and a perambulation. After that come the outer areas, excluding New Town districts: N and E (Padgate, Paddington, Martincroft and Woolston), s to the Ship Canal (Wilderspool and Latchford), s of the Ship Canal (Appleton, Grappenhall, Stockton Heath, Thelwall and Walton), and w (Bank Quay, Liverpool Road, Bewsey, Great Sankey and Penketh). Lastly, the New Town.

TOWN CENTRE

Places of Worship

ST ELPHIN, Church Street. This is a unique, and mysterious, dedication. No one knows who St Elphin was, nor even if Elphin derives from a British name (Alphinus?) or the Saxon, Ælfwine. The church is large, with a splendid climax in the magnificent spire: at 281 ft (86.5 metres) the third-highest parish steeple in the country, and a landmark in the flat Mersey valley. Though there is evidence of a late C12 predecessor church (fragments in Warrington Museum), and though the chancel is essentially mid-C14, nearly everything else, including the spire, is due to *Frederick & Horace Francis* and their rebuilding and restoration of 1859–67 for the Rev. William Quekett (who had employed them at his previous parish, St George-in-the-East, London). It is one of their best works.

Of the surviving C14 fabric there are: bits of the N transept E wall; a crypt (rediscovered in 1824) beneath the E bay of the chancel; the projecting N spiral staircase to the crypt from the chancel; and the chancel itself, though the SEDILIA etc. are a

---

* Not that this is new: Thomas Patten made Bank Quay a warehousing and distribution centre for sugar and tobacco at the end of the C17.

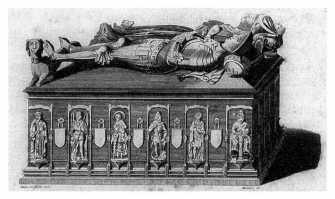

Warrington, St Elphin,
tomb of Sir John Boteler (†1463) and his wife.
Engraving by Birrit after Moses Griffith, before 1819

C19 wood and plaster copy, the ceiling is 1841, when the walls
were raised, and the W bay was rebuilt with the tower. The
chancel side windows have interesting tracery, an ingeniously
twisted variety of reticulation. In the crypt five of the six worn
head corbels seem mid-C14, but the sixth, and the ribbed
vault, date from the mid-C19 restoration. The floor tiles are
Victorian. The S vestry is 1740, the N, 1912.

Most of the rest of the church was post-medieval when the
Francises arrived to investigate the failing C14 crossing piers.
All was swept away for their nave, aisles (with conventional
reticulation), transepts, tower and spire. The latter was not part
of their initial scheme, but planned only once it was clear that
the crossing was beyond repair and would have to be replaced,
along with the late C17 tower above. Construction began
c. 1865. Local wags quipped that Quekett's motto was 'always
to a-spire'. All that remains of the pre-Francis fabric is the S
wall of the 1770 nave, re-erected further S in 1832–3 to accommodate an aisle, and retained by the Francises as an economy
measure; the non-alignment of the string courses where 1770
meets 1860 indicates that this must only have been considered
temporary. Two tiers of windows signal its galleried interior.
The Gothick tracery is unmoulded on the outside, though the
internal moulding is more correct. Door with flat ogee lintel
moved from the nave N wall.

The Francises' INTERIOR is impressive, a broad nave and
broad aisles with quite splendid neo-C13 crossing piers. The
transepts are chapels. Since the plaster was stripped out an
almost Stygian gloom has descended, into which disappears
the high hammerbeam roof over the nave. It springs from
corbels which alternately form the capitals of shafts set against
the spandrels of the arcades. The aisles have GALLERIES. Such

ecclesiologically abhorred features are surprising for the date, but the extra seating was essential. They are set back uncertainly behind the arcades on quatrefoil cast-iron columns, as if the architects did not know quite how to incorporate them. Equally unexpectedly, the gallery PEWS still have doors. There are head corbels everywhere, local and national figures selected by the rector; he and his wife frame the E window, the two architects the E window of the N transept. – REREDOS and ALTAR. The angel-topped reredos is 1933; both decorated in 1999 by *Ronald Sims* with red and green and plenty of gilding, the reredos with characteristic abstract Celtic designs. – PULPIT. C19. The best bit is the fluid, foliate brass balustrade. – SCREEN. Across the W end, a Gothic *tour de force* of *William & Segar Owen*, as late as 1909. Canopied stalls and central door crowned by angels supporting most of the organ. – LIGHTS, above the choir stalls in iron (as hanging lanterns) and in the nave in wood, are *Sims*, 1999 again, in the manner of his master, George Pace. – STAINED GLASS. Chancel E window, N 1st from E, and S 1st and 2nd from E, with remnants by *A. W.N. Pugin*, made by *Hardman*, re-set after Second World War bomb damage. E window, large figures: Christ flanked by the Four Gospels. Chancel S, 3rd from E signed *A. Gibbs* of London. Henry Quekett, the rector's son, †1860. Gibbs probably did the other two in the chancel too. W window, seven apostles, by *Gibbs* also. Commissioned by the Duke of Sussex (for where?), and bought by Quekett, who had the window made to fit it. S aisle W also *Gibbs*, 1864. Also noteworthy: S aisle 1st from E, a First World War memorial, including the mysterious St Elphin; and N aisle, 1947, by *Shrigley & Hunt*. From the destroyed St Peter, Warrington, re-set here 1986. – MONUMENTS. Many tablets, including Dr Thomas Percival, †1804, by *H. Rouw*, with urn. Thomas Lyon, †1818 and family by *Webster* of Kendal. From Frances Legh, †1727, to her family, signed *Benjamin Palmer*, with splayed pilasters.

REGIMENTAL CHAPEL, i.e. the N transept. The chapel of the South Lancashire Regiment since 1943, but founded as a chantry, probably in the C14, for the Botelers, lords of the manor. The earliest surviving fragments are MONUMENTS. An effigy of Lady Alicia Boteler, defaced, early C14, and the lower stages of its wall recess and that of a lost companion knight. Sir John Boteler, †1463, and his wife. An excellent alabaster piece, with effigies (with recarved faces?), he in armour, and fifteen wonderful statuettes on three sides of the tomb – angels, saints etc., also a Crucifixion, an Assumption and a Holy Trinity. They are framed, not under tabernacles or arches, but under billowing banners, or fabric canopies, supported by sculpted poles. Where are similar examples? – Over it is a canopy forming a screen, part of a suite of mid-C20 oak FURNISHINGS including panelling, altar, etc. for the new regimental role in a curious Neo-English Renaissance style by *Seely & Paget*. – More conventional is the Gothic SCREEN to the N aisle, a Boer War memorial of 1903 by *William & Segar*

p. 605

Owen. – Good STAINED GLASS by *Hugh Easton*, 1947, especially the dynamic E window, a Second World War memorial.

ST ANNE'S CHAPEL, i.e. the S transept and adjacent aisle bay. Originally the Mascy chapel, possibly C15, then through marriage to the Pattens of Bank House in the C18. Rebuilt and extended in C18 and C19 before the brothers *Francis* gave it its present form. – Neo-Restoration sanctuary, 1966, with a fine inlaid walnut COMMUNION TABLE, given in 1720 for the chancel. – Many Patten MONUMENTS, including Thomas Patten, †1772, a restrained Adamish tablet with lamp by *John Francis Moore*. Dorothea Patten, †1799, by *Thomas King* of Bath, with a standing allegorical figure in the Bacon style. Thomas Wilson-Patten, †1819. Exceptionally fine, very Roman relief of four figures. He died in Naples: was it made in Italy? Anna Maria Wilson-Patten, †1846. Large tomb-chest, and on it *H.H. Armstead*'s recumbent effigy of John Wilson-Patten, Lord Winmarleigh, †1892. Excellent naturalism of fabric and face.

The CHURCHYARD was scraped of its gravestones and most MONUMENTS in the 1960s, and a broad, dark pavement created from the former. The best of the remaining monuments includes William (†1773), and John (†1793) Hesketh, a small sarcophagus on a pedestal supported in the corners by detached volutes. – At the entrance, a fine pair of GATEPIERS with striking cast-iron GATES dated 1791. Are they really this early? *See* Town Centre Perambulation, p. 616, for the cottages immediately beyond them.

HOLY TRINITY, Sankey Street. Subscriptions raised in 1758, consecration in 1760. Founded as an oratory in 1709 by Peter Legh (of Lyme Park), partly because of the inconvenience of St Elphin. The site was even more constrained in 1758, when Sankey Street was narrower still. The façade to that street, of red sandstone, consists of four superimposed layers to break up the preaching-box form: a banded rusticated plinth, then the lower tier of windows with Gibbs surrounds, and a Doric doorcase, and standard rustication, then upper windows with keyed-in arches divided by Ionic pilasters against the same background, and finally the cornice and parapet. Nevertheless it is still quite flat. In the E wall, a Venetian window. The whole is in the Gibbs style, who was here a decade before at Bank Hall (now the Town Hall, *see* p. 611), but is unlikely to be by him. He surely would have introduced far more dramatic modulation into the street façade, to invigorate what could only be viewed obliquely. The building accounts (now lost) made reference to one *James Meredith*, paid £78 10s. for 'drawing and his attendance at the site'. Is he, an unknown, the author? The slim ogee-capped W tower, with cast-iron octagonal and square stages, is by *W.P. Coxon*, Borough Surveyor, 1862. It belongs to the town, not the church. It is at least the third; the first had a big stone cupola.

The INTERIOR has broad galleries on three sides, carried on panelled piers, from which rise Corinthian columns to the roof supporting a cornice which defines the central body of the church. The galleries are approached in an uncommonly monumental way by an axial staircase starting in one flight and returning in two. An organ originally occupied a second W gallery (it is now in the N gallery). Good Rococo plasterwork enriches the E window. The S aisle was screened in 1974 to create a parish room and vestry; the N lobby was remodelled in 1988. – REREDOS. A First World War memorial by *E. Carter Preston*, 1920. Convincingly C18-style oak panelling. – COMMUNION TABLE. A splendid Rococo piece with marble top, from the first chapel. – FONT. A plump C18 baluster with good Arts and Crafts cover. – PULPIT. C18. It originally stood, conventionally, against the NE pier and was put centrally in front of the reredos and rebuilt with two flanking flights of steps when the chancel was reordered in the 1990s. – BOX PEWS survive throughout, one or two in the galleries still with doors. – ALTAR PAINTING, now in the W gallery. A copy after Andrea del Sarto's Holy Family by a local artist, *James Cranke, c.* 1776. – A marvellous CHANDELIER. Brass, two tiers of arms, the body of a usual Baroque shape. It came from the old House of Commons and was given in 1801.

ST ALBAN (R.C.), Bewsey Street. Warrington's oldest Catholic chapel. 1823, by *Edward Alcock*, replacing an earlier chapel in the street. At heart, typical of pre-Emancipation chapels in S Lancashire – chapel and presbytery set back-to-back within a gabled brick box standing reticently back from the road. But this is now partly disguised by crude buttresses, Romanesque windows of 1900 in place of the original N and S sashes, and the present W façade, of 1909. This has three tall round-arched windows with Venetian tracery and colonnettes, above a porch with feeble carving. Further changes inside, including a much smaller W gallery for the organ of 1909. But the gently coved ceiling remains, and the Corinthian pilasters and chancel arch of the E wall, into which in 1893 *Pugin & Pugin* (which means Peter Paul Pugin at this time) set a new apsidal sanctuary, with a hidden light source satisfyingly illuminating his incongruous Romanesque ALTAR, TABERNACLE and REREDOS. Heavily marble and alabaster (also the ALTAR RAIL). – In blank arches around the reredos are good PAINTINGS, scenes from the life and martyrdom of St Alban, by *Joseph Pippet* of Birmingham. Far less accomplished is the painting under the 1823 chancel arch, by *Richardson & Son* of Warrington, 1923. – OUR LADY ALTAR. 1890, *Pugin & Pugin* also. It has lost its canopy and crenellation. – STAINED GLASS by *Hardman*. 1st and 2nd windows from E on both sides, 1900. Excellent: beautifully composed and framed. W windows, six saints of 1909. – A couple of early C19 TABLETS.

ST MARY (R.C.), Buttermarket. Designed by *E. W. Pugin*, begun in 1875 shortly before his death, and completed by *Peter Paul Pugin* (as Pugin & Pugin) in 1877. Peter Paul's slender SW tower is 1906. One of their finest churches, with characteristic external motifs, an accomplished interior and lavish altars.

Quarry-faced pale Pierpoint and red Runcorn stone, making quite a sickly combination. Typical of E.W. Pugin are: the twin w windows; the profusion of round windows on gable ends, of original design, e.g. in the E wall with elaborate X-pattern tracery; the aisle windows with signature heads of open cusping with pointed trefoils above; and the closely spaced clerestory of sexfoil windows (cf. Our Lady of Reconciliation, Eldon Street, Liverpool, p. 485), two to a bay, here with paired quatrefoils beneath. On the N side the same tracery is strikingly smooth and flush, completely without moulding, as if the windows have been extruded and sliced. Peter Paul's tower, with a parapet spelling AVE MARIA, is perhaps not massive enough (a spire was first planned). The interior has more characteristics of E.W. Pugin: a w porch beneath a w organ gallery; wide arcades to enhance sight lines; deep plinths, squat shafts and heavy naturalistic capitals; confessionals integrated into the N wall; and a tripartite E end with Sacred Heart Chapel, N, and Lady (now English Martyrs) Chapel, S, either side of a square, rather than the usual apsidal chancel (because of a constricted site?). Overall, it is airy and spacious, with a satisfying spatial richness achieved by the interaction of the transepts with the chapels, chancel and nave. Deep N and S chancel windows illuminate the High Altar. Also of note, the simply stencilled panelled ceiling, the delightful row of clerestory windows, the clustered chancel arch, and the angels supporting busts of English saints set against the arcade spandrels. The First World War Memorial Chapel, NW, is an addition of 1923 by *Pugin & Pugin*. The wooden cross is from Flanders.

FITTINGS. All designed by *Peter Paul Pugin*, the carving executed by his normal collaborator *Boulton*. – ALTARS. Of Portland and Bath stones. The most splendid is the High Altar, of the benediction type (i.e. with pinnacled throne over the central tabernacle). With three great canopies, the l. and r. sheltering semi-relief alabaster groups of the Adoration of the Shepherds and of the Kings. Above are four statues of saints; flanking are canopied statues of St Joseph and Our Lady and the Holy Child. The altar table and tabernacle are 1877, the rest 1885. Our Lady (1889) and Sacred Heart (1890) altars good too. Unobtrusive recent celebrant altar, on a stage between the transepts. – PULPIT and COMMUNION RAIL. 1883–4. Hefty. Marble. – PARCLOSE SCREENS. 1890. Stone, quatrefoils and slender angels. – CHOIR STALLS. 1890. Oak. Good. – PEWS. Benches with excellent cast-iron frames. – Expansive ORGAN CASE, *c.* 1887. – STATIONS OF THE CROSS, in recesses. Caen stone. – SCULPTURE. Against the chancel arch: St Benedict and St Scholastica. 1891. Our Lady of Lourdes, N aisle, by *Philip Lindsay Clark*. Impressively severe and graceful. The Holy Family, S transept, by *Josefina de Vasconcellos*. Fibreglass copy after the original formerly in St Martin-in-the-Fields, London; another in Liverpool's Anglican Cathedral. – Good *Minton* TILES flooring the chancel, 1877. Lily design, by *C. W. Pugin*. – STAINED GLASS. S aisle 1st from

E, a memorial to John Ashton, the principal benefactor, by *Hardman*, 1877. With the Pugins one would expect the glass in the E windows above the altars to be Hardman too. The best, indeed the highlight of the church, however, is the superb *Harry Clarke* work, 1931, in the S chapel, and S aisle 1st and 2nd from W. The Annunciation and Visitation in the chapel, Christ and the Raising of Lazarus, and Thomas à Becket and St Augustine of Canterbury in the aisle. Rich, glowing blues and reds, thickly textured and heavily worked like an oil painting.

PRESBYTERIAN CHAPEL (former), Winwick Street. Italianate, with Venetian tracery in the windows. It began in 1807 as the Countess of Huntingdon's Connexion but became Presbyterian in 1854. The new front was put on then.

UNITARIAN CHAPEL, Cairo Street. 1745, on a site occupied since 1703. A brick box, much of the present appearance the result of alterations in the early 1860s when the chapel was reorientated, e.g. the Perp wooden tracery of the two layers of four windows. Originally the pulpit was placed centrally against the long W wall, facing a gallery on the E side, with an entrance from Sankey Street in the N wall (surviving). The gallery was removed, new seating introduced facing N, and two S entrances with Doric doorcases opened up, onto the then recently laid-out Cairo Street. Between these is a round-headed window with Gothick tracery. – MONUMENTS. Wall tablets, many reflecting the close connection with the War-rington Academy. The best are to: Edward Garlick, †1758, an elegant tablet with cheeks and open pediment. He was a student from Virginia; and John Andrews Wilson, †1760, another student. Elaborately framed, and surmounted by obelisk with portrait roundel and urn finial. – BURIAL-GROUND WALL. Brick, panelled. 1745, presumably.

WESLEYAN CHAPEL, Bold Street. A prominent plot on the corner of Palmyra Square filled by a fairly rigorous multi-purpose brick box by the *Mason Richards Partnership*, 1975, with a two-storey hall over the two-storey chapel. It replaced a good large chapel of 1850.

WYCLIFFE CONGREGATIONAL CHAPEL, Bewsey Street. 1873, by *George Woodhouse* of Bolton, based on the Hope Chapel in Oldham. Brick. It was big, with round-arched windows and a square NW tower with pyramid roof. Not any more. The present peculiar appearance, as if it has been deflated, is explained by the demolition of the tower in 1984 and later the upper half of the chapel, so that now the lintels of the retained lower windows arch way above the eaves of the new roof. Nothing remains of the galleried interior.

FRIENDS' MEETING HOUSE, Academy Street (set back out of sight through gates on the W side). 1829–30, replacing a build-ing of 1725. A clean brick block with big sashes, including a recessed tripartite, segment headed main window, and a projecting semicircular porch on the S front. Usual plan with men's meeting house, E, and smaller women's meeting house (now social room), W, separated by a passageway with hung shutters above the dado which could be opened to enable the two rooms to be used together. A curved staircase in the porch leads to a gallery or 'loft', now partially blocked off, which is raked above the women's section facing the men's. The sun-washed men's meeting house has original panelled dado, benches and stand; the women's has fantastically attenuated cast-iron Doric columns supporting the loft (and recently discovered evidence of a stand). Charmingly understated joinery throughout. The buildings fronting Academy Street are a former MEETING HOUSE, thought to have served a Southcottian congregation in the early C19 and later a school, and a COTTAGE.

Public Buildings

TOWN HALL, Sankey Street. Designed by *James Gibbs* and built 35 as Bank Hall in 1749–50, for Thomas Patten. The finest house of its date in S Lancashire. Gibbs is reported to have considered it one of his best; it was also one of his last. It stood on what was then the edge of the town, more a suburban residence than a country house, imposing but not pretentious. This subtly reflected the status of the Pattens – Warrington's most influential C18 family – who were wealthy industrialists by 1750, but not yet landed. Thomas' father made the lower-Mersey navigable and established a copper-smelting operation at Bank Quay on the Mersey ¼ m. W, clearly visible across the fields from the house. This was literally built on the business: the foundations and cellars are made up of blocks of lustrous copper slag. In addition, the glazing bars are made of a copper-iron alloy. In 1872 the Hall was sold to the borough to become the Town Hall, and limited alterations were subsequently made by successive Borough Surveyors.

EXTERIOR. The S façade is of three storeys and nine bays and essentially brick, though the ground floor, treated as a basement, is painted rusticated ashlar (it was painted by 1772 at least). So too are the middle three bays, which are embossed with an attached tetrastyle portico of giant Composite columns and pediment containing the Patten arms. An open two-arm staircase with a fine wrought-iron balustrade leads to the *piano nobile*. On this level the window surrounds are enriched by pediments of alternating shape in the outer bays and arched Gibbs surrounds between the columns. The returns, five bays with arched staircase windows centrally, and the N façade, pediment over slightly projecting centre three bays, are all brick above the ground floor and altogether quieter. By 1772 one-bay ground floor extensions had been made to E and W. The house is flanked by detached service wings, to which it is linked by quadrant screens. Unusually, the wings do not project forward to create a *cour d'honneur*, but equally both fore and aft about the central axis. Dr Friedman has pointed out that this is unique in Gibbs' work and recalls Palladio's Villa Godi. Their wings have rusticated and pedimented three-bay, three-storey centres, and two-storey brick side parts. The E is offices, of thirteen bays, the W, stables, of nine (though both the same length). The rustication is powerful and ruggedly simple, appropriately for their use and status, and feels noticeably more Baroque. The stables have been substantially altered as council offices (see the W façade).

INTERIOR. Altogether the internal scale of the house is nowhere monumental, but there is good plasterwork and joinery throughout. The planning is the most interesting feature. The outer staircase leads to a spacious but not at all monumental entrance hall which is flanked by two lateral staircases of identical size in the middle of the sides. Beyond, on the garden front, from W, is what is known as the music room, then the saloon, now knocked into one, and then, apparently, an apartment. Flanking the hall on the entrance front are, E, the dining room and, W, another apartment, now the Mayor's Parlour. The arrangement is most similar to an unexecuted design of 1728 in Gibbs' *Book of Architecture*, but with the music and dining rooms in the place of two further apartments. Thus, at Bank Hall the two apartments are in opposite corners of the house, so presumably intended for separate individuals. Was the SW one, with Rococo plasterwork and overlooking Bank Quay, for Thomas Patten, a widower by 1749? And the plainer NE one for his daughter? These rooms, of intimate proportions, have coved ceilings. Not so the entrance hall, which has a fine stone chimneypiece, and a late C19 tessellated floor and draught-lobby. Lincrusta dados and ceilings were introduced here and elsewhere e.g. the dining room, which has a marble chimneypiece with excellent Bacchic tablet, and a later vine cornice. The music room and saloon have Rococo ceilings, but the identical rinceau friezes could be C19. The egg-and-dart edging of the fireplace in the saloon matches the mouldings of the music-room joinery, from where it has presumably come. The best and most abundant Rococo plaster-
36 work is on the walls and ceilings of the main, W, stair. The dado (later? It clips the plasterwork in places) is mahogany, a single magnificent 18 ft (5.5 metre) plank to each flight. Both cantilevered staircases have excellent lyre-pattern wrought-iron balustrades. Upstairs were bed- and dressing rooms, now offices; on the ground floor is still a kitchen, and the servants' hall.

Nothing remains of the C18 GARDENS, with lake and rustic boathouse, but fronting Sankey Street are the splendidly heavy,
94 lavish and gloriously gilded cast-iron GATES. They were made by the *Coalbrookdale Company* and designed there by *Kershaw* and *Crook*. The four statues of Nike that crown the posts are by *John Bell*. The whole lot was exhibited at the 1862 London Exhibition, but it is not clear who or what they were made for. Possibly they were commissioned by a City livery

company as a gift to Victoria for Sandringham, hence the Prince of Wales feathers and motto. They languished at Coalbrookdale until erected here in 1895. They have regretfully been isolated since the *Coalbrookdale*'s flanking railings were removed in the Second World War. A cast-iron case for reinstatement.

NEW TOWN HOUSE, Scotland Road. *See* Perambulation, p. 617.

LAW COURTS, Kendrick Street. One of the better of the breed of combined court centres, by *Howell, Killick, Partridge & Amis*, 1992. Brick, slate roofs, glazing in generous grids. Principal block with top-lit courtrooms, lower office wing. Less pompous or domineering than some courts of its date, despite the drawbridge and turret references of the entrance front.

POLICE STATION, Arpley Street. Long, low eclecticism by *R. Burns Dick*, completed in 1900. Terracotta trimmings, dormers with big semicircular pediments and turrets with Mogulish cupolas. The taller Wilson Patten Street wing contained a Police Court on the first floor, and a Coroner's Court to the l.

MUSEUM AND LIBRARY, Bold Street. One of the first purpose-built rate-supported libraries or museums in the country, erected in 1855–7 to the designs of *Thomas Stone* of Newton-le-Willows. An uncommonly dignified building in brick, with stone dressings, unbroken cornice, tripartite ground-floor windows, and above, blank panels intended for relief scenes. The municipal Museum and Library first opened in 1848 in a converted house. In 1853 *John Dobson* was commissioned to design a purpose-built home, partly paid for by rates raised under the provisions of the 1850 Public Libraries Act. But the borough baulked at the cost, paid off Dobson and appointed Stone. He saved money by cutting out Dobson's basement (with gallery), reducing the amount of ancillary accommodation, and leaving the lecture theatre proposed for the NW corner to be built as a later phase (it never was). Dobson's concept of ground-floor library and first-floor, top-lit galleries was kept, but the entrance was moved from the narrow s façade to the E, with a big pediment over the door. Little was retained from Dobson's elevations except an astylar classicism and the first-floor panels. Stone's building is now the Bold Street elevation and the first three bays on Museum Street. The matching five w bays are of 1877, by *R. Vawser*, Borough Engineer, to house a new art gallery. Behind this and in parallel are the vaulted lending library, and then another gallery built in 1929–31 by the Borough Engineer *Andrew M. Kerr*, so completing a circuit of first-floor galleries. That, with a w extension of the 1960s, finishes the building as it is now.

INTERIOR. Often rearranged. On the ground floor, most impressive is the 1931 lending library, with fat square columns and vaulted ceiling. In the library entrance is an excellent marble STATUE of Catherine Macaulay by *John Francis Moore*. It was unveiled at St Stephen Walbrook, London, in 1778, but banished shortly after, and given to the library in 1872.

Macaulay was a celebrated writer and historian in her time, and she is portrayed with the instruments of her art. The great joy is the three first-floor museum galleries in the 1850s section. Top-lit, with narrow mezzanine galleries on cast-iron brackets around the walls and polished specimen cabinets stuffed with curiosities, they belong to an age of curatorship a world away from the breathless, interactive expectations of our century. The cases and galleries are late C19 (the gallery brackets, though, were in place in 1857 in anticipation); the display is essentially of 1933, including back-lit illustrated panels, advanced for their time.

PYRAMID ARTS CENTRE, Palmyra Square South. A confident reworking by *Studio BAAD* of the former County Court and Inland Revenue Offices of 1897–8 by *(Sir) Henry Tanner* of the Office of Works. A pleasingly public new use for a redundant public building. Tanner's handsome building is red brick and yellow terracotta. Bits of Jacobean and bits of Frenchy Gothic, pleasingly varied and gabled, and softly coloured (now cleaned). Lottery funding for the conversion was awarded in 1998, and work finished in 2002. Jutting out onto the pavement between Tanner's building and the Technical School gymnasium to the E – also part of the scheme – is a full-height, glass-walled entrance to signal the reincarnation (something of a Lottery-architecture cliché). This new space, with 'feature' giant scissors-brace behind the glass façade, is the principal circulation area. It is finished with a combination of a robust industrial aesthetic and archaeologically exposed Victorian fabric that is maintained throughout the building. Off it, flexible performance spaces have been created in the C19 buildings, e.g. in the two courtrooms on the second floor (the Registrar's Court is behind the Frenchy gables). The light well has been enclosed, and sliding screens in place of walls on the ground floor ingeniously enable it to be combined with adjacent rooms. Unexpected bridges across voids and views opened up through glass walls, and constant changes of level, all create spatial stimulation. At the rear, an overhanging translucent wall wraps up the new work.

PARR HALL, Palmyra Square South. *William Owen*, 1895. Brick. Very plain, with a big hipped roof with a cupola, but containing an extremely important (because so little altered) organ by the master Parisian builder *Cavaillé-Coll*. Made 1870, installed with its fine Gothic oak case here in 1926.

TECHNICAL SCHOOL (former), next to Parr Hall. Now council offices. 1900–1, by *William & Segar Owen*. Imposing symmetrical façade of eleven bays, the centre an ebullient stone frontispiece with a big semicircular pediment on paired and engaged columns and, beneath, a voluptuous ensemble of deep doorway hood on huge brackets rising from the curling steps parapet. Names of famous scientists in terracotta aprons under the first-floor windows. Inside, a hall with heavy, Neo-C17 detailing, especially the wild doorcases, and a big mullioned-

and-transomed window with stained glass lighting a broad staircase.

SCHOOL OF ART, Museum Street. *William Owen* again, 1883. Red brick, the two first-floor studios expressed externally by their very tall windows, arching up into the dormers. Artisan-Mannerist detailing inside, e.g. staircase and doorcases.

SIR THOMAS BOTELER HIGH SCHOOL. *See* Outer Warrington, south, p. 625.

WARRINGTON HOSPITAL. *See* Outer Warrington, west, p. 632.

CENTRAL STATION, Winwick Street. 1873, for the Cheshire Lines Committee. Low façade to the station approach. Brick and stone dressings, central pediment. Non-matching entrance and booking hall of 1983, in brick and timber, to Winwick Road. N is the impressively four-square, polychromatic brick WAREHOUSE, 1882. Three big storeys. The names of the CLC's constituents are emphatically spelled out in huge concrete or render panels.

GENERAL POST OFFICE (former), Springfield Street. *See* p. 619.

RAILWAY STATION (former), Tanner's Lane. Now the Three Pigeons pub, this two-storey brick building on the corner with Dallam Lane is in fact one of the earliest railway stations in the world, built in 1831 as the booking office of the Warrington & Newton Railway, which opened that year. This was only a year after the Liverpool & Manchester Railway, to which it was connected. There is little to distinguish it from standard domestic structures of the period, particularly since a pub front was inserted later in the C19. At this very early stage, small station buildings had yet to develop a distinctive plan or architectural language.

MERSEY BRIDGES. There is no evidence that the Romans built a bridge at Warrington, though the suspicion persists. The first mention of a bridge at BRIDGE FOOT to replace the ancient fording point further upstream is in 1285; the present structure, of 1911–15, by the engineer *John J. Webster*, is the sixth on the site. Reinforced concrete; guarded by lamps on tall pedestals. It was supplemented immediately upstream by a second BRIDGE in the mid 1980s. A late C19 proposal for a second bridge shrank in execution in 1912 to become the HOWLEY FOOTBRIDGE, Parr Street, an elegant suspension bridge straight out of the *David Rowell & Co.* catalogue. Then, in 1931–4, came the KINGSWAY BRIDGE by *H. W. Fitzsimmons*, a bypass further E. Ferro-concrete, with classical lamp standards. In the 1960s the A6 was superseded by the M6, which crosses the Mersey on the THELWALL VIADUCTS. The W was completed in 1963, the E in 1994. These are massive structures, utterly without art or grace. Yet they are so prominent that they should have been designed with flair, or at least simple good manners.

OTHER BRIDGES. The Grand Junction Railway's WARRINGTON VIADUCT, 1837, 1 m. S of Bank Quay station, is sandstone, with big voussoirs. *Joseph Locke* was the railway's chief engineer.

Only five of the twelve arches remain, but these include the two graceful segmental examples over the river. The TRANS-PORTER BRIDGE, ¼ m. W of Slutchers Lane. Designed by *William Henry Hunter* and built by *Sir William Arrol & Co.* in 1911–15, to carry goods, originally by rail only, to the works of Joseph Crosfield & Sons. S of the Mersey (*see* p. 633 for the factory). Steel. 200 ft (62 metres) between the towers. One of only three such bridges remaining in the United Kingdom.*

MANCHESTER SHIP CANAL. Begun in 1887 and completed six years later. (Sir) *Edward Leader Williams* was the chief engineer. Cutting through rock along the S edge of Warrington, it offers a heroically scaled vista of locks and bridges. There are two swing-bridges, and four high-level bridges: three dynamically skewed railway viaducts of the hog-backed girder type, the other a cantilevered road bridge. The high-level bridges are mainly steel, the low-level, cast-iron. The Latchford Locks are of the canal's standard concrete design.

Town Centre Perambulation

This begins at the PARISH CHURCH (*see* p. 604), standing slightly forlornly as it was described in 1553, at the 'tail end of the town'. It was built close to the ancient ford across the Mersey (the remains of a Roman road were found in the churchyard), but this was abandoned for the present bridging point further downstream in the C13, pulling the town irrevocably W away from CHURCH STREET. In the C19 and C20 this area was an important industrial quarter, but the street is a sad sight. On the S side, much altered, the RING O'BELLS pub, C18 and earlier, forming a pleasant group with COTTAGES (with some horizontal sashes) at the churchyard gates. Is the mid-C19 Gothic pair, in the same red sandstone as the church, by its restorers, *Frederick & Horace Francis*? On the N side W of the Sainsbury supermarket** is No. 88, erroneously known as CROMWELL'S HOUSE (he may have stayed at a nearby inn). An early C17 timber-framed building, with jetty and later nogging. Subsequently divided into three cottages, in the 1930s it was heavily restored, creating a two-bay hall open to the roof; one fireplace has an overmantel with stylised foliage (cf. Speke Hall, Liverpool, pp. 466–7). Across the street, the MARQUIS OF GRANBY pub, also C17 and timber-framed. Cross-wing, and C19 vine-pattern bargeboards. Next to it, incorporated into a recent apartment block, the rather fortress-like Tudor Revival façade of the former NATIONAL SCHOOL, 1833, with central canted bay beneath a gable, flanked by octagonal towers, marked, l., for boys and, r., for girls. The rest was demolished in the 1980s. The BULL'S HEAD pub may also have C17 parts, under the concrete render. Church Street is severed from the

---

*The others, much larger, are at Middlesbrough and Newport.
**Behind until 2003 stood *John Douglas'* minimally Gothic Boteler Grammar School, 1864.

town centre by miserable MERSEY STREET, part of the New Town road system.

DIAL STREET and its extension the BUTTERMARKET, across the roundabout, have a little group of Georgian buildings around St Mary's church (*see* p. 608). On the N side are some detached houses, the former METHODIST SUNDAY SCHOOL, dated 1817 in the gable, and the former TRUSTEES SAVINGS BANK, 1829–31, with pilasters over ground-floor rustication, and later porch. The statelier of the two big buildings set back W of the church, with Doric pedimented door surround and Gothick fanlight, is the former DISPENSARY of 1819. Then on the N side the unredeemingly brutal NEW TOWN HOUSE of the 1970s. It is on the corner of the New Town's inner circulatory road, here ACADEMY STREET–SCOTLAND ROAD, with shopping centres and retail sheds either side. The central arcade of the COCKHEDGE CENTRE, N of New Town House, is formed of elegant elements (dated 1853) of the cast-iron frame of the eponymous cotton mill that stood here.

W across Academy Street the Buttermarket is lined with Neo-Georgian façades of the 1930s. Most sophisticated is the former PELICAN INN by *Wright & Hamlyn*, on the N side, with Mannerist keystones and a bright-eyed sculpture of the said bird perched on the entablature. These buildings form part of a scheme to alleviate chronic traffic congestion by widening the town's four principal streets, begun in the 1880s. The centrepiece of the plan is MARKET GATE, where the four meet at the heart of the town. It was laid out as a circus from 1914–15. Of this date are the SE and SW segments, by *J.E. Wright, Garnett & Wright* in a pleasant mid-C17 style, i.e. alternating pediments over cross-windows. The design won a 1908 competition judged by Professor Charles Reilly (*see* p. 254). His assertion that Georgian was the most suitable style for Warrington, because it corresponded 'to the best period of its history', would establish the aesthetic of redevelopment until the Second World War. The NE quadrant was designed in-house by *Burtons* in the late 1930s; the final, NW, piece wasn't completed until the Golden Square shopping centre was constructed (*see* p. 620). A fountain in the centre of Market Gate is the focal element of a scheme of STREET DESIGN by *Landscape Design Associates* with the American artist *Howard Ben Tre*, completed in 2002. It is hefty and very fussy, and the bulging columns quite baffling, but at least some of it seems robust (e.g. granite benches).

BRIDGE STREET, dropping S down the hill from Market Gate to the Mersey, was widened and extensively rebuilt from the 1880s to 1908, a process that swept away a warren of yards. It is now Warrington's best street, and the best section is the top of the W side: a frothy 1900s group in assorted styles, with lots of terracotta and faience. The narrow and freely – but distinctly – Art Nouveau Gothic façade is the most interesting; the two to its l. are by the *Owens*. The curious sculpture in the middle of the street is a MEMORIAL to the victims of the 1993 IRA bombing here, River of Life by *Stephen Broadbent*, 1996. Water trickles from a rock down a raised, curving bronze trough decorated with friezes depicting the course of the Mersey. On the E side near here is the HOWARD BUILDINGS of *c.* 1906, or at least its fanciful terracotta façade, minus the originally vigorous roofscape. Two friezes depict the work of the prison reformer John Howard, who lodged on the site in 1777 whilst his influential book, *The State of the Prisons*, was published in the town. On the same side, the former LION HOTEL (now a night club), the last of the town's coaching inns, and at the end of the C18 its most important. Behind its early C19 façade are remnants from the C18. Through the archway is a wing with assembly room. On the corner of Rylands Street on the opposite side is the *c.* 1900 half-timbered CO-OPERATIVE BANK, built as Martin's Bank, with disappointingly flat façades but high-quality carved detailing. The next street off to the W is FRIARS GATE, commemorating the house of the Austin Friars (*see* p. 602). On it, a typically exuberant Edwardian variety theatre, the former PALACE THEATRE AND HIPPODROME by *George F. Ward* of Birmingham, opened 1907.

Back on Bridge Street, the best buildings of its rebuilt lower reaches are pubs: the Queen Anne FEATHERS, W, and the former ROYAL OAK by *William & Segar Owen*, E, in a muscular Edwardian Tudor, all buff terracotta gables and chimneys. Next to it are some very modest C18 remnants. Set back opposite is a facsimile of the mid-C18 building which first housed the WARRINGTON ACADEMY (*see* p. 603). The original building and its panelled interiors were disgracefully destroyed in the 1980s; the replacement was given a new W wing in a grander Neo-Georgian style on BRIDGE FOOT (*see* p. 615 for the bridges). In front of this is a statue of Cromwell, by *John Bell*, displayed by the *Coalbrookdale Co.* at the 1862 London Exhibition (*see* p. 612). Walking W along Bridge Foot, past the TELEPHONE EXCHANGE extension of 1911 with relief concrete façades, is STANLEY STREET, a small fragment of Georgian Warrington set amongst trees. It is possible that the developer was the artist *Hamlet Winstanley*, who named it in honour of his patron the Earl of Derby. Three houses, possibly of the 1740s, remain, with quoins and the rusticated wedge lintels typical of the area. No. 25, of four bays, is the best.

The end of Stanley Street backs on to BOLD STREET, part of a C19 residential development (on Legh family land) centred on the modestly pleasant PALMYRA SQUARE. The square became home to many of the town's public buildings. The exotic street names (Suez, Palmyra, etc.) commemorate colonial battles fought by local regiments. The best houses, of the mid C19, flank Bold Street N of the Museum and Library (*see* p. 613). On the E one carved panels, of the Bold family griffin, a Pegasus, etc., copies of originals removed from a house near the market dated 1682, which was demolished. Palmyra Square was laid out as QUEENS GARDENS in 1897 and the STATUE is a Boer War memorial by *Alfred Drury*, 1906, immortalising

Lt-Col. O'Leary as the very model of the Imperial hero. The gardens were replanned in 2004.

w of the Square at the end of Palmyra Square South is Winmarleigh Street, and on it the MASONIC HALL by *Albert Warburton*, 1932–3. Later extension, r. Warburton's sober brick façades are the backdrop to some unusually public Masonic iconography, which is normally reserved for interiors. Flanking the door are two giant, free-standing columns. These are masonry's Two Pillars, the columns called Jachin and Boaz which stood at the entrance of Solomon's Temple. Jachin, l., was associated with foundations, Boaz, r., with strength. The capitals are a conjectural reconstruction after descriptions in the Bible and elsewhere with palm fronds and flowers around basketwork. Surmounting each is a globe – one celestial and one terrestrial. These represent the Supreme Being, and indicate the universal claims of the Craft and the need for charity. The netting draped over each is another element of the Biblical description of the Solomonic pillars. On the first floor inside are two lodge or temple rooms, windowless as usual, with coffered ceilings, reached by a top-lit Imperial staircase. Throughout, a canted-head motif is employed, e.g. with the window surround above the door.

Back at the NW corner of Palmyra Square is SPRINGFIELD STREET and the former GPO of 1908 by *W. Potts* of the Board of Works. Three-and-a-half storeys with a roof-line of towers and dormers. Brick and stone. With stripped-down, squared-off, free C17 detailing. Some of it quite Mannerist, e.g. guttae under some window sills, and aprons pushed up into and out from the surrounds of other windows. Also, lovely Art Nouveau lettering. At the top of Springfield Street is SANKEY STREET, the principal westward thoroughfare, with the Town Hall (*see* Public Buildings) and a number of Georgian buildings, grander on the N side and mostly more modest on the S. Heading E back towards Market Gate on the N side is BANK HOUSE, of two phases, the first with canted bay and the second, C19, with segmental. Then No. 84 and No. 86, almost a pair. Both detached, of five bays and two-and-a-half storeys, with pretty doorways and enriched surrounds above. No. 86 has a three-bay pediment as well. They are later C18. Next comes an Edwardian block of shops, but still daintily Norman-Shavian with its stuccoed gable and oriel windows. By *J.E. Wright, Garnett & Wright*. Across Legh Street is another fragment of the Neo-Georgian C20 replanning, by the *Owens*, partially completed in 1929. Then, on the S side beyond Bold Street is *Albert Warburton*'s Co-operative Building, now T.J. HUGHES. The principal block is 1909, bullishly and freely Wrenaissance with curious round turrets, and tall gabled windows lighting a second-floor hall that seated seven hundred. The ground and first floors were formerly almost entirely plate glass and iron. The NATWEST BANK was built as the District Bank in 1847 by *Edward Walters* of Manchester.

The façade is unusual, with first-floor columns standing on ground-floor Venetian pilasters projecting forward between the windows. The sculptor *Warrington Wood* was a stonemason's apprentice on this job. Next to it is WOOLWORTHS. 1864, designed by *John Douglas* as the showrooms of the furniture makers Robert Garrett & Sons (the water tower of their workshops behind is prominent). It is one of his earliest and very best works, an exceptionally refined secular Gothic façade articulated by pairs and triplets of lancets with free-standing granite columns, and high-quality foliate carving. The arcaded shopfront is destroyed. The other part of Woolworths is their original, typically confident, inter-war store.

Forming the N side of the street opposite all of this is the GOLDEN SQUARE SHOPPING CENTRE, by *Ardin & Brookes & Partners*, 1973–83, the principal architectural impact of the New Town on the town centre, realised at the expense of a picturesque pattern of ancient streets and the old market. The mid-C19 FISH MARKET, an iron frame with roof (and foliate capitals), is retained as the centrepiece of the square itself, around which the centre is arranged as an internal street under a glazed barrel vault. Lining the W side of the square is a row of fatuous replica façades resembling the C18 and C19 buildings that stood here, including the pedimented old Town Hall. The one genuine survival is the BARLEY MOW pub on the N side, though it has suffered one too many facelifts over the years. Late C16 with two jettied gables, three storeys and lots of elaborate timber framing, e.g. quatrefoil panels. Amongst the jumble of fake panelling inside is some that is genuinely C17, which once lined a first-floor room. Aside from the theme-park replications and the destruction of streetscape, Golden Square may be seen as a successful example of its type. The brick architecture, with its rows of oriels, if not exciting is at least inoffensive, and the scale is human and respects the neighbouring buildings. The square itself is an animated, happily sized space, and the location ensures that the town centre remains Warrington's retail heart. In 2005 a large extension was being built N and W on the site of Golborne Road, a 1970s access road.

Leave Golden Square by Lyme Street in the NW corner, and turn N up HORSEMARKET STREET to where at the crossroads it becomes WINWICK STREET, the principal road N. Here is a little group of Georgian houses. No. 3 is of five bays and three storeys with a tall pedimented doorcase. The details of this and the lugged window surrounds suggest an earlier C18 date. Next to it is the NATWEST BANK, built as the headquarters of one of its constituents, Parr & Co., founded on the site in 1788 (a later and much grander headquarters is at Liverpool, *see* p. 312). The present building is of 1877 by *Thomas Beesley*, substantial but not very beautiful, with some superimposed pilasters and a little pedimented gable. At the rear, however, is the best interior in the town, a splendid banking hall. Eight red granite Corinthian columns support a coved and beamed ceiling between, with aisles either side, a superb cornice all round, outrageous pedimented double doorcases and copious gilding. Is it a later addition by a more talented hand? Disappearing NW under the bridges opposite the bank is the beginning of BEWSEY STREET. On this Georgian extension some late-period houses remain, e.g. No. 93 and a multi-phase late C18 row on the N side, much of it now replica. More early C19 houses on its continuation, BEWSEY ROAD, briefly a fashionable suburb.

OUTER WARRINGTON

North and East: Padgate, Paddington, Martincroft and Woolston

CHRIST CHURCH, Station Road, Padgate. 1838, chancel and vestries 1882–3, by *William Owen*. Brick. Bellcote and lancets; aisleless. Late C20 W porch, clumsily attempting to ape the C19 work. The spidery roof trusses, with open lancet framing, are odd, but attractive. An elegant reordering of 1963–71 by *George Pace* includes a screen below the W gallery, and the re-sited altar W of the chancel. – Rectilinear Modernist FURNISHINGS, mainly stained oak and metal. Best are the FONT and the CHOIR STALLS around the three walls of the chancel. – Better still are his characteristic flowing, sinuous glazing bars in the nave lancets. – Pretty C19 FONT in the porch, on huddled marble colonnettes. – Reasonable STAINED GLASS in the E lancets, of the 1870s and 1880s. – Big RECTORY, of c. 1840.

ST ANN (former), Winwick Road. 1866–8. An impressively forceful High Victorian work by *John Douglas*, bold and uncompromising. The quality of composition and detailing emerges with careful study. Dark brick, including detailing. Lancets and plate tracery. Tower with steep hipped roof and a round stair-turret reaching up into the roof zone. Round apse. Powerful buttresses, which project internally with arches spanned between them, as at Albi Cathedral. Redundant and gutted, it became a climbing centre in 1996. The bizarre juxtaposition of luridly coloured and textured climbing walls, all zigzagging angles and flimsily stage-set thin, and the dense, carefully considered C19 architecture is strangely enjoyable. A mezzanine has been put in the chancel. All this is 'reversible', according to that sacrosanct tenet of conservation. – PAINTINGS of the Apostles around the apse by *Westlake*, 1868, repainted by *T. Hesketh* in 1894.

The SETTING, once industrial, was in 2003–4 crassly transformed by the construction of a Rugby League stadium and supermarket. This bounds the church tightly on three sides: the supermarket itself against the N side, the car park behind the W end, and a petrol station flanking the S side. Scarcely believable.

ST MARGARET AND ALL HALLOWS, Orford Green, Orford. 1906–8. A modest but pleasant exercise by *Albert Warburton*, somewhat in the manner of Paley & Austin. Brick, N tower,

Warrington, St Ann, by John Douglas, 1866–8.
(*Building News*, vol. 17, 1869)

lots of roof. The tracery in the chancel windows has cusping with rose stops. Low nave with arch-braced roof, s passage aisle, and a barrel-roofed chancel. – Carved ALTAR FRONTAL. A Second World War memorial, from *Oberammergau*. – Chancel FURNISHINGS. 1931. – Chancel SCREEN. 1924. A First World War memorial. – STAINED GLASS. A number by *Morris & Co.*, including the excellent E window. Creation and Christ in Majesty, with a bluish-purple palette.

ST BENEDICT (R.C.), Longford Street. By *Matthew Honan*. Designed 1911 and built 1914–15 (though the PRESBYTERY went up straight away). Byzantine. Three gabled masses – N and S chapels flanking the body of the church – and a little, narrow NW tower. Brick, some herringbone pattern, stone banding, double-corbelled eaves, arched windows. Smooth plastered interior with barrel vault and a subtle sequence of arched openings, recesses and fenestration. A gallery over the narthex. Narrow passage aisles. The plan is more complex and thoughtful than it may at first appear. – Marble Benediction ALTAR, and MOSAIC of the Crucifixion on the E wall behind.

ST OSWALD (R.C.), Padgate Lane, Padgate. 1965, by *L.A.G. Pritchard & Son*. Big brick T-plan barn, with the ALTAR at the junction. Attached to the N side of the W end is a tall, thin campanile. – STAINED GLASS with abstract doves.

ST PETER AND ST MICHAEL (R.C.), Weir Lane, Martincroft. 1834–5. A simple rendered chapel by *John Smith* of Liverpool, for his friend Edward Stratham. Presbytery attached to the E end. Thin lancets. Little apsidal chancel and deep W gallery on Doric columns. W porch, reordering and redecoration, 1985, by the *Pozzoni Design Group*.

PADGATE WESLEYAN CHURCH, Padgate Lane, Padgate. 1874–5, by *C.O. Ellison* of Liverpool. Yellow stone and a lot of roof. Lancets and flat plate tracery. Quite pretty, though the little octagonal belfry and spirelet above the S porch is a bit odd. A simple hammerbeam roof. Unusually for Methodists, it is filled completely with memorial STAINED GLASS, but none is of any quality.

CEMETERY, Manchester Road (A57). Consecrated 1857. Only one of *Thomas D. Barry*'s three CHAPELS survives. This is, as is usual for him, quite quirky. C13, lots of gables, a spire. Quarry-faced buff stone. Bashed-up Tudor Gothic LODGES by *Barry* too. Fine RAILINGS on Manchester Road with crowns under Gothic canopies. – MONUMENT. George Formby Sen., †1921 (and George Formby Jun., †1961, added), comedians, with of course theatrical motifs. A marble aedicule containing relief mask between drawn curtains. Also the masks of comedy and drama. By *Alberti & Lupton* of Manchester.

ST BENEDICT'S PRIMARY SCHOOL, Quebec Road. By *Brock Carmichael Associates*, 1991. The junior and infants' classrooms flank the central multi-purpose hall in lower, canted wings, forming a sweeping, embracing S façade.

PADGATE COTTAGE HOMES (former), Green Lane, Padgate. Built 1880–1 for orphans and the children of the adult poor by the Warrington Poor Law Union. Brick, terracotta detailing, thinly Old English style. The porter's lodge is prettiest. Boys' blocks now offices. These formed one side of a court; the reflecting girls' accommodation to the E and a school to the S now demolished.

PADGATE STATION, Station Road. 1872. The same standard Cheshire Lines Committee design as Widnes (*see* p. 656). And a neat white row of one-and-a-half-storey COTTAGES.

HOUSING. Fisher Avenue and Crow Avenue, Longford. The same flat-roofed 1940s semis as at Fowley Common, Culcheth (q.v.).

125 ROYAL MAIL RAIL TERMINAL, Eagle Park Drive. This is the best Warrington building of the last twenty years. It is by *Austin-Smith:Lord* and was completed in 1997. It is in essence another large (5,000 sq. metres) portal-frame distribution warehouse, for the exchange of mail between road and rail, but the type's characteristics of scale and simplicity have been made virtues in marvellously dramatic form by wrapping it in a single silvery seamed-aluminium skin that sweeps to the ground, curling in on itself in semicircular profile. The shed is integrated with similarly skinned projections from either end over the railway platforms, an elegant ribbed tube. Celebrating scale, expressing function and exploiting the repetition of standard utilitarian components with panache, it is a worthy heir to the C19 functional tradition. A shame it is so obscurely located.

WINWICK QUAY and HOWLEY QUAY are the most interesting of the few remaining relics of Warrington's long history of water transportation. Winwick Quay, W of Mill Lane, was a small repair yard on the Sankey Brook Navigation canal (*see* p. 52), now filled in here. To the N are cottages, possibly once an inn, then two ranges around a yard. The main workshop, dated 1841, has a gable to the canal and round-arched windows set out in an attractive rhythm. Further S, on what was the opposite bank, is a barge-sized DRY DOCK. Howley Quay, Howley Lane, is Warrington's last warehouse on the Mersey. A mid-C19 cast-iron structure with a roof that oversails the river to form a loading canopy, attached to an C18 agent's house.

South to the Ship Canal: Wilderspool and Latchford

CHRIST CHURCH, Wash Lane, Latchford. By *Kennedy & Rogers*, 1861. Rock-faced. Early C14 style, with an independent SW steeple attached only by a link and a big N aisle. NE vestry and organ chamber, by *Tate & Popplewell*, added 1875. A homely interior. The nave roof has a double hammerbeam; the chancel roof charming collars made of pairs of angels clasping an iron rod between them. – All the CHANCEL FURNISHINGS of oak, following a 1940s fire. – SCREEN, N aisle. A First World War memorial. – Some decent STAINED GLASS, e.g. the W window by *Walter Tower*, and N aisle E, to Harold Broadbent, †1905, by *Edward Frampton*. Pre-Raphaelite style.

SCHOOL, to the S, once pretty, now bashed up. Opposite the church used to stand the timber-framed Plague House of 1656. The plague of development has spirited it away.

ST JAMES, Wilderspool Causeway. Upright Gothick by *Samuel Rowland*, 1828–30, superseding an apparently impressive chapel of 1777. Red ashlar, with tall pointed windows filled with intersecting wooden tracery. Short narrow chancel.

Handsome W front with polygonal buttresses at the angles and the angles of the tower that half projects from the centre. All with uncrocketed finials. The interior is peculiarly unecclesiastical and very ungainly, a big, broad aisle-less barn with a simple flat ceiling and a little chancel. It misses the galleries, N, S, W and across the chancel arch, that gave structure to the space. They were taken out in 1897. Now, peculiar flimsy eight-foot-high screens at the E end form enclosures and create a little choir between. At the W end odd high arches are thrown up at either side of the tower, forming a kind of screen. Beneath these since 1897 are the entrances; the old entrance, beneath the tower, is now the baptistery. – ALTAR and REREDOS. 1967. – Six PAINTINGS, scenes from the Life of Jesus, by *Alfred O. Hemmings*, late C19. They do not appear to have been commissioned for here. – Three STAINED GLASS windows by him too.

OUR LADY OF THE ASSUMPTION (R.C.), St Mary Street, Latchford. A church by *Robert Curran*, 1901–2, that sorely misses its never-built NW steeple. Yellow and red stone like St Mary, Buttermarket (*see* p. 609). Nave, aisles and apsidal chancel, tall roof. Handsome W window with intersecting tracery. Projecting W gallery, vestibule under. Polished granite piers, but only one capital carved before the money ran short. A PAINTING of the Assumption, donated in 1915 and optimistically attributed to Guercino, is framed by the dignified REREDOS of square-panelled oak by *F.E. Massey*, 1950 (the Portland stone HIGH ALTAR is part of the same scheme). – STAINED GLASS around the apse by *Margaret Agnes Rope*, 1932 and 1924.

BETHEL BAPTIST CHAPEL, Wash Lane. 1860. A pedimented brick box with pilaster strips. School alongside of 1878, 1902 and 1929.

SIR THOMAS BOTELER HIGH SCHOOL, Grammar School Road, Latchford. 1937. Inter-war scholastic classicism. Two storeys, seventeen bays to the main front, five broken forward with Ionic pilasters, entablature and straight-backed cupola.

MANCHESTER SHIP CANAL. *See* p. 616.

CENTRE PARK, Park Boulevard, Arpley Meadows. The first phase of this business park opened in 1990 with *ORMS* as architects and *Creative Landscaping* as landscape consultants. The ecological landscaping, with pond, may be a bit fussy, but is of higher quality and better managed than most public spaces today. Of the architecture, there are the usual brick-and-tinted-glass offices, a cod-vernacular hotel (1992) so spectacular that it leaves one speechless, and – easily the best – the crisp NORTH WEST REGIONAL DEVELOPMENT AGENCY OFFICES by *Dyer Associates*, 2001–2. Fully glazed. A court plan, the E side closed by a two-storey bridging wing set well back within a frame.

GREENALL, WHITLEY & CO. BREWERY (former), Wilderspool Causeway, Wilderspool. A brewery was here from the C18 to 1988. The principal C19 buildings were converted into offices

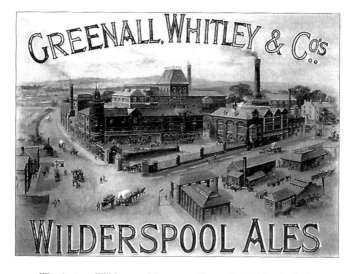

Warrington, Wilderspool Brewery (Greenall, Whitley & Co.).
c19 advertisement

in 1996–8 by *ORMS*, with confident understatement. They were designed by the brewery specialists *R. Davison, Son & Mackenzie* (later *Inskipp & Mackenzie*). To the N, the modified 1877 brewhouse with base but no chimney and, behind, the malt store and boiler house with mansard roof, built in the late 1880s when the brewery was reconstructed. ORMS inserted five floors into the 55-ft (17-metre) malt bins; light enters through three vertical slots, with robust recessed balconies, cut into the exterior. You might not suspect initially they were new. A hop store with prominent clock tower is as yet unrestored. To the W is WILDERSPOOL HOUSE, once home of the Greenall family, now offices. c18 core, but much and incoherently extended. Render, sashes, bay windows and modern cupola. A supermarket now occupies the rest of the site. Across Wilderspool Causeway from the brewery is the SARACEN's HEAD pub, built in the 1880s as the brewery's showpiece. For once the interior is reasonably well preserved, with mosaic flooring, robust woodwork, and fireplaces. Upstairs room with exposed trusses.

LATCHFORD VILLAGE, around Knutsford Road and Thelwall Lane, but overwhelmed as a one-way system now. Some c19 HOUSES and some pubs, e.g. on Knutsford Road, the CHESHIRE CHEESE, probably c18, and THE RAILWAY, a Greenall's building of 1914, with excellent Northern Renaissance terracotta and faience.

THE OLD WARPS, Weir Lane, Victoria Park, Latchford. A house, the home of the Faircloughs, seed millers, of c. 1800. Or earlier? The back is a jumble, and compare the rusticated wedge lintels here with Stanley and Bewsey streets (*see* Town Centre Perambulation, p. 618), which are at least twenty years earlier. So the front, seven sparse rendered bays, plus two to the r., may be a tidying up. Slight central projection with slighter pediment, pilasters at the angles and broad pedimented porch on paired Ionic columns. Handsome fanlight. Almost nothing C18 survives inside. The grounds are now Victoria Park.

ROMAN SITES. *See* pp. 15 and 601.

South of the Ship Canal: Appleton, Grappenhall, Stockton Heath, Thelwall and Walton

This is old Cheshire, but is included because it was designated as part of the New Town (*see* New Town, p. 634). From the middle of the C19 Warrington's more affluent colonised the strip between the Ship Canal and the Bridgewater Canal and the most affluent built on the leafy slopes of Walton rising up from the valley floor. Parts of Appleton and Stretton lying without the New Town are not included here. Churches are described last.

APPLETON has no ancient village, but dotted about are a number of C17 timber-framed buildings. Most are outside the New Town boundaries; an example inside is GREEN LANE FARMHOUSE. Frame exposed at rear; baffle-entrance plan.

GRAPPENHALL has Victorian and early C20 suburban semis and villas N of the Bridgewater Canal, e.g. in Chester Road and Hill Top Road. *William Owen*'s own house, Newholme, of the 1870s, is on Alexandra Road. But S of the canal is still a quiet, attractive little village centre at the church, in spite of the inexorable envelopment by Warrington.

STOCKTON HEATH is almost entirely suburban. At Victoria Square, the crossroads at the centre, the MULBERRY TREE, a very big Greenall's pub of 1907 by *William & Segar Owen*. The Free Style is coarse, and the 'knapped' stone pieces downright odd, so that the erudition of the porch columns is unexpected.

THELWALL remains villagey, if only at the E end of Thelwall New Road, where there are cottages and the PICKERING ARMS INN. This and IVY COTTAGE on Ferry Lane, are C17, with square-panelled timber frames, and later nogging and other alterations. THELWALL OLD HALL next to Ivy Cottage is of sandstone, five bays including a two-storey porch and cross-wing. Mullioned windows, original and renewed, and decent C20 timber casements. E on Lymm Road, CHAIGELEY SCHOOL occupies Thelwall Hall, a good brick house, probably built for Thomas Pickering after 1747. Now altered and extended, but despite the C19 bay windows the Georgian provenance of the five-bay front is immediately evident. Little pediment; also pedimented doorcase. E again on the N side, OLD HALL FARMHOUSE dated 1655, a timber frame rebuilt in brick and false-framed in the C19, and off the S side, HOME FARMHOUSE, dated 1692 and 1745. Of which date the mullioned windows, all wooden and of two lights, all of upright form, and all with raised stone frames?

WALTON, both Lower Walton but especially Higher, are populated by late C19 and Edwardian villas, many in suburban Free
Style or Old English. Amongst these is WALTON HOUSE on
Walton New Road. Late C18. Brick, three storeys and two bays,
with small recessed wings. Ionic porch. (Good plasterwork
inside. DCMS.)

WALTON HALL, Walton Lea Road, off Chester New Road (A56).
A dullish Elizabethan Revival house built in 1836–8 for Gilbert
Greenall M.P., the brewer. Of brick and stone dressing, with
thin, octagonal, ogee-capped turrets, and gables, on the S and
W sides crowstepped Flemish fashion. Those on the W side
apparently moved from the E elevation. Alterations and
enlargements of 1869–70, including a new entrance on the E
side and a new W wing for guests and billiards. This wing is
now reduced, leaving scars, and a slender (also ogee-capped)
clock tower isolated. What date are the bay windows on the S
front, which are of a different colour sandstone? Jacobethan
entrance hall, fully panelled with an Imperial staircase. This all
looks 1870 or later; the more delicate plaster ceiling of the
1830s. One room has a marble overmantel of 1871 by *Warrington Wood*, the sculptor, showing Diana hunting. – Extensive
outbuildings include a dilapidated, but impressive, iron-framed
PALM HOUSE. – LODGE on Chester Road, ½ m. NNE, at the
entrance to the crematorium. Of *c.* 1838. Loudonesque Jacobethan, one storey.

The ESTATE VILLAGE, on and off Old Chester Road, is late C19
and early C20, in various Free Style forms and freely arranged.
Brick, stone, render and half-timbering all employed. Best is
Nos. 138–146, a resourcefully asymmetrical group in which one
arm is roughcast with mullioned windows and the other half-
timbered over brick. The Greenalls' brewery employed both
J.E. Wright, Garnett & Wright, and *William & Segar Owen* to
design pubs; one or both of these were probably the architects
here.

ALL SAINTS, Thelwall New Road, Thelwall. 1843, by *J. Mountford Allen*. The nave is of that date, with a long side of single
lancets *à la* Commissioners, and a bellcote. The nave was
lengthened E and the present chancel added in 1857; the N aisle
and no doubt the porch and probably the W end of the nave
are by *William Owen*, of 1890. All is rock-faced red sandstone.
– WALL PAINTINGS in chancel and baptistery by *Shrigley &
Hunt*. – MEMORIAL to King Edward the Elder, who is
supposed to have founded Thelwall in 923. Designed by
F.C. Eden, made by *Heifor Bros.* 1907. A triptych, with its
middle pediment like a small Venetian altarpiece. *Eric Gill*
executed the lettering.

ST CROSS, Appleton Thorn. 1886–7, by *Edmund Kirby & Sons*,
and better than one expects them to be – the church could be
by Paley & Austin. Little and squat, but with a sufficiently
dominant central tower. The style chosen is Dec. Snug interior
under a barrel roof. Aisle-less nave, and low W baptistery with
a big rose window over. Chancel with organ chamber on the

N side. On the S side is the vestry. – Stone PULPIT attached to the side of the chancel arch with access through an arch from the organ chamber. – STAINED GLASS. E window by *Harcourt M. Doyle*, 1970. The rose-window glass is by *Celtic Studios* of Swansea, 1986. – In 2004 a PARISH ROOM by *Buttress Fuller Alsop Williams* was planned, linked to the SW corner.

ST JOHN EVANGELIST, Higher Walton. 1882–5, by *Paley & Austin* at the expense of Sir Gilbert Greenall, the Warrington brewer. A glorious estate church, exquisitely detailed and composed. Not so large, with no aisles, with an imposing crossing tower crowned by a recessed spire. Austin designed some magnificent towers; this is one of the best. The decoration by chequerwork and flushwork was liked by him. The windows are mainly free Dec, some of them squarely framed, in a virtuoso variety of designs. Fine S side with porch, transept, and vestry. The timber framing of the porch, of course beautifully detailed, is a wonderful touch. Inside there is a little less to note, though the tower has a stone rib-vault on shafts starting from leaf corbels on the sturdy crossing piers. Barrel roof with stencilled panels. Unlike other Paley & Austin churches with crossing towers (e.g. St Matthew Highfield, Wigan), St John has a real crossing, i.e. not with choir beneath it. In the chancel the stepped PISCINA, SEDILIA and vestry door, all square-headed, make a beautiful group. – Excellent FITTINGS by the architects include a Derbyshire marble FONT, a PULPIT and an ORGAN CASE. – LIGHTING. Splendidly Art Deco fittings of 1934 by *Troughton & Young*. Unexpectedly harmonious. Including a spray-shaped light above the W window and a flat circular light with star under the tower vault. – STAINED GLASS by *Shrigley & Hunt*. Also a *Morris & Co.* window of 1929, S transept E. – Good LYCHGATE by the architects.

ST MATTHEW, Stretton Road, Stretton. 1870, by *G.G. Scott*, replacing a Commissioners' church of 1826–7 by *Thomas Hardwick*. The ever-observant Goodhart-Rendel noticed that the chancel (with its plate tracery) does not look like Scott, yet cannot be of 1826. Was there then someone else involved, say about 1860? Scott's work is E.E. W tower, nave and aisles. Scott could be depended on to do an earnest and dignified job, provided the money available was adequate. Goodhart-Rendel called the church 'solid, decent, well designed and unamusing'. – STAINED GLASS. W window by *Trena M. Cox*, 1939.

ST THOMAS, Stockton Heath. 1867–8, by *E.G. Paley*. A large church with a big SE tower. The church is faced with small, squared stones like tiling, and the tracery style is of *c.* 1300. Inside is white-painted brick and stone dressings. Only a S aisle (a N aisle was planned), the arcade with stiff-leaf capitals, and only a N transept, with odd details of the arch springing. – PAINTING. The chancel roof is decorated with panels incorporating six excellent life-sized angels by *Mary Farren* of Cambridge, of 1877. – The *Minton* TILE DECORATION of the chancel is the one thing one will remember most – unexpected

but not exactly attractive. 1877, designed by *R. Reynolds Rowe*.
– STAINED GLASS in the transept by *Hardman*, 1868. Elsewhere work by *Heaton, Butler & Bayne* and *Clayton & Bell*, of
the same date. Good Annunciation window by *Shrigley &
Hunt*, 1903.

ST WILFRED, Church Lane, Grappenhall. An interesting
church. The earliest part is the Norman corbel table preserved
in parts in the nave S wall and visible from the S aisle. Then
follows that part of the S aisle incorporating a chapel with
square-headed reticulated windows. A chantry was indeed
founded *c.* 1334 by William Boydell. The E of the two S windows
is a copy from 1850 when the chapel was extended one bay E;
the present E window replicates the original. A Boydell MON-
UMENT is in the chancel, an effigy of a knight, cross-legged.
Very heavily restored in the C19. Also preserved, though in bits
and pieces, is the STAINED GLASS of the chapel (in the most
easterly S window), plenty of parts of figures (including John
Baptist, St Bartholomew carrying his skin, and Mary Magda-
lene), and plenty of characteristic C14 green and yellow.

All the rest of the church was rebuilt about 1529–39. First
the W tower and the N aisle and arcade, and the chancel. Later
the S chapel was incorporated into a S aisle: a date of 1539 is on
one S arcade pier. Seven bays; no chancel arch. Octagonal piers,
clumsy capitals, double-chamfered arches. The arcades are of
different heights. The clerestory was added in 1833. Windows
are mainly elementary, square-headed with uncusped round-
headed lights, but in the W window and chancel E window
Perp is treated with proper panel tracery of a late form.
However, the present form of the E window may be of 1873–4,
when *Paley & Austin* restored the church. The N vestry is of
1851. – FONT. Norman, big, rectangular, with crude blank
arcading. Discovered buried under the floor in the C19 and
restored on new base. – CHEST. Extremely primitive parish
chest, simply a hollowed oak trunk. C12? – STOCKS. Inside;
replicas now in position outside the churchyard gates. – Victorian STAINED GLASS. Three S aisle windows by *Mayer* of
Munich, 1887. S aisle W, Adoration of the Lamb, 1890, by
Shrigley & Hunt.*

Across Church Lane, which retains cobbled paving, is the
OLD RECTORY, early C19 Gothic, stuccoed, with two canted
bay windows and Gothic treatment of the doorway too.

BRIDGEWATER CANAL. The Runcorn branch meanders from
E to W along a contour line up above the Ship Canal and
parallel to it. Construction here was *c.* 1769–71; the route was
complete in 1772; *James Brindley*, Chief Engineer. Many
single-arch BRIDGES and AQUEDUCTS (e.g. Lumb Brook
Bridge, Stockton Heath) carrying roads over and under, of
brick and stone in varying proportions.

THELWALL VIADUCTS. *See* p. 615.

---

*A sundial in the churchyard dated 1741 has been stolen.

West: Bank Quay, Liverpool Road, Bewsey,
Great Sankey and Penketh

The industrial development of Warrington began at Bank Quay at the end of the C17 (*see* p. 602). Liverpool Road is a C19 industrial district with bits and pieces of C19 works remaining. Great Sankey was a small village.

ST MARY, Liverpool Road (A57), Great Sankey. Brick; aisle-less. The body, with the polygonal W end beneath the tower, is 1767–9, the chancel and porch are *William Owen*, 1883, the strangely un-English bell-turret is 1868–9, and the tracery, of course, is C19 too. A surviving example of the C18 intersecting tracery in the W end. The interior is C19 as well. W gallery on spindly cast-iron Doric columns. Handsome, broad roof trusses, with kingposts, pierced and cusped panels and billeted tie-beams. – Big, artless PULPIT. Marble. 1883. – STAINED GLASS. The best is N, 1st W, by *Jones & Willis*. No date. – MONUMENTS. Of the few tablets, the best is to the Rev. Edward Lloyd, †1815. Putto beside an urn on a pedestal.

ST BARNABAS, Lovely Lane, Bewsey. *William Owen*, 1879. Clearly incomplete: it is missing planned aisles, chancel and SW spire. Simple, brick, triple lancets. – Superb *dalle de verre* STAINED GLASS, by *P. Fourmaintreaux* of *Whitefriars Glass*, 1963. Six windows, illustrating scenes from the life of St Barnabas. Primitivism; wonderful palettes (cf. the Whitefriars glass at St Helens Crematorium, p. 564). – The PULPIT, 1878, came from the first Christ Church, Waterloo (q.v.).

ST LUKE (former), Old Liverpool Road, Sankey Bridges. By *Bodley & Garner*, 1892–3. Now used for storage. One of the practice's most experimental and extraordinary designs. The church is small, stone and has no tower, just a bellcote with ogee-headed opening above the E gable of the nave. It does, however, have two naves, like e.g. Hannington in Northants (late C13), something the practice tried at two other churches as well. The twin naves have not two roofs but one, so that the very large five-bay arcade between them, with nobly slender Dec piers, rises to the ridge. This thoroughly offended Goodhart-Rendel, who thought it 'like some monstrosity crushed into a barn for storage'. There is also a N aisle, an addition which was made to look like an addition: with barrel roof, square piers and low arcade. But how to get two naves into one chancel? The architects' solution was to stop the E arch of the arcade just beyond its apex, where it is met by the apex of the chancel arch. There is a boldly carved angel where arch meets arch, but the junction remains problematic. The chancel itself is narrow with an elevated sanctuary and a flowing Dec window high in the E wall.

SACRED HEART (R.C.), Liverpool Road. 1894–5, by *Sinnott, Sinnott & Powell*. A strong, straightforward design, inspired no doubt by Bodley. Brick, W tower, broader than it is deep, with lancet windows in pairs and triplets above a big W window, but now missing its steep saddleback roof. W porch with passages to the entrances l. and r. Short chancel. s chapel with a hipped roof. Uninteresting, bare interior, but curious arcade capitals, like manicured leaves. w, organ, gallery. – Unusual early C20 STAINED GLASS (e.g. palette) in the E lancets, by *John Richardson* of Warrington.

FRIENDS' MEETING HOUSE (former), Meeting Lane, Penketh. The first, 1681, was replaced by the present in 1736, though you would struggle to guess that, given the utterly unsympathetic late C20 alterations and extensions.

BETHANY PENTACOSTAL CHURCH, Old Liverpool Road, Sankey Bridges. Dated 1905. Hard red brick, small. Minimally Gothic with flèche.

WARRINGTON HOSPITAL, Lovely Lane, Bewsey. On the E side of the site is the former Warrington Union WORKHOUSE. It is of 1851, E-plan and brick, with occasional label mouldings. N of it is the former workhouse infirmary, now the Kendrick Wing, by *William & Segar Owen*, 1899. Ward pavilions flank the administration block, which has terracotta pediments and a Baroque door surround. Inside this are delightful ceramic commemorative panels. The nurses' home on Lovely Lane is by *Geoffrey Owen* (younger son of Segar), 1939.

SANKEY STATION, Station Road, Great Sankey. Of *c.* 1873, the type of Widnes (*see* p. 656).

p. 21 BEWSEY OLD HALL, Bewsey Farm Close, E of Cromwell Avenue. In 2005 empty. Archaeology suggests that the first building, possibly a hunting lodge, was C12. From C13 it was the home of the Botelers, lords of the manor of Warrington until 1586. What one sees now is only the brick s wing, early C17 or possibly of before 1587 (though that would make it exceptionally early for brick in Lancashire). To the N was a medieval hall range, rebuilt in the C17 with porch and wing to create an E-plan, rebuilt again in the C18, and demolished *c.* 1830. The remaining s wing is of three storeys and two bays, the s bay projecting E under a gable. Details of the s wall suggest that it was originally only two storeys high, and that another wing was attached to it (e.g. truncated string courses, blocked first-floor door). Large mullioned-and-transomed windows, of eight or ten lights, and one of sixteen on the second floor. Those below on the s front are C19. In the gable is a stepped three-light window, a type more frequent in Yorkshire. The N wall, with two-storey porch in imitation of the C17 E one, is of *c.* 1830. Attached to the W is a Late Georgian wing, latterly a farmhouse, and to the s by a single-storey link, a C19 kitchen. Little of interest inside has survived alteration, dereliction and post-1978 stabilisation work, though there is evidence that a second-floor room was hastily fitted up in the early C17 with a partition and elaborate finishes, possibly for the use of James I during his stay here in 1617. The remnants of wall decoration are very sweet.

The house is surrounded by a MOAT, now dry to the E. A gatehouse was shown in 1724 guarding a bridge across this arm. Archaeology has revealed traces on the platform of subsidiary buildings N and possibly S, and a terraced C17 garden. The site is part of the Sankey Valley Park (*see* p. 639).

BEWSEY NEW HALL, W of Camp Road. Part of the W wing of this half-timbered monstrosity, largely demolished in the 1940s. 1860–1, almost certainly by *W.G. Habershon* for the 4th Lord Lilford. His wife, evidently a woman of taste, disliked it so much that she refused to live in it.

THE BLACK HORSE pub, Old Liverpool Road, Sankey Bridges. Built as a yeoman's house, with a timber-framed cross-wing dated 1632. The truss exposed in the gable combines a king-post and a herringbone pattern of raked struts – typical of Lancashire – with upper cruck. The other part of the house, of two bays, is a different phase; the rendered brick probably disguises another timber frame. A blocked door in the centre, in front of back-to-back fireplaces. Inside, many heavy beams.

CROSFIELD'S FACTORY (former), Liverpool Road, Bank Quay. Company offices, 1885, by *William Owen*. Freely Wrenaissance, of three storeys and three bays, with a door hood below a flush balcony in the centre, and flanking this big open pediments. JOSEPH CROSFIELDS & SONS LTD. emblazoned in tesserae beneath the cornice. Two-storey wing, r., and attached to that a horizontally sleek silver-panelled new wing, 1994 by *Brock Carmichael Architects*, pivoting about a drum. Thomas Patten began Warrington's industrialisation here in the 1690s (*see* p. 602). Joseph Crosfield started making soap on the site in 1815. It still produces detergents.

PENKETH HALL, Hall Nook, Penketh. Farmhouse. 1757 according to a now lost internal datemark. Five bays, two storeys, brick. How old are the worn sandstone lower walls of the farm building to the SW?

TIM PARRY JOHNATHAN BALL YOUNG PEOPLE'S CENTRE, S end of Cromwell Avenue (A574). A memorial to the two boys killed by the 1993 IRA bomb. The building, by *Graham Locke* of *Buttress Fuller Alsop Williams*, 1999–2001, is refreshingly good, designed with a light and generous touch inside and out following consultation with children, so as not to intimidate. Thus, to break up the deceptively large bulk (which contains offices, a café, games room, a hall, and accommodation for forty-two), the basic plan is a gentle S, and the roof-line is broken up. The wide-eaved, standing-seam zinc monopitch roofs, one half pitched one way and the other half the opposite, are fractured outwards and upwards by low towers, some with gull-wing roofs, and other sections. Walls are clad in weathered timber and have crisp fenestration. This extends from floor to ceiling for full-height spaces, such as the entrance hall which extends through the middle of the building, with a no-nonsense steel bridge across it. Grounds landscaped for play.

WARRINGTON GARDEN SUBURB. A company was established in 1907 and two sites selected, but only one begun, on a triangular plot in the junction of Liverpool and Penketh Roads. Only twenty-three houses were completed by 1914, of which

the first and best are Nos. 17, 19, 21 and 23 PENKETH ROAD.
The architects were *J. E. Wright, Garnett & Wright* and the foundation stone was laid by Ebenezer Howard himself in 1908. A
terrace of four cottages, looking more like a prosperous pair.
In characteristic Garden Suburb style: bays, gables, big chimneys, tiled roofs and roughcast. The result is extremely handsome, particularly the forest of chimneys, and marred only by
replacement windows.

WARRINGTON NEW TOWN

Warrington New Town was designated in 1968, twenty-two years
after Stevenage, the first. Earlier New Towns were intended
primarily to house 'overspill' population generated by slum
clearances (cf. Skelmersdale), but by 1970 the function had
shifted to managing the development of natural growth spots,
and to attracting industry and investment. This element was
particularly important in the North West as a cornerstone of
policy intended to reverse population drift away from the
region. Thus Warrington was designated to accommodate
Mancunian overspill, but by the time the Outline Plan was
approved in 1973 the primary purpose had become managing
growth. The town's situation on main railway and canal routes
midway between the two major regional centres caused it to
be identified as a principal regional growth centre; more significantly, it was also to be a hub of the new motorway network,
at the convergence of the M6, the M62 and M56 opened from
1963. Extensive derelict or soon-to-be-vacated Ministry of
Defence sites also provided thousands of acres for redevelopment. No other New Town appeared so certain of growth.

The change of emphasis between 1968 and 1973 created different PLANNING approaches. Dropping the overspill requirement meant voluntary rather than enforced population growth,
with an emphasis on private housing for sale as against Development Corporation housing for rent, whilst, as managing
natural growth was considered less predictable, a fluid,
flexible outline plan was prepared rather than a rigid masterplan. Warrington New Town was one of only three New Towns★
to be grafted onto a substantial existing town. This meant that
the Development Corporation had to work with county and
rural district councils and the County Borough, and was able
to exercise direct control only over the outer districts. In contrast to earlier Development Corporations, it saw its main
functions as co-ordination, monitoring and stimulation. It
could set an example with housing and industrial schemes, but
the all-important central shopping, cultural and transport
infrastructure was the responsibility of the County Borough.

The 1973 OUTLINE PLAN foresaw a rise in population
from 130,000 to 200,000 by 1991. Adopting the land-use and

★Along with Peterborough and Northampton.

transportation proposals of *Austin-Smith:Lord*'s 1969 Draft Master Plan, it divided the designated area of 18,612 acres (7,532 hectares) into five districts determined by natural and transport features rather than by artificial concepts of ideal township size. They are: BIRCHWOOD, E of the M6 on the site of the Risley Ordnance Factory; PADGATE, W of the M6, making substantial use of an old RAF camp; WESTBROOK, W of the existing town, including the vast RAF Burtonwood complex; OLD WARRINGTON (*see* p. 603); and BRIDGEWATER, S of the Manchester Ship Canal. A network of urban expressways was proposed, and each district was to have a district centre and smaller local centres providing shops and services, linked by a system of footpaths. No housing was to be more than four hundred metres along a path from one of these centres. *Hugh Canning*, from 1976 the Development Corporation's second chief architect and planning officer, wanted to break from the conventions of New Town housing – Radburn-type segregation of vehicles and pedestrians, the rigid hierarchy of distributor and access roads – and reintroduce street frontage schemes (a policy he called 'Come back street, all is forgiven'). He adopted ideas from the Dutch Woonerf system to overturn the supremacy of the car in residential areas. Tenants moving from inner cities wanted suburban housing, and so densities were kept low and houses were provided with large private gardens and parking spaces rather than service courts and back yards (cf. Skelmersdale), minimising the traditional differences between public housing and private development. To the non-expert visitor Canning's vision is not immediately apparent: Warrington is still very much a New Town – overwhelmingly low-density, abundantly landscaped, very disorientating, and car-dependent.

Development has in general followed the 1973 plan, though thankfully some aspects of the road system (especially the fly-overs planned at Bridge Foot) were not realised. The County Borough's contribution was principally expanded town-centre shopping facilities and a 'cultural quarter' around Palmyra Square, which took twenty-five years to get under way. The impact on old Warrington is discussed above. In the 1970s the outlook for manufacturing was grossly overestimated, but conversely the phenomenal growth in distribution systems and services and the retail sector was not fully anticipated. Warrington, with its excellent transport links, has thrived as a centre for these since 1980 in ways few other parts of the North West have, and they now make up the bulk of the land designated for employment uses. The Development Corporation was wound up in 1989, having combined with Runcorn in Cheshire a few years earlier, and its responsibilities were transferred to various local authorities and Government agencies.

During his tenure Hugh Canning attempted to raise design standards, believing good ARCHITECTURE to be fundamental to attracting investment, and for a while the town rivalled Milton Keynes as the most progressive public patron in the

country. At the forefront were housing by *Richard MacCormac*
and *Terry Farrell* at Birchwood and industrial units by *Nicholas
Grimshaw* at Winwick Quay, flagship projects intended to set
standards for future development. In the long term this failed.
Some of the most recent private housing schemes are pleasantly planned, but architecturally they are the usual pastiche
boxes. Offices, warehouses and retail outlets are almost without
exception the styleless, scale-less, nowheresville sheds that are
the norm of contemporary motorway society.

A greater achievement has been the LANDSCAPE DESIGN,
which has matured impressively to bring structure and soft-
ness to a decidedly uninspiring canvas – flat, featureless and
blighted by extensive derelict military installations. From the
outset the landscaping was an integrated element of planning,
with landscape architects embedded in design teams. The concepts adopted were typical of the third-generation New Towns.
The landscapes of early New Towns – sycamores, poplars and
swathes of grass – proved to be expensive to maintain, so a new
approach was developed based on woodland and hardy shrubs.
The framework of naturalistic linear parks along existing
waterways, corridor-planting the length of highways, and
woodland shelter belts was intended to create a continuous
backcloth of landscape that knitted together the settlement and
defined its parts. This approach blended with an emerging
interest in ecological landscaping – conserving and restoring
the natural landscape – to create an environment far removed
from the manicured tradition of municipal parks and gardens.
The idea was explored to its fullest at Warrington, particularly
at the Risley Moss Nature Reserve, an ecologically important
site of peat bog and restored woodland. More recent parts,
e.g. at Westbrook, are more formal, with avenues etc., but well
implemented.

BIRCHWOOD

The greater part of this district, bounded by the M6 to the w
and the M62 to the n, was made up of the former Risley Royal
Ordnance Factory, built 1939–41 and largely abandoned in 1961.
The district plan of 1974 was organised around the UK Atomic
Energy Research Establishment facility, established on part of the
factory site after the Second World War. This became the focus
of one of the United Kingdom's first Science Parks, intended to
attract research and development operations. Around this are the
district centre and three residential areas: Locking Stumps (w),
Gorse Covert (e), and Oakwood (s).

BIRCHWOOD DISTRICT CENTRE, Dewhurst Road. The
lynchpin is the SHOPPING CENTRE, 1980, low and deep with
bright enamel panelling and an internal street. Library, school,
sports centre and health centre are also included. It is located
in the sw corner of Birchwood for the admirable purpose of
integrating it with a new railway station. But the planning is

all wrong, with the parts isolated from one another by the dominating car parking and distributor road, and the whole thing lacks a sense of place.

OAKWOOD LOCAL CENTRE, Admiral's Road. A church, a school and some shops. In other countries they would be grouped compactly around a little paved and tree-lined square.

RISLEY MOSS VISITORS' CENTRE, s end of Moss Gate. By the *Building Design Partnership*, 1980. A timber building buried in the woods on the edge of the Risley Moss Nature Reserve. In plan, five octagons, some stretched. The rather bland, boarded elevations appear to float on the concrete substructure.

HOUSING. KINGSALE DRIVE, Locking Stumps, begun 1974, was one of the first phases, a private development by *Whelmar*, who were also required to create the adjoining golf course as bait for golf-loving middle managers. Architecturally far more interesting are two subsequent and parallel developments in OAKWOOD which have matured well. *MacCormac & Jamieson*'s scheme on Redshank Lane off Ordnance Avenue and *Terry Farrell*'s (of the *Farrell & Grimshaw Partnership*) lanes s of Admiral's Lane, public housing projects both designed in 1978, make an interesting comparison. They respond to the policy of Hugh Canning, the Development Corporation's Chief Architect, to introduce street frontage schemes (*see* p. 635), though neither abandons separate pedestrian routes; MacCormac's scheme has a particularly complex network. The architects took very different approaches to the requirement to anticipate the needs and desires of the (then unknown) tenants.

Richard MacCormac produced a 'perimeter development' evolved from earlier schemes of his such as Pollards Hill, South London. Six U-plan four-storey 'chalets' front the district distributor road to the N to establish a substantial N boundary, introducing verticality and a sense of enclosure in the drab landscape. The architect patronisingly declared these suitable for the elderly because they afforded views of pedestrians and vehicles. In the shelter of the chalets, terraces of two-storey monopitch houses are grouped around the access road – these are Canning's street frontages – and parallel courts. All the buildings have brick ground floors and timber upper stages clad in enamel panels with vertical wooden strips, like a sort of bizarre mock timber framing: MacCormac adopted an unashamedly middle-class ideal of stockbroker Tudorbethan (albeit as ordered and reassembled by a Modernist), to appeal to the aspirations of tenants. Plans arc based on half-levels. The mock-Tudor style attracted criticism when new, but the chalets were well built, the established landscaping has softened the initially stark perimeter blocks, and the humanly scaled courts combine in a satisfyingly intricate layout where the car is definitely subordinated to the pedestrian.

Farrell took Canning's ideas one step further by doing away with access roads altogether. The distributor road is fronted by cheerful enamel-panelled three-storey flats with external steps to the first floor, though as the neighbouring local centre was never built up to similar heights as planned, they stand out slightly awkwardly. Behind these, four parallel lanes are carefully and charmingly extended amongst trees, petering out into woodland to the s. The lanes are lushly leafy and intimate – without separate pavements, after the Woonerf concept – and seem to capture the intimacy and friendliness of idealised village lanes. Farrell's intention to make them communal spaces inhabited by all, not public space shunned by all, appears to have been realised. The houses, in pairs and fours, are enlivened by wooden trellises, verandas and screens. These are applied to a 'universal core' of services, kitchen and bathroom, to which a standard timber-framed skin could be expanded by occupiers to meet their individual needs. Though this adaptability lay at the heart of the architect's approach, few seem to have taken advantage of it.

BIRCHWOOD PARK. The former United Kingdom Atomic Energy Research Establishment (from 1954, the Atomic Energy Authority) site E of Faraday Street retains the grid layout of the Royal Ordnance Factory. 1950s sawtooth-roofed laboratories, and a big blank former reactor block. Its two six-storey slab offices on the W side of the street are of *c.* 1956 by *T.L. Viney* and *R.S. Brocklesby* and absolutely of their date. The rest of Birchwood was conceived by the Development Corporation as a Science Park along US lines, with pavilions set in leafy parkland, like a campus. Of this early, optimistic phase the best building, designed by *Chamberlin, Powell & Bon* like a Modernist peripteral temple, has been demolished. On Birchwood Park Avenue is British Nuclear Fuels' HINTON HOUSE, 1984, by *DEGW*, the most inventive building. The bulk is to a certain extent broken up by a W-plan and tiered wings. This, along with the gablets and deep eaves of the roofs and numerous planted roof terraces, creates a presumably intentional pagoda aesthetic. Dense, award-winning landscaping, though the hoped-for hanging gardens do not really hang. Elsewhere, design has descended since the 1980s into the usual business-park collection of brick-and-tinted-glass offices (now routinely with brises-soleil, and cladding instead of brick), with increasing densities squeezing out landscaping. A recent example is ERLANG HOUSE for Vodafone, by *BDP*. The area E of the UKAEA site has been colonised by vast distribution warehouses and parades of ribbed business-unit sheds.

PADGATE

Much of the development here took place on the site of a Second World War RAF camp N of the small village of Padgate (Outer Warrington, North and East). The development at CINNAMON BROW has good landscaping, and some quite successful HOUSING, e.g. the first phase by *Austin-Smith:Lord*, in collaboration with the Development Corporation, on the streets surrounding the junction of Enfield Park Road and Crab Lane. 1980. Simple brick houses pleasantly composed on serpentine cul-de-sacs in small staggered or grouped terraces, with broken roof-lines and dense, enclosing landscaping, creating some lovely little compositions. The Development Corporation wanted to remove the stigma attached to public housing, such as this, by minimising the differences with private developments. Here the game is given away only by the absence of garages and the smaller size of private gardens, sacrificed to allow more generous public space within the density target of twelve houses per acre. Pedestrian routes snaking through secluded planting and little parks are pleasantly leafy in the summer, but surely threatening on a dark winter's night.

s of the railway is the GRANGE EMPLOYMENT AREA, the first industrial area to be developed by the Development Corporation. Big distribution sheds, but also, on Kingsland Grange, the intriguing BARCLAYS BANK PAPER AND METAL STORE, c. 1979, by the bank's architect *Don Collins*, with the structural engineers *White, Young & Partners*. A building guaranteed to instil peace of mind in Barclays' customers. The unexceptional-sounding 'paper and metal' is of course cash, and this building, though very sculptural, is an utterly functional fortress designed with the help of the Ministry of Defence to withstand military-scale attack, with massive windowless concrete walls and rounded corners (to deflect missiles, apparently). But the dominant feature is the flamboyant double-curved roof. This is a concrete hyperbolic paraboloid shell, a structure chosen to meet the demanding requirement for an assault-proof structure requiring no intermediate support.

WESTBROOK

Substantially a redevelopment of the vast RAF Burtonwood site. The airfield's main runway now forms the foundations of the M62 w of the Sankey Brook. In 2005 five hangars of c. 1939 were still standing on the undeveloped section to its N. A masterplan by *RTKL* would complete redevelopment of the airfield by extending Westbrook w on both sides of the M62 for mixed uses. To the s the district merges with Great Sankey (Outer Warrington, West).

SANKEY VALLEY PARK. An attractive naturalistic park created in the little valley through which the disused SANKEY BROOK NAVIGATION canal of 1757 (*see* p. 52) runs N–S. It incorporates the grounds of Bewsey Old Hall.

BURTONWOOD MOTORWAY SERVICES, Junction 9, M62. [124] 1972–4, by *Patrick Gwynne* for the Ministry of Transport and Trust Houses Forte. A more famous work by Gwynne for Forte is The Dell restaurant in Hyde Park (1965); though this commission lacks the delicacy of The Dell, it is an interesting variation on it, fleetingly bringing imagination to a normally derided building type. Two identical free-standing pavilions flank the motorway like a gateway (to where – Liverpool?), each single-storeyed and octagonal in plan, with dramatic ribbed copper-panelled roofs that sweep up into central chimneys inspired, one presumes, by medieval kitchens such as Wells. Inevitably, they are known locally as the witches' hats. Inside, before alteration, there were restaurants, and separate cafeterias for lorry drivers, with open roofs exposing the concrete beams.

WESTBROOK CENTRE, Westbrook Crescent. A district centre (i.e. shops, offices, cinemas, schools etc.), illustrating how the New Town's architecture has descended into a brick sub-Postmodern vernacular since the early 1980s. Here car is king: this is a giant car park that planting can't disguise, with buildings scattered about. The pompous pedestrian entrance, a Postmodern propylaeum, is therefore a rather redundant gesture.

GEMINI BUSINESS and RETAIL PARKS, along Europa Boulevard parallel to the M62. The usual big crimpled-skin sheds and business units, with tinted-glass cutaway corners, but also a modern cultural icon, the UK's first IKEA FURNITURE STORE, completed in 1987. In line with the Swedish firm's then policy, the outline design was prepared by the *IKEA In-house Design Team* in order to maintain brand identity, and implemented by a local practice, here *Kingham Knight Associates*. The structure is a conventionally clad steel shed, but handled confidently to make virtues of the big, blank, boxy shape. Bold use of colour (Sweden's colours, blue and yellow) and simplicity and crispness are keynotes, since marred by alterations. Contrast this with the fussiness that attempts to hide the scale and true nature of the Marks & Spencer store to the w.

HOUSING, substantially private, is the usual developers' brick boxes, but the plan is often thoughtfully and successfully constructed by developing existing watercourses and ponds as informal foci, e.g. along Kingsdale Road. Standards have been maintained with the most recent developments, along Kingswood Road: housing pleasantly grouped around new greens, e.g. Castle Green and Tourney Green, a good avenue along Westbrook Way, and a new tree-ringed platform at Kingswood Green.

WINWICK QUAY INDUSTRIAL ESTATE, s of the M62, w of Winwick Road (A49). The first building, of 1979, was WINWICK QUAY 4, on Chetham Court off Calver Road. By *Nicholas Grimshaw*, then of the *Farrell & Grimshaw Partnership*. The brief was for a highly adaptable industrial building that would establish an exciting image for the estate, a former refuse tip. The result was one of a sequence of industrial buildings by Grimshaw that began with the Herman Miller factory, Bath, in 1976, with a simple steel frame to which easily adjustable internal divisions and standardised, interchangeable aluminium cladding panels are attached. The concept was of a plan that could be rearranged quickly and simply to increase building efficiency and lifespan; at Winwick this was extended to embrace multiple occupancy. Stainless-steel toilet modules

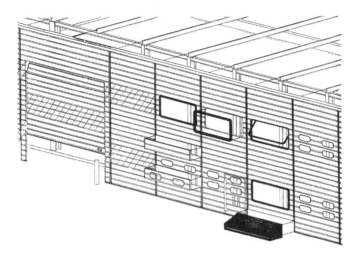

Warrington, Winwick Quay 4 industrial unit,
by Nicholas Grimshaw, 1979. Detail of cladding system

that could be plugged in at any point around the perimeter
attracted particular attention. The exterior is a clean box, 110
by 70 metres (358 by 228 feet), with a flat roof and rounded
corners and eaves. When completed this was crisp and gleam-
ing and elegant, but the cladding is battered and stained now,
and planting rather hides it.

To the N on Calver Road are the three units of *Grimshaw*'s (by
then *Nicholas Grimshaw & Partners*) second phase, WINWICK
QUAY 7, 1983, aesthetically similar but without No. 4's inter-
changeable panels. Beyond them, the eight units of WINWICK
QUAY 5 by the *Warrington New Town Development Corporation
Architect's Department*, more conventional.

BARROW OLD HALL, Barrow Old Hall Lane. The house has
gone, but the medieval MOAT remains water-filled on three
sides.

BRIDGEWATER

Entirely residential, and the least developed New Town district
by 2004. Grafted onto existing suburban settlements – Stockton
Heath, Thelwall and Walton (*see* Outer Warrington, S of the Ship
Canal). At PEWTERSPEAR GREEN ROAD in 2005, a most unreal
sight – Neo-Georgian terraces, of three storeys, rising amidst
fields. These are part of a *Bryant Homes* development, and the
proportions are not bad. Tuscan porches. The landscaping is generous – the distributor road is a broad sweeping avenue of oaks
and pleached beeches – but the Corinthian columns flanking the
bottom of Pewterspear Green Road are verging on the kitsch.

WATERLOO

At the mouth of the Mersey. Nothing survives of the hamlet of
Crosby Seabank, which grew in the C19 into the 'flourishing sea-
bathing place' of Waterloo. The arrival of the railway in 1848
accelerated development as a middle-class seaside suburb of
Liverpool, and today it is contiguous with Great Crosby and
Blundellsands to the N (qq.v.).

CHRIST CHURCH, Waterloo Road. 1891–4. Tower, 1899. One of
Paley, Austin & Paley's very finest,★ replacing an unsound
church of 1840. Red stone. Five-bay nave and clerestory, aisles,
chancel, N transept and mighty NE tower. This with stern rectangularity and magnificent belfry stage (see the depth and
tracery of the openings), set off by a thin pinnacled stair-turret.
A strictly symmetrical W end with porches flanking the aisles
and a baptistery bulging out beneath the window. The vocabulary is very characteristic: a free Perp style; inventive tracery
with Dec elements, e.g. the great W window; distinctly Art
Nouveau details, e.g. on churchyard wall gatepiers, above
doorways and in aisle windows; the extensive use of the texts
Laus Deo and Laudate Dominum to embellish doorways and
the tower parapet; and an overall rectangularity. The INTERIOR
is equally majestic, enhanced by the richly striated stone. The
absence of fittings (they disappeared after redundancy in
1982)★★ creates a romantic, melancholy atmosphere. Round
arcade piers with four fillets, arches dying into imposts and big
springers. Their mouldings suggest a fan-vault, but the roof is
a wooden sexpartite vault: unusually for the practice, which
favoured open roofs. Chancel arch almost as wide as the building. Two-bay chancel with broad seven-light window. To the r.,
a chapel, to the l., a complex composition of N transept and
organ under the tower. Its most surprising and prominent
member is a tremendous inner buttress for the tower treated
in a way Lutyens would have done later. – STAINED GLASS. E
and W windows (Te Deum and the Twelve Apostles respectively), but also clerestory, by *Shrigley & Hunt.* – The chancel
S clerestory windows have glass of *c.* 1855 from the old church.
    The church is surrounded by streets of post-1850 middle-
ranking HOUSES, the earliest still quite Georgian in character
and of chequered brickwork, e.g. in Waterloo Road itself.

ST FAITH, Crosby Road North. By *Grayson & Ould.* Built
1898–1900 at the expense of Douglas Horsfall (*see* p. 251). It
is a large edifice of red Accrington brick and red sandstone
dressings, with an octagonal SE turret capped by a pointy roof.
Free Geometrical tracery, e.g. in the big W window facing the
road. Flying buttresses over the aisles. Effective and atmospheric interior of brick with simple sandstone dressings. Broad
nave with narrow passage aisles, clerestory, and fine hammer-

---

★ Though the competition was won by *Birkett & Langham.*
★★ The church was subsequently vested in the Churches Conservation Trust and
restored in the 1990s.

beam roof. Transepts. The chancel is partially aisled and is narrower than the nave. – REREDOS. A magnificent triptych by *Salviati*, in a frame carved in Suffolk. Installed in 1901. With masses of Dec tracery and gold leaf. The panels are glass mosaic; the central panel is the Crucifixion and the wings have lovely angels. – FONT. Veined marble; octagonal on a cluster of five shafts. – PULPIT. Large, with Early Renaissance tendencies. – CHANCEL SCREEN. By *Giles Gilbert Scott*, installed in 1921 in memory of Horsfall's son, killed in the First World War. Perp, refined and delicate. – Beautiful brass ALTAR LAMPS. 1900. – STAINED GLASS. The best is the N aisle, 1st from E, by *John Wimbolt* in the workshop of *Herbert Bryans*. To Ferdinand Anderton Lathom, 1902. S aisle, various inter-war windows by *James Powell & Sons*.

ST JOHN, St John's Road. 1864–5, by *William Culshaw*. Coursed, quarry-faced buff sandstone. Lancets. No aisles; a lower chancel. Bellcote over the W gable; flèche over the E end of the nave now missing. Odd dormers. Matching transepts of 1869. Hammerbeam roof. – CHANCEL FITTINGS by *F.H. Crossley*, 1936. – STAINED GLASS. One window by *Henry Holiday*, 1885. To Rowland Crawford Armour.

ST MARY, Park Road, Waterloo Park. Built 1882–3 to the designs of *W.B. Habershon* to serve the residential estate of Waterloo Park (*see* p. 645). E.E., cruciform, with a very squat crossing tower where a steeple was intended. Narthex added 1906–7. The main windows are emphasised by shafting; the triplets in the transepts and the E end are really quite handsome. Not much else is. Local purply-red sandstone – quarry-faced – for the walling, Bath and Corsham stone for dressings. Clustered arcade piers.

ST THOMAS (R.C.), Great George's Road. Opened 1877. By *Edmund Kirby*. Coursed buff sandstone. No tower. The W front, to the street, combines Geometrical plate tracery (in the round window in the gable) with Geometrical bar tracery (in the tall two-light windows beneath). Between is a statue of St Thomas in a niche. Below all this is a central gabled portal projecting up from a low lean-to roof. Aisles with lancets either side. – ALTAR. Designed by the architect, 1893.

WATERLOO UNITED FREE CHURCH, Crosby Road North. 1891 etc., by *George Baines & Sons*. Red brick with sandstone dressings. An attractive street front in Arts and Crafts Gothic. It consists of: r., the W end of the church with a large, freely Dec window and flanking projections containing entrances and gallery stairs; and, l., a smaller version which is the hall, with the same Art Nouveau-ish finials and the same narrow square turrets, but with more archaeologically correct tracery in the W window, and catslide projections like the ends of aisles. Inside, light and bright, with slender metal columns supporting exposed roof trusses. – PULPIT, combining Gothic panelling with Arts and Crafts-style steps (e.g. cut-out hearts).

TOWN HALL (former), Great George's Road. Built in 1862 for the Waterloo-with-Seaforth Local Board of Health. By *F.S.*

Spencer Yates, a surveyor. It looks like a big classical villa. Three bays of rock-faced stone and ashlar dressing, with a Doric porch and ground-floor entablature. First-floor windows with pediments, eaves cornice with both dentils and modillions. Attached to the rear, a higher block of 1892, forming a T-plan, with a hall on the upper storey. A low mid-C20 Neo-Georgian extension sticks out from the back of this.

LIBRARY and CIVIC HALL, Crosby Road North. By *G. Ronald Mason*. Low and mainly brick. The two-storey library wing facing the road, of 1964–8, is almost fully glazed, with only a low masonry plinth and first-floor timber dado. The entrance is at the r. end in a broad round corner tower carrying a beacon. Extending back from this is the hall wing, opened 1975, with blank brick walls expressing the form of the 400-seat auditorium.

ADULT EDUCATION CENTRE, Cambridge Road. *See* Waterloo Grammar School, below.

WATERLOO GRAMMAR SCHOOL (former), Cambridge Road. Now an Adult Education Centre. Opened 1912. Brick with stone dressings. Wrenaissance detailing. Cupola.

CHRIST CHURCH NATIONAL SCHOOL (former), Great George's Road. 1842. Single-storey, brick. Stone cross-windows in incongruous surrounds under label moulds.

FIRST WORLD WAR MEMORIAL, Great Crosby Road. By *Francis W. Doyle*. Unveiled 1921.

POTTER'S BARN, Crosby Road South. *See* Seaforth.

SEAFRONT. Waterloo exists because it has the nearest seafront to Liverpool. This is less evident today because of the construction over the sands of municipal gardens and a large marine lake, and because of the looming cranes and wind turbines of the Royal Seaforth Dock, created on reclaimed land at the N extremity of the Liverpool dock system (*see* p. 278). The name is taken from the Royal Waterloo Hotel, which opened in 1816 as the start of an intended sea-bathing resort. Now called the ROYAL HOTEL, it is at the S end of Marine Terrace at the corner with Great George's Road. Nine bays, two-and-a-half storeys, rendered and quite plain. The middle three bays are recessed slightly; the r. return of five bays has a pediment over the projecting middle three (and there is another on the E end of this wing). Next comes MARINE TERRACE itself, begun 1822 at the N end, but still incomplete in 1850. More a row than a terrace, of prettily painted little two-storey houses with delicate filigree cast-iron verandas to the ground floors; that to No. 4 in a charming Craggesque (*see* p. 65) Gothic. Many of the houses with bracketed eaves. Right behind are two fifteen-storey blocks of flats of the 1960s. Next is MARINE CRESCENT, begun in 1826, which is not a crescent, but a slightly canted row of more modest, frequently altered cottages. Stuccoed too, and most with iron verandas in a variety of patterns; those to Nos. 11–16 similar to that already seen at No. 4 Marine Terrace.

Then, across Wellington Street, is ADELAIDE TERRACE, begun in the early 1830s but not complete by 1850 either. Here the houses are again of two storeys and mainly three bays. Very nearly regular, and dignified and unified by entablature mouldings and giant Doric pilasters, but not the pediments shown in a prospectus. Painted assorted pastel shades, seaside fashion. The prospectus described the terrace as only the southern section of a larger scheme. Neither the 'extensive hotel' nor the matching N wing materialised. In their stead, N of Blucher Street, is BEACH LAWN, where restrained Regency gives way to a riot of mid-Victorian gables, bays and brackets and enriched architraves to windows of all shapes and sizes. Mostly the features are Italianate, but also (e.g. No. 1 of 1867) Gothic. The common vocabulary and the varied tones of stucco maintain a sense of harmony in the staggered façades. There are lovely cast-iron verandas again too. The houses were built from the early 1860s to the mid 1870s. Thomas Henry Ismay, founder of the White Star Line (of *Titanic* fame), built No. 13 for himself in 1865, and was one of the developers behind some of the others.* The architect *J.F. Doyle* had some involvement too. The greatest misfits are the end two, Nos. 16 and 17. By *Henry Sumners* for Dr Drysdale, 1861. Altered; originally both of unpainted brick and High Victorian Gothic, and quite wild in their details. They contained systems of central heating (by hot water) and ventilation which Dr Drysdale and his friend Dr Hayward advocated for healthy living (*see* p. 374).

Running behind the seafront terraces are streets with C19 cottages. The most charming, and amongst the earliest, are Nos. 2–14 MERSEY VIEW, a bit further N. Brick, with casements with Y-tracery in simple stone surrounds. Dated 1823.

WATERLOO PARK. A residential development with a picturesque layout, begun 1864. Considerable infill and redevelopment (including hospitals), but some big, three-storey houses remain from the first ten years, e.g. No. 5 BRAMHALL ROAD – brick, some Gothic details – and opposite, on Park Road, STONEHOUSE – rock-faced stone with Gothic columns for jambs.

WESTHEAD *see* ORMSKIRK

WHISTON

4090

In the SE corner of the old Lancashire coalfield. Once a colliery village, now suburban sprawl merging with Prescot and Rainhill (qq.v.).

ST NICHOLAS, Windy Arbor Road. 1864–8, by *G.E. Street*. An earnest work of architecture with nothing done just to please. Buff sandstone with red sandstone dressings. The porch tower stands S of the S aisle and is unfortunately incomplete. Lancets, stepped lancet lights, and some plate tracery. Inside, rock-faced

---

*In 1885 he moved to Dawpool, a house by *Norman Shaw* on the Wirral. This is now demolished.

stone is exposed. The piers are round. To the s chapel, which externally has its own roof, there are two openings filled with large-scale tracery in the style of *c.* 1300. – STAINED GLASS. The s chapel E window, 1873, W windows, 1897, and the s chapel s windows, 1898, all by *Morris & Co.* The W lancets with angels and a youthful Christ high up in the centre of a small rose window. The 1873 lancets, with angelic musicians, are by *Morris* himself; the 1898 lancets, with saints and musical angels, are by *Burne-Jones.* E window no doubt by *Clayton & Bell.*

WHISTON HOSPITAL, Warrington Road, 1 m. NE of St Nicholas. A large site, begun as the Prescot Union Workhouse in 1842–3. On the s side of the road are, E, parallel ward blocks dated 1888, and, W, a low and long range with label moulds, dated 1897. Little CHAPEL dated 1881. On the N side more C19 brick blocks incorporating an early C19 three-bay house. This has a porch with pairs of Corinthian columns, and a door with a big fanlight.

CARR HOUSE FARMHOUSE, Windy Arbor Road, ½ m. SW of St Nicholas. Two phases, both C17. The r. one, dated 1660 over a blocked doorway, of two bays including a cross-wing. Some windows altered, some mullioned. The l. part, of Coal Measures stone, one bay, with altered mullioned windows. Also a stone BARN and attached farm buildings. There is a datestone of 1653 on a now internal gable wall in the barn. The present external appearance dates from 1819, when it was extended and altered. The date is carved on a door lintel. Also another datestone, of 1506, *ex situ.*

HALSNEAD PARK, E of St Nicholas. *Sir John Soane*'s only house in Lancashire was demolished in 1932 to make way for a colliery. Built 1789, it was surprisingly conventional, the façade without obvious Soanisms. The LODGES are not his, but early C19. There is one on Arbor Road opposite St Nicholas and a better one on Fox's Bank Lane. Single-storeyed with pyramid roof. Crude label moulds, round-headed mullioned windows and an odd porch – stone, unmoulded and round-arched. It stands inside rusticated GATEPIERS with big ball finials.

OLD HALSNEAD, W of Fox's Bank Lane, 1 m. SE of St Nicholas. Mid- to late C17. Four bays, baffle-entry plan, rendered. The third bay has a two-storey porch with round-arched entrance. Regular five-light mullioned windows; the ground-floor ones originally with transoms?

WIDNES

Widnes had only 2,209 inhabitants in 1841. In 1847 John Hutchinson established alkali works, and the town grew rapidly into a centre of the chemical industries. By 1891 30,000 were living there. Incorporation came in 1892. In 2000, with extended boundaries, the population was nearly 55,000. Hutchinson was drawn by the excellent communications: in 1833 the rival St Helens & Runcorn Gap Railway and Sankey Brook Navigation

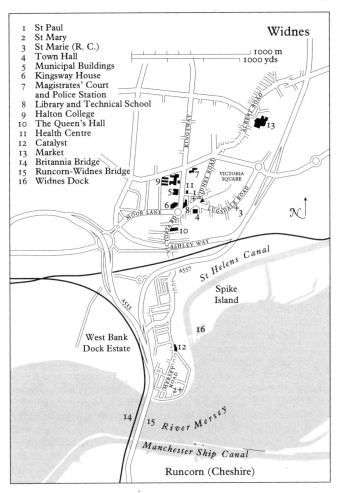

1 St Paul
2 St Mary
3 St Marie (R. C.)
4 Town Hall
5 Municipal Buildings
6 Kingsway House
7 Magistrates' Court
  and Police Station
8 Library and Technical School
9 Halton College
10 The Queen's Hall
11 Health Centre
12 Catalyst
13 Market
14 Britannia Bridge
15 Runcorn-Widnes Bridge
16 Widnes Dock

Widnes

canal arrived in the salt marshes facing Runcorn across the Mersey, establishing small docks for the export of coal. This is what made the town. Today the chemical industry is still the most important employer, though a fraction of its former size: new processes took it to new locations, some visible on the Cheshire bank.

In 1888 the *Daily News* called Widnes 'the dirtiest, ugliest and most depressing town in England'. Some may still agree, though the dirt has gone. Widnes apparently developed almost without design or structure, and the centre is drab and incoherent, though since 2000 attempts have been made to improve it. The town falls into three parts: West Bank at the Mersey bridgehead, where industrial development began; the town proper a little to the N; and the mainly C20 suburban sprawl overtaking villages and hamlets on higher ground. The chemical-laden atmosphere made hardwearing brick and terracotta popular building materials and they have lasted surprisingly well. If anything can be said to characterise the architecture of Widnes, it is their sharp reds and hard edges. Throughout the town there are also substantial late C19 and early C20 pubs built by the brewers Greenall, Whitley & Co. in Domestic Revival styles.

WEST BANK

p. 59 Rural West Bank was a popular destination for early C19 day trippers from Liverpool. The great change was in 1847 when Hutchinson built his alkali works beside the canal. Housing on a grid was put up in the 1860s–70s, and much more industry settled, also on the West Bank Dock Estate w of the railway bridge, which was developed from a salt marsh from the mid 1860s. Much of this industry has gone and the land reclaimed for leisure, and Pevsner's dreary uniform streets of 1969 have been extensively pocked by clearance and redevelopment.

St Mary, St Mary's Road. 1907–10, by *Austin & Paley*, a splendid building of red stone, big, majestic and full of imagination in the magnificent interior. The money – £16,669 – came inevitably from the chemical kings. It is the last of the firm's great urban churches, designed in a squarish free Perp style. There is a substantial tower, as the architects liked. This one is at the w end, and has corner buttresses. It is embraced by the aisles, there are porches N and S, high transepts and freely Perp windows (square-headed in the clerestory; five substantial lights with reticulated tracery E and w). Many of the firm's favourite motifs, e.g. the Te Deum inscription frieze running around the tower and below the parapet of the s side and E end. Everywhere, too, the characteristic richly textured masonry and expertly balanced asymmetry, e.g. the porches – the s one perpendicular to the nave, the N one angled, with chequered stonework; and the different N and s projections, E of the nave.

The INTERIOR has exposed stone of the same mix and the internal expression of the external asymmetry: the chancel is flanked by two totally different appendices, a typical Austin & Paley arrangement creating a delicious variety of spaces and vistas. The N organ chamber is huge, with lofty arches, one to the chancel and two narrower to the transept; the Lady Chapel, s, is low and of three bays beneath soaring Perp windows. Powerful but elegantly designed PISCINA and SEDILIA. The chancel arch, with big, round, panelled piers, responds to the mighty tower piers at the other end of the five-bay nave. Underneath the tower is a fine ribbed vault. The roof, enhanced by excellent modern lighting, is a fitting climax; kingpost principals with collars and braces, intermediates with arching tie-beams.

FURNISHINGS. REREDOS, a First World War memorial. The rest, of high-quality oak, are all of a piece and designed by the architects. – PARCLOSE SCREEN and large ORGAN CASE, freely detailed with suggestions of Art Nouveau. – Darley Dale stone PULPIT and FONT, massively and elaborately panelled, the former a drum, the latter a cuboid, etc. – STAINED GLASS. E window, Ascension and Apocalyptic Vision, a competent early C20 piece by *Shrigley & Hunt*. – Outside, a contemporary matching stone WAYSIDE PULPIT by *Austin & Paley* with text band.

BRIDGES. A ferry here across the Runcorn Gap was first recorded in 1178. In 1799 Ralph Dodd proposed a bridge or tunnel across this narrowest point on the lower Mersey, an idea revived fifteen years later, when a committee anxious to improve communications to Liverpool selected *Thomas Telford*'s scheme for a suspension bridge with an unprecedented principal span of 1,000 ft (308 metres). This was abandoned when the promoters couldn't raise the necessary £84,000. Thus, the London & North Western Railway's BRITANNIA BRIDGE was first across, in 1864–8, designed by the railway's engineer *William Baker*. Three huge iron lattice-truss spans, each 300 ft (92 metres) long, are clasped onto 75-ft (23-metre) stone pylons by crenellated iron half-towers. Stone 'barbicans' with secondary towers, crenellations and machicolations, buttress the spans at the ends of the brick approach viaducts. The height was dictated by shipping. A transporter bridge of 1905 for road traffic (engineers *Webster & Wood*) was closed in 1961, and demolished soon after. The BRIDGE APPROACH and former POWER HOUSE survive at the end of Mersey Road. Of red sandstone, the power house dainty and Frenchy, with banded masonry, Gibbs surrounds and twin, finialled, steep hipped roofs.

The transporter bridge was replaced in 1956–61 by the present ROAD BRIDGE, between it and the Britannia Bridge. By *Mott, Hay & Anderson*. It is a vast steel bowstring arch rising elegantly into the air and carrying, hanging from it, the roadway. The structure consists of two arches connected by diagonal bracing. The inner arch springs from the piers below the road deck; the outer is a double curve above it, slightly concave before it becomes convex – an evolved form of bowstring truss. A suspension bridge was considered, but rejected after wind-tunnel tests. The span is 1,028 ft (316 metres), the total length 1,628 ft (193 metres). It was the largest steel arch in Europe when it was built, and the third largest in the world. Deck widened 1977.

VICTORIA PROMENADE. 1900, by *John S. Sinclair*, Borough Surveyor. On the riverside under St Mary, with an upper and lower terrace separated by stone wall. A modest attempt at improvement.

INDUSTRIAL REMAINS. The beginnings of industry were at SPIKE ISLAND E of Mersey and Waterloo roads, where the canal and the railway arrived in 1833 and Hutchinson established his alkali plant (*see* p. 646). Others followed, but in the C20 the Island fell into polluted dereliction. In 1981 it was reclaimed and reinvented as a pleasant country park. The

CANAL of 1833 survives for pleasure craft, widening at its lowest part for quays on either side. Hutchinson's works were on the E quay. One chamber of the DOUBLE LOCK to the river has been restored. Patched sandstone. To the E is WIDNES DOCK, 1833, the barge dock built by the railway company for coal transhipment: modest perhaps, but the first purpose-built railway dock in the world. Filled remains of the lock in the SW corner. W of the canal is the site of the Gossage Soap Factory, established as an alkali plant in 1850, closed 1933. All that remains is GOSSAGE'S TOWER, on Mersey Road. Built *c.* 1860 as offices and laboratories for Hutchinson & Co., acquired by William Gossage in 1908 and extended. Square, rendered, four storeys, Italianate detailing. Gossage extension, N, two-storey. Now home to CATALYST, a museum of the chemical industry. *Brock Carmichael Associates* added a glass lift and enclosed glazed roof-top observation deck, 1989, and, in 1994–5, a further extension N. This is chunky, with heavy inverted pitched roof: more theme-park multiplex than industrial aesthetic.

¼ m. N on the corner of Waterloo Road and Pitt Street is the former Mersey Power Co. ELECTRICITY SUBSTATION. 1911, *Merz & McLellan.* A brick box, with two little tower-louvres sprouting from the hipped roof. N again, where Waterloo Road meets Hutchinson Road, are the former ICI OFFICES, 1934 by *ICI Estates Winnington.* Brick. Four storeys and shallow wings.

WEST BANK DOCK ESTATE, W of the bridges. Little remains of the dock, opened 1864, other than the filled-in river entrance. Gates *in situ.* Some reclamation and landscaping, including a river walk up and along a heap of chemical waste, known locally as GALLIGU, now forming a cliff almost a hundred feet high where in 1850 it was salt marsh – an unconsidered but dramatic re-engineering of the landscape.

CENTRAL WIDNES

The first industrial housing was N of West Bank in Newtown, before 1860. Soon a slum for the Irish chemical workers, much of it was demolished in the C19 for railways. The town developed N of here in the late C19, linked under railway lines to West Bank by Victoria Road. This street was the town's main artery, terminating in VICTORIA SQUARE, the civic centre which emerged from the 1880s. The square is not remotely square, but it is the only coherent architectural space in Widnes, its disparate buildings held together by common materials – red brick and terracotta. Between the wars the Kingsway N from Victoria Road and a housing estate to the E were laid out, Widnes' only large-scale piece of town planning; the civic centre has expanded onto the bottom of Kingsway. Also in the C20 the retail centre moved N of Victoria Square to Albert Road, dislocating the centre of town. The 1990s shopping centres, supermarkets and market hall are detailed in pastiche, though the MARKET HALL does at least capture the form of an aisled Victorian iron structure. West Bank is now isolated by a bypass where the railways once were, and Victoria Road is deserted; Victoria Square is in turn separated from the current shopping area by the desolate Widnes Road. In 2005 work was under way to try and knit these two back together.

ST PAUL, Victoria Square. 1883–4, by *Henry Shelmerdine*; the SE tower completed 1907. Brown brick with red brick detailing (including all the tower). Big, with Geometrical tracery, and handled without much sensitivity. Spacious inside, with exposed brick and terracotta trimmings, not all Gothic. Quite stygian – a good cleaning would transform it. Four-and-a-half-bay nave, transepts, chancel and aisles. Polygonal barrel vault on thin ribs. – PULPIT. Good; finely detailed terracotta, with a statuette in a columned niche on every side. – FONT. Substantial red sandstone, supported on cusped and pierced panels. Pulpit and font share strong similarities with those at St Ambrose, Halton View (*see* p. 656). – STAINED GLASS. Good five-light E window with grisaille background; central light a later insertion (dated 1896). The VICARAGE to the NE, rather plain with mullioned-and-transomed windows, is *Shelmerdine* also, 1901.

ST MARIE (R.C.), Lugsdale Road. 1865, by *E. W. Pugin*, at his least effusive. With a pretty bellcote and a polygonal apse, but otherwise severe, especially the W end. Banded brick and some red sandstone trim. Lancets; aisles. Thin sandstone piers inside. The capitals are typical of the architect.

ST RAPHAEL (R.C.), Liverpool Road. 1960, by *Dawbarn & Blair*. A limited site, from which came the layout around a fore-court with presbytery to l. and the W end of church and hall side-by-side to the r., pivoting around the tower between and all joined together. Brick, boxy.

PUBLIC BUILDINGS and the rest of the TOWN CENTRE are described topographically, together.

TOWN HALL, Victoria Square. 1885, by *F. & G. Holme*. Symmetrical, brick and terracotta, in a free Northern Renaissance style. Nine bays, the outer ones projecting slightly as gabled wings. A pleasant composition with lots of lively terracotta detailing, e.g. ornate pedimented and pilastered entrance with griffins above, and Dutch gables with finials and panels bearing the town arms. However, the design sags slightly in the centre for want of the planned tower.

FREE LIBRARY AND TECHNICAL SCHOOL, Victoria Road, next to St Paul. By *Woodhouse & Willoughby* 1894–6; enlarged by *Henry Littler*, County Architect, 1909–10. Free Jacobean. It exploits its angular site with a busy asymmetrical plan and staggered façade, in red brick with copious, and excellent, terracotta detailing on ten gables and a tower. Littler's extension in St Paul's Road is matching, but quieter.

Completing VICTORIA SQUARE are late C19 shops and public houses. The best is the RUNCORN WHOLESALE CO-OPERATIVE CENTRAL STORES on the corner of Lugsdale Road,

1904–5, by *W. D. T. Mundford* of Preston. In 2002–3 the square was re-landscaped with refreshing restraint.

The civic centre has spread onto the bottom of the KINGSWAY. On the E SIDE the WIDNES HEALTH CENTRE, 1938–9, by the *Borough Surveyor*. A little essay in Art Deco, with bands of glazing, shallow wings with radial quadrant corners and a glazed stair hall thrusting above the parapet in the centre. Further N, the MAGISTRATES' COURT AND POLICE STATION. 1966–7, by *Roger Booth*, County Architect. The police have a curtain-walled slab raised on pilotis, typical for a small office block, but the Magistrates' Court in front, also raised on pilotis, is low and horizontal. The *piano nobile* walls are faced with reconstructed marble and the courtroom top-lit by a clerestory under a crimpled roof. Pevsner in 1969 considered it rather gay for its purpose; the current miserable condition of the marble and glazing has corrected that.

On the W SIDE, MUNICIPAL BUILDINGS, completed 1967, and HALTON COLLEGE, 1953–61, both by *M. Nevile Player* (his swimming baths opposite are demolished). The Municipal Buildings, a disciplined block of six storeys on a podium raised on pilotis, with consistent white apron bands, has lasted well. Both compare very favourably with the Council's cowardly KINGSWAY HOUSE next door at the bottom of Kingsway, dating from the 1990s. An offensive and illiterate brick lump with pediments, presumably in attempted sympathy for Victoria Square. All the confidence of thirty years before has gone.

THE QUEEN'S HALL, Victoria Road. A spectacularly unsympathetic conversion in 1956–7 of a Wesleyan Methodist Chapel of 1864. The cornice, and the pediments over the windows on the side elevations, are about all the remains of the C19 detailing. The street façade had three large aediculed windows and twin pediments. Nothing of the raked interior remains.

SEWER VENT, Mill Brow, off Albert Road. Like a little brick factory chimney. Last survivor of seven, part of a system of *c.* 1893 designed to channel chemical effluent to the Mersey.

OUTER WIDNES

Suburban expansion into neighbouring villages and hamlets began in the C19 and continues in the C21, especially in Upton.

APPLETON (N)

A scattering of houses until built up in the late C19 with bylaw terraces and middle-class villas.

ST JOHN, Fairfield Road. 1963. A simple but pleasant brick A-frame. At ground level the sides are cut back for deep windows between the frames which thus take on the appearance of triangular buttresses.

ST BEDE (R.C.), Appleton Road. By *Weightman & Hadfield*, completed 1847. A convincing and comfortable work in red sandstone. Sizeable, with a broad W tower with angle buttresses and gargoyles, aisles and the tripartite E end frequent in Catholic churches of the time. Windows are paired lancets to the aisles, trefoils to clerestory and curvilinear to the chancel. A cosy interior. Arcade of deep arches on alternate round and octagonal piers. Nave roof with scissor bracing; to the chancel, braced collar trusses on hammerbeams. – ALTAR. It appears to be an C18 frontal chest. The Gothic retable, with canopy, is C19. Is it the one designed by *A. W.N. Pugin* and supplied in 1850? Celebrant altar on a platform, from reordering in 1991. – ORGAN, handsomely large, in a loft under the tower with cusped-panel front. – STAINED GLASS. E window and chancel N and S, looking like the glass supplied by *Pugin* in 1850. – The PRESBYTERY attached, of harsh red brick, is *Sinnott, Sinnott & Powell*'s, 1892.

WADE DEACON GRAMMAR SCHOOL, Birchfield Road. Good, solid inter-war scholastic Georgian, by *Stephen Wilkinson*, 1930–1. An impressively long façade, forty-three bays wide, with end pavilions and pilastered centre broken slightly forward. Brick with stone dressings. Good detailing, e.g. Ionic capitals, squarish cupola, and railings and gates with County Council cipher.

VICTORIA PARK, Fairfield Road. 1897, expanded 1900. The grounds of the C19 Appleton House, demolished. The WAR MEMORIAL is impressive and dignified. 1920–1, by *Harold E. Davies*; the sculptor was *H. Tyson Smith*. A Portland stone obelisk on an inscribed pedestal above a broad square base bearing the names of the fallen on bronze plaques.

Around Birchfield Road are a few reminders of pre-industrial Widnes, e.g. on HIGHFIELD ROAD a pair of houses (now four, later doors squeezed in), *c.* 1830. Brick, label moulds, Tudor Gothic windows. Possibly built as the Appleton Academy.

FARNWORTH (N)

The principal settlement before the arrival of chemicals, built around a medieval chapel of ease. Now solidly suburban.

ST LUKE, Pit Lane. Until 1859 St Wilfrid. Red sandstone, much pleasantly worn. This is evidently a church of some antiquity. But what features belong to what date? The W wall is partly late C12, says the VCH, on the strength of walling below the floor. But some of the stonework above is typically Norman too. This belongs to the first, aisle-less chapel. To this a tower was added, probably in the mid C14. Towards the nave this is now 6 ft (1.8 metres) out of axis, as can be seen from the scars on the inner face of the W wall left by the earlier roof and N and S walls. Seemingly within a few decades the S aisle was added: the details of the octagonal piers are pre-Perp C14, and so is the doorway with its broad, continuous mouldings; the W window N of the tower, intersecting the roof scar, looks mid-C14 too. However, the N arcade and aisle were described as early Dec, i.e. C13, before they were rebuilt by *William Culshaw* in 1855. Were they, then, moved N to their present position in the C14 after the tower was built, possibly when the S aisle was added? The chancel and S chapel (now organ chamber) on the other hand are late C15 Perp, with a handsome panelled roof of heavily moulded beams and the griffin of the Bold family (though their family chapel was at the N, *see* below). The chancel arch is presumably late C15 too, and joins rudely with the aisles. The S transept is of *c.* 1500. It was a family chapel – see its separate entrance from the W – built by Bishop Smith of Lincoln for the inhabitants of Cuerdley, his birthplace. Rough original roof. The C17 seems to have been at work as well – see the S porch entrance and some of the windows of the E end with their uncusped round arches in the lights. An interesting feature of the C15 or C17 is the timber-framed gables of the chancel and S transept, as they appear behind the battlements; another – of what date? – is the wide channels to some of the masonry. In addition to the N aisle wall and arcade, *Culshaw* entirely rebuilt the C15 Bold Chapel, with an oak SCREEN, at the E end of the N aisle in C13 style; replaced the nave and N aisle roofs (the S aisle roof looks essentially original); rebuilt the chancel E wall; and restored windows e.g. the E window. A second restoration by *Paley, Austin & Paley*, 1894–5, ripped out W and S galleries, box pews and the stately double-decker pulpit (requiring the replacement of the S arcade capitals with faithful copies), and included new vestries, N.

FITTINGS. FONT. Plain, octagonal, possibly C15. – ALTAR. With linenfold panelling (and Tudor roses) from the dismantled S transept screen. – COMMUNION TABLE, Bold Chapel. Early C17. Cup-and-cover legs. – SCREEN. Under the tower arch; charming C17, with balusters in the upper part. – WAINSCOT, in the aisles, S transept and under the tower; C17 and later. Originally pews, and copiously carved with their owners' names (earliest dated 1668); in the chancel is the best, early C18 and geometrically panelled, from the gallery fronts. – PEW, behind the pulpit. Dated 1607. Plain. – COMMUNION RAIL made of reused C18 gallery staircase balusters; turned, good. – BREAD SHELF, under the tower. Dated 1724, but still entirely in the Jacobean tradition. – An impressive series of seven Bold HATCHMENTS, the earliest 1762. – BOOK DOOR, i.e. a concealed door with dummy books in the Bold Chapel, *c.* 1810, from the library of Bold Hall (q.v.). – STAINED GLASS. N aisle, W, by *Morris & Co.*, 1876, the three white figures of Shadrach, Meshach and Abednego standing in the writhing flames of the furnace. Chancel E window by *Burlison & Grylls*. W window and S transept E window (memorial, 1917) by *Shrigley & Hunt*.

MONUMENTS. Nearly all in the Bold Chapel, one of the best collections in the county. – Pretty crude effigy of a knight holding a book. Meant to look *c.* 1500, but almost certainly of Richard Bold, *c.* 1602. Original colouring revealed in restoration. – Richard Bold, 1635. Standing alabaster effigies of him and his wife, a rare arrangement for this date if they were intended to stand, not lie. – Yet another Richard Bold, 1704. Pretty cartouche with cherubs. – Peter Bold, 1762. Fine, large tablet by *B. Bromfield* of Liverpool. – Anne Maria Bold, 1813, tablet by *G. Bullock* of the Mona Marble Co., London. – Peter Patten Bold. Signed by *Francis Chantrey* and dated 1822. White marble. Mourning young woman kneeling over a pedestal. – Mary Bold, Princes Sapieha (a Lithuanian family), 1824. By *Pietro Tenerani*, made in Rome. Tenerani was a pupil of Thorwaldsen. Large relief, with the young woman on a couch, her sorrowful husband standing by her head, an angel at her feet. Sentimental of course, but very competently done. – Alice Houghton, 1852. Behind the altar. White effigy; asleep. – In the chancel, John and Edward Atherton, 1826 and 1820 respectively. Fine, large simple sarcophagus in relief by *T. Franceys & Spence*, Liverpool.

In the churchyard, E, an exceedingly fine C18 SUNDIAL from Bold New Hall (q.v.), quite possibly by its designer, *Leoni*. Also, SE the LOCK-UP, marked Bridewell 1827. A simple stone shed, heavily restored.

ST PIUS X (R.C.), Sefton Avenue off Birchfield Road. 1960, by *Felix A. Jones* of Jones & Kelly, Dublin, engaged through their – very different – work at St Patrick, Newton-le-Willows (q.v.). A very satisfying little brick church with a 70 ft (21.5 metre) campanile. This, a clean elongated cuboid with deep belfry slots, stands in the NE, aligned slightly off axis. This brings welcome movement, and makes it prominent at the top of Birchfield Road – but why is the angle not enough to align with it, so that belfry slots open up all the way through to people travelling up the road? The exterior is clean too, a nave and lower chancel under pitched roofs with buttresses, both subtly angled. Five-light window over a modish W entrance. The interior is a delight, an intimate space like an undercroft, with a vault defined by brick arches made without reinforcement, which divide the nave into six bays. Spanning 40 ft and 40 ft (12.3 metres) high, these spring from the floor with continuous radii. This motif unifies the interior: the side windows are of similar form, and at the E end there is one large arch like this and flanked by two small ones, for the chancel and N and S altars. The chancel is shallow, and lit by hidden side windows; the E wall is blank. – STAINED GLASS. In each window a mosaic of a rich red cross on dying orange. – The design of the ALTARS, LECTERN and FONT, faced in clunky limestone rubble, with mosaic panels, has not aged as well as the building, though some, no doubt, would consider them very retro-chic.

WESLEYAN METHODIST CHAPEL, Derby Road. By *W. Verity* of Wigan, 1891. An unremarkable little chapel, with banded brickwork and Dec tracery and a simple but little-altered interior, and one surprise – a cut-down late C17 or early C18 tripledecker PULPIT from the old parish church of Runcorn in Cheshire, demolished *c.* 1847. Given by Thomas Hazlehurst, a local soap manufacturer, who presented it to the Methodists of Farnworth because Wesley was reputed to have preached from it. Only the pulpit stage remains, without its tester, but nevertheless of recognisable quality. Swelling sides inlaid with IHS in a sunburst. Utterly out of place and far too big for the space, but wonderfully so.

WIDNES CEMETERY, Birchfield Road. Laid out from 1896, chapels and entrance gates 1897–8. By *John S. Sinclair*, Borough Surveyor. Thin Gothic entrance; three arches; pinnacles; red sandstone. The Anglican and Nonconformist chapels are one building, two identical gabled chapels flanking a short tower with stumpy spire, forming an H-plan. Late C13 style. Now the crematorium. The R.C. chapel is demolished.

WIDNES STATION, Birchfield Road. 1872, of a type frequent on the Cheshire Lines Committee's Liverpool line and very similar to the house style of the Manchester, Sheffield & Lincolnshire Railway, a CLC constituent. Brick, pointed lintels, tapered chimneystacks. Gables with a variety of bargeboard patterns and cast-iron canopies with dagger, trefoil and diamond motifs.

LIVERPOOL CATHOLIC REFORMATORY ASSOCIATION NAUTICAL SCHOOLS (former), Norland's Lane, ¾ m. N. An all-too-bleak brick quadrangle by *Edmund Kirby*, begun 1904. Now offices.

Farnworth Street and Derby Road retained a village character well into the late C20, now eroded by demolition and alteration. Late Georgian houses survive on the N side of Derby Road. On Norland's Lane N of the Nautical Schools is NORLAND'S HOUSE, an early C18 farmhouse. Sashes replaced with uPVC double-glazing with the usual distressing results.

HALTON VIEW and MOSS BANK (E)

ST AMBROSE, Halton View Road. By *James F. Doyle*. Begun 1879, finished by 1883. Stock brick and red brick trim. Also red terracotta. Aisles, but no tower, though apparently a NE tower was planned. The windows are mostly lancets, but the first and last bays of the clerestory are singled out by more elaborate plate tracery. Why? Polygonal apse of the same height as the nave. A clean-cut, spacious interior. Brick is exposed, with round red sandstone nave piers and terracotta trimmings. Cross-braced roof and wooden chancel arch. – PULPIT. By *Doyle*, very good. Rich terracotta, with sandstone apostles in marble-columned niches. Clearly related to that at St Paul (*see* p. 651). – FONT. 1881. Red sandstone with flowers intertwined on a grid. Again, the same hand as at St Paul? – COMMUNION RAIL, flowing wrought iron. – STAINED GLASS. E, three lancets: l. and r. First World War memorial; centre, a good Good Shepherd. W, three lancets by *Caroline Townshend* and *Joan Howson*, 1928, a memorial to Eliza Kidd. Illustrating the work of women in Christ's ministry. Strikingly blue tones, but stiffly and naïvely modelled close up. S aisle, second from W, St Boniface (patron saint of

Germany) by *Trena M. Cox*, 1947. Given by German prisoners of war in thanks for humane treatment.

s of Halton View, is MOSS BANK, created from the C19 from salt marsh, now with semi-abandoned industry. A 1930s MEDICAL CENTRE on Tan House Lane, Art Deco, and a WASTE PROCESSING STATION, 1998 by *Austin-Smith:Lord* on Johnson's Lane. With curved roofs. Essential industrial parts (e.g. tanks) gathered artfully. This hardly ever fails: the sheer scale of industrial plant ensures at least a certain drama.

DITTON, HOUGH GREEN and UPTON (NW)

ST MICHAEL, Ditchfield Road, Hough Green. 1870, by *G.E. Grayson*. Rock-faced red sandstone. Aisle-less. Bellcote astride the ridge between nave and chancel. Grayson can be a lot better than this mean and hard building.

ST MICHAEL (R.C.), St Michael's Road, Ditton. 1876–9, by *Henry Clutton*. The church is strikingly big for its surroundings and would have been more so when all around was fields. It was erected at the instigation of Lady Mary Stapleton-Bretherton of Ditton Hall for Jesuits expelled by Bismarck from Germany (cf. St Helens, Portico, p. 570). She paid for it all, £16,000.* Quite a brute, of smooth red sandstone with a huge and assertive w tower with steep saddleback roof. Bell-stage of three lancets framed by shafts with shaft-rings. Lancet windows and rose windows to the transepts, as Clutton liked them. Very Cluttonian also the E wall with two windows separated by a big shaft.

INTERIOR. Spacious and airy, cool and as self-confident as the tower. Bath stone, in contrast to the exterior. Tall, slender columns coupled in depth with shaft-rings and startlingly French Early Gothic crocket capitals. The arcade runs though from w to E, with eight bays, taking no notice of the transepts, and the chancel projects beyond by only some 8 ft (2.5 metres). The roof is a barrel-vault of varnished oak. Orderly overall dimensions: the tower at 120 ft (37 metres) is exactly as high as the building is long and the width of the nave and aisles is exactly half. Reordered by *Bartlett & Purnell*, 1979, in keeping with the dignified austerity of the structure. Theirs are the Clipsham stone ALTAR and LECTERN pushed forward into the crossing on a platform. Much of the elaborate late C19 work made by the German lay brothers was lost in the process. Survivals include the TESTER of the pulpit, now tabernacle canopy, intricately carved, all arcades, crockets and domes, and the simple wooden ALTAR in the Lady Chapel, s. The alien-looking STAINED GLASS is indeed from Cologne.

---

*In the 1850s Clutton had rebuilt the Sacred Heart chapel at the Jesuits' English mother church in Farm Street, London, and designed a school for them at St Francis Xavier, Liverpool (*see* p. 418).

CHURCH OF OUR LADY OF PERPETUAL SUCCOUR (R.C.),
Mayfield Avenue, Hough Green. 1960. The sides are rows of
tall glazed gables.

HOUGH GREEN STATION, Liverpool Road. 1872. Of the same
type as Widnes (*see* p. 656).

DITTON HALL, St Michael's Road. In the shadow of St Michael
is the last remaining of the half-dozen or so minor gentry
houses that stood in Widnes in the C19. There was probably a
manor house here from the Middle Ages, but the present core
is likely to be Late Georgian; its s façade would seem to be the
projecting sections around the ground-floor Tuscan portico *in
antis* which we see now. Extended after 1845, which would
explain the bulk of the rendered house today, unified by a modillion cornice and window architraves. Inside is some plasterwork and two confusing staircases with cast-iron balusters.
These are stylistically correct for *c.* 1850, but may have been
altered, possibly after 1903 when the house became a boys'
home run by the Sisters of Nazareth. For this the grimly institutional brick wings to the w, the nearer of 1911–14 by *Pugin
& Pugin*, that beyond of 1939. Also a CHAPEL by *Pugin &
Pugin*, 1931–2, at the NE corner. Eclectic Gothic, brick.
Chancel with separate s choir for the Sisters at right angles to
the chancel, separated by a screen.

HALE BANK (SW)

Farmland and marsh until the St Helens & Runcorn Gap
Railway extension to Garston arrived in 1852. On a spur from
it was established the Ditton Iron Foundry, 1862, where the
Ditton Brook meets the Mersey. Since then it has become a
little satellite of Widnes, with working-class housing of all
dates from the late C19. In the village, on Hale Road, a simple
brick METHODIST CHAPEL, 1861, with a little embattled
tower and windows under arched Gibbs-style heads.

5000   WIGAN

Wigan is not a *parvenu* of the Industrial Revolution. The site of
the Roman settlement of COCCIUM lies under the town (*see* Perambulation and Introduction, p. 16), on the road from the
Mersey at Warrington to the Ribble at Walton-le-Dale. The parish
church is first mentioned in 1199, the town was made a Royal
Borough in 1246 and the grant of a market in 1258, and there
are minimal features of the C13 in the parish church. What made
modern Wigan is coal and cloth. The word *secole* appears in Wigan
deeds of 1350 (it is even possible that workings uncovered in the
1850s were Roman mines);[*] in 1635 the town was wealthier than
either Liverpool or Manchester, paying more in Ship Money, and

---

[*] Cannel coal was found in Roman furnaces in The Wiend (*see* p. 16) in 1983.

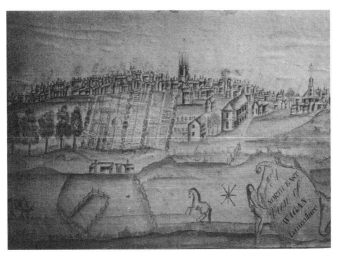

Wigan, a north-east view.
Early C19 drawing

a centre of the woollens, iron, brass and especially pewter industries. By 1784 a cloth hall was opened. But the population in 1801 was only 11,000. By 1911, after the semi-urban extension of Pemberton W of the River Douglas had been absorbed, it was 89,000, and Wigan was one of the centres of the Lancashire coalfield. With dozens of cotton mills, ironworks and squalid slum housing as well, the town was much maligned as the *ne plus ultra* of Lancashire gloom. That was probably unfair even when George Orwell was making Wigan notorious, but it is true that the town in the prosperous Victorian decades showed no outstanding architectural enterprise. It is certainly not true now that all the mines and the mills have closed, and the vigorous façades of red terracotta and brick and local buff-coloured sandstone lining the streets of the pleasantly hilly town centre shine in clean post-industrial air. A small group of local architectural practices at the end of the C19 and beginning of the C20 was predominantly responsible for rebuilding the town centre, including *W. E. V. Crompton* (later architect to the Bedford Estate in London, and to Barclays Bank), *W. Verity*, and above all *Heaton, Ralph & Heaton.*[*]

Churches are described first, then public buildings, and then a town-centre perambulation. Industrial buildings and transport structures have a separate section. Finally, everything else in the outer areas.

---

[*] *William Chasen Ralph* was articled to E.G. Paley in 1864, and remained with him (and Hubert Austin from 1868) until 1875, when he became assistant to John Douglas for fifteen years.

CHURCHES

ALL SAINTS. A big handsome church of buff Coal Measures sandstone, on top of the little hill on which the settlement was founded. It is largely of 1845–50, by *Sharpe & Paley*. In style it is much more like Paley than like Sharpe, and indeed one of his earliest works. However, it is in fact a rebuilding, and a faithful one at the express wish of the parishioners, of the apparently largely late Perp church. This must already in the C16 have been about as large as it is now, for the broad N tower, the two rood turrets, and the N chapel (Walmesley or Gerard Chapel) are original. The tower dates from the later C13 in its lower parts (see the W window of three stepped lancet lights and the arch towards the S). The present belfry stage was added in the earlier C16 if the design of the paired, uncusped three-light openings is a guide. In 1861 Paley topped it off with an arcaded clock stage and pinnacles. The N chapel is of uncertain date. It has windows of five stepped lights with uncusped round heads and a two-bay arcade to the nave which is Perp in its details. Is it mid-C16?

The rebuilding of 1845–50 was largely inspired by the churchwarden, the Hon. Colin Lindsay, a son of the 24th Earl of Crawford. The structure had been declared ruinous by inspecting architects, and all but the tower and N chapel were taken down to the foundations and rebuilt. Paley said that in dimensions the new building was the same as the old and that as far as practicable the old style was preserved; a contemporary account noted that his features and proportions were 'in a better style and made more beautiful in their detail'. The cost was a little over £15,000. It is probably more impressive outside than inside, adorned with plenty of pinnacles and rood stair-turrets, and big regular Perp windows. Those of the first building appear from illustrations to have been simple, uncusped, late Perp: in the aisles, of multiple round-headed lights as still in the N chapel; in the clerestory with intersecting tracery like that of Sefton (q.v.); the present 'correct' windows are Paley's. The windows suggest that the body of the church was rebuilt and the tower raised *c.* 1525–50. The clerestory is of sixteen windows either side, two to a bay, and extends over both nave and chancel. Narrow nave; the C19 arcades have six bays with piers of a Perp section familiar from Sefton church. The shafts and corbels for the roof are typical 1840s stuff, but the roof itself – panelled, with heavy moulded beams – and also those of the aisles reuse medieval timbers.

FITTINGS. REREDOS. By *Paley*. *Opus sectile* panels of 1891 by *Powell & Sons*. – FONT. Fragment of the C14 or C15: an octagonal bowl with quatrefoil frieze. – PULPIT. *Paley*. Stone. – Superb CHANCEL SCREEN of 1901 by *W.D. Caröe*, based on the C16 screen at Sefton (q.v.), with intricate cresting. Coloured and gilded in 1957. – STALLS for Mayor and Corporation. At the W end, rising in tiers. They date from the C19 rebuilding and are heavily carved. – SCULPTURE. A Roman altar is built into the splay of the N window. Found during the rebuilding. – Good *Minton* TILES in the chancel and baptistery. – STAINED GLASS. Late C15 fragments reassembled in the N chapel windows by York Minster glaziers under the direction of *Eric Milner-White* in 1956–7. They include heads, and a roundel depicting the Five Wounds of Christ and Passion implements. E window (1847), W window (1849), and the window W of the font (1845) by *Wailes*. The E window still entirely pictorial, whereas the W window is with twelve upright saints. S chapel windows by *Heaton, Butler & Bayne*. The outstanding E window (1847, figures, border of grisaille scenes) is said to have been conceived by Lady Jane Evelyn Lindsay. Three S aisle windows by *Hardman*, 1855–66. Baptistery S wall, window of 1866 by *Lavers & Barraud*. S aisle 3rd from W is a *Morris* window, St Christopher and four angels, 1868. Strong colouring. Four windows by *Clayton & Bell*, N aisle and NE chapel (Legh Chapel), 1872–99. Tower N wall, 1891, by *Burlison & Grylls*.

MONUMENTS. The monuments in the S chapel (Bradshaigh or Crawford Chapel) said to represent Sir William de Bradshaigh and Lady Mabel, his wife, who founded a chantry in the church in 1338, are in a sad state. The female effigy was re-cut and the male effigy copied by *John Gibson*, c. 1850. The original, defaced male effigy is next to the couple. Priest, only the head visible, on the sill of the tower N window. James Bankes, †1689, attributed to *John Nost*, and John Baldwin, †1726, both S aisle and both good. The Bankes monument a plaque revealed by drawn drapes, with a skull below and two cherubs. On the E wall of the S chapel are two large Gothic marble monuments to the 23rd Earl of Crawford, †1825, and his wife, and to the wife of the 24th Earl, †1850. They are by *Felicie* and *Hippolyte de Fauveau*, made in Florence.

The CHURCHYARD has been cleared and made into public gardens, opened in 1909. In the little section S of the church a fine WAR MEMORIAL by *Sir Giles Gilbert Scott*, erected 1925. It is high and impressive, an octagonal pillar with a delicately traceried lantern exquisitely carved, and in a Gothic similar to that of late works of Voysey.

Former RECTORY or WIGAN HALL, New Market Street, below the church. By *G.E. Street* for the rector, G.T.O. Bridgeman, whose family, the Earls of Bradford, were employing him at Weston Park, Staffs. The rectors were also lords of the manor of Wigan and lived in a large manor house here, rebuilt in 1695 by Bishop Stratford. Undermined by coal workings, this was pulled down by Street, who built afresh in 1875–6 the present Gothic house. It is approached through a GATEHOUSE of stone below, half-timbering above. The house itself is similarly constructed, but with nogging to the timber framing. It is masterfully composed and detailed, and far more fanciful than one expects of Street, e.g. the charming little half-timbered oriel on the S side. And of course, with the half-timbering, tile-hung gables, and handsome star-section chimneys, it is very much a part of the Domestic Revival too. The service wing was demolished in 1956; a datestone of Bishop Stratford's house is reset in the new N gable.

The centrepiece of the interior is the large stair hall, with a complex wooden Gothic staircase. Elsewhere some good doors and panelling, incorporating several older parts (maybe from the previous house), e.g. a Jacobean overmantel, panels of old STAINED GLASS fragments, some Swiss of *c.* 1540–50. The once extensive grounds of the Hall were whittled away in the C20 for Wigan Technical College (*see* p. 667) and the DEANERY CHURCH OF ENGLAND HIGH SCHOOL (1930s Neo-Georgian, 1970, etc.), leaving little more than the drive on one side and a terrace on the other.*

ST ANDREW, Waterloo Street, Springfield, ¾ m. NW. 1882, by *F. W. Hunt* of London. Thin, tall brick single vessel, with aisles and a NW turret, in an intriguing roguish Gothic. – *Opus sectile* PANELS either side of the chancel by *Powell & Sons.* – STAINED GLASS. E window by *Abbott & Co.*, 1917.

ST ANNE, Beech Hill Lane, Beech Hill, 1¼ m. NW. By *Quiggin & Gee*, built 1953. Cost £39,000. A simple plan – no tower or aisles or transepts, and a short chancel. Its purity derives from the device of a two-centred arch springing directly from the ground. The interior is a series of such arches, in concrete; this structure is expressed in the unadorned brick exterior by the curve of the roof above eaves height and by the W façade. Here the arch sweeps up in the brickwork to form a large gable, and a big mullioned window repeats the motif.

ST CATHARINE, Lorne Street, Scholes, ¾ m. E. By *Edmund Sharpe*, 1839–41. The church was built for the Commissioners and cost £3,180. Billinge sandstone. A restless and unbalanced W tower with four gables to mediate to a tall octagonal belfry stage which has eight gables to mediate to a spire, a typical example of the undisciplined inventiveness of church architects of the C19 before Pugin. It is remarkable how ignorant Sharpe was only nine years before the publication of his Gothic source-book, *Architectural Parallels*. The steeple is altogether and quite awkwardly too big for the church, which has the usual sides with thin buttresses and pairs of lancets. Short chancel, three trefoil-panelled galleries on cast-iron columns. – BOX PEWS still in place, except at the W end which is partitioned off by a glazed screen. – VICARAGE, brick and classically minded.

ST GEORGE, Church Street. 1781. A simple brick box delicately enlivened by the triglyph frieze and the shaped gable of the W front, incorporating a bellcote. The shaped gable is very odd for the date. Under that is a big doorway with broken pediment on columns, recessed under a depressed arch. The sides have four bays of arched windows in two tiers. A disastrous fire destroyed the interior, which had giant columns separating the

---

* A church infants' school of 1867 by *Street* on New Market Street was demolished in 1985 to make way for the bus station.

short chancel from the nave (and a w gallery only). Re-roofed, refitted and refurnished by *Anthony Grimshaw Associates c.* 1982–4. The good, stark modern woodwork (ash) is in contrast to the exterior. A large PAINTING on the w wall of St George slaying the dragon, by *Barbara M. Grimshaw*, 1986, and STAINED GLASS by *John Hayward*, 1982.

ST JAMES, Hardman Street, Poolstock, ¾ m. SSW. 1863–6 by *E. G. Paley*. Paid for by J.C. Eckersley, colliery proprietor, M.P. for Wigan and member of the mill-owning family (*see* p. 675). It was the centrepiece of a workers' industrial village (*see* p. 676). The estimate was for over £15,000. Parbold sandstone. Large, with a w tower, nave and aisles, clerestory of pairs of two-light windows, a lower chancel and a s appendix with rose window, with, in its tracery, the Star of David. The period motifs are Dec. It is precise and careful, either dignified or cold. A big, tall nave in bare ashlar, with high, elegant five-bay arcades. The piers alternate between octagonal and quatrefoil; the capitals are good. The pairs of clerestory windows have detached marbled shafts, with shaft-rings, between them. Kingpost principal trusses. Not reordered. s chapel, for the Eckersley family; fitted up with FURNISHINGS from the demolished church of St Thomas, Caroline Street. – FONT moved from under the tower; this now screened off as a choir vestry. – The ornate stone REREDOS with two tiers of Ghibertesque figures in niches l. and r. of the E window is of 1876–7. Under the window, in an arcade, a relief scene. The chancel DECORATION of the same date is no longer complete. – STAINED GLASS. N and s chancel windows by *Hardman*.

ST JOHN THE DIVINE, Church Street, Lamberhead Green, 2½ m. WSW. Pemberton's parish church is a simple Commissioners' job by *Thomas Rickman & Henry Hutchinson*, 1830–2. It cost £4,913. Brick and stone dressings. Narrow bays of lancets and buttresses (cf. their St David, Haigh, on the other side of Wigan), a shallow chancel with stepped lancets and a w front with three lancets and large, square embattled pinnacles at the corners pierced by narrow louvred openings. These are like ears. Very odd. Three galleries on cast-iron columns. Flat ceiling.

The former NATIONAL SCHOOL on Fleet Street faces St John at the other end of the short Church Street. 1833, by *Rickman & Hutchinson* as well. Brick. Five pointed windows on each floor. Altered.

ST MARK, Victoria Street, Pemberton, 1¼ m. SW. Largely 1891–2, by the leading local practice of *Heaton & Ralph*. A good honest job. Square and coursed Coal Measures stone with red Runcorn dressings. Geometrical tracery. Good E and w windows, s transept and stocky SE tower. The chancel and vestries not added until 1901, the belfry stage of the tower not until 1927 (a spire was originally intended). – SCREEN. By *Robin Wolley*, 1988.

ST MATTHEW, Billinge Road, Highfield, 2 m. SW. 1892–4, by *Paley, Austin & Paley*, one of their first flight. Built at the expense of Col. Henry Blundell, who owned the Pemberton Colliery, in memory of his wife. Yorkshire E.E. style. Striated red Runcorn sandstone, with a strong, taut crossing tower with recessed spire and beautifully placed lucarnes at its foot. The nave with a few lancets placed up high. There is a s aisle of five bays, but a N aisle of only two bays w of the transept. Three bays of the s aisle and one bay of the nave were not built until 1909–10. As the practice liked (cf. Kirkby and Mossley Hill, Liverpool), the crossing is actually the choir. The N transept a chapel, the s transept the organ loft. The chancel N side has three shafted windows; the s side has none, but the group of the SEDILIA instead. The E wall has a triplet of lancets in deeply moulded reveals. All these chancel parts have trefoil heads. – FURNISHINGS. Typically good stuff by the architects, including a REREDOS of 1917, stout FONT and PULPIT, and woodwork in a variety of styles. – STAINED GLASS. Good *Hardman* glass in the E window (1917), and the N aisle transepts (1920s). Three windows by *Harold Harvey* of York, 1976–92.

ST MICHAEL, Swinley Road, Swinley, ⅔ m. N. 1873–8, by *G.E. Street*, but not a major work. Nave, aisles and chancel, bellcote between them. E.E.; rock-faced coursed sandstone. Five-bay arcade of cylindrical piers. – Alabaster REREDOS of 1884 by *A.E. Street*. – FONT and PULPIT of 1878 by *G.E. Street*. – Early C20 Perp chancel SCREEN.

ST PAUL, St Paul's Avenue, Worsley Mesnes, 1½ m. SW. 1913–15, by *W. Chasen Ralph & Son*. Red sandstone, with a sturdy w tower and a good interior. Handsome, very much in the Dec–Perp style of Paley & Austin. Indeed so much so one would be forgiven for thinking it was one of theirs.

ST STEPHEN, Balcarres Avenue, off Whelley, 1 m. NE. 1930–8, by *Austin & Paley*. So the firm kept up the Paley & Austin style that long (*see* also Abram church, p. 121). Brown and red stone. An excellent E view with vestry and bellcote facing E on the l. of the chancel E window. Inside, arcade piers with arches dying into them. But the 1930s were an on odd time calmly to do this 1880s-style work. The stonework suggests it was built in two phases.

ST CUTHBERT (R.C.), Sherwood Drive, Pemberton, 1⅔ m. WSW. 1965–7, by *Reynolds & Scott* of Manchester. STAINED GLASS by *Joseph E. Nuttgens*. The present building replaced an extraordinary iron church of 1887 supplied by *Messrs Bruce & Still* of Liverpool. This would have made a good-sized masonry building, being fifty feet from floor to roof ridge, with aisles, clerestory, transepts, chancel and iron hammerbeam roof.

ST JOHN (R.C.), Standishgate. A Jesuit church of 1818–19. Set back down a passageway is a wide, grey ashlar front with a porch of six unfluted Ionic columns. Three arched windows above. A cupola on the SE corner. Exposed from the s by demolitions, showing the large round-arched windows, buttresses and hipped roof. Inside is big and broad. The ample apse comes into its own with attached, truly giant marbled

Corinthian columns. This order wraps around the church; the cornice is continuous and there are pilasters (of 1849) along the side walls. The w gallery is on Corinthian columns too. To reach it, sweeping flying staircases in the corners. Coved and beamed ceiling, retaining C19 stencilled DECORATION in muted tones. Sanctuary refurbished by *J.J. Scoles* in 1834–5 with an elaborate circular BALDACCHINO over the Exposition throne. Reordered *c.* 1994 by *Anthony Grimshaw Associates*, with the big ALTAR RAILS moved out into the nave around a new ALTAR, on a platform. Around this benches are rearranged. A carpet reproduces the pattern of the TILES preserved beneath.

CROSS, in front of the church. 1852. By *A. W.N. Pugin*, according to Goodhart-Rendel. On the base are shields and the symbols of the Four Evangelists. At the top are the Virgin and St John, free-standing figures keeping close to the Crucifixus. Above the cross a crocketed gable. – Fronting the passageway a possible presbytery, certainly later a SCHOOL. About contemporary with the church. Brick, six bays, pedimented. Good doorcase.

ST JOSEPH (former, R.C.), Caroline Street. 1878, by *Goldie & Child*. Polychromatic brick. E.E. The usual urban R.C. plan for the date. w end to street with idiosyncratic bellcote at the gable apex capped by an oversized, steep mansard roof. Linked PRESBYTERY.

ST JUDE (R.C.), Poolstock Lane, Worsley Mesnes, 1½ m. SSW. 1963–4, by *L.A.G. Prichard & Son*. Pevsner's put-down – 'overloaded with the pet motifs of the sixties to a pitch which cannot do good to a contemplative state of mind' – seems unduly unkind now. The plan is like an isosceles triangle with the corners cut off, and the altar at the centre of the very broad base so that the church is much wider than it is deep. Big expressed concrete frames fan out from the long E wall to meet uprights or fins set against the rear walls. The two central roof beams cross over each other, and a clerestory above them floods the altar with light. The spaces between the uprights on the rear walls are filled from floor to ceiling with twelve staggered STAINED GLASS windows, six either side of the porch and baptistery, which project from the centre. The windows consist of superb, swirling abstract *dalle de verre* by *Robin Riley*. Each is made up of six panels. A vestigial spire rises from within the baptistery, which has a clerestory with more *Riley* glass. Semicircular SEATING. – MOSAIC. Excellent Crucifixus panel above the altar designed by *Hans Unger* and made by *Eberhard Schulze* of Germany. This was their first church commission; they came to the attention of the architects for their work for London Transport.

ST MARY (R.C.), Standishgate. 1818. Very close in date and in location to St John, a rival foundation built by secular priests, deliberately one assumes, in very different style. A Perp ashlar front of three bays with battlement and pinnacles and a middle gable with bellcote. Tudor-arched doors in the outer bays, and in the centre a huge and handsome Perp window. The front is surprising for the date; the sides are much more as expected, flat with uncusped window tracery. Chancel windows with cusped lights, but the tracery odd and eclectic. Is it original? Inside, slender quatrefoil piers, one part iron and three parts timber, and two-centred arches. Galleries on three sides, with traceried panelled fronts. Canted ceiling with moulded diagonal ribs and bosses, and closed trusses decorated with blank tracery. A short chancel. – Celebrant ALTAR. 1969. – Good encaustic TILES throughout. – FONT. Good, marble and square; *c.* 1912. – STAINED GLASS in the aisles windows with poor panels by *William Gardner* of St Helens, 1877. – BRASS. Rev. Charles Middlehurst, †1848. Figure in vestments under a Gothic canopy.

ST PATRICK (R.C.), Hardybutts, Scholes, ½ m. E. 1880, by *James O'Byrne* of Liverpool. Single vessel in brick with stark sides punctured by small lancets. No tower, but a bellcote over the W gable. Narthex. Presbytery attached to the E end.

LOCH STREET METHODIST CHURCH, Loch Street, Pemberton, 2 m. WSW. Little Victorian brick chapel, of no interest except for the lovely foliate capitals of the W door. The former SUNDAY SCHOOL of 1895 behind on Fleet Street is bigger.

MOUNT ZION INDEPENDENT METHODIST CHURCH, Ormskirk Road, Pemberton, 2 m. WSW. A little Perp chapel in shiny red brick with stone dressings. It is hard to believe it is really as late as 1934. Earlier church now church hall.

QUEEN'S HALL METHODIST MISSION, Market Street. *See* Perambulation, p. 671.

TRINITY METHODIST CHURCH, Fleet Street, Pemberton, 2⅓ m. WSW. 1851. Debased Gothic, brick with stone trimmings, the façade asymmetrical with a jolly NW tower wearing a stumpy, slated splayed spire.

ST PAUL'S CONGREGATIONAL CHURCH (former), Standishgate. By *F. W. Dixon*, 1902–3. Lancet Gothic, with a thin pyramid-hatted SW tower. Quarry-faced stone. Now a hotel, with remarkably few external changes because it always had tiers of windows.

PUBLIC BUILDINGS

TOWN HALL, Library Street. The former Mining and Technical College of 1900–3 by *Briggs & Wolstenholme*, and the grandest public building in Wigan. Three-and-a-half big storeys. Very large, of red brick and red terracotta, with Edwardian Baroque motifs such as alternately blocked columns and stocky little cupolas. Lots of shaped gables too. Extended in similar style at the rear in 1928 by *Briggs, Wolstenholme & Thornely*. The N side contains a large hall (now council chamber) with STAINED GLASS commemorating Arts, Sciences and Industry. Above, the steeply glazed roofs of the original art studios. Also inside, a lobby with tiles and mosaic, and an imperial staircase.

TOWN HALL (former), King Street. *See* Perambulation.

MUNICIPAL BUILDINGS, Library Street. *Bradshaw & Gass,* 1900. Built by the Royal London Friendly Society as seven shops with chambers above. Two extremely flamboyant façades of red terracotta in a Flemish Renaissance style. Hardly a plain bit of walling in sight – gables, balustrades, bay windows, pilasters, mermen, cornices, finials etc., and a tremendously lavish foliate frieze. The corner turret has a balcony but has lost its dome. Also a generous amount of glazing, essentially continuous mullioned windows on all three floors. Quieter extension to the Hewlett Street façade, dated 1939 on the rainwater hoppers.

COUNCIL OFFICES, Millgate. 1971. Built of a pre-cast concrete panel system. Dour. On an awkwardly sloping site.

MAGISTRATES' COURTS, Darlington Street. By the *Wigan Metropolitan Borough Council Architect, c.* 1992. Façade with relief figure of Justice in carved brick by *Christine Ward.*

COUNTY AND MAGISTRATES' COURTS (former), Crawford Street. *See* Perambulation, p. 672.

POLICE STATION, Harrogate Street. Of *c.* 1974. One of series designed by *Roger Booth,* Lancashire County Architect, employing the County Council-devised Lancashire Rationalised Building Method, a system of lightweight pre-cast concrete panels. Another is at Skelmersdale, *see* p. 588. A pale cuboid of textured concrete panels modulated by narrow vertical strips containing tinted windows.

POLICE STATION, Ormskirk Road (A577), Pemberton, 2 m. WSW. Edwardian, with Wrenaissance detailing. Shiny brick, and stone dressings.

THE HISTORY SHOP, Library Street and Rodney Street. *Alfred Waterhouse*'s former Free Library of 1878, now a local history library and gallery. Gothic of course, and an economic and eloquent essay. Brick with stone dressings. Stepped window lights in the Library Lane part, corbelled-out chimney on its Rodney Street gable. The high ground floor of the Rodney Street wing is now an open exhibition space, with cast-iron columns. Up a staircase with iron balustrade is the little-altered reading room above the exhibition space, with original shelving and a complex arrangement of galleries, the bays of which are integrated with the posts of the arch-braced roof trusses.

CARNEGIE LIBRARY (former), Ormskirk Road, Pemberton. *See* Outer Wigan.

SWIMMING BATHS, Rodney Street. *See* Perambulation, p. 673.

WIGAN AND LEIGH COLLEGE, Parson's Walk. Built as the Technical College and Linacre School in 1950–4. By *Howard Lobb* and *Grenfell Baines & Hargreaves,* and of little architectural interest.

BLUECOAT SCHOOL (former), Bishopsgate (just NW of the church). *See* Perambulation, p. 671.

MESNES HIGH SCHOOL (former), Parson's Walk. 1935–7, by *A.E. Munby.* Now the Wigan Infirmary Outpatients' Department. An uncomfortable mix of Moderne and Neo-Georgian motifs, three sides of a courtyard with a chunky clock tower and Crittall glazing. Brick varied in colour and bond.

ROYAL ALBERT EDWARD INFIRMARY, Wigan Lane (N). The core is by *Thomas Worthington*, opened in 1873. Red brick, with blue brick trim, symmetrical, the front range not large, but with a tower. Gothic. This is the administration block, with the kitchens in a rear wing. The Outpatients' Department, by *W. Chasen Ralph & Co.*, is of 1915 and has Jacobean and Wrenaissance features. Many alterations and subsequent phases, often obscuring the earlier buildings; that completed in 2004 feebly apes Worthington.

MESNES PARK. Opened 1878. A competition in 1877 was won by *John McClean*, a landscape gardener of Castle Donington. The area was on the small side, yet there is a serpentine lake. In the centre of the park, atop terracing, is an awkward octagonal PAVILION of yellow and red brick with iron porches and a big glazed lantern. It is by *W.H. Fletcher* of London. There is a proposal to remove the 1960s gallery-level floor, opening up the ground floor to the lantern. Also by Fletcher, a half-timbered LODGE and a COTTAGE inside the Mesnes Park Terrace gates. Iron BANDSTAND with tent roof, supplied by *George Smith & Co.* of Glasgow in 1890. – Seated bronze STATUE of Sir Francis Sharpe Powell, 1910, by *E.G. Gillick*.

WALLGATE STATION. *See* Perambulation, p. 672.

TOWN CENTRE PERAMBULATION

A circuit of the medieval town, which was built in the cruck of the River Douglas as it descends down from the N out of a dene and loops around to the NW. Much of the street plan remains, and combined with the topography this creates an attractive townscape of incident and variety. The tower of the parish church is the backdrop to many vignettes.

Start in the triangular MARKET PLACE at the top of the hill, where the four main streets of medieval Wigan meet: Wallgate, Standishgate, Millgate and Hallgate. At the SW corner on an awkward site alongside the narrow alley is MOOT HALL CHAMBERS, 1884, by *Issitt & Verity*, ashlar and classical, but missing its lively roofscape. Here stood the Moot Hall, first mentioned in 1422. When it all but fell down in 1719 it was replaced by the New Town Hall (demolished 1882), two stories and cupola, on the W side of the market. On the N side stands a handsome row of shops and chambers of 1904–6 by *Heaton, Ralph & Heaton*, the dominant building of the Market Place. Stripey; a corner turret with copper cupola at one end, and along the front six half-timbered gables, and another three down the side. The Market Place was re-landscaped in 1997 with the best intentions, but without a lightness of touch. At the centre a large MOSAIC by *Sebastian Boyesen* and local schools, including the seal, a cross, and illustrations of the town's history.

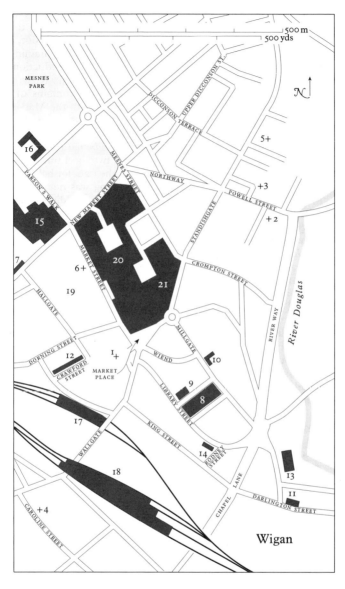

500 m
500 yds

MESNES PARK

16

PARSON'S WALK

15

MESNES STREET

NEW MARKET STREET

NORTHWAY

DICCONSON TERRACE

UPPER DICCONSON ST.

5+

+3

POWELL STREET

+2

STANDISHGATE

7

MARKET STREET

6+

20

21

CROMPTON STREET

RIVER WAY

River Douglas

HALLGATE

19

DORNING STREET

12

CRAWFORD STREET

MILLGATE

MARKET PLACE

1+

WIEND

10

LIBRARY STREET

9

8

17

KING STREET

WALLGATE

18

14

RODNEY STREET

CHAPEL LANE

13

11

DARLINGTON STREET

CAROLINE STREET

+4

Wigan

N

1	All Saints	11	Magistrates' Court
2	St George	12	County and Magistrates' Courts (former)
3	St John (R. C.)	13	Police Station
4	St Joseph (R. C.)	14	The History Shop
5	St Mary (R. C.)	15	Wigan and Leigh College
6	Queen's Hall Methodist	16	Mesnes High School (former)
	Mission (former)	17	Wallgate Station
7	Wigan Hall	18	North Western Station
8	Town Hall	19	Bus Station
9	Municipal Buildings	20	The Galleries Shopping Centre
10	Council Offices	21	Markinson Arcade

THE WIEND leading off the E side is a narrow winding medieval alley. On the S side, some mid-C18 houses, now a pub, on the N side some late C17 cottages. Where The Wiend opens out, a ROMAN ROAD of the C1 and remains of workshops containing iron slag and coal were excavated in 1983 (*see* Introduction, p. 16). Return to the Market Place along COOPERS ROW, a medieval yard. The JOHN BULL on the S side contains C17 fabric. The building beyond it on the corner with the Market Place is mainly Georgian (dated 1759), and was the Earl of Derby's Wigan residence. Facing this across the Market Place is the MARKETGATE CENTRE of 1990 by *Edmund Kirby*, with diamond-patterned gables. It reinterprets two local traditions, one for arcades, the other, an odd one of the C20, for half-timbered façades. Odd, because timber framing was not part of the Wigan townscape by the C20. But the re-cladding seems to have generated its own momentum earlier in the century, especially in STANDISHGATE; e.g., W.H. SMITH on the corner with Station Road illustrates, r., before (1893 by *Heaton, Ralph & Heaton* as the Royal Hotel) and, l., after (1925). Amongst this rash on the W side some better architecture. MARKINSON ARCADE by *Heaton, Ralph & Heaton*, 1897–8, is the best of three arcades connecting the street with the markets area behind (*see* below). Front of brick and red terracotta in a style of French and English C16 elements (the canopy is modern), with a simple, little-altered two-storey interior. The NATWEST BANK, built as Parr's Bank in 1898 by *William Owen*, is the best commercial building in Wigan. A tall, haughty French Renaissance façade, expertly proportioned and beautifully detailed, with gable and pyramid roof. Irregularly shaped pilastered banking hall. The Neo-Tudor MARKS & SPENCER on the E side is by *Norman Jones*, 1931.

200 yards N Standishgate is severed in two by POWELL STREET, the inner ring road, with much destruction. Beyond it, the WHITESMITHS ARMS, with its three gables, the last, largely intact C17 house in the town. Brick exposed on the r. return, with brick hoodmoulds. Stair-tower at the rear. (Inside, a raised cruck in the roof, and an urn-baluster dog-leg staircase: Philip Powell.) Next to it the vigorous free Baroque façade of THE GRIFFIN HOTEL, by *Ralph & Heaton*, dated 1905, then the street climbs out of the town centre past the two R.C. churches of St John and St Mary (*see* pp. 664–5) with a number of large Georgian town houses, e.g. the group of Nos. 134 (probably 1780s or later), 136 (1755) and 138. Three storeys and three or four bays. The latter two are now the MABS CROSS HOTEL. The street was for long the best address. On it, MAB'S CROSS, the stump of a probably C13 cross, one of a series of four (*see* Standish for the others). According to legend, from 1323 until her death Lady Mabel Bradshaigh did penance for bigamy by walking barefoot from Haigh Hall (q.v.) to this cross once a week.

The W extension of Powell Street is NORTHWAY, with a pastiche Georgian terrace, shown up by the genuine and very regular Late Georgian terrace houses of DICCONSON STREET, next door, going around the corner into UPPER DICCONSON

Street. Tuscan doorcases. Across Northway from here is Mesnes Street, with on the r. the bulk of The Galleries Shopping Centre, by *Leach, Rhodes & Walker*, 1985–c. 1990. A very large complex of some 70,000 sq. metres, built on the site of Wigan's C19 markets, containing shopping arcades, supermarket and covered market. Turn r. down Hindley Walk to enter. The cast-iron canopy at the entrance to the market hall is reused from its predecessor of 1877. Hindley Place opens out into Wigan Square at the heart of the development, an open-air market square enclosed entirely by brick façades with Postmodern half-timbered galleries (more of that half-timber disease) and overlooked by higher set-back walks and a tall, bold clock tower, like some weird film set (the tower inspired by mill water-towers). Off it is a sequence of arcades, e.g. Leigh Arcade, high and lined with pastiche Italianate walls and covered by a Neo-Victorian glass-and-iron roof. As a place it all works, because of the variety and interaction of spaces and levels, and the humane scale of most of them.

Leave Wigan Square on the w side by Orrell Arcade to Market Street. The style of The Galleries façade may not be to everyone's taste, but it largely succeeds in breaking down a massive structure into something that does not overpower the street. Opposite is the front only of the Queen's Hall Methodist Mission by *Bradshaw & Gass* (1907–8). Brick and buff terracotta Wrenaissance with a big – indeed far too big – but quite splendid terracotta domed lantern. Attached columns, pediments etc., and topped by a globe. The huge hall itself was demolished in 1985; the foyer now forms the chapel and the new ground-floor façades are by *Anthony Grimshaw*. Beyond the Mission on the same side is Hallgate, and off it on the r. Jaxon Court, which contains the last former back-to-back cottages in Wigan (these of the early C19). When Hallgate turns r., continue straight on down Dorning Street past the Grand Hotel, a Temperance hotel of the 1880s, to the unmissable bulk of the former Coop's Suit Factory, now a business centre and apartments. Four steepling parts to the street (the centre of a U-plan complex). The earliest section, r., is of 1871, by *R. Todd* of Southport; the middle parts, slightly projecting, are of 1888, by *Issitt & Verity*; and the l. section is of 1892, by *Verity* alone. Eighteen bays in all, four to six storeys high. Cream and red brick on a stone plinth. Superimposed giant blank arcades running all the way across, each with two storeys of windows recessed within each bay. One of the middle parts with enriched arcades, a Romanesque portal with clustered shafts, and a balustrade parapet. The l. return has twenty-three matching bays. The factory was established by Timothy Coop and James Marsden to employ girls made redundant by the Lancashire cotton famine in the 1860s.

King Street West starts opposite the factory, and l. off that climbs Crawford Street. All the way up the n side is the former Magistrates' and County Courts. The Magistrates' Court is the e part, of 1888, by *Henry Littler*; the County Court is the w section, of a decade later. But both are Elizabethan-style, in brick with stone dressings, and the differences between them minimal. Seventeen bays with corner turrets at either end, each with pointy hats; a rhythmic ascending row of gables and chimneys. At the top of the street near the W end of the PARISH CHURCH (*see* p. 660) is the former BLUECOAT SCHOOL, founded 1773. No more than a stone cottage, and it still has mullioned windows. Later a garage. The school moved to a plain new building in Hallgate in 1825 (demolished). Around the SW corner of the church to the war memorial (*see* p. 661), in a little court with the church on one side and the backs of the buildings of WALLGATE on the others. On the SW side is a small mid-C19 former tower BREWERY for the Dog and Partridge pub (now Last Orders, *see* below), a reminder of the industrial character of many burgage plots.

Through the S passage to WALLGATE itself, with on the r. a three-storey, three-bay late C18 or early C19 pub, now called the LAST ORDERS. Tuscan doorway. Then the POST OFFICE, 1884, of red brick and red sandstone and some Queen Anne features. Beyond that a former BANK, 1890 by *Issitt & Verity*. Free Renaissance, more luxuriant. Next, two pubs, one either side. On the E side, the former MINORCA HOTEL of *c.* 1820; on the W, the CLARENCE HOTEL, of red brick and matching terracotta in an attractively boxy, eclectic C17 style, with cross- and mullioned windows and a broad doorway of Doric columns and segmental pediment carrying a projecting bay. On down the hill to WALLGATE STATION, of 1896, for the Lancashire & Yorkshire Railway by their architect, *Henry Shelmerdine*. Extensive iron and glass porte cochère. Shelmerdine built chambers on the opposite side of the street too. Below the station on the same side is the VICTORIA HOTEL, 1894, by *Heaton, Ralph & Heaton* with an energetic frontage, and beyond that the long and equally lively eclectic terracotta façade of TOWER BUILDINGS, by *Bradshaw & Gass* of Bolton (1898). Huge amounts of glazing, much of it in bay windows, and missing its dome. Finally the SWAN AND RAILWAY HOTEL, also in red brick and terracotta, but altogether a more subtle building. 1898, by *W.E.V. Crompton*, exhibiting the influence of the Arts and Crafts Movement, e.g. the convex oriels. Quite a bit of the interior survives too.

Retrace steps to the former Minorca Hotel and turn r. into KING STREET, laid out in 1791 and Wigan's first post-medieval excursion into town planning. Some red brick Georgian houses survive, e.g. Nos. 21–25, five bays with a good Tuscan door-case. Nos. 26–34 are 1851 but remarkably Georgian still, and with odd pedimented bay windows. Next to them the GRIMES ARCADE of 1870 by *R.T. Johnson*, with a rather spreading free Venetian Gothic front in buff ashlar. King Street had a number of theatres and cinemas, and though they are all closed and many demolished it remains a focal point of Wigan nightlife, with its numerous cavernous bars. The former COUNTY PLAYHOUSE has a façade of white faience dated 1916. The ROYAL COURT THEATRE (in 2004 the Springbok bar) could seat 5,000. 1886, by *R.T. Johnson*; remodelled by *J.P. Briggs*, 1899. Red brick and terracotta front. The projecting part is

Briggs, with sparse Renaissance motifs on the first floor, and contains a fine marble-clad foyer and staircase. The auditorium has elements from different phases, including its conversion to a cinema in 1930 (by *Gray & Evans*), e.g. two balconies, some Adam-style plasterwork, and the proscenium arch. A little, pale sandstone palazzo of 1891 by *W. Verity* stands out on the w side, built as the Wigan Savings Bank. At the bottom of the street on the corner with RODNEY STREET is the former MUNICIPAL OFFICES, police station and court of 1866–7 by *Nuttall & Cook*. Later the Town Hall; at the time of writing half-demolished. Ashlar below, brick above. Italianate. On the N side of Rodney Street, The History Shop, i.e. the old library (*see* Public Buildings, p. 667).

On LIBRARY STREET around the corner is the SWIMMING BATHS of 1965–6. Not of architectural interest, but all credit to Wigan: it was only the fifth in Britain to go in for Olympic dimensions. Library Street was developed mainly between 1895 and 1905 and mainly in exuberant red brick and terra-cotta. On the E side, the TOWN HALL, and next to it across Hewlett Street, the MUNICIPAL BUILDINGS (*see* pp. 666–7). (At the end of Hewlett Street on MILLGATE is a mid-C18 house, of five bays with keyed lintels and a pedimented door-case with Ionic columns.) Beyond that come the former PRUDENTIAL ASSURANCE BUILDINGS by *Heaton, Ralph & Heaton*, 1905, in Flemish Transitional Gothic style infused with Art Nouveau, then a row of seven shops by the same practice built 1899–1903, three- and four-gabled bays with English Renaissance motifs. Thence back to the MARKET PLACE. On the N corner, the MANCHESTER AND COUNTY BANK, now a pub with 1990s ground-floor elevations, but pretty, original Loire-style sandstone uppers by *Mills & Murgatroyd*, of 1890 to the Market Place and 1895 to Library Street, each with frilly gables, the older with an off-set oriel. On the other corner the Queen Anne-style HSBC BANK of 1895 by *W.B.V. Crompton*.

TRANSPORT AND INDUSTRY

LEEDS AND LIVERPOOL CANAL and WIGAN PIER. The River Douglas was improved under the Douglas Navigation Act between the 1730s and 1742, by Wigan men wanting to make easier the export of local coal to the growing markets of Liverpool and beyond. The Navigation was incorporated in the first parts of the Leeds and Liverpool Canal in 1774, and the river entirely superseded in 1777. The final section of the canal opened in 1816, through Ince immediately E of Wigan (*see* p. 211), linking it with East Lancashire and Leeds.

The BASIN at WALLGATE is the termination of the 1774 works. A long slide into dereliction was reversed from 1982 with a programme of restoration and reuse, and the basin was relaunched as WIGAN PIER. Over the E end is a WAREHOUSE, No. 1 Wigan Pier, probably dating from *c.* 1815. Stone, two-storeyed, with a double barge hole under twin gables. Reconstructed as offices by *M. S. Churchward* in 1984. On the N quay, a number of warehouses, now a pub, museum, etc. The one of stone is probably the original terminal warehouse of *c.* 1770s; the others brick, are of the 1880s and 1890s, with timber-clad hoist towers, and one with a canopy oversailing the quayside. Also restored C19 offices, cottages and bridges and, under the road bridge on the canal opposite Tencherfield Mill, a DRY DOCK with cast-iron columns supporting a roof.

Opinions differ on the real identity of Wigan Pier, that butt of musical-hall jokes. The balance favours an overhead coal tramway demolished in 1910. After that the name was attached to the splendidly underwhelming upturned rails on the S quay of the basin, where coal trucks were emptied into barges from *c.* 1822 until 1929.

WALLGATE STATION. *See* Perambulation, p. 672.

RAILWAY BRIDGE, S of Wallgate on the line to Up Holland. Called the Adam Viaduct. One for the historians of civil engineering: an under-bridge of 1946 within an embankment that was the first pre-stressed reinforced concrete railway bridge in England. By the London, Midland & Scottish Railway, chief engineer *W. K. Wallace.*

MINE SHAFTS numbering 1,100 have been found within a four-mile radius of the town centre, and hundreds more are suspected. Early pits were dug within the town itself. Now there is little above ground to tell of the industry, except for spoil tips and the subsidence lakes, or 'flashes', S and SW of the town (*see* also Aspull and Haigh).

COTTON MILLS. From the C15 to the C17 Wigan was celebrated for its woollen bedding, then in the C18 cotton production started. By 1818 there were eight cotton mills, and by 1870 twenty-six, both spinning and weaving. The survivors are exclusively big Victorian and Edwardian structures.

GIDLOW MILL, Bridgeman Terrace. Now part of Wigan College. A model integrated mill of 1863–5 by *George Woodhouse* for Rylands & Sons, with integral boiler and engine house at the W end, chimney and weaving sheds. Low and long main range of three storeys and thirty-six bays, now with a carbuncle of the 1980s attached rudely to it. Small turrets. White and blue brick dressings employed to relieve the ordinary red. It was one of the most expensive mills ever built because of the completely fireproof construction, and the need for massive iron reinforcing ties. Unusually the cotton was received on the top floor, and processed down through the levels; Dacca-brand calico emerged from the weaving sheds. The design was reproduced in the United States by Woodhouse.

TRENCHERFIELD MILL, Pottery Road. Spinning mill of 1907–8 by *Potts, Son & Hennings*, for William Woods & Son. Spinning ceased in 1968. It stands alongside the Leeds and Liverpool Canal and in the 1980s was put to multiple new uses, including a museum, as part of the Wigan Pier regeneration project (*see* above). In 2005 work commenced to refurbish the building, with e.g. apartments. Red brick walling on an iron and steel frame. Four storeys and fifteen bays. Thin Edwardian Baroque detailing in yellow terracotta to the top floor and the tower, which has a pyramid roof. The engine house retains in working order its original 1906 triple-expansion STEAM ENGINE by *J. & E. Woods* of Bolton, though the chimney was demolished in 1975.

VICTORIA MILL, Miry Lane and Wallgate. Remnants of this mill of *c.* 1840 by *William Fairbairn* exhibit his characteristic severe pilastered style. An early survivor, for Wigan.   101

WESTERN MILLS, Swan Meadow Road. A colossal assemblage of three mills, two of them integrated (and two others demolished), and associated structures just S of Wigan Pier, all by *Stott & Sons* for ffarington Eckersley Ltd. They housed over 200,000 spindles and employed over 2,000 at the peak, and the whole is considered along with the Atlas Mills in Bolton to have been the largest textiles complex in the country. Each mill four-storeyed, of brick with minimal sandstone dressings, with cast-iron columns. Floors of different construction, illustrating the evolving attempts to produce structures that combined light weight (which made them cheaper to build) with as little interruption of the floorspace (i.e. as few columns) as possible (in order to maximise operating efficieny and minimise lighting costs). No. 1 Mill, 1884, has cast-iron beams and *Stott*'s patent double-jack-arch floors; No. 2 Mill, 1888, has steel beams and *Stott*'s patent triple-jack-arch floors; and No. 3 Mill, 1900 (the year ffarington Eckersley merged with neighbouring James Eckersley & Son to form Eckersley Ltd) has reinforced concrete floors and steel joists. More decorative are the offices dated 1904 and 1912, and a workers' welfare building of *c.* 1920. The demolished mills were James Eckersley & Son's Old Mill of *c.* 1830 and Large Mill of 1838 (the E part of the BOILER HOUSE to No. 1 Mill was built for the former). Of the WEAVING SHEDS, only No. 1 along Pottery Terrace survives intact. Weaving finished in 1988; now warehousing and workshops.

COOP'S SUIT FACTORY (former), Dorning Street. *See* Perambulation, p. 671.

H.J. HEINZ & CO. FACTORY, Spring Road, 2½ m. WNW. 1954–9, by *J. Douglass Mathews & Partners* in association with *Skidmore, Owings & Merrill*, who brought the latest American know-how. A vast building – originally 26,000 square yards. It is difficult to muster all of Pevsner's enthusiasm of 1969, perhaps because the crispness of the design is now harder to comprehend under incremental disfigurement.

OFFICES of GKN REINFORCEMENT (former), Woodhouse Lane, 1¼ m. NW. 1961. GKN were one of the biggest suppliers of reinforced concrete to the building industry in the 1960s. Slender, cigar-shaped external posts. Wall panels pre-cast, columns and floors cast *in situ*. The floors are of the firm's patent hollow-mould design, in section like the negative of a chocolate bar.

OUTER WIGAN

Areas include Whitley, Whelley, Scholes, Poolstock, Worsley, Winstanley, Pemberton, Lamberhead Green, Kit Green and Beech Hill. With the possible exception of Winstanley, none of these was a village before being absorbed into Wigan; none have pre-C19 churches. For churches *see* p. 660; for industry and transport, *see* p. 673. Areas SE of the Leeds and Liverpool Canal are in Ince-in-Makerfield (q.v.).

C19 working-class housing engulfs the town centre from the NW around to the S, and to the E across the River Douglas in SCHOLES, where Irish Catholics settled in the 1840s and 1850s. Much of their notorious housing was cleared and redeveloped with mainly medium-rise blocks and low-rise terracing. These areas were all pitted with coal mines well into the C20. The more genteel suburb was a strip N from the centre along the A49, especially in Swinley, though there are very few surviving villas of merit. The Eckersley family, owners of the Swan Meadow Mills (*see* p. 675), developed a model village at Poolstock from the 1850s, N and W of the church of St James (*see* p. 663), which they paid for. Ironically, most of the housing was demolished *c.* 1980 as unfit. Beyond, the usual C20 sprawl in most directions, extending as far to the SW as Winstanley, 2½ m. from the town centre.

CARNEGIE LIBRARY (former), Ormskirk Road, Pemberton, 1¾ m. WSW. 1906–7, by *J.B. & W. Thornely*. Brick and stone, in a conspicuous position on the main A577 road rising W out of Wigan where it divides either side. Symmetrical mullioned-and-transomed windows, but Baroque motifs as well, especially in the gabled front with superimposed orders facing down the hill. Converted to offices 2000.

ROYAL ALBERT EDWARD INFIRMARY, Wigan Lane, Swinley. *See* p. 668.

THE ELMS, Wigan Lane, Swinley, 1 m. N. A five-bay brick house of *c.* 1820–40 just N of the Infirmary (*see* p. 668), now used by the NHS. Doric stone porch.

MARYLEBONE HOUSE, Marylebone Place, Swinley, 1 m. N. Near the Elmes, an intact classical villa of the 1850s.

SWINLEY ROAD, Swinley. 1 m. N. Some big brick terraces, of the later C19. (No. 21 DICCONSON ROAD. Once the home of W.H. Lever, later Lord Leverhulme, with good Japanese interiors.)

GATEWAY AND LODGES, Wigan Lane, 1 m. N. The main entrance to Haigh Hall (*see* p. 187). Contemporary with the Hall, that is of *c.* 1827–44, and presumably therefore by the *7th Earl of Balcarres*, who apparently designed his own house. An impressive ensemble with central stone arch flanked by lodges, all in austere Neoclassical style. The arch has paired Doric pilasters either side; the lodges have set-back Tuscan columns, two to the outside and two to the park side.

HALL LANE COTTAGES, Pemberton Road, 3 m. SW. Probably late C17 or early C18. Dressed stone, flat-mullioned windows and labels.

JJB STADIUM, Robin Park, 1 m. w. By *Atherden Fuller Leng*, opened 1999. One of the better of the post-Hillsborough-disaster all-seater stadia. For Rugby League and football. It retains the traditional plan of four separate stands, rather than an uninterrupted bowl, allowing tantalising glimpses at the corners through into the ground. As the stadium fills, these views help to generate the sense of anticipation that is an integral part of spectator sport. Was this deliberate, or a happy by-product? The stands are not stand-alone – they are tied together by four giant bowstring trusses supporting the roofs, which spring from massive piers in the front corners of the end stands. These trusses give the stadium a strong identity. The detailing of their bearings stands out: crisp and bold, gigantically scaled.

The rest of ROBIN PARK is anonymous silvery-panelled sheds housing shops, cinemas, restaurants, a sports centre etc. The athletics GRANDSTAND has more character, with the same cladding. Buildings and roads are arranged confusingly and apparently haphazardly, when even an elementary plan – say, an avenue culminating in the stadium – could have bestowed some dignity and made the whole much more than the sum of its parts.

Two of the grandest PUBS are by *Heaton & Ralph*, ¾ m. NW of the town centre. The SPRINGFIELD HOTEL, Springfield Road, is dated 1903. Hard red brick and orange terracotta. Free Renaissance frills, gables on both façades and a little cupola'd turret. The lush interior is largely intact. Elaborate central counter. The PAGEFIELD HOTEL, Park Road and Gidlow Lane, also has much of its original interior, including a good staircase.

TYLDESLEY MONUMENT, Wigan Lane, Swinley, 1 m. N. A square pillar with a ball on top. It commemorates the spot where Sir Thomas Tyldesley was fatally injured in the Civil War. Erected in 1679 and later rebuilt.

WINSTANLEY HALL, w of Pemberton Road (A571), 3 m. SW. *p. 35* Actually in Billinge-with-Winstanley (q.v.). Elizabethan. Bought in 1595 by James Bankes, a London goldsmith, and still in the possession of the family, though disused at the time of writing. The original façade (E) is much like those of Birchley Hall – which seems to have come first – and Bispham Hall, both very near (*see* pp. 150–1). Two projecting wings and a recessed centre with square projections in the re-entrant angles, one obviously the hall bay, the other originally almost certainly the porch (cf. Bispham, p. 151). The gables were replaced in the early C19 by a parapet by *Lewis Wyatt*, who worked at Winstanley in 1818–19. Ground-floor windows with transoms, lighting the hall. The centre one is of ten lights with a king mullion. Most of the others are mullioned only. The entrance was in the r. re-entrant projection, in the conventional position for the screens passage. Round the corner on the s side is the present main entrance, in a four-storey central tower. This front, with its Doric-columned doorway and label-moulded mullioned-and-transomed windows, is by *Wyatt*. On the sw corner is a canted bay of 1780 (raised by

Lewis Wyatt). Plans were supplied by *L. Robinson*. More of the gabled W side, with its varied windows, is part of this work too, and has a datestone. Assorted C19 extensions to the N end are of after 1819 (datestones of 1843 and 1889), but incorporate some C17 work. The interior is of disappointingly little interest.

STABLE YARD. W block of 1834. Five bays. Outer bays concave and with arched entrances, centre bay with cartway bowed and projecting out and up. Incorporated at the rear is a BARN, probably C17, with strutted trusses. S block probably early C19. Some mullioned windows with pointed lights. Middle bay raised as a low clock tower with pigeon loft. N block rock-faced stone, possibly *c.* 1859. Canted ends, centre projecting and raised. Two- and three-light windows with canted heads; above, octagonal and square pitching eyes. Two Tuscan cupolas. In the centre of the yard is a big NEPTUNE FOUNTAIN of *c.* 1830 by *William Spence*. Stone, with rearing horses etc. Elaborate iron GATES and stone piers, dated 1859. Also ESTATE OFFICE and MALT HOUSE (both 1884), and DAIRY HOUSE (late C18). – LODGE and GATEPIERS, Pemberton Road. Of *c.* 1818, with mullioned-and-transomed windows and presumably by *Lewis Wyatt*. – The secluded PARK is severed by the M6 in a cutting. It includes a walled garden. A MOAT lies ⅓ m. NW of the hall (the manor is first mentioned in 1212). (Philip Powell reports in the park ¼ m. N a *cottage orné* for an estate official, looking of the early C19.)

WINWICK

Winwick is not an attractive village, but it has a large and handsome church atop a slight wooded hill, the spire rising from the trees. The centre of a large pre-Domesday parish on the route of a Roman road (*see* p. 15), in the early C19 Winwick was reckoned to be the wealthiest living in the country.

ST OSWALD. An impressive, evidently medieval church, with some great puzzles and a chancel by *A.W.N. Pugin* of 1846–9. Only the W tower is now convincingly old. This has satisfyingly massive stepped diagonal buttresses and a sturdy stone spire (rebuilt in Austin & Paley's restoration, 1869). The details are mid-C14, something seemingly confirmed by the now lost twin carved shields of Sir Gilbert de Haydock and Sir Gilbert de Southworth on the tower: they were both alive *c.* 1358. Pretty niches l. and r. of the reticulated W window; they now contain figures of St Oswald and St Anthony, 1973. To the r. of Anthony is his pig, a small panel known as the Winwick Pig. There are such panels in Norman sculpture, but this is likely to be later and merely primitive. One explanation has it that it is a sow, an anagram of St Oswald Winwick. The N aisle E and W walls, S aisle W wall and SW turret are also of worn original sandstone. Around the SW corner of the S aisle is a (renewed) inscription commemorating King Oswald of Northumbria,

according to one tradition killed near here in 642 (*see* St
Oswald's Well, Newton-le-Willows, p. 531), and the date 1530
for the *renovatio* of this wall by the priest Henry Johnson. But
much of the present stonework must date from the 1869
restoration. The tracery was also renewed then, apparently
accurately. It is Late Perp, with round-headed uncusped lights
like those at Lydiate and Sefton (qq.v.) and others of this group
of C16 churches in SW Lancashire. An interesting feature is the
embattled super-transoms, with Tudor roses at the intersections with the verticals. The N aisle tracery (with plaques
carved IHS in place of roses) is almost identical, suggest this
was put up, or rebuilt, at or about the same time. The boxy S
porch was built or rebuilt in 1721. It is embattled and has angle
buttresses, but the gaping segmental-headed doorway and the
mouldings are as unmedieval as one would expect of the date.

The INTERIOR is handsome, but contains the puzzles. The
S arcade with quatrefoil piers is evidently early C14 in style,
though rebuilt in 1836 by *John Palmer*, but the N arcade is very
odd, with clumsy big piers, far wider than their arches. The
arches are probably late C16 – the moulding is comparable with
Standish (q.v.) – but the weird piers, with attached shafts and
hollows and crudely carved capitals, could conceivably be
Perp. More remarkably, the octagonal bases appear to be C12
or C13 capitals reused, each with engaged shafts and four primitive heads, two of them with bishops' mitres. Some of the
stone is quite worn, and none of the elements fits together at
all convincingly. So what to make of this? Are the bases reused?
And the piers too? And were they installed before or after, or
at the same time as the arches they support? The clerestory is
Late Perp, as the C14 nave roof-line inside against the tower
shows, though the fenestration is different N and S. The
arrangement of rounded-headed lights in the three N windows
compares with the *c.* 1530 aisle tracery; the uncusped pointed
lights of the six S windows compare with the original windows
of Wigan parish church (q.v.), which are possibly mid-C16. The
two E bays of the aisles are the Gerard Chapel, N, and Legh
Chapel, S. The Legh Chapel (founded in 1330 by Sir Gilbert
de Haydock) has different Perp fenestration and external
details from the rest of the aisle, from which it is separated by
an arch.* It has the best of the CEILINGS, a fine Tudor panelled job with angels. The Gerard Chapel ceiling is C19. The
massive roofs over the aisles and the nave are another puzzle.
Superficially they are similar – panelled, slightly canted, with
thickly moulded beams. The aisle roofs appear genuinely Perp.
The N one is quite a bit coarser with wall-posts crudely hacked
off, this because neither roof is set out to space with the arcades
or windows (corbels remain in the S aisle for an earlier roof).
Do the dates 1699, S, and 1700, N, carved on them, along with
the names of the churchwardens, commemorate repairs? The

---

*Until 1848 there was a chapel screen dated 1471. Could this be the date of the
fabric?

nave roof is similarly dated 1701 and 1702 with a list of names
including the rector, the Hon. Henry Finch (who paid for it).
However, it looks all right for something of that date made to
match the others, only to be undone by some unmedieval
moulding e.g. the beaded secondary ribs. Nevertheless, if it is
all of that date, and not a rebuilding, it is a striking, early
example of historicism. One boss is carved with an Eagle and
Child, the emblem of the Stanleys, Earls of Derby and patrons
of the living since the C15.

For the CHANCEL we are on much safer ground. *Pugin*
rebuilt it in 1846–9 – one of six Anglican church jobs undertaken by this arch-Catholic. Despite the strain caused by
working with the always right and ever obsessive Pugin, there

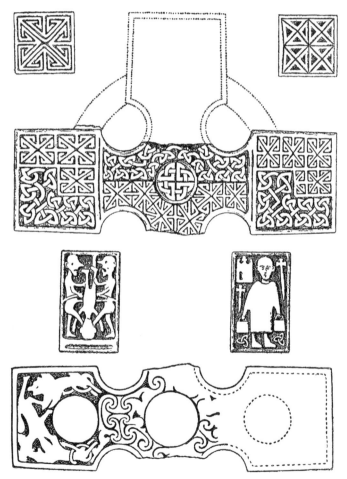

Winwick, St Oswald. Anglo-Saxon cross fragment.
(*Victoria County History of Lancashire*, vol. 1, 1906)

seems to have been a deep understanding between the architect, aged thirty-four, and the Rev. J.J. Hornby, aged sixty-nine, who was honoured to be working with the man he considered the world's greatest artist. The style is Dec, in unapologetic contrast to the nave, but apparently following the replaced chancel in form and detail pretty accurately: Pugin called it the 'best restoration that has hitherto been accomplished', and described the four-light E window as an exact copy (elsewhere we are told that it had been mutilated). Rosettes around the window and in the cornice replicate the medieval work. The roof is steep-pitched like its predecessor, but higher – rising above that of the nave – because Pugin raised the floor level, adamant that the chancel would appear sunken otherwise. The ogee SEDILIA, the ALTAR and REREDOS are of course Pugin's too, but the first we are told are a copy of the original, as are the doors. It is all exquisitely composed. The roof has a rich paint scheme restored in 1970; the internal walls are limewashed. Also the VESTRY, characteristically Pugin, with its tall castellated chimneystack. Inside the vestry, a Pugin fireplace.

OTHER FITTINGS. In the N chapel, a fragment of a big Perp FONT. – PULPIT. Wooden, dated apparently 1849. *Pugin* proposed stone, but if the date is correct this must be his. – In the vestry one beam from the medieval ROOD LOFT, with vine frieze and eleven statue brackets. – The beautiful present SCREEN and STALLS are by *Pugin*. Pugin fervently believed in screens. – IRON SCREENS to the two chapels of 1848 too. – An elegant COMMUNION TABLE, now in the Gerard Chapel. Dated 1725. Cabriole legs; inlaid top with rector's monogram and the churchwardens' initials. – CROSS. In the same chapel the cross-bar of an amazingly large ring-headed C10 cross – the bar is more than 5 ft (1.5 metres) long, which would have made the complete cross the largest known anywhere in England. It has on the front divers interlace patterns and on the back large blobs and animals. Most intriguing and unusual are the arm ends, whose interpretation has been a matter of debate. New research by Prof. Richard Bailey, however, suggests that one shows a priest holding bells, with a church in the corner, and the other a naked soul being tortured in hell – held side down and prodded – by two ferocious figures. The ornament and iconography are strongly influenced by the Celtic world. One shows two rather ferocious men holding a third upside down between them; they appear to be sawing him in half. – CHANDELIER. Of brass, probably C18. – PLAQUE, by Pugin, 1848. Charming, brass, with Gothic script. In the chancel to commemorate its rebuilding. – CHARITY BOARD. S aisle. Early C19, large, five ogee-arched panels. – STAINED GLASS. The fine chancel windows are to *Pugin*'s designs and made by *Hardman*. Mostly large individual figures. Those in the E (the Apostles) were given by the 13th Earl of Derby.* S aisle W, a good Jesse

---

* The E window was mismeasured and had to be cut down; Pugin wrote that he 'never took so much pain with a window in my life'.

window, †1890, by *Shrigley & Hunt*. N aisle E, *Powell & Sons* of Whitefriars, 1937.

MONUMENTS. In the N chapel, an impressive brass to Piers Gerard, †1492. A 4ft 5in. figure (1.4 metres), though badly rubbed, under a triple canopy. He wears broad-toed shoes, an early case. – Most of the rest in the s, the Legh, chapel: a brass to Sir Peter Legh, †1527 and his wife. 30 in. (75 cm.) figures. He wears the vestment of a priest under his armour, as he was ordained after the death of his wife. – Carved panels, some heraldic, from an early C17 alabaster tomb, now set against the wall. – Richard Legh, †1687. Attributed to *John Nost*. Two free-standing busts against baldacchino drapery. One of the most extravagant in the county and of superior quality, but pretty stiff composition. – Benet Legh, †1755, aged eight. Allegorical female figure leaning over a medallion. – Mrs Ellen Legh, †1831. By *R.J.Wyatt*, made in Rome. Relief scene. An angel is ready to take her away. Grieving husband and baby are left behind. – Many more tablets, including N aisle, W wall, aedicule with engaged columns, Rev. John Stanley, †1781, by *B. Bromfield* of Liverpool.

MANOR HOUSE, Golborne Road, Opposite the church. Now four bays. The cartouche of the heavily voussoired lintel is dated 1717. This is right for the pedimented Doric surround and some of the flush sash boxes. The two bays to the l. have been made one, perhaps a century later, and the furthest l. bay is clearly a C19 extension (along, surely, with the unified roof). But on the exposed brick rear elevation are windows with brick labels, which must be C17. On the r. return are two plaques – WWW 55 and WWW 57 – 1655 and 1657? (Inside are stone cellars and a dog-leg newel stair. DCMS.)

One or two altered houses and cottages survive around the church, such as the C17 CHURCH HOUSE FARMHOUSE, Golborne Road, which may have a timber frame beneath the brick and pebbledash.

WINWICK PARK, Newton Road (A49). Begun *c.* 2000. An upmarket development of 'executive' semis and detached houses, in a range of biscuit-tin Neo-Georgian styles. Some are more New England than s Lancashire, but they are more correct than the norm, e.g. sliding (uPVC) sashes, Regency balconies (reconstituted stone), Tuscan porticoes (but plastic slates and stretcher-bond brick). Designed by the developers, *Countryside Properties*. Down the centre is Winwick Park Avenue, opening into a square where for once the house types are consistent. It's easy to be snooty about these aspirational estates and often illiterate theme-park architecture, but this is well cared for (so far), well planted and, significantly, not 'gated', so does not feel defensive or insular. It occupies the site of the huge Lancashire County Asylum, principally 1897–1902, by *W.S. Skinner, Crisp & Oatley* of Bristol. Its R.C. CHAPEL remains, now a nursery. Arts and Crafts-influenced Perp, tracery with Art Nouveau touches. Some thoughtful moments (e.g. the bellcote). Some later, typical early C20 ward blocks survive to the W as part of an NHS unit. The hospital was built, in its turn, on the site of the early C18 Rectory (or Hall).

MYDDLETON HALL, 1 m. E on Delph Lane. The modest building we see now is nearly back to what was in the C17, after the demolition of domineering C19 W and N extensions. Brick, three bays and two storeys. Dated 1658 over the door. Gables to the cross-wings with C19 bargeboards. Labelled many-light mullioned-and-transomed windows, some replacements. To the r. is a twin-gabled C19 addition, in romantic keeping, but subservient. C20 diagonal chimney flues. The N wall with round-headed window, 1960s, encases the retained C19 staircase behind the hall. The rich Neo-C17 Victorian panelling in this room is a recent incorporation. A little C19 gabled LODGE at the junction of Delph Lane and Myddleton Lane. The Delph, the quarry which supplied the stone, remains as part of the garden.

MYDDLETON HALL FARMHOUSE. Across the lane from the Hall. Brick, dated 1657, with three storeys and gable to the road, extended and altered and now divided in two. With a little raised brick decoration and sandstone plinth and quoins. The picturesque collection of windows has been ignorantly replaced with uPVC.

(LOWER ALDER ROOT FARMHOUSE, Hollins Lane, ½ m. w. The DCMS reports, behind an unremarkable pebble-dashed exterior, a sixteen-panelled ceiling to the parlour, of possibly C16 date, with heavily moulded beams.)

BARROW, Highfield Lane. See p. 165.

WOOLDEN

Eccles

On the W edge of Chat Moss, along the negligible valley of the Glaze Brook. No village.

GREAT WOOLDEN HALL, Woolden Road. Now three dwellings. Brick, mostly of the early to mid-C17, and probably encasing a timber frame. Five irregular bays, the outer ones with gables of different sizes; the W bay is an addition, probably late C17. The other four form a half-H-plan, with wings projecting on the N side. This is now the rear, with additional irregular gabled projections (the second from the E of the mid C18, containing a staircase of that date), but it may once have been the front. Predominantly, ugly C19 casement windows on all sides. A number of blocked windows of conflicting arrangement, and some blocked brick-mullioned windows in the E return. Big chimneystacks, apparently C19 rebuilds. The lateral stack, which has an embattled base, fixes the position of the hall as the second and third bays from the E; the screens and front door (now blocked) were at the W end with the kitchen beyond. The E bay was the parlour. In the roof above the former hall is an arch-braced collar truss, suggesting that the hall was originally open. To confuse matters, the timber-framed cross-wall between the hall and the kitchen bay at first-floor level has a doorway with an ogee head, a style which may date it to the late C15–early C16; if *in situ*, this implies that there was a floor over the hall at that time. There are similar lintels in another timber-framed wall. In a room above the hall now, panelling probably of the mid C17, a time when the best room was often a first-floor great or dining room above the hall.

LITTLE WOOLDEN HALL, E, off Holcroft Lane. Brick; *c.* 1800. A seven-bay front with the three middle bays a little recessed. Niches l. and r. of the doorway. There was a castellated porch. The back is not nearly as regular, suggesting that this may be a surviving part of the previous house (possibly early C18), which was apparently destroyed by fire.

IRON AGE FARMSTEAD, ¼ m. W of Great Woolden Hall. Above the river; nothing visible. Occupied in at least three phases between 500 B.C. and A.D. 200. Finds of both Roman and Cheshire stone pottery. With embankment and ditches (*see* also Introduction, p. 14).

WOOLSTON *see* WARRINGTON, p. 621

5000

WORTHINGTON

No village.

MANOR HOUSE, Chorley Lane (A5106). A cruck-framed yeoman's house modernised in the C17–C18 by adding a parlour and rebuilding in stone and brick. Five bays. The date of 1671 on the doorway is when the upper end was rebuilt with a porch and a two-and-a-half-storey parlour wing with mullioned windows. The rest was re-clad in the following decades. Inside, one fine cruck truss survives, with mouldings and an arch-braced collar suggesting it was central to a two-bay hall (cf. Peel Hall, Ince-in-Makerfield, p. 211), but the scale suggests non-gentry origin. A late C15 date has been put forward by Gary Miller for this, and on the basis of its quarter-round beams an early C17 date for the inserted ceiling. The beams rest on a moulded firehood bressumer. There is a turned spere post and, projecting out from one side of the inglenook, a snug little bay window with benches and panelling round the walls.

MILL BRIDGE FARMHOUSE, W off Chorley Lane (A5106). A much bashed-about brick baffle-entry house of 1694 with parlour wing. Interesting porch – external archway and two inner doors side-by-side, for separate entry to the house body and parlour.

WORTHINGTON HALL, W off Chorley Lane (A5106). A fragment, dated 1577 on the lintel. Four bays. Elaborate timber framing survives only to the entrance bay, with panels with crosses and knobbly saltires. First floor jettied out on a carved bressumer, blocked timber-mullioned hall window below (the porch is recent). The stone E bay is the kitchen, of *c.* 1700. W end shortened by removing the parlour bay, and rebuilt in brick in the C20. The back is C18 stone, now mostly rendered. Inside, stairs now occupy the screens passage, against which is a cross-axial fireplace in the former hall with a beefy bressumer. C16 trusses, one a kingpost, others with collars.

On PLATT LANE an early C19 stone laith house; N off it, BLACK LAWYERS, now essentially late C20, but dereliction in the 1980s revealed high quality works.

MILE POST. On the Chorley Road, A5106, N of Red Rock Lane. Delightful cast-iron sign on stumpy flat fluted post, cast by the *Haigh Foundry* (*see* p. 187) in 1837 for the turnpike.

Three large Victorian VILLAS E of the A1508.

GLOSSARY

Numbers and letters refer to the illustrations (by John Sambrook)
on pp. 696–703.

ABACUS: flat slab forming the top of a capital (3a).

ACANTHUS: classical formalized leaf ornament (4b).

ACCUMULATOR TOWER: *see* Hydraulic power.

ACHIEVEMENT: a complete display of armorial bearings.

ACROTERION: plinth for a statue or ornament on the apex or ends of a pediment; more usually, both the plinth and what stands on it (4a).

AEDICULE (*lit.* little building): architectural surround, consisting usually of two columns or pilasters supporting a pediment.

AGGREGATE: *see* Concrete.

AISLE: subsidiary space alongside the body of a building, separated from it by columns, piers, or posts.

ALMONRY: a building from which alms are dispensed to the poor.

AMBULATORY (*lit.* walkway): aisle around the sanctuary (q.v.).

ANGLE ROLL: roll moulding in the angle between two planes (1a).

ANSE DE PANIER: *see* Arch.

ANTAE: simplified pilasters (4a), usually applied to the ends of the enclosing walls of a portico *in antis* (q.v.).

ANTEFIXAE: ornaments projecting at regular intervals above a Greek cornice, originally to conceal the ends of roof tiles (4a).

ANTHEMION: classical ornament like a honeysuckle flower (4b).

APRON: raised panel below a window or wall monument or tablet.

APSE: semicircular or polygonal end of an apartment, especially of a chancel or chapel. In classical architecture sometimes called an *exedra*.

ARABESQUE: non-figurative surface decoration consisting of flowing lines, foliage scrolls etc., based on geometrical patterns. Cf. Grotesque.

ARCADE: series of arches supported by piers or columns. *Blind arcade* or *arcading*: the same applied to the wall surface. *Wall arcade*: in medieval churches, a blind arcade forming a dado below windows. Also a covered shopping street.

ARCH: Shapes *see* 5c. *Basket arch* or *anse de panier* (basket handle): three-centred and depressed, or with a flat centre. *Nodding*: ogee arch curving forward from the wall face. *Parabolic*: shaped like a chain suspended from two level points, but inverted. Special purposes. *Chancel*: dividing chancel from nave or crossing. *Crossing*: spanning piers at a crossing (q.v.). *Relieving or discharging*: incorporated in a wall to relieve superimposed weight (5c). *Skew*: spanning responds not diametrically opposed. *Strainer*: inserted in an opening to resist inward pressure. *Transverse*: spanning a main axis (e.g. of a vaulted space). *See also* Jack arch, Triumphal arch.

ARCHITRAVE: formalized lintel, the lowest member of the classical entablature (3a). Also the moulded frame of a door or window (often borrowing the profile of a classical architrave). For *lugged* and *shouldered* architraves *see* 4b.

ARCUATED: dependent structurally on the arch principle. Cf. Trabeated.

ARK: chest or cupboard housing the

tables of Jewish law in a synagogue.

ARRIS: sharp edge where two surfaces meet at an angle (3a).

ASHLAR: masonry of large blocks wrought to even faces and square edges (6d).

ASTRAGAL: classical moulding of semicircular section (3f).

ASTYLAR: with no columns or similar vertical features.

ATLANTES: *see* Caryatids.

ATRIUM (plural: atria): inner court of a Roman or C20 house; in a multi-storey building, a toplit covered court rising through all storeys. Also an open court in front of a church.

ATTACHED COLUMN: *see* Engaged column.

ATTIC: small top storey within a roof. Also the storey above the main entablature of a classical façade.

AUMBRY: recess or cupboard to hold sacred vessels for the Mass.

BAILEY: *see* Motte-and-bailey.

BALANCE BEAM: *see* Canals.

BALDACCHINO: free-standing canopy, originally fabric, over an altar. Cf. Ciborium.

BALLFLOWER: globular flower of three petals enclosing a ball (1a). Typical of the Decorated style.

BALUSTER: pillar or pedestal of bellied form. *Balusters*: vertical supports of this or any other form, for a handrail or coping, the whole being called a *balustrade* (6c). *Blind balustrade*: the same applied to the wall surface.

BARBICAN: outwork defending the entrance to a castle.

BARGEBOARDS (corruption of 'vergeboards'): boards, often carved or fretted, fixed beneath the eaves of a gable to cover and protect the rafters.

BAROQUE: style originating in Rome *c.*1600 and current in England *c.*1680–1720, characterized by dramatic massing and silhouette and the use of the giant order.

BARROW: burial mound.

BARTIZAN: corbelled turret, square or round, frequently at an angle.

BASCULE: hinged part of a lifting (or bascule) bridge.

BASE: moulded foot of a column or pilaster. For *Attic* base *see* 3b.

BASEMENT: lowest, subordinate storey; hence the lowest part of a classical elevation, below the *piano nobile* (q.v.).

BASILICA: a Roman public hall; hence an aisled building with a clerestory.

BASTION: one of a series of defensive semicircular or polygonal projections from the main wall of a fortress or city.

BATTER: intentional inward inclination of a wall face.

BATTLEMENT: defensive parapet, composed of *merlons* (solid) and *crenels* (embrasures) through which archers could shoot; sometimes called *crenellation*. Also used decoratively.

BAY: division of an elevation or interior space as defined by regular vertical features such as arches, columns, windows etc.

BAY LEAF: classical ornament of overlapping bay leaves (3f).

BAY WINDOW: window of one or more storeys projecting from the face of a building. *Canted*: with a straight front and angled sides. *Bow window*: curved. *Oriel*: rests on corbels or brackets and starts above ground level; also the bay window at the dais end of a medieval great hall.

BEAD-AND-REEL: *see* Enrichments.

BEAKHEAD: Norman ornament with a row of beaked bird or beast heads usually biting into a roll moulding (1a).

BELFRY: chamber or stage in a tower where bells are hung.

BELL CAPITAL: *see* 1b.

BELLCOTE: small gabled or roofed housing for the bell(s).

BERM: level area separating a ditch from a bank on a hill-fort or barrow.

BILLET: Norman ornament of small half-cylindrical or rectangular blocks (1a).

BLIND: *see* Arcade, Baluster, Portico.

BLOCK CAPITAL: *see* 1a.

BLOCKED: columns, etc. interrupted by regular projecting

blocks (*blocking*), as on a Gibbs surround (4b).

BLOCKING COURSE: course of stones, or equivalent, on top of a cornice and crowning the wall.

BOLECTION MOULDING: covering the joint between two different planes (6b).

BOND: the pattern of long sides (*stretchers*) and short ends (*headers*) produced on the face of a wall by laying bricks in a particular way (6e).

BOSS: knob or projection, e.g. at the intersection of ribs in a vault (2c).

BOWTELL: a term in use by the C15 for a form of roll moulding, usually three-quarters of a circle in section (also called *edge roll*).

BOW WINDOW: see Bay window.

BOX FRAME: timber-framed construction in which vertical and horizontal wall members support the roof (7). Also concrete construction where the loads are taken on cross walls; also called *cross-wall construction*.

BRACE: subsidiary member of a structural frame, curved or straight. *Bracing* is often arranged decoratively e.g. quatrefoil, herringbone (7). See also Roofs.

BRATTISHING: ornamental crest, usually formed of leaves, Tudor flowers or miniature battlements.

BRESSUMER (*lit.* breast-beam): big horizontal beam supporting the wall above, especially in a jettied building (7).

BRICK: See Bond, Cogging, Engineering, Gauged, Tumbling.

BRIDGE: *Bowstring*: with arches rising above the roadway which is suspended from them. *Clapper*: one long stone forms the roadway. *Roving*: see Canal. *Suspension*: roadway suspended from cables or chains slung between towers or pylons. *Stay-suspension* or *stay-cantilever*: supported by diagonal stays from towers or pylons. See also Bascule.

BRISES-SOLEIL: projecting fins or canopies which deflect direct sunlight from windows.

BROACH: see Spire and IC.

BUCRANIUM: ox skull used decoratively in classical friezes.

BULL-NOSED SILL: sill displaying a pronounced convex upper moulding.

BULLSEYE WINDOW: small oval window, set horizontally (cf. Oculus). Also called *œil de bœuf*.

BUTTRESS: vertical member projecting from a wall to stabilize it or to resist the lateral thrust of an arch, roof, or vault (IC, 2c). A *flying buttress* transmits the thrust to a heavy abutment by means of an arch or half-arch (IC).

CABLE OR ROPE MOULDING: originally Norman, like twisted strands of a rope.

CAMES: see Quarries.

CAMPANILE: free-standing bell-tower.

CANALS: *Flash lock*: removable weir or similar device through which boats pass on a flush of water. Predecessor of the *pound lock*: chamber with gates at each end allowing boats to float from one level to another. *Tidal gates*: single pair of lock gates allowing vessels to pass when the tide makes a level. *Balance beam*: beam projecting horizontally for opening and closing lock gates. *Roving bridge*: carrying a towing path from one bank to the other.

CANTILEVER: horizontal projection (e.g. step, canopy) supported by a downward force behind the fulcrum.

CAPITAL: head or crowning feature of a column or pilaster; for classical types see 3; for medieval types see Ib.

CARREL: compartment designed for individual work or study.

CARTOUCHE: classical tablet with ornate frame (4b).

CARYATIDS: female figures supporting an entablature; their male counterparts are *Atlantes* (*lit.* Atlas figures).

CASEMATE: vaulted chamber, with embrasures for defence, within a castle wall or projecting from it.

CASEMENT: side-hinged window.

CASTELLATED: with battlements (q.v.).

CAST IRON: hard and brittle, cast in a mould to the required shape.

Wrought iron is ductile, strong in tension, forged into decorative patterns or forged and rolled into e.g. bars, joists, boiler plates; *mild steel* is its modern equivalent, similar but stronger.

CATSLIDE: *See* 8a.

CAVETTO: concave classical moulding of quarter-round section (3f).

CELURE OR CEILURE: enriched area of roof above rood or altar.

CEMENT: *see* Concrete.

CENOTAPH (*lit.* empty tomb): funerary monument which is not a burying place.

CENTRING: wooden support for the building of an arch or vault, removed after completion.

CHAMFER (*lit.* corner-break): surface formed by cutting off a square edge or corner. For types of chamfers and *chamfer stops see* 6a. *See also* Double chamfer.

CHANCEL: part of the E end of a church set apart for the use of the officiating clergy.

CHANTRY CHAPEL: often attached to or within a church, endowed for the celebration of Masses principally for the soul of the founder.

CHEVET (*lit.* head): French term for chancel with ambulatory and radiating chapels.

CHEVRON: V-shape used in series or double series (later) on a Norman moulding (1a). Also (especially when on a single plane) called *zigzag*.

CHOIR: the part of a cathedral, monastic or collegiate church where services are sung.

CIBORIUM: a fixed canopy over an altar, usually vaulted and supported on four columns; cf. Baldacchino. Also a canopied shrine for the reserved sacrament.

CINQUEFOIL: *see* Foil.

CIST: stone-lined or slab-built grave.

CLADDING: external covering or skin applied to a structure, especially a framed one.

CLERESTORY: uppermost storey of the nave of a church, pierced by windows. Also high-level windows in secular buildings.

CLOSER: a brick cut to complete a bond (6e).

CLUSTER BLOCK: *see* Multi-storey.

COADE STONE: ceramic artificial stone made in Lambeth 1769–*c.*1840 by Eleanor Coade (†1821) and her associates.

COB: walling material of clay mixed with straw. Also called *pisé*.

COFFERING: arrangement of sunken panels (coffers), square or polygonal, decorating a ceiling, vault, or arch.

COGGING: a decorative course of bricks laid diagonally (6e). Cf. Dentilation.

COLLAR: *see* Roofs and 7.

COLLEGIATE CHURCH: endowed for the support of a college of priests.

COLONNADE: range of columns supporting an entablature. Cf. Arcade.

COLONNETTE: small medieval column or shaft.

COLOSSAL ORDER: *see* Giant order.

COLUMBARIUM: shelved, niched structure to house multiple burials.

COLUMN: a classical, upright structural member of round section with a shaft, a capital, and usually a base (3a, 4a).

COLUMN FIGURE: carved figure attached to a medieval column or shaft, usually flanking a doorway.

COMMUNION TABLE: unconsecrated table used in Protestant churches for the celebration of Holy Communion.

COMPOSITE: *see* Orders.

COMPOUND PIER: grouped shafts (q.v.), or a solid core surrounded by shafts.

CONCRETE: composition of *cement* (calcined lime and clay), *aggregate* (small stones or rock chippings), sand and water. It can be poured into *formwork* or *shuttering* (temporary frame of timber or metal) on site (*in-situ* concrete), or *pre-cast* as components before construction. *Reinforced*: incorporating steel rods to take the tensile force. *Pre-stressed*: with tensioned steel rods. Finishes include the impression of boards left by formwork (*board-marked* or *shuttered*), and texturing with steel brushes (*brushed*) or hammers (*hammer-dressed*). *See also* Shell.

CONSOLE: bracket of curved outline (4b).

COPING: protective course of masonry or brickwork capping a wall (6d).

CORBEL: projecting block supporting something above. *Corbel course*: continuous course of projecting stones or bricks fulfilling the same function. *Corbel table*: series of corbels to carry a parapet or a wall-plate or wall-post (7). *Corbelling*: brick or masonry courses built out beyond one another to support a chimney-stack, window, etc.

CORINTHIAN: *see* Orders and 3d.

CORNICE: flat-topped ledge with moulded underside, projecting along the top of a building or feature, especially as the highest member of the classical entablature (3a). Also the decorative moulding in the angle between wall and ceiling.

CORPS-DE-LOGIS: the main building(s) as distinct from the wings or pavilions.

COTTAGE ORNÉ: an artfully rustic small house associated with the Picturesque movement.

COUNTERCHANGING: of joists on a ceiling divided by beams into compartments, when placed in opposite directions in alternate squares.

COUR D'HONNEUR: formal entrance court before a house in the French manner, usually with flanking wings and a screen wall or gates.

COURSE: continuous layer of stones, etc. in a wall (6e).

COVE: a broad concave moulding, e.g. to mask the eaves of a roof. *Coved ceiling*: with a pronounced cove joining the walls to a flat central panel smaller than the whole area of the ceiling.

CRADLE ROOF: *see* Wagon roof.

CREDENCE: a shelf within or beside a piscina (q.v.), or a table for the sacramental elements and vessels.

CRENELLATION: parapet with crenels (*see* Battlement).

CRINKLE-CRANKLE WALL: garden wall undulating in a series of serpentine curves.

CROCKETS: leafy hooks. *Crocketing* decorates the edges of Gothic features, such as pinnacles, canopies, etc. *Crocket capital*: *see* 1b.

CROSSING: central space at the junction of the nave, chancel, and transepts. *Crossing tower*: above a crossing.

CROSS-WINDOW: with one mullion and one transom (qq.v.).

CROWN-POST: *see* Roofs and 7.

CROWSTEPS: squared stones set like steps, e.g. on a gable (8a).

CRUCKS (*lit.* crooked): pairs of inclined timbers (*blades*), usually curved, set at bay-lengths; they support the roof timbers and, in timber buildings, also support the walls (8b). *Base*: blades rise from ground level to a tie- or collar-beam which supports the roof timbers. *Full*: blades rise from ground level to the apex of the roof, serving as the main members of a roof truss. *Jointed*: blades formed from more than one timber; the lower member may act as a wall-post; it is usually elbowed at wall-plate level and jointed just above. *Middle*: blades rise from half-way up the walls to a tie- or collar-beam. *Raised*: blades rise from half-way up the walls to the apex. *Upper*: blades supported on a tie-beam and rising to the apex.

CRYPT: underground or half-underground area, usually below the E end of a church. *Ring crypt*: corridor crypt surrounding the apse of an early medieval church, often associated with chambers for relics. Cf. Undercroft.

CUPOLA (*lit.* dome): especially a small dome on a circular or polygonal base crowning a larger dome, roof, or turret.

CURSUS: a long avenue defined by two parallel earthen banks with ditches outside.

CURTAIN WALL: a connecting wall between the towers of a castle. Also a non-load-bearing external wall applied to a C20 framed structure.

CUSP: *see* Tracery and 2b.

CYCLOPEAN MASONRY: large irregular polygonal stones, smooth and finely jointed.

CYMA RECTA and CYMA REVERSA: classical mouldings with double curves (3f). Cf. Ogee.

DADO: the finishing (often with panelling) of the lower part of a wall in a classical interior; in origin a formalized continuous pedestal. *Dado rail*: the moulding along the top of the dado.

DAGGER: *see* Tracery and 2b.

DALLE-DE-VERRE (*lit.* glass-slab): a late C20 stained-glass technique, setting large, thick pieces of cast glass into a frame of reinforced concrete or epoxy resin.

DEC (DECORATED): English Gothic architecture *c.* 1290 to *c.* 1350. The name is derived from the type of window tracery (q.v.) used during the period.

DEMI- or HALF-COLUMNS: engaged columns (q.v.) half of whose circumference projects from the wall.

DENTIL: small square block used in series in classical cornices (3c). *Dentilation* is produced by the projection of alternating headers along cornices or stringcourses.

DIAPER: repetitive surface decoration of lozenges or squares flat or in relief. Achieved in brickwork with bricks of two colours.

DIOCLETIAN OR THERMAL WINDOW: semicircular with two mullions, as used in the Baths of Diocletian, Rome (4b).

DISTYLE: having two columns (4a).

DOGTOOTH: E.E. ornament, consisting of a series of small pyramids formed by four stylized canine teeth meeting at a point (1a).

DORIC: *see* Orders and 3a, 3b.

DORMER: window projecting from the slope of a roof (8a).

DOUBLE CHAMFER: a chamfer applied to each of two recessed arches (1a).

DOUBLE PILE: *see* Pile.

DRAGON BEAM: *see* Jetty.

DRESSINGS: the stone or brickwork worked to a finished face about an angle, opening, or other feature.

DRIPSTONE: moulded stone projecting from a wall to protect the lower parts from water. Cf. Hood-mould, Weathering.

DRUM: circular or polygonal stage supporting a dome or cupola. Also one of the stones forming the shaft of a column (3a).

DUTCH or FLEMISH GABLE: *see* 8a.

EASTER SEPULCHRE: tomb-chest used for Easter ceremonial, within or against the N wall of a chancel.

EAVES: overhanging edge of a roof; hence *eaves cornice* in this position.

ECHINUS: ovolo moulding (q.v.) below the abacus of a Greek Doric capital (3a).

EDGE RAIL: *see* Railways.

E.E. (EARLY ENGLISH): English Gothic architecture *c.* 1190−1250.

EGG-AND-DART: *see* Enrichments and 3f.

ELEVATION: any face of a building or side of a room. In a drawing, the same or any part of it, represented in two dimensions.

EMBATTLED: with battlements.

EMBRASURE: small splayed opening in a wall or battlement (q.v.).

ENCAUSTIC TILES: earthenware tiles fired with a pattern and glaze.

EN DELIT: stone cut against the bed.

ENFILADE: reception rooms in a formal series, usually with all doorways on axis.

ENGAGED or ATTACHED COLUMN: one that partly merges into a wall or pier.

ENGINEERING BRICKS: dense bricks, originally used mostly for railway viaducts etc.

ENRICHMENTS: the carved decoration of certain classical mouldings, e.g. the ovolo (qq.v.) with *egg-and-dart*, the cyma reversa with *waterleaf*, the astragal with *bead-and-reel* (3f).

ENTABLATURE: in classical architecture, collective name for the three horizontal members (architrave, frieze, and cornice) carried by a wall or a column (3a).

ENTASIS: very slight convex deviation from a straight line, used to prevent an optical illusion of concavity.

EPITAPH: inscription on a tomb.

EXEDRA: *see* Apse.

EXTRADOS: outer curved face of an arch or vault.

EYECATCHER: decorative building terminating a vista.

FASCIA: plain horizontal band, e.g. in an architrave (3c, 3d) or on a shopfront.

FENESTRATION: the arrangement of windows in a façade.

FERETORY: site of the chief shrine of a church, behind the high altar.

FESTOON: ornamental garland, suspended from both ends. Cf. Swag.

FIBREGLASS, or glass-reinforced polyester (GRP): synthetic resin reinforced with glass fibre. GRC: glass-reinforced concrete.

FIELD: *see* Panelling and 6b.

FILLET: a narrow flat band running down a medieval shaft or along a roll moulding (1a). It separates larger curved mouldings in classical cornices, fluting or bases (3c).

FLAMBOYANT: the latest phase of French Gothic architecture, with flowing tracery.

FLASH LOCK: *see* Canals.

FLÈCHE or SPIRELET (*lit.* arrow): slender spire on the centre of a roof.

FLEURON: medieval carved flower or leaf, often rectilinear (1a).

FLUSHWORK: knapped flint used with dressed stone to form patterns.

FLUTING: series of concave grooves (flutes), their common edges sharp (arris) or blunt (fillet) (3).

FOIL (*lit.* leaf): lobe formed by the cusping of a circular or other shape in tracery (2b). *Trefoil* (three), *quatrefoil* (four), *cinquefoil* (five), and *multifoil* express the number of lobes in a shape.

FOLIATE: decorated with leaves.

FORMWORK: *see* Concrete.

FRAMED BUILDING: where the structure is carried by a framework – e.g. of steel, reinforced concrete, timber – instead of by load-bearing walls.

FREESTONE: stone that is cut, or can be cut, in all directions.

FRESCO: *al fresco*: painting on wet plaster. *Fresco secco*: painting on dry plaster.

FRIEZE: the middle member of the classical entablature, sometimes ornamented (3a). *Pulvinated frieze* (*lit.* cushioned): of bold convex profile (3c). Also a horizontal band of ornament.

FRONTISPIECE: in C16 and C17 buildings the central feature of doorway and windows above linked in one composition.

GABLE: For types *see* 8a. *Gablet*: small gable. *Pedimental gable*: treated like a pediment.

GADROONING: classical ribbed ornament like inverted fluting that flows into a lobed edge.

GALILEE: chapel or vestibule usually at the W end of a church enclosing the main portal(s).

GALLERY: a long room or passage; an upper storey above the aisle of a church, looking through arches to the nave; a balcony or mezzanine overlooking the main interior space of a building; or an external walkway.

GALLETING: small stones set in a mortar course.

GAMBREL ROOF: *see* 8a.

GARDEROBE: medieval privy.

GARGOYLE: projecting water spout often carved into human or animal shape.

GAUGED or RUBBED BRICKWORK: soft brick sawn roughly, then rubbed to a precise (gauged) surface. Mostly used for door or window openings (5c).

GAZEBO (jocular Latin, 'I shall gaze'): ornamental lookout tower or raised summer house.

GEOMETRIC: English Gothic architecture *c.* 1250–1310. See also Tracery. For another meaning, *see* Stairs.

GIANT or COLOSSAL ORDER: classical order (q.v.) whose height is that of two or more storeys of the building to which it is applied.

GIBBS SURROUND: C18 treatment of an opening (4b), seen particularly in the work of James Gibbs (1682–1754).

GIRDER: a large beam. *Box*: of hollow-box section. *Bowed*: with its top rising in a curve. *Plate*: of I-section, made from iron or steel plates. *Lattice*: with braced frame-work.

GLAZING BARS: wooden or some-times metal bars separating and supporting window panes.

GRAFFITI: *see* Sgraffito.

GRANGE: farm owned and run by a religious order.

GRC: *see* Fibreglass.

GRISAILLE: monochrome painting on walls or glass.

GROIN: sharp edge at the meeting of two cells of a cross-vault; *see* Vault and 2c.

GROTESQUE (*lit.* grotto-esque): wall decoration adopted from Roman examples in the Renaissance. Its foliage scrolls incorporate figur-ative elements. Cf. Arabesque.

GROTTO: artificial cavern.

GRP: *see* Fibreglass.

GUILLOCHE: classical ornament of interlaced bands (4b).

GUNLOOP: opening for a firearm.

GUTTAE: stylized drops (3b).

HALF-TIMBERING: archaic term for timber-framing (q.v.). Sometimes used for non-structural decorative timberwork.

HALL CHURCH: medieval church with nave and aisles of approxim-ately equal height.

HAMMERBEAM: *see* Roofs and 7.

HAMPER: in C20 architecture, a visu-ally distinct topmost storey or storeys.

HEADER: *see* Bond and 6e.

HEADSTOP: stop (q.v.) carved with a head (5b).

HELM ROOF: *see* 1c.

HENGE: ritual earthwork.

HERM (*lit.* the god Hermes): male head or bust on a pedestal.

HERRINGBONE WORK: *see* 7ii. Cf. Pitched masonry.

HEXASTYLE: *see* Portico.

HILL-FORT: Iron Age earthwork en-closed by a ditch and bank system.

HIPPED ROOF: *see* 8a.

HOODMOULD: projecting moulding above an arch or lintel to throw off water (2b, 5b). When horizontal often called a *label*. For label stop *see* Stop.

HUSK GARLAND: festoon of stylized nutshells (4b).

HYDRAULIC POWER: use of water under high pressure to work machinery. *Accumulator tower*: houses a hydraulic accumulator which accommodates fluctuations in the flow through hydraulic mains.

HYPOCAUST (*lit.* underburning): Ro-man underfloor heating system.

IMPOST: horizontal moulding at the springing of an arch (5c).

IMPOST BLOCK: block between abacus and capital (1b).

IN ANTIS: *see* Antae, Portico and 4a.

INDENT: shape chiselled out of a stone to receive a brass.

INDUSTRIALIZED or SYSTEM BUILDING: system of manufac-tured units assembled on site.

INGLENOOK (*lit.* fire-corner): recess for a hearth with provision for seating.

INTERCOLUMNATION: interval be-tween columns.

INTERLACE: decoration in relief simulating woven or entwined stems or bands.

INTRADOS: *see* Soffit.

IONIC: *see* Orders and 3c.

JACK ARCH: shallow segmental vault springing from beams, used for fireproof floors, bridge decks, etc.

JAMB (*lit.* leg): one of the vertical sides of an opening.

JETTY: in a timber-framed building, the projection of an upper storey beyond the storey below, made by the beams and joists of the lower storey oversailing the wall; on their outer ends is placed the sill of the walling for the storey above (7). Buildings can be jettied on several sides, in which case a *dragon beam* is set diagonally at the corner to carry the joists to either side.

JOGGLE: the joining of two stones to prevent them slipping by a notch in one and a projection in the other.

KEEL MOULDING: moulding used from the late C12, in section like the keel of a ship (1a).

KEEP: principal tower of a castle.

KENTISH CUSP: *see* Tracery and 2b.

KEY PATTERN: *see* 4b.

KEYSTONE: central stone in an arch or vault (4b, 5c).

KINGPOST: *see* Roofs and 7.

KNEELER: horizontal projecting stone at the base of each side of a gable to support the inclined coping stones (8a).

LABEL: *see* Hoodmould and 5b.

LABEL STOP: *see* Stop and 5b.

LACED BRICKWORK: vertical strips of brickwork, often in a contrasting colour, linking openings on different floors.

LACING COURSE: horizontal reinforcement in timber or brick to walls of flint, cobble, etc.

LADY CHAPEL: dedicated to the Virgin Mary (Our Lady).

LANCET: slender single-light, pointed-arched window (2a).

LANTERN: circular or polygonal windowed turret crowning a roof or a dome. Also the windowed stage of a crossing tower lighting the church interior.

LANTERN CROSS: churchyard cross with lantern-shaped top.

LAVATORIUM: in a religious house, a washing place adjacent to the refectory.

LEAN-TO: *see* Roofs.

LESENE (*lit.* a mean thing): pilaster without base or capital. Also called *pilaster strip*.

LIERNE: *see* Vault and 2c.

LIGHT: compartment of a window defined by the mullions.

LINENFOLD: Tudor panelling carved with simulations of folded linen. *See also* Parchemin.

LINTEL: horizontal beam or stone bridging an opening.

LOGGIA: gallery, usually arcaded or colonnaded; sometimes freestanding.

LONG-AND-SHORT WORK: quoins consisting of stones placed with the long side alternately upright and horizontal, especially in Saxon building.

LONGHOUSE: house and byre in the same range with internal access between them.

LOUVRE: roof opening, often protected by a raised timber structure, to allow the smoke from a central hearth to escape.

LOWSIDE WINDOW: set lower than the others in a chancel side wall, usually towards its W end.

LUCAM: projecting housing for hoist pulley on upper storey of warehouses, mills, etc., for raising goods to loading doors.

LUCARNE (*lit.* dormer): small gabled opening in a roof or spire.

LUGGED ARCHITRAVE: *see* 4b.

LUNETTE: semicircular window or blind panel.

LYCHGATE (*lit.* corpse-gate): roofed gateway entrance to a churchyard for the reception of a coffin.

LYNCHET: long terraced strip of soil on the downward side of prehistoric and medieval fields, accumulated because of continual ploughing along the contours.

MACHICOLATIONS (*lit.* mashing devices): series of openings between the corbels that support a projecting parapet through which missiles can be dropped. Used decoratively in post-medieval buildings.

MANOMETER or STANDPIPE TOWER: containing a column of water to regulate pressure in water mains.

MANSARD: *see* 8a.

MATHEMATICAL TILES: facing tiles with the appearance of brick, most often applied to timber-framed walls.

MAUSOLEUM: monumental building or chamber usually intended for the burial of members of one family.

MEGALITHIC TOMB: massive stone-built Neolithic burial chamber covered by an earth or stone mound.

MERLON: *see* Battlement.

METOPES: spaces between the triglyphs in a Doric frieze (3b).

MEZZANINE: low storey between two higher ones.

MILD STEEL: *see* Cast iron.

MISERICORD (*lit.* mercy): shelf on a carved bracket placed on the underside of a hinged choir stall seat to support an occupant when standing.

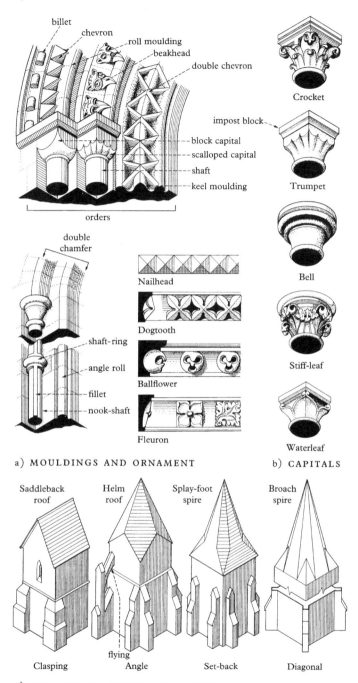

a) MOULDINGS AND ORNAMENT   b) CAPITALS

c) BUTTRESSES, ROOFS AND SPIRES

FIGURE 1: MEDIEVAL

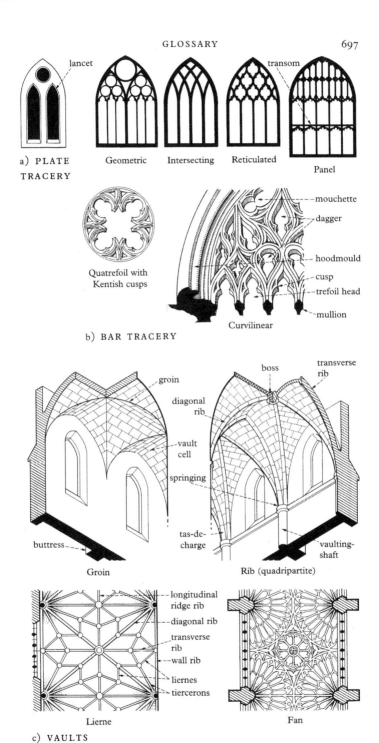

a) PLATE TRACERY

lancet

Geometric   Intersecting   Reticulated

transom

Panel

b) BAR TRACERY

Quatrefoil with Kentish cusps

mouchette
dagger
hoodmould
cusp
trefoil head
mullion

Curvilinear

c) VAULTS

groin
diagonal rib
vault cell
springing
tas-de-charge
buttress

boss
transverse rib

Groin

vaulting-shaft

Rib (quadripartite)

longitudinal ridge rib
diagonal rib
transverse rib
wall rib
liernes
tiercerons

Lierne   Fan

FIGURE 2: MEDIEVAL

ORDERS

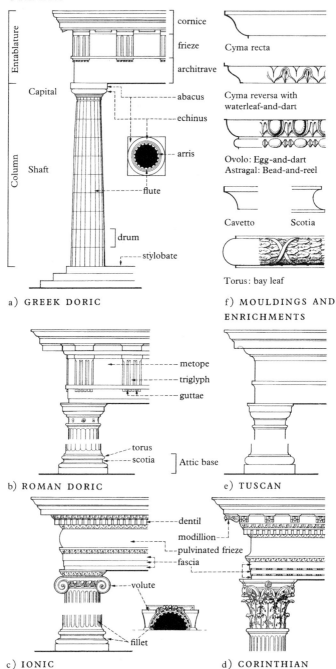

a) GREEK DORIC

f) MOULDINGS AND ENRICHMENTS

Cyma recta

Cyma reversa with waterleaf-and-dart

Ovolo: Egg-and-dart
Astragal: Bead-and-reel

Cavetto   Scotia

Torus: bay leaf

Entablature
cornice
frieze
architrave

Capital
abacus
echinus
arris

Column
Shaft
flute
drum
stylobate

b) ROMAN DORIC

metope
triglyph
guttae
torus
scotia
Attic base

e) TUSCAN

c) IONIC

dentil
modillion
pulvinated frieze
fascia
volute
fillet

d) CORINTHIAN

FIGURE 3: CLASSICAL

a) PORTICO

Distyle in antis   Prostyle

Anthemion & Palmette   Guilloche   Key pattern

Rinceau   Husk garland   Vitruvian scroll

Console   Diocletian window   Acanthus

Broken pediment   Lugged architrave

Segmental pediment   Shouldered architrave

Venetian window

Open pediment   Swan-neck pediment   Gibbs surround

b) ORNAMENTS AND FEATURES

FIGURE 4: CLASSICAL

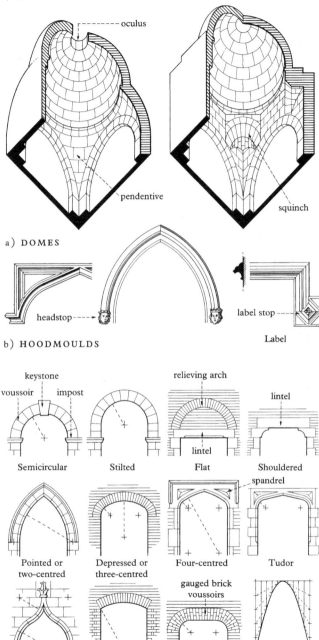

a) DOMES

b) HOODMOULDS

Label

c) ARCHES

FIGURE 5: CONSTRUCTION

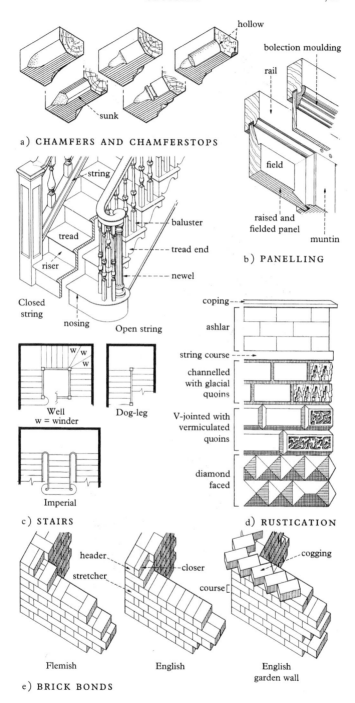

a) CHAMFERS AND CHAMFERSTOPS

b) PANELLING

c) STAIRS

d) RUSTICATION

e) BRICK BONDS

FIGURE 6: CONSTRUCTION

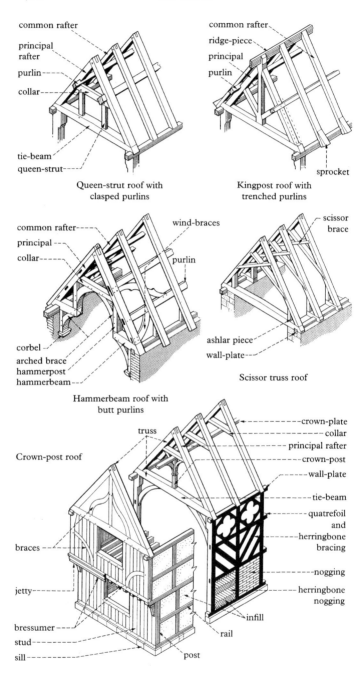

Queen-strut roof with
clasped purlins

common rafter
principal rafter
purlin
collar
tie-beam
queen-strut

Kingpost roof with
trenched purlins

common rafter
ridge-piece
principal
purlin
sprocket

Hammerbeam roof with
butt purlins

common rafter
principal
collar
wind-braces
purlin
corbel
arched brace
hammerpost
hammerbeam

Scissor truss roof

scissor brace
ashlar piece
wall-plate

Crown-post roof

truss
braces
jetty
bressumer
stud
sill

crown-plate
collar
principal rafter
crown-post
wall-plate
tie-beam
quatrefoil and herringbone bracing
nogging
herringbone nogging
infill
rail
post

Box frame: i) Close studding   ii) Square panel

FIGURE 7: ROOFS AND TIMBER-FRAMING

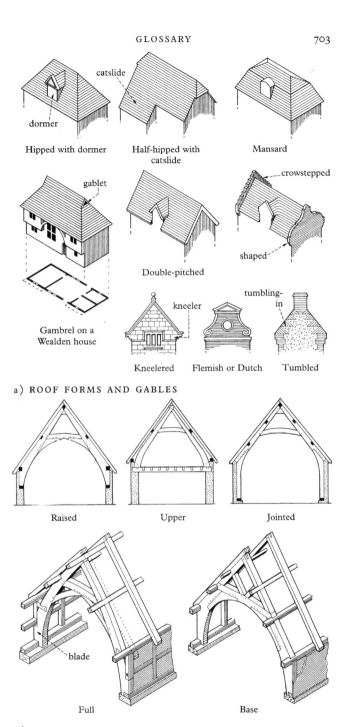

a) ROOF FORMS AND GABLES

b) CRUCK FRAMES

FIGURE 8: ROOFS AND TIMBER-FRAMING

MIXER-COURTS: forecourts to groups of houses shared by vehicles and pedestrians.

MODILLIONS: small consoles (q.v.) along the underside of a Corinthian or Composite cornice (3d). Often used along an eaves cornice.

MODULE: a predetermined standard size for co-ordinating the dimensions of components of a building.

MOTTE-AND-BAILEY: post-Roman and Norman defence consisting of an earthen mound (motte) topped by a wooden tower within a bailey, an enclosure defended by a ditch and palisade, and also, sometimes, by an internal bank.

MOUCHETTE: see Tracery and 2b.

MOULDING: shaped ornamental strip of continuous section; see e.g. Cavetto, Cyma, Ovolo, Roll.

MULLION: vertical member between window lights (2b).

MULTI-STOREY: five or more storeys. Multi-storey flats may form a *cluster block*, with individual blocks of flats grouped round a service core; a *point block*, with flats fanning out from a service core; or a *slab block*, with flats approached by corridors or galleries from service cores at intervals or towers at the ends (plan also used for offices, hotels etc.). *Tower block* is a generic term for any very high multi-storey building.

MUNTIN: see Panelling and 6b.

NAILHEAD: E.E. ornament consisting of small pyramids regularly repeated (1a).

NARTHEX: enclosed vestibule or covered porch at the main entrance to a church.

NAVE: the body of a church W of the crossing or chancel often flanked by aisles (q.v.).

NEWEL: central or corner post of a staircase (6c). Newel stair: see Stairs.

NIGHT STAIR: stair by which religious entered the transept of their church from their dormitory to celebrate night services.

NOGGING: see Timber-framing (7).

NOOK-SHAFT: shaft set in the angle of a wall or opening (1a).

NORMAN: see Romanesque.

NOSING: projection of the tread of a step (6c).

NUTMEG: medieval ornament with a chain of tiny triangles placed obliquely.

OCULUS: circular opening.

ŒIL DE BŒUF: see Bullseye window.

OGEE: double curve, bending first one way and then the other, as in an *ogee* or *ogival arch* (5c). Cf. Cyma recta and Cyma reversa.

OPUS SECTILE: decorative mosaic-like facing.

OPUS SIGNINUM: composition flooring of Roman origin.

ORATORY: a private chapel in a church or a house. Also a church of the Oratorian Order.

ORDER: one of a series of recessed arches and jambs forming a splayed medieval opening, e.g. a doorway or arcade arch (1a).

ORDERS: the formalized versions of the post-and-lintel system in classical architecture. The main orders are *Doric*, *Ionic*, and *Corinthian*. They are Greek in origin but occur in Roman versions. Tuscan is a simple version of Roman Doric. Though each order has its own conventions (3), there are many minor variations. The *Composite* capital combines Ionic volutes with Corinthian foliage. *Superimposed orders*: orders on successive levels, usually in the upward sequence of Tuscan, Doric, Ionic, Corinthian, Composite.

ORIEL: see Bay window.

OVERDOOR: painting or relief above an internal door. Also called a *sopraporta*.

OVERTHROW: decorative fixed arch between two gatepiers or above a wrought-iron gate.

OVOLO: wide convex moulding (3f).

PALIMPSEST: of a brass: where a metal plate has been reused by turning over the engraving on the back; of a wall painting: where one overlaps and partly obscures an earlier one.

PALLADIAN: following the examples and principles of Andrea Palladio (1508–80).

PALMETTE: classical ornament like a palm shoot (4b).

PANELLING: wooden lining to interior walls, made up of vertical members (*muntins*) and horizontals (*rails*) framing panels: also called *wainscot*. *Raised and fielded*: with the central area of the panel (*field*) raised up (6b).

PANTILE: roof tile of S section.

PARAPET: wall for protection at any sudden drop, e.g. at the wall-head of a castle where it protects the *parapet walk* or wall-walk. Also used to conceal a roof.

PARCLOSE: *see* Screen.

PARGETTING (*lit.* plastering): exterior plaster decoration, either in relief or incised.

PARLOUR: in a religious house, a room where the religious could talk to visitors; in a medieval house, the semi-private living room below the solar (q.v.).

PARTERRE: level space in a garden laid out with low, formal beds.

PATERA (*lit.* plate): round or oval ornament in shallow relief.

PAVILION: ornamental building for occasional use; or projecting subdivision of a larger building, often at an angle or terminating a wing.

PEBBLEDASHING: *see* Rendering.

PEDESTAL: a tall block carrying a classical order, statue, vase, etc.

PEDIMENT: a formalized gable derived from that of a classical temple; also used over doors, windows, etc. For variations *see* 4b.

PENDENTIVE: spandrel between adjacent arches, supporting a drum, dome or vault and consequently formed as part of a hemisphere (5a).

PENTHOUSE: subsidiary structure with a lean-to roof. Also a separately roofed structure on top of a C20 multi-storey block.

PERIPTERAL: *see* Peristyle.

PERISTYLE: a colonnade all round the exterior of a classical building, as in a temple which is then said to be *peripteral*.

PERP (PERPENDICULAR): English Gothic architecture *c.* 1335–50 to *c.* 1530. The name is derived from the upright tracery panels then used (*see* Tracery and 2a).

PERRON: external stair to a doorway, usually of double-curved plan.

PEW: loosely, seating for the laity outside the chancel; strictly, an enclosed seat. *Box pew*: with equal high sides and a door.

PIANO NOBILE: principal floor of a classical building above a ground floor or basement and with a lesser storey overhead.

PIAZZA: formal urban open space surrounded by buildings.

PIER: large masonry or brick support, often for an arch. *See also* Compound pier.

PILASTER: flat representation of a classical column in shallow relief. *Pilaster strip*: *see* Lesene.

PILE: row of rooms. *Double pile*: two rows thick.

PILLAR: free-standing upright member of any section, not conforming to one of the orders (q.v.).

PILLAR PISCINA: *see* Piscina.

PILOTIS: C20 French term for pillars or stilts that support a building above an open ground floor.

PISCINA: basin for washing Mass vessels, provided with a drain; set in or against the wall to the S of an altar or free-standing (*pillar piscina*).

PISÉ: *see* Cob.

PITCHED MASONRY: laid on the diagonal, often alternately with opposing courses (*pitched and counterpitched* or *herringbone*).

PLATBAND: flat horizontal moulding between storeys. Cf. stringcourse.

PLATE RAIL: *see* Railways.

PLATEWAY: *see* Railways.

PLINTH: projecting courses at the

foot of a wall or column, generally chamfered or moulded at the top.

PODIUM: a continuous raised platform supporting a building; or a large block of two or three storeys beneath a multi-storey block of smaller area.

POINT BLOCK: *see* Multi-storey.

POINTING: exposed mortar jointing of masonry or brickwork. Types include *flush*, *recessed* and *tuck* (with a narrow channel filled with finer, whiter mortar).

POPPYHEAD: carved ornament of leaves and flowers as a finial for a bench end or stall.

PORTAL FRAME: C20 frame comprising two uprights rigidly connected to a beam or pair of rafters.

PORTCULLIS: gate constructed to rise and fall in vertical grooves at the entry to a castle.

PORTICO: a porch with the roof and frequently a pediment supported by a row of columns (4a). A portico *in antis* has columns on the same plane as the front of the building. A *prostyle* porch has columns standing free. Porticoes are described by the number of front columns, e.g. tetrastyle (four), hexastyle (six). The space within the temple is the *naos*, that within the portico the *pronaos*. *Blind portico*: the front features of a portico applied to a wall.

PORTICUS (plural: porticūs): subsidiary cell opening from the main body of a pre-Conquest church.

POST: upright support in a structure (7).

POSTERN: small gateway at the back of a building or to the side of a larger entrance door or gate.

POUND LOCK: *see* Canals.

PRESBYTERY: the part of a church lying E of the choir where the main altar is placed; or a priest's residence.

PRINCIPAL: *see* Roofs and 7.

PRONAOS: *see* Portico and 4a.

PROSTYLE: *see* Portico and 4a.

PULPIT: raised and enclosed platform for the preaching of sermons. *Three-decker*: with reading desk below and clerk's desk below that. *Two-decker*: as above, minus the clerk's desk.

PULPITUM: stone screen in a major church dividing choir from nave.

PULVINATED: *see* Frieze and 3c.

PURLIN: *see* Roofs and 7.

PUTHOLES or PUTLOG HOLES: in the wall to receive putlogs, the horizontal timbers which support scaffolding boards; sometimes not filled after construction is complete.

PUTTO (plural: putti): small naked boy.

QUARRIES: square (or diamond) panes of glass supported by lead strips (*cames*); square floor slabs or tiles.

QUATREFOIL: *see* Foil and 2b.

QUEEN-STRUT: *see* Roofs and 7.

QUIRK: sharp groove to one side of a convex medieval moulding.

QUOINS: dressed stones at the angles of a building (6d).

RADBURN SYSTEM: vehicle and pedestrian segregation in residential developments, based on that used at Radburn, New Jersey, USA, by Wright and Stein, 1928–30.

RADIATING CHAPELS: projecting radially from an ambulatory or an apse (*see* Chevet).

RAFTER: *see* Roofs and 7.

RAGGLE: groove cut in masonry, especially to receive the edge of a roof-covering.

RAGULY: ragged (in heraldry). Also applied to funerary sculpture, e.g. *cross raguly*: with a notched outline.

RAIL: *see* Panelling and 6b; also 7.

RAILWAYS: *Edge rail*: on which flanged wheels can run. *Plate rail*: L-section rail for plain unflanged wheels. *Plateway*: early railway using plate rails.

RAISED AND FIELDED: *see* Panelling and 6b.

RAKE: slope or pitch.

RAMPART: defensive outer wall of stone or earth. *Rampart walk*: path along the inner face.

REBATE: rectangular section cut out of a masonry edge to receive a shutter, door, window, etc.

REBUS: a heraldic pun, e.g. a fiery cock for Cockburn.

REEDING: series of convex mouldings, the reverse of fluting (q.v.). Cf. Gadrooning.

RENDERING: the covering of outside walls with a uniform surface or skin for protection from the weather. *Limewashing*: thin layer of lime plaster. *Pebbledashing*: where aggregate is thrown at the wet plastered wall for a textured effect. *Roughcast*: plaster mixed with a coarse aggregate such as gravel. *Stucco*: fine lime plaster worked to a smooth surface. *Cement rendering*: a cheaper substitute for stucco, usually with a grainy texture.

REPOUSSÉ: relief designs in metalwork, formed by beating it from the back.

REREDORTER (*lit.* behind the dormitory): latrines in a medieval religious house.

REREDOS: painted and/or sculptured screen behind and above an altar. Cf. Retable.

RESPOND: half-pier or half-column bonded into a wall and carrying one end of an arch. It usually terminates an arcade.

RETABLE: painted or carved panel standing on or at the back of an altar, usually attached to it.

RETROCHOIR: in a major church, the area between the high altar and E chapel.

REVEAL: the plane of a jamb, between the wall and the frame of a door or window.

RIB-VAULT: *see* Vault and 2c.

RINCEAU: classical ornament of leafy scrolls (4b).

RISER: vertical face of a step (6c).

ROACH: a rough-textured form of Portland stone, with small cavities and fossil shells.

ROCK-FACED: masonry cleft to produce a rugged appearance.

ROCOCO: style current *c.* 1720 and *c.* 1760, characterized by a serpentine line and playful, scrolled decoration.

ROLL MOULDING: medieval moulding of part-circular section (1a).

ROMANESQUE: style current in the CII and CI2. In England often called Norman. *See also* Saxo-Norman.

ROOD: crucifix flanked by the Virgin and St John, usually over the entry into the chancel, on a beam (*rood beam*) or painted on the wall. The *rood screen* below often had a walkway (*rood loft*) along the top, reached by a *rood stair* in the side wall.

ROOFS: Shape. For the main external shapes (hipped, mansard, etc.) *see* 8a. *Helm* and *Saddleback*: *see* 1c. *Lean-to*: single sloping roof built against a vertical wall; lean-to is also applied to the part of the building beneath.
Construction. *See* 7.
Single-framed roof: with no main trusses. The rafters may be fixed to the wall-plate or ridge, or longitudinal timber may be absent altogether.
Double-framed roof: with longitudinal members, such as purlins, and usually divided into bays by principals and principal rafters.
Other types are named after their main structural components, e.g. *hammerbeam*, *crown-post* (*see* Elements below and 7).
Elements. *See* 7.
Ashlar piece: a short vertical timber connecting inner wall-plate or timber pad to a rafter.
Braces: subsidiary timbers set diagonally to strengthen the frame. *Arched braces*: curved pair forming an arch, connecting wall or post below with tie- or collar-beam above. *Passing braces*: long straight braces passing across other members of the truss. *Scissor braces*: pair crossing diagonally between pairs of rafters or principals. *Wind-braces*: short, usually curved braces connecting side purlins with principals; sometimes decorated with cusping.
Collar or *collar-beam*: horizontal transverse timber connecting a pair of rafter or cruck blades (q.v.), set between apex and the wall-plate.
Crown-post: a vertical timber set centrally on a tie-beam and supporting a collar purlin braced to it longitudinally. In an open truss

lateral braces may rise to the collar-beam; in a closed truss they may descend to the tie-beam.

Hammerbeams: horizontal brackets projecting at wall-plate level like an interrupted tie-beam; the inner ends carry *hammerposts*, vertical timbers which support a purlin and are braced to a collar-beam above.

Kingpost: vertical timber set centrally on a tie- or collar-beam, rising to the apex of the roof to support a ridge-piece (cf. Strut).

Plate: longitudinal timber set square to the ground. *Wall-plate*: plate along the top of a wall which receives the ends of the rafters; cf. Purlin.

Principals: pair of inclined lateral timbers of a truss. Usually they support side purlins and mark the main bay divisions.

Purlin: horizontal longitudinal timber. *Collar purlin* or *crown plate*: central timber which carries collar-beams and is supported by crown-posts. *Side purlins*: pairs of timbers placed some way up the slope of the roof, which carry common rafters. *Butt* or *tenoned purlins* are tenoned into either side of the principals. *Through purlins* pass through or past the principal; they include *clasped purlins*, which rest on queenposts or are carried in the angle between principals and collar, and *trenched purlins* trenched into the backs of principals.

Queen-strut: paired vertical, or near-vertical, timbers placed symmetrically on a tie-beam to support side purlins.

Rafters: inclined lateral timbers supporting the roof covering. *Common rafters*: regularly spaced uniform rafters placed along the length of a roof or between principals. *Principal rafters*: rafters which also act as principals.

Ridge, ridge-piece: horizontal longitudinal timber at the apex supporting the ends of the rafters.

Sprocket: short timber placed on the back and at the foot of a rafter to form projecting eaves.

Strut: vertical or oblique timber between two members of a truss, not directly supporting longitudinal timbers.

Tie-beam: main horizontal transverse timber which carries the feet of the principals at wall level.

Truss: rigid framework of timbers at bay intervals, carrying the longitudinal roof timbers which support the common rafters. *Closed truss*: with the spaces between the timbers filled, to form an internal partition.

See also Cruck, Wagon roof.

ROPE MOULDING: *see* Cable moulding.

ROSE WINDOW: circular window with tracery radiating from the centre. Cf. Wheel window.

ROTUNDA: building or room circular in plan.

ROUGHCAST: *see* Rendering.

ROVING BRIDGE: *see* Canals.

RUBBED BRICKWORK: *see* Gauged brickwork.

RUBBLE: masonry whose stones are wholly or partly in a rough state. *Coursed*: coursed stones with rough faces. *Random*: uncoursed stones in a random pattern. *Snecked*: with courses broken by smaller stones (snecks).

RUSTICATION: *see* 6d. Exaggerated treatment of masonry to give an effect of strength. The joints are usually recessed by V-section chamfering or square-section channelling (*channelled rustication*). *Banded rustication* has only the horizontal joints emphasized. The faces may be flat, but can be *diamond-faced*, like shallow pyramids, *vermiculated*, with a stylized texture like worm-casts, and *glacial* (frost-work), like icicles or stalactites.

SACRISTY: room in a church for sacred vessels and vestments.

SADDLEBACK ROOF: *see* 1c.

SALTIRE CROSS: with diagonal limbs.

SANCTUARY: area around the main altar of a church. Cf. Presbytery.

SANGHA: residence of Buddhist monks or nuns.

SARCOPHAGUS: coffin of stone or other durable material.

SAXO-NORMAN: transitional Romanesque style combining Anglo-Saxon and Norman features, current *c.* 1060–1100.

SCAGLIOLA: composition imitating marble.

SCALLOPED CAPITAL: *see* 1a.

SCOTIA: a hollow classical moulding, especially between tori (q.v.) on a column base (3b, 3f).

SCREEN: in a medieval church, usually at the entry to the chancel; *see* Rood (screen) and Pulpitum. A *parclose screen* separates a chapel from the rest of the church.

SCREENS or SCREENS PASSAGE: screened-off entrance passage between great hall and service rooms.

SECTION: two-dimensional representation of a building, moulding, etc., revealed by cutting across it.

SEDILIA (singular: sedile): seats for the priests (usually three) on the S side of the chancel.

SET-OFF: *see* Weathering.

SETTS: squared stones, usually of granite, used for paving or flooring.

SGRAFFITO: decoration scratched, often in plaster, to reveal a pattern in another colour beneath. *Graffiti*: scratched drawing or writing.

SHAFT: vertical member of round or polygonal section (1a, 3a). *Shaft-ring*: at the junction of shafts set *en delit* (q.v.) or attached to a pier or wall (1a).

SHEILA-NA-GIG: female fertility figure, usually with legs apart.

SHELL: thin, self-supporting roofing membrane of timber or concrete.

SHOULDERED ARCHITRAVE: *see* 4b.

SHUTTERING: *see* Concrete.

SILL: horizontal member at the bottom of a window or door frame; or at the base of a timber-framed wall into which posts and studs are tenoned (7).

SLAB BLOCK: *see* Multi-storey.

SLATE-HANGING: covering of overlapping slates on a wall. *Tile-hanging* is similar.

SLYPE: covered way or passage leading E from the cloisters between transept and chapter house.

SNECKED: *see* Rubble.

SOFFIT (*lit.* ceiling): underside of an arch (also called *intrados*), lintel, etc. *Soffit roll*: medieval roll moulding on a soffit.

SOLAR: private upper chamber in a medieval house, accessible from the high end of the great hall.

SOPRAPORTA: *see* Overdoor.

SOUNDING-BOARD: *see* Tester.

SPANDRELS: roughly triangular spaces between an arch and its containing rectangle, or between adjacent arches (5c). Also non-structural panels under the windows in a curtain-walled building.

SPERE: a fixed structure screening the lower end of the great hall from the screens passage. *Spere-truss*: roof truss incorporated in the spere.

SPIRE: tall pyramidal or conical feature crowning a tower or turret. *Broach*: starting from a square base, then carried into an octagonal section by means of triangular faces; and *splayed-foot*: variation of the broach form, found principally in the south-east, in which the four cardinal faces are splayed out near their base, to cover the corners, while oblique (or intermediate) faces taper away to a point (1c). *Needle spire*: thin spire rising from the centre of a tower roof, well inside the parapet: when of timber and lead often called a *spike*.

SPIRELET: *see* Flèche.

SPLAY: of an opening when it is wider on one face of a wall than the other.

SPRING or SPRINGING: level at which an arch or vault rises from its supports. *Springers*: the first stones of an arch or vaulting rib above the spring (2c).

SQUINCH: arch or series of arches thrown across an interior angle of a square or rectangular structure to support a circular or polygonal superstructure, especially a dome or spire (5a).

SQUINT: an aperture in a wall or through a pier usually to allow a view of an altar.

STAIRS: *see* 6c. *Dog-leg stair*: parallel flights rising alternately in opposite directions, without an open well. *Flying stair*: cantilevered from the walls of a stairwell, without newels; sometimes called a *Geometric* stair when the inner edge describes a curve. *Newel stair*: ascending round a central supporting newel (q.v.); called a *spiral stair* or *vice* when in a circular shaft, a *winder* when in a rectangular compartment. (Winder also applies to the steps on the turn.) *Well stair*: with flights round a square open well framed by newel posts. *See also* Perron.

STALL: fixed seat in the choir or chancel for the clergy or choir (cf. Pew). Usually with arm rests, and often framed together.

STANCHION: upright structural member, of iron, steel or reinforced concrete.

STANDPIPE TOWER: *see* Manometer.

STEAM ENGINES: *Atmospheric*: worked by the vacuum created when low-pressure steam is condensed in the cylinder, as developed by Thomas Newcomen. *Beam engine*: with a large pivoted beam moved in an oscillating fashion by the piston. It may drive a flywheel or be *non-rotative*. *Watt* and *Cornish*: single-cylinder; *compound*: two cylinders; *triple expansion*: three cylinders.

STEEPLE: tower together with a spire, lantern, or belfry.

STIFF-LEAF: type of E.E. foliage decoration. *Stiff-leaf capital see* 1b.

STOP: plain or decorated terminal to mouldings or chamfers, or at the end of hoodmoulds and labels (*label stop*), or stringcourses (5b, 6a); *see also* Headstop.

STOUP: vessel for holy water, usually near a door.

STRAINER: *see* Arch.

STRAPWORK: late C16 and C17 decoration, like interlaced leather straps.

STRETCHER: *see* Bond and 6e.

STRING: *see* 6c. Sloping member holding the ends of the treads and risers of a staircase. *Closed string*: a broad string covering the ends of the treads and risers. *Open string*: cut into the shape of the treads and risers.

STRINGCOURSE: horizontal course or moulding projecting from the surface of a wall (6d).

STUCCO: *see* Rendering.

STUDS: subsidiary vertical timbers of a timber-framed wall or partition (7).

STUPA: Buddhist shrine, circular in plan.

STYLOBATE: top of the solid platform on which a colonnade stands (3a).

SUSPENSION BRIDGE: *see* Bridge.

SWAG: like a festoon (q.v.), but representing cloth.

SYSTEM BUILDING: *see* Industrialized building.

TABERNACLE: canopied structure to contain the reserved sacrament or a relic; or architectural frame for an image or statue.

TABLE TOMB: memorial slab raised on free-standing legs.

TAS-DE-CHARGE: the lower courses of a vault or arch which are laid horizontally (2c).

TERM: pedestal or pilaster tapering downward, usually with the upper part of a human figure growing out of it.

TERRACOTTA: moulded and fired clay ornament or cladding.

TESSELLATED PAVEMENT: mosaic flooring, particularly Roman, made of *tesserae*, i.e. cubes of glass, stone, or brick.

TESTER: flat canopy over a tomb or pulpit, where it is also called a *sounding-board*.

TESTER TOMB: tomb-chest with effigies beneath a tester, either free-standing (tester with four or more columns), or attached to a wall (*half-tester*) with columns on one side only.

TETRASTYLE: *see* Portico.

THERMAL WINDOW: *see* Diocletian window.

THREE-DECKER PULPIT: *see* Pulpit.

TIDAL GATES: *see* Canals.

TIE-BEAM: *see* Roofs and 7.

TIERCERON: *see* Vault and 2c.

TILE-HANGING: *see* Slate-hanging.

TIMBER-FRAMING: *see* 7. Method of construction where the structural frame is built of interlocking timbers. The spaces are filled with non-structural material, e.g. *infill* of wattle and daub, lath and plaster, brickwork (known as *nogging*), etc. and may be covered by plaster, weatherboarding (q.v.), or tiles.

TOMB-CHEST: chest-shaped tomb, usually of stone. Cf. Table tomb, Tester tomb.

TORUS (plural: tori): large convex moulding usually used on a column base (3b, 3f).

TOUCH: soft black marble quarried near Tournai.

TOURELLE: turret corbelled out from the wall.

TOWER BLOCK: *see* Multi-storey.

TRABEATED: depends structurally on the use of the post and lintel. Cf. Arcuated.

TRACERY: openwork pattern of masonry or timber in the upper part of an opening. *Blind tracery* is tracery applied to a solid wall. *Plate tracery*, introduced *c.* 1200, is the earliest form, in which shapes are cut through solid masonry (2a). *Bar tracery* was introduced into England *c.* 1250. The pattern is formed by intersecting moulded ribwork continued from the mullions. It was especially elaborate during the Decorated period (q.v.). Tracery shapes can include circles, *daggers* (elongated ogee-ended lozenges), *mouchettes* (like daggers but with curved sides) and upright rectangular *panels*. They often have *cusps*, projecting points defining lobes or *foils* (q.v.) within the main shape: *Kentish* or *split-cusps* are forked (2b). Types of bar tracery (*see* 2b) include *geometric(al)*: *c.* 1250–1310, chiefly circles, often foiled; *Y-tracery*: *c.* 1300, with mullions branching into a Y-shape; *intersecting*: *c.* 1300, formed by interlocking mullions; *reticulated*: early c14, net-like pattern of ogee-ended lozenges; *curvilinear*: c14, with uninterrupted flowing curves; *panel*: Perp, with straight-sided panels, often cusped at the top and bottom.

TRANSEPT: transverse portion of a church.

TRANSITIONAL: generally used for the phase between Romanesque and Early English (*c.* 1175–*c.* 1200).

TRANSOM: horizontal member separating window lights (2b).

TREAD: horizontal part of a step. The *tread end* may be carved on a staircase (6c).

TREFOIL: *see* Foil.

TRIFORIUM: middle storey of a church treated as an arcaded wall passage or blind arcade, its height corresponding to that of the aisle roof.

TRIGLYPHS (*lit.* three-grooved tablets): stylized beam-ends in the Doric frieze, with metopes between (3b).

TRIUMPHAL ARCH: influential type of Imperial Roman monument.

TROPHY: sculptured or painted group of arms or armour.

TRUMEAU: central stone mullion supporting the tympanum of a wide doorway. *Trumeau figure*: carved figure attached to it (cf. Column figure).

TRUMPET CAPITAL: *see* 1b.

TRUSS: braced framework, spanning between supports. *See also* Roofs and 7.

TUMBLING or TUMBLING-IN: courses of brickwork laid at right-angles to a slope, e.g. of a gable, forming triangles by tapering into horizontal courses (8a).

TUSCAN: *see* Orders and 3e.

TWO-DECKER PULPIT: *see* Pulpit.

TYMPANUM: the surface between a lintel and the arch above it or within a pediment (4a).

UNDERCROFT: usually describes the vaulted room(s), beneath the main room(s) of a medieval house. Cf. Crypt.

VAULT: arched stone roof (sometimes imitated in timber or plaster). For types see 2c. *Tunnel* or *barrel vault*: continuous semicircular or pointed arch, often of rubble masonry.

Groin-vault: tunnel vaults intersecting at right angles. *Groins* are the curved lines of the intersections.

Rib-vault: masonry framework of intersecting arches (ribs) supporting *vault cells*, used in Gothic architecture. *Wall rib* or *wall arch*: between wall and vault cell. *Transverse rib*: spans between two walls to divide a vault into bays. *Quadripartite* rib-vault: each bay has two pairs of diagonal ribs dividing the vault into four triangular cells. *Sexpartite* rib-vault: most often used over paired bays, has an extra pair of ribs springing from between the bays. More elaborate vaults may include *ridge ribs* along the crown of a vault or bisecting the bays; *tiercerons*: extra decorative ribs springing from the corners of a bay; and *liernes*: short decorative ribs in the crown of a vault, not linked to any springing point. A *stellar* or *star* vault has liernes in star formation.

Fan-vault: form of barrel vault used in the Perp period, made up of halved concave masonry cones decorated with blind tracery.

VAULTING SHAFT: shaft leading up to the spring or springing (q.v.) of a vault (2c).

VENETIAN or SERLIAN WINDOW: derived from Serlio (4b). The motif is used for other openings.

VERMICULATION: *see* Rustication and 6d.

VESICA: oval with pointed ends.

VICE: *see* Stair.

VILLA: originally a Roman country house or farm. The term was revived in England in the C18 under the influence of Palladio and used especially for smaller, compact country houses. In the later C19 it was debased to describe any suburban house.

VITRIFIED: bricks or tiles fired to a darkened glassy surface.

VITRUVIAN SCROLL: classical running ornament of curly waves (4b).

VOLUTES: spiral scrolls. They occur on Ionic capitals (3c). *Angle volute*: pair of volutes, turned outwards to meet at the corner of a capital.

VOUSSOIRS: wedge-shaped stones forming an arch (5c).

WAGON ROOF: with the appearance of the inside of a wagon tilt; often ceiled. Also called *cradle roof*.

WAINSCOT: *see* Panelling.

WALL MONUMENT: attached to the wall and often standing on the floor. *Wall tablets* are smaller with the inscription as the major element.

WALL-PLATE: *see* Roofs and 7.

WALL-WALK: *see* Parapet.

WARMING ROOM: room in a religious house where a fire burned for comfort.

WATERHOLDING BASE: early Gothic base with upper and lower mouldings separated by a deep hollow.

WATERLEAF: *see* Enrichments and 3f.

WATERLEAF CAPITAL: Late Romanesque and Transitional type of capital (1b).

WATER WHEELS: described by the way water is fed on to the wheel. *Breastshot*: mid-height, falling and passing beneath. *Overshot*: over the top. *Pitchback*: on the top but falling backwards. *Undershot*: turned by the momentum of the water passing beneath. In a *water turbine*, water is fed under pressure through a vaned wheel within a casing.

WEALDEN HOUSE: type of medieval timber-framed house with a central open hall flanked by bays of two storeys, roofed in line; the end bays are jettied to the front, but the eaves are continuous (8a).

WEATHERBOARDING: wall cladding of overlapping horizontal boards.

WEATHERING or SET-OFF: inclined, projecting surface to keep water away from the wall below.

WEEPERS: figures in niches along the sides of some medieval tombs. Also called mourners.

WHEEL WINDOW: circular, with radiating shafts like spokes. Cf. Rose window.

WROUGHT IRON: *see* Cast iron.

INDEX OF ARTISTS, ARCHITECTS, PATRONS AND RESIDENTS

The names of architects and artists working in the areas covered by this volume are given in *italic*. Entries for partnerships and group practices are listed after entries for a single surname. Minor differences in title are disregarded.

Indexed here are also the names/titles of families and individuals (not of bodies or commercial firms) recorded in this volume as having owned property or commissioned architectural work. It includes monuments to members of such families and other individuals where they are of particular interest.

Abbey Holford Rowe 330
Abbott & Co. 97, 198, 202, 230
Abercrombie, Patrick 578
Adam, Robert 46n., 217n., 246, 509–10
Adams, G.G. 296
Adams-Acton, John 296
Adderley, Hubert B. 471
Adshead, Mary 103, 255, 393
Adshead, Stanley D. 301
AEW Architects 599
AFL 115, 278, 396, 676
Aikin, Edmund 63, 246, 316, 377, 379
Airey, Sir Edwin 191
Alberti & Lupton 623
Aldridge, Charles 93, 479
Aldridge & Deacon 155, 411, 436, 437, 479, 489, 545, 570
Allcard 527
Allen, C.J. 82, 83, 94, 251, 252, 294, 321, 328, 331, 332, 337, 363, 364, 365, 375, 450, 451, 454, 475
Allen, J. Mountford 66, 628
Allford Hall Monaghan Morris 313
Allom, Thomas 298
Almquist, Carl 181
Alsop, Will 115
Amschewitz, J.H. 289
Anderson, C.J. 158
Anderson, J. Macvicar 84, 406, 407–8
Anderson, C.J., & R.S. Crawford 81, 181, 430
Anderton, James 150
Anderton, Roger 34, 151
André, Edouard 75, 250, 391, 453, 454
Ansell, W.H. 361
APEC 112, 556
Aquila Consultancy Services 496
Architects Design Partnership 364
Ardin & Brookes & Partners 110, 620
Argent, Edward 421

Armstead, H.H. 97, 607
Armstrong, William 168
Arrol (Sir William) & Co. 616
Artificers' Guild 450
Arup Associates 257, 332, 383
Ashcroft, James 339
Ashton, Nicholas 509
Ashurst family 170
Ashworth (T. Arnold) & Sons 325
Astley, Ralph 138–9
Atherden Fuller Leng see AFL
Atherton, Jacob 204
Atherton, John 139
Atherton, Robert Vernon 138
Atherton, William 139
Atkins, David 358, 359
Atkins (W.S.) & Partners 310
Atkinson Bros 579
Atkinson, C.A. 172, 173
Atkinson, Frank 83, 86, 98, 154, 334, Pl. 108
Audley, George 454
Audsley, G.A. 454
Audsley, W. & G. 85, 89, 94, 95, 250, 251, 281, 309, 376, 382, 393, 473, 474, 476, 541, 542, Pl. 76
Austin, Hubert (James) 88, 91, 96, 103, 121, 198, 210, 223, 659n.
Austin, Thomas 91
Austin & Paley 25, 92, 99, 103, 121, 124, 137, 142, 144, 210, 224, 229, 231, 345, 517, 537, 589, 591, 648, 664
see also Paley & Austin
Austin-Smith:Lord 107, 113, 115, 257, 278, 301, 302, 325, 336, 338, 367, 372, 373, 463, 624, 638, 657, Pl. 125

Backhouse, David 272, 327
Bacon, John, Jun. 68, 592, Pl. 46

Bacon, Percy (Bros) 399, 411, 471, 501
Badger, F.E.G. 404, 446
Baguley (G.J.) & Son 410
Baines (George) & Sons 643
Baker, Sir Herbert 456n.
Baker, Michael 188
Baker, William 54, 304, 649, Pl. 100
Balcarres, Alexander Lindsay, 6th Earl of 58, 128, 184, 187
Balcarres, Alexander Lindsay, 8th Earl of 186
Balcarres, James Lindsay, 7th Earl of 62, 128, 132, 183, 186, 187, 188, 676, Pls. 53, 54
Balcarres, Earls of 50, 60, 87, 131
Ballantine & Gardiner 598
Balmer, Clinton 475
Balmer, Peter 95, 534
Bankes family 530, 677
Banner, E.H. 79, 85, 475
Banner & Rhind 454
Banner, E.H. 79, 85, 475
Bannister, H. 112, 564
Bannister Storr Associates 270
Bare, H. Bloomfield 83, 252, 375, 512
Barkentin & Krall 97, 471
Barker, E.H. 196
Barker, Richard & Paul 436
Barnett, James 360
Barnish, Leonard 308
Baron, J.A. 560
Barratt 378
Barry, Thomas D. (& Son) 76, 138, 152, 210, 394, 427, 429, 479, 563, 623
Bartlett & Purnell 112, 657
Basil, Victor 313
Bateson, W.G. 390
Baxter, Henry 548
BDP/Building Design Partnership 123, 258, 270, 271, 325, 344, 380, 558, 572, 637, 638
Beattie, E., Jun. 83, 561
Beckett, R.T. 322, 432
Beech, Gerald R. 106, 109, 256, 367, 368, 388, 434n., 476–7, 514, Pl. 120
Beech (Gerald) Partnership 369
Beecham, Thomas 58, 558
Beesley, Thomas 72, 73, 529, 620
Bell, John 82, 612, 618
Bell, Robert Anning 252, 286, 298, 449
Ben Tre, Howard 114, 617
Bennett, William 289
Bennett (T.P.) & Son 110, 160
Bentley, J.F. 95, 102, 400, 472
Bernasconi, Francesco 290
Berrington, John Arthur 262, 271, 274, 279
Berry, Henry 52, 260, 273, 565, 566
Bews, Philip 273
Bibby, John 96, 386–7
BIQ Architecten 303

Biram, Frank S. 560, 564, 570
Biram & Fletcher 559, 560, 564, 576
Birch, C.B. 82, 297
Bird, John 540
Birkett & Langham 642n
Bisbrown, Cuthbert 49, 245, 469, 470
B.I.S.F. 105, 200
Bispham, William 151
Bland, James 389
Blease, C.W. 505
Blomfield, Sir Reginald 100, 210, 395
Bloomfield, Edward 98, 254, 457, 458, Pl. 116
Blore, Edward 66, 164
Blount, Gilbert 526
Blundell family (of Crosby) 46, 80, 86, 152, 196, 240
Blundell family (of Ince Blundell) 205, 206, 240
Blundell, Bryan 302
Blundell, Col. Henry 664
Blundell, Henry 45, 47, 194, 204, 205–9
Blundell, Robert 205
Blundell, William 152, 240
Blythin, Charles F. 333
Boddy, J.W. 105, 256
Bodley, G.F. 91, 93–4, 96, 251, 345, 351, 398, 448, 477, 479, Pl. 62
Bodley & Garner 93, 631
Boehm, J.E. 451
Bold, Peter 154, 219
Bold, Richard 29, 654–5
Bold, Sir Thomas 162
Bolland, Sidney 402
Bonomi, Joseph 207
Booth, Roger 108, 109, 442, 588, 652, 667
Bootle, Sir Thomas 224
Bor, Walter 105, 256
Boteler, Sir John 27–8, 605, 606
Boult, Joseph 318
Boulton 95, 419, 420, 472, 556, 579, 609
Boulton & Watt 55
Bourne, J.H. 98, 569
Bower, S.E. Dykes 478
Bowes, James L. 476, 515
Boyesen, Sebastian 114, 668
Bradbury, George 418
Bradbury, Ronald 105, 106, 108, 109, 215, 256, 276, 298–9, 302, 333, 338, 372, 387, 388, 395, 400, 403, 405, 409, 432, 434, 455, 504
Bradbury (George) & Sons 121
Bradford, Earls of 661
Bradley, Arthur W. 565
Bradley, Henry A. 513
Bradley, J. 325
Bradshaigh, Dorothy, Lady 188
Bradshaigh, Lady Mabel 670
Bradshaigh, Sir Roger 50, 188
Bradshaw, J.J. 83, 235

Bradshaw & Gass 95, 99, 138, 285, 596, 667, 671, 672, Pl. 73
Bradshaw, Gass & Hope 56, 238
Bradshaw, Rowse & Harker 107, 256, 318, 319, 336, 451, 486
Brakspear, W.H. 549
Brancker, P.W. 71, 248, 486
Bratt 230
Bridgeman, G.T.O. 661
Bridges, Peter 112, 556
Bridgewater, Francis Egerton, 3rd Duke of 52
Bridgwater, Shepheard & Epstein 367
Brierley, R. 526
Brierley & Rutherford 525
Briggs, J.P. 83, 672
Briggs & Thornely 364
Briggs, Thornely & McLaughlin 159
Briggs & Wolstenholme 71, 79, 81, 253, 331, 557, 559, 560, 561, 666, Pls. 1, 83
Briggs, Wolstenholme & Thornely 80, 98, 253, 343, 363, 364, 490, 494, 666, Pl. 82
Bright, Henry Arthur 438
Brindley, James 52, 523, 630
British Rail London Midland Region 305
British Railways London Midland Region, Architect's Department 415
Broadbent, John 65, 67, 247, 484, 487
Broadbent, Stephen 310, 317, 459, 617
Brock, David Le Marchant 370–1
Brock, Thomas 335, 454
Brock Carmichael Architects/Associates 112, 114, 115, 257, 266, 268, 270, 310, 321, 325, 330, 333, 337, 353, 371, 372, 374, 402, 468, 476, 507, 623, 633, 650, Pl. 59
Brocklebank, Sir Thomas 392
Brocklehurst, A. 150, 383
Brocklehurst, E. 233
Brocklesby, J. Sydney 102, 125, 126, 568, Pl. 114
Brocklesby, R.S. 638
Brodie, J.A. 87, 98, 100, 254, 306, 404
Bromfield, B. 41, 138, 655, 682
Bromsgrove Guild 326, 332, 341, 352, 454
Brooks, Joseph and Jonathan 307
Brothers, Colin S. 337
Brotherton & Partners 123
Brown, Helen 304
Brown, John William 97, 102, 352
Brown, Joseph 290
Brown, Lancelot 'Capability' 47, 222
Brown, Philip 427
Brown, W. Raffles 398, 418, 424
Brown, William 298
Bruce & Still, Messrs 664
Brumby, Robert 359
Brunlees, James 305

Brunner, Sir John 450
Bruxby & Evans 393
Bryans 448
Bryans, Herbert 643
Bryant Homes 641
Budden, L.B. 98, 100, 297, 367
Building Design Partnership see *BDP*
Bullen, Alfred 457
Bullock, George 467, 655
Bulmer, Hubert E. 157
Burgess, Brian 284
Burlison & Grylls 96, 353, 411, 419, 654, 661
Burmantofts 300, 335, 363, 365
Burn, William 47, 62, 204, 217, 217n., 222, 224
Burne-Jones, Sir Edward 96, 192, 251, 386, 436, 479, Pl. 67
Burnet, Sir John 457n
Buro Happold 362
Burrows, William 571
Bushe, Frederick 371
Butler, Edward C. 111, 284
Buttress, Donald 439
Buttress Fuller Alsop Williams 115, 501, 629, 633, Pl. 126
Buxeby & Evans 189
Bylander, Sven 103, 430, Pl. 127

Cain, Robert 83, 326, 455
Campbell (D.A.) & E.H. Honeybourne 102, 254, 387
Campbell Smith 471
Campbell, Smith & Co. 515
Camus 105, 424
Canning, Hugh 107, 635, 637
Capronnier, J.B. 180, 507, 592
Capstick, George T. 98, 306, 323, 332, 341
Carlhian 221
Carnegie, Andrew 81, 138, 181
Caröe, W.D. 70, 92, 94, 95, 103, 153, 286, 312, 553, 554, 581, 582, 583, 660, Pl. 75
Carter, Mr 547
Carter's (of Poole) 335
Cartwright Pickard Architects 161
Casolani, M. 555
Cass Associates 302
Casson, John Whiteside 379, 444
Cavaillé-Coll 614
Cawthra, Herman 157
Celtic Studios 629
Central Electricity Generating Board 166
Chadwick & Watson 84, 326
Chalk, Tim 305
Chamberlin, Powell & Bon 113, 638
Champigneulle, C. 592
Champneys, Basil 92, 597, Pl. 4
Chandra, Avinash 574
Chantrey, Sir Francis 67–8, 82, 290, 296, 361–2, 655

Chapman, Taylor & Partners 203
Charlewood, H.C. 591
Charnock, Robert 590
Charoux, Siegfried 323
Chavalliaud, Léon-Joseph 454
Cheesman, Kenneth 571
Chisnall, Edward 592, Pl. 23
Churchward, M.S. 673
Chute, John 173
Ciminaghi, Virginio 359
City Architect's Department (Liverpool)
    395, 462, 495
City Housing Department 461
Clark (Anthony) Partnership 422
Clark, Philip Lindsay 609
Clarke, Geoffrey 370
Clarke, Harry/Harry Clarke Studio 102,
    103, 125, 126, 127, 610, Pl. 115
Clarke, John (architect) 340, 343
Clarke, John (banker) 61, 538
Clarke, Joseph 177
Clarke, Thomas C. 328, 339
Clayton, Sarah 45, 48, 316
Clayton & Bell 96, 198, 251, 471, 583,
    646, 661
Clemens, James 438-9
Clutton, Henry 79, 89, 172, 419, 657
Coalbrookdale Company 82, 442,
    612-13, 618, Pl. 94
Cobham, Sir Alan 457n
Cockerell, C.R. 63-4, 70, 71, 238, 246,
    247, 291, 294, 295, 296, 297, 307n.,
    311, 318, Pls. 78, 89
Cockerell, F.P. 318
Colling, J.K. 68-9, 329
Collins, Don 113, 639
Combaz, M. 454
Comper, Sir Ninian 479
Cook (David) Architects 535
Cook, Thomas 364, 372
Cooksey, May L.G. 429, 472, 579
Cookson, Edward H. 505
Coop, Timothy 671
Cooper, Andrew 305
Copnall, Bainbridge 393, 412, 445-6
Corbett, Edward 70, 249, 321
Corbett (iron-founder) 187
Cornish & Gaymer 581
Corsi, Vincenzo 488
Corson & Aitken 556
Countryside Properties 682
County Planning Officer 215
Court, W.R. 76, 253, 495
Courtaulds Technical Services (Ltd) 228,
    363
Cox, Stephen 310
Cox, Thomas 284
Cox, Trena M. 629, 657
Coxon, W.P. 607
Crace, J.G./Messrs Crace 84, 89, 205,
    206, 208, 401, Pl. 105
Cragg, John 62, 65, 247, 375, 381, 384,

417, Pl. 45
Cragg, Tony 271
Crake 194
Crane, Thomas 522
Creative Landscaping 625
Cripps, John 308
Crompton, Albert 173
Crompton, W.E.V. 672, 673
Cronshaw, Edward 315
Crook 612, Pl. 94
Crossley, F.H. 198, 643
Crossley, John 549
Crowther, J.S. 231
Cubbon, T.W. 196
Cullearn & Phillip 234
Culshaw, William 78, 172, 307, 309,
    317, 324, 334, 337, 368, 374, 425,
    443, 470, 491, 502, 514, 534, 643,
    654
Culshaw & Sumners 71, 343, 389, 442,
    448, 491, 504
Cunliffe, Mitzi 369
Cunliffe Surveyors 207
Cunningham, John 79, 238, 309, 323,
    371, 374, 379-80, 413, 414
Cunningham & Holme 66, 304, 309,
    380
Curran, Robert 625
Currey, Henry 452
Curtin (W.G.) & Partners 114, 268
Curtis, Ward & Hughes 598
Cutts, J.E.K. 469
CZWG 325

Dagnall, Thompson W. 566
Dalwood, Hubert 370
Dane Ashworth Cottam 461
Danson & Davies 375
Darby, Abraham 442
Darbyshire, Thomas 151
David Marks Julia Barfield Architects
    114, 258, 263, 273
Davies, Sir Alan Hudson 572
Davies, Harold E. 100, 653
Davies, Harold Hinchliffe 99, 255, 323,
    374, 403
Davies (Harold E.) & Son 374, 403,
    482, 483, 512
Davies (Patrick) Architecture 274
Davioud, Gabriel 315
Davis, Arthur J. 71-2, 253, 332, 333,
    430, 431, Pl. 1
    see also Mewès & Davis
Davison (R.), Son & Mackenzie 58,
    626
Dawbarn & Blair 651
Dawson, Joshua 67, 547, Pls. 49, 50
Deacon, Charles E. 73, 80, 93, 198, 336,
    397, 411
    see also Aldridge & Deacon
Deacon (C.E.) & Sons 103, 402, 437
Dean, William 291

DEGW 638
Della Robbia Pottery 436
Demaine & Brierley 93, 524
Department of Health and Social
   Security Architects 491
Derby, Thomas Stanley, 1st Earl of 28,
   30, 225, 226, 227
Derby, 9th Earl of 217, 226
Derby, 10th Earl of 217, 218–19, 220,
   221
Derby, 11th Earl of 148
Derby, 13th Earl of 222, 224, 681
Derby, 14th Earl of 223, 224
Derby, 17th Earl of 217
Derby, 18th Earl of 222
Derby, Countess of 533
Derby, Earl(s) of 221, 223, 227 8, 599,
   618, 670
   see also Stanley family
Design Lights 127, 129, 137
Design Shed 317, 324
Design Studio 343
Dick, R. Burns 74, 613
Dixon, F.W. 364, 427, 666
Dixon Jones 316
Dobie, Glen 402
Dobson, John 81, 613
Dod, Edwin J. 162, 196
Dod, Harold 98, 254, 313, 365
Dodd, Ralph 649
Dooley, Arthur 284, 327, 359, 476
Doubleday, John 327
Douglas, John 72, 84, 89, 92, 179, 195,
   409, 616*n.*, 621, 659*n.*, Pl. 66
Douglas & Fordham 92, 94–5, 181, 195
Doulton, Sir Henry 564
Doultons 342
Downey, Archbishop Richard 354, 356
Downie, George 446
Downs Variava 419
Doyle, Francis W. 644
Doyle, Harcourt M. 129, 284, 629
Doyle, James F. 71, 82, 87, 93, 181, 238,
   249, 250, 308, 325, 328, 339, 365,
   398, 423, 428, 440, 454, 475, 479,
   483, 489, 504, 519, 656, Pl. 91
Doyle, Sidney W. 77, 365
Drabkin, Johnathon 327
Drake, Sir James 107, 585
Dressler, Conrad 294, 419
Drury, Alfred 82, 618
Drysdale, Dr 645
DTR Sheard Walshaw 272
Duckworth & Metcalfe 427
Dudok, W.M. 98, 104
Duffy, Terry 373
Duhamel Marrelle 198
Dunbar, George 377
Duncan, Thomas 76, 253, 422
Dyer Associates 625

Earle, Richard 204

Earley Studio 420, 489
Earp 291
Easton, Hugh 607
Eckersley family 86, 663, 675, 676
Eckersley, James Carlton 121, 663
EDAW 459, 462
Eddy, H.T. 430
Eden, F.C. 628
Edmund Percey Scherrer & Hicks 307,
   334
Edmundson (R.B.) & Son 474
Edward, Prince of Wales 451
Edwards, Carl 112, 352, 440
Edwards, J.C. 326
Edwards, Mr 281
Egerton, Elizabeth 29, 167
Ellard, Lyle 330
Ellis, Anthony 440
Ellis, Peter 69, 248, 317, 342, Pl. 90
Ellison, C.O. 77, 78, 157, 378, 437, 473,
   508, 509, 623
Elmes, Harvey Lonsdale 63–4, 78, 79,
   81, 85, 115, 247, 291–6, 391, 421,
   438, 515, Pls. 77, 78, 81
Emerson, William 345
Enfield & Schmidt 178
Epstein, Jacob 104, 335
Esher Street Marble Works 185
Evans, David 353, 381
Eve (Gerald) & Co. 159
Everard, William 47, 207
Eyes, Charles 308
Eyes, John 40, 197, 287

Fabiani, Frederigo 387
Fairbairn, William 675
Falconer Chester Architects 113, 258,
   319, 325, 333, 338, 340, 343, 357,
   367, 423, 458, 459
Farey, Cyril 354
Farmer 285
Farmer & Brindley 304, 363
Farmer & Dark 108, 300, 330
Farrell, Terry 107, 636, 637–8
Farrell & Grimshaw Partnership 637,
   640
Farren, Mary 96, 629
Faulkner, Howard 360
Fauveau, Felicie and Hippolyte 661
Ferrers, William de 19
Field, Horace, Sen. 309
Finch, Hon. Henry 680
Fink, Peter 462
Finlay, Thomas 159
Flatz, Gebhard 89, 208
Fleetwood, J.M. 511
Fleetwood-Hesketh, Peter 190
Fleischmann, Arthur 567
Fletcher, Jacob 390
Fletcher, Ralph 87, 136, 137
Fletcher, W.H. 75, 668
Fletcher, Burrows & Co. 136, 139, 140

Foley, J.H. 450, 454
Fontana, G.G. 82, 296
Fordham, D.P. 92
Formby, John 173
Forrest 208
Forrest, Marianne 372
Forrest & Son 296
Forsyth, James 433, 503
Foster, John, Jun. 53, 62, 63, 64, 67, 75,
    77, 104, 110, 123, 174–5, 217, 220,
    221, 246–7, 281, 293, 303, 304,
    307n., 310, 316, 320, 336, 361, 368,
    375, 379, 413, 414, 513, Pl. 107
Foster, John, Sen. 45, 51, 61, 63, 236,
    246–7, 248, 260, 276, 277, 281, 286,
    288, 290, 303, 309, 310, 313, 321,
    322n., 323, 368, 379
Foster, Stephen 359
Foster, Thomas 513
Foster & Griffin 281
Fourmaintreaux, P. 112, 631
Fox, Charles Douglas 54, 305
Frampton, Edward 180, 181, 624
Frampton, Sir George 82, 333, 335, 363,
    449, 560
Franceys, S. &. J. 418, 542, 545, 583
Franceys & Spence 583, 655
Francis, Frederick & Horace 88, 604,
    607, 616
Franklin, Joseph 67, 247, 285, 308,
    Pl.48
Franklin Stafford Partnership 114, 266,
    268, 422
Fraser, Frederick G. 329
Fraser, Gerald de Courcy 98, 103–4,
    314, 315, 334, 343, 416, Pl. 117
Fraser, Gilbert 375
Fraser, W.G. 94, 153
Fraser, Son & Geary 322, 334
Freeman, F.R. 147
Fright, J. 305
Frimston, Ethel 367
Frink, Elisabeth 350, 359
Fry, Arthur P. 451, 494, 503
Fry, E. Maxwell 364, 371, 572
Fry, Drew & Partners 110, 572, Pl. 122
Fry, H. & A.P. 79, 470
Furber, E.R. 160
Furse, Charles Wellington 290
Fyfe 527

Gamble, David 81, 552, 557, 563
Gamble, Josiah Christopher 57
Gandy, J.M. 290, 382, 417
Gandy, James 563, 566
Gardner, William 666
Gardner-Medwin, Robert 370, 425
Garner 595
Garnett & Sons 232
Gay, William 76, 394
Gee, Ernest 226, 308, 445
Gee, H. 89, 239

Geflowski, E.E. 418
George (Sir Ernest) & H.A. Peto 85,
    250, 399, 433, 434
Gerard family 127
Gerard, Sir John 62, 175, 563
Gerard, Piers 28, 682
Gerard, Sir Thomas 25, 563
Gibberd, Sir Frederick 111, 255, 353,
    356–60, Pls. 118, 119
Gibbs, A. 418, 606
Gibbs, Charles A. 493, 501
Gibbs, James 45, 73, 611, Pls. 35, 36
Gibbs & Canning 340
Gibson, John 67, 82, 247, 296, 322,
    361, 362, 377, 450, 583, 661
Gilbert, Alfred 454
Gilbert, Walter 352, 353, 453
Gilby (Peter S.) & Associates 111, 427
Gill, Eric 628
Gillebrand, George 281
Gillick, E.G. 82, 668
Gilling, M.G. 442
Gilling, Dod & Partners 376, 442
Gilling Dod Partnership 366
Gillow 506
Gladstone, A.C. 456n
Gladstone, John 337, 578
Gleichen, Count Victor G. 363, 432
Glen, William R. 99, 326
Glenn Howells Architects 326
Goetze, Sigismund 507
Goldie & Child 665
Goldie, Child & Goldie 420
Goodden, R.Y. 359
Goodhart-Rendel, H.S. 350, 382
Goodison, G.W. 86, 153
Goodwin, J. 129
Gorvin, Diane 273
Gospel Oak Iron Works 267
Gotch & Partners 305, 337
Gott, Joseph 67–8, 362
Gough, William 352
Graffenried, Mark de 272
Gray, Mr 385
Gray & Evans 561, 673
Grayson, G.E. 69, 79, 92–3, 249, 251,
    308, 309, 311, 312, 324, 328, 337,
    340, 386, 423, 477, 487, 657
Grayson, George Hastwell 308
Grayson & Barnish 339
Grayson & Ould 70, 77, 93, 249, 311,
    312, 319, 327, 341, 377, 389, 483,
    507, 642
Green, Samuel 41, 229
Green & Parslow 481
Green, Russell & Knowle 502
Greenall family 87, 552
Greenall, Sir Gilbert 62, 92, 628, 629
Greenall, Peter 552, 570
Gregory, Paul W. 393
Grenfell Baines & Hargreaves 667
Grey Wornum & Louis de Soissons 446

Griffith, Edward O. 332, 340
Grime, Paul 305
Grimshaw (Anthony) Associates 169,
    479, 528, 537, 663, 665, 671
Grimshaw, Barbara 169, 663
Grimshaw, Nicholas 113, 636, 640
Grimshaw (Nicholas) & Partners 109,
    203, 641
Grosvenor Group 115
Grüner, Ludwig 295
Guest, Robert 55, 236
Gunton & Gunton 109, 159, 322, 325
Gwynne, Patrick 108, 639, Pl. 124

Habershon, W.G. 633, 643
Hadfield, Charles 156
Hadfield, M.E. 156
Hadfield (M.E.) & Sons 377
Haigh, Bartin 303
Haigh Foundry 185, 267, 270, 594, 685
Haigh, Thomas 504
Haigh (Thomas) & Co. 69, 250, 315,
    509–10
Hales Associates 362
Hall, O'Donahue & Wilson 256, 301
Halliday, Edward 313
Halsall, Bill 477
Halsall, Richard 193
Hanley, Mr 472
Hansom, Charles 88, 95, 412
Hansom, Joseph 91, 198, 231, 542, 546,
    Pl. 60
Hansom, J. & C. 377
Harding & Horsman 518
Hardman, John and James 392
Hardman & Co. 96, 103, 149, 193,
    208, 400, 412, 448, 489, 501, 534,
    542, 579, 606, 610, 630, 661, 664,
    681
Hardman (John) & Co. 194, 556
Hardman & Powell 419
Hardwick, Philip 266–7, 269–70, 279
Hardwick, Thomas 629
Hare, H.T. 478, 479
Harris, George 558
Harris, Jethro 196
Harris & Hobson 446
Harrison, John 182, 473, 569
Harrison, Thomas 62, 63, 65, 113, 246,
    247, 248, 281, 307, 390, 491
Harrison, Thomas Fenwick 479, 496
Harrisson, Thomas Harnett 84, 383
Harry Clarke Studio see Clarke, Harry
Hartley, Henry 58, 325, 339, 424
Hartley, J.B. 261, 279, 486
Hartley, Jesse 51, 53, 248, 260, 261,
    263–77, 279, 280, 386, 527, 548, Pl.
    96
Hartley, Sir William 87, 427, 428
Harvey, Harold 664
Harvey, Harry 193
Hatch, Messrs 450

Hatton, William 189
Hausman Group 269
Hawkes (Thomas) & Co. 291
Hawkshaw, John 486
Haworth Tompkins 325
Hay, John 324, 393
Hay, W. & J. 89, 95, 143, 144, 195, 373,
    451, 472, 493, 502, 511, 526, 566
Haydock, Sir Gilbert de 679
Hayes & Finch 548
Hayley & Son 95, 451
Hayward, Christopher F. 318
Hayward, Dr J.W. 374
Hayward, John 663
Hazlehurst, Thomas 655
Head Wrightson 132
Headley, W.R. 559
Heaton, George 76, 159, 199
Heaton, Butler & Bayne 96, 131, 179,
    183, 386, 399, 436, 476, 479, 507,
    630, 661
Heaton & Ralph 659, 663, 677
Heaton, Ralph & Heaton 72, 73, 122,
    177, 198, 199, 210, 211, 659, 668,
    670, 672, 673
Heenan, Cardinal John 356
Heesom, Patrick Glyn 330
Heffer, E.A. 89, 474, 493
Heifor Bros. 628
Helberg, Rolf 441
Hemm, Gordon 363
Hemmings, Alfred O. 625
Hems, H. 436
Hendrie, Herbert 112, 352
Hennebique 278
Hepworth, Barbara 369
Herbert & Co. 548
Hermann, Charles Z. 444, 454
Heseltine, Michael 114
Hesketh, T. 621
Hesketh (W.) & Co. 423
Hetherington, William 290
Hewett, Bertram 306
Heywood, John Pemberton 501
Hicks (Derek) & Thew Partnership 496
Hikins, James Bain 302
Hill, Sandy & Norris 387
Hiller, H. Gustave 97, 232, 326, 382,
    440, 448, 493, 583
Hiller, H.G. & Co. 592
Hillier, Parker, May & Rowden 315
Hind, Mr 497
Hind & Lumb 161
Hind Woodhouse Partnership 109, 160,
    Pl. 123
Hines, Edward 196
Hitch, Nathaniel 447–8
Hobbs & Thornely 71, 253, 331, Pl. 1
Hodder Associates 203
Hodel, Joseph A. 81, 372, 451, 479, 490
Hogan, James H. 102, 352
Holcroft family 175

Holford, William 108, 255, 362, 369
Holford Associates 109, 114, 256, 268, 421
Holford (William) & Associates 313
Holiday, Henry 95–6, 202, 214, 439, 470, 489, 520, 534, 568, 583, 598, 643
Holland, Sir Robert de 597*n*
Holme, Arthur Hill 79, 89, 246, 250, 308, 311, 372, 374, 375, 380, 413, 443, 444, 452, 517, Pl. 59
Holme, F.U. 455
Holme, George 89, 180
Holme, A. & G. 89, 180
Holme, F. & G. 73, 74, 77, 83, 249, 300, 317, 320, 340, 376, 505, 513, 651
Holme, S. & J. 71, 248, 373–4, 384, 486
Holme, S. & Son 517
Holt, Alfred 76, 85, 173, 250, 443
Holt, Emma 444
Holt, Felix 210, 311
Holt, George 443, 444
Holt, Mrs George 450
Holt (Alfred) & Co. 341
Honan, Matthew 94, 360, 419, 623
Honan, Patrick 579
Hooper & Webb 338
Hope, John 39, 207, 246, 492
Hope, Samuel 49, 310
Hopkinson, Frederick 578
Hornblower, Lewis 75, 250, 314, 453
Hornby, Hugh Frederick 299
Hornby, Rev. J.J. 681
Horner, H.P. 503
Horsburgh, William P. 320, 375
Horsfall, George 447, 448
Horsfall, H. Douglas 89, 251, 447, 479, 642
Horsfall, Robert 89–90, 447, 470, 471
Hough, Henry T. 455
Houghton, John 320
Hoult & Wise 339
Housman, John 417
Howard, Ebenezer 87, 634
Howard, F.E. 177
Howe, Percy 568
Howe brothers 102, 125, 126
Howell, Killick, Partridge & Amis 108, 613
Howson, Joan 103, 427, 434, 656
Hughes, David 327
Hughes, John 101, 102, 254, 379
Hughes, R.W. 507
Hughes (Robert) & Sons 185
Hunt, F.W. 662
Hunter, William Henry 616
Huskisson, William 361, 527
Huson, Thomas 83, 375
Huss, Henry 250
Hussey, Christopher 463

Hutchins, James B. 99, 313, 335, 339
Hutchinson, Henry 66
Hutchinson, John 646
Huws, Richard 337

ICI Estates Winnington 650
IDC Ltd 371
IKEA In-house Design Team 640
Imrie, Amy Elizabeth 93, 419–20
Induni, P. 353
Innes Wilkin Ainsley Gommon 455
Insall (Donald W.) & Associates 288–9
Inskipp & Mackenzie 58, 626
Ireland, Lawrence and Eleanor 518
Ismay, Thomas Henry 86, 645
Issitt & Verity 668, 671, 672, Pl. 103
Ives, E.W. 304

Jackson, Sir T.G. 148–9
Jackson & Edmonds 216
James & Bywaters 342
Jee, John Denison 76, 378, 410
Jeffery, J.R. 314, 509
Jenkins, Albert D. 338, 367, 458, 482, 491, 496
Jessop, William 277
John, King 19
John of Kirkby 22
John, David 526
John, William Goscombe 100, 306, 333, 335, Pl. 110
Johnson, Henry 679
Johnson, John 73, 158
Johnson, R.T. 83, 672
Johnson, Thomas 287
Johnston, Philip 125, 207
Jones, Alfred 77, 333
Jones, Allen 317
Jones, Felix A. 111, 526, 655
Jones, Jonah 548
Jones, Mike 375
Jones, Norman 670
Jones, Ronald P. 368, 376, 450
Jones (Leslie) Associates 561
Jones & Kelly 111, 526
Jones & Willis 131, 223, 501, 631
Joy, Albert Bruce 296, 335, 363
Joyon, M. 297

Kavanagh, Peter 361
Kayll & Co. 566
Keay, Sir Lancelot 100, 203, 214, 254, 379, 389, 404–5, 427, 438, 446, 456, 460, 461, 462, 491–2, 500, 506
Keef, H.W. 79, 475
Kemp, Edward 76, 250, 394, 395–6, 426
Kempe, C.E. 91, 97, 137, 142, 153, 202, 229, 353, 399, 448, 478, 507, 542
Kennedy & Rogers 624
Kennington, Eric 366
Kerr, Andrew M. 613

Kershaw 612, Pl. 94
Keyser, Nicaise de 472
Kighley, Henry 178
Kilpin, J.A. 315
Kindersley, Richard 300
King, Dave 257, 369
King, John 376
King, Phillip 370
King McAllister 367
Kingham Knight Associates (KKA) 110, 113, 263, 274, 278, 279, 280, 286, 322, 329, 338, 378, 560, 640
Kirby, Edmund 80, 85, 93, 251, 325, 327, 377, 419, 420, 489, 491, 517, 534, 549, 570, 596, 643, 656, 670
Kirby (Edmund) & Sons 78, 122, 319, 343, 365, 374, 506, 549, 628
Kirkegaard (Lawrence) Associates 372
Kissack, Thomas 224
KKA see Kingham Knight Associates
Knight, Frank 359
Knowles, Thomas 210
Knowsley Estate Surveyor 220, 223
Kossowski, A. 457
Krolow, H. V. 58, 558
Kurtz, A.G. 444

Lace, Ambrose 376, 514
Lancashire County Council, Architect's Department 216
Lancaster, Charles H. 78, 428, 502
Landscape Design Associates 114, 617
Langford, Rev. William 190
Langton, Walter de 597
Lanyon, Peter 364
Lasdun (Denys) & Partners 256, 367
Lathom, 1st Earl of 224
Lathom, 3rd Earl of 102, 227
Lathom, Henry de 23
Lathom, Isabel 217*n.*
Lathom, James 504
Lathom, Sir Thomas de 20
Lavers & Barraud 223, 661
Law & Dunbar-Nasmith 299, 300
Lawson, Andrew 82, 300
Lawson, George Anderson 82, 300
Lawton, Joseph 181
Layland, Thomas 474
Le Brun, Christopher 352
Leach, Rhodes & Walker 110, 671
Leach Rhodes Walker Architects 459
Leathart, Granger & Webber 99, 443
Leather, Joseph 390
Lee, Thomas Stirling 82, 294, 312
Legé, Frederick 288, 307
Legh family 524, 528, 618
Legh, Ellen 68, 682, Pl. 47
Legh, Sir Peter and Lady 28, 30, 163, 682
Legh, Peter (of Lyme Park) 44*n.*, 607
Legh, Richard 29, 682, Pl. 24
Leifchild, H.S. 424

Leigh, Robert Holt 130
Leigh, Roger 128
Leitch, Archibald 491
Lennon, Cynthia 327
Lennon, John 102, 327
Leoni, Giacomo 41, 44, 45, 47, 48, 102, 154–5, 219, 224, 227, 228, 655, Pls. 32, 33
Leslie, John 224
Lethaby, W.R. 345
Lever, William 81, 604
Leverhulme, Lord (W. H. Lever) 676
Lewis, David 474
Leyland, Frederick 463–4, 468
Liénard, Paul 82, 300
Lightoler, Timothy 39, 335
Lilford, 4th Lord 633
Lillie Reed 348
Lindsay, Hon. Colin 660
Lindsay, Lady Jane Evelyn 661
Litchfield, Messrs 221
Littler, Henry 74, 81, 528, 529, 651, 671
Littlewoods Department of Architecture & Planning 330
Lobb, Howard 667
Locke, Graham 633
Locke, Joseph 615
Lockwood & Mawson 80, 181
Lombardi, Giovita 454
Longbotham, John 52, 195, 523
Lonsdale, H. W. 436
Lonsdale, Walter 479
Lovejoy (Derek) & Partners 353
Lowe, James 357
Lowndes, Mary 399
Lucy & Littler 76, 312, 394, Pl. 88
Lugar, Robert 241
Lutyens, Sir Edwin 100, 102, 111, 255, 354–6, 395
Lyon, John 555
Lyons, Israel, Ellis & Partners 109, 538, 539
Lyster, A. G. 51–2, 261, 262, 276, 277, 278, 279
Lyster, G.F. 51–2, 248, 261, 262, 270, 272, 274, 276, 277, 280, 452, Pl. 97

McAllister, Rod 257, 369
McAslan (John) & Partners 115, 310, 577
Macaulay, Catherine 41, 613
Macbride, J.A.P. 362
McCarthy, John 371
McCartney, Paul 106
McClean, John 75, 668
MacCormac, Richard 107, 636, 637
MacCormac & Jamieson 637
McCormick, William 486
McCormick Architecture 370, 459
McCorquodale, George 524
McDonald, Terry 373
Macfarlane's 329

McGhie, Robin 361
McGovern, J.H. 417
Mackay, John 552
Mackenzie & Moncur 75, 396, 454, Pl.87
Mackmurdo, A.H. 86, 173, 469
McLaughlan, Stewart 316
MacNair, Herbert 445
McTavish, Keith 313
Maddox & Pearce 471
Mallett, R.A. 108, 557
Mangnall, W.M. 150
Manning & Clamp 109, 441
Manning Clamp & Partners 367
Manning, Don 535
Mansell, John 19
Marko, Igor 462
Marsden, James 671
Marsh family 212
Marsh, George 570
Marshall, J.E. 98, 367
Martin, Alfred R. 319
Martin, Ken 114, 343
Martin, W. Alison 475
Marton, George Mayer 359
Martyn, H.H. (& Co.) 334, 352, 450
Mason, G. Ronald 108, 644
Mason Richards Partnership 112, 610
Mason, W.I. 251, 373, 425, 473
Massey, F.E. 625
Massey & Massey 122
Matcham, Frank 83, 416, 560
Matear & Simon 253, 322, 329
Mathews (J. Douglass) & Partners 110, 675
May, Harry 58, 558
Mayer, Charlotte 379
Mayer & Co. 153, 156, 165, 231
Medcalf, W.J. 144
Medcalf & Medcalf 322, 494
Melling, Richard 188
Mellor (Tom) & Partners 369, 370, 371
Mercer, William 287
Meredith, James 607
Meredith, Peter 185
Merz & McLellan 650
Mewès & Davis 103, 228, 332, 430, Pls. 1, 127
    see also Davis, Arthur J.
Middleton, John 189
Migos, Athanassios 279
Milburn, W. & T.R. 99, 326
Mill, Donald 345
Miller, Bernard A. 103, 254, 393, 445, 448, 456
Mills, D.H. 320
Mills & Murgatroyd 72, 673
Mills Beaumont Leavey Channon 115, 203, 373
Milner-White, Eric 661
Ministry of Public Building and Works 109, 157, 160

Minoprio, Anthony 99, 375
Minoprio & Spencely 254
Minton 96, 295, 629, 661
Mitchell, William 233, 358, 376
Moffat, John 39
Moira, Gerald 94, 251, 450, Pl. 72
Mole, C.J. 325
Molyneux family 30, 406, 521, 580–2
    see also Sefton, Earls of
Molyneux, 3rd Viscount 245, 326
Molyneux, 4th Viscount 42, 406
Molyneux, 5th Viscount 43, 509
Molyneux, 7th Viscount 576
Molyneux, Anne 582
Molyneux, Anthony 580, 581
Molyneux, Edward 580, 581
Molyneux, James 26, 580, 582
Molyneux, Sir Richard (d. 1568) 28, 583
Molyneux, Sir Richard (fl. 1575–1605) 406, 469
Molyneux, Thomas 426
Molyneux, Sir William 27, 28, 583
Moore, A.L. (& Son) 124, 519
Moore, Albert 408
Moore, Edward 137, 142
Moore, John Francis 41, 607, 613
Mordaunt, Charles 195
Morgan, William de 549
Morley (David) Architects 366
Morley (W.J.) & Sons 239
Morris, John Grant 391
Morris, Thomas 260, 273
Morris, William 192, 386–7, 533, Pl. 67
Morris & Co. 96, 191, 230, 251, 353, 386, 411, 432, 436, 439, 440, 443, 450, 466, 479, 507, 542, 622, 629, 646, 654, 661, Pl. 67
    see also Morris, William
Morrison, William 154
Mort, Adam 132
Morter, Pelham 402
Morter & Dobie 340, 342
Morton, F.W. 596
Moseley, William 78
Moser & Co. 290
Mott, Basil 98, 306
Mott, Hay & Anderson 108, 649
Mouchel, Louis Gustave 278
Mountford, E.W. 80, 298, Pl. 79
Munby, A.E. 99, 667
Mundford, W.D.T. 652
Murphy, Tom (sculptor, active 1930s-80s) 360
Murphy, Tom (sculptor, b. 1949) 284, 315, 459
Murray, Frank 311
Murray, Thomas E. 83, 319
Muspratt, James 57

Nagington & Shennan 488
Nall-Cain, Sir Charles 495

Nash, John 62, 74, 190, 399
Naylor, Peers 524
Naylor, R.C. 329
Neale, G. Hall 375
Nelson & Parker 106, 154, 504
Nesfield, Eden 84, 408–9, 503
Newton-Dawson, Forbes & Tate 329
Nicholl, S.J. 419
Nicholl, W.G. 294, 297, 318
Nicholson, A.K. 231
Nicholson (A.K.) Studio 471
Nicholson, Sir Charles 231, 345
Nicholson, F.W. 427
Nightingale, Florence 76, 365
Noble, Matthew 97, 223, 296
Nollekens, Joseph 592
Norbury, Alfred 474
Norbury, Frank 96, 281, 403
Norbury, Paterson & Co. 420
Norbury, Upton & Paterson 378
Norreys, John and Nicholaa de 463
Norris, Edward 32, 398, 463, 465,
    466, 467
Norris, Henry 467
Norris, Margaret 465, 467
Norris, Sir William 32, 467
Norris, William II 463
Northcroft, George 468
Nost, John 661, 682, Pl. 24
Nuttall, Jonas 574
Nuttall & Cook 673
Nuttgens, Joseph E. 381, 664
Nuttgens, Patrick 534

Oboussier, Claire 508
O'Byrne, James 377, 471, 472, 592,
    599, 666
Office of Works 336
Ogle, Sir John 29, 542
Oldham, F.H. 124
Oliver & Lamb 370
O'Mahoney, Richard 172
O'Mahony Fozzard 358
OMI Architects 315
O'Neill, J. 444
Orlit 105, 200
Ormrod & Partners 320, 371, 558
ORMS 625, 626
Ould, Edward 93, 507
Owen, Geoffrey 165, 632
Owen, R. Wynn 493
Owen, Richard 162
Owen, William 72, 81, 604, 614, 621,
    627, 628, 631, 633, 670
Owen Ellis Partnership 274, 334, 503,
    508, 535
Owen (R.) & Son 157, 494
Owens (R.) & Sons 470
Owen, William & Segar 81, 83, 525,
    604, 606–7, 614, 617, 618, 619, 627,
    628, 632
Owens, Richard 318

Pace, George 533, 591, 592
Page & Park 258, 325
Paley, E.G. 91, 198, 210, 223, 534, 629,
    659n., 660, 663
    see also Austin, Hubert (James);
    Austin & Paley etc.
Paley & Austin 87, 91–2, 96, 136, 137,
    141, 189, 192, 193, 198, 213, 220,
    223, 229, 230, 231, 251, 439, 440,
    533, 629, 630, Pls. 63–5
Paley, Austin & Paley 223, 567, 642,
    654, 663
Palmer, Benjamin 606
Palmer, John 66, 174, 679
Palmer & Holden 341
Papworth, Wyatt 452
Pardo, Jorge 343
Parkwood PFI Projects 153
Parr, Thomas 246, 316, Pl. 37
Pasmore, Victor 574
Patten, Thomas 45, 604n., 611
Pattesson, James & Samuel 138, 360
Pawle, H.L. 471
Paxton, Joseph 75, 250, 451, 452
Payton, F. Bartram 405
Peace, David 284
Pearce, Walter J. 230
Pearson, John Loughborough 89, 251,
    447, 456, 581, Pl. 68
Pegram, Henry 333
Peirce, Charles James 74, 249, 490,
    Pl. 86
Pendle Glass 592
Penfold, J.W. 370
Penketh, John 577
Penn-Smith & Weston 112, 577
Pennethorne, James 75, 250, 451, 452
Pennington, R. 538
Perry (Martin) Architects 241
Peskett, Eric 371
Phaophanit, Vong 508
Phillimore, Claud 106, 217, 218–19,
    221, 222
Phillips, Joseph 323, 351, 353
Phyffers, Theodore 377
Pickard Finlason Partnership 122
Pickles Martinez Associates 257, 373
Picton, J.A. (Sir James) 51, 69, 94, 249,
    284, 312, 313, 319, 323, 339, 372,
    389, 497, 499, 526
Picton (J.A.) & Son 94, 420
Picton, W.H. 318, 339, 466, Pl. 14
Pilkington family and firm 552, 559,
    565, 567, 571–2
Pilkington, R.A. 578
Pilkington, Col. Richard 85, 196, 546
Pilkington, Col. William 559
Pinckney, Roger 350
Piper, John 112, 255, 358
Pite, Beresford 345
Player, M. Nevile 108, 652
Pointer, William 595

Poitou, Roger de 18
Pomeroy, F.W. 80, 296, 298, 335
Pope, Nicholas 333
Porter, Adrian J. 277
Posford, Pavry & Partners 462
Potter, T. Wickford 224
Potter, William 579
Potts, A. 619
Potts, W. 74
Potts, Son & Hennings 674
Powell, Charles B. 102, 555, 556
Powell, David 429
Powell & Powell 599
Powell (James) & Sons (Whitefriars)
    97, 112, 121, 198, 223, 231, 352, 434,
    440, 534, 564, 583, 591, 643, 660,
    662, 682
    see also Whitefriars Glass
Pozzoni Design Group 231, 623
Preedy, Frederick 432
Prescott, John 168
Prescott, Seth and Frances 584
Preston, Edward Carter 102, 339, 350,
    351, 352, 353, 488
Preston, J.S. 231
Prestwich, Harold 228
Prestwich, James Caldwell 72, 73, 80, 138,
    228, 232, 233, 234, 236, 238, Pl. 85
Prestwich (J.C.) & Sons 73, 99, 139,
    141, 228, 233, 234, 235–6
Prichard, L.A.G. 239
Prichard (L.A.G.) & Son 111, 202,
    255, 405, 431, 494, 576, 623, 665
Priddle, William 314
Priestley, Joseph 603
Prioleau, C.K. 368
Pritchard, H.W. 389
PSA Projects, Birmingham 114, 273
Pugh, Frederick G. 360
Pugin family 93
Pugin, A.W.N. 85, 88, 96, 251, 354,
    400, 401, 480, 481, 542, 606, 653,
    665, 678, 680–1
Pugin, C.W. 609
Pugin, E.W. 69, 88, 89, 93, 95, 251,
    285, 313, 354, 400, 401, 420, 480,
    485, 507, 532, 609, 651, Pl. 61
Pugin, Peter Paul 93, 95, 124, 129, 383,
    412, 435, 609, Pl. 61
Pugin & Pugin 78, 93, 124, 181, 377,
    383, 412, 419, 420, 471, 485, 489,
    502, 563, 566, 567, 609, 658
Purcell 599
Purcell Miller Tritton 296
Purdie, A.E. 153
Purdy, Martin 112, 556

Queen, James 291
Quekett, Rev. William 604
Quiggin & Gee 103, 111, 153, 308, 311,
    327, 338, 404, 445, 488, 662
Quirke, E. 571

Radcliffe, Richard 483
Radcliffe, Richard, Jun. 484
Rainey, Clifford 305
Ralph, William Chasen 72, 659n.
Ralph (W. Chasen) & Co. 668
Ralph & Heaton 670
Ralph (W. Chasen) & Son 664
Rampling, Clark 246, 378
Rankin, H. 340
Rankin's Union Foundry 329
Rannigar, Timothy 185, 186
Rathbone, Edmund 378, 454
Rathbone, Hannah 442
Rathbone, Richard Llewellyn 94, 251,
    252, 289, 450
Rathbone, William 441
Rathbone (Joseph) & Fawcett (William)
    442
Rattee & Kett 352
Rawlinson, Robert 291, 294, 295
Rayner, Lloyd 441
Reade, Rev. J.C. 477
Reade, T. Mellard 80, 86, 153–4, 196,
    252, 397, 413, 475
Reade, William 196
Redford, Dianne 305
Redford, James 477
Redmayne, G.T. 79, 317
Reed, Charles 85, 564
Reed, Lillie 348
Rees & Holt 378
Rees-Thomas, Gillian 369
Reeve, John Elliott 321, 498
Reid, Dr Boswell 297
Reid (Geoffrey) Associates 114, 316, 558,
    559
Reilly, Sir Charles 72, 97, 98, 254, 345,
    366, 367, 492, 493, 513, 617
Reilly, Budden & Marshall 368
Rennie, John 51, 262, 270, 277
Repton, Humphry 47, 175
Repton, Thomas 226
Reynolds, F. 387
Reynolds, Francis and James 448
Reynolds, W. Bainbridge 352
Reynolds & Scott 664
Reyntiens, Patrick 112, 255, 358, 437
Rhind, James 70, 76, 395, 416, 443,
    444
Rhind, William Birnie 329, 364
Rhind & Banner 85
Rice, A.E. 371
Rice, Sean 359, 393
Richards, Ceri 359
Richardson, John 632
Rickman, Thomas 65, 66, 67, 182, 202,
    281, 284, 316, 382, 417, 514
Rickman, Thomas, & Henry Hutchinson
    183, 663
Ridsdale, G.H. 546
Rigby, Alfred 360
Rigby, Edward 287

Riley, Robin 111, 665
Rimmington, Frank 489, 535
Ripley, Thomas 43, 303
Robarts, Rev. Frederick Hall 94, 420
Robbia, Giovanni della 352
Robbins (W.H.) & Associates 160
Roberts, David 442
Roberts, Gareth 304
Roberts, James A. 110, 256, 335
Robertson, Eric 374
Robertson, John 452
Robertson Young & Partners 378
Robinson, C.B. 542
Robinson, L. 678
Robson, E.R. 73, 75, 249, 291, 395, 426
Rochdale, Robert 217
Rogerson, Joseph 284, 318
Rollett, G.H. 301
Romaine-Walker, W.H. 84, 217, 219, 220, 221, Pl. 31
Romaine-Walker & Jenkins 289, 290
Rope, Margaret Agnes 625
Roscoe, William 48, 62, 63, 246, 379, 392
Rose, James 512
Ross, Eduard 114, 263, 278
Ross, Henry William 513
Rossi, J.C. 288
Roughley, Thomas 568
Rouw, H. 606
Rowe, R. Reynolds 96, 630
Rowell (David) & Co. 615
Rowland, Samuel 64, 65n., 247, 249, 318, 360, 379, 624
Rowlandson, C.A. 305
Rowse, Herbert J. 97–8, 254, 306, 314, 328, 332, 335, 341, 371, 571, 583
Ruabon Terracotta Works 325
Rutherford, Rosemary 129

Sale, John 29, 167
Salisbury, Frank O. 289
Salomons, Wornum & Ely 310
Salviati, Messrs 95, 311, 493
Sandy & Norris 480
Saunders Bell 112
Saunders Boston 112, 180
Saunders & Boston 374
Saunders, Boston & Brock 370
Scarisbricke, James 149
Scarratt, William 291
Scheffer, Ary 419
Schofield, W.H. 98
Schulze, Eberhard 134, 665
Schulze, Edmund 198
Scoles, J.J. 67, 80, 84, 92n., 206, 208, 209, 251, 418, 517, 555, 665, Pl. 30
Scott, Adrian Gilbert 111, 356, 480
Scott, Sir George Gilbert 85, 88, 91, 96, 250, 251, 389, 501, 629
Scott, G.G., Jun. 501

Scott, Sir Giles Gilbert 94, 96, 97, 97n., 99, 103, 112, 253, 255, 344, 345–53, 398, 479, 494, 643, 661, Pls. 70, 71, 112
Scott, J. Oldrid 96, 405, 501
Scott, Walter 506
Scriven, Robert 535
Seddon, J.P. 324
Seddon, William 226
Seely & Paget 606
Sefton, Earl of 453
Sefton, 4th Earl of 406
Sefton, 7th Earl of 213, 215
Seifert (R.) & Partners 326
Sephton, Daniel 41, 542, 592
Sephton, Henry 39–40, 43, 148, 205, 218, 407, 541, Pls. 30, 39
Seward (A.) & Co. 167
Sewell, Fr Nicholas 570
Seymour Harris Partnership 257, 316
Shallcross, T. Myddelton 308
Shand, William 392
Shanghai Linyi Garden Building Co. Ltd. 327
Shankland, Graeme 105, 256
Shankland Cox & Associates 310
Sharpe, Edmund 66, 88, 223, 662
Sharpe & Paley 25, 567, 660
Sharples, Henry 400
Sharples, James 400
Shaw, George 556
Shaw, (Richard) Norman 70, 71, 85, 249, 250, 312, 325, 328, 345, 448, 645n
Shed KM 115, 257, 258, 320, 324, 388, 421, 430, 431, 437, Pls. 81, 127
Shellard, E.H. 175, 229
Shelmerdine, Henry 54, 93, 320, 338, 339, 451, 651, 672
Shelmerdine, Thomas 74, 76, 77, 81, 249, 253, 289, 299, 302, 335, 367, 412, 420, 428, 429, 435, 453, 468, 475, 481, 482, 495
Shelmerdine, E. & H. 340
Shennan, Alfred E. 99, 315, 423, 439, 451, 479, 497, 503
Shennan (Alfred) & Partners 321, 496
Shepheard & Bower 304
Sheppard Robson Architects 363
Sheridan, J.G.R. 122
Sherlock, Cornelius 81, 191, 249, 250, 299, 339, 431, 432, 433, 434, 443, 499, Pl. 80
Shipway, Lawrence 26, 590
Shoolbred, James N. 299
Shrigley & Hunt 96, 137, 165, 172, 174, 181, 193, 223, 229, 239, 382, 418, 429, 448, 502, 505, 524, 525, 537, 563, 567, 576, 589, 592, 606, 628, 629, 630, 642, 649, 654, 682
Shuttleworth, Richard 238
Simmonds, William G. 126

Simon, Frank W. 364
Simpson, Frederick Moore 82, 289, 321, 364, 376
Sims, Ronald 592, 606
Sinclair, John S. 649, 656
Sinnott, Dan 579
Sinnott, J. & B. 394, 435, 494
Sinnott, Sinnott & Powell 93, 180, 400, 571, 579, 631, 653
Skeaping, John 99, 375
Skelmersdale Development Corporation Architects Department 588, 589
Skidmore, Messrs 471
Skidmore, Owings & Merrill 110, 675
Skinner, Peter 112, 136, 137
Skinner (W.S.), Crisp & Oatley 78, 682
Slater, Sir Henry 177
Slater, John 67, 247, 284, 472
Slater, William 307
Slater & Carpenter 155
Slater & Moberly 99, 401
Smirke, Sir Robert 65, 66, 595
Smirke, Sydney 147, 194, 535, 536
Smith, A. W. 524
Smith, Bishop of Lincoln 654
Smith, Gerald E.R. 471
Smith, Herbert Tyson 100, 156, 254, 297, 304, 308, 313, 314, 315, 322, 333, 341, 387, 395, 403, 445–6, 459, 493, 598, 653, Pls. 111, 113
Smith, J. Myrtle 81
Smith, Roger 427
Smith, Stanley H. 333
Smith (George) & Co. 668
Smith, William and Alexander 384
Snape, Alan 534, 537
Soane, Sir John 46, 646
Sorocold, George 260
Spence, Basil 255, 370
Spence, Benjamin Edward 296, 299, 454
Spence, William 48, 150, 284, 360, 387, 412, 520, 678
Spence (Basil), Glover & Ferguson 370
Spencely, Hugh Greville 99, 375
Spencer, Joseph 419
Stammers, J.H. 129, 592
Standish, Edward 591, 592
Stanley family 62, 148, 217, 224, 225, 227, 533, 599
    see also Derby, Earls of
Stanley, Sir Edward 148
Stanley, Sir John 217n., 243
Stanley, Peter 146
Stanley, Thomas 20, 226
Stapleton-Bretherton, Lady Mary 65,
Stark, Malcolm 345
Steele, Tommy 340
Steers, Thomas 39, 43, 51, 52, 260, 303, 320
Stephen, J.H. 80, 133
Stephens, E. N. 295

Stephenson, George 53, 60, 526–7, 548, Pl. 98
Stephenson, Gordon 369
Stephenson, Robert 530
Stephenson, William 287n
Stephenson (Derek) & Partners 325
Stephenson, Young & Partners 370
Stevens, Alfred 295, 504
Stevenson, F. 54, 304, Pl. 100
Stevenson, W.L. 156, 330
Stewart, Daniel 66, 161, 361
Stirling, Edwin 223, 318, 389
Stirling, James 114, 257, 269
Stirling, Wilford & Associates 269
Stirrup, John 530
Stockley, N.H. 310
Stokes, Leonard 93–4, 251, 448, 449, Pl. 69
Stone, Thomas 81, 528–9, 613
Stott, Abraham Henthorn Jun. 56, 237
Stott & Sons 56, 58, 200, 237, 545, 675, Pl. 101
Stratton, Arthur 375
Street, A.E. 664
Street, George Edmund 85, 89, 96, 251, 470, 489, 645, 661, 664
Strong, James 330
Stuber, M. 62, 185
Studio BAAD 114, 614
Sugden (William) & Son 87, 428
Sullivan, W.H. 192
Sullivan & Sweetman 399
Sumners, Henry 73, 91, 95, 251, 307, 317, 322, 335, 378, 385, 410, 472, 557, 564, 645, Pl. 74
Sussex, Duke of 606
Sutcliffe, G.L. 87, 500, Pl. 109
Sutherland, John 284
Sutton, H. Havelock 470
Swiercynski, Jan 137, 162
Swire, Henry 98

TACP Design 561
Tanner, Sir Henry 40, 75, 412, 614
Tapper, W.J. 345
Tarbock, Sir Henry de 22
Tarbock, Richard de 22
Tate, Sir Henry 77, 450, 5
Tate & Lyle Engineering Dept 110, 280, Pl. 121
Tate & Popplewell 624
Taylor, Isaac 140, 559
Taylor, J. Medland 57, 85, 131, 141, 546, 559, 566, 571
Taylor, Samuel 66, 576, 577–8
Taylor, J. Medland & Henry 87, 90–1, 96, 128, 130–1, 141, 183, 570
Taylor Young 278
Telford, Thomas 649
Temperley (G.) & Son 139
Tenerani, Pietro 68, 362, 655
Thearle, Herbert 400, 435

Thearle (Herbert) & Partners 109, 388
Theed, William, the Younger 296
Thicknesse, Philip 96, 403
Thomas, Dewi Prys 514
Thomas, F.G. 350
Thomas, Walter Aubrey 71, 253, 316, 319, 324, 327, 331, 342, 432, Pls. 1, 92
Thomas, Walter W. 83, 252, 253n., 326, 375, 423, 497, 498, Pl. 95
Thomas (Percy) Partnership 373, 437
Thomas (Sir Percy) & Son 110, 216
Thompson, C.E. 82, 299, 430, 475
Thompson, Edmund C. 98, 170, 306, 314, 323, 332, 341, 342, 372
Thompson, Henry Yates 396, 454
Thompson, Jabez 423
Thomson, Mr 448
Thomson, James 486
Thomson (Eric) & Associates 197
Thornely, Arnold 94, 98, 153, 254, 299, 341, 364, 571
Thornely, J.B. & W. 81, 127, 676
Thornycroft, Hamo 475
Thornycroft, Thomas 82, 297
Threadgold, Robert 423
3XNielsen 115
Tillemans, Peter 219
Tite, William 304
Todd, R. 671
Tomlinson, Arthur 240
Tower, Walter 624
Towneley, Charles 47, 207
Townshend, Caroline 103, 427, 434, 656
Traherne, Margaret 359
Travers & Ramsden 167
Traves, Henry 176-7
Tripe & Wakeham 109, 153, 256, 330
Troughton & Young 629
Turner, Arthur 352
Turner, C.A. 430
Turner, Richard 304
Twist & Whitley 371
Tyrrell, Thomas 353

Ugolino, Fr 449
Unger, Hans 134, 665
Union North 115, 313
Unit Construction Ltd 215
United Kingdom Atomic Energy Authority 370
Unsworth, Thomas 555
Unwin, Raymond 87, 100, 252, 500, 565
Urban Splash 114-15, 257, 340, 343, 430
Urmston, Frances 238

Vale, H.H. 81, 203, 249, 299, 343, 361, 376
Vasconcellos, Josefina de 352, 609
Vaughan, Fr Richard, SJ 419

Vawser, R. 613
Velarde, Francis Xavier 103, 111, 126, 156, 199, 254, 403, 526, 598
Velarde (F.X.) Partnership 563
Verity, W. 655, 671, 673
Viney, T.L. 638
Vis Williams Prichard 358
Voysey, C.F.A. 482

Waddington (William) & Son 95, 161, 199
Wade, Herbert 199
Wailes, William 96, 401, 501, 502, 661
Wainwright (T.) & Sons 99, 313, 335
Wakefield, William 44, 140, 141
Walker, Andrew Barclay 80, 85, 203, 250, 299
Walker, David 435
Walker, Derek 344
Walker, Peter 321
Walker, William Hall 433
Wallace, W.K. 674
Walmsley, John 306
Walters, Edward 72, 619
Walters, Barker & Ellis 72
Walton, Linda 419
Warburton, Albert 72, 98, 619, 621
Ward, Christine 667
Ward, George F. 618
Ward, Ashcroft & Parkman 268
Ward & Hughes 137, 592, 598
Ward, W.H., & W.G. Cogswell 427
Waring & Gillow 352
Warrington, William 399
Warrington New Town Development Corporation Architect's Department 641
Waterhouse, Alfred 76, 77, 78, 79, 80, 83, 85, 210, 250, 304, 319, 335, 363, 364, 365, 390-1, 425, 441, 452, 475, 667, Pls. 84, 93, 106
Waterhouse, Paul 319, 364
Watt, Adelaide 463, 464
Watt, Richard 68, 463, 466, 467, 468, 592, Pl. 46
Webb, Aston 317
Webb, John 47, 241
Webb, William 500
Webster of Kendal (mason) 606
Webster, David 327
Webster, John J. 615
Webster & Wood 649
Weddle, A.E. 160
Weightman, John 73, 74, 81, 249, 291, 298, 301, 490, Pls. 79, 86
Weightman & Bullen 109, 111, 255, 364, 365, 401, 432, 437, 457, 482, 507, 508, 516
Weightman & Hadfield 88, 240, 485, 534, 566, 652
Weingartner, Louis 352, 353, 543
Welch, E. 88, 546, 547

Weld, Thomas 205, 206
Westlake 621
Westmacott, J.S., Sen. 144
Westmacott, Sir Richard 68, 82, 246, 323, 423, 542
Westmacott, Richard, Sen. 288
Westwood, Bryan 371
Westwood, Bryan & Norman, Piet & Partners 108, 256, 369, 560
Whelmar 637
Whiffen, Charles E. 312
Whistler, Hector 371
Whistler, J.A.M. 464
White, Sir Thomas 457
White, Young & Partners 113, 639
Whitefriars Glass 399, 631
Whitley (C.T.) & Fry 525
Wigan Metropolitan Council Architects Department 186, 667
Wilbraham, Mary Charlotte Bootle 226
Wilford (Michael) & Partners 269
Wilkinson, C.P. 315
Wilkinson, Horace 555
Wilkinson, Stephen 99, 535, 653
Wilkinson, Walter 583
Wilkinson Eyre 115, 258, 273, 306
Wilkinson Hindle Halsall Lloyd 106, 322, 487
Wilkinson, Hindle & Partners 477
Williams, Messrs 315
Williams, Sir Edward Leader 551, 616
Williams (Ellis) Architects/Partnership 373, 485, 560, 571
Williams, Arthur Yates & George 66, 191, 247, 469, 557
Williams (Alan) & Partners 561
Williams & Watkins 494
Williamson, F.J. 338
Williamson, Joseph 415
Willink & Dod 99, 323, 442
Willink & Thicknesse 70, 71, 81, 82, 155, 172, 249, 253, 312, 321, 332, 364, 372, 376, 385, 410, 416, 454, 475, 492, Pl. 1
Wilson, Mr 353
Wilson, G.W. 352
Wilson, Sir Hugh 107, 586–7
Wilson, J.M. 560, 562
Wilson, Richard 206
Wilson, William 112, 352
Wilson (J.M.) & Son 456
Winstanley, Hamlet 48, 618

Wolley, Robin 112, 202, 663
Wood, Derwent 329
Wood, John 45, 245, 286–7, 289, Pl. 34
Wood, John Warrington 299, 533, 620, 628
Woodall, Noel 157
Woodford, James 375n., 496
Woodhouse, George 55, 610, 674
Woodhouse & Willoughby 81, 651
Woodroffe, Paul 444, 542
Woods, Edward 304
Woods, J. & E. 675
Woolfall & Eccles 172, 329, 451
Woolner, Thomas 489
Woore, Edward 542
Wordley, W.H. 293, 296
Worthington, Percy 94, 449
Worthington, Thomas 77, 78, 81, 200, 508, 668
Worthington (Thomas) & Son 94, 251, 449
Worthy, M.J. 360
Wortley, William 405, 427
Wragge, George 289, 331
Wright, Professor H. Myles 160
Wright (J.E.), Garnett & Wright 83, 604, 617, 619, 628, 634
Wright & Hamlyn 617
Wrightington, Edward 29, 592, Pl. 22
Wroot, Ian 278
Wyatt, James 45, 245, 246, 286, 288–91, 322n., Pls. 34, 56
Wyatt, Lewis 62, 677, 678
Wyatt, Matthew Cotes 82, 246, 290, 323
Wyatt, R.J. 68, 682, Pl. 47
Wyatt, Thomas Henry 84, 168, 225, 322n., 406, 407
Wylie, Thomas 373

Yates, F.S. Spencer 73, 643–4
Yates, Richard Vaughan 451, 452, 454
Yeatman-Biggs, Colonel 468
Yorke, Rosenberg & Mardall 108, 256, 366, 369
Young, R.R. 366
Young, W. 88, 230
Young (Bryan) & Associates 415

Zaccagnini 420
Zammit, Rosario 432

INDEX OF PLACES

Principal references are in **bold** type; demolished buildings are shown in *italic*. Liverpool is indexed in three separate entries: Liverpool centre, Liverpool docks and Liverpool suburbs.

Abram 73, 87, 103, **121–2**, 664
    Brookside Farmhouse 37, **122**
    Platt Bridge **121–2**
Aigburth *see* Liverpool suburbs
Aintree *84*, 104, **122–3**
Appleton *see* Warrington; Widnes
Ashton-in-Makerfield *16, 17*, 57, 81, **123–7**, 174
    Bryn **124–5**, **127**
    churches 93, **124–7**
        Park Lane Chapel 29, **127**
        St Oswald and St Edmund
          Arrowsmith (R.C.) 102, **125–7**, 568, Pls. 114, 115
    Haydock Park Racecourse and *Haydock Lodge 46*, **127**, **528**
Aspull 50, 60, **127–32**
    churches **128–9**, **130–1**
        St Elizabeth 90–1, 96, **128–9**
        St John Baptist 91, **130–1**
    Colliers Arms 42, **131**
    Gidlow Hall 32, 34, **129–30**
    Hindley Hall 44, **130**
    Kirkless Hall 30, 33, **131–2**, 211, 212
    New Springs 91, **130–2**
    Pennington Hall and Green 37, *128*, **130**
    Walker's Higher Farm 42, **129**
Astley 60, 87, **132–5**
    Astley Green 50, 55, **132**
    Astley Hall *11*, 34, 35, **132–3**
    Higher Green Lane cottages 55, **132**
    Manor House Farm 42, **134**
    Morley's Hall 31–2, 33, **134–5**
    Old Vicarage 42, **133–4**
Astley Green *see* Astley
Atherton 2, 17, 50, 86, **135–42**
    Alder House 36, 42, **138–9**
    Atherton Hall 44–5, 46, **140–1**
    Chowbent 40, 57, 135, **137–8**
    churches etc. 76, **136–8**, **141–2**
        St John Baptist 92, 112, **136–7**, Pl. 63
        St Michael and All Angels 92, 97, 136, **141–2**
    Collier Brook Bolt Works 57, **139**

Howe Bridge 87, 92, 97, 136, **141–2**
    Gibfield Colliery baths 87, **139**
Howe Bridge Mills 56, **140**
    obelisk 47, **138**
    public buildings 73, 75, 81, 99, **138**, **141**
Aughton 1, 18, 84, **142–7**
    almshouses 79, **144–5**
    Aughton Old Hall 31, 33, **145**
    churches 66, **142–4**
        St Michael 23, 25, 26, **142–4**, 192, 531, 532
    Moor Hall 34, **145–6**
    waterworks 76, **147**
    West Tower 85, **146–7**
Aughton Hall *see* Ormskirk

Bedford *see* Leigh
Beech Hill *see* Wigan
Bewsey *see* Warrington
Bickershaw 38, **147**
Bickerstaffe 45, **147–8**
Billinge 17, 36, **148–52**
    Birchley Hall 34, **150–1**, 677
    Bispham Hall 34, **151**, 170, 677, Pl.17
    St Aidan 39, **148–50**, 164, 166, Pl. 3
    Winstanley Hall *see* Wigan
Birchley Hall *see* Billinge
Bispham Hall *see* Billinge
Blackbrook *see* St Helens
Blundellsands 1, 86, 94, **152–4**
    Maeldune 106, **154**
    Redcot 86, **154**, Pl. 108
Bold *30, 33*, 41, 44, 47, 48, **154–5**, **654**
    see also St Helens
Bootle 1, 86, 104, 105, 106, 109–10, **155–61**
    churches **155–7**
        St Monica (R.C.) 103, **156–7**, 598
    docks *see* Liverpool docks
    gasholders 58, **160**
    public buildings 108, **157–9**
        Bootle Borough Hospital 77, **157**
        Civic Centre 73, 76, **157–9**
        National Giro Centre 109, **157**

Stanley Precinct 105, 109, **159–60**
streets **157–61**
Triad Building 109, **160**,
 Pl. 123
Bradley Old Hall *see* Burtonwood
Bridgewater Canal 52, 132, 229, 245,
 272, 551, 627, **630**
Broad Oak *see* St Helens
Bryn *see* Ashton-in-Makerfield
Burscough 66, **161–2**, 523
 Burscough Priory *see* Lathom
 Martin Hall 38, **162**
Burtonwood 40, **162–3**
 Bradley Old Hall 21, 29–30, 32,
 163
 Motorway Services 108, **639–40**,
 Pl. 124
 RAF Burtonwood 635, **639**

Calderstones *see* Liverpool suburbs
 (Allerton)
Childwall *see* Liverpool suburbs
Chowbent *see* Atherton
Clock Face *see* St Helens
Clubmoor *see* Liverpool suburbs
Cowley Hill *see* St Helens
Crawford 87, **163–4**
 Manor House 42, **163–4**, 166,
 Pl. 26
Cressington Park *see* Liverpool sub-
 urbs (Aigburth)
Croft 66, **164–5**
 Southworth Hall *11*, **165**
Cronton 17, 43, 164, **166**
Crosby Hall *see* Little Crosby
Croxteth *see* Liverpool suburbs
Cuerdley Cross **166**
 Fiddler's Ferry Power Station 110,
 166
Culcheth 17, 29, 78, **167–8**, 624
 Kenyon Hall 62, **167–8**

Dalton 2, 38, **168–70**
 Ashurst Hall 38, **169**, 170
 Prior's Wood Hall 37, **170**
 Stone Hall 42, **170**, Pl. 25
Denton's Green *see* St Helens
Dingle *see* Liverpool docks
Ditton *see* Widnes
Downholland **170–1**
 Haskayne 37–8, **171**

Earlestown *see* Newton-le-Willows
Eccleston *see* St Helens
Edge Hill *see* Liverpool suburbs
Everton *see* Liverpool suburbs

Fairfield *see* Liverpool suburbs
Farnworth *see* Widnes
Fazakerley *see* Liverpool suburbs
Fiddler's Ferry Power Station *see*
 Cuerdley Cross

Formby 86, **171–3**
 churches 40, 89, **171–2**
 Formby Hall 46, **173**
 Sandhills Cottages 86, **173**

Garston *see* Liverpool suburbs
Garswood 47, 62, 66, **173–5**
Gateacre *see* Liverpool suburbs
Gathurst *see* Orrell
Gathurst Hall *see* Shevington
Gin Pit *see* Astley
Glazebrook **175**
Glazebury 55, **175–7**
 Hurst Hall Barn 31, 32–3, **175–6**,
 Pl. 12
 Light Oaks Hall 33, 35, 36, **176–7**
Golborne 40, 60, **177–9**, 515
 Lawson's Farmhouse 36, 37, **178**
 Lightshaw Hall 33, 46, **178–9**,
 550
Grappenhall *see* Warrington
Great Altcar **179–80**, Pl. 2
 St Michael 92, **179–80**, 195,
 Pl. 66
Great Crosby 1, 81, **180–2**
 churches 94–5, **180–1**
 St Luke 89, 112, **180**
 Merchant Taylors' Schools 39, 80,
 181–2
Great Sankey *see* Warrington

Haigh 60, **183–8**, 211
 Great Sough 50, **183**
 Haigh Hall and Estate 47, 50, 62,
 75, 150, **183–8**, 488, **676**, Pls. 53,
 54
 Haigh Foundry 58, **187–8**
 Receptacle, The 46, **188**
 school 80, **188**
 wind pump 58, **188**
 St David 66, **183**, 663
Hale *12*, 19, 38, **188–91**
 church 24, 40, **189**
 Manor House 42, **189–90**, 509,
 Pl. 27
 Old Hutte 30
 prefabs 105, **191**
Hale Bank *see* Widnes
Halewood 106, **191–2**
 Brook House Farm site *13*, *192*, 228
 church 66, 96, **191–2**
 Court Farm site *16*, *17–18*, *192*
 Halewood Car Plant *see* Liverpool
 suburbs (Speke)
Halsall 9, *11*, 30, 38, 52, **192–5**
 church 23, 24, 25, 26, 28, 142,
 192–4, 596, Pl. 5
Halsnead Park *see* Whiston
Halton View *see* Widnes
Harrington *see* Liverpool suburbs
 (Toxteth)
Haskayne *see* Downholland

Haydock 52, 77, 87, 92, **195–6**
  Haydock racecourse and *Haydock Lodge see* Ashton-in-Makerfield
  theatre 83, **195**
Hightown *10–11*, 86, **196–7**
Hindley 105, **197–200**
  churches **197–9**
    All Saints 40, **197–8**
    St Benedict (R.C.) 91, **198–9**
    St John Evangelist 93, **198**
    St John Methodist Church 95, **199**
    St Peter 88, **198**
  public buildings 75, **199–200**
    District Council offices 73, **199**
    Hindley and Abram Grammar School (former) 80, **200**
    Library and Museum 81, **200**
Hindley Green *see* Hindley
Hindley Hall *see* Aspull
Hollins Green 40, **201**
Hough Green *see* Widnes
Howe Bridge *see* Atherton
Hunt's Cross *see* Liverpool suburbs
Hurst Hall Barn *see* Glazebury
Hurst House *see* Huyton
Huyton 84, **201–4**
  churches 94, 111, **201–2**, 203
    St Michael 23, 24, 25, 26, 27, 28, 29, 40, 96, **201–2**, 542
  Hazels, The 45, **204**
  public buildings 106, 108, 110, **202–4**
    Heatwaves Leisure Centre, Stockbridge Village 109, **203–4**
    library 115, **203**
    school 80, **203**
  Roby 18, 19–20, **202–3**

Ince Blundell 1, *16*, 79–80, **204–9**, 241
  Cross Barn 38, **209**
  Ince Blundell Hall 43, 45, 84, 89, **204–9**, Pls. 30, 105
    Pantheon etc. 47–8, 84, 205, **206–8**, Pls. 51, 52
Ince-in-Makerfield *17*, 50, 58, 73, 87, **210–12**
  churches etc. 76, **210**
    St Mary 189, 210
    Wigan Borough Cemetery 76, 100, **210**
  Ince Hall 34, 211
  Peel Hall 30, 31–2, 33, 36, **211–12**, 684

Kensington *see* Liverpool suburbs (Edge Hill)
Kenyon **212**
Kirkby 2, *12*, 18, *22*, **213–17**, 256
  church 23, 92, 96, **213–14**, 439, 664, Pl. 3
  Civic Centre 108, **216**

dovecote 38, **216**
Kirkby Industrial Park 110, **216**
Kirkby Town 106–7, 110, 213, **214–16**
Simonswood Hall **216–17**
Kirkdale *see* Liverpool suburbs
Kirkless Hall *see* Aspull
Kit Green *see* Wigan
Knowsley 80, **217–24**
  Knowsley Hall 1, 20, 22, 43–4, 45, 46n., 47, 62–3, 84, 106, **217–23**, 407, Pls. 31, 107
    New House 106, **222**
    park 1, 22, 30, 46–7, 219, **221–3**, 545
  St Mary 88, 97, **223**

Lamberhead Green *see* Wigan
Langtree *see* Standish
Latchford *see* Warrington
Lathom 80, **224–8**
  Blythe Hall 102, **227**
  Burscough Priory 23, 26, 28, *224*, 226, 532, 534
  Duttons Farm site *13–14*, *15*, *16*, *228*
  Lathom House *20*, *30*, *44*, 47–8, 102, **224–6**, 228, Pls. 32, 33
  Lathom Park 22, **226–8**
  Lathom Park Chapel 23, 25, 26, **226–7**, Pl. 8
  Lathom Park House **226–7**
Lea Green *see* St Helens
Leigh 2, 49–51, 52, 55, 59, 72, 75, 114, **228–39**
  churches **228–32**
    St Joseph (R.C.) 91, *95*, **231–2**, Pl. 60
    St Mary 25, 26, 29, 41, 46, 92, **228–9**
    St Paul, Westleigh 88, **230**
    St Peter, Westleigh 92, 96, **230**
  industrial architecture 52, 55–6, 58, **236–7**
  public and commercial buildings **232–6**
    Boar's Head 82, **233**
    Co-op Central Buildings 72–3, **234**
    Conservative Club 83, **234–5**
    park (Atherton) 75, **140–1**
    Public Library and Technical School 80–1, **233**
    Town Hall 73, **232–3**, Pl. 85
    War Memorial 99–100, **233**
  streets and houses 86, **233–6**, **237–8**
    Bedford Hall 36, **237–8**
    Bradshawgate 55, 59, 73, **234**, 236
    Higginson Street 55, **236**
    Market Place 47, 229, **233–4**
    Wild's Passage (Robert Guest's house) 55, **236**

Bedford 228, **231–2**, **238–9**
Pennington **229–30**, **235**
Westleigh *212*, 228, **230**
Lightshaw Hall *see* Golborne
Litherland 82, 89, 93, 95, **238–9**
Little Crosby *9*, *10*, *12*, **240–1**
  Crosby Hall 1, 38, 46, 47, **240–1**
  Harkirk 18, **241**
  St Mary (R.C.) 40, 88, 97, **240**
Liverpool centre 1, 2–3, 19, 48–9, 51,
  60, 68–115, **242–80**
  castle 19, *29*, *243*, *310*, *320*
  cathedrals:
    Anglican Cathedral 6, 94, 97,
      102, 112, **253**, **344–53**, 507,
      Pls. 70, 71; furnishings **352**,
      398, 609; monuments 97n.,
      102, **353**; stained glass 97, 102,
      112, **352–3**
    Metropolitan Cathedral (R.C.)
      102, 111–12, 255, **353–60**, Pls.
      118, 119; *C19 R.C. cathedral 89*,
      354
  churches etc. 64–8, 75, 110–11, *245*,
    247, **281–6**, 354, **360–2**
    Chatham Street Welsh
      Presbyterian Chapel **370**
    Great George Street
      Congregational Church 67,
      247, **285–6**, Pl. 48
    Gustav Adolfs Kyrka, Park
      Lane (Swedish Seamen's
      Church) 95, **286**, 475, Pl. 75
    Holy Innocents, Grove Street 197
    Methodist Central Hall,
      Renshaw Street 95, **285**, Pl. 73
    Notre Dame Convent **377**
    Our Lady and St Nicholas 65,
      111, 243, 247, **281–4**
    St Andrew, Rodney Street
      (Scottish Presbyterian) 67,
      247, **361**, 372
    St Bride, Percy Street 64–5,
      247, **360**, 379
    St Catherine, Abercromby
      Square *368*
    St George, Derby Square *19*, *39*,
      320
    St James's Cemetery 63, 67–8,
      247, **361–2**
    St John, Old Haymarket 39, *294*,
      297, *335*, *345*, *360*
    St Luke 110–11, 247, **281**, Pl. 44
    St Mary del Key 243, *281*
    St Nicholas (C14) *281*
    St Nicholas, Berry Street 65
    St Nicholas (R.C.), Hawke
      Street *354*
    St Patrick (R.C.) *see* Liverpool
      suburbs (Toxteth)
    St Paul, St Paul's Square *39*, *40*,
      41, *480*

St Peter, Church Street 39, 41,
  245, *303*, *313–14*, *344*, 378, **402**,
  576
St Peter (R.C.), Seel Street 40,
  245, **284–5**, 354, 472
St Philip, Hardman Street *375–6*
St Philip Neri (R.C.),
  Catharine Street 94, **360–1**
*St Saviour, Upper Huskisson
  Street 172*
St Thomas, Park Lane *39*
St Vincent de Paul (R.C.), St
  James Street 251, **285**
Synagogue, Hope Place (now
  Unity Theatre) **373**
Third Church of Christ
  Scientist **361**
Unitarian Chapel, Renshaw
  Street *376*, 450
Victoria Chapel **318**
public and commercial buildings
  63–4, 64, 68–72, 73–84, 97–100,
  107–10, **286–306**, **362–73**
  Adelphi Hotel 83, 98, **334**
  Adult Deaf and Dumb Institute
    see Liverpool suburbs
    (Toxteth)
  Albany Building 68–9, **328–9**
  Argyle Street warehouses 71,
    306, 325, Pl. 102
  Art House Square **336**
  Athenaeum *63*, 98, **313**
  banks 64, 69–70, 246, 249;
    Adelphi Bank 69, **312**; Bank of
    England 69, 249, **311**, Pl. 89,
    Heywood's Bank, Brunswick
    Street 64, 246, **309**, Pl. 38;
    HSBC, Dale Street 256, **318**;
    Martins Bank, Water Street
    98, 254, **341**; North and South
    Wales Bank, Derby Square 69,
    249, **321**; North and South
    Wales Bank (HSBC), Bold
    Street **308**; Parr's (now
    NatWest) Bank, Castle Street
    69–70, 249, **312**; Royal Bank
    249, **318**
  Barned's Buildings 64, 248, **337**
  Blackburne Arms 99, **374**
  Blackburne House (women's
    training centre) 257, **373**
  Blue Coat School *see* Bluecoat
    Chambers *below*
  Bluecoat Chambers (first Blue
    Coat School) 43, 104, 166,
    245, **302–4**, 495, Pl. 29
  Bon Marché 98, **315**
  *Botanic Gardens, Mosslake Fields
    63*, *246*, *413*
  Bridewell, Campbell Square
    310, Pl. 102
  Bridewell, Cheapside 74, **301**

Brown's Buildings 389
Brunswick Buildings 68, 248
Cavern Walks 327
Central Station 54, 107, 305, 334
Central Station (underground)
  305, 334
Chancery House (Gordon
  Smith Institute for Seamen)
  79, 330
City Education Offices 73, 336
City Tramway Offices 74, 302
College of Commerce 338
College of Technology 109, 302
Commutation Plaza 316-17
Compton House (Marks &
  Spencer) 69, 250, 314-15, 509
Conservation Centre (former
  Midland Railway goods ware-
  house) 71, 114, 343
Conservative Club 83, 320
Consumption Hospital 77, 377
Corn Exchange 255, 323-4
Cotton Exchange 253, 329
County Sessions House 74,
  249, 300
Cripps's shop 250, 308
Crown Street station 304, 413, 415
Cunard Building 7, 72, 253-4,
  332, Pl. 1
Custom House (Foster Jun.) 63,
  104, 247, 310, 322
Custom House (Ripley) 43, 303
docks see Liverpool docks
Elkington's shop 250, 314
Empire Theatre 99, 326
Exchange Buildings 45, 63, 246,
  322-3
Exchange Station 54, 107, 338, 486
Eye and Ear Infirmary 77, 378
FACT 115, 258, 301, 309
Fire Station, Hatton Garden
  74, 250, 302
Forum Cinema 99, 326
Fowler's Building 249, 339
Futurist Cinema (City Picture
  House) 83-4, 326
General Post Office 75, 340,
  343
George's Dock Ventilation and
  Control Station 332-3
Goree Warehouses 64n., 337
Granite Buildings 69, 249, 337
Hahnemann Homeopathic
  Hospital 77, 376
Harold Cohen Library see
  University of Liverpool below
Hornby Library 249, 299
Imperial Chambers 248, 320
India Buildings 98, 254, 341
International Garden Festival
  see Liverpool suburbs
  (Aigburth)

James Street Station 305, 341
Lewis's department store 98,
  104, 334-5
Lime Street Station 53, 54, 83,
  107, 293, 304-5, 413, 414, Pls.
  93, 100
LIPA see Mechanics' Institution
  below
Liverpool & London Insurance
  Co. 71, 248, 309, 318
Liverpool Art School 81, 372
Liverpool Central Technical
  School see Museum and
  Library below
Liverpool Community College
  Arts Centre 373
Liverpool Institute of
  Performing Arts (LIPA) see
  Mechanics' Institution below
Liverpool John Moores
  University 109, 115, 258;
  Aldham Robarts Learning
  Resource Centre 115, 258,
  372; Avril Robarts Learning
  Resource Centre 302, 338;
  Byrom Street buildings 109,
  258, 302; Dean Walters
  Building 379-80; Joe H.
  Makin Drama Centre 373;
  Notre Dame Convent and
  Teacher Training College 377;
  Peter Jost Enterprise Centre
  258, 302
Liverpool Prison see Liverpool
  suburbs (Walton Prison)
Liverpool Royal Institution 63,
  246, 316, Pl. 37
Liverpool Women's Hospital
  373
Lyceum 63, 113, 246, 257,
  307-8
Lying-In Hospital 77, 378
Magistrates' Courts 74, 301
Mechanics' Institution (LIPA)
  63, 114, 246, 257, 372, 421,
  Pl. 59
Medical Institution 63, 246,
  378
Mersey Docks and Harbour
  Board (Port of Liverpool
  Building) 71, 253, 331, Pl. 1
Mersey Mission to Seamen 79,
  324
Mersey Road Tunnel
  (Queensway) 98, 107, 254,
  306, 310, 328, 332-3, 335
Merseyrail underground system
  107, 305, 319
Merseyside Trade Union,
  Community and Unemployed
  Resource Centre 375
Met Quarter 343

Midland Railway warehouse (Conservation Centre) 70, 114, **343**

Millennium House **340**

monuments see sculpture and monuments *below*

Moorfields Station **319**

Municipal Buildings 73, 249, **291**

Museum and Library (with Museum Extension and Central Technical School) 5, 80, 81, 104, 249, **298–9**, Pl. 79

Music Hall **308**

Musker's Buildings (Junior Conservative Club) 83, **319–20**

National Museums Liverpool offices **320**

Oriel Chambers 69, 248–9, 311, 317, 318, **342**, Pl. 90

Philharmonic Hall 98, 99, 254, **371–2**

Philharmonic Hotel 83, 252, **375–6**, Pl. 95

Picton Reading Room 81, 249, **299**, Pl. 80

Pier Head see *under* streets and houses *below*

Playhouse 83, 256, **301**

police stations **302**

Postal Sorting Office **371**

Premier Buildings 98, **315**

Queen Elizabeth II Law Courts 108, **300**, 321

Royal & Sun Alliance (formerly Royal Insurance) 109–10, 256, **328–9**

Royal Court Theatre 99, **335**

Royal Infirmary 77, *245, 293, 297*, **365**

Royal Infirmary Medical School 364

Royal Insurance head office 71, 82, 249, **328**, Pl. 91

Royal Liver Building 71, 253, **331–2**, Pl. 1

Royal Liverpool University Hospital see Liverpool suburbs (Everton)

sailors' homes 79, 113

St George's Hall 5, 63–4, 74, 82, 110, 247, 249, 256, **291–7**, 336, 453, Pls. 77, 78

St John's Market 75, 110, 247, 256, 336

St John's Precinct 110, 256, **335–6**

School for the Blind 79, 96, 99, 254, **375**, **403**, **496–7**

sculpture and monuments 82, 246, 252, 254; Cenotaph 100, 254, **297**, Pl. 111; Heroes of

the Marine Engine Room 100, **333**, Pl. 110; Alfred Jones Memorial 82, **333**; Nelson Monument 82, 246, **323**; St John's Gardens 82, **335**; Steble Fountain 82, **300**; Queen Victoria Monument, Derby Square 82, **321**; Queen Victoria, Prince Albert and Disraeli, St George's Plateau 82, **297**; Wellington Monument 82, **300**

Seel's Building 69, **313–14**

Sheltering Home for Destitute Children **378**

State House 8, **319**

Tate & Lyle Sugar Silo see Liverpool docks

Theatre Royal 63

Tower Buildings **342**, Pl. 92

Town Hall (and Exchange) 45, 73, 245, **286–91**, Pls. 34, 56

Union News Room 63, 246, 298, **321–2**

Unity Theatre **373**

University of Liverpool 108, **362–71**; Abercromby Square 108, **368–9**; Arts and Law buildings 108, 256, **369–70**; Ashton Building 80, **364**; Catholic Chaplaincy **360**; Chadwick Laboratory 255, **370**; Electrical Engineering and Electronics 108, 256, **366**; Guild of Students 97, 257, **366**; halls of residence see Liverpool suburbs (Mossley Hill); Harold Cohen Library 98, 254, **365–6**; School of Architecture (Leverhulme Building) 98, 257, **368–9**; School of Tropical Medicine 77, **364–5**; Senate House **369**; Sports Centre 108–9, 256, **367–8**; Victoria Building 80, **363**, Pl. 84

Vines, The 83, **326**

Walker Art Gallery 5, 81, 249, **299–300**

Wapping Goods Station 53, **305–6**, 415

Wellington Rooms 63, 246, **377–8**

West Africa House 98, **343**

White Star Line 71, 249, **325–6**, 328

Workhouse 78n., 354, 362

Workshops for the Outdoor Blind 79, **317**

Roman Catholic Cathedral see cathedrals *above*

streets and houses *19*, 60, 60–1, 61, 64, 100–2, 245, 252, **306–44**, **373–80**

Abercromby Square 61, 108–9, 248, 255, 362, **368–9**
Argyle Street 70, **306**, Pl. 102
Bedford Street South **369**
Benson Street **373–4**
Berry Street **306–7**
Bixteth Street **307**
Blackburne Place and Terrace **374**
Bold Street **307–9**
Bridgewater Street **330**
Brownlow Hill 354, 362–3, 368
Brunswick Street 64, **309**, 331
Button Street **309–10**
Byrom Street 298, **302**, **310**
Campbell Square **310**
Canning Place 79, 243, **310**
Canning Street **374**
Castle Street 49, 69–70, 243, 246, 249, **310–13**
Catharine Street **360**, **374**
Cathedral precinct **353**
Chapel Street 243, **313**
Chatham Street **370**
Cheapside **313**
Church Alley **313**
Church Street 250, **313–15**
Clarence Street **377**
Clayton Square *48*, *245*, 257, **316**
Cleveland Square 113
College Lane 64n., **316**
Colquitt Street 246, **316**
Commutation Row **316–17**
Concert Square and Street 114, 257, **317**
Cook Street 69, **317**
Cornwallis Street **317**
Crosshall Street **317–18**
Dale Street 243, **318–21**
Derby Square 243, 255, **320–1**
Duke Street 48, 60, 64, 245, **321–2**, 325
Edmund Street **322**
Egerton Street **374**
Exchange Flags 246, **322–3**
Exchange Street East **323**
Falkner Square and Street 248, 368, **374**
Falkner Terrace **380**
Fenwick Street **323–4**
Fleet Street **324**
Gambier Terrace 61, 248, **376**, Pl. 57
Great Crosshall Street **324**
Great George Place **324**
Great George Square 61, 248, **324**
Grove Street **374**
Hanover Street 243, **324–5**
Hardman Street **374–5**
Harrington scheme *see* Liverpool suburbs (Toxteth)

Hatton Garden 74, **325**
Henry Street 71
High Street 243
Hockenhall Alley **320**
Hope Street and Place **375–6**, Pl. 57
Houghton Street **325**
James Street **325–6**
Lime Street **326**
Lord Street 104, 255, **326–7**
Mathew Street **327**, 339
Minster Court **378**, 379
Mosslake Fields *63*, *246*, 248, 368, *413*
Mount Pleasant 246, 357, **366–7**, **376–8**
Mount Street **378**
Myrtle Street **378**, 379
Nelson Street **327–8**
North John Street 64, **328**
Old Church Yard **328**
Old Hall Street 243, 256, **328–30**
Old Haymarket 243
Pall Mall **338**
Paradise Street 110, 243, 258, 306, **310**, 316, 325, 327, **330**, 337
Parliament Street 71, **330**
Percy Street 61, 248, **378–9**
Pier Head 71, 76, 82, 100, 114, 115, 252, 253, 258, **330–3**, Pls. 1, 110
Plateau, The 293, **297**
Pleasant Street **379**
Preston Street **320**
Queen Avenue **311**
Queen Square **333**
Queen's Walk **353**
Rainford Square and Gardens **309–10**, **327**
Ranelagh Place **334**
Ranelagh Street **334–5**
Renshaw Street **376**
Rodney Street 48–9, 61, 246, **379**, 416
Roe Street **335**
Ropewalks Square 114, **309**
Rumford Place **335**
St Andrew's Gardens 102, 254, **379**
St George's Plateau 293, **297**
St John's Gardens 82, 252, **335**
St John's Lane **335**
Seel Street 48, **336**
Seymour Street **379**
Sir Thomas Street **336–7**
Slater Street **337**
South John Street **337**
Stanley Street **337**
Strand, The **337**
Sweeting Street 64, 248, **337**

Tempest Hey **337**
Temple Court **327**, **339**
Tithebarn Street 243, **338**
The Tower (*Stanley family house*)
    243, *342*
Trueman Street **320**
Union Street **329**
Upper Duke Street **379–80**
Upper Parliament Street 248,
    380
Victoria Street **338–40**, 343
Wapping **340**
Water Street 8, 97–8, 243, 331,
    340–3
Watkinson Street **330**
Whitechapel 243, 340, **343**
William Brown Street 5, 81,
    297–300
Williamson Square 245, **343**
Wolstenholme Square 245, **343**
Wood Street **343–4**
York Street **344**
Liverpool docks 2, 51–2, 70, 98, 104,
    107, 245, 248, 257, **259–80**, 337
    Albert Dock and warehouses 51,
        58, 114, 248, 257, 261–2, **263–70**,
        293n., Pl. 96
    Alexandra Dock 51–2, **277**
    Brunswick Business Park **274**
    Brunswick Dock 261, 263, **270–1**
    Canada Dock 261, **277**
    Clarence Dock 261, **277**
    Customs and Excise Building 114,
        273
    Dingle Tunnel 54, **272**
    Dock Traffic Office (Granada TV
        News) **269–70**
    dock wall **276**
    Duke's Dock 52, 260, 262, **272**
    Garston *see* Liverpool suburbs
        (Garston)
    George's Dock 330–1
    Gladstone Dock 52, 98, 261, **277**
    Harrington Dock **274**
    Herculaneum Dock 262, **272**,
        382
    King's Dock 261, *262*, 263, **272–3**
    Liverpool Overhead Railway 54,
        262–3, 272
    Liverpool Watersport Centre 114,
        258, 263, **273**
    Merseyside Maritime Museum
        114, **268**, 270
    Museum of Liverpool Life **271–2**
    North Docks **276–80**
    Old Dock 247, **260**, *310*
    Pier Head *see* Liverpool centre
        (streets and houses)
    Prince's Dock 51, 114, 258, 260,
        263, **276**, **277–8**
    Queen's Dock *see* Liverpool
        Watersport Centre *above*

Royal Seaforth Dock 107, 262,
    278, 578, 644
Salthouse Dock 262, **273**
South Docks 257, **263–74**
Stanley Dock 261, 262, **279**, **486**
Stanley Hydraulic Power Centre
    (accumulator tower) 261, **279**
Tate & Lyle Sugar Silo 110, 255,
    262, **279–80**, Pl. 121
Tate Liverpool 114, 257, **269**
Tobacco Warehouse 52, 262, **279**
Toxteth Dock **274**
Wapping Dock 262, **274**
Wapping Hydraulic Power Centre
    (accumulator tower) 261, **274**
Wapping Policeman's Lodge 261,
    274
Wapping Warehouse 257, 263, **274**
warehouses 70–1, 114, 248, 262
Waterloo Dock 52, 248, 261, 263,
    280, Pl. 97
Liverpool suburbs 48–9, 60–1, 70,
    73–4, 78, 81, 84, 100–2, **380–515**
    Aigburth 62, **380–6**
        Aigburth Grange *see* Granary,
            The *below*
        churches **380–3**; Aigburth
            Methodist Church 103, **383**; St
            Anne 66, 247, **380**;   St
            Austin (R.C.) and schools 67,
            80, 97, **382–3**; St Mary,
            Grassendale 89, **380–1**, 385; St
            Michael-in-the-Hamlet 65,
            247, **381–2**, 384
        Cressington Park 250, **385**
        Fulwood Park 84, 250, **384**
        Granary, The 20, 30, **385–6**
        Grassendale Park 250, **384–5**
        public buildings etc. 80, **383–4**;
            Bank of Liverpool 70, 249,
            385; Cressington Station 54,
            383; Liverpool Cricket Club
            84, **383**; Liverpool
            International Garden Festival
            (site and Festival Hall) 257,
            272, 310, 317, 333, **383**
        St Michael's Hamlet 62, 247,
            381–2, **384**
        streets and houses 62, 70, 250,
            384–6
    Alder Hey *see* West Derby
    Allerton 85, **386–92**
        Calderstones and Park 11–12,
            75, 248, 386, **389**, 396
        churches etc. **386–7**; All
            Hallows 92–3, 96, 251, **386–7**,
            Pl. 67; All Souls 102–3, 254,
            387; cemetery 76, **387**
        houses 62, 85, 106, 248, 250,
            386, **388–92**; Allerton 62, 248,
            390; Allerton Hall 44–5, 46,
            47, 62, 246, 386, 387, **390**,

392; Allerton Priory 85, 250, **391**, Pl. 106; *Hart Hill 389*; New Heys 85, **390–1**; Paul McCartney's 106; Springwood 62, 248, **391–2**
public buildings 108, 109, **387–9**; Wyncote Sports Pavilion 109, 256, **388**, Pl. 120
Anfield 86, **392–7**
churches etc. **393–4**; City of Liverpool Cemetery 76, 251, 387, **394–5**, 405, Pl. 88; St Columba 103, 255, **393**, 412
public buildings **395–7**; Board Schools 80, 252, **397**; Liverpool Football Club **396–7**
Stanley Park 75, 250, **395–7**, 426, 435
Calderstones Park *see* Allerton *above*
Childwall 17, 84, **397–402**
Childwall Hall 62, 399
churches etc. **397–9**, **402**; All Saints 23, 24, 28, 65, 243, **397–9**, 466; Bishop Eaton Monastery 88, 95, 96, **400**; St David 41, 103, **402**
Oswaldcroft (St Joseph's Home) 85, 251, **400–1**
public buildings **401–2**, 495, **496**; Liverpool Hope University (former Christ's College and St Katharine's College teacher-training colleges) 99, 109, 111, 255, **401–2**
Clubmoor 108, **402–5**
churches **402–3**; St Andrew 96, **402–3**; St Matthew 103, 254, **403**
Queens Drive and Muirhead Avenue housing 87, 100, 254, **404**
Cressington Park *see* Aigburth *above*
Croxteth 106, **405–9**, **409**
Croxteth Hall 36, 42–3, 47, 48, 75, 84, 243, 246, **406–9**, 501, 509, Pl. 28
West Derby Cemetery 76, **405**
Edge Hill (and Kensington) **409–17**
churches etc. **410–12**; Christ Church, Kensington 89, **410**; Jewish Cemetery 63, **413**; St Anne (R.C.), Edge Hill 88, **412**; St Cyprian 91, 112, **410**; St Dunstan 89, **411**, 479, 489; St Mary, Edge Hill 247, **411–12**
housing *43*, 86, 248, 409–10, **416–17**; Clare Terrace 248, **417**

public buildings etc. **412–16**; Bank of Liverpool 70, **416**; Botanic Gardens and Wavertree Park 63, 250, 392, **413**; Chatsworth School 80, **413**; fire and police station 74, **413**; library 250, **412**; Littlewoods Building 103–4, **416**, Pl. 117; Olympia Theatre 83, **416**; *Post Office 75, 412*; railway structures, Waterloo Tunnel and Edge Hill station 53, 54, 248, 304–5, **413–15**, Pl. 99; Wavertree Park *see* Botanic Gardens *above*; West Derby Union Offices 78, **413**; Williamson's Tunnels **415–16**
Edge Lane *see* Edge Hill; Fairfield
Everton **417–24**
churches etc. 354, **417–20**; Cemetery *see* Fazakerley *below*; Richmond Baptist Church 94, **420**; Sacred Heart (R.C.) 95, **420**; *St Benedict* 180, *411*; *St Chad with Christ Church* 403; St Francis Xavier (R.C.) 79, 93, 95, 113, 251, 257, **418–19**, 657n.; St George 65, 247, 382, **417–18**, Pl. 45; St John Chrysostom 112, **418**; St Mary of the Angels (R.C.) 93, **419–20**; Shaw Street Baptist Chapel 94, 251, **420**
Ogden's Tobacco Factory 58, **424**
public buildings **420–4**; Collegiate Institution 79, 115, 247, **421**, Pl. 81; Everton Football Club, Goodison Park *see* Walton *below*; George III statue 82, 246, **423**; Library 81, 250, **420–1**; lock-up 46, **424**; Royal Liverpool University Hospital 109, 256, **421–2**; St Francis Xavier College (Liverpool Hope University College) 79, **419**; Water Works 253, **422**
streets and houses 105, 256, 417, **422–4**, *506*; London Road 82, **422–3**
Fairfield **424–6**
Newsham House and Park 45, 75, 79, 250, 395, 425, **426**
Royal Liverpool Seamen's Orphan Institution 79, **425**
Fazakerley 22, **427–9**
churches etc. **427**; Everton Cemetery 76, **427**; Holy Name (R.C.) 111, **427**; Kirkdale Cemetery 76, **427**

Hartley's Factory and village 87, **428–9**
public buildings **427–8**; New Hall 78, **428**; University Hospital Aintree 77, **428**
Fulwood *see* Aigburth *above*
Garston **429–31**
docks 52, 60, 429, **431**
Francis Morton & Co. foundry 58
library 81–2, **429**
Mersey Match Factory (The Matchworks) 103, 115, 257, **430–1**, Pl. 127
St Michael 28, 430n., 468
Gateacre **431–4**
Gateacre Brewery 58, **432**
Gateacre Chapel 40, **431**
Gateacre Grange 85, 250, 399, 432, **433–4**
St Stephen 96, **431–2**
Grassendale *see* Aigburth *above*
Greenbank *see* Mossley Hill *below*
Harrington *see* Toxteth *below*
Hunt's Cross **434–5**
Kensington *see* Edge Hill *above*
Kirkdale **435–6**
cemetery *see* Fazakerley *above*
Gordon Working Lads' Institute 79, **435**
New Bridewell (police and fire station) 74, **435**
Knotty Ash **436–9**
Ash Grange 115, 258, **437–8**
Broad Green Hospital 78, 413, **437**
churches **436–7**; Holy Spirit 103, 402, **437**; St John Evangelist 66, 247, **436–7**; St Margaret Mary (R.C.) 111, 255, **437**
Dovecot Estate 100, **438**, 446
Thingwall Hall 18, **438**
London Road *see* Everton *above*
Mossley Hill **439–45**
churches 93, **439–40**; Mossley Hill Baptist Church 95, **440**; St Matthew and St James 92, 96, 112, 251, **439–40**, 664, Pls. 64, 65
public buildings **441–3**; Carnatic Halls 109, 256, **441**; Liverpool College 99, **442–3**; Liverpool Marsh Campus **442**; University of Liverpool halls of residence 99, 109, 256, **441–2**
villas/houses 85, 250, **443–5**; Crofton 85, 250, **443**; Greenbank 62n., 109, 247, **442–3**, Pl. 55; Holmestead 85,

250, **443**; Mossley House 391, **441**; Sudley House **444–5**
Newsham House and Park *see* Fairfield *above*
Norris Green 100, **445–6**, 460
churches **445–6**; Christ Church 103, **445**; St Christopher 103, 255, **445–6**
Old Swan *see* Tue Brook *below*
Prince's Park *see* Sefton Park *below*
Princes Road *see* Toxteth *below*
Queen's Drive *see* Clubmoor *above*, Walton *and* Wavertree *below*
Royal Liverpool University Hospital *see* Everton *above*
St Michael's Hamlet *see* Aigburth *above*
Sandfield Park *see* West Derby *below*
Sandown Park *see* Wavertree *below*
Sefton Park and Prince's Park 84, 105, **447–55**
churches etc. **447–51**; Methodist (Independent Baptist) 95, **451**; St Agnes and vicarage 85, 89–90, 251, **447–8**, 456, Pl. 68; St Clare (R.C.) 93–4, 251, **448–9**, Pl. 69; *St Paul, Prince's Park 381, 452*; Unitarian 94, 95, 251, **449–51**, Pl. 72; Welsh Presbyterian *see* Toxteth *below*
houses 250, **452–3**, **454–5**; Gledhill and The Towers 250, **454–5**
Prince's Park 75, 250, 447, **451–3**
Sefton Park 75, 250, 295, 395, 396, 397n., 447, **453–5**, Pl. 87
Sheil Park 250
Speke 100, 104, 106, 254, **455–68**
Boulevard Industry Park 113, **463**
churches **456–7**, 461; St Ambrose (R.C.) 111, 255, 437, **457**, 516
Estuary Commerce Park 113, 456, 458, **459**
Halewood Car Plant 30n., 110, **462–3**
housing 100, 106, 213, 215, 254, **460–1**
Liverpool Airport 98, 100, 113, 254, 258, 456, **457–9**, 468, Pl. 116
Speke Hall 20, 21, 28, 32–6, 38, 243, 455, **463–8**, Pls. 14–16, 518, 616
Stanley *see* Tue Brook *below*
Stanley Park *see* Anfield *above*
Stoneycroft *see* Tue Brook *below*

Thingwall *see* Knotty Ash *above*
Toxteth 256, 285, **469–77**
  Cain's Brewery 58, **477**
  churches etc. 417, **469–74**, **476**;
  Ancient Chapel 40, 243,
  472–3; Our Lady of Lourdes
  and St Bernard (R.C.) 112,
  471; St Clement 66, 67, 247,
  469–70; St James 39, 245, **470**;
  St Margaret of Antioch 89–90,
  96, 97, 251, 447, **470–1**; St
  Nicholas (Greek Orthodox)
  95, 251, **472**, Pl. 74; St
  Patrick (R.C.), Park Place 67,
  247, 354, **472**; Synagogue,
  Princes Road 95, 251, **473–4**,
  Pl. 76; Toxteth Park Cemetery
  75–6, 394, **474**; Toxteth
  Tabernacle 251, **473**; Welsh
  Presbyterian 94, 251, **473**
  Harrington scheme 49, 245,
  469
  housing and streets 106, 469,
  476–7; Princes Road **476–7**
  public buildings **474–6**; Adult
  Deaf and Dumb Institute 79,
  475; docks *see* Liverpool
  docks; Florence Institute for
  Boys 79, **475**; Park Hill
  Reservoir 76, 253, **476**; Steble
  Street baths (now Park Road
  Sports Centre) 76, 253, **475**;
  Turner Memorial Home 78–9,
  475–6
  Toxteth Park 22, 469
Tue Brook, Old Swan, Stanley and
  Stoneycroft **477–84**
  churches **477–81**; St John the
  Baptist and vicarage 85, 91,
  96, 251, **477–9**, Pl. 62; St
  Oswald (R.C.) and Convent
  of Mercy, Old Swan 88, 111,
  251, **480–1**; St Paul,
  Stoneycroft 41, 94, 96, 253,
  479–80
  Gardener's Arms, Old Swan
  99, 403, **483**
  public buildings **481–3**; Lister
  Drive Baths 76, 253, **481–2**;
  Lister Drive School 80, **482**;
  Rathbone Hospital (City
  Hospital East) 77, **482**
Vauxhall 60, **484–7**
  churches **484–5**; Our Lady of
  Reconciliation (R.C.) 89, 251,
  485, 609; St Alban (R.C.) 88,
  485; St Anthony (R.C.),
  Scotland Road 67, 247, 354,
  484–5; St Sylvester (R.C.) **485**
  docks *see* Liverpool docks
  housing 86, *252*, 484, **487**;
  Bevington Street 252, **487**;

Eldon Grove 252, **487**;
  Eldonian Village 106, **487**
  Mersey Road Tunnel
  (Kingsway) 107, 484, **486**
  warehouses 71, 248, 484, **486**;
  Clarence Warehouses (P.W.
  Brancker) 71, 248, **486**
Walton 17, 18, **487–92**
  churches **487–90**, **491**; St
  Francis de Sales (R.C.) 93,
  489–90; St Mary (parish
  church) and rectory 23, 65,
  111, 247, **487–9**, **491**
  public buildings **490–2**;
  Arnot Street Schools 80, **491**;
  Bank of Liverpool 70, 249,
  492; Everton Football Club,
  Goodison Park 397, 489, **491**;
  Old Grammar School 39,
  490–1; Walton Prison 74, 249,
  490, Pl. 86; Workhouse 78, **491**
  Queen's Drive 254, **491–2**
Wavertree *11*, 61, 83, **492–500**
  churches **492–4**; Christ the
  King (R.C.), Queen's Drive
  111, 405, **494**; Holy Trinity 39,
  97, 100, 245–6, 254, **492–3**,
  Pl. 113; St Bridget 89, 95, **493**
  houses and streets 84, 248, 492,
  497–500; Olive Mount 45,
  246, **498–9**; Sandown Park
  etc. 61, 250, **499**; Wavertree
  (Liverpool) Garden Suburb
  87, 252, **500**, Pl. 109
  public buildings **494–8**; Abbey
  Cinema 99, **497**; Blue Coat
  School 80, 253, **495–6**, Pl. 82;
  lock-up 46, **497**; Olive Mount
  Cutting 53, **497**; Royal School
  for the Blind 79, **496–7**;
  Technical Institute 80, **495**;
  Wavertree Park *see* Edge Hill
  above
West Derby 18, 19, 20, *22*, 84,
  501–6
  castle 18, 29, *501*
  churches etc. **501–2**; cemetery
  see Croxteth *above*; St James
  88, 96–7, **501–2**; St Mary 88,
  96, 251, 405, **501**
  houses and streets 250, **503–6**;
  Sandfield Park 62, 250, **505**
  public buildings **502–3**, **505–6**;
  Alder Hey Children's Hospital
  78, **502**; Court House 38, **507**;
  St Vincent's School for the
  Blind 79, **502**
Woolton 84, 375n., 386, **506–15**
  churches **507–8**, **511**; St Peter
  93, 97, 100, 112, **507**
  houses and streets 106, 250,
  510–15; John Lennon's house

(Mendips) 102, 507;
Strawberry Field 515n. ;
Woolton Tower 146, **513**
public buildings **508–9**, **511–12**;
Liverpool Convalescent
Institution 78, **508–9**
Woolton Hall 43, 46n., 75, 246,
509–10
Lower Ince *see* Ince-in-Makerfield
Lowton 41, 55, 111, **515–16**
Byrom Hall 42, **516**
Lunt *see* Sefton
Lydiate **516–18**
churches 25, 26, 66, **517**, 679
Lydiate Hall 33, 467, **517–18**, 582
Scotch Piper Inn 38, **518**

Maghull 23, 93, **518–20**
Manor House 45, 79, **519**
Manchester Ship Canal 54, 259, 551,
602, **616**
Martincroft *see* Warrington
Melling 17, 66, **520–1**
Micklehead Green 21
Moss Bank *see* St Helens
Mossley Hill *see* Liverpool suburbs
Mote Hill *see* Warrington

Netherton 106, 359, **521–2**
St Benet 41, 126, **521–2**, Pl. 40
New Springs *see* Aspull
Newburgh 19, 43, **522–3**
Moorcroft House 42, 134, 166,
522–3
Woodcock Hall 42, **523**
Newton-le-Willows 15, 17, 19, 22, 38,
523–31
castle (Castle Hill) 18–19, 29, 530
churches 66, 111, **524–6**
Congregational 94, 97, **526**
Emmanuel 66, **525**
St Patrick (R.C.) 111, **526**, 655
St Peter 93, **524–5**, 529
Earlestown 53, 47, 60, 73, 111, 524,
525–6, **527**, **529**
Haydock Lodge gateway 46, **528**
Newton Hall 35, 524
Newton Park Farm and barn 38,
45, 529, **530–1**
public buildings, transport struc-
tures etc. 74, 81, **526–9**
Earlestown Station 53, **527**
Sankey Viaduct 53, **526–7**,
Pl. 98
Town Hall 73, **529**
racecourse 84, 529
St Oswald's Well **531**, 679
Vulcan Foundry and Village 60, **530**
Wargrave 66, 524, **525–6**, **530**

Old Swan *see* Liverpool suburbs (Tue
Brook)

Ormskirk 1, 18, 19, **531–7**
churches **531–4**, **536–7**
Emmanuel Methodist 95, **534**
St Anne (R.C.) 88, **534**
St Peter and St Paul 23, 25, 28,
29, 40, 41, 92, 142, 143, 192,
229, **531–4**, 596, Pls. 7, 20;
Derby Chapel 23, 28, 29, 531,
532–4
folly 46, **536**
public buildings 74, 75, 78, 80,
534–7
Dispensary 64, **536**, Pl. 58
Edge Hill College 99, **534–5**
streets and houses 48, 55, 64,
535–6
Aughton Hall **536**
Westhead **536–7**
Orrell 2, 50, 53, 60, **537–40**
Abraham Guest and Up Holland
High Schools 109, **539**
Ackhurst Hall 33, 34, **539**
churches 103, 121, **537**
Gathurst Fold 42, **539**
Mount, The 61, **538**

Paddington *see* Warrington
Padgate *see* Warrington
Parr *see* St Helens
Peasley Cross *see* St Helens
Peel Hall *see* Ince-in-Makerfield
Pemberton *see* Wigan
Penketh *see* Warrington
Pennington *see* Leigh
Pennington Green *see* Aspull
Pimbo *see* Up Holland
Platt Bridge *see* Abram
Poolstock *see* Wigan
Portico *see* St Helens
Prescot 19, 20, 49–50, 57, **540–5**
churches 17, **540–3**
Our Lady Immaculate (R.C.)
91, **542**
St Mary 28, 29, 39, 41, 68, 96,
201, **540–2**, 544, Pl. 21
public buildings etc. 35, 48, 64,
100, **543–4**
Court House or Town Hall 46,
113, *543*, 544
Derby Street 20, 64, **543**
watch-making buildings 57–8, 543,
544–5

Rainford **545–6**
Guild Hall Farmhouse 37,
545–6
Rainford Hall 85, **546**, 559
Scythe Stone Delph Farm 42, **546**
Rainhill **546–50**
churches **546–8**
St Bartholomew (R.C.) 67,
547–8, Pls. 49, 50

houses **548–50**
  Loyola House **548**
  Manor House 36, **549**
  Rainhill Old Hall 21, 31,
    549–50
  Tower, The 85, **548–9**
  station and bridge 53, 546, **548**
  West Derby County Asylum 78, *546*
Rainhill Stoops *see* Rainhill; Widnes
Ravenhead *see* St Helens
Risley *see* Warrington
Rixton 32, **550–1**
Rixton-with-Glazebrook *see*
  Glazebrook; Hollins Green
Roby *see* Huyton
Roby Mill *see* Up Holland
Runcorn bridges *see* Widnes

St Helens 2, 49–50, 57, 58, 59, 72, 83,
  551–78
  churches etc. (centre) 552, **553–7,**
    562–3, 566, 567–8, 570–1
    Borough Cemetery and
      Crematorium 76, 112–13,
      563–4, 631
    Chapel of St Thomas
      (Windleshaw Abbey) 25, 76,
      563–4
    Christ Church, Eccleston 29,
      66, 67, **576**
    Friends' Meeting House 29,
      556–7
    Holy Cross 92n., **555**
    Holy Trinity, Traverse Street
      89, **566**
    Methodist Church, Eccleston
      112, **577**
    Methodist Church, Nutgrove
      94, **571**
    Our Lady Help of Christians
      (R.C.), Portico 40–1, **570**, 657
    St Helen 103, 241, *551*, **553–5,**
      576
    St Mary 553
    St Mary Lowe House (R.C.)
      102, 103, **555–6**
    St Nicholas, Sutton 88, **567–8**
    St Teresa of Avila (R.C.),
      Eccleston 111, **576–7**
    St Theresa (R.C.), Sutton
      Manor 102, 126, **568**
    Sutton Oak Welsh Chapel 94,
      568
    United Reformed 112, **556**
  glass industry 56–7, 552, 558–9,
    567, **571–4**
    Cowley Hill Glass Works 57,
      552, **565**
    No. 9 Tank House **559**
    Pilkington Glass, Ravenhead
      56–7, 98, 110, 552, **571–4,**
      Pl. 122

houses:
  borough and industrial 60, 100,
    564–5, 566, **568–9, 572, 578**
  Cowley House 85, **564**
  Eccleston 20–1, 46, **577–8**
  Eltonhead Farm 46, **574**
  Scholes, The 30, 34, 570, **575–6**
  villas **569, 575**
public and commercial buildings
  (centre) 72, 83, 105, 108, 552,
    557–61, 564
  Beecham's Factory *see* St
    Helens College *below*
  Church Square Shopping
    Centre 110, 553, **560–1**
  Citadel (Theatre Royal) 83, **561**
  Gamble Institute 81, **557**
  Law Courts 108, **557–8**
  Rugby League Ground,
    Knowsley Road 84, **578**
  St Helens College (Beecham's
    Factory) 58, **558**
  Town Hall *64*, 73, 74, **557**
  Queen Victoria statue 82, **560**
  World of Glass 114, **558–9**
  YMCA 79, **561**
Blackbrook 61, 78, **566–7**
Bold **569**
Broad Oak **566–7**
Clock Face 87, 98, **567–9**
Cowley Hill 57, 552, **562–5**
Denton's Green **562–5**
Eccleston 17, 46, 552, **576–8**
  churches 29, 66, 67, 112, **576–7**
  De la Salle School, Centre for
    Arts 115, **577**
  Eccleston Hall 20–1, **577–8**
Moss Bank **562–5**
Nutgrove 94, **569, 574**
Parr 52, **566–7**
  Old Double Dock 52, **566**
  St Peter, Parr 90, **566**
Peasley Cross **567–9**
Portico 40–1, 240, **569–76**
Ravenhead 56–7, 60, 552, 567,
  569–76
Sutton 21, **567–9**
  Burtonhead *22*
  churches 88, 94, 102, **567–8**
  collieries **569**
  Lea Green 21, **569**
  St Helens Junction Station 53,
    568
  Sutton Hall Cottages 38, **569**
Sutton Heath 551, **569**
Thatto Heath 57, **569–76**
Windle **562–5**
  Windleshaw Abbey 25, 75,
    563–4
St Michael's Hamlet *see* Liverpool
  suburbs (Aigburth)
Sankey Viaduct *see* Newton-le-Willows

Scholes *see* Wigan
Seaforth 83, 93, 387, **578–9**
   Royal Seaforth Dock *see* Liverpool
     docks
Sefton 18, 23, 106, **579–84**
   Lunt **584**
   St Helen 24–8, 92, 143, 517, 518,
     532, 553, **580–3**, 660, 679, Pl. 9;
     screens and other furnishings
     26, 29, 41, **581–3**, 660, Pls. 10, 19
   Sefton Old Hall 30, 406, 407n., *584*
Seneley Green *see* Garswood
Shevington **584–5**
   Club House Farmhouse 36, 37, 38,
     584–5
   Crooke 87, **584**
   Forest Fold Farm 38, **585**
   Gathurst Viaduct 108, **585**
Simonswood *see* Kirkby
Simonswood Moss 9
Skelmersdale 2, 107, 168, 256, **585–90**,
   600
   New Town plan 107, 585–9,
     600
   public buildings 108, 109, **587–9**
Southworth Hall *see* Croft
Speke *see* Liverpool suburbs
Standish and Langtree 46, 64,
   590–4
   Bradley Hall 31, 33, 36, **593**
   Giant's Hall Farmhouse 36, **594**
   St Wilfrid 23, 26, 99, 142, **590–2**,
     679, Pls. 11, 13; furnishings 29,
     41, **591–2**, 598; monuments 27,
     29, 68, **592**, Pls. 22, 23, 46
   Standish Hall 33, 35, 593
Stanley *see* Liverpool suburbs (Tue
   Brook)
Stockbridge Village *see* Huyton
Stockton Heath *see* Warrington
Stoneycroft *see* Liverpool suburbs
   (Tue Brook)
Sutton *see* St Helens
Swinley *see* Wigan

Tarbock 12, 16, 22, **594–5**
   Brunt Boggart 22
   Daggers Bridge Farm 21
   Ochre Brook 16–17
   Tarbock Hall Farmhouse 38,
     594–5
Thatto Heath *see* St Helens
Thelwall *see* Warrington
Thelwell Viaducts *see* Warrington
   (centre: public buildings)
Toxteth *see* Liverpool suburbs
Twiss Green 21
Tyldesley 2, 49, 64, 86, **595–7**
   churches 40, 65–6, **595–6**
   Garrett Hall Farmhouse 36, **596**
   New Hall 32, **596**
   see also Astley

Up Holland 29, 60, 587, **597–601**
   churches **597–600**
     St Teresa (R.C.) 111, **598–9**
     St Thomas (and *priory*) 23, 28,
       29, 92, 96, **597–8**, Pl. 4
   Derby House 38, **599**
   Douglas Bank Farmhouse **600**,
     Pl. 18
   Holland Lees **600**
   Johnson's Farmhouse 30, **601**
   Knight's Hall and Roby Mill 134,
     163, 174, **601**
   Old Grammar School 39, **600**
   Pimbo 587, **601**
   Up Holland High School *see* Orrell
Upper Ince *see* Ince-in-Makerfield
Upton *see* Widnes

Vauxhall *see* Liverpool suburbs
Vulcan Village *see* Newton-le-Willows

Walton *see* Liverpool suburbs;
   Warrington
Wapping *see* Liverpool docks
Wargrave *see* Newton-le-Willows
Warrington 2–3, 16, 19, 50, 55, **601–41**
   castle (Mote Hill) 18, 29, 602n.
   churches etc. (centre) **605–11**
     Austin Friary 23–4, 602, 618
     Cemetery 76, **623**
     Friends' Meeting House 67,
       610–11
     Holy Trinity 39, 41, **607–8**
     Masonic Temple 98, **619**
     Sacred Heart (R.C.), Liverpool
       Road 93, **631–2**
     St Ann, Winwick Road 89, 90,
       621–2
     St Benedict (R.C.), Longford
       Street 94, **623**
     St Elphin (parish church) 24–5,
       40, 41, 88, 97, 598, 602,
       605–7, 616; monuments 27–8,
       68, **606–7**
     St Luke, Sankey Bridges 93,
       631
     St Mary (R.C.) 93, 95, 96,
       102n., **608–10**, 625, Pl. 61
     St Peter 606
     Unitarian Chapel 40, **610**
     Wesleyan Chapel 112, **610**
   industry and transport 57, 58, 71,
     113, 602, **615–16**, **624**, **633**
     Barclays Bank Store 113, **639**
     Bridgewater Canal **630**
     Greenall, Whitley & Co.
       Brewery 58, 604, **625–6**
     Manchester Ship Canal 54,
       602, **616**
     Royal Mail Rail Terminal 113,
       624, Pl. 125
     Winwick Quay 52, **624**, 636

public and commercial buildings
35, 64, 71–2, 76, 83, **611–21**
  Boer War memorial 82, **618–19**
  bridges 602, **615–16**, 618
  Cromwell Statue 82, **618**
  Fish Market 75, **620**
  Golden Square Shopping
    Centre 110, 617, **620**
  GPO 75, **619**
  Law Courts 108, **613**
  Museum and Library 41, 81,
    603, **613–14**
  parks 75, **612**, 618
  Parr Hall 81, **614**
  Police Station 74, **613**
  Pyramid Arts Centre (former
    County Court) 74, 114, **614**
  School of Art 81, **615**
  stations 53, 70, **615**, 623, 632
  Technical School 81, **614–15**
  Thelwall Viaducts 108, **615**
  Tim Parry Johnathan Ball
    Young People's Centre 115,
    633, Pl. 126
  T.J. Hughes (Warrington Co-
    operative Building) 72, **619**
  Town Hall (Bank Hall) 45, 47,
    73, 75, 82, **611–13**, 620, Pls. 35,
    36, 94
  Warrington Academy 113, 603, 618
  Warrington Hospital (former
    workhouse) 77–8, **632**
  Warrington Union (former) 78,
    623
  Woolworths (Garrett & Sons)
    72, **620**
Roman (*see also* Wilderspool *below*)
  16, 601, 615, *616*
streets and houses (centre) 48, 60,
  72, 84, **616–21**, 624, 627
  Bewsey Street 48, 61, 602, **621**,
    627
  Bridge Street 72, 602, **617–18**
  Church Street 602, **616**
  Cromwell's House 35, **616**
  Market Gate 72, 114, 602, **617**
  Palmyra Square 84, 602,
    618–19, 635
  Stanley Street 48, **618**, 627
  Winwick Street 48, **620**
Appleton 602, **627–30**
Bank Quay 604n., 611, 612, **631–4**
Barrow Old Hall 21, 641
Bewsey 112, **631–4**
  Bewsey Old Hall 21, 30, 36,
    632–3, 639
Birchwood 635, **636–8**
  Hinton House (British Nuclear
    Fuels) 113, **638**
  UK Atomic Energy Research
    Establishment (former) 167,
    636, **638**

Bridgewater 635, **641**
Burtonwood Motorway Services
  108, **639–40**, Pl. 124
Gorse Covert 636
Grappenhall 602, **627–30**
  St Wilfred 23, 26, 28, **630**
Great Sankey 40, **631–4**
IKEA 113, **640**
Latchford 602, **624–7**
  Peel's Cotton Works 55
  Plague House 624
  St James 65n., **624–5**
Liverpool Road **631–4**
Locking Stumps 636, **637**
Martincroft **621–4**
New Town 2, 107, 113, 603, **617**,
  627, **634–41**
Oakwood 636, **637**
Orford **621–2**
Paddington **621–4**
Padgate 78, 111, 175, **621–4**
  New Town 635, **638–9**
Penketh 17, **631–4**
RAF Burtonwood 635, **639**
Risley:
  Old Abbey Farm 21, 30
  Risley Moss Nature Reserve
    636, **637**
  Risley Remand Centre *see*
    Culcheth
  Risley Royal Ordnance Factory
    (former) 636, **638**
Sankey Bridges **631–4**
Sankey Valley Park 633, **639**
Science Park 113, **638**
Stockton Heath *15*, 602, **627–30**
  St Thomas 88, 96, **629–30**
Stretton **629**
Thelwall 66, **627–30**
Walton **627–30**
  Estate Village 87, **628**
  St John Evangelist 92, **629**
Walton Hall 62, **628**
Warrington Garden Suburb 87,
  633–4
Warrington New Town *see* New
  Town *above*
Westbrook 636, **639–41**
Wilderspool *15, 16, 17*, **601**, **624–7**
Winwick Quay 52, **624**, 636, **640–1**
Woolston **621–4**
Waterloo 1, 62, 83, 86, **642–5**
  Beach Lawn 86, **645**, Pl. 104
  churches 92, 93, 95, 103, *631*,
    642–3
  public buildings 53, 73, 108, **643–4**
Wavertree *see* Liverpool suburbs
West Bank *see* Widnes
West Derby *see* Liverpool suburbs
Westhead *see* Ormskirk
Westleigh *see* Leigh
Whelley *see* Wigan

Whiston *78*, **645–6**
　Halsnead Park *46*, *646*
Widnes 2, 19, 50, 57, 60, **646–58**
　castle 29
　chemical industry 57, 647–8, **650**
　churches (centre and West Bank)
　　648–9, **651**, 652
　　St Mary 92, **648–9**
　　St Paul 93, **651**, 656
　housing:
　　council and industrial 100, 650,
　　　658
　　suburban 84, 648, 653, **656**, **658**
　public buildings etc. (centre and
　　West Bank) 649, **650–2**
　　Britannia Railway Bridge 54,
　　　649
　　Catalyst (museum) 57, 114,
　　　650
　　Free Library and Technical
　　　School 81, **651**
　　Liverpool Catholic
　　　Reformatory Association
　　　Nautical Schools 78, **656**
　　Mersey Road Bridge 108, **649**
　　promenade 75, **649**
　　pubs 83, 648
　　Runcorn-Widnes road bridges
　　　54, **649**
　　Town Hall 73, **651**
　　war memorial 100, **653**
　　Widnes Health Centre 99, **652**
　　Widnes Station 54, **656**
　Appleton 100, **652–3**
　　St Bede (R.C.) 88, **653–4**
　　Wade Deacon Grammar
　　　School 99, **653**
　Ditton **657–8**
　　Ditton Hall 78, **658**
　　St Michael (R.C.) 89, 112, **657**
　Farnworth 19, **653–6**
　　churches **653–6**; St Luke 23,
　　　24, 26, 29, 41, 68, **653–5**; St
　　　Pius (R.C.) 111, **655**; Wesleyan
　　　Methodist Chapel 41, **655–6**
　　public buildings **656**; Liverpool
　　　Catholic Reformatory
　　　Association Nautical Schools
　　　78, **656**; lock-up 46, **655**;
　　　Widnes Station 54, **656**
　Hale Bank **658**
　Halton View **656–7**
　　St Ambrose 93, 651, **656–7**
　Hough Green **657–8**
　Moss Bank **657**
　Spike Island **649–50**
　Upton 652, **657–8**
　West Bank 59, 92, 647, **648–50**,
　　651
Wigan 2, *15–16*, *17*, 19, 49–50, 55–6,
　658–78
　churches etc. 103, **660–6**, **671**

All Saints (parish church) and
　Wigan Hall 23, 25–6, 27, 85,
　88, 96, 99, 229, 658, **660–2**,
　679, Pl. 112
Queen's Hall Methodist
　Mission 95, **671**
St George 40, **662–3**
St James, Poolstock 88, **663**
St John the Divine (Pemberton
　parish church), Lamberhead
　Green 66, **663**
St John (R.C.), Standishgate
　66–7, **664–5**, Pl. 42
St Jude (R.C.) 111, **665**
St Mary (R.C.), Standishgate
　66–7, **665–6**, Pls. 41, 43
St Matthew, Highfield 92, 629,
　663–4
St Thomas, Caroline Street 663
Wigan Borough Cemetery
　(Ince) 76, 100, **210**
housing (council and industrial)
　60, 86, 105, 659, 676
industry and transport 53, 55, 56,
　58, 115, 658–9, **673–5**
　coal mines 53, 62, 658, **674**
　Coop's Suit Factory 58, **671**,
　　Pl. 103
　gasworks 58
　Gidlow Mill 55, **674**
　Heinz Factory 110, **675**
　Victoria Mills 55, **675**
　Western Mills 56, **675**, Pl. 101
public and commercial buildings
　666–73
　banks 72, **670**, **672**, **673**
　cloth hall 55, 659
　council offices 108, **667**
　Galleries shopping centre 110,
　　671
　History Shop (former Free
　　Library) 81, **667**
　hotels and pubs 83, **670–2**, **677**
　Magistrates' and County
　　Courts 74, **671**
　Mesnes High School (Wigan
　　Infirmary Outpatients' Dept)
　　99, **667–8**
　Mesnes Park 75, 82, **668**
　Moot Hall 668
　Municipal Offices 73, **673**
　New Town Hall 45–6, 73, 668
　police stations 108, **667**
　Robin Park JJB Stadium 115,
　　677
　Royal Albert Edward Infirmary
　　77, **668**
　Royal Court Theatre 83, **672–3**
　schools 99, **662**, **663**, **667**, **671**
　Town Hall (former Mining and
　　Technical College) 81, **666**,
　　Pl. 83

Wigan Pier 52, 114, **673–4**
Roman remains (*Coccium*) 15–16,
    17, 658, **670**
streets and houses 60–1, 72, 84,
    115, 591, 659, **668–73**
    King Street 49, 83, **671, 672**
    Market Place 72, 114, **668–70,
    673**
    Millgate Street 48
    Standishgate 48, 61, 66, **670**
    Wallgate **671–2**
    Wigan Hall 85, **661–2**
Beech Hill **662**
Highfield 92, **663–4**
Lamberhead Green **663**
Pemberton 659
    churches 66, **663, 664, 666**
    library 81, **676**
Poolstock 86, 88, **663, 676**
Robin Park 115, **676–7**
Scholes 66, 67, 88, 105, **662, 666,
    676**
Springfield **662**
Swinley **664, 676–7**
Whelley **664**

Winstanley 676, **677**
Winstanley Hall 34–5, 47, 48, 62,
    677–8
Worsley Mesnes **664, 665**
Wilderspool *see* Warrington
Windle *see* St Helens
Windleshaw Abbey *see* St Helens
    (Windle)
Winstanley *see* Wigan
Winstanley Hall *see* Wigan
Winwick 11, 15, 16, 18, **678–83**
    Lancashire County Asylum 78, **682**
    St Oswald 17, 24, 25, 26, 28, 88,
        142, 174, 525, **678–82**, Pl. 6;
        furnishings 41, 96, **680–2**;
        monuments 27–8, 29, 41, 68,
        682, Pls. 24, 47
Woolden **683–4**
    Great Woolden Hall 14, 31,
        683–4
Woolston *see* Warrington
Woolton *see* Liverpool suburbs
Worsley *see* Wigan
Worthington 37, 46, **684–5**
    Worthington Hall 35, **684–5**